FAR WEST

FODOR'S TRAVEL PUBLICATIONS

are compiled, researched, and edited by an international team of travel writers, field correspondents, and editors. The series, which now almost covers the globe, was founded by Eugene Fodor in 1936.

OFFICES

New York & London

Fodor's Far West:

Editor: Christopher Caldwell
Area Editors: Barry and Hilda Anderson, Ruth Armstrong, Curtis Casewit, Toni Chapman, Ralph Friedman, Marael Johnson, Jane Lasky
Editorial Contributor: Cecelia Caso
Drawings: Sandra Lang
Maps: Pictograph

FODOR'S®

FAR WEST 1988

ARIZONA
CALIFORNIA
IDAHO
MONTANA
NEVADA
OREGON
UTAH
WASHINGTON
WYOMING

FODOR'S TRAVEL PUBLICATIONS, INC.
New York & London

 Published in the United States by Fodor's Travel Publications, Inc., a subsidiary of Random House, Inc., New York, and simultaneously in Canada by Random House of Canada Limited, Toronto. Distributed by Random House, Inc., New York.

ISBN 0-679-01501-9
ISBN 0-340-41881-8 (Hodder & Stoughton)

MANUFACTURED IN THE UNITED STATES OF AMERICA
10 9 8 7 6 5 4 3 2 1

CONTENTS

Map of the Far West, viii

FACTS AT YOUR FINGERTIPS 1

When to Go, 1; Planning Your Trip, 1; Packing, 2; Insurance, 2; Tips for British Visitors 3; What It Will Cost, 3; Hints to the Motorist, 4; Far West by Train 5; Traveling with Pets 6; Accommodations, 6; Restaurants, 8; Liquor Laws, 9; Time Zones, 9; Summer Sports, 9; Winter Sports, 9; Roughing It, 10; Tipping, 10; Hints to Handicapped Travelers, 11

THE FAR WEST, STATE BY STATE

ARIZONA—Fun on the Range 13

Map of Arizona, 15
Exploring Phoenix, 20
Map of Phoenix, 21
Practical Information for Phoenix, 23
Exploring Arizona, 32
Map of Grand Canyon National Park, 33
Map of Indian Reservations, 38
Map of Tucson, 50
Practical Information for Arizona, 57

SOUTHERN CALIFORNIA—Surf, Sand, and Spectaculars 73

Exploring the Los Angeles Area, 73
Map of Los Angeles, 74–75
Map of the Los Angeles Area, 81
Practical Information for the Los Angeles Area, 86
Exploring San Diego, 107
Map of San Diego, 108
Practical Information for San Diego, 110
Exploring Southern California, 122
Map of Southern California Beaches, 123
Practical Information for Southern California, 138
Map of California, 160–161

NORTHERN CALIFORNIA—Magic and Majesty 162

Exploring San Francisco, 162
Map of San Francisco, 164–165
Practical Information for San Francisco, 168
Exploring Northern California, 179
Map of the Bay Area, 180
Map of Marin County (Southern Half), 182

Map of Monterey Peninsula, 185
Map of Napa and Sonoma County Wineries, 188
Map of Yosemite National Park, 190
Map of the Reno–Lake Tahoe Area, 194
Practical Information for Northern California, 193

IDAHO—Outdoor Life—Mountain Style 210

Map of Boise Area, 211
Map of Idaho, 214
Map of Sun Valley Area, 221
Practical Information for Idaho, 222

MONTANA—Riches in the Hills 253

Map of Montana, 255
Map of Helena Area, 261
Map of Glacier National Park, 264
Practical Information for Montana, 266

NEVADA—Entertainment Capital of the World 283

Map of Nevada, 284
Practical Information for Nevada, 287
Map of Las Vegas, 289
Map of Hoover Dam–Lake Mead Area, 299

OREGON—The Sedate Frontier 308

Map of Portland, 310
Map of the Oregon Coast, 312
Map of Crater Lake National Park, 322
Map of Oregon, 331
Practical Information for Oregon, 340

UTAH—The Outdoor Amphitheater 388

Map of Salt Lake City, 390
Map of Utah, 394
Map of Bryce Canyon and Zion National Parks, 401
Practical Information for Utah, 402

WASHINGTON—The Mountains and the Sea 418

Exploring Seattle, 419
Map of Seattle, 421
Map of Mt. Rainier National Park, 425
Practical Information for Seattle, 427
Exploring Washington, 438
Map of Washington, 442
Map of the Puget Sound Area, 448
Map of North Cascades National Park, 454
Practical Information for Washington, 470

WYOMING—The Cowboys Still Ride 497

Map of Yellowstone National Park, 500
Map of Grand Teton National Park, 502
Map of Wyoming, 504
Practical Information for Wyoming, 507

Index 521

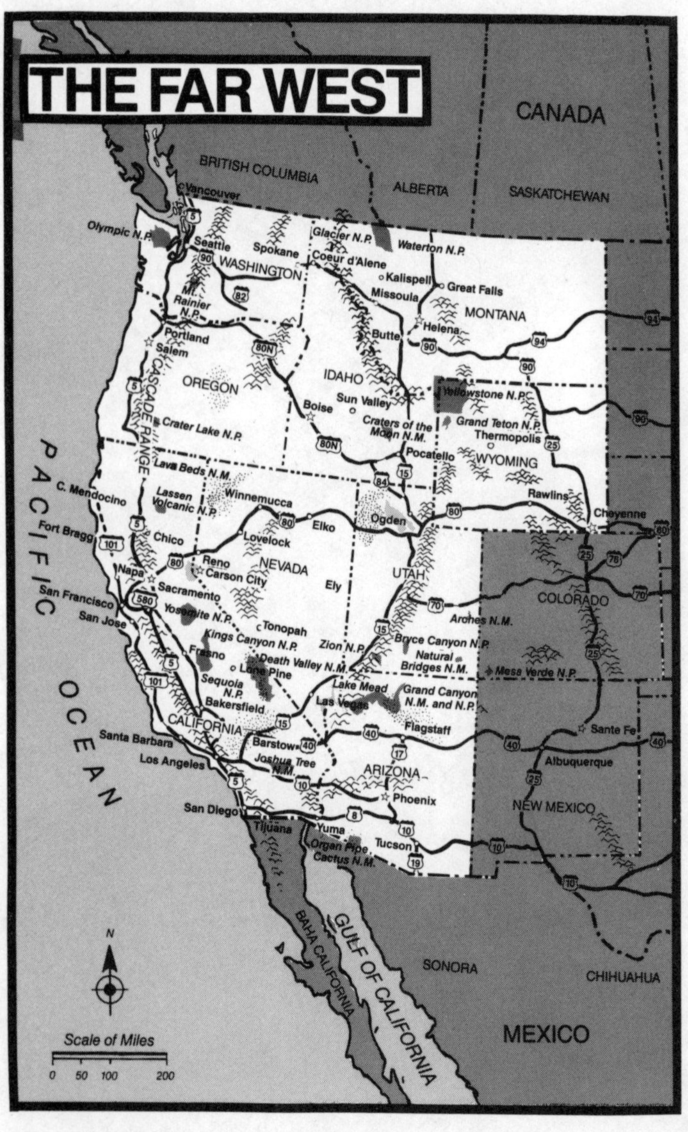

THE FAR WEST
CANADA
BRITISH COLUMBIA
ALBERTA
SASKATCHEWAN
Vancouver
Olympic N.P.
Seattle
Spokane
WASHINGTON
Glacier N.P.
Waterton N.P.
Coeur d'Alene
Kalispell
Great Falls
Missoula
Mt. Rainier N.P.
MONTANA
Helena
Butte
Portland
Salem
OREGON
CASCADE RANGE
IDAHO
Sun Valley
Boise
Yellowstone N.P.
Grand Teton N.P.
Thermopolis
Craters of the Moon N.M.
Crater Lake N.P.
Pocatello
WYOMING
PACIFIC
Lava Beds N.M.
C. Mendocino
Lassen Volcanic N.P.
Winnemucca
Rawlins
Cheyenne
Fort Bragg
Chico
Elko
Ogden
Lovelock
NEVADA
Reno
Carson City
Napa
Sacramento
Ely
UTAH
San Francisco
COLORADO
San Jose
Yosemite N.P.
Tonopah
Arches N.M.
Kings Canyon N.P.
Zion N.P.
Bryce Canyon N.P.
Fresno
Death Valley N.M.
Natural Bridges N.M.
Lone Pine
Mesa Verde N.P.
OCEAN
Sequoia N.P.
Lake Mead
Grand Canyon N.M. and N.P.
Bakersfield
Las Vegas
CALIFORNIA
Flagstaff
Santa Barbara
Barstow
Sante Fe
Los Angeles
Joshua Tree N.M.
Albuquerque
ARIZONA
Phoenix
San Diego
NEW MEXICO
Tijuana
Yuma
Tucson
Organ Pipe Cactus N.M.
GULF OF CALIFORNIA
BAHA CALIFORNIA
SONORA
CHIHUAHUA
N
MEXICO
Scale of Miles
0 50 100 200

FACTS AT YOUR FINGERTIPS

WHEN TO GO. With the Humboldt current (cold) swirling toward the south of this region, and the Japanese current (warm) nudging northern coastal strips, with America's highest, coolest mountains and its deepest, sun-sizzled valleys, the humidity and temperature readings in this region are as varied as the patterns on your grandmother's favorite patchwork quilt. Here and there sea breezes cause a temperature variance of as much as five to 15 degrees within the limits of a single city.

Southern California knows no season as far as tourism and weather are concerned. Though the first three months of the year may be cold, windy, and damp along the coast, at that time the mountain regions call hunters and skiers.

Coastal California north of Sacramento should be visited in summer, as temperatures are relatively low. California's mountains are usually cool, but its deserts are considered too hot (often over 100 degrees) for summer vacationing.

Best seasons for Oregon, Washington, and Idaho, are late spring, summer, and early fall, though ski resorts are luring more and more winter visitors. Nevada, with its many deserts, is generally considered too hot in summer but delightful from October through April.

There are travelers who find the desert areas of Utah too hot in summer, while many others revel in the region's clear, hot days—its cool, cool nights. Visitors may, of course, plan off-to-the-hills activities for the daytime hours, returning in the evening for a dip in that pool which is almost certain to be found at their hotel or motel.

From Thanksgiving to the middle of April there is some of the best skiing in the country at places like Alta and Snowbird near Salt Lake City. There is even year-round skiing on glaciers in Montana.

PLANNING YOUR TRIP. A travel agent won't cost you a cent, except for specific charges like telegrams. He gets his fee from the hotel or carrier he books for you. A travel agent can also be of help for those who prefer to take their vacations on a "package tour"—thus keeping your own planning to a minimum. If you prefer the convenience of standardized accommodations, remember that the various hotel and motel chains publish free directories of their members that enable you to plan and reserve everything ahead of time.

If you don't belong to an auto club, now is the time to join one. They can be very helpful about routings and providing emergency service on the road. Two such are: the *American Automobile Association,* 8111 Gatehouse Rd., Falls Church, VA, 22047; and the *Amoco Motor Club,* Box 9014, Des Moines, IA, 50306. In addition to its information services, the AAA has a nation-wide network of some 26,000 service stations which provide emergency repair service. The *Exxon Travel Club,* 4550 Deoma, Houston, TX 77092, provides information, low-cost insurance, and some legal services. The *National Travel Club,* 51 Atlantic Ave. Travel Building, Floral Park, NY 11001 offers information services, insurance, and tours. Some of the major oil companies will send maps and mark preferred routes on them if you tell them what you have in mind. Try: *Exxon Touring Service,* Box 3663, Houston, TX 77092; *Texaco Travel Service,* Box 538, Comfort, TX 78013. In addition, most states have their own maps, which pinpoint attractions, list historical sites, parks, etc. City chambers of commerce are also good sources of information. Specific addresses are given under *Tourist Information* in the individual state chapters. The *American Automobile Association* (AAA) offers both group personal accident insurance and bail bond protection as part of its annual membership. Today, most people who travel use credit cards for major expenses such as gas, repairs, lodgings, and some meals. Consider converting the greater portion of your trip money into travelers' checks. You might want to leave a neighbor your itinerary (insofar as possible), car license number, and a key to your home (and tell police and firemen who has it). Since some hotel and motel chains give discounts (10%–

25%) to Senior Citizens, be sure to have some sort of identification along if you qualify. Usually AARP or NRTA membership is best. (See below at the end of the hotels and motels section.)

PACKING. *What to take, what to wear.* Make a packing list for each member of the family. Then check off items as you pack them. It will save time, reduce confusion. Time-savers to carry along include extra photo film, suntan lotion, insect repellent, sufficient toothpaste, soap, etc. Always carry an extra pair of glasses, including sunglasses, particularly if they're prescription ones. A travel iron is always a good tote-along, as are some transparent plastic bags (small and large) for wet suits, socks, etc. They are also excellent for packing shoes, cosmetics, and other easily damaged items. If you fly remember that despite signs to the contrary airport security X-ray machines do in fact damage films in about 17 percent of the cases. Have them inspected separately or pack them in special protective bags. Fun extras to carry include binoculars, a compass, and a magnifying glass—useful in reading fineprint maps.

All members of the family should have sturdy shoes with nonslip soles. Keep them handy in the back of the car. Carry rain gear in a separate bag in the back of the car (so no one will have to get out and hunt for it in a downpour en route).

Women will probably want to stick to one or two basic colors for their wardrobes, so that they can manage with one set of accessories. If possible, include one knit or jersey dress or a pants suit. For dress-up evenings, take along a couple of "basic" dresses you can vary with a simple change of accessories. That way you can dress up or down to suit the occasion.

Be sure to check what temperatures will be like along the route. Traveling in mountains can mean cool evenings, even in summer—and so can traveling through the desert. An extra sweater is always a safe thing to pack, even if just to protect you from the air conditioning.

Men will probably want a jacket along for dining out, and a dress shirt and tie for formal occasions. Turtlenecks are now accepted almost everywhere and are a comfortable accessory. Don't forget extra slacks.

Planning a lot of sun time? Don't forget something to wear en route to the pool, beach, or lakefront, and for those first few days when you're getting reacquainted with sun on tender skin.

One tip for frequent motel stops along the road is to pack two suitcases—one for the final destination, and the other with items for overnight stops: pajamas, shaving gear, cosmetics, toothbrushes, fresh shirt or dress. Put the overnight luggage into the trunk last, so it can be pulled out first on overnight stops. A safety hint: Don't string your suits and dresses on hangers along a chain or rod stretched across the back seat. This obstructs vision and can cause accidents.

INSURANCE. In planning your trip, think about three kinds of insurance: property, medical, and automobile. The best person to consult about insuring your household furnishings and personal property is your insurance agent. For Americans, he is also the person to ask about whatever special adjustments might be advisable in medical coverage while traveling. Foreigners visiting the United States should bear in mind that medical expenses in this country can be astronomical compared to those elsewhere, and that the kind of protection that some countries (Britain, for example) extend not only to their own nationals but to visiting foreigners as well simply does not exist here.

Every state has some sort of Financial Responsibility law establishing minimum and maximum amounts for which you can be held liable in auto accidents. Most states require insurance to be offered, and many states require you to have it in order to register a car or get a license within their jurisdictions. In any case, it is almost essential to have third party coverage, or "liability insurance," as claims can run very high for both car repairs and, particularly, medical treatment. Insurance premiums vary according to place and person; they are generally highest for males under 25 and for drivers who live in large urban areas.

One possibility is the *American Automobile Association* (AAA), which offers both group personal accident insurance ($3,000) and bail bond protection up to $5,000 as part of its annual membership (fee $36). The AAA can also arrange the validation of foreign driving permits for use in the United States. Foreigners should consider getting their insurance before leaving their own countries since short-term tourists will find it difficult and expensive to buy here. For the AAA, write to *AAA,* 8111 Gatehouse Rd., Falls Church, VA 22047. Travel insurance is also offered by the *Exxon Travel Club,* 4550 Decoma, Houston, TX 77092; and by the *National Travel Club,* 51 Atlantic Ave., Travel Holiday, Floral Park, NY 11001. Persons over 50 who are members of NRTA/AARP may join that organization's motoring plan which offers, among other things, reimbursement for legal fees, hospital emergency room bonding, arrest bonding, and emergency breakdown service. Write to: *NRTA/AARP Motoring Plan,* 3200 E. Carson St., Lakewood, CA 90712.

Trip cancellation insurance is also available (usually from travel agents) to protect you against losing any advance payments should you have to cancel your trip at the last moment.

TIPS FOR BRITISH VISITORS. Passports. You will need a valid passport and a U.S. Visitor's Visa (which can only be put in a passport of the 10-year kind). You can obtain the visa either through your travel agent or directly from the *United States Embassy,* Visa and Immigration Department, 5 Upper Grosvenor St., London W1A 2JB (01–499 3443). Allow 4 weeks if applying to the Embassy by mail; if you apply in person, your visa can be obtained in about 3 hours.

No vaccinations are required for entry into the United States.

Customs. If you are 21 or over, you can take into the U.S.: 200 cigarettes, or 50 cigars, or 2 kilos of tobacco; 1 U.S. quart of alcohol. Everyone is entitled to take into the United States duty-free gifts to a value of $100. Be careful not to try to take in meat or meat products, seeds, plants, fruits, etc. And avoid narcotics like the plague.

Insurance. We heartily recommend that you insure yourself to cover health and motoring mishaps, with *Europ Assistance,* 252 High St., Croydon CRO INF (01–680–1234). Their excellent service is all the more valuable when you consider the possible costs of health care in the United States.

Tour Operators. The price battle that has raged over transatlantic fares has meant that most tour operators now offer excellent budget packages to the U.S. Among those you might consider as you plan your trip are:

American Airplan, Marlborough House, Churchfield Rd., Walton-on-Thames, Surrey KT12 2TJ.

Cosmos Air Holidays Ltd., 1 Bromley Common, Bromley, Kent BR2 9LX.

Intasun Holidays, Intasun House, Cromwell Ave., Bromley, Kent BR2 9AQ.

Kuoni Travel, Kuoni House, Dorking, Surrey RH5 4A2.

Speedbird, 152 King St., London W6 0QU.

Trekamerica, Trek House, The Bullring, Deddington, Oxford, Oxon OX5 4TT.

Air Fares. We suggest that you explore the current scene for budget flight possibilities, including *People Express* and *Virgin Atlantic Airways.*

Some of these cut-rate fares can be extremely difficult to come by, so be sure to book well in advance. Be sure to check on APEX and other money-saving fares, as, quite frankly, only business travelers who don't have to watch the price of their tickets fly full-price these days—and find themselves sitting right beside an APEX passenger!

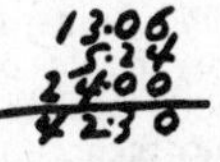

WHAT WILL IT COST? This is obviously a crucial question and one of the most difficult.

In some areas you can cut expenses by traveling off season, when hotel rates are usually lower. The budget-minded traveler can also find bargain accommodations at tourist homes or family-style YMCA's and YWCA's. Some state and federal parks also provide inexpensive lodging.

Another way to cut down on the cost of your trip is to look for out-of-the-way resorts. Travelers are frequently rewarded by discovering very attractive areas which haven't as yet begun to draw quantities of people.

If you are budgeting your trip, don't forget to set aside a realistic amount for the possible rental of sports equipment (perhaps including a boat or canoe), entrance fees to museums, amusement areas, historical sites, etc. Allow for tolls for bridges and superhighways (this can be a major item), extra film for cameras, and souvenirs.

After lodging, your next biggest expense will be food, and here you can make very substantial economies if you are willing to get along with only one meal a day (or less) in a restaurant. Plan to eat simply, and to picnic. It will save you time and money, and it will help you enjoy your trip more. That beautiful scenery does not have to whiz by at 55 miles per hour. Many states have picnic and rest areas, often well-equipped and in scenic spots, even on highways and thruways, so finding a pleasant place to stop is usually not difficult. Before you leave home put together a picnic kit.

Sturdy plastic plates and cups are cheaper in the long run than throw-away paper ones; and the same goes for permanent metal flatware rather than the throw-away plastic kind. Pack a small electric pot and two thermoses, one for water and one for milk, tea, or coffee. In other words, one hot, and one cold. If you go by car, take along a small cooler. Bread, milk, cold cereal, jam, tea or instant coffee, bouillon cubes and instant soup packets, fruit, fresh vegetables that need no cooking (such as lettuce, cucumbers, carrots, tomatoes, and mushrooms), cold cuts, cheese, nuts, raisins, eggs (hard boil them in the electric pot in your room the night before)—with only things like these you can eat conveniently, cheaply, and well.

Even in restaurants there are a number of things you can do to cut costs. 1) Order a complete dinner; a la carte *always* adds up to more. If the place doesn't have complete dinners, don't eat there. 2) If there is a salad bar, you can fill up there and save the price of dessert and/or extras. 3) Ask about smaller portions, at reduced prices, for children. More and more places are providing them now. 4) Go to a Chinese restaurant and order *one less* main dish than the number of people in your group. You'll still come away pleasantly full. 5) Always stop at the cash register and look over the menu *before* you sit down. 6) Ask for the Day's Special, the House Special, Chef's Special, or whatever it's called. Chances are that it will be better and more abundant than the other things on the menu. 7) Remember that in better restaurants lunch may be more of a bargain than dinner.

If you like a drink before dinner or bed, bring your own bottle. Most hotels and motels supply ice free or for very little, but the markup on alcoholic beverages in restaurants, bars, lounges and dining rooms is enormous, and in some states peculiar laws apply regarding alcohol consumption. And in any case, a good domestic dry white wine makes a fine aperitif and can be far cheaper than a cocktail.

HINTS TO THE MOTORIST. Probably the first precaution you will take is to have your car thoroughly checked by your regular dealer or service station to make sure that everything is in good shape. Second, you may find it wise to join an auto club that can provide you with trip planning information, insurance coverage, and emergency and repair service along the way. Third, if you do find yourself in need of repairs on the road, consider hunting up a mechanic certified by the National Institute for Automotive Service Excellence. They test mechanics' competence regularly.

Shortly after you pass the ranger station a brief distance inside the comparatively new Canyonlands National Park in southern Utah, you encounter a sign, stuck in the sand. It reads: "Four-wheel drive vehicles only beyond this point." This is wild, rugged country, where you follow routes, not roads, through shifting sand, up trickling stream beds which can turn into raging torrents during a sudden storm, where the wheels of even four-wheel drive vehicles can sink hopelessly into the sand if they don't move along briskly, and where you climb a 27-degree face of sheer rock as part of getting over Elephant Hill. The Rockies and Plains area is the country of the Badlands of North and South Dakota, the mule-riding country of the Grand Canyon, the country of towering mountains interspersed with the broad flat spaces of the Plains—an area where, off the well-traveled, well-kept main roads, the motorist can have virtually any driving experience he cares to meet.

DESERT DRIVING

You will encounter long stretches of desert driving in the southern portions of this area. Better cars, better roads, and more service facilities make desert driving less a hazard than it once was. A principal point to check before crossing the hot desert is your tires. Put them at normal driving pressure or slightly below. Heat builds pressure. If your car seems to be bouncing too readily, stop to let your tires cool. If you have a good radiator, don't worry about extra water, but keep an eye on the water gauge. Be alert for sudden sandstorms and rainstorms. If you have a car radio, keep it tuned to local stations for information about unusual road conditions. In spite of its dryness, the desert, in a flash flood, can become a death trap. In sandstorms, pull off the road and wait it out.

MOUNTAIN DRIVING

Unless you venture onto exotic mountain roads, you should have little trouble with mountain driving. Today's mountain roads are engineered for the ordinary driver. They are normally wide, well graded, and safe. Be especially wary of exceeding the speed limits posted for curves. Keep to the right. If your normal driving is at low altitudes, have a garage mechanic check your carburetor. It may need adjusting for mountain driving. Use your motor for downhill runs, second or low gear to save your brakes. If your car stalls, and your temperature gauge is high, it could mean a vapor lock. Bathe the fuel pump with a damp cloth for a few minutes.

If you get stuck on any kind of road, pull off the highway onto the shoulder, raise the hood, attach something white (a handkerchief, scarf, or a piece of tissue) to the door handle on the driver's side, and sit inside and wait. This is especially effective on limited-access highways, usually patrolled vigilantly by state highway officers. A special warning to women stalled at night: Remain inside with the doors locked, and make sure the Good Samaritan is indeed what he seems. It is easier to find telephones along the major highways these days, since their locations are more frequently marked than they used to be. If you're a member of an automobile club, call the nearest garage listed in your emergency directory. Or ask the operator for help.

FAR WEST BY TRAIN. *Amtrak* is the semi-governmental corporation that has taken over passenger service on most of the nation's railroads. At present the system has some 26,000 miles of track linking over 500 cities and towns in 44 states (except Maine, New Hampshire, Oklahoma, South Dakota, Alaska, and Hawaii). Amtrak's equipment, at best, is among the most modern and comfortable anywhere in the world; not all of the equipment is up to this standard, however; and the condition of the tracks and the adequacy of the auxiliary services (stations, meals, punctuality, etc.) is highly uneven. On medium and longer runs the advantages of rail travel are in the spaciousness of the cars (against the cramped immobility of bus and plane) and the chance to enjoy the changing American landscape.

The simplest train accommodation is the day coach. There you ride in reclining seats, which may be reserved, with ample leg room, never more than two abreast. Next up is the leg-rest coach with (of course) leg rests, head rests, and deeper cushioning for the simplest kind of long distance nighttime accommodation. Slumber-coaches have lounge seats that convert into either a single bed or upper berths at night. For more space and privacy, a roomette gives a sitting room by day and at night a sleeping room with a full-length bed, and private toilet facilities. Bedrooms have two separate sleeping berths and private washing and toilet facilities. Superliner cars, operating between Chicago and the West Coast, also have family bedrooms that can sleep up to two adults and two children. Other types of special cars include dining cars, of course, and tavern lounges—an informal setting for a quiet drink, a game of cards, or just conversation. Some trains, especially where the scenery is best, have dome lounge cars, which give a great view of the countryside through high glass domes.

Amtrak serves most major cities in the far west and offers passengers a number of vacation packages which may include meals, siteseeing excursions, hotel accommodations and even car rental at your final destination. If you contact Amtrak with a rough itinerary a tour desk representative can help design a package that suits your needs. During the summer months escorted tours of the western states are also offered, particularly popular are those covering the Grand Canyon and the national parks.

The reservation system is computerized and operates nationwide. Call 800–USA–RAIL. Amtrak has about 75 different package tours in addition to its regularly scheduled service. The tours may include hotels, meals, sightseeing, even tickets to Broadway shows. Write to *Amtrak,* Western Folder Distribution Co., Box 7717, 1549 Glen Lake Ave., Itasca, IL 60413, for brochures on the package tours available in the part of the country to which you are traveling.

Senior citizens, handicapped travelers, and families should inquire about discounts.

TRAVELING WITH PETS. Traveling by car with your pet dog or cat? More and more motels accept them but be sure to check before you register. Some turn them down, some want to look first, some offer special facilities. If it's a first-time trip for your pet, accustom it to car travel by short trips in your neighborhood. And when you're packing, include its favorite food, bowls, and toys. Discourage your dog from riding with its head out the window. Wind and dust particles can permanently damage its eyes. Don't leave your pet in a parked car on a hot day while you dawdle over lunch. Keep his bowl handy for water during stops for gas; gasoline attendants are usually very cooperative about this. Make sure your pet exercises periodically; this is a good way for you and the kids to unwind from long stretches of unbroken traveling, too.

ACCOMMODATIONS. *General Hints.* Don't be one of those who take potluck for lodgings. You'll waste a lot of time hunting for a place, and often won't be happy with the accommodations you finally find. If you are without reservations, by all means begin looking early in the afternoon. If you have reservations, but expect to arrive later than five or six P.M., advise the hotel or motel in advance. Some places will not, unless advised, hold reservations after six P.M. And if you hope to get a room at the hotel's *minimum* rate be sure to reserve ahead or arrive very early.

If you are planning to stay in a popular resort region, at the height of the season, reserve well in advance. Include a deposit for all places except motels (and for motels if they request one). Many chain or associated motels and hotels will make advance reservations for you at affiliated hostelries along your route.

A number of hotels and motels have one-day laundry and dry-cleaning services, and many motels have coin laundries. Most motels, but not all, have telephones in the rooms. If you want to be sure of room service, however, better stay at a hotel. Many motels have swimming pools, and even beachfront hotels frequently have a pool. Even some motels in the heart of large cities have pools. An advantage at motels is the free parking. There's seldom a charge for parking at country and resort hotels.

Hotel and motel chains. In addition to the hundreds of excellent independent motels and hotels throughout the country, there are also many that belong to national or regional chains. A major advantage of the chains, to many travelers, is the ease of making reservations en route, or at one fell swoop in advance. If you are a guest at a member hotel or motel, the management will be delighted to secure you a sure booking at one of its affiliated hotels for the coming evening at no cost to you. Chains also usually have toll-free WATS (800) lines to assist you in making reservations on your own. This, of course, saves you time, worry, and money. In some chains, you have the added advantage of knowing what the standards are all the way. The insistence on uniform standards of comfort, cleanliness, and amenities is more common in motel than in hotel chains.

However, many travelers prefer independent motels and hotels because they are more likely to reflect the character of the surrounding area. There are several aids to planning available in this sphere. *The Hotel and Motel Redbook,* published annually by the American Hotel and Motel Association, 888 Seventh Avenue, New York City, NY 10019, covers all of North America and sells for around $60.00. *Hotel and Travel Index,* published quarterly by Ziff-Davis, sells for about $35.00. These are probably best consulted at your travel agent's office. On a more modest scale, the AAA supplies, *to its members only,* regional *Tour Books* that list those establishments recommended by the Association.

The main national motel chains are Holiday Inn, Howard Johnson's, Quality Hotels, Ramada Inns, Sheraton Motor Inns, and TraveLodge. Alongside the style that these places represent, however, are others, less luxurious and less costly. Here are some national chains and their toll-free numbers: Comfort Inn/Quality Hotel (800–228–5050), Days Inn (800–325–2525), Econo Lodge (800–446–6900), Holiday Inn (800–HOL–IDAY), Howard Johnson (800–654–2000), La Quinta (800–531–5900), Quality International (800–228–5151), Ramada (800–228–9898), Super 8 (800–843–1991), and TraveLodge (800–255–3050).

Prices in the budget chains are fairly uniform, but this is not the case in chains such as Ramada, Quality, Holiday Inns, Howard Johnson's and TraveLodge. Their prices vary widely by region, location, and season. Among the national non-budget chains the most expensive are Hilton, Marriott, and Sheraton; the middle range includes Holiday Inns, Howard Johnson, Quality Inns, and TraveLodge; and the least expensive are usually Best Western, Ramada, and Rodeway (mainly in the South).

Price Categories. Hotels and motels in all chapters are divided into five categories, based on the average cost of a double room. Although the names of the various hotel and motel categories are standard throughout, the prices listed under each category may vary from area to area. This variance is meant to reflect local price standards, and take into account that what might be considered a *moderate* price in a large urban area might be quite *expensive* in a rural region. In every case, however, the dollar ranges for each category are clearly stated before each listing of establishments.

Free parking is assumed at all motels and motor hotels; you must pay for parking at most city hotels, though certain establishments have free parking, frequently for occupants of higher-than-minimum-rate rooms. *Baby sitter* lists are always available in good hotels and motels, and *cribs* for the children are always on hand—sometimes at no cost, but more frequently at a cost of $1 or $2 per night. The cost of a *cot* in your room, to supplement the beds, is around $3 per night, but moving and *extra single bed* into a room costs around $7 in better hotels and motels.

Senior citizens may in some cases receive special discounts on lodgings. The Days Inn chain offers various discounts to anyone 55 or older. Holiday Inns give a discount to members of the NRTA (write to National Retired Teachers Association, Membership Division, 3200 East Carson St., Lakewood, CA 90712) and the AARP (write to American Association of Retired Persons, Membership Division, 3200 East Carson St., Lakewood, CA 90712). Members of the AARP, the NRTA, the National Association of Retired Persons, The Catholic Golden Age of United Societies of U.S.A., and the Old Age Security Pensioners of Canada, and similar organizations benefit increasingly from a number of discounts, but the amounts, sources, and availability of these change, so it is best to check with either your organization or the hotel, motel, or restaurant chain you plan to use. The *National Council of Senior Citizens,* 925 15th St. N.W., Washington, DC 20005, 202–347–8800, works especially to develop low-cost travel possibilities for its members.

The bed-and-breakfast, a mainstay of European travel, is fast becoming a popular alternative for U.S. travelers as well. Most are private homes and apartments or small guest houses that have one or more rooms available, usually with shared bath, on a nightly basis. Breakfast, as might be expected, is included in the charge. The quality of accommodations and the range of prices vary widely, but at least one national and many regional organizations exist to help tourists sort out the type of lodging they want.

Bed & Breakfast Registry, Box 8174, St. Paul, MN 55108; 612–646–4238. This is a reservation service covering North America. Prices range from $22–$150 per night, with the Registry requiring the first night's rate plus $10 per room/night deposit. The deposit is refundable if the traveler is not satisfied with the accommodations after inspection, or if cancellation is made 7 days in advance. Also worth contacting is the *American B & B Association,* Box 23294, Washington, D.C. 20026; 703–237–9777. Their publication *A Treasury of Bed and Breakfasts,* available for $14.95 plus $3 postage and handling, lists over 3,000 establishments in the U.S.A. and Canada. They also operate the Evergreen B & B Club for over fifties. Those with rooms to let might consider joining *InnTer Lodging Co-op,* Box 7044, Tacoma Washington 94807; 206–756–0343. InnTer Lodging is a network of bed-and-breakfasts (alas, often without the breakfasts). You pay $45 to be listed in a directory, agree to accept guests for three months out of the year, and you are entitled to guest privileges for $4–$5 per night in the homes of other registrants. The network covers most of the U.S., Canada, and parts of Europe. *Sweet Dreams & Toast, Inc.,* Box 4835–0035, Washington, D.C. 20008; 202–483–9191. This service provides current listings of local B & B networks by state for $3.00.

Fodor's Bed & Breakfast Guide gives a close look at 750 of the best B&Bs on the continent, with a generous sampling of fine lodgings in the Western states. It is available at most bookstores and from Fodor's Travel Publications, Inc. 201 E. 50th St., New York, NY 10022. Periodically updated directories of bed-and-breakfast establishments include: *Bed & Breakfast International,* 151 Ardmore Rd., Kensington, CA 94707, (415) 525–4569; *Bed & Breakfast Homes Directory for the West Coast,* by Diane Knight, Knightime Publications, Box 591, Cupertino, CA 95015; *Bed & Breakfast U.S.A.,* by Betty Rundback and Nancy Ackerman, E.P. Dutton, 2 Park Ave., New York, NY 10016; and *Bed & Breakfast American Style,* by Norman T. Simpson, Berkshire Traveller Press, Pine St. Stockbridge, MA 01262. Always call ahead to make sure the home you've selected is still open to guests, to insure availability of a room and to find out if references or deposits are required.

In larger towns and cities a good bet for clean, plain, reliable lodging is a YMCA or YWCA. These buildings are usually centrally located, and their rates tend to run to less than half of those of hotels. Nonmembers are welcome, but may pay slightly more than members. A few very large Ys may have accommodations for couples but usually sexes are segregated. Decor is spartan and the cafeteria fare plain and wholesome, but a definite advantage is the use of the building's pool, gym, reading room, information services, and other facilities. For a directory, write to YMCA of the USA, 356 W. 34th St., New York, NY 10001; and the National Board of the YWCA, 726 Broadway, New York, NY 10003.

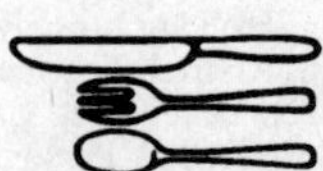

RESTAURANTS. For evening dining, the best advice is to make reservations whenever possible. Most hotels and farm-vacation places have set dining hours. For motel stayers, life is simpler if the motel has a restaurant. If it hasn't, try to stay at one that is near a restaurant.

Some restaurants are fussy about customers' dress, particularly in the evening. For women, pants and pants suits are now almost universally acceptable. For men, tie and jacket remains the standard. Shorts are almost always frowned on for both men and women. Standards of dress are becoming more relaxed, so a neatly dressed customer will usually experience no problem. If in doubt about accepted dress at a particular establishment, call ahead.

Roadside stands, turnpike restaurants, and cafeterias have no fixed standards of dress.

If you're traveling with children, you may want to find out if a restaurant has a children's menu and commensurate prices (many do).

When figuring the tip on your check, base it on the total charges for the meal, not on the grand total, if that total includes a sales tax. Don't tip on tax.

Price Categories. Restaurants are divided into price categories as follows: *super deluxe, deluxe, expensive, moderate,* and *inexpensive.* As a general rule, expect restaurants in metropolitan areas to be higher in price, but many restaurants that feature foreign cuisine are surprisingly inexpensive. We should also point out that limitations of space make it impossible to include every establishment. We have, therefore, listed those which we recommend as the best within each price range. Although the names of the various restaurant categories are standard throughout this series, the prices listed under each category may vary from area to area. This variation is meant to reflect local price standards and take into account that what might be considered a *moderate* price in a large urban area might be quite *expensive* in a rural region. In every case, however, the dollar ranges for each category are clearly stated before each listing of establishments.

LIQUOR LAWS. In all but one of the United States, you must be at least 21 to buy or drink alcoholic beverages. In Wyoming, the legal drinking age is 19. Specific laws governing drinking and the sale of package goods are listed in the Practical Information section for each state.

TIME ZONES. Time zones do not follow state lines throughout the Rockies and Plains states. All of Montana, Wyoming, and Colorado are on Mountain Time, as are the western halves of South Dakota and Nebraska. All of North Dakota and the eastern halves of South Dakota and Nebraska are on Central Time. In Utah, the western third is on Pacific Time and the rest on Mountain Time.

SUMMER SPORTS. *Swimming* is invigorating in many of the lakes and reservoirs and relaxing in the hot springs pools in Wyoming, Montana, Colorado, and South Dakota. The Great Salt Lake offers something quite different, salt water that is more buoyant than the oceans. Water skiing and sailing are popular on the larger lakes. Sailing is available on the lakes created by the many dams and on some reservoirs as well.

The many rivers and streams offer exciting possibilities for *canoeing, kayaking,* and *rafting.*

The Rocky Mountains offer ample opportunity for *hiking, backpacking,* and *mountain climbing* or *horseback riding.* Many areas are accessible only on foot or by horse.

Fishing in this area is very popular and the system of waterways quite extensive; whether your pleasure is fly fishing the rivers and streams for trout or fishing the lakes for the larger walleye, bass, and northern pike, you're certain of great sport and much excitement.

In light of this area's western frontier heritage, it's not surprising that *rodeo* is the most pervasive of the spectator sports throughout this region. In general the season runs from late spring into early fall; whether it takes place in Nebraska, where rodeo was born, in Wyoming, where Frontier Days attracts national champions, or at a small county fair, it's sure to be action-packed.

There are many fine *golf* courses throughout the area, such as the splendid layout at Jackson Hole in Wyoming. *Tennis* is also a popular sport, and courts are found at virtually every major resort or urban area.

WINTER SPORTS. *Skiing* is without a doubt the major winter sport of this area. New areas continue to be developed throughout the Rocky Mountains, especially Aspen and Vail in Colorado, and near Salt Lake City in Utah. Cross-country skiing, or *ski touring,* is becoming increasingly popular as both a means of escape from the cost of lift tickets and the ever-longer lift lines, and also as a means of enjoying the breathtaking scenery.

Each year, *snowmobiling* attracts more and more people who enjoy the thrill of speeding along snow-covered mountain trails or over open meadows. Many areas have organized rallies and races.

Ice skating on frozen lakes and ponds, or in year-round rinks, also has its share of enthusiasts.

Hunting for deer, antelope, elk, moose, and even bear brings hunters from all over into this area. There are also seasons for waterfowl, pheasant, quail, partridge, and grouse. In some cases, nonresidents are permitted to hunt the less populous of these species only with bow and arrows.

ROUGHING IT. More, and improved, camping facilities are springing up each year across the country, in national parks, national forests, state parks, in private camping areas, and trailer parks, which by now have become national institutions. Farm vacations continue to gain adherents, especially among families with children. Some accommodations are quite deluxe, some extremely simple. Here and there a farm has a swimming pool, while others have facilities for trailers and camping. For a directory of farms which take vacationers (including details of rates, accommodations, dates, etc.), write to *Adventure Guides, Inc.,* 36 East 57 Street, New York, NY 10022, for their 224-page book *Farm, Ranch, & Country Vacations,* $12.00.

Because of the great size of the United States and the distances involved, youth hostels have not developed in this country the way they have in Europe and Japan. In the entire 3½ million square miles of the U.S. there are upwards of 200 youth hostels and because they are, in any case, designed primarily for people who are traveling under their own power, usually hiking or bicycling, rather than by car or commercial transportation, they tend to be away from towns and cities and in rural areas, near scenic spots. In the U.S. they are most common and practical in compact areas like New England. Although their members are mainly younger people, there is no age limit. You must be a member to use youth hostels; write to *American Youth Hostels, Inc.,* Box 37613, Washington, DC 20013–7613. A copy of the Hostel Guide and Handbook will be included in your membership. Accommodations are simple, dormitories are segregated by sex, common rooms and kitchen are shared, and everyone helps with the cleanup. Lights out 11 P.M. to 7 A.M., no alcohol or other drugs allowed. Membership fees: ages 18–65, $20; over 65 or under 18, $10; family-$30. Hostel rates vary from about $4 to $10. In season it is wise to reserve ahead; write or phone to the particular hostel you plan to stay in.

Useful Addresses: *National Parks Service,* U.S. Dept. of the Interior, Washington, D.C. 20240; *National Forest Service,* Box 2417, U.S. Dept. of Agriculture, Washington, D.C. 20013. For information on state parks, write *State Parks Dept., State Office Building* in the capitol of the state in which you are interested.

The National Campers & Hikers Assoc., 7172 Transit Rd., Buffalo, NY 14221. Commercial camping organizations include *American Camping Assoc., Inc.,* Bradford Woods, Martinsville, IN 46151. Also *Kampgrounds of America, Inc. (KOA),* Box 30558, Billings, MT 59114.

TIPPING. Tipping is supposed to be a personal thing, your way of expressing your appreciation of someone who has taken pleasure and pride in giving you attentive, efficient, and personal service. Because standards of personal service in the United States are highly uneven, you should, when you get genuinely good service, feel secure in rewarding it, and when you feel that the service you got was slovenly, indifferent, or surly, don't hesitate to show this by the size, or withholding, of your tip. Remember that in many places the help are paid very little and depend on tips for the better part of their income. This is supposed to give them incentive to serve you well. These days, the going rate for tipping on *restaurant* service is 15% on the amount *before* taxes. Tipping at counters is not universal, but many people leave $0.25 on anything up to $1, and 10% on anything over that. For *bellboys,* 50¢ per bag is usual. However, if you load him down with all manner of bags, hatboxes, cameras, coats, etc., you might consider giving an extra quarter or two. For one-night stays in most *hotels* and *motels,* you leave nothing. But if you stay longer, at the end of your stay leave the maid $1–$1.50 per day, or $5 per person per week for multiple occupancy. If you are staying at an *American Plan* hostelry (meals included),

$2–3 per day per person for the waiter or waitress is considered sufficient, and is left at the end of your stay. If you have been surrounded by an army of servants (one bringing relishes, another rolls, etc.), add a few extra dollars and give the lump sum to the captain or *maître d'hôtel* when you leave, asking him to allocate it.

For the many other services you may encounter in a big hotel or resort, figure roughly as follows: doorman, 50¢ for taxi handling, $1 for help with baggage; bellhop, 50¢ per bag, more if you load him down with extras; parking attendant, $1; bartender, 15%; room service, 10–15% of that bill; laundry or valet service, 15%; pool attendant, 50¢ per day; snackbar waiter at pool, beach, or golf club, 50¢ per person for food and 15% of the beverage check; locker attendant, 50¢ per person per day, or $2.50 per week; masseur or masseuse 20% of the bill; golf caddies, $1–$2 per bag, or 15% of the greens fee for an 18-hole course, or $3 on a free course; masseurs and masseuses, 20%; barbers, $1; shoeshine attendants, 50¢; hairdressers, $2; manicurists, $1.

Transportation. Give 25¢ for any taxi fare under $1 and 15% for any above; however, drivers in New York, Las Vegas, and other major resorts *expect* 20%. Limousine service, 20%. Car rental agencies, nothing. Bus porters are tipped 50¢ per bag, drivers nothing. On charters and package tours, conductors and drivers usually get $10 per day from the group as a whole, but be sure to ask whether this has already been figured into the package cost. On short local sightseeing runs, the driver-guide may get 50¢–$1 per person, more if you think he has been especially helpful or personable. Airport bus drivers, nothing. Redcaps, in resort areas, 50¢ per suitcase, elsewhere, 25¢. Tipping at curbside check-in is unofficial, but same as above. On the plane, no tipping.

Railroads suggest you leave 10–15% per meal for dining car waiters, but the steward who seats you is not tipped. Sleeping-car porters get about $1 per person per night. The fee you pay a railway station baggage porter is not a tip but the set fee that he must hand in at the end of the day along with the ticket stubs he has used. Therefore his tip is anything you give him above that, 25–50¢ per bag, depending on how heavy your luggage is.

HINTS TO HANDICAPPED TRAVELERS. One of the newest, and largest, groups to enter the travel scene is the handicapped, literally millions of people who are in fact physically able to travel and who do so enthusiastically when they know that they can move about in safety and comfort. Generally their tours parallel those of the nonhandicapped traveler, but at a more leisurely pace, and with all the logistics carefully checked out in advance.

Louise Weiss's *Access to the World: A Travel Guide for the Handicapped,* published by Henry Holt & Co., New York, gives valuable information about facilities for the handicapped. It can be ordered only through your local bookstore; the company will not accept orders from individuals. Two other important resources are: 1) the *Travel Information Center,* Moss Rehabilitation Hospital, 12th St. and Tabor Rd., Philadelphia, PA 19141; and 2) *Easter Seal Society for Crippled Children and Adults,* Director of Information and Education Service, 2023 West Ogden Ave., Chicago, IL 60612. In Britain, there are *Mobility International,* 62 Union St., London SE1 (01–403 5688); and *The Royal Association for Disability and Rehabilitation,* 25 Mortimer St., London W1 (01–637 5400).

The President's Commission on Employment of the Handicapped, along with the Easter Seal Society, has put together a series of guide books for every major city in the United States and a special book called *Guide to the National Parks and Monuments.* Each book lists only those places that are reasonably accessible to the handicapped or are so well known that information is frequently requested. The Commission has also issued a guide to over 330 roadside rest-area facilities considered "barrier free" for the disabled. Write to the Commission at Washington, DC 20210.

Lists of commercial tour operators who arrange or conduct tours for the handicapped are available from the *Society for the Advancement of Travel for the Handicapped,* International Office, 26 Court St., Suite 1110, Brooklyn, NY 11242. The Greyhound Bus system has special assistance for handicapped travelers. International Air Transport Association (IATA) publishes a free pamphlet entitled *Incapacitated Passengers' Air Travel Guide.* Write IATA, 2000 Peel St., Montreal, Quebec H3A 2R4. For a copy of the *Handicapped Driver's Mobility Guide,* contact your local AAA club (95 cents, ask for Stock No. 3772).

The Itinerary, which bills itself as "the magazine for travelers with physical disabilities," is published bimonthly by Whole Person Tours. Useful articles describe accessible destinations and devices that aid travel. Subscriptions cost $7 a year. Write Box 1084, Bayonne, NJ 07002.

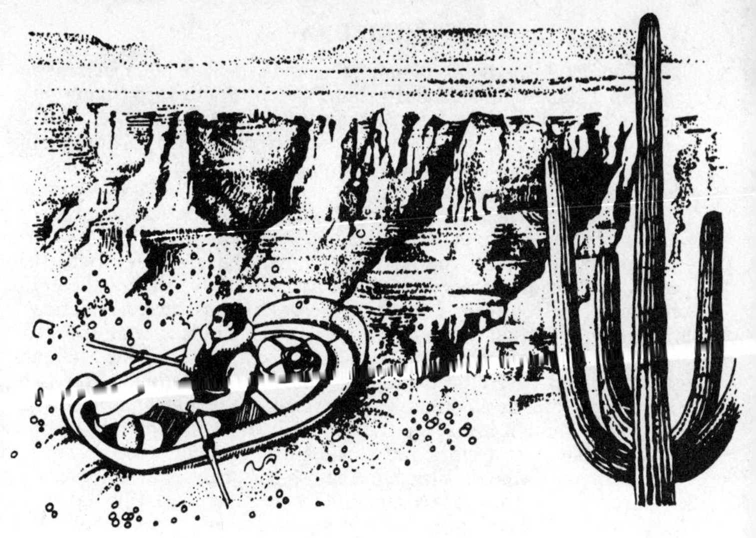

ARIZONA

Fun on the Range

by
RUTH ARMSTRONG

Ruth Armstrong, who writes about all of the West, has written travel articles for newspapers and magazines as well as several books.

To most travelers Arizona is a question mark, a contradiction, a study in contrasts. They know it is a winter vacation spot, they know about Phoenix and Tucson, but the rest remains pretty much a mystery. It is, indeed, a land of contrasts: desert and mountains, cactus and wild columbine, sand dunes and ski slopes, sparkling modern cities and ancient Indian ruins, home of the respected national statesman, Barry Goldwater, and the locale of the famous film shootout at a well-known corral. It is as new as space-age industry and as old as the Grand Canyon, as up-to-date as a sophisticated Scottsdale, and as down-home as a ranch near Wilcox.

Here, within some 114,000 square miles of the nation's sixth largest state, is a virtual magician's box of visual wonders created by man and nature. Across the northern part of the state, high plateaus and mountains reaching twelve thousand feet look down on gorges where rock formations dwarf some New York skyscrapers. Mesas and buttes like those of Monument Valley sometimes resemble a surrealist's dream.

Thick, graceful woodlands of pines, firs, and aspen are but a jack rabbit jog from eroded badlands and painted desert. Southward, mountains and plateaus rise above forests, rangelands, and canyons. Even the desert is patched with swaths of emerald, irrigated farms. Throughout the regions, sights change and intermingle like patterns in a kaleidoscope: ghost towns, open-pit copper mines, Indian villages, Spanish missions, dam-formed lakes, trading posts, former frontier forts, world-famous resorts, and much, much more.

Throughout history, the land and climate have affected both the people and the area's development. From the 12th through the 14th centuries, the Hohokam Indians of the desert constructed America's first known irrigation canals to bring water to their fields. Many of their original ditches formed the pattern for current Valley of the Sun and other irrigated desert farm projects. Indeed, even today, water is a controlling factor in the state's economy. For where one finds adequate water, even though it may be transported many miles by canals, one also finds the biggest cities and greatest development.

Three main elements—Indian, Spanish-Mexican, and American—run through the story of Arizona, influencing the present just as they did in the past. The longest, extending back to prehistoric days, has been that of the Indians. Most dynamic has been the American, particularly in its many present forms.

Because of the findings at Ventana Cave, northwest of Tucson, archaeologists believe that human beings have resided in what is now Arizona for at least ten thousand years and possibly twenty thousand years or longer. This site, however, is the exception. The majority of excavated sites are ancient, providing a rich and varied Indian background and stretching from prehistoric Basket Maker cultures through the Great Pueblo period to the Hohokam era before coming into the time of recorded history, when the Spaniards arrived.

The most memorable reminders of these ancient cultures come from the Hohokam and Pueblo days, which lasted from about 800 to 1500 A.D. They can be seen in cliff dwellings and other ruins in national monuments like Navajo, Wupatki, Walnut Canyon, Tuzigoot, Montezuma Castle, Tonto, and Casa Grande. Numerous museums, in addition to those at these monuments, feature a wide variety of artifacts from all the ages. The three foremost showplaces of this type are the Museum of Northern Arizona in Flagstaff, the Heard Museum in Phoenix, and the Arizona State Museum on the University of Arizona campus in Tucson.

Arizona's Indian Heritage

Beginning at the end of the last Ice Age, at least 10,000 years ago, prehistoric Indians lived in what is now Arizona. They were the descendants of early hunters who followed mammoths, mastadons, and bison across the tundra down from the Bering Strait. They learned to gather wild grains and fruits to supplement their meat diet. Slowly through the centuries they learned that seeds, when planted and watered by rain, would sprout and produce, eliminating the need always to be on the move. Thus was born the first agricultural society in North America, and in the Southwest.

By the beginning of A.D. they had developed into several distinct cultures, primarily thc Hohokams in central and southern Arizona, the Anasazi in northern Arizona and northwestern New Mexico, the Sina-

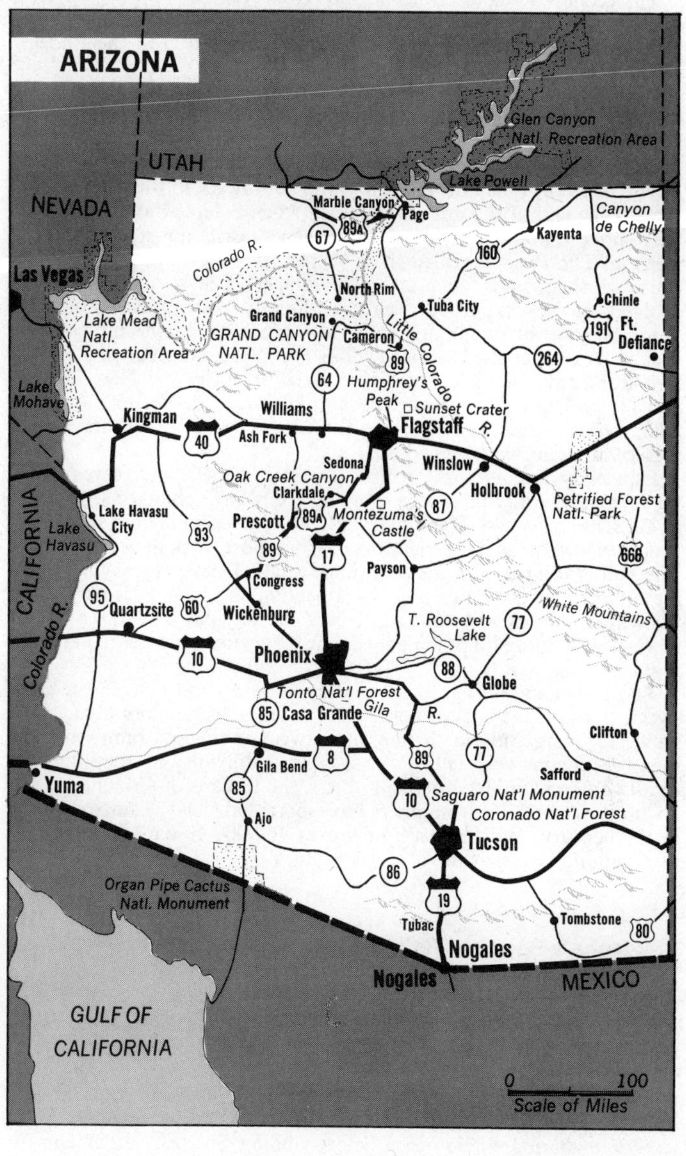
ARIZONA
UTAH
NEVADA
Glen Canyon
Natl. Recreation Area
Lake Powell
Marble Canyon
Page
Canyon de Chelly
Kayenta
Colorado R.
Las Vegas
North Rim
Tuba City
Chinle
Lake Mead Natl. Recreation Area
Grand Canyon
GRAND CANYON NATL. PARK
Cameron
Little Colorado R.
Ft. Defiance
Lake Mohave
Humphrey's Peak
Sunset Crater
Williams
Kingman
Ash Fork
Flagstaff
Sedona
Winslow
Oak Creek Canyon
Clarkdale
Holbrook
Petrified Forest Natl. Park
Lake Havasu City
Lake Havasu
Prescott
Montezuma's Castle
CALIFORNIA
Payson
Congress
Quartzsite
Wickenburg
White Mountains
T. Roosevelt Lake
Colorado R.
Phoenix
Globe
Tonto Nat'l Forest
Gila R.
Casa Grande
Clifton
Gila Bend
Safford
Yuma
Saguaro Nat'l Monument
Coronado Nat'l Forest
Ajo
Tucson
Organ Pipe Cactus Natl. Monument
Tombstone
Tubac
Nogales
Nogales
MEXICO
GULF OF CALIFORNIA
0 100
Scale of Miles

gua and the Salado in south-central Arizona, and the Mogollon in southeast Arizona.

The Indians along the Gila and Salt rivers near Phoenix dug a system of irrigation ditches used later by 19th-century homesteaders, and which, in fact, are still the major source of irrigation in the Phoenix valley.

Pueblo Indians of Arizona are scattered from the Hopi villages in the north to the Havasupais along the Colorado River in the west, to the Pimas and Papagos in the south. Except for the Hopis, most of the Anasazi migrated toward the Rio Grande in New Mexico.

The peaceful Pueblo Indians had the Southwest to themselves until toward the end of the fifteenth century when a fierce, nomadic people who spoke the Athabascan tongue began to drift down from central Canada. The Pueblos called them "Apaches," meaning "enemy," because of their raids on crops and villages. The nomads gradually evolved into several groups, scattered loosely over hundreds of thousands of acres of mountains and plains. In Arizona the largest tribe became known as the Navajos. Today their reservation covers 16 million acres, two-thirds of which is in Arizona, a third in New Mexico, and a bit in Utah. Other groups became known as the Western Apaches who, today, occupy the adjoining San Carlos and Fort Apache Indian Reservations in west-central Arizona.

Especially among the Pueblos, customs, beliefs, and ceremonials became deeply ingrained and in many cases have changed little from a thousand years ago. The Pimas and Papagos near Phoenix still weave beautiful baskets as their ancestors did, but most work in nearby towns. The Hopis still perform the traditional Snake Dance atop a high bleak mesa, but they also value modern education and have adapted well to the white man's world. And while Navajos may pay a visit to a doctor in a hospital, they still prefer a medicine man when it comes to performing a healing chant.

The Indians are often torn between tradition and convenience, between their old ways and the new ones. The schism is not always just between young and old. It may be between individual family or clan members, or between entire clans. Despite difficulty in adapting to a totally different civilization from theirs, the Indians of Arizona are not a vanishing race. Their numbers have increased steadily since the turn of the century, and there are now over 160,000 Indians living on 17 reservations in Arizona.

Arizona's Spanish Heritage

The first person of European descent to set foot in what is now Arizona was a Franciscan padre, Fray Marcos de Niza, in 1539, an advance scout for the Coronado Expedition that followed the next year. They were looking for the Seven Cities of Cibola, where gold grew on trees according to stories passed on by four shipwrecked Spaniards who had wandered across the deserts of southern Texas and northern Mexico for eight incredible years before finding Spanish settlements in Mexico. Coronado and several later exploring parties failed to find gold, but they did find a well-established civilization along the Rio Grande in New Mexico, where people lived in great communal four- and five-story houses and cultivated fields of corn, beans, and squash. They established a Spanish colony in New Mexico in 1598, but no permanent settlements were made in Arizona for more than a hundred years.

Most notable of the Arizona colonizers was the tireless trekker Father Eusebio Francisco Kino, a Jesuit born in Trent, Austria. In twenty-four years of service, up to his death in 1711, he founded two dozen missions in northern Mexico and southern Arizona. The greatest remaining monuments to his efforts are the missions of San Xavier del Bac, still in use near Tucson, and Tumacacori, whose battered and partially restored ruins are now part of a national monument north of Nogales.

The first permanent settlement came with the founding of the Spanish presidio at Tubac in 1752. Tubac was a community destined in its vicissitudes to make even the proverbial cat with nine lives an envious creature. The presidio, however, was removed to Tucson in 1776, and what was to become Arizona's second largest city began its life.

Americanizing the Great West

Spain's hold on the area lasted until 1821 when Mexico won its independence from the mother country. Mexico's grip was even less durable. With the end of the Mexican War in 1848, the region became a territory of the United States. Gradually, the more enterprising pioneers—mountain men who trapped for furs, a few silver and gold prospectors, and a handful of cattlemen—began to explore and homestead the region. But to most Americans, it was the Great Wilderness, a frightful desert which one should avoid or, at best, traverse as quickly as possible. Despite vicious Apache and Navajo raids, swooping like dust devils out of the hills and deserts, settlement continued to grow. The lure of gold, especially, was too great to resist, in spite of the hardships.

In 1854 Arizona and New Mexico were lumped together as New Mexico Territory. For a few months in 1861 the southern half of the territory (both states) became Confederate territory while the northern half remained loyal to the Union, but though sympathetically in the Confederate column, Arizona was still Union land. The war was so remote, in fact, that only one skirmish was fought on Arizona soil—the brief 1862 engagement between Union and Confederate forces in Picacho Pass, north of Tucson.

The Apaches, however, took advantage of the withdrawal of Federal troops caused by the national conflict; they became bolder and more effective, in their raids. Chieftains like Cochise and Geronimo continually harassed the settlers. Many of the pioneers were driven away or killed; others, like Pete Kitchen, became legends in their fight against Indian marauders. In 1886, though, it was all over, with Geronimo surrendering for the last time.

By then, notorious communities like Tombstone had passed their heyday. Gradually, peaceful development increased. In 1889, the Territorial Capital was moved from Prescott to Phoenix, the last of several political chess maneuvers that had, in previous years, shifted the seat of government all the way from Prescott to Tucson and back.

Prescott had another distinction, though, during the Spanish-American War of 1898. A well-known localite, Capt. William "Bucky" O'Neill, was the founder of Teddy Roosevelt's famed Rough Riders; he died charging up San Juan Hill, and his memory is perpetuated today in an equestrian statue in Prescott's Courthouse Plaza.

Phoenix's stature as the regional capital has continued as the capital city ever since. A year earlier, Theodore Roosevelt Dam on the Salt River was completed—the country's first federal reclamation project—to provide better irrigation for the Phoenix area. It was these two events that marked the beginning of Arizona's—and Phoenix's—rise to national prominence.

Nonetheless, the first 60 years of American influence had brought only gradual change, and the next 35 years or so did not greatly alter that rate of change. The real catalyst was World War II, with its military, research, and industrial endeavors and its uprooting of people. Many of those who were assigned to duty in Arizona liked what they saw and returned with their families when the war ended. Industry, too, realized the value of the climate and other favorable natural factors. By 1950, rapid expansion was a reality; it still is.

Cattle, Cotton, Copper, and Climate

The completion in 1911 of the Roosevelt Dam had made feasible, on a larger scale, what the Hohokam had shown was possible more that 600 years earlier: that given water, even desert regions could produce bountiful crops. The early pioneer attempts at farming (Phoenix began as a hay camp to supply forage for cavalry horses at nearby Fort McDowell) finally had a chance to expand on a reliable basis. Succeeding years brought more dams on the Salt and Verde rivers. There are now seven dams and a steady growth of agriculture and cattle raising. The four C's—cattle, cotton, copper, and climate—became the economic mainstays. Copper had replaced the early gold- and silver-mining endeavors, and climate would prove to be the basis for the important tourist industry.

Until the 1950s, many residents considered industry and manufacturing of little economic importance. By 1953, however, manufacturing had matched the income produced by agriculture and had surpassed that from mining or tourism. Thus, Arizona has been the scene of a modern industrial revolution that has accentuated growth and brought profound changes in both the region's way of life and traditional pioneer philosophy.

Today another big bonanza, matching the multi-billion dollar income from industry, is the tourist business, which ranks with manufacturing as the state's top revenue producer. Many visitors to Arizona later return to become residents.

When the state's original constitution—with provisions for recall, referendum, and the initiative—was drawn up, many conservative Easterners felt it was exceptionally radical. In such respects, the progressive, even aggressive, pioneer spirit of Arizona was ahead of the times, even so during the 1940s and 50s. To some extent, it still is today. But time has begun to catch up with the state. Conservatism, brought by the Southerners and Midwesterners, has altered the early attitudes. Like the young, poor liberal who has grown wealthy in middle age, Arizona has changed its opinions and reactions in many ways. As one Phoenix resident summed it up: "We've grown too fast too quickly; we haven't been able to absorb the newcomers and still keep the old ways."

The old ways—the informality, friendliness, and hospitality of the Old West—are different. But like the Indian and Spanish traditions, they have been modified, not completely transformed. The changes have been subtle, perhaps recognized mainly by residents who arrived before the 1950s. Indeed, Easterners continue to be delighted by the friendliness and easy-going manner of most Arizonans. Tourists may express wonder at not seeing Indians in full-feathered regalia, without stopping to realize that such outfits were the attire of Plains Indians, not those of Arizona. An authentic Hopi ceremonial, though, can quickly fulfill expectations. So can a cowboy in beat-up Stetson and scuffed boots, whether seen on the range, walking down a city street or bending an elbow at a bar. These elements—so essential to the picture-book atmosphere of the West—are still prevalent in Arizona. But so are more Eastern ways and manners, and sometimes the Old West feeling gets squeezed out.

Perhaps, in more than any other field, this transformation, this mixture, is portrayed in cultural attributes. In the 1880s, Tombstone—despite its outlaw element—rivaled San Francisco as a center for the performing arts. It was high-life in those days; by today's standards it might seem crude. But at least it was a start. In the intervening years, and particularly over the last decade or so, cultural factors have reached maturity. Today, Arizona—though still feeling its way along—is a center for both fine arts and the fine art of living; however, local artists, often exceptional, despite national recognition fail to get much showing in the Phoenix Art Museum.

Artists, writers, poets, singers, dancers, actors, actresses, lecturers, and other cultural contributors—many of them home-grown or self-adopted natives—not only consider Arizona a source for fulfillment, but, equally important, contribute to the increasing stature of the state as a creator of rather than merely a receptacle for works produced elsewhere.

Appropriately, the strain of Indian, Spanish-Mexican, and American influences continues—sometimes in altered or diluted forms, sometimes in more original purity. There has been a borrowing, however, and the interweaving and overlapping has enriched the scene. Drawing on traditional forms and methods, craftsmen, for example, have created excitingly different designs. What may have been antiquated has become revitalized. And the old, just as nature ordained, has become the parent of the new. The relationship is unmistakable even if the offspring appears dissimilar.

Through the ages, and we suspect this was true even in the days when cave dwellers were chiefly concerned about the next meal, the state's multitude of astounding magnets has always attracted travelers seeking the unusual. Today, the more familiar lures have been added to so that the selection of sightseeing and recreation is wider than ever, from those created by nature to man-made enticements that include a splendid array of special events.

A Modern Cornucopia of Diversions

Let's consider a few of the diversions. Like to fish? Unlike early pioneers, you can do it in the desert—thanks to dam-formed lakes—even in sections where the surrounding land seems drier and tougher than hardtack. Golf? You can bat the ball year-round, and in the Phoenix area play on a different course every day during a month's vacation. Want the pleasure of warmth in winter but still desire to take in winter sports? Simple. Stay in Tucson or Phoenix. From the former, the ski area atop Mt. Lemmon is about an hour's drive away; from the latter, skiing at Flagstaff is less than three hours away. You can, quite literally, go from palms to pines and back, from skiing and swimming, in the same day smack in the middle of winter.

Recreation in Arizona is outdoor and year-round. From archery to shuffleboard, there are more than two dozen pastimes all year. Around Phoenix, just in the so-called winter season from October to April, there are more than five hundred special events to enliven anyone's stay. Each year, the list gets larger. Activities include art shows, operas, symphonic concerts, gold treks, rodeos, theatrical productions, exhibition major league baseball games, livestock shows, golf tournaments (with the world's top pros), cactus exhibits, Indian ceremonials (including strange Yaqui Easter rites), boat races, horse and dog meets, fairs and scores of other occasions. Diversity is the theme, and pleasure is the dividend.

Such is Arizona. In many respects, it defies description or comparison. Yet it is extraordinarily familiar, thanks to novels, movies, and television. Even so—no matter how much one may have read, how much one may have looked at movies and photographs—Arizona and its people still come as a surprise. The first-time visitor may be startled at times, but, like so many others, will probably leave with an intense liking for the state and its residents. For Arizona has a profound effect on most travelers. Some can take it and leave it. Many more cannot; and they eventually return as residents rather than tourists.

And what is the fascination? No one can truly say, since the reason given by one person may be at pole's end from that of another. Yet there is an affinity, even though one does not realize it. Call it what you wish, but to most people—residents or travelers—there is a common bond.

It is this: bygone days—Indian, Spanish and American—continue to enrich the present. Even still-life ruins assume a role that enlivens today. Landscapes, despite their awesome qualities, usually end up instilling profound inspiration. The scope of sightseeing, terrain and traditions may seem too gigantic to assimilate but one inevitably gains a deep affection and understanding that transcend the momentary reaction. A spirit of vibrancy prevails, in spite of the growing conservatism, and this is the key to the future. On the whole, a friendly, informal mood prevails. And the lock, which may appear complicated at first, becomes, on closer inspection and familiarity, a gateway to a moving human experience and an unforgettable vacation.

EXPLORING PHOENIX

Phoenix, with surrounding Maricopa County, is the heart of Arizona—politically, economically, population-wise, and in just about every other way. The so-called Valley of the Sun—which stretches from about Apache Junction west to Gila Bend and from Chandler north to Wickenburg—is also a winter resort, famed for its generally mild temperatures and sunny skies. Here, in addition to Phoenix, are tourist-popular communities like Scottsdale, Tempe, Mesa, Chandler, Litchfield Park, Glendale, Wickenburg, Sun City, Cave Creek, and Carefree.

The miracle of irrigation has been the lifeblood of the Phoenix area's development. All the growth has come as a direct result of reclamation projects that began with Roosevelt Dam in 1911. Agriculture was the first economic endeavor of importance; it remains significant today

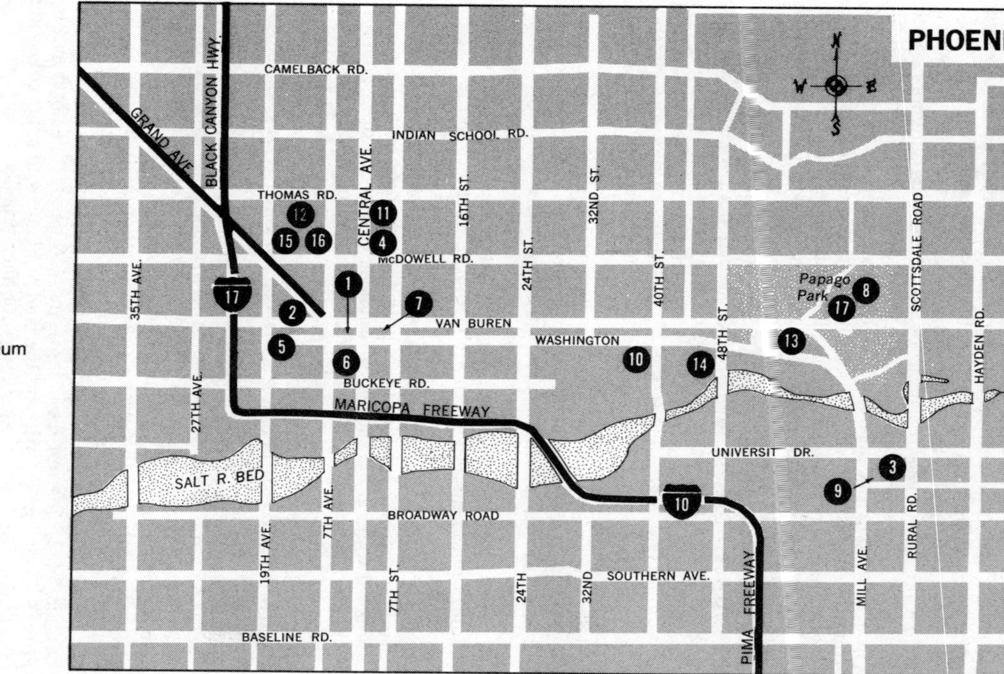

Points of Interest

1) Arizona Historical Society Museum
2) Arizona Museum
3) Arizona State University
4) Art Museum
5) Capitol Building
6) City-County Complex
7) Civic Plaza
8) Desert Botanical Garden
9) Grady Gammage Memorial Auditorium
10) Greyhound Park (Dog Racing)
11) Heard Museum
12) Mineral Museum
13) Municipal Stadium
14) Pueblo Grande
15) State Fairgrounds
16) Veteran's Memorial Coliseum
17) Phoenix Zoo

although industry and tourism rank higher. Research, electronics, and aircraft have been prime movers in making manufacturing one of the state's, and Phoenix's, foremost income producers.

Phoenix and its satellites are modern, airy, attractive cities where the bulk of growth has been outward rather than upward. However, high-rise apartments and office buildings now are part of the city whose skyline previously was the network of surrounding mountains with landmarks like Squaw Peak and Camelback Mountain. The city's green appearance contrasts sharply with the arid brownness of desert land around the valley. Nowhere is this more vivid than in Encanto Park, a mid-town section of winding, palm-shaded lagoons, golf courses, gardens, band concerts, picnicking, and recreation from boating to shuffleboard and swimming.

A few blocks west, the Arizona State Fairgrounds is the site of the huge Arizona Veterans Memorial Coliseum, built in 1965, and the Arizona Mineral Museum (having extensive collections of ores and minerals), and thus is a year-round attraction in addition to the time of the state fair each autumn. Speaking of special events, the Phoenix area puts on some five hundred each winter season, from October through April.

From the Coliseum, the Arizona State Capitol stands almost due south, at 17th Avenue and Washington Street. Exemplifying both old and new, it is set in a large park containing native flora. The central, domed part, built from Arizona stone, was constructed as the Territorial Capitol in 1900; the newer, flanking wings and nearby state office buildings reflect more modern architectural designs. The old Capitol has been restored to its 1912 appearance with the original Senate and Governor's rooms, Indian basketry, and historic portraits, documents, relics, photos and exhibits pertaining to Arizona's past. There are conducted tours at 10 and 2:30 weekdays, or you can do it yourself.

On the eastern side of Phoenix, Papago Park—marked by eroded red sandstone hills—is a tourist lodestone. Hiking and riding trails thread through desert terrain that overlooks the main city area. An 18-hole municipal golf course challenges the average golfer. The Phoenix Zoo features both native and foreign birds, reptiles and animals in a 125-acre layout. And the Desert Botanical Garden, covering more than 150 acres, offers hundreds of species—easily seen along paved paths—of desert flora from all over the world. Pottery shards from former Hohokam homesites can still be found in the park. However, the best place to get a glimpse of this prehistoric civilization is at nearby Pueblo Grande, which has a good museum and partially excavated ruins. Nearby are Phoenix Municipal Stadium for baseball games, the Royal London Wax Museum depicting some 450 years of historic events, Phoenix Greyhound Park, and the Hall of Flame with a fine collection of old-time fire-fighting equipment and memorabilia.

For another, more illuminating insight to past cultures, visit the Heard Museum, two blocks north of the Civic Center. This is one of the Southwest's most comprehensive showplaces dealing with anthropology, archeology and ethnological materials. The displays cover all phases of Arizona's history plus certain fields of aboriginal culture in other parts of the world. Among its many priceless collections is that of over 400 Hopi Kachinas, donated by Senator Barry Goldwater, of which about 170 are on display. The museum also stages illustrated programs, and sponsors arts and crafts classes.

The Civic Center, just south at Central Avenue and McDowell Road, is the home of the main Phoenix Library, the energetic Phoenix

Theater Center, and the Phoenix Art Museum, one of the more prominent in the Southwest. Its collections deal with all important schools, and also stress the role of Western artists (even youngsters) in American culture.

Other noteworthy Phoenix points are: the Phoenix Indian School with about 500 students from 12 tribes; the Bayless Cracker Barrel Store, which recreates an 1890s general store; South Mountain Park, whose nearly fifteen thousand acres make it the nation's most extensive city-owned park, with desert-mountain picnic sites and a scenic drive to Dobbins Lookout; the Arizona Museum, exhibiting Salt River Valley material; Taliesin West, now an architectural school for disciples of Frank Lloyd Wright; Paolo Soleri's Cosanti Foundation, which gives another slant on modern architecture; and North Mountain Park, with its valley vistas and picnic *ramadas.*

Scottsdale

Though the state's fifth city in terms of population, adjacent Scottsdale—while maintaining its own identity—is so closely wrapped up in the Phoenix resort picture as to be an integral part of it. In fact, many of the so-called Phoenix resorts are actually in Scottsdale where city lines meet around Camelback Mountain. A short motor swing around the reddish rock mountain lets one see a majority of the posh and varied resorts catering to many winter vacationers. Scottsdale, in addition, is a thriving art and crafts center. The downtown section retains a pseudo-Old West appearance given by porch-fronted buildings, but the rest of town reflects newer ideas in smart stores, art galleries, crafts shops, and outstanding restaurants. Many of the homes are luxurious. One of the most elaborate is the $5.8-million McCune estate, near Barry Goldwater's home, off Lincoln Drive. Special events of note in Scottsdale are Parada del Sol and an All-Arabian Horse Show.

PRACTICAL INFORMATION FOR PHOENIX

WHEN TO GO. Phoenix is one of the nation's sunniest spots, with 86 percent overall sunshine. That translates into over 300 sunny days per year and an annual average of 7 inches of rain. There are two rainy seasons, July and August, which is called "monsoon" season for the late afternoon dust devils that combine swirling dust with thundershowers; and November through January, when there may be a few cloud-filled days.

But warm, sunny and dry is the usual report. In fact, the average temperature for June, July, and August is 102 degrees, with 99 percent sunshine. Low humidity makes the summer heat comfortable, and when the sun goes down, you may wish for a sweater if you're poolside, even though temperatures only cool off to about 95 degrees.

Winters are mild, pleasant, and the best time for visitors and residents alike. Daytime temperatures hover right around 70 degrees, with lows of about 40 degrees. You can work on your tan during the day and curl up to a roaring firepit at night.

The tourist season lasts from November until Easter, with the busiest months being January and February. Much of Phoenix is booked during the beginning of the year, and so it is wise to make reservations far in advance. There is no real agreement among hotels and resorts as to when the "season" begins and ends, but with respect to rates there are three general categories: January 1 through April 30, when the highest rates are in effect; May 1 through September 30, when rates are the lowest; and October 1 through December 31, when rates fall in the middle.

HOW TO GET THERE. By Plane. Phoenix Sky Harbor International Airport is relatively new, has excellent facilities for handicapped persons, and is within a half hour from most points in Phoenix. It has three terminals and is served by all major carriers, including *American, Braniff, Continental, Delta, Eastern, TWA, United,* and *USAir,* which bring visitors from all over the United States. Regional airlines are *America West,* which is based in Phoenix and flies to San Diego, Palm Springs, Albuquerque, El Paso, and Kansas City; *Southwest,* flying to many of the same cities; *PSA,* a California carrier; and *Alaska Airlines.*

By Bus. Phoenix is on *Greyhound* and *Trailway's* major routes from Dallas to Los Angeles. Greyhound has a clean and modern terminal and restaurant in the heart of downtown, 5th St. and Washington, within walking distance of the Convention Center, Symphony Hall, and the major downtown hotels. For fares and schedule information, call 602–248–4040. The Trailways terminals are not as conveniently located, north of city center at 5005 N. Black Canyon Highway or nearer to Sky Harbor airport, 321 S. 24th St. Their fares and information numbers are 602–246–4341 and 602–267–8741, respectively.

By Car. The main north-south route through Arizona is I-10, which runs from Tucson north to Phoenix and west from Phoenix to Los Angeles. I-17 runs north to Flagstaff. Another Interstate, I-8, cuts southwest from I-10 south of Phoenix to Yuma and San Diego.

A free illustrated Arizona state road map is available from the Arizona Department of Transportation by writing to *Arizona Highways Magazine,* 2039 West Lewis Ave., Phoenix, AZ 85009.

By Train. Amtrak serves Phoenix with a downtown passenger station at 401 W. Harrison (602–253–0121). The toll-free information and reservations phone number is 800–USA–RAIL. Amtrak's Sunset Ltd. route starts in New Orleans and winds its westerly way through Houston, San Antonio, and El Paso, arriving in Phoenix 36 hours later before going on to Yuma and Los Angeles. The Southwest Ltd. takes 28 hours from Chicago through Kansas City, Albuquerque, and Flagstaff, where you must obtain bus tickets for the final stretch into Phoenix (140 miles).

ACCOMMODATIONS. Hotels and motels in the Phoenix area range from ultra-posh resorts to little mom 'n pop places. There are more luxury resorts here than in most cities, because this is such a popular winter-vacation destination. Every place is air-conditioned, and all listed here have swimming pools. Telephones and TV are standard except in a few bare-bones budget operations. Hotels that cater to conventions and corporate travelers have extensive sports facilities, such as golf courses, tennis and racquet ball courts, spas, and jogging paths, and some on the outskirts of the city have equestrian trails and stables.

Prices are always highest Jan.–Mar., often dropping as much as 50 percent in the summer. Some larger hotels have special weekend packages at about half price except during peak seasons. A few offer senior-citizen discounts. Price categories listed here are based on double occupancy during peak seasons and do not include lodger or other taxes: *Super deluxe,* $150 and up; *Deluxe,* $110–$150; *Expensive,* $80–$110; *Moderate,* $50–$80; and *Inexpensive,* less than $50. Most places don't fit neatly into these categories but overlap on one end or the other. We have aimed for averages.

PHOENIX

Super Deluxe

Arizona Biltmore. 24th & Missouri Ave., Phoenix, AZ 85016 (602–955–6600). A 5-star resort, historic stone architecture, was once out of town, now engulfed by city, but on 39 acres of exquisitely landscaped grounds.

The Pointe at Squaw Peak. 7677 N. 16th, Phoenix, AZ 85020 (602–997–2626) (800–528–0428). Complimentary breakfast and cocktails, all rooms are suites or villas. In foothills, has stables. Two other Pointes in area.

Deluxe

Embassy Suites Camelhead. 1515 N. 44th St., Phoenix, AZ 85008 (800–447–8483). Convenient to industrial parks of Tempe.

Gateway Park Hotel. 320 N. 44th, Phoenix, AZ 85008 (602–225–0500). All suites, complimentary breakfast, cocktails, near airport, limousine service.

Hyatt Regency. 122 N. 2nd St., Phoenix, AZ (602–252–1234). Mobil 4 Star and AAA 4 Diamond ratings. Downtown, across from Civic Plaza. Fine revolving rooftop restaurant.

Expensive

Grace Inn at Ahwatukee. Airport Hwy. (602–893–3000). Elegant Southwestern decor, dining, in-room bar. Near airport.

Phoenix Hilton. 111 N. Central, Box 1000, Phoenix, AZ 85001 (602–257–1525). Mobil 4 Star and AAA 4 Diamond ratings. Downtown, across from Civic Plaza. Limo to airport, 3 miles.

Crescent Hotel. 2735 E. Camelback, Phoenix, AZ 85016 (602–954–0084). Caters to conferences, with state-of-the-art facilities. Health club.

Executive Park Hotel. 1100 N. Central, Phoenix, AZ 85004 (602–948–1167). Luxury hotel for business travelers, many special services and amenities. Midway between downtown and midtown.

Phoenix Metrocenter Holiday Inn & Holidome. 2532 W. Peoria, Phoenix, AZ 85029 (602–943–2341). Luxury conference and convention center, indoor/outdoor pools, complete indoor recreation center.

Hotel Westcourt. 10220 N. Metro Pkwy. E, Phoenix, AZ 85051 (602–997–5900); (800–858–1033). Luxury conference center, shops, night clubs, restaurants, entertainment.

Moderate

Continental Inn Phoenix. 1500 N. 51st Ave, Phoenix, AZ 85035 (602–233–2672). Southwestern decor, four-story atrium lobby with waterfall. Diningroom, lounge.

Sheraton Airport Inn. 2901 Sky Harbor Blvd., Phoenix, AZ 85034 (602–993–0800). On airport grounds, shops, restaurant, lounge.

Holiday Inn Financial Center. 3600 N. 2nd Ave., Phoenix, AZ 85013 (602–248–0222). Across from Park Central Mall, near Civic Plaza.

Heritage Hotel. 401 N. 1st St., Phoenix, AZ 85004 (602–258–3411). Close to convention center, courtesy car to airport.

Royal Palms Inn. 5200 E. Camelback Rd., Phoenix, AZ 85018 (602–840–3610). Large, well-landscaped grounds on slopes of Camelback Mountain. Near Scottsdale, shops, restaurants.

Park Central Motor Hotel. 3033 N. 7th Ave., Phoenix, AZ 85013 (602–277–2621). Large suites, studio units, kitchenettes, near shopping, parks.

Inexpensive

Comfort Inn Airport. 4120 E. Van Buren, Phoenix, AZ 85008 (602–275–5746). Newly decorated, with kitchenettes, near airport and major attractions.

Rodeway Inn-Grand Avenue. 3400 Grand Ave., Phoenix, AZ 85017 (602–264–9164). Free movies, special weekend rates.

Days Inn. 2735 W. Sweetwater Ave., Phoenix, AZ 85029 (609–993–7200). Part of a chain catering to seniors. Off I-17 at Thunderbird exit. Attractive, comfortable.

Kon Tiki Hotel. 2364 E. Van Buren, Phoenix, AZ 85006 (602–244–9361). Polynesian decor, free continental breakfast, lounge, restaurant. Not far from airport, limo service.

LaQuinta Inn-Coliseum. 2725 N. Black Canyon Hwy., Phoenix, AZ 85009 (602–258–6271). Just off I-17 at Thomas Rd. exit. Part of a chain with no frills, but attractive, clean, convenient rooms.

Los Olivos Resort Hotel. 202 E. McDowell, Phoenix, AZ 85004 (602–258–6911). Suites with kitchens, garden courtyard, close to museums and theaters, with restaurant and lounge.

Quality Inn-Desert Sky. 3541 E. Van Buren St., Phoenix, AZ 85008 (602–273–7121). Attractive units on well-landscaped grounds, near botanical garden, zoo.

Allstar Inn. 4130 N. Black Canyon Hwy., Phoenix, AZ 85017 (602–277–5501). Near fairgrounds, recently redecorated.

Best Western Bell Motel. 17211 N. Black Canyon Hwy., Phoenix, AZ 85023 (602–983–8300). Large, spacious. Near horse racing. Easy access to Scottsdale and Sun City.

Newton's Inn. 917 E. Van Buren, Phoenix, AZ 85006 (602–258–8131). Large rooms, refrigerator in each, 4 blocks to Convention Center.

Airport Central Inn. 2247 E. Van Buren, Phoenix, AZ 85006 (602–244–9341). Courtesy limo to airport. Tennis and golf nearby.

Ambassador Inn. 4727 E. Thomas Rd., Phoenix, AZ 85018 (602–840–7500). Newly remodeled, spa, kitchenettes, complimentary breakfast.

Arizona Ranch House Inn. 5600 N. Central Ave., Phoenix, AZ 85012 (602–279–3221). Family units with kitchenettes, spa. Quiet, secluded location.

Best Western Airport Inn. 2425 S. 24th St., Phoenix, AZ 85034 (602–273–7251). Senior citizen discount off season. Racquetball and hot tub, near golf and shopping.

SCOTTSDALE

Super Deluxe

Stouffer Cottonwoods Resort. 6160 N. Scottsdale Rd., Scottsdale, AZ 85253 (602–991–1414). One of Scottsdale's newest and most luxurious. Restaurants, shopping. Suites with hot tubs.

John Gardner's Tennis Ranch. 5700 E. McDonald Dr., Scottsdale, AZ 85253 (602–948–2100). Tennis packages include lessons by top pros, meals, lodging, other amenities.

Marriott's Camelback Inn. 5402 E. Lincoln Dr., Box 70, Scottsdale, AZ 85252 (602–948–1700). Mobil 5 Star and AAA 5 Diamond ratings. All resort facilities.

Marriott's Mountain Shadows. 5641 E. Lincoln Dr., Scottsdale, AZ 85253 (602–948–7111). 70 Exquisitely landscaped acres at foot of Camelback Mountain. All resort facilities.

Sheraton Scottsdale Resort. 7200 N. Scottsdale Rd., Scottsdale, AZ 85251 (602–948–5000). Restaurants, lounges, five pools, stocked bars in rooms.

The Registry Resort. 7171 N. Scottsdale Rd., Scottsdale, AZ 85253 (602–991–3800). Luxury golf and tennis resort, several restaurants, lounges, spa.

Deluxe

Camelview (Raddison). 7601 E. Indian Bend Rd., Scottsdale, AZ 85253 (602–991–2400). 2- and 3-story complex, extensive recreational facilities.

Clarion Inn at McCormick Ranch. 7401 N. Scottsdale Rd., Scottsdale, AZ 85253 (602–948–5050). AAA 4 Diamond rating. Refrigerators and mini-bars in rooms and villas.

Paradise Valley Resort. 5401 N. Scottsdale Rd., Scottsdale, AZ 85253 (602–947–5400). All resort and conference facilities in botanical garden landscaping.

Scottsdale Conference Resort. 7700 E. McCormick Pkwy., Scottsdale, AZ 85258 (602–991–9000). Full resort and conference facilities.

Scottsdale Embassy Suites. 5001 N. Scottsdale Rd., Scottsdale, AZ 85253 (602–949–1414). All rooms are suites, complimentary breakfast and cocktails.

Scottsdale Hilton. 6333 N. Scottsdale Rd., Scottsdale, AZ 85253 (602–948–7750). Near shopping, several restaurants, lounges, live entertainment.

Sunburst Resort Hotel. 4925 N. Scottsdale Rd., Scottsdale, AZ 85251 (602–948–7666). Near shopping and center of town, contemporary architecture.

Expensive

Hospitality Inn. 409 N. Scottsdale Rd., Scottsdale, AZ 85257 (602–949–5115). Free breakfast, poolside cocktails, some kitchens, courtesy limo to airport.

Ramada Valley Ho Resort Hotel. 6850 Main St., Scottsdale, AZ 85251 (602–945–6231). Lighted tennis courts, three pools, spa. Golf and stables nearby.

Moderate

Shangrila Resort. 6237 N. 59th Pl., Scottsdale, AZ 85253 (602–948–5930). Small, quiet place, just 10 units. Some kitchens.

Best Western Papago Inn. 7017 E. McDowell Rd., Scottsdale, AZ 85257 (602–94[illegible]–7335). Walking distance to two malls. Restaurant and lounge.

Doubletree Hotel at Scottsdale Mall. 7353 E. Indian School Rd., Scottsdale, AZ 85251 (602–948–2109). Near good shopping, art and gallery district.

Holiday Inn. 5101 N. Scottsdale Rd., Box 1806, Scottsdale, AZ 85251 (602–945–4392). Near shopping, golf, tennis.

Rodeway Inn. 7110 E. Indian School Rd., Scottsdale, AZ 85251 (602–946–3456). Walking distance to shops, restaurants. Courtesy car to airport.

Scottsdale's Fifth Avenue Inn. 6935 5th Ave., Scottsdale, AZ 85257 (602–994–9461). In the heart of Scottsdale's famous shopping district.

OTHER AREA ACCOMMODATIONS

Super Deluxe

The Boulders. 34801 N. Tom Darlington Rd., Box 2090, Carefree, AZ 85377 (602–488–9009). A Rockresort, in desert foothills, 25 miles north of Scottsdale.

The Wigwam. 17 miles west of Phoenix, Box 278, Litchfield Park, AZ 85340 (602–935–3811). A premier resort with several golf courses, shops, all recreational facilities. Spread out over large acreage. Mobil 5 Star and AAA 5 Diamond ratings.

Inexpensive

Allstar Inn. 513 W. Broadway Rd., Tempe, AZ 85282 (602–967–8696). Newly redecorated. Near ASU.

Franciscan Inn. 1005 E. Apache Blvd., Tempe, AZ 85281 (602–968–7871). Near ASU, restaurants, shopping.

Motel 6. 6848 E. Camelback Rd., Scottsdale, AZ 85251 (602–946–2280). In heart of Scottsdale, near shops, restaurants, attractions.

YOUTH HOSTELS. Hostels provide inexpensive, simple, clean lodging for people usually traveling by bicycle or hiking, regardless of age.

To stay in American Youth Hostels, one must be a member (about $20 a year). Though Arizona's hostels are too far apart for biking or walking, they are fine for bus or car travel. The only one near Phoenix is *Valley of the Sun Intnl. Hostel,* 1026 N. 9th St., Phoenix, AZ 85006. Others are located in Flagstaff, Grand Canyon, Holbrook, Lakeside, Tucson, and Williams. For more information write to Arizona State Council of the American Youth Hostels, Box 10217, Scottsdale, AZ 85271.

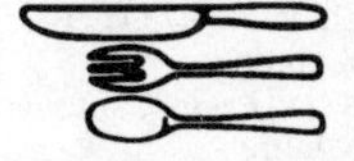

RESTAURANTS. This is a touchy subject. You know the old saying: "one man's meat . . . " We have listed just a few of the hundreds of restaurants in the Phoenix/Scottsdale area. You may want to try some of these, or explore on your own. These are listed according to price: *Deluxe,* $18 and over; *Expensive,* $12–$18; *Moderate,* $8–$12; *Inexpensive,* under $8. This does not include tax, tip or alcoholic beverage, and restaurants may serve meals in one of the other categories.

Deluxe

The Citadel. 8700 E. Pinnacle Peak Road, Scottsdale (994–8700). Contemporary southwestern dining.

Marriott's Mountain Shadows Dining Room. 5641 E. Lincoln Dr., Scottsdale (948–7111). Elegant resort at foot of Camelback Mountain. Continental, American, and French cuisine.

Oscar Taylor, Butcher, Bakery and Bar. 2420 E. Camelback Rd., Phoenix (956–5705). In Biltmore Fashion Park. 1920s Chicago atmosphere, features prime aged beef, barbecued pork, fresh-baked breads and pastries. Reservations suggested.

Pointe of View. 7677 N. 16th, Phoenix (997–5859). At the luxury resort, The Pointe at Squaw Peak. Relaxed but elegant ambiance. Fine continental menu. Also at Squaw Peak is **Beside the Pointe** in a garden setting. At The Pointe at Tapatio Cliffs, 11111 N. 7th, Phoenix, 866–7500, are **Pointe in Thyme** with a varied cuisine, and **Different Pointe of View,** featuring a French menu and panoramic views.

Expensive

Avanti. 3102 N. Scottsdale Rd., Scottsdale (949–8333), and also at 2728 E. Thomas Rd., Phoenix (955–9977). Outstanding continental cuisine served in sophisticated elegance. Entrees include traditional recipes from Spain, Italy, France.

Beef Eaters. 300 W. Camelback Rd., Phoenix (264–3838). Traditional English atmosphere, featuring prime rib. Live entertainment.

Cherry Blossom Chinese Restaurant. 3402 N. Central, Phoenix (277–9118). Gourmet Szechuan and Mandarin food.

El Chorro. 5550 E. Lincoln Dr., Scottsdale (948–5170). Long-time local favorite, American cuisine. Good art used in decor, fireplaces in some rooms. Outside patio.

Hungry Tiger. 702 W. Camelback Rd., Phoenix (264–6636). Also at 5350 S. Lakeshore Dr., Tempe (western metropolitan Phoenix area). Features live Maine lobster and other fresh seafood, oyster bar, steaks, and chicken. Entertainment and dancing.

La Chaumiere. 6910 Main St., Scottsdale (946–5115). Fine French cuisine served in elegant surroundings.

Navarre's. 52 E. Camelback Rd., Phoenix (264–5355). International cuisine, French provincial decor.

Timothy's. 6335 N. 16th St., Phoenix (277–7634). A cozy cottage atmosphere, serving fine American cuisine.

Trader Vic's. 7111 5th Ave., Scottsdale (945–6341). One of a small chain of fine restaurants featuring continental and Polynesian cuisine, lamb and veal dishes. Exotic Polynesian decor.

Vincent's French Cuisine. 8711 E. Pinnacle Peak Rd., Scottsdale (998–0921). Fine dining enhanced by European decor. Dinner only, reserve in advance.

Moderate

Black Angus. Three locations: 10021 Metro Pkwy. East, Phoenix (944–1517); 2125 E. Camelback Rd., Phoenix (955–9741); 6300 N. Scottsdale Rd., Scottsdale (948–4272). A popular Southwestern chain of good restaurants specializing in steak and prime rib, also seafood.

Bobby McGee's Conglomeration. 7043 E. McDowell Rd., Scottsdale (947–5757). Also at 8501 N. 27th, Phoenix (995–5982). General American cuisine, costumed waiters, antique decor, fun place with good food and service.

Capn's Oyster Dock. 3313 N. Hayden Rd., Scottsdale (947–9737). Fresh seafood with a southern flair, oyster bar, indoor/outdoor dining.

China Doll. 3336 N. 7th Ave., Phoenix (264–0538). Specializes in Cantonese entrees. Reservations suggested. Has drive-up take-out window.

Emperor's Garden. 7228 E. 1st Ave., Scottsdale (946–6564). Oldest Chinese restaurant in Scottsdale. Mandarin and Cantonese dishes.

Garcia's. Three locations: 7633 E. Indian School Rd., Scottsdale (945–1647); 4420 E. Camelback Rd., Phoenix (952–8031); 3301 E. Peoria, Phoenix (866–1850). Part of a small Southwestern chain specializing in Mexican entrees and drinks, exotic decor.

Giorgio's Ristorante. 322 E. Camelback Rd., Phoenix (248–8813). Pasta, veal and seafood.

Macayo. Two locations: 7005 E. Camelback Rd., Scottsdale (947–7641); and 4001 N. Central Av., Phoenix (264–6141). Serves good Mexican food.

Pinnacle Peak Patio. 10426 E. Jomax Rd., Scottsdale (563–5133). In foothills, fantastic view of valley. Western flavor in mesquite-broiled steaks. Casual, fun-filled atmosphere.

Rawhide. 23023 N. Scottsdale Rd., Scottsdale (563–5111). Golden Belle restaurant in movie-set town of Rawhide. Great place for the family—rodeo museum, panning for gold, hayrides, burro rides, other western fun. Steaks, barbecued ribs, chicken

Inexpensive

Los Olivos Mexican Patio. 7328 E. 2nd St., Scottsdale (946–2256). Features old Mexican favorites, such as enchiladas, tamales, chimichangas, and margaritas. Entertainment and dancing on weekends.

Ristorante Pronto. 3950 E. Campbell Ave., Phoenix (956–4049). Italian cuisine, interesting decor. Locally popular, reservations suggested.

The Spaghetti Company. 1418 N. Central Ave., Phoenix (257–0380). Family restaurant featuring Italian cuisine. 1980s decor.

TOURIST INFORMATION. For a complete visitor's guide, contact the Phoenix and Valley of the Sun Convention and Visitors Bureau, 505 N. Second St., Suite 300, Phoenix, AZ 85004 (602–254–6500). For help with reservations, call 800–528–0483.

SEASONAL EVENTS. *January:* Arizona National Livestock Show; Phoenix Open Golf Tournament. *February:* Turquoise Classic (LPGA tournament); Cactus Show; All-Arabian Horse Show in Scottsdale. *March:* Jaycee Rodeo of Rodeos; Major League baseball spring training; *April:* West Is Best Fair. *May:* Scottsdale Chef's Fiesta. *June-August:* No major events scheduled, but there are special exhibits at museums and zoos. *October:* Arizona State Fair; Cowboy Artists of America Annual Exhibit. *November:* Gems of the Golden West Show. *December:* Annual Indian Market; Annual Fiesta Bowl Parade.

MUSEUMS. The *Arizona Museum* at 1002 W. Van Buren (253–2734) displays relics of Arizona's pioneer days, specimens of Indian arts, and historic maps. The *Heard Museum* offers fine collections of Indian arts and crafts. It is located at 22 E. Monte Vista Rd. (252–8848). The *Phoenix Art Museum* at 1625 N. Central Ave. (257–1222) sponsors special exhibits and an annual western art show. It also has collections of European, American, and Far Eastern art. The *Arizona Historical Society Museum,* 1242 N. Central (255–4479), has exhibits including a general store, pharmacy, and toy store. *Heritage Square,* 127 N. 6th (262–5071), and 1894 restored mansion, has period exhibits, shops, and restaurants. The *Hall of Flame,* 6101 E. Van Buren, (275–3473). Largest collection of fire-fighting apparatus and equipment in the world.

TOURS. Many tour companies operate in Phoenix/Scottsdale. A few are: *All 'round Valley Tours* (951–2110); *Arizona Awareness* (947–7852); Arizona Desert *Mountain Jeep Tours* (860–1777); *Mansion Club Tours* (955–4079); *Windows of the West* (840–8245).

Trolley Tours. A fun way to get around Phoenix is by *Great Western Trolley,* which travels through the Central and Camelback corridors from Nov. through April, stopping at shopping centers, banks, hotels, restaurants, and museums. Pick it up anywhere by waving at the conductor. Fare is 25¢. A free booklet of a dozen special tours, from bicycle to stagecoach, is published by the Tucson Convention and Visitors Bureau, 450 Paseo Redondo, Ste. 110, Tucson 86701 (624–1817).

GARDENS AND ZOOS. *Desert Botanical Garden,* 1201 N. Galvin Pkwy. (941–1225). Thousands of desert plants, lectures, tours, and shows. *Phoenix Zoo,* 5810 E. Van Buren (273–1341). 1,000 animals, 125 acres. Guided train safari, children's zoo, special Arizona fauna exhibit.

GOLF. Golf and tennis are two of the main reasons why people visit the Phoenix area in the winter. The Phoenix Open is the largest of several golf tournaments held in Phoenix every winter. Major resorts frequently have as many as three courses for their guests and will sometimes welcome non-guests if not busy. Listed here are municipal courses and a few other public courses: *Ahwatukee Lakes Country Club,* 13431 S. 44th (275–8009), executive course; *Cave Creek Golf Course,* 15202 N. 19th Ave. (866–8076), municipal; *Encanto 1 & 2* 2705 N. 17th (253–3963), municipal; *Papago Golf Course,* Papago Park at east end of Van Buren (275–8428), municipal; Thunderbird Country Club, 701 E. Thunderbird Tr. (243–1262); *Marriott's Camelback Inn,* 7847 N. Mockingbird Ln. (948–6770), Scottsdale; call for tee-off times, fees, and availability.

TENNIS. Tennis courts are at practically every motel and inn as well as the larger resorts, some of which, like John Gardner's Tennis Ranch, offer weekly packages including accommodations, meals, instruction, and play. Listed here are public courts: *Encanto Park,* 15th Av. and Encanto Dr. (262–8870), municipal; *Granada Park,* 6505 N. 20th St., municipal; *Phoenix Tennis Center,* 6330 N. 21st Ave. (249–3712); *Indian School Park,* 4289 N. Hayden Rd. (994–2740), Scottsdale; *Paradise Valley Resort,* 5401 N. Scottsdale Rd. (947–5400) Scottsdale; *Palute Park,* 6535 E. Osborn Rd., Scottsdale (994–2360).

SPECTATOR SPORTS. Phoenix has its own professional basketball team (Phoenix Suns) and baseball team (Giants) and hosts the Chicago Cubs, Oakland Athletics, Milwaukee Brewers, and Seattle Mariners for spring training. Collegiate football at Arizona State University culminates in the Fiesta Bowl on Jan. 1. Phoenix's Turf Paradise provides a pastoral setting for Thoroughbred horseracing; several tracks in the area offer greyhound racing; and two raceways host professional auto racing. Seasons run October through May.

CHILDREN'S ACTIVITIES. Picnic in any of the dozens of city parks. *Phoenix Zoo,* 5810 E. Van Buren (273–1341), has jaguars, leopards, gorillas, orangutans, ocelots, and 1,000 more animals and birds. A miniature train takes kids and parents on a safari through the zoo, which covers a 125-acre park. *Big Surf,* 1500 N. Hayden Rd., Tempe (947–7873). Create big waves in a man-made ocean. *Rawhide,* 23023 N. Scottsdale Rd. (563–5111), has a bit of the glamour of the Wild West with rinky-tink piano music, gun fights, replicas of frontier buildings, and stagecoach and burro rides. There's *horseback riding* in South Mountain Park, about 10 miles south of the city on Central Avenue. Hiking trails, picnic tables.

HISTORIC SITES. The Pueblo Grande Museum, at 4619 E. Washington St. (275–3452), is a Hohokam ruin, thought to have been occupied 200 B.C. to 1400 A.D. The excavation is under the direction of Phoenix city's archeologist.

Taliesin West is the western architecture school and was the winter home of the late noted architect Frank Lloyd Wright. It is a striking study in desert architecture. Located off Shea Blvd. on 108th St. (948–6674). Admission fee.

Old State Capitol. 1700 W. Washington St. (255–4581). Restoration has returned this handsome building to the way it way in 1901. Open to the public as a free museum on weekdays.

MUSEUMS AND GALLERIES. Phoenix: *Arizona Historical Society Museum,* [illegible] N. Central Ave. 85004 (255–4479). *The Arizona Museum,* 1002 W. Van Buren St., 85007 (253–2734). *Arizona Museum of Science and Technology,* 80 N. 2nd St., 85004 (256–9388). *Desert Botanical Garden,* 1201 N. Galvin Pkwy., 85008 (941–1225). *Heard Museum,* 22 E. Monte Vista Rd., 85004 (252–8848). One of the best in the southwest. *Phoenix Art Museum,* 1625 N. Central Ave., 85004 (257–1222). *Phoenix Zoo,* 5810 E. Van Buren, Box 5155, 85010 (273–1341).

Tempe: Tempe Historical Museum, Tempe Community Center, 3500 S. Rural Rd. (966–7902).

MUSIC. Musical entertainment in Phoenix runs the gamut from symphony and opera to jazz, blues, and rock in the valley's many nightclubs. For more complete listings, check the Arizona *Republic,* the Phoenix *Gazette,* and the *New Times,* a weekly alternative paper.

The **Phoenix Symphony Orchestra,** which has recently achieved major status, plays classical, pops, chamber, and special Christmas concerts at Symphony Hall, 2d St. and Adams, from Oct.–May. For ticket information, call 264–4754; single ticket prices start at $5.50.

People's Pops Concert Series are performed on a monthly basis year-round at Symphony Hall, 2d St. and Adams (262–4634). For no charge, you can enjoy members of the Phoenix Symphony playing light classics and popular music; concerts also feature aspiring musicians, singers, and dancers.

You can get the scoop on **jazz** concerts in the valley by calling a 24-hour hotline at 254–4545. There are a number of clubs around town offering jazz, folk, and rock performances; for show times and cover charges, check local newspapers.

STAGE. Phoenix Little Theater, 25 East Coronado (254–0688), is the nation's longest continuously running theater. Performances include musicals, premieres, and dramas directed and acted by local talent. Matinees are generally less expensive. With more than 20 companies performing in the area visitors can choose almost any type of theater. *The Arizona Opera* has achieved a solid reputation for good performances. The *Gammage Center for the Performing Arts* and *Celebrity Theatre* are among several spectacular concert sites. Rock, western, jazz, or classical, it's all in the Phoenix area. Telephone 252–5588 for a two-minute recorded message about current activities and events.

SHOPPING. As one would expect in a metropolitan area with a population well over a million, most well-known department-store chains are represented here, such as Bullock's, I. Magnin's, Mervyn's, Saks, Goldwater's, Joske's, Penney's, Sears, and Montgomery Ward. Major shopping malls, all climate-controlled, are located in all parts of the valley and are usually anchored by two or three large stores in addition to dozens of smaller stores, specialty shops, restaurants, and theaters. Some of the malls are: *Biltmore*

Fashion Park, 2470A E. Camelback Rd. (955–8400); *Camelview Plaza,* 6900 E. Camelback Rd., Scottsdale (947–7521); *Fiesta Mall,* 1445 W. Southern Ave., Mesa (833–5450); *Los Arcos Mall,* 1315 N. Scottsdale Rd., Scottsdale (945–6376); *Metro Center,* 9617 Metro Parkway West, Phoenix (99METRO); *Park Central Mall,* 3121 N. 3rd Ave. (863–1955); *Scottsdale Fashion Square,* 7000 E. Camelback Rd., Scottsdale (990–7800).

NIGHTLIFE. Some of the major hotels and resorts with live entertainment in their lounges are: (in Phoenix) *Arizona Biltmore,* 24th and Missouri; *Camelback Sahara,* 502 W. Camelback Rd.; *Embassy Suites Camelback,* 2630 E. Camelback Rd.; *Gateway Park Hotel,* 320 N. 44th; *Heritage Hotel,* 401 N. 1st St.; *The Pointe at Squaw Peak,* 7677 N. 16th; *The Pointe at Tapatio Cliffs,* 11111 N. 7th; *Royal Palms,* 5200 Camelback Rd.; (in Scottsdale) *Camelview* (Raddison), 7601 E. Indian Bend Rd.; *Clarion Inn at McCormick Ranch,* 7401 N. Scottsdale Rd.; *The Cottonwoods* (Stouffer), 6160 N. Scottsdale Rd.; *Marriott's Camelback Inn,* 5402 E. Lincoln; *Marriott's Mountain Shadows,* 5641 E. Lincoln; *The Phoenician,* 6255 E. Phoenician Blvd.; *The Registry,* 7171 N. Scottsdale Rd. A few special night spots are: *Toolies,* 4231 W. Thomas Rd., Phoenix, 272–3100, Arizona's newest and largest country/western club, seven nights; *Funny Fellows,* 1814 W. Bethany Home Rd.; *Mr. Lucky's,* 3660 Grand Ave.; *Seekers Comedy Night Club,* 4519 N. Scottsdale Rd.

EXPLORING ARIZONA

Too many short-term visitors follow only one route across the state, and all too frequently it is either Interstate 40 in northern Arizona or Interstate 10 and 8 in the southern portion. Neither route gives a complete picture or even an adequate cross-section of Arizona terrain, sights, and people. Such sightseeing leaves a traveler with the wrong impression.

There are three roads that not only reveal the many diverse landscapes, from southern deserts through the higher plateaus and grass prairies to pine-clad mountains, but also are a key to many of the state's major cities, unusual sights, sports, and historic locales. They are I–19, US 89, and 89A, which go north from the Mexican border at Nogales through Tucson, Phoenix, and Prescott, thence past ghost towns, cattle lands, piney mountains, and Indian ruins to Flagstaff, and then across the Navajo Reservation to Page and Glen Canyon Dam. No other Arizona highways match their variety and magnitude of lures.

LAKE MEAD AND NORTHWESTERN ARIZONA

In the northwestern section of Arizona, the Lake Mead National Recreation Area (Hoover Dam) is about a 4½-hour drive from Flagstaff. One of the most tourist-frequented locales in Arizona, it is a superb example of how man can transform barren desert and stark mountain-canyon lands, and even change the pattern of regional life forms.

Partly because of its proximity to Las Vegas, but also because of its scenic and recreational outlets, Lake Mead attracts millions of visitors annually. Though its main section is around 115-mile-long Lake Mead, formed by inverted, bell-shaped Hoover Dam plugging Black Canyon between Arizona and Nevada, the preserve stretches for about 240 miles along the Colorado River from Grand Canyon National Park to the southern end of Lake Mohave. There is also a detached section on

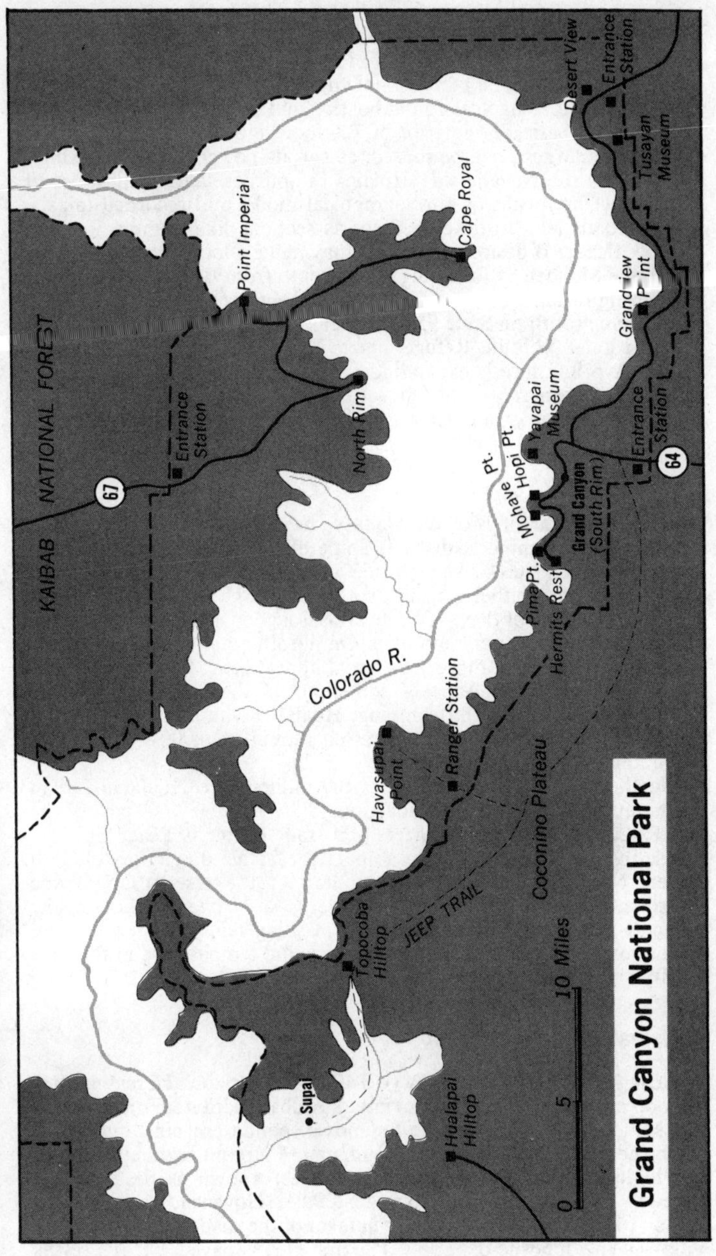
Grand Canyon National Park
KAIBAB NATIONAL FOREST
67
Entrance Station
Point Imperial
Cape Royal
North Rim
Desert View
Entrance Station
Tusayan Museum
Grand View Point
Yavapai Museum
Hopi Pt.
Mohave Pt.
Pima Pt.
Hermits Rest
Grand Canyon (South Rim)
Entrance Station
64
Colorado R.
Ranger Station
Havasupai Point
Ranger Station
Coconino Plateau
JEEP TRAIL
Topocoba Hilltop
Supai
Hualapai Hilltop
0
5
10 Miles

part of Grand Canyon National Park's northern boundary. From a purely practical point of view, Hoover and Davis dams have been prominent features in the program to provide power and irrigation to the Southwest. From a recreational angle, they have also proven to be a big boon, affording year-round boating and angling for catfish, trout, crappie, and bass. The interior of 726-foot-high Hoover Dam, one of the world's largest, can be toured, as can its power plant. An exhibit building on the Nevada side explains the purpose and significance of the project by means of a topographical model and recorded talks.

Side roads lead to developed sports sections like Temple Bar and Willow Beach. If desired, motorists may make a loop around the river and Lake Mohave by following US 95 south from Boulder City, Nevada, through California, and Calif. 163 and Ariz. 68 back to Kingman, or continue south on State 95, which can mean jaunts to Lake Havasu and National Wildlife Refuge, above Parker Dam on the Colorado River. A prime lure is expanding Lake Havasu City, where London Bridge has been reconstructed with an adjoining "English Village," state park facilities, water sports and other recreation add much appeal.

Kingman

Kingman, seat of Mohave County, has long been famous as the center of a rich mineral district. Some of the mining continues, but many of the old sites—like Chloride, Goldroad, Oatman, White Hills, and others—are either ghost towns or semi-ghosts. Tourists have picked over many of these—White Hills is a good example—until little remains of the former communities. On the other hand, the semi-ghosts like Chloride retain a more substantial appearance. The Mohave Museum of History and Art tells something of the pioneer glory. For sports like picnicking and camping, Hualapai Mountain Park, about fourteen miles south, offers a forested retreat at 6,000-to-8,400-foot elevations in the Hualapai Range.

Northeast of Kingman stretches the million-acre Hualapai Indian Reservation, which can be reached via State Highway 66 (part of the old Route 66). The headquarters and trade center is Peach Springs. These Indians are related to the Yuma tribe farther down the Colorado River. Near the southeastern boundary of the reservation, beside Arizona 66, are the Grand Canyon Caverns, some twenty stories below ground, and having a mile of trails revealing many-colored mineral formations. Take a wrap since the year-round temperature in the cave is fifty-six degrees.

Kaibab National Forest

Near Ash Fork, the highway (US 40, which Arizona 66 rejoins after its loop north to the reservation) enters Kaibab National Forest, which has some of the state's loveliest stands of ponderosa pine and aspen. Soon the 9,264-foot bulk of Bill Williams Mountain rears up south of the highway, and you enter Williams, best known as the southern gateway for Grand Canyon National Park. However, there is good reason to shun the paved highway in favor of the road south to Perkinsville—in the opposite direction. The first part is paved, but the rest is either generally good dirt or graded surface. First target is the old Mount Williams Ski Area, which has slopes for beginners and advanced intermediate skiers. Farther along, a spur road to the east leads to tree-rimmed White Horse Lake with fishing and shoreside picnic and camp facilities. Still another side road ambles to the edge of little-visited Sycamore Canyon, with red-wall cliffs some 2,500 feet high, hiding numerous Indian ruins. The most satisfactory way to see it is to arrange a pack trip into its depths. Ask at USFS District Ranger Station.

THE GRAND CANYON

The arrival at Grand Canyon, north via State 64 from Williams or US 180 from Flagstaff, is breath-taking since thick pine forests give little hint of the awesome gorge until you are almost on its southern edge. While most of the 277-mile-long canyon is within the park area and visible from the South and North Rims, it is the most spectacular part, with widths varying from one to fourteen miles between rims and with depths of up to 5,750 feet from North Rim points that are most accessible to visitors. The climate change within the canyon—it has six of the Northern Hemisphere's seven botanical life zones—is, from top to bottom, the same as one would encounter traveling from Canada to Mexico. However, without doubt, the most striking feature of Grand Canyon is its geological story and scenery. There is nothing like it anywhere else on earth. Its saga is estimated to be one and one-half billion years old; some of the multi-colored strata, for instance, took more than one hundred seventy million years to be formed, and each layer was built upon the top of a lower one that took about as long for its creation. Parts of it even formed the bed of an ancient sea, and one can see marine fossils along Bright Angel Trail as it snakes from Grand Canyon Village down to the Colorado River.

If the mighty gorge seems unbelievable, like a two-dimensional stage backdrop, don't be surprised. It may even cause shock or wonderment on first contact. Only through repeated meetings can one begin to appreciate its vastness. A trip into its heart—via foot or mule—helps to reveal many aspects hidden from the rims and to create a greater sense of reality. Even so, one can leave wondering if all the scenes were not just part of some fantastic dream. If you can choose the time to go, make it in autumn—after the summer crowds are gone and before the first snow falls. It's then that the crisp air and the chance for solitude heighten the gorge's grandeur like some muted theme that suddenly bursts into symphonic brilliance. It's then, too, that one can more quickly gain at least a preliminary understanding of the scope of this natural wonder.

The majority of travelers view Grand Canyon only from the South Rim, since it is open year-round and is most accessible from the major northern Arizona tourist centers. To reach the North Rim, only fourteen miles away, means a circuitous two-hundred-mile drive, unless one wants to hike or ride a mule on a jaunt of at least two days to canyon bottom, across the river, and up the other side. But, assuming it is not the season (from October to April) when heavy snows prevent a visit, try to include it. For the North Rim vistas—from highpoints like Point Imperial, Cape Royal, Point Sublime, and others—lend an entirely different interpretation to Grand Canyon's depths and citadel-like formations.

The South Rim

On the South Rim, the focal point is Grand Canyon Village, with an assortment of accommodations, nature walks, forest bridle trails, and two popular points overlooking the canyon. One lookout point, near El Tovar Hotel, is Hopi House, a curio shop built to resemble the Hopi pueblo homes. The other is Lookout Studio, where you can view the canyon through a telescope.

From the South Rim you can either hike or take a mule (if you are over 12 years old and weigh less than 200 pounds) down to Phantom Ranch at the bottom of the canyon. Consider it a two-day trip either way, and remember to talk to rangers about safety precautions, including taking plenty of water. At Phantom Ranch there are campsites, rather primitive accommodations, a dining hall, and ranger station. Reservations are necessary. If you don't care to trek all the way down (and up), Plateau Point is only halfway down the canyon.

The big sightseeing attractions on the South Rim are two scenic drives. The eight-mile West Rim Drive goes by several panoramic sights and ends at Hermit's Rest, with its curio/snack shop. Built in 1912 (and rebuilt in 1919), the road is not equipped to carry large numbers of tourists and their cars. In the summer, it can only be traveled by foot or free shuttle bus.

The twenty-five mile East Rim Drive, along Arizona 64, from Grand Canyon Village to Desert View, is a real motoring gem. There are about a half dozen major lookout points. The most stunning—for its expansive vistas up and down the canyon-cutting Colorado far below—is Yavapai Point. It has a series of binoculars aimed at important gorge features, a small museum dealing with fauna and flora, a relief map of the canyon, and wonderful ranger-naturalist talks on the creation of the canyon. This point is about a half-mile east of the Visitor Center, with another, larger museum describing all aspects of the region. About three miles before reaching Desert View, the Tusayan Ruin and Museum, near the south side of the road, gives an insight into how early man lived in the area and how he built his small stone pueblos. At Desert View, the Watchtower overlooks canyon views as well as part of the western section of the Painted Desert. The tower's lower section is mainly a souvenir shop; the upper part of the stone structure contains Indian pictographs, and paintings by the noted Hopi artist Fred Kabotie. Nearby is a curio shop—cafe.

NORTHERN ARIZONA

Tourists seeking remote, off-the-beaten-path locales should make a memo about Havasu Canyon south of the middle portion of the national park. Access, via a good-to-rough sixty-two-mile road, is best from US 66 about five miles east of Peach Springs. Entrance to this isolated canyon—where Havasupai Indians live amid dashing streams, waterfalls, green fields and ruby walls—is at Hualapai Hilltop. From here, you can hike or take a horse down the twisting, eight-mile trail to Supai, the main village, where only recently has the white man's civilization begun to make an impression. Some people have called this canyon America's Shangri-la; certainly there's no better place to completely get away from the sometimes frantic tempo of today—if you don't mind plain accommodations or, more likely, camping out. It is *essential* that you make reservations ahead if you want to visit this section. Contact the Havasupai Tourist Enterprise, Supai, AZ 86435, 602–448–2121; there is a fee for hiking, and one for horse-rental (if you wish to ride).

Now, let us return to Flagstaff, the starting point for trips in northern Arizona. It's less than a two-hour drive, via US 180, from Grand Canyon Village.

Flagstaff, cuddling up to the Elden Mountains and San Francisco Peaks, is the biggest city of northern Arizona. As such, it's the seat for Coconino County, the nation's second largest, and a tourist-trade center. Lumbermen, cowboys, Hopi and Navajo Indians, railroad men, and even southern Arizonans converge here, especially on weekends. The city is a popular outdoor locale and the home of Northern Arizona University. Meadows and tall ponderosa pines (part of the most widespread stand of such trees in the country) radiate from town and lend a lush look that's lacking in southern desert sections and even in the rough plateau country northward. Indeed, it is a rare traveler who fails to be captivated by Flagstaff's scenic appeal.

But for tourists—and residents—there's quite a bit more than scenery. The salient sights on the edge of town are two. One is Lowell Observatory, where the planet Pluto was discovered in 1930; today it is a leader in assimilating data on the Moon and Mars. The other is the Museum of Northern Arizona, about three miles northwest on Fort Valley Road, where the whole picture of this region—from prehistoric Indians through geology to natural science and modern crafts—is vividly revealed. What's more, it is a place to witness such annual summer displays as those by Hopi and Navajo craftsmen (who demonstrate their techniques), and to purchase, at moderate prices, from a choice selection of handicrafts produced by northern Arizona Indians.

There's more, though. The Pioneers Historical Museum, near the Museum of Northern Arizona, exhibits displays of local frontier times. Up on the towering San Francisco Peaks, reached via US 180 and a spur road, is the Arizona Snow Bowl. It is the most consistent of all Arizona winter sports areas, generally having skiing from December to March. Facilities are the best in the state: a chair lift that rises to an elevation of 11,800 feet, platter pull, Poma lift, ski shop, lodge, and slopes to suit every type of skier from novice to expert. In this same vicinity, the Schulz Pass Road (best traversed from late spring to autumn) offers a scenic drive between the San Francisco Peaks and Elden Mountains. It joins US 89 north of town, providing a circle trip.

South of Flagstaff, the principal routes are US 89A and I-17, the latter being part of the high-gear Black Canyon Highway to Phoenix. A short distance south of town, a marked but unnumbered road (Lake Mary Rd.) runs southeast about 45 miles through forest and lake country to connect with State 87. 40 miles farther, at Payson, the road joins US 260. 87 continues south to Phoenix, and 260 turns east across the Mogollon Rim, a high plateau covered by pine forests, lakes, and meadows. This is Zane Gray country. The cabin of that immortal creator of western fiction is a small private museum. This route across the Mogollon Rim is one of the surprising delights of traveling in Arizona.

Cliff Dwellings and Canyons

I-17 is fast despite the rugged terrain, and can easily carry you swiftly past two points. Don't neglect them. One is Montezuma Castle National Monument, having a detached portion nearby called Montezuma Well. Principal feature is the five-story, twenty-room cliff dwelling built into the face of a steep limestone wall; it is one of the

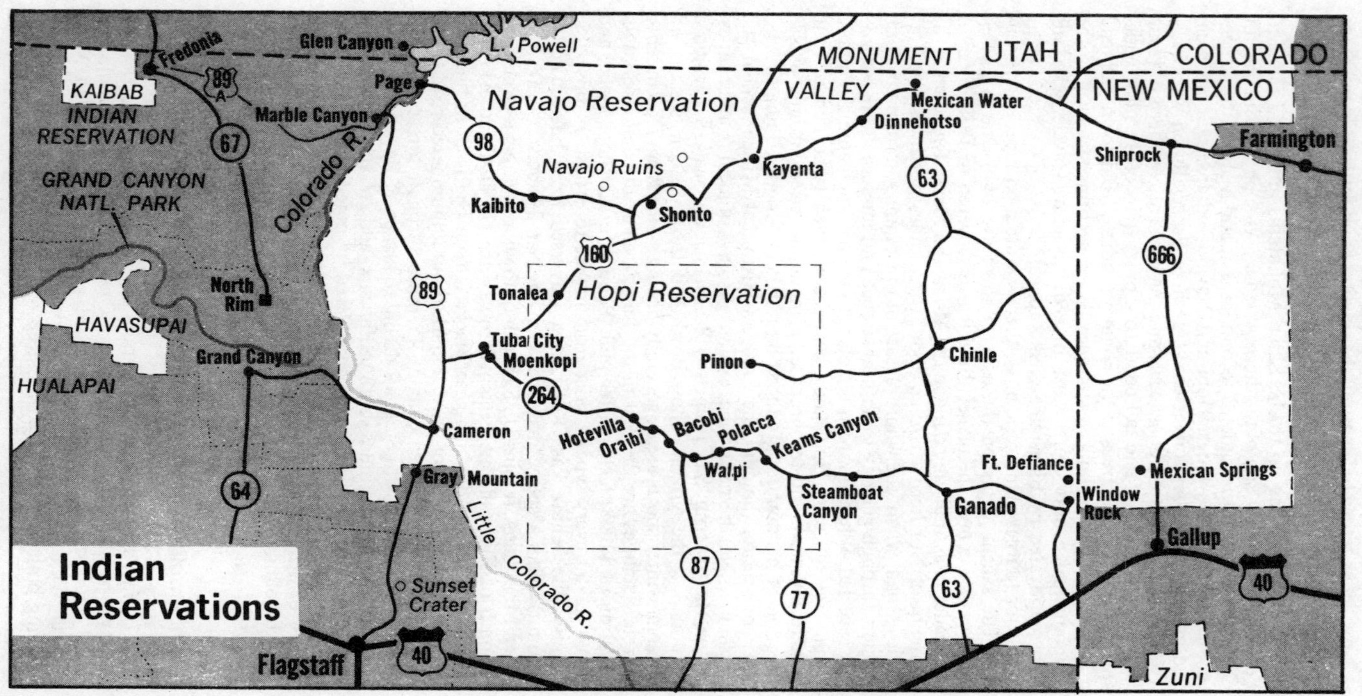
Indian Reservations
UTAH
COLORADO
NEW MEXICO
MONUMENT VALLEY
Navajo Reservation
Hopi Reservation
Navajo Ruins
KAIBAB INDIAN RESERVATION
GRAND CANYON NATL. PARK
HAVASUPAI
HUALAPAI
Zuni
L. Powell
Colorado R.
Little Colorado R.
Glen Canyon
Fredonia
Page
Marble Canyon
North Rim
Grand Canyon
Kaibito
Shonto
Kayenta
Mexican Water
Dinnehotso
Tonalea
Tuba City
Moenkopi
Pinon
Chinle
Shiprock
Farmington
Cameron
Gray Mountain
Hotevilla
Oraibi
Bacobi
Polacca
Walpi
Keams Canyon
Steamboat Canyon
Ganado
Ft. Defiance
Window Rock
Mexican Springs
Gallup
Sunset Crater
Flagstaff
89 A
67
98
160
89
264
64
87
77
63
666
40

Southwest's best-preserved 13th-century Pueblo structures of its type, being about 90 percent intact. The self-guiding Sycamore Trail allows one to explore lower ruins and also to get acquainted with local flora and fauna. Some seven miles northeast, Montezuma Well is a round limestone sinkhole having smaller cliff home ruins. The other place is Camp Verde, where the Fort Verde Museum, now a state park in part of the original army outpost, displays Indian, military, and pioneer relics.

The slow-poke route—partly because of its winding nature, but chiefly because of its scenery and recreation—is US 89A southward through Coconino National Forest and Oak Creek Canyon, called by many residents the most beautiful in the state. Reddish brown and grayish white, weather-sculptured rock formations rise dramatically above the pine and oak forests, campgrounds, rustic lodges and the dashing creek, to form a gorge some 1,500 feet deep and about twelve miles long. It opens around Sedona into a gorgeous amphitheater with monumental, brilliantly tinted formations all around. This section may look familiar to first-time visitors, and with good reason. It has been, for years, one of Hollywood's favorite locales for making western movies in color. It was also the setting for Zane Grey's book *Call of the Canyon.*

In addition to being a movie and tourist town, Sedona also is an art and writing colony. The Arts Center, with both crafts instruction and rotating exhibits by Arizona artists, is located in The Barn, on the north edge of town and just off the east side of the highway. On the south edge, the wonderfully re-created Mexican-style center called Tlaquepaque is another excellent locale for many forms of arts, crafts, and dining. The local scenery inspires many of the works and also acts as a springboard for fresh concepts. The surrounding landscapes actually pull one toward them, demanding closer and longer acquaintance. From the center of Sedona—at the junction of US 89A and State 179—quite a few diverse sights are an easy drive. They include the vista-filled drive up Schnebley Hill, Baldwin's or Red Rock Crossing, where one fords the creek, Shrine of the Red Rocks with its giant hand-hewn cross and scene of annual Easter Sunrise Services, sites of former movie sets, and the contemporary-style Chapel of the Holy Cross atop red stone formations just off State 179, about five miles from Sedona.

Rose-orange Tints and the Tall House

North from Flagstaff, US 89 leads to Lake Powell and Glen Canyon Recreation Area, and US 160 and State 264 turn east through the Navajo and Hopi reservations. Less than a half-hour's drive from Flagstaff via US 89, and about four miles east of it, is Sunset Crater National Monument, where a rose-orange tinted cinder crater, almost perfect in symmetry, juts about one thousand feet above the surrounding terrain of lava fields, grassy meadows, and pine forests. Scientists say the last eruption occurred in 1064. For closer inspection, one may follow the easy nature trail—past fumeroles, squeeze-ups, and perpetual ice caves—through the Bonito lava flow. A paved loop drive swings north and west through nearby Wupatki National Monument before returning to US 89. This latter preserve is another treasure of prehistoric culture and homes. In its more than 35,000 acres, it protects some eight hundred ruins, the majority of them dating from the 12th century.

The most arresting is the Tall House that gives the monument its name; a self-guiding trail goes through this former apartment house with more than one hundred rooms built on a red sandstone ledge, and past a rare ball court, and ceremonial amphitheater. Another self-guiding trail takes one through the smaller Nalakihu pueblo and the forty-room Citadel constructed atop a lava-capped sinkhole. The three-story Wukoki Ruin, which retains much of its original appearance including defensive works, is one of the better preserved but frequently is missed by visitors.

US 89 enters the Navajo Reservation just north of Gray Mountain. About ten miles farther on is Cameron, on the banks of the Little Colorado River. State 64, west from near here, reveals views of the river's steep-walled canyon gashing a fairly flat plateau before the stream joins the bigger Colorado in Grand Canyon National Park. Moenkopi Plateau above Cameron is inhabited by lonely Navajo settlements with roaming herds of sheep and tiny cornfields. About sixty miles north of Cameron, US 89 divides. The alternate route crosses the Colorado over Navajo Bridge, 467 feet above the river; at the northern end, a picnic area-viewpoint affords a relaxing spot to gaze at Marble Canyon, part of the Park area, with its sheer eight-hundred-foot high cliffs. The highway continues along the foot of the aptly named Vermilion Cliffs, through House Rock Valley, which is the home of one of the state's few remaining buffalo herds, past Jacob Lake where State 67 runs south to the North Rim of Grand Canyon, and on to Fredonia, just below the Utah line. State 389 westward traverses the Kaibab Indian Reservation, gives access to the pioneer Mormon fort built about 1871, at Pipe Spring National Monument, before it turns north into Utah.

State 89 continues north to Page and the Glen Canyon National Recreation Area, fastest growing vacation region in the state. Page was first constructed as a base for crews building seven-hundred-foot-high Glen Canyon Dam on the Colorado River; it is now an attractive tourist center and headquarters community for Bureau of Reclamation offices.

Glen Canyon National Recreation Area contains 186-mile Lake Powell with a shoreline of about 1,800 miles, much of it accounted for by an incredible number of side canyons that create imposing landscapes for boaters. The lake has exceptional bass fishing in addition to both pleasure boating and sightseeing trips. The latter include excursions up to Rainbow Bridge National Monument in Utah, reached via a short hike from the shore of the lake.

Main center for recreation is Wahweap Basin, National Park Service headquarters site, northwest of Page. Just below the dam, Glen Canyon Bridge, world's highest steel arch-type, carries US 89 some seven hundred feet above the river. At one end stands the Carl Hayden Visitor Center with exhibits about the dam, bridge, and surrounding area; the Center also is the starting point for self-guided tours inside the dam. Southwestward, reached from Marble Canyon off US 89A, is Lee's Ferry, once an important crossing point and now—with picnic and camp facilities, and a boat launching ramp—the area's sole below-dam recreational spot.

Two long loop trips, using US 89 north from Flagstaff, can reveal widespread portions of the Navajo and Hopi reservations. One route would be US 89, US 160 (with a side trip on US 163 to Monument Valley), to the Four Corners, then New Mexico 504 and US 666 to the Gallup area, thence west via New Mexico and Arizona 264 through the

Hopi Reservation and back to Flagstaff on US 160 and US 89. The other loop would follow this latter routing to Gallup, and return to Flagstaff on I-40 through Holbrook and Winslow.

Tuba City and Navajo Cliff Dwellings

US 160 running northeastward to the Four Corners area (the only place in the United States where four state lines meet) rolls over vast, lonely expanses dotted with occasional Navajo hogans and sheep herds. The first real settlement east of US 89 is Tuba City, where there are trading posts, shopping center, hospital, boarding school, modern community center, and a motel. About a mile south, just off State 264, lies Moenkopi, a Hopi village with typical stone pueblo homes, small orchards and sandy cornfields, and nearby (inquire locally for location) dinosaur tracks imprinted some one hundred million years ago in sandstone. It was founded by residents from Old Oraibi to take advantage of the waters of Moenkopi Wash, and is the one sizable Hopi village off that tribe's reservation lands. East of Tuba City is the former uranium processing plant of Rare Metals, Inc., and nearby—to the southeast—one can see sections of Blue Canyon, whose blue-gray, erosion-shaped formations resemble those in Bryce Canyon, differing only in color.

Past the trading post at Red Lake, two massive rocks stand hard by the west side of the highway. These are the Elephant Feet, appropriately named. 30 miles northwest of Red Lake State 564 leads to Betatakin and Keet Seel ruins in Navajo National Monument, containing some of the best preserved and most beautiful 13th-century cliff dwelling ruins. Easiest to reach is the Betatakin Area, in a spur of Segi Canyon, where a steep trail of slightly more than a mile leads from the monument Visitor Center to a prehistoric apartment house that probably had 135 rooms. Many of the roofs made by the original builders are still in place. Another branch of the canyon, which is a strenuous eight-mile walk from Betatakin, hides the Keet Seel Area, the best in the preserve, where large dwellings have been dated to as early as 1116. Information about a guided horseback ride may be obtained at the Visitor Center, and require a day's advance notice. A third part of the monument, Inscription House, is presently closed to the public. In spite of the name, Navajo National Monument, and its location in the Navajo Reservation, the early inhabitants of the cliff dwellings were Anasazi, ancestors of the Pueblo Indians, not Navajo.

Kayenta, once just a trading post, is both a junction and accommodations point for trips into scenic Monument Valley. Excursions by four-wheel-drive vehicles into the valley—the recommended way to explore it—can be arranged here or at Goulding's Lodge farther north. About a mile south of Kayenta proper, US 163 runs almost due north from US 160. This route continues into Utah and to Mexican Hat on the San Juan River. Just east of it near the Utah line are headquarters for Monument Valley Navajo Tribal Park, which contains the more imposing red sandstone buttes, pinnacles, arches, and other formations, as well as more remote and not so well-known Cane and Mystery valleys.

One of the prominent, though less startling, landmarks is Hoskinini Mesa, named after a chief who led his people into this area when Kit Carson made the historic Navajo roundup at Canyon de Chelly in 1863–64. Hoskinini's followers were among those who returned from internment at Bosque Redondo. Surprisingly, their numbers had increased by over a thousand during those trying times. Two impressive squarish buttes—Mitchell and Merrick—have more tragic connotations, having been named after two prospectors who discovered rich silver in the region, but who were killed on their second expedition for more ore. The mine apparently has never been found again. Among the more famous formations are the Mittens, within sight of the park headquarters, with its small tribal displays. From this visitor center, a self-guiding drive over dirt roads reveals some of the other landmarks. But for really intimate looks at the Totem Pole, Three Sisters, sand dunes at whose foot water trickles, cliff dwellings, petroglyphs, Navajo hogans with women weaving or tending sheep nearby, and other attractions of this fascinating area, plan on taking a tour with a Navajo guide. The investment brings many, often unexpected, dividends. For campers, there are developed sites near the Visitor Center.

From Kayenta US 160 continues east to Four Corners National Monument where the boundaries of Arizona, Utah, New Mexico, and Colorado meet. This is lonely land, not for the timid tourist. The high, barren plateaus rise in timbered hills in some places. Watch for an occasional trading post where you may find good buys in authentic Navajo rugs, but don't expect them to be cheap; each rug takes hundreds of hours of painstaking work. About 40 miles east of Kayenta, US 191 turns south for 62 miles to Chinle, headquarters of Canyon de Chelly National Monument, one of the most spectacular groups of prehistoric cliff dwellings in the world. US 191 continues south to connect with State 264. About 5 miles from the junction near Ganado is Hubbell Trading Post National Historic Site, one of several posts started by the Hubbell family over 100 years ago.

Coal Canyon and the Dance of the Mad Woman

The middle route—State 264—leaves US 160 at the junction near Tuba City and Moenkopi. In a curlicue fashion, it runs almost due east to Window Rock, just west of the New Mexico line. After a drive east from Moenkopi of a little more than a half hour, watch for a sign that points to the short, dirt road (it is clearly marked) that leads to the edge of Coal Canyon. This handsomely eroded gorge, which also resembles, but for its tints, parts of Bryce Canyon in its stone sculptures, is very frequently overlooked. It should not be, even if one merely views it from the rim where the road ends. What's more, it is a legendary setting—a place, where according to the Hopis, the luminous figure of a mad woman dances under the ghostly light of a full moon.

Motoring eastward, one meets the Hopi villages of Hotevilla and Bacobi. These are very conservative communities. Hopis are probably descendants of the Anasazis, early men who settled the area in the last Ice Age and occupied the cliff dwellings until mysteriously disappearing. Most of the stone, mud-plastered homes are one story, and the women weave a twined type of basketry. Old Oraibi, at the other edge of the mesa, is more imposing despite being partially deserted. It lays claim to being the oldest continuously inhabited town in the country, dating back to about 1100. Some of the older structures, which are beginning to crumble with disuse, are terraced and rise to two or three stories. Check on arrival whether you may visit the village; policy changes. If it's "go," by all means go. Between Oraibi and Shongopovi on the Second Mesa, just off the north edge of the road, stands the workshop and showroom of Fred Kabotie's Hopi Silversmith Guild. Mr. Kabotie, a noted artist, has revived interest in, and expert production of, overlay silverwork in many forms. Other types of Hopi crafts—basketry, pottery, Kachina dolls, and some leatherwork—also are on sale. Not far away is the Hopi Cultural Center, not to be missed, with coffee shop and a good modern motel.

Principal Second Mesa villages are Shongopovi and Mishongnovi, both known for their pulsating ceremonials, including the famous Snake Dance, which are staged regularly throughout the year. Main handicraft items here are the excellently made coiled baskets and plaques in Kachina or geometric designs. As in other villages, kivas or underground ceremonial chambers are quite numerous. Tourists are not allowed in them, so stay away to avoid any misunderstandings. You can recognize the kivas by long-pole ladders sticking above the flat roofs.

For the most part, even in the more conservative villages, you'll find that the Hopi people are among the friendliest residents of Arizona. At times, they may seem shy or reserved, but an amiable approach is almost always reciprocated. For the Hopis are known as the Peaceful People, and they are—to an extent that their philosophy, though not actually Christian, is often more Christlike than that practiced by some conscientious church-goers.

This is particularly true of the residents on the First Mesa, where the schism between the old and new is most apparent. From Polacca on the highway, a swing-back road up the rocky mesa goes, in safe though often scary fashion, to Hano. If you are driving, park your car here and walk the rest of the way to the end of the mesa. Hano blends into Sichomovi so closely they seem like one long village of back-to-back, one-story homes. Pottery and Kachina dolls can be found for sale at some of the homes, and often only a kind word and smile are needed for an invitation to come inside. Contradicting the old traditions, however, are the tall, dark poles—sticking up like sore thumbs above the houses—that bring in the modern convenience of electricity.

Continue on to the narrow saddle, about ten feet wide and deeply rutted (despite recent sand fill-ins) by wagons and pickup trucks over the years. Just beyond, rising like a mystic, terraced Near Eastern village, is Walpi, where homes are often built into the mesa rock. Hopis have lived here for three hundred years amid natural air-conditioning and tremendous views that include the San Francisco Peaks near Flagstaff. The path around the village often borders the sheer cliff, and retaining fences are reassuring. Kivas line sections of the precipice and are only an arm touch away.

Eastward, Keams Canyon is the Hopi Indian Agency headquarters. As such, it is rather uninspiring compared to the villages already seen. Its setting within a small rocky gorge is interesting, but hardly causes one to gasp with astonishment after having been to the three Hopi mesas. Less than ten miles beyond, State 77 bee-lines south toward Holbrook and can be a compromise, short-cut route. It passes Navajo hogans, tinted deserts, jutting mountains and long, long vistas of the storybook West.

East on State 264 is Window Rock, capital of the Navajo nation. Visitors' facilities include a restaurant, motel, a museum, and a library devoted to the history and culture of this, America's largest Indian tribe.

Fort Defiance

About five miles north, Fort Defiance, at the mouth of Canyon Bonito, has had a checkered history. A former Navajo rendezvous, an army outpost which Indians attacked about 1860, abandoned, reestablished, abandoned again, and once more brought to life in 1868, Indian agency headquarters, and then the location of a tuberculosis sanitorium and a hospital—this is a capsule account of its more than one hundred years of existence. Farther north, the community of Sawmill, with its lumber operations, is representative of Navajo tribal efforts to improve living and economic conditions throughout the reservation.

I-40, east of Flagstaff, despite its popularity with tourists, has less to offer than the two more northern routes. About ten miles southeast of Flagstaff, and reached via a spur road off I-40, is Walnut Canyon National Monument. More than three hundred pint-sized cliff dwellings, used by Sinagua Indians from about 1100 to 1275, are sandwiched in corrugated limestone cliffs around a horseshoe-shaped gorge whose rims are pine-covered. Many have been damaged by vandals, but enough of the original structures remain to help one conjure up visions of bygone days. A self-guiding trail takes visitors past some two dozen of the better ruins; a canyon-top museum reveals more of the section's past, and a nice picnic area under the pines makes a pleasant spot for a coffee break or meal.

About twenty-two miles west of Winslow, a paved, six-mile road runs south to Meteor Crater. Scientists say that the 570-foot-deep, 4,150-foot-wide circular depression was formed by a giant meteor crashing into the earth about fifty thousand years ago. The terrific impact actually pushed the crater's rim some 150 feet above the adjacent plateau. There is a viewpoint on the north rim, plus a museum and curio shop. Winslow itself is a stopover point, Indian trade center, and Amtrak division terminal. State 87 southward is a fairly scenic route, especially in the Mogollon Rim area, to Payson and Phoenix.

Holbrook, a former cowtown, retains a faint resemblance of frontier days. The community is the best base for exploring Petrified Forest National Park. Less than a half hour's drive to the east, this preserve can be approached from I-40 or US 180. For a short loop trip, we suggest taking the former route, following the Painted Desert rim drive, then the main road through Petrified Forest, and US 180 back to Holbrook.

Fossils Tell the Story

It's difficult to realize that this section was a swamp some one hundred ninety million years ago, but fossils show it was. The stone logs were once giant trees that floated from mountain areas to this basin. With the passage of time, the logs were buried, their fibers replaced by minerals, the land uplifted, and then eroded. And so, now, the stone trees—many of them especially colorful—are sprinkled over badlands and other unlikely spots. Each year, erosion brings forth new petrified trees that have remained hidden for millennia. Chief districts in the park are the Painted Desert, Blue Mesa, Jasper, Crystal, Long Logs, and Giant Logs. Of these, the area around Rainbow Forest Museum and the Jasper section are the most highly colored. Other attractions include the ruins of ancient Indian villages, Newspaper Rock with numerous petroglyphs or stone writings, 111-foot Agate Bridge spanning a wind-swept arroyo, and the Rainbow Forest Museum with its displays of polished petrified wood. *A word of warning:* don't pick up even a chip of stone wood to cart away. Spot checks are made by rangers and the penalty isn't worth the risk. This stringent form of protection has been made necessary by thoughtless tourists in the past. Indeed, it's estimated that if every visitor took away a specimen—whether large or minute—there would be no such thing as the petrified forest within twenty-five years. You can buy specimens, collected outside the preserve, at the park's curio shops.

There's been unearthing of a different nature between Lupton and Houck where archeologists have excavated pueblo and earlier ruins some 1,200 years old. This was done by the Smithsonian Institution and other groups, and may be viewed by getting off the main highway. Almost due south of here is the county seat of St. Johns, near which there are extinct volcanoes and lava beds, Lyman Lake State Park for water sports, and the semi-ghost town of Concho.

Westward to Retirement and Mirages

West of Phoenix, US 60 is a chief route, and it leads to several varied points. A short distance beyond Glendale, center of a widespread irrigated agricultural district, are Sun City, Sun City West, and Youngtown, leaders in the retirement concept that oldsters need not be farmed out but can reap the harvest of their golden years through active living, mingling with their own age group, and taking part in hobby, sports, entertainment, art, and crafts programs.

The greater portion of this segment of US 60, past Wickenburg, crosses desert lands where phantasmal mountains frequently create mirages on the horizon. Salome came to national attention in the 1920s when humorist Dick Wick Hall and his Laughing Gas Service Station created a bright spot on an otherwise bleak drive. Near Granite Pass, which the highway crests at 1,925 feet, you can inspect more Indian pictographs doodled on rocks. State 72 heads northwest to Parker, above which Lake Havasu offers diversified water recreation as well as migratory fowl hunting in season.

Quartzsite brings additional diversions. In the old cemetery, one can see the Hi Jolly Memorial, erected to honor Hadji Ali, one of the few Arabs who stuck out the unsuccessful attempt to adapt camels to transportation in the Arizona desert. The beasts' major accomplishments were to get sore feet and to scare whatever cattle or horses happened to meet them. Westward, a few remains can still be found of the once prosperous mining towns of La Paz and Ehrenberg, near the Colorado River. South of Quartzsite, accessible via spur roads, rise the rugged Kofa Mountains, named after the fabulous King of Arizona mine. Most of the range is within the Kofa Game Refuge, home for desert bighorn sheep. Tucked within the peaks is Palm Canyon, reached by a strenuous hike, where some two score palm trees thrive. They are the only native palms in Arizona. In this same region are some of the state's best rock-hunting areas, especially for those seeking quartz crystals and semi-precious stones. One section, known as the Crystal Hills Recreation Area, has been set aside for the use of rock hobbyists.

State 85, as it goes west from Phoenix, has just a few sights, but they are worth mentioning. From Avondale, drive a couple of miles north and you'll come to Litchfield Park, locale of The Wigwam, one of the valley's top resorts. Nearby is Luke Air Force Base. Northwest of Gila Bend is Painted Rocks State Historic Park with a good assortment of ancient Indian stone writings. And the Yuma area, reached on I-8, boasts of many historic, scenic and recreational enticements, including the big Territorial Prison, now a state park site.

North of Phoenix to Gold Country

Now, let's look at an easy one-day loop trip north from Phoenix, following US 89 through Wickenburg and Prescott, US 89A into the Verde Valley, and the Black Canyon Highway (I-17) back to Phoenix.

Wickenburg, which came into prominence more than a century ago when the Vulture Gold Mine was discovered southwest of the townsite, has gone from mining days to its current dude ranch era. The Vulture was one of the state's leading producers, and many people still feel that lots of gold remains undiscovered in nearby hills. Today, though, Wickenburg—on the banks of the upside-down river called the Hassayampa (it's claimed that anyone drinking the stream's water is forever after a liar)—depends on tourists who like to soak up real ranch atmosphere. The main part of town, incidentally, heightens the Old West mood with porch-fronted buildings that seem much more authentic than those of Old Scottsdale. A Wishing Well on the bank of the Hassayampa tells the legend, while a couple of blocks away the Jail Tree illustrates how lawbreakers were chained out in the open air before a jail with cells was built.

Around Congress, pastimes are quite varied. You might explore ghost towns like Octave and several others, search in washes for gold dust, or drive out US 93 for a look at the state's only Joshua Tree forest. Past Congress, US 89 speedily swings up Yarnell Hill, affording extensive desert-mountain panoramas, and at Yarnell offers a side trip to the Shrine of St. Joseph of the Mountains, with Stations of the Cross, a chapel, and replicas of the Garden of Gethsemane and the setting of the Last Supper. Northward, rolling, hilly cattle lands give way to the pines of Prescott National Forest. A roundabout way, past former Indian battlegrounds like Skull Valley, storybook range country, and scenic forests, can be made from Kirkland Junction to Prescott.

The old territorial capital of Prescott still reflects the mining, farming, and ranching endeavors that made it important in the late 1800s. Indians and cowboys are common sights in town, and the Smoki Ceremonials and Frontier Days Rodeo each summer intensify the atmosphere of yesteryear. Old Prescott, with the log Governor's Mansion, Fort Misery, Sharlot Hall Museum, and other lures, is one of the state's foremost centers for viewing the paraphernalia of frontier days in a setting where the first Territorial Legislature met over one hundred years ago. The Smoki Museum, maintained by the Smoki, a group of white people whose ceremonials often seem more authentic than some current Indian rites, is housed in a pueblo-type building that exhibits ceremonial costumes and numerous artifacts from regional ruins. For fishing, boating, swimming, picnicking, and communing with nature, make a note of these places in the vicinity: aptly named Thumb Butte; Granite Basin, with a small lake at the base of a rugged mountain; Granite Dells, a virtual rock wonderland; and the Lynx Creek section with a recreation lake, and many sites for gold-panning.

Ghost Town on the Go

Across Lonesome Valley and up over piney Mingus Mountain with its small, sky-high recreation area, US 89A snakes down into the former copper mining community of Jerome, a spectral town clinging to the side of Cleopatra Mountain. Nowhere in the United States will you find another settlement comparable to this one. Vistas far down to the Verde Valley and far out to the distant Coconino Plateau are tremendous. Homes and other buildings stand askew, often roof-to-basement, as the town slithers down the mountainside. And truly it is moving—very slowly, to be sure, but decidedly—ever since a too-potent dynamite blast was set off in the Black Pit in 1925. In the old days, Pancho Villa and his henchmen hauled in water for the inhabitants, who had the lusty philosophy of the frontier. Today, part of the town is a state historical park, part is an artist colony, part is a retirement locale. The drive through Jerome descends 1,500 feet from top to bottom of the town, giving plenty of glimpses of one of America's most fantastic places.

Down in the Verde Valley, the former smelter town of Clarkdale has one tourist distinction. It is Tuzigoot National Monument. This pueblo-citadel, overlooking the Verde River and dating to about 1400, is exceptional. One can trace some three hundred years of development, see ancient Indian home burials, look at reconstructed rooms, and examine a particularly good collection of Indian artifacts. Past here, State 279 leads to the Black Canyon Highway back to Phoenix, affording a side trip north to Montezuma Castle National Monument.

As one moves into central and eastern Arizona, loop trips from Phoenix become more numerous and exciting. The most widely-known one is over the Apache Trail (State 88). The usual one-day, two-hundred-mile loop goes from Phoenix through Tempe, home of Arizona State University (on whose campus the Grady Grammage Auditorium is the last major work of Frank Lloyd Wright), and Mormon-built Mesa with its imposing white Mormon Temple amid exquisitely landscaped grounds. The scenic drive begins at Apache Junction, near the foot of jutting Superstition Mountain, whose craggy recesses supposedly hide the Lost Dutchman Gold Mine. Canyon, Apache and Roosevelt lakes are prime goals for boaters, water-skiers and fishermen seeking bass or bluegill. The widespread panoramas of mountains, canyons like that of Fish Creek, lakes, and desert growth are numerous and noteworthy. A few miles past Roosevelt Dam, Tonto National Monument—having 14th-century Salado Indian cliff dwellings—looks out on an exceptional vista of Tonto Basin and the Sierra Anchas. The return through the copper mining towns of Miami and Superior goes past more arresting scenery, especially around Devil's and Queen Creek canyons, with their fanciful stone figurines, pinnacles and other formations. Just west of Superior, the Boyce Thompson Southwestern Arboretum State Park, hard by massive Picket Post Mountain, has thousands of different species of desert country flora from all parts of the world. Foot trails wind through a sizable section of the preserve.

Apache Domain

If one were to stop in Globe rather than return to Phoenix, another, bigger circle could be added. It would be into the heart of Apache and former Spanish domains, and the routing would be US 60 north, State 73 and 260 to the Springerville region, US 666 south to Safford, and US 70 west to Globe. The 13th- to 15th-century Beshba-Gowah pueblo ruins, one mile south of this town, allow a look into bygone days. Quickly, though, one enters the present Indian era in the cattle lands, rugged mountains and ponderosa pine forests of the San Carlos and Fort Apache reservations. A major sight on US 60 is huge Salt River Canyon, which, if Grand Canyon were elsewhere, would probably be the state's most tourist-frequented gorge. Unfortunately, it is not well known. But it is one of the few deep-cut canyons where one can drive from rim almost to bottom and back—a twisting five miles down to the Salt River and a similar distance up the opposite rim.

Prior to Springerville, northern end of the scenic Coronado Trail (US 666), sights include brush wickiups used in summer by the Apaches, historic Fort Apache, the 11th-to-14th-century Indian village known as Kinishba Ruins, the former lumber town of McNary, and summer-popular vacation locales like Hawley Lake, and other White Mountain recreation sections.

The Coronado Trail, named in honor of the Spanish explorer whose expedition of 1540 cut across this region, is almost wholly within Apache-Sitgreaves National Forest, South to Clifton, it rolls and curls through meadows and mountains, and down the sharp Mogollon Rim, for about 117 miles. The drive is, unquestionably, one of Arizona's stand-out motor trips, and offers widespread vistas, fishing and hunting. From Clifton, a short side trip may be made up the mountain to see the giant copper pit mine at Morenci, one of the state's leading copper producers. In the center of Clifton, the odd, two-cell Cliff Jail and the antiquated Coronado locomotive are reminders of frontier times when prospectors honeycombed the hills in search of gold.

Safford, as the center of the Gila River Reclamation Project, is a bright, well-farmed oasis amid tawny desert hillocks. To the southwest rises 10,720-foot Mt. Graham, which Coronado called Sierra del Flora. The peak is surrounded by a segment of Coronado National Forest, and its summit is reached via the view-filled Swift Trail that curls up through five different climatic zones. Beyond the mountain is Fort Grant, a former frontier post now a Dept. of Corrections facility. Northwest of Safford, Apaches have settled at the San Carlos Reservation, and now raise some of the nation's highest-grade beef cattle. Near the southern end of the reservation is Coolidge Dam.

Two other scenic loops from Phoenix have in common State 87 through the Fort McDowell Indian Reservation and Tonto National Forest, and over the Mazatzal Range, to the lumber-cattle-sportsmen-town of Payson below the Mogollon Rim. One goes northwest through Pine—and past the entrance to Tonto Natural Bridge, a 183-foot-high, 400-foot-long tunnel and down a spur canyon of the Mogollon Rim to Camp Verde. The other runs eastward, along the Rim, near the cabin where Zane Grey wrote *Under the Tonto Rim,* then follows State 288 south through Young and Pleasant Valley, principal locale for the Graham-Tewksbury feud or Pleasant Valley Cattle War of the late 1880s, and joins the Apache Trail east of Roosevelt.

Still another circle drive from Phoenix might follow US 60 to Superior, then State 177 southward, with a return through Florence, Coolidge, and Chandler. In addition to some mighty mountainous-canyon scenery whose massiveness is sometimes overwhelming, one can look at the Kennecott Copper Company's giant open mine at the former townsite of Ray, and at the smelter operations in nearby Hayden. Just outside Coolidge, Casa Grande National Monument is one of the choicest surviving remnants of the Hohokam culture that flourished more than six hundred years ago. The main ruin, a four-story observatory-watchtower, is protected by a huge steel "umbrella." Tours through this Big House reveal such things as calendar holes, strange designs, pioneer inscriptions, the waist high passageways between the maze of rooms, and even the handprints of some of the builders. A deep appreciation of the area, its people and their civilization can be obtained by examining exhibits in the Monument's museum. Returning to Phoenix, one passes through the Gila River Indian Reservation, a desert-mountain domain where Pimas, believed to have descended from the Hohokams, live in adobe homes. The women, incidentally, produce fine basketwork, some of which can be purchased at the Gila River Arts and Crafts Center. Also here is the new Gila Heritage Park, a living museum of Indian culture. (Open during fall and winter.)

TUCSON AND THE SOUTH

The vacation lures of southern Arizona—for which Tucson is the touring center—are much more concentrated, the majority of them located in and around Old Pueblo's environs, and in the region southeastward. Many of them are along or quite near the principal routes: Interstate 10, 8, and 19, US 80 and 89. Yet numerous secondary highways and byways tempt auto explorers.

Yuma, at the western end of this southern region on the bank of the lower Colorado River, has grown from a lonely river port and crossing site to one of the state's outstanding cities. It is the hub of a large and rapidly expanding agricultural region, made fertile by Colorado River waters. It is also a prime vacation base for Colorado River recreation, rockhunting, and even journeys to Mexico. Without irrigation, the land is among the most arid in Arizona, often receiving less than three inches of rain annually. Westward, in California, sand dunes are so desert-like that Hollywood movie companies use them instead of the Sahara. Yet the mountain-ringed Yuma area is more green than brown, thanks to water, and clearly shows how this apparently sterile land is actually made very fertile.

Yuma Indians formerly lived on both sides of the Colorado, though today their reservation is in California. Fathers Kino and Garces did missionary work here, the latter being massacred in a Yuma uprising of 1781. Fort Yuma was founded in 1856, but pioneers knew the city by several other names. In 1875, Yuma became the location of the Territorial Prison, now a state historical park, which was constructed through the labors of the inmates themselves. Many frontier desperadoes were housed within its thick stone-and-adobe-walled cells. The new Yuma Crossing National Historic Landmark Park is also located here.

North of Yuma, Martinez Lake and Laguna Reservoir are particularly good for fishing, while migratory waterfowl like to gather at Imperial National Wildlife Refuge farther north. East of this preserve are the Kofa Game Refuge and Palm Canyon, already mentioned. South from Yuma, the twin towns of San Luis on the Mexican border afford an interesting and peaceful glimpse of international life.

Interstate 8 and 10 are rapid routes to Tucson, but several points call for attention. Parts of the highways parallel the old Butterfield Stage Route, but very few remnants exist. Near Gila Bend, one can see the scene of the Oatman Massacre in 1851, when a westward-bound family

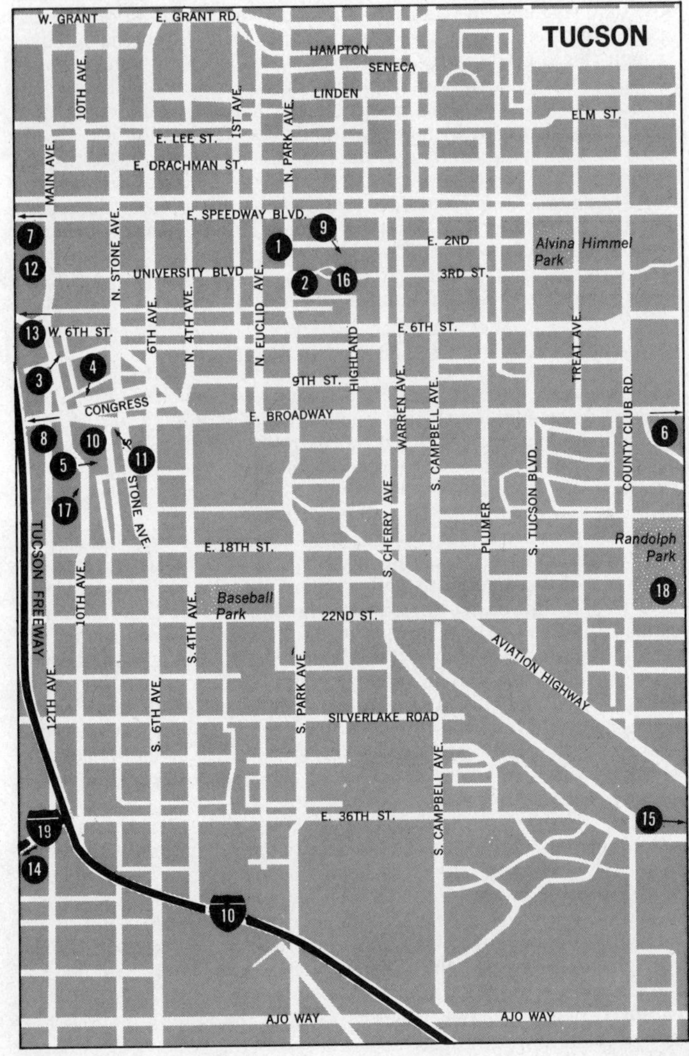

Points of Interest

1) Arizona Historical Society
2) Arizona State Museum
3) Art Center
4) City Hall
5) Community Center
6) Colossal Cave
7) Desert Museum
8) Garden of Gethsemane
9) Mineralogical Museum
10) Music Hall
11) Old Adobe
12) Old Tucson
13) Pima College
14) San Xavier Mission
15) Tucson Botanical Gardens
16) University of Arizona
17) Wishing Well
18) Zoo

was partially wiped out by Apaches. The older girl, Olive, who was captured, became a *cause celebre* until she was finally released about five years later. Slightly more than twenty-five miles northwest of Gila Bend is still another reminder of past years. It is Painted Rocks State Historic Park, where prehistoric residents doodled on gray rocks that pioneers used as navigational landmarks across the desert. Two more places of interest are the San Francisco Giants' major and minor league spring training complex about four miles west of Casa Grande, and the sharp volcanic crag of Picacho Peak, near whose base was fought the only Civil War battle in Arizona.

If one decides on a southerly route from Gila Bend, quite a few additional possibilities develop. The route goes through an Air Force gunnery range and rather quickly comes to Ajo, where a Phelps Dodge Corporation open copper pit covers some four hundred acres. Now closed, this place has two distinctions: it was worked by Spaniards in the 1750s; and, under American development, it not only started production about 1855, but was also the birthplace of the modern process by which very low-grade ore is mined profitably to produce high-grade anodes.

South of Ajo, State 85 bisects Organ Pipe Cactus National Monument, which protects about 516 square miles of desert-mountain terrain along and above the Mexican border. Several rare species of fauna and flora can be found here. Among them are the cactus that gives the preserve its name, desert bighorn sheep and the Gila monster, a poisonous lizard whose reputation is worse than its bite. The main monument route goes due south to Lukeville, then across the border to Sonoita, and on to ocean sports at Rocky Point (Puerto Penasco) on the Gulf of California. Other roads within the area provide diverse sights. These include the fifty-one-mile Puerto Blanco Drive, the self-guiding, twenty-one-mile Ajo Mountain Scenic Loop, and even traces of the Camino del Diablo first blazed by Father Kino in 1698.

From Why, State 86 swings eastward across the two-and-one-half-million-acre Papago Indian Reservation. Queer-sounding names are common here, and most of them mark small adobe and mud-brush homes in tiny villages. Some of the sights are obvious, some are not. In the former category are tribal headquarters of Sells, where each autumn an Arts and Crafts Exhibit and Rodeo are staged; the thumb-like projection of 7,864-foot-high Baboquivari Peak; and Kitt Peak, on whose summit sits a national observatory, one of the Tucson area's top travel targets, with the world's largest solar telescope, several other scopes, and a museum whose exhibits give greater insight into the universe. Regional panoramas from the summit are extraordinary. Less noted—to cite two examples—are the Well of Sacrifice and Ventana Cave, north of Quijotoa. At the former, located just west of the village of Gu Achi (Santa Rosa), *ocotillo* fences enclose a rock-covered hole where, according to legend, four Papago children were sacrificed to stop a flood. The good dirt road west, which leads to the well, continues on to the vicinity of Ventana Cave, site of the oldest known human habitation in Arizona.

The Spanish Mood of Tucson

And so we come to Tucson, where the Spanish influence can still be seen and felt despite rapid development as a winter resort and its rank as Arizona's number two city. Many sections of Tucson are browner than any in Phoenix since there is not the same widespread irrigation system. The desert comes closer to the city's mid-section, yet it's a generally pleasing, not harsh, meeting. Moreover, the mountains—much higher than around Phoenix—appear nearer, a more integral part of the settlement.

Tucson's central area has the greenest look, and one of the nicest spots is the 312-acre University of Arizona campus. The university was founded in 1885, the first in the state, and is still a leader. Architecture ranges from territorial to modern. Points of interest on the campus are the Arizona State Museum, with its comprehensive archeological exhibits; the Student Union Memorial Building, in which is the bronze bell of the *USS Arizona* (sunk in the attack on Pearl Harbor); the University Art Gallery, which features the Kress Collection of Renaissance Art; the Grace B. Flandrau Planetarium; and the Mineral Museum, with a collection of specimens from all over the world. Across from the campus, the Arizona Historical Society warrants the attention of anyone seeking a complete Southwestern research library and pioneer museum. Nearby is the Center for Creative Photography with important collections of famed photographers' pictures and memorabilia.

Though a somewhat Spanish-colonial mood prevails in and around the downtown section, modern department stores, hotels, Community Center, and other city facilities are but a step away. Some of the adobe buildings from the early American period—when architecture more closely reflected the heritage from south of the border—still stand. The most famous is called The Old Adobe Patio, now an historic site. It was erected in 1868 and shows the charm of pioneer patio-style living. Another early landmark is the restored 19th-century John C. Fremont House. A few blocks away, the Wishing Shrine, its adobe bricks covered with candle soot, perpetuates a Mexican love legend that claims one's wish will be granted if a candle placed there burns through the night.

More than all else, though, Tucson is a town for exploring—for getting out and around the fringes where a small bonanza of sights and pastimes await. The Santa Catalina Mountains, rising up to the 9,157-foot summit of Mt. Lemmon, and their foothills, hide a wealth of vacation pursuits. The mountain itself embraces a pine-forested recreation area in which there's frequently skiing from about January to March. Both the Hitchcock Highway up to it and the back road on the other side curl past vast views and changing flora and fauna that add lots of beauty to the drive. Beneath the summit lies rocky Sabino Canyon, another pleasant spot where tall pines shade trout pools, a cool clear stream, picnic and camp facilities, and nature trails that give intimate glimpses of the countryside. Within the shadow of the range are two different attractions. One is old Fort Lowell Museum, a key point in the Apache warfare during the 1870s and 1880s. It has been partially restored, though many adobe walls still stand. The other is artist Ted DeGrazia's Mission in the Sun, constructed by him and Yaqui Indians entirely from desert materials. The mission is part of the artist's gallery. DeGrazia, who died Sept. 17, 1982, was one of the Southwest's leading painters.

On the Tucson west side, Tucson Mountain Park, which encompasses thirty thousand acres of rugged peaks, thick desert growth like the big saguaro cactus, and sweeping vistas, is a triple target. First goal could be the Arizona-Sonora Desert Museum, where emphasis is placed on desert life. Larger animals are kept in open paddocks while smaller ones—insects, reptiles, and the like—are ingeniously shown in three-dimensional dioramas. Trails lead through a desert garden, a walk-in aviary, along Water Street, an underground cave-geology replica of wet and dry caverns, the above- and underground Beaver-Otter-Bighorn Sheep complex, and into the Tunnel exhibit, where visitors can watch animals living underground as they normally do. Other exhibits, from fish to minerals, also are featured.

Next goal might be Old Tucson, first erected for filming of the movie *Arizona* in 1940 to duplicate in adobe and wooden structures what Tucson supposedly looked like about 1860. The place is now a television set-amusement area with simulated gunfights, stagecoach, pony and frontier train rides, and an assortment of typical frontier-period buildings. The third target can be the thirty-five-mile scenic park drive or some of the seventeen miles of hiking and bridle trails to such points as Indian pictographs, former mines, and splendid cactus forests that are a part of Saguaro National Monument.

The White Dove of the Desert

South of the park, Mission San Xavier del Bac—the White Dove of the Desert—stands as a monument to religious works by man. Founded about 1700 by Father Kino, it represents a major breakthrough in early missionary work, and has remained important ever since it was created. The present structure dates to 1783, and is a gem of Spanish colonial architecture with carved stone portals, Indian-painted murals, and elaborate altar. It fell into disrepair in later years, but now has been faithfully restored. Special fiestas are staged annually, on the eves of October 4 and December 3, in honor of the two St. Francises.

Former Apache battle locales, a large cavern, and desert flora are the lures on a short loop east of Tucson, following I-10 to the Vail cut-off, near which pioneers and Apaches often fought, and taking the Spanish Trail north and west back to town. Colossal Cave is a huge limestone cavern with many rooms and formations carved by nature inside the Rincon Mountains. Though never fully explored, it must have entrances other than the main one, since bandits hiding out there in the 1880s escaped a sheriff's posse through another opening. This is a so-called dry cave with constant seventy-two degree temperature. It has lighted paths for easier sightseeing.

A few miles away, the main portion of Saguaro National Monument protects some of the most magnificent stands of the big saguaro that grows only in the southern Arizona and northern Mexican desert. This species may grow to more than fifty-foot heights, and live for more than two hundred years. Its pointing, curving, looping, and twisting arms can provide an endless source of delight for imaginative photographers. The Cactus Forest Loop Drive, together with nature trails and the visitor center, lets one see more than two dozen kinds of cactus, desert birds and animals, and interesting geological scenes.

The former El Camino Real, which pioneers dubbed the road to "Tucson, Tubac, Tumacacori, and To Hell," and whose modern counterpart is I-19, offers a pleasant drive up the fertile, mountain-rimmed Santa Cruz Valley, where 9,453-foot Mt. Wrightson atop the Santa Rita Range dominates the landscape. This range, incidentally, is the locale of the Madera Canyon Recreation Area. Though part of the route is through desert, a sizable portion is bordered by farmlands irrigated by water from deep wells. At Amado, there's a greyhound track for parimutuel dog races. And Green Valley is a pseudo-Spanish-style retirement community with nearby copper mines and pecan groves.

About two-thirds of the way along Int. 19 to Nogales, the Spanish presidio of Tubac is now the setting for a state historic park, with a museum on the old fort grounds. A writing and art colony has developed here, too, and one may inspect or purchase works of the latter. The Tubac Country Club with its eighteen-hole golf course is great for playing, and the clubhouse serves fine meals. Southward, also on the east side, just off Int. 19, stands Tumacacori National Monument. It protects a massive mission constructed by Franciscans in the late Spanish period. By the 1850s, though, the mission was deserted. Apaches preyed on it, fortune hunters gouged the walls and grounds searching for reputed treasure, and it was even used as a stable. A legend claims that the mission's lost bells, said to have been buried in the desert, still peal their melodious notes late at night to lonely wayfarers. Partially restored, it gives a good chance—with its quiet patio garden, mission ruins, museum, and remnants of other church buildings—to conjure up visions of the past. For water recreation, State 289 runs west from the main highway to hill-enclosed Pena Blanca Lake.

Ambos Nogales Contrasts

Ambos Nogales—both Nogaleses, as they are sometimes called—are not exactly typical border communities. There are certain characteristics—like the curio shops, liquor stores, and weekend pleasures—but the two cities are completely different from other Mexican border towns. They blend yet contradict each other. The American side looks more prosperous, yet it is hardly glittering despite being one of the most important points of entry on the American-Mexican border. Something of frontier days lingers on. The Mexican side presents the sharp contrast so frequently seen south of the border. Crude, hill-clinging adobe homes, dirt streets and hovels seem to blanket the land just beyond the shops, restaurants, night clubs, and the super-highway that marks the start of the West Coast route to Mexico City. But just a few blocks away, one passes elaborate villas. For a brief visit, formalities are at a minimum, and bargains in Mexican products, plus a certain *mañana* mood in spite of the bustle of the stores, make even a short stay fun. So do the people.

Ghost Trail Along the Border

Since we are at the international line, we'd like to tell you about an off-the-beaten-path trip that even many natives have never taken. Yet it ranks among the state's most interesting because of the scenic, historic and recreational opportunities it offers. We call it the "Ghost Trail Along the Border." The unnumbered route begins about five miles north of Nogales, off State 82 at a country school. From here to Douglas should take a full day if all attractions are to be enjoyed. These include storybook cattle ranches, golden grass and emerald hills, farms, ghost mining-community sites like Washington Camp and Duquesne, Lochiel and its monument commemorating the entry into Arizona of Fray Marcos, Parker Canyon and its lake and shoreside sports, the high Huachuca Mountains, and Coronado National Memorial, which honors the explorer while offering far-flung panoramas of Arizona and

Mexico. Nature trails, with exhibits and lots of exceptional bird-watching, meander through this high part of piney Coronado National Forest.

The trail meets State 92, bypasses old copper operations at Bisbee, offers a side trip to Naco in Mexico (which Pancho Villa liked to raid), and continues eastward to Douglas, largest Cochise County community, smelter site, and neighbor of Agua Prieta, Mexico, where Villa was also prone to be and which today has a few stores for tourist shopping.

Douglas, still retaining something of frontier days and full of friendly people, can be a base or stopping point. Between here and Tucson—up and down and across Cochise County—are some of the most famous and little-known segments of the old and new West. East of town, for example, US 80 looks placid, yet south of it, in 1886 at Skeleton Canyon, Geronimo surrendered for the last time. Go north on US 666 up grassy Sulphur Spring Valley with its large ranches, and a detour at the junction of State 181 brings big dividends. This road angles up to Chiricahua National Monument, full of amazing stone pinnacles, figurines, balanced rocks, and tight crevice canyons where Apaches—who once lived here—continue to haunt the scene and seem ready to jump out at each bend in the many riding or hiking trails. Another portion of Coronado National Forest borders the area and extends over much of the Chiricahua Range, which nears 9,800 feet. Within the national forest are outdoor sports at Rucker Canyon, the tinted rock drive through lonely Cave Creek Canyon to Portal, and ghost towns like Paradise.

State 186 ripples over hills and past ranches to the cattle-agricultural town of Willcox. A good spur road to the northeast runs through 5,175-foot-high Apache Pass—a notorious ambush spot in pioneer days—and past what is left of Old Fort Bowie, now a national historic monument amid low, rough mountains. The main road to Willcox continues on, through the semi-ghost town of Dos Cabezas, where adobes, both occupied and abandoned, still stand and where a boothill cemetery adds an authentic Old West touch. It's worth a halt for at least picture-taking.

If one wants to backtrack from Chiricahua National Monument, US 666 leads toward Cochise Stronghold, named in honor of one of the most significant of all Apache chieftains. The angular road west from US 666 is straight and fast. It soon enters still another section of Coronado National Forest. This portion is granite-rugged, so much so that one can easily understand how the Indians could stand off superior forces trying to dislodge them. Though the camp-picnic ground is peaceful, one can't help wondering whether, somewhere nearby, the ghost of Cochise wanders. (His grave was trampled by horses to obliterate its location.)

There is a spider web of roads west of here, and some of your destinations might include the stone fantasy of Texas Canyon on I-10; Patagonia, in hilly cattle terrain where the movie *Oklahoma!* was filmed; the Army electronic proving ground at Fort Huachuca (one of the state's oldest, and having a delightful picnic area and informative museum); plenty of ghost towns, and an abundance of bygone mines *(for safety's sake, stay out of old shafts).*

However, as one swings back toward Tucson on US 80, two towns are paramount. The first is Bisbee, a community which has acquired a special identity over the years. In some respects, buildings scrambling up the steep hillside remind one of Jerome, but the town is not yet a ghost, even if yesteryears live in its narrow streets and old structures.

Built around Mule Pass Gulch, Bisbee was a prominent mining town since the 1880s, having produced more than a billion dollars' worth of copper, gold, silver, and other ores. But copper was always the main mineral. The Bisbee Civic Center and Mining and Historical Museum give interesting background. You can now make a tour, too, of the old underground Queen Mine. On the north side, and traversed by US 80, the immense, terraced Lavender Pit was scooped out for its forty-one million tons of copper ore. An overlook permits viewing of the site, and pit tours are conducted each day at noon.

Tombstone

Over the Mule Mountains and across the rolling brown land lies Tombstone, which proudly calls itself the town too tough to die. Much has been written and filmed about this former silver camp that rivaled San Francisco during its heyday in the 1880s; most of it has been fictitious. But the reputation of Tombstone has been established as a symbol of the lusty, lawless frontier, and that's the image on which it survives today.

Tombstone now is a national historical site, and private enterprise has restored many of the frontier buildings to a semblance of their original appearance. The once-rich mines like the Lucky Cuss, Goodenough, and others became flooded about a half-dozen years after the boom began. The Goodenough is near the so-called Million Dollar Stope, a caved-in mine tunnel near the edge of the business district, and trips are conducted through its upper levels.

Most of the sights are conveniently grouped within a few blocks so that a walking tour of Tombstone is both practical and profitable. Toughnut, Allen, and Fremont Streets are the main ones, and most of the places to see are along them. The Bird Cage Theater, erected in 1881, is said to be the West's last genuine honky-tonk where many noted entertainers played. A block away is the Crystal Palace, a popular saloon. The OK Corral, supposed scene of the notorious gun battle between the Earps and Clantons, has been enhanced with a general store, old vehicles, life-size figures of the gunslingers, and a movie depicting the event. The Camillas Fly Studio recreates a boardinghouse and frontier photographer's shop. The home of "Historama," which tells the town's story, is in a building next to the OK Corral. The Tombstone Courthouse State Historical Park contains pioneer collections, rooms where many well-known pioneer trials were held, and even a replica of the gallows on which convicted culprits were given elevated status. Another interesting showplace of the past is the Wells Fargo Museum, actually a series of museums portraying almost every aspect of the Southwest. Also of interest are the giant rose tree, office of the *Tombstone Epitaph,* and St. Paul's Episcopal Church, the state's oldest Protestant church still in use. Boothill Cemetery, where almost two hundred of the early town's residents are buried beneath headboards that succinctly describe their demise, is just off US 80 on the north edge of Tombstone.

Remember, as you go around Tombstone and the rest of the state, that Arizona is a vacationland that calls for lingering to savor fully its varied holiday treats. One can take in the principal sights and even indulge in various forms of recreation on a time-limited trip. But a lengthy visit or repeated ones are more rewarding, for there is so much, all over Arizona, to do and see. Indeed, the state's motto of *Ditat*

Deus—God enriches—can be amended to apply to this region of contrasts. For Arizona enriches any traveler who chooses to meet it.

PRACTICAL INFORMATION FOR ARIZONA

FACTS AND FIGURES. Arizona probably derives its name from *ali-shoñak,* Papago Indian for "place of little springs." Its nicknames are: *Grand Canyon State* and *Copper State. Ditat Deus* ("God Enriches") is the state motto, and "Arizona" the state song. The state flower is the white blossom of the saguaro cactus; palo verde is the state tree; the cactus wren is the state bird; and the bola tie (in any form) is the official necktie. Phoenix, the state's biggest city, is also the capital. Arizona, one of the nation's fastest growing states, now has a population of over 2,700,000. Fourteen separate Indian tribes occupy more than 19 million acres of Arizona land, with a population of over 100,000.

HOW TO GET THERE. By Plane. The busiest terminal is Phoenix Sky Harbor International Airport (see Practical Information for Phoenix, above).

The only Arizona city of size south of Phoenix, Tucson enjoys air service exceeding that of other cities of similar size. Airlines serving Tucson are *Aeromexico, Alaska Airlines, America West, American, Eastern, Frontier, Northwest Orient, PSA, Republic, TWA, United,* and *Western.*

Smaller Arizona towns, such as Sedona, Prescott, Bisbee, Douglas, Sierra Vista, Flagstaff, Winslow, Seligman, Kingman, and Page, are served by regional airlines, including *Air Sedona, Golden Pacific, Sierra Vista Aviation, Skywest Airlines,* and *Sun West.*

The Grand Canyon Airport is served by *Scenic Airlines* and *Air Nevada* from Las Vegas and by *Sun West* from Phoenix and Flagstaff.

By Bus. Arizona is served by *Trailways* and *Greyhound* as well as by regional lines.

By Train. Amtrak's *Sunset Limited* travels from New Orleans to Los Angeles, stopping in Benson, Tucson, Phoenix, and Yuma. The legendary *Super Chief,* now known as the *Southwest Limited,* comes from Chicago and stops in Winslow, Flagstaff, Seligman, and Kingman. Winslow is about 28 hours from Chicago.

By car. The interstate highway system serves the state fairly well. I–40, which follows the route of fabled old US 66, passes through the Navajo Reservation, then on through Winslow, Flagstaff and Kingman. It crosses the Colorado River to Needles, California. I–10 traverses the southern tier, from El Paso, Texas, and Las Cruces, New Mexico, through Tucson to Casa Grande, where I–8 takes over for the trip into Calif. via Gila Bend and Yuma. I–10, zigs north to the Phoenix-Scottsdale-Mesa-Tempe area, then zags west through desert and mountain ranges to Blythe, California. North-south routes are good, too. US 93 is the road from Las Vegas almost all the way to Phoenix. US 89 comes out of Salt Lake City, Utah, to Flagstaff; then you can use I–17 to Phoenix, I–10 to Tucson and I–19 to Nogales and the Mexican border. The fastest route from Denver is I–25 to Albuquerque, New Mexico, then I–40 west. The major Mexican highways up to Arizona are # 8 from Puerto Penasco, # 2 from Caborca and # 15 from Magdelena.

ACCOMMODATIONS. Hotels and motels in Arizona usually come equipped with swimming pools, sun patios, cabanas, poolside service. Most resorts are around Tucson and Phoenix-Scottsdale, though there are some in other areas. Principal types of places: resorts; small inns or guest lodges; resort hotels; guest (dude) ranches; motor hotels or motels; trailer parks. Rates are generally on a seasonal basis, with reductions of 25 to 50 percent out of season (generally winter in northern areas and summer in southern sections). Fringe periods—spring and fall—are between the highs and lows. Some resorts and dude ranches operate on the American Plan (meals included with price of room) though there is a trend away from strict AP rates lately.

The price categories reflect the cost of a double room during the high season (winter in the south, summer in the north). Though they may overlap at either end, they will average as follows: *Super Deluxe,* $150 and up; *Deluxe,* $90–150; *Expensive,* $60–90; *Moderate,* $40–60; and *Inexpensive,* below $40. Taxes are not included.

APACHE JUNCTION. Resort at Gold Canyon, *Expensive–Deluxe.* 6210 S. Kings Ranch Rd., Apache Junction, AZ 85220 (602–982–9090). Pool, golf, tennis, riding, dining room.

BISBEE. Copper Queen Hotel. *Moderate.* 11 Howell Ave., Bisbee, AZ 85603 (602–432–2216). World War I period piece. Restaurant, bar; pool.

BULLHEAD CITY. Lake Mohave Resort & Marina. *Moderate.* On Katherine Landing, Bullhead City; AZ 86430 (602–754–3245). Boat rentals, store, restaurant, slips, beach.

Clearwater Motel. *Moderate–Inexpensive.* 381 Main St., Bullhead City, AZ 86430 (602–754–2201). Some kitchenettes. Boat, fishing dock, some riverfront rooms.

CAREFREE. Carefree Inn & Resort. *Super Deluxe.* Mule Train Rd., Box 708, Carefree, AZ 85377 (602–488–3551). Tennis, golf, stables, three dining rooms.

Adobe Inn. *Expensive–Deluxe.* Elbow Bend and Sidewinder Rds., Box 1081, Carefree, AZ 85377 (602–488–4444). Continental breakfast, dining, tennis; some rooms with wet bars and fireplaces.

CASA GRANDE. Boots & Saddle Motel. *Inexpensive.* 509 W. 2nd St., Casa Grande, AZ 85222 (602–836–8249).

CHANDLER. Aloha Motel. *Inexpensive.* 445 N. Arizona Ave., Chandler, AZ 85224 (602–963–3403).

COTTONWOOD. Las Campanas. *Moderate.* 302 W. Hwy. 89A, Cottonwood, AZ 86326 (602–634–4287). Dining room, near golf.

DOUGLAS. The Gadsden Hotel. *Moderate.* 1046 G Ave., Douglas, AZ 85607 (602–364–4481). Dining room, golf. National historic site.

FLAGSTAFF. Junipine Resort. *Expensive.* Box 300, Oak Creek Route, Flagstaff, AZ 86001 (602–774–9637). Condos can accommodate four.

Little America, *Expensive.* 2515 E. Butler Ave., Flagstaff, AZ 86001 (602–779–2741). Large motel at edge of town, landscaped grounds. Shops, restaurant, lounge.

Quality Inn. *Expensive.* 2000 S. Milton Rd., Flagstaff, AZ 86001 (602–774–8771). Restaurant, pool.

Continental Inn. *Expensive.* 2200 E. Butler Ave., Flagstaff, AZ 86001 (602–779–6944). Indoor pool, coffee shop, lounge.

Holiday Inn. *Expensive.* 1000 W. Highway 66, Flagstaff, AZ 86001 (602–774–5221). Dining room, lounge, pool.

Arizona Mountain Inn. *Moderate–Expensive.* 685 Lake Mary Rd., Flagstaff, AZ 86001 (602–774–8959). Family units, cottages, fireplaces, playground.

Best Western King's House Motel. *Moderate.* 1560 E. Santa Fe, Flagstaff, AZ 86001 (602–774–7186). Continental breakfast, limo to airport and Amtrak.

Evergreen Inn. *Moderate.* 1008 E. Santa Fe, Flagstaff, AZ 86001 (602–774–7356). Pool, spa.

Quality Inn. *Moderate.* 2000 S. Milton Rd., Flagstaff, AZ 86001 (602–774–8771). Pool.

Ramada Inn East. *Moderate.* 2610 E. Santa Fe, Flagstaff, AZ 86001 (602–526–1399). Pool, restaurant, lounge.

Western Hills Motel. *Moderate.* 1612 E. Santa Fe, Flagstaff, AZ 86001 (602–774–6633). Dining room, lounge, pool.

La Quinta Motor Inn. *Moderate.* 2350 E. Lucky Lane, Flagstaff, AZ 86001 (602–779–3614).

Best Western Pony Soldier Motel. *Inexpensive–Moderate.* 3030 E. Santa Fe, Flagstaff, AZ 86001 (602–526–2388). Dining room, pool.

Comfort Inn. *Inexpensive.* 914 S. Milton Rd., Flagstaff, AZ 86001 (602–774–7326).

Imperial 400 Motor Inn. *Inexpensive.* 223 S. Sitgreaves, Flagstaff, AZ 86001 (602–774–5041).

GILA BEND. Best Western Space Age Lodge. *Moderate.* 401 E. Pima St., Box C, Gila Bend AZ 85337 (602–683–2273). Pool, spa, coffee shop.

GLOBE. El Rey Motel. *Inexpensive–Moderate.* 1201 Ash St., Globe AZ 85501 (602–425–4427).

GOODYEAR. Best Western Crossroads Inn. *Moderate.* 1770 N. Dysart Rd., Goodyear AZ 85338 (602–932–9191). HBO, heated pool, spa, some suites, continental breakfast, lounge. Cable TV.

GRAND CANYON. At the North Rim: **Grand Canyon Lodge.** *Moderate–Expensive. c/o TW Services,* Box 400, Cedar City, Utah 84720, (801–586–7686). Beautiful lodge in the grand old style of national parks, with shops, dining room, lounge, verandas; some cabins more rustic.

At the South Rim: The following seven lodges are managed by Grand Canyon Natl. Park Lodges, Box 699, Grand Canyon, AZ 86023 (602–638–2401). Reservations for any of these may be made at the above address or telephone number, between 8 A.M. and 5 P.M., Mon.–Sat.

El Tovar Hotel. *Deluxe.* Another of the grand old lodges of yesteryear, recently refurbished; on the rim, though not all rooms overlook the Canyon. Shops, elegant dining room, coffee shop, visitor programs.

Thunderbird and **Kachina Lodges.** *Deluxe.* Identical lodges, built more recently. Half the rooms overlook the Canyon, other half the village and forest. Located between Bright Angel and El Tovar. Easy walking to restaurants and other facilities.

Bright Angel Lodge. *Moderate–Expensive.* Many years old, but well-maintained. Stone lodges, good dining room, and steak house; near the rim, some rooms with view of Canyon.

Maswik Lodge. *Moderate–Expensive.* Newer lodge, not on the rim, but within easy walking distance. Dining room, gift shop, lounge.

Yavapai Lodge. *Moderate–Expensive.* Newer, not on the rim, but within easy walking distance. Cafeteria, lounge.

Moqui Lodge. *Moderate–Expensive.* Dining room, lounge, shop, horseback riding, tennis. The only one of the Grand Canyon Lodges operated by the above company that is not within the Park, but located just outside the Park entrance.

The following three lodges are individually owned and operated, and all are outside the Park entrance:

Grand Canyon Inn. *Moderate–Expensive.* Box 702, Williams, AZ 86046 (602–635–9203). Coffee shop, dining room, lounge, 28 miles from Canyon rim.

Grand Canyon Squire Inn. *Moderate–Expensive.* Best Western. Box 130, Grand Canyon, AZ 86023 (602–638–2681). Dining room, coffee shop, lounge, gift shop, pool, tennis, bowling, spa, billiards, game room. 7 miles from Canyon rim.

Quality Inn Red Feather Lodge. *Moderate–Expensive.* U.S. 64 and 180, Box 520, Grand Canyon, AZ 86023 (602–638–2673). Dining room, coffee shop, lounge, pool, gift shop. 8 miles from Canyon rim.

HOLBROOK. Best Western Adobe Inn. *Moderate.* 615 W. Hopi Dr., Holbrook, AZ 86025 (602–524–3948). New, with pool, dining room, lounge. 18 miles to Painted Desert and Petrified Forest.

Best Western Arizonian Inn. *Moderate.* 2508 E. Navajo Blvd., Holbrook, AZ 86025 (602–524–2611). Pool, dining room.

KAYENTA/MONUMENT VALLEY. Holiday Inn. *Moderate–Expensive.* At junction of US 160 and 163, Box 307, Kayenta, AZ 86033 (602–697–3221). 35 miles to Monument Valley, 29 miles to Navajo National Monument. Navajo jewelry shop.

Wetherill Inn Motel. *Moderate.* on US 163, 1 mile north of US 160, on Navajo Reservation. Box 175, Kayenta, AZ 86033 (602–697–3231). Nearest to Monument Valley (5 miles) except for Gouldings Lodge, which is in Utah Box 7, Monument Valley, UT 84536 (801–727–3231).

KINGMAN. Quality Inn. *Moderate.* 1400 E. Andy Devine Ave., Kingman, AZ 86401 (602–753–5531). Restaurant, pool, gift shop, lounge, fitness room, spa.

Rodeway Inn. *Inexpensive–Moderate.* 411 W. Beale St., Kingman, AZ 86401 (602–753–5521). Coffee shop, laundry, pool.

Comfort Inn Holiday House. *Inexpensive.* 1225 W. Beale St., Kingman, AZ 86401 (602–753–2153). Pool, coffee shop, laundry.

Hill Top Motel. *Inexpensive.* 1901 E. Andy Devine Ave., Kingman AZ 86401 (602–753–2198).

LAKE HAVASU CITY. Nautical Inn Resort. *Expensive–Deluxe.* 1000 McColloch Blvd., Lake Havasu City, AZ 86403 (602–855–2141). Pool, cocktail lounges, restaurants, golf, tennis, live entertainment.

Best Western Lake Place Inn. *Moderate.* 31 Wings Loop, Lake Havasu City, AZ 86403 (602–855–2146). Pool, coffee shop, lounge.

Sands Vacation Resort. *Moderate.* 2040 Mesquite, Lake Havasu City, AZ 86403 (602–855–1388). Pool, tennis, continental breakfast, cocktails, driving range, spa, putting green, shuffleboard, horseshoes.

Pioneer Hotel. *Moderate.* 271 S. Lake Havasu Ave., Lake Havasu City, AZ 86403 (602–855–1111). Coffee shop, dining room, spa, live country western music Tues.–Sat.

Sandman Inn. *Inexpensive.* 1700 McColloch Blvd., Lake Havasu City AZ 86403 (602–855–7841). Dining room, cocktails, laundry, kitchenettes, pool.

LITCHFIELD PARK. The Wigwam. See Phoenix "Other Area Accommodations."

MESA. Raddison Hotel Centennial. *Deluxe.* 200 N. Centennial Way, Mesa, AZ 85201 (602–898–8300). Restaurants, lounge, tennis.

Saguaro Lake Guest Ranch. *Deluxe.* 13020 Bush Hwy., Mesa, AZ 85205 (602–984–2194). Horses, tubing on Salt River, pool, restaurant, lounge.

Golden Hills Golf Resort. *Expensive–Deluxe.* 425 S. Power Rd., Mesa, AZ 85208 (602–832–3202). Kitchenettes, 1- and 2-bedroom units, golf course casitas, lighted tennis courts, restaurants, lounge, other recreational facilities.

Hilton Pavilion. *Expensive–Deluxe.* 1011 W. Holmes Ave., Mesa, AZ 85202 (602–833–5555). Restaurants, lounge, pool, shop.

Best Western Dobson Ranch Inn. *Expensive.* 1666 S. Dobson Rd., Mesa, AZ 85202 (602–831–7000). Spas, suites, restaurant, lounge, patio dining.

Lexington Hotel Suites. *Moderate–Expensive.* 1410 Country Club Dr., Mesa, AZ 85202 (602–964–2897). Hot tub, laundry, pool, continental breakfast.

Best Western Mesa Inn. *Moderate.* 1625 E. Main St., Mesa, AZ 85204 (602–964–8000). Coffee shop, some non-smoking rooms.

Mezona Best Western Motel. *Moderate.* 250 W. Main St., Mesa, AZ 85201 (602–834–9233). Health facilities, restaurant, lounge.

MIAMI. Best Western Copper Hills Inn & Resort. *Moderate.* on US 60, Rte. 1, Box 506, Miami, AZ 85539 (602–425–7151). Restaurants, lounge.

NOGALES. El Dorado. *Moderate–Expensive.* 1001 Grand Ave., Nogales, AZ 85621 (602–287–4611). Some apartments, pool, restaurants, lounge.

Americana Motor Hotel. *Moderate.* 850 Grand Ave., Nogales, AZ 85621 (602–287–7211). Restaurant, lounge, entertainment, beauty shop.

Best Western Time Motel. *Inexpensive.* 1200 Grand Ave., Nogales, AZ 85621 (602–287–4627).

PAGE. Ramada Inn. *Moderate.* 716 Rim View Dr., Box C, Page, AZ 86040 (602–645–2466). Restaurant, lounge, spa, cable TV, some suites.

Holiday Inn. *Moderate.* 287 N. Lake Powell Blvd., Page, AZ 86040 (602–645–8851). Restaurants, lounge, fishing.

Wahweap Lodge. *Moderate–Expensive.* About 10 miles northeast of Page, at the main marina on Lake Powell, Box 1597, Page AZ 86040 (602–645–2433). Boat dock, boat tours, rentals. Pool, restaurant, lounge, dinner cruises.

PARKER. Kofa Inn. *Inexpensive.* 1700 California Ave., Parker, AZ 85344 (602–669–2101). Pool, coffee shop.

PRESCOTT. The Hassayampa Inn. *Moderate–Deluxe.* 122 E. Gurley St., Prescott, AZ 84301 (602–778–9434). Restaurants, lounge, bakery.

Sierra Inn. *Moderate–Expensive.* 809 White Spar Rd., Prescott, AZ 86301 (602–445–1250). Pool, fireplaces, spa, kitchenettes.

SAFFORD. Best Western Sandia Motel. *Inexpensive.* 520 E. Hwy. 70, Safford, AZ 85546 (602–428–1621). Pool, restaurant, lounge adjacent.

SEDONA. Los Abrigados. *Deluxe–Super Deluxe.* 160 Portal Lane, Sedona, AZ 86336 (602–282–1777), pool, dining room, tennis, golf.

Poco Diablo Resort. *Deluxe.* Hwy. 179, 2 miles south of town, Box 1709, Sedona, AZ 86336 (602–282–7333). Fireplaces, tennis, golf, pools, hot tubs, restaurant, lounge.

Best Western Arroyo Roble Hotel. *Expensive.* 400 N. Hwy. 89A, Sedona, AZ 86336 (602–282–4001). Pool, restaurant.

Bell Rock Inn. *Moderate–Expensive.* Hwy. 179, Sedona, AZ 86336 (602–282–4161). Pool, tennis, restaurants, lounge, health club, and golf privileges.

SHOW LOW. Best Western Maxwell House. *Moderate.* Box 2437, Show Low, AZ 85901 (602–537–4356). Pool, restaurant, lounge, private fishing, spectacular fall colors.

TOMBSTONE. Best Western Lookout Lodge. *Moderate.* Hwy. 80 West, Tucson, AZ 85638 (602–457–2223). Pool, continental breakfast.

TUCSON. All places listed for Tucson have air-conditioning, pools, phones, and most have lower rates from April 15 to Oct. 1. Most guest ranches close in summer.

Loews Ventana Canyon Resort. *Deluxe–Super Deluxe.* 7000 N. Resort Dr., Tucson, AZ 85715 (602–299–2020). Golf, tennis, disco, gourmet restaurant, all resort facilities.

The Westin La Paloma. *Deluxe–Super Deluxe.* 3800 E. Sunrise Dr., Tucson, AZ 85704 (602–742–6000). New with restaurants, lounge, golf, tennis, all luxuries.

Hotel Park. *Deluxe.* 5151 E. Grant Rd., Tucson, AZ 85712 (602–323–6262).Restaurants, lounge.

Airport Embassy Suites Hotel. *Expensive–Deluxe.* 7051 S. Tucson Blvd., Tucson, AZ 85706 (602–573–0700). Spa, restaurant, lounge, complimentary cocktails/breakfast.

Arizona Inn. *Expensive–Deluxe.* 2200 E. Elm St., Tucson, AZ 85706 (602–325–1541). Old favorite. Dining room, lounge, tennis, quiet reading room, shady patios.

Aztec Inn. *Expensive–Deluxe.* Best Western. 102 N. Alvernon Way, Tucson, AZ 85711 (602–795–0330). Suites with kitchenettes, gift shop, beauty shop, dining room, lounge, shuffleboard.

Raddison Suite Hotel. *Expensive–Deluxe.* 6555 E. Speedway, Tucson, AZ 85710 (602–721–7100). Golf, tennis, restaurants, lounge.

Westward Look Resort. *Expensive–Deluxe.* 245 E. Ina Rd., Tucson, AZ 85704 (602–297–1151). In foothills of Santa Catalina Mnts. three pools, three spas, tennis, putting green, lounge.

Doubletree Hotel. *Expensive.* 445 S. Alvernon Way, Tucson, AZ 85711 (602–881–4200). Restaurants, lounge, spa, golf, tennis.

Quality Inn Tanque Verde. *Expensive.* 7007 E. Tanque Verde, Tucson, AZ 85715 (602–298–2300). In restaurant/entertainment district. Cocktails and breakfast included.

Smuggler's Inn. *Expensive.* 6350 E. Speedway Blvd., Tucson, AZ 85710 (602–296–3292). Restaurant, lounge, golf, tennis, private patios.

Sheraton Tucson El Conquistador. *Moderate–Super Deluxe.* 10000 N. Oracle Rd., Tucson, AZ 85704 (602–742–7000). Restaurants, lounge, golf, tennis, horseback riding, spa, boutiques.

Lodge on the Desert. *Moderate–Deluxe.* 306 N. Alvernon Way, Box 42500, Tucson, AZ 85733 (602–325–3366). In-town resort. European and American Plan available. Lounge, complimentary breakfast.

Cliff Manor Inn. *Moderate–Expensive.* 5900 N. Oracle Rd., Tucson, AZ 85704 (602–887–4000). Spa, lounge, restaurant, golf, tennis.

Lexington Hotel Suites. *Moderate–Expensive.* 7411 N. Oracle Rd., Tucson, AZ 85704 (602–575–9255). All suites. Large patio, putting green, other resort facilities. Breakfast included.

Ghost Ranch Lodge (Best Western), *Moderate.* 801 W. Miracle Mile, Tucson, AZ 85705 (602–791–7565). Laundry, kitchenettes, restaurant, lounge, putting green.

Santa Rita Hotel. *Moderate.* 88 E. Broadway, Tucson, AZ 85701 (602–747–7581). Spa, restaurant, lounge. Complimentary golf and tennis available.

Royal Sun Inn (Best Western). *Moderate.* 1015 N. Stone Ave., Tucson, AZ 85705 (602–622–8871). Saunas, shuffleboard, coffee shop, dining room, lounge, spa.

Continental Inn. *Moderate.* 750 W. 22nd St., Tucson, AZ 85713 (602–624–4455). Coffee shop, weight room.

Tucson Desert Inn. *Inexpensive.* 1 N. Freeway, Tucson, AZ 85745 (602–642–8151).

GUEST RANCHES IN THE TUCSON AREA. **Hacienda del Sol.** *Super Deluxe.* 5601 N. Hacienda del Sol Rd., Tucson AZ 85718 (602–299–1501). In Catalina foothills. Exercise center, horseback riding, tennis, putting green. American Plan.

La Madera Ranch and Resort. *Deluxe.* 9061 E. Woodland Rd., Box 60280, Tucson, AZ 85751 (602–749–2773). Dining room, cocktails, tennis.

Lazy K Bar Ranch. *Deluxe.* 8401 N. Scenic Dr., Tucson, AZ 85743 (602–297–0702). Horseback riding. Guests met at airport. American Plan.

Tanque Verde Guest Ranch. *Super Deluxe.* 8 miles east to end of Speedway Blvd., Box 66, Tucson, AZ 85748 (602–296–6275). Indoor/outdoor pools, putting green, stables, other ranch activities, playground, spas, tennis. Downtown. Olympic pool, coffee shop.

White Stallion Guest Ranch. *Super Deluxe.* 9251 W. Twin Peaks Rd., Tucson, AZ 85743 (602–297–0252). 3000-acre ranch. Riding, tennis, rodeos, therapy pool, cookouts, hayrides. Open Oct. 1 to May 1. No credit cards. American Plan.

WICKENBURG. Rancho de los Caballeros. *Super Deluxe.* Off US 60, Box 1148, Wickenburg, AZ 85358 (602–684–5484). Ranch resort in desert setting. Playground, children's counsellor, riding, tennis, golf, skeet. Open Oct. 15 to May 1. No credit cards. American Plan.

Flying E Ranch. *Deluxe.* 15 miles west of town off US 60, Box EEE, Wickenburg, AZ 85358 (602–684–2690). 21,000-acre working cattle ranch. Private dining room, tennis, all ranch activities. American Plan.

Kay El Bar Guest Ranch. *Deluxe.* 3 miles north of town on Rincon Rd., Box 2480, Wickenburg, AZ 85358 (602–684–7593). Horseback riding, pool. Open Oct. 15 to May 1. American Plan.

Wickenburg Inn Tennis and Guest Ranch. *Deluxe.* Box P, Wickenburg, AZ 85358 (602–684–7811). Luxury cabanas on a hillside near a desert wildlife preserve.

WILLCOX. Best Western Plaza Inn. *Moderate–Expensive.* 1100 W. Rex Allen Dr., Willcox, AZ 85643 (602–384–3556). Restaurant, pool, lounge.

WILLIAMS. Travelodge Downtown. *Inexpensive–Moderate.* 430 E. Bill Williams Ave., Williams, AZ 86046 (602–635–2651).

WINSLOW. Motel 6. *Inexpensive.* 725 W. 3rd St., Winslow, AZ 86047 (602–289–3903). Budget chain, but clean and adequate.

YUMA. Stardust Resort Motor Inn. *Moderate–Expensive.* 2350 4th Ave., Yuma, AZ 85364 (602–783–8861). Spa, putting green, laundry, restaurants, lounge.

Best Western Chilton Inn. *Moderate.* 300 E. 32nd St., Yuma, AZ 85364 (602–344–1050). Pool, coffee shop, lounge.

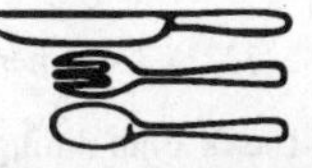

RESTAURANTS. Dining out in Arizona means chiefly American cuisine to travelers, but you can also find Mexican, German, Chinese, Italian, and Polynesian foods and more. By the way, "chicken fried steak" on the menu is breaded beef, not fowl. Categories indicate the cost of a full meal for one, without beverage, tax, or tip included. The price categories are: *Deluxe,* over $18; *Expensive,* $12–18; *Moderate,* $8–12, and *Inexpensive,* under $8.

CASA GRANDE. Ochoa's. *Moderate.* 512 E. Cottonwood Ln. (836–9867). Excellent chimichangas. Closed Sun.

FLAGSTAFF. Black Bart's Steakhouse & Saloon. *Moderate–Expensive.* 2760 E. Butler Ave. (779–3142). A fun place, good food, Old West dinner theater.

Mama Luisa. *Moderate.* Kachina Shopping Center at Santa Fe and Steves streets (526–6809). Italian food.

Mandarin Garden. *Moderate.* 3518 E. Santa Fe St. (526–5033). Chinese food, pleasant surroundings.

El Chilito. *Moderate–Inexpensive.* 1551 S. Milton Rd. (774–4666). Mexican food.

HOLBROOK. Butterfield Stage Co. *Moderate.* 609 W. Hopi Dr. (524–3447).

JEROME. English Kitchen. *Moderate.* 119 Jerome Ave. (634–2132). In spite of the name, the specialty is Chinese food.

House of Joy. *Expensive.* Hull Ave. (634–5339). It's a restaurant, but it used to be just what it sounds like. Popular, make advance reservations.

KINGMAN. Angel's. *Moderate.* 927 Andy Devine Rd. (753–9832). Italian food.

La Poblanita. *Inexpensive.* 1921 Club Rd. (753–5087). Mexican food.

LAKE HAVASU CITY. London Arms. *Expensive–Moderate.* At the end of the bridge (855–4081). In a complex of buildings recreating a bit of merry olde England on the desert. Continental cuisine.

Casa de Miguel. *Inexpensive.* 1556 S. Palo Verde (453–1550). Mexican food.

MESA. Lakeshore Inn. *Moderate.* 14011 Bush Hwy. (984–5311). At Saguaro Lake Marina, about 20 miles northeast of town. Steak, seafood, chicken, outdoor lounge.

Marshals USA. *Moderate.* 1235 E. Main (890–0000). Steak and prime rib.

NOGALES. La Fuente. *Moderate–Expensive.* 1001 Grand Ave. (287–4611). International menu, lounge.

PRESCOTT. Pine Cone Inn. *Moderate–Expensive.* White Spar Rd. (445–2970). American cuisine, cocktails, music, dancing.

SAFFORD. Golden Corral. *Moderate.* In Gila Valley Plaza in Thatcher, 3 miles north of town on US 70 (428–4744). Family dining.

Tiki Restaurant & Lounge. *Inexpensive.* at Desert Inn Motel, 1391 Thatcher Blvd. (428–0521). American and Chinese entrees.

SEDONA. The Atrium. *Expensive.* (282–5060). One of several nice places in Tlaquepaque Plaza at south end of town.

The Coffee Pot. *Moderate.* 2445 W. Hwy. 89A (282–6226). Family dining. Over 100 kinds of omlettes.

The Happy Cooker. *Moderate.* Castlerock Plaza (284–2240). Nouvelle cuisine.

Fournos. *Moderate–Expensive.* 3000 W. Hwy. 89A (282–3331). Continental cuisine.

L'Aberge de Sedona. *Expensive.* 301 Little Lane (282–1661). Fine dining in luxury resort, small and intimate.

SHOW LOW. Asia Gardens. *Moderate.* 59 W. Duece Clubs Ave. (537–4383). Good Chinese food.

TUCSON. The Eclectic Cafe. *Expensive.* 7053 E. Tanque Verde (885–2842). Excellent nouvelle cuisine.

The Good Earth Restaurant and Bakery. *Moderate.* 6266 E. Broadway (745–6600). Beef, chicken, fresh seafood.

El Adobe Mexican Restaurant. *Moderate.* 40 W. Broadway (791–7458). Authentic Sonoran Mexican cooking, outdoor garden patio, and indoor adobe dining rooms. Historic site.

Katherine and Company. *Expensive.* 2574 N. Campbell Ave. (327–3086). Charming outdoor cafe with European atmosphere, gourmet food.

Silver Saddle Steak House. *Moderate–Expensive.* Fourth Ave. at I–10 (622–6253). Mesquite-broiled steaks, ribs, chicken, and seafood.

Samaniego House Restaurant. *Moderate–Expensive.* 222 S. Church St. (622–7790). Historic adobe house, fireplaces, courtyards.

La Fuente. *Moderate.* 1749 N. Miracle Mile (623–8659). Mexican food, mariachi music.

Mama Luisa's. *Moderate.* 2041 S. Craycroft Rd. (790–4702). Italian food, locally popular. Homemade pasta.

Po Folks Family Restaurant. *Inexpensive–Moderate.* 5632 E. Speedway (748–2700). Country cooking, large portions. American cuisine.

WICKENBURG. Frontier Inn. *Moderate to Expensive.* 466 E. Center (684–2183). Western atmosphere, American menu, specializing in smoked meats. Closed summers.

Gold Nuggett. *Moderate.* 222 E. Center (684–2858). General menu, western decor.

WILLIAMS. Rod's Steak House. *Moderate.* 301 E. Bill Williams Ave. (635–2671). Charcoal-broiled steaks, chicken.

WINSLOW. The Entre Restaurant and Motel. *Moderate.* on W. Hwy. 66 (289–2140). Family dining. Chinese and American food.

YUMA. El Charro. *Moderate–inexpensive.* 601 W. 8th St. (783–9790). Mexican food a specialty, also cocktails.

HOW TO GET AROUND. By Rental Car. National and independent car rental agencies are located in all major towns and airports. Some companies offer special packages for a weekend, week, or longer.

By Bus. Bus service links many of the communities. For local sightseeing, however, the main source is *Gray Line,* which offers 4-hour and 4-day escorted tours. Tucson: 180 W. Broadway Blvd., Box 1991 (622–8811). Flagstaff: Box 339 (774–5003).

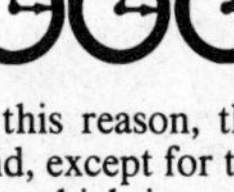

TOURIST INFORMATION. *Arizona Office of Tourism,* Suite 180, 1480 Bethany Home Rd., Phoenix, AZ 85014 (602–255–3618). *Metropolitan Tucson Convention and Visitors Bureau,* 450 W. Paseo Redondo, # 110, Tucson, AZ 85705 (602–624–1817). See also under "Practical Information for Phoenix."

TIME ZONE. Since most of Arizona's population lives in the desert, saving daylight in summer was not of great concern. Most desert dwellers can't wait for the sun to go down in the summertime so things can cool off a little. For this reason, the state elected to stay on *Mountain Standard Time* year-round, except for the Navajo Indian Reservation in the northeastern part of the state, which is on *Mountain Daylight Time.*

TELEPHONES. All Arizona is within area code 602. Directory assistance is 1411. Pay phones cost 25¢. **Emergency telephone numbers:** *Poison Control,* 800–326–0101; *Community Information and Referral Services,* 263–8856; *Crisis Services,* 249–1749; *FBI,* 279–5511; *Department of Public Safety* (Highway Patrol), to report an accident, 262–8011.

SEASONAL EVENTS. Here are just a few events, mostly those that have been in operation several years. Dates may vary, so check locally or write for a complete statewide list: Arizona Office of Tourism, Suite 180, 1480 E. Bethany Home Rd., Phoenix 85014. Or call 602–255–3618.

January. *Tempe:* Fiesta Bowl football game. *Phoenix:* National Livestock Show, American Indian Market, Phoenix Open Golf Tournament. *Apache Junction:* Rock & Mineral Show, Lost Dutchman Days. **February.** *Quartzite:* Gem & Mineral Show. *Wickenburg:* Gold Rush Days. *Phoenix:* Square Dance Jubilee, Annual Cactus Show and various programs at Botanical Garden. *Scottsdale:* Arabian Horse Fiesta. *Flagstaff:* Ski Carnival. *Safford:* Old Time Fiddlers

Contest. *Tucson:* Winter Classic Horse Show, Fiesta de Los Vaqueros (big rodeo). **March.** *Phoenix:* Heard Museum Indian Fair, Jaycee Rodeo, American Indian Spring Festival and Fair, Heritage Square Arts and Crafts Festival. *Tombstone:* Territorial Days. *Lake Havasu City:* Sailboat Regatta. *Tucson:* Livestock Show, Pioneer Days. *Mesa:* Square and Round Dance Festival. **April.** *Scottsdale:* Spring Arts Festival (juried), Outdoor Jazz Festival. *Lake Havasu City:* London Bridge Regatta. *Tucson:* Celebrity Tennis Tournament. **May.** *Tucson:* Cinco de Mayo Festival (also held in many other towns). *Kingman:* Horse Racing. *Sedona:* Senior Open Tennis Tournament. *Jerome:* Historic Home Tour. *Tombstone:* Wyatt Earp Days. *Springerville:* John Wayne Days. **June.** *Fort Huachuca:* Cavalry Olympics. *Sonoita:* Quarter Horse Show (one of oldest in nation). *Prescott:* Folk Art Fair. *Flagstaff:* Rodeo. *Holbrook:* Old West Days. **July.** All towns and cities celebrate the Fourth in various ways. *Prescott:* Frontier Days. *Globe/Miami:* Old Time Fiddlers Contest. *Payson:* Loggers Festival. **August.** *Flagstaff:* Navajo Crafts Exhibition. *Whiteriver:* Tribal Fair & Rodeo. *Williams:* Mountain Men Rodeo. *Tombstone:* Wild Bunch Wild West Days. *Oatman:* Gold Camp Days. **September.** *Window Rock:* Annual Navajo Tribal Fair. *Sedona:* Festival of the Arts. **October.** *Tombstone:* Helldorado Days. *Lake Havasu City:* Sailboard Regatta. *Phoenix:* Cowboy Artists of America Annual Awards and Exhibit. **November.** *Wickenburg:* Bluegrass Festival. *Phoenix:* Gems of the Golden West Show. **December.** *Page:* Festival of Lights on Lake Powell. *Tumacacori:* Mission Festival. *Phoenix:* Annual Indian Market, Fiesta Bowl Parade. *Tucson:* Christmas Kingdom.

NATIONAL PARKS. Grand Canyon National Park. This is one of the most popular national parks in the United States. In few places of the world has nature flaunted herself to the degree found here. Located about 60 miles north of the town of Williams, Grand Canyon varies in width from one to 14 miles and is about a mile deep. From the top, the Colorado River appears to be a winding ribbon cutting through the canyon floor amid the constantly changing hues of the canyon walls as the sun's rays bounce off its sculptured faces. The *North Rim* is the least developed side of the canyon but there are roads along part of the rim for the traveler wishing to see the most. Overnight guests at the Ranch are welcome; advance reservations are a "must." *Point Imperial* and *Point Sublime* offer the best North Rim views of the canyon. The National Park Service provides lectures and nature walks around the area. Because of the snows, the North Rim is closed usually from October to May.

The canyon's *South Rim* is the busiest sightseeing area, open year-round and with some 35 miles of good paved roads. Foremost sightseeing trips are the 8-mile *West Rim Drive* and 25-mile *East Rim Drive,* both offering exceptional views. The Fred Harvey Company runs sightseeing trips on these drives to *Hermit's Rest* and *Desert View.* Most outstanding viewpoints and museums dealing with the gorge's story are at the *Visitor Center, Yavapai Point, Desert View* and the *Tusayan* (Indian) *Ruin.* Other points of interest include Hopi House. *NOTE:* In late spring, summer, and early fall, advance reservations and permits are *essential* for *all* accommodations, mule trips, camping; the West Rim Drive is closed in summer to cars—free shuttle-bus service is provided.

For information, write to the Superintendent, Grand Canyon National Park, AZ 86023 or call 602–638–7888.

Petrified Forest National Park. Situated 15 miles east of Holbrook, this park is one of the most unusual national parks in the country. Ancient trees which have turned to rock are colored with every hue of the rainbow. The park is divided into six general areas: *Long Logs, Giant Logs, Rainbow Forest, Blue Mesa, Crystal,* and *Jasper Forests.* Rainbow has stone logs more than 100 feet long. The petrified wood is protected against pilferage by park authorities. Pieces from other areas can be purchased at one of the shops. The petrified wood can also be gathered outside the preserve. It is not the only item of interest here. *Agate House,* constructed by Indians from petrified wood more than 900 years ago, is of interest, as is *Newspaper Rock,* which contains petroglyphs of an ancient civilization. *Puerco Ruin* here is the remains of a 14th-century Indian village. *Rainbow Forest Museum* contains fossilized skulls found in the vicinity in addition to fossils, minerals, and other artifacts. The area is open only during daylight hours.

The *Painted Desert,* that portion of the park north of I–40, is an awesome landscape of eroded shales, sandstones, and marls, with exposed bands of grey, red, brown, yellow, and mauve.

For information, contact the Superintendent, Petrified Forest National Park, AZ 86208 (602–524–6228) or the Holbrook/Petrified Forest Chamber of Commerce, 100 E. Arizona, Holbrook, AZ 86025 (602–524–6558).

You can also contact the *National Park Service* at 115 N. First St., Phoenix, AZ 85004 (602–261–4956).

Glen Canyon National Recreation Area encompasses most of the 150,000-acre Lake Powell, on the Colorado River. Fishing and houseboating are popular, and the scenery is spectacular. The main gateway is in Page, Arizona, but the lake lies mostly in Utah. For information write Box 1507, Page, AZ 86040.

NATIONAL MONUMENTS. These parks are administered by the National Park Service and preserve places of scenic, geological, or anthropological interest almost —but not quite—as important as national parks. A partial list of national monuments in Arizona:

Canyon de Chelly. Box 588, Chinle, AZ 86503 (602–674–5436). Seventy-five miles north of I–40 at Chambers, this park includes two deep red canyons containing prehistoric Indian cliff dwellings. It is on the Navajo Reservation though they are not the descendants of the cliff dwellers. Navajo guides must accompany all jeep and horseback parties into the monument, except on one foot trail that goes to White House Ruin. A scenic drive goes along the rims of the canyons with good overlooks of the canyons and ruins.

On the way to Canyon de Chelly, at forty miles north of Chambers is **Hubbell Trading Post National Historic Site,** Box 388, Ganado, AZ 86505 (602–755–3254). It is well worth a stop. Since 1874 it has been an important post on the Navajo Reservation. It is still an active trading post with one of the finest collections of rugs and jewelry in the southwest.

Montezuma Castle. Box 219, Camp Verde, AZ 86322 (602–567–3322). Twenty miles south of Sedona off I–17, Montezuma Castle preserves cliff dwellings built between 1100 and 1400 A.D., abandoned 600 years ago. A detached portion is *Montezuma Well,* five miles north, a limestone sinkhole with smaller ruins.

Navajo National Monument, Tonalea, AZ 86044 (602–672–2366). Thirty-one miles southwest of Kayenta are the magnificent prehistoric cliff dwellings at Betatakin, reached by a lovely canyon trail, and at Keet Seel, reached only by a rugged 8-mile foot or horseback trail.

Organ Pipe Cactus National Monument, Box 38, Aho, AZ 85321 (602–387–6849). 30 miles south of Aho on AZ 85. The largest stand of this stately cactus in the world is here. The monument is bordered on the south by Mexico and on the east by the Papago Indian Reservation. Few roads, no facilities, inquire locally and take water.

Saguaro National Monument. Rte. 9, Box 905, Tucson, AZ 85743 (602–883–6366). The monument is in two sections, a few miles east and west of Tucson. The saguaro cactus is a recognized symbol of Arizona. When the blossom, the state flower, blooms in May and June, it is a glorious sight. The Arizona-Sonoran Desert Museum (883–1380), hiking trails, and the famous movie town, Old Tucson, are in the western portion, but the largest saguaros grow in the eastern portion.

Sunset Crater National Monument. Tuba Star Rte., Flagstaff, AZ 86001 (602–527–7042). Ten miles north of Flagstaff on US 89. An almost perfect cinder cone rises a thousand feet above the surrounding lava beds, glowing burnt orange in the sunlight. The last eruption was in 1064, and pine trees and shrubs are slowly reclaiming the land. Good paved trail to the top of the cone goes past interesting volcanic formations.

Tuzigood National Monument. Box 68, Clarkdale, AZ 86324 (602–634–5564). Twenty miles southwest of Sedona on US 89A. Built by prehistoric Sinagua Indians in the 13th century, this 100-room pueblo on top of a hill commands a view of the Verde Valley where they once farmed. Visitor center, trail to the ruins.

Walnut Canyon National Monument. Rte. 1, Box 24, Flagstaff, AZ 86001 (602–526–3367). Three miles south of I–40 at the eastern edge of Flagstaff. Preserved cliff homes built 800 years ago by the Sinagua Indians. Delightful trail through shady canyon overlooking canyon.

Wupatki National Monument. Tuba Star Rte., Flagstaff, AZ 86001 (602–527–7040). Thirty miles north of Flagstaff on US 89. Some 800 ruins are scattered on this 35,000-acre preserve. Most were built in the 12th century. A trail goes to the largest ruin of over 100 rooms and to a few smaller sites including an ancient ball court, a ceremonial amphitheater, and other pueblos.

NATIONAL FORESTS. Though most people think first of Arizona's deserts, six large national forests lie within its borders on millions of acres of mountains, canyons, and plateaus. If you plan to camp, hike, or backpack in any forest, we suggest you write for a map that will show roads, trails, campgrounds, wilderness areas, and geographic features. It's well worth the $2–3 price. Always check in with a local forest ranger before backpacking or hiking any great distance. District offices are located in a nearby town, and ranger stations are usually near the high-use areas.

Apache/Sitgreaves National Forest. So. Mountain Ave., Hwy. 180, Box 640, Springerville, AZ 85938 (602–333–4301). In east central Arizona.

Coconino National Forest. 2323 E. Greenlaw Ln., Flagstaff, AZ 86001 (602–527–7400). On both sides of I–40, north and south of Flagstaff.

Coronado National Forest. Federal Bldg., 300 W. Congress, Tucson, AZ 85701 (602–629–6483). 12 separate units in southeastern and south central Arizona.

Kaibab National Forest. 800 S. 6th St., Williams, AZ 86046 (602–635–2681). In three sections north and south of Grand Canyon, including the North Rim. This section has the largest virgin ponderosa pines in the United States.

Prescott National Forest. 344 S. Cortez St., Prescott, AZ 86301 (602–445–1762). In all directions from Prescott.

Tonto National Forest. 2324 E. McDowell Rd., Box 5348, Phoenix, AZ 85010 (602–225–5200). Northeast of Phoenix. With almost 3 million acres, this is the largest of Arizona's national forests, and includes the fabled Mogollon Rim, site of Zane Grey's novels and his home.

STATE PARKS. There are state parks throughout Arizona at sites of scenic, historical, or recreational value. Many have campgrounds and other facilities. For a list of parks, rates, restrictions, and nearby points of interest, contact Arizona State Parks, 1688 W. Adams, Room 122, Phoenix, AZ 85007 (602–255–4174).

CAMPING OUT. With 72 percent of Arizona's land federally or state owned and in Indian reservations, a half dozen national forests, some twenty national parks, monuments and recreation areas, and a state park system that has over 15 preserves plus more than two hundred roadside parks (many equipped for camping), anyone who wants to camp out has no problem. In addition, there are many private facilities, especially for trailer camping. Most federal and state sites—fairly evenly distributed around the state but chiefly in mountain, canyon, forest and lake country—have set fees and camping time limits, and most require advance reservations, especially during summer months. Campground lists and information are available from the Arizona Office of Tourism, 1480 E. Bethany Home Rd., Suite 180, Phoenix, AZ 85014. This office can also provide a list of contacts for tribal offices. Several tribes maintain campgrounds, especially the Navajo.

TRAILER TIPS. Trailer living is a popular way of life in the Grand Canyon State with both residents and visitors. Facilities in national and state preserves have been greatly improved in recent years. The network of privately operated trailer camps and parks is extensive and particularly well-developed in areas of greatest tourist interest. Ranging from plain to deluxe, they are likely to have many conveniences—such as swimming pools, recreation or community centers, laundries, rest rooms, game areas and other facilities—above the basic ones like electric hookups and sewer outlets. Among the top ones are those affiliated with KOA. Greatest concentration of parks and camps are in the Valley of the Sun around Phoenix, in the Tucson areas and along the Colorado River. However, no section of the state lacks good sites, either on the spot or relatively close. Hauling hazards are few—chiefly the desert heat in summer and mountain snows in winter. Some highways with numerous mountains—such as I-17, US 89 and US 60—mean slower travel, but all Federal and State highways are geared for use of average-size trailers. Without a special permit, state maximum size restrictions are 40 feet in length (65 feet for overall combination), 13½ feet high and 96 inches wide.

GUEST RANCHES. This popular western pastime has been brought to a fine art in Arizona, whether the place is rustic or deluxe. Emphasis is on informality, fresh-air recreation; there's no need to go horseback riding unless desired since there are plenty of other sports. Main centers are Tucson and Wickenburg; there are also scattered dude ranches in other locales such as Patagonia and the region around Douglas. Except for sports clothes and blue jeans, don't bring "western attire;" you'll do better to buy it in Arizona, where it's authentic rather than "rodeo riot" in design. *Note:* In recent years, dude ranches have stressed less cow and more comfort in modern amenities, though informality still prevails.

A complete list of guest ranches is available from the state Office of Tourism, 1480 E. Bethany Home Rd., Phoenix, AZ 85014.

INDIANS. There are 17 reservations and over 100,000 Indians in Arizona. Chiefly of interest for the tourist are *Navajo Reservation* in the northeastern part of the state, a land of vast spaces, *Monument Valley,* national monuments and hogans. Crafts for sale include rugs and silver jewelry. *Hopi Reservation.* This is located inside the big *Navajo Reservation;* one can sometimes see authentic dance ceremonials, and may purchase ceremonial sashes, Kachina dolls, pottery, silver jewelry and baskets. In *Havasupai Reservation,* south of the middle part of *Grand Canyon National Park,* the Indians live in a canyon "Shangrila," the most remote tribe in the state and least affected by the white man's ways. Lovely waterfalls are to be seen here. *Fort Apache* and *San Carlos Indian Reservations* in east central Arizona have the popular *White Mountain* recreation area, *Salt River Canyon,* wickiups, some ceremonials, basketry and other crafts. *Gila River (Pima)* and *Papago Reservations* are in desert sections with adobe and squat brush-wattle homes, few ceremonials. Best craft is basketry. Many of the Arizona Indians, particularly the Hopi, do not like to have their photographs taken so it is wise to ask permission before aiming the camera. Ceremonials are almost never subject matter for photographs.

The Navajo Tribal Fair, with parades, ceremonial dances, rodeos, and exhibits, takes place in early September. For more information, contact the Tribal Visitor Service, Box 308, Window Rock, AZ 86515 (871–4941).

MUSEUMS AND GARDENS. Flagstaff: *Lowell Observatory,* one mile west of center of town (774–3358). Astronomers here discovered Pluto in 1930. Lecture tour daily at 1:30, evening programs on Friday during summer. *Museum of Northern Arizona,* three mi. north of town on US 180 (774–5211). Anthropology, geology, and biology of northern Arizona. *Pioneer Historical Museum,* two miles north of town on US 180 (774–6272).

Glendale: *Wildlife World Zoo,* Rte. 1, Box 152, on Northern Ave., 85301 (935–WILD).

Jerome: Jerome Historical Society *Douglas Mining Museum,* Box 156, 86331 (634–7349).

Superior: *Southwest Arboretum,* Box AB, 85273 (689–2811).

Sedona: This town at the end of Oak Creek Canyon is the art center of Arizona and has dozens of galleries representing prestigious artists.

Tucson: *Arizona-Sonora Desert Museum,* Rte. 9, Box 900, 85743 (883–1380). World famous. *Garden of Gethsemene,* at Congress Exit off I–10 (791–4873). Statuary garden. *Kitt Peak National Observatory,* 950 N. Cherry, 85726 (325–9204). Observatory located 53 miles west of Tucson. Research in astronomy, open to the public daily except Christmas. *Pima Air Museum,* 6400 S. Wilmot, 85706 (574–0462). Traces history of aviation in America. *Reid Park Zoo,* Randolph Way and E. 22nd St., 85716 (791–4002). *Tucson Botanical Garden,* 2150 N. Alvernon Way, 85712 (326–9255). *Arizona State Museum,* Univ. of Ariz. Campus (621–6302). Cultural history of the southwest. *Mineral Museum,* Univ. of Ariz. Campus (621–4227). *Tucson Museum of Art,* 140 N. Main Ave., 85701 (624–2333).

PARTICIPANT SPORTS. Boating. Boating on the man-made desert lakes is popular. Along the Colorado River are lakes Martinez, Havasu, Mohave, Mead, and Powell; along the Salt River are lakes Saguaro, Canyon, Apache, and Roosevelt. Other areas with lakes are the Mogollon Rim and the White Mountains regions. Houseboating is popular on Lakes Mead and Powell. For a list of boat rentals at Lake Mead, write Superintendent, 601 Nevada Highway, Boulder City, NV 89005. For complete information on Lake Powell, write Glen Canyon National Recreation Area, Box 1507, Page, AZ 86040.

Fishing. Bass crappie and catfish in lakes and streams. Remote rivers in the Grand Canyon and lakes in the mountains are excellent for trout.

Hunting. Fall and winter are the seasons for big game; predatory animals are in season year-round.

Golf: The state abounds with over 150 good courses, most open year-round. Many resorts have them. Most open on reciprocal basis, some are entirely public. Others may be public if not busy. Check with local tourist bureaus regarding which courses are open to travelers, and about times, cost, conditions, etc. Without difficulty, you can play on a different course every day for a month or more.

Tennis. Resorts and city parks offer hundreds of courts.

SKIING. The *Arizona Snow Bowl* near Flagstaff has five rope tows, Poma lift, double chair lift and over 20 miles of ski trails. *Mount Lemmon,* only an hour's drive from Tucson, has a rope tow and Poma double chair lift. *Sunrise Ski Area* outside Springerville is owned and operated by the White Mountain Apache Tribe and features three double chair lifts and tow for beginners.

CHILDREN'S ACTIVITIES. Every youngster who ever watched television already knows the town of *Tombstone,* featured in so many westerns. All of the famous landmarks are clearly marked such as the *OK Corral, Wells Fargo Office, Boothill,* and many other equally familiar places around which stories have been told and retold.

Any of the numerous Indian villages are always of interest to children, particularly those of the *Hopi Indians,* where the child may see tribal dances, staged almost every weekend during summer. Trips to these villages are worth the effort. Indian trading posts in various communities offer colorful wares which never fail to lure youngsters.

There are also the ghost towns, various frontier forts, the old jails like those in *Wickenburg, Clifton* and *Yuma,* the *Smoki Museum* at *Prescott. Old Tucson,* a converted movie set outside the city of Tucson, is a favorite of children because of the various western-style amusements and staged gunfights in the streets. So is the nearby *Arizona-Sonora Desert Museum.*

Grand Canyon Caverns, west of *Williams* and *Colossal Cave,* east of *Tucson,* provide interesting views of nature's handwork in sculptured rock and variegated stone formations, stalagmites and stalactites.

HISTORIC SITES. Some historical and archaeological sites are listed above under "National Monuments." Here are more: **Casa Grande Ruins National Monument.** Supt., Box 518, Coolidge, AZ 85228 (723–3172). One mile north of Coolidge on AZ 87, halfway between Phoenix and Tucson. Includes ruins of a 4-story pueblo built about 600 years ago by Indians of the Gila Valley. Visitor center, trails to other sites.

Fort Bowie National Historic Site. Box 158, Bowie, AZ 85605 (847–2500). Twenty-five miles south of I–10 at Bowie in southeast corner of the state. Unpaved road. Ruins of a fort and stagecoach stop on the old Butterfield Trail used to protect and supply pioneers and military parties before the Civil War. A cold natural spring made it a campsite of the Apaches, and bloody battles ensued over its use.

Chiricahua National Monument. Dos Cabezas Star Rte., Wilcox, AZ 95643 (824–3560). Thirty-three miles southeast of Wilcox via AZ 186. In Coronado National Forest, these rugged mountains and canyons were hide-outs and the last bastion of the Apaches. Visitor Center, trails, scenic drives, camping.

Pipe Spring National Monument. Moccasin, AZ 86022 (643–7105). Located in the "strip"—that isolated part of Arizona north of Grand Canyon—which is more easily reached from Utah. If you are going to the North Rim or to Utah, this will be an interesting stop on AZ 389. It is the site of a large stone fort built by Mormans in 1870 to protect pioneer settlers farming in the lush valley watered by Pipe Spring. It is within the Kaibab Indian Reservation whose ancestors have lived there since Basket Maker times.

Tombstone. Tombstone Tourism Assn., Box 917, Tombstone 85638 (457–2227). The entire town is a historic site with many restored buildings and activities to recall days of the Frontier West, including the gunfight at the OK Corral.

Heritage Square. 127 N. 6th St., Phoenix 85004 (262–5071). In the early days of Phoenix this was a square of important homes and buildings. Victorian architecture is highlighted in the restored 1894 Rosson House and in museums, shops, and other buildings.

El Presidio. Adjacent to Tucson Museum of Art, 140 N. Main Ave., Tucson 85701 (624–2333). Restored buildings once part of the first military quarters are here.

John C. Fremont House. 151 S. Granada, Tucson 85701 (622–0956). The Restored home of Gov. Fremont now houses the Arizona Historical Society. Open to the public Wed.–Sat. Tours led through Tucson's historic district on Sat. mornings with advance reservations.

Old Tucson. 201 S. Kinney Rd., Tucson 85746 (883–0100). About eight miles west of downtown, adjacent to the Arizona/Sonora Desert Museum in Saguaro National Monument. The Old West is kept alive with re-enactments, decor in shops and restaurants, costumes, and sound stage tours.

TOURS AND SIGHTSEEING. A free booklet published by the Phoenix and Valley of the Sun Convention and Visitors Bureau, 505 N. 2nd St., Ste. 300, Phoenix 85004, (602–254–6500), lists 45 tour companies that take individuals or groups on regular or charter tours anywhere in the state.

MUSIC. *Arizona Opera Company,* 3501 N. Mountain Ave., Tucson 85701 (293–4336), presents four performances from Oct.–March. *The Tucson Symphony Orchestra,* 443 S. Stone Ave., Tucson 85701 (882–8585), presents concerts of classical and pop music Oct.-May. Student and faculty concerts with guest artists are presented throughout the academic year at the *University of Arizona,* Tucson 87521 (621–1302).

STAGE. *Arizona Theater Co.* in Tucson, 56 W. Congress 85701 (622–2823) presents performances Tues.-Sun. at Tucson Community Center Little Theatre, 260 S. Church, Tucson (791–4266). At Tucson Community Center Music Hall a special Easter pageant with a full orchestra and 100-member cast is held, free admission (327–5560). *University of Arizona* drama department, Tucson, offers productions throughout the academic year (621–1302).

SHOPPING. Arizona is the place to indulge your whims in western clothing, whether it's a pair of jeans or a tailored gabardine suit with matching boots. Women, too, can find suits, skirts, shirts, and every kind of casual western wear. Indian jewelry, especially Navajo and Hopi, can be found in shops throughout the state and on the reservations. If you do not know the craft, rely on established merchants. The Pima and Papago Indians in southern Arizona are known for their exquisite basketry. Sedona is the center for art, and its dozens of galleries handle the best known artists. Art galleries can also be found in Phoenix, Tucson, and Flagstaff, and most other towns of any size. There are big shopping malls with major department stores and all kinds of specialty shops in various parts of Tucson and Phoenix.

RECOMMENDED READING. Zane Grey's *Under the Tonto Rim* and *Call of the Canyon* were set in Arizona and make interesting reading to go along with your tour of the Grand Canyon. Also interesting are: *All About Arizona* and *All The Southwest* by Thomas B. Lesure; *Arizona—A State Guide; Arizona—Its People and Resources; Arizona Place Names; Arizona Highways,* a monthly magazine, Phoenix.

NIGHTLIFE. In Tucson: *Bobby McGee's,* 6565 E. Tanque Verde, 85715 (886–5551). Costumed characters, music, dancing, great salad bar and soup. *Bum Steer,* 1910 N. Stone, 85705 (884–7377). Live entertainment, lots of activity. *Houlihan's,* 410 N. Wilmot Rd., 85711 (886–8885). Dancing, good food. *Roxy Night Club,* 144 W. Lester 85705 (622–6363). Live country-western music Wed.–Sun. Drink specials on Tues.; closed Mon. *Gaslight Theatre,* 7000 E. Tanque Verde, 85715 (886–9428). Live theater, comedy, melodrama, family fun. Wed.-Sun. Reservations. Dinner at adjacent restaurant. *Triple C Ranch,* 8900 W. Bopp Rd., 85746 (883–2333). Barbecued-beef dinner and Old West show. Reservations. **In Tombstone** try the *Crystal Palace Saloon* where you might find a live gunfighter or rustler.

LIQUOR LAWS. Alcoholic beverages may be legally consumed in any licensed bar, restaurant, hotel or inn from 6 A.M. to 1 A.M. weekdays and from noon to 1 A.M. on Sundays. Most open about 9 or 10 A.M. Personal supplies may be obtained from regular package stores, drugstores or markets, most of which close about 9–11 P.M. There are no state liquor stores. No minor under 21 may be served legally.

SOUTHERN CALIFORNIA

Surf, Sand and Spectaculars

EXPLORING THE LOS ANGELES AREA

Los Angeles is the heartbeat of Southern California, but its pleasures are not limited to the city limits. Los Angeles proper is a microcosm. It is California's largest city—more than 464 square miles—with countless things to see and do. But Los Angeles is only the center of a much larger area, the Los Angeles basin. You can travel the 25 miles from city hall and still remain within the boundaries of the city; travel less than three miles from city hall and end up in a totally different town. The area extends arms into Los Angeles County, into Ventura, Orange, Riverside, and San Bernardino counties, and offers no end of scenic attractions.

For example, Disneyland is not in Los Angeles. It is in Anaheim, 30 minutes away by high-speed freeway. Is Mt. Wilson in Los Angeles? No, again. The famed observatory is in Los Angeles County, but is located high in the adjacent San Gabriel Mountains, much nearer Pasadena.

But the name, Los Angeles, is the magnet, to be sure. L.A. is the place to go, the heart, the nerve center.

Reborn, revitalized downtown Los Angeles includes such noted attractions as the Civic Center, which is not far from the original site of the city and the Old Plaza. Remnants of the city's romantic past are here, yet to see this monumental civic-center complex of theaters,

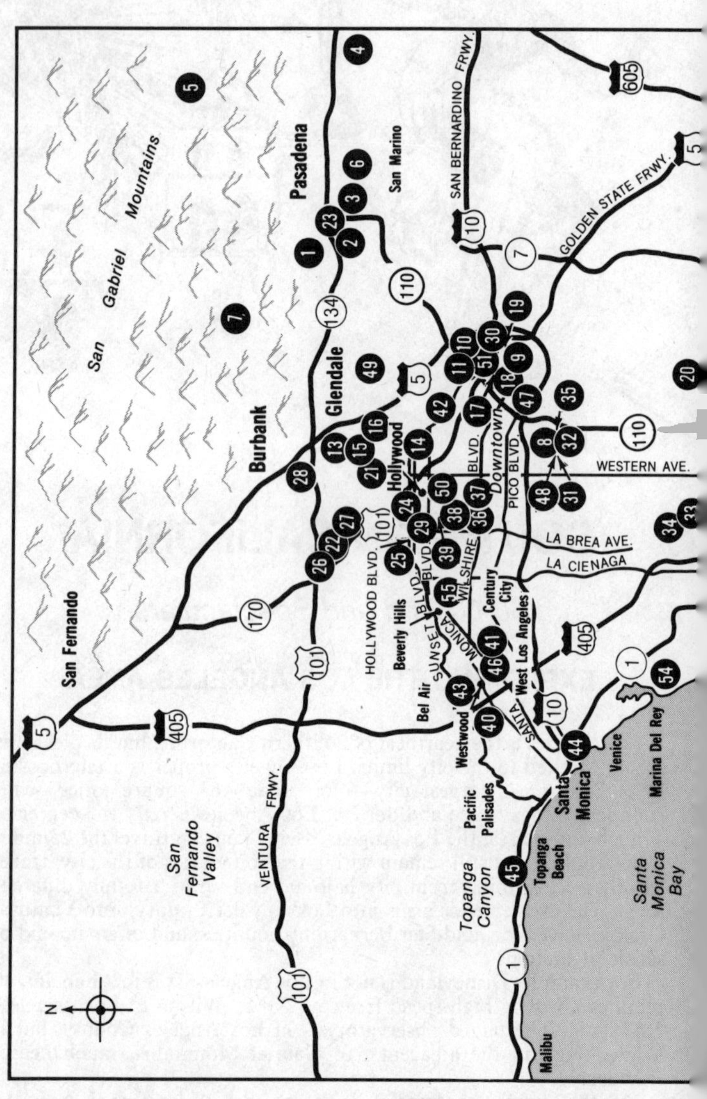
San Gabriel Mountains
San Fernando
Burbank
Glendale
Pasadena
San Marino
San Fernando Valley
VENTURA FRWY.
HOLLYWOOD BLVD.
Hollywood
Beverly Hills
Bel Air
Westwood
SUNSET BLVD.
SANTA MONICA BLVD.
WILSHIRE BLVD.
Century City
West Los Angeles
Downtown
PICO BLVD.
WESTERN AVE.
LA BREA AVE.
LA CIENAGA
SAN BERNARDINO FRWY.
GOLDEN STATE FRWY.
Pacific Palisades
Topanga Canyon
Topanga Beach
Santa Monica
Venice
Marina Del Rey
Santa Monica Bay
Malibu
N

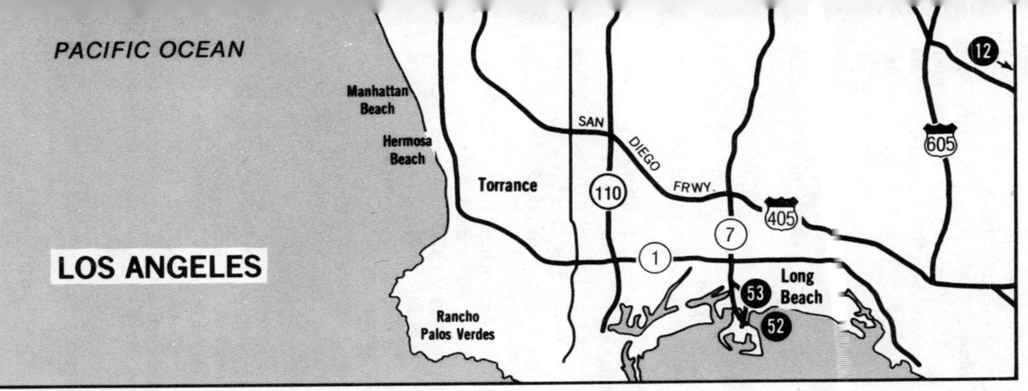

Points of Interest

1) Rose Bowl
2) Norton Simon Museum
3) Pasadena Civic Auditorium
4) Santa Anita Racetrack
5) Mt. Wilson Observatory
6) Huntington Library Gallery
7) Descanso Gardens
8) USC Campus & Medical Center
9) Little Tokyo/Museum of Contemporary Art
10) Chinatown
11) Dodger Stadium
12) Anaheim Stadium, Disneyland, Knott's Berry Farm, Anaheim Convention Center
13) L.A. Zoo
14) Barnsdall Park
15) Griffith Park
16) Greek Theater
17) Civic Center
18) Music Center
19) City Hall
20) Watts Towers
21) Griffith Park Observatory
22) Hollywood Sign
23) Hollywood Bowl
24) Pantages Theater
25) Mann's Chinese Theatre
26) Universal Amphitheatre
27) Universal Studios
28) NBC Studios
29) James A. Doolittle Theatre
30) Union Station
31) Coliseum
32) Exposition Park
33) Hollywood Park Racetrack
34) The Forum
35) Shrine Auditorium
36) L.A. County Art Museum
37) La Brea Tar Pits
38) Farmer's Market
39) CBS TV City
40) Pacific Design Center
41) Shubert Theater
42) ABC Entertainment Center
43) UCLA
44) Santa Monica Civic Auditorium
45) J. Paul Getty Museum
46) Mormon Temple
47) Los Angeles Convention Center
48) California Museum of Science and Industry
49) Forest Lawn Memorial Park
50) Paramount Studios
51) Olvera St.
52) Queen Mary/Spruce Goose
53) Long Beach Convention Entertainment Center
54) L.A. Int'l Airport
55) Beverly Center

industry and commerce is to feel the vigor and vitality of this young city. It has the largest concentration of public buildings west of Washington, D.C.

Downtown's skyline has been dramatically altered in just the past decade. Contemporary hotels like the ultra-modern Westin Bonaventure and multi-story office building complexes have sprouted everywhere. Several 50-story-plus towers now punch the air.

One of the country's most enlightened municipally supported developments—the Los Angeles County Music Center for the Performing Arts—is the jewel of downtown. Composed of three handsomely designed buildings, it is interconnected by a large landscaped plaza and crowned by Jacques Lipchitz's symbol of peace, an impressive sculpture entitled *Peace on Earth.*

The splendid Dorothy Chandler Pavilion is the winter home of the Los Angeles Philharmonic, where opera, ballet, symphonies, and musical comedies are performed.

The Mark Taper Forum is an intimate theater-in-the-round; the presentations are experimental and original. A number of the Taper's productions—for instance, *Children of A Lesser God*—go on to Broadway. Also at the Taper are chamber music, operas, and lectures.

The Ahmanson Theater features the Civic Light Opera, musical dramas, plays, and the Joffrey Ballet, now a resident company. In fact, it's the city's major center of popular entertainment.

To become oriented with Los Angeles you can go up to the 25th-floor observation area in the City Hall. On a clear day there is a panorama of the entire city—of Mt. Wilson in the San Gabriel Mountains, the Pacific Ocean, and the Los Angeles Harbor.

Close at hand, facing the plaza, is Olvera Street, part of El Pueblo de Los Angeles State Historic Park. Some 88 shops are jammed with souvenirs, hand-blown glass objects, pottery pinatas, Mexican fashions and jewelry. It is no wonder that this is one of the city's top tourist attractions, for Los Angeles holds the honor of having the second-largest Spanish-speaking population of any city in the world. Many of this metropolis' Spanish-speaking community live in East Los Angeles, where murals of famous Chicano artists adorn the walls, speaking in vibrant colors of California's heritage, her people's struggles, hopes, and dreams.

Nearby, at First Street, is Little Tokyo, the Japanese quarter of downtown Los Angeles. The city has one of the largest Japanese populations in the United States. There are unusual giftshops, an ornate Buddhist temple, a few Oriental food markets, fine Japanese book stores and good restaurants and sushi bars throughout the area. Weller Court, adjacent to the luxurious New Otani Hotel, boasts fine department stores, specialty shops and restaurants.

A new highlight of the redeveloping downtown is The Museum of Contemporary Art. MoCA is a two-location museum: The main space, at California Plaza and designed by controversial architect Arata Isozaki, opened in December 1986 while the auxiliary exhibition area is a refurbished 1940s warehouse on the edge of Little Tokyo.

Chinatown, located off North Broadway near College Street, is a collection of Chinese curio shops, restaurants, and bustling businesses. The restaurants range from mediocre to excellent. Some are so popular that long waits are required for tables, increasing the popularity of local picture galleries, curio shops, and the typical amusement-park entertainment. Travelers can find excellent values in fine silk (by the yard), brocades, lacquerware, soapstone and jade novelties, and kimonos. It is not quite as exciting as the New York or San Francisco Chinese quarters, but the Los Angeles Chinatown has a lively night scene.

Other points of interest downtown are the bustling Grand Central Market, Arco Plaza and the World Trade Center.

Stadiums and Museums

Major-league baseball games in Los Angeles now are played at Dodgers' Stadium, a beautiful ball park on a bluff in Chavez Ravine, overlooking downtown Los Angeles. The view is spectacular. The California Angels use Anaheim stadium, at 2000 State College, for their home games.

Equally noteworthy in the downtown Los Angeles area, in Exposition Park at Exposition Dr. and Figueroa St., is the Los Angeles Memorial Coliseum. Built in the twenties, the Memorial Coliseum is the scene of the home football games of the University of Southern California Trojans and University of California at Los Angeles Bruins, the Rams' professional football games, fêtes, and rodeos.

New facilities were built to accommodate the XXIIIrd Olympiad in 1984. The McDonald's Swim Stadium now serves youthful swimmers from the L.A. area. The new Olympic Velodrome, a $3 million complex at California State University-Dominique Hills, was the site of the cycling competition. There's a new weight lifting area at Loyola Marymount College and new field tracks at the Coliseum.

Also situated in Exposition Park is the Sports Arena. Modern, completely enclosed, air-conditioned, the Sports Arena plays host to hockey games, ice extravaganzas, track and field events, as well as shows and festivals.

Opposite the Sports Arena is a pair of museums, the Los Angeles Museum of Natural History and the California Museum of Science and Industry. The former has four fine animal-habitat halls of mammals and birds from Africa and North America. (Its fine displays of reconstructed prehistoric skeletons have been moved seven miles northeast to the magnificent George C. Page Museum in Hancock Park, site of the La Brea Tar Pits, the original source of the skeletons.) The California Museum of Science and Industry exhibits scientific wonders—many that you can operate yourself. The mathematics, electricity, aviation, and space displays are fascinating. Changing exhibits include industrial design, graphic and advertising art. An upright Titan missile towers outside over the landscape.

Across the street from Exposition Park is the University of Southern California, founded in 1876. It has several highly regarded graduate schools—medicine, dentistry, pharmacy—and an outstanding cinema department. Located on the campus is the Fisher Art Gallery—sixteenth- and seventeenth-century Dutch and Flemish painting.

Traveling from Downtown northwest toward Hollywood, it is necessary to pass the edge of Griffith Park, the country's largest city park, with more than 4,000 mountainous acres. Griffith Park boasts an imposing observatory-planetarium (seen from all points of the city and an easily recognizable white art-deco building), the open-air Greek Theater, set in a natural canyon below pine-covered mountains, where summer performances play to capacity audiences; golf courses; tennis courts; baseball fields; and miles of hiking and riding trails. In the center of the park is the Los Angeles Zoo, with its 2,000 citizens. They are grouped by their five continental origins in areas resembling their natural environments. There's also a Children's Zoo. The vast park harbors Travel Town with vintage transportation; children can explore a Victorian railroad station, antique trains, planes, cable cars, and a swimming pool. Ferndell, a lovely green spot, has paths shaded by ferns, sycamore and oak trees, waterfalls, running streams, and a Nature Museum with plant and animal exhibits.

The Los Angeles Municipal Art Gallery is in Barnsdall Park, corner of Hollywood Blvd. and Vermont Ave., cached in Frank Lloyd Wright-designed Hollyhock House.

Hollywood is still synonymous with films, television and entertainment. As the glamour capital of the world, it retains much magic because of the stars who work, live, and play in this vicinity. For anyone who has not been into a large motion-picture studio, Universal Studios invites you into Never-Never Land (you can catch Hollywood in the act, for a price). Guided tours through the back lot and sound stages run continuously. Burbank Studios (Warner Brothers) also offers tours.

Hollywood's Boulevards: Hollywood Boulevard—a mere mention of the name—brings to mind visions of glamour and excitement few hometowns can equal. Some visitors are disappointed by its honky-tonk. Others are thrilled by famous names and places they've heard of but never seen. With eyes wide, they stroll the Walk of Fame, a roll call of entertainment's "greats," commemorated in concrete and bronze stars in miles of sidewalks. At Christmastime, the boulevard is transformed into Santa Claus Lane. When in town, check to see when the next unveiling of a new star along the boulevard will take place. A media event, open to the public, the Greater Los Angeles Visitors and Convention Bureau (at 213–624–7300) can tell when and who is set to star next on Hollywood Boulevard's sidewalks.

The celebrated Mann's Chinese Theatre (formerly Graumann's) 6925 Hollywood Boulevard, started the dramatic custom of preserving concrete foot- and handprints of theatrical celebrities back in 1927 with Norma Talmadge. By now millions of tourists have matched their footprints with those of leading cinema personalities ranging from Judy Garland to the cast of *Star Wars.* Nearby on Hollywood Blvd. is C.C. Brown's Ice Cream Parlor, said to be the home of the original hot-fudge sundae.

The Lasky-Demille barn now stands directly across from the Hollywood Bowl and in the Fairfield parking lot; that's where the first major motion picture, *The Squaw Man,* was made.

The famous Hollywood sign, standing 45 feet high and weighing over 480,000 pounds, watches over the city from atop the Hollywood Hills. First erected in 1928, the sign fell into disrepair over the years. Its significance to the community, however, was not forgotten, and a massive fund-raising campaign to reconstruct the sign was launched by the Hollywood Chamber of Commerce, Hugh Hefner, Alice Cooper, Warner Brothers Studios and other institutions and celebrities. The new sign was officially rededicated in 1978.

La Cienega Boulevard, north from Wilshire Blvd. to Santa Monica Blvd., is well known for its "Restaurant Row" of dining spots and art galleries. Tuesday evenings find Los Angeles area art buffs prowling. Some galleries serve snacks and libations. Nearby (Fairfax Blvd. at Third St.) is Farmers' Market, a bustling complex of food stalls and restaurants that is a long-time favorite with visitors. CBS Television City is right next door.

You'll pass many attractions by driving leisurely along Wilshire Boulevard, one of the longest streets in Los Angeles, which stretches from downtown Los Angeles to the clifftop Palisades Park in Santa Monica above the Pacific.

Southwest of Los Angeles is Inglewood and the famed Hollywood Park Race Track, with its regular 55-day season, opening in May. It is located on Century Boulevard, off the southward-running Harbor Freeway. Hollywood Park opens its gates early in the morning for railbirds who like to watch the horses work out. Also in Inglewood is The Forum, home of the Lakers basketball team, and high-decibel rock concerts.

A few miles beyond Hollywood Park, off Century Boulevard, is the Los Angeles International Airport, known locally as LAX. Landmarks include the high-arching modern restaurant and the multiple supersonic-jet landing strips. This airport has the distinction of being the only U.S. airfield served by *all* trunk lines.

In Highland Park, a suburb of Los Angeles, is the Southwest Museum and Heritage Park, 234 Museum Dr. Perched high on a hill overlooking the Pasadena Freeway, the museum contains extensive collections of Indian relics and artifacts from North, South, and Central America. It has an outstanding collection of California Indian baskets, material gathered by several archeological expeditions into the field of California, and Plains Indian materials. It plays host to a large number of Southern California schoolchildren, all of whom study the California Indians as a regular part of their curriculum.

The Los Angeles County Museum of Art is located at the edge of Hancock Park, on Wilshire Blvd. near Fairfax Blvd. It is evidence of the city's significance as an art center, for its exhibitions, lectures, films and concerts are of great aesthetic and educational value to the community. It draws students, art lovers, and scholars from all over the world. The handsome, four-building complex is surrounded by fountains and tree-lined plazas. Ahmanson Gallery displays the permanent collection, spanning over 5,000 years, from ancient to avant-garde works. Major traveling exhibitions accompanied by lectures, films and special programs are shown in the Frances and Armand Hammer Wing. The Leo S. Bing Center has a cafeteria, art rental gallery, and the Bing Theater, which features various cultural programs. The glass-brick Robert O. Anderson Building houses the museum's most contemporary works.

The George C. Page Museum with more than 1,000 displays is also in Hancock Park, along with the original La Brea Tar Pits where its prehistoric animal specimens were captured and preserved. The large asphalt sink still is murky and bubbly as it was 35,000 years ago.

The western section of the city includes Beverly Hills, Westwood, Brentwood, and Bel-Air. These suburbs became part of the vast Los Angeles metropolis in the early 1900s. Most visitors to Southern California have a great desire to see TV and movie stars, and they are likely to be seen in the chic shops, supermarkets, and celebrity haunts of the elegant communities. Starting from the early 1920s, many showpeople from the movie colony moved to these suburbs (Harold Lloyd, Mary Pickford, Gloria Swanson and many others), and it is still a popular area with TV, theatrical and rock personalities. A popular evening stroll is the stretch along Wilshire Boulevard and Rodeo Dr. in Beverly Hills, an area that is perfectly safe at night.

Visit the Otis Art Gallery, 2401 Wilshire Blvd., located on the site of "Bivouac," former home of General Harrison Gray Otis, pioneer publisher of the *Los Angeles Times.* Focuses on works by contemporary artists. J. Paul Getty Museum, 17985 Pacific Coast Hwy., Malibu (parking limited; reservations are required. Call 213–458–2003): Housed in a recreation of a first-century Roman villa, the renowned museum's collection includes Greek and Roman statuary, magnificent eighteenth-century French furniture and European paintings from fourteenth to nineteenth centuries. One of the most generously-endowed and impressive museums anywhere.

Century City is a pacesetter for urban development; it is a handsome, well-planned "city within a city" just west of Beverly Hills. This complex includes: Century Plaza Hotel, an extensive shopping mall (a great place to find trendy Los Angeles fashions and great chic gifts all under one roof), the ABC entertainment center, towering office buildings, restaurants, and movie theaters. This complex is built on the grounds that were once part of Twentieth Century-Fox Studios.

Northwest of Los Angeles, near Beverly Hills, is Westwood, a unique cosmopolitan center that has retained much of the village atmosphere, with fifteen movie theaters and a variety of restaurants. It is the focal point of much of Los Angeles' nightlife, where strolling musicians, mimes and jugglers add color and charm to the village streets.

One block north of the village is the sprawling campus of the University of California at Los Angeles. UCLA has outstanding departments of medicine, chemistry, theater arts, environmental design and athletics. For a special afternoon, walk through the University's Franklin D. Murphy Sculpture Garden, the Japanese Gardens and the Frederick S. Wright Art Galleries, which display contemporary and historical art, archeological and anthropological artifacts and the renowned Grunwald Collection.

West of the village are Santa Monica and Venice, two popular beachside communities which offer an exciting variety of activities ranging from body surfing and roller skating to antique shopping, and nighttime entertainment and dining on charming Main Street.

The San Fernando Valley is a vast bedroom community across the low hills from central Los Angeles. In addition to a growing number of good shops and better restaurants, the "Valley" has attractions such as Magic Mountain (amusement park with thrill rides), Busch Bird Sanctuary, NBC Studios and Mission San Fernando.

From Pasadena to San Gabriel

Pasadena is located northeast of Los Angeles and is the well-known home of the annual Tournament of Roses, the Rose Bowl, each January 1. The city is famed for its fine residential district, stately old homes, leisurely and aristocratic way of life, and the sprawling Huntington-Sheraton hotel, built at the turn of the century by railroad tycoon Henry Huntington.

The site of the Rose Bowl—open throughout the year in the bottom of the Arroyo Seco just west of town—and of the California Institute of Technology, on California Boulevard at Hill Avenue, Pasadena has become even more famous recently as the home of NASA's Jet Propulsion Laboratory. Many of the complicated moon- and Mars-scanning satellites sent aloft were designed at Pasadena's Jet Propulsion Laboratory by local technicians. Pasadena is also the home of the magnificent Norton Simon Museum. The thrust of the changing exhibits is toward outstanding contemporary art and its origins.

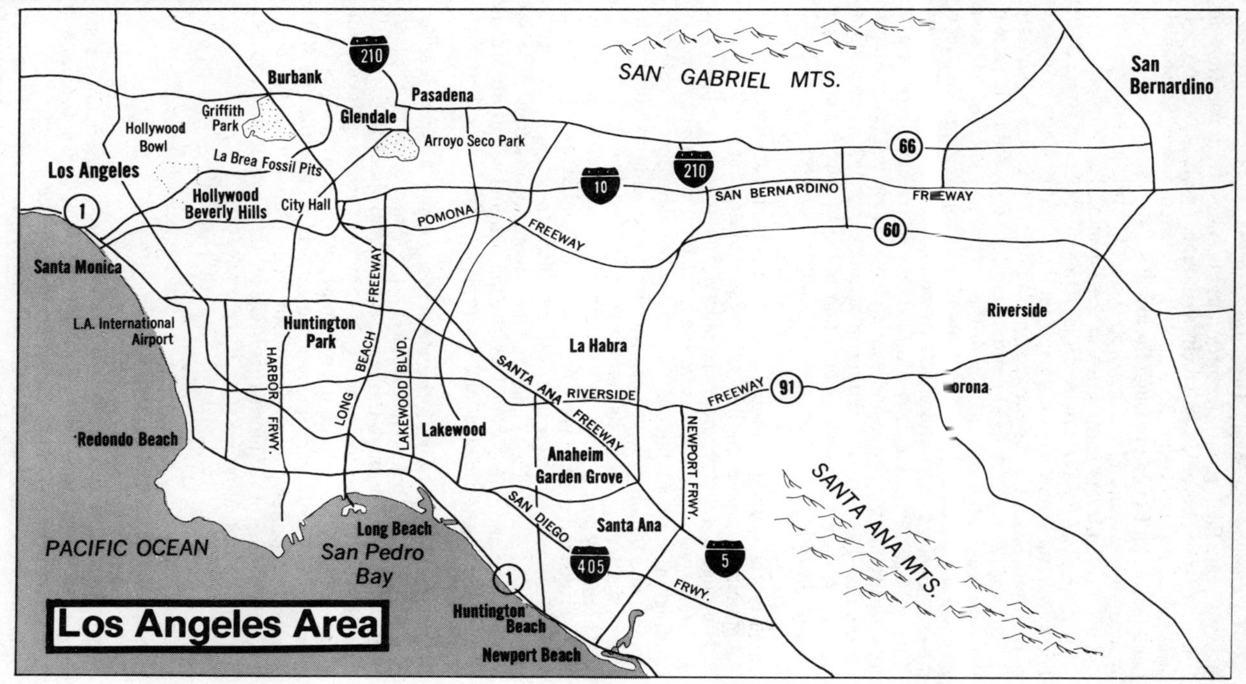
210
Burbank
Pasadena
SAN GABRIEL MTS.
San Bernardino
Griffith Park
Glendale
Hollywood Bowl
Arroyo Seco Park
La Brea Fossil Pits
Los Angeles
Hollywood
Beverly Hills
City Hall
10
210
SAN BERNARDINO
66
60
1
POMONA
FREEWAY
Santa Monica
L.A. International Airport
Huntington Park
LONG BEACH FREEWAY
HARBOR FRWY.
LAKEWOOD BLVD.
La Habra
Riverside
SANTA ANA FREEWAY
RIVERSIDE FREEWAY
91
Lakewood
Redondo Beach
Anaheim
Garden Grove
NEWPORT FRWY.
SANTA ANA MTS.
SAN DIEGO
405
FRWY.
Santa Ana
5
Long Beach
PACIFIC OCEAN
San Pedro Bay
1
Los Angeles Area
Huntington Beach
Newport Beach

In La Canada are lovely Descanso Gardens, 1418 Descanso Dr., open all year. Each month features floral beauties, from camellias in January to roses, begonias, and fuchsias in June. The 165-acre horticultural haven is part of Rancho San Rafael, located on a 1784 Spanish Land Grant. Paths wind through the lovely woods, which are threaded by a running stream. More than 150 species of birds find refuge here and visitors can relax and sip tea in the Japanese Tea Garden.

To the east of Pasadena is Arcadia, home of the Santa Anita Race Track, with its annual season starting on the day after Christmas. One of the most beautiful race tracks in California, this one is lavishly planted with flowers. A local custom: gardners dig up the plants and give them away on a first-come basis the day the season ends. The new year will see the track decorated with a fresh crop. Also in Arcadia is the Los Angeles County and State Arboretum. Formerly part of the old "Lucky" Baldwin estate, it was turned over to the two agencies as a growing ground for native and exotic plants. There is a palm-fringed lagoon that has been the setting in a hundred jungle-story motion pictures. A tram takes visitors on a tour of the site. Artists come here to paint the old Queen Anne Cottage, built by Baldwin, and to sketch the Hugo Reid adobe, a Spanish-period structure which has been restored on the grounds and given a museum-display treatment.

Adjoining Pasadena on the south is San Marino, home of the Henry E. Huntington Library and Art Gallery. Situated on a hillside and beautifully planted, this 200-acre site is the former home of Henry E. Huntington, railroad builder and real-estate developer. The home grounds and buildings have been converted into an extraordinary art gallery, displaying among its famous paintings *The Blue Boy* and *Pinkie.* The library has a renowned collection of rare books and printed manuscripts and draws visitors and scholars from all over the world. Among the works of greatest interest: fifteenth-century Gutenberg Bible, Shakespeare's First Folio, and the original manuscripts of Benjamin Franklin and Edgar Allen Poe. The surrounding botanical gardens are famed for their camellias and desert plants, while everywhere there are giant oaks.

Adjacent to San Marino is the fine old San Gabriel Mission, founded in 1771, ten years before the settling of Los Angeles, along the main north-south route through California. Completed about 1800, it is still a parish church in the community. It has a fine mission garden, complete with tame doves, and a small museum, once the padre's living quarters. The great arrangement of ancient bells high on the side of the mission wall is often photographed. San Gabriel Mission was the fourth mission founded in California; San Diego, the Carmel site, and San Antonio de Padua, near King City, preceded it.

Hills and Mountains

Hills ring the Los Angeles basin. Most of them have names, some do not. They are the barrier that keeps out the desert influences and makes Southern California such a delightful place to live.

Immediately north of the basin are the Santa Monica mountains, running north along the coast as far as Oxnard and sorting the seaward breezes.

In the Hollywood-Santa Monica area, stilt-supported homes have been placed on hundreds of lots whittled from hillside sites, which afford an aerial view of the Southland. By night and without smog it is a fairyland of lights and colors.

There are scenic drives that cross along this mountain area. Mulholland Drive is the most famous of these. It can be reached most easily from the Hollywood Freeway. Near the beginning of Mulholland Drive, in the area where the Hollywood Freeway cuts through the hills, is the Hollywood Bowl, which offers a gala summer season of rock to classical music. This natural amphitheater is built against a hillside and the acoustics are excellent. The Bowl's grounds are so inviting in this woody dell that picnickers tote gourmet suppers, complete with wine, candles, and tablecloths.

The larger San Gabriel Mountain Range, which separates the Los Angeles basin from the Mojave Desert, is one of the state's most notable transverse ranges. The San Gabriels start at Interstate 5—the main freeway that reaches north and south through the center of the state—and stretch east for well over fifty miles. Lifting to close to two miles high at their tallest peaks, the San Gabriels are considered Los Angeles' mountain playgrounds and are within the Angeles National Forest, one of the most heavily used national forests in the United States.

Along the Angeles Crest Highway—the main road into the mountain area which starts at La Canada—are a number of fine mountain campgrounds: Chilae, Charlton Flats, Buckhorn, Horse Flats, and a number of lesser picnic sites. Good paved roads and dirt roads crisscross the mountain country. Some of the mountain lands facing the Los Angeles basin are closed to public entry during the summertime because of high fire hazard.

The principal scientific outpost in the San Gabriel Mountains is the Mt. Wilson Observatory. A crude road up from Pasadena originally brought the astronomical equipment to this mountain site. It was chosen around 1904 (before smog devoured the area) because of the unparalleled viewing from the site. Here are a small astronomical museum, the giant 100-inch Hooker telescope, a smaller 60-inch telescope, and a trio of solar telescopes. There is a good road now up to the observatory site from Red Box on the Angeles Crest Highway, and parking is provided.

Valleys, Gardens and Show Farms

East of Los Angeles, the San Gabriel Valley, the Pomona Valley, and eventually the San Bernardino Valley, separated only by low ridges of hills, form the arm of the Los Angeles basin that reaches in that direction.

East of Pasadena is Claremont, noted for its collection of colleges—Scripps College, Claremont Men's College, Pomona College, Harvey Mudd College, and Claremont Graduate School—and the exceptional Santa Ana Botanic Gardens, a wonderland of native plants.

In Pomona is the Los Angeles County Fairgrounds, where each September the Los Angeles County Fair is staged. In this corner of the Pomona Valley, around Cucamonga and Guasti, are miles of vineyards. There are numerous wineries in the area, most with tasting rooms. It is a colorful sight in the fall to watch the grapes being harvested, and at the winery you can smell the perfume of the new wine. At Pomona is California Polytechnic College and the Kellogg Arabian Horse Ranch, where demonstrations by the fine horses are given. Also to be seen in this eastern San Gabriel Valley-Pomona

Valley-San Bernardino Valley complex are the last of the great groves of citrus that once blanketed all of this area. Each spring, San Bernardino hosts an 11-day National Orange show.

Knott's Berry Farm, on Beach Boulevard in Buena Park, is an amusement center built up from the original industry of raising boysenberries and selling boysenberry jam and pies from a roadside stand. Today the spreading farm has restaurants, still featuring the famous berry pies, and a host of amusement-park rides and is the third best-attended attraction in the United States. Shops and rides have a frontier motif. Fiesta Village is a highlight of the park with two unique rides: the Soapbox Races and the Dragon Boat, a Viking-style ship which carries brave passengers on an unforgettable ride.

Also on Beach Boulevard in Buena Park is the Movieland Wax Museum and Palace of Living Art, a collection of more than 230 waxen images of famous motionpicture and TV stars in actual onstage settings. Walk through the original set of Doctor Zhivago or stroll down the Yellow Brick Road with Dorothy and the Tin Man.

Fabulous Disneyland

Disneyland, in Anaheim, off the Santa Ana Freeway not far from Buena Park, was inspired by the genius of the late Walt Disney. Located on 74 acres at 1313 Harbor Blvd., the "Magic Kingdom" has appealed to visitors of all ages since it opened in 1955. From the entrance into Main Street, a typical thoroughfare in the United States in the 1890s, the various "lands" of Disneyland—Tomorrowland, Frontierland, Fantasyland, Adventureland, and New Orleans Square—open up. Tomorrowland is typified by the great gleaming monorail that whisks passengers around the park. The Star Tours ride allows visitors to climb aboard their Star Speeder and travel to a far-off galaxy, courtesy of a flight simulator. The 3-D music video *Captain E-O* features Michael Jackson. Pinocchio In Fantasyland offers a daring journey; the Peter Pan Flight has ocean waves and a fly-through waterfall; and in Snow White's Scary Adventures, logs turn into crocodiles.

Frontierland caters strongly to yesterday. There is a train ride that takes you back into Gold Rush days, past a drowsy little mining camp, into the desert, and through a mine lit with myriad-colored waterfalls. There are rivers of America on which two boats, the stern-wheeler *Mark Twain* and the sailing vessel *Columbia,* take visitors on a tour around Tom Sawyer Island. There are burro-back rides, rides on rafts and canoes, caves to explore, Indians to fight. During the summer there are entertainers on the dock and on the two big boats that sail around the lagoon.

In Adventureland the most popular rides are the Jungle River Cruise and the Pirates of the Caribbean. Another favorite adventure is a climb into a tremendous tree, like the one in Disney's *Swiss Family Robinson* movie. This one has three tree-houses to poke through. Throughout the park there are curio shops, some with inexpensive gifts, some with exquisite items. There are all manner of eating spots from fancy restaurants to refreshment stands.

No matter when you come—winter (open only weekends) or summer, early morning or late evening—Disneyland looks as though it has just been freshly painted, scrubbed, and swept. The late Walt Disney's promise that "Disneyland will continue to grow, to add new things, as long as there is imagination left in the world" is still the theme.

More visitors than ever from all over the world visited this area for the 1984 Summer Olympics, and Orange County geared up with new hotels, restaurants and attractions. Raging Waters, an aquatic recreation park, and the 15,000-seat Pacific Amphitheater at the Orange County Fairgrounds are among the additions.

South Coast Metro, which includes South Coast Plaza shopping center, is fast becoming urbanized, offering visitors high-calibre shopping as well as cultural attractions such as the Noguchi Sculpture Gardens in Koll Center and the Orange County Peforming Arts Center, with state-of-the-art theaters offering the world's best acoustical system.

Well within the Los Angeles basin is the seaside community of Long Beach, originally named Iowa-by-the-Sea because of the midwesterners who arrived in great numbers in the 20s and 30s. The city boasts a five-mile beach, inside the harbor breakwater, with excellent swimming, pier and deep-sea fishing offered. Harbor cruises and helicopter rides leave from Pier A-West and Pierpoint Landing for views of California's fifth largest city. Pierpoint Landing is one of the largest sportsfishing bases in the area. It is adjacent to the large U.S. Navy installation in Long Beach. The historic *Queen Mary* has a permanent home in Long Beach Harbor, berthed on Queensway Bay. Tours of the 81,000-ton former Cunard liner are conducted every day.

Nearby is the world's largest airplane—Howard Hughes's *Spruce Goose,* also a touring facility. The plane is housed under a gigantic geodesic dome; inside, visitors enjoy exhibits of Hughes's flying accessories and some background on the billionaire's life.

The new $51 million Performing Arts & Convention Center gives Long Beach magnificent facilities for plays and concerts (3,141-seat Terrace Theater), smaller presentations (862-seat Center Theater) and a 14,000-seat sports arena for basketball, hockey, circuses and rock concerts.

San Pedro, overlooking Los Angeles Harbor from the west, is America's second largest deep-sea port. Tuna boats and luxury cruise ships anchor here before setting off for ports in Mexico and Alaska. From Wilmington, northeast, boats leave for Catalina (also from Long Beach).

Ports O'Call Village is a yesterday-flavored, marine-salted attraction with shops and restaurants along the main channel of Los Angeles Harbor. Everytime a cruise ship leaves, Ports O'Call hails its farewell to the passing liner.

North, along the Pacific are a number of beach communities: Redondo, with a marina and a fine fishing and restaurant pier; Hermosa, also with a fishing pier; Manhattan, likewise with a pier. Venice, once designed to look like the Old World site with canals and gondolas, has become the home of artists, poets and writers.

Santa Monica has many beaches, excellent sport- and pier-fishing and a Civic Auditorium, where many popular and classical productions are staged. It is a lively little city perched on bluffs above the Pacific. Many expatriate Englishmen now live in Santa Monica, so it has pubs, darts and even an old-fashioned English music hall, the Mayfair.

North lies the movie beach-colony of Malibu, with its picture-postcard bay and dramatic jagged cliffs and the coast highway north to Oxnard and Ventura.

PRACTICAL INFORMATION FOR THE LOS ANGELES AREA

HOW TO GET THERE AND HOW TO GET AROUND. By Plane. Among the four airports that serve the Los Angeles area, Los Angeles International Airport (LAX) is the largest. Close to 100 airlines fly into this active hub. Airport access is on two levels: Arrivals for the most part enter from the top, departures from the bottom. For additional information, call 213–646–5252.

Airport services at LAX are about as complete as any other in the country: Restaurants, news stands and even a place for transit passengers to shower and relax (its called Skytel, located next to the Air France ticket counter in the Tom Bradley International Terminal on the upper level. Luxuriate in a compact cruise ship-style cabinette, complete with bed, bathroom, and workspace. Rent by the half hour. Call 213–417–0200.)

Ontario International Airport, 35 miles east of L.A., serves the Riverside-San Bernardino area with about a dozen regional and national carriers. Call 714–983–8282.

Burbank operates a smaller domestic terminal in the San Fernando Valley with short-haul and a few coast-to-coast flights. Airlines that serve Burbank are *AirCal, Alaska, American, America West, Continental, Mid-Pacific, PSA, Sun-Aire,* and *Western.* Call 818–840–8847.

John Wayne Orange County Airport is another point of entry for the Los Angeles area, 14 miles south of Anaheim, with daily local flights from San Diego, Los Angeles, Denver, Salt Lake City, Seattle, Phoenix, and other major cities. The airport services *American, Air Cal, Delta PSA,* and *Western,* among others. Call 714–834–6649.

To accommodate those travelers who require transportation to and from LAX, try the *Super Shuttle* (9625 Ballanca Ave., L.A., 213–777–8000). Price varies depending on mileage from the airport and size of party. Plan at least two hours for the trip to the airport. Upon arrival, after picking up baggage, use the terminal's courtesy phone to request shuttle service for outbound trips from the airport. The vehicle will arrive within 10 minutes.

There are convenient shuttle buses and comfortable air-conditioned motor coaches traveling from both LAX and John Wayne Orange County airports to designated stops and hotels in Orange County. Call *Airport Service Motor Coach* (714–776–9210) or *Air Link* (714–635–1390).

By Rental Car. Avis and Hertz have offices at all the airports, as well as at: Anaheim, Beverly Hills, Burbank, Hollywood, Los Angeles (in town), Pasadena, Santa Monica and Thousand Oaks. Budget, Avis, Hertz and/or Dollar-A-Day also have offices at the Burbank and Long Beach Airports.

By Bus. *Trailways* (213–742–1200) and *Greyhound* (213–620–1200) operate out of the central bus terminal in L.A. at 6th and Los Angeles streets, as well as out of Hollywood, Santa Monica, and other locations. Municipal bus lines operate on frequent schedules to local destinations. In Los Angeles, call RTD at 213–626–4455. In Orange County, call the Orange County Transit District at 714–636–RIDE.

By Train. Los Angeles's Union Station, one of the last grand railroads to be built in this country, is located at 800 N. Alameda Street. Transcontinental Amtrak trains as well as the Coast Starlight from Seattle stop here. There is also service to San Diego, with numerous daily departures. The run takes 2 hours, 35 minutes and stops in San Clemente, Santa Ana, Fullerton, and San Juan Capistrano. Fullerton and Santa Ana stops are convenient to Anaheim. Los Angeles' Union Station at 800 North Alameda is an attraction itself, with 52-foot high ceilings and beautiful carved wood. It is one of the country's last grand railroad stations. For Amtrak scheduling and information call 800–USA–RAIL.

By Taxi. To hire a taxi, phone ahead because you are unlikely to find a cruising cab. Companies include *Independent Cab Co.* (213–385–8294) and *United Independent Taxi* (213–653–5050).

ACCOMMODATIONS. For convenience in locating hotels in the confusing megalopolis sprawl that makes up the city of Los Angeles, we have divided the hotel listings into several sections: first is the downtown (central) area of the city, followed by the leading outlying areas and distinctive neighborhoods, such as Hollywood, Beverly Hills, West Los Angeles, and Santa Monica, listed in alphabetical order. Listings are in order of price category. For a more complete explanation of hotel and motel listings see Far West *Facts At Your Fingertips*. Based on double occupancy, the price categories and ranges are as follows: *Deluxe* $110 and up; *Expensive,* $70–110; *Moderate,* $35–70; and *Inexpensive,* under $35.

DOWNTOWN/WILSHIRE AREA

Deluxe

The Biltmore Hotel. 515 South Olive St., L.A., CA 90013 (213–624–1011; 800–421–0156 nationwide 800–252–0175 inside CA). Downtown Los Angeles historical landmark. Opposite Pershing Square. Completely refurbished older hotel with great touches. Beauty shop. Elegant seafood restaurant. Cocktail lounge, coffee shop, dining rooms.

Hyatt Regency Los Angeles. 711 South Hope St., L.A., CA 90017 (213–683–1234; 800–228–9000). Big, airy, 25-story, 500-room hotel built into the Broadway-Plaza shopping complex. Revolving rooftop restaurant, glass-enclosed skylight, great view.

Hyatt Wilshire. 3515 Wilshire Blvd., L.A., CA 90010 (213–381–7411; 800–228–9000). Pleasant Hotel in the Wilshire Blvd. business area. Good restaurant. Pool.

The New Otani Hotel and Garden. 120 S. Los Angeles St., L.A., CA 90012 (213–629–1200; 800–421–8795 nationwide; 800–252–0197 in CA). Grand luxury 448–room hotel in the middle of downtown Little Tokyo. Many Japanese features, including gardens and restaurants, plus New World features like refrigerators in tastefully decorated rooms, jacuzzi, and airport bus service. Downtown's most peaceful hotel.

Sheraton Grande Hotel. 333 S. Figueroa St., L.A., CA 90071 (213–617–1133; 800–325–3535). New 14-story 550-room mirrored hotel near Dodger Stadium, Chinatown, Music Center in the Bunker Hill district. Outdoor pool, limo service.

Westin Bonaventure. 404 S. Figueroa St., L.A., CA 90071 (213–624–1000; 800–228–3000). Impressive round-towered jewel of downtown. You've seen the circular towers in movies. Pool. Elegant and all the amenities. 1,500 rooms and meeting space for 3,000.

Expensive–Deluxe

University Hilton. 3540 S. Figueroa, L.A., CA 90007 (213–748–4141). Comfortable hotel near the University of Southern California campus. Free shuttle service downtown. Same-day valet service. Pool, jacuzzi. Nightly entertainment.

Expensive

Ambassador. 3400 Wilshire Blvd., L.A., CA 90010 (213–387–7011). Large grounds. Putting green, heated pool, health club, tennis, sauna, and masseurs. Cafe and lounge, dancing and entertainment.

Los Angeles Hilton. 930 Wilshire Blvd., L.A., CA 90017 (213–629–4321). Pleasant, large 1,200-room hotel. Dining rooms, cafe and bar. Barber and beauty shops. Airport bus available. Heated pool and poolside service. Within walking distance of convention center.

Moderate

New Seoul Hotel and Shopping Center. 2666 W. Olympic Blvd., LA 90006 (213–381–5777). A ground-floor shopper's mecca gives way to a 50-room hotel, modestly furnished with amenities like courtesy coffee, free parking. Korean restaurant.

Holiday Inn–Convention Center. 1020 South Figueroa St., L.A., CA 90015 (213–748–1291; 800–238–8000). Family type accommodations with comfortable attractive rooms. Heated pool, coin-operated laundry, dining room and bar.

Howard Johnson's Hotel. 1640 Marengo Dr., L.A., CA 90033 (213–223–3841; 800–654–2000). The closest hotel in the city to Dodger Stadium. Also near Chinatown. Restaurant, lounge, babysitting services. Most pets allowed.

Inexpensive

Orchid Hotel. 819 S. Flower St., L.A., CA 90017 (213–624–5855). One of the smaller downtown hotels, this one is very reasonably priced. No frills but clean. Laundromat on premises. Parking in nearby lot.

Royal Host Olympic Motel. 901 W. Olympic Blvd., L.A., CA 90015 (213–626–6255). Clean, friendly atmosphere. Convenient to the Convention Center. 52 rooms.

Stillwell Hotel. 838 S. Grand Ave., L.A., CA 90017 (213–627–1151). One of Los Angeles's oldest hotels, the Stillwell has kept its charm throughout the years. On-premises Indian and American restaurants. Parking nearby. 250 rooms. Low weekly rates.

WEST LOS ANGELES

Deluxe

Bel-Air Hotel. 701 Stone Canyon Rd., L.A., CA 90077 (213–472–1211). Charming secluded hotel, lovely gardens, trees, flowers, and a creek afloat with swans. Dining room with Old World atmosphere, cocktail lounge, entertainment. Fine service. Distinctively furnished room and suites. Heated pool.

Bel-Air Sands. 11461 Sunset Blvd., L.A., CA 90049 (213–476–6571; 800–421–6649 nationwide; 800–352–6680 in CA). The Bahamas in Bel Air. Two-story motel with well-landscaped grounds. Heated pool, playground shuffleboard. Free transportation. Barber and beauty shops, bar.

Westwood Marquis. 930 Hilgard Ave., L.A., CA 90024 (213–208–8765; 800–352–7454 in CA; 800–346–0410 nationwide). Elegant property attracts corporate and entertainment personalities. Near UCLA campus. Pool, sauna, refrigerators, bathroom phones. 256 suites, no two alike.

Expensive

Holiday Inn–Brentwood/Bel–Air. 170 N. Church Lane, L.A., CA 90049 (213–476–6411). Smart, circular building located at the San Diego Freeway. Cafe and lounge, room service, ice on each floor. Heated pool. Cribs no charge. Van shuttle to UCLA.

BEVERLY HILLS AREA

Super Deluxe

Beverly Wilshire Hotel. 9500 Wilshire Blvd., Beverly Hills, CA 90212 (213–275–4282; 800–421–4354 nationwide; 800–282–4804 in CA). European atmosphere and decor with personal service and extras to match. Garden swimming pool. Sauna bath. Award-winning *La Bella Fontana* restaurant. Limousine service to airport, buses to Disneyland, Marineland, and other visitor attractions. Multilingual staff.

Deluxe

Beverly Comstock. 10300 Wilshire Blvd., L.A., CA 90024 (213–275–5575). Small, well-appointed 150-room hotel. All suites.

Beverly Hills Hotel. 9641 Sunset Blvd., Beverly Hills, CA 90210 (213–276–2251). Beautiful grounds with tropical plants. Lovely rooms. Quiet location

Breakfast and lunch are served on the Loggia and adjoining outdoor patio. The famous *Polo Lounge* is here. Tennis courts, poolside service. Lunch and dinner served in the *Coterie Restaurant* overlooking the pool. Heated swimming pool, naturally.

Beverly Hilton. 9876 Wilshire Blvd., Beverly Hills, CA 90210 (213–274–7777). Large hotel complex, 600 well-decorated rooms, wide selection of restaurants and shops. *Trader Vic's* and *L'Escoffier* two of the finest restaurants in Los Angeles. Theater ticket desk. Limousine service. Pool. Free coffee in lobby for hotel guests.

Beverly Rodeo. 360 N. Rodeo Dr., Beverly Hills, CA 90210 (213–273–0300). Intimate yet elegant. 100 units. Pool, European-style garden dining. Lounge. Convenient to fashionable shopping.

Century Plaza Hotel. 2025 Avenue of the Stars, L.A., CA 90067 (213–277–2000; 800–228–3000). Largest hotel in the heart of Century City. Fine style and amenities. 20-story hotel with a newer, 30-story tower, lavishly decorated and furnished like a mansion. Ronald Reagan stays in the Tower. All rooms have refrigerator, lanai and a view. The hotel has several restaurants, including *La Chaumiere* for California/French cuisine, *The Terrace* for American/Continental, the *Garden Pavilion* for spa cuisine, and the *Cafe Plaza,* a French-style cafe for light meals. Dancing and entertainment. Pool. In the heart of Century City.

Four Seasons Los Angeles. 300 S. Doheny Dr., L.A., CA 90048 (273–2222; 800–268–6282). Formal European decorative details are complemented by outpourings of flora, from the *porte-cochère* to the rooftop pool deck. Great location. Outstanding New American cuisine by chef Lydia Shire. Valet parking, concierge, two-line phones, exercise equipment. 287 rooms.

L'Ermitage. 9291 Burton Way, Beverly Hills, CA 90210 (213–278–3344; 800–424–4443). All suites in this small 115-room European-style hotel. Attention to detail is evident. Complimentary continental breakfast, newspaper delivered to rooms. Roof-top dining. Pool.

Le Mondrian Hotel. 8440 Sunset Blvd., West Hollywood, CA 90069 (213–650–8999; 800–424–4443). Not only is this new all-suite business hotel full of fine art works, but the entire structure is a monument to the Dutch artist after whom the hotel is named. Israeli artist Yaacov Agam has actually transformed the exterior of this 12-story hotel into a giant surrealistic mural that is both Mondrianesque and truly Agam. Private, chauffeured limo at each guest's disposal, Cafe Piet with nouvelle cuisine, and convenient to major recording, motion picture and television studios.

Le Parc Hotel. 733 N. West Knoll, West Hollywood, CA 90069 (213–855–8888; 800–424–4443). Intimate European style hotel housed in a modern, lowrise building. All suites with fireplaces and private balcony. *Cafe Le Parc* exclusive to guests. Near Farmer's Market.

Expensive

Beverly Hillcrest Hotel. 1224 S. Beverwil Dr., L.A., CA 90035 (213–277–2800; 800–421–3212 nationwide; 800–252–0174 in CA). Luxurious accommodations. Rooms all have balconies. Suites. Pool (heated). Garage, Restaurant, bar. Dancing and entertainment. Room service.

Moderate

Beverly House Hotel. 140 South Lasky Dr., Beverly Hills, CA 90212 (213–271–2145). Small and friendly, near Century City. Hand-carved Louis XV furniture, finely printed fabrics in bedrooms create homespun atmosphere. Chess and backgammon in the lounge.

HOLLYWOOD

As a general rule, the more expensive Hollywood motels are located in the Sunset Strip area or in West Hollywood, which borders on Beverly Hills.

Deluxe

Chateau Marmont Hotel. 8221 Sunset Blvd., Hollywood, CA 90046 (213–656–1010). Old World elegance, swimming pool. Haunt of many entertainment stars.

Le Dufy. 1000 Westmount Dr., West Hollywood, CA 90069 (213–657–7400; 800–424–4443). Soothing yet sophisticated decor and the comforts you'd find in a fine home. The younger sister of L.A.'s prized luxury hotel, *L'Ermitage,* has charm without the hefty price tag. All suites.

Sunset Marquis Hotel. 1200 N. Alta Loma Rd., Hollywood, CA 90069 (213–657–1333; 800–697–2140 nationwide; 800–858–9758 in CA). Three-story property near the Strip offers nightly entertainment. Lovely landscaping. 115 rooms.

Expensive

Hollywood Roosevelt. 7000 Hollywood Blvd., Hollywood, CA 90028 (213–466–7000; 800–858–2244 nationwide; 800–423–8363 in CA). State-of-the-art Hollywood glamour and luxury on the site of the first Academy Awards. Olympic pool, Tropicana Bar. In a downmarket neighborhood across from the Chinese Theater and its famous footprints. 320 rooms, 90 poolside cabanas.

Hyatt on Sunset. 8401 Sunset Blvd., Hollywood, CA 90019 (213–656–4101; 800–228–9000). Located in the heart of Sunset Strip. A favorite of the music business, rock stars. Penthouse suites and some rooms with private patios. Rooftop pool, garage, parking lot. *Red Roulette* for gourmet dishes. *Cafe Continental,* streetside cafe with Parisian decor.

Moderate

Dunes Motel. 5625 W. Sunset Blvd., Hollywood, CA 90028 (213–467–5171). Across the street from two television stations, so you'll find studio people around.

Inexpensive

Hollywood Highland Motel. 2051 N. Highland Ave., Hollywood, CA 90028 (213–851–3000). 52-room motel. Free continental breakfast. Coffee shop; near the John Anson Ford Theatre and Universal Studios.

Hollywood LaBrea Motel. 7110 Hollywood Blvd., Hollywood, CA 90046 (213–876–8000). Near Walk of Fame and Sunset Strip. Pool.

Hollywood Premier Hotel. 5333 Hollywood Blvd., Hollywood, CA 90046 (213–466–1691). Near the Observatory and Griffith Park. Room service. Chinese staff.

INGLEWOOD (AIRPORT AREA)

Deluxe

Sheraton Plaza La Reina Hotel. 6101 W. Century Blvd., L.A., CA 90045 (213–642–1111; 800–835–3535). Opened in 1981, this modern hotel has a multilingual staff for international visitors. Luxurious, high-class 15-story property.

Stouffer Concourse Hotel. 5400 West Century Blvd., L.A., CA 90045 (213–216–5858; 800–468–3571). A good place to stay if you're looking to be pampered and want to stay close to the airport. Two levels of Club Floors, limousine service, many suites with private outdoor spas. 750 rooms and suites, done in soft pastels. Indoor parking. Expansive lobby. Trattoria Grande pasta and seafood restaurant.

Expensive

Hyatt House Hotel. 6225 W. Century Blvd., L.A., CA 90045 (213–670–9000; 800–228–9000). 630 soundproof rooms. Health club, pool, tennis. Color TV. Near L.A. International Airport. Attractive rooms. Heated pool. No pets. Cafe, lounge with piano bar.

Los Angeles Airport Marriott Hotel. 5855 W. Century Blvd., L.A., CA 90045; 213/641–5700; 800–228–9290. 18-story 1,020-room hotel. Many restaurants, with shows nightly in lounge. Tastefully decorated rooms. Color TV with remote controls. AM-FM radio. Mercedes limousines leave every 15 minutes to and from airport. Poolside service and swim-up bar.

Moderate

Airport Century Inn. 5547 W. Century Blvd., L.A., CA 90045 (213–649–4000; 800–421–3939). Garden atmosphere. Small 150-room hotel with courtesy limo to airport. Coffee shop. Pool.

Amfac Hotel. 8601 Lincoln Blvd., L.A., CA 90045 (213–670–8111; 800–277–1117). Large motor inn with 759 rooms. Close to L.A. International Airport. Suites. Pool, saunas. Transportation to airport. Restaurant, coffee shop, bar.

Quality Inn-Airport. 5249 W. Century Blvd., L.A., CA 90045 (213–645–2200; 800–228–5151). Near L.A. airport. Large attractively decorated rooms. Free garage. Restaurant, bar. Pool (heated).

Ramada Hotel Culver City. 6333 Bristol Pkwy., Culver City, CA 90[illegible]30 (213–670–3200; 800–[illegible]). Double-story motor inn near L.A. International Airport. Restaurant, coffee shop, bar. Pool. Transportation to airport.

Inexpensive

Friendship Inn's Manchester House Motel. 901 W. Manchester, Inglewood, CA 90301 (213–649–0800; 800–453–4511 nationwide; 800–231–2508 in CA). Small, comfortable and hospitable. Limo service to and from LAX.

LONG BEACH

Deluxe

Queen Mary Hotel. Pier J, Box 8, Long Beach, CA 90801 (213–435–3511; 800–421–3732 nationwide). Stay in the cabins of the elegant ocean liner. Several restaurants. Interesting experience; skyline views.

The Viscount. 700 Queensway Dr., Long Beach, CA 90801; (213–435–7676; 800–255–3050). On beach near Queen Mary. All rooms have patios with views. Tennis courts, pool. Shuttle to and from Long Beach Airport.

Expensive

Ramada Inn. 5325 E. Pacific Coast Hwy., Long Beach, CA 90804 (213–597–1341; 800–2–RAMADA). Polynesian mood. TV. Dining room, lounge, heated pool, beauty salon, baby sitters, patio, boat trailer parking.

Rochelle's Motel. 3333 Lakewood Blvd., Long Beach, CA 90808; (213–421–8215). Kitchen facilities come with many of the rooms at this motel. Restaurant, entertainment, swimming pool.

Moderate

Beach Terrace Manor Motel. 1700 E. Ocean Blvd., Long Beach, CA 90802 (213–436–8204). Terraces overlook beach. Near restaurants. No pets.

Holiday Inn. 2640 Lakewood Blvd., Long Beach, CA 90815 (213–597–4401; 800–465–4329). Member of the chain. Attractive multi-story circular hotel. Restaurant, bar. Pool (heated).

Inexpensive

Downtown TraveLodge. 80 Atlantic Ave., Long Beach, CA 90802 (213–435–2471; 800–255–3050). Near ocean, Queen Mary, port. Restaurant. Swimming pool.

MALIBU

Expensive

Casa Malibu. 22752 W. Pacific Coast Hwy., Malibu, CA 90265 (213–456–2219). Private beach, sweeping view. Weekly rates in winter.

Moderate

Tonga Lei Motor Hotel. 22878 Pacific Coast Hwy., Malibu, CA 90265 (213–456–6444). Nine-unit motel right on the sand. Polynesian-style.

MARINA DEL REY

Deluxe

Marina City Club Resort Hotel. 4333 Admiralty Way, Marina del Rey, CA 90292 (213–822–0611; 800–882–4000 nationwide; 800–862–7462 in CA). Lovely 30-acre site on the water. Full recreational facilities. Three restaurants, disco, 24-hour security.

Marina Del Rey Hotel. 13534 Bali Way, Marina del Rey, CA 90292 (213–822–1010; 800–882–4000 nationwide; 800–862–7462 in CA). In midst of huge marine complex. Good views, restaurants. Pool. Free service to airport.

Marina del Rey Marriott Inn. 13480 Maxella Ave., Marina del Rey, CA 90292 (213–822–8555; 800–228–9290). Nice hotel in Marina area. Heated and hydrotherapy pools. Walking distance to Fox Hills shopping mall.

Expensive

Marina International Hotel. 4200 Admiralty Way, Marina del Rey, CA 90292 (213–822–1010; 800–882–4000 nationwide; 800–862–7462 in CA). Good location in marina near airport. 110 rooms, many with waterfront views. Secluded hotel, with 25 individually designed villas with 110 rooms.

Pacifica Hotel. 6161 W. Centinela Ave., Culver City, CA 90231 (213–649–1776). New resort atmosphere. Large rooms (375) with color TV. Los Gauchos dining room for continental lunch and dinner; Casa del Cafe or pool patio for all meals. Tennis, pool (heated), sauna, bicycle path, and jogging walk surround 5-acre tract of hotel. Free parking and airport buses. On the fringe of Marina del Rey near airport.

PASADENA

Reservations mandatory during *Tournament of Roses* and *Rose Bowl Game* on New Year's Day.

Expensive

Huntington-Sheraton. 1401 S. Oak Knoll Ave., Pasadena, CA 91109 (818–792–0266; 800–325–3535). Picturesque old building with elegant past. Dine overlooking pool. Tennis courts. Free garage. Limo to LAX and Burbank airports. Putting green. Pets welcome. Secluded hotel with 95 rooms.

Pasadena Hilton. 150 S. Los Robles, Pasadena, CA 91101 (818–577–1000). 253 rooms. Pool. Free parking. Hilton Skylights Restaurant and disco. Fanny's piano bar in lobby. Boutiques.

Moderate

Vagabond Motor Hotel. 2863 E. Colorado Blvd., Pasadena, CA 91107 (818–449–3020; 800–522–1555). Pleasant decor. Restaurant. Pool (heated).

Holiday Inn at Pasadena Center. 303 E. Cordova St., Pasadena, CA 91101 (818–449–4000; 800–HOLIDAY). Downtown Pasadena. Convenient to Rose Bowl. Tennis.

SANTA MONICA

Deluxe

Miramar-Sheraton. 101 Wilshire Blvd., Santa Monica, CA 90401 (213–394–3731). Landscaping incorporates gigantic rubber tree. Pool, restaurant, drugstore, beauty shop. Where Wilshire meets the sea, across the street from Pacific Palisades Park.

Expensive

Holiday Inn. 120 Colorado Ave., Santa Monica, CA 90401 (213–451–0676; 800–HOLIDAY). Branch of chain. Large facility with comfortable rooms, many with ocean view. Restaurant, bar. Pool (heated). Pets accepted. Free coffee in rooms.

Oceana Hotel. 849 Ocean Ave., Santa Monica, CA 90403 (213/393–0486). Combined resort and commercial hotel. Ocean view from most units. Housekeeping units. Color TV, heated pool, free garage. Seasonal rates.

Santa Monica TraveLodge. 1525 Ocean Ave., Santa Monica, CA 90401 (213–451–0761). Overlooks the ocean and Palisades Park. TV. Heated pool. Seasonal rates. Several restaurants nearby.

Inexpensive

Stardust Motor Hotel. 3202 Wilshire Blvd., Santa Monica, CA 90403 (213–828–4584). Near UCLA, Westwood Village. 33-room inn with multilingual staff, ample parking, and a pool.

SAN FERNANDO VALLEY

Expensive

Sheraton-Universal Hotel. 333 Universal Terrace Pkwy., Universal City, CA 91608 (818–980–1212; 800–325–3535). Large, multi-story hotel overlooking Hollywood, Universal Studios, San Fernando Valley. Barber and beauty shop, three restaurants, bar, heated pool.

Moderate

Holiday Inn. 8244 Orion Ave., Van Nuys, CA 91406 (818–989–5010). Multi-story hotel near Magic Mountain and Universal Studios. Lovely outdoor pool. Free bus to Van Nuys Airport. Restaurant, bar.

La Maida House. 11159 La Maida St., North Hollywood, CA 91601 (818–769–3857). This lovely villa is a historic landmark located near Universal City and Burbank Airport. Built in the early 1920s by Italian immigrant Antonio La Maida. His home, now a bed-and-breakfast inn, has plenty of marble, oak, mahogany, tile, and stained glass. 10 guest accommodations.

Sportmen's Lodge Inn. 12833 Ventura Blvd., Studio City, CA 91604 (818–984–0202). An attractive motor hotel. 193 pleasant rooms. Heated pool, cocktail lounge. Popular restaurant, beautiful gardens.

Valley Hilton. 15433 Ventura Blvd., Sherman Oaks, CA 91403 (818–981–5400). 200 attractive rooms with dressing areas and balconies. Heated pool and sauna. Cafe, lounge (open 11 A.M.–2 A.M.), dancing, entertainment. Ice machine on each floor. Golf and tennis privileges. Plush executive suites.

Inexpensive

Best Western Mission Hills Inn. 10621 Sepulveda Blvd., Mission Hills, CA 91345 (818–891–1771; 800–352–5670). Two-story motel on pleasant grounds. Cafe open 24 hours. Heated pool. Close to Magic Mountain, Busch Bird Sanctuary, San Fernando Mission.

Chalet Lodge. 19170 Ventura Blvd., Tarzana, CA 91356 (818–345–9410). 50 units, 10 minutes to Hollywood. Close to Universal Studios. Coin laundry nearby.

Royal Oaks Motel. 4747 Sepulveda Blvd., Sherman Oaks, CA 91403 (818–789–7131). Pleasant motel, big rooms, some with kitchenettes. Heated pool, children's playground.

Sierra Lodge Motel. 4781 Sepulveda Blvd., Sherman Oaks, CA 91403 (818–788–3200). Fine for families and extended stays. No pets.

Town House Motel. 6957 Sepulveda Blvd., Van Nuys, CA 91405 (818–782–8800). Modest 32-room motel. Family operated. Near attractions.

HOSTELS. Los Angeles International Hostel. 3601 S. Gaffey Street, Bldg. 613, Angel's Gate Park, San Pedro, CA 90731 (213–831–8109). Self-service kitchen, television room, French and German staff.

ANAHEIM

Deluxe

Anaheim Hilton and Tower. 777 Convention Way, Anaheim, CA 92802 (714–750–4321; 800–HILTONS). Opened in 1984, the 15-floor, 1,600-room hotel boasts three restaurants, lounges, and full health club.

Disneyland Hotel. 1150 W. Cerritos Ave., Anaheim, CA 92802 (714–778–6600; 800–854–6165). 1,100 rooms. Air-conditioning, TV, pool, driving range, golf course, gardens, free parking. No pets. Monorail to Disneyland. Eight restaurants, authentic Oriental gardens, nightly entertainment in a fantasy atmosphere. A great place for family fun.

Grand Hotel. 7 Freedman Way, Anaheim, CA 92802 (714–772–7777; 800–421–6662 nationwide; 800–352–6686 in CA). Close to Disneyland. Rooms are attractively decorated. Pool (heated), sauna. Play area. Restaurant, bar. Entertainment. Nightclub. Transportation to Disneyland. Beauty and barber shop.

Hyatt Anaheim. 1700 S. Harbor Blvd., Anaheim, CA 92802 (714–772–5900; 800–228–9000). Across from Disneyland. Olympic pool. disco, homey atmosphere. Daisy's Market restaurant has just about anything you'd like.

Expensive

Anaheim Holiday Inn. 1850 S. Harbor Blvd., Anaheim, CA 92802 (714–750–2801; 800–972–7349 nationwide; 800–624–6730 in CA). Disneyland close by. Large hotel. Member of the chain. Restaurant, bar. Pool (heated), Jacuzzi.

Anaheim TraveLodge. 1166 W. Katella Ave., Anaheim, CA 92802 (714–774–7817; 800–255–3050). Attractive motel with restrt. nr. Close to Disneyland. Pool (heated). Free coffee in rooms.

Sheraton-Anaheim Motor Hotel. 1015 W. Ball Rd., Anaheim, CA 92802 (714–778–1700; 800–325–3535). Close to Disneyland with free bus to and from Disneyland. Large, tastefully decorated rooms. Restaurant, bar. Dancing.

Moderate

Alpine Motel. 715 W. Katella Ave., Anaheim, CA 92802 (714–535–2186; 800–772–4422 in CA only). Near Disneyland. Swimming. Sitter list. Steam baths. Across the street from the Anaheim Convention Center.

Stovalls Best Western Inn. 1110 W. Katella Ave., Anaheim, CA 92802 (714–778–1880). Close to Disneyland. Nice garden with topiary trees. Pool, sauna, whirlpool.

Magic Lamp Motel. 1030 W. Katella Ave., Anaheim, CA 92802 (714–772–7242). 80 modern rooms. Apartment-style property with restaurant adjacent.

BUENA PARK

Deluxe

Buena Park Hotel and Convention Center. 7675 Crescent Ave., Buena Park, CA 90620 (714–995–1111). 13-story hotel with 320 rooms next to Knott's Berry Farm. Free shuttle to Disneyland. Bar with 50s-60s theme. Many suites. Pool.

Moderate

Buena Park Quality Inn. 7555 Beach Blvd., Buena Park, CA 90620 (714–522–7360; 800–228–5151). Two-story hotel has 150 rooms, exercise room, cable television, pool, sauna, Jacuzzi.

Farm de Ville Friendship Inn. 7800 Crescent Ave., Buena Park, CA 90620 (714–527–2201). Swimming pool, sauna. Modern decor. 130-room Friendship Inn.

Inexpensive

Best Inn Capri Motel. 7860 Beach Blvd., Buena Park, CA 90620 (714–522–7221). Jacuzzi suites. 400 feet from Knott's Berry Farm. Pool and kitchenettes so good for the family.

Covered Wagon Motel. 7830 Crescent Ave., Buena Park, CA 90620 (714–995–0033). One-story L-shaped motel. Modern and modest. Opposite Knott's Berry Farm's southern entrance. Pool.

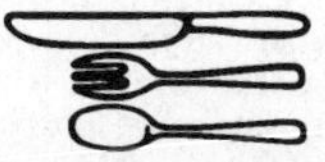

RESTAURANTS. Not many years ago, Los Angeles was considered a gastronomic wasteland; if you were in a restaurant and were served a steak the way you ordered it, you were considered a lucky individual. Ethnic restaurants were a rarity, and it was the general consensus that New York was the only city where you could eat your way around the world.

In the last decade, there has been a tremendous growth in the restaurant industry of Los Angeles. Chinese restaurants now include Szechuan, Hunan, Cantonese, and Mandarin restaurants, categorized by the region of the country. Italian restaurants also became specialized and now serve either northern- or southern Italian cuisine. There grew to be representation of other countries as well: Hungary, Jordan, Israel, Ethiopia, Morocco, Spain, Germany, and Jamaica. Ethnic bistros, offering home-style food at budget prices, much like those in New York City, are now in every corner of the city.

French restaurants have also undergone growth. When *nouvelle cuisine* became the vogue, French restaurants in Los Angeles, such as Ma Maison and L'Orangerie, offered this distinctive cuisine on their menu at practically the same time as the rage hit Paris. Los Angeles, along with San Francisco, is where California cuisine (featuring regional produce) was born, and here too, is the place where Franco-Japanese meals first were eaten.

Price categories are approximate and generally are set for a three-course meal—appetizer, entrée, and dessert—per person. The price does *not* include cocktails, wine, tax, or tip. Fifteen percent is the expected tip, 20 percent for very fine service or for a dinner at the city's most expensive restaurants. An *expensive* dinner runs $30 and up. A *moderate* meal usually costs between $12 and $30 per person. An *inexpensive* dinner runs less than $12.

American

California Pizza Kitchen. *Moderate.* 207 South Beverly Dr., Beverly Hills (213–272–7878). Memphis look at this uptown gourmet pizza parlor with eccentric pies of all description: Rabbit sausage, spinach, garlic and sun-dried tomatoes is one.

The Egg and The Eye. *Moderate.* 5814 Wilshire Blvd. (213–933–5596). Pleasant lunch spot featuring dozens of omelets and homemade desserts. Across from the Los Angeles County Museum of Art. L, Tues.–Sun. AE, MC, V.

Womp's. *Moderate-Inexpensive.* 100 Universal City Plaza, Universal City; (818–777–3939). A great place to bring the family. MCA built this restaurant out of authentic barnwood to resemble an 1880s wagon factory. Buffalo-meat chili is a must to try; it's robust, hearty, and rich with spices. There are many barbequed items as well as steaks, salad plates, and sandwiches. Country-and-western entertainment after 9:00 P.M. during the summer only. L, D, daily. All major credit cards.

The Hard Rock Café. *Inexpensive.* 8600 Beverly Blvd., West Hollywood (213–276–7605). A vintage '59 Cadillac jets out of the roof, Elvis's motorcycle hangs on the wall, and the waitresses are dressed in appropriate threads of the fifties. The menu consists of burgers, baby back ribs basted in watermelon barbecue sauce, and apple pie. Fast becoming an L. A. landmark. L, D, daily. AE, MC, V.

Johnny Rockets. *Inexpensive* 7505 Melrose, West Hollywood (213–651–3361). Always fun and lively, this 50s-style diner has 20 seats at the counter and some of Hollywood's juiciest burgers. Try the sizzling fries smothered in chili. Open daily. No credit cards.

Phillippe's Original Sandwich Shop. *Inexpensive.* 1001 N. Alameda St. (213–628–3781). A 76-year-old cafeteria close to Union Station. Giant haunches of meat rest on a long counter where they are sliced into thick and juicy roast-beef sandwiches. Stew, soup, salads, and chili are also on the menu, but the sandwiches are the real draw. Dining is communal; everyone eats together at long tables. Coffee is still 10¢ a cup! B, L, D, daily. No reservations. No credit cards.

Vickman's. *Inexpensive.* 1228 E. 8th St. (213–622–3852). All the action starts here at the improbable hour of 3:00 A.M., when this restaurant opens its doors. It's by the downtown produce mart, and its customers are truck drivers, delivery men, and insomniacs. The fare is plain and wholesome American food, including an excellent assortment of freshly baked goods. The strawberry pie is not to be missed, and the Danishes are sheer heaven. Ham, omelettes, poached salmon, and stuffed pork chops are satisfying. Mon.-Fri., 3:00 A.M. to 3:00 P.M. Sat., 3:00 A.M. to 1 P.M. No reservations. No credit cards.

California

L. A. Nicola. *Moderate.* 4326 Sunset Blvd., Hollywood (213–660–7217). California/International cuisine and high-tech decor. Great hors d'oeuvres, and chef-owner Larry Nicola excels with fish and chicken dishes. Around the corner from ABC Studios. Features an airy outdoor café and up-tempo lounge. Closed Sundays. L, Mon.-Fri.; D, Mon.-Sat. AE, MC, V.

Spago. *Moderate.* 1114 Horn Ave., just off Sunset Strip., West Hollywood (213–652–4025). Owner Wolfgang Puck is the "golden chief" of Los Angeles, and this California-style restaurant is innovative, creative, and unique, featuring produce, poultry, and seafood native to California. Wood-burning ovens cook your meals right in the dining room as a bit of a show. Many unusual combinations of pizza. There are also Santa Barbara shrimp, California goat cheese, homemade duck sausage, and pastas with seafood. The fresh fish is served strict and pure, grilled with butter only. The restaurant, decorated in a beige color scheme, has small tables and ice-cream-parlor chairs and fine art on the walls. You'll see rows of Rolls-Royces and Mercedeses in the parking lot; this is a restaurant patronized by the elite—great for celebrity spotting. Interesting wine list. The pastry chef prepares flaky tarts, cakes, and other pastries, many with fresh fruit and liqueurs. Valet parking. D, nightly. Reservations absolutely necessary. Phone between 3 and 8 P.M. All major credit cards.

Chinese

Abacus Chinese Seafood Restaurant. *Expensive–Moderate.* 11701 Wilshire Blvd., Brentwood (213–207–4875). Mandarin and Szechuan cuisine dished up in an upscale environment. Emphasis on seafood and Peking duck, available with one hour's notice.

Lew Mitchell's Orient Express. *Moderate.* 5400 Wilshire Blvd. (213–935–6000). This is no ordinary neighborhood Chinese restaurant. It's chic and sophisticated, with bentwood chairs, a plethora of potted palms, and ivy-covered trellises in the windows. In other words, no one will throw you your chopsticks here. Specialties include sesame beef, thin-sliced steak glazed with honey and sesame seeds, tea-smoked duck, beggar's chicken, and Peking duck (the latter requiring 24-hr. notice). Szechuan dishes are predominant, but Mandarin cooking is featured as well. For the timid there is even a Western-style menu. The dessert menu is eclectic. L, Mon.-Fri.; D, Mon.-Sat. AE, CB, MC, V.

Continental

Camille's. *Expensive-Moderate.* 13573 Ventura Blvd., Sherman Oaks (818–995–1660). One of the most romantic restaurants in the Valley. Rose-colored walls, an eclectic assortment of antique mirrors and paintings, trailing plants, and a lot of lattice work provide a sentimental Art Deco-Victorian ambience. Chef-coowner Peter Schawalder is Swiss; his creations are individualistic as well as poetic in presentation. Entrées are often garnished with carrot stars, olives hold enoki mushrooms, and strawberries are sculptured into blossoming roses. Entrées include sautéed whitefish and grapefruit, veal steak with mushroom puree, and roasted duckling and apple and chestnut puree. The soup of the day is always fresh, and their desserts are worth giving up a diet for. L, Tues.-Fri.; D, Tues.-Sat. All major credit cards.

French

L'Ermitage, *Expensive.* 730 N. La Cienaga Blvd. (213–652–5840). One of LA's most refined French restaurants. Brought to great heights by its late owner, Jean Bertranou, L'Ermitage's beautiful ambience is complimented by such entrées as breast of chicken with goose liver and port wine, and sautéed veal loin with green apples. Creativity reigns in chef Michel Blanchet's capable kitchen. L, Mon.-Fri. D, Mon.-Sat. Valet parking. All major credit cards.

Les Freres Taix. *Moderate.* 1911 Sunset Blvd., L.A. (213–484–1265). Near downtown, although not in the greatest neighborhood. One of the oldest French restaurants and easily the finest value in the city. Food is simple and good Tureen of soup and salad with entree. One of best and least expensive wine lists in town. Special every evening.

La Petite Chaya. *Expensive.* 1930 Hillhurst Ave., Hollywood/Los Feliz (213–665–5991). Highly touted Franco/Japanese restaurant serving the newest in-vogue cuisine. French-trained Japanese chef is very imaginative, service is impeccable and decor is simple yet elegant. Enclosed porch makes for a very romantic dining spot. Near ABC Studios. Lunch Mon. through Friday, dinner daily. Valet parking. Full bar. All major credit cards.

Le St. Germain. *Expensive.* 5955 Melrose Ave., Hollywood (213–467–1108). A serene restaurant, decidedly French and decidedly chic. One of the restaurants to see and be seen in. The menu is elegant, and the specials of the day are always the best. The service is impeccable. The presentation of the plates is a joy to behold. The surroundings are formal, despite a casual ambience. Salmon with a sorrel cream sauce and roast chicken in a champagne sauce are noted entrées. Fresh berry fruit tarts are the best bet for dessert. L, Mon.-Fri.; D, Mon.-Sat. No CB.

Indian

Indian Bombay Palace. *Moderate–Expensive.* 8690 Wilshire Blvd., Beverly Hills. (213–659–9944). Mouthwatering tandoori dishes served against an elegant Art Deco backdrop. Try the onion kulcha bread with murgh tikka masala. Open daily for lunch and dinner. All major credit cards.

Bengal Tiger. *Inexpensive.* 1710 N. Las Palmas Ave., Hollywood (213–469–1991). This tiny Indian and Pakistani restaurant consistently prepares authentic cuisine from its corner of the world. Mulligatawny soup is a spicy specialty, and curries will be prepared just as hot as you can stand them. Breads are truly delights; the *poori,* deep-fried puffed wheat bread, and *parathas,* flaky layered, crisp bread stuffed with potatoes or vegetables, are some of the best prepared Indian breads in the city. Wine, beer. L, D, daily, AE, MC, V.

Italian

Cardini. *Expensive.* 930 Wilshire Blvd., downtown (213–227–3464). A big surprise in the Los Angeles Hilton, this fine restaurant resembles an Italian village, post-modern style. Unusual pastas and tasty risotto plus daily specials.

Celestino. *Expensive.* 236 South Beverly Dr., Beverly Hills (213–859–8601). Co-owner Celestino Drago creates northern Italian food that's perfect: fresh pasta, beautifully designed appetizers served in a low-key setting.

La Scala. *Expensive.* 9455 Santa Monica Blvd., Beverly Hills (213–275–0579). One of Los Angeles' trend setters in bringing fine Italian cuisine to this city. Specialties include smoked Scottish salmon, zuppa all' Ortolana, fettuccine Leon, calf's liver all' Veneziana, and homemade ice cream. Valet parking. L, Mon.-Fri.; D, daily except Sun.

Harry's Bar. *Moderate.* 2020 Avenue of the Stars. In the ABC Entertainment Center near the Shubert Theater, Century City (213–277–2333). Fashioned after the world-famous restaurant in Florence, Italy. The specialties are veal dishes and fettucine Alfredo. Closed Sun. for lunch. All major credit cards.

The MoCA Cafe-Il Panino. *Inexpensive.* The Museum of Contemporary Art, 250 South Grand Ave., in California Plaza (213–617–1844). Euro-style sandwich bar. Italian breads baked on the premises are used in imaginative menu items named for legendary Italian destinations. Cappuccino, too (of course). Open Tues.–Sun. No credit cards.

Japanese

Restaurant Katzu. *Expensive.* 1972 N. Hillhurst Ave., Los Feliz (213–665–1891). A stark hi-tech interior and exterior (no sign indicates that there's a restaurant inside) provides a great showplace for some of the city's most imaginative sushi. Owner-designer-sushi chef Katzu never compromises on his own tastes; all sushi orders are authentic. There's no physical menu to glance over, but be assured that you'll be able to order anything Japanese in this restaurant. Wine and beer. L, D, daily except Sun. AE, MC, V.

Imperial Gardens. *Expensive-Moderate.* 8225 Sunset Blvd., West Hollywood; (213–656–1750). A gathering spot for entertainment-industry sushi freaks as well as restaurateurs who come here on their nights off. Different dining rooms feature tempura, teriyaki, and *shabu-shabu. Tatami* room. Valet parking. L, Mon.–Fri.; D, daily. All major credit cards.

Horikawa Restaurant. *Moderate–Expensive.* 111 South San Pedro St. (213–680–9355). Los Angeles's most impressive Japanese restaurant offers everything from sushi to *teppan* dining. Private Japanese rooms have *tatami* matting and offer *ryotei* for up to 24. Reservations recommended. L, Mon.–Fri.; D, daily. All major credit cards.

Yoriki. *Inexpensive.* 4057 W. Third St., L.A. (213–388–8983). Featured here is Kushikatsu, a chef's selection of fresh foods that are lightly breaded and deep-fried on a skewer. Those with adventurous palates should try the turtle soup. L, Mon.-Fri.; D, Mon.-Sat. MC, V.

Mexican

Antonio's Restaurant. *Moderate-Inexpensive.* 7472 Melrose Ave., L.A. (213–655–0480). The usual Mexican fare, with the addition of more complex specialties. Jicama salad with fresh exotic fruits and chicken with an intriguing mole sauce excel. Authentic ropa vieja. Mariachi music. L, D, daily Tues.–Sun. Valet parking at night only. AE, MC, V.

El Cholo. *Inexpensive.* 1121 S. Western Ave., L.A. (213–734–2773). Attentive service, a huge menu, and giant portions characterize this comfortable Mexican restaurant. Great for families, starving artists, and virtually everyone who thinks spending a lot of money to eat out is ridiculous. L, D, daily. AE, MC, V.

The Gardens of Taxco. *Inexpensive.* 1113 N. Harper Ave., L.A. (213–654–1746). This restaurant represents the best of Mexico City cuisine. The *quesadillas* are splendid, the chicken mole is terrific, and there are at least ten desserts to choose from, including the flan and bananas in a creamy custard. D, daily except Mon. AE, MC, V.

Lucy's El Adobe. *Inexpensive.* 5536 Melrose Ave., Hollywood (213–462–9421). An intimate Mexican restaurant that is a music-industry hangout. Reportedly was a rendezvous for Gov. Jerry Brown and Linda Ronstadt. *Arroz con pollo,* enchiladas rancheros, and enchiladas verdes are specialties. L, D, Mon.-Sat. MC, V.

Moroccan

Moun of Tunis. *Moderate.* 7445½ Sunset Blvd., Hollywood (213–874–3333). Like your neighborhood Casbah. Enter through an arched door leading to small rooms with cushioned benches and round, low tables. Waiters and waitresses in traditional garb. Several choices of full-course meals; *b'stilla* is wonderful, as is the lemon chicken with almonds, which literally falls apart in your fingers because it's so moist. A mixed salad plate includes a couple of hot salads; be prepared to breathe fire. Belly dancing nightly. D, daily. All major credit cards.

Thai

Tommy Tang's. *Moderate.* 7473 Melrose Ave., Hollywood (213–651–1810). This trendy Thai bistro caters to the entertainment industry with a punkish flair. Thai cuisine has an American flavor. Try the spicey barbecued chicken, squid with mint leaves and chili, and *mee krob.* Sushi bar. L, D, Mon.–Sat. All major credit cards.

Chao Praya. *Inexpensive.* Corner Yucca and Vine at 6307 Yucca, Hollywood (213–466–6704). This earthy restaurant is set smack in the middle of Hollywood, cater-cornered from the Capital Records Bldg. The delicious Thai cuisine is served in an extremely casual manner. Highlights: beef and pork *stay, mee krob,* barbecued and garlic chicken dishes. Generous portions. L, D, daily. All major credit cards.

TOURIST INFORMATION. The *Greater Los Angeles Convention and Visitors Bureau,* in downtown L.A. at 505 S. Flower St., level B, Atlantic Richfield Plaza (213–624–7300) provides brochures, pamphlets, regional maps, events calendars, and TV-show tickets at no cost. If you would like to obtain information through the mail, write to the bureau at 515 S. Figueroa St., L.A., CA 90071. Another branch is at 6541 Hollywood Blvd. (213–461–4213).

Anaheim Area Visitors and Convention Bureau is at 800 W. Katella Ave., Anaheim, CA 92803 (714–999–8999).

Beyond these two main bureaus, each individual community maintains either a specialized tourism bureau or a chamber of commerce. Here is a sampling.

Oxnard Convention and Visitors Bureau is at 400 Esplanade Drive, Suite 100, Oxnard 93030; (805–485–8833).

Santa Monica Visitor Information Center is at 1430 Ocean Ave. in Palisades Park; (213–393–7593).

Long Beach Convention and Visitors Bureau is at 180 E. Ocean Blvd., Suite 150, Long Beach 90802 (213–436–3645).

Santa Catalina Island visitor information is handled by the *Catalina Island Chamber of Commerce,* Box 217, Avalon 90704 (213–510–1520). Write ahead as accommodations are scarce and reservations should be made in advance; the chamber will give you a listing of what's available.

Palm Springs Convention and Visitors Bureau, 255 N. El Cielo, Suite 315, Palm Springs, CA. 92262 (619–327–8411) has multi brochures available in offices only 300 yds. north of the Palm Springs Airport on El Cielo.

Beverly Hills Visitor & Convention Bureau, 239 S. Beverly Dr., Beverly Hills 90212 (213–271–8174).

Malibu Chamber of Commerce is at 22235 Pacific Coast Highway 90265; (213–456–9025).

Pasadena Convention and Visitors Bureau, 171 S. Los Robles, Pasadena, CA 91101, south of the Pasadena Mall (818–795–9311).

Ventura Visitor and Convention Bureau, 785 S. Seaward, Ventura 93001 (805–648–2075). Take the Seaward off-ramp off US 101.

Because Los Angeles covers such a large area, telephone assistance can save the visitor considerable time and energy. For *beach and surfing conditions,* call 213–451–8761; for *road conditions,* call 213–626–7231; and for the *weather,* call 213–554–1212.

California, Los Angeles, L.A. Style, and *Valley* magazines are published monthly and incorporate extensive listings of restaurants, shopping, museums, children's activities, theater events, and films as well as happenings in the art, music, and dance worlds.

This sprawling city also offers three daily newspapers, the *Los Angeles Times, The Daily News,* and the *Los Angeles Herald Examiner.* They keep up with the metropolitan area's goings-on from day to day. The *Times'* Calendar section gives information on films, theater events, and so on, with the same information provided in the *Herald's* Style section.

Two free newspapers, the *Los Angeles Weekly* and the *Los Angeles Reader,* are excellent sources of information on scheduled events. These publications can be found in many stores and neighborhood restaurants as well as in bookstores and movie theaters.

TELEPHONES. The area code for central Los Angeles is 213. Northern area communities of the San Fernando Valley, including Glendale, Pasadena, and Burbank, are in the 818 area. Central and coastal Orange County is 714. Dial 411 for directory assistance, and be aware that there are many telephone directories for the area. When direct-dialing long distance, first dial the number 1, then the area code and number. For operator assistance on credit, collect, or person-to-person calls, dial 0, then 1, then the number. Pay phones start at 20 cents.

EMERGENCY TELEPHONE NUMBERS. In the Los Angeles area, dial the universal emergency number 911. The number for *police* in Los Angeles is 625–3311; *fire,* 384–3131; *medical emergencies,* 483–6721; *poison information,* 484–5151; *daytime medical referral service,* 483–6122. These are all in the 213 area code.

HINTS TO MOTORISTS. Now that other cities are crisscrossed by freeways, driving in Los Angeles may not seem like such a dreaded ordeal. Freeways do provide faster and usually safer travel over the area's great distances—the 30 miles from Los Angeles Airport to Disneyland, for instance. There are more than 30 freeways. Eight radiate from Los Angeles' downtown freeway loop. All are named for their destinations, with the exception of the Golden State Freeway. A map is essential, and should be studied before arrival if possible. When driving, always plan freeway routes, identify interchanges, and note exits before setting out.

HINTS TO HANDICAPPED TRAVELERS. All facilities at Los Angeles International Airport are accessible, and free wheelchair lift service is provided between the eight terminals. Call 213–646–6402 or 646–8021. All major public buildings and downtown intersections have access ramps. The *Rapid Transit Districts* (RTD) operates 100 buses with handicapped access, but considering the size of Los Angeles, they may be miles away. Most larger, newer hotels, especially the Ramada Inn and Holiday Inn chains, are accessible. For a list of historic sites that can accommodate wheelchair visitors, write for the brochure "Round the Town With Ease" from the *Junior League of Los Angeles,* Third and Fairfax St., Los Angeles, CA 90036. Enclose a self-addressed, stamped envelope. *Independent Living Centers* in the area may be able to answer questions by phone; among them the *Westside Community Center* (213–836–1075).

TOURS AND SPECIAL-INTEREST SIGHTSEEING. The *Gray Line* offers the widest range of bus tours, including Pasadena, Hollywood, Beverly Hills. Buses pick up visitors at more than 300 hotels. There are half-day and day-long excursions. For information in Los Angeles, telephone 213–481–2121. In Orange County, contact Gray Line, 6333 W. Third St. (714–778–2770).

The Los Angeles Conservancy 849 S. Broadway, M22, Los Angeles, CA 90014 (213–623–2489). A non-profit group saving the city's historic buildings it conducts walking tours Sat., 10 A.M.–12:30 P.M. downtown. Five separate tours cover the area around Pershing Square, the Broadway movie theater district, the commercial arena, Art Deco buildings, and the old financial district along Spring St. Reservations required; $5 adults.

The Music Center. 135 N. Grand, downtown L.A. (213–972–7483). The Symphonians, a dedicated group of volunteers, conduct free tours of all three theaters (the Mark Taper Forum, the Dorothy Chandler Pavilion, and the

Ahmanson Theater) during the week, and focus on the Dorothy Chandler Pavilion on Saturday.

Round Town Tours (213–836–7559) leads ethnic-neighborhood tours through Chinatown, Little Tokyo, Little Armenia.

Santa Catalina Island, the scenic resort 21 miles off the coast, offers swimming, hiking, glass-bottom boat cruises, and a museum and landmark movie palace in the town of Avalon. Two cruise lines provide the two-hour voyage: *Catalina Cruises,* Box 1948, San Pedro, CA 90733 (213–514–3838), sails from San Pedro and Long Beach; *Catalina Channel Express,* Box 1391, San Pedro, CA 90733 (213–519–1212), sails from San Pedro to two ports on Catalina.

HOLLYWOOD AND THE STARS. Hollywood Fantasy Tours, 1721 N. Highland Ave. near Hollywood Blvd., Hollywood, CA 90028 (213–469–8184) offers two-hour tours in double-deck, open-top buses, including stars' homes and such final resting places as Rudolph Valentino's grave.

Hollywood on Location 8644 Wilshire Blvd., Beverly Hills, CA 90211 (213–659–9165), provides new lists each weekday of movie and TV series in production around Los Angeles, with exact locations and names of stars. The $19 fee covers everyone going in one car, and includes a specific map and route.

Starline Sightseeing Tours, Mann's Chinese Theatre, 6845 Hollywood Blvd., Los Angeles, CA 90028 (213–463–3131), offers bus tours of Hollywood landmarks and a drive past stars' homes.

Maps of stars' homes are sold by street vendors and Hollywood bookshops. Most homes are in Beverly Hills and Bel Air. The ultimate guide is *The Movie Lover's Guide to Hollywood* by Richard Alleman, a paperback published by Harper Colophon Books. It includes everything from Pickfair, the Mary Pickford and Douglas Fairbanks mansion (1143 Summit Dr., Beverly Hills) to the house where Marilyn Monroe died (12305 5th Helena Dr., Brentwood).

Hollywood and its filmmaking image are more glamorous in legend than the reality of the famous intersection, Hollywood Blvd. and Vine St. Paramount Pictures is the only major studio still with its headquarters here, at 5451 Marathon St. The Walk of Stars, however, continues to add celebrities' names to the sidewalks on Hollywood Blvd. between Sycamore and Gower, and Vine between Sunset and Yucca. Dedication ceremonies, with stars usually attending, are held monthly; for dates and times call the Chamber of Commerce, (213–469–8311).

Other Hollywood attractions: Mann's (originally Grauman's) Chinese Theatre with stars' footprints and autographs in cement, 6925 Hollywood Blvd.; Hollywood Museum, with actual movie props and costumes, 7051 Hollywood Blvd.; Max Factor Building and Beauty Museum, 1666 N. Highland Ave.; Hollywood Wax Museum, 6767 Hollywood Blvd.; Musso & Frank Grill, an old-fashioned favorite since 1919, 6667 Hollywood Blvd. The Hollywood sign in the hills above the city, off Beachwood Dr., originally promoted the *Hollywoodland* housing development. It was restored in 1978.

Cemeteries in Los Angeles surprise visitors with their park-like settings including chapels, reproductions of famous artworks, and mottos such as "a place for the living to enjoy." Forest Lawn, 1712 S. Glendale Ave., Glendale, has a stained-glass reproduction of *The Last Supper;* the Wee Kirk of the Heather Church where Ronald Reagan married Jane Wyman in 1940; and memorials to Clark Gable, Carole Lombard, Errol Flynn, and Walt Disney. Others include Hollywood Memorial Park, 6000 Santa Monica Blvd., Hollywood: memorials to Rudolph Valentino, Tyrone Power: Westwood Memorial Park, 1218 Glendon Ave. off Wilshire Blvd., Westwood: Marilyn Monroe, Natalie Wood, Darryl Zanuck: Holy Cross Cemetery, 5835 W. Slauson Ave., Culver City; Bing Crosby, Rosalind Russell, Mario Lanza.

STUDIO TOURS AND TV SHOWS. Universal Studio Tour. 2900 Lankershim Blvd., Universal City, CA 91608 (818–508–9600). An industry of its own, this narrated tram tour takes visitors through the movie and TV studio, displaying special effects and a stunt show. It's been updated to illustrate recent hit movies. Summer, holidays, open at 8 A.M., other periods at 10 A.M., to 6 P.M. Adults, $15.95; children 3–11, $11.95; seniors, $11.50.

Burbank Studios VIP Tour. 4000 Warner Blvd., Burbank, CA 91522 (818–954–1744). A behind-the-scenes look at the TV and movie studio shared by Warner Bros. and Columbia. Mon.-Fri., 10 A.M.–2 P.M., additional summer tours, closed holidays. No children under 10, no cameras. Admission, $20.

NBC Studio Tours. 3000 W. Alameda Ave., Burbank, CA 91523 (818–840–3537). Hour-long tour includes studio sets and special effects demonstrations; you can also see yourself on camera. Mon.-Fri., 9 A.M.–4 P.M.; Sat., 10 A.M.–2 P.M.; Sun., 10 A.M.–2 P.M. Closed most major holidays. Adults, $5.50; children, $3.50.

Television Shows. Free tickets are available the days shows are videotaped at the downtown Los Angeles Visitors and Convention bureau, and at the studios, usually beginning at 9 A.M. Call ahead for availability: ABC, 4151 Prospect Ave., Hollywood (213–557–7777); CBS, 7800 Beverly Blvd., Los Angeles (213–852–2455); NBC, 3000 W. Alameda Ave., Burbank (213–840–3537).

PARKS AND GARDENS. Barnsdall Art Park. 4800 Hollywood Blvd., Los Angeles, (213–662–7272). It contains the restored Hollyhock House built by Frank Lloyd Wright. Free.

Descanso Gardens. 1414 Descanso Dr., La Canada. Thousands of azaleas, camelias, and roses in a site once part of the vast Spanish Rancho San Rafael. Adults, $1.50; children, 75 cents.

Griffith Park. Los Feliz Blvd. and Riverside Dr., Los Angeles. 4,000 acres for hiking, tennis, golf, picnics, plus Griffith Observatory and Planetarium. Park is free, admission charge to planetarium.

Los Angeles State and County Arboretum. 301 N. Baldwin Ave., Arcadia. The jungle setting for TV's *Fantasy Island* is here, plus home demonstration gardens, tropical greenhouse, orchids. Adults, $1.50; children, 75 cents.

Will Rogers State Historical Park. 14253 Sunset Blvd., Pacific Palisades (213–454–8212). The humorist's ranch is open, with daily house tours, 10 A.M.–5 P.M. Fee $2 per car.

ZOOS. The Los Angeles Zoo. 5333 Zoo Dr. in Griffith Park (213–666–4090). The zoo contains 2,000 animals, including 78 endangered species. Special attractions are a koala house and bird and elephant shows. Open daily except Christmas, 10 A.M.–5 P.M., until 6 P.M. in summer. Adults, $4.50, children, $1.50.

Baby strollers and wheelchairs can be rented. A tram service tours the zoo's perimeter. Snack stands and two picnic areas are located on the grounds.

PARTICIPANT SPORTS. Jogging is a city-wide activity. Beaches and adjacent pathways are ideal. Popular routes are along San Vicente Blvd. from Brentwood to Santa Monica, then through palm-lined Palisades Park. On the walkways between Santa Monica and Venice, joggers manage to share space with bike riders and roller skaters.

Tennis courts are in most major parks, lighted at night, and more readily available when local residents are busy elsewhere: mid-day on weekdays, evenings on weekends. Try Griffith Park's well-lit courts near the intersection of Los Feliz and Riverside Dr. Except from 11 A.M. to 3 P.M., the courts are often unoccupied. Be prepared to pay an hourly fee anywhere, unless courts are available at your hotel.

Golf is another year-round activity, and golfers from harsher climates may enjoy the novelty of playing in mid-winter. There are three public courses in *Griffith Park* alone, and other popular courses include *Rancho Park,* 10460 W. Pico Blvd., Los Angeles, and *Penmar,* a 9-hole golf course at 1233 Rose Ave., Venice. For information on other golf courses, tennis courts, swimming pools and hiking trails, contact the *Los Angeles City Parks and Recreation Dept.* (213–485–5555) or *County Parks and Recreation Dept.* (213–738–2961).

SPECTATOR SPORTS. Baseball. The National League Dodgers play at Dodger Stadium in Chavez Ravine above downtown Los Angeles Apr.-Sept. (213–224–1500). The American League California Angels play at the Anaheim Stadium in Orange County (714–634–2000).

Basketball. The Lakers play their home games at the Forum in Inglewood (213–673–1300). The Clippers play at the Sports Arena in Los Angeles (213–748–8000).

Football. The Raiders make their current home at Memorial Coliseum, site of two Summer Olympics in Los Angeles (213–322–3451). The Rams play in Anaheim Stadium (714–937–6767).

Thoroughbred racing takes place late Apr. to late July, Nov. and Dec. at Hollywood Park in Inglewood near Los Angeles International Airport (213–419–1500) and Dec.-Apr., Oct.-Nov. at Santa Anita Park in Arcadia (818–574–7223).

BEACHES. Los Angeles County operates more than 40 miles of beaches along 76 miles of coastline, from Nicholas Canyon Beach in the north to San Pedro's Cabrillo Beach in the south. At these county beaches, lifeguards are on duty all year during daylight hours. Beachgoers are advised to check with lifeguards on arrival to learn of unusual surfing conditions or beach hazards. Pets, alcoholic beverages, and bonfires are prohibited. Public parking, for a fee, is available at most beaches.

For information on county-operated beaches and the recreation boating harbor at Marina del Rey, just north of Los Angeles Airport, contact the *Marina del Rey Information* Center, 4701 Admiralty Way (213–822–0119). Open daily, 9 A.M.–5 P.M.

Traveling from north to south, popular beaches include: Zuma Beach, with extensive parking, and Surfrider Beach with its Sept. surfing contest in Malibu; Santa Monica city beaches, family favorites; Venice, with its colorful characters and the bodybuilders' "Muscle Beach"; Marina del Rey, a dock for thousands of boats and site of many restaurants; Manhattan, Hermosa, and Redondo Beaches, clean sand and pleasant settings.

THEME PARKS. Disneyland. Box 3232, Anaheim, CA 94803 (714–999–4565). From Los Angeles, drive south on I-5, the Golden State Freeway, which becomes the Santa Ana Freeway. The Disneyland exit is in Anaheim. In the mid-1950s filmmaker Walt Disney's vision turned a 76-acre orange grove into an entertainment center. Today, the seven theme areas remain as fresh and colorful as Disney envisioned. Recent additions include Star Tours and *Captain E-O,* a video starring Michael Jackson.

Open year-round, Mon.-Fri. 10 A.M.–7 P.M.; Sat.-Sun., 10 A.M.–6 P.M. Extended summer hours, mid-June to mid-Sept., Mon.-Fri. 9 A.M.–10 P.M.; Sat. to midnight; Sun. to 10 P.M. Admission, $10–$15 a day. Discounts on two-day and three-day passes.

Knott's Berry Farm. 8039 Beach Blvd., Buena Park (714–220–5200). Take State Rte. 91 east from the Golden State Freeway (I-5). Western and Gold-Rush themes carry through this 150-acre family park and its 165 rides. They include Montezooma's Revenge and the Corkscrew roller coaster with two 360-degree loops. In the Camp Snoopy area, Charles Schulz's "Peanuts" cartoon characters do their best to match the Disney appeal. Winter hours: Mon., Tues., Fri., 10 A.M.–6 P.M.; Sat., 10 A.M.–10 P.M.; Sun., 10 A.M.–7 P.M.; open additional days during school vacations. Summer: Sun.-Thurs., 10 A.M.–11 P.M.; Fri. to midnight, Sat. to 1 A.M. Admission $11.95–$16.95.

Transportation among Anaheim attractions is provided by the Fun Bus, with a route to major hotels, Disneyland, Knott's Berry Farm, Movieland Wax Museum, Anaheim Convention Center. Buses operate hourly year-round. Round trip, about $18.50. Information and hotel pick-up requests, 714–635–1390.

Six Flags Magic Mountain. 26101 Magic Mountain Pkwy. (exit from Golden State Freeway), Valencia (805–255–4111). Located a half-hour drive north of Hollywood, this park boasts a $35-million upgrading and rides that youngsters consider the most thrilling, including the Colossus roller coaster and Jet Stream water ride. There is a Wizard's Village for younger children. Open Sat., Sun., holidays (except Christmas) year-round, 10 A.M.–8 P.M. Open until 10 P.M. Sept.-Oct. Extended schedule Memorial Day-Labor Day, 10 A.M.–midnight daily.

HISTORIC SITES AND HOUSES. **Bradbury Building.** 304 S. Broadway, Los Angeles (213–489–1893). Restored five-story 1893 office building with inner court, skylight, ornate railings on balconies. Open Mon.-Sat., 10 A.M.–6 P.M. $2 admission.

Bullocks-Wilshire department store. 3050 Wilshire Blvd., Los Angeles (213–382–6161). If the 1920s are considered history in Los Angeles, then this 1928 Art Deco and Moderne building must be a historical site. The grand entrance is from the rear parking lot. There is a spacious tea room on the fifth floor.

El Pueblo de Los Angeles. Bounded by Alameda, Arcadia, Spring and Macy Sts. (213–628–1274). This 44-acre state historical park displays the roots of Los Angeles history. The Avila Adobe dates from 1818; Old Plaza Church, *Nuestra Senora la Reina de Los Angeles,* from 1822; and the Pico House, once a hotel, was built in 1870 by the last Mexican governor of California. Olvera Street, created from a slum in the 1930s, is lined with souvenir shops and restaurants. Free admission.

Gamble House. 4 Westmoreland Pl. off N. Orange Grove Blvd., Pasadena (818–793–3334). This rambling bungalow built by architects Charles and Henry Greene in 1908 is a masterpiece of the Arts and Crafts movement, with every detail finely crafted. Open Tues. and Thurs., 10 A.M.–3 P.M.; Sun., noon–3 P.M. One-hour tours. Admission, $4.

Mission San Fernando Re de Espana. 15151 San Fernando Mission Blvd., Mission Hills (818–361–0186). Restored 1797 church, monastery, workrooms in a garden setting. A 35-bell carillon rings hourly, 10 A.M.–6 P.M. Open Mon.-Sat., 9 A.M.–4:30 P.M.; Sun. and holidays, 10 A.M.–5 P.M. Admission, $1.

Mission San Gabriel Arcangel. 537 W. Mission Dr., San Gabriel (818–282–5191). Founded in 1771, this restored mission and its grounds are among the best representations of California life during the Spanish era. Open 9:30 A.M.–4:15 P.M. daily; closed Easter, Thanksgiving, Christmas. Admission, $1, 50 cents for children.

MUSEUMS AND GALLERIES. Los Angeles museums maintain fine permanent collections and display significant changing exhibitions. *Los Angeles* and *California* magazines and the *Los Angeles Times* provide information on current exhibits, lectures, films, dance, and special museum programs. Here are specifics on some major museums:

California Museum of Science and Industry. 700 State Dr., L.A. (213–744–7400). Located in the Exposition Park neighborhood, southeast of downtown. Hands-on computer exhibit, animal husbandry exhibits, with 150 chicks hatching daily; economic exhibits on labor, trade, and banking. Aerospace museum in separate building with IMAX Theater showing three films daily. Gift shop, MacDonald's.

The J. Paul Getty Museum. 17985 Pacific Coast Hwy., Malibu 90265 (213–458–2003). This replica of a first-century Roman villa was completed in 1974 to house the collection (Greek and Roman antiquities, European paintings from the thirteenth to nineteenth centuries) begun by the famous oil magnate in the 30s. Reservations are required so write or call ahead.

The Huntington Gallery. 1151 Oxford Rd., San Marino (818–405–2100). Sharing the ground with the Huntington Library and Botanical Gardens are 18th- and 19th-century British and European works of art, including perennial favorites like Gainsborough's *Blue Boy* and Lawrence's *Pinkie.* Book and plant stores, snack bar. Reservations required on Sundays.

Los Angeles County Museum of Art. 5905 Wilshire Blvd., L.A. (213–927–2590). Established in 1965, this museum completed a renovation in 1987 which included the addition of a five-story glass brick facade housing a four-tiered cascading waterfall and new modern art collection in the Robert O. Anderson wing. LACMA is composed of four buildings with a spectacularly full range of art covering the entire world. Important traveling exhibits. Gift shop, cafeteria.

Museum of Contemporary Art (MoCA). 250 S. Grand Ave., L.A. 90012 (213–626–6222). A permanent collection of international scope representing modern art, beginning in the 1940s and continuing through to the present. Main facility at California Plaza; adjunct Temporary Contemporary at 152 N. Central in Little Tokyo.

The Natural History Museum of Los Angeles County. 900 Exposition Blvd., L.A. (213–744–3411). Opened in 1913, this striking Spanish Renaissance building houses permanent and temporary exhibits, including some of the finest fossils discovered in the La Brea Tar Pits. Gift shop, bookstore, cafeteria.

Pacific Asia Museum. 46 N. Los Robles Dr., Pasadena (818–449–2742). Patterned after a Chinese imperial palace, this museum was built in the early 1920s to display Grace Nicholson's collection of Far Eastern art. Bookstore, original art sold in Collectors Gallery.

George C. Page Museum of La Brea Discoveries. 5801 Wilshire Blvd., L.A. (213–936–2230). In front of the Page Museum are the La Brea Tar Pits, where prehistoric animals became mired in the sticky asphalt while hunting or drinking. Inside are some of the remains of these animals recovered from the pits, including saber-toothed cats, and wolves. Paleontological Laboratory, educational films. Gift shop.

Norton Simon Museum. 411 W. Colorado Blvd., Pasadena (818–449–3730). Once the Pasadena Museum of Modern Art, this museum now displays art spanning more than 2,000 years. Gift shop. Hours vary, call ahead.

Galleries exist all over the area. Of particular note are the many that operate along La Cienega Blvd. in Beverly Hills, as well as in downtown Los Angeles, Venice, and Laguna Beach.

MUSIC. Today, the traveler to Los Angeles has a broad range of musical choices: at indoor auditoriums or amphitheaters, at the universities—recitals, operas, musical comedy, concerts, rock and jazz festivals, symphony. Concerts are held frequently all over Southern California and Los Angeles, which is headquarters for the recording industry; consult the Sunday *Los Angeles Times* "Calendar" section. Here's a sampling of what to expect:

Classical. *The Dorothy Chandler Pavilion.* 135 N. Grand Ave., downtown (213–972–7211). Winter home of the Los Angeles Philharmonic and showcase for the Los Angeles Civic Light Opera and the Joffrey Ballet.

The Hollywood Bowl. 2301 N. Highland Ave., Hollywood (213–850–2000). Open since 1920, one of the world's largest natural amphitheatres. In a park surrounded by mountains, trees, and gardens, it is said to be acoustically perfect. Summer home of the Los Angeles Philharmonic. Other concerts draw big names. Many patrons picnic beforehand.

The Greek Theater. 2700 N. Vermont Ave., L.A. (213–216–6666). In Griffith Park. Everything from the classics to rock, pop, and country is heard in this concert hall under the stars.

Orange County Performing Arts Center. 600 Town Center Dr., Costa Mesa (714–556–2121). Opened in late 1986 to feature prominent companies like the Los Angeles Philharmonic, the Pacific Symphony, and the New York City Opera.

Jazz. *Nucleus Nuance.* 7267 Melrose Ave., Hollywood (213–939–8666). Art-Deco restaurant offers 30s and 40s jazz making for a great evening.

Memory Lane. 2323 W. Martin Luther King Blvd., L.A. (213–294–8430). Owned by actress Marla Gibbs (*The Jeffersons*), here sample jazz and blues for easy listening in a clubby atmosphere.

Jax. 339 N. Brand Blvd., Glendale (818–500–1604). An intimate club serving up food and fun. Live music daily.

Folk/Pop/Rock. *The Palace.* 1735 N. Vine St., Hollywood (213–462–3000). "In" spot for the upwardly mobile. With plush Art-Deco interior, a great environment for big names.

Vine Street Bar and Grill. 1610 N. Vine St., Hollywood (213–463–4375). Elegant club in the heart of Hollywood. Italian food served.

Gazzarri's. 9029 Sunset, West Hollywood (213–273–6606). Sunset Strip landmark serving up pure rock and roll. Casual dress, no credit cards.

Country. *The Palomino.* 6907 Lankershim Blvd., North Hollywood (818–764–4010). Good old boys and hip cowboys meet here for a good time.

SHOPPING. In the vast Los Angeles area, shopping runs the gamut from high-priced quality department stores and trendy boutiques to inexpensive national chain stores. What has been called "urban sprawl" (decentralization of living, away from a downtown section) has brought about shopping centers throughout Southern California. In them you'll find department stores (*Bullock's, I. Magnin's, Robinson's, Saks, Broadway, Buffums,* and *May Co.*), chain stores, boutiques, bookstores—everything from health foods to furniture to garden shops—all grouped together around landscaped malls and plazas. Browse, shop, lunch, see a fashion show. But downtown is still a major shopping area, with shopping complexes such as Citicorp Center.

Beverly Hills is a mecca for shoppers; on Wilshire Blvd. starting at Beverly Dr., and running west is where you'll find *Bonwit Teller's, Tiffany and Co., Neiman Marcus, Mark Cross, Cartier's, Saks Fifth Avenue, I. Magnin* and *J. W. Robinson's.* For shopping or being tempted, walk along Rodeo (probably the densest concentration of chic boutiques in the world), Camden, Bedford Drives. Many of the stores are as handsome as their merchandise especially in the swank new section dubbed "The Rodeo Collection." For women's chic, high-priced clothes, accessories and jewelry: *Gucci's, Hérmes, Courréges, Céline, Giorgio,* (complete with a full service bar), *Matthews, Theodore, Right Bank, Bally, Van Cleef and Arpels, Omega,* superb collection of pearls. Elegant men's clothiers: *Mr. Guy, Bijan, Carroll & Co., Jerry Magnin.*

The mile-and-a-half of Melrose Avenue stretching from a few blocks west of La Brea to a few blocks west of Crescent Heights in West Hollywood is where you'll find whatever's next in style. Flashing neon and technicolor hairstyles set off tiny boutiques like *Wild Blue,* a contemporary gallery of wearable art; *Art Deco L.A. Antiques,* filled with authentic treasures from the 30s and 40s; and *Black Salad,* an off-beat collection of shoes, hats, jewelry, lighters and hairdryers.

Miracle Mile, between La Brea and Fairfax, is not the major shopping center it once was. Branches of *May Co., Silverwood's* and *Desmond's.*

Westwood Village has *Bullock's Westwood, Desmond's* and many boutiques patronized by faculty and students from adjacent U.C.L.A., and by residents of Brentwood and Westwood.

In Brentwood, the *Del Mano Gallery and Studio* (11981 San Vincente Blvd. near Bundy) offers unique and exclusive American crafts, handmade gifts and wearable collectibles.

Shopping Centers: *Century City,* 10250 Santa Monica Blvd., West L.A., is dominated by *Bullock's* and the *Broadway* as well as a collection of trendy shops under one roof with convenient underground parking. Closer to Hollywood is the *Beverly Center,* built in 1982, with fabulous shops and convenient cafés, including Bullocks, the Broadway and numerous small boutiques. *Fox Hills Mall,* 200 Fox Hills Mall, Culver City, has over 100 stores including *Penney's, May Company* and *Broadway. Santa Monica Place* opened in 1980 with 160 shops just a stone's throw from the Ocean. Between 2nd and 4th Sts., Colorado Ave. and Broadway in Santa Monica. *Marina Pacifica Shopping Village,* 6346 C Pacific Coast Hwy., Long Beach. Over 100 shops, 6 restaurants located in the marina. *Fashion Square,* Sherman Oaks, in the San Fernando Valley. *I. Magnin's* and *Bullock's.* Good parking facilities. *Glendale Galleria,* between Brand and Central in Glendale, is a large, suburban-style mall with lots of department stores and boutiques. *Fisherman's Village,* a re-creation of Cape Cod, has specialty shops and restaurants. Overlooking the main channel at Marina del Rey. 13755 Fiji Way.

STAGE. Los Angeles benefits from the box-office appeal and talent of the film and television industry's actors "between engagements." Among the local companies the **Los Angeles Theatre Center,** 514 S. Spring St., Los Angeles, CA 90013 (213–627–5599), has expanded to four stages within a remodeled bank building downtown. It presents new and recent plays, with music and poetry series on the plays' dark nights.

Other local theaters, also emphasizing new works: The **Mark Taper Forum** at the Music Center, 135 N. Grand Ave., Los Angeles (213–972–7654); **L.A. Public Theater** at the Coronet, 366 N. La Cienega Blvd., West Hollywood (213–659–6415).

Touring plays and musicals are housed at the Ahmanson Theater in the Music Center, the Pantages, and the Shubert and Henry Fonda theaters, all in Los Angeles; the James A. Doolittle in Hollywood; and the Wilshire in Beverly Hills. Check newspapers for current attractions. For ticket information, call *Ticketron, at* 213–216–6666.

There's humor at the *Comedy Store,* 8433 Sunset Blvd., West Hollywood (213–656–6225) and improvisational theater and satire at *The Improvisation,* 8162 Melrose Ave., West Hollywood (213–651–2583).

BARS. Despite its well-publicized penchant for hedonism, Los Angeles is not a saloon town like New York City or San Francisco. But although the sprawl of the city has stunted the growth of a true saloon society, hundreds of cozy bars, lively pubs, and festive watering holes do quench the thirst in Los Angeles—they are simply not confined to a particular neighborhood. In all areas, most hotels and restaurants have bars or lounges, for a convivial cocktail—some are lively, others are private and secluded. You'll find them attractively decorated in all conceivable motifs. Try *L.A. Nicola Bar,* 4326 Sunset Blvd., L.A. (213–660–7217), or the *Rangoon Racquet Club,* at 9474 Little Santa Monica Blvd. (213–274–8926). Other possibilities: *Scandia Restaurant,* 9040 Sunset Blvd., Hollywood (213–278–3555); *Cock 'n Bull Restaurant,* 9170 Sunset Blvd., Hollywood (213–272–1397), the journalists' haunt; and *Polo Lounge,* in the Beverly Hills Hotel (213–276–2251), crowded with celebrities. *Tom Bergin's,* 840 S. Fairfax Ave. (213–936–7151), is a popular meeting spot, as is *Casey's Bar,* downtown at 613 S. Grand Ave. (213–629–2353).

EXPLORING SAN DIEGO

San Diego, the country's southwesternmost city, considers itself the only area in the United States with perfect weather. San Diego Bay ranks second among California's natural harbors. Now the second most populous city in California (surpassing San Francisco), San Diego is also home port for the Eleventh Naval District and 130 active U.S. Navy ships. Cabrillo National Monument, on the tip of Point Loma, is one of the most popular national monuments, giving even the Statue of Liberty a run for its money.

The fist of the southeastern arm protecting the bay is North Island, power-packed with the U.S. Naval Air Station. Super aircraft carriers call here. The community of Coronado, favorite anchorage for retired Naval officers, adjoins. "The Del," the dowager queen of California hotels, has crowned Coronado since 1888. Formally known as the Hotel del Coronado, it has been a royal resort and convention site.

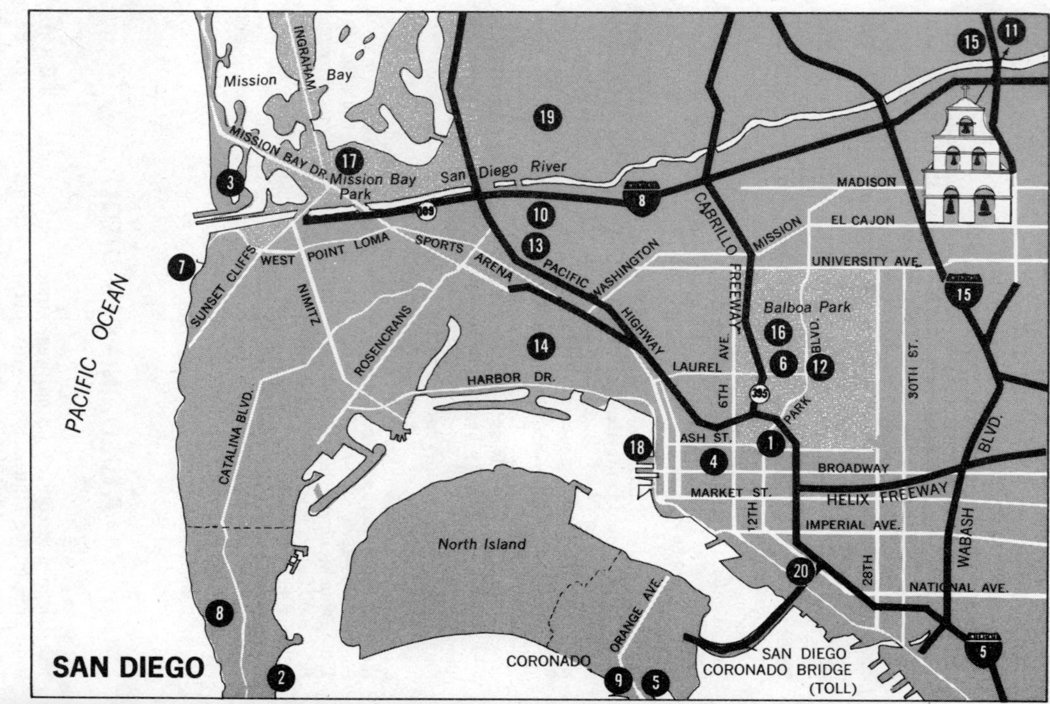

Points of Interest:

1) Balboa Stadium
2) Cabrillo Monument
3) Mariner's Basin
4) City Hall
5) Coronado Beach, Glorietta Bay
6) Fishing Pier
7) Fort Rosencrans National Cemetery
8) Hotel Coronado
9) Junipero Serra Museum
10) Mission San Diego de Alcala
11) National History Museum
12) Old Town State Park
13) San Diego International Airport
14) San Diego Museum of Art
15) San Diego Stadium
16) San Diego Zoo
17) Sea World Aquatic Park
18) Star of India
19) University of San Diego
20) Seaport-Village

Guests have included the Prince of Wales, the Maharajah of Jaipur, and eight presidents of the United States. Southward, the skinny arm extends toward the city of Imperial Beach, and along the way offers the beach facilities of the Silver Strand State Park.

Mission Bay is a 4,600-acre, city-owned, $60 million aquatic playground with nearly 30 miles of free beaches and half-a-dozen resort-type hotels. It's 10 minutes from downtown San Diego and has swimming, sailing, boating, golf and tennis.

The Coronado Bay Bridge connects San Diego and Coronado. From the Broadway pier, climb aboard a harbor excursion boat for a one- or two-hour cruise around San Diego Harbor. You will head out toward Shelter Island and Point Loma, pass by the cargo vessels and Navy ships.

The *Star of India,* launched in 1863 and now the oldest iron sailing ship afloat, has been restored to her best appearance and is moored alongside the Embarcadero, along with sister ships *Berkeley* and *Medea.*

Much of San Diego's cultural and recreational life centers on Balboa Park, a 1,400-acre garden spot. Here, in one of the country's finest city parks, are buildings of gracious Spanish Baroque design that house the park's many attractions. These include the Fine Arts and Timken Galleries, showing Old Masters' works, Russian icons, exceptional changing exhibitions, the new Reuben H. Fleet Space Theater and Science Center, Museum of Man, Natural History Museum, and the Botanical Building. The Spreckels organ, with 5,000 pipes, is one of the world's largest outdoor organs. The House of Pacific Relations is a quaint collection of 15 cottages representing 20 nationalities.

Old Town, 10 minutes from modern San Diego's downtown, is where the white man first established himself in California 200 years ago. The four square blocks of Old Town Park now boast a new, grassy Plaza Square reminiscent of those so popular in many Mexican towns.

Located in the shadow of the San Diego-Coronado Bridge at the foot of Harbor Drive and Pacific Highway, Seaport Village has three connected sections: Old Monterey, Victorian San Francisco and traditional Mexico. Appropriate architecture pinpoints each section and a northern Pacific-style five-story lighthouse guards the edge of a quarter-mile boardwalk. Featured are 50 boutiques and a barrage of restaurants. Adjacent is the eight-acre Embarcadero Marine Park.

The San Diego Zoo, in Balboa Park, boasts approximately 3,200 animals of 800 species, the largest collection of wild animals in the world. Most live outdoors in simulated natural habitats. There are huge walkthrough, free-flight cages for viewing some of the zoo's 1,800 birds.

San Diego Wild Animal Park, 30 miles northeast of downtown but still within the city, has 2,200 animals in near-natural habitats on a 1,800-acre site. An electric monorail train takes visitors through the park.

Presidio Park and the Junipero Serra Museum of historical relics of the Southwest mark the stop where the Spanish padres founded the first mission of their California chain in 1769. Relocated later, Mission San Diego de Alcala is five miles up Mission Valley, the original five old bells still hanging from the belfry. Fascinating artifacts are showing up from the archaeological research being done by the University of San Diego, and are shown in the mission's museum.

Across the border is the Mexican city of Tijuana, offering a wide variety of colorful shops, restaurants, Mexican festivals and sporting events. The bright red Tijuana Trolley connects the city with San

Diego. The Tijuana Cultural Center is a magnificent complex, which displays Mexico's cultural heritage. An Omnimax theatre employs state-of-the-art technology to project images of Mexico on a 180-degree screen.

PRACTICAL INFORMATION FOR SAN DIEGO

HOW TO GET THERE AND AROUND. By Plane. Most major airlines and some low-cost regional ones serve San Diego, with frequent special fares available. San Diego International Airport is near the downtown area; transportation from the airport is available via taxi, city bus, hotel limo, and rental car.

By Bus. The *Greyhound* and *Trailways* bus stations are both located downtown and have daily arrivals and departures to most major cities in the U.S. Both lines offer occasional special fares. For Greyhound, call 239–9171; for Trailways, 232–2001.

San Diego Transit operates buses throughout the county, but schedules and transfers can be complicated unless you are staying downtown or at the Hotel Circle. Many hotels, train and bus stations, and tourist information centers have bus schedules and route maps. Call 233–3004 for specific route information or schedules, but be prepared to redial often. The fare is 80 cents (exact change only) for regular routes and $1 (exact change only, no bills) for express routes, and transfers are usable for only a half hour or until the next available bus. Senior citizen fares are 50 cents during nonpeak hours. Some buses have bike racks; 20 are equipped for handicapped riders.

By Train. Long-distance Amtrak routes reach San Diego through interchanges in Los Angeles and arrive at the downtown Santa Fe station. Daily trains serve San Diego and Los Angeles with stops along the coast and inland. Promotional fares are sometimes available during the winter. The toll-free number for fares and information is 800–872–7245.

By Trolley. The San Diego Trolley's bright red electric cars travel south through downtown to the Mexican border. The trolley doesn't reach any of the major tourist attractions but is an inexpensive way to reach the border; from there, Tijuana is a short walk or taxi ride away. Each stop has a map and ticket machines, which take only quarters for the $1.50 fare from downtown to the border. Some major stops have change machines. Call 231–1466.

By Taxi. The average taxi fare in San Diego is $2 for the first mile and $1 for each additional mile. Since the mileage between attractions can be considerable (15 miles from downtown to La Jolla, for example), it is best to use cabs only for short jumps. Cab companies are listed in the Yellow Pages; be sure to ask about fares and whether the company serves only a particular area.

By Car. The major routes into San Diego are Interstate Highway 5, running north-south through most of California; Interstate 8/U.S. 80, running east-west to the coast; Highways 163 and 15, the inland north-south route; and U.S. 94, from the eastern desert. Interstate 805 intersects with Highway 163 and Interstate 5 north of San Diego and provides an alternative route to the Mexican Border.

ACCOMMODATIONS. There is a "peak" season during June, July, and August. January and February are also considered "peak" season at many hotels. During these months, hotel and motel rates increase, sometimes by a large amount. This varies from hotel to hotel. To assure yourself of accommodations, reserve early. In general, San Diego is not as expensive as many other cities. The guest pays more for a view of the ocean or the bay than for room appointments.

The price categories are based on the cost of a double room. Because establishments often offer a range of prices (and even these will vary), the categories here overlap somewhat. They are: *Deluxe,* \$90–\$200; *Expensive,* \$70–\$150; *Moderate,* \$40–\$70; *Inexpensive,* under \$45. There is a 7-percent tax on all hotel and motel rooms. Because deluxe hotels are relatively well-priced when compared to comparable hotels elsewhere, you will need to make reservations especially early.

Deluxe

Hotel Del Coronado. 1500 Orange Ave., Coronado (435–6611). Built in 1888, the Hotel Del Coronado is the last of its kind anywhere in California. Steeped in glamour and tradition, the hotel offers rooms and suites that were once occupied by the Duke and Duchess of Windsor, a number of U.S. presidents, countless movie stars, and other celebrities. A designated historical landmark, the white frame Victorian structure, with its cupolas and distinctive red roofing, has been maintained scrupulously to retain the flavor of its era. For the guest who prefers a newer room, there's a high-rise wing adjacent to the original building. The Crown Room Restaurant is well known, and there is entertainment nightly in one of the hotel's bars. With full amenities including pool and tennis courts, the hotel is also located on one of San Diego's most beautiful beaches.

Horton Grand Hotel. 311 Island Ave., downtown (544–1886). This charming 100-year-old restored Victorian hotel is in the Gaslamp Quarter. The 110 rooms are furnished with period antiques, ceiling fans, and gas-burning fireplaces. A Chinatown Museum, restaurant, tea room, and bar/lounge are on the premises.

Hotel Inter-Continental San Diego. 333 West Harbor Dr., San Diego (234–1500), or (800–327–0200). This high-rise on the San Diego Harbor has a marina, four restaurants, a health club, and luxurious suites. Room rates escalate with the floor and view.

Hyatt Islandia. 1441 Quivira Rd., Mission Bay (224–1234), or (800–228–9000). Located in the middle of one of San Diego's most beautiful seashore areas, Mission Bay Park, the Islandia has lanai-style units and a high-rise. Landscaping is beautiful and the room decor is tastefully modern, with dramatic views. The restaurant offers an elegant atmosphere and gourmet cuisine, plus splendid Sunday brunch.

La Costa Hotel & Spa. Costa del Mar Rd., Carlsbad (438–9111). This internationally known spa resort is the place where the well-to-do and well-known come to shed unwanted pounds at the health spa and relax in the sunshine. The resort offers tennis, golf, and a gymnasium. There are six restaurants, plus bars and a movie theater, in this 340-unit resort located 30 miles north of San Diego and far enough inland to be almost perpetually sunny. La Costa is the site of celebrity golf and tennis tournaments throughout the year.

La Valencia. 1132 Prospect St., La Jolla (454–0771). A tradition for many long-time visitors to La Jolla, this European-style, pink stucco hotel was haven for movie stars of the 1930s and '40s. It has a courtyard for patio dining and a quiet, elegant lobby where guests congregate in the evenings to enjoy the spectacular view of the ocean while sipping cocktails, reading, or listening to music. The clientele tends to be older, except in the Whaling Bar, which is a gathering spot for all ages. The restaurants have excellent food, and the hotel is ideally located for walking to La Jolla Cove Beach, shopping, and restaurants.

Rancho Bernardo Inn. 17550 Bernardo Oaks Dr. in the North County area (487–1611), or (800–854–1065) for reservations. This rambling, Spanish-style resort is located 30 miles northeast of downtown San Diego in a scenic inland valley. The Inn is famous for its tennis college, which features the latest in professional instruction, including videotapes of your game and lessons for players at all levels. Championship golf courses, riding, and swimming are also available for guests, and the restaurant is excellent. It is far away from the beach and tourist attractions, but there's plenty to do—and the community of Rancho Bernardo, where it is situated, offers many good restaurants and movies, and a lot of entertainment.

Sheraton Harbor Island. 1380 Harbor Island Dr. (291–6400) or (800–325–3535). Built on the lot that provides the best view of man-made Harbor Island and within walking distance of Lindbergh Field, the international airport, this is not a typical airport hotel. Located on the Bay, it offers attractive rooms with a smashing view of the downtown area, yacht harbor, and surrounding areas. The restaurants are good and the lounges offer top local entertainment (especially fine jazz Sunday evenings). Don't let the proximity to the airport scare you off—the rooms are well-insulated against jet noise. Recently remodeled into two separate hotels: *Sheraton East* offers a private deck and luxury suites; the *West* has water views from every room.

U. S. Grant Hotel. 326 Broadway, downtown (232–3121). This historic hotel has undergone a complete renovation. Facing downtown's new centerpiece, Horton Plaza, the Grant is elegant and formal, with marble floors and glistening chandeliers. Butlers and concierges serve guests splendidly. There are two restaurants, the Garden Room and the Grant Grill, a long-time favorite of high-powered business types.

Westgate. 1055 Second Ave., downtown (238–1818). Easily the most formal of San Diego's hotels, from its lobby, with French provincial decor and chandeliers, to the opulently decorated rooms and white-gloved waiters in the dining room. Its clientele tends toward business travelers and international tourists. The Westgate is the only hotel in its class in the downtown area, and it's close to theater and convention facilities, transportation, and the rapidly developing Gaslamp Quarter, a project to re-create downtown the San Diego of the late 1800s.

Expensive

Blue Sea Lodge—Best Western. 707 Pacific Beach Dr. (483–4700), or (800–258–3732). All suites are located directly on the beach at this new, tastefully decorated hotel, San Diego's first fully solar-powered hotel or motel. It caters strictly to visitors since there are no convention or meeting facilities. There is no restaurant or cocktail lounge, but there are kitchen units, and best of all, the beach and lots of sunshine.

Britt House. 406 Maple St., downtown (234–2926). This charmingly restored Victorian house is San Diego's first bed-and-breakfast hostelry. Its owners have lavished loving care on the decor and service, which includes home-baked goodies for breakfast daily. Located near downtown, the Zoo, and Balboa Park, it's well worth the price, but you must have reservations if you want to be assured of one of Britt House's nine rooms.

Colonial Inn. 910 Prospect St., La Jolla (454–2181) or (800–832–5525). A tastefully restored turn-of-the-century building, this hotel is in the midst of La Jolla's shopping and dining attractions. You can walk among the boutiques, galleries, and cafés to nearby La Jolla Cove. The restaurant on the premises offers the same historic, but rather stolid, decor.

Dana Inn & Marina. 1710 Mission Bay Dr. (222–6440), or (800–445–3339). This hotel, which has an adjoining marina, offers the best bargains in the Mission Bay Park area. The accommodations are not as grand as in some of the other hotels, but they're perfectly fine for visitors who don't plan to spend much time cooped up in a room.

Glorietta Bay Inn. 1630 Glorietta Blvd., Coronado (435–3101 or 800–854–3380). Built around the mansion of the Spreckels family—who once owned most of downtown San Diego, Coronado, the transit company, and both daily newspapers—this spotlessly maintained hotel offers 100 rooms in an Edwardian mansion, circa 1908. This low-rise structure is across the street from the Coronado small-craft harbor on one side, and the Hotel Del on the other, and around the corner from Coronado Village, which has many fine restaurants and quaint shops. The Inn has no coffee shop or bar, though a continental breakfast is served to guests. There are plenty of dining and drinking spots within a block.

Half Moon Inn. 2303 Shelter Island Dr. (224–3411), or (800–542–7401). This rustic, two-story resort hotel has rental bicycles, shuffleboard, a putting green, and ping-pong, plus usual features. The setting is South Seas-restful, and the place has a relaxing, out-of-the-way feeling, although it is in the middle of Shelter Island, an artificial island on San Diego Bay not far from Harbor Island. Its restaurant, Humphrey's, has an attractive nautical/garden decor, sponsors outdoor jazz concerts in the summer, and is popular with locals.

Hanalei Hotel. 2270 Hotel Circle N. (297–1101), or (800–854–2608). Despite the architect's failure to make the place look like an authentic South Seas spot, as its name suggests, the rooms are attractively decorated. There is a new tower section. The restaurant and bar also are good, and the Mission Valley location is convenient for fanning out by car to all sections of the city rapidly and efficiently.

Holiday Inn at the Embarcadero. 1355 N. Harbor Dr. (232–3861), or (800–465–4329). Right on the bay and just across the street from the Maritime Museum, this inn is less than three miles from the airport. It's also near the Amtrak depot and downtown, and has the most scenic location of any downtown hotel. The hotel is large—600 units—and caters to both business groups and individual travelers. The bayside rooms offer a spectacular view, and there is a restaurant and lounge. Within walking distance of many other seafood restaurants, and ideal for strolls along the Embarcadero.

Kona Kai Club. 1551 Shelter Island Dr. (222–1191 or 800–325–2218). A private club, the Kona Kai does rent rooms to visitors who are nonmembers. Located at the tip of Shelter Island, the Kona Kai has tennis courts, racquetball, and a private beach. The accommodations are not grand, but the Hawaiian-influenced decor is quiet and tasteful. The restaurant and bar provide good fare.

San Diego Hilton. 1775 E. Mission Bay Dr. (276–4010 or 800–445–8667). Located between Interstate and the east shore of Mission Bay, this Hilton has convenience and a spacious, parklike setting. The hotel is a resort-style set-up, with spacious, gorgeously landscaped grounds and only one unit of high-rise rooms; the rest of the accommodations are lanai-style units. It features a jogging track, tennis courts, and the Cargo Bar, a locally popular night spot with live entertainment. Also a hotel yacht.

San Diego Princess Resort. 1404 W. Vacation Rd. (274–4630 or 800–542–6275). Another of the seaside resort facilities in Mission Bay Park, the grounds are so beautifully landscaped that Vacation Village has been the setting of many movies. The atmosphere is relaxing, the grounds are extensive, and cottage units with kitchens and bay views are available. It offers full amenities, including a restaurant and bar, bicycles, and boat rentals; favored by families, particularly during the summer.

Seapoint Hotel. 4875 N. Harbor Dr. (224–3621 or 800–762–8899). Recently acquired by the Great Pacific Hotels Chain, this small, comfortable spot is conveniently located near the airport and major attractions.

Summer House Inn. 7955 La Jolla Shores Dr. (459–0261 or 800–223–7896). A pleasant, modern, medium-rise hotel located five-minutes from the center of La Jolla's commercial district. It has all standard amenities, and Elario's Restaurant offers a spectacular view of the Pacific, gourmet cuisine, and live jazz entertainment most nights. $74–87.

Town and Country. 500 W. Hotel Circle North (291–7131), or (800–854–2608). With 1,000 rooms, the Town and Country is the biggest single hotel-motel complex in town. It's so big, in fact, that a guest can get lost rather easily. It is beautifully landscaped and centrally located in Mission Valley. With the city's largest private convention facilities, it caters to convention and meeting groups, but is resortlike enough to appeal to tourists too. Guests have their choice of two-story units or a room in one of the two towers. The sprawling layout has several bars, discos, and restaurants, plus a Country-Western lounge. A large shopping center and golf course are within walking distance. Access to Atlas Health Club.

Moderate

Andrea Villa Inn. 2402 Torrey Pines Rd., La Jolla, CA 92037 (619–459–3311, 800–367–6467). A medium-sized attractive La Jolla motel. It has a swimming pool and restaurant.

Catamaran Hotel. 3999 Mission Blvd., Pacific Beach, CA 92109 (619–488–1081, 800–821–3619). In Mission Beach, not far from the ocean, Mission Bay Park, Sea World, and other attractions. The rooms are large, airy and pleasant. There is a coffee shop and a restaurant-bar with live entertainment and dancing.

Circle 8 Motor Inn. 543 Hotel Circle South, San Diego, CA 92108 (619–297–8800, 800–227–4743). A large complex located in Mission Valley, with pool, coffee shop, and small refrigerators in all rooms. Weekly rates available.

Ebb Tide Hitching Post. 5082 West Point Loma Blvd., Ocean Beach, CA 92107 (619–224–9339). Only a block from the ocean and a half block to the bay. Some units have kitchens. Weekly rates available.

Fabulous Inns of America. 2485 Hotel Circle Pl., San Diego, CA 92108 (619–291–7700, 800–824–0950). A family-oriented Mission Valley motel with swimming pool and game room. Golf course and tennis courts adjacent.

Harbor View Holiday Inn. 1617 First Ave., San Diego, CA 92101 (619–239–6171, 800–465–4329). This Holiday Inn is located between downtown and Balboa Park, near the airport and the ocean. The view from the bar and restaurant at the top is one of the best downtown.

Holiday Inn Mission Valley. 595 Hotel Circle S., San Diego, CA 92108 (619–291–5720, 800–HOL–IDAY). This nondescript hotel is a pleasant, predictable, reliable place to stay.

Hotel San Diego. 339 West Broadway, San Diego, CA 92101 (619–234–0221, 800–621–5380 nationwide, 800–824–1244 in CA). This old hotel has been restored tastefully, giving it the glitter it enjoyed when it opened in 1912. The rooms are nicely done; the dining is average. Senior citizen and government discounts available.

Mission Valley Inn. 875 Hotel Circle S., San Diego, CA 92108 (619–298–8281, 800–854–2608 nationwide, 800–542–6082 in CA). A comfortable low-rise facility offering the convenience of proximity by car to practically everything in town. Liquor store, coffee shop, and deluxe Mexican restaurant on the premises. Senior citizen and government discounts offered.

Outrigger Motel. 1370 Scott St., Point Loma, CA 92106 (619–223–7105). Just across from sport fishing docks, 2 miles from the airport. All units have full kitchens. Shops and restaurants within walking distance. Swimming pool.

Pacific Shores Inn. 4802 Mission Blvd., San Diego, CA 92109 (619–483–6300, 800–854–3380). A large motel for this area, a half block from the beach. Nicely decorated with most amenities, including a pool. Accepts pets; $50 deposit required.

Quality Inn. 2901 Nimitz Blvd., Point Loma, CA 92106 (619–224–3655, 800–228–5151 nationwide, 800–352–1222 in CA). Between Mission Bay Park and San Diego Bay, a good close-in location for visitors. Accommodations are good. Senior citizen discount available.

Santa Clara Motel. 839 Santa Clara Place, Mission Beach, CA 92109 (619–488–1193). Small hotel a block from beach, shops, and restaurants. Kitchens available, but no frills.

Surfer Motor Lodge. 711 Pacific Beach Dr., Pacific Beach, CA 92109 (619–483–7070). Right on the beach; has a restaurant and cocktail lounge as well as a swimming pool and kitchens. Senior citizen and government discounts available.

Tradewinds Motel. 4305 Mission Bay Dr., San Diego, CA 92109 (619–273–4616). Near Mission Bay Park; motel offers a view of the bay as well as the golf course. Weekly and monthly rates.

TraveLodge—Balboa Park. 840 Ash St., San Diego, CA 92101 (619–234–8277, 800–255–3050). Convenient downtown location for walking to the park and zoo; has swimming pool and kitchens.

TraveLodge—Civic Center. 1505 Pacific Hwy., San Diego, CA 92101 (619–239–9185, 800–255–3050). A small motel with no restaurant or bar. Senior citizen and government discounts available.

TraveLodge—La Jolla. 1141 Silverado St., La Jolla, CA 92307 (619–454–0791, 800–255–3050). Its best feature is the location, right in the heart of La Jolla's shopping and restaurant district. Kitchens are available as well as senior citizen and government discounts.

TraveLodge—San Diego Downtown. 1345 Tenth Ave., San Diego, CA 92101 (619–234–6344, 800–255–3050). Basic motel with a pool; kitchens available.

Vagabond Motor Hotel. 625 Hotel Circle S., San Diego, CA 92108 (619–297–1691, 800–522–1555). Rooms are clean, neat, and comfortable. No restaurant or bar on the premises but several close by.

Inexpensive

La Jolla Palms Inn. 6705 La Jolla Blvd., La Jolla, CA 92037 (619–454–7101, 800–367–6467). Friendly atmosphere, attractive landscaping. One block from beach and walking distance from nearby restaurants. Has a pool, restaurant, cocktail lounge, kitchen units, weekly rentals. Accepts pets.

Loma Manor Motel. 1518 Rosecrans St., Point Loma, CA 92106 (619–223–8391). Centrally located, not too far from beaches. Weekly rates offered.

Mission Bay Motel. 4221 Mission Blvd., San Diego, CA 92109 (619–483–6440). Close to ocean and bay, within walking distance of restaurants. Swimming pool, kitchens available.

Point Loma Inn. 2933 Fenelon St., Point Loma, CA 92106 (619–226–9333 800–225–9610 nationwide, 800–824–3051 in CA). Near Shelter Island, downtown, and harbor areas.

Townhouse Lodge—A Friendship Inn. 810 Ash St., San Diego, CA 92101 (619–233–8826, 800–982–2020). A basic two-story motel with a pool. Central downtown location.

BED AND BREAKFAST. **Carolyn's Bed and Breakfast Homes.** 416 Third Ave., Chula Vista, CA 92010. (619–435–5009). Finds accommodations in private homes and cottages. Rates range from $35 to $75 per night.

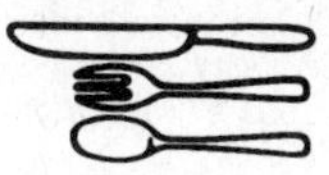

RESTAURANTS. Visitors to San Diego will discover an unusually broad range of choices for dining. The oceanside location of the city means a ready supply of fresh, delectable seafood, and the proximity to the Mexican border accounts for the spicy Mexican influence. San Diego is a sophisticated city whose eating establishments reflect its cosmopolitan heritage.

Price categories for recommended restaurants are based on the price of a complete meal for one, without beverage, tax, or tip. They are: *Expensive,* $20 and up; *Moderate,* $10–$20; and *Inexpensive,* $10 and under.

Expensive

Anthony's Star of the Sea Room. 1360 Harbor Dr., at Ash St. on Embarcadero (619–232–7408). This family-owned restaurant is perhaps the best seafood establishment in Southern California. Extraordinary specialties, not the least of which is a sensational abalone in garlic butter, served in a luxurious, gold-toned setting overlooking San Diego Bay.

Elario's Restaurant. In the Summer House Inn, 7955 La Jolla Shores Dr. (459–0541). Continental Cuisine in La Jolla with panoramic Pacific view. Specialties: Beef Wellington, filets de sole Victoria.

Fontainebleau Room. In the Westgate Hotel, 1055 2nd Ave., at Broadway (238–1818). Gourmet French cuisine served in the Continental manner. The kitchen is top-flight, and the Beef Wellington is a super specialty. Very elegant.

Lubach's. 2101 N. Harbor Dr. (232–5129). One of the city's favorite lunch spots, and a cozy place for dinner, too. Delicious continental cuisine that is simple, timeless, and well-executed. Pepper steak is highly recommended.

Piret's. 902 W. Washington St., Hillcrest (297–2993). This eaterie mixes elements of boulangerie, charcuterie and patisserie to come up with a charming place to dine. Goat cheese quiche, cabbage tart, and elaborate salads adorn the menu. The pastries are fancy and irresistible.

Reuben E. Lee. 880 E. Harbor Island Dr. (291–1880). Seafood served aboard an old Mississippi sternwheeler docked in San Diego Bay.

Sheppard's. In the Sheraton Harbor Island East Hotel, 1380 Harbor Island Dr. (619–692–2255). Beautiful dining, gracious service, nouvelle cuisine and American regional fare. Jackets required for men.

Moderate

Antony's Fish Grotto. A few locations: 1360 N. Harbor Dr. (232–5103); 9530 Murray Dr., La Mesa (463–0368); 215 Bay Blvd., Chula Vista (425–4200). Owned by the Star of the Sea people but about half the price. A San Diego institution. Excellent family dining, but there are often long lines.

Bali Hai. 2230 Shelter Island Dr. (222–1181). The emphasis is on Cantonese specialties, all served in a pleasant environment overlooking the bay. Got Let Chicken and Chicken of the Gods are favorites; also char-broiled steak and lobster. Long and exotic drink list provides a pleasant complement to dining. There's also a Polynesian floor show. Located close to many hotels.

Cafe Pacifica. 2414 San Diego Ave., Old Town (619–291–6666). Fresh fish, prepared simply, in a stylish restaurant with a patio. L, Mon.–Fri.; D, daily. AE, MC, V.

Crown Room, Hotel del Coronado. 1500 Orange Ave., Coronado (619–435–6611). Magnificent main dining room of the Victorian-era hotel. Continental cuisine, inexpensive early dinner. L, D, daily; brunch Sun. All major credit cards.

Harbor House. Seaport Village, Pacific Hwy. at Harbor Dr. (619–232–1141). Fresh fish is the specialty of this beautiful restaurant. Simply prepared dishes are recommended. L, D, daily; brunch Sun. All major credit cards.

Papagayo. Seaport Village, Pacific Hwy. at Harbor Dr. (619–232–7581). Mexican-style seafood in an elegant dining room, harbor view. L, D, daily; brunch Sun. All major credit cards.

El Torito. 1590 Harbor Island Dr. (299–3464). This is the place in town to see and be seen. Waiters, believe it or not, ride tricycles or unicycles. A mariachi band plays aluminum bowls filled with bottle caps. Bells ring, horns toot, feet stamp. This is the Barnum and Bailey of the burrito world. The menu's mostly Mexican tamed for American tastebuds but fresh and very tasty.

Mandarin House. 6765 La Jolla Blvd. (454–2555). La Jolla's "in" Oriental experience.

Old Town Mexican Cafe. 2489 San Diego Ave., Old Town (619–297–4330). Carnitas (roast meat) is the specialty; empanadas and burritos are also very good. The bar can be noisy and crowded. L, D, daily until 11 P.M. All major credit cards.

Inexpensive

Kansas City Barbecue. 610 W. Market St. (619–231–9680). Ribs and chicken served in a typical cafe that served as one of the locations for the film *Top Gun.*

TOURIST INFORMATION. The *San Diego Convention and Visitors Bureau* publishes a general brochure on San Diego available in English, Japanese, Spanish, French, and German along with maps and pamphlets on various vacations, including a monthly publication *What's Doing in San Diego,* listing special activities and information on all major tourist attractions. Write or call the bureau for free information at 1200 Third Ave., Suite 824, San Diego, CA 92101 (232–3101); for a 24-hour information recording, call 239–9696; for a 24-hour arts and entertainment hotline, call 234–ARTS.

The *Mission Bay Visitors Information Center,* 2688 East Mission Bay Drive, San Diego, CA 92109 (276–8200,) located in Mission Bay off Interstate 5 at the Clairemont Drive exit, is open from 9:00 A.M. until dark and offers a full range of tourist services including hotel reservations, information and maps for all tourist attractions, bus schedules, and information on Mexico.

The *Plaza Information Booth,* located downtown in the Community Concourse, 202 C Street, dispenses general information and bus schedules daily 9 A.M.–6 P.M.

The *Mission Bay Harbor Patrol* has a telephone recording of current beach and weather conditions for surfers, sailors, snorkelers, and swimmers. Call 224–1862.

The *Mexican Consulate,* 1333 Front St., San Diego, CA 92101 (231–8414), has information on traveling into Mexico.

San Diego magazine, the San Diego *Union, Evening Tribune,* San Diego edition of the Los Angeles *Times,* and the free weekly *Reader* all carry listings of current events. Many hotels and motels supply free tourist publications, and some carry Tele-Vu, a televised overview of San Diego attractions.

HINTS TO HANDICAPPED TRAVELERS. The *Community Service Center for the Disabled,* 2864 University Ave., San Diego, CA 92103 (293–3500), has information on hotels, motels, and attractions with access for the handicapped. San Diego does not have any wheelchair-accessible beaches, but most have cement walkways bordering the beach. Handicapped parking spaces are available at all attractions and are closely policed by parking patrols.

TOURS AND SPECIAL-INTEREST SIGHTSEEING. **Walking.** *Walkabout International* (223–9255) offers free imaginative walks through San Diego's neighborhoods at all hours of the day and night, led by volunteers with ample information on the area. *Elegant Ambles Travel Service* (222–2224) provides travel and walking tours of the world. The *Gaslamp Quarter Association* (233–[illegible]) has tours of downtown's renovated Gaslamp Quarter, and the *Natural History Museum* (232–3821) has hikes through nearby canyons.

Boating. A variety of boats leave the downtown Embarcadero for narrated tours of the harbor, including the *Harbor Excursions* (233–6872) and the *Invader* sailing schooner and *Showboat* paddlewheeler (298–8066), with fees ranging around $7 for an hour. The winter migration of the California gray whales is particularly popular from December through February; the tour boats above offer special **whale watching trips,** as do *H&M Landing* (222–1144) and *Islandia Sportfishing* (222–1164). The *Bahia Belle* paddlewheeler offers moonlight cruises through Mission Bay during the summer months (488–0551).

Bus. *Gray Line Sightseeing Tours* (231–9922) has half-day tours throughout the city for about $15 and longer tours to Tijuana and Disneyland. *Mexicoach* (232–5049) offers tours to Tijuana and Baja. *San Diego Mini Tours* (234–9044) charges $10 to $30 for trips to local attractions. The *Molly Trolley*'s (233–9177) open-air cars travel along the waterfront from Shelter Island to Seaport Village with stops at Sea World and Hotel Circle. Fare is $4.

PARKS AND GARDENS. There is no shortage of parkland in San Diego, starting with **Cabrillo National Monument,** the most frequently visited monument in the country. Located on a high cliff at the tip of Point Loma, this is a prime whale watching spot and offers a remarkable view of the San Diego Harbor and the Coronado Islands. The Visitor's Center offers a museum, theater, gift shop, and narrated tours of the monument, including the old Point Loma Lighthouse, built in 1854. A small paved road right before the entrance leads down to marine research labs with dolphins and seals swimming in enormous tanks. Cabrillo Monument is open daily year-round, and there is no admission fee. Call 557–5450 for information.

Closer to sea level there's the 4,600-acre **Mission Bay Park,** a waterfront wonderland that is overrun by bicyclists, roller skaters, joggers, picnickers, kite flyers, Frisbee throwers, and all sorts of outdoor enthusiasts. Sections of the bay are partitioned for swimming and wading, waterskiing, and sailing. Within the park there are miniature and professional golf courses, tennis courts, resort hotels, a campground, boat rentals, sport fishing charters, a jogger's paracourse, restaurants, all sorts of seasonal events, and plenty of free parking.

Balboa Park's 1,400 acres were first designated as a city park in 1835, but it took the Panama-California Exposition of 1915 and the California Pacific International Exposition of 1935 to transform the park into the city's cultural and recreational center. Many of the museums and theaters listed elsewhere are located in the park, along with the world's largest outdoor pipe organ at the Spreckels Organ Pavilion, where free Sunday afternoon concerts are held during the summer. Musicians, mimes, jugglers, and other performers appear on most of the park's grassy lawns; restaurants and outdoor vendors provide nourishment to keep you going. One can easily spend an inexpensive day or two roaming the park; there's plenty of space for impromptu picnicking and enough free sights to please everyone.

BEACHES. With 70 miles of coastline, San Diego offers almost every ocean pleasure possible, from skin diving to midnight campfires. Ocean temperatures average around 62 degrees, with lows in the fifties during winter months and highs in the seventies usually by the middle of July. Some of the most popular beaches have lifeguards year-round; many have rest rooms, showers, and changing rooms. Camping, pets, and glass containers and dishes are prohibited on all beaches, and ticket writers bearing coolers concealing their official papers wander the sand in the summer. Police officers patrol the boardwalks on bicycles and the beaches in jeeps. Picnicking is allowed on all beaches, but fires are prohibited except in established fire pits, which dot the coastline. On almost any beach you'll find surfing (body, board, and wind), swimming, and the most popular pastime of all, sunbathing. You'll also find crowds and a scarcity of parking spaces during the summer.

Different types tend to gather at different beaches, though the trends vary from year to year. *Imperial Beach, Coronado, Ocean Beach, Mission Beach,* and *Pacific Beach* all have long stretches of sand for volleyball games, sunbathing, and people watching; plenty of waves for surfers and swimmers; and crowds as varied as the general population. Small neighborhood beaches favored by locals curve into the coastline along *Sunset Cliffs* and the rocky strip between *Pacific Beach* and La Jolla. *La Jolla Cove*'s underwater preserve is the place for snorkeling, diving, and wave-free swimming; its narrow cliffside beaches fill up quickly on sunny summer weekends.

North of the cove, *La Jolla Shores* has a long stretch of uninterrupted beach sectioned off for swimmers, body surfers, boogie boarders, and surfers; its northern end leads past spectacular oceanfront homes to the Torrey Pines Glider Port atop the rising cliffside. The beach gets very narrow here and is passable only during the lowest of tides, and the cliffs are highly unstable. The area just under the glider port was once a popular "swimwear optional" beach called *Black's Beach,* but the cliffside paths down to it have eroded with time, making it dangerous to reach; once there, you may be cited if not dressed. Black's can be reached more safely by walking (almost an hour) south from *Torrey Pines State Beach,* another good sunning, swimming, and surfing beach beneath the cliffs of vegetation of the state reserve. North County's beaches are as popular as the rest, but it is possible to roam far enough away from the crowds to find your own cliffside niche.

San Diego's waves are said to rival those of Hawaii, and they draw scores of surfers who prefer *Windansea* in La Jolla, *La Jolla Shores,* and *Pacific, Mission,* and *Ocean* beaches.

ZOOS. The 100-acre **San Diego Zoo,** in Balboa Park (234–3153), is a botanist's delight, with lush tropical vegetation that is an unusual and fascinating as the 5,000 animals that inhabit the park. The quickest way to tour the zoo is on a double-decker guided tour bus, but it is much more rewarding to wander the winding paths over bridges, past waterfalls, and through the junglelike terrain filled with all sorts of exotic species. The Children's Zoo has a nursery where baby chimps play with educational toys and goats and sheep roam freely, helping themselves to any edibles you may be carrying. The zoo is open daily 9 A.M.–dusk. Adults, $6.50; children, $2.50; military in uniform free.

The Zoo's **San Diego Wild Animal Park** (619–234–6541) is a 1,800-acre animal preserve designed to allow endangered and nearly extinct breeds of animals to roam and reproduce. The park's highlight is the electric monorail safari through exhibits that recreate the terrain of north, south, and East Africa and the Asian plains and swamps, where giraffes, gazelles, antelope, and other animals gallop, graze, and mingle as they would in the wild. The ride is particularly impressive during the early evening feeding times. Within the park there are impressive, informative animal shows, a fascinating children's zoo, and a hiking trail through an east African setting. On summer evenings, bluegrass, jazz, and rock concerts are held in the park's outdoor amphitheater. The Wild Animal Park is about 30 miles northeast of downtown but well worth the drive if you prefer seeing animals allowed to roam free. The park is open from 9 A.M. until dusk during the winter and until 11 P.M. in the summer. Adults, $12.95, children, $6.50.

The **Scripps Institute of Oceanography Aquarium** is filled with fish tanks displaying an incredible array of freshwater and saltwater inhabitants. An outdoor man-made tidal pool displays many of the sea creatures found off San Diego's coastline, including sea anemones, starfish, octopus, and garabaldi. The aquarium is located at 8602 La Jolla Shores Dr.; a donation is requested for admission. Call 452–4085 for information.

At the south end of Mission Bay lies **Sea World,** Sea World Dr., off I–5, a 100-acre marine park with exhibits, shows, petting pools, and Cap'n Kid's World, a wonderful self-contained playground. The park's new Penguin Encounter contains hundreds of penguins in a simulated Arctic environment, and Shamu the whale puts on a great show. The PSA Sky Tower rises 320 feet into the air for a full-circle view of San Diego, Sea World, and the Atlantis restaurant across Mission Bay. During December, Sea World's Snow World gives southern California kids a chance to slide down snowy hills, build snowmen, and throw snowballs at adults. Allow at least half a day to tour the park, longer if you're interested in browsing through the many good gift shops. The park is open daily year-round from 9:00 A.M. until dusk. Full admission to Sea World including rides is $17.95 for adults and $11.95 for children ages 3 to 11. Discounts are available for seniors and active military personnel. Call 222–6363 for information.

PARTICIPANT SPORTS. Because of San Diego's consistently excellent weather, the city is alive with sporting enthusiasts and sporting opportunities. With more than 70 distinctive courses in the country, it's little wonder **golf** is popular. Green fees range from $11 to $14 at the frequently used municipal courses. A few courses are: *Balboa Park Municipal* 18-hole course, Golf Course Drive (232–2470); *Balboa Park Municipal* 18-hole course, Golf Course Drive (232–2470); *43Coronado Golf Course,* 2000 Visalia Row (435–3121); *Mission Bay Golf Course,* 2702 N. Mission Bay Dr. (273–1221); and *Torrey Pines Municipal Golf Course,* 11480 N. Torrey Pines Rd. (453–0380).

Jogging. The pathways along the beaches and through all of the parks as well as the beaches themselves are great for jogging. *Fiesta Island* in Mission Bay is also a runners' and bike riders' favorite.

Tennis. There are numerous public tennis courts maintained by the city of San Diego that are available free or for a minimal fee. Courts at local colleges or high schools are usually open to the public when classes are not in session. Here are just a few: *Mission Bay Youth Field,* 2639 Grand Ave. (273–9177); *La Jolla Recreation Center,* 615 Prospect St. (454–2071) (free); and *Morley Field-Love Tennis Center,* in Balboa Park (298–0920).

Bicycling. The parks and beach areas all have paths that are wonderful for bicycle riding. There are rentals available along the beach areas.

Sailing, wind surfing, and rowboating. Mission Bay is the most popular boating place, but both Shelter and Harbor islands are crowded with marinas. Instruction and rentals are available. Prices vary, but you should be able to find windsurfers for around $10 and Hobie Cats for $16 per hour. *California Pacific Catamaran Rental and Inc.,* 2211 Pacific Beach Dr., Pacific Beach (270–3211). *Harbor Sailboats,* 2040 Harbor Island Dr. (291–9568). *Mission Bay Sports Center,* 1010 Santa Clara Pl., Mission Beach (488–1004).

Scuba diving and snorkeling. *La Jolla Shores, La Jolla Cove,* and *Scripps Pier* are good spots for both scuba and snorkeling. These areas are all within the *La Jolla Shores Ecological Reserve* and are closed to hunting and fishing. For further information about the reserve and other diving areas, call local dive shops: *The Diving Locker,* 1020 Grand Ave., Pacific Beach (272–1120); *New England Divers,* 3860 Rosecrans St. (298–0531); and *San Diego Divers Supply,* 7522 La Jolla Blvd. (459–2691).

Fishing. San Diego is a haven for sport fishers. Boats set off for all types of fishing trips. In the summer, the catch includes marlin, bonito, barracuda, and tuna; in the winter, ling cod, black fish, and rock cod. Naturally, fishermen must have the proper license, which is sold at bait shops, boat landings, the Department of Fish and Game Offices, and many sporting goods stores. Half-day and full-day trips are offered by *Seaforth Sportfishing,* 1717 Quivira Rd. (224–3383); *H&M Landing,* 2803 Emerson St. (222–1144); and *Islandia Sportfishing,* 1551 West Mission Bay Dr. (222–1164).

Horseback riding. San Diego, especially the hilly outlying areas, has many stables and lovely riding areas. For information and rates, call one of these listed numbers or check the phone book for others: *Hilltop Stables,* 2671 Monument Rd., San Diego (428–5441); and *Rancho San Diego Stables,* 11990 Campo Rd., Spring Valley (463–2836).

Raquetball. Racquetball has always been a favorite in San Diego, and there is a choice of court space around town. *San Diego State University* has courts that are available for less than those at most other clubs; for court times and reservations, call 265–6492. A partial listing of San Diego's public courts follows: *Courtsports of San Diego,* 3443 India St. (294–9970); *Jack LaLanne Sports Center,* 3666 Midway Dr. (223–5581); *YMCA of San Diego,* Copely Family Branch, 3901 Landis (283–2251); and La Jolla Family Branch, 8355 Cliffridge Ave. (453–2144).

Swimming. There are all of the fabulous beaches for swimming with water temperatures up to 73 degrees in the summer, but there are also a number of pools run by the city of San Diego's Park and Recreation Department: Clairmont, 3600 Clairmont Dr. (273–9540).

SPECTATOR SPORTS. Football. The *San Diego Chargers* evoke a blue-and-gold fever that pervades the town during football season, and tickets are hard to get. Some 11 home games (regular and preseason) are played at Jack Murphy Stadium, which will hold the *1988 Super Bowl.* Tickets cost $8 to $19; information is available by calling 280–2111. If you do get tickets, plan to tailgate at the parking lot before the game like the locals do—it saves some of the aggravation of sitting in a line of cars as the game begins and gives you the chance to see how Charger fans party.

Baseball. The National League *Padres* rallied forth to win the 1984 Western Division championship, and now tickets are not as easy to come by as they once were. The Padres play at Jack Murphy Stadium from April through September; tickets cost $4 to $6.50, and information is available by calling 283–4494.

Horse racing. The *Del Mar Thoroughbred Club* brings legal betting to the Del Mar Fairgrounds for the 43-day season beginning in late July. Nine races are run daily except Tuesday, with gates opening at noon. Opening day at Del Mar is always a San Diego summer highlight, with celebrity fans mingling with the local elite in a high society show. Admission is $2.50 to $5; call 755–1141 for information.

Golf. The *Isuzu Andy Williams San Diego Open* puts golf in the forefront the last weekend in January at the Torrey Pines Golf Course, call 453–8148 for information. In April, the *MONY Tournament of Champions* brings together tour champions at the La Costa Hotel and Spa; call 438–9111 for information.

HISTORICAL SITES. The **San Diego Historical Society** operates the **Serra Museum** in Presidio Park, housing a collection of maps, documents, and records from San Diego's early days. The museum is open daily; for information, contact the historical society at 297–3258.

The Gaslamp Quarter, along Fourth and Fifth avenues downtown, contains many of San Diego's historic buildings; the Gaslamp Quarter Association offers guided tours of the area and historical information. Call 233–5227.

Old Town State Historic Park contains much of San Diego's original settlement, with historical buildings and displays, new shops, and an abundance of Mexican restaurants lining San Diego Ave. to the Bazaar Del Mundo, a popular dining and shopping square. **Heritage Park,** a collection of historic Victorian buildings, and other shopping complexes line the side streets, and there are plenty of grassy park areas for picnics and people watching.

MISSIONS. San Diego must be the mission capital of the nation, starting with the **Mission San Diego de Alcala,** established by Padre Junipero Serra in 1769. The mission is located at 10818 San Diego Mission Road, near Mission Valley, and is open 9 A.M.–5 P.M. daily; services are held every Sunday in the original mission chapel. The Father Luis Jayme Museum features relics of early mission days and is the only permanent ecclesiastical art museum in southern California. Call 281–8449 for information.

Mission San Luis Rey, 4050 Mission Ave., San Luis Rey, is the largest of the 21 Franciscan California missions and was once the home of 3,000 Indians. On the 50-cent self-guided tour you can explore the Spanish, Mexican, and Moorish architecture and the cloister garden, Indian cemetery, archaeological excavations, and a large collection of Spanish vestments. The mission is located about 40 miles from downtown, east of Oceanside. Call 757–3250 for information.

The Assistencia de San Antonio de Pala (Pala Mission) is located in the back country of North County and is still used as a school and church by the Indians. Call 742–3317 for information. Mission Santa Ysabel, an original assistencia to San Diego de Alcala, is located 50 miles outside the city and is best reached during a drive through the mountains. Call 765–0810 for information.

MUSEUMS. Most of San Diego's museums are gathered along Balboa Park's El Prado. All have free admission on the first Tuesday of each month and discounts for seniors, students, and military personnel. The gift shops can be visited without paying the admission fee, and they carry an unusual collection of gift items. Starting at the Laurel Street Bridge end of El Prado, the museums are the following:

The Hall of Champions and Hall of Fame honors the country's great athletes and is popular with sports fans. Open daily 10:00 A.M.–4:30 P.M. except major holidays; admission free.

The Museum of Man (239–2001) is housed under the California Tower and includes exhibits of the anthropology and archaeology of man in the western Americas and artifacts from Indian and Mexican cultures. The "Wonder of Life" exhibition housed across the street is a multi media presentation of human reproduction and birth. Adults, $2, with discounts for students, seniors, and military personnel; children under 16, 25 cents. Open 10 A.M.–4:30 P.M. except on major holidays.

The Museum of Natural History (232–3821) contains permanent collections on the Southwest, Baja, and the desert and an excellent scientific library. The museum holds nature walks throughout the country, whale watching trips, weekly films, children's classes, and minerology displays. Open 9:30 A.M.–5 P.M. daily except major holidays. Adults, $3; children 6–18, $1.

Museum of Photographic Arts (239–5262) presents various photography exhibits. Admission is $2, and the museum is open Tues.–Sun. 10 A.M.–5 P.M.

The Reuben H. Fleet Space Theater and Science Center (238–1168) has the largest projection dome in the country, where films on space and nature are shown throughout the day. The Science Center contains hands-on exhibits that explain scientific principles. Admission to the theater and science center is $4 for adults and $2.50 for juniors (5 to 15) and seniors. Open daily 9:45 A.M.–9:30 P.M.

The San Diego Aerospace Museum (234–8291) is south of El Prado in the renovated Ford building, an impressive circular structure with neon outlining. The museum houses old military planes, Lindbergh's *Spirit of St. Louis,* and an Aerospace Hall of Fame. Open daily 10:00 A.M.–4:30 P.M. Adults, $3.50; children under 17, $1.

San Diego Art Institute (234–5946) sponsors monthly shows covering nearly every medium. Open Tues.–Sun. 10:00 A.M.–4:30 P.M.; admission free.

The San Diego Museum of Art (232–7931) features a permanent collection of Old Master paintings and American and Asian arts and popular traveling shows including the Muppet exhibit and the Golden Treasures of Peru. Adjacent to the museum is the outdoor Sculpture Garden and Cafe, serving French specialties. Open 10 A.M.–5:00 P.M. Tues.–Sun.

The Timken Art Gallery (239–5548) houses a collection of American and European art including paintings by Rembrandt and Cezanne. Open 10:00 A.M.–4:30 P.M. Tues.–Sat.; admission free.

MUSIC. The **San Diego Symphony** (699–4200), under the direction of maestro David Atherton, appears throughout the city with major productions at the Civic Center (236–6510), located at Third and C streets downtown. The Symphony's popular **summer pops series** is held at Hospitality Point in Mission Bay.

The **San Diego Opera** (544–7827) season runs from mid-October until May, with the annual June Verdi Festival a particularly popular event. Most performances are at the Civic Center. The **San Diego Civic Light Opera Association** (231–1333) presents a series of outdoor musicals in the outdoor Starlight Bowl in Balboa Park during the summer.

STAGE. The most celebrated theater in San Diego is the **Old Globe Theater** in Balboa Park, a replica of the Shakespearean Theater at Stratford-on-Avon. The Old Globe is part of three interconnected stages known as the Simon Edison Centre for the Performing Arts. The popular summer Shakespearean festival takes place on the outdoor Festival Stage, and the Old Globe and Cassius Carter stages host major productions throughout the year. Call 239–2255 for ticket information.

The **San Diego Repertory Theatre** (235–8025), a local production company, performs year-round in their new theater in Horton Plaza, downtown. The **Marquis Theaters** (295–5654) are three stages that hold contemporary, experimental, and original plays at 3717 India St., near downtown. The **Gaslamp Quarter Theatre** (234–9583) holds contemporary plays in an intimate 90-seat historical site at 547 Fourth Ave., downtown. The **Coronado Playhouse** (435–4856), located near the historic Hotel Del Coronado, presents about five plays.

EXPLORING SOUTHERN CALIFORNIA

Southern California is divided up by north-and-south mountain ranges. So, except for jaunts over the mountain passes, the handiest way to explore the area is by slices peeled off inland, away from the seacoast. Along the ocean, though, visitors can experience up close the magic of the American Riviera.

The South Coast

Heading south from Los Angeles along the ocean you first encounter *Santa Catalina Island,* 22 miles offshore and reached by boat or amphibian airlines from Long Beach and San Pedro. Crossing time is about two hours. Motor cruisers and frequent flight schedules provide transportation to the island. Avalon is the main settlement and sportfishing capital: a quiet crescent bay, the village climbing up the slopes inland.

The flying fish (May to October) are, according to authorities, the world's largest. Some grow 18 inches long and are colored blue-green with iridescent "wing" fins. When frightened by a hungry swordfish or a ship, they spurt out of the water and slide through the air for as far as 75 yards. A nighttime launch trip with a powerful searchlight brings them aloft by the silvery thousands. You can buy a frozen flying fish

Southern California Beaches
Avila Beach
San Luis Obispo
Pismo Beach
Point Sal Beach
Lompoc
Gaviota Beach
Refugio Beach
El Capitan Beach
Goleta Beach
Santa Barbara
San Miguel
Santa Rosa
Carpinteria Beach
Emma K. Wood Beach
Ventura
Santa Cruz
San Buenaventura Beach
McGrath Beach
Oxnard
Point Mugu Beach
Leo Carillo Beach
Pt. Dume Beach
Malibu Beach
Santa Monica
Hollywood
Los Angeles
San Nicolas
PACIFIC OCEAN
Long Beach
Santa Catalina
Huntington Beach
San Clemente
Doheny Beach
San Clemente Beach
San Onofre Beach
Solana Beach
San Diego
Silver Strand Beach
Border Field Beach
N
W
E
S

from the fish market at the end of the recreation pier. They are prized as swordfish bait.

Glass-bottom boats cruise over the California State Marine Preserve, covering a scenic underwater stretch where all sea life is protected. Fish seem to know they are safe, and congregate here by the hundreds. Most spectacular are the foot-long saltwater goldfish, the sparkling electric perch, and swarms of other fish in brilliant blue and green. A big fellow may ease up and lazily eye the windows from a few feet away. Kelp seaweed 70 feet long waves in the water currents like treetops of a forest in a breeze.

From the Seal Rocks, hundreds of seals bark and splash into the water as the cruise launch approaches; some graying old-timers stay their ground for a close view. Some bus trips do the high arc of the Avalon Terrace hills; others climb into the mountainous interior (the island is a drowned mountain) to see the cattle herd, the buffalo left over from a movie set, wild boar, wild goats, and a ranch of superbly trained Arabian horses. The famed Bird Farm has been dismantled, but most of its former 650 exotic residents may be visited at their new L.A. Zoo home.

Back on the mainland and traveling south along the coast, the oil wells walk in a straight line beside the highway at *Huntington Beach.* The holes don't go straight down, but slant out to drain submarine oil pools far out under the ocean waves. Huntington Beach is the site of the Surfboard Championships, which take place in September.

Newport Beach and Harbor are next. Most people live on seven islands dotting the bay. Harbor cruises offer 45-minute Bay views of waterfront homes of celebrities and the yacht basins.

Newport's boat population is more than 8,000, not counting the little ones. There are seven yacht clubs. Weather permitting, and it usually is, there is a regatta virtually every weekend of the year. The Flight of the Snowbirds Regatta, held in July, is a race of about 150 little Snowbird-class catboats, mostly skippered by youngsters.

The annual Character Boat Parade is held in late summer. Best description of a "character boat" is Edgar Bergen's: "a Monterey double-ender purple cabin with ivy twining up the antenna, puffing old steam engine, and shrieking steam whistle." Moored here and there are some 50 of them, ranging from a steam-powered replica of a river sidewheeler to a launch shaped like a sea horse.

About a mile from the Balboa Pier is *Balboa Island.* This picturesque man-made island, shaped like a parallelogram, is reached by means of a 3–car ferry. The streets are kept immaculately by some 5,000 residents who make their home on thoroughfares named for gemstones: Amethyst, Onyx, Diamond, Ruby. Restaurants are as quaint as the town. Only one, the Village Inn, serves liquor.

Laguna Beach, with its flowery studio-clustered seacliffs and French seaport flavor, has been compared to the coast of Normandy. The late Richard Haliburton had his home here, a concrete lookout high up on the point surveying the coast each way for miles. Laguna Beach is an informal place. Instead of wasting land on sidewalks, the Lagunatiks (as some locals like to call themselves) often plant more flowers, which grow lush in the sea air. They have seen nothing unusual in the fact that a world-famous sculptor operated a hot dog stand on the boardwalk in the summer. After all, this has been a favorite haunt for artists since 1900.

The artists operate their own community art gallery, which is worth a visit. In the summer they hold the Festival of Arts, which grew from a little sidewalk showing of their paintings during the depression of the '30s. Out of doors, artists display their paintings, sculpture, ceramics and handicrafts.

Drive on past *Dana Point,* overlooking the blue-green cove where Richard Henry Dana, Jr., in his book *Two Years Before the Mast* told of loading stiff cattle hides tossed over the cliff by the Spanish California rancheros and the Capistrano Mission padres. The new Mariner's Village complex offers restaurants, shops and a marina for sport fishing boats.

The Swallows of Capistrano

A few miles beyond is the *Mission San Juan Capistrano,* founded by the Spanish Franciscan padres in 1775. It gained fame for the legend that its flock of swallows always flew off on the mission patron saint's day, October 23, and returned "miraculously" on St. Joseph's Day, March 19. Local Spanish California natives believed in the miracle but an inquiring young priest studied swallows and found that they *all* come and go at fairly regular dates. The flower gardens of the moldering old ruin, toppled in an early earthquake, bloom most of the year. Inside the mission, a new visitors' center was opened in 1982 to inform those who come to see this historic park.

On down the coast past the awesome San Onofre nuclear plant is the town of *San Clemente,* which once was restricted to Spanish-style red-tiled roofs and white walls; many of which still dot the town. Ex-President Nixon's former home, La Casa Pacifica, is rather inaccessible but visitors may inspect Nixon memorabilia at the Nixon Museum. The four-mile stretch of broad sand along the beach has idyllic conditions for sunbathing and picnics. The fishing pier is a favorite for anglers of perch and halibut the year round. Marines, their combat equipment, and barracks line the next 20 miles—this is *Camp Pendleton,* biggest of all Marine Corps bases and a troop takeoff point for the Pacific in World War II and during the Korean and Vietnam wars. Marines storm ashore from landing fleets seen offshore, struggle over the camp's three mountain ranges and through five lakes and over 250 miles of training roads.

The waves rolling in at *Oceanside* are just right for surfing; some 300 members of the local surfing club celebrate Christmas Day by lining up on the beach for a forenoon dip in the Pacific. Four miles inland is *Mission San Luis Rey* (1798). Waxy green groves covering the nearby inland valleys grow most of the California avocado crop.

In a scenic setting beside the sea is the Spanish-styled horse racing track at *Del Mar,* founded by Bing Crosby and Pat O'Brien. Outside of thoroughbred racing season, trotting and pacing horses can be seen training here. The gnarled trees making a forest of nearby Torrey Pines State Park grow only here and on an offshore island. Gliders soar over Torrey Pines bluff during the Annual Torrey Pines Soaring Contest in late March and every weekend, weather permitting. The last Sunday in April, the Jumping Frog Jamboree is held at the county fairgrounds. The Southern California Exposition (formerly San Diego County Fair) is a huge celebration held in June and July with a national horse show and carnival.

La Jolla is next; no one seems to know for certain how the resort and art colony got its name. It may come from the Spanish "La Joya," meaning "The Jewel," because of its gemlike setting on a rocky peninsula; or from the Indian *Hut La Hoya,* meaning "Place of the Caves." Seven caves have been carved out of the soft cliffs by the ocean waves over the centuries. One may be explored via an inland tunneled stairway, and the other six must be entered from the ocean. Windansea is one of the best beaches anywhere on California's coastline.

Alligator Head, which looks like just that, protects the blue-green La Jolla Cove, where every September some 150 swimmers start and end the Rough Water Swim. The race has been held since 1916. Buster Crabbe and channel swimmer Florence Chadwick have been winners.

For generations, La Jolla has been a tennis center. The venerable La Jolla Tennis Tournament, also held since 1916, includes some 40 events for all ages—youngsters to grandparents. The La Jolla Beach and Tennis Club has ten championship tennis courts. In the oceanside Marine Room restaurant and Spindrift lounge, picture windows of quarter-inch tempered plate glass are slapped by Pacific waves, which are illuminated at night. At the entrance a tank of live sea horses greets patrons.

The La Jolla Museum of Contemporary Art often has 30 exhibits during a year. It focuses these changing exhibits on outstanding contemporary works.

The aquarium museum at Scripps Institution of Oceanography, 8602 La Jolla Shores Dr., features more than 50 oceanographic exhibits, including an onshore tide pool and 22 marine-life tanks. Visitors are welcome. Picnic areas and beaches are nearby.

Mission Bay Park's 4,600-acre city-owned aquatic wonderland is a sunny playground between La Jolla and San Diego. The bay area, the marine parks, the grassy, tree-lined coves, and the resort hotels offer boating, swimming, fishing, water-skiing, day or night golfing, camping and trailer sites.

Sea World is one of the highlights at Mission Bay. Children are captivated by this oceanarium that features Shamu the killer whale and trained dolphins who star at the Theater of the Sea. Also on exhibit are walrus and an impressive colony of penguins. The panorama of Mission Bay Park can be enjoyed by taking a skyride, a hydrofoil ride or catching the 360-degree view from the skytower.

Southern Backcountry

The southern "backcountry," as it is called, is Indian country. Interstate 8, heading inland from San Diego and at times almost touching the Mexican border, received a high rating among veteran travel editors in a poll as one of the most scenic highways they had seen. It rambles through rugged mountains and drops through the In-Ko-Pah Gorge, seemingly tiled with a mosaic of flat rocks, in the Jacumba Mountains, so rugged that the nearby railroad has to snake through 11 tunnels to make 12 miles.

Julian, farther north, celebrated its centennial in 1970. It was a Gold Rush town until its mines played out. False-fronted buildings from the late 1800s are still there and relics of Gold Rush days are on view at the town museum. You can still stay in the old 14-room Julian Hotel.

At *Santa Ysabel,* seven miles northwest, the general store's sign reads: "Established 1879—I think." Priests of Santa Ysabel chapel, with its windmills beside the floor of the old mission ruins dating back to 1818, serve 7 Indian tribes on ten reservations.

Pala is an Indian village on a reservation where the tribal council still makes the laws. About 300 Indians of 7 tribes live in the not very prosperous-looking dwellings (most have TV antennas, however), although the younger tribesmen are leaving for better prospects elsewhere. The little Mission San Antonio de Pala, which is the only mission still at its original assignment of serving the Indians, has an unusual detached bell tower. The annual Corpus Christi fiesta is held at Pala in June.

Indians once warred over the warm sulphur springs that still pour out 300,000 gallons a day at the *Warner Springs* Guest Ranch, 55,000 acres spreading over the entire valley with picturesque abodes dating back to 1830. Today the springs fill the swimming pools and water the golf course.

From Warner Springs it's a 30-mile climb to one of the world's biggest telescopes, on *Palomar Mountain.* The giant silver dome bursts into view—high as a 12-story building. Viewed from the glassed-in balcony inside, the massive telescope itself is eight stories high and weighs 500 tons. It is so delicately mounted that a slight push can move it. How far does the 200-inch Hale Telescope reach? It would take an astronaut more than a billion years to get there—if he could travel at the speed of light (186,000 miles per second)! A loudspeaker tells the story of the telescope and drawings explain its working.

East and Southeast of Palomar Mountain is Anza-Borrego Desert State Park. The winter weather here is great. You can camp (at a developed campground with running water and other amenities, or at primitive camp sites in one of the steep sided canyons surrounding the central valley) or stay in the slowly developing resort town of Borrego Springs, where there are several golf courses and restaurants.

Hike a short distance up a canyon to see a natural stand of native palms. They look nothing like the skinny, out-of-place palms you see in the center of so many lawns throughout the state. The rangers lead interesting geological tours culminating at an overlook above the badlands. The park is not highly developed.

The Imperial Valley

The *Imperial Valley,* with *El Centro* as its largest city, claims the largest population on earth living below sea level. Easily reached from San Diego, the land climbs back to minus one foot and then plus one foot at the twin towns at the Mexican border that have related names, Calexico and Mexicali. They share problems and fiestas, they elect both a valley girl and a Mexican señorita as beauty queens, all parades cross the border (as you may do), and wind through both towns.

Salton Sea sparkles in Imperial Valley, where crops are harvested in midwinter. Farmers from other states are astounded at seeing a lush green section of alfalfa in December and learning that here they get seven cuttings of hay a year. Winter farms will be blue with flax flowers, red with mass harvests of tomatoes and carrots, white with cotton. Melons go east by the trainload. Convenient highways encircle Salton Sea, Calif. 86 on the west, and Calif. 111 on the east. *Brawley,* which has the largest cattle-feed lot in the world, is the site of the Imperial Valley Rodeo and Cattle Call in November.

Irrigation canals, frequently crossed when driving, extend for more miles than the highways. It seldom rains in the valley; a heavy rain is so rare, in fact, that when one does come, the schools may declare a "mud holiday" because the farm roads are mired. So, as the farmers put it, "we get our rain by telephone," from the giant man made All-American Canal. This great ditch, 200 feet wide, stretches 80 miles to the Colorado River, and by an intricate system of subcanals, it waters every farm in the valley.

The canal and freeway cut through the *Algodones Sand Hills,* their yellow blur on the horizon becoming a range of enormous dunes, wind-blown and tawny as a lion's hide. They hump high as eight-story buildings, dune-buggy riders roll over them, and they are a treat for youngsters to climb and slide down.

Palm Springs

The last geographic section of Southern California inland from the ocean is the land of the deserts, southernmost of which is the warm, low-level *Colorado Desert,* with its Sunshine Strip of resorts like *Palm Springs, Palm Desert, Indian Wells,* and *La Quinta.* From this vacation oasis, the desert stretches east to the Colorado River and south to the Mexican border.

The Colorado Desert is reached from the Los Angeles or Santa Ana areas by a nonstop freeway. It passes through the naval-orange country and below the flat-topped wall of the *San Bernardino Mountain* range, where there is a chain of resort lakes and winter snow slopes along the mile-high Rim o' the World Highway. This mountain playground is reached by two excellent mountain highways.

San Gorgonio Pass, dividing the desert from the orange country, is a great trough providing an easy grade route for highway and railroad to travel, beneath mountain peaks towering more than two miles high.

Palm Springs nestles in the lee of one of the peaks, Mt. San Jacinto, rising 10,831 feet in the steepest mountain escarpment in the United States. "Old San Jack," as it is called, protects the resort from the wind blasts that sometimes whistle down the pass. The melting snows from its summit supply water for the resort's numerous pools and green grass golf courses.

Palm Springs, 110 miles east of Los Angeles, is a celebrity playground attracting visitors from all over the world. In fact, they've counted 700 millionaires living there. The climate in Palm Springs is warm and dry; average daytime high is 88 degrees, nighttime average is 55 degrees. (Remember, though, that in the summer, the thermometer more often than not exceeds the 100-degree mark.)

The Palm Springs Aerial Tramway climbs 8,516 feet to the top of Mt. San Jacinto, in just 14 minutes. It's an entirely different world once you reach the top. You're suddenly in an Alpine-type forest, and it's 40 degrees cooler than the desert. There are a restaurant, gift and apparel shops, game room and picnic area.

The Moorten Botanical Gardens display 2,000 varieties of desert plants, Indian lore, petrified wood and relics.

Much of Palm Springs' life centers around more than 7,000 swimming pools of all shapes and sizes. Some pools are entirely enclosed by the home. There was the case of the pool that extended from the living room to the outdoors. It was considered a happy innovation until aquatic burglars swam in and ransacked the place. One home owner wanted a pool so badly that he had it blasted out of the solid rock of his site on the lower slope of San Jacinto. A pool builder once advertised: "Wall to wall water."

Palm Springs has more than 50 grass golf courses within a 15-mile area, and has become known as the "Golf Capital of the World." This is a favored golfing site for political figures and Hollywood motion-picture and television stars. Palm Springs is also a major tennis center, with 120 courts open to the public.

The local Chamber of Commerce issued a list of more than 100 Hollywood personalities having homes in Palm Springs. They head the Palm Springs Mounted Police and Desert Circus parades as grand marshals.

Shopping in Palm Springs' many exclusive shops, a number of them branches of Los Angeles' larger stores, can be done in casual clothes. Desert Fashion Plaza and the Palm Springs Mall are both air-conditioned, enclosed, complete shopping areas for value-conscious consumers. The Courtyard at the Bank of Palm Springs Centre is a tri–level shopping mall with exclusive boutiques centered around landscaped courtyards and open air atriums. The street lights of the main thoroughfare of the village shine out through the fronds of the tall palm trees to which they have been anchored.

Other activities at Palm Springs include scenic horseback and chuck-wagon breakfast rides, tennis, hikes, drives over the nearby desert to such spots as *Palm Canyon,* fishing at nearby Whitewater Canyon for mountain trout, and power speedboating at Salton Sea. At Palm Canyon a grove of 3,000 palms along a trickling stream is mute testimony to the great groves that once covered much of this country in prehistoric times.

Since Palm Canyon is on a reservation, an Indian tollkeeper collects a nominal fee at the gate. But in recent years, this fee has become very small change for what now are widely known as the "richest Indians in California." About 30,000 acres of the Palm Springs desert is reservation land, some of it right downtown. An act of Congress freed it for sale or lease. Now 140 members of the Aqua Caliente band of the Cahuilla Indians own land worth several million dollars. A syndicate leased eight acres of the Indians' land for a two-million-dollar spa utilizing the ancient Indian springs, which is the Spa Hotel right downtown.

Well worth visiting is the Palm Springs Desert Museum, unique for its desert collections and authoritative lectures and literature, as is Cabot's Indian Pueblo, a four-story building with 35 rooms, constructed single-handed by Cabot Yerxa over a 20-year period.

"Arabia of America"

An alternative and very scenic route to Palm Springs is over the Pines-to-Palms Highway. This starts near *Riverside* at *Hemet,* where hundreds of townsfolk take weekend roles in the Ramona Outdoor Play, staged in a mountainside bowl each spring. The story dramatizes Helen Hunt Jackson's novel of the California *rancho* girl and her Indian lover. The highway climbs a shoulder of Mt. San Jacinto, circles around the mountain, and affords a magnificent view over the warm, yellow desert, then zigzags down Seven Level Hill.

The country called the "Arabia of America" starts a few miles from Palm Springs. Here they grow better dates than Arabia, hold camel races every winter, and even have a town called *Mecca.* This is the *Coachella Valley,* which grows most of America's commercial dates. *Indio,* in the Palm Springs area, is the "Date Capital" and site of the

National Date Festival, held in February. Year-round, visitors to the area enjoy the town's primo drink, the date shake.

What looks like a soft green cloud on the horizon turns out to be the even tops of tall date palms laid out in precise rows. This is called a date palm "garden," not an "orchard" or a "grove." Dates are usually harvested in November and December, and since they ripen one by one, they must be picked in this same fashion, which means 10 to 20 trips up to each cluster by the date pickers. Pickers ride moving platforms, hang from harnesses, climb 40-foot ladders on circular tracks, or are seated at the ends of long mechanical booms.

Packing plants and roadside establishments sell fresh dates, date malted milk, date cookies, date cake, date pudding, and date sugar.

After leaving Palm Springs, you may notice the land has been dropping in elevation. Now and then the highway signs that usually tell the height of the road above sea level now tell the depth below. It is 22 feet at Indio. *Calipatria* posts a sign calling itself the "Lowest Down City in the Western Hemisphere" and manages to fly its flag at sea level only because the Stars and Stripes are at the top of what's reputed to be the tallest of all flagpoles, exactly 184 feet high.

The blue shimmering on the yellow horizon is *Salton Sea,* the lowest dip, 235 feet below the surface of, and almost exactly as salty as, the Pacific Ocean, 80 miles away. This body of water, about 24 miles long and 10 miles wide, was formed when the Colorado River broke loose in 1905 and flooded Salton Sink, the lowest part of the valley. Today Salton Sea is a favorite for warm winter boating and water skiing, and fishing for the corvina. This sporty fish was transplanted from the Gulf of Baja, California, and since has multiplied by the thousands. There is a state park on the shore, and boating-fishing resorts are becoming numerous.

A visit to the *Joshua Tree National Monument,* northeast, is absolutely fascinating. This monument was established to protect the fast-diminishing stands of the strange Joshua tree, a species of the lily family, which grows 20 to 40 feet high, sending roots deep into the sands, and is estimated in some cases to be as much as 300 years old. Joshua Trees are not cactus, as is popularly believed. The Joshuas bloom with heavenly waxy greenish-white flowers in March and April. Joshuas are havens for interesting desert life—lizards, wood rats, and birds.

In the monument area, Joshuas grow in the Wonderland of Rocks, where desert winds and temperatures have shaped the rocks into weird skulls, loaves of bread with slices gone, ships and prehistoric monsters. The monument is not far from *Twenty-nine Palms,* which calls itself the "northernmost oasis in America," or the town of *Joshua Tree,* where in May they hold the Grand National Desert Turtle Sweepstakes. There is also an entrance from the Colorado Desert 53 miles southeast from Palm Springs and 30 miles from Indio.

The High Desert

The northernmost desert in this area is the *Mojave* (pronounced *mo-hav-ee*), called "a great and mysterious wasteland, a sun-punished place" by novelist John Steinbeck and known as the "High Desert" because of its elevation, ranging up to more than 6,000 feet. Broad sandy basins alternate with bleached salt flats and rough mountain terrain.

The vast arid stretch of the Mojave Desert starts just over the mountain range north of Los Angeles and sweeps eastward to the Colorado River. It begins at the west with the *Antelope Valley,* named so for the huge herds of antelope that once roamed the area. The Mojave Desert offers vast expanses of rich natural desert beauty, traces of century-old ghost towns, wildlife, and softly hued plants. In the spring of a rainy year the stands of California golden poppies are so big that their flashy color can be seen 10 miles away.

Antelope Valley raises a superior quality of alfalfa, and each September a festival is held at the town of *Lancaster.* A highlight of the event is the Rural Olympics, when alfalfa farmers and their wives race "hopped-up" farm tractors and snake them through obstacle courses of alfalfa bales. The fastest farm tractor is then matched against a quarter horse—and the horse usually wins.

Much of the Mojave Desert is mining country. Near the town of Mojave, once the terminus of the 20-mule-team borax wagons out of Death Valley, is the lonesome hump of Soledad Mountain, pocked by the shafts of mines that are now closed after giving up millions in gold.

Beyond the mountain, *Tropico Mine,* Southern California's largest standing gold mill, is now a visitors' attraction. Tickets are sold for a tour through a 900-foot shaft and a look at "pay-dirt" ore that would be mined today were the price of gold higher. Crushed ore is available for panning and gold-ore chunks can be taken home as souvenirs. A Gold Town and museum of relics of the old days are interesting to explore.

On the way to the gold town of *Randsburg* there's another kind of mining. What looks like a snowstorm on the desert beside the road is Koehn Dry Salt Lake. The salt is almost pure enough to serve at the dinner table.

Strung along the slope of Red Mountain, old Randsburg is about what a movie set of a past day's mining town ought to look like. Some of the walls of the buildings are made of old dynamite boxes. Named for the famed mining town in South Africa, Randsburg boomed for a time, but faded away when the Yellow Aster mine played out after yielding $16 million in gold. The Old Time Mining Celebration is held in late August, with rock-drilling and gold-panning contests. Admission to the Desert Museum is free.

At *Boron,* borax is mined in an open pit 3,000 feet across and 350 feet deep. Visitors can stand behind the fence at the brink and watch the borax blasted loose and brought up in oversize truckloads on a road spiraling around the sides.

The old silver town of *Calico* was crumbling to ruin until Walter Knott of Knott's Berry Farm fame bought it out of sentiment; he had worked in the mines as a youth. In their heyday, the Calico mines yielded $80 million in silver. The ghost town has now been restored as a visitors' attraction.

A few miles south is the dude and guest ranch country in the *Lucerne* and *Apple* valleys at the foot of the San Bernardino mountains.

At Edwards Air Force Base, just southeast of the Mojave, thousands gathered to watch the Columbia space shuttle make more than a half dozen landings since 1981. The country's second-largest airforce base was made famous in the book and film, *The Right Stuff;* this is where the sound barrier was first broken. Each May on Armed Forces Day, civilians can catch a glimpse of what goes on when the Edwards flight line is opened to the public.

Lowest, Hottest, and Driest

Death Valley, north of the Mojave Desert, is the lowest and, in summer, one of the hottest and driest spots in the United States. At more comfortable times of the year, many regard the valley as one of the more geologically fascinating places on earth.

Third largest of the national monuments, Death Valley is a trough in the northern reaches of the Mojave Desert, 140 miles long and six to 20 miles wide. The rainfall averages only about two inches a year, and the National Park Service has recorded the hottest summertime temperature ever.

The sun-blasted valley was called Tomesha, which means "ground afire," by the Panamint Indians. Its present name is supposed to have originated in 1849 when a party of gold-rushers were rescued after wandering the sea of salt for 80 days. One emaciated emigrant is supposed to have looked back and said, "Goodbye, Death Valley!"

Today the valley is a well-supervised monument, with excellent highways, plenty of water, and a wide range of accommodations.

Among the interesting features to be seen in Death Valley are brilliantly colored canyons and mountains, freakish natural formations, and authentic artifacts of the Old West. Zabriski Point is an awesome lookout over miles of golden-brown hills.

The colors of Golden Canyon range from a deep purple to a rich gold, according to the changing angles of the sun passing overhead. The Grapevine Mountains are colored red and black, while the Funeral Mountains are a hot tan and rosy brown. The Black Mountains are strangely streaked with rose, fawn, and milky green shades. Badwater, a salty pool 282 feet below sea level, is the lowest-lying water in America.

Mosaic Canyon has varicolored pebbles embedded in the gray rock of the floor. They have been polished by the wind to resemble mosaic patterns. The Devil's Golf Course is a bed of rugged salt crystals rising to pinnacles as high as four feet and still growing. (On a still day you can hear them snap.) Ubehebe Crater is now an 800-foot-deep pit formed by a volcanic eruption between 1,000 and 2,000 years ago.

Sand dunes are the beach line of an ancient sea that covered this once-lush area before the rise of the Sierra Nevada mountains cut off the rain. The Gnomes' Workshop consists of acres of odd alkaline formations. Natural Bridge is an arch over a canyon in the Black Mountains.

At the Harmony Borax Works in Mustard Canyon, old machinery that supplied the borax for the 20-mule-team wagons is on display. Stone beehive-shaped kilns, in Wildrose Canyon, once made charcoal for the mine smelters in the nearby Panamint Mountains. "Dante's View" is the name of the spot where a tilt of the head allows you to take in the lowest point in the U.S.A., Badwater (282 feet below sea level), as well as the highest point in 49 states, Mt. Whitney (14,495 feet).

There are luxury quarters at Furnace Creek Inn, where the big Travertine spring pours out a generous supply of water at a steady 70 degrees, and more modest accommodations for several hundred at the nearby Furnace Creek Ranch. The Furnace Creek golf course holds the world's lowest-down tournament each year, played at 178 feet below sea level. A visitor's center in Furnace Creek provides exhibits, an hourly slide program, evening naturalist programs, guided walks and a variety of publications to help orient the traveler.

The National Park Service maintains the Death Valley Museum at Death Valley National Monument, featuring natural-history exhibits, charcoal kilns, and the Harmony borax works.

Scotty's Castle, at the northern end of Death Valley, has been opened to visitors for tours. The fabled character Death Valley Scotty made headlines by hiring a private train for a speed record to Chicago and was supposed to have built the elaborate castle in Grapevine Canyon with the proceeds of a secret gold mine. The fact is that the place was owned by Albert M. Johnson, a wealthy Chicago businessman who came to the desert for his health and became a fast friend of Scotty's.

There are also accommodations at Stovepipe Wells, so named for the old prospectors' habit of marking springs with sections of stovepipe stuck into the sands.

The San Joaquin Valley, southern arm of the vast Great Valley of California, is walled off from the Los Angeles basin by the high and rugged Tehachapi Mountains. Until recent years, the Tehachapis were a stubborn barrier. Travel over them could be a rugged ordeal of steep grades and winding roads. Today, a modern freeway makes the trip easy.

Inland and North

The most direct route from Los Angeles is the Ridge Route, Interstate 5. The freeway sweeps over high cattle ranges, through cuts into convulsed rock formations, below brooding peaks. An interesting stop is the restored *Fort Tejon State Historic Park,* open year-round. Established in 1854 as headquarters of the U.S. Army's First Dragoons, it was assigned here to stop cattle rustling and protect the nearby Indians. It became a station for the Butterfield Overland Route in 1858. What used to be the tortuous Grapevine stretch is now a "million-dollar-a-mile highway"—eight lanes, two exclusively for trucks.

A second route is the Tehachapi Pass from the Mojave Desert; this is also an engineering marvel. In the early days of railroading, the Southern Pacific tracks that parallel the new freeway came to Walong Mountain and couldn't get through. So they went around, in the Walong Loop. You see a train heading into a tunnel and, while the cars are still worming in below, the locomotive pops out around the mountain and crosses over its caboose, 77 feet below. It is an old railroad joke that the engineer waits for the Loop to reach into the caboose for his lunch pail.

The *San Joaquin Valley* grows large-scale crops under irrigation. Cotton and potato fields and grape vineyards stretch by the mile. During harvest time the potatoes go out by the trainloads. During the cotton harvest in early winter you may pick a cotton boll for a souvenir, follow a "train" of cotton trailers to a gin and there watch the seeds picked out of the snowy crop, which is then baled up and stacked by the mile.

A worthwhile stop is Kern County Museum and Pioneer Village in *Bakersfield.* It is a complete 12-acre village of the Old West, which includes 40 restored buildings, a log cabin, an 1891 Victorian mansion, a wooden jail, a horse-drawn fire engine, an old steam locomotive (1898), and a keg of square nails! The adjoining museum has a collection of Indian artifacts, minerals and gems. Bakersfield is also the country-music capital of the west.

At *Wasco,* 27 miles northwest, the commercial nurseries present a glorious spring sight—900 blooming acres of roses.

At 954-acre *Tule Elk Reserve State Park,* 26 miles south and west of Bakersfield near Tupman, the last of the big herds of the diminutive Tule Elk are preserved, in the rather bleak but rich oil country in the western San Joaquin Valley. At times the elk can be seen in the afternoon at feeding hours.

The Eastern High Sierra

Once in the northern part of the San Joaquin at Bakersfield, it is an easy drive along Calif. 178 to the *Sierra Nevada* and then a spectacular drive north on U.S. 395 along the mountain's eastern flank. (You could take 395 back south through the Mojave Desert.)

This was once volcanic country and the remains are seen in the pinkish, purplish lava cones along the way. Almost-dry *Owens Lake* was once well filled; legend says that a small steamer carrying silver bars across it from now defunct Gerro Gordo mine sank in its mud and was never raised.

At intervals along the lower slopes of the mountains to the left will be seen the Los Angeles aqueduct, which carries water from this valley, which receives its water from the snowy crests of the Sierra.

The town of *Lone Pine* looks up at *Mt. Whitney,* 14,495 feet high, and topped in the United States only by peaks in Alaska. Close by are Mt. Williamson, 14,384 feet. Mt. Russell, 14,190 feet, and Mt. Muir, 14,015 feet. A trail that cost $25,000 to build climbs Mt. Whitney from the end of the auto road at Whitney Portal. Every summer thousands make the hike to the "attic" of the continental U.S.A., a near-plateau of three or four acres at the summit.

At the base of the mountain, the queer and rugged formations of the *Alabama Hills* may look familiar to television viewers. Many TV Westerns are filmed in the canyons twisting through these rocks.

At *Independence,* 16 miles north, the Eastern California Museum in the basement of the courthouse displays antiquated firearms used in the Indian wars, old sidesaddles, candle and mullet molds, and Indian relics. Admission is free.

The *Palisade Glaciers* overlooking Big Pine, 28 miles north, small as glaciers go, have the distinction of being the southern-most "living" glaciers on this continent; a "living" glacier is one that is continually cracking off and melting at its lowest fringe, supplied anew at its upper level by the winter snows. These glaciers are at about the same latitude as the palm trees in the San Joaquin valley on the other side of the range. The glaciers cover about two square miles. Guided pack trips to the glaciers start at Glacier Lodge, at the end of the auto road.

Bishop, another 15 miles north, is an outfitting center for hunters and fishers, who cast in some 2,000 trout-filled lakes and streams. Every notch in the great mountain wall is marked by a trout stream trickling down to the highway. The prized golden trout, found in few other places, is caught in the higher waters. Five miles northeast of Bishop is the Laws Railroad Museum of railroading, containing a five-room station agent's house, mining exhibits, Western movie set, and period antiques.

Sequoia and Kings Canyon National Parks

This pair of natural beauties, running wild from the gentle foothills of the San Joaquin Valley to the splintered crest of the Sierra Nevada, were established 50 years apart, but they adjoin and are referred to as a team. Their combined area covers 1,314 square miles.

Sequoia Park's noble stands of its namesake tree *(Sequoia gigantea)* began reaching for the California heavens about the time Troy fell to the Greeks. Largest of the park's sequoias is the General Sherman Tree in the Giant Forest, over 36 feet through and 101 feet around at the base. It soars to just over 272 feet—higher than a 20-story office building—and is estimated to be 3,500 years old. A man could lie crosswise on some of its massive branches. The tree's weight has been estimated at 2,145 tons (heavy as a small ocean-going steamship) and it also has been estimated that the General Sherman Tree could produce 600,000 board feet of lumber—enough to build a small town.

Kings Canyon Park also has giant sequoias. The General Grant Tree is only 5 feet shorter than the Sherman and exceeds the Sherman's base circumference by 6 feet. In 1965 Kings Canyon Park, already noted for its lakes, canyons, waterfalls, and rushing rivers, was greatly enhanced when President Johnson signed into reality the dream of naturalist John Muir, adding the Cedar Grove tract and the Tehipite Valley to the national park area.

Other notable sights in these parks include Tharp Log (where the road goes through, rather than around, the trunk), the Fluted Columns and Chimney Tree. Morro Rock, climbed by a safe, 300-foot stairway for a view over the Great Western Divide, and Crystal Cave, a marble cave with elaborate limestone formations, may also prove fascinating. Open during the summer; guide service is available.

There is a museum at the ranger station. Stop by the Lodgepole and Grant Grove Visitor Centers for expert advice on organizing your sightseeing, park data, and campfire talks information. Highways to the parks are kept open the year round and there are year-round accommodations. Bus tours are available from *Tulare* and *Visalia.*

Along the North Coast

It is a seacoast drive for much of the way from Los Angeles along Highway 101. Oxnard is a small city on the Pacific with interesting motels and recreational facilities. Fisherman's Wharf, located at Channel Islands Harbor, is reminiscent of New England, with shops, restaurants and a seafood market. Seaside *Ventura* is known as the "Poinsettia City." If you are there in winter, the crimson blooms will be everywhere, in long hedges and giant clumps sprouting high as the bungalow eaves. Millions of beautiful Monarch butterflies come to the city and surrounding countryside in October to stay the winter. Mission San Buenaventura was founded in 1782. Its museum is excellent, and the city is developing the site into an archeological park. Lake Casitas, 8 miles north, has fishing, boats for rent. In late fall and winter (usually October, November and December) Ventura is deluged with its annual, mysterious "blizzard" of beautiful Monarch butterflies. An unforgettable natural show.

Lemon groves cover the valleys a few miles inland. Lemon trees like even milder weather than do oranges. They are known as the "hardest-working" trees because they bear sweet-smelling blossoms and ripen fruit simultaneously the year round. Lemons are picked every six weeks; in a year a single well-bearing tree may produce 3,000 lemons! The "square" trees you see, giving you the impression that you could walk across the flat top of a grove, are trimmed to increase the yield. The world's largest lemon grove, of 1,800 acres, is near *Santa Paula,* known as the "Lemon Capital."

Ojai Valley (pronounced *Oh High*) is supposed to have been named for the Indian word for "nest," and the view from the top of the Dennison grade over the bowl, with its ranches and trim rows of citrus trees, may well confirm this belief.

Ojai village, with its colonnaded business district and oak-dotted estates, is favored by artists, writers, and showpeople.

On up the coast, a letter mailed at *Santa Claus* will bear this holiday postmark. The bulky-looking things offshore are steel "islands" for seagoing oil wells. One is an actual man-made island, even planted with palm trees. The extremely long surf at Rincon Point offers an unusual surfing sight—as many as two dozen surfers riding the waves at the same time.

Mountains rising out of the sea leave just enough room to squeeze in the highway and the railroad tracks. On a breezy day, salt spray may coat the windshield.

Spanish Santa Barbara

At the approach to *Santa Barbara,* wealthy *Montecito* covers the lower mountain slopes and canyons with wooded estates. Almost every Sunday, matches take place on the polo field beside the highway. To many the stretch of freeway entering the city is regarded as the most beautifully landscaped in the California system.

Santa Barbara climbs the mountain slopes from the yacht harbor and palm-fringed beach, almost all of it a grassed-over public park. This was the gracious social center of old Spanish California, and today's residents, many of them wealthy, retired Easterners, have attempted to retain the old atmosphere.

The Spanish-Moorish County Courthouse is perhaps one of the most beautiful of public buildings in North America. Among those red-tiled towers, bright window boxes, and sudden balconies, it is hard to believe that somewhere, there has to be a jail.

The Santa Barbara Museum of Art has excellent exhibits and is noted for its Greek, Roman, and Egyptian sculptures, set in the central gallery and highlighted by natural light from skylights, as well as for its rich glassware collection. The Museum of Natural History, in a wooded canyon back of the Mission, is notable for, among many things, the mounted specimens of the California Condor, largest flying bird in North America. Deep in the rugged mountains back of Santa Barbara, is a special sanctuary, a forlorn band of these 10-foot winged giants is making a last stand to escape the fate of the dodo. The Alhecama Players here offer serious drama in the Lobero Theater. The Theater is a very important part of Santa Barbara's cultural life.

California plants of sea coast, valley, mountain, and desert grow in the pleasant canyon of the Botanic Gardens.

Mission Santa Barbara is the only California mission having twin towers and is regarded by many as the most beautiful. It is notable for the fact that since its founding in 1786, the altar light has never been extinguished. Brown-frocked brothers lead guided tours. Santa Barbara's civic events, such as the colorful Old Spanish Days Fiesta in August.

The many Spanish adobes in the city were built by the Indians of massive bricks, made of local adobe clay. The rounded red-clay roof tiles were molded on the thighs of Indian women. Numerous adobes are in active community use today.

The local visitor's bureau offers a leaflet with a "Red Tile Walking Tour" and there's a marked "Scenic Drive Tour."

The Spanish influence is everywhere in street names such as Indio Muerte (Dead Indian) Street, Los Olivos (The Olives) Street, Camino Cielo Street (Street of the Sky), to name but a few.

Up the coast a few miles, the University of California campus, overlooking the sea at Goleta, is a gem of California architecture. The mild, sunny climate is utilized to the utmost for an open-air reading balcony off the library, plazas and landscaped squares, where art and drama classes can be held out-of-doors. There are numerous art exhibits and dramas by the college students in the campus theater. At Goleta you can tour the Dos Pueblos Orchid Ranch, free of charge.

San Marcos Pass is an easy jump inland, with panoramic marine views over the coast and Channel Island Chain, opening into the Santa-Ynez Valley, where palamino parade horses were first bred systematically at Rancho San Fernando Rey.

Denmark in California

The village of *Solvang,* meaning "Sunny Valley," at the end of the valley, has sought to make itself a bit of transplanted Denmark. The village was founded by Lutheran clergymen who liked the valley and called for Danes all over the country to come and found an old-country type "folk" school here. Danish festivals are held every September. Here, you can buy real Danish pastries and imported goods.

For a scenic and leisurely trip to *Pismo Beach,* home of giant clams, Route 1 is recommended. Years ago the beach at Pismo literally was paved with clams, and farmers plowed them up for chicken and hog feed. Today there's a daily limit, and no clam less than five inches in diameter can be taken. Local shops and motels offer the schedule of tides and limits.

San Luis Obispo, beneath the brooding peaks of four volcanic cones, is an old town, as epitomized by the Sinsheimer Brothers Drygoods Store, founded in 1876 and still doing business with the same old fixtures. This is the home of the California State Polytechnic College, which has model stock farms worth seeing. Visitors are welcome on the 3,500-acre campus. The San Luis Obispo Nuclear Center has many exhibits and a nuclear theater presenting a 14-minute program on how nuclear power is used to generate electricity. Buses leave the center throughout the day for a 1½-hour tour to Diablo Canyon, where the Pacific Gas and Electric Company is constructing nuclear power generating units. Also well worth a visit are the Mission San Luis Obispo de Tolosa and the County Historical Museum.

As Calif. 1 leaves San Luis Obispo and nears the coast at *Morro Bay,* the huge landmark on the horizon becomes Morro Rock, rearing 576 feet above the surf and called the "Gibraltar of the Pacific." Hundreds of artists display their work in the shops and galleries along the Embaracadero. At the Museum of Natural History are interesting displays, lectures, and movies. Farther along the coast is *Cambria,* a resort and an artists' and writers' colony. This route, skirting blue-green coves and rocky headlands, is scenic all the way to Carmel.

Watch the mountains for the first sight of what looks like a towered European castle. La Case Grande *(San Simeon)* is just that, being the famed castle built by the late William Randolph Hearst and depository of millions of dollars' worth of his art collection from around the world. Travelers once had their nearest view of La Casa Grande through coin-in-the-slot telescopes beside the beach at the village of San Simeon. Now it is a state historical monument, presented to California by the Hearst family and open to the public. Escorted buses tour the 123-acre estate.

San Simeon crowns *La Cuesta Encantada* (the Enchanted Hill), in the Santa Lucia Range. It is reached by traveling five miles up a one-way winding road through the former Hearst ranchland populated by Herefords and a game preserve of zebra, fallow deer, aoudads, axis and sambar deer and tahr goats.

One of the floors of the castle is Pompeiian mosaic tile dating to 60 B.C. Some of the carved and decorated panel ceilings were dismantled in Europe and shipped here to be reassembled by European craftsmen. The Assembly Room is 84 feet long and 35 feet wide, marked by marble medallions weighing one ton each. There are 100 rooms (not all open), of which 38 are bedrooms, 31 are bathrooms and 14 are sitting rooms. Tours are scheduled daily.

The beautiful valley area inland of San Luis Obispo is particularly colorful in spring; hundreds of acres of grapevines supply several wineries, and there are a few wine-tasting rooms in Paso Robles. Lakes San Antonio and Nacimiento offer excellent boating, fishing and camping facilities; Los Padres National Forest affords scenic camping and hiking grounds; while at Lopez Lake, just twenty minutes out of town, in addition to the usual water sports, there are hot springs and a unique 600-foot waterslide.

PRACTICAL INFORMATION FOR SOUTHERN CALIFORNIA

HOW TO GET THERE. If you are traveling to Southern California by plane, bus, or train, you will probably be heading for Los Angeles or San Diego. See the "How to Get There" sections above for information. Palm Springs airport is served by *American Eagle, Continental, States West, Trans World Express, United Express,* and *Western Express* airlines, as well as commuter airline *Sun Aire.* Santa Barbara has the major airport north of Los Angeles, with service from *American, American Eagle, Continental, Sky West Trans World Express, United,* and *United Express. American Eagle, Sky West,* and *United Express* serve San Luis Obispo.

If you are driving across the desert to Southern California, be sure to take adequate precautions. See the "Desert Driving" section in *Facts at Your Fingertips.*

ACCOMMODATIONS. Hotels and motels in Southern California are plentiful, so you are apt to find some good bargains. Few motels try to compete for the tourist trade without at least one swimming pool—several have three! In this section we list establishments alphabetically by location. Los Angeles area and San Diego accommodations are listed in the two preceding practical information sections.

The price categories, based on the cost of a double room, are: *Deluxe,* $100 and up, *Expensive,* $75–100, *Moderate,* $50–75; *Inexpensive,* under $50.

AVALON (SANTA CATALINA ISLAND). Las Casitas Garden Hotel. *Deluxe.* Box 278, Avalon, CA 20704 (213–510–2226). At Avalon and Tremont roads. 34 cottages, surrounded by gardens, with kitchens, private patios, pool with large deck, tennis court, and children's playground. Next to golf course and near beach. Built in the 1930s, Las Casitas has a rustic look. Seasonal rates.

Villa Portofino. *Deluxe.* Box 127, Avalon, CA 90704 (213–510–0555). At 111 Crescent Ave. Mediterranean-style. 33 rooms (one with private pool), some overlooking the bay. Cafe, bar.

Zane Grey Pueblo. *Deluxe.* Box 216, Avalon, CA 90704 (213–510–0966). The former home of Zane Grey is still a favorite spot. Horses, stables, bikes available. Fireplace, pool table, organ, and piano in lounge. Pleasant accommodations. View of the bay.

Atwater Hotel. *Expensive.* Box 737, Avalon, CA 90704 (213–510–1788). Avalon's largest hotel, with 100 rooms. Family-oriented, half a block from the beach.

BAKERSFIELD. Best Western Casa Royale Motor Inn. *Moderate.* 251 S. Union Ave., Bakersfield, CA 93307 (805–327–3333). Comfortable accommodations at this double-story motel. Restaurant, coffee shop. Bar with entertainment and dancing. Shuffleboard. 119 rooms.

Holiday Inn. *Moderate.* 2700 White Lane, Bakersfield, CA 93304 (805–832–3111; 800–465–4329). Branch of chain. Attractive rooms and nicely kept grounds. Suites. Waterbeds. Pets permitted. Restaurant, bar. Pool (heated); service at poolside. Transportation to airport. 152 rooms.

Kern River Motor Inn. *Moderate.* 2620 Pierce Rd., Bakersfield, CA 93308 (805–327–9651). Pleasant, large, double-story motel. Restaurant, bar with dancing and entertainment. Room service. Pets accepted. Pool (heated).

BARSTOW. Desert Inn Motel. *Moderate.* 1100 E. Main, Barstow, CA 92311 (619–256–2146). Excellent. Pool. Free coffee in rooms. Seasonal rates.

Howard Johnson's Motor Lodge. *Moderate.* 1431 E. Main, Barstow, CA 92311 (619–256–0661). Comfortable rooms with balconies or patios. Restaurant, bar. Wading pool, pool. Pets permitted.

Sunset Inn. *Moderate.* 1350 W. Main, Barstow, CA 92311 (619–256–8921). Double-story motel with cheerful decor. Restaurant nearby. Sauna. 41 rooms.

BIG BEAR LAKE. For lodging assistance in this mountain resort, call the Tourist and Visitor's Bureau at 714–866–4601.

Knickerbocker Mansion. *Deluxe.* 869 S. Knickerbocker Rd., Big Bear, CA 92315 (714–866–8221). Ten-room 1920s bed and breakfast near downtown.

Big Bear Inn. *Expensive.* 42200 Moonridge Rd., Big Bear, CA 92315. (800–BEAR INN). Get the feeling of Switzerland at this mountaintop retreat. Health club, swimming pool.

BISHOP. Best Western Motel Bishop. *Moderate.* 150 E. Elm St., Bishop, CA 93514 (619–873–3564). Updated 54 room hotel with pool. Near restaurant. Airport bus. Some water beds.

High Sierra Lodge. *Moderate.* 1005 N. Main St., Bishop, CA 93514 (619–873–8426). Rustic wood hotel with two buildings, 51 rooms, indoor jacuzzi. Heated pool, fishing facilities.

Town House Motel. *Moderate.* 625 N. Main St., Bishop, CA 93514 (619–872–4541). Swedish chalet-style inn with 35 rooms. Air-conditioning, TV. Heated Pool. Fish cleaning, freezer facilities.

BLYTHE. Rodeway Inn. *Moderate.* 401 E. Hobsonway, Blythe, CA 92225 (619–922–2184). 53 rooms. Pleasant accommodations. Coffee shop. Bar. Pool (heated). Play area, putting green, bicycles.

BORREGO SPRINGS. La Casa del Zorro. *Moderate.* Box 127, Borrego Springs, CA 92004 (619–767–5323). Pleasant accommodations in this desert resort in the middle of the vast Anza-Borrego State Park in either the motel or one- or two-bedroom cottages. Restaurant, bar, heated pool, play area, putting green, lighted tennis court. Golf nearby.

BRAWLEY. Brawley Travel Lodge. *Moderate* 300 W. Main St., Brawley, CA 92227 (619–344–2810). 42 rooms. Attractive motel. Heated pool. Complimentary coffee in rooms. Pets. Cafe nearby.

BUELLTON. Windmill Country Inn. *Expensive.* 114 East Hwy. 246, Buellton, CA 93427 (805–688–8448). A huge windmill in front will help you spot this 107-room Danish-style property. Pool, jacuzzi, some refrigerators in rooms.

COSTA MESA. The Westin South Coast Plaza Hotel. *Deluxe.* 666 Anton Blvd., Costa Mesa, CA 92626 (714–540–2500; 800–228–3000). Big, posh hotel of the Westin chain near Newport Beach and South Coast Plaza, a great shopping center. Tennis courts, pool, restaurants. San Diego Frwy. 394 rooms.

DEATH VALLEY. Furnace Creek Inn. *Deluxe.* Box 1, Death Valley, CA 92328 (619–786–2345). This ranch-style property is a true oasis in the heart of the desert. Private sun decks, tennis courts, riding, gift shop, beauty salon, pool, nearby golf course, dancing nightly except Sun. Good restaurant. Open Nov. to April (but the Ranch keeps some rooms open in the summer).

Stove Pipe Wells Village. *Moderate.* State Hwy. 190, Death Valley, CA 92328. To call, ask operator to connect you to Stove Pipe Wells Toll Station #1. Motel open Oct.–Apr. Some summer accommodations. Restaurant, pool, gift shop.

DESERT HOT SPRINGS. Desert Inn. *Moderate.* 10805 Palm Dr., Desert Hot Springs, CA 92240 (619–329–6495). Whirlpool, sauna, massage. Olympic pool, patios, beauty shop. Golf privileges, massage available, entertainment, dancing. 50 rooms.

EL CENTRO. Ramada Inn. *Moderate.* 1455 Ocotillo Dr., El Centro, CA 92243 (619–352–5152). Large motor inn with 150 rooms. Member of chain. Restaurant, bar. Pool (heated). Wading pool. Putting green, shuffleboard.

HUNTINGTON BEACH. Best Western Huntington Beach Inn. *Deluxe.* 21112 Pacific Coast Hwy., Huntington Beach, CA 92648 (714–536–1421). On beach. Excellent service, pool, 24-hour cafe, superb dining and cocktails. Three-par golf course.

Huntington Shores Motor Hotel. *Deluxe.* 21002 Pacific Coast Hwy., Huntington Beach, CA 92648 (714–536–8861). Situated opposite beach. Pleasant rooms. Some with view of the Pacific. Restaurant nearby. Pool (heated).

IDYLLWILD. Bluebird Hill Lodge. *Moderate.* 26905 Hwy. 243, Box 963, Idyllwild, CA 92349 (714–659–2696). View of San Jacinto Mountains. Play area, ping-pong, many fireplaces. 26 rooms.

LAGUNA BEACH. Eiler's Inn. *Deluxe.* 741 S. Coast Hwy., Laguna Beach, CA 92651 (714–494–3004). Bed and breakfast inn with live entertainment on weekends. Flower-laden atrium and fountain. 13 rooms.

Surf and Sand Hotel. *Deluxe.* 1555 S. Coast Hwy., Laguna Beach, CA 92651 (714–497–4477). The largest hotel in town right on its own private beach. Sauna, swimming pool. Spectacular Art Deco restaurant. *The Towers,* at the top, with a great view.

Seacliff Motel. *Expensive.* 1661 S. Coast Hwy., Laguna Beach, CA 92651 (714–494–9717). Under the same management for 20 years, the Seacliff has many rooms overlooking the Pacific. Private sun decks, heated pool, in-room coffee.

LAGUNA NIGUEL. Ritz Carlton Laguna Niguel. *Deluxe.* 33533 Shoreline Dr., Laguna Niguel, CA 92677 (714–240–2000; 800–241–3333). Resort on 17½ acres overlooking the Pacific. Mediterranean architecture, extensive landscaping, beach access. Jacuzzi, two pools, two restaurants, three lounges. Adjacent to 18-hole golf course. 393 rooms.

NEWPORT BEACH-BALBOA BAY. Reservations necessary in summer and during Easter Week, when teenagers take over the town.

Four Seasons Hotel. *Deluxe.* 690 Newport Center Drive, Newport Beach, CA 92660 (714–759–0808; 800–332–3442). Posh 296-room high rise with many amenities and excellent service. Southwestern decor. Fine restaurant, swimming pool.

Hotel Meridien Newport Beach. *Deluxe.* 4500 MacArthur Blvd., Newport Beach, CA 92660 (714–476–2001; 800–543–4300). Located in the Koll Center, this ultra-modern hotel is shaped like a pyramid with a six-story atrium lobby. Concierge, cafe, gourmet restaurant and full-service health club.

Mariott Hotel and Tennis Club. *Deluxe.* 900 Newport Center Dr., Newport Beach, CA 92660 (714–640–4000; 800–228–9290). Tennis, golf privileges, pool, hydrotherapy pool. Restaurant, entertainment, dancing. Spectacular ocean view.

The Newporter Resort. *Deluxe.* 1107 Jamboree Rd., Newport Beach, CA 92660 (714–644–1700). Elegant. Air-conditioning. TV. Heated pool, shuffleboard, golf course, helicopter service. *John Wayne* tennis club with cocktail bar overlooking the courts. The Duke was often seen playing backgammon here. Fine dining, lounge, dancing. Villas with private pools.

Sheraton Newport Beach. *Expensive.* 4545 MacArthur Blvd., Newport Beach, CA 92660 (714–833–0570; 800–325–3535). Newest in area. Expanded to 360 rooms. Pool, jacuzzi, tennis courts. Near Orange County Airport. Free coffee and *Wall Street Journal.*

OJAI. Ojai Valley Inn. *Deluxe.* 1203 W. Ojai, Box L, Ojai, CA 93023 (805–646–5511). Splendid view, golf course, heated pool, tennis courts. Excellent dining room. Barbecues, box lunches. Popular for conventions. 61 units.

Capri Motel. *Moderate.* 1180 E. Ojai Ave., Ojai, CA 93023 (805–646–4305). Pool, whirlpool. Terrific mountain view.

Ojai Rancho Motel. *Moderate.* 615 W. Ojai Ave., Ojai, CA 93023 (805–646–1434). Rustic place with large heated pool, outdoor barbecue, cable TV.

OXNARD. Casa Sirena Marina Hotel. *Deluxe.* 3605 Peninsula Rd., Channel Islands Harbor, Oxnard, CA 93035 (805–985–6311). Attractive double-story motel overlooking the marina. Suites and efficiency units. Restaurant, bar with entertainment and dancing. Offers pool, sauna, jacuzzi, tennis courts, game room, fishing.

Mandalay Beach Resort. *Deluxe.* 2101 Mandalay Beach Road, Oxnard, CA 93035 (805–984–2500). All-suite hotel. Each unit has a micro-kitchen and lavish marble bath. At the edge of the Pacific, with tennis on premises and golf nearby.

Oxnard Hilton Inn. *Moderate.* 600 Esplanade Dr., Oxnard, CA 93030 (805–485–9666; 800–445–8667). Near beach, boating, golf. Tennis. Pool, poolside eating. Beauty shops.

PALM SPRINGS AND VICINITY. Don't attempt to visit this famous resort during holiday season without advance reservations. From L.A. call for Palm Springs information and reservations (619–325–1577). Excellent rates and an abundance of availability in summer, from June 1 to September 15.

Americana Canyon Hotel Racquet & Golf Resort. *Deluxe.* 2850 S. Palm Canyon Dr., Palm Springs, CA 92262 (619–323–5656). Elegantly decorated rooms with luxurious furnishings. Kitchen suites available. Restaurant, bar. Three heated pools and therapy pools. Tennis. Riding, golf and health spa available. Barber shop and beauty salon.

Desert Princess. *Deluxe.* Vista Chino at Desert Princess Dr., Cathedral City, CA 92234 (619–322–7000). This new luxury resort hotel managed by Princess Cruises has 385 rooms and suites and a full slate of amenities: 18-hole championship golf course, tennis and racquet courts, pools, spas and health club. Has three restaurants, including gourmet dining room.

Gene Autry Hotel. *Deluxe.* 4200 E. Palm Canyon Dr., Palm Springs, CA 92264 (619–328–1171). Luxury accommodations. Suites available. Restaurant, bar. Transportation to airport. Tennis, 3 pools.

Grand Champions. *Deluxe.* 44–600 Indian Wells Lane, Indian Wells, CA 92210 (619–341–1000). Rambling Moorish spread on 35 acres with every conceivable luxury—even personal butlers in some of the 340 guest quarters. Championship tennis and golf, excellent restaurant with menus designed by Wolfgang Puck of Spago restaurant fame.

Ingleside Inn. *Deluxe.* 200 W. Ramon Rd., Palm Springs, CA 92262 (619–325–0046). Charming old hacienda-style place with 26 memorable rooms furnished with antiques. Pool. Complimentary continental breakfast. No children. Great restaurant and bar. Garbo slept here.

La Siesta Villas. *Deluxe.* 247 W. Stevens Rd., Palm Springs, CA 92262 (619–325–2269). Lovely one- and two-bedroom villas with kitchens and fireplaces. Patios overlook nicely landscaped grounds. Children must be at least 14 years old. Pool (heated).

La Mancha Villas and Private Club. *Deluxe.* 444 N. Avenida Caballeros, Palm Springs, CA 92263 (619–323–1773). Fully-equipped condominium-like villas with daily maid service. Facilities include sauna, therapy pools, paddle tennis courts, tennis, 65-foot long pool, gym. Continental breakfasts daily, weekend gourmet dinners, European-style dining in the club, snack bar. You can cook for yourself (each Villa is fully-stocked with the necessary utensils), dine at the club or in nearby (walking distance) restaurants.

Maxim's. *Deluxe.* 285 N. Palm Canyon Dr., Palm Springs, CA 92262 (619–322–9000; 800–MAXIMS nationwide; 800–533–3556 in CA). Located center stage in the heart of downtown shopping, the new Maxim's has 194 luxurious suites and is part of the Desert Fashion Plaza. Striking 6-story asymmetrical lobby is an architectural marvel. Two restaurants and a popular sidewalk cafe. Health club, pool facing Mt. San Jacinto.

The Palm Springs Marquis/A Harbaugh Hotel. *Deluxe.* 150 S. Indian Ave., Palm Springs, CA 92262 (619–322–2121). New $28-million downtown hotel with underground parking. 262 rooms and villas, gourmet restaurant, cafe, meeting and convention facilities.

Sheraton Plaza. *Deluxe.* 400 E. Tahquitz Way, Palm Springs, CA 92262 (619–320–6868; 800–325–3535). The cool, white marble elegance of this plant-filled 263-unit resort hotel just off Palm Canyon Drive, plus its two superb restaurants make this a top choice for the city. Tennis, swimming, Jacuzzi.

Spa Hotel and Mineral Springs. *Deluxe.* 100 N. Indian Ave., Palm Springs, CA 92262 (619–325–1461). Gym, mineral baths, therapeutic pool, 35 swirlpool tubs, massages, entertainment.

Jerry Buss' Ocotillo Lodge. *Expensive.* 1111 E. Palm Canyon Dr., Palm Springs, CA 92262 (619–327–1141). An elegant, relaxing hostelry nestled at the foot of the San Jacinto Mts. Suites, bungalows, villas, (each has own sitting-room bedroom, kitchen, and patio or lanai). Restaurant, cocktail lounge, poolside bar, tennis, and golf privileges nearby.

Tiki Spa Hotel & Apts. *Moderate.* 1910 S. Camino Real, Palm Springs, CA 92262 (619–327–1349). Sauna, hot tub, family-owned business with small restaurant—serves breakfast and lunch.

Villa Royale. *Moderate.* 1620 Indian Trail, Palm Springs, CA 92264 (619–327–2314). Small and charming with 21 units each individually decorated in an international theme.

RIVERSIDE. Holiday Inn. *Moderate.* 1200 University Ave., Riverside, CA 92507 (714–682–8000). Branch of chain. Pleasant rooms. Suites. Restaurant, bar. Pool (heated). Pets accepted. 207 rooms.

Howard Johnson's Motor Lodge. *Moderate.* 1199 University Ave., Riverside, CA 92507 (714–682–9011). Double-decker motel with nicely furnished rooms. Restaurant, bar. Pool (heated), wading pool.

Park Inn International. *Moderate.* 1150 University Ave., Riverside, CA 92507 (714–682–2771). Tastefully decorated rooms. Restaurant, bar with dancing. Pool (heated).

SAN BERNARDINO. Inland Empire Hilton. *Expensive.* 285 E. Hospitality Lane, San Bernardino, CA 92408 (714–889–0133). 245 luxurious rooms, pool, jacuzzi, French restaurant. Luxurious rooms, in-room steam baths. Rim o' the World Highway is a 45-mile mountain highway to Big Bear Lake and Lake Arrowhead.

SAN JUAN CAPISTRANO. Best Western Capistrano Inn. *Deluxe.* 27174 Ortega Hwy., San Juan Capistrano, CA 92675 (714–993–5661). 108-room two-story property with pool, whirlpool. Some pets. 24-hour restaurant adjacent.

Country Bay Inn. *Deluxe.* 34862 Pacific Coast Hwy., Capistrano Beach, CA 92624 (714–496–6656). Bed and breakfast. Wood-burning fireplaces in each room. Brass headboards, balconies, patios. Jacuzzi. Gracious hospitality. Capistrano Beach.

SAN LUIS OBISPO. San Luis Bay Inn. *Deluxe.* Box 189, Avila Beach, CA 93424 (805–595–2333; 800–592–5928). A classic seaside resort with rooms and suites offering breathtaking views. Sunken tubs, 18-hole golf course, pool. Seafood and steak restaurant. 76 rooms.

Country House Inn. *Expensive.* 91 Main St., Box 179, Templeton, CA 93465 (805–434–1598). Built in 1886, this quaint village inn boasts 11 foot ceilings and is filled with antiques and fresh flowers. Lovely gardens. No smoking except out on the porch. Six rooms.

Heritage Inn. *Expensive.* 978 Olive Ave., San Luis Obispo, CA 93401 (805–544–7440). Turn-of-the-century bed-and-breakfast offers rooms packed with antiques. Continental breakfast. Nine rooms, one with private bath; the rest are shared.

Madonna Inn. *Expensive.* 100 Madonna Rd., San Luis Obispo, CA 93401 (805–543–3000). Favorite place for honeymoon couples and those who love kitch. One of a kind, very fantasy-oriented with themed rooms—some rather garish. 109 rooms. Four restaurants, lounge, candy bar for kids.

SAN SIMEON. Reservations advisable during summer season, when tourists flock to see Hearst Castle.

Cavalier Inn Best Western. *Expensive.* 9415 Hearst Dr., San Simeon, CA 93452 (805–927–4688). Two heated outdoor pools, a spa, patios, fireplaces. 5 minutes from Hearst Castle. Restaurant. 3½ miles south of town on Hwy. 1.

Friendship Inn Silver Surf Motel. *Moderate.* 9390 Castillo Dr., San Simeon, CA 93452 (805–927–4661). Three miles south of the castle. Garden patio motel in ocean setting, indoor pool, Jacuzzi, restaurants nearby. 72 rooms.

San Simeon Lodge. *Moderate.* 9520 Castillo Dr., San Simeon, CA 93452 (805–927–4601). 3½ miles south of town on Hwy. 1. Close to Hearst Castle. Overlooks ocean with nearby deep-sea fishing, abalone hunting, swimming pool.

SANTA BARBARA. Besides plenty of major hotels in this lovely city, there are many bed & breakfast establishments. For a complete list, write Bed &

Breakfast Innkeepers Guild of Santa Barbara, Box 20246, Santa Barbara, CA 93120.

Four Seasons Biltmore. *Deluxe.* 1260 Channel Dr., Santa Barbara, CA 93108 (805–969–2261). Luxurious accommodations in traditional elegant style. Hotel rooms and cottages, private beach (across street), two pools, complementary bicycles, golf & tennis privileges. Famous, aristocratic hotel opened in 1927, recently renovated.

The Old Yacht Club Inn. *Expensive.* 431 Corona Del Mar, Santa Barbara, CA 93103 (805–962–1277). Bed-and-breakfast half block from the beach. Fresh flowers, sherry in each of the nine rooms.

The Glenborough Inn. *Expensive-Moderate.* 1327 Bath St., Santa Barbara, CA 93101 (805–966–0589). Charming inn with beautiful antiques and decor. Complimentary breakfast includes freshly squeezed juices and fresh-baked breads. Hot tub. Nine rooms.

The Parsonage. *Expensive-Moderate.* 1600 Olive St., Santa Barbara, CA 93101 (805–962–9336). This quaint bed & breakfast establishment was built in 1892 as a parsonage. Nice view of the harbor, private solarium. Six rooms.

El Escorial Hotel. *Moderate.* 625 Por La Mar Circle, Santa Barbara, CA 93101 (805–963–9302). Near beach and golf. Tennis, pool, Jacuzzi, rec room with billiards, bicycles. 312 suites with balconies.

Santa Barbara Inn. *Moderate.* 435 S. Milpas St., Santa Barbara, CA 93104 (805–966–2285). Triple-story motel on the ocean. Distinctively decorated rooms with balconies. Don the Beachcomber restaurant. Entertainment and dancing. Room service. Pool (heated) with service at poolside. Game room. Wheelchair unit. 71 rooms.

VENTURA. Holiday Inn Beach Resort. *Deluxe.* 450 E. Harbor Blvd., Ventura, CA 93003 (805–648–7731). One of chain. On beach. Pool. Rooftop revolving restaurant. 260 rooms, saunas.

Best Western Ventura Motor Lodge. *Moderate.* 708 East Thompson Blvd., Ventura, CA 93001 (805–648–3101). One block to fishing pier and beach. Pool. 75 rooms.

Pierpont Inn. *Moderate.* 550 San Jon Rd., Ventura, CA 93001 (805–653–6144). Walking distance to the beach. Tennis at adjacent tennis club. Excellent restaurant.

Visalia

Lamp-Liter Inn. *Moderate.* 3300 W. Mineral King Ave., Visalia, CA 93291 (209–732–4511). Air conditioning.TV, pool, dining room, coffee shop, lounge.

Travel Lodge Motel. *Moderate.* 4645 W. Mineral King Ave., Visalia, CA 93291 (209–732–5611). Pool, coffee shop and dining room.

GUEST RANCHES. Circle Bar B Guest Ranch. 1800 Refugio Rd., Goleta, CA 93117 (805–968–1113). On the mountainside 3 miles up Refugio Canyon, 22 miles north of Santa Barbara, where a car meets you.

Apple Valley Inn. 20600 Hwy. 18, Apple Valley, CA 92307 (619–247–7271). Five miles from Victorville on California 18. At the foot of the San Bernardino Mountains in the high desert country. Luxurious accommodations. Swimming, golf, horseback riding, fishing, boating, hayrides, dancing, rifle ranges, etc. Special events with a Western flavor are campfire steak fries, stagecoach rides and hunt breakfasts. World's largest display of mounted longhorns plus a large collection of paintings, hunting trophies and mementoes of Roy Rogers and Dale Evans.

San Ysidro Ranch. 900 San Ysidro Lane, Montecito, CA 93108 (805–969–5046). A secret hideaway nestled in the foothills of the Santa Ynez Mountains, about 15 minutes from the heart of Santa Barbara. It is here that John and Jackie Kennedy honeymooned. Exquisite cottages offer complete privacy and panoramic mountain views.

Cholame Creek Ranch. Box 8-R, Cholame, CA 93451 (805–463–2320). A 5,000-acre homestead about three hours north of Los Angeles. Ranch house or bunkhouse lodging. Summer for children only, balance of year for all ages. All kinds of ranch chores: branding, camping, nearby Indian sites.

The Alisal. 1054 Alisal Rd., Solvang, CA 93463 (805–688–6411). On 100,000 acres of rolling hills. Situated in the Santa Ynez Valley, the guest ranch offers swimming pool, 18-hole golf course, riding horses, sailing, fishing and even weddings and receptions.

Zaca Lake Resort. Box 187, Los Olivos, CA 93441 (805–688–4891). About 40 miles north of Santa Barbara. A quiet retreat with *no* phones or TV; instead you'll find cozy log cabins with fireplaces, tennis, hiking, swimming, fishing, horses, row boats and candlelight dining.

HEALTH SPAS. Southern California boasts more health and reducing spas per potbelly and double chin than any other state in the nation. There's a spa tailored to fit every bulging waistline and budget, and to cater to almost all your needs. If your shape could use some remodeling—and your body a little rejuvenation—a visit to one of the area's top spas could be just what you need. Prices range from super-expensive, $1500-per-week luxury establishments, to moderately-priced $29-a-day economy spas. Be sure to make reservations well in advance as these are among the most popular spas in the world.

The Golden Door. *Super Deluxe.* Box 1567, Escondido, CA 92025 (619–744–5777). Probably the most expensive spa in the world $3000 a week. Designed as a Japanese Honjin Inn, Deborah Szekely's posh retreat—a 40-minute drive from San Diego Airport—caters to the rich and famous. Sunday-Sunday week includes individualized exercise schedules, beauty treatments (facials to pedicures), low-calorie gourmet meals, and endless pampering. Co-ed programs offered six times a year. Men's weeks number eight. Women only otherwise.

La Costa Resort Hotel & Spa. *Super Deluxe.* 2100 Costa Del Mar Rd., Carlsbad, CA 92009 (619–438–9111). An hour from San Diego. Another posh retreat with rates from $130 to $750 a day. Weekly rate is $2000 per person, single occupancy and $1,500 per person, double occupancy. Price includes exercise classes, beauty treatments, low-calorie gourmet meals, lodging, golf and tennis fees. Nightlife at La Costa is more active than at most spas. Dine among strolling violinists and dance to band music.

The Ashram. *Expensive.* 2025 McKain St., Box 8009, Calabasas, CA 91302 (818–888–0232). Hidden in hills above famous Malibu Beach. For staunch fitness/health buffs only who can endure Dr. Anne-Marie Bennstrom's rigorous daily routine—hiking, calisthenics, jogging. Also yoga, meditation, and massage are included in the weekly rate, which is about $1,500, along with low-calorie vegetarian diet.

Monaco Villa Reducing Resort. *Expensive.* 371 Camino Monte Vista, Palm Springs, CA 92262 (619–327–1261). Features a variety of low-calorie, fitness and exercise programs as well as hot therapy and massages. Cost: $95 per person, per day. Seven units.

The Palms at Palm Springs. *Moderate to Expensive.* 572 N. Indian Ave., Palm Springs, CA 92262 (619–325–1111). This spa shares many similarities with the Oaks at Ojai. Slightly higher rates; location a big plus. All shopping, sports and sightseeing activities nearby in Palm Springs. Twelve fitness programs each day together with personalized attention and healthy food.

Zane Haven. *Moderate-Expensive.* Box 2031, Palm Springs, CA 92263 (619–323–7486). Weight training and fitness program. Aerobics and stretching in a fully equipped gym. Nutritional counseling too. Sessions limited to eight people. Facilities include swimming pool, sunbathing deck and sauna. Zane Haven is a 15-minute walk from downtown Palm Springs.

Meadowlark Health and Growth Center. *Moderate.* Meadowlark Center for Holistic Health, 26126 Fairview Ave., Hemet, CA 92344 (714–927–1343). One- or two-week rejuvenation programs on this 20-acre country estate at the foot of the San Jacinto Mountains. Cottages, rest, exercise, dining. A host of activities include medically supervised fasting, body awareness, nutrition classes, yoga, meditation.

Rancho La Puerta. *Moderate.* Located in Tecate, Baja, Mexico. For reservations, write to 3085 Reynard Way, San Diego, CA 92103 (619–294–8504). Just south of the San Diego border in a sleepy little Mexican village is this coed fitness ranch—operated by Golden Door's Deborah Szekely. Offers a "Sunday Check-in" for a five or seven day stay. Rates start at $1039 per person weekly. You're on your own to partake of fitness classes that run round the clock from 6:30 A.M.–5 P.M. Daily rate includes any/all classes, vegetarian diet, and use of all facilities. Massage, facials, etc. are extra.

The Oaks at Ojai. *Expensive.* 122 East Ojai Ave., Ojai, CA 93002 (805–646–5573). Daily rates include accommodations, medical supervision, low-cal meals, personalized weight control program, and use of all facilities. About an hour from Santa Barbara this elegant hotel was first built in 1920 and recently reconstructed.

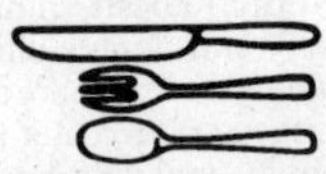

RESTAURANTS. Dining out in Southern California is bound to be as exotic culinary experience—with hundreds of elaborate and chic restaurants to choose from for lunch or dinner. Since you're near Mexico, try some south of the border dishes; and since you're on the Pacific coast, look for specialties from China, Japan, and Polynesia, too. Restaurants are listed alphabetically according to location and then according to price category. The categories, based on the cost of a complete meal for one, without beverage, tax, or tip, are: *Expensive,* $16 and up; *Moderate,* $10–$16; and *Inexpensive,* under $10.

BAKERSFIELD. Maison Jaussaud. *Expensive.* 1001 South Union Ave. (805–327–3041). Continental menu, steak, prime rib, Rock Cornish hen specialties. Background music, dancing, entertainment in lounge. A warm, romantic (candle-lighted) setting.

BUELLTON. Pea Soup Andersen's. *Expensive.* 376 Avenue of Flags (805–688–5581). A great split-pea soup started it all. Chicken Forester and other specialties expand the reputation. Good breakfasts. Cocktails, wine cellar. Gift shop.

CORONA DEL MAR. Five Crowns. *Expensive.* 3801 E. Pacific Coast Hwy. (714–760–0331). English-American. Fine restaurant. Prime rib. Replica of a 12th-century inn at Hurly-on-Thames. Fine premium California wines, English beer.

CUCAMONGA. Magic Lamp Inn. *Moderate* 8189 Foothill (714–981–8659). Charcoal-broiler cuisine. Old English atmosphere. Closed Mon.

HEMET. The Embers. *Moderate.* 828 W. Florida Ave. (714–658–2242). Steak and prime ribs are house staples. Buffet lunch weekdays; Sun. brunch.

LAGUNA BEACH. The Towers Restaurant. *Expensive.* 1555 South Coast Hwy. (714–497–4477). Intimate dining with a view of the ocean. Specialties: Steak, rack of lamb, totuava sea bass. In the Surf and Sand Hotel. Reservations please!

Las Brisas. *Expensive-Moderate.* 361 Cliff Dr. (714–497–5434). Right off the Coast Hwy., north of the junction with Route 133. On the cliffs for Mexican cuisine. Lots of seafood and veal dishes. If you can book reservations at sunset, do so. The view of the ocean at that time's spectacular.

The Beach House. *Moderate.* 619 Sleepy Hollow Lane (714–494–9707). Ocean views. Serving fresh seafood: fish, lobster, and steamed clams.

The Cottage Restaurant. *Moderate.* 308 N. Coast Hwy. (714–494–3023). Real home cooking in a folksy 70-year old landmark building, formerly the residence of a pioneer area developer. Great breakfast, but crowded. Best brunch place in entire area. But dinner's quite good, too.

OJAI. L'Auberge Restaurant. *Expensive.* 314 El Paseo St. (805–646–2288). French cuisine cooked to perfection. Extensive wine list. Reservations recommended.

The Ranch House. *Moderate-Expensive.* 102 Besant Rd., Ojai (805–646–2360). Superb restaurant hidden in back streets. Wine deck, concerts. People travel 100 miles to dine here. Reservations essential.

The Gaslight Restaurant. *Moderate.* 11432 N. Ventura Ave., Ojai (805–646–5990). Veal, steak, fresh seafood and German dishes are specialties. Reservations recommended.

Ojai Valley Inn and Country Club. *Moderate.* Country Club Dr., Ojai (805–646–5511). Fine country club-style dining room with American specialties.

ORANGE. Chez Cary Restaurant. *Expensive.* 571 S. Main St., Orange (714–542–3595). Plush red-velvet and walnut-decorated dining room. Fresh flowers and an air of quiet splendor. Continental cuisine attractively served. Musical quartet weekdays. Fine wine list. Flaming desserts.

The Hobbit. *Expensive.* 2932 E. Chapman Ave., Orange (714–997–1972). Continental-style dining in a charming house. Champagne and hors d'oeuvres in the wine cellar. Art gallery. Reservations must usually be made four to five months in advance.

OXNARD/CHANNEL ISLANDS Lobster Trap. *Moderate.* 3605 Peninsula Rd. (805–985–6361). In the Casa Sirena Marina Hotel. Features owner's "catch-of-the-day," oyster steak, stuffed abalone. Champagne brunch Sun. View of marina.

Mandarin House. *Moderate.* 475 W. Channel Islands Blvd. (805–985–5955). Mandarin as well as Szechuan selections.

Reubens. *Moderate.* 3910 W. Channel Islands Blvd., Channel Islands (805–985–3922). Dine on the docks in full harbor view. Fresh seafood eaten amid nautical decor. Fisherman's Wharf.

The Whale's Tail. *Moderate.* 3950 Bluefin Circle (805–985–2511). Elaborate Salad Boat and menu of beef and seafood along with nightly entertainment is offered at this Channel Islands Harbor restaurant.

PALM SPRINGS AND VICINITY. Mancuso's. *Expensive.* 72–281 Highway 111, Palm Desert (619–340–6610). Northern Italian, French, and continental cuisines served in an elegant environment enhanced with royal-blue velvet and fine crystal. Veal dishes are recommended. Valet parking.

Melvyn's Restaurant, Ingleside Inn. *Expensive.* 200 W. Ramon, Palm Springs (619–325–2323). Trés elegant atmosphere with fine, gourmet food to match. Indoor or outdoor dining, piano bar, lounge, weekend brunch. Be sure to dress up for this one. Terrific place.

Trattoria. *Expensive.* At Grand Champions, 44–600 Indian Wells Lane, Indian Wells (619–341–1000). Excellent informal eatery built around an exhibition kitchen. A wood-burning oven beckons with the pleasant aroma of scorched mesquite. Imaginative pizzas, pastas.

Alfredo's. *Moderate.* 292 E. Palm Canyon Dr., Palm Springs (619–320–1020). This used to be a neon-and-linoleum pizza and sub parlor, and regulars are amazed at how cleverly it's been converted into a new pint-size dining spot smacking of big-city style. Salads are great, as are chicken wings with mild-to-hot sauce.

Las Casuelas Nuevas. *Moderate.* 70–050 Highway 111, Rancho Mirage (619–328–8844). Mexican. Delicious food served in a fun and traditionally Mexican ambiance.

Lyon's English Grille. *Moderate.* 233 E. Palm Canyon Dr., Palm Springs (619–327–1551). Dinner reservations suggested. English décor, menu, and serving wenches. Hearty 18th-century fare.

Two Bunch Palms. *Moderate.* 67–425 Two Bunch Palms Trail, Desert Hot Springs (619–329–8791). This is the kind of place you like to keep secret because it's small and so good crowds are bound to spoil it. It's a hideaway health resort that asks 24-hour notice for dinner, but the bother is worth it. Meals are prepared by a fabulous chef and served in a quiet, lodgelike room filled with antiques.

SAN BERNARDINO. The Gourmet. *Moderate.* 1445 E. Highland Ave. (714–883–2613). Delightful restaurant. Greek cuisine. Entertainment. Children's portions.

SAN JUAN CAPISTRANO. El Adobe. *Moderate.* 31891 Camino Capistrano (714–830–8620). Early California cuisine. Historic structure. Mexican dance band weekends. Reservations.

Walnut Grove Restaurant. *Inexpensive.* 26871 Ortega Hwy. (714–493–1661). Family-type foods. Own pastry. Spanish-style setting.

SANTA BARBARA. Four Seasons Biltmore Restaurant. *Expensive.* 1260 Channel Dr. (805–969–2261). Excellent gourmet dining in elegant atmosphere. Lamb specialty as well as prime rib and beef bourguignon.

The Plow and Angel. *Expensive.* 900 San Ysidro Lane, Montecito (805–969–5046). At the San Ysidro Ranch. An exquisite French restaurant. Intimate, decorative and what's more, excellent cuisine.

Casa del Sevilla. *Moderate.* 428 Chapala St. (805–966–4370). Comfortable dining featuring Spanish-style and Continental cuisine.

SOLVANG. Ballard's Store. *Moderate.* 2449 Baseline (805/688–5319). This former country store roams the world with delights like Long Island duckling and beef roulade.

Continental Inn. *Moderate.* 1646 Copenhagen Dr. (805–688–5410 or 688–9077). Danish from appetizers to dessert. Hearty breakfast, lunch, and dinner menu.

Danish Inn. *Moderate.* 1547 Mission Dr. (805–688–4813). Delicious smorgasbord. Reservations suggested.

Mollenkroen Restaurant. *Inexpensive.* 435 Alisal Rd. (805–688–4555). Modeled after a European sidewalk cafe, this bistro features Belgian waffles. Solvang fruit wines.

VENTURA. Hungry Hunter. *Moderate.* 2046 E. Harbor (805–648–5146). Prime ribs and steaks set the mood.

Pierpont Inn. *Moderate.* 550 San Jon (805–653–6144). Overlooks the ocean. Fine prime ribs, seafood, entertainment some evenings, cocktails. Rustic decor.

El Torito. *Moderate.* 770 S. Seaward Ave. (805–648–5219). Old-world Mexican restaurant where terrific Sonora-style Mexican food is served. Try a Margarita.

TOURIST INFORMATION SERVICES. Some useful material can be obtained from The Greater Los Angeles Visitors and Convention Bureau, 505 S. Flower St., L.A. 90071. Good information also available from the visitors' bureaus of Palm Springs, Oxnard, Ventura and Santa Barbara. See "Tourist Information" in the Los Angeles Practical Information section. For information on the National Forest Campgrounds in California write the Regional Forester, 630 Sansome St., San Francisco, CA 94111 (415–556–0122). For a small fee you can obtain a booklet about California's 800 historical landmarks from the Division of Beaches and Parks, P.O. Box 2390, Sacramento, Calif. 95814. Pacific Gas and Electric Co., San Francisco, issues an excellent booklet, *California's Historical Monuments.*

SEASONAL EVENTS. *January:* Tournament of Roses, 391 S. Orange Grove, Pasadena. Annual parade of floats and femininity the morning of New Year's Day, followed by the Rose Bowl football game that afternoon. Reserved seats may be bought. Many people camp out with stoves, sleeping bags, chairs, etc., on the sidewalk a day in advance to secure ideal viewing sites. If you're in town a few days before the parade, visit car barns throughout Pasadena to watch around-the-clock crews attach flowers to the floats, and to see where the drivers sit and what their view looks like. Chinese New Year, Los Angeles Chinatown. Horse Racing, Santa Anita Park, Arcadia. Los Angeles Philharmonic Orchestra Season, Los Angeles Music Center. Andy Williams-PGA Golf Tournament, San Diego. San Diego National Symphony Orchestra Season, San Diego. Sled Dog Races, Aerial Tramway, Palm Springs. Colgate Triple Crown Women's Golf Tournament, Palm Springs, Mounted Police Rodeo of Stars, Palm Springs, National Intercollegiate Tennis Classic, Palm Springs.

February: Bob Hope Desert Golf Classic, Palm Springs. Laguna Beach Winter Festival, Laguna Beach. Whale migration, San Diego and Los Angeles viewing points. National Date Festival, Indio, with a Slave Girl Mart, camel races nightly. Michelob Pro-Celebrity Tennis Tournament, La Costa Country Club, La Costa. Glen Campbell-Los Angeles. A premier tennis match, the Pilot Pen Classic, Indian Wells (Palm Springs).

March: Annual All City Kite Tournament, Long Beach. Fiesta de Golondrina, San Juan Capistrano. (Return of the Swallows). National Orange Show, an 11-day event in San Bernardino, features crafts exhibits, flower shows, sports events and live entertainment. Annual Michelob Desert Polo Classic, Eldorado Polo Club, Palm Springs.

April: Dodger Baseball, Dodger Stadium, Los Angeles (through Sept.). Stewart's Annual April Orchid Festival, San Diego. Thoroughbred Racing, Hollywood Park, Inglewood (through July). Blessing of the Animals, Los Angeles. Easter Sunrise Services, Hollywood, San Diego, and Palm Springs. Tournament of Champions Golf Classic, La Costa Golf Resort, La Costa. Annual Ramona Pageant, in Ramona Bowl, about two miles southeast of Hemet; late April-early spring. Renaissance Pleasure Faire, Paramount Ranch, Agoura (thru May).

The young set captures the Faire's Medieval and Renaissance spirit by wearing costumes. You'll have great fun sampling the foods, and taking in the crafts, plays, and music.

May: L.A. Civic Light Opera, Music Center, L.A. (thru Oct.). Cinco de Mayo, Los Angeles, San Diego, and Knott's Berry Farm, Buena Park. Westwood Sidewalk "Living Crafts Show," Westwood Village. Ojai Music Festival, Ojai. Turtle Races, Joshua Tree. Paso Robles Wine Festival.

June: Annual All City Outdoor Art Festival, Los Angeles. Highland Gathering and Games, Santa Monica. Southern California Exposition (a giant country fair), Del Mar. San Diego National Shakespeare Festival begins performances with flourishes of trumpets and banners amid sunshine and palm trees to recreate a bit of American Merrie Olde England's theater. Prior to performances, singing and dancing, in the sixteenth-century manner, are presented "on the green." Mid-June through Sept. Redlands Bowl Summer Musical Festival, Redlands. "Semana Nautica" Summer Sports Festival, Santa Barbara. Sports from speedboat races to sports-car racing.

July: Greek Theatre Outdoor Summer Concerts, Greek Theatre, Los Angeles (through Aug.). Hollywood Bowl Summer Concerts, Hollywood Bowl, Los Angeles (through Sept.). Festival of the Arts at Laguna Beach. This noted art colony puts on a splash of art display during July and half of Aug. Its Pageant of the Masters recreates famous paintings and sculptures life-size with residents posed as the subjects of the great art works. Del Mar Turf Club Thoroughbred Racing Season (through Sept.). Indian Dance Festival, Mission Santa Barbara, Santa Barbara. Over-the-Line Softball Tournament, San Diego. Miss Tramway Beauty Pageant, Aerial Tramway, Palm Springs.

August: California International Sea Festival, Long Beach. Old Spanish Days Fiesta transforms the city into Old Spanish atmosphere and mood, Santa Barbara. World Tournament Softball Championships, Long Beach. Mozart Festival, San Luis Obispo. Morro Bay's annual three-day antique show, first weekend of month.

September: Night Harness Racing, Hollywood Park, Inglewood (through Dec.). Los Angeles County Fair, Pomona. Danish Days in Solvang, Solvang. Westwood Village Art Festival, Westwood Village. L.A. Rams football, Los

Angeles Coliseum. Kern County Fair, Kern County Fairgrounds, Bakersfield. Fireman's Challenge, Morro Bay.

October: Oak Tree Thoroughbred Racing, Santa Anita Park, Arcadia. San Antonio Winery's Anniversary Festival, Los Angeles. Space Fair, Naval Air Station, Point Mugu. Open House, University of California at Los Angeles, West Los Angeles, usually takes place on a Sun. in late Oct. It offers fascinating glimpses into what is being researched and accomplished in higher education in our society today and displays of exact replicas of Leonardo da Vinci's inventions and experiments. Come early: it's mobbed.

November: Fiesta de la Cuadrilla, San Diego: *Los Angeles Times* NASCAR 500, Ontario Motor Speedway. National Senior Hardcourt Tennis Championships, La Jolla Beach & Tennis Club. Santa Claus Lane Parade, in the heart of downtown Hollywood, features Tinsel Town celebrities, lavish floats and, of course, Saint Nick himself. Fun for kids and adults alike.

December: Christmas Float Parade, San Pedro. Horse Racing, Santa Anita Park, Arcadia. Naples Christmas Parade of Lighted Boats, Alamitos Bay, Long Beach. Mission Bay Christmas Parade, Mission Bay, San Diego. Las Posadas, Olvera St., Los Angeles. Pageant depicting journey of Joseph and Mary to Bethlehem, mid-Dec. to Christmas Eve.

NATIONAL PARKS AND MONUMENTS. California counts her blessings in having seven National Parks and eight National Monuments. How many of these are located in Southern California depends on whose north-south demarcation is considered. Many writers, historians and politicians use the east-west Tehachapi range, northeast of Santa Barbara, as the dividing line. Others claim the ten counties whose northern boundaries parallel the 36-degree latitude shortly to the north. And there are those who include the four counties bordering the southern ten. The California Information Almanac, a state textbook, excludes Santa Barbara and San Luis Obispo counties and a portion of Kern county. It includes Inyo and part of Mono county. This interpretation extends a panhandle of Southern California on the east all the way north to a parallel with San Francisco!

Sequoia and Kings Canyon National Parks are in Southern California when one of the more generous measures mentioned above is applied. Sequoia has a Visitor Center that will provide you with advice on sightseeing. Helpful data and photographs are displayed. Campfire gatherings at night. Housekeeping cabins (European plan) at Camp Kaweah, where there are also a coffee shop, grocery store, gas, gift shop, all open all year. Giant Forest Lodge (American and European plan) and Giant Grove Lodge (European plan) open about May 24 to Oct. 25. At Kings Canyon, the lodge, cabins and housekeeping cabins keep approximately the same dates and have similar facilities. For additional information write: Sequoia Kings Canyon National Parks, Three Rivers, Calif. 93271.

Death Valley National Monument, awesome and historic, bakes up in the Southern California panhandle that pokes northward in the east. It's weird, spooky, and memorable and covers almost two million acres. Death Valley is actually a lively place with many facilities from rough to resort. The Visitor Center (619–786–2331) is open year around.

Joshua Tree National Monument, a 557,992-acre sprawl, preserves the unique yucca species, named by pioneering Mormons to whom its arms seemed raised in supplication, in the manner of Joshua in the Bible. The Visitor Center (619–367–7511) is at Twenty-nine Palms, and there are more than a dozen campgrounds on the valley floor. Fill the tank before entering.

The Channel Islands of Anacapa, Santa Barbara, Santa Cruz, Santa Rose and San Miguel now comprise California's newest National Park, consisting of some 18,000 acres. Anacapa and Santa Barbara were set aside in 1936 by President Roosevelt as a National Monument. On March 5, 1980, President Carter signed Public Law 96–199 establishing the Channel Islands National Park. At the Park headquarters in Ventura Harbor, there is a small visitors' center with a slide presentation showing the pinnipeds (seals and sea lions), other fauna and flora, and the beauty of the Park islands (805–642–8618). All-day boat trips are scheduled from the Ventura Harbor aboard Island Packer Cruises (1867 Spinnaker Dr., Ventura CA 93001, (805–642–1393).

Cabrillo National Monument is without doubt in Southern California. It's a memorial, in the form of the Old Point Loma Lighthouse, to Juan Rodriguez Cabrillo, the Portuguese mariner serving Spain who discovered present San Diego Bay. The ocean view is top mast, and whale-watching is another exciting pleasure from mid-December through mid-February. Pack a picnic—it'll never taste better (619–557–5450).

One warning: If you're hiking without a guide, go prepared with map and compass. Trail guides and maps can be purchased at visitor centers. For safety, register at trailheads. Tell a responsible person where you are going and when you can be expected to return. On long hikes carry rainwear, extra woolen clothing, and food. If lost, hurt, or caught by fog or darkness, don't panic. Just wait. Don't go rushing off. Wait. Before you do anything, collect yourself. If you keep your cool, the chances of being found soon are excellent. Build a fire and stay by it. Rescuers will find you. This cautionary note applies to all other national parks, national forests, and other wilderness areas.

For a free booklet on camping in California's national park system, write to the U.S. National Park Service, 22900 Ventura Blvd., Suite 140, Woodland Hills, CA 91364.

NATIONAL FORESTS. California is 18½ times blessed with National Forests. Their nearly 20 million acres are outnumbered nationally only by those of Idaho and Alaska. Southern California has a couple million acres less than the northern part of the state. All the forests are open for picnicking and camping with more than 1,000 campgrounds on a first-come, first-camp basis. Licensed fishing and hunting are permitted. The areas also offer swimming, boating, hiking, rockhounding, horseback riding, sightseeing, and snoozing. Their winter sports often attract more winter visitors than summer.

Inyo National Forest (619–347–2480) in the northeastern panhandle of Southern California, is the largest in the Southland. It has approximately 1,891,000 acres and pokes a bit into Nevada. Inyo contains Palisades Glacier. This is the farthest south glaciers venture into this country. Among Inyo's winter playgrounds are *McGee Mountain, Mammoth, Big Pine,* and *June Lake.*

Sierra National Forest's (209–487–5456) ponderosa pines and blue oaks begin where Inyo leaves off. The area presents winter and summer recreation in rough or resort fashion. *Sequoia and King's Canyon National Park,* (209–565–3341) Sierra's neighbor to the south, is another million-acres-plus attraction, with reason to attend every season.

Los Padres National Forest (805–245–3449) switches the forest scenery to the Pacific coast, with *Mt. Pinos* and *Mt. Abel* for winter people, and ocean swimming and jade-hounding for summer folk. There's a Wild Area for the robust. *Angeles National Forest,* (818–574–1613) inland from Los Angeles, is a ski-see and sun-fun place.

San Bernardino National Forest (714–383–5588), one of the smaller in acreage, is big in vistas with its *Rim of the World Drive.* For the wintry elves there's *Snow Valley* (714–867–5111) *Big Bear,* and others. Winter-summer visitors enjoy sporty-resorty *Lake Arrowhead* (714–866–3671).

Cleveland National Forest, (619–293–5050) deepest in the California Southland, intrigues with ocean-desert sights. *Laguna Mt. Recreation Area* (619–473–8533).

STATE PARKS. The nation's first state park was established in California in 1864–65 after Congress issued a grant, signed by President Abraham Lincoln, permitting the state to maintain the famed Yosemite Valley and the Mariposa Grove of giant sequoias for perpetual public use. Four decades later, California added the land to the surrounding Yosemite National Park created in 1890.

Today, California's State Park system involves more than 200 units spread over 850,000 acres of mountains and valleys, lakes and plateaus, rivers and deserts, forests and beaches. It also embraces many famous landmarks of the state's historical heritage.

Two types of campgrounds exist in the parks. *Developed* sites include hot showers, laundries, stoves, tables, piped drinking water, and flush toilets. *Primitive* campsites offer a central water supply, tables, pit toilets. Maximum stay is 15 days, less in smaller camping areas and during peak summer months. Dogs, on leash, permitted during daylight hours only. At night your dog must stay inside your tent or in an enclosed vehicle.

Among the varied designations of California's state parks are Ocean, Ocean-Beach, Scenery, Ocean-Scenery, Desert-Scenery, Mountain-Scenery, Redwoods, Historical, Forest, Foothills-Forest, River, Lake, Coastal, Reserve, Wild and Wilderness. (However, California's 12 Wild and five Wilderness Areas are all within National Forests.) About half of the state parks are in Southern California, mostly strung along the Pacific Coast as beach parks. Using one of the controversial Southern California measures, the beach parks form a seashell bracelet from *San Simeon Beach* down to San Diego's *Silver Strand* and *Imperial Beach,* a hot-tamale toss from Old Mexico.

Reservations for state parks at Ticketron at Sears, Broadway Dept. Stores, Montgomery Ward; or write Ticketron, P.O. Box 2715, San Francisco, CA 94126.

Anza-Borrego Desert Park, (619–767–5311) 94 miles northeast from San Diego, reigns as the state-park system's undisputable giant. Its nearly half-million acres boast 183 campsites and 34 picnic sites stashed amidst its virgin wilderness. Illustrated lectures and guided nature walks are conducted by state-park naturalists on weekends, Oct. through May. Most popular self-guided hike is the one to Palm Canyon, where the only variety of palms native to California flourishes a thousand strong. Elephant trees trod the terrain. "Flaming Swords" slash crimson the vistas. These are only three among the 500 flora species in this native habitat of the Borrego desert bighorn sheep.

Cuyamaca Rancho State Park, (619–765–0755) between San Diego and Borrego, offers forested mountains, hiking, fishing, winter sports, 179 campsites and 142 picnic facilities, at 4,960 feet.

Salton Sea State Recreation Area, (619–393–3052) beyond Borrego, a water and sand playpen at 234 feet below sea level, was formed by the overflowing Colorado River in 1905. It has become the most important inland boating center. Camping, water-skiing, swimming, fishing. Very high summer temperatures. Heavenly early and late in the year.

Will Rogers State Historic Park, (213–454–8212) 14253 Sunset Blvd., Pacific Palisades, enshrines the beloved cowboy philosopher's ranch home and mementos. "Never met a man I didn't like," said Will. Folks must feel likewise toward him. Over 225,000 visitors come callin' at his house yearly. Open daily from 8 A.M. to 7 P.M.

A current California State Park Camping Guide is available for $2 at most state park units or from the Department of Parks and Recreation, P.O. Box 2390, Sacramento, CA 95811 (916–445–6477). Reservations may be made by applying in person to any local Ticketron outlet.

CAMPING OUT. Californians think nothing of traveling several hundred miles for a week-end trip that in the East would take you across several state borders. Since the state also attracts a large mobile population from the rest of the U.S. as well, there are many state parks that offer camping facilities. A complete list is available free from the *Division of Beaches and Parks,* State Dept. of Parks and Recreation, P.O. Box 2390, Sacramento 95811. Information by phone: Los Angeles, (213–620–3342) (Division Parks and Recreation), San Diego, (619–237–7411).

The state has approximately 8,500 campsites, and Southern California's share is many and varied. San-duned *Pismo State Beach* (805–489–2684) south of San Luis Obispo, contains 143 campsites and 89 trailer units tucked amidst shrubs and trees along its six-mile beach.

At *Carpinteria Beach State Park* (805–684–2811), 12 mi. east of Santa Barbara, 92 sites and 25 trailer units invite campers. Grunion runs are among the best in the state; also fishing and swimming.

Leo Carillo State Beach Park, (818–706–1310) 12 mi. west of Malibu, scatters 140 sites throughout its 1,500 acres. Great surfing and fishing.

Doheny Beach State Park, (714–496–6171) an hour south of Los Angeles, has 120 campsites perched on its sea walls. Excellent surfing, fishing, swimming.

Nearby *San Clemente Beach State Park* (714–492–3156) presents fantastic cliff-top seascapes from its 83 sites and 70 trailer units. Fine fishing, swimming, skin-diving, beach-combing. Picnic sites and trailer facilities.

The *Cleveland National Forest* (619–293–5050) (San Diego) has 20 campgrounds; most are open all year, with 14-day limit. Some have trailer space. Open April–November, famed *Palomar Observatory* (619–742–3476) has 44 campsites. Reservoirs are stocked with bass and trout. Hunting outside of the game refuge.

"Old Baldy" (altitude: 10,080 ft.) towers over the *Angeles National Forest* (818–574–1613) (Pasadena), which claims approximately 46 campgrounds, most with trailer facilities. Spectacular mountain views, fishing, hunting lure the visitor to this area.

The *San Bernardino National Forest* (714–383–5588) is a study in awesome contrasts with burning desert areas—minutes away from snowcaps. 34 campgrounds, few with trailer facilities.

Generally, admission to State Parks of California costs $1.50 per car for day facilities, $2.00 for overnight in "primitive" areas, $4.00 (overnight) for "developed" areas and $5.00 with hookups (water, electricity, etc.). Facilities include: campgrounds, hot water, showers, trailer hookups and general store.

TRAILER TIPS. *Desert Hot Springs:* Golden Lantern Trailer Lodge, Dillon Rd., therapeutic pools. *Los Angeles:* Inglewood Rolling Homes, Inc., 5875 Rodeo Rd. *North Hollywood:* Valley Trailer Park, 8250 Lankershim Blvd. Adults only, no pets. *Oceanside:* Mission View Mobile Manor, 140 N. River Rd. *Oxnard:* Wagon Wheel Trailer Lodge, 2851 Wagon Wheel Rd. *San Diego:* De Anza Trailer Harbor, 2727 De Anza Rd.; Parking on Mission Bay. *Santa Barbara:* Rancho Santa Barbara, 333 Old Mill Rd. Adults only, no pets. *Santa Monica:* Beck's DeLuxe Trailer Park, 2818 Colorado Ave. Adults only, small pets. *Anaheim:* Vacationland, Ltd., 1343 S. West St., across from Disneyland.

For trailer service and repair: Southwestern RV Repair, E. Cajon (619–561–1880). Thomson's Trailer & Camper Service, 7982 Dagget, San Diego (619–279–7070).

MUSEUMS AND GALLERIES. *Bakersfield:* Kern County Museum, 3801 Chester Ave. Indian artifacts, firearms. *Death Valley:* Death Valley National Monument (619–786–2331): Natural History Museum, charcoal kilns, Harmony Borax Works and Scotty's Castle. *Desert Hot Springs:* Cabot's Old Indian Pueblo 67–616 East Desert View (619–329–7610), is a Hopi-Indian-style structure with a museum, art gallery, and trading post. *Independence:* Eastern California Museum, 155 Grant St. (619–878–2010). Indian artifacts, narrow-gauge steam locomotive. *San Luis Obispo:* County Historical Museum, 696 Monterey St. (805–543–0638).

Art. *Laguna Beach:* Laguna Beach Museum of Art, 307 Cliff Dr. (714–494–6531). Paintings by early California artists. *Santa Barbara:* Santa Barbara Museum of Art, 1130 State St. (805–963–4364).

Special Interest. *Bishop:* Laws Railroad Museum. 5 miles Northeast of Bishop on US 6 (619–873–5950). *Port Hueneme:* Civil Engineer Corps Seabee Museum (805–982–5163). A fascinating memorial to the U.S. Navy Construction Battalions. *Palm Springs:* Desert Museum, 101 Museum Dr. (619–325–7186), has exhibits devoted to the desert. *Santa Barbara:* Museum of Natural History, 2559 Puesta del Sol Rd., County Courthouse, 1120 Anacapa and Anapamu streets (805–682–4711). Spanish-Moorish structure. *Victorville:* Roy Rogers and

Dale Evans Museum, 15650 Seneca Rd., (619–243–4547). You'll see unique memorabilia collected by the handsome duo, such as a $50,000 silver saddle, prize trophies, guns, and longhorns.

HISTORIC SITES. Scattered along the 780-mile length of California are about 44 official State Historical Monuments and approximately 800 Historical Landmarks. Hundreds of federal, private and municipal historic sites also mark the path of California's trek into the present. There is also the "Father Junipero Serra rosary" of 21 missions. Southern California is richly endowed with relics of prehistoric days, of the diverse Indian culture, of the golden age of Spaniards, and of the American pioneers.

Be sure to visit Santa Barbara's adobe Casa de la Guerra, of 1826 vintage. It is in the center of El Paseo, a quaint restoration of an old Spanish shopping center at 19 E. de la Guerra St.

Laws Railroad Museum and Historical Site in Bishop is built on the site of the Old Laws Railroad Depot and Agent's house (619–873–5950). The Depot is filled with many artifacts of the old railroad days, including *Locomotive Number 9* and its little string of cars standing on the original tracks, switches and bunkers. Free.

In Ventura, visit the Archaeological Site and Interpretative Center. At 113 East Main Street, "3,500 years in a city block" includes two audio-visual shows, the exposed foundation of a previously unknown site of Mission San Buenaventura, early Chinatown exhibits and Chumash Indian artifacts. Free; open daily 10–5 except Monday.

Hearst San Simeon State Historical Monument (805–927–4621) has castles, mansions, statuary, art treasures, historical structures, an indoor gold-inlaid Roman pool, magnificent gardens, all on 123 acres. It should be on your "must see" list.

Ft. Tejon, Ft. Tejon State Historical Park, Lebec. See "Missions."

TOURS. By Boat. Sightseeing boat trips are available from the piers and docks at Santa Barbara, Balboa, Marina del Rey, Ventura, Oxnard, Santa Barbara, Long Beach, San Pedro, and Newport Beach. Underwater sea life may be observed on glass-bottom-boat cruises over the California State Marine Preserve. Hydrofoil rides are offered at Mission Bay.

Funicular Rides. Palm Springs Aerial Tramway, located at Tramway Dr. Chino Canyon, (619–325–1391) off Hwy. 111 north. There are special ride and dinner tickets. In summer there are gondola rides up Mammoth Mt. The tram operates a Nordic ski center in the winter months which offers cross-country skiing, equipment rental and instruction.

By Balloon. Tours over the desert are launched from Palm Springs' La Quinta Hotel. Sunrise Balloons, 82–550 Airport Blvd., Thermal, CA 92274 (619–346–7591).

SPECIAL INTEREST TOURS. *Hearst San Simeon State Historical Monument,* Hwy. 1, San Simeon, (805–927–4621) offers a large variety of tours of this magnificent 123-acre estate. Much walking and climbing. Yr. round, except for major holidays. Reservations in advance by mail at Ticketron, P.O. Box 2715, San Francisco, CA 94126.

Lovers of the grape have a new wine-growing area extending from Paso Robles south to Santa Barbara. Hoffman Mountain Ranch has a tasting room in Paso Robles. Solvang is the home of Santa Barbara Winery at 1656 Mission Drive as well as their Santa Barbara winery at 202 Anacapa Street. Dee's Tours offers a complete wine-tasting tour through various wineries in the villages of the valley. 1324 State Street, Suite C, Santa Barbara, CA 93101; (805) 962–9624.

OLD MISSIONS. On Calif. 76, a replica of Mission San Antonio de Pala (Pala Mission Road, Pala 8942300 (619–742–3300) originally Las Asistencia, or outpost, of the Oceanside Mission, still serves the Indians' religious needs and provides schooling for seven neighboring reservations. Thus, it is the only California mission still serving its original purpose.

Mission San Buenaventura, at Ventura, was the ninth mission founded and the last to be dedicated by the Franciscan padre, Father Serra. The date was Easter Sunday, 1782, two years before his death.

Mission Santa Barbara, (2201 Upper Laguna St., Santa Barbara 93015; (805–682–4713) "Queen of the Missions," on a height overlooking sea and city, is considered the state's most photographed building. Its museum and gardens are outstanding. This is the only one of California's missions never abandoned by the Franciscans. A candle has been kept burning on the altar since December 4, 1786.

Mission Santa Inés (Box 408, Solvang 93463 (805–688–4815) 35 miles north of Santa Barbara, is only a bell's call from the Danish-inspired town of Solvang. The beautifully restored mission housed California's first seminary, the College of Our Lady of Refuge. Santa Inés was founded in 1804 and dedicated to the martyred Saint Agnes. Still in use are carved wooden crucifixes, hand-hammered copper and silver altar pieces, and other religious articles crafted on the premises by Indian neophytes. The original mural decorations are rivaled only by those at San Miguel.

Mission La Purísma Concepción, RFD 102, Lompoc 93436 (805–733–3713) is a faithful restoration of the impressive mission that was sadly neglected after the Mexicans sold it at auction in 1845 for $1,000. When the mission was being restored in the 1930s, young men of the Civilian Conservation Corps (CCC) molded more than 100,000 adobe bricks in the manner of the original Indian builders. The mission was founded in 1787, but the original buildings were destroyed in an 1812 earthquake. The hero of the earthquake, Father Mariano Payeras, is buried on the premises.

San Luis Obispo de Tolosa, (Box 1483, San Luis Obispo 93406 (805–543–1034), in the center of the city of San Luis Obispo, was Father Serra's fifth mission, dedicated in 1772. It is believed that tile roofs had their beginning here after the flaming arrows of Indians continually set fire to the original roofs of tule, or rush. Father Serra's vestments and other rare religious items are preserved in the mission museum.

San Miguel Arcángel Mission (Box 69, San Miguel 93451, 805–467–3256) about 10 miles north of Paso Robles, adjacent to the town of San Miguel, is noted for its murals, arches, and for a donkey named Ramona. It is the sixteenth mission, founded in 1797.

San Juan Capistrano (Box 697, San Juan Capistrano 92693, 714–493–1111) south of Los Angeles on the Pacific, the "Jewel of the Missions," founded in November 1776, is known the world over for the legend of its swallows, which hopefully return to the mission ruin every St. Joseph's Day (March 19th). The classic beauty of the mission, its gardens and its flocks of white pigeons attract visitors and photographers in great numbers. Inside, a new visitor's center for the town has been opened.

Also see *Old Missions* in Los Angeles and San Diego sections.

GARDENS. Rancho Santa Ana Botanic Gardens, 1500 No. College Ave., Claremont, (714–625–8767) has an extensive collection of flowers and plants native to California. Shield's Date Gardens, 80–225 Hwy. 111, Indio, (619–347–0996) presents a free 30-minute color slide show on the "sex life" of dates. Moorten Botanical Gardens, 1701 So. Palm Canyon Dr., Palm Springs (619–327–6555) boasts more than 2,000 varieties of plants from the world's deserts. The Gardens also has a Palm Springs outlet at 364 N. Palm Canyon Dr. (805–682–4726) Santa Barbara Botanic Garden. Plan about an hour to take a leisurely self-guided tour through this magnificent 50-acre garden. Plants and trees indigenous to California grow in this natural setting—colorful wildflowers, redwoods, brilliantly flowering shrubs and desert plants. Trail direction can be obtained at the Information Center. Guided tour on Thurs. The Dos Pueblos Orchid Ranch, Goleta (805–968–3535) has free daily tours.

MUSIC. Idyllwild Art Foundation (714–659–2171) presents the University of Southern California's summer showcase of fine music and dramatic productions in a 250-acre mountain site. Both the renowned faculty and the students create a cultural United Nations in this remote village, in the remote mountains about 100 miles east from Los Angeles. In Palm Springs, the Palm Springs Friends of the Los Angeles Philharmonic provides a consistently rewarding repertoire of classical works, with highly regarded Sunday afternoon concerts.

One of the highlights for Southern California music lovers is the Ojai Music Festival, Ojai. See also Los Angeles and San Diego sections. Presented in May at the Festival Bowl.

STAGE AND REVUES. Santa Barbara has created on the site of its first theater, built about 1873 by Jose Lobero, its present county-owned playhouse, the Lobero Theater, which houses local products as well as national touring groups, 33 E. Canon Perdido St.

At the annual Ramona Pageant almost 400 thespians take part in a dramatization of Helen Hunt Jackson's immortal love story of early California. Performances are given in Ramona Bowl, about 2 miles southeast of Hemet. Late April to early May. See also Los Angeles and San Diego sections. The Palm Springs Center Theater presents legitimate theater, including comedy, light musicals and some drama.

Laguna Moulton Playhouse at 606 Laguna Canyon Rd. in Laguna presents dramas, comedies and musicals, and also boasts a children's theater.

See also Los Angeles and San Diego Sections.

LIQUOR LAWS. California drinking laws are rigidly enforced. Youthful looking men and women are often asked for identification cards to establish that they are 21, the legal drinking age. Liquor may be sold and served in stores and bars from 6 A.M. to 2 A.M. every day, including all holidays.

CASINOS. The town of Gardena is a miniature Las Vegas, about 20 miles south of L.A. Relatively low-stakes card games only. For nongamblers, a visit to these places can be of interest for sociological observation and research. *Horseshoe Club,* 14305 S. Vermont (213–323–7520) has one-dollar and two-dollar games in poker, low ball and a special "jackpot" card game. *The Eldorado,* 15411 S. Vermont Ave. (213–323–2800). A high-rollers club, the only card room has a $100–$200 limit game going nonstop.

SUMMER SPORTS. *Watersports:* Year round water sports may be enjoyed along the southeast border of California, from Parker to Blythe, and—amongst many other places at Salton Sea, Lake Gregory, Lake Arrowhead, Big Bear Lake and June Lake. The Pacific, however, is too cool for swimming except in the summer. You can dig for clams at Morro Bay; for giant clams at Pismo Beach; snatch grunion (bare hands and fishing license required) as the tiny fish spawn at low tide during the full moon.

Fishing: Inland, the lakes reservoirs, rivers and mountain streams yield bluegill, bullheads, channel and white catfish, crappie and rainbow trout. There is trout fishing also at Whitewater Canyon and Bishop. The "Sea in the Desert," Salton Sea, is populated with corvinas up to 15 lbs. Oxnard is a favorite bon-voyage port for fishing the Channel Islands for halibut, the size fishermen tell tall tales about. Bass, swordfish and even sharks are taken offshore. Surf fishing is popular.

Ocean sportfishing services are offered by H & M Sportfishing, Breakwater, Santa Barbara. Other boats leave from Avila Beach, Morro Bay, Port Hueneme, San Simeon, and Ventura. There is good sportfishing at Catalina Island.

Surfing: Surfing has become a big sport in Southern California in recent years. There are about 125 beaches between Morro Bay and San Diego. For exciting observation or participation in the skills of surfing and the "surfing scene," head out to the beaches bright and early (best time is between 6 and 9 A.M.) Expert surfers follow the tide conditions and swell directions in choosing their day's beach. In the arty community of Laguna, you'll find lots of surfers during the summer; the main spot is at Thalia St. During the winter (it's a year-round sport) at Rincon in Ventura, some of the world's best surfers ride huge Hawaii-type waves. In Santa Barbara, Jalama State Park has waves so large that dozens of ships have crashed on the rocks. It's a beautiful drive down to the sea through verdant, lush valleys. In the San Diego area, it's Pacific Beach in La Jolla.

Swimming: Open all year, the Palm Springs Swim Center in Sunrise Plaza Community complex features a 50-meter, Olympic-sized swimming pool, a separate swimming section for children, and more than 20,000 square feet of spacious lawns and sundeck. Swimming lessons are on-going.

Boating: There are boat marinas and yacht harbors surrounding the Salton Sea State Recreational Area, which is California's most popular boating park. The Colorado River is also popular with boaters; marinas with boats for rent sprinkle the river. Marina Del Rey, Los Angeles, is one of the largest boating centers in the world. Santa Barbara and Ventura also have facilities. San Diego's Mission Bay is alive with pleasure craft.

Golf: Southern California is literally teeming with courses. The Palm Springs area alone has 37. Among the best are: *Alisal G.C.,* a resort course at Solvang; *Ojai Valley C.C.,* also a resort course at Ojai; *Valencia G.C.,* Valencia, a semi-private rugged Trent Jones course; *Apple Valley Inn,* Apple Valley, a sprawling resort course; *Hesperia G. & G.C.,* Hesperia, semi-private; *Spring Valley Lake G.C.,* San Bernardino, semi-private short course on lake; *Massacre Canyon Inn,* Gilman Hot Springs, with many trees; *Soboba Springs C.C.,* San Jacinto, challenging Muirhead creation; *La Quinta C.C.,* La Quinta, a private course; *Palm Springs C.C.,* Palm Springs, private, but open to members of out-of-town clubs; *Riviera Hotel & C.C.,* Palm Springs, a resort course, open to the public; *Biltmore Hotel C.C.,* Palm Springs, open to the public; *Canyon C.C.* (North) Palm Springs, private, but open to members of out-of-town clubs; *Canyon C.C.* (South) Palm Springs, a challenging layout, open to the public during slow seasons; *Palm Springs Municipal Golf Course,* Palm Springs, an outstanding course; *Mission Hills G. & C.C.,* Cathedral City, private, open to visitors by invitation; *Shadow Mountain C.C.,* Palm Desert, private, but open to members and guests of some hotels; *Del Safari C.C.,* Palm Desert, private, but open to out-of-town club members; *Palm Desert C.C.,* Palm Desert, semi-private, excellent greens; *Desert Island C.C.,* Cathedral City, private Muirhead course, open to out-of-town club members; *Indian Wells C.C.,* Indian Wells, private, open to out-of-town club members; *Bermuda Dunes C.C.,* Bermuda Dunes, open to visiting club members; *Westward Ho C.C.,* Indio, semi-private, but public welcome; *Pala Mesa Inn & G.C.,* Fallbrook, a championship course; *San Vincente C.C.,* Ramona, semi-private Ted Robinson course; *Lake San Marcos G.C.,* Lake San Marcos, flat, open course; *Rancho California G.C.,* Temecula, new resort course; *Rancho Santa Fe G.C.,* Santa Fe, an interesting course. Also see L.A. and San Diego Sections.

Bicycling: There are many bicycling clubs in Southern California, most of them affiliated with the American Youth Hostels. In Santa Barbara, Hazard's Bike Shop, 115 La Guerra, has been well-known for rentals and repairs since 1914. Palm Springs has 14 miles of bike trails. Los Angeles, San Diego, and Santa Barbara have numerous trails. For Los Angeles information, contact Los Angeles Wheelman's Assn., 213–533–1707. In Palm Springs, stop by Burnett's Bicycle Barn for an up-to-date area bicycle path map.

Hiking: Hiking trails lead through beautiful palms at Andreas, Murray and Palm Canyons in Palm Springs. Sturdy shoes recommended. You can also hike up to the summit of Mt. Whitney. Hiking is excellent all over Southern California and ranges from the most precipitous peaks to the flattest coast.

Horseback riding: Smoke Tree Stables in Palm Springs rents horses for the novice and the expert. Miles of bridle trails take riders onto Indian reservation land and into rugged foothills for spectacular views of the desert.

Jai Alai (pronounced Hi Lie): This fast game, in which players hurl and catch a hard-as-granite ball from large clawlike devices strapped to their wrists, draws crowds every Thurs. through Mon. night to the Fronton Palacio, Tijuana, Mexico, 16 mi. below San Diego. Betting is heavy.

Tennis: Southern California is the tennis capital of the world. Thousands of courts dot the landscape, many of them lighted for night play. They range from the most exclusive private clubs, to pay-for-play, to public. Palm Springs has 27 public courts, all but nine are free.

WINTER SPORTS. *Skiing:* There are more than 20 established ski areas in Southern California, half of them within a two-hour drive from Los Angeles. Depending on the weather, the season is Nov.-March. In the Ontario/Riverside/San Bernardino areas, snow sports may be enjoyed at Lake Arrowhead and Big Bear Lake. Several ski resorts are north of Ventura. Laguna Mountain is east of San Diego.

SPECTATOR SPORTS. *Races:* Ontario Motor Speedway, 3901 East "G" St., Ontario, California "500," Grand Prix Motorcycles, N.H.R.A. Supernationals Drag Race; Miller 500 Stock Car Race. Year round. Riverside Raceway, 22255 Eucalyptus Ave., Riverside. Five major races a year in Jan., Apr., June, Oct. and Nov. Camel and ostrich races every winter during National Date Festival in Indio, a few miles from Palm Springs. The Long Beach Grand Prix is held in early spring.

Golf: Palm Springs/Palm Desert have more than 100 tournaments in the area annually, including the Bob Hope Desert Classic. Eisenhower Heart Fund Tournament, Palm Springs City Championship, Baseball-Celebrity Golf Classic, American Cancer Society's Women's Golf Classic, Senior Golf Tournament, the Chuck Connors Invitational, and the Nabisco Dinah Shore Invitational. There is an Annual Salton City Pro-Am Tournament. The Glen Campbell-Los Angeles Open is one of the most important tournaments.

Tennis: The annual Ojai Tennis Tournament is held in April and the Pilot Pen Classic, held in Palm Springs at La Quinta, attracts the biggest names in tennis competition as well as top prize money.

Boating: The Flight of the Snowbirds Regatta, in which Snowbird-class cat-boats participate is held at Newport in July; "Character Boat Parade" in August.

Baseball, Football, Basketball, Hockey. San Diego and Los Angeles have several professional teams.

Rose Bowl. In Pasadena every New Year's Day (or the following day if it's a Sunday). The Nation's top two collegiate football teams meet. The world-famous parade precedes the game.

Polo: Played at Will Rogers State Historic Park in Pacific Palisades. Games are usually played Thurs. and Sat. Polo matches also at Eldorado Polo Club, Palm Springs.

CHILDREN'S ACTIVITIES. Zoological Gardens, 500 Ninos Dr., Santa Barbara (805–962–6310), is a unique park, playground and zoo, designed with children in mind. Popular is the Sealarium, with underwater portholes for viewing. A miniature railroad rides around the park.

Hope Town Movie Ranch (805–526–1147) five miles east of Santa Susana on Calif. 118, is a 2,000-acre spread where movies and TV shows are filmed. Sets include an Old Western town, Ft. Apache, a Mexican street, a Corsican village, Sherwood Forest, Robin Hood Lake. Demonstrations of movie-making are presented with mock cowboy gunfights, bank robberies, and stage holdups. Free picnic sites (except Sun.) with fireplaces. Also chuckwagons, restaurant.

In Palm Springs, some fourteen miles of trails may be enjoyed by cyclists, who can pedal past celebrity homes, the Palm Springs Desert Museum (619–325–7186) (where children six and under are admitted free), shops, and into the desert.

At the Palm Springs Swim Center (619–323–8278) an Olympic-sized public swimming pool has a separate swimming section for children only. Swimming instruction available for all ages. Entrance fee.

Calico Ghost Town (619–254–2122), 10 miles north of Barstow, was the site of the west's richest silver strike, in 1881. It brought in some $66 million. Relive the raucous days of the Old West via mine tours, train rides and stage shows.

See also Los Angeles and San Diego sections.

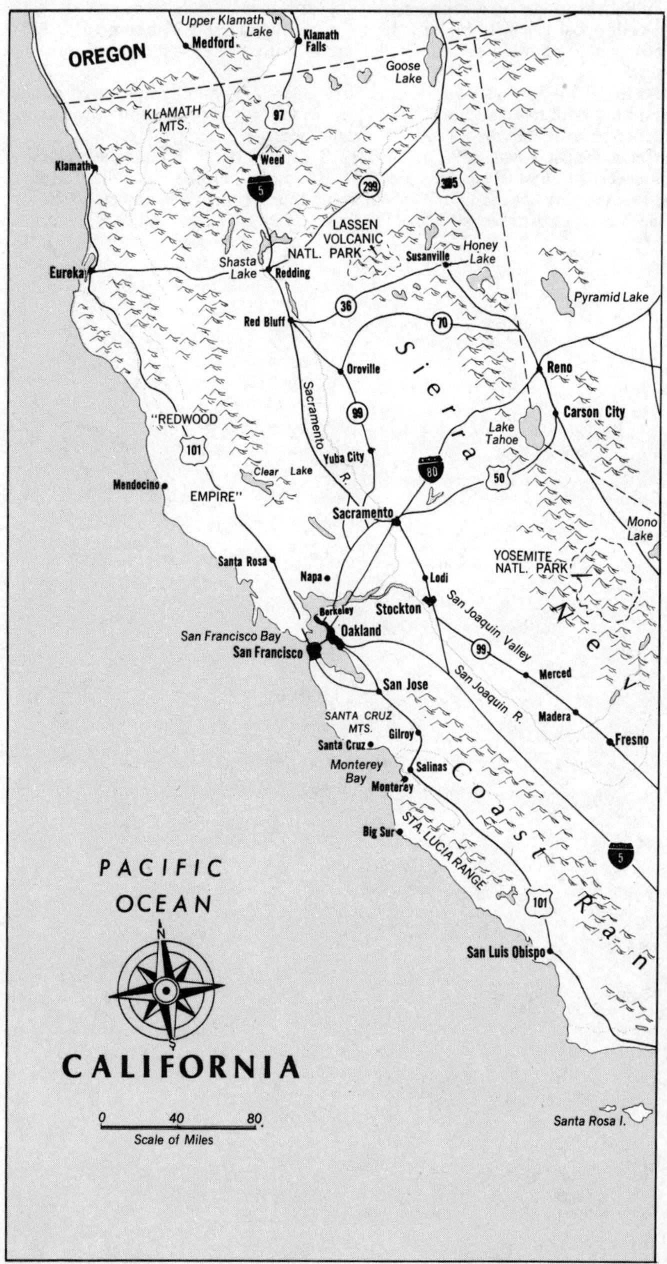

OREGON
Upper Klamath Lake
Medford
Klamath Falls
Goose Lake
KLAMATH MTS.
97
Weed
Klamath
5
299
395
LASSEN VOLCANIC NATL. PARK
Susanville
Honey Lake
Shasta Lake
Redding
Eureka
36
Pyramid Lake
Red Bluff
70
Sierra
Oroville
Reno
Sacramento R.
99
Carson City
"REDWOOD
Lake Tahoe
101
Yuba City
80
Clear Lake
50
Mendocino
EMPIRE"
Sacramento
Mono Lake
YOSEMITE NATL. PARK
Santa Rosa
Napa
Lodi
Nev
Berkeley
Stockton
San Joaquin Valley
San Francisco Bay
Oakland
San Francisco
99
Merced
San Jose
San Joaquin R.
SANTA CRUZ MTS.
Madera
Gilroy
Fresno
Santa Cruz
Monterey Bay
Salinas
Monterey
Coast Ran
STA. LUCIA RANGE
Big Sur
5
PACIFIC OCEAN
101
San Luis Obispo
N
S
CALIFORNIA
0 40 80
Scale of Miles
Santa Rosa I.

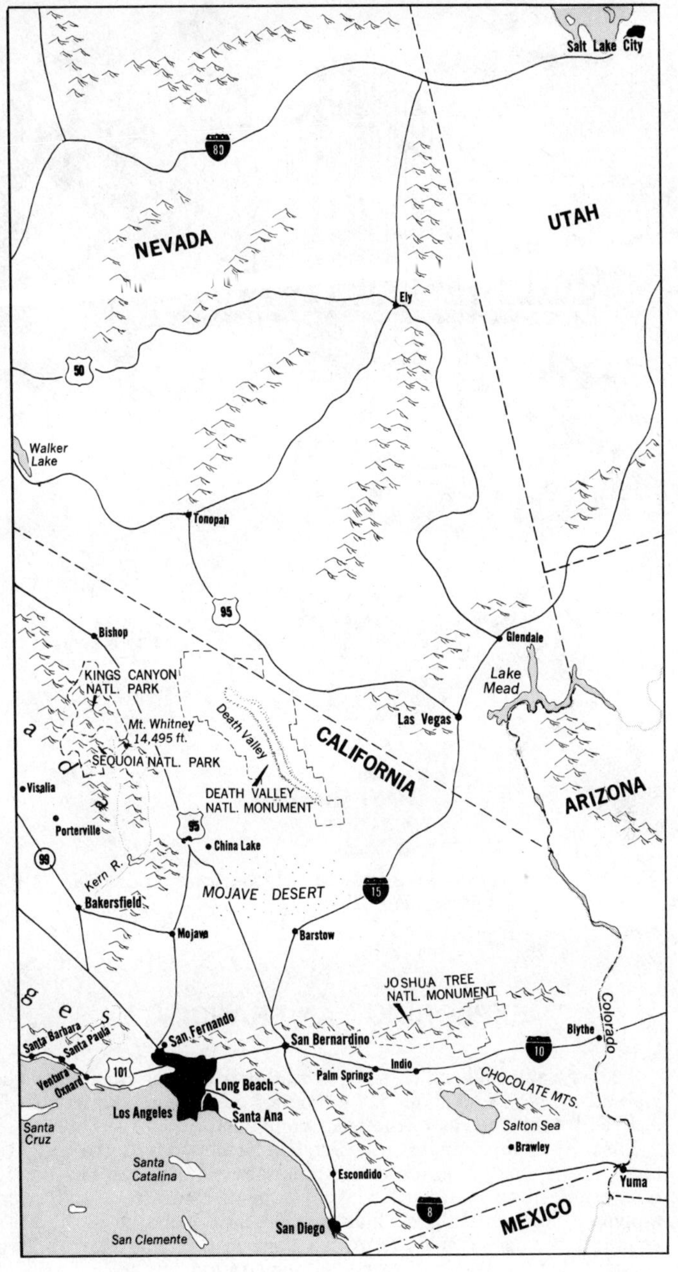

Salt Lake City
80
UTAH
NEVADA
Ely
50
Walker Lake
Tonopah
95
Bishop
Glendale
KINGS CANYON NATL. PARK
Lake Mead
Las Vegas
Mt. Whitney 14,495 ft.
Death Valley
CALIFORNIA
SEQUOIA NATL. PARK
Visalia
DEATH VALLEY NATL. MONUMENT
ARIZONA
Porterville
95
China Lake
99
Kern R.
MOJAVE DESERT
15
Bakersfield
Mojave
Barstow
JOSHUA TREE NATL. MONUMENT
Colorado
San Fernando
Santa Barbara
Santa Paula
San Bernardino
Blythe
10
Ventura
Oxnard
101
Palm Springs
Indio
Long Beach
CHOCOLATE MTS.
Los Angeles
Santa Ana
Santa Cruz
Salton Sea
Brawley
Santa Catalina
Escondido
Yuma
8
MEXICO
San Diego
San Clemente

NORTHERN CALIFORNIA

Magic and Majesty

by
TONI CHAPMAN

Toni Chapman, a free-lance writer and broadcaster based in San Francisco, is an expert on the Far West.

EXPLORING SAN FRANCISCO

Today, California can be reached readily from every quarter of the globe. Tourists spend about $27 billion for the style and variety of life enjoyed by the citizens of the most populous state in the Union.

For the nostalgic-minded traveller, San Francisco is Mecca. Surprisingly, it is a small city. 45 square miles above water and another 55 square miles underwater. It is a cityscape of contrasts. Coit Tower, topping Telegraph Hill, was built in 1934, as a memorial to the city's volunteer firemen. Inside are murals done in the same year by local artists under the Works Projects Administration.

The downtown skyline is dominated by the 52-story carnelian granite-clad tower of headquarters of the world's largest bank, Bank of

America. The elegant Carnelian Room crowns the building, offering superb dining and a magnificent view.

Wide media exposure has made the 853-foot Transamerica Pyramid recognizable in "the city that everyone loves" just as the Opera House's soaring wings identify Sydney's harborscape.

Almond-hued homes march up the hills which surround the city. San Francisco's Victorian homes are quite unique—interesting, grotesque, amusing, pretentious, stately—they reflect the highly individualistic folk who called them home. Minuscule gardens are treasured and come in many moods, from Old English country style to sparse Japanese-oriented bonsai and rock-strewn enclosures.

Street corner flower stalls attest to the natives' love for all things green. Ferny dells delight in restaurants and family flats. No matter how tight the budget, there are always a few dollars for a flower or a plant.

In the summer of 1984, San Francisco's 110-year-old cable car system reopened after a 20-month, $58.2 million rehabilitation. The look of the cable cars did not change. But the cable and pulley systems which enable the cars to function has been completely overhauled. New tracks have been installed, involving all sixty-nine blocks along the routes. The cable car is a living, working part of the city. Today, San Francisco is the only city in the world that operates the sturdy little hillclimbers.

Just a mile from the downtown's major shopping scene (Union Square) is Nihonmachi, or Japantown. More than 60,000 Japanese-Americans live in the Bay Area. The five-acre $15 million "Little Tokyo" houses two fine hotels—*The Miyako,* noted for its traditional Japanese suites with tatamis (floor mats), sliding shoji panel doors, indoor rock and bamboo gardens, and futons (Japanese-style beds). The *Kyoto Inn* offers steam baths in some rooms.

The 100-foot Peace Pagoda is a gift of friendship from the people of Japan. During Spring Cherry Blossom Festival and Fall Festival (Aki Matsuri) there are folk song and dance programs as well as judo, karate, kendo (Japanese fencing), and Ikebana (flower arranging) exhibits.

Stop in a *sushi* restaurant and sample *nigiri-zushi*—a two-bite sized mound of vinegar-flavored rice covered with a fresh slice of *sashimi* (raw fish). *Sashimi* is fresh morsels of tuna, shrimp and bass which are dipped into a soy sauce spiked with green horse radish. Try a steaming bowl of *soba,* noodles in a chicken or fish broth, topped with bits of vegetables and onion. Heavier fare includes *tempura* (shrimp, fish, and vegetables deep-fried in batter) with hot *sake* on the side.

Return downtown, via Geary Street. Don't miss the dramatic St. Mary's Cathedral atop Cathedral Hill at Gough Street. It is one of the most striking contemporary structures in The City.

With the U.S. normalization of relations with the People's Republic, there is a new emphasis and awareness of the culture of China. Current Chinese population figures range from 75,000 to over 120,000 and the dialects of Canton, Shanghai, and Mandarin are in the air.

Almost three million visitors pass under the green tile gate at Bush Street, into the world of Suzie Wong. If possible, join the Saturday afternoon walking tour offered by the Chinese Cultural Foundation in the Holiday Inn at Kearny Street. Stroll Grant and Stockton. Shops bulge with trinkets and treasures from Hong Kong, Peking, Taipei. New and old jade, ivory, porcelain, wood carvings, embroideries jostle with plastic and machine-made "authentic reproductions."

Points of Interest

1) Alcoa Building
2) Balclutha
3) Bank of America
4) Cannery
5) City Hall
6) Civic Center
7) Coit Tower
8) Curran Theater
9) Embarcadero Center
10) Ferry Building
11) Fisherman's Wharf
12) Flood Building
13) Geary Theater
14) George R. Moscone Convention Center
15) Golden Gate Center
16) Grace Cathedral
17) Hilton Hotel
18) Hyatt Hotel
19) Hyde Street Pier
20) Lotta's Fountain
21) Maritime Museum
22) Municipal Pier
23) Museum of Modern Art
24) Old U.S. Mint
25) Opera House
26) Pier 39
27) St. Mary's Cathedral
28) St. Patrick's Church
29) Stock Exchange
30) Transamerica Pyramid
31) Victorian Park
32) Visitor Information Center

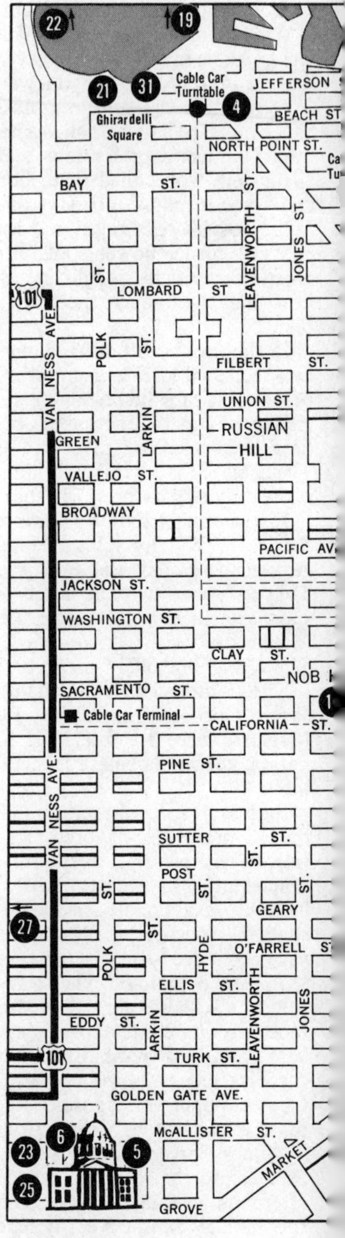

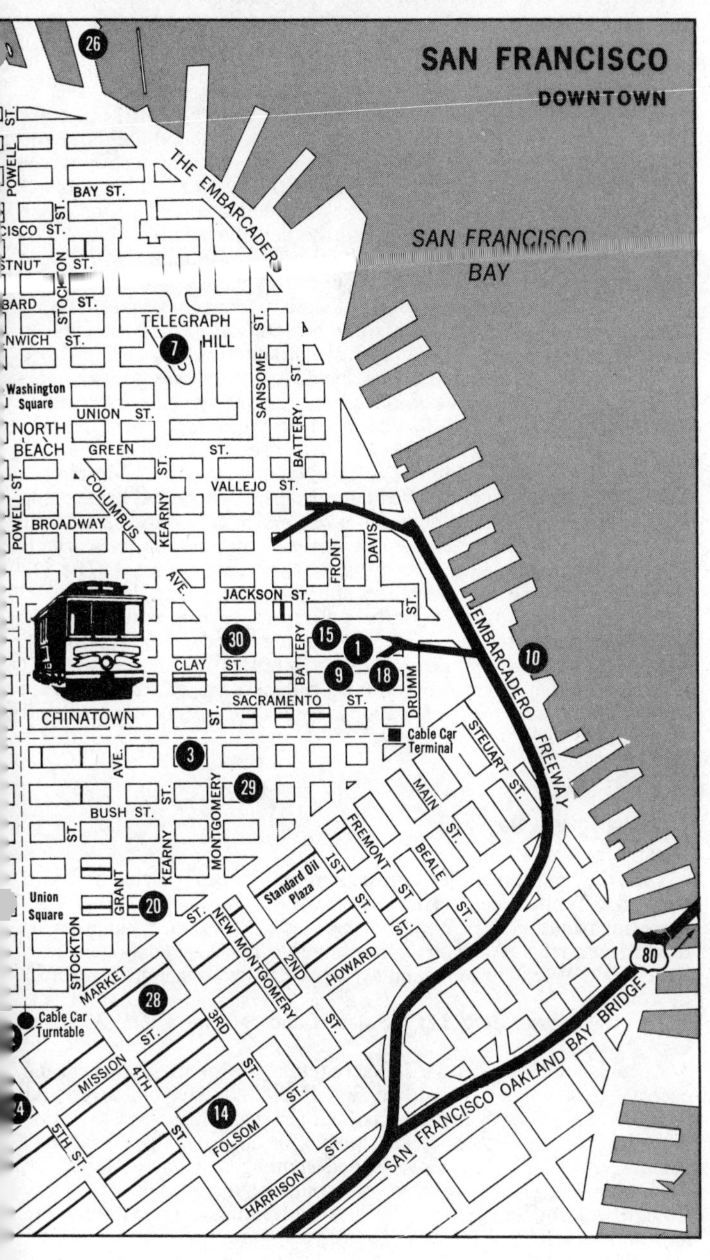

SAN FRANCISCO
DOWNTOWN
SAN FRANCISCO BAY
THE EMBARCADERO
TELEGRAPH HILL
Washington Square
NORTH BEACH
CHINATOWN
Union Square
Cable Car Terminal
Cable Car Turntable
Standard Oil Plaza
EMBARCADERO FREEWAY
SAN FRANCISCO OAKLAND BAY BRIDGE
80
BAY ST.
UNION ST.
GREEN ST.
VALLEJO ST.
BROADWAY
COLUMBUS AVE.
JACKSON ST.
CLAY ST.
SACRAMENTO ST.
BUSH ST.
MARKET ST.
MISSION ST.
HOWARD ST.
FOLSOM ST.
HARRISON ST.
POWELL ST.
STOCKTON ST.
GRANT AVE.
KEARNY ST.
MONTGOMERY ST.
SANSOME ST.
BATTERY ST.
FRONT ST.
DAVIS ST.
DRUMM
STEUART ST.
MAIN ST.
BEALE ST.
FREMONT ST.
1ST ST.
2ND ST.
3RD ST.
4TH ST.
5TH ST.
NEW MONTGOMERY
26
7
30
15
1
9
18
10
3
29
20
28
14

Inspect the colorful rows of oranges, tangerines, snow peas, winter melons, and ginger roots piled in windows and on counter-tops. Examine the tanks full of fish and the neighboring butcher with his line of glazed ducks strung across his window.

Both Chinatown and its neighbor, North Beach, should be seen on foot. Washington Square, at Columbus and Union, is a UN plaza of ethnic groups daily sunning, swapping tales of the good old days, and warily eyeing the T-shirt and jeans-wearing newcomers sharing the turf. All around "Little Italy" live more than 100,000 inhabitants of Italian descent. Try a cappuccino or get the fixings for a picnic lunch at one of the famed delicatessens in the neighborhood.

The Barbary Coast entertainment strip along Broadway introduced "topless" in the 1960s. The 70s brought the massage parlor. By daylight, you'll see three blocks or so of shabby, porno-type clubs with a few old-time favorite restaurants like *Vanessi's* at 498. Nighttime is a blaze of neons, loud music and brash barkers hawking the so-called shows. Recently, local authorities have closed several establishments after repeated complaints of customers ranging from overpricing to threats of physical harm. Stay away or be prepared, is our advice.

For the sight, sound, and smell of the sea, hop the #15 bus at Fisherman's Wharf. Reminisce at the National Maritime Museum, a storehouse of elaborately-carved figureheads, anchors and ornate ship models. Step aboard the *Balclutha,* a restored square-rigger, last of the Cape Horn fleet. The Wharf, hosting over 12 million visitors yearly, is second only to Disneyland as the state's top tourist mecca. The $12 million Anchorage complex offers shopping and dining delights.

Pier 39, a turn of the century waterfront village, hosts over 100 shops, a dozen restaurants, free wine tasting and daily entertainment.

Inspect the red-brick 19th century Ghirardelli Square complex. It houses a myriad of fine restaurants, galleries, ethnic bazaars and a cinema. Sample at *Almond Plaza,* a handsome setting for great gift selections of California almonds.

Cruising the Bay

Take the spectacular Bay Cruise. Anytime is the right time to board the Red & White Fleet, berthed at Pier 41, or the Blue and Gold Fleet departing from Pier 39's West Marina. Red & White Fleet boats depart from Fisherman's Wharf, daily in summer to Tiburon and Angel Island State Park. Weekend and holiday service only; from mid-September thru May.

Carry a sweater or jacket, headscarf and camera. There are snack bars aboard.

Angel Island State Park, a 740-acre retreat for hikers, picnickers and cyclists, is the largest island in San Francisco Bay, and overlooks Alcatraz. California's only state park is open daily from 8 A.M. to sunset. A useful map and brochure is available for 50¢, and there is a small visitors center at Ayala Cove. Good sunning at Quarry Beach but swimming is unsafe. A narrated train tour recounts the island's history from Miwok Indian villages to its 20th-century use as a detention camp for Chinese immigrants (1882–1943).

Explore the Cannery, at the foot of Columbus, the City's second melange of fascinating shops and restaurants. Sit and sun in the courtyard of the former Del Monte Fruit Cannery. Enjoy people-watching, as well as the special street entertainers performing under the almost-century old olive trees.

Be sure to make advance reservations, if you wish to visit Alcatraz. The Rock is now part of the 72,815-acre Golden Gate National Recreation Area. A 1 ½-hour tour departs from Pier 41. Very popular. A bit strenuous while walking on the island. Warm jacket, comfortable shoes a must. Park rangers provide historic and comic comments on the occupants of the legendary 12-acre fortress.

Sidewalk stalls of fish, shrimp and crabs attract crowds of people to the Wharf. Sample San Francisco specialties including abalone steak meuniere, poached salmon, broiled petrale sole, crab cioppino

San Francisco's Civic Center, located within the triangle formed by Market Street, Van Ness Avenue and McAllister Street, is a tribute to the turn-of-the-century, City Beautiful Movement. Seven Beaux Arts buildings grace the complex. The gray California granite City Hall is a gem—don't miss the rotunda. The Opera House, birthplace of the UN charter in 1945, is modeled on Garnier's Paris Opera.

A dream to walk is Union Street from Van Ness to Steiner. Originally dubbed Cow Hollow, the first dairy was established here in 1861 and the cows grazed here till 1900. There is no doubt that this area itself has a youthful exuberance that draws both tourists and Bay Area residents.

Contemporary fashions, often unisex; elegant antiques; galleries and book shops geared to browsers; unusual and casual saloons, coffee houses, and ethnic eateries attract all ages.

To continue city touring, tackle a bit of Golden Gate Park. Over one thousand acres offer something for everyman, from art to the Steinhart Aquarium's three-story, $1.2 million "Roundabout" ocean fish tank, and a mock tide pool full of small, touchable creatures. On entering the new concrete structure, visitors first see a shallow "touch tank" filled with organisms typical of tide pools along California's central coast. Children will be encouraged to handle the inhabitants—hermit crabs, starfish and sea urchins. A spiral ramp leads to the "Roundabout"—a huge showspace for the hundreds of open sea species who are in continuous motion—swimming past the 36 three-inch Plexiglass windows. The new Penguin Environment in the California Academy of Science presents the birds in a natural setting that also includes fish, plants, and invertebrates.

It was a Scotsman, John McLaren, who became manager of the park in 1887 and transformed the sand into the green civilized wilderness we enjoy today. There are tennis courts, a polo field, a buffalo paddock and the often photographed conservatory, a copy of the greenhouse at Kew Gardens, England. The framework for the Conservatory, left among the property of James Lick, San Francisco's early, eccentric benefactor, was bought by public-spirited citizens and erected in the park. Mr. Lick's estate, valued at $3.5 million when he died in 1876, was used to establish or aid a variety of cultural institutions, many of which operate today. First among these is Lick Observatory, now under the auspices of the University of California. Many significant astronomical discoveries have been made there.

Visit the de Young Museum's smashing new American Wing. Browse thru the fabulous displays of Asian treasures and the world-renowned Avery Brundage Collection of Oriental Art. Relax over jasmine tea and fortune cookies at the neighboring Japanese Tea Garden. Modest entrance fee.

San Francisco's dramatic new Moscone Center opened in 1981. The convention center features a 270,000-square-foot exhibit floor that is 37 feet below street level and 11 feet below the water table. Long-range redevelopment plans have been made for a 24-acre Yerba Buena Gardens. The $750-million complex will include a 1,500-room Marriott Hotel, near Fourth and Market streets, scheduled for completion in late 1988.

San Francisco's best kept secret, for the time being, is the renaissance of the area south of Market Street, the city's new SoMa, our answer to New York's South of Houston of a decade ago. Jack London wrote of the division of San Francisco between "North of the Slot" and "South of the Slot," where "were the factories, slums, laundries, machine shops, boiler works and the abodes of the working class."

Today trendy, upscale art galleries and artists' lofts, cafes and bistros serving Californian and continental cuisine are flourishing. Though many of the bars and clubs attract a gay clientele, there is a growing "yuppie" invasion on weekends. It reminds old-timers of North Beach during the early days of the beats.

Slip away some early morning to Lincoln Park. Enjoy the silence and splendor of this special spot. Observe the fog rolling through the Golden Gate and the dramatic Marin headlands. Warm up (after 10 A.M.) and wander thru the California Palace of the Legion of Honor, modeled after the 18th century Paris landmark. In addition to its fine French works, there is an important Rodin collection, and the little-known Achenbach Foundation graphics collection, the largest representation in the western U.S.

PRACTICAL INFORMATION FOR SAN FRANCISCO

HOW TO GET THERE. By Plane. *Eastern, TWA, United, USAir, American, Delta, Alaska, Pan Am, Northwest, Continental,* and *Republic* service San Francisco from various parts of the United States. Regional service is provided by *Piedmont, United,* and *AirCal,* among others. (See "Practical Information for Northern California.")

By Car. From the east, Interstate 80 will take you to San Francisco. Interstate 5 runs from Washington through California, east of San Francisco. If you want to drive up from Los Angeles on Highway 101 or even I–5, remember that its a *long* day's drive. You won't be able to drive up comfortably and see anything along Highway 1 in under 3 days.

By Train. *Amtrak's* newly refurbished trains travel into Oakland and passengers transfer to buses for the trip into the Trans-Bay Terminal in San Francisco.

By Bus. *Greyhound* and *Continental* both operate transportation to San Francisco.

ACCOMMODATIONS. In 1986, tourists and business visitors spent nearly $1 billion in San Francisco, while delegates to 770 conventions, trade shows, and professional meetings spent another $576 million. The city's 25,000 rooms range from deluxe to basic. Reservations are suggested year-round; check current rates, senior discounts, and weekend and special packages. There are a number of smaller, recently renovated hotels in central locations near the Financial District, Market Street, and Union Square. All rates are subject to a 11 percent occupancy tax.

Hotel rates are based on double occupancy, with no meals. Categories, determined by price, are: *Super Deluxe:* $135 and up; *Deluxe,* $115–135; *Expensive;* $90–115; *Moderate,* $60–90; and *Inexpensive,* under $60.

Super Deluxe

Campton Place. 340 Stockton, Union Square (415–781–5555). Elegant.

Donatello. 501 Post. (415–441–7100). Quiet elegance.

Fairmont Hotel & Tower. Nob Hill, at California & Mason. (415–772–5000). Restaurants include the *Squire Room, Canlis', Venetian Room* and the *Fairmont Crown,* a spectacular cocktail lounge.

Four Seasons/Clift. Geary St. at Taylor. (415–775–4700). Fortune magazine named it one of the world's eight great small hotels.

Huntington. 1075 California. (415–474–5400). Popular with diplomatic missions. Its *Big Four* restaurant, handsomely appointed, recalls the era of the four Nob Hill railroad nabobs.

Hyatt on Union Square. 345 Stockton (415–398–1234). Near fine shops, theaters.

Hyatt Regency. 5 Embarcadero Center. (415–788–1234). Glass elevators, atrium lobby. Revolving rooftop lounge. Friday tea dancing.

Mandarin. 222 Sansome St. (415–885–0990). Opulent Oriental property. Spectacular views and service.

Mark Hopkins. Nob Hill, at California & Mason. (415–392–3434). Boasts the *Top of the Mark* and superb dining in the *Nob Hill* restaurant.

Marriott. Fisherman's Wharf. (415–775–7555). Multilingual staff.

Meridien. 50 Third Street. (415–974–6400). Superb service and cuisine.

Nikko. 1 Halladie Plaza (415–394–1111). Japanese high rise near Union Square.

Portman. 500 Post St. (415–771–8600). Member of the famed Peninsula Group, Hong Kong.

Ramada Renaissance. 55 Cyril Magnin St. (415–392–8000). 32-story art-filled hostelry.

The Stanford Court. 905 California (415–989–3500; 800–227–4736). An outstanding "European-type" hostelry.

Westin St. Francis. Union Square. (415–397–7000). Stately grande dame. Fascinating people watching at the Art-Deco *Compass Rose* lounge.

Deluxe

Bed & Breakfast Inn. 4 Charlton Court, off Union St. (415–921–9784). Nine Victorian charmers, continental breakfast.

Handlery Motor Inn. 260 O'Farrell. (415–986–2526). Heated pool.

Holiday Inn-Civic Center. 50 Eighth St. (415–626–6103). Pool. Pets.

Holiday Inn-Fisherman's Wharf. 1300 Columbus. (415–771–9000). Close to *The Cannery,* Ghirardelli Square and Fisherman's Wharf.

Holiday Inn-Golden Gateway. 1500 Van Ness. (415–441–4000). Heated pool. Room service.

Holiday Inn-Union Square. Sutter at Powell. (415–398–8900). Restaurant highly recommended for fare and decor. *S.S. Holmes, Esq.,* San Francisco's Sherlockian pub, now housed on the 30th floor.

Cathedral Hill. Van Ness and Geary. Civic Center (415–776–8200). Heated swimming pool. Attractive restaurant.

Mansion. 2220 Sacramento. Pacific Heights (415–929–9444). Victorian ambience. *Bufano* sculpture garden.

Miyako. 1625 Post. In Japantown. (415–922–3200). Sauna. Japanese decor.

Raphael. 360 Geary. (415–986–2000). Charming small hotel. Close to shops, theaters. New upscale 24-hour coffee shop, *Vincent's* has a select menu.

Sheraton-Fisherman's Wharf. 2500 Mason. (415–362–5500). Handsome building and landscaping.

Sheraton-Palace. 639 Market. (415–392–8600). Near Financial District.

Sir Francis Drake. 450 Powell. (415–392–7755). Popular spots include the famed *Starlite Roof,* The new *Crusty's Sourdough Cafe* serves creative California cuisine. and home of the much photographed Beefeater doormen.

Expensive

Bedford. 761 Post. Near Union Square shops, theaters (415–673–6040).

Bellevue. 505 Geary. Union Square area (415–474–3600). 24-hour coffee shop.

Beresford. 635 Sutter. Art gallery area. (415–673–9900). Also the *Beresford Arms,* 701 Post St. Ideal for families; some suites with kitchenettes.

Californian. 405 Taylor. Union Square area (415–885–2500). A block from airline terminal.

Canterbury/Whitehall. 750 Sutter. (415–474–6464). Home of *The Greenhouse,* dining in a bower of plants and flowers and wicker furnishings.

Cartwright. 524 Sutter. (415–421–2865). Pay garage. Full service.

Cecil. 545 Post. Near Union Square (415–673–3733). Coffee shop.

Chancellor. 433 Powell. (415–362–2004). Cable car at the door.

Chelsea Motor Inn. 2095 Lombard. (415–563–5600). Reservation deposit required. Very attractive.

Comfort Inn. 240 Seventh St. (415–861–6469). Civic Center area. Newly refurbished; free airport pickup; free parking. Spa, sauna, cafe.

Commodore International. 825 Sutter. Union Square a short walk (415–885–2464).

Cow Hollow Motor Inn. 2190 Lombard. (415–921–5800). Exceptional accommodations reservation deposit required. Convenient to restaurants.

De Ville Motel. 2599 Lombard. (415–346–4664). Van Ness area.

El Cortez. 550 Geary. (415–775–5000). Excellent location, fine family accommodations.

Galleria Park. 191 Sutter. (415–781–3060). $10 million renovation. Adjacent shopping mall.

Juliana. 590 Bush. (415–392–2540). suites named for art dealers.

Kyoto Inn. 1800 Sutter (415–921–4000). In Japantown. Indoor free parking. Restaurant serves Japanese cuisine.

Laurel Motor Inn. 444 Presidio (415–567–8467). Kitchenettes. Complimentary continental breakfast.

Lombard. 1015 Geary. (415–673–5232). Civic Center/theaters near. *Gray Derby* restaurant.

Roberts-at-the-Beach. 2828 Sloat Blvd. (415–564–2610). Near Zoo. Kitchenettes.

Rodeway Inn Downtown. 895 Geary. (415–441–8220). Walking distance to Union Square.

Royal Pacific Motor Inn. 661 Broadway. (415–781–6661). Convenient to North Beach, Chinatown, Fisherman's Wharf.

San Remo. 2237 Mason (415–776–8688). North Beach. Restored Victorian hotel/restaurant.

Stewart. 351 Geary. (415–781–7800). Union Square. Connected to the Handlery Motor Inn, use of their pool and service.

Vagabond Downtown. 2550 Van Ness. (415–776–7500). Heated pool.

Villa Florence. 225 Powell (415–397–7700). Formerly the Manx; refurbished with European ambience.

Vintage Court. 650 Bush. (415–392–4666). European-style accommodations with an elegant restaurant.

York. 940 Sutter. (415–885–6800). Home of the *Plush Room,* popular cabaret. Hitchcock's *Vertigo* filmed here in 1955. Very attractive property.

Moderate

Grant Plaza. 465 Grant (415–434–3883). Chinatown. Newly renovated; near cable car lines; three blocks to Union Square.

King George. 334 Mason. (415–781–5050). Attractive tea room. Union Square area.

Mark Twain. 345 Taylor. (415–673–2332). Charming atmosphere. Near Downtown Airlines Terminal.

Oasis Motel. 900 Franklin. (415–885–6865). Civic Center. Pets. Sundeck.

Inexpensive

Adelaide Inn. 5 Adelaide Pl., between Geary and Post. (415–441–2474). Tiny B & B; shared bath. Great location.

Embarcadero Y.M.C.A. Center. 166 The Embarcadero. (415–392–2191). Co-ed, pool, athletic facilities. Shared bath.

Oxford. Mason at Market St. (415–775–4600). Near Union Square and Moscone Center. Restaurant.

HOSTEL: American Youth Hostels. Golden Gate Council. Building 240, Fort Mason. Dormitory, family room accommodations. First-come, first-served basis.

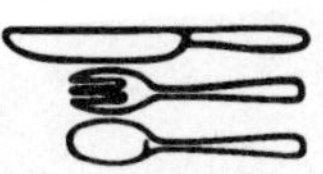

RESTAURANTS. San Francisco's more than 4,000 restaurants offer visitors a round-the-world ticket to dining pleasure. Practically every ethnic taste can be satisfied, with establishments in every price range. Among the unique regional foods to be sampled are abalone, Dungeness crabs, sand dabs, bay shrimp, crusty sourdough French bread, artichoke dishes and excellent cheeses. All these can be accompanied by fine California wines, grown within an hour and half of San Francisco.

Restaurants are listed according to the price of a complete dinner: *Deluxe,* $25 and up; *Expensive,* $20–$25; *Moderate,* $10–$20; *Inexpensive,* under $10. A la carte will, of course, be more expensive.

Editor's Choices

Rating restaurants is, at best, a subjective business, and obviously a matter of personal taste. It is, therefore, difficult to call a restaurant "the best," and hope to get unanimous agreement. The restaurants listed below are our choices of the best eating places in the Greater San Francisco area, and the places we would choose if we were visiting this area.

Campton Place. *Deluxe.* 340 Stockton (781–5155). Nationally acclaimed Bradley Ogden's innovative classic American menu. Memorable breakfast specials.

Castagnola's. *Moderate.* Fisherman's Wharf (775–2446). Great views of city's fishing fleet. Try the fresh sand dabs, a local treat. Coffee reputed to be the best in town.

Donatello. *Expensive.* Donatello Hotel, Post & Mason Sts. (441–7100, ext. 881). Northern Italian classics in an intimate, luxurious setting.

Fournou's Ovens. *Expensive.* Stanford Court Hotel, Nob Hill (989–1910). The charming dining room is designed around the blue and white Portuguese tiled ovens. Delicious roast rack of lamb and boned duckling.

Hunan. *Moderate.* 924 Sansome (956–7727). Modest decor but Henry Chung's cooking is anything but. Accompany it with Wan Fu, a white table wine from France.

MacArthur Park. *Moderate.* 607 Front (398–5700). Trendy, up-scale clientele. Garden surroundings. Superb steaks and ribs—and decadent desserts.

Sam's. *Moderate.* 374 Bush (421–0594). A landmark; noted for its fine seafood selection. Lunch is jammed. Try early dinner.

Trader Vic's. *Deluxe.* Emeryville (653–3400). Dining with a view. Indulge in the Indonesian rack of lamb with peanut sauce and the wicked "Scorpion" garlanded with a gardenia.

Other Recommended Restaurants

Deluxe

Alexis'. 1001 California. Continental (885–6400). *Rack of Lamb Karski* and *Chicken Kiev* are exceptional choices.

Ernie's. 847 Montgomery. French (397–5969). Haute cuisine and turn-of-the-century decor complement each other.

Fior D'Italia. 621 Union St. (986–1886). This century-old Italian favorite overlooks Washington Square Park.

French Room. Four Seasons/Clift Hotel (775–4700). Superb prime rib or Maine lobster.

L'Etoile. 1075 California, Nob Hill (771–1529). Elegant. The fresh Dover sole meunière is perfection.

Masa's. 648 Bush (989–7154). Acclaimed French cuisine. Small. Advance reservations required.

Pierre. Meridien Hotel, 50 Third St. (974–6400). Classic French specialties.

Nob Hill, Mark Hopkins (392–3434). Elegant dining. An outstanding selection of wines by the glass.

Expensive

Bardelli's. 243 O'Farrell. Continental (982–0243). Seafood fanciers should go for abalone or sand dabs.

California Culinary Academy. 625 Polk, Civic Center area (771–3500). The city's prestigious training ground for great chefs.

Empress of China. 838 Grant (434–1345). Manchurian beef and lobster Cantonese will transport you to the Orient.

Gaylord's. Ghirardelli Square (771–8822). North India cuisine. Handsome decor and Bay view.

Harris'. 2100 Van Ness (673–1888). Prime beef specialists.

Harry's Bar and American Grill. 500 Van Ness Ave. (864–2779). Great pastas as well as Florentine and Venetian specialties. Near Davies Symphony Hall.

Imperial Palace. 919 Grant (982–4440). Cantonese specialties include squab with plum sauce, lichee chicken and lobster Imperial.

Jack's. 615 Sacramento (421–7355). French. Old San Francisco atmosphere. A favorite for many years.

Kan's. 708 Grant (982–2388). Cantonese cuisine at its best.

L'Olivier. 465 Davis Court, Golden Gateway Center (981–7824). Classic French Provincial fare and setting.

La Mere Duquesne. 101 Shannon Alley (776–7600). French Country cooking. The *Coquille* (veal mousse on creamed spinach topped with scallops and a rich sauce) stands apart.

Le Central. 453 Bush St. (391–2233). Very Gallic; long-aproned waiters, blackboard menus.

Mandarin. Ghirdardelli Sq. (673–8812). Northern Chinese. Opulent menu, view, and decor. Sweet-sour fish and Mongolian Fire Pot are the best this side of the Orient.

Maxwell's Plum. Ghirardelli Square (441–4140). Hollywood-glitzy decor; menu ranges from burgers to Chateaubriand.

Modesto Lanzone's. Ghirdardelli Square (771–2880). Great views, pastas and Italian favorites. Also at Opera Plaza, Civic Center area (928–0400).

Monroe's. 1968 Lombard (567–4550). Continental dishes served to perfection in a cozy, other-century house.

North Beach. 1512 Stockton (392–1700). Outstanding cuisine. Try their seafood/pasta establishment, *Basta Pasta,* at Vallejo and Grant streets (434–2248).

Prego. 2000 Union (563–3305). Trendy Northern Italian trattoria.

Square One. 190 Pacific Ave. (788–1110). Joyce Goldstein's acclaimed cooking. Reservations essential.

Vanessi's. 498 Broadway (421–0890). Long-time favorite.

Victor's. St. Francis Tower (956–7777). Rack of lamb and veal Jerez vie with the view for attention.

Washington Square Bar & Grill. 1707 Powell (982–8123). North Beach Italian ambience. Menu specialties change daily, but you usually can count on salmon in sorrel sauce and a Livornese fish stew.

Moderate

A. Sabella's. 2766 Taylor, Fisherman's Wharf (771–6775). Italian-seafood specialties. Watch the fish come in right off the boat.

Alfred's. 886 Broadway (781–7058). Italian-style steak house.

Balboa Cafe. 3199 Fillmore (921–3944). American cuisine.

Caffe Sport. 574 Green (981–1251). North Beach funky decor, crowded. Reputed to be the best Sicilian fare in the world.

Caravansary. 310 Sutter (362–4640). Middle Eastern specialties include moussaka, tabaka (boned chicken breast), shish kebob and change-of-pace quiches.

Celadon. 881 Clay (982–1168). Award-winning Chinese cuisine.

Coffee Cantata. 2030 Union (931–0770). After-theatre desserts and coffee specialties.

Courtyard. 2436 Clement (387–7616). Sunday brunch.

Doidge's. 2217 Union (921–2149). Specializes in all the breakfast favorites—French toast, buttermilk pancakes, omelets.

Elite Cafe. 2049 Fillmore (346–8668). New Orleans-style creole cuisine. Some expensive meals.

Enrico's. 504 Broadway (392–6220). San Francisco's original sidewalk cafe. People-watching point. Newly refurbished.

Fog City Diner. 1300 Battery St. (982–2000). Reservations essential at this trendy dining car. Light creative menu.

Franciscan. Pier 43½, Fisherman's Wharf (362–7733). Seafood. Family-style.

Golden Phoenix. 728 Washington (989–4400). Noted for steamed fish, sesame noodles.

Greenhouse. 740 Sutter, Hotel Canterbury (474–6478). Garden atmosphere. Great for Sunday brunch. Very popular.

Greens. Fort Mason, Bldg. A (771–6222). Marina area. Vegetarian menu with home-baked breads and pastries.

Hayes Street Bar & Grill. 324 Hayes St. (863–5545). Seafood.

Iron Horse. 19 Maiden Lane (362–8133). The accent is Italian. Veal dishes excel. Near Union Square.

Ivy's. 398 Hayes, in The Performing Arts Center (626–3930). Daily menu features California cuisine and wines.

Kimball's. 300 Grove (861–5555). Oyster bar, jazz.

Kuleto's. 221 Powell (397–7720). Reputed to be the city's best-designed eatery. Northern Italian favorites.

Lafayette. 290 Pacific (986–3366). French fare modestly priced. Piano bar.

La Traviata. 2854 Mission (282–0500). Long-time Italian dinner house with recorded opera classics.

L'Entrecote de Paris. 2032 Union (931–5006). Chic Parisian ambience accompanies sumptuous entrees.

Mama's. 1701 Stockton (362–6421). North Beach breakfast/lunch rendevous.

Max's Opera Cafe. 601 Van Ness (771–7300). Popular after theater/concert stop. Noted for ribs and corned beef sandwiches.

New San Remo. 2237 Mason (673–9090). Old San Francisco mood and menu.

Phil Lehr's Steakery. Lower level, Hilton Hotel Tower, 330 Taylor (673–6800). The weight of your steak determines your complete dinner price. The house specialty (peach beef Wellington) would grace any house.

Rosalie's. 1415 Van Ness (928–7188). Trendy decor, clientele, menu. Sample their Hawaiian steak.

Sears. 439 Powell (986–1160). Breakfast served until 3 P.M. Famous for its pancakes and fresh fruits and vegetables.

Scott's. 2400 Lombard (563–8988). Also, 3 Embarcadero (981–0622). No reservations. Plan a late lunch or after six, be prepared to wait. Try the Fisherman's Stew for sharing.

Teddy Bears. 131 Gough (621–6766). Delight in the 2600 adopted bears in the lounge and savor the carefully prepared specialties. Great brunch.

Yet Wah. Pier 39 (434–4430). Every province stars on this sumptuous menu.

Inexpensive

Bull's. 25 Van Ness Ave. (864–4288). Southwestern motif. Menu greats include ribs, chile, burgers. Busy bar.

Capp's Corner. 1600 Powell (989–2589). A North Beach institution. Locals and visitors rave about the Italian family-style dining; under $10.

Clown Alley. 42 Columbus (421–2540 Columbus) & 2499 Lombard. (931–5890). Favorite hamburger scene.

Il Pollaio. 555 Columbus Ave. (362–7727). In rural Italy, *friggitoria* or "fry shop" feature roast meats, especially chicken. North Beach's new "chicken coop" *Il Pollaio* offers a memorable, inexpensive dinner.

Lefty O'Doul's. 333 Geary (982–8900). Downtown hofbrau. Children welcome.

Golden Turtle. 308 5th Ave., near Clement (221–5285). Award-winning Vietnamese restaurant serving marinated meats cooked over charcoal.

Magic Pan. 341 Sutter (788–7397) and Ghiradelli Square (474–6733). Entree & dessert crepes. Feather-light and tempting. Steak kebobs and salads offer change-of-pace possibilities.

Salmagundi. 442 Geary (441–0894); 2 Embarcadero Center (982–5603); and 1236 Market Street (431–7337). Soups, salads, quiche, Espresso and Cappucino.

Zim's. Six locations: check directory. Breakfast and hamburger stop.

TOURIST INFORMATION SERVICES. General information is available from San Francisco Convention and Visitors Bureau, Swig Pavilion, Hallidie Plaza, Powell & Market Streets. For bus tours contact: Gray Line of San Francisco, 420 Taylor St., San Francisco.

HOW TO GET AROUND. San Francisco is surprisingly compact. Many of its most interesting sights are within easy walking distance of each other. From Union Square, it's an easy stroll through Chinatown to Jackson Square and North Beach—and wherever you are there are things to see.

By Car: If you are driving your car during your stay in San Francisco, there are three points to remember: 1) cable cars have the right of way, 2) cars parked on any grade or hill must have wheels set to the curb to prevent rolling, 3) watch parking signs: there are many tow-away zones during certain hours, and cars illegally parked are towed away.

You'll have to pay a toll to drive over one of the bridges: 75¢ westbound on the long San Francisco—Oakland Bay Bridge, free eastbound; $1 weekdays, $2 weekends on the Golden Gate Bridge to Sausalito and Marin County.

By Bus: The most economical way to reach points in the city beyond walking distance is cable cars, streetcars and buses. Bus maps are at the front of the Yellow Pages in the telephone book; free transfers at many points.

Beyond the city limits trains and buses will carry you most anyplace. The Bay Area Rapid Transit System (BART) now operates; Greyhound Lines offer regular commuter service to most points. AC Bus Transit System operates between San Francisco and many points in the East Bay.

By Ferry: *Golden Gate Ferries* depart daily to Sausalito from the Ferry Building, at the foot of Market Street. *Larkspur* has a Monday-Friday commuter service. *Red & White Fleet* operates daily to Sausalito from Pier 41. Fare: $3.50 one way; 5–11, $1.75 when accompanied by an adult. Week-day commuter service to Tiburon is from the Ferry Bdlg.; week-ends from Pier 43½. Fare: $3.50 one way; children under 5 free. Week-end and holiday service to Angel Island from Pier 43 ½. Fare: $6.10 round-trip; children $3.30 (5–11).

By Cable Car: By the summer of 1984, San Francisco's three cable car systems were in operation again. The 21-month project cost $75 million according to some sources, others insist $58.2 million. On June 21, 1984, Mayor Feinstein, Tony Bennett and 100,000 party-minded people celebrated with an all city parade and picnic. Both the Powell-Mason (#59) and the Powell-Hyde

(#60) terminate at Fisherman's Wharf. The California (#61) runs east-west to Van Ness Ave. Adult fare: $1.50 with transfer 75¢.

MUSEUMS AND GALLERIES. There are several fine arts museums in the city. In the Civic Center is the *San Francisco Museum of Art,* which has frequently changing exhibits. The *M.H. deYoung Museum* is in Golden Gate Park. Its spacious galleries enclose a landscaped court. Paintings by Rembrandt, El Greco, Titian, Rubens, etc. Open 10 A.M. to 5 P.M.; closed Monday and Tuesday (415–558–2887). The magnificent collection of Asian arts, one of the finest in the western world, donated by Avery Brundage, late president of the International Olympic Committee. The collection is housed in the Asian Art Museum, a wing of the deYoung building. The *California Palace of the Legion of Honor* is in Lincoln Park, at the end of California Street. A beautiful museum, recently renovated, it has a magnificent view of the city from the terrace. There's a small restaurant. It's worthwhile to get out to the *Oakland Art Museum,* 10th and Oak Sts., Oakland; excellent cafe. Large collection of California art, including early engravings by the Spanish explorers, and Gold Rush paintings. Open Wed.-Sat. 10 A.M.–5 P.M.; Sun noon–7 P.M. (415–893–4263).

Arts and crafts may be seen at the *Union Street* galleries, between several unusual restaurants. *Images of the North,* 1782 Union, is the city's only gallery specializing in Native North American art. Traditional Eskimo themes appear in stone carvings and colorful prints; there is also Southwest Indian pottery and jewelry. The *Mexican Museum,* Fort Mason, Building D, is one of the few of its kind in the United States. It houses Mexican colonial and folk art and the works of contemporary Mexican and Chicano artists. *The San Francisco Crafts and Folk Art Museum,* 626 Balboa St. (415–668–0406) exhibits work from state and international artists. Open Wed.-Fri., 1 P.M.–5 P.M.; Sat.-Sun., 1 P.M.–4 P.M. Closed Mon.-Tues.; major holidays.

Other kinds of exhibits may be seen at these museums: *Wells Fargo History Room,* at 420 Montgomery St., in the Wells Fargo bank. Varied collection of objects that figured in the development of the West. Open 9–5 weekdays. There is the *Academy of Sciences* in Golden Gate Park, housing a collection of American and African mammals (mounted), as well as the *Steinhart Aquarium* with its great fish collection, and *Morrison Planetarium.* Open daily. The *Maritime Museum,* foot of Polk Street. Seafaring exhibits with model ships, old figureheads, etc. Open daily 10–5. The *Museum of Paleontology,* at the University of California in Berkeley (Hearst Memorial Building and Bacon Hall). Largest collection of its type on the Pacific Coast. A good geology museum with displays of rocks, minerals, and dioramas depicting what life was like in the various prehistoric ages. Open daily 9–4; 9-noon Saturdays.

The *Balclutha* Pier 43 (415–929–0202), last of the square-sail fleet that sailed around Cape Horn to San Francisco in the late 19th century. Exhibits include photo displays and relics. Open 9 A.M.–9 P.M. The *Cable Car Barn* Washington & Mason (415/474–1887), has a visitors' gallery and museum with 19th-century photos of the cars that are the only national landmark on wheels. Open daily 10 A.M.–5 P.M. The *California Historical Society,* 2090 Jackson St., (415–567–1848), has a library and small museum. Open Wed., Sat.-Sun., 1 P.M.–4:30 P.M.

HISTORIC SITES. San Francisco itself has the *Presidio,* the *Mission Dolores,* and the *Opera House,* important because it is where the United Nations was officially organized. Ft. Point, the city's most northern point, was built to protect the Bay during the Civil War. Unique architecture lying beneath the Golden Gate Bridge. Superb views. *Portsmouth Square* is a small historic park in Chinatown, where the U.S. flag was raised in July 1846.

GARDENS. The *sidewalk flower stands* of San Francisco have been a tradition since the 1880s. Specialties are daphne in the spring, tiny Pinocchio roses in summer, chrysanthemums in fall, holly in winter. At *Golden Gate Park,* see the *Japanese Tea Garden,* with its camellias, magnolias, red-leafed Japanese maples. It's a fairyland of *cherry blossoms* in the spring (usually at their best in early April). See also the *Conservatory.* Modeled after Kew Gardens in England, it's a fascinating hothouse in a fascinating setting—the sections of the building were brought around the Horn by clipper ship. Out front a floral design honors contemporary events of local or national importance. In South San Francisco, see *Rod McLellan Gardens,* at 1450 El Camino Real. *Orchids,* as far as the eye can see; also greenhouses filled with carnations, gardenias, anthuriums and poinsettias, all aligned in uniform rows under laboratory-like conditions. Open from 8 A.M. to 5 P.M., with tours at 10:30 A.M. and 1:30 P.M. The gardens at *Sunset Magazine,* Menlo Park (down the Peninsula), have all the outstanding trees, shrubs and flowers native to all sections of the Pacific coast. There are tours, or you can stroll about on your own. *Lakeside Nursery Gardens,* at Lake Merritt, Oakland, have a show garden and a propagating nursery for the many Oakland parks. In Santa Cruz *(Antonelli Bros.),* and in Capitola *(Vetterle & Reinelt Hybridizing Gardens),* begonia nurseries are at their most spectacular in August and September. Capitola has a *Begonia Festival* every September.

TOURS. *Gray Line* offers a variety of tours, from a deluxe 3½-hour comprehensive view to an all-day city, Sausalito, Muir Woods, and Bay Cruise excursion. Half-day trips to Muir Woods and the famous giant redwoods in the 550–acre National Monument are very popular. Daily day-long excursions to the Napa and Sonoma Valleys include a performance of "Napa Valley Show" at Vintage 1870, a restored shopping and restaurant complex. Special stops are made at two wineries. Wine tasting not allowed to persons under 21. Reservations are a must. Another scenic route is south to Monterey, charming Carmel and a picturesque drive thru privately owned Del Monte Forest. Though a long day, there is a lunch at Monterey's Cannery Row and the new Monterey Bay Aquarium. New limo service is available for all tours. *California Parlor Car Tours* offers three-to-five day tours to Yosemite, Lake Tahoe, Monterey, Carmel, and the Hearst Castle at San Simeon.

Red & White Fleet Harbor Tours sightseeing boats make short 1 ¼-hour cruises around San Francisco Bay constantly, every day, all year around. Departures from Fisherman's Wharf. Telephone 415–546–2896 for time/price. Weekends, June to October, both the *Red & White Fleet* and the *Blue & Gold Fleet* offer cruising with dining, dancing and entertainment. For details phone: Red & White: 415–546–2896; Blue & Gold: 415–781–7877. The commuter ferries listed under "How to Get Around" are also pleasant ways to tour the Bay.

SPECIAL EXHIBITS. The following sites are a bit off the usual tourist trek, but worth the effort. Famed and photogenic *Coit Tower,* atop Telegraph Hill, houses fascinating murals by WPA artists of the '30s. Visit the *Musée Mécanique,* at the Cliff House. This is a fascinating collection of old arcade games dating from the 17th century to modern-day video era. Free. A challenge to young and old are the more than 400 science-oriented exhibits at *Exploratorium,* at 3601 Lyon Street. *Ft. Point National Historic Site* at Golden Gate Bridge, features free tours of the three-tiered brick structure from 10–5. *The American Carousel Museum,* 633 Beach St., displays vintage carousel figures and ongoing figure-carving and restoration demonstrations.

MUSIC. All year, there are free *band concerts* in San Francisco's *Golden Gate Park* on Sunday and holiday afternoons; *organ recitals* on Saturday and Sunday afternoons in the *Palace of the Legion of Honor* (free, after paying museum entrance fee). Oakland also offers free concerts by the *Municipal*

Band Sunday afternoons at the bandstand at Lake Merritt. *San Francisco Opera* season opens in mid-September annually, and runs for thirteen weeks. San Francisco's first Summer Festival, May 28–August 15, 1982 was a dazzling line-up of grand opera including Handel's *Julius Caesar* and Puccini's *Turandot,* both sellouts. San Francisco's *Symphony* subscription season is Sept-May; Davies Hall. During July the symphony can be heard in a lighter role—in pops concerts. Sunday afternoons in summer there's free opera, symphony, or ballet in the *Sigmund Stern Grove,* out past Golden Gate Park, and also *chamber music* concerts at the *Paul Masson Vineyards* high on a mountaintop in Saratoga (down the Peninsula).

STAGE AND REVUES. The *American Conservatory Theater,* Geary Theater, is a resident repertory company with a regular season extending from late October into May. The *Curran, Golden Gate and Orpheum Theaters* offer the best-of-Broadway musicals and dramas. The *San Francisco Ballet* has two principal seasons: Winter and Spring.

NIGHTCLUBS. San Francisco is a swinging city, and the choice of after dark entertainment is broad. Tour buses still frequent Broadway, their passengers herded into *Finocchio's,* with its lavish revue of female impersonators. Most of the other clubs are run-down, shady operations where you are on your own. Beware. The "topless, bottomless" clubs have overexposed their product and those surviving attract undesirables.

Jazz is popular and old and new names appear at *Bajone's, Kimball's, Milestones, Pier, 23,* and *Pearl's,* the Hotel York's *Plush Room* and Bill Graham's new *Wolfgang's* at 901 Columbus.

Dancing is very much in. From the elegant *Venetian Room* in the Fairmont which features headline entertainment and ballroom dance music by Dick Bright, to *Henri's* on the 46th floor of the Hilton, it's the return of the light fantastic. "Disco" dancing stars at Hyatt Union Square's *Reflections,* the *Holiday Inn,* Van Ness Avenue, and the *Bay Street Bar & Grill,* Ramada Inn. *Barnaby's,* One Embarcadero Center, jumps with three rock bands, three dance floors with music and dancing from 5 until 2 A.M. Tuesday thru Saturday. *Hyatt Regency* has big-band dancing Friday, 5:30–8:30 P.M. and free jazz concerts Saturday and Sunday afternoons. *Oz,* on the 32nd floor of the *Westin St. Francis,* is a mirrored and glass fantasy forest for disco fans. Salsa swingers pack *Cesar's Palace,* 3140 Mission Street.

BARS. As in many other areas, San Francisco's bars have style. For those wishing a view, the skyrooms are spectacular spots for wining and dining. The *Carnelian Room* crowns the 52-story Bank of America Center. The *Equinox* is a revolving restaurant atop the Hyatt Regency. Long-time favorites are the Fairmont *Crown Room,* the *Henri's at the Hilton* and the *Top of the Mark* in the Mark Hopkins.

In recent years, there has been instant success in "singles" establishments, many Victorian in decor, all with great ambiance. Referred to by some critics as "body shops," essentially they are boy meets girl places. Most famed is *Perry's* on Union Street. *Lord Jim's, Balboa* and *Harry's Bar* all attract crowds nightly. A favorite of media and arty types is North Beach's *Washington Square Bar & Grill.* Union Square's *Lefty O'Doul's* is a family spot featuring a photo gallery of sports figures and a sing-along piano bar. The *Hard Rock Cafe,* 1699 Van Ness, a clone of Peter Morton's London success, is packed with younger yuppies.

Popular Union Square bars are *Napper Tandy,* in the Hyatt Union Square, Irish pub informality, fine for lunch. Across the park in the St. Francis is *Dewey's* and the new Art Deco rendezvous, *Compass Rose.*

SUMMER SPORTS. *Golf:* The Olympic Club ranks among America's greatest courses. There are four public golf courses—Harding Park, Lincoln Park, Golden Gate Park and Sharp Park in Pacifica.

Tennis: There are more than 100 tennis courts throughout the city, maintained by the San Francisco Recreation & Parks Department (415–566–4800). With the exception of the 21 courts located in Golden Gate Park, all are free.

San Francisco Bay offers *sailing* all year round, and there's also sailing in the Oakland Estuary, and on Lake Merced, Lake Merritt, Richardson Bay, Tomales Bay and at Palo Alto and Redwood City. If you like to *fish,* just go casting off San Francisco's municipal pier at Aquatic Park (all-year, no license), or at Lake Merced.

Numerous *bicycle* and roller skate rental agencies are located at main entrances to Golden Gate Park.

SPECTATOR SPORTS. Professional matches of the *football-playing 49ers,* the *Giants baseball* team, *basketball* games of the *Pioneers,* and Saturday afternoon *rugby* matches. The *Annual Open Skeet* and *Trap Shoot* of the Pacific Rod and Gun Club takes place at Lake Merced in late April. For *horse racing, Bay Meadows* is the major spot. It has three seasons: roughly, mid-January through February, mid-May to mid-June, and early November to mid-December. There is also racing in the East Bay at *Golden Gate Fields* from Feb. to June. See the *Annual Pacific Coast International Tennis Championships* at the Berkeley Tennis Club in September. *Rodeo* buffs will want to see the *Grand National,* in October. *Opening Day yachting parade* is held in late April and early May. This traditional and festive occasion dating from the early 1900s opens with the blessing of the fleet of Tiburon. Good vantage points are along the Marina or the Vista View area on the Sausalito side of the Golden Gate Bridge. In October there's the *Transamerica Open Tennis Championships* at the Cow Palace.

SHOPPING. Podesta & Baldocchi, the famed florists, have moved to 2525 California, near Steiner. A tradition since 1907, their trademark creations have involved unusual arrangements in unlikely containers. Always a fantasyland, especially during the Christmas season. The Grant Avenue shops and bazaars in Chinatown are fascinating, with their plastic ivory and jade-like collectibles, their brocade material, basketry, teak furniture.

Union Square and its environs is the center of an extensive, smart shopping area that includes large department stores and specialty shops for both men and women. Nordstrom, Bullock & Jones, I. Magnin, Macy's, Saks Fifth Avenue and Neiman-Marcus are some of the larger stores. On Post Street, nearby, are several unique luxury shops including Gump's, Alfred Dunhill, Arden's, Shreve's, Brooks Brothers, Gucci, Jaeger and Roberts Furs. They're all in the "200" block of Post. Gump's is unique for exotic and useful imports, with heavy accent on the Oriental (ask to see the jade collection, worth, in individual pieces, up to $100,000. It is kept behind locked doors but will be shown to anyone interested). This store got its start as a bric-a-brac shop!

Down in the Fisherman's Wharf area explore the city's newest complex, Pier 39, boasting over one hundred shops, galleries, and restaurants. Several interesting shops at The Cannery and Ghirardelli Square, which are a must to see. For antiques, the Jackson Square area, Union Street, between Franklin and Steiner, and upper Sacramento Street. The best of the best are Hardy, John Doughty, Dolphin Antiques, Postlethwaite, and Arbes & Co. Check opening times.

For fine art, Sutter Street has several important galleries: Walton-Gilbert, Maxwell, Janet Steinberg, John Pence, and Maiden Lane's Moss and Conacher, John Berggruen, Hansen, Harcourts, and Union Street Graphics (original prints and posters from 1880 to the present). Also worth a visit are Vorpal and Hoover galleries. You can also buy one thousand paintings of San Francisco, but many of them are turned out in assembly-line fashion. Great ice cream at Häagen-

Dazs (Union and Columbus). Sample California wines—some of the best can be purchased only here, or at the wineries, offering estate-bottled classics.

CHILDREN'S ACTIVITIES. Stroll across the *Golden Gate Bridge.* Try to time your walk for when a ship will be sailing beneath. Then you'll realize how very high you are (220 feet), and how very huge the bridge is. Take them aboard the *Balclutha,* the handsome old three-masted sailing ship near Fisherman's Wharf. Inspect the wheelhouse, the red-plus chart house, the captain's cabin, the ship's gallery. Open 9 A.M. to 10 P.M. Show them the *buffalo* in the paddock at Golden Gate Park. They seem to be roaming at large. Take them to the *San Francisco Zoo.* Easiest way to get about is by the *Zebra Zephyr* leaving the Giraffe Barn every half hour between 10 A.M. and 6 P.M. Visit the new $2-million Gorilla World, rare white tigers and [illegible]. Take them sailing on easy-to-navigate *Lake Merritt* in Oakland, or *Lake Merced* in San Francisco.

Marina Green is a grassy waterfront recreation area with a beautiful view of the Bay. *James D. Phelan Beach,* at 28th and Sea Cliff Avenue, is a 6-acre park with beach frontage, for sunbathing and picnics. *Ocean Beach* has plenty of sand and surf and a superb view. *Lake Merced* offers boating and fishing within the city.

EXPLORING NORTHERN CALIFORNIA

Oakland and Berkeley

Oakland is much more than home base for the Oakland Athletics baseball franchise. Kaiser Industries World Headquarters splash the skyline. The Port of Oakland is #2 in containerized cargo. Controversial BART (Bay Area Rapid Transit), a 75-mile inter-city train system, links 15 bedroom communities with San Francisco.

Culturally, the city is alive and thriving. Visit the award-winning 3-terraced Museum, a storehouse of California lore. Inspect the new Natural Sciences Gallery, dedicated to increasing our understanding of the environment. Snack at the bar or linger over a gourmet lunch, with California wine, at the attractive Museum restaurant, staffed by local volunteers.

Pop into the Paramount Theatre, Broadway at 21st Street. This gilded Art Deco showplace is a State Historical Landmark as well as being listed in the National Register of Historic Places. It was restored to its original opulence in 1973, by Skidmore, Owings & Merrill, and is one of the last remaining 1930-vintage movie palaces. It is now the home of the Oakland Symphony. Three public tours are scheduled each month: on the first Monday at 2 P.M., and on the second and fourth Tuesdays at 11 A.M. There is a modest admission charge.

Oakland's sparkling Lake Merritt was declared a State Game Refuge in 1870—making it the oldest wildlife refuge on the North American continent. Along its shoreline and on man-made islands, thousands of migratory waterfowl spend the fall and winter months. Almost one hundred species of bird—both migratory and permanent residents—have been observed. Daily lectures are offered by park naturalists at the feeding grounds.

Lakeside Park, including the lake, consists of 277 acres and three miles of shoreline. Popular for jogging, strolling, boating, and bicycling. A summer Sunday afternoon draws as many as 50,000 people, without crowding.

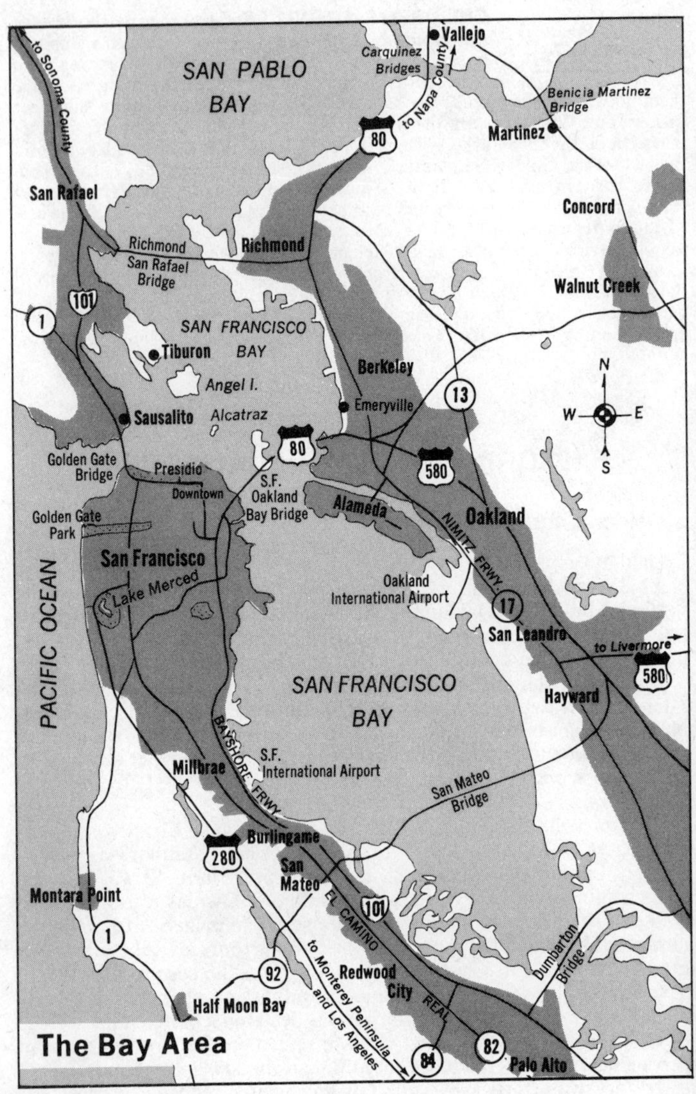
SAN PABLO BAY
Vallejo
Carquinez Bridges
to Napa County
80
Benicia Martinez Bridge
Martinez
to Sonoma County
San Rafael
Concord
Richmond
Richmond San Rafael Bridge
Walnut Creek
101
1
SAN FRANCISCO BAY
Tiburon
Angel I.
Berkeley
13
N
W
E
S
Sausalito
Alcatraz
Emeryville
80
580
Golden Gate Bridge
Presidio
Downtown
S.F. Oakland Bay Bridge
Alameda
Oakland
Golden Gate Park
NIMITZ FRWY.
San Francisco
Lake Merced
Oakland International Airport
17
PACIFIC OCEAN
San Leandro
to Livermore
580
SAN FRANCISCO BAY
Hayward
BAYSHORE FRWY
Millbrae
S.F. International Airport
San Mateo Bridge
280
Burlingame
San Mateo
Montara Point
EL CAMINO REAL
101
1
Dumbarton Bridge
92
to Monterey Peninsula and Los Angeles
Redwood City
Half Moon Bay
The Bay Area
84
82
Palo Alto

Close by the bandstand is Children's Fairyland, the pioneering playland conceived about 25 years ago and now consisting of some 60 settings based on fairy stories and Mother Goose Rhymes. Especially popular with the young at heart are their puppet and magic shows.

We mentioned Jack London Square previously. Its prime attraction is the *First and Last Chance Saloon,* a mini-museum cum bar crammed with memorabilia from the life and times of London.

Star gaze at the Chabot Science Center, 4917 Mountain Boulevard, the Bay Area's oldest observatory, built in 1913. Its 20-inch refractor telescope is the largest open year-round for public viewing.

Berkeley is a blend of old and new, ugly and attractive. The city developed out of two separate and distinct communities; the western flatland area oriented to Oakland and the Bay and the hillside community oriented to the university.

The Berkeley campus is one of nine of the University of California's institutions. Student population is about 30,000. Its first class graduated in 1873. The University Art Museum, 2626 Bancroft Way, has an outstanding permanent collection of Hans Hofmann and its changing exhibits feature ceramics, collages, paintings, and photos of contemporary artists as well as earlier periods.

For the sights and sounds of now, stroll along Telegraph Avenue to where it meets Bancroft Way. En route, street artisans set up shop offering the usual leather, pottery, and tie-dye fashions. Ethnic eating spots and Little Theater offerings are popular. Dress is highly original or banal (the jeans syndrome).

Gastronomic fans crowd two local restaurants: John Hudspeth's American classics at Bridge Creek, and Alice Waters Chez Panisse.

The dominant architectural character of north Berkeley is eclectic—little-boxes-on-stilts-on-the-hillside, multi-versions of Swiss Chalets, informal shingled structures, fantasy Spanish castles, and modest cottages.

A must for scholars is The Judah L. Magnes Memorial Museum (the Jewish Museum of the West), 2911 Russell Street. In addition to one of the nation's largest collections of Jewish ceremonial objects, the Museum has a general library, as well as archives on Jews living on the West Coast. Phone 415–849–2710 for hours.

The Lawrence Hall of Science in the East Bay hills at Centennial Drive exhibits scientific displays aimed at educating visitors of all ages. Computer games draw a faithful following. Phone 415–642–5132 for information.

Meanwhile, in Marin County

Crossing the Golden Gate Bridge (opened in 1937) is a visual adventure. The United States Travel Service rated it as the country's premier man-made attraction. Panoramic views of the 456-square-mile area that is San Francisco Bay plus the steep and rocky headlands, often shrouded in summer fog, dazzle viewers. The Verrazano-Narrows Bridge, between Staten Island and Brooklyn, N.Y., has a suspension span of 4,260 ft., longest in the world and exceeding the Golden Gate Bridge by 60 feet.

Early-day San Francisco's water supply came from willow-shaded springs on the Marin shore, and was carried in barrels, aboard rafts to the city. Sausalito (a corruption of the Spanish *Salcedo,* meaning willow) is a delightful excursion. A bit like villages on the French Riviera,

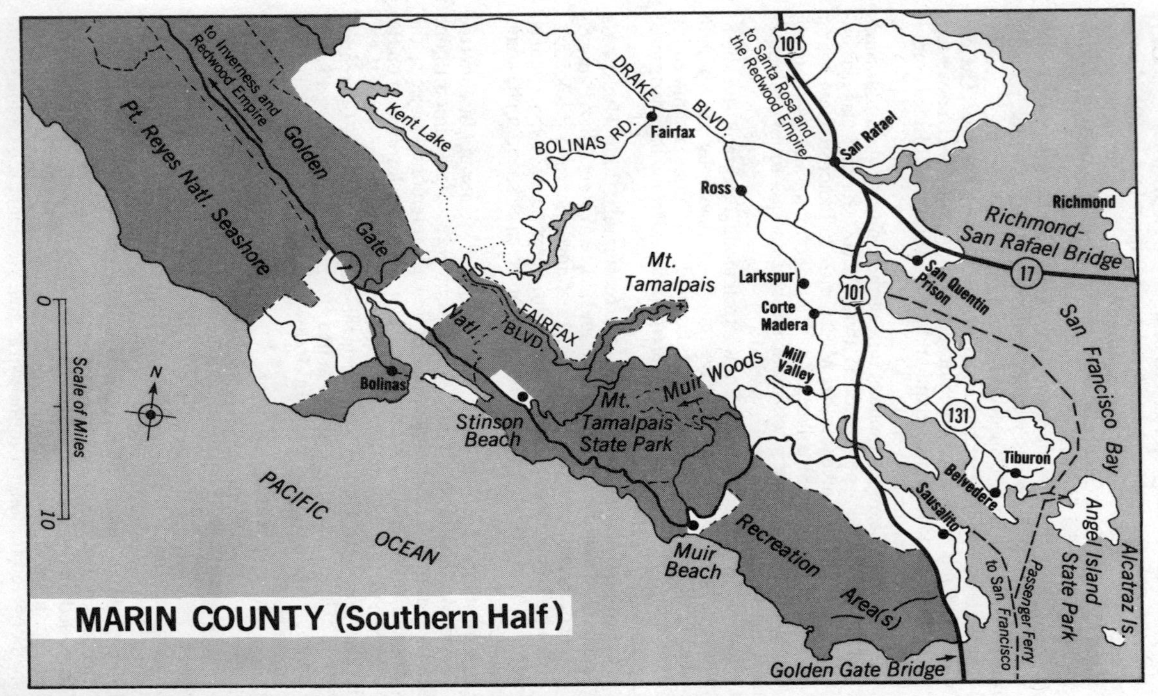
MARIN COUNTY (Southern Half)
to Inverness and Redwood Empire
Pt. Reyes Natl. Seashore
Golden
Gate
1
Kent Lake
DRAKE
BLVD.
BOLINAS RD.
Fairfax
101
to Santa Rosa and the Redwood Empire
San Rafael
Ross
Richmond
Richmond-San Rafael Bridge
17
San Quentin Prison
Mt. Tamalpais
Larkspur
Corte Madera
FAIRFAX
BLVD.
Natl.
Mill Valley
Muir Woods
Muir
Mt. Tamalpais State Park
San Francisco Bay
131
Tiburon
Belvedere
Sausalito
Bolinas
Stinson Beach
N
Scale of Miles
0
10
PACIFIC
OCEAN
Muir Beach
Recreation
Area(s)
Angel Island State Park
Alcatraz Is.
Passenger Ferry
to San Francisco
Golden Gate Bridge

sun, scenery (the view of San Francisco is smashing) swank shops, several superb restaurants. Sausalitans seem to tolerate tourists and share they will, part-time.

One of the loveliest spots in Sausalito for brunch (weekday, if possible), is the hillside hotel *Alta Mira.* From its terrace, scan the San Francisco skyline, savoring their special Eggs Benedict. Watch out for the Ramos fizzes (gin, cream, egg white, lemon, sugar, curaçao)—potent brew. For a very special evening, dine at *Ondine.*

San Rafael is the county seat of "Marvelous Marin." One of the local marvels is the 1957 Frank Lloyd Wright Civic Center. Its golden spiked tower, graceful arches, and lavish indoor and outdoor landscaping are much photographed.

Believe-it-or-not creator Robert L. Ripley is honored in his hometown, Santa Rosa, by the Church of One Tree Museum. The church is built of one redwood tree which grew near Guerneville. A favorite stop is State Historical Monument 19, the home and gardens of Luther Burbank. The famed naturalist worked for over fifty years in the area in plant research and experimentation. He died in 1926, at the age of 77. In June 1977, his widow and former secretary, Elizabeth, died at the age of 89. She had outlived her "plant wizard" by 51 years.

Santa Rosa is the gateway for the Russian River area, as Napa is for the Napa Valley wineries.

In 1769 Father Junipero Serra and his followers brought wine grape vines and seeds with them from Mexico and planted them as they built their 21-mission chain as far north as Sonoma. The wine industry based at these missions thrived until the 1830s. By that time, commercial vineyards were beginning to flourish, especially in Los Angeles.

During the early 1850s, immigrant Hungarian County Agoston Haraszthy imported some 100,000 cuttings of 300 European grape varieties. More than 125 principal varieties thrive today and new varieties are constantly being developed, especially at the Davis Campus of the University of California.

The "Count" settled briefly at historic Buena Vista Ranch, near Sonoma. Most of the state's present ten thousand growers operate vineyards smaller than Haraszthy's original acreage.

Visit a family-operated spread like the 350-acre Sebastiani Vineyard. The late Don August Sebastiani proudly rejected impressive offers to buy the thriving operation. More than a million cases of wine are shipped yearly from this winery.

Chateau Souverain in Geyserville is the design of Sausalito architect John Marsh Davis. In addition to the tours and tastings, lunch and dinner are served in the Souverain Restaurant. Call for reservations.

A special side-trip is a pilgrimage to Glen Ellen, in the Valley of the Moon. Jack London is buried under a red lava boulder. Admirers from around the globe seek this shrine. Some come to gaze and study the personal possessions on view. Most hike to the haunting ruins of Wolf House, his dream castle burned the night after it was finished.

Northern California's Redwood Highway starts at the Golden Gate Bridge; 200 miles north one meets the giant 2,000-year old redwoods. John Steinbeck called the tall trees "Ambassadors from another time . . ." From southwestern Oregon to California's Big Sur splendor, there are 181,000 acres of preserved *Sequoia Sempervirens.*

Muir Woods National Monument, a 550-acre grove, forty minutes drive from San Francisco, hosts over a million visitors yearly. Most linger an hour or two, follow nature trails to Cathedral Grove, with its plaque commemorating a visit in 1945 of United Nations delegates.

There is a "Braille Trail" for blind visitors. There is a restaurant and souvenir shop as well as nearby picnic grounds on 2,600-foot Mt. Tamalpais.

From three to five days are needed for extended trips north through Ft. Ross (an early Russian outpost), the rugged coast, and picturesque Mendocino village. Born in the Gold Rush clamor, today it is a charmer—an internationally recognized art colony with a strong streak of New England "down east" manners and mores. Once a thriving logging and fishing center, boasting 3,500 residents, 8 hotels, 17 saloons and perhaps 15 to 20 bordellos, contemporary Mendocino offers limited and unspoiled vacationing.

Heritage House, at Little River, is a quiet country inn, informal, handsome accommodations, a gourmet dining room and lots of paths along the beaches and thru the forests. Many of the scenes in the film *Same Time Next Year* were shot at this charming resort. Fort Bragg, north of Mendocino, is the terminus of the famous "Skunk" railroad excursions. A must for railroad buffs, camera clickers and all the family. The round trip takes about six hours and one crosses thirty-one bridges and trestles thru redwoods.

The Big Daddy of them all is Redwood National Park, established in 1968, near Crescent City, close to the Oregon border.

The Old and the New in Monterey

Monterey, the legendary first capitol of California, is about two hours south of San Francisco.

The new Monterey Bay Aquarium, a $40 million, state-of-the-art facility opened in the fall of 1984 on Cannery Row. It offers a fish-eye look into the underwater wonders of Monterey Bay and is a marine research center as well as a "hands-on" experience for the public.

The best way to explore Monterey is on foot. In 1938, the city adopted the "Path of History" plan. A circular route, 2.8 miles long, with a red-orange line painted on the streets, leads to many of the historical landmarks. The Chamber of Commerce provides a free map plotting the route.

Begin at Custom House, one of the ten buildings and sites combined in the Monterey State Historic Park. On July 7, 1846, Commodore John Sloat raised the 28-star U.S. flag over the Plaza, which had previously hosted the standards of Spain, Mexico and the short-lived Bear Republic.

Nearby, the Casa Del Oro showcases the utilitarian objects of the business and social life of the community. It was a leading saloon in the fishing port.

In 1845, Thomas Oliver Larkin spent $8,000, and the labor of Indians, military deserters and civil prisoners who quarried the stone, to complete the first wharf.

The Larkin House, built in the 1830s, is a gracious two-storied adobe, which served as the U.S. Consulate in 1843–46, when the former Bostonian became the first and only Consul to Mexico in Monterey. The home became the prototype of the popular "Monterey" style of architecture.

For Robert Louis Stevenson buffs, a stop at the former rooming house where he autumned in 1879 is mandatory. The author did a series of articles for the local papers to earn his bed and one full meal daily. Payment—$2 weekly! In "Across The Plains" he wrote: "On no

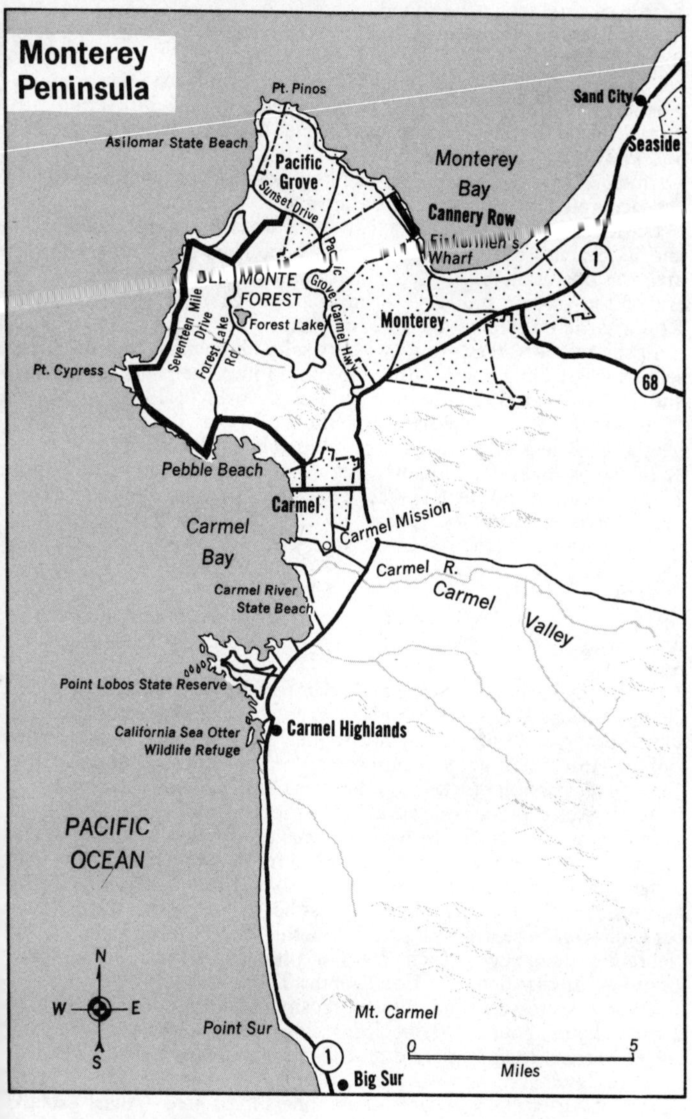
Monterey Peninsula
Pt. Pinos
Sand City
Asilomar State Beach
Seaside
Pacific Grove
Monterey Bay
Sunset Drive
Cannery Row
Wharf
1
MONTE FOREST
Seventeen Mile Drive
Forest Lake
Pacific Grove Carmel Hwy
Monterey
Forest Lake Rd.
Pt. Cypress
68
Pebble Beach
Carmel
Carmel Mission
Carmel Bay
Carmel R.
Carmel Valley
Carmel River State Beach
Point Lobos State Reserve
California Sea Otter Wildlife Refuge
Carmel Highlands
PACIFIC OCEAN
N
W
E
S
Mt. Carmel
Point Sur
0
5
Miles
1
Big Sur

other coast that I know shall you enjoy, in calm, sunny weather, such a spectacle of ocean greatness, such beauty of changing color, or such degree of thunder in the sound."

The Presidio, founded in 1770 as a garrison for Spanish soldiers, today headquarters the Defense Language Institute.

The Great Conquistador of the Cross, Padre Junipero Serra, founded Mission San Carlos in 1770. Fourteen years later, he died and was buried inside the sanctuary of the Carmel Mission, dedicated in 1775 and known today as the Basilica of Mission Carlos Borromeo del Rio Carmelo. The church is one of the finest examples of the ornate Mexican decorative architecture in California.

Until the turn-of-the-century, Monterey was a booming whaling port and its beaches were white with whalebone. The first cannery in the area was operating in 1895, packing salmon mostly. The 1930s was the era of the sardine industry. From about 1921 thru 1946, Cannery Row's sardine spree netted a $22-million catch.

In the mid-40s, the "Row" with its salty characters, colorful purse seiners (big fishing boats with nets) passed into the pages of Pulitzer and Nobel Prize winner John Steinbeck's work. In 1945, his novel, "Cannery Row" was released and the world was introduced to the people, buildings and the spirit of adventure of the Wharf.

Salinas is Steinbeck-land. His maternal grandparents settled on a 1,700-acre grain and cattle spread, a few miles south of King City. This ranch served as model for "Trask" in "East of Eden." In 1952, the film was shot on location. As in "Cannery Row," "Tortilla Flat" and "Sweet Thursday" some actual sites still exist, but often not in the locations the author described.

On his death in 1968, the "hometown boy" was buried at 768 Abbott. Visit the Steinbeck Library, 110 W. San Luis, with its memorabilia.

Each July, Salinas' California Rodeo recaptures the thrills and excitement of the Western Frontier. Top cowboys compete in bareback, saddle-bronc and bull riding, calf roping, steer wrestling and Roman riding. Most times, a TV or movie star lends additional glitter.

September spotlights the Monterey Jazz Festival. Annual since 1957, it has attracted old and new names in the music galaxy.

In fall, nearby Pacific Grove is the main attraction with the return of millions of orange monarch butterflies from summering in Canada.

Spectator sports bring visitors all seasons. From January's AT&T Pro-Am Golf Tournament to the newest heady experience, the December California Wine Festival, the follow-the-sport set are offered motor car rallies, polo, rugby, yacht races and the jet-set frolic, July's Clint Eastwood Invitational Celebrity Tennis Tournament.

Carmel is crowded and colorful, cosmopolitan and quaint. It is a community of about 5,000 full-time residents with perhaps a like number of tourists each week-end and all summer. It is a collage of art galleries, fascinating shops and restaurants, seascapes and serendipity.

Two of America's premier photographers lived here—Ansel Adams and Edward Weston. Collectors should seek out the Weston Gallery which displays prints of both artists. The distinguished Pasquale Iannetti Gallery exhibits prints and drawings from 16th-century and contemporary masters.

A must is the 17-mile Drive through Del Monte Forest, an unforgettable landscape of Monterey cypress. The wind-twisted trees are unique to this area and Point Lobos. The snowy sand dunes and the elegant and eclectic architecture are fascinating. Entrance fee is $5 per car; unless one is visiting friends in the distinguished private community.

There are 34 miles of bridal paths in the forest. Pause at Seal and Bird Rocks to film and observe the antics of the shore birds and the offshore herds of sea lions.

Along the peninsula's south shore is Pebble Beach, one of the top ten golf courses in the U.S. Many celebrities call the Monterey Peninsula home. Most agree with Clint Eastwood's statement: "There's not a place in the world I'd rather live than on the Monterey Peninsula. I plan to stay forever."

Currently, Doug McClure, Merv Griffin, Kim Novak and cartoonist Gus Ariola enjoy a special lifestyle in this wild and beautiful land. Unfortunately, Big Sur's great photographer Ansel Adams died in May 1984.

A few miles south of Carmel, is Point Lobos Reserve State Park, over a thousand acres of coastal and inland territory established to protect the California sea otter and insure a breeding ground for the California brown pelican, considered an endangered species. Early morning tidepool walks are offered during low tide periods. Because of mass collecting of specimens and the disturbance of habitat, alarming declines in the population of many species have been noted. In order to protect fragile marine organisms, attendance at the tidepool walks is limited to 50. Check with Rangers.

Robert Louis Stevenson visited Point Lobos (the early Spanish named it Punta de los Lobos Marinos—Point of the Sea Wolves) in 1879 and it is said he found inspiration for Spyglass Hill in "Treasure Island" here. In November, the reserve offers a vantage point for the viewing of the migrating California gray whale. This large mammal, up to 40 tons and 50 feet long, can be seen as it travels close to shoreline.

Big Sur Country, approximately 150 miles south of San Francisco, is a 94-mile stretch from Carmel south to the Hearst Castle at San Simeon. Scenic Highway I with its winding, narrow road offers some of the most dramatic and awesome views of the Pacific and the wilderness areas of the Los Padres National Forest. A number of state parks offer picnicking, some camping, hiking, and just quiet among the redwoods and pines. For further information contact Pfeiffer-Big Sur State Park, P.O. Box A, Big Sur, CA 93920 (408–667–2315).

North to Napa . . . and a Wine Experience

The rich Napa-Solano-Sonoma district, 90 minutes northeast of San Francisco, is the heart of Northern California's traditional premium wine-growing areas. Today, over 400 wineries are concentrated in Napa and Sonoma Counties. Most offer tasting rooms, quite a few offer tours. Wine may be purchased at almost all wineries. Several provide picnic areas, as well.

Visitors may sip and sightsee from northern Mendocino county south almost to the Mexican border in San Diego. Monterey has noted vineyards—Mirassou and Paul Masson—and even tiny Carmel-by-the-Sea has a mini-winery.

Eight miles north of the town of Napa is Yountville. A stop at mellowed-brick Vintage 1870 is a must. The complex restored first in 1966–67 is a labyrinth of charming shops and eateries. In addition the town's two hotels are furnished in 19th-century antiques. Summer

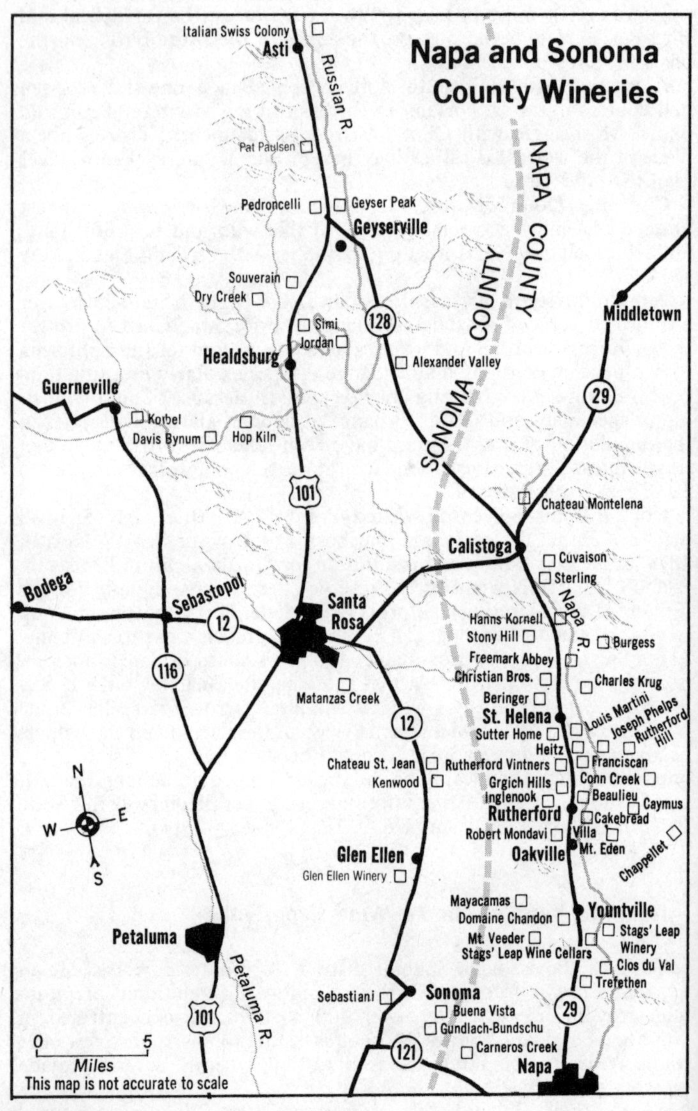
Napa and Sonoma County Wineries
Italian Swiss Colony
Asti
Russian R.
Pat Paulsen
Pedroncelli
Geyser Peak
Geyserville
Souverain
Dry Creek
128
Simi
Jordan
Healdsburg
Alexander Valley
SONOMA COUNTY
NAPA COUNTY
Middletown
29
Guerneville
Korbel
Davis Bynum
Hop Kiln
101
Chateau Montelena
Calistoga
Cuvaison
Sterling
Napa R.
Bodega
Sebastopol
12
Santa Rosa
Hanns Kornell
Stony Hill
Burgess
Freemark Abbey
Christian Bros.
Charles Krug
116
Matanzas Creek
Beringer
12
St. Helena
Louis Martini
Joseph Phelps
Rutherford Hill
Sutter Home
Heitz
Chateau St. Jean
Rutherford Vintners
Franciscan
Kenwood
Grgich Hills
Conn Creek
Inglenook
Beaulieu
Caymus
Rutherford
Cakebread
Robert Mondavi
Villa
Mt. Eden
Oakville
Chappellet
Glen Ellen
Glen Ellen Winery
N
E
W
S
Mayacamas
Domaine Chandon
Yountville
Petaluma
Mt. Veeder
Stags' Leap Winery
Stags' Leap Wine Cellars
Clos du Val
Trefethen
Petaluma R.
Sebastiani
Sonoma
29
Buena Vista
101
Gundlach-Bundschu
0 5
Miles
This map is not accurate to scale
121
Carneros Creek
Napa

months a professional repertory group presents a program of nationally acclaimed plays, as well as works by new California playwrights.

Hidden in the hills west of Napa is one of the three wineries operated in the Napa Valley by the Christian Brothers. Mont La Salle Vineyard is a 500-acre estate; corporate headquarters of the Brothers' vineyards, and produces many of the fine red and white table wines from superior grapes such as Pinot Saint George, Sylvaner and Grey and Johannisberg Rieslings.

In 1950, the Brothers purchased "Greystone," an imposing and picturesque landmark stone winery in St. Helena. This is a very popular tourist attraction. If possible, purchase a bottle or two of Estate Bottled classics. The author highly recommends the Pineau de La Loire, a crisp chablis type and the fine Pinot St. George. Many Californians are partial to a dessert-type product, Chateau La Salle, fine before or after dinner and smashing over fresh berries or peaches.

For cheese, bread and wine picnickers, visit St. Helena's Pasta Prego or the Oakville Grocery, to add one or two special cheeses to the basket. Sample a rich Brie, a pungent Stilton or our own Monterey Jack.

Perhaps one of the most beautiful and certainly one of the most unusual wineries is Sterling Vineyards. This hilltop winery resembles a Moorish citadel or a Greek monastery, gleaming white and accessible only by an aerial tramway. In addition to tasting, some wineries offer picnic and barbecue facilities. Usually, week-ends are crowded. Often wineries close certain legal and religious holidays. Write for the free brochure from the Wine Institute, 165 Post Street, San Francisco, CA 94108; supplement this with a current California road map. Check the yellow pages of the San Francisco telephone directory for additional information.

We suggest limiting your wine touring and tasting to two establishments, though there are dozens of big and small wineries offering their wares to taste and to buy in Wine Country, USA.

Yosemite

Yosemite National Park can be reached using California Highway 120. The western Big Oak Flat entrance, is open all year, while the Tioga Pass Road and the west entrance from Lee Vining are closed during the winter. In addition, both the Merced route, State Highway 140, and the Fresno route, State Highway 41, are also open all year. The entrance to the Park on Highway 41 is called, quite simply, "South Entrance." After entering the Park, one can turn east for approximately a seven-minute drive to the Mariposa Grove of Big Trees (it is on a spur road, not Highway 41). Similarily, Wawona is located north, about a 15-minute drive from the South Entrance.

Although Yosemite National Park includes the meadow-like Yosemite Valley, it is by no means the entire Park. There are nearly 1,200 square miles in the National Park itself; of this, only ten square miles are located in Yosemite Valley. In-park tours include a two-hour Valley Floor Tour (in an open-air tram), a four-hour tour to Glacier Point, a six-hour tour to the Mariposa Grove of Big Trees, and an eight-hour tour combining the Glacier Point and Mariposa Grove tours. Tours are available from the Yosemite Transportation System. They also offer a Merced Day Tour, which leaves Merced at 11:15 A.M., includes lunch and a tour of the Valley, returns at 6:45 P.M., and connects directly with Amtrak's "San Joaquin" train to Oakland-San Francisco.

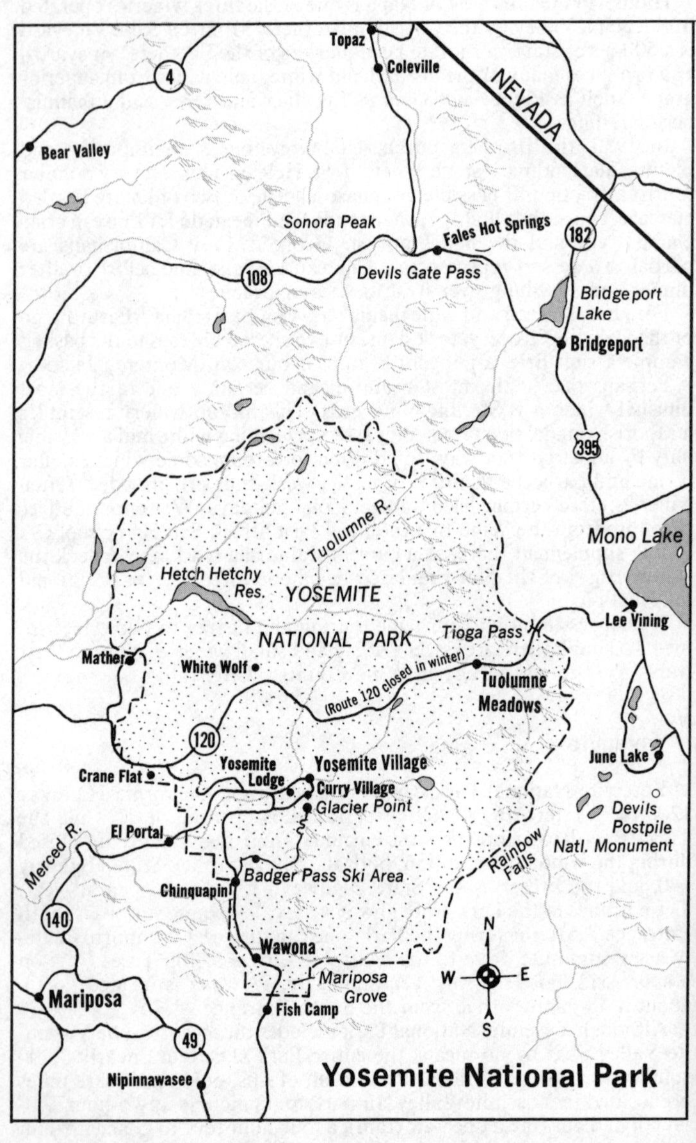
Topaz
Coleville
NEVADA
4
Bear Valley
Sonora Peak
Fales Hot Springs
182
108
Devils Gate Pass
Bridgeport
Lake
Bridgeport
395
Tuolumne R.
Mono Lake
Hetch Hetchy
Res.
YOSEMITE
NATIONAL PARK
Tioga Pass
Lee Vining
Mather
White Wolf
(Route 120 closed in winter)
Tuolumne
Meadows
120
June Lake
Crane Flat
Yosemite
Lodge
Yosemite Village
Curry Village
Glacier Point
Devils
Postpile
Natl. Monument
Merced R.
El Portal
Rainbow
Falls
Badger Pass Ski Area
Chinquapin
140
N
W
E
S
Wawona
Mariposa
Grove
Mariposa
Fish Camp
49
Nipinnawasee
Yosemite National Park

The Ahwahnee Hotel is open year-round. However, the Wawona Hotel is open only from April to Dec. Other year-round accommodations include Yosemite Lodge and Curry Village. Advance reservations are necessary, especially in summer. Phone reservations may be made: 209–252–4848. The High Sierra Camps are also very popular, and visitors wishing to use the camps the following summer should write for reservations in December.

Besides dining at the hotels, Yosemite Lodge has two restaurants and a cafeteria. Curry Village has a cafeteria, Yosemite Village offers the Loft Restaurant and several fast-food services.

If you want to do the Yosemite High Sierras on foot you join one of the guided hiking expeditions. There are some seven day ones in summer, weekly. The seven-day hikes, and other High Sierra Camp trips begin at Tuolumne Meadows.

Bicycles may be rented at the Yosemite Lodge Bike Stand and the Curry Village Bike Stand. The Stables, which are located at Yosemite Valley, Wawona, Tuolumne Meadows, and White Wolf, offer horses, pack service and walk-and-lead burros and ponies.

Best season to visit the park? Autumn or spring. Next best, winter. Beginning skiers find the Badger Pass slopes superb. Summer is Yosemite's least enjoyable visiting season, simply because it is so crowded with tourists. The park hosts over two million visitors annually.

Mother Lode Country and More

Historic Sacramento is one spot to start a pilgrimage thru the ghost towns and gold camps of the Sierra Nevada foothills.

Old Sacramento Historic Area is the new gold rush find. The 28-acre recreation of mid-1800's frontier began in 1965. Today, there are 250 specialty shops and 30 restaurants, as well as major sites such as the Pony Express, the Old Eagle Theatre, and the Central Pacific Passenger Station.

Opened in 1981 the $14 million California State Railroad Museum has 40 historic interpretive displays, 21 pieces of rolling stock and railroad memorabilia. Visitors are greeted by a $100,000 film featuring the romance of railroading. The "Big Four" (Charles Crocker, Leland Stanford, Mark Hopkins and Collis Huntington) all Sacramento businessmen, were responsible for the transcontinental railroad project, which on May 10, 1869 linked the nation.

Captain John Augustus Sutter, with a small crew, voyaged up the Sacramento in the summer of 1839. On a land grant of 44,000 acres which Sutter, a naturalized Mexican citizen, received in June 1841, he established Sutter's Fort.

Visit the fort and with the aid of electronic headsets relive the excitement of the discovery of gold in 1848 and the toil and hardship of the thousands of "Forty-niners" passing through.

With the price of gold moving close to $450 an ounce, a new epidemic of gold fever is sweeping the Mother Lode, that fabulous mineral deposit about 50 miles wide and 300 miles long, stretching from Oroville in the north to Yosemite National Park in the south. Miners from Sonora, Mexico gave the name *vena madre* (mother lode) to the area because of the incredibly rich quartz veins they found. Amateurs lined riverbanks last summer, swirling their $3.99 plastic gold pans. Vacationers pan gold successfully, especially along the Mokelumne and Stanislaus Rivers.

Other finds in the Gold Country are spectacular spring wildflower displays, nostalgic remnants of mining towns and picturesque restorations like Sonora, Jamestown and Sutter Creek. An easy weekend excursion from San Francisco east to Highway 49 (the Mother Lode Highway) offers glimpses of the rich farming and cattle country as well as detours to photogenic gems like the covered bridge at Knight's Bridge and the nearby ruins of its jailhouse and Masonic Hall.

A number of charming inns are tucked away en route. Sonora's Gunn House, an adobe inn flavored with Victorian icing, dominates busy Main Street. By contrast, the 13-room Sutter Creek Inn offers a gentle haven admidst antique shops, restaurants and bars. The Hotel Leger, a favorite of desperado Joaquin Murrieta, in Mokelumne Hill (Mok Hill) is complete with a Frontier Saloon and a 20th-century swimming hole. Jackson is home of the famed National Hotel as well as nearby Daffodil Hill, a carpet of yellow each spring.

About 70 percent of Coloma is included in Marshall Gold Discovery Historic Park. An outstanding attraction is a full-size replica of Sutter's Mill, along with other outdoor and museum mining displays.

No automobiles are allowed in reconstructed Columbia, a State Historic Park. The City Hotel, built in 1856, provides lodging and libations.

All in all, a fascinating area, demanding several mini-motortrips for full appreciation.

Lassen Volcanic National Park

The season is important, because this park is snowed in most of the year and the highway is impassable. It was back in May of 1914 that Lassen Peak, up until then merely a landmark named for the pioneer emigrant leader Peter Lassen, first exploded. Throughout that summer and fall it erupted more than a hundred times. In May of 1915 it came alive with such violence that the snows melted, causing an avalanche. As far away as Reno, streets were buried under inches of ash. Lessening eruptions continued into 1917, and since then the mountain has been peacefully dormant. It's California's smallest National Park. Entering at West Sulphur Creek and exiting at Manzanita Lake, you pass close by the major attractions. You can drive it in an hour, though it would be a shame to rush so fast. Highlights are the Chaos Crags and Chaos Jumbles, Bumpass Hell (it gurgles, hisses, boils and gives off a rotten-egg odor) and violently roaring hot springs like Steam Engine and Big Boiler. The park is dotted with good fishing lakes annually stocked with rainbow, eastern brook and German brown trout, and hiking is great. Accommodations in the vicinity of the park are rare, aside from campsites. A much wider range of overnight facilities and restaurants are available in nearby Redding, Red Bluff and Chester.

From Lassen take Calif. 89 to see the 14,162-foot-tall landmark, Mt. Shasta, which is visible for more than a hundred miles in each direction. "A moving picture in the sky," remarked Jack London. It has a popular ski resort. On the way, you pass the McArthur-Burney Falls State Park, with picnic and camping facilities and the photographic split waterfall fed by an underground river. US 99 takes you through Castle Crags, sheer rocks rising 6,000 feet, the Lake Shasta Caverns, which can be reached only by boat, and the Shasta Dam, with its reservoir. It's the world's second highest and it's backed up a 47-square-mile lake whose shoreline runs in and out a mile for every day in the year. And if you ever dreamed that maybe someday you'd like to live on a houseboat and laze and loaf around the way they do in the Vale of Kashmir, well, now you've arrived at the time and the place. Because here on Shasta the houseboats, for rent, are waiting for you. They called them "Floatels," and you'll agree when you check their housekeeping hostelry accommodations. They have icebox, cooking range (butane gas), water heater, cooking pans, all table accessories. Also freshwater tank, lights, of course, and all modern toilet arrangements. Regular beds (sleeps six). And a convertible sofa. You bring linen, bed blankets and—to supplement your food, which also you must bring—fishing tackle.

Lake Tahoe and Reno

Straddling the California and Nevada border, 6,230-foot Lake Tahoe provides exciting High Sierra vacations. In summer there's water sports, camping, hiking, and fishing. A number of lake cruises offer visitors views of some of the secluded estates and resorts. In winter there are 19 downhill ski resorts to enjoy, along with ice skating, snowmobiling, and sleigh riding.

From Tahoe City on the lake you take Calif. 89 if you want to go to the one-time (1960) Winter Olympic site—Squaw Valley. Ski lifts operate here in summer. Two miles south of Squaw Valley you'll find its sister resort Alpine Meadows, offering fine powder skiing. And way down south on Tahoe's shores, right where you came in, is Heavenly Valley, the nation's only two-state ski resort. Ride the aerial tramway here up 8,300 feet above the mountain and you'll get the finest view of all of the lake. It's breathtaking.

Neighboring Reno has changed greatly in recent years. A $400-million expansion has added six plush casinos and almost 2,000 hotel rooms to the rustic community. Don't miss Bally's Grand Hotel (it was the MGM), a glitzy array of shopping, high-stakes gaming, and headline entertainers.

PRACTICAL INFORMATION FOR NORTHERN CALIFORNIA

HOW TO GET THERE. See under "Practical Information for San Francisco," above.

ACCOMMODATIONS. Hotels and Motels in Northern California range from the plush accommodations of the seaside establishments to the cozy chalet-type digs you will find in Carmel, as well as the rustic and far-from-rustic rooms to be had in and near the national parks. For double occupancy, prices are as follows: *Deluxe:* $100 up; *Expensive:* $75–$100; *Moderate:* $50–$75; *Inexpensive:* under $50. For a more complete explanation of hotel and motel categories refer to Far West *Facts at Your Fingertips.*

BERKELEY. Berkeley Marina Marriott. *Deluxe.* 200 Marina Blvd. (415–548–7920). Resort facilities. Tennis. Sauna.

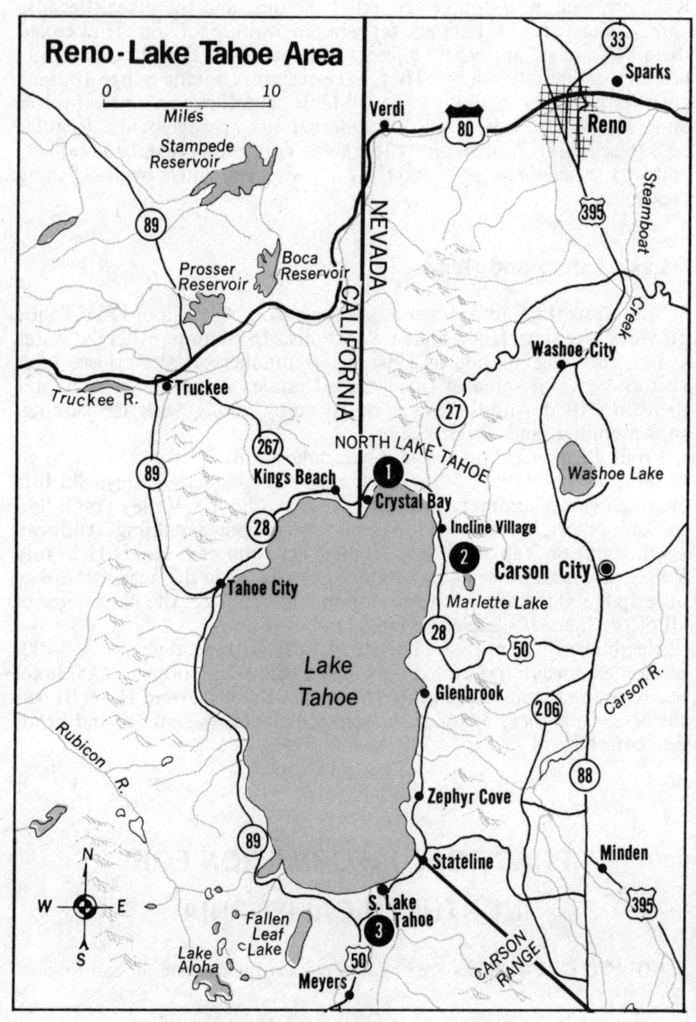

RENO-LAKE TAHOE AREA

Major Hotel/Casinos

1) Tahoe Sands Resorts, CharmeyChalet Resort, Tahoe Vista
2) Club Tahoe, Incline Village
3) Caesar's Tahoe, Harrah's, Harvey High Sierra, Inn by the Lake, Station House Inn

Claremont Resort Hotel. *Deluxe.* Domingo & Ashby Aves. (415–843–3000). Pool & tennis spa. 22 acres with superb San Francisco Bay View. Gourmet dining.

Gramma's Bed & Breakfast Inn. *Expensive.* 2740 Telegraph (415–549–2145). 19 rooms in a Tudor charmer.

CARMEL. Adobe Inn. *Deluxe* (408–624–3933). Short walk to shops, galleries, beaches. Fireplaces, heated pool and sauna. Fine family dining in pub restaurant.

Highlands Inn. *Deluxe* (408–624–3801). 4 miles south of Carmel on Coast Highway. Over 70 "spa suites" with hydromassage tubs. Fine dining in the *Pacific Edge* restaurant.

Quail Lodge. *Deluxe* (408–624–1581). A mile south of Carmel on the Carmel Valley Golf & Country Club property. Distinguished resort. Tennis. The *Covey* restaurant serves fresh Monterey Bay seafoods in season.

Rosita Lodge. *Expensive.* Box 2077, 4th Ave. and Torres (408–624–6926). Charming. Free continental breakfast and daily newspaper. Fireplaces.

Tickle Pink. *Expensive.* 4 miles south of Carmel on Coast Highway (408–624–1244). Secluded, smashing views.

Pine Inn. *Moderate* (408–624–3851). Victorian decor. Center of town. No pets. Superb Garden Restaurant.

LAKE TAHOE AREA. Bally's Grand. *Deluxe.* 2500 E.2nd St. (800–648–5080). Reno's 2,000-room showplace, casino.

Caesar's Tahoe. *Deluxe.* Stateline (702–588–3515). Health club. Entertainment. World-class hotel.

Harrah's. *Deluxe.* Stateline (702–588–6611). Resort-type amenities. Health club.

Harvey's Hotel. *Deluxe.* Box 128, Stateline, NV 89449 (702–588–2411).

High Sierra. *Deluxe.* Box C, Stateline, NV 89449 (702–588–6211). casual western image with a Chuckwagon buffet.

Tahoe Beach & Ski Club. *Deluxe.* Box 1267, South Lake Tahoe, CA 95705 (916–541–6220). Fine resort, private beach.

Forest Inn. *Expensive.* Box 4300, South Lake Tahoe, CA 95729 (916–541–6655). 2 pools. 1–2 bedroom apts. Over 18 only.

Best Western Lake Tahoe Inn. *Moderate.* Box 11, South Lake Tahoe, CA 95729 (916–541–2010). 1 mile to Heavenly Valley Ski Resort.

Flamingo Lodge. *Moderate.* Box 4028, South Lake Tahoe, CA 95729 (916–544–5288). Walk to casinos.

Inn by the Lake. *Moderate.* Box 849, South Lake Tahoe, CA 95705 (916–542–0330). Attractive family-type accommodations. Spa.

Tahoe Marina Inn. *Moderate.* Box 871, South Lake Tahoe, CA 95705 (916–541–2180). On lake.

LOS GATOS. La Hacienda Inn. *Expensive.* 18840 Saratoga-Los Gatos Rd. (408–354–9230). Excellent restaurant.

Los Gatos Lodge. *Expensive.* 50 Saratoga Ave. (408–354–3300). Charming landscaping.

MENDOCINO AND FT. BRAGG. Heritage House. *Deluxe.* Little River (707–937–5885). Some cottages overlook rugged surf. Reserve at least six months in advance.

Hill House. *Deluxe.* Box 625, Mendocino, CA 95460 (702–937–0554). Victorian charmer seen in TV's "Murder, She Wrote."

Harbor Lite Lodge. *Moderate.* 120 N. Harbor Drive. Ft. Bragg, CA 95437 (707–964–0221). Overlooks Noyo Harbor and fishing fleet.

Mendocino Hotel. *Moderate.* 45080 Main Street, Mendocino, CA 95460 (707–937–0511). Restored 1878 Victorian with 50-plus rooms; attractive restaurant.

Pine Beach Inn. *Moderate.* Box 1173, Fort Bragg, CA 95437 (707–964–5603). Tennis. Beach.

MONTEREY. Hyatt Regency Monterey. *Deluxe.* 1 Old Golf Course Rd. (408–372–1234). 14 acres of resort amenities.

Monterey Plaza. *Deluxe.* 400 Cannery Row (408–646–1700). Elegant decor. Superb dining at *Delfino's.* Near new aquarium.

Spindrift Inn. *Deluxe.* 652 Cannery Row (408–646–8900). Elegant, antique-accented ambience.

Doubletree Inn. *Expensive.* 2 Portola Plaza (408–649–4511). At Fisherman's Wharf. Excellent restaurants, very handsome property.

Monterey Bay Inn. *Expensive.* 242 Cannery Row (408–373–6242). Spa, diving facilities. Low-keyed quiet ambience.

Best Western Monterey Inn. *Moderate.* 825 Abrego St. (408–373–5345). Well-maintained attractive rooms. Convenient location.

Casa Munras. *Moderate.* 700 Munras Ave. (408–375–2411). Pleasant setting, restaurant. Excellent winter rates.

OAKLAND. Hyatt Regency. *Deluxe.* 1001 Broadway (415–893–1234). Adjacent to Convention Center, Chinatown, Jack London Square, BART to San Francisco.

Holiday Inn-Bay Bridge. *Expensive.* 1800 Powell St., Emeryville (415–658–9300).

Hyatt at Oakland International Airport. *Expensive.* 455 Hegenberger Rd. (415–562–6100). *Duck's Inc.* for dining.

Oakland Airport Hilton. *Expensive.* 1 Hegenberger Rd. (415–635–5000).

Best Western/Thunderbird Motor Lodge. *Moderate.* 233 Broadway (415–452–4565). Near BART to San Francisco; walk to Jack London Square.

PALO ALTO. Holiday Inn. *Deluxe.* Opposite Stanford University (415–328–2800). Attractive grounds, usual Holiday Inn services.

Hyatt Palo Alto. *Deluxe.* 4290 El Camino Real (415–493–0800). Health Club.

Best Western Creekside Inn. *Moderate.* 3400 El Camino Real (415–493–2411).

Stanford Terrace Inn. *Moderate.* 531 Stanford Ave. (415–857–0333). Opposite Stanford University. Sauna.

PEBBLE BEACH. The Lodge at Pebble Beach. *Deluxe* (408–624–3811). Golf privileges at Pebble Beach or Spyglass Hill, the classic Pro-Am course. Gourmet dining, *Club XIX.*

SACRAMENTO. Capitol Plaza Holiday Inn. *Expensive.* 300 J Street (916–446–0100). downtown highrise, adjacent to Old Sacramento.

Red Lion Motor Inn. *Expensive.* 2001 Point West Way (916–929–8855). Fine restaurant.

Sacramento Inn. *Expensive.* 1401 Arden Way (916–922–8041). 3 pools, putting green.

Beverly Garland Motor Lodge. *Moderate.* 1780 Tribute Rd. (916–929–7900). Great value.

Clarion Hotel. *Moderate.* 700 16th St. (916–444–8000). Opposite historic Victorian Governor's Mansion. Garden courtyard.

Vagabond. *Moderate.* 909 3rd St. (916–446–1481). Walking distance to Capitol and Old Sacramento.

Woodlake Inn. *Moderate.* 500 Leisure Lane. 3 miles north off 160 (916–922–6251). Resort motel. Family-oriented. All sports.

SAN JOSE. Hyatt San Jose. *Expensive.* 1740 N. First St. (408–298–0300). Heated pool. Cafe—24 hrs. *Hugo's* for dining.

Red Lion Motor Inn. *Expensive.* 2050 Gateway Place (408–279–0600). Very attractive property.

Best Western Sandman. *Moderate.* 2585 Seaboard Ave. (408–263–8800). Heated pool. Therapy pool, sauna. There is a downtown location as well as one 5 min. from airport and Great America.

Vagabond Inn. *Moderate.* 1488 N. First St. (408–294–8138). Cable TV, pool. Pleasant rooms.

SANTA CRUZ. Holiday Inn. *Expensive.* 611 Ocean St. (408–426–7100). Summer reservations suggested in this popular family resort area, two hours from the Bay Area. Heated pool.

SANTA ROSA. Sheraton Round Barn Inn. *Deluxe.* 3555 Round Barn Blvd. (707–523–7555). Elegant resort built around historic barn.

El Rancho Tropicana. *Expensive.* 2200 Santa Rosa Ave. (707–542–3655). 25 relaxing acres, playground. Near Convention Center and Fairgrounds.

Los Robles Lodge. *Moderate.* 925 Edwards Ave. (707–545–6330). In-room movies. Heated & wading pools. Friday night seafood buffet.

SAUSALITO. Casa Madrona. *Expensive.* 801 Bridgeway (415–332–0502). Restored Victorian landmark. Country French dining.

TIBURON. Tiburon Lodge. *Expensive.* 1651 Tiburon (415–435–3133). Heated pool. Restaurant.

YOUTH HOSTELS. California has 25 of the 300 U.S. hostels. The six Bay Area hostels, including two lighthouses account for 20 percent of overnight stays in U.S. hostels. Ft. Mason hostel expects 50,000 visitors yearly. Cooking, cleaning and general chores are shared by users. American Youth Hostels (AYH), a branch of the international organization, was founded in 1934. The aim is to provide cheap and safe sleeping accommodations for people hiking, biking, skiing. Although used by young people mostly, youth hostels enforce no maximum age.

For information on AYH, please mail a self-addressed, stamped envelope to: AYH, Box 37613, Washington, D.C. 20013–7613. Also check telephone directory.

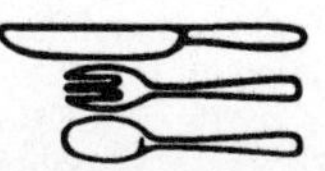

RESTAURANTS. Dining out in Northern California can give the tourist a good insight into the justifiable chauvinism of most Californians. Generalizing is impossible: you can find French cooking; pleasant, good plain cooking like Boston-baked beans; barbecued meat Western-style; Viennese and Czech food; and everywhere, fish, fish and more fish, topped by the hard-to-find abalone, the specialty of many seaside restaurants. Settings for California's unusual variety of cooking styles and fare range from the waterfront to an old firehouse, tea rooms to old Spanish missions and restaurants with stagecoachy Western decor.

Restaurants are listed according to categories: *Deluxe* restaurants charge from $25 and up for a complete dinner; *Expensive* $20–$25; *Moderate* $10–20; *Inexpensive* under $10. A la carte meals will of course cost more. For a more complete explanation of restaurant categories see *Facts At Your Fingertips* at the front of this volume.

BERKELEY. Chez Panisse. *Expensive.* 1517 Shattuck Ave. (415–548–5525). Continental. Elegant Sunday brunch. A one-acre organic garden in Amador County raises much of the produce.

Fourth Street Grill. *Moderate to Expensive.* 1820 4th (415–849–0526). California mesquite-grilled fresh fish, pastas, steaks. No credit cards.

Santa Fe Bar & Grill. *Moderate to Expensive.* 1310 University (415–841–4740). Restored railway depot serving fresh fish and pasta specialties.

Spenger's Fish Grotto. *Moderate.* 1919 4th St. (415–845–7771). Extremely popular, no reservations. Expect a wait. Nautical Museum to glance through while waiting.

Siam Cuisine. *Inexpensive.* 1181 University Ave. (415–548–3278). Thai family-style, excellent.

CARMEL. Andre's. *Expensive.* 3770 The Barnyard, Carmel Valley (408–625–0447). Continental cuisine. Reservations suggested.

Simpson's. *Expensive.* Carmel Sands Motel (408–624–1255). Specialties: prime rib and fresh seafood.

Bully III. *Moderate to Expensive.* 8th & Dolores, Adobe Inn (408–625–1750). Prime rib specialties.

The Carmel Butcher Shop. *Moderate.* Ocean & Lincoln (408–624–2569). Prime rib and Beef Wellington vie for attention with chicken Davidian and tournedos Zarounian. Fireplace. Reservations advised.

Clam Box. *Moderate.* Mission, south of 5th (408–624–8597). Seafood specialties abound, but there will be chicken and pot roast on hand for landlubbers.

French Poodle. *Moderate.* 5th & Junipero (408–624–8643). For a perfect meal, order *Le Filet de Sole Marinette.* Chef owned. Reservations required.

Raffaello. *Moderate.* Mission, north of 7th (408–624–1541). Italian specialties abound. Concentrate on *Cannelloni Raffaello* or *vitello Piemontese.*

Rio Grill. *Moderate.* The Crossroads, Hwy. 1 (408–625–5436). Informal, eclectic menu from cheeseburgers to grilled rabbit.

Pablo's. *Inexpensive.* 3670 The Barnyard, Carmel Valley (408–624–1446). Mexican favorites, including Pacific red snapper.

Tuck Box. *Inexpensive.* Dolores St. (Ocean & 7th Aves.) (408–624–6365). Tasty lunch and tea stop.

LAKE TAHOE. The Dory's Oar. *Expensive.* 1041 Fremont Ave., South Lake Tahoe (916–541–6603). The "down East" New England mood is reflected in the fare. Live Maine lobster, Eastern clams, and oysters as well as aged beef. Reservations suggested.

Bacchi's Inn. *Moderate.* 2 miles N.E. of Tahoe City, off Hwy. 28 (916–583–3324). Family style Italian-Continental.

Swiss Chalet. *Moderate.* on US 50, four miles west of Stateline (916–544–3304). Continental. Sauerbraten, fondue and St. Moritz steak are recommended. Closed Mon.

LOS GATOS. La Hacienda. *Expensive* (408–354–6669). Continental. Varied menu highlights chicken kiev, shish kebob and veal scallopini. Country inn ambience.

Villa Felice. *Moderate.* 15350 Winchester Rd. (408–395–6711). Seafood and steak are staples. Reservations suggested.

MONTEREY. Delfino's. *Deluxe.* Monterey Plaza, 400 Cannery Row (408–646–1706). Superb Northern Italian cuisine served in an elegant room. Unusual open Genovese stove with rotisseries and brick oven.

Sardine Factory. *Expensive.* 701 Wave St. (408–373–3775). Continental. Seafood, but pastas enjoy equal renown. Try veal or prawns.

The Rogue. *Expensive.* Fisherman's Wharf #2 (408–372–4586). Great view; good family dining. Seafood, chicken and steak selections.

Whaling Station Inn. *Expensive.* 763 Wave (408–373–3778). Cannery Row. Dinner only; reservations required. Features seasonal fresh fish.

OAKLAND. Trader Vic's. *Deluxe.* 9 Anchor Dr. (415–653–3400). Original Trader Vic's was in Oakland. Chinese and Indonesian dishes lead an extensive parade of international specialties. Beautiful decor, Bay viewing. Host Freddy Fung will help you select. Reservations necessary.

Scott's. *Expensive.* 73 Jack London Square (415–444–3456). Seafood selections superb.

El Caballo. *Moderate.* 67 Jack London Square (415–835–9260). The mood and food of Mexico.

Gallagher's. *Moderate.* 86 Jack London Square (415–893–5292). Very attractive decor featuring carrousel horses and circus art.

Gulf Coast Oyster Bar and Specialty Company. *Moderate.* 736 Washington St. (415–839–6950). Oysters galore plus gumbo, corn bread.

PALO ALTO (REDWOOD CITY, SUNNYVALE). Barbarossa. *Expensive.* 3003 El Camino Real, Redwood City (415–369–2626).

Chantilly. *Expensive.* 530 Ramona Palo Alto (415–321–4080). Fine French cuisine.

Mac Arthur Park. *Moderate.* 27 University Ave., Palo Alto (415–321–9990). Mesquite-grilled fresh fish, great baby back ribs.

Velvet Turtle. *Moderate.* DeAnza Sq. (408–738–4070). steaks and seafood.

Village Pub. *Moderate.* 2967 Woodside Rd., Redwood City (415–851–1294). Fine food, warm atmosphere.

SACRAMENTO. Aldo's. *Expensive.* Town & Country Village (916–483–5031). Popular local favorite. Extensive wine list. Suggest reservations.

Cafe La Salle. *Expensive.* 1028 2d St., in Old Sacramento (916–442–9000). California French cuisine in a charming old-world atmosphere. Terrace dining.

The Firehouse. *Expensive.* In Old Sacramento. 1112 Second St. (916–442–4772). With 24-hour notice you can feast on a suckling wild boar roast. Excellent service. Popular. The courtyard is lovely for lunch.

Frank Fat's. *Moderate.* 806 L St. (916–442–7092). Favorite of politicians and lobbyists. Where the Legislature meet over kwok or chop suey. Cantonese.

ST. HELENA. Miramonte. *Expensive.* 1327 Railroad Ave. (707–963–3970). Reservations; dinner Wed.-Sun. A country inn for sophisticated dining.

Rose et Lefavour. *Expensive.* 1420 Main St. (707–963–1681). Updated French cuisine with an elegant Thai touch.

SAN JOSE. Hugo's. *Expensive.* Hyatt San Jose, 1740 N. First St. (408–298–0300). Continental. Elegant contemporary decor matches a varied menu that includes many flaming dishes.

Le Pavillon. *Expensive.* Le Baron Hotel. 1350 N 1st St. (408–288–9200). Sunday brunch scene.

Paolo's. *Moderate.* 12th & E. Santa Clara (408–294–2558). A potpouri of Italian favorites includes chicken tripiano with zucchini, mushrooms and peas, and chicken Bellini with white wine, asparagus and artichoke hearts.

Original Joe's. *Inexpensive.* 301 S First St. (408–292–7030). Italian. Pastas naturally play an important role. The veal scallopini also merits attention.

SANTA CRUZ. Hotel La Rosa. *Expensive.* 308 Wilson St. (707–579–3200). Small Victorian hotel with nostalgic dining room.

Shadowbrook. *Expensive.* 1750 Wharf Rd., Capitola (408–475–1511). Delightful atmosphere with plants and flowers in profusion. Abalone and scampi are recommended, as is everything else that swims.

SANTA ROSA. John Ash and Company. *Moderate.* Vinters Inn, 4350 Barnes Rd. (707–575–7350). Country French air, fine wines, interesting menu. Open daily, reservations suggested.

SAUSALITO. The Spinnaker. *Moderate.* 100 Spinnaker Dr. (415–332–1500). On the water; superb view. Seafood, American menu. Open daily, reservations suggested.

SONOMA. Au Relais. *Expensive.* 691 Broadway (707–996–1031). French. Lamb shanks, a rare delight. Reservations suggested. Adjacent bed & breakfast inn.

Starmont, Meadowood. *Expensive.* 900 Meadowood Lane (707–963–3646). Innovative cuisine and select Napa Valley wines make dining memorable in this secluded resort.

California Cafe. *Moderate.* Cement Works,/Hwy. (707–963–5300). Contemporary decor with a menu that is conservative nouvelle.

La Belle Helene. *Moderate.* (707–963–1234). Sunday brunch includes homemade croissants. Choice California wine list. Art gallery on second floor.

YOUNTVILLE. Domaine Chandon. *Expensive* (707–944–2880). Elegant dining; home of the Museum of Champagne, and one of the area's newest and most prestigious wineries.

The French Laundry. *Expensive.* Washington & Creek Streets (707–944–2380). Open Wed.-Sat; one seating from 7–8:30 P.M. Reservations required.

Mama Nina's. *Moderate.* 6772 Washington St. (707–944–2112). Homemade pastas and northern Italian favorites.

Mustards. *Moderate.* Hwy. 29, just north of Yountville (707–944–2424). Mesquite grill; imaginative salads and a well-chosen wine list have made this a must-stop in the Napa Valley.

HOW TO GET AROUND. By Plane. Aside from San Francisco, a number of Northern California cities (particularly San Jose and Sacramento) are served by national carriers such as *American, Continental,* and *United.* Regional airlines like *USAir* and *Air Cal* also fly between many towns.

On Horseback. There are many pack trips to take in Northern California, not only in Yosemite, but also in *Stanislaus National Forest, Lassen Volcanic National Park, Six Rivers,* and *Klamath, Shasta-Trinity, Modoc, Mendocino, Lassen, Plumas, Tahoe,* and *El Dorado national forests.* Write California Chamber of Commerce for their *Packers and Pack Trips* booklet, which gives particular names and addresses.

By Boat. On the *Sacramento River* (the Delta), you can rent a *houseboat* and tie up at night to any convenient tree. There are many primeval water mazes where you'll hear nothing but the bulrushes clattering softly in the wind. Ocean-going freighters use the Delta too! For more information write S & H Boat Yard, Box 514-A, Antioch, CA 94509 or Herman & Helen's Marina, Venice Island Ferry, Stockton, CA 95209.

By Train. Two *Super Skunk* locomotives wind through redwood forest, through tunnels, and over many bridges, from *Fort Bragg* to *Willits* (and vice versa) one or more times a day, depending on the season. 8–9 hours round-trip. Another interesting old train: the *Roaring Camp & Big Trees Railroad,* operating out of Felton in the *Santa Cruz Mountains.* Six-mile round trip takes an hour. In Sonoma, tour *Train Town's* mini-world on board the mini-steam railroad.

TOURIST INFORMATION SERVICES. General information is available from *San Francisco Convention & Visitors Bureau,* Swig Pavilion Information Center, in Hallidie Plaza, at Powell & Market Streets. Take escalator to lower plaza. Phone 391–2000 for daily-events information. The *Redwood Empire Association* welcomes visitors at #1 Market Plaza, 10th floor. Most local Chambers of Commerce will send you material on their city. Information on specific subjects may be obtained from such services as these: *Wine Institute,* 165 Post St., San Francisco; *Shasta-Cascade Wonderland Association,* Redding; *Lake Tahoe Chamber of Commerce,* P.O. Box 884, Tahoe City; *Golden Chain Council of the Mother Lode,* Soda Springs, CA 95728; and (for tours) *Gray Line of San Francisco,* 420 Taylor St., San Francisco.

SEASONAL EVENTS. In San Francisco: *February:* Golden Gate Kennel Club All Breed Dog Show, Cow Palace. Chinese New Year Celebration, Chinatown. *March:* St. Patrick's Day Celebration, week-long festivities, ending with parade on St. Patrick's Day. *April:* Cherry trees in bloom, Japanese Tea Garden, Golden Gate Park. Bay Area Science Fair, Calif. Academy of Sciences, Golden Gate Park. Cherry Blossom Festival, Japantown and

Japan Center, parade. Grand National Junior Livestock Exposition and Horse Show, Cow Palace, Macy's Easter Flower Show, Stockton & O'Farrell St. *Early May:* Peak blooming of rhododendrons in Golden Gate Park. *June:* The Gay Freedom Day Parade attracts 100,000-plus participants. *Mid-June:* Upper Grant Avenue Street Fair. *July:* Fourth of July Celebration and Fireworks Display, Candlestick Park. *Late August:* San Francisco Flower Show, Hall of Flowers, Golden Gate Park. *September:* San Francisco Municipal Outdoor Art Festival, Civic Center Plaza. *October:* Blessing of Fishing Fleet, Church of SS Peter and Paul and Fisherman's Wharf. Columbus Day Celebration and Parade, North Beach and Aquatic Park. Grand National Livestock Exposition, Horse Show and Rodeo, Cow Palace.

SPRING

San Francisco's annual Chinese New Year celebration in late January or early February is a crowded, colorful nine-day festival. In early March, Sacramento holds its annual Camellia Festival. San Francisco's *St. Patrick's Day* parade, nearest Sunday to March 17th, is colorful, with all sorts of marching bands, Irish pipers, Chinese girls. In late March the *cherry trees* blossom in the Japanese Tea Garden in Golden Gate Park (sometimes these wait until early April to come out).

April is a month filled with blossoms, of course, so there are plenty to see: the *Easter Floral Display* in Mill Valley; an *April Blossom Festival and Orchard Tour* in Sebastopol. At *Easter,* sunrise services are held at Mount Davidson in San Francisco—a foot pilgrimage at dawn. The *baseball season* opens for the Giants at Candlestick Park, and *boat racing* begins officially with a gala regatta beneath Golden Gate Bridge.

May is so busy you'll have to keep to a rigorous schedule in order to get a taste of even a few of its many events. Early in the month Willow Creek in Humboldt county has *White Water Races;* in mid-May, the *Luther Burbank Rose Festival and Parade* in Santa Rosa. The month draws to a close; there'll hardly be time for the *Jumping Frog Jubilee* at Angels Camp (yes, it is a frog-jumping contest, with international participants, plus other entertainment, such as circus acts, a rodeo); the *Shasta County Sheriff's Posse Parade and Rodeo* in Redding.

SUMMER

If you're not exhausted by that season's activities, summer should finish you off—unless you just read about all the fun in store. June brings Cloverdale's *Ram Sale & Sheepdog Trials,* Eureka's *Redwood Acres Fair,* and, from June to August, the *Festival of the Arts* at Stanford University with major guest symphonies, soloists, groups, and drama and films. Starting in mid-June and running all the way through October are the open air *musical and dance performances* Sundays in Sigmund Stern Grove in San Francisco. The *Days of Kit Carson* occur late in the month in Jackson; there are a fast-gun contest, a beard contest, an antique fire-engine fight, and other such stimulating tests going on here. And starting in late June, running through early July, Vallejo presents the *Solano County Fair,* with horse racing, rodeo, horse shows, parades.

July 4th: Sonora has the *Mother Lode Fair,* with a queen contest, a variety show, a horse rodeo show, a rodeo, and a lumberjack contest. There's a *Fiesta Rodeo* in San Juan Bautista which has a barbecue and a horse show. In the middle of the month Murphys stages a *Homecoming Parade and Old Timers' Picnic,* and Salinas holds the *California Rodeo.* Mid-month on through early September there's the *Marin Shakespeare Festival* in Ross. And also mid-month there are outdoor *fashion shows* in Union Square, San Francisco, exhibiting what local manufacturers are producing for fall wear. Or perhaps you'd like to sit down at one of the lighthearted *pops concerts* given by the *San Francisco Symphony* during July and August. Santa Cruz area's *Cabrillo Music Festival* is held in late August.

In August: Napa has the *Town & Country Fair.* Susanville has the *Lassen County Fair,* with horse show, livestock sale, destruction derby, loggers' show, rodeo. The *Eldorado County Fair,* with horse show, auto races, rodeo, wheelbarrow races, is in Placerville. Ukiah combines the *Redwood Empire County Fair* and *Sports Show.* The *San Joaquin County Fair* is in Stockton, with pari-mutuel betting, horse show, rodeo. The *Del Norte County Fair,* with its own rodeo, is in Crescent City; and Monterey holds the *Monterey County Fair.*

FALL AND WINTER

September brings the beginning of the fall season, and a few more fairs. The *California State Fair* in Sacramento. The *Tulelake Butte Valley Fair,* with parade, horse show, livestock auction, and, wonderfully enough, the world championship syphon-tube-setting contest. The *Mendocino County Fair* and *Apple Show,* in Boonville, has the seemingly ubiquitous horse show and rodeo, plus vaudeville entertainment and sheep-dog trials. Lodi has a *Grape Festival and National Wine Show,* and Sonoma has the *Valley of the Moon Vintage Festival,* with blessing of the grapes and a barbecue, and Capitola its annual *Begonia Festival.* Musical events include the *Jazz Festival* at Monterey in September, which attracts audiences, soloists, and groups from all over the world, and the opening of the *opera season* in San Francisco.

October opens with the old time *World Wrist Wrestling Championships* at Petaluma's Veteran's Memorial Building and Salinas's spectacular *International Airshow.* Dazzling aero-feats by acclaimed U.S. and international performers, including the precision flying expertise of the U.S. Navy's Blue Angels. Late October features the *Grand National Livestock Exposition, Rodeo and Horse Show,* held in San Francisco's Cow Palace.

By Thanksgiving, San Franciscans are tuned into Yuletide specials. The city's first *Santa Claus Parade,* in 1981, will hopefully become a yearly tradition à la Macy's New York. Other city Christmas treats are the Union Square display windows and decorations; the rainbow dazzle of Nob Hill's hotels and residences and the treasure of tree decorations available year-round at Pier 39's S. Claus, including San Francisco theme ornaments.

NATIONAL AND STATE PARKS. *Lava Beds National Monument* is in northeastern California, near Tulelake. Open all year. Visitor center, campground, picnic area. Self-guiding trails; 19 caves open for visits and exploration. Pictographs, petroglyphs, Indian artifacts. Fascinating caves, including several ice caves, were formed when frothy lava flowed from deep volcanic cracks in the earth's crust. The surface hardened upon exposure to the air, but the hot lava beneath continued to flow, forming cavelike lava tubes.

Muir Woods National Monument, named after John Muir, early California wilderness explorer and advocate of national parks, is a magnificent grove of redwoods, some more than 2,000 years old and up to 240 feet in height. It's 10 miles north of San Francisco across the Golden Gate Bridge in Mill Valley.

Point Reyes National Seashore is up the coast 40 miles from San Francisco. In the 19th century, it was a familiar area to American, British, Mexican, and Russian whalers and fur traders. Rum runners during Prohibition knew it well, too. Created by the San Andreas Fault (major cause of most California earthquakes), the peninsula is of rocky granite entirely unrelated to the mainland just across Tomales Bay. It is very wooded, very unspoiled, and the beach is beautiful. Ideal for outings in August, September, or October—but uncomfortable in summer, when it's shrouded in fog. *No swimming—the surf is treacherous!*

Yosemite National Park is a meadowlike valley threaded by mountain streams, noble groves of trees and waterfalls, and surrounded by almost vertical walls taking shapes of great domes and pinnacles. Summer is *not* the best time—very crowded then. The two major hotels in the valley, the Ahwahnee and the Wawona, are open most of the year.

Big Basin Redwoods State Park, the first of redwood groves to be declared a protected state park, is usually visited en route to Carmel. You can hike, picnic, or camp here, take advantage of planned recreation facilities, or just enjoy the magnificent giant trees.

Caswell Memorial State Park is five miles west of US 99, 16 miles south of Stockton. One of the few remaining primeval groves of the valley oaks that once were abundant in the Great Central Valley. Spring and fall best climate-wise.

Del Norte Coast Redwoods State Park, 8 miles south of Crescent City, offers camping, stream and surf fishing plus a fascinating trail, Damnation Creek, a one-mile thousand-foot descent to the sea.

Henry Cowell Redwood State Park, just south of Felton, is another serene preserve. Don't forget to ride the old train.

East Bay Regional Parks are more than 34,000 acres of beautiful California countryside set aside for daytime recreation. Many miles of hiking and bridle trails, picnicking spots. Try *Charles Lee Tilden Regional Park* (with the most recreational facilities), *Lake Temescal Regional Park,* and *Chabot* (camping, fishing, boating, riding).

Humboldt Redwoods State Park is 35 miles of forest bordering US 101 between Garberville and Redcrest. Highlights are the *Rockefeller Forest, Founder's Grove,* and the *Avenue of the Giants.*

Mount Diablo State Park is behind Oakland. According to Indian superstition, the mountain was the dwelling place of an evil spirit, a *puy.* Bret Harte stated that the peak was named when a Mexican muleteer on a missionary expedition first espied it and cried: "*Diablo!*" (Devil). The Marsh Creek-Clayton Road gives the most diabolical impression—dark shadows in deep ravines, sharp and craggy contours.

Mount Tamalpais is back of Mill Valley, across the Golden Gate Bridge from San Francisco. One of the few places close to downtown that can really be called pastoral. You may drive to the top, but it's easily hiked. Part of the land is in *Muir Woods National Monument;* the rest is state park.

Russian Gulch State Park is along the coast just north of the town of Mendocino. It has a wave-scarred headland pocked with coves, pools with good campsites, and the lure of skin diving for abalone. Usually foggy in summer. A more protected park a few miles inland, *Paul M. Dimmick Wayside Camp* is nine miles from the coast on Calif. 128, and is open for camping from spring until fall.

Salt Point State Park is California's newest preserve, two hours' drive north of San Francisco, north on the coast from Jenner. Super for skindiving, shelling, or the study of sealife.

Sonoma Coast Beaches State Park is great for views of the Pacific, especially from the Russian River approach at Jenner, where Calif. 12 and Calif. 1 intersect.

CAMPING OUT. *Bucks Lake* is in the Feather River country. The south shore of the lake is a developed resort area, with boating, swimming, water skiing, fishing. The north shore is a virtual wilderness, but with excellent camping and fishing spots. No roads. You cross over by boat (which can be rented). Campsites at *Mill Creek* are the best. Bring a horse, or plan to hike; there are many lakes and streams to explore.

Take Calif. 29 to Kelseyville, then follow the signs for *Clear Lake State Park. Soda Bay* has the largest number of facilities for camping, trailer space, etc.

Castle Crags State Park is 48 miles north of Redding. Great camping in a setting of gray-white granite domes and spires rising out of an evergreen forest. Good hiking trails.

The ill-fated Donner Party camped at the site of *Donner Memorial State Park* during the winter of 1846–47. Forty-two of the 90 persons in the party died before the winter was out. Today, there are campsites in the same area, much in demand, especially in summer! Donner Lake offers excellent picnic facilities and fishing, but is really too cold for swimming.

Mt. Diablo is in the East Bay, behind Oakland. If the weather is superb, you'll find picnicking and camping sites with magnificent views at *Juniper,* 3 miles below the summit. For good views, plus protection from the weather, try the *Pioneer* and *Blue Oak* areas on the south slopes. Modest fees.

Eagle Lake is a formerly isolated valley with excellent forest campgrounds and marina. Close to Susanville. It's California's second largest natural lake and offers great trout fishing, swimming, water skiing, and boating. It is home to the Eagle Lake trout, a fish native only to this lake.

Emigrant Wilderness is just north of Yosemite Park. Combines the best features of high-country magnificence and low-country warmth. No improved campgrounds, but plenty of people camp anyway, especially at *Cow Meadow* (good fishing, and the campsites are protected by a high granite ridge from the wind).

Fremont Peak State Park is between Monterey and San Benito counties, 11 miles south of San Juan Bautista via San Juan Canyon-State Park Road. An off-the-beaten-track retreat with valley white and California black oaks shading the picnic and camping area. Modest fees.

Lassen Volcanic National Park offers 150 miles of trail, seven campgrounds, Visitor Center with guided walks in summer and evening talks. In winter, only ski area accessible for cross-country, downhill skiing and snowshoe exploring.

Near the beach, just north of Eureka, is *Patrick's Point State Park.* Complete facilities for campers and picnickers. The park is a California "rain forest": the native growth is so dense it screens the campsites from each other. Hiking trails lead to the bluff above the sea.

Prairie Creek Redwoods State Park has a beautiful creek, and a magnificent meadow where herds of Roosevelt elk live. For campers, this is as pleasant a place as you can find. (Within boundaries of Redwood National Park.)

Pfeiffer Big Sur State Park has good hiking, camping, picnicking, fishing, riding (saddle horses for rent). South of Carmel on State 1. Avoid summer if you can: the campgrounds are very crowded then and you're liable to be turned away.

Pinnacles National Monument is off State 25, 35 miles south of Hollister. Offbeat trails for hiking in fantastically carved and jumbled terrain with natural staircases, caverns, moats. Only a short walk from the *Bear Gulch* campgrounds.

Richardson Grove State Park is in Humboldt County. Highly developed campgrounds with swimming holes, along the Eel River's South Fork. Restaurant, grocery store, and 10 miles of hiking trails, plus a state naturalist who conducts trail walks during the summer season.

There are many campgrounds in the *Trinity Alps* along the Trinity River west from Weaverville to Willow Creek.

Thousand Lakes Wild Area is north of Lassen Volcanic Park. Especially great for knapsack carriers and horse-packers seeking solitude. Undisturbed fishing in eight upland lakes, and wildflower meadows to hike. (Twin Lakes-Magee Lake are the most free of mosquitos.)

Yosemite National Park's very popular five *High Sierra Camps* (Glen Aulin, Vogelsang, May Lake, Merced Lake, and Sunrise) are surrounded by fish-filled streams and lakes, lush meadows and walls of rugged peaks. All are situated from 7,000–10,000 plus feet elevations, and are walk-in from Tioga Pass Road. Accommodations are dorm-style cabins; guests segregated by sex; no private tents available. All camp opening dates are subject to snow melt, late June-mid-July and closed in mid-September.

FARM VACATIONS AND GUEST RANCHES. These popular family-oriented vacation destinations offer maximum opportunities to loll, fish, swim, hike and ride in usually remote wilderness areas at moderate cost. Some ranches allow guests to help with chores; others leave one almost totally alone. After-dark activities include steak fries, square dancing, swapping tales round a campfire, studying the Milky Way.

Just fourteen miles from the southern entrance to Yosemite National Park, is the scenic Pines Resorts. Handsome two-story chalets come equipped with kitchens; children under 16 are free guests. Sport activities abound—tennis courts, great fishing in Bass Lake, horseback riding and golf. Fitness fans flock to the exercise room and sauna/Jacuzzi. Two restaurants with cocktail lounges plus cable TV offer P.M. diversions.

Try a wilderness adventure at the *Muir Trail Ranch,* P.O. Box 269, Ahwahnee, Ca. 93601. Board a ferryboat at Florence Lake, ride horseback to a corral surrounded by glacier-carved peaks. Photograph some of the 60 varieties of wildflowers. Delicious family-style food. Log cabins, campsites.

Trinity County invites with many ranches; more than 100 miles of streams, famous for salmon and steelhead fishing; the pristine Trinity Alps, and historic Jackson and Weaverville. *Coffee Creek Guest Ranch,* Trinity Center, CA 96091, handles only 50 guests, and in season offers hunting and cross-country skiing; secluded cabins.

The M Bar J Guest Ranch, Box 121–G, Badger, Ca. 93603, is open from April-October 31. Eight cabins in a secluded oak-studded valley. Cross-country skiing in nearby Sequoia National Park is through April.

Eight miles south of Garberville on Hwy. 101, 30-acre *Hartsook Inn,* Piercy, CA 95467 adjoins Richardson Grove State Park (redwoods). Attractive cabins and home-cooked meals.

Advance reservations are necessary at all these ranches, especially for the summer season.

HEALTH SPAS. The principal one is *Calistoga,* north of St. Helena on State 29. The entire region has a scattering of hot springs, mineral springs, and steaming geysers. California's newest luxury health club/spa is situated in the heart of the wine country in the Sonoma Mission Inn. The pink-hued art deco showplace attracts vacationers who prefer quiet country life with a dash of sunning, tennis and gourmet dining as well as those seeking a spartan fitness regime. Other popular resorts are *Dr. Wilkinson's Hot Springs,* at 1507 Lincoln Ave., and *Calistoga Spa,* at 1006 Washington St. Both provide mud and mineral baths, massage, hot mineral pools, and motel accommodations. Busy on weekends.

MUSEUMS AND GALLERIES. Auburn: *Placer County Museum,* 1273 High St. Memorabilia of pioneer life and mining in area.

Berkeley: *Judah L. Magnes Memorial Museum,* 2911 Russell St., houses an impressive collection of Jewish ceremonial art, rare books. *University Art Museum,* 2626 Bancroft Way, offers guided tours and gallery talks, paintings, sculpture, drawings, prints. Carmel: *Carmel Mission and Gift Shop,* 3080 Rio Rd., is a historical museum, with sculpture, Indian artifacts and textile collections. *The Gallery of Fine and Comic Art,* southwest corner of Dolores and Fifth, exhibits and sells original drawings by Gus Arriola *(Gordo),* Pulitzer Prize winner Gary Trudeau *(Doonesbury),* Charles Schulz *(Peanuts),* and other name cartoonists. Crescent City: *Del Norte County Historical Society,* 710 H St., is housed in an old jail building. Eureka: *Clarke Memorial Museum,* 240 E. St. has anthropology, archaeology, costume, Indian lore, and natural history exhibits.

Fresno: *Arts Center,* 3033 E. Yale Ave. *Kearney Mansion Museum,* 7160 W. Kearney Blvd., is a general history museum with a blacksmith shop, carriage house and 1890s home.

Monterey: *Allen Knight Maritime Museum,* 550 Calle Principal. *Monterey Peninsula Museum of Art,* 559 Pacific St. *Old Monterey Jail,* Dutra St., Civic Center. *Robert Louis Stevenson House,* 530 Houston St. *San Carlos Cathedral,* 550 Church St., offers guided tours of its 18th- and 19th-century Spanish religious painting and sculpture. *United States Army Museum,* Presidio of Monterey, is housed in a 1908 cavalry-supply depot. The new Historical Wax Museum, Cannery Row, recalls Old Monterey.

Palo Alto: *Stanford University Museum of Art.* Redding: *Museum and Art Center,* specializes in Indian and pre-Columbian art.

Sacramento: *California State Indian Museum,* 1218 K St., is located on the site of Sutter's Fort. *E. B. Crocker Art Gallery,* 216 O St. *Governor's Mansion,* 16th and H Sts., an ornate 23-room Victorian Gothic charmer. *California State Historic Railroad Museum & Central Pacific Passenger Station,* Old Sacramento.

San Jose: *The Rosicrucian Egyptian Museum and Art Gallery,* Park Avenue, contains the largest ancient Egyptian and Babylonian collection in the Western

United States, plus the Vadenais Collection of 18th century French decorative art and furnishings. *State University Art Gallery,* 20th-century painting, sculpture, graphics. *Civic Art Gallery,* 100 S. Market St. Regional artists. *Historical Museum,* 635 Phelan Ave. Mining, transportation, historic houses. Stockton: *Pacific Center for Western Historical Studies,* Univ. of the Pacific. Western Americana, John Muir papers. *Pioneer Museum and Haggan Galleries,* 1201 N. Pershing Ave.

HISTORIC SITES. *Columbia,* 4 miles from Sonora, is the best preserved of the Gold Rush towns. All buildings in the town are marked for easy identification. Excellent museum. *Donner Memorial State Park* is two miles west of Truckee on US 40. The park is a memorial to members of the Donner party, who camped here during the winter of 1846–47. Very impressive monument. Try to see the old part of *Monterey,* as it was when it was Spanish capital of Alta California. *San Juan Bautista State Historical Monument,* off US 101 between Gilroy and Salinas, is a chapter of early California history that ended with the coming of the railroad. And do see *Sutter's Fort* in *Sacramento,* where gold was discovered. It's at 28th and L Streets, carefully reconstructed, with California's greatest collection of Gold Rush and pioneer relics.

TOURS. 3-day Wine Country-Lake Tahoe, four- and five-day circle tours of *Yosemite, Monterey* and *Carmel* are offered weekly, all year, by *California Parlor Car Tours Co.* (modern air-conditioned motor coach). Also a six-day trip combining the above with *Lake Tahoe,* plus *Santa Barbara* and *Los Angeles* in Southern California. The latter offered weekly in summer only. The *California Western Railroad* offers trips on the *Skunk,* a small train making scenic 80-mile round trips through redwood forests, over 33 bridges and trestles, and through two tunnels. It shuttles all year between *Ft. Bragg* and *Willits;* one round trip daily, except in summer, when there are two or more. Four-day tours of the *Redwood Empire* are offered monthly in July, August, and September by *Western Greyhound Lines.* The trip covers Frank Lloyd Wright's *Marin Civic Center, Sonoma, St. Helena, Santa Rosa, Mendocino, Ft. Bragg, the Avenue of the Giants, the Pacific Lumber Mill* at Scotia, *Eureka,* and the *Rockefeller Redwoods State Park.*

SPECIAL-INTEREST TOURS. Explore Northern California's wilderness wonders on an organized *llama trek.* Shasta Llamas, Box 1137E, Mount Shasta, CA 96067 (916–926–3959) schedules hikes in the Trinity Alps and the Marble Mountains from mid-June to mid-Sept. Plan about five to ten miles of daily walks with lots of rest periods to photograph, soak in the pristine landscapes, or nap. Prices range from $255 for a three-day trip to $400 for a five-day trek.

There are guided seven-day *hiking trips* around Yosemite Park, leaving Yosemite Valley every Sunday in summer. Guided six-day *horseback trips* around the High Country of the park leave the valley several days a week in summertime. There's also *rafting* down the *Klamath River.* Way up past Yreka, close to the Oregon border, this is a real adventure in the wilderness. Two- or three-day weekend trips offered during the summer months. Write Wilderness Waterway, 4 Live Oak Circle, El Sobrante, Calif. A different kind of tour may be taken by those interested in *lighthouses.* See *Point Arena,* on the Mendocino Coast, from 1 to 4 P.M. weekends and holidays, and *Point Cabrillo,* five miles north of Mendocino.

THE CALIFORNIA MISSIONS. In 1768, when the Russian interest in Alaska was seen as a possible prelude to southward expansion, King Charles of Spain ordered the colonization of California. The king's decree launched the missions, which provided the seminal growth for California. Under the astute leadership of Father Junipero Serra and Father Fermin Lausen—each founded nine missions—the gray-robed Franciscans moved slowly northward. By 1823 a chain of twenty-one missions extended 600 miles from San Diego to Sonoma. Approximately a day's travel apart (30 miles in those days), the missions dotted the coastal route called El Camino Real. Today, US 101 closely parallels the historic Mission Trail, one of the state's most popular tourways. To view them and explore them is the keystone to the history of California.

GARDENS. In Carmel Valley, see *Hanssens' Begonia Gardens,* a riot of color in summer. A mile east of San Juan Bautista on Hollister Rd. is the *Ferry-Morse Flower Farm.* Nine hundred acres of splendid blooms are at their best from mid-July to September. Open 9 A.M. to 5 P.M. weekdays, Saturdays until noon. *Capitol Park,* Sacramento, has camellias (more than 800 varieties) in bloom during February and March. *Fresno Underground Gardens,* 7 miles north of Fresno, is a maze of trees, shrubs, vegetables, flowers, and vines, all planted underground and flourishing.

In and around Santa Rosa, visit the *Luther Burbank Memorial Gardens* in town. Visit *Hakone Gardens,* 21000 Big Basin Wy., hidden in the hills on the road to Big Basin in the Saratoga area. A miniature city park, complete with wooden Japanese houses, quiet pools, and wandering walks, designed by the son of a court gardener to the Emperor of Japan.

MUSIC. A big event for jazz buffs is the annual Monterey Jazz Festival in mid-September. There's always an abundance of name talent. In Saratoga, Villa Montalvo has a cultural center and annual music festival, from May through June, which features opera, chamber music and recitals. In 1987, the Carmel Bach Festival celebrated its 50th season. This major musical bacchanalia, starting in mid-July, includes daily recitals, a children's concert; opera symposium. Phone 408–624–1521 for information.

STAGE AND REVUES. The Concord Pavilion (45 minutes from San Francisco), has a year-round series of musicals, plays, and personality shows. Stanford University at Palo Alto, and the University of California at Berkeley, have regularly scheduled theatrical productions.

DRINKING LAWS. You must be 21—and if you look young, be sure to always carry proof of your age, for you're bound to be challenged to show it. Legal hours for dispensing drinks in public places are from 6 A.M. to 2 A.M.

CASINOS. You'll find them only on the Nevada side of Lake Tahoe. Most of the casinos are on the south shore. In recent years, Reno has added six new casinos and renovated its international airport. Ten million tourists seek million-dollar jackpots yearly. *Bally's Grand Hotel* hosts the "Hello Hollywood, Hello!" extravaganza.

Lake Tahoe, at 6,000 ft. offers year-round attractions including water and snow skiing, golf, tennis, fishing and hunting, and top-name entertainment.

SUMMER SPORTS. For *skiing* and *boating* in general, California is loaded with lakes; some major ones are *Tahoe, Berryessa* and *Mendocino.* At Clear Lake the *Hot Boat and Ski Races* are held in May, on July 4, and over Labor Day. Here also are the *Pacific Coast Water Ski Open Racing Championships* in late July.

For *fishing* there are *Lake Tahoe* and the *Upper Sacramento River* from north of Dunsmuir to south of Shasta Lake, with many choice fishing spots in the *Castle Crags State Park area.*

White water enthusiasts can run the Tuolumne River in 2, 3 or 4 days; and outings are offered on the Stanislaus, Sacramento, and American rivers. The American River Touring Association, 445 High Street, Oakland, CA 94612 (tel. 415–465–9355) can offer suggestions.

Golf: Northern California has some outstanding courses. According to "Golf Digest" the Pebble Beach G.C., Pebble Beach, ranks among the first ten of America's 100 greatest courses; Spyglass Hill G.C., Pebble Beach, among the fourth ten; Cypress Point Club, Pebble Beach, among the fifth ten; Stanford Univ. G.C., Stanford, among the second fifty.

Other courses recommended by "Golf Digest" are: Lake Shastina G.C., Mt. Shasta, a Robert Trent Jones course; Silverado C.C., Napa, open to guests staying on premises; Alameda G.C., Alameda, a renovated course with five artificial lake hazards; Las Positas G.C., Livermore, a municipal course with water hazards; Sunol Valley G.C., Sunol, a semi-private course; Pasatiempo G.C., Santa Cruz, overlooking Monterey Bay; Laguna Seca G.C., Monterey, a Trent Jones course; Rancho Canada G.C., Carmel Valley, a public course; Del Monte G.C., Monterey, a semi-private course; Pacific Grove G.C., Pacific Grove, a short, municipal course; Carmel Valley G. & C.C., Carmel, flat course; San Luis Bay Inn & G.C., Avila Beach, a resort course.

WINTER SPORTS. *Skiing* is another big sport in the mountains of California. Good areas are *Squaw Valley* off State 89, 8 miles from Tahoe City; *Alpine Meadows,* a mile south of the Squaw Valley turnoff; *Heavenly Valley,* at Bijou on the south end of Lake Tahoe; *Sugar Bowl; Badger Pass,* in Yosemite; *Northstar-at-Tahoe,* near Truckee, a year-round resort, noted for its cross-country skiing tours; and *Mount Shasta Ski Bowl.* Slaloms and other competitions rotate among all these areas from January through March. There's also *Tahoe-Sierra Sled Dog Racing* at Lake Tahoe in mid-March.

SPECTATOR SPORTS. California is second only to Texas in number of *rodeos.* There are over 60 sanctioned each year by the Rodeo Cowboys Association. Major ones are at *Red Bluff* in April. *Angels Camp* in May, *Livermore* in June, and the biggest of them all at *Salinas* in July (the *California Rodeo*). This last is one of the Big Four of the rodeo world, ranking with the Calgary Stampede, the Pendleton Round-up, and Cheyenne Frontier Days.

Other *equestrian events* are offered, too. There's the interclub horse show at *Carmel Valley Trail and Saddle Club* grounds in early May. Redding has the *Shasta Wonderland Three-day Non-Competitive Trail Ride* in mid-July. Mid-August sees the *Carmel Valley Horsemen's Roundup.* There's the *High Sierra Trail Horseback Ride* at Twain Harte in mid-August. And the *Equestrian Trails and Western American Cup,* preceded by a big public breakfast and a parade, are held at the Pebble Beach Stables in early September.

WHAT TO DO WITH THE CHILDREN. Visit *Santa Cruz Beach-Boardwalk,* the state's finest seaside playground, reminiscent of pre-Disneyland amusement parks. Old-fashioned rides, games, restaurants, amusements and a mile-long beach. Open daily in summer, weekends in winter. If you like, you may let them flip fish to baby seals and pet the ponies, donkeys, lambs, goats and ducks in *Happy Hollow Park* in San Jose. It's fun to herd them through *Winchester Mystery House* in San Jose, the ultimate in haunted houses: a 160-room rambling wooden dwelling with trapdoors, secret passageways, and stairs that go nowhere.

Great for kids are float trips thru the *Redwood National Park.* For reservations write to Redwood National Park, 1111 Second Street, Crescent City, CA. 95531. Or carry an inner tube to Yosemite and float anywhere between Pines

Campgrounds and El Capitan Bridge. Life jackets are advisable. Never tube alone.

Great America Theme Park, at I–101 in Santa Clara (408–988–1776), offers entertainment for the family. Six areas of the U.S. are showcased. Thirty-one rides (eight for kids) include the Revolution and the Blue Streak, a mini roller-coaster. Younsters delight in Hanna-Barbera's Smurf Woods and the dolphin and sea lions' antics. Three stage shows, a giant-screen movie, and 20 restaurants and snack shops please all ages. Closed winter; spring, fall, only weekends. In addition to the famed thrill rides, five theaters offer different types of entertainment. About 45 miles south of San Francisco.

Other favorite spots for youngsters include Lake Merritt's *Children's Fairyland,* with rides and puppet shows. Open Wed. through Sun, 10 A.M.–4:30 P.M. At Grand Avenue near Bellevue. Phone 415–452–2259 for more information.

The *Oakland Zoo* is a 100-acre [illegible] in Oakland's Knowland Park, with over 300 animals and birds. Open daily, 10 A.M.–4 P.M.; weekends until 4:30 P.M. Take 98th Avenue Exit from I–580. Phone 415–568–2470 for current information.

Visit the *Marine Mammal Center,* Fort Cronkhite, Marin Headlands, where injured or orphaned sea lions and seals are cared for and returned to the wild. Open daily, 10 A.M.–4 P.M. Phone 415–331–SEAL for more information.

IDAHO

Outdoor Life—Mountain Style

by
RALPH FRIEDMAN

Ralph Friedman is a freelance writer and teacher living in Portland, Oregon. He is the author of ten regional books, a newspaper columnist, and a contributor to many publications. Mr. Friedman has taught freelance writing and Oregon folklore for Portland Community College.

Boise is the capital and largest city of Idaho. A flourishing agricultural, horticultural, and stock-raising region lies about the city, and rich mines pocket the surrounding mountains. It is also one of the most important trade centers for wool in the United States. Though it lies in the southwest section of the state, it is the hub of tourism and will be our starting and finishing point for tours around Idaho.

Standing on the Boise River, at the upper end of the green Boise Valley, this capital is basically a residential city of homes and trees. It was named by French-Canadian voyagers who, after plodding for weeks through gritty, dust-choked wastelands, cried out, upon seeing trees: "*Les Bois!*" Boise is pronounced either *Boy-see* or *Boy-zee;* local ears hear both so often they cannot distinguish the difference.

The city boasts a four-year college; a regionally famous philharmonic orchestra, with a resident conductor; a virile Little Theater; the Boise

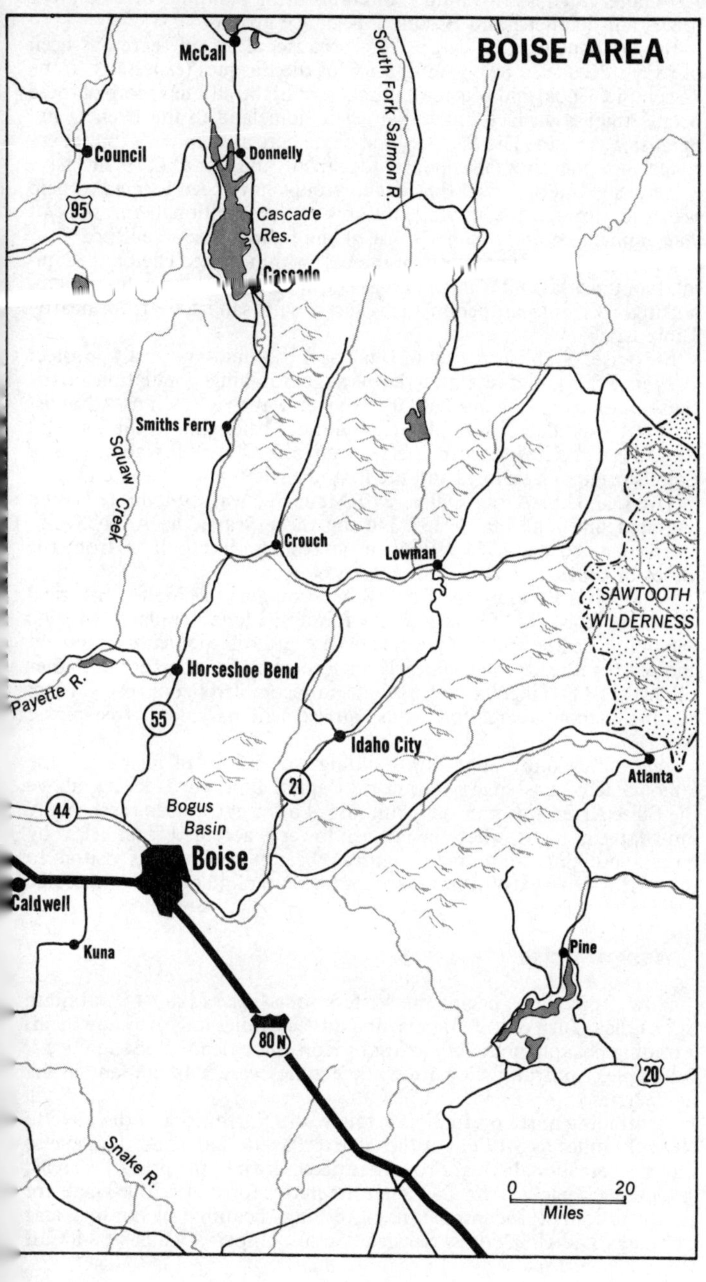
BOISE AREA
McCall
Council
Donnelly
South Fork Salmon R.
95
Cascade Res.
Cascade
Smiths Ferry
Squaw Creek
Crouch
Lowman
SAWTOOTH WILDERNESS
Horseshoe Bend
Payette R.
55
Idaho City
21
Atlanta
44
Bogus Basin
Boise
Caldwell
Kuna
Pine
80N
20
Snake R.
0
20
Miles

Art Gallery, whose traveling exhibitions bring paintings to a hundred towns and hamlets; and Basque folk-dance groups.

Basque dancing is a feature here because, although there has been of recent decades a heavy emigration of the Basques (especially to the Argentine, Cuba, and Mexico), the state of Idaho still has more of these people than any place other than their homeland in the French and Spanish Pyrenees. The Basques first came here as shepherds, but open-range sheepherding has greatly declined, and most of them have become so Americanized that dance groups have been formed to help preserve, through the stirring rhythms of the traditional *Auresku, La Jota,* and *Purrusalda,* some spirit of the fading Basque culture.

And there are other points of interest within Boise. The State Capitol, monumental and classical in aspect, with Corinthian columns supporting a Corinthian pediment, is faced with sandstone from nearby Table Rock.

Ft. Boise, established July 4, 1863, as a U.S. military post to protect Oregon Trail emigrants and the new gold-mining population of the Boise Basin from Indians, has largely given way to a Veterans Administration Hospital, but several early buildings belonging to the fort still stand near the hospital. In the same area is O'Farrell Cabin, one of Boise's original dwellings and the first to shelter women and children.

The Old U.S. Assay Office, 210 Main St., was built in 1871 and operated until the mid-1930s. During those years, the Assay Office received more than $75 million in gold and silver bullion from the mines of southern Idaho and eastern Oregon.

Julia Davis Park, by the Boise River, contains the Idaho Historical Museum; Boise Art Gallery; State Library; Pioneer Village, with its 1863-built Pearce and Coston cabins (the latter fashioned of driftwood and put together with pegs); early stagecoaches, fire engines, and other vehicles; "Big Mike," a powerful steam locomotive; zoo; rose garden; boating lagoon; recreation fields; amusement park; and free picnic grounds.

One of the more appealing buildings to visit is, of all places, the Union Pacific Passenger Station on Capitol Boulevard. Rising above the Boise River, this imposing building of brick and stucco is especially impressive at night, when the tall bell tower is accented from below by large floodlights. Man-made "natural" beauty also attracts visitors to the nearby Howard V. Platt Gardens displays of plants and waterfalls.

West of Boise

Now, from Boise, begins the western tour. Take Idaho 44, out State St., 8 miles. Turn onto Idaho 55, and drive 20 miles to Horseshoe Bend, a trading post of about 700. (West of Horseshoe Bend, along Idaho 52, rolls a pleasant fruit valley. Emmett, 20 miles west, is Idaho-famous for its cherries.)

Continuing north on Idaho 55, follow the North Fork of the Payette River 79 miles to McCall, at the edge of Payette Lake and the Payette Lakes Recreational Area. From here planes fly into the primitive areas; several back-packers' headquarters are in this town of 2,200. There are excellent tourist accommodations, fishing, boating, swimming, and camping. The U.S. Forest Service "Smokejumper" Center at McCall welcomes visitors.

From McCall, roads lead deep into the wilds of the Payette National Forest. One picks its way 31 miles north to Burgdorf Hot Springs, where there are a swimming pool, campsites, cabins, and, of course, thermal springs.

Another road, graded, cuts a swath through the woods 52 miles to Yellow Pine, on the East Fork of the South Fork of the Salmon, where there is a typical dude ranch. Guides are available for fishing and hunting trips. Hunters go after mountain sheep or goats, or, on a deluxe expedition, elk, deer, and bear.

Beyond McCall, Idaho 55 jaunts through a round meadowed valley 12 miles to New Meadows, where the road runs out. To the south are dairy farms, gentle plateaus, and forests of yellow pines; to the north are the barren mountains and the shadowy canyons of the Little Salmon River. There is only one road north at this point, US 95. Riggins, 35 miles above New Meadows, lies in a T-shaped canyon at the confluence of the Little Salmon and Salmon rivers. To the west, 15 miles as the crow flies, is Hells Canyon, deepest gorge on the continent. Between Riggins and the gorge rise the Seven Devils, snow-capped most of the year. High on the slopes and in the saddles are glinting blue lakes encircled by evergreen pine, fir, spruce, and tamarack clusters.

Where Indians Feared to Tread

The Salmon River is the mythical "River of No Return," so named by the Indians, whose bravest of the brave were turned back by the steep canyon walls and rapids. But though the myth persists, the boats of the white man now travel upriver as well as downstream. Each year an increasing number of boats do try the Salmon, enjoying the adventure of riding the turbulent rapids. A few hermits live along it, in a mode more common to the nineteenth than the twentieth century.

A dirt road runs 20 miles up the Salmon from Riggins. The terrain is wild, scary, and photogenic. Nine miles up this trace from US 95 is a hot springs, with swimming pool, cabins, and picnic area.

Now, beyond Riggins, the highway swings alongside the lusty Salmon River. The deep, steep canyon cut by the stream is sometimes, near noon, sprinkled with sunshine, but more often it is carpeted by the cool shadows of twilight, though twilight may be hours above the canyon walls.

Emerging from the chasm, the road is accosted by steep mountains, on whose lower slopes cling tiny farms. These massifs give way to mountains where beetling rocks crop through the brown parchment of the vegetation, while below, the Salmon bubbles along as it hurries to join the Snake. At White Bird, 29 miles above Riggins, it veers westward, to keep its ancient rendezvous.

It was in White Bird Canyon, north of this hamlet, that the first battle in the Nez Percé war was fought, in 1877, when the people of Chief Joseph repulsed the efforts of soldiers to stomp them into the ground.

Beyond White Bird village the historic road climbs almost 3,000 feet. At the summit there are panoramas of the Seven Devils, blue-misted canyons, and ranges to the east lost in purple obscurity. The descent is down slopes of gay and fragrant wildflowers and onto a sweeping plateau of amber grain-fields, whose center is Grangeville, 21 miles north of White Bird.

Today Grangeville is the marketplace of the lovely Camas Prairie, a realm of gold minted by seed and sun. But in the 1860s the town was the jumping-off point to a dozen gold camps. Some of these, far back,

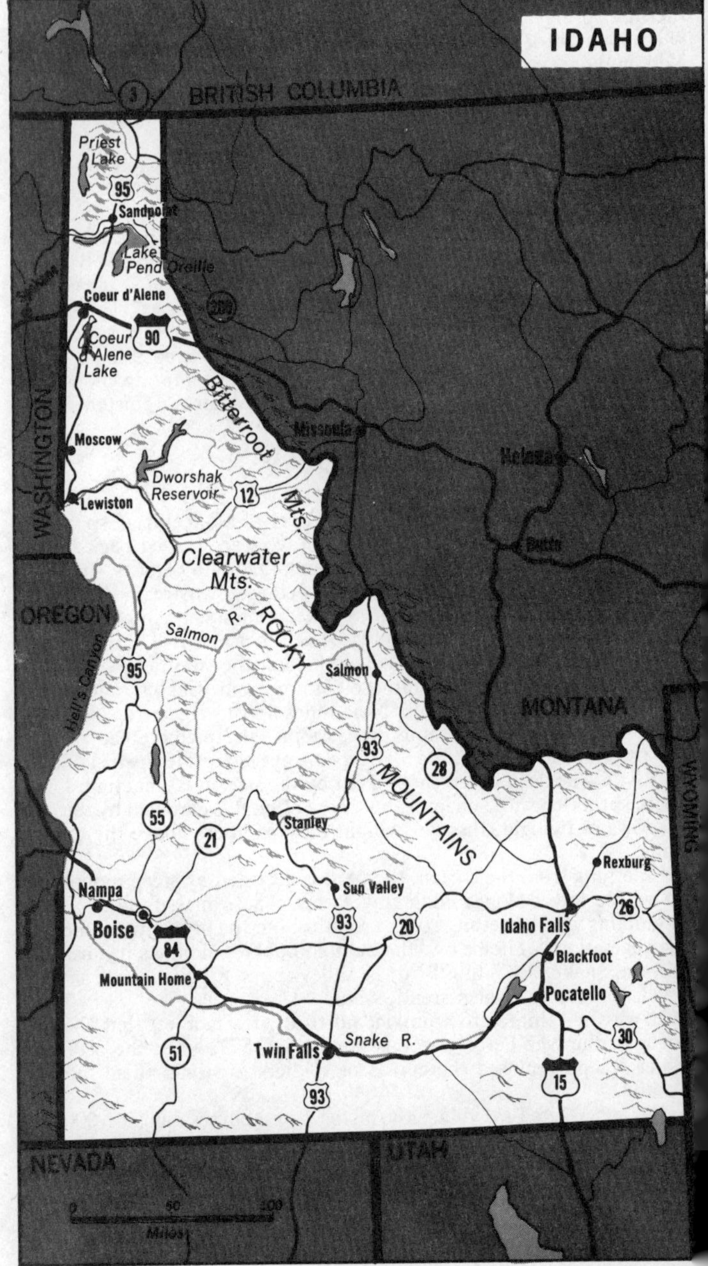
IDAHO
BRITISH COLUMBIA
Priest Lake
95
Sandpoint
Lake Pend Oreille
Coeur d'Alene
90
Coeur d'Alene Lake
Bitterroot Mts.
Missoula
Helena
Moscow
Dworshak Reservoir
Lewiston
12
WASHINGTON
Butte
Clearwater Mts.
OREGON
Salmon R.
ROCKY
Hell's Canyon
95
Salmon
MONTANA
93
MOUNTAINS
28
WYOMING
55
21
Stanley
Rexburg
Nampa
Sun Valley
Boise
93
20
Idaho Falls
26
84
Blackfoot
Mountain Home
Pocatello
30
Snake R.
51
Twin Falls
15
93
NEVADA
UTAH
0 50 100
Miles

are touched by saddle trips through the Selway-Bitterroot Primitive Area. For up-to-date particulars, write Nez Percé National Forest Service Headquarters or Chamber of Commerce, both at Grangeville ID 83530.

A secondary road south ends in 4 miles at Mt. Idaho, where the first Republican convention in Idaho Territory was held. Today it is another ghost town.

A more ambitious drive is up the Clearwater River to Elk City, 61 miles east of Grangeville via Idaho 14. This is an area of densely wooded canyon walls hovering above the tumultuous river, of glistening evergreens and ferns, and of wildflowers, miles of them, that launch wave after wave of almost suffocating fragrance.

Elk City, near the lip of Salmon River Breaks and Idaho Primitive Areas, is at the end of the paved road. The settlement actually numbers 450 persons, a veritable metropolis in these parts, where a collection of 20 souls constitutes a social center. Yet Elk City held 20,000 when it was a roaring gold camp. Nearby, as distance in these parts is measured, is the resort of Red River Hot Springs.

Razor Edge Ridges

Another route from Grangeville might be to follow Idaho 13 to Kooskia, 26 miles to the northeast. Now you are in Lewis and Clark country. The explorers staggered out of the mountains here in the autumn of 1805, half-starved and half-frozen after a frightful crossing over the icy and snow-covered razor-edge ridges.

Early in the 1960s, US 12, which parallels this Lolo Indian trail, was finally completed as a direct route between Lewiston and Missoula. In the 100 miles between Kooskia and the Montana border there is only one hamlet, Lowell (population 30), 23 miles east of Kooskia. But there are numerous campsites along the Lochsa River, the mountains roll away in all directions, and just above, and sometimes at roadside, is the treacherous path followed by Lewis and Clark. This is history close up.

North of Kooskia, follow US 12 for 7 miles to Kamiah, where the oldest Protestant church in Idaho stands. The front, mounted on two columns, looks like one birdhouse built on top of another. Near Kamiah is the East Kamiah Site of the Nez Percé National Historical Park.

Continue along the Clearwater for 15 miles to the junction with Idaho 11. This road jogs 30 miles through immense stands of yellow pine, white pine, and fir to Pierce, where gold was first discovered in Idaho, in 1860. For decades the town looked like a Western movie-set; but now it's changing, and the population has soared from 500 to 1,100—about what it held as a rough mining camp in 1861. (It was to get a lot bigger before the placer gold ran out and the miners departed.)

From Pierce, backtrack on Idaho 11 for 12 miles to Weippe, near where the Lewis and Clark party first encountered the Nez Percé, and then another 18 miles to Greer, a tiny hamlet at the junction of US 12. Eight miles north, up US 12, stands gold rush Orofino, which had 12,000 people in 1861, with all their belongings and necessities for building a town brought in by pack train, which was for two years the only form of transportation. Orofino today has 3,700 population and is built on industry, agriculture, and tourism. A few miles below Orofino is the Lewis and Clark Canoe Camp, where the Nez Percé taught the elkskin-clad trailblazers how to make canoes by burning out fallen trees. It was in these canoes that the explorers made their way to the Pacific.

From Orofino, US 12 follows the Clearwater downstream about 40 miles to Lewiston, one of Idaho's most historic and interesting cities. At the confluence of the Snake and Clearwater, and flanked by steep hills, it is as much a trading center today for the rich grainlands and fruit orchards which slope high above it in three directions as it was a frenetic supply and transportation hub for the upstream gold rush town of the 1860s. For many years practically all the stores in this city of 28,000 were on one long street, but in recent years shopping centers have been built on the nearby plateaus.

Idaho's only seaport (some ocean-going vessels come up the Columbia and Snake to dock here), Lewiston is at the lowest elevation in the state, only 738 feet. It is also one of the warmest places in the state and has been called Idaho's "Banana Belt."

From Lewiston Hill, there are panoramas of rivers, forests, waves of wheatland, and the city itself below.

Potlatch Corporation offers free tours of its giant sawmill complex. Luna House Museum, in a pioneer residence, displays native art from early American civilizations. One of the most famous rodeos in the West, the Lewiston Roundup, is held in the first weekend after Labor Day.

River Boat Trips

One of the outstanding river boat trips in the West begins and ends here. A mail-supply boat, which plies up the Snake River almost to the gates of Hells Canyon, carries passengers and is also used solely for excursions. (For up-to-date fares and schedules, write: Chamber of Commerce, Lewiston, ID 83501.)

Nez Percé National Historical Park, at Spalding, site of Old Lapwai Mission, founded in 1836, is 10 miles from Lewiston. An interpretive center is worth the trip. Here, too, is the Spalding Area of the park. Three miles on is Lapwai, headquarters of the Nez Percé Indian Reservation. Visitors welcome.

Back at Lewiston, cross the Clearwater and take Idaho 3 to Genesee, Juliaetta, Kendrick, Deary, Santa, and on to St. Maries, a combined distance of about 100 miles. The road travels over, through, and past undulating prairie lands, long hills that seem in the distance like a succession of ocean swells, benchlands, and deep gorges. Juliaetta, with a population of about 500, is the home of the fine Arrow Museum, a collection of Indian artifacts.

St. Maries, a rustic county seat stretched out on softish hills, is the southern terminus of freight and passenger boats plying the St. Joe River, said to be the highest navigable stream in the world. It is called "shadowy St. Joe" by residents, because of the brooding, shifting reflections cast on the still surface of the stream by lovely foliage.

From St. Maries, boats go to Heyburn State Park (12 miles via Idaho 5), and some boats cruise into Coeur d'Alene Lake and up to its northern shore. Many shaded campgrounds are along the river and the lake.

Idaho 3 travels west of St. Maries for 11 miles and then northeast 22 miles, to Cataldo Mission, the oldest building in the state. You are now on I-90. Turn east and drive 12 miles to Kellogg, in the Coeur d'Alene mining district. A cornucopia of lead, silver, gold, and zinc (and an occasional scene of tragedy), it is neat and bustling, totally unlike the typical slag-ugly mining town. The soaring price of silver revived Kellogg and other towns in the Coeur d' Alené Mining District, bringing back the Boom Days. But then the prices plummeted, and in 1982 mines were closed and the disaster of hard times struck heavily, casting a pall over the former bonanza towns. The future now seems uncertain.

Wallace, 10 miles east of Kellogg and 7 miles west of Mullan, and Burke, 7 miles north of Wallace, are on the axis of a large silver and lead mining area. Burke, with a population of 80, is the most colorful of the mining towns. Its one street is pressed against the side of a deep gulch.

Backtrack to the junction of Idaho 3 and Idaho 97, and follow the latter road 43 miles north up the east shore of Coeur d'Alene Lake to the town of Coeur d'Alene.

Coeur d'Alene's Lovely Lake

This drive ought to be made slowly and with frequent pauses at the turnoffs, for there is enchantment every yard of the winding overlook. The lake is lovely to the point of disbelief. At times it appears to be a cloud floating off into space, one moment it may look like a field of windblown poppies, and the next like acres of glittering diamonds. Within a 5-mile stretch it can be violet-tinted, rose-hued, and orange blossomed. No lake in the Northwest evokes such imagery, has such a color range, or seems so ethereal.

Coeur d'Alene is the largest city in the Idaho panhandle, with tourist accommodations ranging from the elegant to the simple. No one ought to come here without taking the excursion boat ride to Heyburn State Park.

Follow US 95 north 18 miles, through crisp woods, vales, and lakes, to Bayview turnoff. Eight miles east, at Bayview, is the southern extremity of Lake Pend Oreille (pronounced *pon-duh-ray*), the largest lake in Idaho. Fabled for its fishing, it is the home of the Kamloops trout, biggest in the world. Four mountain ranges press against the lake, and the waters are broken by numerous isles. Bayview has cottages, apartments, campsites, trailer parks, stores, restaurants, rental boats, and a beach.

Return to US 95 and motor 28 miles, through woods brightened by small lakes, to Sandpoint, a cedar-shipping center on Pend Oreille Lake.

However, the lake is seen best by paved road from Idaho 200 (which skirts it for 25 miles) to Clark Fork, on the eastern side of the lake. Just west of here is the site of the first trading post (1809) in the Oregon Country.

From Sandpoint follow US 2 along the Pend Oreille River to Priest River—a delightful half-hour-or-so drive—and turn north on Idaho 57 to Coolin turnoff, 19 miles. Go east 4 miles to Priest Lake and up 4 miles to the Priest Lake Recreational Area. Priest is a "primitive" lake. The only settlement close to it is Nordman, 15 miles above the Coolin junction on Idaho 57; it has only 50 people. Even unpaved roads to the lake are few, and Upper Priest Lake is reachable only by boat.

The thrust of the Selkirk Mountains is shrouded by forests, hemming Priest in with lofty stands of virgin fir, pine, and spruce; ferns, shrubs, and wilderness weave intricate patterns between the trees. The forest contains bear, deer, elk, and wildcat. The recreational area has campsites, and there are resorts near Coolin.

Return to Priest River and take US 2 seven miles west to Albini Falls Dam, always impressive. Turn south on Idaho 41 and breeze through more lake country to Coeur d'Alene, 47 miles.

Now ride US 95 for 68 miles through the golden wheatlands of the western Palouse Hills to Moscow. Here on a slope is the University of Idaho campus, a landscaping masterpiece.

The road continues south to the summit of Lewiston Hill, where it spins down to Lewiston, 35 miles below Moscow.

Continuing south, US 95 lances pastoral hillsides and tablelands, where every farm is a sylvan setting and wildflowers lie in ambush among the pastures, springing up where least expected. So the road goes to Grangeville, 72 miles. Then it winds down White Bird Hill, through the shadows of Salmon River Canyon, past the meadowlands of the Little Salmon, and on into New Meadows, 87 miles.

At Council, 25 miles south, a gravel road meanders 41 miles to Cuprum, gateway for awesome views of Hells Canyon. Modest accommodations there. At Cambridge, 23 miles farther south, a paved road of 29 miles reaches at Hells Canyon dam.

Now US 95, leaving the blue haze of mountains, enters grain and dairy and then orchard country, reaching Weiser in 32 miles.

About 125 years ago the site was known to Oregon Trailers as a fording point on the Snake River. Today Weiser is the center of rich fruitland and has earned a regional reputation for its nearby water recreation spots, the closest being only half-a-mile west of town, at the Idaho Power Co. boat dock.

From Weiser, follow US 95 and then I–84, south and east through numerous fruit, dairy, and industrial villages and towns, to Nampa, 56 miles, where the colorful Snake River Stampede is staged each mid-July. Lake Lowell, 6 miles southwest, harbors millions of migratory birds. There is boating, swimming, fishing, and picnicking.

From Nampa, it is 20 miles to Boise via I–84.

Eastern Tour

Back again at Boise, the futuristic freeway Interstate 84 strides boldly eastward across prairie terrain, as we reverse the path taken by the covered wagons on the Oregon Trail. In 42 miles the road reaches Mountain Home, once a bleak clump of shacks scrounging for life on a sagebrush flat (an Air Force base was built nearby, and now the modern town has a population of 7,500). Here U.S. 20 breaks off from I–84 for its eastward course.

Eighteen miles from Mountain Home the highway meets the Snake River, and 9 miles farther, at Glenns Ferry, is Three Island Ford, an historic crossing on the Oregon Trail. Twenty miles on, at Bliss, a hamlet of about 200 souls, U.S. 26 and U.S. 30, which have been riding I–84, break off, U.S. 26 heads straight east, and U.S. 30 twists south. Gooding, 11 miles east of Bliss on US 26, is the gateway to Mammoth Cave, Shoshone Ice Caves, Sun Valley, and Craters of the Moon.

From Bliss, US 30 travels 19 miles to Thousand Springs, cascading down the glistening banks above the road. The sprays and gushes are believed to be the outlet of Lost River, or of several buried rivers.

Ten miles more—and Buhl. Lying under the breaks of a deep canyon eroded by the Snake is the world's largest trout hatchery, which produces annually more than 1.5 million pounds of Rocky Mountain Rainbows. Visitors are cordially welcomed.

On a further side trip, take the county road due south 11 miles to Castleford. Follow directions 5½ miles to Balanced Rock, awesome among even the fantastically shaped pillars and colonnades in Devils Creek Gorge. The 40-foot tower resting on a tiny block of stone looks as though a feather would knock it over—but it has stood this way for eons.

Twin Falls, 15 miles east of Buhl, is southcentral Idaho's largest city, with a population of some 26,000. Idaho's most beautiful bridge, a cantilever span 1,350 feet long and 476 feet high, and part of US 93 just north of town, affords a striking view of the Snake River canyon.

Shoshone Falls, about 4 miles northeast of Twin Falls, is spectacular in the spring, when the Snake at full water takes a sheer 212-foot drop over the basaltic horseshoe rim nearly 1,000 feet wide. During the summer, when water is diverted for irrigation, the river trickles rather than plunges, but the naked rimrock is not without its own stark beauty.

From Twin Falls, US 30 furrows the Snake River plain, a basin of prosperous farms. Burley, 40 miles east, is a potato-products center, with large processing plants.

Now turn south on Idaho 27 to Oakley, 22 miles. This town has fewer than 700 persons, but its Pioneer Days Rodeo, in late July, was long one of the state's liveliest. From Oakley follow a gravel road southeast 22 miles to the Cassia City of Rocks, a 25-square-mile area of eroded stones resembling a scattered village. There is immense historical significance here, too, for this silent "city" was the junction of two famous trails—the Sublette Cutoff (to Oregon) and the California Trail. Here the wagons divided and many an adieu was said at the foot of the eroded cathedrals, towers, and shattered walls. Upon the walls are recorded thousands of names and dates, as well as messages left for those not yet arrived. Below the "city" is Almo, whose 40 persons are blessed by an abundance of gorgeous scenery. A paved road leads 16 miles to Idaho 77. Albion, 11 miles onward, is a tiny former college town whose charm lies in its decaying buildings, repositories of pioneer lore.

Continue north 12 miles to I–84 again. Turn east, at a point 9 miles east and 2 miles north of Burley. Forty-eight miles farther on, past a turnoff to Minidoka Dam and past Massacre Rocks, lies American Falls (on I–86, formerly U.S. 30), settled during the days of the Oregon Trail. In 1900, the area from American Falls to 170 miles west of it supported little more than sagebrush, coyotes, cheat grass, and lizards. Today it is all one huge irrigated garden. Within a few minutes' drive of the city is the mile-wide American Falls Dam and its 36-mile-long reservoir. The reservoir recreation area offers boating, swimming, fishing, and picnicking.

The indoor pool at Indian Springs, 4 miles south on Idaho 37, is one of Idaho's finest. Pocatello, 24 miles east of American Falls, is eastern Idaho's largest city (with a population on its way toward 50,000) and the seat of Idaho State University. Along the Portneuf River, which flows through the west side of the city, beaver-workings are still observable. In Ross Park there is evidence of Indian art work carved into stone cliffs.

Thirty-three miles southeast of Pocatello, on I–15, is Lava Hot Springs, one of Idaho's many wonders. Mineral waters boiling out of lava rocks—each spring with a different mineral content—form the basis for a state-owned resort consisting of mineral plunges and natatoriums. Accommodations are nearby. Up the cold Portneuf River, within easy hiking distance of the village, are 50 small waterfalls and the smoke holes of old volcanoes.

Return to Pocatello, turn north on US 91, and drive 11 miles to Ft. Hall, agency headquarters for the Shoshone and Bannock tribes on the Ft. Hall Indian Reservation. In July the famed Sun Dances, religious observances followed by buffalo feasts, are held at Ross Fork and Bannock Creek. In early August the reservation stages the exciting 4-day Shoshone-Bannock Indian Festival, complete with historical pageant, war and social dancing, Indian games, parade, all-Indian rodeo, displays, buffalo feast, and crowning of Miss Shoshone-Bannock.

Idaho Falls, 39 miles north of Ft. Hall, and on I–15, is a lovely city, its beauty enhanced by a low but turbulent 1,500-foot-wide waterfall in the Snake River, which hums through the city. A landscaped picnic area drapes the river banks. A significant fraction of the trout stocking in the state comes from Sportsman's Park on the Snake River, where half a million fish are raised annually. Tautphaus Park features a campground and rodeo area.

Although the Mormon Temple, a superb piece of architecture, is not open to the public, the visitors' center offers slides and guided tours of the area. Idaho Falls reflects the agricultural wealth of the upper Snake River Valley in its many products: seed-pea, potato, beet, honey, dairy, flour. Its stockyards are Idaho's largest. To the northwest is located the central control of the Atomic Energy Commissions's National Reactor Testing Center.

East of Idaho Falls, US 26 runs through pleasant vales and woods, and in 72 miles the road reaches the Wyoming border. The last 30 miles run first along the Snake River trench; then past earth-filled Palisades Dam, 270 feet high and 2,100 feet long; then past the dam's reservoir, a camping and boating area. At Alpine, on the border, follow US 89 to Jackson, Wyoming (29 miles), gateway to the Tetons and Yellowstone. Turning west at Jackson on Wyoming 22, cross 8,429-foot Teton Pass, and 24 miles from Jackson reach Victor, Idaho, where old-fashioned melodramas are presented at Pierre's Summer Playhouse.

A World-Famous Resort

The Highway south of Stanley passes roads to several lakes, including the well-known Redfish and Alturas, before climbing 8,701-foot Galena Summit. From this "top of the world" drive the Sawtooths seem close enough to touch. Sixty miles from Stanley, Idaho 75 comes to Sun Valley.

Long recognized as one of the world's famous winter resorts, Sun Valley has for some years also been popular as a summer playground. Sun Valley is a village unto itself, with even its own hospital. In addition to the usual ice skating, swimming, riding, tennis, and fishing, there are mind-shattering trips into the wilderness.

A mile below Sun Valley is Ketchum, the last home of Ernest Hemingway, who wrote some sections of *For Whom the Bell Tolls*—"The part with all the snow in it," as he recalled years later—in Room 205 of the Sun Valley Lodge. He lived in a house on the Wood River, supped at the Christiana Inn the night before his death, and his body now lies in the town's rustic cemetery.

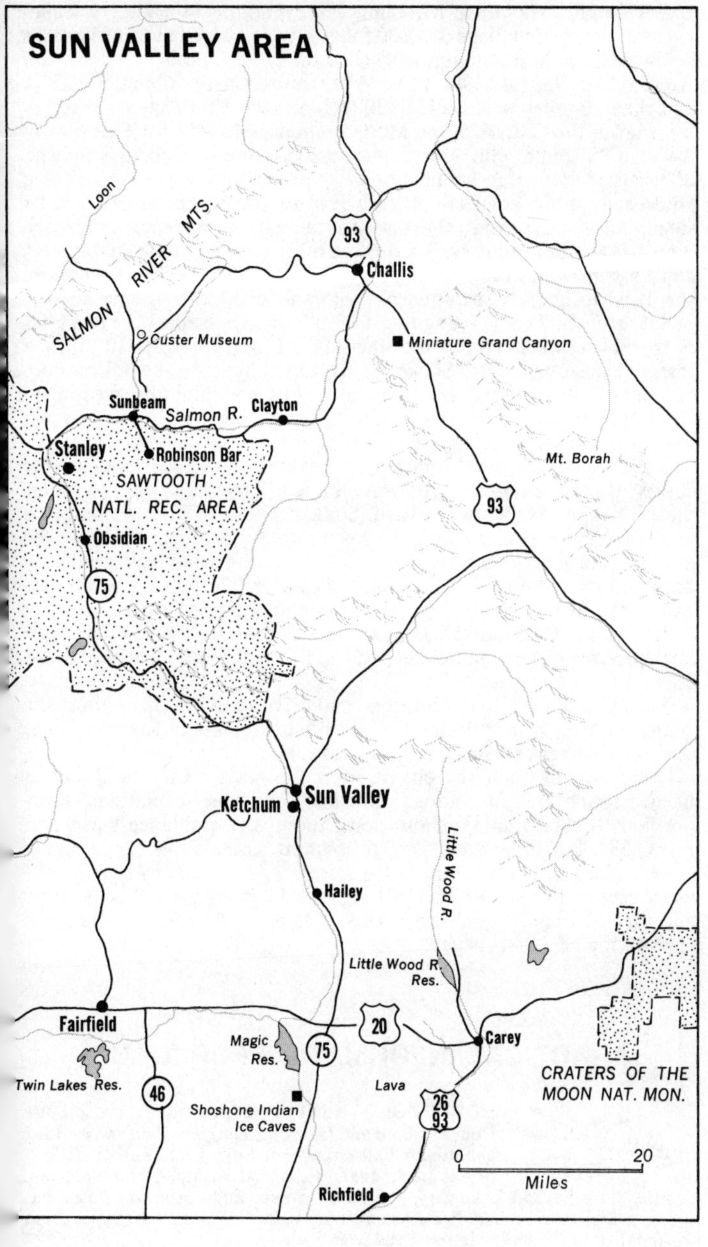
SUN VALLEY AREA
Loon
SALMON RIVER MTS.
93
Challis
Custer Museum
Miniature Grand Canyon
Sunbeam
Salmon R.
Clayton
Stanley
Robinson Bar
SAWTOOTH
NATL. REC. AREA
Mt. Borah
93
Obsidian
75
Sun Valley
Ketchum
Little Wood R.
Hailey
Little Wood R.
Res.
Fairfield
20
Magic
Res.
75
Carey
Twin Lakes Res.
46
Lava
CRATERS OF THE
MOON NAT. MON.
Shoshone Indian
Ice Caves
26
93
0
20
Miles
Richfield

Twelve miles south along the Wood River is Hailey, site of the fine Blaine County Historical Museum. Four miles below Hailey is Bellevue, a sweet rustic village of 1,000 folks, give or take a few, and 10 miles below Bellevue is a junction with U.S. 20. To reach this junction from Arco, on US 93, travel 44 miles southwest to Carey, a hamlet of 300, and then 20 miles west on U.S. 20 to Idaho 75. US 93 passes through a corner of the Craters of the Moon National Monument. This utterly desolate 83-square-mile area is a fantastic, grotesque Dante's inferno of basaltic features. A 7-mile loop drive passes by some of the volcanic landscapes, while a variety of trails lead to others. The loop drive, its side roads, and several short walks can all be made in about one hour—if you're in a hurry. Visitors are often surprised to see a few trees and hosts of wildflowers in this universe of death. They are even more surprised to learn that quite a few animals make their home here.

South of the U.S. 20 junction, Idaho 75 leaves behind the shadows of the Sawtooths and rolls into the Snake River Plain. At 10 miles, a turnoff leads one mile to Shoshone Ice Caves, lying in the hollow core of a once molten river of lava. Above-ground you might be sweating—this is hot summer country—but in the caves a few feet below you will need a warm sweater.

Idaho 75 leads south 17 miles to Shoshone, market center of a large sheep-raising area. (Along the way, the road passes a turnoff to Mammoth Cave, a mile from the road. Some people consider Mammoth a more awesome and remarkable cavern than Shoshone.) As can be guessed, not everyone pronounces Shoshone the same way; evidently both *Sho-shone* and *Sho-shonee* are acceptable. The name is an Americanization of the Indian *Shoshoni,* meaning "Great Spirit."

At Shoshone, Idaho 75 has its southern terminus. US 93 comes into Shoshone from Arco and Carey, and south of Shoshone the road is US 93.

Turn west on US 26 at Shoshone and drive 16 miles to Gooding, the center of the bountiful Big Wood and Little Wood River Valleys, prairies that remind Midwesterners of home.

More famous than the city itself is the nearby City of Rocks, a 6-square-mile area of colored shale and sandstone formations. As is peculiar to such rock configurations, there is resemblance to ancient ruins: battered pillars and jagged columns, tumbled castles, sagging towers, shattered cathedrals, fallen spires, sagging balconies, and stairways broken in two. From Gooding it is 11 miles via US 26 to Bliss and then an easy 90-minute (or less) drive on I–84 to Boise, where our exploration of Idaho began.

PRACTICAL INFORMATION FOR IDAHO

HOW TO GET THERE. By Plane. *United* flies to Boise from Portland and Denver. *Delta/Sky West* serves Boise and Idaho Falls from Salt Lake City. *Alaska Airlines* flies to Boise, Idaho Falls, and Pocatello from Portland, Seattle, Spokane, Salt Lake City, and Pasco, Wash., and during ski season has nonstop flights from San Francisco to Sun Valley. *PSA* flies to Boise from Portland. *Pioneer* serves Idaho Falls from Denver.

By Train. The daily *Empire Builder* stops at Sandpoint on the Seattle-Chicago run. *Pioneer* (also Amtrak), on the Portland-Salt Lake City run, stops daily at Nampa/Caldwell, Boise, Mountain Home, Shoshone, and Pocatello.

By Car. From Utah: Interstate I–84 to Rupert and Burley; Interstate 15 to Pocatello. From Nevada; US 93 to Twin Falls. From Oregon: US 95 to Caldwell; Interstate I–84 to Caldwell, Nampa, and Boise. From Washington: Interstate 90 to Coeur d'Alene; US 2 to Sandpoint; US 12 and US 195 to Lewiston; Wash. 270 to Moscow. From Montana: US 2 to Bonners Ferry; Interstate 15 to Idaho Falls; US 12 to Kamiah; US 93 to Salmon; Interstate 90 to Wallace and Kellogg. From Wyoming: US 20 to St. Anthony; US 26 to Idaho Falls. From Canada: Canada Route 21 from Creston to border and Idaho 1 to Bonners Ferry; Canada Route 3 to border and US 95 to Eastport and Bonners Ferry.

By Bus. Greyhound reaches all major cities: Trailways' route is across Interstate I–84, the heartland of Idaho.

Empire serves Coeur d'Alene, Lewiston, and Boise. *Sky West* serves Pocatello, Idaho Falls, and Twin Falls. *Horizon* serves Idaho Falls, Twin Falls, and Pocatello.

ACCOMMODATIONS. In addition to the many hotels and motels that are operated by regional and national chains, there are a number of attractive independent hostelries in Idaho. They cater, with equal enthusiasm, to vacationers and traveling business people. Rates tend to be less expensive than in heavily populated states, so you may well find deluxe accommodations for less than deluxe prices. Based on double occupancy, categories and price ranges are as follows: *Deluxe,* over $50; *Expensive,* $35–50; *Moderate,* $25–35; and *Inexpensive,* under $25.

American Falls. Best Western Hillview Motel. *Moderate.* E. Interchange I–86, 83211 (208–226–5151). Single- and two-story sections, spacious, comfortable units. Heated pool; 24-hour restaurant.

Arco. Lazy A Motel. *Moderate.* 318 W. Grand, 83213 (208–527–8263). Queen beds; courtesy coffee. 20 units.

Ashton. Rankin Motel. *Moderate.* 120 Yellowstone Hwy., 83420 (208–652–3570). Small, cheerful, neighborly. Facing beautiful vistas; close to cafes.

Four Seasons Motel. *Moderate.* 112 Main St., 83420 (208–652–7769). Small motel on main business route, some units with kitchens. Folksy.

Blackfoot. Best Western Riverside Inn. *Expensive.* 1229 Parkway Dr., 83221 (208–785–5000). Comfortable units, some king-size, some with wet bar. Pool, restaurant, and lounge on premises. Lake nearby. Golf available.

Boise. Compri Hotel at Park Center. *Deluxe.* 475 Park Center Blvd., 83706 (208-345-2002). A new hotel with pool, spa; restaurant nearby.

Holiday Inn. *Deluxe.* 3300 Vista Ave., 83705 (208–344–8365). Huge motel near airport with elevator, heated indoor pool, therapy pool, sauna, play area, recreation rooms, exercise room, miniature golf. Dining room and cocktail lounge.

Owyhee Plaza. *Deluxe.* 1109 Main, 83702 (208–343–4611; 1-800–233–4611). Large, multi-story motel; some rooms with balconies. Two fine restaurants. Two lounges with entertainment.

Red Lion Inn-Downtowner. *Deluxe.* 1800 Fairview, 83702 (208–344–7691). Large motor hotel, many conveniences, including heated pool, dining room, coffee shop, cocktail lounge, entertainment. Beauty salon, barber shop. Airport courtesy car. Close to all downtown facilities.

Red Lion Motor Inn-Riverside. *Deluxe.* 2900 Chinden Blvd., 83704 (208–343–1871). Large, well-appointed rooms, sunken tubs, king beds, 2 restaurants, (one poolside), coffee shop, lounge, whirlpool, wading pool. Award-winning landscape.

Rodeway Inn. *Deluxe.* 1115 N. Curtis Rd., 83706 (208–376–2700). Excellent accommodations, beautiful grounds adjacent to St. Alphonsus Hospital. Some units have sunken tubs, fireplaces, wet bars. Heated pool, therapy pool, two restaurants, coffee shop, cocktail lounge, entertainment. Skiing, tennis, golf available. Airport courtesy car.

Statehouse Inn. *Deluxe.* 981 Grove St., 83702 (208–342–4622). Close to Capitol and Boise State Univ. Suites with whirlpool baths. Garage, airport transportation, restaurant and lounge. Red carpet treatment.

Best Western Vista Inn. *Expensive.* 2645 Airport Way, 83705 (208–336–8100). All the comforts of modern motels, including heated indoor pool, exercise room, sauna. Restaurant adjacent.

Idanha Hotel. *Expensive.* 928 Main St., 83702 (208–342–3611). Comfortable, roomy units. Coffee shop, cocktail lounge, coin laundry. Landmark hotel featuring antique and modern decor. Chauffeur-driven limousine service to airport in a vintage automobile.

Landmark Inn. *Expensive.* 2155 North Garden, 83702 (208–344–4030). 52 units with 25 unit ambiance. Restaurant adjacent. Courtesy car to airport. On US 20–26, at I–84.

Littletree Inn. *Expensive.* 2717 Vista Ave., 83705 (208–343–7505; 1–800–325–3738). Spacious rooms with king or queen sized beds. Two blocks from Boise Airport. Kitchenettes, lounge. Great for the fly-folks.

University Inn. *Expensive.* 2360 University Dr., 83706 (208–345–7170). Large motel with heated pool, coffee shop, and lounge. Suites available; pets OK. Airport transportation. Near Boise State University.

Boise TraveLodge. *Moderate.* 1314 Grove St., 83702 (208–342–9351; 1–800–255–3050). Good family motel, near airport. Heated pool. Unobtrusive informality.

The Boisean Motel. *Inexpensive.* 1300 S. Capitol Blvd., 83706 (208–343–3645). Opposite Boise State University. Medium-size motel with garden setting. Four restaurants within block.

Sands Motel. *Inexpensive.* 1111 W. State, 83702 (208–343–2533). Comfortable small motel with all basic conveniences and an adjacent restaurant. Downtown.

Seven K Motel. *Inexpensive.* 3633 Chinden, 83704 (208–343–7723). Comfortable family motel on lovely landscaped grounds, with convenient grassy play area for children across the street. Heated pool.

Skyline Motel. *Inexpensive.* 3209 Federal Way, 83705 (208–344–2557). Small motel with comfortable units. Weekly rates only.

Sunliner Motel. *Inexpensive.* Oversize beds, near race track, fairgrounds, restaurants. 3433 Chinden Blvd., 83704 (208–344–7647).

Bonners Ferry. Best Western Kootenai River Inn. *Expensive.* (208–267–8511). A brand-new, 48-unit motor inn on the Kootenai River. Suites, units with fireplaces available. Heated indoor pool, spa, steam room. Restaurant and lounge on premises.

Deep Creek Inn. *Expensive.* Route 1, 83805 (208–267–2373). 13-unit motel on shady grounds near a cool mountain stream. A few 2-room units. Most units with kitchenettes. Heated pool, restaurant, cocktail lounge. Seven miles south of town. Fishing nearby.

Valley Motel. *Expensive.* Route 1, Box 382, 83805 (208–267–7567). On the south side of US 95. Small, but comfortable. Restaurant adjacent.

Buhl. Oregon Trail Motel. *Moderate.* 510 S. Broadway, 83316 (208–543–8814). Kitchenettes, neat, cheery management.

Burley. Best Western Burley Inn. *Expensive.* 800 N. Overland Ave., 83318 (208–678–3501; 1–800–635–4952). Large, swank. Coffee shop, dining room, lounge with entertainment. Pool, children's playground.

Budget Motel. *Moderate.* 900 N. Overland Ave., 83318 (208–678–2200; 1–800–634–4592). 100 neatly kept units accommodate families, nonsmokers, handicapped. Pets OK. Restaurant adjacent.

East Park Motel. *Moderate.* 507 E. Main St., 83318 (208–678–2241). Small, comfortable motel, across from city park. Restaurant nearby. Quiet and tranquil.

Greenwell Motel. *Moderate.* 904 E. Main St., 83318 (208–678–5576). Another small motel with pleasant, comfortable units, refrigerators in rooms. Personalized service.

Lampliter Motel. *Inexpensive.* 304 E. Main St., 83318 (208–678–0031). Small 17-unit motel with pool and cable television.

Caldwell. Sundowner Motel. *Moderate.* 1002 Arthur, 83605 (208–459–1585). Fairly large motel with pool. Easy access to restaurant. Relaxed mileu. Continental breakfast.

Challis. Challis Lodge. *Moderate.* Box 944, 83226 (208–879–2251). Medium-size, within walking distance of all shopping; cozy.

Northgate Inn. *Moderate.* HC 63, Box 1665 (208–879–2490). Seasonal, weekly, and monthly rates available at this 56-unit motel.

Village Inn. *Inexpensive–Moderate.* Box 6, 83226 (208–879–2239). Cable TV; cooking facilities; cafe; pets allowed. Friendly place.

Coeur d'Alene. The Coeur d'Alene Resort. *Deluxe.* 115 S. 2nd Ave., 83814 (208–765–4000). Posh facilities at this lakefront lodge. Large motor hotel with two heated pools (one indoors), wading pool, therapy pools, saunas, health club, beach, marina, fishing, waterskiing, bowling. Two restaurants, three lounges. World's longest floating boardwalk.

Holiday Inn of Coeur d'Alene. *Deluxe.* 414 Appleway, 83814 (208–765–3200). Very large, two-story motel with family-size units available. Heated pool, restaurant, cocktail lounge.

Flamingo Motel. *Expensive.* 718 Sherman Ave., 83814 (208–664–2159). Small, home-like, pin-neat.

Garden Motel. *Moderate–Deluxe.* 1808 NW Blvd., 83814 (208–664–2743). 1 22-unit motel off I–90. Rates are good for up to six persons in some units. Heated indoor pool. Senior discount.

Cedar Motel. *Moderate-expensive.* 319 S. 24th St., 83814 (208–664–2278). 16 units. Heated pool, game room, kitchenettes, laundry. Adjoining RV park with winter hook-ups.

Pines Resort Motel. *Moderate.* 1422 N.W. Blvd., 83814 (208–664–8244). Medium-size, off-highway motel with variety of units, including older remodeled ones and classy, spanking-new ones, situated on hill boasting view of Lake Coeur d'Alene and Spokane River. A good family spot with playground, heated pool, restaurant and lounge.

Star Motel. *Moderate.* 1516 Sherman Ave., 83814 (208–664–5035). A 10-unit motel, caringly managed. Five mini-kitchenettes; one suite. Color cable TV with HBO. Family, weekly rates, Cafe nearby. Small pets OK.

State Motel. *Moderate.* 1314 Sherman Ave., 83814 (208–664–8239). All 13 units are decorated in knotty pine. Some suites.

Siesta Motel. *Inexpensive.* 2115 Sherman Ave., 83814 (208–664–5412). Large picnic area.

Driggs. Best Western Teton West Motor Inn. *Expensive.* 476 N. Main St., 83422 (208–354–2363; 1–800–528–1234). Modest size but a variety of accommodations including some family-size units with kitchens. Twelve miles from Grand Targhee Ski Resort; 35 miles to Jackson Hole, Wyo. Seasonal rates.

Grangeville. Crossroads Motel. *Moderate.* W. Main & B Sts., 83530 (208–983–1420). Individual air conditioning and electric heat. Home-style friendliness.

Monty's Motel. *Moderate.* 700 W. Main St., 83530 (208–983–2500). Small motel, open year-round, with heated pool.

Idaho Falls. Best Western Driftwood Motel. *Expensive.* 575 River Parkway, 83402 (208–532–2242). A large motel overlooking river and falls and offering many conveniences. Heated pool; river boat fishing. Guest laundry. Restaurant near. Seasonal rates.

Littletree Inn. *Expensive.* 888 N. Holmes, 83401 (208–523–5993). All units in this large motel have either king-or queen-size beds. Charming landscaped courtyard gives touch of isolation from highway. Golf course and Elks adjacent. Pool, restaurant, and lounge on premises. Coin laundry; in-room movies. Airport transportation.

Quality Inn Westbank. *Expensive.* 475 River Parkway, 83402 (208–523–8000). Huge motel with varied accommodations, lovely view of river and falls. Heated pool. Popular coffee shop, restaurant and lounge on premises. Seasonal rates.

Thrifty Lodge. *Moderate.* 255 E. St., 83401 (208–523–2960). Quiet comforts in a good medium-size motel, handy to downtown, with restaurant close by.

West Motel. *Moderate.* 1540 Broadway, 83402 (208–522–1112). Recreation area, queen beds, kitchenettes. Latch-string welcome.

Weston's Lamplighter. *Moderate.* 850 Lindsay Blvd., 83402 (208–523–6260). Htd. pool; cafe; bar; entertainment. Free airport, RR station, bus depot transportation. Oversize beds. Overlooking river. Pets OK.

Jerome. Holiday Motel. *Moderate.* 401 W. Main St., 83338 (208–324–2361). Medium-size motel with heated pool, some family-size units. Neat and clean.

Ketchum-Sun Valley. Best Western Christiania Lodge. *Deluxe.* 651 Sun Valley Rd., 83340 (208–726–3351). Fine motel in center of Ketchum, with a variety of accommodations, some with fireplaces, views of Mt. Baldy. Heated pool, whirlpool. Restaurants and other city facilities within a few blocks. Seasonal rates.

Elkhorn Resort at Sun Valley. *Deluxe.* Box 6009, Sun Valley, 83354 (208–622–4511; 1–800–635–9356). Think of all things luxurious and this is it.

Heidelberg Inn. *Deluxe.* Warm Springs Rd., Box 304, Sun Valley, 83353 (208–726–5361). Attractive motel built in Bavarian style; refrigerators in all units. Coin laundry. Heated pool, sauna and hot tub. Golf course across the way; easy walk to trout stream. Seasonal rates.

Sun Valley Lodge. *Deluxe.* One mile north of Ketchum, off SR 75 on Sun Valley Rd. US 75, 83353 (208–622–4111; 1–800–632–4107). Huge facility with hundreds of units and wide variety of accommodations, including many sizes of apartments and suites. Many kitchens, three heated pools. Varied recreational facilities available, including children's program, iceskating, fishing, skiing, golf, tennis, riding. Four dining rooms, two restaurants, coffee shop, two cafeterias. Seasonal rates.

River Street Inn. *Deluxe.* 100 River St. W., 83353 (208–726–3611). A new country inn with eight lovely units.

Tamarack Lodge. *Deluxe.* Sun Valley Rd., Box 2000, Sun Valley 83353 (208–726–3344). Medium-size motel with enclosed courtyard, units with private balconies or patios, some with fireplaces. Glassed-in heated swimming pool. Seasonal rates.

Bald Mountain Hot Springs. *Expensive-Deluxe.* 151 S. Main St., 83340 (208–726–9963). Moderate-sized facility with a hint of luxury at popular rates. Charming rooms; Olympic-sized natural hot-water pool. Easy access to ski areas; adjacent to restaurants and shopping.

Lava Hot Springs. Lava Spa Motel. *Inexpensive.* 318 E. Main St., 83246 (208–776–5589). Medium-size motel with family-size units as well as smaller ones, near park and recreation areas, and across from hot springs.

Lewiston. Best Western Tapadera Motor Inn. *Expensive.* 1325 E. Main St., 83501 (208–746–3311). Large, multi-story motor inn with comfortably furnished rooms and some suites. Heated pool. Cocktail lounge overlooking pool. Restaurant adjacent; 24-hour tavern opposite.

Pony Soldier Motor Inn. *Expensive.* 1716 Main St., 83501 (208–743–9526; 1–800–635–2062 in Idaho). Heated pool, suites, courteous personnel.

Sacajawea Lodge. *Expensive.* 1824 Main St., 83501 (208–746–1393). Large motel with variety of units, many with refrigerators. Heated pool, whirlpool. Fine restaurant on premises.

El Rancho Motel. *Moderate.* 2240 3rd Ave. N., 83501 (208–743–8517). Quiet, modest-size motel with heated pool. Some units with kitchens.

Holywood Inn. *Moderate.* 3001 N.S. Hwy., 83501 (208–743–9424). Enjoy a view of the Clearwater River as well as convenience of heated pool, restaurant and lounge before bedding down in your comfortable room.

McCall. Shore Lodge. *Deluxe.* Warren Wagon Rd., 83638 (208–634–2244). Large resort facility with both winter and summer recreational opportunities. Beach, two heated pools, waterskiing, fishing, tennis. Some lakefront units. Dining room, coffee shop, lounge.

Malad City. Southgate Motel. *Moderate.* At Malad Exit I–15, 83252 Box 166 (208–766–4761). Medium-size motel with well-furnished units. Management takes personal interest in guests.

Montpelier. Best Western Crest Motel. *Expensive.* 243 N. 4th St., 83254 (208–847–1782). Medium-size motel with pleasant, comfortable rooms. Restaurant near. Exercise room, therapy pool. Golf available nearby.

Park Motel. *Moderate.* 745 Washington St., 83254 (208–847–1911). Smaller motel in downtown location, near restaurant. Spacious, sparkling clean.

Budget Motel. *Inexpensive.* 240 N. 4th St., 83254 (208–847–1273). A 24-unit motor inn with fishing, playground, barbecue along a mountain stream. Some kitchens; refrigerators. Restaurant.

Moscow. Best Western University Inn. *Deluxe.* 1516 Pullman Rd., 83843 (208–882–0550). New facility adjoining University of Idaho and Kibbie Dome, with pool, restaurant and lounge, live entertainment, 24-hour coffee shop.

Cavanaugh's Motor Inn. *Expensive.* 645 Pullman Rd., 83843 (208–882–1611; 1–800–541–6800, ID MT, N.CA.). Large. Therapy pool. Lovely setting. Immaculate. Informal.

Mark IV Motor Inn. *Expensive.* 414 N. Main St., 83843 (208–882–7557). Deluxe spot with separate recreation building featuring indoor heated pool, restaurant, lounge, and entertainment.

Royal Motor Inn. *Moderate.* 120 W. 6th St., 83843 (208–882–2581). Medium-size motel with comfortable units, heated pool.

Hillcrest Motel. *Inexpensive.* 706 N. Main St., 83843 (208–882–7579). Choose your favorite bed size for a quiet night's sleep in this medium-sized motel with one and two room-units and some with kitchenettes. Heated pool. Cable television.

Motel 6. *Inexpensive.* 101 Baker St., 83843 (208–882–5511). Medium-size, clean, well-kept hostelry with comfortable accommodations.

Mountain Home. Hilander Motel. *Moderate.* Hwy. 30E and Air Base Rd., 83647 (208–587–3311). Medium-size motel with pool, restaurant, and cocktail lounge.

Towne Center Motel. *Moderate.* 410 N. 2nd E., 83647 (208–587–3373). All the comforts and conveniences of more expensive facilities. Pool.

Motel Thunderbird. *Inexpensive.* Highway 30 W., 83647 (208–587–7927). Smaller motel, conveniences and comfort throughout. Pool. Restaurant short walk away.

Nampa. Best Western Desert Inn Motel. *Expensive.* 115 9th Ave. S., 83651 (208–467–1161). Medium-size motel conveniently located downtwon, with heated pool, restaurant nearby.

Pocatello. Best Western Cotton Tree Inn. *Expensive–Deluxe.* 1415 Bench Rd., 83201 (208–237–7650). Swim for fun or therapy in heated pools here, enjoy a round of golf nearby or a fast game of tennis before stretching out in one of the well-appointed units. Restaurant and lounge on premises.

Pocatello Quality Inn. *Expensive–Deluxe.* 1555 Pocatello Creek Rd., 83201. (208–233–2200). Large establishment, formerly Hilton Inn. Sound-proof luxury in posh decor. Indoor swimming pool, sauna, whirlpool, luxurious dining, lounge with live entertainment.

Holiday Inn. *Expensive.* 1399 Bench Rd., 83201 (208–237–1400). Huge motel with variety of units, free transportation from airport. Heated pool. Restaurant, coffee shop, cocktail lounge, entertainment. The usual Holiday efficiency.

Bidwell Motel. *Moderate.* 1335 S. 5th Ave., 83201. (208–232–3114). Small motel across from Idaho State University. Indoor heated pool. Restaurant nearby. Families can find larger units here, some kitchens.

Oxbow Motor Inn. *Moderate.* 4333 Yellowstone Ave. 83202. (208–237–3100). Heated pool, sauna, whirlpool; many kitchens available. Restaurant and lounge. Airport transportation.

Sundial Inn. *Moderate.* 835 S. 5th Ave., 83201. (208–233–0451). Across from Idaho State University and next to well-known restaurant.

Howell Motel. *Inexpensive.* 1230 Yellowstone, 83201 (208–237–4523). Commercial rates, kitchens, cable TV, quiet.

Idaho Motel. *Inexpensive.* 1159 S. 5th Ave., 83201 (208–232–1160). Across from Idaho State University. Insulated. Some kitchens.

Thunderbird Motel. *Inexpensive.* 1415 S. 5th Ave., 83201. (208–232–6330). Medium-size motel near city park and Idaho State University. Heated pool. A nice place for families with children.

Rexburg. Best Western Fantastic Inn. *Expensive.* 450 W. 4th St. S., 83440 (208–356–4646). Large facility south of town, with heated indoor pool, and restaurant on premises. Near Ricks College. Charming place.

Viking Motel. *Moderate.* 271 S. 2nd W., 83440 (208–356–9222). Medium-size motel near city park. Heated pool. Management eager to please.

C. Rex's Motel. *Inexpensive.* 357 W. 4th St. S., 83440 (208–356–5477). Small, modest facility with comfortable units.

St. Anthony. Best Western Weston Riverview. *Moderate.* 115 S. Bridge St., 83445 (208–624–3711). Location on Henry's Fork River, across from city park, gives this motel special attractiveness. Restaurant and coffee shop.

St. Maries. Pines Motel. *Moderate.* 1117 Main St., 83861 (208–245–2545). Located downtown, this medium-size motel is comfortable and convenniet to city facilities, restaurants. Municipal park and pool across street. Tennis half a block away, golf one mile.

Salmon. Stagecoach Inn. *Expensive.* 201 Hwy. 93 N., 83467 (208–756–4251). Comfortable units in this medium-size motel with heated pool, private patios, river view. Cafe near. Wholesome atmosphere.

Best Western Wagons West. *Moderate–Expensive.* Hwy. 93 N., 83467 (208–756–4281). Cooking units available. Restaurant, lounge.

Suncrest Motel. *Moderate.* 705 Challis St., 83467 (208–756–2294). Smaller motel with a few kitchen units. Playground for youngsters. Near cafe.

Motel DeLuxe. *Inexpensive.* 112 S. Church St., 83467 (208–756–2231). Medium-sized, with built-in hospitality. Kitchen units, in-room coffee. Restaurant nearby; downtown.

Sandpoint. Edgewater Lodge. *Expensive–Deluxe.* 56 Bridge St., 83864 (1–800–635–2534). Located on Lake Pend Oreille, and close to downtown, this medium-size motel offers comfortable units with private patios affording magnificent views of lake and mountains and easy access to shopping, restaurants, beach, boating facilities. On-premises conveniences include health spa, sauna, therapy pool, dining room, cocktail lounge. Seasonal rates.

Best Western Connie's Motor Inn. *Expensive.* 323 Cedar St., 83864 (208–263–9581). Downtown and on Lake Pend Oreille. Heated pool, spa, dining room, coffee shop. Elegant plus.

Quality Inn Sandpoint. *Expensive.* 807 N. 5th, 83864 (208–263–2111). Heated indoor pool, spa; restaurant and lounge.

Lakeside Motel. *Moderate–Expensive.* 106 Bridge St., 83864 (208–263–3717). A block from downtown business area, this medium-size motel on Lake Pend Oreille has large, comfortable units, easy access to city beach and park, and to tennis courts. Some suites and efficiency units are available. Recreation room. Cafe nearby. Seasonal rates.

Soda Springs. J-R Inn. *Moderate.* 179 W. 2nd S., 83276 (208–547–3366). Medium-size motel two blocks west of town, cafe a few minutes away. In historic Oregon Trail country.

Lakeview Motel. *Inexpensive.* 341 W. 2nd St., 83276 (208–547–4351). Small and neat. Cooking units.

Stanley. Mountain Village Lodge. *Expensive.* Junction Hwy. 75 and 21, 83278 (208–774–3661). Formerly Armada Motel, this comfortable, medium-size facility is located between Salmon River and the Sawtooth Mountain Range, and affords good view of mountains. Restaurant. Seasonal rates.

Redwood Motel. *Moderate.* Hwy. 75, Lower Stanley, 83278 (208–774–3531). Small motel on Salmon River, in lovely picnic spot. Several units with kitchens.

Sun Valley. (See "Ketchum-Sun Valley".)

Twin Falls. Best Western Apollo Motor Inn. *Expensive.* 296 Addison Ave. W., 83301 (208–733–2010). Medium-size motel with heated pool. Golf, cafe nearby. Seasonal rates.

Best Western Canyon Springs Inn. *Expensive.* 1357 Blue Lakes Blvd. N., 83301 (208–734–5000). Pool-side dining, lounge and entertainment. Transportation to airport. Senior discount.

Best Western Weston Inn. *Expensive.* 906 Blue Lakes Blvd. N., 83301 (208–733–6095). Large, two-story motel with heated pool. Free coffee. Near several restaurants.

Holiday Inn. *Expensive.* 135, Blue Lakes N., 83301 (208–733–0650). Another huge facility, with heated pool, health-club facilities, cafe, dining room, bar, dancing, entertainment. Seasonal rates.

Imperial "400" Motel. *Moderate.* 320 Main Ave. S., 83301 (208–733–8770). Medium-size, motel in downtown location. A few family units. Heated pool. Near restaurant.

Monterey Motor Inn. *Moderate.* 433 Addison Ave. W., 83301 (208–733–5151). Medium-size, quiet motel on spacious two acres. Family units. Heated pool, picnic and playground areas add to warm family atmosphere.

Twin Falls Super 8 Motel. *Moderate.* 1260 Blue Lakes Blvd. N., 83301 (208–734–5801). A medium-size motel near restaurant and Magic Valley Shopping Center.

Twin Falls TraveLodge. *Moderate.* 248 2nd Ave. W., 83301 (208–733–5630). Medium-size motel with heated pool. Near cafe. Seasonal rates.

Capri Motel. *Inexpensive.* 1341 Kimberly Rd., 83301 (208–733–6452). Medium-size motel with emphasis on comfort. The usuals—with unusual care.

Wallace. Stardust Motel. *Moderate.* 410 Pine, 83873 (208–752–1213). Downtown motel, medium-size, convenient to restaurant and coin laundry. Family units. Ski-waxing room. Free coffee.

Weiser. Colonial Motel. *Moderate.* 251 E. Main St., 83672 (208–549–0150). Smaller motel with comfortable units, some kitchens, and located close to restaurant and coin laundry.

YOUTH ACCOMMODATIONS. Many youngsters traveling through Idaho on their own make full use of the numerous campgrounds in national forests and state parks. But there is a scarcity of established inexpensive lodgings. There are only two YWCAs which have rooms for transient women. These are in Boise (at 720 Washington) and in Lewiston (at 300 Main St.). None of the YMCAs has a hotel, but they are usually good sources for recommendations of local spots where one may secure inexpensive overnight accommodations. The only hostel in the state listed by American Youth Hostels is at Sandpoint, the Whitaker House Home Hostel, 410 Railroad Ave., #10, Sandpoint 83864 (208–263–0816). Cost is $10 per night.

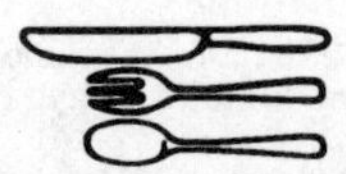

RESTAURANTS. Idaho exudes Western informality, and dining out in Idaho is an experience in keeping with that atmosphere. The emphasis is on good-sized portions of hearty, tasty fare, cheerful atmosphere, and quick service, rather than on exotic dishes and extensive imported wine lists. Sport or casual dress is acceptable in all but the top clubs and city restaurants. High on the popularity list for native Idahoans is a thick, juicy steak with potatoes (Idaho, of course), vegetable, and salad, topped off with a slab of homemade pie. Of course, there are exceptions. For decor, many Idaho restaurants take advantage of the state's natural beauty by providing luscious views of the immediate area to whet the appetite of their patrons and to complement the good food. There is often fine food and relaxing atmosphere in restaurants connected with hotels or motels. Restaurants are listed by categories: *Expensive* $8 to $12; *Moderate* $4 to $8; *Inexpensive* under $4.

Boise. The Gamekeeper. *Expensive.* 1109 Main St. (344–7361). Located in the Owyhee Plaza Hotel, this award-winning restaurant offers fine food with a flair. Dramatic flaming dishes, superb steaks and seafood, excellent wine cellar are top features here. Live entertainment nightly.

Peter Schott's Continental Restaurant. *Expensive.* 10th & Main (336–9100). In the historic Idanha Hotel. Flair, flamboyance and excellently prepared food.

Brick Oven Beanery. *Moderate.* 501 Main (342–3456). Country hearth baked bread, slow roasted meats; always cordial.

Lugenbeel's. *Moderate.* 981 Grove (342–4622). Continental cuisine in an intimate atmosphere.

Kowloon Family Restaurant. *Moderate.* 10332 Fairview Ave. (375–0342). Experience in Cantonese dining.

Nam King. *Moderate.* 4624 W. State (345–0260). Chinese and American, with emphasis on Chinese. Try the combination dinner of Egg Flower Soup, pork chow mein, fried shrimp, sweet and sour pork, and fried rice.

Red Robin. *Moderate.* 211 W. Park Center Blvd. (344–7471). Valley-famous for luscious burgers. Outdoor dining; overlooking pond. Children's menu. Swift, smiling service. Great place for kids.

Heart Break Cafe. *Moderate.* 607 Main (345–5544).All baked goods made fresh on premises.

Coeur d'Alene. The Cedars. *Expensive.* One-quarter mile south of I–90 on US 95; US 95 exit (664–2922). Located on Lake Coeur d'Alene, this floating restaurant and cocktail lounge features Hawaiian-style broiled chicken and biergarten steak among its specialties.

North Shore Plaza Restaurants. *Moderate.* 115 S. 2nd Ave. (664–9241). Whether you want plush rooftop dining as offered by the Cloud 9 restaurant atop the North Shore Motel, or the more casual atmosphere of the Shore Restaurant where pancakes and a salad bar are among the features, or chicken-to-go from Templin's you'll find it at this lakeshore complex.

Osprey. *Moderate.* 1000 W Hubbard (664–2115). Overlooking Spokane River; royal dining.

Idaho Falls. Barn Stormer. *Moderate.* Municipal Airport (529–2255). Aviation theme restaurant priding itself in steaks and seafood.

Marie Callender. *Moderate.* 530 E. Anderson (529–0306). The Idaho place for homemade pies and cornbread. Omelettes are great, too.

Smitty's Pancake and Steak House. *Moderate.* 645 Broadway (523–6450). Strong on family dining; waffles and pancakes particularly good. Cordial service.

Ketchum-Sun Valley. The Ore House. *Moderate.* Sun Valley Mall (622–4363). On the mall, this place has attained regional fame for make-it-yourself salads, coldwater lobster, corn-fed beef, and Coffee Nudge.

Warm Springs Ranch. *Moderate.* 1801 Warm Springs Rd. (726–8238). Outdoor dining with a mountain view, and specialties which include trout, sourdough scones, and barbecued ribs.

Lava Hot Springs. Chuckwagon Restaurant. *Moderate.* 206 E. Main St. (776–5626). Memorable seafood, delicious homemade pies and bread.

Lewiston. Cedars III. *Moderate.* 701 6th (758–7951). Dress casually, serve yourself at the salad bar, then sit back to enjoy one of the hand-cut steaks that are a specialty here.

Helm. *Moderate.* 1824 Main St. (743–5111). In Sacajawea Lodge. Steaks and seafood specialties served against attractive marine decor.

Kosher House/London Pub. *Moderate.* Morgans Alley (743–7719). In Morgan's Alley. Different and delightful. The best of two worlds.

Nampa. HasBrouck House. *Moderate–Expensive.* 1403 12th Ave. S. (467–7375). Terrace dining in restored turn-of-century house. Gourmet dining with a vengeance.

El Charro Cafe. *Moderate.* 1802 Franklin Rd. (466–9852). South-of-the-border specialties such as *chalupas, chiles rellenos,* and *chile verde* draw those seeking a tangy menu change.

Pocatello. Elmer's Pancake and Steak House. *Moderate.* 851 S 5th Ave. (232–9114). Twenty-one varieties of pancakes to choose from, as well as ever-popular steaks, chicken, seafoods, and salads. Across from Idaho State University.

Salmon. Salmon River Coffee Shop. *Moderate.* 606 Main (756–3521). Home baking here, which makes the cinnamon rolls just about irresistible. Fine steaks and seafood. Music, dancing, entertainment.

Shady Nook Lounge and Supper Club. *Moderate.* Hwy. 93 N. (756–4182). Steaks, seafoods (a specialty is shrimp in a beer batter), and home baking make this cafe on motel premises a popular dining spot.

Sandpoint. Garden Restaurant. *Moderate.* 15 E. Lake St. (263–5187). Outdoor dining, homebaked breads and desserts are among the attractions here, where the chef-owner takes pride in serving specialties ranging from fresh seafoods to roast duck and Oriental-style dishes. Lakeside view.

Twin Falls. Depot Grill. *Moderate.* 545 Shone St. S. (733–0710). Since 1927. Smorgasbord in the Caboose Room.

HOW TO GET AROUND. By Plane. *Sky West* serves Pocatello, Idaho Falls, and Twin Falls.

By Car. One of early America's most important thoroughfares, the Oregon Trail, traversed the broad southern part of Idaho, and today interstate highways follow the Oregon Trail closely, as well as the Mullan Road, in the Idaho Panhandle, at the top of the state. Improved transportation is a factor in bringing together this state that has for so many years been divided geographically, commercially, and even politically. The slow spiral routes on US 95 have been straightened, many highways have been widened, new roads have been built—all since 1967. Interstate 90 has superseded US 10 across the panhandle; Interstate I–84 and Interstate 15 has replaced US 30 along much of the Oregon Trail route; Interstate 15 has succeeded US 91 in eastern Idaho. The route followed by Lewis and Clark across north-central Idaho is paralleled by US 12 and that, too, is relatively new, as roads go. Before it was built there was only wilderness. Even today there is no vehicle service available on this road for about 75 miles. US 93 from Shoshone to Stanley and on to Challis has been redesignated Idaho 75, and has been named the Sawtooth Scenic Highway. In addition, US 93A from north of Shoshone via Arco to a junction south of Challis has been redesignated US 93. Magnificent scenery, from 8701-foot Galena Summit to Sawtooth Mountain valleys and along the Salmon River, make renamed Idaho 75 a popular tourist run. US 95, cutting along the western part of the state, from Canada to Oregon, is the longest road and touches the most varied scenery.

Car Rental. Avis and Hertz have car rental offices in Boise, Hailey, Idaho Falls, Pocatello, Sun Valley, and Twin Falls. Hertz has additional offices in Caldwell and Lewiston.

By Bus. A dozen bus lines operate in this far-flung state. Connecting bus or limousine service is available at points served by airlines.

Access to the vast primitive areas of the state is principally by pack horse and charter plane. Guides are widely utilized by big-game hunters. There are also many wilderness trails that have known only the tread of moccasin or boot.

TOURIST INFORMATION SERVICES. Best all-around source of information is *Idaho Travel Council,* Room 108, Capitol Building, Boise 83720 (tel. 208/334–2470), or out of state (800–635–7820). The local chambers of commerce are good sources on individual communities (in Boise, tel. 208/344–7777). A number of roadside information booths are staffed in summer.

SEASONAL EVENTS. Idaho's seasonal attractions are strongly tied to the heritage of the land, the people being more interested in celebrating themselves than in crowing for tourists. This indigenous folk spirit makes the events more charming to outsiders. Special festivals and celebrations generally begin in May and extend thru mid-September. For up-to-date information on specific dates (which sometimes change from year to year), write: Idaho Tourism, Capitol Building, Boise, ID 83720.

May: *Boise,* Birds of Prey Festival Week; *Sandpoint,* Kamloops & Kokanee Week, fishing derby; *Priest Lake,* Spring Festival and Flotilla; *St. Anthony,* Fisherman's Breakfast; *Payette,* Apple Blossom Festival; *Lewiston,* Orchards Blossom Festival; *Riggins,* Salmon River Rodeo; *Cottonwood,* Folk Life Festival.

June: *Massacre Rocks,* Trapper Rendezvous; *Kamiah,* Clearwater Valley Rodeo; *Murphy,* Outpost Day; *Coeur D'Alene,* Summer Theatre; *American Falls,* Opening of Crystal Ice Caves; *Weiser,* National Old-Time Fiddlers Contest; *Burley,* Burley Speedboat Regatta; *Meridian,* Pancake Feed and Dairy Show; Picnic, featuring noon buffalo barbecue; *Craigmont,* Talmaks Annual Camp Meeting, religious revival for Nez Percés of region; *Rexburg,* International Folk Dance; *Orofino,* Mule Days.

July: *Lapwai,* Chief Joseph Memorial, Four Nation Pow Wow; *Sandpoint,* Blue Grass Festival; *Rupert,* 4th of July, 3 nights of rodeos, 4 days horse racing, street dances; *Hailey,* Days of the Old West, including rodeo and lamb barbecue; *Worley,* Coeur D'Alene Tribal Pow Wow; *Boise,* Basque Picnic; *Buhl,* Sagebrush Days, including free barbecue; *Winchester,* Winchester Days, including fiddlers' contest; *Soda Springs,* 4th of July Old West Days: 3-day celebration, followed by Bear River Rendezvous; *Fort Hall,* Sun Dance, War Dances and Indian games (no cameras permitted); *Sun Valley,* Western Art Auction; *Shoshone,* Old Time Fiddler's Jamboree; *Nampa,* Snake River Stampede; *Bonners Ferry,* Kootenai River Days, including lumberjack competition and rodeo; *Boise,* Streets for People; *Cataldo,* Old Mission State Park Historic Skills Fair; *Kooskia,* Kooskia Days, includes fiddlers' jamboree; *Moscow,* Idaho State Square & Round Dance Festival; *Cascade,* Thunder Mountain Day; *Weiser,* Hell's Canyon Rodeo; *Preston,* Preston Famous Night Rodeo; *Elk City,* Elk City Days; *Wood River,* Music Festival; *McCall,* Folk Music Festival; *Soda Springs,* Bear River Rendezvous; *Gooding,* Annual Basque Picnic.

August: *Idaho Falls,* War Bonnet Roundup; *Driggs,* Pierre's Hole Rendezvous, old-fashioned melodrama accompanied by buffalo barbecue, parade of Indians, fiddling, Indian exhibition dancing, and rodeo; *Kellogg,* Miners Day Picnic, 10-day celebration; *Kamiah,* Looking glass Pow Wow, three days of Native American hoopla; *Cataldo,* yearly pilgrimage to Old Cataldo Mission and Catholic Mass held by Coeur d'Alene Indians in ancient tongue; *Hailey,* Northern Rocky Mountain Folk Festival; *Boise,* Western Idaho State Fair.

September: *Blackfoot,* Southeastern Idaho State Fair; *Coeur D'Alene,* North Idaho Fair and Rodeo; *Fruitland,* Fall Harvest Festival; *Orofino,* Lumberjack Days; *Fort Hall,* Shoshone-Bannock Indian Day; *Gooding,* Spud Festival; *Ketchum,* Wagon Days; *Lewiston,* Lewiston Round-Up; *Boise,* Art in the Park.

TOURS. *By boat.* There are so many kinds of trips on the Snake River and through Hells Canyon that you can accumulate a small library of literature on the subject. (For details, write Greater Lewiston Chamber of Commerce, 1030 F St., Lewiston, ID 83501 (208–743–3531).

Accommodations on Snake River trips range from very comfortable rustic lodges to camping as you can on the shore or returning to your motel after a one-day trip. (For information on jet and paddle rides on the Middle Fork of the Salmon and the swift Selway River write Idaho Outfitters and Guides Association, Box 95, Boise, ID 83701.)

On a more placid note, excursion boats operate in the summer months from the city dock of Coeur d'Alene for cruises on Lake Coeur d'Alene and the St. Joe River. Helicopter flights over the lake range from 15 minutes to 1 hour and reveal 125 miles of lakeshore as well as smaller lakes in the area. (For up-to-date schedules, write: Coeur d'Alene Chamber of Commerce, Box 850, Coeur d'Alene, ID 83814 (208–664–3194).

SPECIAL-INTEREST TOURS. With so much of Idaho swift stream, high lake, and mountain country, it is natural that most special-interest tours feature the rugged and off-the-beaten path. Practically every guest ranch offers a variety of these trips. Rates vary and are, of course, subject to change. To be on the safe side, estimate from $85 a day, including meals and saddle horse, on fishing trips, to $2,100 per person for 9 days on fly-in hunts for elk and deer.

Few guides list prices; you have to contact them individually. For more detailed information, and for free catalog, write: Idaho Outfitters and Guides Association, Box 95, Boise, ID 83701.

Ice Caves: Minnetonka Cave in the Cache National Forest, near Paris, in the southeast corner of the state, is open daily from mid-June through Labor Day. Guided tours begin on the hour from 10–5. Jackets advisable, temperature in cave is 40°F. Shoshone, Ice Caves, Idaho 75, 17 miles north of Shoshone, is open May thru Sept. from 8 A.M. to 8 P.M. Guided tours every 20 minutes. Crystal Ice Cave, North Pleasant Valley Road, American Falls, is open daily May–Oct. from 7 A.M.–sunset. Guided tours. Mammoth Cave, located 7 miles north of Shoshone on Idaho 75, has similar schedule to Shoshone Ice Caves.

Old Idaho Penitentiary, built in 1870, has guided 30-minute walking tours of the former state prison and grounds. Sat. 10–4; all other days, noon–4. Comfortable walking shoes suggested.

Idaho State Capitol, built in 1905, and constructed of native sandstone and marble from Alaska, Georgia, and Vermont, has weekday tours, with emphasis on exhibits of agricultural, mineral, and timber products.

INDIANS. Idaho has a rich Indian heritage. The Indians lived almost entirely upon fish and plants, preferred the portable tepee, used skins instead of cloth, made little pottery, and did not practice agriculture. The horse probably reached the Idaho region before 1751. These tribes were able to become excellent nomadic horsemen, and the acquisition of horses was the most important factor in Indian life before the coming of the whites. Horses revolutionized Indian warfare and transportation; permitted wider and more frequent migration, leading to tribal wars—though these have been grossly exaggerated by white historians; and, especially, enabled Indians to fight the whites in more equitable battles. The horse also changed the Indian mode of hunting and could not help but have a strong effect upon Indian culture.

The friendliest and most helpful Indians Lewis and Clark met on their long trek to the Pacific and back to St. Louis were the Nez Percé.

Not until hordes of white settlers began usurping the Indian lands did Idaho's Indians retaliate with gun and arrow.

However, only three red-white wars were fought in Idaho, and all were caused by forcing the Indians to move to reservations. The Nez Percé War in 1877 was the largest. The next year the Bannocks, under Chief Buffalo Horn, fought to retain rights on the Camas Prairie, near Fairfield. The last battle was fought in the Sheepeater War by the Lemhis in 1879.

The Nez Percé have been eulogized by historians since the journals of Lewis and Clark were made public, and their heritage is honored and preserved in this nation's first National Historic Park, unique in that it is a scattered sanctuary of 22 bits and parcels of land, all in Idaho.

Spreading from Spalding on the west to Lolo Pass on the east, and as far south as the White Bird Battlefield (US 95), the park, with headquarters at Spalding, near Lewiston, brings together separate sites of historical significance.

In recent years, Idaho archeologists have discovered "buffalo jumps" in the Owyhee breaks and near Challis, some dating back less than 150 years. Excavations of ancient campsites have been made by researchers from the University of Idaho, Idaho State University, and Boise State College. These official digs throughout the state have found layered remains dating back some 10,000 years, to the time of the atlatl. To preserve this Indian heritage, only surface finds may be kept by individuals, and digging is prohibited by law.

Indian petroglyphs are found primarily along the Snake River and to the south and west. Near Melba is a "map rock" which has been studied by ethnologists.

There are many small collections of Indian artifacts spread about Idaho. Major collections include: Spalding Museum, Juliaetta Arrow Museum, Owyhee County Historical Museum at Murphy, Herrett Arts and Science Center in Twin Falls, and Idaho State University at Pocatello. Tepees of the Bannock tribe are on view at the replica of Old Fort Hall in Pocatello's Ross Park.

Idaho's Indian people have six languages, spoken with numerous dialects. One, the Salishan, ties the Coeur d'Alene—whose own name was Skitswish—with tribes as far away as southeastern Alaska. Culturally, the Indians of Idaho were closely identified with those of neighboring areas: Great Basin, Columbia Plateau, and Great Plains.

Five tribes can be found today in Idaho: Kutenai, Coeur d'Alene, and Nez Percé in the north, and Shoshone-Bannock and Paiute in the south.

The Lower Kutenai own 3,985 acres of treaty land in the Bonners Ferry area, and have a population of 75.

Of the four reservations in the state, the largest is Fort Hall, in southeastern Idaho, where a treaty signed more than 110 years ago set aside 1.8 million acres for the Shoshone and Bannock tribes. The reservation has dwindled to 524,557 acres, including government-owned land within the boundaries. In addition, about 50 miles of the Old Oregon Trail cross the reservation. Present population is about 3,100. In July the reservation Indians hold their Sun Dances and religious observances, at Ross Fork and Bannock Creek. Both include a buffalo feast. In August, the Shoshone-Bannock Indian Festival and Rodeo, at Fort Hall, includes 4 days of activities: historical pageant, war and social dancing, Indian games, parade, all-Indian rodeo, displays, buffalo feast, and the crowning of Miss Shoshone-Bannock. On the last weekend of October, Indian Days is held at Fort Hall, with a varied program. Indian exhibits, dances, and horse races are featured at the Eastern Idaho State Fair (in Blackfoot) in early September, with strong Shoshone and Bannock participation.

In the panhandle, about 35 miles south of the city of Coeur d'Alene, is the Coeur d'Alene Reservation, with some 58,000 acres mingled in a checkerboard pattern with non-allotment lands. Current population is about 1,500. In mid-July, Whaa-Laa Days, a celebration centered on Indian games and dancing, is held in the reservation town of Worley. In late July, Plummer, the reservation headquarters, is the site of Indian Days, a Pow-wow and festival, with a parade, and held in conjunction with Plummer Days. The big attraction is the annual Tepee Town gathering. In mid-August, at the yearly Pilgrimage to Old Cataldo Mission, the first Catholic Mission in Idaho, a Catholic Mass is held by the Coeur d'Alene in their ancient tongue. The public is welcome to the services and to the "friendship" lunch that follows.

Northcentral Idaho is the home of the Nez Percé tribe, which once ranged over the entire region. With headquarters at Lapwai, the reservation contains almost 88,000 acres, and has a population of about 1,600. Lincoln's Birthday Celebration, with Nez Percé games and war dances, is held at Kamiah. From mid-June to July 4, the Talmaks Annual Camp Meeting is held at Craigmont. Religious services begin at 6 A.M. and continue all through the day and evening. Games and races are held on July 4. The meeting includes all six reservation churches. In the second week of August, at historic Lapwai, the Nez Percé hold their Pi-Nee-Waus Days, with soul music—Indian style—for the modern touch, plus dancing, Friendship Feast barbecue, parade, races, exhibits, and Indian games. In the third week of August the Nez Percé go to their Mud Springs Camp, near Craigmont, for Indian games and feasting.

The Paiute occupy some 290,000 acres in Duck Valley, part of which lies in southern Owyhee County. Headquarters are at Owyhee, Nevada. About 200 Paiutes live on the Idaho part of the reservation. No Paiute ceremonials are held in Idaho.

NATIONAL FORESTS. Visitors to Idaho are amazed at how much of the state is still unspoiled, though environmentalists are constantly battling to prevent ruination everywhere. Eight national forests lie entirely within the boundaries of Idaho and seven others partly within the boundaries, giving the state about 21 million acres of National Forest lands. (In addition, there is a National Grasslands of approximately 50,000 acres.) Within the national forests are the *Selway-Bitterroot Wilderness Area,* with almost 1 million acres; the Sawtooth National Recreation and Wilderness Area, with more than 750,000 acres; the *Idaho Primitive Area,* with more than 1,230,000 acres; adjoining the Idaho Primitive Area, the *Salmon River Breaks Primitive Area,* with almost 220,000 acres; the *Hells Canyon-Seven Devils Scenic Area,* with 130,000 acres; the *Middle Fork of the Salmon Wild River;* the *Middle Fork of the Clearwater Wild River;* and the 1978-established *Gospel-Hump,* with 206,000 acres. Within the national forests of Idaho are about 20,000 miles of trails and more than 400 campgrounds, with a total of about 5,000 campsites. The recreational opportunities are as sophisticated as water-skiing at well-developed lakes and as primitive as backpacking in the wilderness area.

Major forests include: *Boise,* the largest in Idaho, with almost 3 million acres. Highways reaching the forest are US 20, US 95, I–84 and Idaho 21 and 55. Nearby towns are Boise, Cascade, Emmett, Idaho City, and Mountain Home. Attractions include the Sawtooth Wilderness Area and other rugged backcountry; abandoned mines and ghost towns; virgin stands of ponderosa pine; scenes of early Indian camps and red-white battles; Arrowrock, Anderson Ranch, Cascade, Deadwood, and Lucky Peak Reservoirs, and scores of lakes; the headwaters of the Boise and Payette Rivers; scenic drives in Payette and Boise River canyons, along the Boise Ridge and edge of Sawtooth Wilderness Area; lake and stream fishing for trout and salmon. The forest has 825 miles of trail, suitable for foot and horse travel, 97 developed camp and picnic grounds, and contains resorts, motels, dude ranches, and the Bogus Basin Winter Sports Area. *Boise National Forest,* 1750 Front St., Boise, ID 83702 (208–334–1516).

Caribou: Practically all of it is in Idaho, about 1 million acres in the state. Highways reaching it are I–15, US 26, 30, and Idaho 34 and 36. Nearby towns are Idaho Falls, Montpelier, Pocatello, Malad City, Soda Springs, and Franklin. Attractions include towering mountain ranges divided by lovely valleys, historic markers and trails, natural soda springs, rushing streams and waterfalls, and many scenic drives, including the Snake River-McCoy Road along the south bank of the South Fork of the Snake River. The forest has 1,220 miles of trail, 28 camp and picnic grounds, a winter sports area, and contains resorts and motels. *Caribou National Forest,* Suite 294, Federal Bldg., 250 S. Fourth Ave., Pocatello, ID 83201 (208–236–6700).

Challis: The second largest national forest in Idaho, with about 2.5 million acres. Highways reaching the forest are US 20 and 93, and Idaho 75 and 22–33. Nearby towns are Challis, Salmon, and Stanley. Attractions are so numerous and so awesome as to stupefy the researcher. Outstanding are White Cloud Peaks; Lost River Range, with Mt. Borah, at 12,662 feet the highest peak in Idaho; Salmon River and White Knob Mountain Ranges; Sawtooth National Recreation Area; riding and hiking trails, and wilderness boating and packing trips. The forest has nearly 1,600 miles of trails and 40 developed campsites and picnic grounds, and dude ranches, with commercial packers and guides available. *Challis National Forest,* Box 404, Challis, ID 83226 (208–879–2285).

Clearwater: Large stands of white pines are scattered through the approximately 1.7 million acres. Reached by US 12 and Idaho 8 and 11. Nearest towns are Kooskia, Kamiah, Orofino, and Lewiston. Attractions include the historic Lolo Trail, over which the Lewis and Clark party struggled in blizzards; Selway-Bitterroot Wilderness; scenic drives on the North Fork of the Clearwater River and US 12; trout and salmon fishing. The forest has more than 25 camp and picnic grounds and several for picnic only, and contains motels and cabins. Pack-trip outfitters available. *Clearwater National Forest,* 12730 Highway 12, Orofino, ID 83544 (208–476–4541).

Coeur d'Alene (about 725,000 acres), in the northern part of the state, is reached by US 95, Interstate 90, and Idaho 3. Nearby towns are Coeur d'Alene, Kellogg, Spirit Lake, and Wallace. Attractions include the 1846-built Cataldo Mission and 30-mile long (104 miles of shoreline) Coeur d'Alene Lake. The forest has more than 10 camp and picnic grounds, several for picnic only, and Lookout Pass Winter Sports Area, and resort hotels and cabins. *Idaho Panhandle National Forests,* 1201 Ironwood Drive, Coeur d'Alene, ID 83814 (208–765–7233).

Kaniksu, The northernmost of the forest, reaches to the Canadian border, with about 900,000 acres. It is accessible by US 2 and 95, and Idaho 57 and 200. Nearby towns are Bonners Ferry, Priest River, and Sandpoint. Attractions include two magnificent lakes, Pend Oreille and Priest; the 107-mile Pend Oreille Loop Drive; Selkirk Mountain Range; historic Kullyspell House; Roosevelt Ancient Grove of Cedars; Chimney Rock; Cabinet Mountain Wilderness; lake and stream fishing; and a lot of rugged backcountry. The forest has about 30 camp and picnic grounds, about a dozen for picnic only, and three swimming sites. It also contains the Schweitzer Basin Winter Ski Area, resorts, hotels, lodges, and cabins. *Idaho Panhandle National Forests,* 1201 Ironwood Drive, Coeur d'Alene, ID 83814 (208–765–7233).

Nez Percé, in the western part of the state, has more than 2 million acres. Reaching it are US 95 and 12, and Idaho 13 and 14. Nearby towns are Grangeville, Kooskia, and Riggins. Attractions include the Selway-Bitterroot Wilderness; Salmon River Breaks Primitive Area; Seven Devils Range, between the Salmon and Snake Rivers; Red River Hot Springs; historic Elk City; lake and stream fishing; hiking and horse trails; wilderness pack trips and scenic drives along the Lochsa, Salmon, and Selway Rivers. The forest has 28 campgrounds,

4 picnic areas, a documentary site, a boating site and a private hot springs resort. It also contains hotels and cabins. Pack-trip outfitters are available. *Nez Perce National Forests,* Route 2, Box 475, Grangeville, ID 83530 (208–983–1950).

Payette, just south of the Nez Percé National Forest, has about 2.4 million acres and is reached by US 95, and Idaho 55. Nearby towns are Cascade, Council, McCall, New Meadows, and Weiser. Attractions include Hells Canyon-Seven Devils Scenic Area (Hells Canyon is the deepest gorge on the continent), Payette Lakes Recreational Area, more than 150 fishing lakes, more than 1,500 miles of fishing streams, trout and salmon fishing, scenic drives, and wilderness trips. The forest has more than 2,400 miles of trail, 25 camp and picnic grounds, and includes the Payette Lakes Winter Sports Area and dude ranches. *Payette National Forest,* P.O. Box 1026, McCall, ID 83638 (208–634–8151).

Salmon, in the sparsely settled eastern part of the state, has almost 1.8 million acres. It can be reached by US 93 and Idaho 28. Nearby towns are Salmon and Leadore. Attractions include the Idaho Primitive Area, Big Horn Crags, historic Lewis and Clark Trail, Salmon River Canyon, Salmon River and Panther Creek forest trails, and boat trips on the "River of No Return." The forest has 1,100 miles of trail, 21 developed camp and picnic grounds, and contains dude ranches. Pack-trip guides and outfitters available. *Salmon National Forest,* Box 729, Salmon, ID 83467 (208–756–2215).

St. Joe National Forest, just below the panhandle, with about 900,000 acres, is reached by Interstate 90 and Idaho 3. Nearby towns are Moscow, Potlatch, and St. Maries. Attractions include the wild Bitterroot Range of the Idaho-Montana divide, St. Maries River Valley, canyon area of the Little North Fork of the Clearwater River, the Clearwater-St. Joe River divide, the Palouse River area, virgin stands of white pine, large timber operations, scenic drives along the St. Joe River from source to mouth in Coeur d'Alene Lake, and lake and stream fishing. The forest has more than 20 camp and picnic grounds, a fine network of trails, a swimming site, and the North-South Winter Sports Area. Dude ranches are nearby, and there are cabins on the St. Joe River. *Idaho Panhandle National Forests,* 1201 Ironwood Dr., Coeur d'Alene, ID 83814 (208–765–7223).

Sawtooth, in the south central part of the state, has more than 1,700,000 acres in Idaho and may be reached by Interstate 84, Interstate 15, US 93, and Idaho 37, 27, 81 and 77. Nearby towns are Burley, Gooding, Ketchum, and Twin Falls. Attractions include Sun Valley, Sawtooth Wilderness Area, panoramic views of the Snake River Valley, the incredibly eroded "Silent City of Rocks" (famous as a dividing point of the Oregon and California Trails); hot springs, multicolored mountains, charming lakes, fishing, scenic drives, and saddle and pack trips. The forest has more than 1,500 miles of trails, 90 developed camping and picnic grounds, one swimming site, and eight winter sports areas, including Magic Mountain. Mt. Harrison, Soldier Creek, and Sun Valley, and contains many dude ranches, camps, and motels. *Sawtooth National Forest,* 1525 Addison Ave. East, Twin Falls, ID 83301 (208–733–3698).

Targhee, pressed against Wyoming (and close to Grand Teton National Park), has more than 1.3 million acres. It is reached by US 20 and 26, Interstate 15, and Idaho 31, 32, 33 and 47. Nearby towns are Ashton, Driggs, Dubois, Idaho Falls, Rexburg, St. Anthony, and Victor. Attractions include Island Park Reservoir, Grand Canyon of the Snake River, Cave Falls, Falls River, Palisades Dam, scenic drives, lake and stream fishing, and riding and hiking trails into the untrammeled mountains. The forest includes about 1,500 miles of trails, 33 developed campsites and picnic grounds, and contains three winter sports areas (Bear Gulch, Moose Creek, and Pine Basin), as well as resorts, motels, dude ranches, fishing camps, and boating facilities. Pack outfits for hunting parties are available. *Targhee National Forest,* Box 208, St. Anthony, ID 83445 (208–624–3151).

For detailed information on national forests, write: Forest Service Intermountain Region, Federal Office Building, Ogden, UT 84401, and U.S. Forest Service, Northern Region, Missoula, Montana 59801.

STATE PARKS. The Idaho State Department of Parks and Recreation maintains 19 parks, ranging from undeveloped, natural areas to full scale recreation areas, and totaling almost 29,000 acres. Located in all sections of the state, these areas provide more than 2,500 day-use sites and about 950 camping sites. (The Idaho Department of Transportation—formerly Idaho State Highway Department—administers 111 safety rest-areas for the convenience and comfort of the motoring public. Located on the major highways throughout the state, most safety rest-areas provide rest stations, drinking water, and picnic tables under shade trees or sun shelters.)

Included in the Idaho State Park System are: *Priest Lake,* with three camping units (Lion Head, 45 sites, without hookups; Indian Creek, 60 tent sites, 22 trailer sites; and Dickensheet, 10 tent sites), 37 miles north of the town of Priest River, at road end, and in thick woods on the east shore of dreamy Priest Lake. Boating, fishing, swimming, and nature hikes. *Round Lake,* 10 miles south of Sandpoint and 2 miles west of US 95, near Pend Oreille Lake, has 53 RV sites, no hookups. *Farragut,* on the shore of fish-famous Pend Oreille Lake, has 145 sites, 22 foot maximum RV length, 100 no hookups. *Old Mission,* historic missions at Cataldo on Interstate 10, 10 miles west of Kellogg, has picnic sites, guided tours, and museums. *Heyburn,* on Idaho 5 between Plummer and St. Maries, and near the entry of the St. Joe River in Coeur d'Alene Lake, has 5,505 acres and contains 136 RV sites, most with hookups and picnic tables at all 3 campgrounds. *Hells Gate,* on the Snake River at the southern edge of Lewiston, a gateway to Hells Canyon, has 93 RV sites, 64 with water & elec., and boasts fine swimming, boating and fishing. *Winchester Lake,* a popular fishing lake, and at the edge of the town of Winchester, 40 miles south of Lewiston on old US 95, has 65 sites, all in the woods. *Mowry* is an undeveloped site on Lake Coeur d'Alene accessible only from the water. *Eagle Island* is a day-use park sited between north and south channels of the Boise River, with 15-acre manmade lake and swimming beach. *Ponderosa,* at McCall, on a peninsula at the southern end of Payette Lake, has 106 units with water & elec. and 64 units without, and is in the center of a vast forest and water recreationland. *Veterans Memorial,* in the capital city of Boise, is on the Boise River and has surfaced trails, fishing, and picnicking. *Lucky Peak,* on a reservoir 8 miles east of Boise, on Idaho 21, has a swimming beach, group picnic shelters, boat ramps, fishing, and water skiing. *Bruneau Dunes,* 7 miles northeast of Bruneau on Idaho 51, is a unique sand dune formation near a spectacular deep-canyon area; it has 32 tent, 16 trailer, and 31 picnic sites, offers fishing, hiking, and photographic opportunities. *Three Island Crossing,* at Glenns Ferry, off Interstate 84 is a famous Oregon Trail fording; offers boating, swimming, and history trail; has 50 RV and 27 family-picnic sites and one group-picnic site. *Massacre Rocks,* 12 miles west of American Falls, on Interstate 86, includes an Oregon Trail campsite at Register Rock and has 52 RV and 26 picnic sites. *Bear Lake,* 2 miles east of Idaho 89, on the north shore of Bear Lake, near the Utah border, offers swimming, fishing, and boating. *Henry's Lake,* 17 miles southwest of West Yellowstone, Montana, is on a famous Mountain Man lake; has 32 RV sites without hookups, and is noted for its fishing and boating. *Indian Rocks,* south of Pocatello, has desert flowers into early summer; interpretive center; *Malad Gorge,* near Hagerman, is a 250-ft.-deep scenic gorge with waterfall (footbridge spans gorge), lava formations, picnic area; *Harriman,* north of Ashton, a former cattle ranch is now a refuge for wildlife with lakes & ponds; on Henry's Fork of Snake River.

Camping in season (approximately May 1–Sept. 30). There is a charge for camping with or without hookups; fees change periodically. Persons 65 years of age or older and disabled citizens on Social Security camp at half-price, but they have to be Idaho citizens. Length of stay is 15 days in any 30-day period except at Priest Lake, Farragut, and Ponderosa. These parks have a 10-day limit. And these parks—Priest Lake, Farragut, and Ponderosa—also have reservation systems, with $5 reservation fee per campsite. Contact Regional Office North, 1838 N. Lincoln Way, Coeur d'Alene 83814 (208–667–1511) to obtain reservation forms for Priest Lake or Farragut. For reservations at Ponderosa, contact Ponderosa State Park, Box A, McCall 83638 (208–634–2164).

For detailed information on state parks, write: Idaho Department of Parks & Recreation, 2177 Warm Springs Ave., Boise, ID 83720.

CAMPING OUT. Idaho has campgrounds throughout the state. In the national forests alone there are more than 400 campgrounds, with a total of about 5,000 tent and trailer sites. (For specific forests, see section on *National Forests.*) The state parks of Idaho provide about one thousand campsites in all parts of the state. (For specific parks, see section above, *State Parks.*)

The Bureau of Land Management has 26 recreation sites with developed units, on which there are 278 trailer sites. (For specific information write to Bureau of Land Management, Box 010, Federal Bldg., 550 W. Fort St., Boise, ID 83724.)

The Corps of Engineers has two projects in Idaho, Dworshak Reservoir and Lucky Peak Lake, the latter near Boise. Dworshak Dam, on the North Fork of the Clearwater River, has created a 53-mile-long reservoir that offers diverse recreation opportunities. More than 10,000 acres of land adjacent to the man-made lake are set aside for public use. Free camping areas accessible by boat are located at isolated coves and creek inlets along the reservoir shoreline. One hundred forty of the mini-camping sites have been established at 75 locations. The Nez Perce Tribal Marina at Big Eddy offers moorage rentals for 150 boats. Dents Acres Recreation Area, 19 miles from Orofino, has pull-through facilities for 50 camp trailers. (For specific information, write: U.S. Corps of Engineers, Building 602, City-County Airport, Walla Walla, WA 99362.)

Over 250 public recreation sites have been provided by private companies in Idaho. These parks offer more than 8,000 campsites, as well as the usual range of outdoor recreation activities. Idaho Power Company has 4 campgrounds on the Snake River in the Hells Canyon area: Hells Canyon Park, near Homestead; Copperfield Trailer Park, near Oxbow Dam; McCormick Park, below Brownlee Dam; and Woodhead Park, at Brownlee Dam. All parks have trailer hookups. While the company does not charge for day use, it has broken with its 20-year-old policy of free overnight camping facilities and now charges $1 a night for tent space and $3 per day for RV space. Idaho Power also has picnic-camping areas at C.J. Strike Dam, 10 miles west of Bruneau, and picnic areas at Hagerman Valley, in the Bliss and Hagerman areas, and at Shoshone Falls—American Falls. (For specific information, write: Public Information Dept., Idaho Power Co., Box 70, Boise, ID 83707.)

Craters of the Moon National Monument has a 51-space campground.

Cascade Reservoir, near Cascade (Idaho 55), has 2 campgrounds, Donnelly Park and Cascade Park, with a total of 70 trailer sites.

A number of communities in the state offer overnight camping in their parks. These include Lewiston, whose Kiwanis Park has trailer stalls; Old Fort Boise Park in Parma, also with trailer facilities; and Shoshone Falls Park in Twin Falls, with units for tents and trailers.

KOA Kampgrounds are so many that you can, touring around the state, stay at one every night if you properly arrange your schedule. Included are Arco, Blackfoot, Boise, Bonners Ferry, Burley/Rupert, Caldwell, Coeur d'Alene, Hayden Lake, Idaho Falls, Jerome-Twin Falls, Lava Hot Springs, Lewiston, McCall, Montpelier, Mountain Home, Pinehurst, Pocatello, Sandpoint, Island Park and Victor. Other private campgrounds are peppered throughout the state, so there is never far to look for one.

For more detailed information on city parks and KOA campgrounds, write: Idaho Travel Council. (See *Tourist Information Services.*)

TRAILER TIPS. There are, literally, hundreds of places to park trailers, RVs, and campers. There are many sites in national forests, state parks, Bureau of Land Management facilities, corporation-owned areas, parks in some municipalities, and KOA Kampgrounds. (See section on *Camping Out.*) For more detailed information write to Idaho Tourism. (See *Tourist Information Services.*)

GUEST RANCHES. Idaho has many outstanding guest ranches. Some specialize in pack trips for hunting or fishing, some offer more leisurely enjoyment of the big-sky country, and most are a combination of the two. Because rates change due to inflation, they are not listed here; but it can be said that Idaho guest-ranch rates are no more expensive than most guest ranches in other states. Among the better-known guest ranches are these: *Cook Ranch,* 50 miles south of Elk City. Access in winter by plane or snowmobile; in summer by auto up to two miles and then by wagon or horse. Lodge. Family-style meals. Fishing, horseback riding, etc. Cook Ranch, 5727 Hill Rd., Boise, ID 83703 (208–344–0951). *Harrah's Lodge,* on the Middle Fork of the Salmon. Luxurious retreat. Heated swimming pool, hot springs bathouse (c/o Harrahs, Box 10, Reno, NV 89504.) *Elkins on Priest Lake,* 3 miles east of Nordman, high in the Panhandle, with 31 year-round fully equipped housekeeping cabins, restaurant, store, sandy beach, fish, boat rentals, surf sailers, canoe, cross country ski trails, handicapped access. Rte. 1, Box 40, Priest Lake, ID 83848 (208–443–2432). *Yellow Pine Lodge,* in lovely back country. Family-style meals. Mountain location close to winter recreation, hunting, fishing. Yellow Pine Lodge, Box 77, Yellow Pine, ID (208–382–4336). *Indian Creek Guest Ranch,* located 10 miles down Salmon River from North Fork, ID. Small ranch specializing in individual attention. Family-style meals, 3 miles of trout fishing on property, horseback riding, hiking. Flying customers picked up at Salmon Airport. (Address: Rt. 2, Box 105, North Fork, ID 83466 (208—Salmon operator—ask for 24F211). *Mackay Bar Lodge,* on the "River of No Return," the big Salmon, in the heart of the Chamberlain Basin primitive area. Guest rooms and tent cabins. (Address: 3190 Airport Way, Boise, ID 83705 (208–344–1881). *Salmon River Lodge,* located across the Salmon River from the end of the road, 30 miles below Shoup. Middle Fork and Salmon River float trips, steelhead fishing, primitive area pack trips, Salmon River jet boat trips, big-game hunting in season. (Address: Box 348, Jerome, ID 83338 (208–324–3553). *Mystic Saddle Ranch,* in the Sawtooth Wilderness. Pack trips, trout fishing, big-game hunting in season. (Address: Stanley, ID 83340 (208–774–3591). *Shepp Ranch,* on the banks of the "River of No Return." Jet boating, rafting, nature trips. (Address: Box 3417, Boise, ID 83703; tel. 208–343–7729). *Happy Hollow Camps,* in the Salmon River country. Working ranch vacation, float trips on Mail Salmon, fishing, trail rides, pack trips. (Address: Star Route, Box 14, Salmon, ID 83466 (208–756–3954). *Sulphur Creek Ranch,* on Middle Fork of the Salmon River. Basically for hunters and fishers. (Address: 7153 West Emerald, Boise, ID 83704 (208–377–1188.) *Flying W Ranch,* 110 miles from Cascade. Way back, as indicated by directions: Warm Lake to Landmark to Yellow Pine to Big Creek. Lodge cabins. Family-style meals. Fishing, backpacking, horseback riding, snowmobiling. Reservations only. Flying W Ranch, Box 401, Emmett, ID 83617 (208–365–4946).

CONVENTION SITES. National and international conventions (as well as regional gatherings) are held at Sun Valley. Small national conventions and regional conventions are held at Boise. Scholarly-technical meetings and conventions are held at the University of Idaho (Moscow) and Idaho State University (Pocatello). Regional conventions are staged at McCall, Burley, Idaho Falls, Lewiston, Pocatello, and Coeur d'Alene.

HOT SPRINGS. Idaho has more than a hundred mineral springs, with a variety of facilities and accommodations at the most popular of them. At *Lava Hot Springs,* on the Portneuf River, the state operates a resort. Probably the best-known of the mineral springs are at *Soda Springs,* famous in Oregon Trail lore. The waters of these springs are reputed to contain 22 different kinds of minerals and to possess curative powers. One of the soda springs in this area is Steamboat Spring, which boils up through 40 feet of water and explodes at the surface; another is Mammoth Soda Spring, which is nearly the same size as Mammoth Hot Springs in Yellowstone Park. At *American Falls* there is bathing in mineral pools fed by 30 different springs, from hot to cold. At *Hot*

Creek, near Bruneau Canyon, in southwestern Idaho, hot springs boil out of a ravine, and for a mile the steaming water froths in fury until it tumbles over a fall into a scoured-out cavity, 15 feet across, called Indian Bowl. Near the area are campground and dressing facilities for swimmers. Other hot springs in the state include *Red River,* 27 miles east of Elk City, Idaho 14; *Boulder Creek,* 8 miles south of Pollock, US 95; *Riggins,* 9 miles east of Riggins, US 95; *Sulphur,* 14 miles north of New Meadows of US 95; *Zim's Plunge,* 7 miles north of New Meadows off US 95; *Meadows Valley,* 5 miles north of New Meadows, US 95; *Kreigbaum,* at Meadows, 2 miles east of New Meadows, US 95; *Starkey,* 8 miles north of Council, US 95; *Burgdorf,* 30 miles north of McCall, Idaho 55; *Givens,* 12 miles south of Marsing, near US 95; *Warm Springs Plunge,* 2 miles south of Idaho City, Idaho 21; *Silver Creek Plunge,* 10 miles east of Banks, Idaho 55; *Kirkham,* 4 miles east of Lowman, on Idaho 21; *Grandjean,* 30 miles east of Lowman, Idaho 21; *Hot Spring at Weatherby Sawmill,* near Atlanta, on dirt road near southern edge of Sawtooth Wilderness Area; *Baumgartner,* near Featherville, on gravel road 22 miles south of Atlanta; *Paradise,* on South Fork of the Boise River near Featherville; *Salmon,* 3 miles southeast of Salmon, US 93; *Beardsley,* south of Salmon along US 93; *Sharkey,* 20 miles southeast of Salmon, US 93, and near Idaho 28; *Challis,* on Warm Springs Creek east of Challis, Idaho 75; *Sunbeam,* on Idaho 75, 13 miles east of Stanley; *Mineral,* 2 miles south of Stanley on Idaho 75; *Stanley,* at junction of Valley Creek and Idaho 75; *Clarendon,* 7 miles northwest of Hailey, Idaho 75; *Banbury,* between Buhl and Hagerman on US 30; *Nat Soo Pah,* 6 miles east of Hollister, US 93; *Cedar Creek,* west of Rogerson (US 93) at intersection of road and Cedar Creek; *Murphy,* near Rogerson, US 93; *Magic,* 24 miles southeast of Rogerson, US 93; *Lidy,* 16 miles west of Dubois on Idaho 22; *Green Canyon,* 33 miles southeast of Newdale, Idaho 33; *Heise,* 5 miles east of Ririe, near US 26; *Hooper,* one mile north of Soda Springs, US 30; *Champagne,* near Hooper Spring; *Sulphur,* 8 miles southeast of Soda Springs, US 30; *Vincent,* near Idaho 36 midway between Preston and Mink Creek at southern end of Oneida Narrows; *Downata,* 5 miles south of Downey, US 91; *Pleasantview,* 5 miles west of Malad City, Interstate 15; *Indian,* 3 miles southwest of American Falls, Interstate 15W; *Twin Springs,* east of Atlanta on Middle Fork of Boise; *Maple Grove Hot Springs,* 6 miles south of Cleveland; *Mammoth Soda Spring,* 3 miles north of Soda Spring; *Price's Hot Springs,* near Gwenford; *South North Beach,* east side of Bear Lake.

SUMMER SPORTS. Idaho is a state of mountains, forests, lakes, and streams. Sports are generally of the outdoor type-fishing, hunting, hiking, boating and skiing.

Boating: The lakes and rivers provide water highways for small-boat operators. Days can be spent on inland waters in the north, and Snake River reservoirs provide more-than-adequate water space in the south. Waterskiing is popular at Lucky Peak Reservoir, a short drive east of Boise. Sailboats abound on the Payette Lakes, at McCall, and on Coeur d'Alene Lake, where there is sailboat racing. Dangerous storms can whip up on huge Pend Oreille and other lakes of the panhandle. Boatmen unfamiliar with the lakes should stay within shouting distance of shore. Special thrills are offered on the white-water trips down the Snake, Middle Fork of the Salmon, Main Salmon, and Selway, but these are for the skilled and experienced only. (For guided float and jet boat trips down these rivers, see *Guest Ranches, Tours,* and *Special Interest Tours.*)

Golf: The Sun Valley Golf Club has a beautiful 18-hole course, open May to Oct. One of the most picturesque courses is Blue Lakes Country Club in the Snake River Canyon near Twin Falls. All major cities have golf courses, along with golf shops. There are more than 60 public courses in the state, with 18-holers at these courses open to the public: Shadow Valley and Warm Springs, in Boise; Municipal, in Burley; Purple Sage, in Caldwell; Avondale, in Hayden Lake; Eagle Hills, in Eagle; Pinecrest, in Idaho Falls; Shoshone, in Kellogg; Bryden Canyon, in Lewiston; Municipal, in McCall; Highlands and Riverside, in Pocatello; Elkhorn and Sun Valley, in Sun Valley; Municipal, in Twin Falls.

FISHING. The fishing is good in all parts of Idaho. The rivers, smaller streams, large lakes, mountain pools, and ponds all produce excellent catches. Record-size trout are taken from Lake Pend Oreille, in the north, and the average is also heavy in nearby Priest and Coeur d'Alene lakes. Steelhead and sturgeon challenge the anglers along the Snake and Clearwater Rivers, while the Salmon and its Middle Fork offer solitude as well as top fly fishing.

The general fishing season usually runs from the Saturday before the Memorial Day holiday thru November, when trout and other species may be taken. Special seasons also apply to trout, salmon, steelhead, and a number of other species. Bag limits vary with different species. Non-resident season fishing license is $35.50; non-resident ten-day fishing license is $17.50; non-resident one-day fishing license is $5.50. Fishing licenses may be obtained from vendors in nearly every town in the state.

Forest Service public campgrounds are available along many streams and lakes. Packers and guides may be hired to go into the back country. Idaho has over 1,800 lakes, in addition to rivers, reservoirs, and smaller streams.

For list of regulations and further information, write: Idaho Fish & Game Dept., 600 S. Walnut St., Box 25, Boise, ID 83707.

HUNTING. Big Game: The many miles of wilderness and age-old forests provide a special opportunity for big-game hunting. The inexperienced hunter would be little short of insane not to hire a professional guide before striking out into treacherous terrain. General seasons for deer, elk, and bear extend from mid-Sept. until Nov., though areas and seasons vary throughout the state. Controlled hunts are sometimes established for moose, antelope, mountain goat, and bighorn sheep. Non-resident big-game hunters should contact the Idaho Fish & Game Dept., beginning in Jan., since licenses are obtained on a quota basis. Copies of the official regulations may be obtained without charge from license vendors or from the Idaho Fish & Game Dept. Big-game seasons are set about May 20, and hunting maps are available from the Department after July 1 each year. License fees for non-residents are $85.50 per adult; game tags range up to $235.50 per kill. Since fees are subject to change, for up-to-date information, write: Idaho Fish and Game Dept., 600 S. Walnut St., Box 25, Boise, ID 83707, *Guest Ranches* and *Special Interest Tours,* and write: Idaho Outfitters and Guides Association, Box 95, Boise, ID 83701.

Birds. Hunting seasons of varying length are set for partridge, quail, and grouse, usually in Sept. and Oct.; for pheasant, in specified areas from late Oct. thru most of Nov.; for waterfowl, usually from mid-Oct. thru Dec. Opening dates for upland bird seasons are set in May, with complete regulations established in late August. Licenses may be obtained from vendors in nearly every town in the state. Game tags (for nonresidents) for turkey are $25.50. For regulations and up-to-date information, write: Idaho Fish & Game Dept. For guides, write: Idaho Outfitters and Guides Association.

WINTER SPORTS. *Skiing:* The fastest-growing sport in Idaho, at least as far as facilities are concerned, is skiing. Tow lines and chair lifts now run up many slopes in the state, and the facilities attract skiers from a wide area outside Idaho.

The most famous ski resort is *Sun Valley.* It has been said of Sun Valley, "The first complete ski resort remains the best. The two mountains are the finest in America." With 200 ski instructors, "Sun Valley continues to offer the finest learn-to-ski and ski-improvement program available anywhere," a ski resort expert wrote. *Elkhorn* at Sun Valley is located adjacent to Dollar Mountain, while still convenient to the slopes of Mt. Baldy. Sun Valley offers 3 ice rinks, supervised child-care, and a romantic horse-drawn sleigh ride, in addition to skiing. Elkhorn has its own ice rink. Both have lodging, dining, and entertainment facilities. Ketchum (Idaho 75) is close by, and some people stay there. The city of Ketchum operates buses to Sun Valley and Elkhorn between 7 A.M. and 11 P.M.

One of the most spectacular scenic ski areas in the nation is *Grand Targhee,* 12 miles east of Driggs (Idaho 33) on the western slope of the Tetons, with panoramic views of the awesome range. Although actually in Wyoming, Grand Targhee is included in Idaho because of its proximity to Idaho Falls and nearby communities. Snow here has been described as "limitless in its profusion of Rocky Mountain powder." Snowfall averages 500 inches annually. Operating schedule is daily, November 19 to April 24. Helicopters fly powder enthusiasts to untracked areas in the high mountains. Accommodations are Grand Targhee Resort and Driggs. Ski shop, equipment rental, and full-time nursery. Restaurant at base of chairlifts.

Bogus Basin, 16 miles north of Boise, and a favorite with western Snake River Valley winter sports-minded men and women, is one of the major ski areas in the Pacific Northwest. Copious snowfall and moderate temperatures from Thanksgiving deep into April make Bogus Basin a true winter wonderland. The longest illuminated slope in the country is here—over 1,000 acres; 43 major runs offer a variety of ski terrain with packed and powder slopes. Day and night skiing. Ski area has ski rental shop, inn with 200 beds, 2-day lodges, restaurants, full-time nursery, and professional ski school.

Another magnificently-located ski area is *Brundage Mountain,* 7 miles north of McCall, on Idaho 55. The slopes overlook Payette Lakes and out to a world of silver forests and high, rugged terrain. Two riblet double chairlifts transport skiers a mile to the top of the mountain in approximately 10 minutes (no lift lines here). Total vertical drop on Brundage Mountain is 1,600 feet. An alpine T-bar lift, 1,800 feet long, 450-foot vertical rise, services the more gentle beginner and intermediate slopes. At this high, dry altitude, powder snow is the rule rather than the exception. Ski shop, rentals, ski school, day lodge, cafeteria. Open 7 days a week, mid-Nov.–mid-Apr. Overnight accommodations in McCall.

Other principal ski areas include:

Bald Mountain, 6 miles northeast of Pierce on Idaho 11. Has 3,000-foot T-bar and 3 main runs. Day lodge, snack bar, ski shop, equipment rental. Open weekends and holidays. Overnight accommodations in Pierce and Orofino.

Bear Gulch, 10 miles northeast of Ashton (US 20) and off Idaho 47. From the top of the 5,300-foot mountain, downhillers have 6 slopes and a trail to attack. Day lodge with snack bar. Ski school has family rates. Open Thur.-Sun., Dec. 1–Apr. 1. Overnight accommodations in Ashton and St. Anthony.

Blizzard Mountain, 18 miles west of Arco on US 93–US 20–US 26, and 2 miles from Craters of the Moon National Monument. A 2,500-foot poma lift and rope tow handle the mountain. Day lodge, snack bar, and ski school. Open weekends and holidays. Overnight accommodations in Arco.

Caribou, 6 miles east of Pocatello. Two main slopes and three trails are served by a chairlift. Night skating Wed. thru Fri., Dec.–March. Olympic-size ice rink and skating instructor. Day lodge and snack bar, equipment rental, ski school. Open weekends. Overnight accommodations in Pocatello.

Cottonwood Butte, 5 miles west of Cottonwood off US 95. Six miles of cross-country runs open off the north slope of Cottonwood Butte. Downhill skiers have 3 open slopes, the longest just under 1 mile. Open weekends, holidays, and Wed. nights mid-Dec.–mid-Mar. Day lodge, snack bar, equipment rental, ski school. Overnight accommodations in Cottonwood, Grangeville, and Craigmont.

Flying H Ski Resort, 12 miles north of Coeur d'Alene off US 95. A novice and intermediate ski area with gentle slopes illuminated for night skiing. Open slopes with the longest trail 1,200 feet and 250 feet of vertical drop. Day lodge and snack bar. Rental equipment available. Fri., Sat. & Sun. Overnight accommodations.

Hitt Mountain, 16 miles west of Cambridge (US 95) on Idaho 71. Five trails branch off the top of the 2,500-foot T-bar lift. Day lodge, snack bar, ski school, rental equipment. Open weekends and holidays. Overnight accommodations at Cambridge and Weiser.

Kelly Canyon, 25 miles northeast of Idaho Falls. Three double chairlifts and 1 rope tow. Six open slopes are served by 3 chairs. Longest run is 1 mile in length with a vertical drop of 870 feet. Day lodge, ski school, equipment rental. Open daily except Mon.; night skiing Tues.–Sat. Overnight accommodations in Idaho Falls; Heise Hot Springs and Pizza Parlor are 2 miles away.

Lookout Pass, a short drive east of Wallace on I–90. Excellent snow and gentle (850-foot vertical drop) slopes make it a fine teaching area. Day lodge, cafeteria, and ski rental shop. Open Fris., 7–10 P.M., weekends and holidays. Overnight accommodations in Wallace, Mullan and Kellogg.

Lost Trail, 42 miles north of Salmon on US 93, near Montana border and Continental Divide. Double chairlift. Seven open runs, the longest 6,600 feet in length, and a 10-mile crosscountry area. Day lodge, snack bar, ski school, equipment rental. Open Fri., Sat., Sun., and Mon., also holidays, Thanksgiving to May. Overnight accommodations in Salmon and Lost Trail Hot Springs.

Magic Mountain, 35 miles southeast of Twin Falls. Two separate mountains, 15 runs and 4 trails, with the longest 2 miles in length. Main lift is a 3,000-foot double chair; it and the adjacent 2,500-foot T-bar offer excellent powder runs for advanced skiers. The second mountain is primarily a ski-school slope; skiers move up on a 2,000-foot poma lift. Day lodge with cafeteria, ski school, equipment rental. Open Wed. to Sun., Dec.–Apr. Overnight accommodations in Twin Falls.

Montpelier Ski Area, at the edge of city limits of Montpelier, on US 30. Recreation area for children and teenagers. One rope two climbs an 800-foot hill with slopes for skiers, sleds, and toboggans. Open weekends and holidays. Accommodations in town.

North-South Bowl, 60 miles south of Coeur d'Alene and 45 miles north of Moscow (US 95) on Idaho 6. Popular with students from University of Idaho and Washington State University. Double chairlift and 2 rope tows. Open Fri. night, Sat., Sun. Day lodge with fast foods, ski school, rental equipment. Accommodations at St. Maries and Moscow-Pullman area.

Pebble Creek, 15 miles southeast of Pocatello, off I–15. Open Dec. thru mid-April. 1 D-chair, 1 T-chair, 2 pomas. Vertical drop planned for 3,000 feet. Instruction, day lodge, food, lounge. Lodgings in Pocatello and Lava Hot Springs.

Pomerelle, 29 miles southeast of Burley (I–84) off Idaho 77. A variety of challenging runs over open slopes and trails winding down through the timbered slopes of 8,020-foot Mt. Harrison. Two 4,600-foot double chairs and a beginning rope move skiers up the mountain. Day lodge has cafeteria, ski shop with equipment rental, and ski school. Open 6 days, 5 nights; closed Monday. Nov.–Apr. Overnight accommodations in Burley.

Schweitzer Ski Basin, 11 miles northwest of Sandpoint off US 95-US 2. Has an 7,500-skiers-per-hour-capacity. Seven chairlifts and 1 T-bar move skiers uphill into 2 huge bowls, Schweitzer and Colburn. Almost 40 runs and trails up to 3 miles long. The Lodge, the Outback Inn, and the Powder House serve food and beverages. The Bierstube in the Lodge is a popular after-ski stop. Ski shop and equipment rental in the Alpine Shop at Lodge. Ski school. Open daily late Nov.–mid-Apr.

Silverhorn, 6 miles south of Kellogg off I–90, has 14 major runs which lace Silverhorn's twin peaks, providing deep powder as well as packed powder skiing through wooded and open terrain. Runs range from Stemwinder's 2-mile tour and the winding, gentle Success to free-fall skiing down the Last Chance. A mile-long double chairlift with 2 loading points. Nursery service available. Ski shop, complete with rentals and repair service. *Bierstube,* cafeteria, lounge, ski school. Flanking the lodge are 18 electrical hookups for recreation vehicles. Open Wed. thru Sun. and holidays, Nov.–Apr. Overnight accommodations in Kellogg, Osburn, Wallace and Coeur d'Alene.

Skyline, 15 miles southeast of Pocatello at I–15 Inkom Exit. Great for downhill skiers; with a 1,650-foot vertical drop in its 5,000-foot length. Ten open slopes and 4 trails. Day lodge at the 6,700-foot level on Mt. Bonneville. Food, lounge, ski school, ski shop. Open Tue. thru Sun. Dec.–May. Overnight accommodations in Pocatello.

Snowhaven, 7 miles south of Grangeville (US 95). Local area, with gentle slopes, serving residents of the Camas Prairie. Emphasis on instruction for beginning and intermediate skiers. Four open slopes and 2 trails. Lunch, no rentals, ski school for beginners only. Open Wed., weekends, and holidays Dec. 20–Apr. 1. Overnight accommodations in Grangeville.

Soldier Mountain, 11 miles north of Fairfield. Excellent skiing from late Nov. thru April on the open slopes of the 10,000-foot mountain. More than a dozen packed and powder runs. Day lodge, cafeteria, beer, wine, pizza; equipment rental, ski school. Open Wed., thru Sun. and holidays.

Tamarack, 17 miles northeast of Moscow (US 95); 5 miles north of Troy (Idaho 8). Novice, intermediate, and advanced runs on 2 open slopes and 2 trails serviced by 2 surface lifts. Day lodge, snack bar, equipment rental, ski school, crosscountry. Overnight accommodations at Troy or Moscow.

Taylor Mountain, 13 miles southeast of Idaho Falls, has 6 open slopes and 12 trails. Longest run is 3,500 feet, with 750 feet of vertical drop. Day and night skiing, 6 days and nights. Day lodge, snack bar, lounge, ski school, equipment rental. Overnight accommodations in Idaho Falls and Ammon.

Tours. For information on tour operators serving the ski areas and on prices for tours and lodging, write Idaho Travel Council, Statehouse, Boise, ID 83720 (1–800–635–7820) for a copy of "The Idaho Ski & Winter Sports Directory."

SPECTATOR SPORTS. Rodeos are scheduled throughout summer and early fall, providing excitement for many. (See *Seasonal Events.*) Many colleges as well as the university of Idaho and Idaho State University field football, basketball, baseball, and track teams, along with teams in other sports, with women moving forward strongly in the area of athletics. Boise State College attracts large crowds with its always-formidable football teams. Motorcycle and drag races are held throughout the state. Blackfoot has a Sportsman's Speedway, Boise a Firebird Speedway (as well as Owyhee Motorcycle Races at Peaceful Cove), Lewiston a Banana Belt Speedway, and Meridian a Meridian Speedway. There is parimutuel horse racing April through May at Coeur d'Alene, May thru Labor Day at Boise, May thru Sept. at Pocatello, in July at Jerome, and at Rupert in Sept. Logging contests are staged at Prichard, Deary, St. Maries, Elk City, and Orofino. Then there are snowmobile races in Feb. at Dixie, Ashton, Island Park, and Stanley; dog sled races at Priest Lake in Jan. and McCall and Island Park in March; river raft races at Prichard in May; canoe races at Emmett in July; yacht races at Bayview in July; sailboat racing at McCall in Aug. and Sept.; power boat racing at Burley in July; and porcupine races in Council on the 4th of July.

SHOPPING. The visitor will find interesting craft and gift shops scattered around Idaho, especially at or near major resort areas. Antique hunters will do best at second-hand stores and auction houses in smaller communities. There is no concentration of population to support a metropolitan range of specialty shops, but most Idaho cities offer an adequate selection. Best buys: Western styles. (Caution: Check labels. As in every other state, some "native" products are actually from Japan, Taiwan, and South Korea.)

In Boise, popular general stores are The Bon, 918 W. Idaho (344–5521) and Falk's Idaho Dept. Store, 10533 Overland (376–9372). The style-conscious might try Mode Ltd., 802 W. Idaho (342–4551). Unusual shops include Hobby Horse Antiques and Crafts, 231 Warm Springs Ave. (343–6005); Scientific Wizardry, 9019 Fairview (376–0027); L & L Shirt Shop, 5615 Fairview (376–8881); Brown's Galleries, 1115 Boise (342–6661); and Orient East, 113 N. 11th (344–6232).

In Idaho Falls, Marketplace Books & Art has a good display of Idaho arts and handcrafts at 431 Park Ave. (523–7717), and Country Store Boutique, Hwy. 26 & Crowley Rd. (522–8450), is a cornucopia of antiques and collectibles. Karcher's Mall Nampa, (466–9276), boasts Idaho's largest shopping centers, 60 stores, including fine restaurants.

CHILDREN'S ACTIVITIES. In a state abounding with lakes, streams, woodland trails, ghost towns, deer, old barns, picturesque farmsteads, and charming fences, children will find activity or interest nearly every time the family car pauses. In addition, public parks in Blackfoot, Boise, Caldwell, Coeur d'Alene, Idaho Falls, Pocatello, and other major cities provide playgrounds and pools. There are zoos at Boise, Idaho Falls, and Pocatello, and amusement rides in the parks at Boise, Coeur d'Alene, and Idaho Falls. Children are fascinated by the miniature power station at Trenner Memorial Park at American Falls. Then, of course, there are the county fairs (which always have a lot of things for children), rodeos, horse shows, and Indian festivals, as well as fun theaters popping up here and there. Square dancing, which delights many youngsters, seems to be going on all over the state all the time. Sun Valley is a children's paradise. At Macks Inn, in eastern Idaho's legendary Mountain Man country, the Island Park Music Circus has Mon. thru Sat. performances from mid-June thru Labor Day. Pierre's Summer Playhouse, at Victor, stages "old-fashioned melodramas" Thur. thru Sat., July thru Labor Day—and any one of those ought to send the kids into titters and screams. Finally, there are the magnificent backpacking and trail pack trips deep into the wilderness, where the children come close to nature and, with reasonable luck, will see a variety of wildlife.

MUSEUMS AND GALLERIES. Most of Idaho's museums and galleries in the larger towns are open daily in the summer, from 9 A.M. to 5 P.M., and most are free. In the smaller towns, schedules are often erratic and few museums have telephones.

Historical. *American Falls:* Massacre Rocks State Park, Visitors Center, American Falls, ID 83213, *Arco:* Craters of the Moon National Monument, Visitors Center, Arco, ID 83213. *Athol:* Henley Air Museum, Athol, ID 83801. *Blackfoot:* Bingham County Historical Museum, 190 North Shilling, Blackfoot, ID 83221. *Boise:* Boise Gallery of Art, 670 Julia Davis Drive, Boise, ID 83701; Idaho State Historical Museum, 610 North Julia Davis Drive, Boise, ID 83702 (208–334–2120); Old Idaho Penitentiary, 2445 Old Pen Road, Boise, ID 83702 (208–334–2844); Idaho Transportation Museum, Old Idaho Penitentiary, 2445 Old Pen Road, Boise, ID 83702. *Caldwell:* Orma J. Smith Museum of Natural History, Boone Science Building, College of Idaho, Caldwell, ID 83605; Blanche and David Rosendahl Gallery of Art, Blatchley Hall, College of Idaho, Caldwell, ID 83605; Odd Fellows Historical Building, 920 Grant St., Caldwell, ID 83605; Van Slyke Agricultural Display, Caldwell City Park, Caldwell, ID 83605.

Cambridge: Cambridge City Museum, Cambridge, ID 83610. *Cataldo:* Coeur d'Alene Mission of the Sacred Heart, Box 135, Cataldo, ID 83810. *Clayton:* Custer Museum, mountain man country artifacts, c/o Yankee Fork Ranger Station, Clayton, ID 83227. *Coeur d'Alene:* Fort Sherman Museum, Box 812, Coeur d'Alene, ID 83814 (208–667–3448); Museum of North Idaho, 115 Northwest Blvd., Coeur d'Alene, ID 83814. *Cottonwood:* Idaho County Farm Museum, Cottonwood, ID 83522; St. Gertrude's Museum. Open by appointment, (208–962–7123 or 962–3224). *Custer:* Custer Museum (May thru August), c/o Yankee Fork Ranger District, Clayton, ID 83277. *Donnelly:* Long Valley Museum, Roseberry Townsite, 1½ miles east of Donnelly, 3rd Sunday of May thru 3rd Sunday of Sept. *Dubois:* Heritage Hall Community Museum, Cubois, ID 83423. *Franklin:* Pioneer Relic Hall, Franklin, ID 83237. *Glenns Ferry:* Three Island Crossing State Park Visitors Center, Box 609, Glenns Ferry, ID 83623.

Grangeville: Idaho County Historical Museum, Rte. 1, Box 82, Grangeville, ID 83530. *Hailey:* Blaine County Historical Museum, Box 115, Hailey, ID 83333. *Idaho City:* Boise Basin Historical Museum, 501 Montgomery Street, Idaho City, ID 83631. *Kamiah:* First Presbyterian Church of East Kamiah, Kamiah, ID 83536. *Lava Hot Springs:* Lava Hot Springs Historical Center, Tourist Information Office, Box 387, Lava Hot Springs, ID 83426. *Lewiston:* Lewis-Clark State College Museum, Dr. H.L. Talkington Collection, Lewiston,

ID 83501; Nez Percé County Historical Museum, Third and C Streets, Lewiston, ID 83501 (208–743–2535). *Malad:* Oneida County Relic Room, 270 West 500 North, Malad, ID 83252.

Montpelier: Relic Hall, 420 Clay Street, Montpelier, ID 83254. *Moscow:* Apaloosa Horse Museum, Moscow-Pullman Highway, Box 8403, Moscow, ID 83843; Latah County Historical Society, 110 South Adams, Moscow, ID 83483, (208–882–1004); University Museum, Faculty Office Complex—W, University of Idaho, Moscow, ID 83843 (208–885–6480). *Mountain Home:* Elmore County Historical Foundation, 885 North 10th East, Mountain Home, ID 83647. *Mullan:* Mullan Historical Society, IOOF Hall, Mullan, ID 83486. *Murphy:* Owhyhee County Historical Complex Museum and Library, Murphy, ID 83650 (208–495–2319). *Nampa:* Canyon County Historical Society, 12th Avenue at Front Street South, Nampa, ID 83651 (208–467–7611). *Oakley:* Oakley Pioneer Museum, Main and Center Streets, Oakley, ID 83346. *Orofino:* Clearwater County Historical Society, 315 College Avenue, Orofino, ID 83544.

Payette: Payette County Historical Society Museum, 9th Street and 1st Avenue South, Payette, ID 83661. *Placerville:* Henrietta Penrod Museum, Placerville, ID 83666. *Pocatello:* Bannock County Historical Museum, Center and Garfield, Pocatello, ID 83201 (208–233–0434); Museum of Natural History, Idaho State University, Pocatello, ID 83209. *Rexburg:* Upper Snake River Valley Historical Society, College Avenue, Rexburg, ID 83440 (208–356–7030). *St. Anthony:* Fremont County Historical Society, 4 Village Square, Chester, ID 83421. *Salmon:* Lemhi County Historical Museum, Salmon, ID 83467. *Sandpoint:* Bonner County Historical Society, Ontario and Ella Streets, Sandpoint, ID 83864 (208–263–2344). *Silver City:* Old Schoolhouse Museum, open from June 1 to Oct. 1, Silver City, ID 83650. *Soda Springs:* Caribou County Historical Society, County Courthouse, Soda Springs, ID 83276. *Spalding:* Nez Perce Historical Park Visitor Center, US Highway 95, Spalding, ID 83551 (208–843–2261).

Stanley: Stanley Museum, Box 70, Stanley, ID 83278. *Sun Valley:* Sun Valley Center, Box 656, Sun Valley, ID 83353 (208–622–9371). Troy: Troy Museum and Visitor Center, Troy, ID 83871. *Twin Falls:* The Herrett Museum, College of Southern Idaho, Box 1238, Twin Falls, ID 83301, (208–733–9554–ext. 356); Twin Falls County Historical Society, 542 Addison West, Twin Falls, ID 83301 (208–734–7358). *Wallace:* Coeur d'Alene District Mining Museum, 509 Bank Street, Wallace, ID 83873 (208–753–7151). *Wiser:* Intermountain Cultural Center and Museum, Hooker Hall, Paddock Lane, Box 307, Weiser, ID 83672. *Winchester:* West Lewis County Museum, R.R. 2, Culdesac, ID 83524 (208–924–7773). Many of Idaho's ghost towns are living museums. Among them are Murray, Florence, Bonanza, Custer, Warren, Silver City, Rocky Bar, Atlanta, Shoup, Gibbonsville, Leesburg, Blackbird, Yellowjacket, Roosevelt City, Thunder City, Bullion, Vienna, Sawtooth City, Galena, Eagle City, Moose City, Nicolia, Mount Idaho, and Springtown. Many of the old mining towns are still inhabited, though sparsely, so please respect private property and the rights of others when you come a-visiting.

Religious. There are also a number of religious shrines of strong tourist interest. These include: in Boise, Christ Chapel, St. John's Roman Catholic Cathedral, Latter Day Saint (L.D.S.) Temple, Jewish Synagogue. Idaho City, St. Joseph's Church. Paris, L.D.S. Tabernacle. Idaho Falls, L.D.S. Temple. Rexburg, L.D.S. Tabernacle.

Art. Boise, Boise Gallery of Art, in Julia Davis Park, is the finest in state. Pocatello, Idaho State University Art Gallery, Fine Arts Building, University Campus, displays works of regional artists. Twin Falls, Herrett Arts & Science Center, East Five Points & Kimberly Rd., is focal point of Snake River Valley artists.

Special Interest. Craters of the Moon National Monument, south of Arco, has exhibits explaining the volcanic features, flora and fauna of the area. Boise, Idaho Wild Birds, Science Building, Boise State College. Idaho Falls, Intermountain Science Experience Center. Massacre Rocks, 20 miles southwest of American Falls, has a museum containing displays of fossils and Indian objects. Pollock, Little Canyon River Museum, has exhibits on natural history of area. Shoshone, Shoshone Ice Caves Museum. Stanley, Visitor Center, off Idaho 75, at Redfish Lake, in Sawtooth National Forest, contains exhibits of the flora, fauna, geology, and history of area. Wallace, Coeur d'Alene Mining Museum, has displays of mining equipment and models of famous mines of the area. Caldwell, Van Slyke Agricultural Display in City Park has earth-working implements of white society here going back more than a century. Cottonwood, Idaho County Farm Museum is history of white agriculture in back-country Idaho.

HISTORIC SITES. Many of Idaho's historic sites parallel the trails of history through the state—the *Oregon Trail* in the south, *Lewis and Clark Route* in the north-central section, and *Mullan Road* in the panhandle. The visitor may retrace these famous routes on modern highways, guided by the state's fine graphic historical-sign program.

In the north, along US 10, I–90, the visitor should pause at Cataldo, between Kellogg and Coeur d'Alene, to see the *Mission of the Sacred Heart,* oldest building in Idaho. Construction of this church began in 1846, after the black-robed Jesuits abandoned an earlier mission, founded in 1842 on the shores of Lake Coeur d'Alene. "The Old Mission," as the Cataldo structure is called, is honored by an annual pilgrimage. A few miles west, and just a short walk from the highway, is the stump of the tree blazed with his name by wagonroad-builder Capt. John Mullan on July 4, 1861, which gives the *Fourth of July Canyon* its name. Eighteen miles east of Sandpoint, and near the village of Hope (Idaho 200) and on the shore of Lake Pend Oreille, is the site of *Kullyspell House,* built in 1809 by David Thompson, who opened Idaho's fur trade by constructing the post.

Lewiston, at the junction of US 12 and US 95, was the site of the *first capital of Idaho Territory* in 1863. Only a marker indicates the location. *Luna House Museum,* one of the oldest residences in north Idaho, is a rich repository of Indian artifacts. *Old Fort Lapwai,* at Lapwai, near Lewiston, is one of the sites in *Nez Percé National Park,* the first decentralized park in the nation. Open 8–4:30 weekdays, 9:30–6 weekends in winter. Open daily 8–4:30 in summer. Closed Thanksgiving, Christmas, and New Year's. Other historical sites in the area are the *Craig Donation Land Claim,* five miles south, along US 95, and *St. Joseph's Mission,* 14 miles southeast.

In 1840, a veteran mountain man, Col. William Craig, of Greenbrier, Virginia, beat his way west, until he came to the confluence of the Snake and Clearwater rivers. He liked what he saw and built a good home a few miles from the Spaldings. So he became the first settler and homesteader in Idaho and received the earliest title for a land patent issued. The nearby town of Craigmont was named for him.

Spalding Memorial Park, 11 miles east of Lewiston, is the site of the second mission built by the Rev. Henry Harman Spalding and his wife, Eliza, the first missionaries in what is now Idaho. They came in 1836 with famed Dr. Marcus Whitman (see chapter on *Washington*). The Spaldings built the first church, school, and mills in what is now Idaho and set up the first printing press. Sent originally from Boston to Honolulu, the press arrived at Ft. Vancouver (across the Columbia from present Portland) in 1839 and was delivered to Spalding at Lapwai Mission. There it was set up, and that same year of 1839 the first book was run off, a Nez Percé primer. The memorial park contains the site of the original Nez Percé Indian Agency and the graves of the Spaldings, as well as monuments to them. The memorial park is also the headquarters of the Nez Percé National Historical Park.

Each section of the national historical park reflects in its own unique way the prewhite culture of the Nez Percé people and the emergence of white domination following the Lewis and Clark expedition. *Visitor centers* at *Spalding, East Kamiah* (US 12) and *White Bird Battlefield* present interpretive displays to reveal the influences significant in the molding of this part of the great Pacific Northwest.

Pierce, in 1860 the *scene of the first significant gold discovery in Idaho,* an event that had the most far-reaching effects, including the creation of Idaho as a state, is 80 miles east of Lewiston, reached by US 12 and Idaho 11. Mementoes of the glory days of the 1860s remain.

Eight miles south of Cottonwood in Grave Creek Canyon is *Weis Rockshelter,* in Nez Percé Land, where excavations have found human occupation dating back 8,000 years.

US 12 parallels the *Lewis and Clark trek from Lewiston to Lolo Pass,* on the Montana border. To the north is the perilous Lolo Indian Trail, which put the elkskin explorers to their severest test. *Visitors' Center,* at Lolo Pass, has graphic displays about this portion of the Lewis and Clark trail.

Grangeville, 65 miles below Lewiston, on US 95, was the jumping-off point to many mining communities. *Mt. Idaho,* a few miles southeast, hosted the state's first Republican convention and boasted a hotel. The population is now 75. *Elk City,* 45 miles east of Mt. Idaho, and also on Idaho 14, was a booming gold town, with miners thronging the creeks, ravines, and streets. Today the settlement has fewer than 500 people, and there is more interest in farming than in mining. *Dixie* and *Orogrande,* also born in the gold boom of 1861, are practically ghost towns now, each with a population of about ten. Both are reached by gravel roads from Elk City.

White Bird Battlefield Area, 15 miles south of Grangeville, along US 95, is the site of the first battle of the Nez Percé War.

Six miles northwest of Parma (US 95, 20, and 26) is the site of *Ft. Boise,* established in 1834 as a trading post and later prominent in the annals of Oregon Trail emigrants.

In Caldwell, *Memorial Park* has a pioneer cabin.

In Boise, the *O'Farrell Cabin,* between 5th and 6th on Fort St., is the city's best-known pioneer building. A *pioneer log cabin* stands in Boise's Julia Davis Park.

Idaho City (Idaho 21), 40 miles north of Boise, was the state's biggest *gold-rush* town. In the 1860s it had a population of 40,000 and was the capital of Idaho Territory. It boasts many state firsts, including publication of the first newspaper. The population today is only about 300. Pioneer buildings and miles of dredges remain. Near Idaho City are the *gold ghost towns* of Centerville, Placerville, and Pioneerville, reached by slow, but not exasperating, gravel and dirt roads.

Custer, 24 miles northeast of Stanley (11-mile dirt road from Sunbeam, on Idaho 75), is a shadow of its past as a febrile *gold-mining town.* A tintype of a century gone, as reflected in its rustic museum.

Settlers Cave, on a gravel road southeast of Bruneau (21 miles south of Mountain Home), contains several rooms hollowed from a hardclay hillside by settlers as a retreat from unfriendly Indians.

The *California Land Trailmark,* where the California Trail and a branch of the Oregon Trail divided, is at the Silent City of Rocks, southeast of Oakley (Idaho 27).

A replica of *Ft. Hall,* built in 1834, stands in Pocatello. The original site of Ft. Hall was 11 miles west of the present town of Ft. Hall, which is 10 miles north of Pocatello.

In 1860 a band of Mormons, looking for land to call home and under the impression that they were still within the boundaries of Utah, established the *first agricultural settlement* in Idaho, at Franklin (US 91). The town, regarded as Idaho's oldest, has a pioneer flavor even now.

Pierre's Hole, south of Diggs, was a famous rendezvous of the Mountain Men. It was on the direct road from Jackson Hole, Wyoming, to the Snake River. Through here passed Capt. Bonneville, Nathaniel Wyeth, William Sublette, and a host of other figures famous in Western exploration.

Salmon has history all around it. To the north is the pass where the Nez Percé, led by Chief Joseph, crossed the Continental Divide as they fled pursuing soldiers. Fourteen miles south of Salmon, on Idaho 28, is the *Sacajawea Monument,* marking (approximately) the birthplace of the only woman with the Lewis and Clark party. Six miles below the monument is the village of Tendoy. Ten miles east, on a gravel and dirt road, at Lemhi Pass, is *where Lewis and Clark crossed the Continental Divide* in 1805. Just northwest of Tendoy is the site of *Ft. Lemhi,* a Mormon community established in the 1850s. Two years later, after a grasshopper plague and Indian attacks, the Mormon missionaries were recalled to Utah, putting an end to the colony.

One of the most interesting historical sections of the state is in the southeast, where a tide of gold seekers flooded the Owyhee hills in the 1860s. After the precious metals ran out, or the miners thought they did, or they became too expensive to extract, the miners left, and towns they had populated and frenzied stayed behind, empty and silent. From the top of 8,065-foot War Eagle Mountain, the scene is a panorama. Silver City, at 6,719 feet, is the most unblemished ghost town in the state and has the best representation of the past, though mining has started up again. Other ghost towns in the area are not as large and picturesque, but all are fascinating.

For a list of historical landmarks by town, write: Idaho Travel Council. (See *Tourist Information Services.*)

STAGE AND REVUES. As in every other state, dramatic groups are springing up all over Idaho. Not since the W.P.A. in the Great Depression of the 1930s has there been such a renaissance. Most of the new groups border on the ephemeral, and some are so intimate that only their small circles of friends know them. But, wherever they have sprouted and however long they last, they are adding more strands of culture to the state.

Any place you go in Idaho you may come across the ubiquitous Antique Festival Theatre. Antique plays anywhere–performing in American Legion and Grange halls, state parks, football fields, barns, ranchhouses.

Boise, as to be expected, has the largest number of theatrical groups, including those at or emanating from Boise State College, the cultural pillar and wellspring of the city. Boise Little Theatre, performing in a unique 24-sided building, is a self-supporting community theater that puts on a wide variety of plays. From early July to mid-August, Boise stages a Shakespeare Festival at the Plantation Golf Course. Unique in the state is the Idaho Theater For Youth.

The Coeur d'Alene Summer Theatre Carousel Players bring musical repertory to north Idaho. The season runs from June into September, except Mondays. The University of Idaho Summer Theatre in the Kiva, at Moscow, produces several shows over the summer (late June thru July, Tue. thru Fri.), each playing for several nights. The Lewiston Civic Theatre starts its season in September and runs until the last week of May, with a broad program of presentations. Lewis-Clark State College, also in Lewiston, has a summer theater schedule. Valley Dramatists, a Nampa-Caldwell community group, stages fall plays, usually melodramas, at the Nampa High School Little Theater. Fairyland Park Marionette Theater, in Jerome, is unique in its casting; the actors are not local talent but are manufactured by local talent. The group has been presenting summer marionette shows since 1967. Theater groups from around the state show their stuff at the Idaho City Arts Festival, 1st weekend in August. The Magic Valley Dilettantes have produced a musical comedy in Twin Falls annually since 1958. The Magic Valley Little Theatre, also in Twin Falls, is devoted to legitimate drama. College of Southern Idaho, also in Twin Falls, has a variety of dramatic entertainment, including the Summer Mummers, a training program for Magic Valley High School students. Theatre I.S.U. at Idaho State University, in Pocatello, presents comedies in its summer season, and in the fall and winter turns to more-serious drama. At Salmon, the Salmon River Playhouse offers comedy, drama and melodrama June thru Aug. for evening entertainment. Pierre's Summer Playhouse, in Victor, whoops it up with summer melodrama and there is more melodrama at Pierre's Hole Rendezvous, in Driggs, the first week of August. Island Park Music Circus, at Macks Inn, stages musicals from mid-June thru Labor Day. Harrison has a boisterous theater revue in late July; Preston, a theater festival in mid-August.

Not exactly a stage show or revue, but certainly dramatic and theatrical, is the Coeur d'Alene Indian Pageant, "Feast of the Assumption" at Old Mission State Park at Cataldo.

LIQUOR LAWS. The legal age for consumption of alcoholic beverages is 19. Liquor can be obtained from state liquor stores or by the drink from 10 A.M. to 1 A.M. The sale of liquor is prohibited on Sundays, Memorial Day, Labor Day, until the polls close on Election Day, Thanksgiving, and Christmas.

NIGHTCLUBS. Except for Boise and the college towns, such as Moscow and Idaho Falls, night life in much of Idaho tends to be loud and lively. There are some communities where casual conviviality seems to be the principal industry. Like wildflowers, many nightclubs appear to jump out of nowhere and disappear as quickly.

BOISE. *Red Lion Inn/Downtowner,* 1800 Fairview Ave. (344–7691), draws patrons to its lounge with a congenial atmosphere and live entertainment. *Iron Gate Lounge* of Ramada Inn, 2360 University Dr. (345–7170), attracts a young, bright clientele with its crisp entertainment. *Ranch Club,* 3544 Chinden Blvd. (342–9546), has dancing to live music Mon. thru Sat. Live entertainment nightly in *The Gamekeeper* of the Owyhee Plaza Hotel, 11th and Main (343–4611), downtown. "Happy Hour" Mon. thru Fri. Holiday-Inn Airport, I–80 and Vista Ave. (344–8365), draws more than travelers with its live entertainment nightly in its *Rusty Harpoon Lounge. Peter Schotts,* in Idanha Hotel, 10th and Main (336–9100), draws with live music. Basque songs and dances and Pyrenees ardor are joyfully evident at *Basque Center,* 601 Grove (432–9983). *Fats,* 1124 Front St. (342–9663), is a favorite with young adults.

COEUR D'ALENE: *The Hop,* French Gulch Road (664–3221), relies heavily on well-deserved word-of-mouth praise for trade. Western buffs make for the *Iron Horse,* 404 Sherman (667–7314), a downtown supper club for live country music. North Shore Resort Hotel, 115 S. 2nd, features *Cloud 9* (664–9421), Idaho's only rooftop lounge, with dancing and exciting live entertainment.

IDAHO FALLS: *Matador Lounge,* 840 Northgate Mile (525–9976), is a popular night-out spot for valley folks.

MOSCOW: Professors and students from the University of Idaho mix with wheat farmers, lumbermen, and businessmen to relax jovially at the *Rathskeller Inn,* 101 E. Palouse River Dr. (882–0378).

POCATELLO: *Peg Leg Annie's Lounge* in Cotton Tree Inn, 1415 Bench Rd. (237–7650) has a colorful and relaxed atmosphere.

SANDPOINT: *Cow Girl Corral,* 200 Ponderay Hwy. (263–5193) is alive nightly with country music.

TWIN FALLS: *Holiday Inn,* 1350 Blue Lakes Blvd. (733–0650) offers live entertainment in its lounge. *The Alley,* 1241 4th Ave. S. (733–4613) has live music nightly except Mon.

WORLEY: *Leo's Worley Club* (686–1223) offers live entertainment on weekends, dancing from 8:30 P.M.–12:30 A.M. each Fri. and Sat.

BARS. A Boise favorite is *The Gamekeeper* in the Owyhee Plaza Hotel, 11th and Main (343–4611), downtown. *Art's Rosebud Tavern,* 3931 W. State (342–9093), is one place the locals bring their out-of-town friends to for fun and relaxation. *Desert Edge Tavern,* 4000 Federal Way (344–7559) and *Tom Grainey's Sporting Pub,* 109 S. 6th (345–2505), are great for local folk color. *Hannah's,* 621 Main (345–7557), and *Mort's Bar,* 1413 W. Idaho (342–9402), have the imprint of down-to-earth Boise venacular. In Coeur d'Alene there's always a fresh breeze at *Cedars Floating* Restaurant, Blackwell Island (664–2922). Also in Coeur d'Alene, *North Shore Resort Hotel,* 115 S. 2nd (664–9241), has a lake view. *Seagull Inn* boasts of its roasted chicken, Friday fish fry and fee pool at 816 N. 4th (664–8815). In American Falls, *Star Dust Lounge,* 180 Harrison (226–5272), is a homey place for city folks and farmers. In smaller towns, the bar is sometimes the cultural center, especially for loggers, miners, and farmers. Some examples: *First and Last Chance Beer Parlor* (775–4169) in Post Falls; *Grub Stake Cafe,* Hwy 55 (793–2333) in Horseshoe Bend, is the frontier all gussied up; at *The Pub,* 1601 Hwy. 30 (678–9906), in Burley, cold beer is washed down with small-town humor and folklore; *Linger Longer Bar* (623–2211) at Spirit Lake, jumps with live music on Fri. and Sat. nights. *Johnny's Bar* (784–9321), at Smelterville, is popular with hard-rock miners.

MONTANA

Riches in the Hills

by
CURTIS CASEWIT

Curtis Casewit is a member of the Travel Writers Guild and a specialist in travel writing on the U.S. West.

The Yellowstone River has been the dominant highway of the region for years. Captain William Clark followed it on his way back from the Pacific, and generations of Montanans have looked to it for protection, direction, and a sometimes reliable drink for man, cow, or crop.

From Glendive down I–94 to Miles City, you pass a number of streams flowing northward into the Yellowstone. There's the town of Fallon near O'Fallon Creek, named for Clark's nephew, and Terry, named for General Alfred H. Terry who was Custer's commander. Then comes the Powder River, so named because it often is dried up and dusty. The 91st Division in World War I immortalized the cry, "Powder River, Let 'er Buck." Along the Powder and through all this country were the really big cattle spreads like the LO, Niobrara, Rafter Circle, Diamond Bar, and XIT. Their successors are still there, and water is still their lifeblood.

The Tongue River forks into the Yellowstone at Miles City. Clark camped on its banks in 1806, and Fort Keogh was established here in

1877, the year after Custer's fall. Keogh was a captain who died with him. From Fort Keogh, General Nelson Miles ranged out after the Custer debacle eventually to defeat the Indians.

In Miles' honor, the civilian shacks near the fort took his name, and the settlement grew into a great cowtown. After the Indian wars, it became a northern terminus for longhorn drives up from Texas. Beneath these cottonwoods, that Western tradition is still alive. At the stock yard or on Main Street, Stetsons and sharp-toed boots are part of a Montanan's everyday wardrobe.

Miles City was the home of frontier photographer L. A. Huffman Coffrin. Old West Gallery, the Red Rocks Inn, and Range Riders Museum (west of the city) have good collections of his work as well as range and Indian memorabilia. The U.S. Livestock Experiment Station is at the western city limits.

Fort Peck and the Missouri

Miles City and Glendive offer you the most convenient takeoff for a roundtrip to the north to see Fort Peck Dam and the Missouri River, where Lewis and Clark first entered Montana.

Fort Union, one of the three or four important forts of the trapper's West, stood where the Missouri and Yellowstone Rivers join northeast of Sidney, a center of irrigated sugarbeet farming and extensive oil and coal fields. Fort Union is restored as a national historic site, and has a museum.

On US 2, "The Hi-Line" westward to Fort Peck Dam, you pass Culbertson, named for an old fur trapper. Its economy now is based on wheat, some cattle—although beef ranching is not extensive north of the Missouri—and a new plant to crush oil from safflower seeds. If you have time, drive north of Culbertson to the area of Froid and Medicine Lake where you will see the best examples of the extensive, highly mechanized wheat farming which characterizes this section of Montana. Note the strips of alternately plowed and planted land, widely adopted after the dust storms of the Depression 30's. Alternate planting conserves moisture in the non-planted strip, while the planted strip forms a break to slow wind erosion. The zebra-striped land pattern extends across northern Montana to the mountains.

On US 2, west of Culbertson, you will pass Poplar, headquarters of the Fort Peck Indian Reservation. The agency, as Indian reservation headquarters is called, was set up here in 1876, and it was on this site that Sitting Bull finally surrendered. The Indians are remnants of the Assiniboine tribes who lived in the vicinity when Lewis and Clark first arrived. The reservation is one of seven in the state.

Soon you reach Wolf Point, a former fueling station for steamboats. Now a county seat, Wolf Point gets its name from its early reputation as a hunting spot for wolves. Its Wild Horse Stampede in July is one of the toughest rodeos in the nation.

Fort Peck Lake, 17 miles southeast of Glasgow, is formed by the waters of the Missouri River retained by one of the world's largest earthfill dams, 250 feet above the river surface. The lake is 180 miles long, with 1,600 miles of shoreline, most of which is surrounded by a wildlife refuge. Rock Creek State Recreation Area on the eastern shore and Hell Creek State Recreation Area on the south offer good camping and picnicking facilities, but inquire about road conditions. Drive south to I–94 either at Glendive or Miles City.

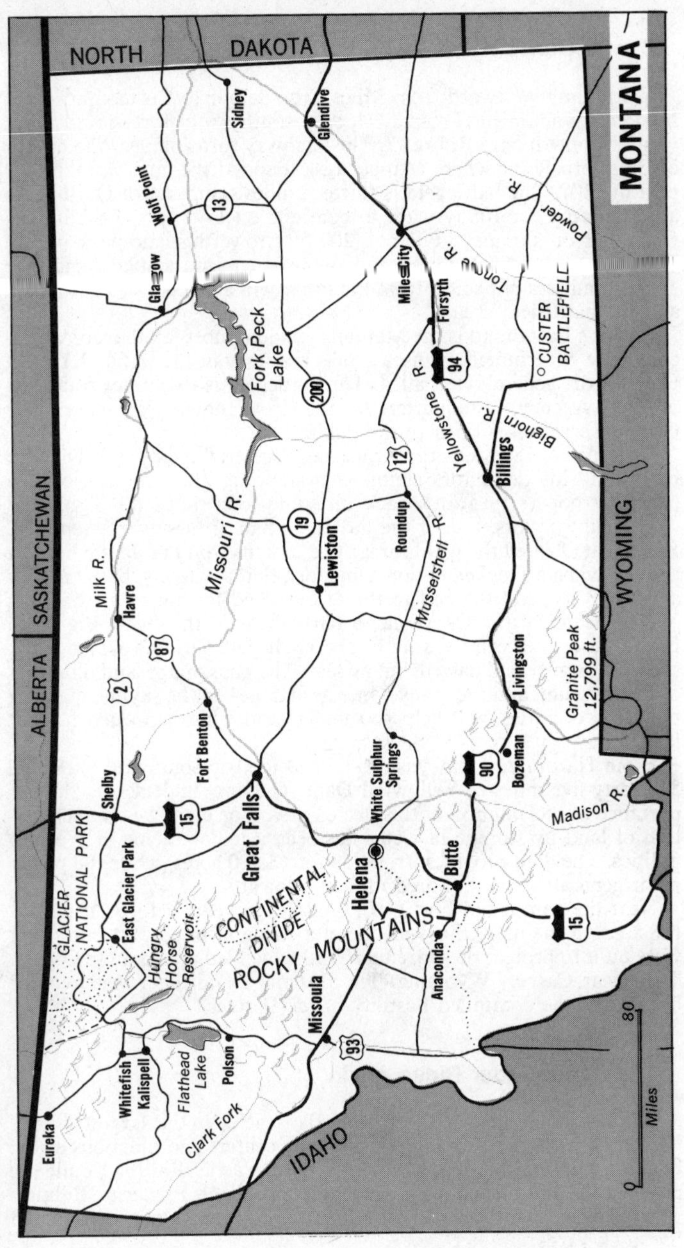
MONTANA
NORTH DAKOTA
SASKATCHEWAN
ALBERTA
WYOMING
IDAHO
Sidney
Glendive
Wolf Point
Glasgow
Miles City
Forsyth
CUSTER BATTLEFIELD
Powder R.
Tongue R.
Fork Peck Lake
Missouri R.
Milk R.
Havre
Yellowstone R.
Bighorn R.
Billings
Roundup
Lewiston
Musselshell R.
Livingston
Granite Peak 12,799 ft.
Bozeman
Madison R.
Fort Benton
Shelby
Great Falls
White Sulphur Springs
Helena
Butte
Anaconda
GLACIER NATIONAL PARK
East Glacier Park
Hungry Horse Reservoir
CONTINENTAL DIVIDE
ROCKY MOUNTAINS
Missoula
Whitefish
Kalispell
Flathead Lake
Polson
Clark Fork
Eureka
Miles
0
80
2
13
15
19
12
87
90
93
94
200

Custer Stood Here

Continuing westward from Miles City, detour to Custer Battlefield National Monument. From I–94, turn south about forty-seven miles west of Forsyth onto Route 47. This highway turns off near the mouth of Big Horn River where Manuel Lisa founded the first Montana fur post in 1807. The battlefield is thirteen miles southeast of Hardin. As an alternative, you may want to continue on I–94 to see the initials Clark left on Pompeys Pillar, a 200-foot towering landmark on the Yellowstone from which the Indians used to send smoke signals. A gravel road straight south from the Pillar will also take you to Hardin and the battlefield area.

Custer's Last Stand is the Montana incident most familiar to Americans. The government's museum tells the story of the ill-fated Yellow Hair, as the general was called. The battlefield is two miles southeast of Crow Agency, headquarters for the Crow Indian reservation. The Crow reservation is open to the public.

On June 25, 1876, George Armstrong Custer, flamboyant Civil War hero and—his detractors claim—a headstrong glory-seeker, led 225 cavalry troopers into an attack on some four thousand Sioux and Cheyenne warriors, one of the largest Indian armies ever assembled. His defeat affected the whole area. The Indians won that battle but lost the war when a shocked nation demanded that the Army, based mostly at Miles City, end the Indian threat once and for all. In 1915, Chief Yellow Hand of the Cheyenne, a participant in the Little Big Horn Battle, described seeing Custer just before he fell. Custer's eyes, he said, showed insanity and hatred, but no fear. The guns, maps, and dioramas of the museum, and the many white headstones on the skyline marking the areas of battle, will help you understand what happened on that fateful day.

From Hardin you may wish to take a side trip southwest on Route 313 forty-five miles to Yellowtail Dam. The dam underscores the importance of reclamation of this barren area. For many years, reclamation of land by storage of water has been a major theme in Western politics. The dam provides irrigation for 43,500 acres, while the power plant generates nine hundred million kilowatts.

Near the dam is old Fort C. F. Smith. Ten years before Custer put the area on the map, this was one of a string of important posts that were built to protect the Bozeman Trail which led up from the Oregon Trail near Casper, Wyoming. The Bozeman Trail later was avoided because of the continued hostility of the Indians.

The Range Rider Rides Again

Billings, northwest of the Custer Battlefield, is the largest city of Montana; it offers several major shopping centers and functions as the banking hub for the region. The Northern Pacific Railroad built the city in 1882 and named it in honor of its president, Frederick Billings. The area has sugarbeet and oil refineries, large shale oil deposits and livestock yards.

Among the Billings' sights is the statue of the Range Rider of the Yellowstone, William S. Hart, cowboy hero of silent movies. This is along Black Otter Trail, which follows the rim above the city to the north. Five miles from Billings, Pictograph Cave shelters the most important scratchings of prehistoric man on the Great Plains.

From Billings turn south on US 212 for a ride along the Beartooth Scenic Highway, which cuts through the western portion of Custer National Forest. If you have the time, call the U.S. Forest Service headquarters in Billings to get information on the many hiking, horseback, and camping possibilities. You will begin to climb sharply after passing the town of Red Lodge. You get to Beartooth Pass (elev. 10,940 ft.) passing alpine meadows, mountain lakes and viewing, off to the west, Granite Peak, Montana's highest at 12,799 feet. The road dips into Wyoming and Yellowstone Park. Here is an excellent opportunity to include this important national park in your tour of Montana. The mountains you spiral around on this trip are the Absaroka, from the Indian word other tribes gave to the Crows: Up-sa-rah-qu, or sharp people. Turn southeast and you will pass Red Lodge, one of Montana's top winter sports areas. In August there's an outstanding nine-day International Festival of Nations, and a summer ski racing camp.

Return to Montana from Yellowstone

You may return to our route swiftly from the Gardiner entrance toward Livingston on I–90. (Or cross the park to the West Yellowstone entrance where, incidentally, an airport receives scheduled service during the summer months.) If you take the Gardiner route (US 89), the area around Emigrant was the site of Yellowstone City, where gold was discovered in 1862.

Back to Livingston, named for a Northern Pacific official. This is a great fishing center. Drive west over Bozeman Pass into the Gallatin Valley, called Valley of the Flowers by the Indians. They weren't far wrong; this is one of the richest agricultural valleys in Montana. Bozeman Pass was the divide between mountain and plains Montana in the old days. East of the pass was Indian country, where white settlement proceeded with great risk; west was mountain country, where mining boomed and brought in trade and towns.

Bozeman, settled in 1864, was named for a frontiersman who founded that short-lived trail north from Wyoming. Today it's the home of Montana State University (with an enrollment of some 11,300 students), headquarters for the 1,700,000-acre Gallatin National Forest, and the center of purebred livestock, small grain farming and dairying. The college fieldhouse and the Museum of the Rockies on the southwest corner of the campus are worth a side trip. If you are interested in grain or cattle farming, the Montana Agricultural Experiment Station is one of the best in the country.

Bozeman is also headquarters for the Montana Wilderness Federation which every summer conducts numerous walking and riding trips for visitors into the remote wilds of the state.

Follow I–90 west from Bozeman to Three Forks. Just north of the town you'll find the Missouri River Headquarters State Park where three rivers meet: the Jefferson, the Madison, and the Gallatin. The waterways were named by Lewis and Clark for their bosses—the President and the Secretaries of State and Treasury—when they reached the forks in late July 1805 after their long struggle upriver. This juncture is the beginning of the Missouri River proper, which then flows east 2,500 miles to the Mississippi at St. Louis.

The Three Forks of the Missouri was a bloody battleground in the early days. Blackfoot Indians from the north, Crows from the east, Snakes from the south, and the Nez Percé and Flatheads from over the divide to the west, all converged on the forks at various times to fight over game or to discourage trappers. Manuel Lisa, aided by John Colter of the Lewis and Clark party, tried to build a post as early as 1810, but this was only one of many attempts that failed because of the Blackfeet.

One of Montana's leading natural attractions, Lewis and Clark Caverns State Park, is thirteen miles further west on your interstate route. This is a safe, underground limestone cavern where guided tours operate daily from May 1 through September 30. The 2-hour walk through this fantasia of stalactites and stalagmites fascinates children and is a refreshing change from Indians, cows, and history.

Turn south from the caverns on US 287. You are following the Madison River trout stream. The most important turnoff is at Ennis west to Virginia City. You can also travel south to the site of the 1959 earthquake on the shores of Hebegen Lake. The U.S. Forest Service has displays and campgrounds here. An 80-million-ton rockslide blocked the river, created Quake Lake, and killed at least twenty-eight people in one of the West's most dramatic natural disasters.

Williamsburg of the West

Now back to Virginia City, a boom town that has been carefully restored. Here you can recapture the feel of those post-Civil War gold rushes which first drew large numbers of people upriver and overland to the mountainous West.

Six prospectors fleeing from the Indians tried to change their luck in Alder Gulch on the Stinkingwater, now more decorously called the Ruby River. It was May 26, 1863. They discovered gold. Within a month, ten thousand people were sweating and snorting in the area. Within a year thirty-five thousand people were working within a ten-mile radius. In the months and years to come, $300 million in gold dust came out of this provincial gravel. Mining operations didn't end until 1937.

Virginia City was the territorial capital for ten years. Here the vigilantes took the law into their own hands after outlaws had murdered two hundred residents. More important, this was the first home for many of the families, businesses, churches, and lodges that later spread over Montana.

At Virginia City, the visitor will see many authentic details of the West's mining frontier, thanks to the late Charles Bovey and his wife, Sue. They have spent a fortune in restoring both Virginia City and neighboring Nevada City. A narrow-gauge railroad operates in the summer months to ferry tourists between the two cities and provide the chance to behold beautiful, untamed country. You can see wooden sidewalks, real saloons, good museums, an old assay office, a Wells Fargo office, and Boot Hill Cemetery—where six of the vigilantes' prey rest. Nearby is the original Robbers' Roost, where the gang of Henry Plummer, the sheriff who turned outlaw, lay in wait.

From Virginia City, rejoin the interstate route for a visit to Butte. Follow Route 287 west from Virginia City to Twin Bridges, drive south on Route 41 to Dillon. This is the site of Western Montana College and headquarters for the Beaverhead National Forest, one of the great hunting and fishing areas of the West. Join I–15 at Dillon and proceed north to Butte.

Bannack, a ghost town twenty miles to the west of Dillon on Route 278 is now a state park. The very first capital, it was also the first camp of any note: gold was struck here in 1862. Lewis and Clark pushed southward into this area from the Three Forks, and it was here that they decided to turn west to cross the Continental Divide. This is less developed than Virginia City, but quaint and quiet.

Butte—the Richest Hill on Earth

Butte was settled in 1864. First gold and then silver were discovered around Butte, but the big fortunes were made after 1870 in copper. The "war of the copper kings" dominated Montana politics for the next three decades.

From beneath these five square miles of bleak hilltop have come more than 20 billion pounds of copper. More than ten thousand miles of mine shafts run below Butte. The underground operations closed some years ago.

Today Butte is an industrial and distributing center, and an international Port of Entry. While you are there, be sure and visit the Old Town and the World Museum of Mining. The early-day displays on the 33-acre mine site will take you back to the frontier days of Montana.

Three big names in Montana history were the copper kings: Marcus Daly, William Andrews Clark, and F. Augustus Heinze. Clark eventually made the U.S. Senate in 1900 after a corrupt election that put Montana on the national political map. Daly, a founder of ACM, lost to Clark in his battle to have nearby Anaconda named capital over Helena, but nonetheless his company was the power in Montana for a half century. Heinze gave the other giants fits with his court cases. He eventually pulled out with $10.5 million, which he later lost in the Wall Street panic of 1907.

Anaconda Co. has produced the biggest share of the state's wealth in the form of copper, zinc, silver, and gold, as well as playing a dominant role in its lumber industry. Today it has diversified with an aluminum plant at Columbia Falls near the west entrance to Glacier Park.

Anaconda, practically a western suburb of Butte, was the site of the Anaconda Smelter, with its 585-foot smokestack, highest in the world. Marcus Daly was determined that Anaconda should be the queen city. The smelter is not currently operating.

Ghost Towns Galore

From Anaconda, drive north on I–90 through Warm Springs to Deer Lodge, one of the earliest mining camps but now the home of the state prison. Here is W. A. Clark's old mansion, at 311 Clark Street. Follow the interstate to Garrison, where you turn eastward on US 12 to climb over McDonald Pass to Helena, the state capital. (You slipped over to the west side of the Continental Divide north of Dillon; now you go back over it.) Just over the Divide you might enjoy Frontier Town's Old West Museum, restaurant, stockade, jail, store, chapel, and bar.

If you are enthusiastic about ghost towns, swing west from Anaconda on Route 10A to Philipsburg, a famous silver-mining center, East of Philipsburg is Granite, an old silver town. Between 1865 and 1913 it produced $32 million. Drive north from Philipsburg between the Flint Creek Range and the John Long Mountains to Drummond. You'll be back on the interstate and can turn east to pick up the route at Garrison, passing Gold Creek, scene of the very first Montana gold strike in 1850. It was developed by the Stuart brothers. Granville Stuart became a leader in mining and cattle and was later appointed Minister to Uruguay. If you should choose the direct route north from Butte to Helena, don't miss the Elkhorn ghost town, just south of Boulder on I–15. It is one of the best-preserved.

The State Capital

Helena got its start when some discouraged miners took their "last chance" in 1864 on what is now the main street of the city—and made a strike. The area subsequently produced $20 million in gold. It is said that by 1888 Helena had fifty millionaires and was the richest city per capita in the country.

The American Smelting and Refining Co. has a plant in East Helena, and the city is a prosperous distributing center for the surrounding Prickly Pear Valley. But the main business of Helena is government, and the trappings of politics are the real attraction. The state capitol is faced with Montana granite, topped by a copper dome, and adorned by Western artists, most notably the Russell masterpiece, *Lewis and Clark Meeting the Flatheads,* on the third floor. In front of the capitol is a statue of Thomas Francis Meagher, an Irish revolutionary of note who somehow harangued his way West to become an "acting" territorial governor of Montana. Amid great mystery, he eventually fell into the Missouri River at Fort Benton and presumably drowned. Some say the vigilantes pushed him.

Some Montanans from time to time bemoan what they consider a cultural lag. But the State Historical Museum, east of the capitol, takes second place to none. It has good dioramas covering the complete story of Montana, an excellent collection of Charles Russell's art, and a comprehensive gun collection. If you get Montana fever, ask to see a copy of the *Montana Magazine of Western History.* The museum offers an excellent research library, too. The Cathedral of St. Helena, replica of the Votive Church of Vienna, is worth seeing.

Politics remains important in Montana. When the legislature is in session, the town fills up with performers and spectators. There are company lobbyists, cattlemen from the plains, grain growers—both the conservatives and the more liberal Farmers Union agents—timbermen, the Butte and Great Falls labor leaders, conservationists and recreationists from the mountainous West, educators and students, plus the ever-watchful eyes of the railroads, oil, mining and trucking interests.

Helena has been the stomping ground for several great senators, including Thomas Walsh, the prosecutor of the Teapot Dome scandals; Burton K. Wheeler, FDR's isolationist opponent of the '30s; Mike Mansfield, former long-time Senate majority leader who came up from the Butte mines; and Jannette Rankin, the country's first congresswoman. If all this seems too political, reflect that Gary Cooper and Myrna Loy were born in the area.

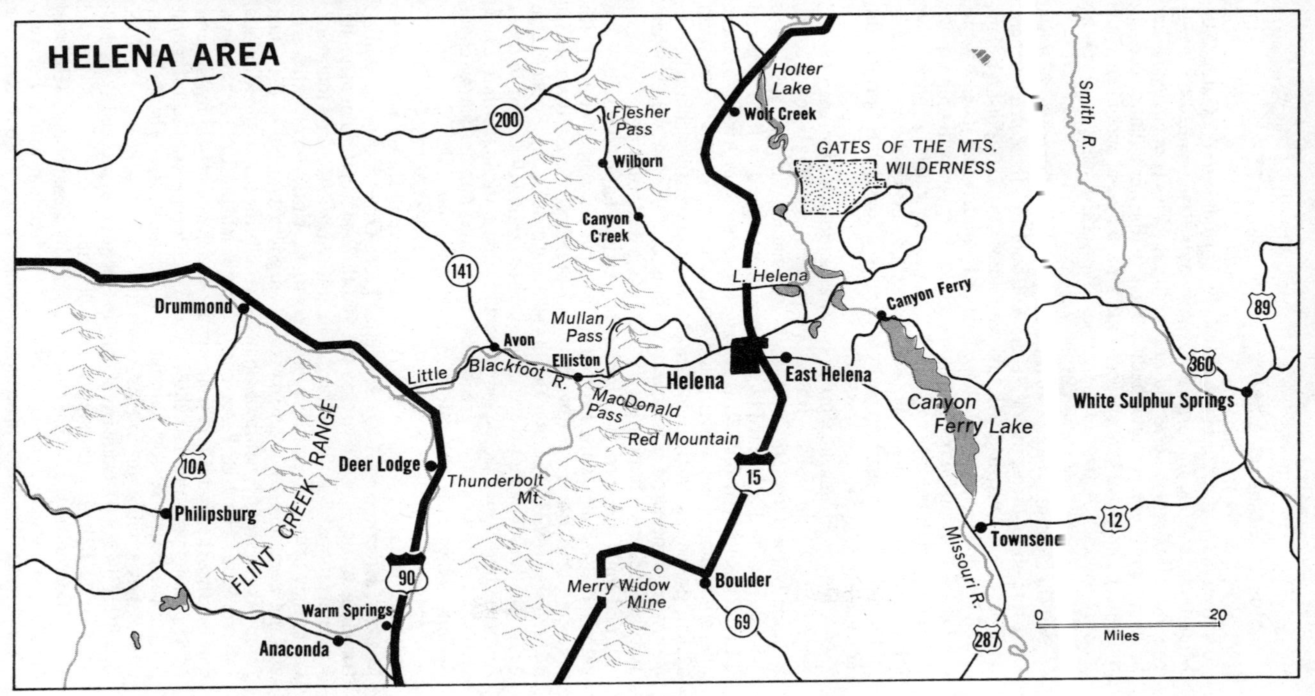
HELENA AREA
200
Flesher Pass
Wilborn
Canyon Creek
Holter Lake
Wolf Creek
GATES OF THE MTS. WILDERNESS
Smith R.
141
L. Helena
Canyon Ferry
89
Drummond
Mullan Pass
Avon
Elliston
Little
Blackfoot R.
Helena
East Helena
MacDonald Pass
Red Mountain
Canyon Ferry Lake
360
White Sulphur Springs
10A
Deer Lodge
Thunderbolt Mt.
FLINT CREEK RANGE
15
Philipsburg
Townsen
12
Missouri R.
90
Merry Widow Mine
Boulder
Warm Springs
69
Anaconda
0
20
Miles
287

Gates of the Mountains

Sixteen miles north of Helena, on I–15, you come to the Gates of the Mountains, a 2,000-ft. gorge in the Missouri River named by Lewis. Nervous about what he would find in the Rockies (remember he had been trudging upriver and hadn't been in the mountains, yet), he thought the gorge "the most spectacular" he had seen, but of "dark and gloomy aspect." A two-hour summer river cruise lets you check his opinion in almost the same setting.

You should also explore Canyon Ferry Dam and Reservoir. The best route is to go southeast out of Helena on Route 287, then turn northeast on Route 284. This road will take you across the 210-foot-high dam, which has created a 24-mile-long lake. As you drive on its east shore, the lake will be on your right hand. To the left you will come to the turnoff for Diamond City which will take you to yet another ghost town and, if you persist, to the old site of Fort Logan, where one building still stands. Return to Helena by way of White Sulphur Springs and Townsend.

North from Helena, keeping to I–15, we approach Montana's second largest city, Great Falls, with 57,000 residents (Billings, pop. 66,800, is actually the largest). Great Falls was named for the falls in the Missouri to the northeast. The area was first mapped by the Lewis and Clark Expedition in 1805. It is the site of Malmstrom Air Force Base, one of the important links in the SAC and Air Defense Command system protecting North America. Minutemen missiles abound hereabouts. Hydroelectric plants near the falls, and a fertile winter wheat and livestock area have made Great Falls a boom town.

Great Falls was home base for cowboy artist Charley Russell. A fine gallery of Russell's work may be seen in his old studio at 1201 4th Avenue North. From this town his fame spread even to Hollywood, but he preferred the Mint Saloon and the leathery cronies of the open-range days. The Rainbow Hotel was a Great Falls landmark similar to other Montana hotels such as the Northern in Billings, the Placer in Helena, or Butte's Finlen. See the "great falls" themselves and the nearby Giant Springs, which flow at a rate of 388 million gallons daily.

If you want to make a side trip to Russell's country, take US 87 southeast of Great Falls to US 191, then drive northward across the Missouri River to join US 2 at Malta. From Great Falls, you will be traveling through the heart of the Judith Basin cattle country, the Russell National Wildlife Refuge, and, in the Little Rocky Mountains, the outlaw camps of Landusky and Zortman. Until recently this area was not accessible by good roads. When you get to US 2, the Chief Joseph Battleground, south of Chinook, recalls the last of the Montana Indian Wars. The Nez Percé chief, Joseph, led the U.S. Army on a chase across the breadth of Montana but was finally caught by General Miles coming up from the Yellowstone. Chief Joseph lost the last round here in the Bear's Paw Mountains in 1877, and said, "Where the sun now stands I will fight no more forever."

Return by US 87 from Havre to Fort Benton or proceed northeast from Great Falls if you skipped the side trip.

Fort Benton, pop. 1,700, now a sometimes bypassed county seat, was once the economic capital of the Rocky Mountain West. For two decades, it was the center of steamboat travel on the Missouri River—a direct link with St. Louis and the "States."

After Lewis and Clark passed by, Fort Benton slumbered until an American Fur Company post was established in 1846 by Alexander Culbertson, a great trader. The steamboat on the Missouri had reached this point by 1860. So when the mining camps sprouted in the mountains to the southwest, Fort Benton merchants were ready with goods to be wagon-hauled to the camps. Hundreds of boats puffed up the Missouri River to serve the gold camps and to link up with the Mullan Road wagon trail over the Rockies to Walla Walla, Washington. In its peak year (1879) Fort Benton docked forty-nine steamboats.

Today Fort Benton has an excellent museum, and you can visualize from its old levees the days when it was a bustling port. Not until the Northern Pacific Railroad pushed through to reach the Pacific Coast in 1883 did Benton and the steamboat era begin to decline. Guthrie's *These Thousand Hills* or Paul Sharp's *Whoop-up Trail* are good reading on Benton.

From Fort Benton, the Missouri moves eastward 180 miles through the untouched Missouri River Breaks to the beginning of Fort Peck Reservoir. Some years ago, a national battle took place over whether this relatively wild waterway was to be preserved as a refuge or dammed for waterpower and irrigation. One part of the land still remains wild and scenic. For the canoeing enthusiast, this stretch of river provides a rare opportunity.

Blackfeet Country

From Fort Benton, turn north and west for the Blackfeet Indian country around Browning, which also is the eastern gateway to Glacier National Park, the Alps of America. You take Route 223 north from Fort Benton to Chester, and then go west on US 2. Near Shelby—where Dempsey fought Gibbons in 1923—and Cut Bank, you pass through one of Montana's prolific oil areas. More than 1,100 oil wells and one hundred gas wells dot the dryland wheat farms of the area.

Browning is the headquarters for the 1,500,000-acre Blackfeet Indian Reservation. In the summer months, the town is alive with the colorful tribesmen, and the second week of July they celebrate North American Indian Days with traditional dances. The Montana event is of great interest to foreign tourists.

The Museum of the Plains Indians, located at US 2 and 89, is open the year-round. The historic and contemporary displays are worth seeing.

Glacier National Park

Located 175 miles north of Great Falls, Glacier National Park remains Montana's great natural "spectacular." Since 1910, the more than 1,600 square miles of jagged mountain scenery have drawn travelers, lured by its many glaciers and alpine lakes, well-developed campgrounds, and motel and hotel accommodations of all types. A quick drive through the park can touch only the highlights, but there are endless opportunities for hiking, camping, and fishing to meet each vacationer's taste and time. The park season runs from June 15 through September 10, when most hotels and cabin camps are open. The main roads, however, may stay clear until mid-October, depending on the weather.

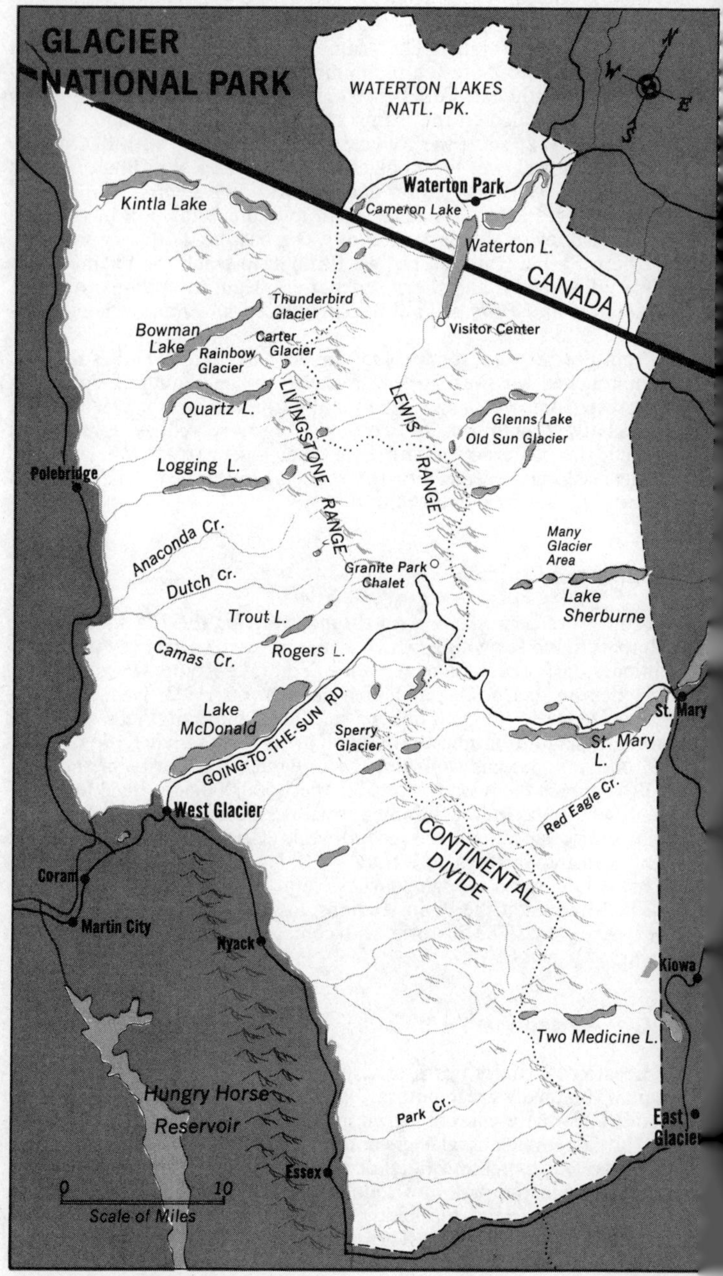
GLACIER NATIONAL PARK
WATERTON LAKES NATL. PK.
N
W
E
S
Waterton Park
Cameron Lake
Waterton L.
CANADA
Kintla Lake
Thunderbird Glacier
Visitor Center
Bowman Lake
Carter Glacier
Rainbow Glacier
Quartz L.
LIVINGSTONE RANGE
LEWIS RANGE
Glenns Lake
Old Sun Glacier
Polebridge
Logging L.
Many Glacier Area
Anaconda Cr.
Granite Park Chalet
Dutch Cr.
Lake Sherburne
Trout L.
Camas Cr.
Rogers L.
St. Mary
Lake McDonald
GOING-TO-THE-SUN RD
Sperry Glacier
St. Mary L.
Red Eagle Cr.
West Glacier
CONTINENTAL DIVIDE
Coram
Martin City
Nyack
Kiowa
Two Medicine L.
Hungry Horse Reservoir
Park Cr.
East Glacier
Essex
0
10
Scale of Miles

Most of Glacier Park is accessible only by its seven hundred miles of foot and horse trails; on-the-spot inquiry and attention to park regulations is essential—this is rugged country. When the park itself is closed, US 2 may be used to the south from Browning to West Glacier. Local inquiry is advisable if the weather looks bad. And, don't feed the bears.

Starting from Browning, you'll visit the Glacier Park Lodge at East Glacier on State 49. This is typical of the huge log hotels developed by the Great Northern Railway in the early days of the century to handle what was primarily wealthy railroad travelers. This hotel offers a variety of riding, hiking, golf, and fishing. Be sure to inquire about guided tours and lectures offered by the National Park Service naturalists. They will increase your enjoyment of this alpine beauty spot.

From St. Mary you can also swing north to Waterton-Glacier International Peace Park in Canada, an extension of the same kind of mountain terrain as you find on the American side, but perhaps less crowded in the peak months. Also note on the north route the access road to Many Glacier Hotel on Swiftcurrent Lake; you leave the highway at Babb and drive a few miles west to what many consider the park's most varied center of activity. All of the recreation activities are developed here, with trails to Grinnell Lake and Glacier. George Bird Grinnell, the naturalist, was instrumental in the establishment of the park.

On a quick tour, you'll want to see Two Medicine Valley and Lake. Turn west about four miles north of East Glacier on State 49. A seven-mile road leads to a lake (launch trips during the season) ringed by high peaks. There is a short, well-marked nature trail at Falls, a safe, quick introduction to Glacier.

There's a campground at St. Mary Lake and another at Rising Sun on the north shore highway. Four miles west of the latter at Sun Point there are both an information station and self-guiding trails. The frontal range of the Rockies at this point is known as Lewis Range.

The most spectacular drive through Glacier is over the Continental Divide via the Going-to-the-Sun road. From Browning and East Glacier, drive north on State 49 and US 89 to St. Mary, and then turn westward for the 50-mile drive over Logan Pass to the west end of the park. If you are hauling a camper, and your rig is over thirty feet in length—including your car—you had better make arrangements to leave your camper and pick it up later. In July and August park rules forbid vehicles over thirty feet long on this highway. Before and after August 3, overall length limit is 35 feet. You will realize why when you begin your climb.

From St. Mary Lake in the east to Lake McDonald in the west the highway crosses 6,664-ft. Logan Pass. It is the great spot to stop and view the park: from here you have 100-mile vistas. There is a large Information Center atop Logan Pass. Ask about Highline Trail to Granite Park, an area of ancient lava flows and glacial valleys.

After Logan Pass, descend west along the Garden Wall, one of America's greatest mountain highways. Below, at Avalanche Campground, there is an easy two-mile trail to Avalanche Basin, a natural amphitheater with walls two thousand feet high and waterfalls for a backdrop. The red cedars and the rushing streams give you a sense of what the park must be like deep in the interior, if you haven't the time for longer hikes or rides.

Lake McDonald is ten miles long and a mile wide. Lake McDonald Lodge, near the head of the lake on our highway, is the center. There are public campgrounds here and at the foot of the lake at Apgar, as well as several classes of accommodations at both spots. The hike to Sperry Glacier and Chalet is popular.

PRACTICAL INFORMATION FOR MONTANA

HOW TO GET THERE. By Plane. *Delta* and *Continental Airlines* have flights to Billings, Bozeman, Great Falls, Kalispell, Missoula, and Helena. *Northwest Orient* serves Billings, Bozeman, Missoula, Helena, and Great Falls. *United* flies to Billings, Great Falls, and Bozeman. *Northwest Airlink* connects most major points and many smaller towns in the state, and can arrange charter flights.

By Train. Amtrak serves Glacier National Park, Havre, Browning, Glasgow, Libby, Malta, Shelby, Whitefish and Wolf Point.

By Bus. Greyhound has buses running to major cities in Montana. Charter buses service all points in Montana.

By Car. I–94 enters Montana from North Dakota in the east, I–90 from Wyoming in the south and from Idaho in the west, and I–15 from Alberta, Canada, in the north and Idaho in the south.

ACCOMMODATIONS. Many new representatives of the national hotel and motel chains are now in Montana, but during the prime tourist season reservations are still advisable. In fact, if you want to stay in or around Glacier or West Yellowstone parks you may well have to book reservations as much as a year in advance. Rates are lower during the off-season. Note: throughout Montana the *area code is 406.*

The price categories in this section, for double occupancy, will average as follows: *Deluxe,* $60 and up; *Expensive* $50–60; Moderate $40–50; and *Inexpensive* under $40. Prices are subject to change.

Unless otherwise indicated, all hotels, motels, and restaurants have a 406 area code.

ANACONDA. Fairmont Hot Springs Resort. *Deluxe.* I–90, Exit 211 (797–3241). Completely up-to-date resort. Outdoor-indoor swimming.

Vagabond Lodge Motel. *Moderate.* 1421 E. Park (563–5152). Cafe.

ASHLAND. Western 8 Motel. *Moderate.* West 212 Hwy., 59003 (784–2400). Pets allowed. Handicapped facilities.

BIG FORK. Marina Cay. *Expensive.* 180 Vista Lane, 59911 (837–5861). On Flathead Lake. Pool, golf, picnic tables. Cafe and bar.

BIG SKY. Huntley Lodge. *Deluxe.* Mountain Village, 59716 (995–4211). 40 mi. S. of Bozeman, 7 miles west of US 191. The late Chet Huntley's ski resort in the heart of the Gallatin Canyon. Large bright rooms, condominiums, loft rooms, outdoor pool, and health club. Open year round.

Telemark Inn. *Expensive.* Meadow Village (995–4269). Pool.

The Mountain Lodge. *Moderate.* Mountain Village (800–831–3509). Open during ski season only. Restaurant and bar.

BILLINGS. Sheraton. *Deluxe.* 27 N. 27th St., 59101 (252–7400). 23 stories. 305 sleekly furnished rooms, three restaurants, many shops. Gratis airport shuttle. Free local calls, parking.

Best Western Northern Hotel. *Expensive.* Box 1296, Broadway at 1st Ave., 59101 North (245–5121). Well-known downtown hotel. Some suites. Shops, good restaurant. Free airport transport.

Cherry Tree Inn. *Expensive.* 823 N. Broadway, 59101 (252–5603). Near downtown, color TV, suites and apartments. Pool and playground nearby.

Dude Rancher Lodge. *Expensive.* 415 N. 29th, 59101 (259–5561).

Best Western Ponderosa Inn. *Expensive.* Box 1791, 2511 1st Ave. N., 59101 (259–5511). Cable TV, pool, sauna, and 24-hour cafe.

Billings Plaza Holiday Inn. *Expensive.* 5500 Midland Rd., 59101 (248–7701). Live entertainment. Indoor pool, restaurant, conference rooms. Convention area.

War Bonnet Inn. *Expensive.* 2612 Belknap, 59101 (248–7761). On I–90, 27th St., Exit 450. Pool, lounge, dancing, entertainment, restaurant, conference rooms. Free airport bus.

Juniper Motel. *Moderate.* 1315 N. 27th St. (245–4128). Cafe. Sundeck. Pleasant rooms, pets allowed.

Regal 8 Inn. *Moderate.* I–90 and Midland Rd. (248–7551). Off Interstate. Pool.

Thrifty Scot. *Moderate.* 1345 Mullowney Lane at I–90 and King Ave. (252–2584). Free local phone calls. Free continental breakfast.

Imperial 400 Motor Inn. *Inexpensive.* 2601 4th Ave. N., 59101 (245–6646). 35 units. Pool, handicapped facilities.

Motel 6. *Inexpensive.* 5400 Midland Rd., RR No. 1 (248–7759). I–90 at exit 446. Good value.

BOZEMAN. The Voss Inn. *Deluxe–Expensive,* 319 S. Willson, 59715 (587–0982). Bed and breakfast in a restored, 100-year old mansion. Six elegant guest rooms, each with private bath.

Best Western City Center Motel. *Expensive.* 507 W. Main St., 59715 (587–3158). Indoor heated pool, sauna, free coffee. 24-hour cafe adjacent. Good restaurant.

Holiday Inn. *Expensive.* 5 Baxter Lane, 59715 (587–4561). 182 rooms, modern meeting rooms. Off interstate.

Imperial "400" Motel. *Moderate to Inexpensive.* 122 W. Main St., 59715 (587–4481). Near University, heated pool, free coffee, cafe nearby.

Western Heritage Inn. *Moderate to Inexpensive.* 1200 E. Main, 59715 (586–8534). Laundry. Restaurant nearby.

Royal 6. *Inexpensive.* 310 N. 7th, 59715 (587–3103).

BUTTE. Best Western Copper King Inn. *Expensive.* 4655 Harrison Ave. S., 59701 (494–6666). Close to airport. Indoor pools, sauna.

Best Western War Bonnet Inn. *Expensive.* 2100 Cornell Ave. at Harrison Ave., 59701 (494–7800). 134-room convention motel. Heated pool, cafe, meeting rooms.

Finlen Hotel and Motor Lodge. *Moderate.* Broadway and Wyoming, 59701 (723–5461). A 100-room motor inn. Bar, beauty shop, meeting rooms, garage.

Mile Hi Motel. *Inexpensive.* 3499 Harrison, 59715 (494–2250). Pool. Pets allowed.

CHINOOK. Bear Paw Court. *Inexpensive.* Box 639, Montana at W. 2nd Ave., 59701 (357–2221). Free coffee, cafe nearby, some kitchenettes.

COOKE CITY. All Season's Inn. *Expensive* (838–2251). Restaurant, bar, indoor pool; skiing and snowmobiling, hunting and fishing available. On Hwy. 212 in center of business district overlooking mountains; 4 miles from Yellowstone.

Hoosier's. *Inexpensive.* Box 1057 on US 212, 59020 (838–2241). On Main Street. Lounge.

DILLON. Best Western Royal Inn Motel. *Moderate.* 650 N. Montana, 59725 (683–4214). Heated pool, cafe. Some suites available.

Creston Motor Inn. *Inexpensive.* 335 S. Atlantic (683–2341). Free coffee, 24-hour cafe one-half mile.

ENNIS. El Western Motel. *Expensive.* On Hwy. 287 S. Box 487, 59729 (682–4217). Cafe nearby. On the Madison River. Hunting, fishing float trips, guides available. Near Virginia City.

Rainbow Valley. *Moderate.* On Hwy. 287 S. Box 26, 59728 (682–4264). Picnic tables, grills, playground, and pool.

ESSEX. Izaak Walton Inn. *Inexpensive.* Off Hwy. 2, 59916 (888–5569). Historic inn near Glacier Park. Open year-round. Many activities. Dining. Lounge.

FORT BENTON. Pioneer Lodge. *Moderate.* 1700 Front St., 59442 (622–5441). Historic building on waterfront.

GARDINER. Westernaire. *Moderate.* On Hwy. 89. Box 20, 59030 (848–7397). Cable TV. Cafe nearby.

GLACIER NATIONAL PARK. Glacier Park Lodge. *Expensive.* (226–9311). Heated indoor pool, playground, restaurant, bar, beauty shop. 9-hole golf course, pitch 'n putt, putting green, shuffleboard, volleyball, pingpong, riding, fishing. Reservations. Open June to Labor Day. 155 rooms.

Lake McDonald Lodge. *Expensive.* (888–5441). Ideal for a tranquil vacation.

Many Glacier Hotel. *Expensive* (732–4411). 12 mi. W of Babb off US 89, on lake. Restaurant, bar, barber and beauty shops, fishing, boating, riding, pack trips (summer and fall only), volleyball. View of Swiftcurrent Lake. Reservations essential.

Village Inn. *Expensive.* Box 115 (888–5632). On lake with beach, fishing, boats available. Open early June to mid-Sept.

Rising Sun Motor Inn. *Expensive–Moderate.* (226–5551). 6 mi. W on St. Mary Park entrance on Going-to-the-Sun Rd. Restaurant, playground, on lake. June 15 to Sept. 3.

Swift Current Motor Inn. *Moderate.* 13 mi. W. of Babb (226–5551). Cafe. In center of park; motel and cabin facilities.

GLASGOW. Campbell Lodge. *Moderate.* 3 blks. S. of US 2 at 3rd Ave. and 6th St. (228–9328). Free Continental breakfast, cafe nearby, sundeck.

Rustic Lodge. *Moderate.* 700 1st Ave. N. (228–2451). Playground, free Continental breakfast, 24-hour cafe nearby, playground.

GLENDIVE. Best Western Holiday Lodge. *Moderate.* Box 741, 222 N. Kendrick Ave., 59330 (365–5655). 3-story motel with indoor pool.

Rustic Inn. *Moderate.* 1903 N. Merrill, 59330 (761–1900). Pool, cafe.

Super Eight. *Moderate.* Box 198, 1904 N. Merrill Ave., 59330 (365–5671). Restaurants nearby.

GREAT FALLS. Sheraton Great Falls. *Deluxe to Expensive.* 400 10th Ave. S., 59405 (727–7200). Skyscraper hostelry en route to airport. (Courtesy bus.) Good café, cocktails, conventions.

Best Western Heritage Inn. *Expensive.* 1700 Fox Farm Rd., 59401 (1–800–528–1234). 232-room motor inn; indoor heated pool, cafe, bar, dancing, entertainment. Many conveniences. Free airport transportation.

Holiday Inn. *Expensive.* 1411 10th Ave. S., 59401 (761–4600). Elevator, heated pool, cafe, bar, dancing, entertainment.

Crestview. *Moderate.* 500 13th Ave. S., 59401 (727–8380). Kitchen units.

Imperial 400. *Moderate.* 601 2nd Ave. N., 59401 (452–9581). Centrally located motel. Nice desks and lights. Popular with salesmen. Indoor pool.

O'Haire Motor Inn. *Moderate.* 17 7th St. S., 59401 (454–2141). Pool. Lounge, Dancing.

Starlit Motel. *Moderate.* 1521 1st Ave. N. 59401 (452–9597). Heated pool, playground, free coffee, 24-hour cafe nearby.

Super Eight. *Moderate.* 1214 13th St. S., 59405 (727–7600). Near shopping center.

Triple Crown Motor Inn. *Moderate.* 621 Central Ave., 59401 (727–8300). Downtown. Many soundproofed rooms. Radios and TV.

Ski's Western Motel. *Inexpensive.* 2420 10th Ave. S., 59405 (453–3281). Open all year. Some two-bedroom units.

HAMILTON. Best Western Hamilton. *Moderate.* 409 S. 1st St., 59840 (363–2142). Scenic valley location. Cafe nearby.

HARDIN. American Inn. *Moderate.* Box 411, at I–90 City Center exit, 59034 (665–1870). Particularly good for families.

Lariat Motel. *Moderate.* 709 N. Center Ave., 59034 (665–2683). Quiet.

HAVRE. Le Havre Inn. *Moderate.* 629 W. 1st St., 59501 (265–6711). Pool, bar, laundry room. 24-hour cafe nearby.

HELENA. Best Western Colonial Inn. *Expensive.* 2301 Colonial Dr., 59601 (443–2100). Heated pool, sauna, cafe, bar, dancing, entertainment, barber and beauty shops. Free airport bus. Convenient. Enjoys much repeat business.

Park Plaza. *Expensive.* 22 N. Last Chance Gulch, 59601 (443–2200). Pool, sauna, airport transportation.

Imperial 400 Motor Inn. *Moderate to Inexpensive.* (442–0600). Centrally located.

Helena Hotel 6. *Inexpensive.* 800 N. Oregon, 59601, I–15 & exit US 12 W. (442–1311). Heated pool. Cafe nearby. Spartam.

KALISPELL. Best Western Outlaw Inn. *Expensive.* 1701 US 93 S., 59901 (755–6100). An elite establishment. Attractive to conventions. Pool. Tennis, Popular restaurant.

Four Seasons Motor Inn. *Moderate.* 350 N. Main St., 59901 (755–6123). Highly rated 101-room establishment. Cafe. Whirlpools.

Vacationer Motel. *Inexpensive.* 285 7th Ave. EN, 59901 (755–7144).

LEWISTOWN. Yogo Inn. *Moderate.* 211 E. Main St., 59457 (538–8721). 85 units. Heated pool, cafe, bar, picnic tables, grill.

Motel Sunset. *Inexpensive.* 115 N.E. Main, 59457 (538–8741). Free coffee, cafe nearby.

LIVINGSTON. Best Western Yellowstone Motor Inn. *Expensive.* 1515 W. Park, 59047 (1–800–528–1234). 100-room, three story motel with all amenities. Indoor garage.

Del Mar Motel. *Moderate.* I–90 Business Loop West (222–3120). Heated pool, playground, free coffee, 24-hour cafe in area. Quiet area.

MALTA. Maltana Motel. *Inexpensive.* 138 First Ave. W., 59538 (654–2610). Playground, free coffee, 24-hour cafe nearby.

MILES CITY. Best Western War Bonnet Inn. *Moderate–Expensive.* 1015 S. Haynes, 59301 (800–528–1234). Heated pool, free Continental breakfast.

Super Eight. *Inexpensive.* I–94 to US 312 S. (232–5261). Cafes nearby.

MISSOULA. Sheraton Inn. *Deluxe to Expensive.* 200 S. Pattee, 59081 (721–8550). Indoor pool, game area, lounge, gift shop. New.

Best Western Executive Motor Inn. *Expensive.* (1–800–528–1234). 201 E. Main St. 3-story, 3-star motel with heated pool, cafe.

Red Lion Motel. *Expensive.* 700 W. Broadway, 59802 (728–3300). Cable TV, heated pool, meeting rooms. Restaurant.

Super Eight. *Moderate.* I–94 & Hwy. 93 S. (251–2255). Pancake House nearby.

City Center. *Inexpensive.* 338 E. Broadway, 59801 (543–3193).

POLSON. Best Western Queen's Court. *Expensive-Moderate.* Hwy. 93, 59860 (1–800–528–1234). Free Continental breakfast, cafe nearby, boats, fishing, water-skiing available. On Flathead Lake.

PRAY. Chico Hot Springs Lodge. *Moderate,* 27 mi. S. of Livingston, 59065 (333–4933). Old resort hotel, swimming, fishing, riding, cafe.

RED LODGE. Best Western Lupine Inn. *Expensive.* (1–800–528–1234). Indoor pool; skiing, snowmobiling available. On Hwy. 212 in Beartooth Wilderness and Ski Mountain area; 50 miles from Yellowstone.

Eagle's Nest Motel. *Inexpensive-Moderate.* 702 S. Broadway, 59068 (446–2312). Pets O.K.

SIDNEY. Angus Ranchouse. *Moderate.* 2350 S. Central, 59270 (1–800–637–1741). 50 rooms. Nearby restaurant.

Park Plaza Motel. *Inexpensive.* 601 S. Central, 59270 (482–1520). Continental breakfast, cafe nearby, park opposite.

VIRGINIA CITY. Fairweather Inn. *Moderate.* Box 338, 59755 (843–5377). On US 287. Coffee house opposite, Old West decor. Melodrama performances.

Virginia Terrace Motel. *Inexpensive.* Wallace St., 59755 (843–5368). Cafe and music hall nearby.

WEST YELLOWSTONE. Stage Coach Inn TraveLodge. *Expensive.* Madison & Dunraven, 59758 (800–255–3050). Sauna, hot tub, indoor pool, some refrigerators. Two bars and lounge with entertainment; restaurants; tennis, skiing, and snowmobiling. At west entrance to Yellowstone.

Big Western Pine Motel. *Moderate.* 234 Firehole Ave., 59758 (646–7622). Heated pool, cafe nearby, tennis, outdoor fireplaces. Open year-round.

Dude. *Moderate.* Box 609, 4 Madison Ave., 59758 (646–7316). Near Yellowstone entrance.

Tepee Motor Lodge. *Moderate.* 205 Yellowstone Ave., 59758 (646–7391). 2½ blocks west of West Gate entrance to Yellowstone Park.

Three Bears Lodge. *Moderate.* 217 Yellowstone Ave., 59758 (646–7353). Two blocks from park entrance.

Starlite. *Inexpensive to Moderate.* 118 Electric St., 59758 (646–7656). 1 block west of West Gate of Yellowstone Park.

WHITEFISH. Alpinglow Inn. *Deluxe.* Box 1670, 59937 (862–6966). Highly rated inn with sauna, adjacent to Big Mountain skiing. Dining. Cocktails.

Viking Lakeshore Inn. *Expensive.* 1360 Wisconsin, 59937 (862–3547). 1¼ mi. N at Whitefish Lake. Own beach, heated pool, sauna, cafe, bar, entertainment, recreation room.

Mountain Holiday Motel. *Moderate.* 6595 W. 93 S., 59937 (862–2548). Free coffee, hot tub, playground. Restaurant nearby.

WOLF POINT. Sherman Motor Inn. *Moderate.* 200 E. Main St., 59201 (653–1100). Restaurant, lounge.

Homestead Inn. *Inexpensive.* 101 Hwy. 2 E., 59201 (653–1300). Pleasant three-story inn.

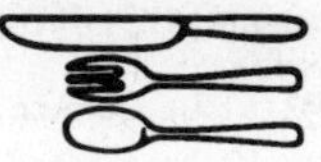

RESTAURANTS. Steak, prime ribs, and lobster are big favorites in the area, and many restaurants cater to this taste. Local game, too, finds it way onto many menus and is worth eating whether it's trout, elk, deer, or buffalo. Prices are for medium-priced items on the menu.

Restaurant categories are as follows: *Deluxe* will average $25 and up; *Expensive* $15–25; *Moderate* $10–15; and Inexpensive under $15. These prices are for *hors d'oeuvre* or soup, *entrée* and dessert. Not included are drinks, tax, and tips. For a more complete explanation of restaurant categories refer to *Facts at Your Fingertips* at the front of this volume.

BIG SKY. Furst Place. *Moderate.* Meadow Village ([illegible]). Fresh fish, venison. Good view. Closed November and May.

BILLINGS. The Alexandria. *Expensive.* 1000 1st Ave. N. (259–1100). On the outskirts of Billings.

Golden Belle. *Expensive.* (245–5121). In the Northern Hotel. Award-winning. A Gay 90s restaurant specializing in steak and seafood. Flambés. Bar.

Dos Machos. *Moderate.* 300 S. 24th St. W. (652–2020). Mexican food with lots of atmosphere. Sunday brunch.

Black Angus. *Moderate to Inexpensive.* 2658 Grand Ave. (656–4949). Steak, seafood, children's menu. Entertainment.

Kings Table Buffet. *Inexpensive.* 411 S. 24th W. (656–7290). Cafeteria-style dining. Variety of dishes.

BOZEMAN. The Overland Express. *Expensive to Moderate.* 15 N. Rouse Ave. (587–7982). Steak and lobster. Open late for meals. Lunches, too.

Black Angus Steak House. *Moderate.* 507 W. Main St., in Best Western (587–0652). Steak and lobster. Locally popular.

Union Hall Restaurant and Bakery. *Moderate.* 238 E. Main St. (587–8920). Fondue, crépes, pastries in historic building.

4 B's Cafe. *Inexpensive.* 421 W. Main St. (587–4661). A restaurant popular locally that serves chicken, roast beef and steak. Open 24 hours.

BUTTE. Lydia's. *Expensive.* 2.5 miles So. on US 10 from I–90. (494–2000). Excellent steak and Italian cuisine, or lobster, chicken. Soft candle lighting.

4 B's Restaurant. *Inexpensive.* Montana and Front St. (782–5311). A locally popular restaurant specializing in chicken and their own desserts.

DILLON. The Bannack House. *Moderate-Expensive.* 33 E. Bannack (683–5088). Italian and American menu with an extensive wine collection.

GLACIER NATIONAL PARK. Glacier Park Lodge. *Expensive.* In the Glacier Park Lodge Hotel (226–9311). On State 49. Complete dinners of prime rib, trout, steak served with their own baked goods.

Many Glacier. *Expensive.* In the Many Glacier Hotel (723–4311). Twelve miles west of Babb off US 89. Complete dinners of prime rib, trout, steak served with their baked goods.

GREAT FALLS. Eddie's Supper Club. *Expensive.* 38th & 2nd Ave. N. (453–1616). T-bones, N.Y. steaks, prime rib, lamb. Large portions. On edge of town.

Black Angus Steak House. *Moderate to Inexpensive.* 3800 10th Ave. S. (761–4550). The motif is Bavarian and the food prime rib, lobster, and steak. A pleasant dining experience.

HAVRE. 4 B's Restaurant. *Moderate.* 604 W. 1st St. (265–9721). Popular with families. Good value.

HELENA. Frontier Pies Restaurant and Bakery. *Moderate.* 1231 Prospect Ave. (442–7437). Home-style cooking with Western motif.

House of Wong. *Moderate.* 2711 N. Montana Ave. (442–3320). Chinese and American dishes.

Jorgenson's. *Moderate.* 1714 11th Ave. (442–6380). This restaurant serves an assortment of good food family style. Children's menus.

KALISPELL. Hennessy's Outlaw Inn. *Moderate.* (755–6100). ¼ mi. S just off US 93. Restaurant in the inn of the same name. Lounge and supper club.

Pancho Magoo's. *Inexpensive.* (755–4778). Mexican food.

MISSOULA. Mansion Overland Express. *Expensive.* 102 Ben Hogan Dr. (728–5132). Good, solid American food in a Victorian setting.

Milwaukee Station. *Moderate–Expensive.* 250 Station Dr. (721–7777). Historic Old Milwaukee Depot Building on Clark Fork River. Outdoor patio open for lunch. Cocktail lounge. Children's menu.

Kings Table Buffet. *Inexpensive.* 3611 Brooks "All you can eat" buffet style. Better than most buffets.

RED LODGE. Red Lodge Cafe. *Moderate.* 16 Broadway (446–2808). Serves buffalo when available. Locally popular.

WEST YELLOWSTONE. Strozzi's Dude Lounge. *Expensive.* 4 Madison Ave. (646–7573). A popular tourist restaurant that serves steak, prime ribs, and lobster. Children's portions.

Rustler's Roost. *Expensive to Moderate.* In the Big Western Pine Motel (646–7585). Buffalo barbecue, scones, chuck wagon stew.

Silver Spur Cafe. *Moderate.* 111 Canyon St. (646–9400). A popular family restaurant serving luncheon, dinners, and a children's menu.

La Dump. *Moderate.* Box 1823 (752–3000), 7 mi. S. on US 935. This popular local spot serves regional specialties. Set in the country with a spectacular view of Flathead Valley.

WHITEFISH. Alpine Glow Inn. *Expensive.* (862–6966). A beautiful view awaits you when you come to the Ptarmigan Room after a day of skiing or boating. Good village location. A diverse menu including steak, lobster, crab. Salad bar.

HOW TO GET AROUND. By Plane. *Delta* and *Continental Airlines* have flights to Billings, Bozeman, Great Falls, Kalispell, Missoula, and Helena. *Northwest Orient* services Billings, Bozeman, Missoula, Helena and Great Falls. *United* flies to Billings, Great Falls, and Bozeman. *Northwest Airlink* services major points in the state, including many of the smaller airports, and can arrange charter flights.

By Train. Amtrak has two lines serving Montana. The "Hi-Line" (which parallels US 2) serves Havre and Glacier Park.

By Bus. Greyhound and Intermountain Transportation are the principal carriers serving the major cities. Rimrock Stage serves Billings, Helena and Missoula. Many charter services are available.

By Car. I–94 runs east-west from Glendive through Miles City to Billings, where I–90 continues to Bozeman, Butte, and Missoula. The northern east-west route, US 2, is the principal access to Glasgow, Havre, Shelby, Glacier National Park, and Kalispell. I–15 runs north-south through Butte, Helena, and Great Falls to Shelby.

TOURIST INFORMATION. For information and brochures about points of interest, travel, and campgrounds in Montana, write Travel Promotion Division, Department of Commerce, Helena 59620. Up-to-date travel information can also be had by calling 800–548–3390.

SEASONAL EVENTS. The Chamber of Commerce in Helena furnishes on request a Calendar of Events folder which gives the exact dates and location of the current year's activities.

Some annual events are:

January: Montana Winter Fair, Bozeman; *Montana Pro Rodeo Circuit Finals,* Great Falls.

February: Sno-Fest, Anaconda; *Winter Carnival,* Red Lodge.

March: Charles Russell Art Auction, Great Falls; *Ski Chase,* West Yellowstone.

April: Renaissance Dinner, Shelby; *Spring Arts Festival,* Libby; *Figure Skating Championships,* Great Falls.

May: Fishing Season open; *Rodeo season* begins last week of month; *Bucking Horse Sale,* Miles City; *Cherry Festival,* near Polson.

June: Glacier National Park and main roads into *Yellowstone* open, and park accommodations are available beginning mid-month; *Big Sky Logging Championships,* Kalispell; *Viking Boat Regetta,* Whitefish; *Marathon and Logger Days,* Missoula; *Red Bottom Indian Celebration,* Frazer; *National Intercollegiate Rodeo Finals,* Bozeman, third week; *Homesteader Days,* Hot Springs; *Jazz Festival,* Helena; *Jazz Festival,* Helena.

July: Fair season begins: *Whitefish Lake Regatta,* Whitefish; *Wild Horse Stampede* at Wolf Point attracts riders from throughout the nation; *Home of Champions Rodeo,* Red Lodge; *Fiddlers' Championships,* Polson; *Homesteader Days Celebration,* Worden; *Indian Powwows* throughout the month; *North American Indian Days* at Browning, the Blackfeet invite other Indians to join a four-day encampment featuring dances, games, races, and a rodeo; *Great Lake to Lake Canoe Race,* Whitefish; *Missoula Rose Show,* Missoula; *North Montana State Fair and Rodeo,* Great Falls.

August: Copper Cup Regatta, Polson; *Festival of Nations,* Red Lodge; *Rodeo,* Billings; *Flathead Lake Sailboat Regatta,* Bigfork; *National Trout Derby* at Livingston offers a heavy purse for the largest trout caught; *Crow Indian Fair and Rodeo,* Crow Agency; *Bozeman Roundup Rodeo,* Bozeman; *Western Montana Fair,* Missoula; *Mineral County Fair,* Zortman. *Western Montana Fair and Horse Racing,* Missoula.

September: Annual Whitefish Summer Games, Whitefish; *Herbstfest,* Laurel; *Threshing Bee,* Culbertson.

October: Bison Roundup, Moiese; *hunting season* begins; *Northern International Livestock Exposition,* Billings; *Electrum,* Helena.

November: Ski season begins.

December. Snowmobile Roundup at West Yellowstone, through Mar.

NATIONAL PARKS AND FORESTS. Glacier National Park, crowning the continent across the Rocky Mountains of northwestern Montana, contains one of the most spectacularly scenic portions of the entire range. Although today there are still some forty glaciers, the park is named for the Ice Age glaciers which carved out the rugged scenery. Covering over 1,600 square miles, it is the U.S. section of the Waterton-Glacier International Peace Park (the rest lies across the Canadian border in Alberta).

The Going-to-the-Sun Road, which links the east and west sides of the park by crossing the Continental Divide at Logan Pass, is one of the most beautiful drives in the world, but the over seven hundred miles of well-kept trails throughout the park are the only access to many isolated and magnificent areas.

For detailed information write Superintendent, Glacier National Park, West Glacier, Montana 59936. (406–888–5441).

Absaroka-Beartooth Wilderness. 920,000 acres astride Yellowstone Park. Comprises the highest and most rugged areas of Montana, 25 peaks over 10,000 feet. Snow is a year-round possibility.

Yellowstone National Park. Three of the five entrances are in Montana: at Gardiner on US 89, the Beartooth Highway (US 212), and US 191 and 287. (See section on Wyoming for detailed information about the park.) Or call 307–344–7381.

Bighorn Canyon National Recreation Area. Focal point of this 63,000-acre area in northern Wyoming and southern Montana is the 71-mile-long Bighorn Lake. Boating, camping and picnic facilities are available. Access is via Hardin. Contact the Superintendent, Bighorn Canyon National Recreation Area, Box 458, Fort Smith, MT 59035 (662–2412).

Beaverhead National Forest, in southwestern Montana east of Divide, is a great hunting and fishing area and one of the few places in the nation where grayling can be caught. In addition to scenic rugged mountains and alpine lakes there are hot springs and winter sports here. Park headquarters are at Skihi St. & U.S. 91, MT41, Box 1258, Dillon, MT 59725 (683–2312). Ranger Stations at Ennis, Sheridan, Dillon, Wisdom, and Wise River.

Bitterroot National Forest, west of the Divide in southwestern Montana, contains the 1,115,000-acre Selway-Bitterroot Wilderness, largest in the U.S. Mountain lakes, hot springs, scenic drives, fishing, hunting, and winter sports are also available. Also has handicapped facilities. Headquarters are in Hamilton. Contact the Forest Supervisor at Bitterroot National Forest. 316 N. 3rd St. (363–3131).

Custer National Forest, located in the southeast, partly in Montana, partly in South Dakota, offers winter sports, and big-game hunting. Granite peak, at 12,799 feet, is the highest point in Montana. There are also primitive areas, alpine plateaus, glaciers, and hundreds of lakes. Grasshopper Glacier has millions of grasshoppers imbedded within its depths. Headquarters are at Billings. Write the Custer National Forest, 2602 1st Ave. N., Billings, MT 59103 (657–6361).

Deerlodge National Forest headquartered at Butte has wilderness areas, alpine lakes, fishing, hunting, and winter sports. Box 400, Butte, MT 59703.

Flathead National Forest, south and west of Glacier National Park, is a heavily timbered area of rugged, glaciated mountains. There are wilderness and primitive areas here and fishing, hunting, boating, swimming, winter sports, and scenic drives. Headquarters are at Box 147, 1935 3rd Ave. E., Kalispell, MT, 59901 (406–755–5401).

Gallatin National Forest in south central Montana includes dramatic quake area camps and the beautiful Beartooth Scenic Highway. One of the gateways to Yellowstone. Headquarters are at the Federal Bldg., Box 130, Bozeman, MT 59715 (587–5271, ext. 4249). The Big Sky ski area is here.

Helena National Forest, straddling the Continental Divide in west central Montana offers almost 1 million acres of fishing, hunting, and wilderness areas. The Gates of the Mountains Wilderness, where the Missouri River begins and pushes through the Big Belt Range, contains a deep gorge lined with 2,000-foot limestone walls. Headquarters are at the Federal Bldg., Drawer 10015, 301 S. Park, Helena, MT 59601 (449–5201).

Kootenai National Forest, in the northwest corner of the state, offers wilderness, beautiful timber (including Giant Cedars), hunting, fishing, and winter sports. Contact headquarters at Box AS, Libby, MT 59923 (293–6211).

Lewis and Clark National Forest in north central Montana contains nearly two million acres of canyons, mountains, meadows, and wilderness. The 1,000-ft.-high, 15-mi.-long Chinese wall will be found here. Headquarters are at Galloway Center, Box 871, Great Falls, MT 59403 (727–0901).

Lolo National Forest, mostly west of the Divide in west central Montana, includes the famed Lewis and Clark Highway over the Bitterroot Mountains, and fishing, hunting, scenic drives and winter sports. Headquarters are located at Fort Missoula, Bldg. 24 (329–3750) or contact the Chamber of Commerce, P.O. Box 7577, Missoula, MT 59807 406–543–6623.

STATE PARKS. The *Lewis and Clark Caverns State Park,* just off I–90 forty-seven miles east of Butte, contains large limestone caverns. Delicate, varicolored stalactites and stalagmites make this one of the most beautiful caverns in the country. Guide service through the caverns is available, May through Labor Day.

Giant Springs State Park, four miles northeast of Great Falls on Missouri River. Here, in the Charles Russell Country, is one of the world's largest freshwater springs—it flows at a rate of 338 million gallons of water per day.

James Kipp Recreation Area, northeast of Lewistown off US 191, is the area said to have provided a hiding place for Kid Curry. Drinking water, stoves, tables, sanitary facilities, fishing, boating, and boat ramp are available.

Missouri Headwaters State Park is near Three Forks, off I–90.

Medicine Rocks State Park, north of Ekalaka off State 7, provides drinking water, stoves, tables, and sanitary facilities amidst 160 acres of weird sandrock formations. Lots of wildlife.

West Shore State Park is 20 miles south of Kalispell on Flathead Lake off US 93. Boating and camping on the lakeshore.

Missouri River Wolf Creek Canyon Recreation Area, can be found twenty-five miles north of Helena. Fishing, picnics, hiking.

For further information on state parks, contact Montana Fish, Wildlife, and Parks, 1420 E. 6th Ave., Helena, MT 59620.

INDIANS. There are seven Indian tribes living in Montana: Blackfeet Reservation, Browning; Flathead Reservation, Confederated Salish and Kootenai Tribes, Dixon; Crow Reservation, Crow Agency; Fort Belknap Reservation, Harlem; Fort Peck Reservation, Assiniboine and Sioux Tribes, Poplar; Northern Cheyenne Reservation, Northern Cheyenne Tribe, Lame Deer; Rocky Boy Reservation, Chippewa-Cree Tribe, Rocky Boy. At various times during the year these reservations hold powwows, dances, celebrations, fairs, rodeos, parades, and craft and art displays.

HOT SPRINGS. *Sleeping Child Hot Springs,* 3 mi. S of Hamilton on US 93, then E on State 38, then 11 mi. SE on County 501, offers swimming in natural hot springs and pool. The *Fairmont Hot Springs* on the edge of Anaconda provides a modern resort for health seekers.

In addition there are hot springs in the Bitterroot National Forest near Hamilton, in the Beaverhead National Forest near Dillon, and locally around such towns as White Sulphur Springs, Hot Spring, and Camas.

CAMPING OUT. Most State Parks and Recreation areas are open from May to Sept. Camping is limited to fourteen consecutive days. Fees are charged per night per vehicle. Complete information and brochures are available from the Montana Department of Fish, Wildlife & Parks, 1420 E. 6th Ave., Helena 59620.

Montana also offers a generous number of National Forest campgrounds, along with those on BLM lands.

Montana has far too many recreation areas to list all, so only information on the principal areas will be given (see also section on State Parks.). "Complete facilities" usually includes drinking water, stoves, tables, sanitary facilities, fishing, boating, swimming, and boat ramps are all available.

Ashley Lake, 15 mi. SW of Kalispell on US 2, then 13 mi. N on an unnumbered road. All facilities.

Big Arm, 12 mi. N of Polson on US 93 along the west shore of Flathead Lake. Complete facilities, including a boat ramp suitable for sailboats.

Bitterroot Lake, 23 mi. W of Kalispell off US 2. No showers.

Canyon Ferry, ten miles east of Helena on US 12, then nine miles north on State 284. Complete facilities.

Clark Canyon Reservoir, 20 mi. S of Dillon on US 91, I–15. Complete facilities.

Cooney Lake, twenty-two miles south of Laurel on US 212 to Boyd then nine miles west. No showers.

Deadman's Basin, 33 miles east of Harlowton off US 12. Complete facilities except drinking water.

Elmo, nineteen miles north of Polson off US 93 on the shore of Flathead Reservoir. Complete facilities.

Finley Point, twelve miles north of Polson off State 35, Complete facilities including golf course, nature program. Seven-day limit.

Fort Peck Dam and Reservoir, twenty miles southeast of Glasgow on State 24, is the world's second largest earth fill dam. Complete facilities.

Hell Creek, twenty-six miles north of Jordan off State 200. Complete facilities including rockhound areas.

Hooper, seventy-three miles east of Missoula off State 200. Drinking water, stoves, tables, sanitary facilities, and rockhound areas.

Lambeth Memory, formerly Lake Mary Ronan, seven miles northwest of Dayton, off US 93. Complete facilities except drinking water. Seven-day limit.

Logan, forty-five miles west of Kalispell off US 2. Complete facilities.

Nelson Reservoir, nineteen miles northeast of Malta on US 2, then north. Complete facilities, but no swimming.

Painted Rocks, twenty miles south of Hamilton on US 93, then twenty-three miles southwest of State 473. Complete facilities.

Rock Creek, fifty miles south of Glasgow off State 24. Complete facilities, except swimming.

Rosebud, at Forsyth on the Yellowstone River. No swimming or drinking water.

Wayfarers, south of Bigfork off State 35. Complete facilities.

Whitefish Lake, out of Whitefish on west shore of lake off US 93. Complete facilities. Seven-day limit.

Woods Bay, seventeen miles southeast of Kalispell off State 35. Complete facilities.

Yellow Bay, fifteen miles south of Bigfork on State 35 along east shore. Complete facilities.

TRAILER TIPS. For information about trailer and campground sites, contact Montana Dept. of Fish, Wildlife and Parks, 1420 E. 6th Ave., Helena 59620

West Yellowstone: Beaver Creek National Forest, 8 mi. N on US 191, has 65 sites with flush toilets and boating. Open June 1 to Sept. 15.

Kalispell: Bitterroot Lake State Park, 20 mi. W on US 2, then 5 mi. N on Marion Rd., 17 miles west on US 287, has 20 sites and swimming, boating, and fishing. Open May 1 to Oct. 30.

East Glacier Park: Two Medicine National Park, 8 mi. NW on State 49 then 4 mi. W on County Rd., has 100 sites, store, snack bar, swimming, boating, fishing.

Fort Peck: Rock Creek, 31 mi. S on State 24 then 5 mi. W on dirt road, has 15 sites and swimming, boating and fishing.

West Glacier Park: Fish Creek National Park, 4 mi. NW on Sun Rd., has 180 sites, flush toilets, swimming, and fishing.

FARM VACATIONS AND GUEST RANCHES. Montana has dozens of first-rate guest or "dude" ranches which are either working ranches with crops and livestock where guests are another source of income, or mountain ranches primarily for guests which run only horses for that purpose. Either type of ranch is an excellent way to get the best of Montana, for you meet congenial and characteristic local types. Ranches furnish the necessary guides for pack trips, fishing, hunting, etc., and can make sidetrips to points of interest. Yet, you have thoroughly modern accommodations on the whole.

Most dude ranches require advance reservations. The best sources of information are the railroads or airlines serving the state or the *Montana Travel Promotion Bureau,* Helena, Montana 59620 (406–444–2654), which will be glad to furnish an up-to-date list of ranches. Most ranches open for June-Sept. season only, and most will meet you at train or plane.

Here is a partial list of suggestions:

Yellowstone Country. *Beartooth Ranch,* Nye, 59016 (406–328–6194 or 328–6205). Fishing, horseback riding, pack trips.

Big Sky of Montana, Box 1, 59716 (406–995–4211), Big Sky. Year-round resort. Golf, tennis, fishing, horses, gondola rides.

Chico Hot Springs Lodge, Pray, 59065 (406–333–4933). Fine dining, riding, fishing.

G Bar M Ranch, Clyde Park, 59018 (406–686–4687). operating stock ranch some thirty miles off I–90 northwest of Livington. Horses and fishing.

Hawley Mountain Ranch, McLeod, 59052 (406–932–5791). Riding, floating, cabins, lodge. Fishing and hunting in season.

Lazy K Bar Ranch, Big Timber, 59011 (406–537–4404). In the Crazy Mountains north of Big Timber.

Mountain Sky Guest Ranch, Box 1128, Bozeman, 59771 (1–800–548–3392). Year-round near Yellowstone.

Parade Rest Ranch, West Yellowstone, 59758 (406–646–7271). Riding in wild area or Yellowstone Park.

Lone Mountain Guest Ranch, Box 69, Big Sky, 59716, (406–995–4644). Forty miles south of Bozeman. Part of the Big Sky complex, this retreat provides summer recreation in an atmosphere typical of a western ranch. Cross-country skiing in winter.

63 Ranch, Livingston, 59047 (406–995–4283). Working stock ranch. Riding, hunting.

Stillwater Valley Ranch, Nye, 59052 (406–932–6108). Float fishing on Yellowstone River. Fly fishing instruction.

Sweet Grass Ranch, Melville Rt., Box 161, Big Timber, 59011 (406–537–4497). Working ranch. Cabins, lodge, family-style meals.

320 Ranch, Gallatin Gtwy. Cabins, riding, pack trips.

X Bar A Ranch, McLeod. Working cattle ranch. Riding, fishing.

Glacier Park Area. *Bear Creek Ranch,* East Glacier Park, 59434 (406–226–4489). five miles west of the Divide off US 2 to the south. Open all season and for fall hunting. Trail rides into the park and Flathead National Forest.

Willow Fire Inn, RR 1, Box 64, Eureka, 59917 (406–889–3343). Working ranch near Kootenai Reservoir. Trail rides, pack trips.

Western Mountain Area. *Flathead Lake Lodge,* (406–837–4391). one mile south of Bigfork on the east shore of Flathead Lake. This dude ranch on a lake has pools, lake sports and rides, horseback riding, barbecues, square dancing.

Diamond Bar X, Augusta, 59410 (406–562–3524). Trail rides, fishing, summer horse camp for kids, fall hunting.

Ford Creek Ranch, Box 329, Augusta, 59410 (406–562–3672). Hunting, fishing, pack trips.

Montana Sports Ranch, Condon, 59868 (406–754–2351). Open year-round for hiking, fishing, riding, cross-country skiing.

Other Areas. *CB Cattle & Guest Ranch,* Box 604, Cameron 59720 (406–682–4954). Working ranch. Fishing, horses.

Canyon Creek Guest Ranch, Box 126M Melrose 59743 (1–800–228–4333). Float trips, jeep rides to ghost towns, trail rides.

MUSEUMS AND GALLERIES. The **Montana Historical Society** at 225 N. Roberts St. in Helena (406–444–2694) presents a capsule history of Montana in dramatic dioramas and a permanent collection of Charles M. Russell's art.

Charles M. Russell Original Studio and Museum at 12th St. and 4th Ave. N. in Great Falls (406–727–8787) exhibits many of the late cowboy artist's oils, watercolors, sketches, letters, and sculptures. The adjacent original log cabin studio contains the artist's easels and other memorabilia, along with Russell's own collection of Indian costumes and gear, watercolors and changing exhibits, lectures, films and children's theatre.

Museum of the Rockies, on the Montana State University Campus in Bozeman, contains Indian and pioneer relics. *Artifacts Gallery,* 308 E. Main, Bozeman, displays craftwork in stoneware, jewelry, fiber, ceramics and mixed media.

Range Riders Museum and Pioneer Memorial Hall, on US 10, 12, west of Miles City, presents exhibits and memorabilia from early range life (406–232–3465).

J. K. Ralston Museum & Art Center, 221 5th St. S.W. in Sidney, exhibits historical artifacts from the region and original Ralston paintings.

The Central Montana Museum, 408 E. Main St. in Lewistown, casts a light on early Montana history via photos and dioramas (406–538–5436).

World Museum of Mining, W. Park St., one mile west of Butte at Golden Girl Mine, has indoor and outdoor displays of mining tools, equipment, and relics.

Museum of the Yellowstone, 124 Yellowstone Ave., West Yellowstone, has Indian artifacts, military memorabilia and wildlife exhibits.

Fort Benton Museum, 1800 Front St. in Fort Benton, has dioramas and displays on steamboats, Indians, and agriculture. Open 10 to 7, June to Aug.; May 19 to 31 and Sept. 1 to 15. 1 to 5 P.M. Closed rest of year.

Beaverhead County Museum, 15 S. Montana St. in Dillon (406–683–5511). offers Indian artifacts, geological displays, and memorabilia of frontier and mining days. Free.

Fort Missoula Museum, southwest of Missoula, was one of Montana's first military outposts. It was built in 1877.

In downtown Billings, the smallish *Yellowstone Art Center,* 401 N. 27th, presents paintings, prints and sculpture of the region.

Copper Village Museum and Arts Center, 110 E. 8th St., Anaconda, will interest mining buffs (406–563–8421).

HISTORIC SITES. Rosebud Battlefield, N of Decker on Rt. 314. This is the site of the largest Indian battle in the U.S.—the battle between Sioux warriors and General Cook's troops in 1876.

Custer Battlefield National Monument. Located in southeastern Montana, this scene of the famous Last Stand memorializes one of the last armed efforts of the Northern Plains Indians to resist the westward march of the white man's civilization. In 1876 in the valley of the Little Bighorn River, several thousand Sioux and Cheyenne warriors did battle with the U.S. Army troops under the command of Lt. Col. George A. Custer. Although the Indians won this battle, killing Custer and all his men, they lost the war against the white man who brought an end to their independent, nomadic way of life. Dioramas, exhibits, and background and history programs are offered.

Big Hole Battlefield National Monument. In August 1877, a force of U.S. Army troops staged a surprise attack against a band of Nez Percé Indians led by Chief Joseph. Having refused reservation life, this nomadic tribe made a courageous though futile attempt to reach Canadian sanctuary. Audio-visual programs and displays of firearms and frontier relics are available at the visitors' center.

Chief Joseph Battlefield, sixteen miles south of Chinook on MT Sec. 240. The site of the final battle and surrender of Chief Joseph of the Nez Percé, which brought an end, in 1877, to Montana's Indian wars.

Old Fort Benton, on the riverfront near Main St. in Fort Benton. The ruins of an old trading post and blockhouse still remain from the frontier days when the town was an important commercial center.

Missouri River Headwaters Monument, thirty-one miles northwest of Bozeman on I–90, near Three Forks. Here Lewis and Clark discovered the Jefferson, Madison, and Gallatin Rivers joining to form the Missouri.

Montana Territorial Prison, 1106 Main St., Deer Lodge, was the first of its kind in the Western U.S. It's now a museum.

Original Montana Governor's Mansion, 304 N. Ewing St., Helena, was built in 1885 and has housed nine governors since 1913.

Pompey's Pillar, near the town of the same name, is a towering sandstone rock, where Capt. Clark carved his name in 1806.

Prehistoric fossil field, south of Fort Peck Dam in the northeastern corner of the state.

Prehistoric Indian site (Hagen), near Glendive off I–94.

Virginia City, southwest of Bozeman on Route 287. Restored early-day mining boom town and political capital.

TOURS. *Glacier Park, Inc.,* offers four-, five- and six-day tours of Glacier National Park and Waterton Lakes National Park, Canada. Tours include lodging, meals, launch cruises, and transportation via scenic coaches. Bus service is also available between hotels, and to and from depots and lakes. This is essentially a scenic tour on the park's lakes and highways. For complete information and rates write Glacier Park, Inc., East Glacier, Montana 59434 (406–226–5551) (summer), or Glacier Park, Inc., Greyhound Tower Sta. No. 5185, Phoenix, AZ 85077 (602–248–6000) (winter).

SPECIAL-INTEREST TOURS. Roaming buffalo, at the *National Bison Range,* at Moiese (south of Charlo and the Nine Pipe National Migratory Waterfowl Refuge), may be seen from June through Labor Day on 19-mile self-guided automobile tours. There is also the possibility of seeing the majestic elk, deer, antelope, mountain goat, and bighorn sheep.

Wilderness walks into many of the remote areas of Montana designed especially for the visitor who may not have the equipment or much stamina are arranged by the Montana Wilderness Assn., Great Falls. If you can, write ahead; if you're passing through and get the urge, call them—they may be able to work you in. These walks have informed guides and are unique. The Association is also represented in Bozeman and other communities. Call 406–761–4434 for more information.

Forest fire fighting is explained in full at the Aerial Fire Depot west of Missoula, Montana, on US 10. Special tours are held from mid-June until Labor Day. Call 406–329–3131 for times.

Earthquake damage explained in self-guiding tour around Hebegen Lake on US 287 between Ennis and West Yellowstone. Contact the Chamber of Commerce, Yellowstone at Canyon, Box 458, 59758.

Missouri River boat cruises, à la Lewis and Clark, are held each June depending on when water is best. They usually take three or more days, and everything's furnished. Contact State Travel Promotion Unit in Helena, or Chamber of Commerce, Fort Benton, 59442, for current information.

Big Mountain Ski Area summer chair lift operates June 15-Labor Day for a high view of the Western Rockies.

Snow-vehicle rides in Yellowstone from West Yellowstone are available in winter. Contact Yellowstone Park Company, Yellowstone National Park, 82190.

Figure Eight Drive scenic tour of mountains and ghost towns every summer day from Helena. Call 406–442–4120.

Last Chance Tour Train and London Bus around Helena on an automotive train explores the city's past and present history, including Pioneer Cabin. Built in 1865, this building has been renovated and furnished with pioneer artifacts. Tours take one and one-half hours and leave from the Montana State Historical Museum several times a day from June 15 to Labor Day. Montana College in Billings also organizes guided tours. Phone 406–443–7641.

FISHING. Seasonal licenses are required for nonresidents and 5-day permits are available. The fishing season traditionally starts the third Saturday in May and ends around Nov. 30. Local inquiry to the State Fish and Game Department will give you further information about laws and locations of the types of fish you want.

Some of the good fishing spots are:

Madison River. One-half mile to twelve miles south of Ennis in southern Montana. Inquire about local restrictions.

Flathead River. Six miles east of Somers at New Holt Bridge (five acres) in western Montana.

Clark Fork River. Rock Creek south of Missoula turnoff on I–90 just east of Clinton (107 acres).

For **lake** fishermen, the state provides public access at these lakes: *Seeley,* ten miles northwest of Ovando; *Sophie,* State 32 NW of Eureka; *Broadview Pond,* near Broadview; *Park Lake,* I–15 south of Helena; *Savage Lake,* near Troy; *Dailey Lake,* 22 miles south of Livingston; *Boot Jack Lake,* US 93 NW of Whitefish; *Skyles Lake,* near Whitefish, *Swain,* six miles east of Big Fork; on 209 near Eureka; *Crystal,* US 2 West of Kalipell.

A quick rundown on respected fishing locations by type of fish: *Big Blackfoot River,* western Montana near Bonner, rainbow and cutthroat trout, sockeye salmon in headwaters.

Big Hole River, southwestern Montana, rainbow, brown, grayling, and cutthroat trout.

Bitterroot River a few miles below Missoula, rainbow, brook, and brown trout.

Clark Fork River, drains west of Missoula, various trout species, with boat fishing on Cabinet Gorge Reservoir for Kokanee salmon as well.

Flathead Lake. Cutthroat, rainbow, Dolly Varden, and sockeye salmon, with some bass in protected bays; salmon plentiful in fall.

Fort Peck Reservoir. Pike, catfish, and other warm-water species.

Gallatin River, near Bozeman, good trout, stream heading toward Yellowstone park.

Georgetown Lake, near Anaconda. Rainbow, and eastern brook trout.

Jefferson River, above Twin Bridges, and the *Madison River* near Ennis, very good for rainbow and brown trout. (Special regulations.)

Judith River, near Lewistown, in central Montana, various trout species.

Kootenai River, near Libby and Troy, cutthroat and Dolly Varden.

Lake Koocanusa, near Libby. Kokanee salmon, whitefish, ling, trout.

Marias River near Shelby and Tiber Reservoir, good trout fishing in both stream and reservoir.

Milk River, Glasgow to Havre, trout near headwaters, tending to crappie and walleye out on plains and in Fresno Reservoir.

Missouri River, trout in the headwaters; boat fishing at Holter, Hauser, and Canyon Ferry Dams, for brown trout, rainbow, and salmon. Downstream harbors sturgeon, walleye pike, northern pike, sunfish, crappies, catfish and perch.

Yellowstone River, good from Yellowstone Park headwaters through southeastern Montana. Cutthroat high in headwaters region, then rainbow, brown and whitefish in Livingston to Columbus area, parallel to I–90. Catfish, and warmer water species take over east of Billings on the hot, dry plains where the river meanders.

HUNTING. Combination Hunting Licenses are expensive for non-residents. Hunting regulations vary according to the game and residence status. The license entitles the hunter to one elk, one deer, one black bear, various birds, plus fishing.

For full hunting details contact the Montana Department of Fish and Game Dept., Helena 59601. The seasons tend to vary from year to year depending on the annual conditions. There is usually an early elk and deer season in the wilder hunting areas (around the wildernesses) in September. The regular deer and elk season begins in late October and generally runs until late November. Antelope hunting, on a drawing-quota basis only, begins one week earlier than deer and elk season and ends around the middle of November. Goat, sheep, and moose, also on the quota system, begin in mid-September and run until mid-November. Black and brown bear season opens around March 15 and runs until mid-November. Bird hunting begins in early September and runs till the end of the year for ducks and geese, November 30 for grouse and pheasant. Special quotas pertain to ducks and geese on the Central Fly Way.

Montana has more than two dozen game preserves, where many special rules apply to each species. Write for full instructions before coming to hunt.

SUMMER SPORTS. Golfing. There are three dozen courses in Montana at most principal cities. Some are public, many private, but easy to get on if you go through your hotel or local tourist center. Your attention is especially called to the beautiful vacation settings at Polson, Kalispell, Whitefish, and Libby, all public. There is a golf course at East Glacier; the nearest to Yellowstone is Bozeman. Billings offers golf as well. Greens fees are moderate and many of the clubs have the normal pro shop services.

Tennis. Billings has more than 30 public tennis courts. Montana's smaller communities all have some facilities. The Big Sky Resort also offers this sport to its summer guests.

Rock Hunting. Montana attracts rockhounds. Sapphires, rubies, garnets, and moss agates are found. The State Advertising Department has a special pamphlet for rockhounds, and agate shops are frequent on the highways.

Boating. Water-skiing and power-boating are common on the larger lakes and reservoirs. Montana boating laws, fairly standard, are available from the State Fish and Game Commission in Helena.

WINTER SPORTS. *Skiing.* For a complete guide on skiing write Dept. of Highways, Helena, Montana 59601, or phone 1–800–548–3390. Major ski areas in Montana are as follows: *Big Sky.* The late Chet Huntley's dream, some forty-five miles south of Bozeman, is one of the keystones of Western skiing. Two passenger gondolas and numerous triple and double chairs span many miles of downhill and cross-country terrain. Mountain village with lodge, shops, and restaurants make this a complete resort. Special beginners package. Write the Big Sky Resort, Box 1, Big Sky, MT 59716 (406–995–4211).

Big Mountain Ski Area. Whitefish, alt. 4,774–7,000 feet. Opens around Thanksgiving, closes around May 1: lodge at area, and hotels and motels are in Whitefish; four triple and two double chair lifts, T-bar, pomalift, and rope tow; excellent runs for all classes; ski patrol, ski school, shops, rental equipment, a cafeteria and restaurant. Write the Big Mountain, Box 1215, Whitefish, MT 59937 (406–862–3511).

Red Lodge Mountain, sixty-five miles southwest of Billings and six miles west of Red Lodge; alt. 7,400–9,400 ft.; season Nov. to May; hotels and motels at Red Lodge; one triple and four double chair lifts, one pomalift; 25 miles of trails and slopes from beginner to high intermediate and expert; access by train or Northwest, Delta, or United to Billings and from there by bus; ski patrol, ski school, rental, and chalet for meals. Summer camp for young racers. Call in-state 446–2503, or toll free out-of-state 800–468–8977.

Other Montana ski areas: All have some kind of lift and generate considerable local activity. *Bear Paw,* 30 miles south of Havre; *Beef Trail,* eight miles southwest of Butte; *Belmont,* 25 miles northwest of Helena; *Bridger Bowl,* sixteen miles northeast of Bozeman; *Deep Creek* on Wise River, 45 miles southwest of Butte; *Red Lodge Mt.,* six miles west of Red Lodge; *Lost Trail,* 45 miles south of Hamilton; *Marshall Mountain,* 7 miles northeast of Missoula; *Maverick Mountain,* 40 miles northwest of Dillon: *Teton Pass,* 23 miles northwest of Choteau; *Montana Snow Bowl,* 13 miles north of Missoula; *Turner Mountain,* 21 miles northwest of Libby; *Discovery Basin,* 18 miles northwest of Anaconda. For some excellent ski touring, enthusiasts travel to *Big Sky, Big Mountain, Essex, Blacktail Mountain* and other areas. For ski conditions and general area information, phone 1–800–548–3390.

CHILDREN'S ACTIVITIES. The extensive parks and recreation areas in Montana give youngsters a chance to run free and to work off their excess energy in the clean air of the mountains, lakes and valleys.

Near Ronan the *Ninepipe* and *Pablo National Wildlife Refuges* has some spots to see waterfowl. Over 185 species have been observed here, including ducks, geese, grebes, bitterns, and cormorants. And at the *National Bison Range,* 300–500 head of buffalo roam over a range of 18,500 acres.

Fish, and trout in particular, of all sizes can be seen at the *Fish Hatcheries* in Bozeman, Great Falls and in Lewistown. Picnic facilities are nearby.

Missoula's *Children's Theater* will delight youngsters.

Ghost towns and restored *frontier towns* give a sense of the frontier and mining past. Maiden, Kendall, and Gilt Edge, all near Lewistown, are ghost towns left over from the mining days of the 19th century. Helena's *Frontier Town* is a replica of a pioneer village, hewn out of solid rock and cut from giant trees. *Virginia City* is a restored gold-boom town with newspaper office, livery stable, general store, blacksmith shop and others. There is a train ride to *Nevada City* where there are authentic replicas of early mining stores, homes, and schools. The Nevada City Depot has a *railroad museum* with antique engines and cars. The *Western Heritage Center* in downtown Billings appeals to youngsters with its Indian and Trappers displays and its cowboy relics.

At the end of a car ride from Butte are *Lewis and Clark Caverns* where children can go underground into a wonderland of colorful rock formations.

STAGE AND REVUES. The University of Montana (Missoula) and Montana State University (Bozeman) are worth checking out. Many student and professional events—including plays, song recitals and ballets—take place during the year, and the prices are usually very reasonable. The hotels in major cities will be aware of any professional shows and local scheduling—such as Community Concert Series. In Billings, the local symphony orchestra performs six times a year.

Summer theater: Bigfork, *Bigfork Summer Playhouse,* weekly musicals beginning in June and running through August usually starts around 8 P.M. Fort Peck, *Fort Peck Summer Theater* presents weekend shows June to August. Admission is charged. Virginia City *Players* present 19th-century melodrama every night June through Labor Day. Helena, the *Grand Street Theatre* offers year-round productions every weekend.

At West Yellowstone's *Playmill Theatre,* college students stage nightly musical comedy and melodrama performances May to September.

MUSIC. The *Symphony Association* at Great Falls sponsors concerts during the late spring and summer. Billings, Missoula, and Helena both have their own symphonies, and during the summer months Helena has *municipal band concerts.*

LIQUOR LAWS. The legal drinking age in Montana is 19 years. Most bars are open until 2 A.M. Monday through Saturday nights. You can buy liquor by the bottle at state liquor stores in each town, as well as from bars, 8–2 A.M. daily. No special license is required. You may order liquor by the drink in Montana bars, and some sell bottles over the counter.

NEVADA

Entertainment Capital of the World

by
MURRAY HERTZ and STEPHEN ALLEN

Murray Hertz is a publisher of magazines. Stephen Allen is a Las Vegas-based freelance travel writer.

If Nevada is a paradox, Las Vegas must truly be seen to be believed. One of the fastest-growing cities in the U.S., the "Entertainment Capital of the World" is engaged in supplying the needs, interests, and amusements of the 13 million visitors who streak in annually.

Glamour and glitter are the passwords in the desert oasis of Las Vegas. Neon lights flash, blink, and perform every possible kind of optical illusion all day long and all night long. World-famous entertainers star in the floor shows, and between shows you may find yourself rubbing elbows with them at the gaming tables.

The Las Vegas "Strip"

In the town itself there are many interesting things to see, among them some of the most luxurious resort hotels in the world. These are concentrated along the "Strip," a three-and-one-half mile boulevard which parallels Interstate 15. Here, stage spectaculars from Broadway

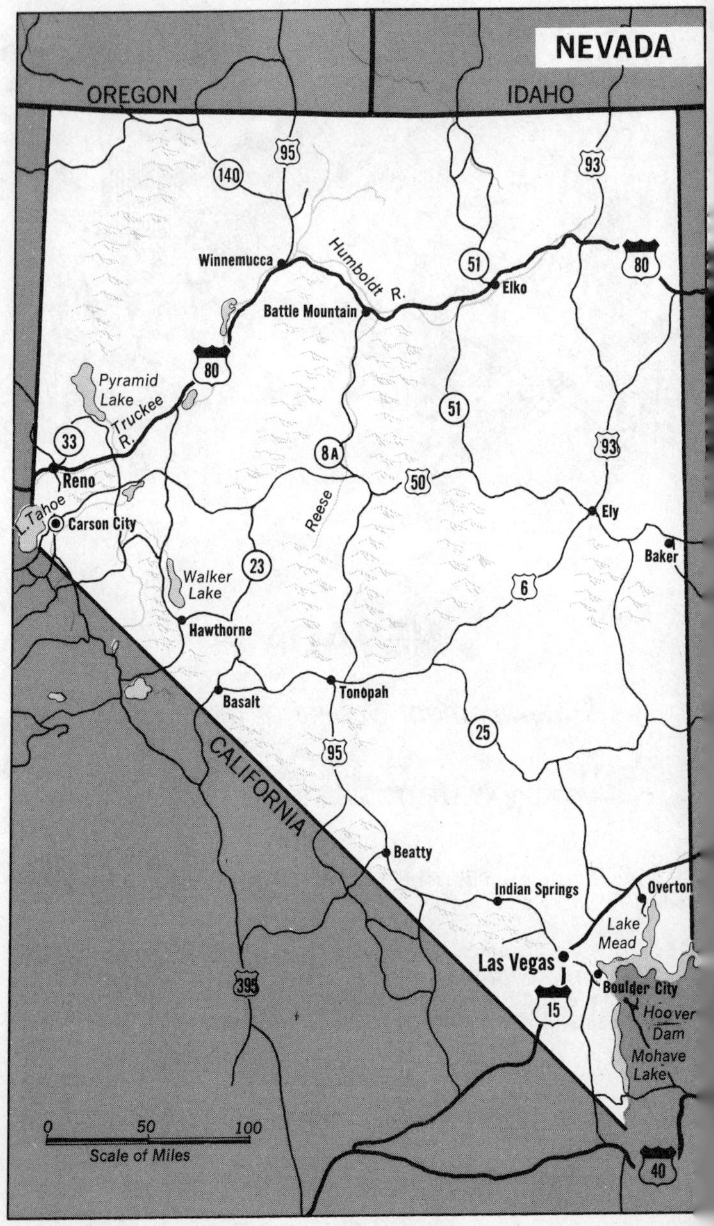
NEVADA
OREGON
IDAHO
95
140
93
Winnemucca
Humboldt R.
51
80
Elko
Battle Mountain
80
Pyramid Lake
Truckee R.
51
33
93
8A
Reno
50
L. Tahoe
Carson City
Reese
Ely
Baker
23
Walker Lake
6
Hawthorne
Basalt
Tonopah
25
95
CALIFORNIA
Beatty
Indian Springs
Overton
Lake Mead
Las Vegas
Boulder City
Hoover Dam
15
395
Mohave Lake
0
50
100
Scale of Miles
40

and Europe spotlight the world's greatest entertainers. Here also is offered fine food and drink and the utmost in comfort and service.

Las Vegas is also one of the world's great convention centers. It has a huge 825,000-square-foot complex built expressly for this purpose—a modern, steel structure resembling a giant flying saucer hovering over the desert. The rotunda seats 7,000 persons at a time.

Bus or air tours of Las Vegas, Hoover Dam, the Grand Canyon or even Death Valley, 145 miles northwest, can easily be arranged from your hotel.

Circle Tour of Nevada

If you can allow a full nine days to explore Nevada, a memorable trip covering every corner of the state awaits you. If you do not have nine days to spare, plan to make your base at any of the stopover points to be designated later and see as much as you can. For reference, consult any good map of the state, such as the official Nevada map that can be obtained by writing the Department of Transportation, 1263 S. Stewart St., Carson City, NV 89712.

Starting from Las Vegas, two one-day excursions are recommended. Begin by driving south from the city on US 93 to charming little Boulder City. Here you can stop at the Visitors' Center for information about Hoover Dam, or at the headquarters of the Lake Mead National Recreation Area, where maps, exhibits, and a schedule of tours and other activities will suggest how best to spend the rest of your day. If you want to explore on your own, start with the tour of Hoover Dam, then drive on to Willow Beach on the Arizona side of Lake Mohave. Here you will develop a fast appreciation for the effort it required to tame the rampant Colorado in such a rugged setting. Return to Hoover Dam and proceed along the shore of Lake Mead to the marina for swimming, boat rides, sweeping views. In March there are superb wildflower displays throughout the countryside. From the marina, return to Boulder City and poke into the desert region south of US 95—Nelson Canyon, site of rip-roaring mining squabbles of the last century, Searchlight, and Davis Dam. Depending on how long you dally, you can be back in Las Vegas in eight hours.

To the Valley of Fire

A rewarding second tour begins with the drive to Henderson on US 95. Here turn left at the junction of Lake Mead Dr. and continue on the scenic highway built by the Lake Mead National Recreation Area to Echo Bay. This paved road takes you through some of the most remote, topsy-turvy mountain and desert country in the West. Stop at Echo Bay (with its motel, dining room, and marina), then proceed on to Overton and visit Lost City Museum of Archeology, where exhibits of ancient Indian dwellings are featured. Backtrack now and enter the Valley of Fire State Park, exploring this magnificent series of red and yellow sandstone natural carvings via a slow-speed paved road through the park. Indian civilizations responsible for the petroglyphs on these rocks are believed to have inhabited the valley about 1500 B.C. You can spend two hours here, or half a day if you wish to poke. The Visitor Center, will provide you with material on the park's attractions, such as Elephant Rock, Mouse's Tank, Atlatl Rock, and the Beehives. An exit from the park puts you on Interstate 15. Turn right if you have two hours to spare, and explore the early Mormon farming towns of Mesquite, Bunkerville, and Logandale. Bunkerville, with its well-preserved early houses, is particularly interesting. Or, by returning directly to Las Vegas from the park, you will have time to see colorful Red Rock Canyon, 15 miles west of town. The entire trip takes about eight hours.

Bombs and Death Valley

Starting from Las Vegas, head out for a long day's drive on US 95 north, detouring 15 miles from town to take State 157 up to Mt. Charleston, the highest range in the vicinity. This road carries you through heavy stands of yucca and cactus up to elevations where evergreens dominate and where substantial snowfall allows skiing in winter. Returning to US 95, continue north past the Department of Energy Nevada Test Site, at Mercury, to Beatty, another old mining town. Recommended now is a loop drive into Death Valley, reached on State 374 from Beatty via the ghost town of Rhyolite (see *Where to Go*) and steep-walled Grapevine Canyon. In Death Valley take State 190 (Calif.) through this famous and desolate desert basin to Scotty's Castle, an odd bit of architecture now open to the public as a museum. You won't want to miss it. From Scotty's return via State 72 into Nevada and proceed to Tonopah. En route you pass through Goldfield, a pitiful remnant of the Tonopah-Goldfield boom nearly 100 years ago. Tonopah, with its imposing old buildings, is still prosperous, and you can spend a lively evening at the town's colorful casinos. Total driving and sightseeing time for the day is eight to ten hours.

Ichthyosaur, Anyone?

Another long driving day and you have several inviting alternate routes, the first being from Tonopah via State 376 through one of Nevada's characteristic, isolated interior basins, Smoky Valley. Detour on State 377 to see the semi-ghost towns of Manhattan and Belmont and, when you reach US 50, a boomtown of a century ago, Austin. Continue west on US 50 past the famous Singing Sand Mountain, the naval air base at Fallon, the rich ranching area fed by Lahontan Dam (first Federal reclamation project in the country) to your overnight stop at either Carson City or Lake Tahoe. (Advance reservations advised in summer.) The second route from Tonopah leads from Luning to Gabbs. Detour here to Berlin-Ichthyosaur State Park over a mostly paved road. The remains of the ancient, sea-going ichthyosaur lie near the bleak ghost town of Berlin. Ichthyosaurs dominated the seas 160 million years ago, ages before the dinosaur, and this deposit of fossilized bones in central Nevada, the only one of its kind in the world, is well worth visiting. Continue on to US 50 via Buffalo Canyon (ask the park ranger), or return via Gabbs, on to Carson City or Lake Tahoe. Third route is via the main highway, US 95, past impressive Walker Lake to Yerington, where you can stop to see Anaconda's big copper operation. Continue via State 208 and US 395 through the pretty ranching towns of Minden and Gardnerville to your destination. You can take a short loop from above Gardnerville to Mormon Station at Genoa, site of the first settlement in the state. Spend the evening seeing the clubs in Carson City, or take in a big Las Vegas-like show at one of the hotel-casinos in Reno, Tahoe or Stateline.

Underground Tour

If you are spending your vacation in the Ely area, you can begin by driving up US 93 to the company plant at McGill to see how copper ore is processed. Next, for a visit to the amazing Lehman Caves, return to Ely and head out via US 50 and State 21 to the entrance to the caves west of Baker. The underground tour of the caves takes at least an hour, and you will be smart to take along warm clothing for the walk through the chilly but spectacular underground caverns.

From Baker you will enjoy taking one of the scenic roads into the high country surrounding Wheeler Peak in the Snake Range, or a hike along one of the many well-tended trails maintained by the Forest Service. This tour eats up most of your day.

Alpine Vistas

One of the most beautiful drives in the world is that around the perimeter of Lake Tahoe, which has been called by many one of the most spectacular lakes on earth. Lake Tahoe is easily accessible from Reno via US 395 and State 28. Passing through unspoiled stands of pine and cedar, you will enjoy breathtaking views of the vivid, blue, freshwater lake—6,000 feet high, second in size and altitude only to South America's Lake Titicaca.

PRACTICAL INFORMATION FOR NEVADA

HOW TO GET THERE. By Plane. Reno and Las Vegas may be reached by American, Continental, Delta, Eastern, Frontier, Northwest Orient, PSA, Republic (Hughes Airwest), Pan Am (National) TWA, United and Western direct flights, as well as by connecting flights from innumerable points in the U.S.A., and Commuter Air Lines. From Calgary, Canada, Republic, and Western fly direct to Las Vegas. From Reno-Cannon International Airport, you can get an Airporter bus to South Lake Tahoe.

By Car. The Reno-Lake Tahoe region is easy to reach via major all-year freeways: scenic U.S. Hwy. 50 and I–80 from San Francisco and Sacramento; U.S. Hwy. 395 from Los Angeles; I–80 from Salt Lake City and points east, and San Francisco and Sacramento from the west. Las Vegas is easily reached by I–15 north from Los Angeles and I–15 south from Salt Lake City. US–93 from Kingman, Arizona, US–95 from Reno and San Francisco.

By Train. Amtrak has service from the East, Midwest, and West to Reno and Las Vegas.

By Bus. Greyhound and Trailways, from all points.

ACCOMMODATIONS. Hotels and motels in Nevada range from the superbly flamboyant ones of Las Vegas to the quiet, plain, but comfortable establishments along the country roads to the north of the city of casinos. Most of Las Vegas' luxury hotels are located on "the Strip." It is in these hostelries that you can wash your shirt, or lose it, depending on how successful you are at beating the house at blackjack, craps, or the roulette wheel. Prices quoted are double occupancy. Most hotel rooms are the same rate single or double. *Deluxe* $60 and up, *Expensive* $50–$60, *Moderate* $30–$50, and *Inexpensive* under $30. Hotels are listed by price category.

All area codes in Nevada are 702.

BOULDER CITY. Boulder Dam Hotel. *Moderate.* 1305 Arizona St., Boulder City, NV 89005 (293–1808). A national historic sight. Charming rooms.

Nevada Inn. *Moderate.* 1009 Nevada Hwy., Boulder City, NV 89005 (293–2044). French provincial decor.

El Rancho Boulder Motel. *Moderate.* 725 Nevada Hwy., Boulder City, NV 89005 (293–1085). Spanish-style motel, some kitchen units.

CARSON CITY. Ormsby House. *Moderate.* 600 S. Carson St., Carson City, NV 89701 (882–1890). Best hotel in Carson City, 200 rooms.

Best Western City Center Motel. *Moderate.* 800 N. Carson St., Carson City, NV 89701 (882–5535).

Carson City TraveLodge. *Moderate.* 1400 N. Carson St., Carson City, NV 89701 (882–3446).

Hardman House Motor Inn. *Moderate.* 917 N. Carson St., Carson City, NV 89701 (882–7744). Queens, kings, and suites.

Frontier Motel. *Inexpensive–Deluxe.* 1718 N. Carson St., Carson City, NV 89701 (882–1377). Room rates to fit every pocketbook.

ELKO. Best Western Marquis Motor Inn. *Moderate.* 837 Idaho St., Eklo, NV 89801 (738–7261). Heated pool, oversized beds.

Esquire Motor Lodge. *Moderate.* 505 Idaho St., Elko, NV 89801 (738–3157). Family rates, in-room coffee.

Holiday Inn. *Moderate.* E. Elko Interchange, Elko, NV 89801 (738–8425). One mile from downtown.

Stampede 7 Motel. *Inexpensive.* 129 W. Idaho St., Elko, NV 89801 (738–8471). Large rooms, refrigerators.

Stockman's Motor Hotel. *Moderate–Deluxe.* 340 Commercial St., Elko, NV 89801 (738–5141). Large, modern operation with casino, dancing, entertainment, pool, golf, tennis, fishing.

ELY. El Rancho Motel. *Inexpensive.* 1400 Aultman St., Ely, NV 89301 (289–3644).

Idle Inn. *Inexpensive.* 150 4th St., Ely, NV 89301 (289–4411). Family units and commercial rates.

FALLON. Fallon TraveLodge. *Moderate.* 70 E. Williams Ave., Fallon, NV 89406 (423–2194). Restaurant one block away.

Western Motel. *Inexpensive.* 125 S. Carson St., Fallon, NV 89406 (423–5118). Restaurant adjacent.

Ranch Motel. *Inexpensive.* 1705 S. Taylor St., Fallon, NV 89406 (423–2277). Kitchenettes available.

HAWTHORNE. Best Western El Capitan. *Moderate.* 540 F. St., Hawthorne, NV 89406 (945–3321). Casino, restaurant, bar, coffee shop, pool, entertainment.

Holiday Lodge. *Inexpensive.* W. 5th & J Sts., Hawthorne, NV 89415 (945–3316).

INCLINE VILLAGE. Cal-Neva Lodge. *Deluxe.* Incline Village at Crystal Bay, NV 89402 (832–4000). Casino. Minutes from many ski resorts. Nine-story hotel with 220 rooms, most with lake views; also cabins, chalets.

Incline Motor Lodge. *Deluxe.* 1003 Tahoe Blvd., Incline Village, NV 89450 (831–1052). Pool.

Hyatt Lake Tahoe Resort. *Deluxe.* Country Club & Lakeshore Drs., Incline Village, NV 89450. Pool, beach, health club.

LAS VEGAS. What is perhaps the greatest concentration of luxury resort hotels is located along 3½ miles of the Las Vegas "Strip" within minutes of one another. Designed to keep the guest inside and entertained 24 hours a day, these elegant establishments feature the ultimate in accommodations and the finest in

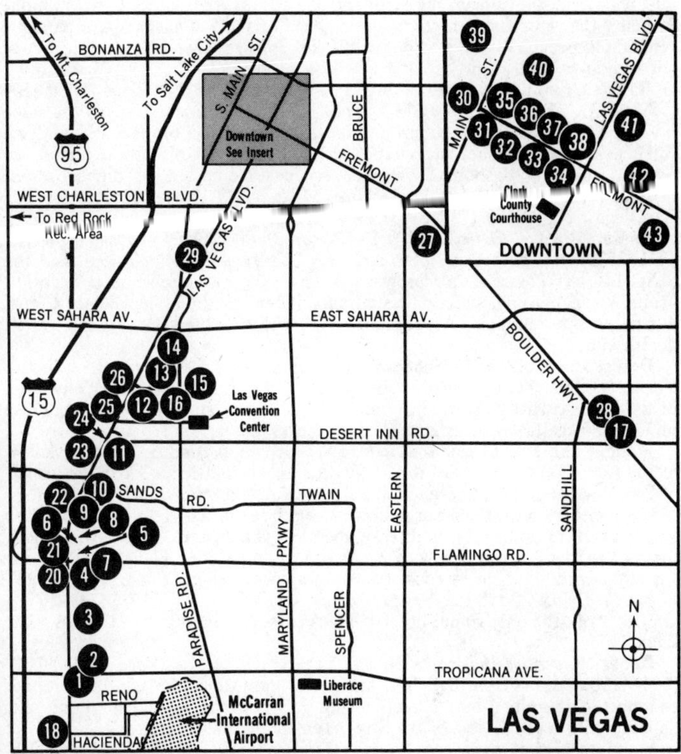

Resort Hotels and Casinos

1) Tropicana
2) Marina
3) Aladdin
4) Bally's Grand
5) Barbary Coast
6) Flamingo Hilton
7) Maxim
8) Imperial Palace
9) Holiday Inn & Casino
10) Sands
11) Desert Inn
12) Riviera
13) El Rancho
14) Sahara
15) Las Vegas Hilton
16) Landmark
17) Nevada Palace
18) Hacienda
20) Dunes
21) Caesar's Palace
22) Castaways
23) Frontier
24) Silver Slipper
25) Stardust
26) Circus-Circus
27) Showboat
28) Sam's Town

Downtown Hotels and Casinos

29) Vegas
30) Union Plaza
31) Golden Gate Casino
32) Golden Nugget
33) Four Queens
34) Sundance
35) Las Vegas Club
36) Mint
37) Horseshoe
38) Fremont
39) Holiday Inn
40) California Hotel
41) Lady Luck Casino
42) El Cortez
43) Western Hotel

cuisine and entertainment. Each has its own casino open 24 hours a day. A brief description of the major hotels follows:

Alexis Park. *Deluxe.* 375 E. Harmon St., Las Vegas, NV 89109 (796–3300). Just a short distance from the Strip and the airport, the Alexis Park is unique in being the only major hotel in the city WITHOUT a casino. A nice, quite refined place, such as you would find in Palm Springs. Excellent food, attractive surroundings. Full resort facilities.

Bally's Grand Hotel. *Deluxe.* 3645 Las Vegas Blvd. S., Las Vegas, NV 89109 (739–4111). This *was* the MGM Grand. It has a new name but it's the same lavish establishment. The largest and most beautiful casino in Las Vegas. Two full-size showrooms offer superstar entertainment plus a big production show. Seven restaurants, 40 shops. Swimming pool, health clubs, tennis, movie theater.

Best Western Royal Las Vegas Hotel. *Deluxe.* 99 Convention Center Dr., Las Vegas, NV 89109 (735–6117). Near center of the Strip.

Caesars Palace. *Deluxe.* 3570 Las Vegas Blvd. S, Las Vegas, NV 89109 (731–7110). At the busiest intersection in Las Vegas, Flamingo Rd. and the Strip. Caesars Palace is the last word in opulence and atmosphere. Beautiful grounds and lighting, superior restaurants, including the famed Palace Court. Superstar entertainment. A pool and setting befitting the gods. Tennis courts, health club.

Desert Inn Hotel and Country Club. *Deluxe.* 3145 Las Vegas Blvd. S, Las Vegas, NV 89109 (733–4444). Probably the most beautiful grounds of any hotel in the city. Attractive golf course and spa facilities unmatched anywhere else in Vegas. Excellent restaurants, outdoor elevators.

Holiday Inn-Hotel Casino. *Deluxe.* 3475 Las Vegas Blvd. S., Las Vegas, NV 89109 (369–5000). Center of the Strip with casino that looks like a showboat.

Las Vegas Hilton. *Deluxe.* 3000 Paradise Rd., Las Vegas, NV 89109 (732–5111). Neither on the Strip nor in downtown, the Hilton is right next to the Las Vegas Convention Center, with easy access to the airport. This is the largest luxury resort in the world, with 3,174 rooms and suites. Eleven restaurants, superstar entertainment. A rooftop swimming pool, tennis, and a Youth Hotel.

Sands. *Deluxe.* 3355 Las Vegas Blvd. S., Las Vegas, NV 89109 (733–5000). On the Strip, the only round hotel in Las Vegas. Famed home of the 50s "Rat Pack."

Dunes. *Expensive-Deluxe.* 3650 Las Vegas Blvd. S., Las Vegas, NV 89109 (737–4110). Across from Bally's Grand Hotel and Caesars Palace. 1,300 rooms and one of the city's best championship golf courses. Excellent dining and dancing with a good view of the Strip. Tennis and swimming.

Flamingo Hilton. *Expensive-Deluxe.* 3555 Las Vegas Blvd. S., Las Vegas, NV 89109 (733–3111). Also near the intersection of Flamingo Rd. and the Strip and across from Caesars. Good Chinese restaurant, ice show. Pool. Don't miss Bugsy Siegel's Rose Garden.

Frontier. *Expensive-Deluxe.* 3120 Las Vegas Blvd. S., Las Vegas, NV 89109 (734–0110). Centrally located and across from the Desert Inn. Both used to be owned by Howard Hughes. Now the home of Siegfried & Roy, superstars of magic, one of the best acts in Las Vegas.

Golden Nugget. *Expensive-Deluxe.* 129 E. Fremont St. Las Vegas, NV 89101 (385–7111). The only first-class hotel in downtown area, with one of the most beautiful casinos in the state. Recently remodeled, now the only home of superstars in the downtown area.

Imperial Palace. *Expensive.* 3535 Las Vegas Blvd. S., Las Vegas, NV 89109 (731–3311). On the Strip, featuring an Oriental decor and a large auto collection.

Maxim. *Expensive.* 160 E. Flamingo Rd., Las Vegas, NV 89109 (731–4300). Across from Bally's Grand Hotel.

Riviera. *Expensive.* 2901 Las Vegas Blvd., Las Vegas, NV 89109 (734–5110). On the Strip, attractive grounds.

Sahara. *Expensive-Deluxe.* 2535 Las Vegas Blvd. S., Las Vegas, NV 89109 (737–2111). At the northernmost end of the Strip, or the beginning of the Strip, depending on how you view it. Good restaurants and top-name entertainment.

Tropicana. *Expensive-Deluxe.* 3801 Las Vegas Blvd. S., Las Vegas, NV 89109 (739–2222). At the corner of the Strip and Tropicana Rd., the "Trop" is the nearest major hotel to the airport. With the creation of the "Island of Las

Vegas," it is now one of the most beautiful hotel properties in the world. Cascading waterfalls. Beautiful casino, good food, and home of the American "Folies Bergere."

Hacienda. *Moderate-Expensive.* 3950 Las Vegas Blbd. S., Las Vegas, NV 89109 (739–8911). Located at the tail end of the Strip, near the Tropicana. Prettiest wedding chapel in Las Vegas on the grounds. Ice Show. Large camperland.

Landmark. *Moderate-Expensive.* 364 Convention Center Dr., Las Vegas, NV 89109 (733–1110). Across from the Convention Center, the most unusual-looking hotel in the city. Beautiful swimming pool and outside elevators.

Las Vegas Strip TraveLodge. *Moderate-Expensive.* 2830 Las Vegas Blvd. S., Las Vegas, NV 89109 (735–4222). Near center of the Strip.

Marina. *Moderate–Expensive.* 3805 Las Vegas Blvd. S., Las Vegas, NV 89109 ([illegible] 1500). Near the Tropicana.

Bali Hai Motel. *Moderate.* 336 Desert Inn Rd., Las Vegas, NV 89109 (734–2141). Only a half block from the center of the Strip. Kitchenettes in some units.

California. *Moderate.* 12 Ogden Ave., Las Vegas, NV 89101 (385–1222). In downtown. Restaurants, lounge, casino.

Circus Circus. *Moderate.* 2880 Las Vegas Blvd. S., Las Vegas, NV 89109 (734–0410). Near the center of the Strip and more fun than a barrel of clowns. This is the one hotel in Las Vegas that caters to the family trade, with a mezzanine full of games and live circus acts. Don't stay here if you don't like kids. Camperland for RVs.

Downtown TraveLodge. *Moderate.* 2028 E. Fremont St., Las Vegas, NV 89101 (384–7540). In downtown.

Four Queens. *Moderate.* 202 E. Fremont St., Las Vegas, NV 89101 (385–4011). In downtown. French Quarter Lounge features best in jazz and Dixieland.

Golden Inn Motel. *Moderate.* 120 Las Vegas Blvd. N., Las Vegas, NV 89101 (384–8204). In downtown.

Mint. *Moderate.* 100 E. Fremont St., Las Vegas, NV 89101 (387–6468). In downtown area. Home of the "Mint 400 Off Road Race" immortalized by Hunter Thompson.

Sam's Town. *Moderate.* 5111 Boulder Hwy., Las Vegas, NV 89122 (456–7777). Not near the Strip nor downtown, but locals and visitors seem to love it. Sam's Town is always full. A western atmosphere, with the best western store in Nevada next door.

Showboat. *Moderate.* 2800 E. Fremont St., Las Vegas, NV 89104 (385–9123). The showboat, on the approach to Las Vegas has been around quite a while. Though not located near anything, families seem to love it. 110 bowling lanes and a sports center for wrestling and boxing.

Stardust. *Moderate.* 3000 Las Vegas Blvd. S, Las Vegas, NV 89109 (732–6111). Located in the center of the Strip. Home of Lido de Paris. Large camperland for RVs.

Sundance. *Moderate.* 301 E. Fremont St., Las Vegas, NV 89101 (382–6111). In downtown area, the tallest building in the state.

Tam O'Shanter. *Moderate.* 3317 Las Vegas Blvd. S., Las Vegas, NV 89109 (735–7331). Motel located near center of the Strip.

Union Plaza. *Moderate.* 1 Main St., Las Vegas, NV 89101 (386–2110). In downtown area, the only hotel/casino in the world with a train station in it! (On the site of the old Union-Pacific station, now Amtrak). Dinner-theatre. Front rooms have a terrific view of downtown.

Vegas World. *Moderate.* 2000 Las Vegas Blvd. S., Las Vegas, NV 89104 (382–2000). Halfway between downtown and the Strip and owned by the "Polish Maverick," Bob Stupak.

Sam Boyd's Fremont. *Inexpensive–Moderate.* 200 E. Fremont St., Las Vegas, NV 89101 (385–3232). In downtown area.

El Cortez Hotel. *Inexpensive.* 600 E. Fremont St., Las Vegas, NV 89101 (385–5200). The oldest still-standing hotel in Las Vegas and now with a new tower.

Travel Inn. *Inexpensive.* 217 Las Vegas Blvd. N., Las Vegas, NV 89104 (384–3040). In downtown.

RENO. Bally's Reno. *Deluxe.* 2500 E. Second St., Reno, NV 89595 (789–2000). Nearest hotel to the airport. With 2,001 rooms, it's Reno's largest hotel and has the largest casino in the world. Seven restaurants, major production show, bowling, tennis, wedding chapel.

Fitzgerald's. *Deluxe.* 255 N. Virginia St., Reno, NV 89501 (786–3663). Downtown. Dinner-theatre.

Harrah's. *Deluxe.* 219 N. Center St., Reno, NV 89520 (786–3232). In the heart of downtown Reno. Headliner entertainment, five restaurants.

Reno Hilton. *Expensive–Deluxe.* 255 N. Sierra St., Reno, NV (322–1111). 599 rooms, three restaurants. Opera House Theatre, downtown area.

Best Western Daniel's Motor Lodge. *Moderate–Expensive.* 375 N. Sierra St., Reno, NV 89501 (329–1351). Downtown.

River House. *Moderate–Expensive.* 2 Lake St., Reno, NV 89505 (329–0036). Near downtown. Overlooking Truckee River. Dining room.

Boomtown. *Moderate.* Interstate 80 West, Reno, NV 89503 (345–6000). Seven miles west of Reno.

Circus Circus. *Moderate.* 500 N. Sierra St., Reno, NV (329–0711). Downtown. Popular with families. Free circus acts and a midway for young people.

Comstock. *Moderate.* 200 W. 2nd St., Reno, NV 89505 (329–1880). Downtown, 300 rooms, all decorated in 1880s style.

Eldorado. *Moderate.* 345 N. Virginia St., Reno, NV 89501 (786–5700). Downtown, 400 rooms. Five restaurants.

Holiday Hotel. *Moderate.* Mill & S. Center Sts., Reno, NV 89501 (329–0411). On the Truckee River, downtown. Nice views.

Onslow. *Moderate.* 133 N. Virginia St., Reno, NV 89501 (786–7310). Downtown. Excellent steak house.

Pioneer. *Moderate.* 221 S. Virginia St., Reno, NV 89501 (329–9781). Downtown.

Ramada. *Moderate.* 6th & Lake Sts., Reno, NV 89504 (788–2000). Downtown, 250 rooms.

Reno Downtown TraveLodge. *Moderate.* 2 Lake St., Reno, NV 89503 (329–3451). Downtown. In-room coffee.

Riverside. *Moderate.* 17 S. Virginia St., Reno, NV 89501 (786–4400). Downtown, 200 rooms.

Sundance Motel. *Moderate.* 850 N. Virginia St., Reno, NV 89501 (329–9248). Downtown.

Tally Ho. *Moderate.* 370 N. Sierra St., Reno, NV 89501 (329–0969). Downtown.

Thunderbird Motel. *Moderate.* 420 N. Virginia St., Reno, NV 89501 (329–3578). Downtown.

Sundowner. *Inexpensive–Moderate.* 450 N. Arlington Ave., Reno, NV 89520 (786–7050). Downtown, 600 rooms.

Wonder Lodge. *Inexpensive–Moderate.* 430 Lake St., Reno, NV 89501 (786–6840). Downtown.

Bonanza Inn. *Inexpensive.* 215 W. 4th St., Reno, NV 89501 (322–8632). Downtown. Parking for RVs.

SOUTH LAKE TAHOE/STATELINE. Caesars Tahoe. *Deluxe.* Stateline, NV 89449 (588–5315). Magnificent rooms with oversized tubs and great views of the lake. Health spa, tennis, racquetball. Seven restaurants, superstar entertainment. Shuttle service to ski slopes.

Harrah's Tahoe. *Deluxe.* Box 8, Stateline, NV 89449 (588–6606). One of the finest hotels in the state. Winner of numerous awards. Five restaurants and coffee shop. Name entertainment. Excellent service. Beautiful views of the lake or forest.

Harvey's. *Deluxe.* Stateline, NV 89449 (588–2411). Highly rated. Live entertainment, 575 rooms, eight restaurants, tennis.

High Sierra. *Deluxe.* Stateline, NV 89449 (588–6211). Highly rated, 537 rooms.

Lakeside Inn. *Deluxe.* Stateline, NV 89449 (588–7777). Live entertainment, pool.

The Ridge Tahoe. *Deluxe.* Stateline, NV 89449 (588–3553). Suites, fitness center, tennis, racquetball, sauna, steam rooms.

SPARKS. Nugget Hotel Tower. *Expensive.* 1100 Nugget Ave., Sparks, NV 89431 (356–3300). Sparks is right next to Reno.

TONOPAH. Mizpah Hotel. *Expensive.* 100 Main St., Tonopah, NV 89049 (482–6202). A restored Victorian retreat into Nevada's past. A beautiful place. Live gaming.

The Station House. *Moderate.* 1100 Erie Main, Tonopah, NV 89049 (482–9777). Unique charm of a turn-of-the-century railroad station. Live gaming

VIRGINIA CITY. Savage Mansion. *Deluxe.* S. D St., Virginia City, NV 89440 (847–0574). Built in 1861. Original furnishings. An appropriate inn for this historic town.

Sugarloaf Motel. *Moderate.* S. C St., Virginia City, NV 89440 (847–0300).

WELLS. Best Western Sage Motel. *Inexpensive–Moderate.* Near Interstate 80 & Hwy. 93, Wells, NV 89835 (752–3353). Small pool.

Ranch House. *Inexpensive.* Interstate 80 & Hwy. 93, Wells, NV 89835 (752–3384). Restaurant open 24 hrs. Comfortable rooms.

Sharon Motel. *Inexpensive.* 633 6th St., Wells, NV 89835 (752–3232). Small motel with comfortable rooms.

WINNEMUCCA. Best Western Red Lion Inn and Casino. *Expensive–Deluxe.* 741 W. Winnemucca Blvd., Winnemucca, NV 89445 (623–2565). 24-hour restaurant.

Nevada Motel. *Moderate.* 635 W. Winnemucca Blvd., Winnemucca, NV 89445 (623–5281). Large rooms.

Winners Hotel. *Moderate.* W. Winnemucca Blvd. & Lay St., Winnemucca, NV 89445 (623–2511). 83 rooms. Live entertainment, live gaming.

Scott Shady Court. *Inexpensive.* Pavilion & W. 1st Sts., Winnemucca, NV 89445 (623–3646). 78 units.

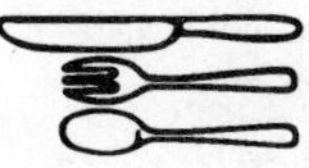

RESTAURANTS. Dining out in Nevada often means dining-dancing-show watching, especially in the gambling towns of Las Vegas and Reno. In Las Vegas, most of the hotels have buffets, where you can eat all you want for a reasonable price. You should also try to sample the cooking of the Basque shepherds in northern Nevada; Elko and Gardnerville have good, representative Basque restaurants. Restaurants are listed by price ranges of a complete meal, without drinks, namely: *Deluxe* $20 and up; *Expensive* $15–$20; *Moderate* $10–$15; and *Inexpensive* under $10. For a more complete explanation of restaurant categories see *Facts At Your Fingertips* at the front of this volume.

CARSON CITY. Dug's West Indies. *Moderate.* 3439 N. Carson St. (882–6565). Cantonese, polynesian, and West Indian cuisine. Mahogany-broiled steaks, tropical drinks.

Enrico's of Carson. *Moderate.* 1801 N. Carson St. (882–6334). An excellent Italian restaurant that has been in Carson City for more than 30 years. Fireplace and candlelight.

El Charro Avitia. *Inexpensive.* 4389 S. Carson St. (883–6261). Good Mexican food, big margaritas.

ELKO. Nevada Dinner House. *Moderate.* 351 Silver St. (738–8485). Family-style Basque dinners.

Star Hotel. *Moderate.* 246 Silver St. (738–9925). One of the best Basque restaurants in Nevada, serving family-style meals. Famous steaks.

FALLON. Nugget Steak House. *Moderate.* 70 S. Maine St. (423–3300). Good food, live entertainment.

GARNERVILLE. J&T Restaurant. *Inexpensive.* 760 S. Main St. (782–2074). Basque menu. Informal family service at long tables.

HAWTHORNE. El Capitan. *Moderate.* 540 F. St. (945–3321). Well-known for its pastries. Open 24 hours.

INCLINE VILLAGE. Hugo's Rotisserie. *Expensive.* Hyatt Lake Tahoe. (831 –1111). Excellent food, with spectacular decor, overlooking Lake Tahoe.

LAS VEGAS. You'll easily fill your appetite's desire in this "super" eating town. The offerings range from exotic and foreign gourmet cuisine to inexpensive breakfast, lunch, and dinner buffets. The restaurants vary in price and menus—you'll find moderately priced cafés, coffee shops, health food store counters, and pancake houses all around town. Food is served at all hours of the day and night.

Many of the hotel showrooms used to offer dinner with the show; few do any more. The Riviera, Las Vegas Hilton, and Tropicana are about the last holdouts. On the other hand, some of the best restaurants in America are to be found in the lavish Las Vegas hotels, particularly Caesars Palace, Bally's Grand Hotel and, across the street, the Las Vegas Hilton and Desert Inn. Here are our half-dozen favorite restaurants, followed by some others.

Palace Court. *Deluxe.* Caesars Palace (731–7547). Quite simply, the best restaurant in Las Vegas. Often cited by gourmet magazines. You can dine on gold plates with gold cutlery—in a decor filled with trees, plants, and flowers. The roof can be rolled back when the weather is nice. The cuisine, as you would expect, is classical French.

Bacchanal. *Deluxe.* Caesars Palace (731–7525). Probably the most unusual dining experience in Las Vegas. Go there hungry but with money (or credit cards). It's a seven-course dinner in a room that would have been right at home in ancient Rome. The wine flows like wine and is poured by beautiful handmaidens (Careful! They belong to Caesar.) Truly, an experience to remember—and to soothe the feelings of one who has lost.

Gigi's. *Deluxe.* Bally's Grand Hotel (formerly the MGM Grand) (739–4651). The closest thing to Maxim's in Las Vegas. Opulent setting and fine classically French food.

Pample Mousse. *Deluxe.* 400 E. Sahara Ave., near the Sahara Hotel (733–2066). Probably the most beautiful restaurant in Las Vegas, and it's just a small place, created by owner Georges LaForge to look like a French country inn. Fine food to match. "Pamplemousse" means "grapefruit"—which they don't serve. Ask Georges the story.

Andre's. *Deluxe.* 401 S. 6th St., near downtown (385–5016). Declared by many to be the BEST restaurant in Las Vegas, and in an odd residential location. Romantic French provincial decor.

Chin's. *Moderate.* 2300 E. Desert Inn Rd. (733–7764). Believed by many to be the best Chinese restaurant in the city—and the secret hideaway of many celebrities.

Other Recommended Restaurants

Alpine Village. *Moderate.* 3003 Paradise Rd., across from the Las Vegas Hilton (734–6888). Lovely Swiss decor. Good German-Swiss food, and a Rathskeller with an omp-pah-pah band downstairs.

Aristocrat. *Moderate.* 850 S. Rancho Dr. (870–1977). An out-of-the-way place, but the locals have voted it the best restaurant in Las Vegas.

Battista's. *Moderate.* 4041 Audrie St., across from Bally's Grand Hotel (formerly the MGM Grand). May be the finest Italian restaurant in the city, certainly the cleanest. And Battista sings opera. All the house wine you can drink with dinner.

Benihana Village. *Expensive.* Las Vegas Hilton (732–5111). Eleven restaurants around a waterfall and a rain forest. What more could you want? The chefs are a show in themselves.

Caruso's. *Expensive.* Bally's Grand Hotel (739–4656). Wonderful Northern Italian food in a sumptuous setting.

Chicago Joe's. *Inexpensive.* 820 S. 4th St., near downtown (382–5246). There's no "mob" in Las Vegas, of course, but if there was, this is where they would eat.

Cosmos' Underground. *Moderate.* 32 E. Fremont St., in downtown (382–0330). Good Italian food, with a tree growing underground.

Facciani's Library. *Expensive.* 200 W. Sahara, near the Sahara Hotel (384–5200). One of the most attractive restaurants in the city. Excellent food.

Golden Steer. *Moderate.* 308 W. Sahara Ave., across from the Sahara Hotel (384–4470). Probably the best place in Las Vegas for good steaks.

Liberace's Tivoli Gardens. *Expensive.* 1775 E. Tropicana Ave. (739–8762). One of the most beautiful restaurants in Las Vegas—and created by the master showman himself.

Mariano's. *Moderate.* 3513 S. Valley View Rd., not far from the Strip (871–4596). In an odd location, but Mariano is doing everything right. Wonderful Italian food, good piano bar. Celebrities love the place.

Old Heidelberg. *Moderate.* 604 E. Sahara Ave., near the Sahara Hotel (731–5310). Fine German food. They make their own sausage in their German deli.

Ricardo's. *Moderate.* 2380 E. Tropicana, at Eastern (798–4515). Many believe this to be the best Mexican restaurant in the city, of which there are many. Beautiful decor and strolling musicians.

The Tillerman. *Moderate.* 2245 E. Flamingo Rd., near Eastern (731–4036). Consistently good seafood in an attractive decor and with pleasant help.

Tracy's. *Moderate.* Bally's Grand Hotel (739–4111). Some have called this the best Chinese food to be found between San Francisco and New York, unusual in a hotel.

MOUNT CHARLESTON. Mount Charleston Restaurant. *Moderate.* Kyle Canyon Rd. (872–5408). If you want to get away from the summer heat of Las Vegas, this is the place to go. Just 30 miles away from town and yet away up in the mountains. Good food, beautiful surroundings.

RENO. In Reno, as with Las Vegas, you will find many of the best restaurants in the city are to be found in the hotels, particularly Bally's Grand Hotel, which is near the airport.

Bundox. *Moderate.* 2 Lake St. (323–0324). Just about an institution in Reno. Fine dining on the river.

Cafe Gigi. *Deluxe.* Bally's Grand Hotel (formerly the MGM Grand) (789–2266). Probably the finest restaurant in Reno, often cited by gourmet magazines. In a beautiful setting, with classical French cuisine.

Caruso's. *Expensive.* Bally's Grand Hotel (789–2267). Just about the best Italian restaurant in the city.

Louis Basque Corner. *Moderate.* 301 E. 4th St. Another Reno institution. Authentic Basque dining.

Top of the Hilton. *Expensive.* Reno Hilton (322–1111). Reno's only skytop dining. Beautiful view of the Sierra Nevada, Truckee River, and the lights of Reno.

SPARKS. John Ascuaga's Nugget. *Moderate.* (356–3300). Eight unique specialty restaurants under one roof. No need to go any further. Sparks is not far from Reno.

VERDI. Donner Trail Dinner House. *Moderate.* 405 Bridge St., Verdi. A historic place, although it does not serve the "fare" for which the Donner party became famous. Closed Mon.

VIRGINIA CITY. Sharon House. *Moderate.* S. C St. (847–0133). So loaded with atmosphere that you'd expect one of the Cartwrights of "Bonanza" fame to walk in. Primarily steaks and prime ribs.

WINNEMUCCA. Winners. *Moderate.* Winners Hotel. Hwys 95–180 (623–2511). Firepit dining room and 24-hour coffeeshop.

HOW TO GET AROUND. By Plane. In the Reno area, you can charter planes at the Reno or Carson airports. In Las Vegas, small planes can be rented or chartered at Hughes Aviation Services, McCarran Field, or North Las Vegas Air Terminal, on the Tonopah Highway, to flightsee Las Vegas.

By Car. Hertz, Avis, Budget and other major car rental companies are at the airport; other car rentals along the Strip and in the major hotels.

By Bus. In Las Vegas, the Strip bus runs every 15 minutes from the downtown Casino Center area to the Hacienda Hotel, at the end of the Strip. Fare $.95.

By Boat. Las Vegas Boat Harbor, on Lake Mead Dr., Henderson, offers boats for rent or lease. Houseboat rentals available at Echo and Callville bays.

TOURIST INFORMATION. You can get information on Las Vegas by writing to the *Las Vegas Chamber of Commerce,* 2301 E. Sahara Ave., Las Vegas, NV 89104 (702–457–4664), or the Las Vegas Convention & Visitors Authority, 3150 Paradise Rd., Las Vegas, NV 89106 (702–733–2323). You can get information on Reno by writing to the *Greater Reno Chamber of Commerce,* 133 N. Sierra St., Reno, NV 89505 (702–786–3030). For North Lake Tahoe ski resort country, write *Incline Village Chamber of Commerce,* Drawer CS, Incline Village, NV 89450 (702–831–4400). For South Lake Tahoe, it's *South Lake Tahoe Visitors Bureau,* Box 17727, South Lake Tahoe, CA 95706 (916–544–5050). Finally, for old Virginia City, contact *Virginia City Chamber of Commerce,* Box 464, Virginia City, NV 89440 (702–847–0311).

SEASONAL EVENTS. In January you may want to attend the *Winter Carnival* in beautiful South Lake Tahoe. The $100,000 Mint 400 off-road desert race is held in Las Vegas in May. In the latter part of April, you may want to attend Henderson's *Industrial Days.* If you're around Elko, Fallon, Ely, Lovelock, or Winnemucca from mid-May to mid-June, watch the ranches for the spring *branding of calves.* Join the community-wide Western celebration during the North Las Vegas *Progress Days*—parades, fairs, a beauty contest—early in May. This is followed late in May by the *Helldorado,* four days when Las Vegas turns back the clock, so don your Western garb. Virginia City holds its annual *May Antique Show* on Memorial Day weekend, with items from all the dealers in surrounding Western States. Also, on Memorial Day weekend, Tonopah hosts *Jim Butler Days,* a celebration with contests that test the skills of miners.

If mid-June finds you driving around remote areas of Nevada, watch for Basque shepherds rounding up sheep. Also in mid-June *Carson Valley Days* are celebrated in Minden-Gardnerville. And in late June there's the *Reno Rodeo,* one of the richest in the West.

You'll do well to spend your time early in July at the *National Basque Festival* in Elko. There's sheep shearing, wood chopping, other feats of endurance and contests of strength to enjoy, and anyone can join in the colorful dancing. July also brings the *annual rodeo* in Tonopah (July 3–4) and the *Boulder Damboree,* in Boulder City on July 4. In mid-July Austin has its *Toiyabe Trail Ride,* and Fallon the *Indian Stampede* (all-Indian rodeo).

Towards the end of August, lots of events take place: *Pony Express Days* are celebrated in Ely; *Wagon Train Race* from Placerville (California) to Lake Tahoe; the *Nevada Fair of Industry* in Ely; Tonopah's *Annual Horse Show.*

From the end of August to October—the *big beef roundup* in the areas of Elko, Fallon, Ely, Lovelock, and Winnemucca.

Plenty of things to do in September, too. Fallon has a *Lion's Stampede and 49er Show* and *Kiwanis Chuck Wagon Breakfast.* On Labor Day weekend, Elko has the *County Fair and Livestock Show.* And the *Nevada Rodeo and Humboldt County Fair,* in Winnemucca, has one of the West's best rodeos—cowboys and Indians come in from the big ranges to test their skills. September is also the month for the *Music Festival* at the University of Nevada in Las Vegas. Gabbs has its *Fall Festival* with old-fashioned mining camp contests. Virginia City is famous for its *camel races;* volunteer riders always welcome. In mid-September, there's the *Nevada State Fair* in Reno. The end of the month brings *hydroplane races* on the south shore of Lake Tahoe.

Boulder City attracts art buffs to their annual *Outdoor Art Festival* the first Sunday in October. The University of Nevada *Homecoming Parade,* in Reno, comes along in late October. October 31st is *Nevada Day Celebration,* commemorated annually in Carson City with a big parade and exhibits.

National Rodeo Finals are held in Las Vegas in December.

TOURS. In Las Vegas several companies offer a wide variety of tours including Hoover Dam, Lake Mead, Death Valley, and the Grand Canyon. *Las Vegas-Tonopah-Reno Stage Line* (384–1230) has daily tours to Hoover Dam and Death Valley. *Gray Line Tours* (384–1234) has daily tours from where you are staying, to the dam or around Las Vegas, and then back in time to get freshened up for a nightclub tour.

Scenic Airlines provides one of the most exciting scenic adventures, a flight from Las Vegas to the South Rim of the Grand Canyon (418-mile round trip). Leave early in the morning in a twin-engine Cessna, fly over the Las Vegas Strip, see awesome views of Lake Mead, Hoover Dam, and the Colorado River. You'll hear a running commentary as the plane dips and soars from 1,000 to 1,500 feet below the Outer Rim of the Grand Canyon—or 800 feet above the Inner Gorge! An extinct volcano, Navajo Waterfalls, Havasupai Indian Village come into view en route to the Grand Canyon Airport. The tour continues with a drive along the South Rim, stopping at vantage points for viewing and experiencing the grandeur of the geological formations, the mule trails, and a visit to the Yavapai Museum. Stop for lunch at a restaurant set in a juniper and ponderosa pine forest. Return to Las Vegas by late afternoon. (Scenic Airlines, P.O. Box 5368, Las Vegas 89102, tel. 702–739–1900. Tour prices range from $119 for a three-hour flyover to $169 for a deluxe air-ground tour that includes a three-hour bus tour of the canyon and a buffet lunch.

Nevada's sightseeing attractions include: the *casinos* and *luxury hotels* of Las Vegas; *Hoover Dam; Lake Mead;* the *Anaconda Copper* operation near Yerington; *Carlin Gold Mine* (no actual tours, but visitors welcome if they've written ahead), *Copper Smelter* at McGill; *Liberty Pit* at Ruth.

Archeological sites: Valley of Fire, near Las Vegas, with Indian petroglyphs; the *Winnemucca Dry Lake Area;* and the *Pyramid Lake Area* (the east shore caves). For details, ask at the State Museum in Carson City. The *Red Rock Canyon* area 20 miles west of Las Vegas offers opportunities for frontier-era pictograph and petroglyph observations as well as a further insight into the 10,000-year history of the desert area.

NATIONAL PARKS AND FORESTS. A peculiarity of Nevada is the span of its two national forests. Toiyabe National Forest is actually four widely separated areas; Humboldt National Forest is five. Between them, there are 4,997,019 acres of mountains providing protected watersheds, grazing lands, spectacular scenery, and recreation areas for the public. For centuries, all this area was Indian territory. The Paiute and Shoshone tribes who roamed the western part of Nevada named that land Toiyab—"Black Mountains." Early-day cowboys with huge herds of cattle and sheep were attracted to the open ranges. And during the Gold Rush numerous mining camps sprang up and flourished. Ghost towns still linger.

The Humboldt National Forest takes its name after the Humboldt River watershed that it embraces. Baron von Humboldt was one of the early explorers. First settlers in this area were latecomers to the Gold Rush who grew travel-weary and decided to settle down. Settlers also came from mining camps, and many were ex-soldiers from Ft. Ruby and Ft. Halleck.

Taking the four parts of **Toiyabe National Forest** in order, you have: (1) 40 miles west of Las Vegas the section with *Mt. Charleston.* Outstanding camp and picnic grounds from May to October, a popular ski area from December to March. The two major canyons are *Kyle* (with skiing, tobogganing, riding, excellent hiking trails to Cathedral Rock and Charleston Peak) and *Lee* (camp and picnic grounds, skiing, hiking). These two canyons are connected by a 16-mile drive over the scenic *Deer Creek Road.* (2) A section of Toiyabe is along the *California-Nevada* border, between (see your road map) Dyer and Wellington. Many *ghost towns* in this area. The *Lucky Boy Pass* (elevation 8,001) leads to the famed California ghost town of *Bodie.* (3) You come upon more Toiyabe in the *Reno/Lake Tahoe* area. Here is where you'll find fine skiing in one of the most beautiful settings in America. (4) Most massive part of Toiyabe is smack in mid-state from (roughly) Austin on the north to (not quite) Tonopah on the south, extending from Gabbs on the West almost as far as Eureka to the east. Outstanding features of this park are the *Ichthyosaur Paleontologic Monument* (see *State Parks*); *Diana's Punch Bowl* in *Monitor Valley,* an extinct geyser cone surrounding hot springs; and the *Hoover Wild Area,* with its *Wild Cat Peak.*

Humboldt National Forest's five vastly separated areas include: (1) a part extending from just below the Oregon border with the *Ft. McDermitt Indian Reservation* and *Paradise Valley;* and (2) a section just below the Idaho border with *Mountain City, Jarbridge Wild Area,* excellent fishing in *Wildhorse Reservoir,* a portion of the *Western Shoshone Indian Reservation,* and a mountain called the *Matterhorn!* There are also (3) the area surrounding the *Ruby Mountains and Lakes,* which is a National Scenic Area in itself (fine fishing and deer hunting); (4) a three-part section with *McGill* and *Ruth* at its center (*copper mines,* skiing at *Ward Mountain,* the *Ward Charcoal Ovens* (see *Historic Sites*), and *Lehman Caves National Monument,* through which guided tours are conducted daily. In summer: 8–5; the rest of the year at 9, 10:30, 12:30, 2:30 and 4. Tour takes one and one-half hours, costs adults about 50¢. The fifth part of Humboldt is a little (speaking colloquially) lone area south of the Pancake Range, to the east of Tonopah, to the north of Las Vegas. Near here is Nevada's most recent volcanic activity—with the *Lunar Crater* and other cinder cones landmarks.

A listing of Nevada's national parks could not be complete without *Death Valley* and *Lake Mead.* A bit of **Death Valley National Monument** extends into Nevada. You'll find it west of Beatty, south of Scotty's Junction. By entering the valley at Beatty (State 374) and exiting at State 267, you can visit *Scotty's Castle,* now a hotel-museum.

The **Lake Mead National Recreation Area** includes *Boulder Beach, Las Vegas Wash,* and the *Overton-Echo* and *Callville Bay* areas, each with boat ramps, boat rentals, camping, and refreshments. At Boulder Beach, park naturalists give daily illustrated talks (but not in winter). At *Lake Mead Marina,* northeast of Boulder City, the Hoover Dam Cruise is of interest; four times a day. *Lake Mohave,* also part of the area, has two recreation developments within Nevada—*Eldorado Canyon* and *Cottonwood Cove,* both with facilities similar to Lake Mead's.

For information and maps on the two national forests, write to U.S. Dept. of Agriculture, Forest Service, Intermountain Region, Ogden, UT.

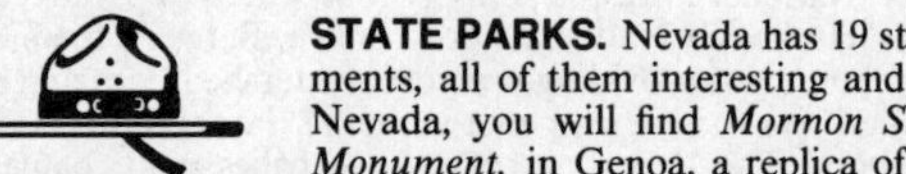

STATE PARKS. Nevada has 19 state parks and monuments, all of them interesting and varied. In northern Nevada, you will find *Mormon Station Historic State Monument,* in Genoa, a replica of a trading post built in 1851 by Nevada's first white settlers; *Lake Tahoe Nevada State Park,* which consists of 13,000 acres of Sierra wilderness; *Washoe Lake State Park,* which offers majestic views of the Sierra Nevadas; *Dayton State Park,* near Dayton, which sits amidst a historic mining area; *Fort Churchill Historic State Monu-*

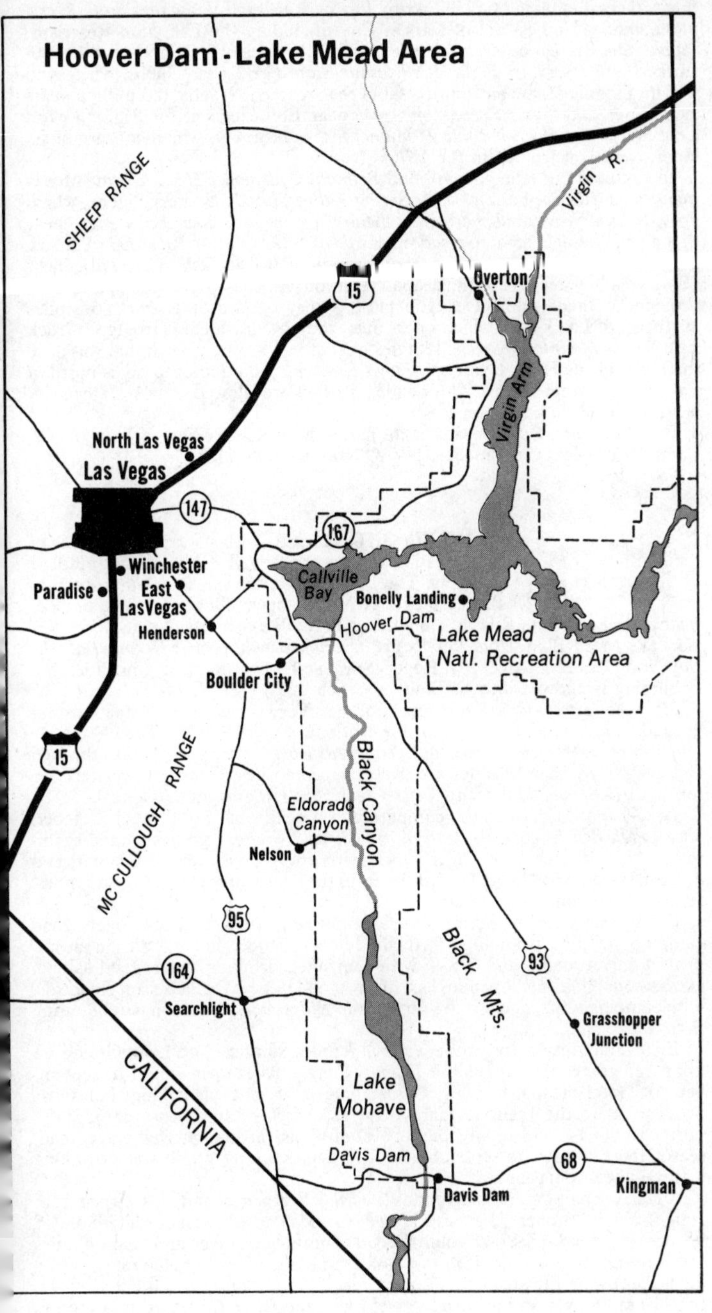
Hoover Dam - Lake Mead Area
SHEEP RANGE
Virgin R.
15
Overton
Virgin Arm
North Las Vegas
Las Vegas
147
167
Callville Bay
Bonelly Landing
Winchester
Paradise
East LasVegas
Henderson
Hoover Dam
Lake Mead Natl. Recreation Area
Boulder City
15
MC CULLOUGH RANGE
Black Canyon
Eldorado Canyon
Nelson
95
Black Mts.
93
164
Searchlight
Grasshopper Junction
CALIFORNIA
Lake Mohave
Davis Dam
68
Davis Dam
Kingman

ment offers remnants of a U.S. Army fort built in 1860; *Lahontan State Recreation Area,* 45 miles east of Carson City, including the Lahontan Reservoir; *Patch State Recreation Area,* 22 miles east of Lovelock, which includes a 10,000-surface-acre reservoir; *Berlin-Ichthyosaur State Park,* near Gabbs, where you will find fossils of ancient Ichthyosaurs that roamed Nevada 180 million years ago; *Cave Lake State Recreation Area,* near Ely, excellent for fishing; *Ward Charcoal Ovens Historic State Monument,* also near Ely, which consists of six large ovens constructed in the 1870s.

In southern Nevada, you will find *Belmont Courthouse Historic State Monument,* a courthouse built in 1874; *Spring Valley State Park,* near Pioche, which provides water-oriented recreation; *Echo Canyon State Recreation Area,* near Pioche, including a 65-acre reservoir; *Cathedral Gorge State Park,* near Panaca, a long narrow valley cut into a clay formation; *Beaver Dam State Park,* near Caliente, a flowing stream and a small reservoir; *Kershaw-Ryan State Park,* near Caliente, a small colorful canyon park; *Valley of Fire State Park,* 55 miles northeast of Las Vegas, which offers fine examples of Indian petroglyphs (rock art); *Spring Mountain Ranch,* 15 miles west of Las Vegas, a ranch that was once the home of the Hope Diamond; *Floyd R. Lamb State Park,* 10 miles north of Las Vegas, a wonderful park for picnicking. Pets are allowed in most state parks, but they must be kept on a leash.

For information on Nevada state parks, write to Division of State Parks, Capitol Complex, Carson City, NV 89710 (702–885–4384).

CAMPING OUT. Nevada, with its acres and acres of wild beauty, is extremely well equipped for outdoor camping. The *Lake Mead National Recreation Area,* to the east of Las Vegas, open all year, offers *Boulder Beach,* on Lakeshore Rd. via US 93, *Las Vegas Wash* on the North Shore Rd. via Lake Mead Blvd. from Las Vegas, *Overton Beach, Rogers Spring, Callville Bay,* and *Echo Bay.* All except Rogers Spring offer boat-launching facilities, but swimming is allowed only at Boulder Beach.

Mt. Charleston, to the northwest of Las Vegas, has several major campgrounds under the jurisdiction of the National Forest Service. The closest, 36 miles away, are *Kyle Canyon* and *Cathedral Rock,* open from May 1 through October 31. Within 10 miles are five other campsites, ranging from rocky to forested: *Hill Top, Mahogany, Deer Creek, McWilliams* and *Dolomite.*

Lake Tahoe has two major campgrounds, open from May through October. At *Nevada Beach,* on U.S. 50, right on the lake, you can go fishing and swimming. The other camp is *Clear Creek* with group areas, drinking water, and campsites—also on US 50, but 5 miles from the lake. Camps are 25 and 15 miles, respectively, from Carson City.

For travelers cutting across state at mid-mark, the Austin area offers good camping facilities, from June through October. Fifteen miles south on an improved gravel road is *Big Creek,* with campsites, drinking water, good fishing, and seasonal hunting. Six miles east of town on US 50 is the *Bob Scott Roadside,* with camping units, and 5 miles farther on, *Kingston* (good fishing and hunting here, too).

Elko, first turnoff for Ruby Valley, 7 miles southeast of Lamoille, on an improved gravel road, offers the *Thomas Canyon* park, open June 1 to September 30. Good fishing, hunting, 28 camping units, and picnicking. For those pressing on to the Wells turnoff, *Angel Lake* is the camp. Located 62 miles northeast of Elko and 12 miles southwest of Wells, on an improved gravel road, season there is July 1 to September 30. It provides fishing, group areas, drinking water and camping units.

A rash of campgrounds surrounds the *McGill-Ely* area, and all are open from June through October. There are *Timber Creek,* 5 miles north of McGill on US 93, then east for 8 miles on a country road of improved gravel, and finally 4 miles south over a dirt road; and *Berry Creek* (same directions but a couple of miles farther on). The Ely area offers *Clear Creek,* 9 miles southeast on US 6–50–93, then 10 miles over an improved gravel road; and *Cleve Creek,* 40 miles to the southeast via US 6–50–93, then 10 miles north on a paved county road and 7 miles more northwest on an improved gravel road. Good fishing, hunting at all 11 camps.

For campers going to the *Lehman Caves,* needless to say, there are no overnight accommodations within the monument, and camping is not allowed. Good campsites are located in a section of *Humboldt National Forest* adjoining the monument, and there are motels in Baker, the nearest town, 5 miles away. Other convenient overnight locations are the *Lehman Creek, Lehman Creek Trailer,* and *Baker Creek* camps 6 miles west of Baker on State 488. *Snake Creek Camp* is also good: 16 miles southeast of Baker, reached by State 488 and an improved gravel road. Hunting, fishing, and 8 camping units.

The *Valley of Fire* also has a good overnight park, run by the Nevada state park system. It can be reached from U.S. 93 at the marker, or from Overton by State 169 (8 miles). It has 24 camping units.

In the state park recreational areas, $5 a night is the users' fee for camping. For a list of all the camping places and information about them, write Dept. of Economic Development, Carson City, NV 89710 (702–885–4322).

For camper equipment: *Vegas Trailer Supply,* 3076 E. Fremont, Las Vegas (457–4265). Disposal station listings: *Mobile Oil Station,* 1004 Nevada Hwy., Boulder City; *Gulf Oil Service,* 14001 Rand St. and Hwy. 50, Carson City; *Gulf Oil Station,* 1600 Idaho St. and Hwy. 40E, Elko; *Gulf Oil Station,* E. Boulder Hwy., US 95, Las Vegas; *Union 76 Station,* Highland and Western, Las Vegas; *Union 76 Station,* 6199 Las Vegas Blvd., Las Vegas; *Union 76 Station,* S. Virginia and Kumie Lane, Reno; *Union 76 Station,* Hwy. 40 and Hwy. 93, Wells.

TRAILER TRIPS. Carson City: *Comstock Country RV Park,* 5400 S. Carson; Reno: *MGM Grand* (460 spaces), 2500 East Second Street; *Four Seasons RV Park,* 13109 S. Virginia; Las Vegas: *Circus Circus Camperland,* 2880 Las Vegas Blvd. S.; *Stardust Camperland,* 3000 Las Vegas Blvd. S.; *Hacienda Camperland,* 3950 Las Vegas Blvd. S.; *Kings Row Trailer Park,* 3660 Boulder Hwy.

FARM VACATIONS AND GUEST RANCHES. Mostly in the Reno area. *Donner Trail Ranch* in Verdi is deluxe type, can be visited casually for meals. *Whitney's Guest Ranch* on Del Monte Lane, Reno; *Pablo Canyon Guest Ranch,* Smokey Valley Rd., Round Mountain. No guest ranches in the Las Vegas area.

HEALTH SPAS. Best are *Carson Hot Springs* in Carson City (pool, baths, motel, and restaurant) and *Steamboat Hot Springs,* at 16010 S. Virginia St., Reno (mineral baths, mudpack, etc.). In Las Vegas, you may want to try the Desert Inn Hotel-Casino, which has the most beautiful spa facilities in the city. The *Las Vegas Sporting House* has, in addition to its athletic facilities, an olympic-size indoor swimming pool and separate whirlpool baths and cold plunges for men and women. Most large hotels also have spa facilities.

SUMMER SPORTS. Boating. Boats are for rent, also boat rides, at the several marinas at Lakes Mead and Mohave in southern Nevada. Same at Lake Tahoe. Boating is very popular on other lakes, Pyramid, Walker, and Lahontan, for example, but for these you should bring your own boat.

Swimming and water sports. There are year-round water sports in southern parts of the state; summer only for Lake Tahoe and other northern regions. Water skiing especially good on Lake Tahoe, and on lakes Walker, Pyramid, Topaz, Mead, and Mojave. For calm, smooth water skiing, try the Lahontan Reservoir between Carson City and Fallon. Ski boats can be rented on Lake Mead.

Golf. The following are among the best local courses: in Las Vegas—*Craig Ranch G.C.,* a short and simple course catering to novices; *Desert Inn C.C.,* a flat tournament course with many trees; *Dunes Hotel & C.C.,* with long par-5s and par-3s and many traps; *Las Vegas G.C.,* a municipal course, with small greens; *Showboat Country Club,* a good tournament course. *Sahara Hotel & C.C.,* recently remodelled, a tough driving course; *Tropicana Hotel & C.C.,* with lots of character; *Desert Rose G.C.* (formerly Winterwood G.C.); *Las Vegas C.C.,* a private course, open to guests of adjacent hotel, a fine desert course. In nearby Henderson, *Black Mountain G. and C. C.* In Reno—*Washoe County G.C.,* a municipal, tree-lined course, easy to walk; *Lake Ridge G.C.,* a semi-private rolling Trent Jones layout, with water and sand; *Brookside G.C.,* semi-private, flat with large greens and some water. At *Lake Tahoe—Incline Village G.C.,* semi-private, a Trent Jones layout in resort development. *Northstar* at Tahoe, 18 holes with lots of variety. In Stateline—*Edgewood-Tahoe G.C.,* in new resort complex; a stiff challenge.

Hiking. Throughout the state, particularly in the national forest areas, where good, established trails await.

Horseback riding. Corky Prunty's Stables, Reno. At Lake Tahoe, it's the Incline Stables, Incline Village. In the Southern portion of the state, horseback riding can be found at the Bonnie Springs Ranch in Blue Diamond, just west of Las Vegas and at Mt. Charleston, 35 miles from Las Vegas.

FISHING AND HUNTING. Fishing. Best from November through April at Pyramid Lake (cutthroat and rainbow trout), Lake Tahoe (giant mackinaw, rainbow, and cutthroat), Walker Lake (cutthroat and Sacramento perch), lakes Mead and Mohave (bass, bluegill, catfish, black crappie, stripers, coho, and rainbow trout). Licenses are $10 for the special three-day visitor's permit, or $20 annually. For Mead and Mohave there are also $3 special-use stamps.

Hunting. Deer hunting lasts from early October through mid-November. Best areas are along the Sierra foothills, all of northern Elko County, and White Pine County. Non-resident hunting licenses $50, plus $50 for a deer tag. Bow-and-arrow hunts held before the regular rifle season, usually the first three weeks of September. (License $50 with a $10 tag fee.) Hunting seasons for ducks and upland game are mid-Oct. until early Jan.; mid-Sept. to late Jan. for small game (except mid-Nov. for pheasant). Major areas are Stillwater Wildlife Management Area in Churchill county, Mason Valley Wildlife Area and Fernley Wildlife Area in Lyon county, Sunnyside Wildlife Area in Nye county, Overton Wildlife Area in Clark county. Other popular areas are Humboldt and Tulon Sink areas in Pershing county, Ruby National Wildlife Area in Elko county (the Ruby lakes are an outstanding migratory waterfowl refuge); the Newark, Diamond, and Reese River valleys in eastern Nevada; the Carson, Truckee, Walker, and Humboldt rivers; and Washoe Lake near Reno.

For additional hunting and fishing information, write to the *Nevada Dept. of Wildlife,* Box 10678, Reno, NV 89520 (702–784–6214).

WINTER SPORTS. *Skiing:* At Lee Canyon on Mt. Charleston near Las Vegas; and in the Reno-Lake Tahoe area, where nearly twenty well-equipped ski resorts lie within an hour's drive from Reno. Among the big ones —Mt. Rose, Slide Mountain, and Ski Incline, Northstar, Heavenly Valley, and Squaw Valley. All in all, they add up to one of the finest ski centers in America.

SPECTATOR SPORTS. *Rodeos:* Helldorado, the big annual Western pageant in Las Vegas, in May; the Reno Rodeo, the state's richest, in June; and the Nevada Rodeo, the biggest and most traditional, in Winnemucca in Sept.

Tennis: In April, the Alan King Tennis Tournament at Caesars Palace in Las Vegas.

SHOPPING. There is no problem in Las Vegas locating attractive shops where you can splurge with your winnings. Most of the major hotels have luxurious stores within. No question that Las Vegas has become a showcase for top designers. Recently opened on the Strip at Spring Mountain Rd. is the lavish Fashion Show Mall with such top-of-the line stores as *Neiman-Marcus, Sak's Fifth Avenue, Bullock's, Goldwater's* and *Diamond's,* plus numerous elegant smaller shops. Exclusive stores also are to be found in such hotels as Caesars Palace, the *Bally's Grand* and the Las Vegas Hilton. The air-conditioned, enclosed *Boulevard Mall* has an assortment of 74 stores, restaurants, and snack bars. The chain stores: *Diamond's, Silverwood's, Penney's, Sears, Broadway. Hickory Farms of Ohio* and *El Poco Candles* carry gift items. A fountain, plants, and parking convenience make the arcade comfortable for shopping. 3528 S. Maryland Pkwy. (tel. 735–8268). The air conditioned, enclosed 2-story shopping center *Meadows Mall* has 110 stores on two levels, including *Diamond's, Sears, Broadway* and *Penney's.* 4300 Meadows Lane (878–4849).

Antiques: If you're "into collecting," prowl and browse around the dozen or more Reno antique shops for anything from Indian artifacts to old cut glass and dishes. In Las Vegas, try *Antique Square and Pavilion* at 2016 E. Charleston, about a mile from the Strip. A collection of more than a dozen unusual shops.

CHILDREN'S ACTIVITIES. Children seem to enjoy the free live circus acts from the mezzanine of the *Circus Circus Hotel.* The Circus Circus is unique in Las Vegas: the entire mezzanine is devoted to the entertainment of children, with more games than you ever thought existed. Other hotels with good game rooms for young people are the *Bally's Grand,* the *Hilton,* the *Sahara* and the *Dunes.* Kids also enjoy the futuristic Omnimax Theatre at *Caesars Palace* and the brand new *Wet 'n' Wild* water theme park, next to the Sahara Hotel.

Ponderosa Ranch, at Incline Village, will interest nostalgia fans of TV's popular *Bonanza.* There's a frontier town, Cartwright ranch, riding trails, and an antique car collection. Snacks and lunch available. Daily in summer, 10–6; winter schedule depends on weather. Adults, $4, under 12, $3, covers all exhibits and rides, except horseback riding.

Hoover Dam is an exciting sightseeing venture; only 25 miles from Las Vegas. The huge dam was constructed in 1931–35 by a small army of workers. It backs up the Colorado River for 115 miles as Lake Mead—one of the largest manmade lakes in the world. Government guides take you on a tour 700 feet into the depths of the dam. Stay on and hear a short talk on the history of the Colorado River. Hours: 8:30–4:15. Adults, $1; under 12, 50¢. On US 93, about 25 miles from Las Vegas. If you prefer a combination land and lake excursion—*Hoover Dam* and *Lake Mead*—it is now being offered by the *Gray Line.* It includes seeing all of the features of Hoover Dam, plus a sail on Lake Mead. The captain will take you to a close-up view of the dam and the intake towers and spillways, then cruise through the Boulder Islands. Lunch is included, also hotel pickup and return service. Children over 12 years may go "on their own." $28.35. About 6 hours.

If parents are absorbed in "Las Vegas games," consider the Youth Hotel at the Hilton. Well-qualified educators, great at handling and involving young people, arrange many activities and provide snacks and meals. Some of the supervised activities for teen-agers can vary from a ski trip at Lee Canyon to experiencing the intrigue of the Valley of the Fire State Parks. Rates: $2.50 per hour or $15 overnight. Only available to guests of the Las Vegas Hilton and Flamingo Hilton.

OUTSTANDING ARCHITECTURE. Las Vegas: The fabulous "Strip" and downtown *"Casino Center"* offer some of the most beautifully designed resort facilities in the world. The Las Vegas Hilton is the largest resort hotel in the world. The nearby *Spring Mountain Ranch,* under State Park Service direction, is open to the public, and the 528-acre oasis in the desert is a beautiful attraction. The *Pioneer Theater Auditorium,* built in 1967; its gold geodesic dome glistens against Reno's skyline. This facility is used for cultural and commercial events; the auditorium and exhibiting space are located underground.

Also the silver-domed *capitol building,* the *museum* and *old homes* at Carson City; the *Pioneer Mormon Buildings* in Mesquite and Bunkerville; the mansions at Virginia City, and private homes in southwest Reno. (Take the Scenic Tour, guided by signs posted along the way.)

In Carson City: *Bowers Mansion,* overlooking Washoe Lake, 10 miles north on US 395, was the home of one of the first men to become a millionaire from the Comstock Lode. It is filled with European furnishings. On this museum's grounds are a swimming pool fed by hot springs, and a picnic area. *Mormon Station,* 1 mi. S of Carson City on US 395. Oldest town in the state, created by the gold rush. The *State Capitol* houses an art gallery and museum. In Ely, the *White Pine Public Museum,* 20000 Aultman St., houses many relics from the Pony Express era. Closed holidays. Free. One more museum of interest is the *Lost City Museum* in Overton. In it are many relics from the advanced pueblo-dwelling Indians, dating back more than a thousand years. Virginia City has *The Castle* and other mansions, with invaluable antiques brought to this country from many foreign lands.

HISTORIC SITES. Historical markers have been erected throughout the state. Bicentennial projects brought about new and interesting markers. For a listing of locations, write the State Park Commission, Carson City 89701.

The Nevada Dept. of Transportation makes it extremely easy to locate the state's many historical sites. Their official highway map, published annually, circles the major places of interest, and, by a dotted trail, pinpoints the early pioneer trails and ghost towns. If you're looking for the latter, the most outstanding are: *Virginia City,* once the richest city in America and now one of the most colorful; *Manhattan* and *Belmont,* on State 376, are semi-ghost towns, relics of past glories and riches; *Austin,* on U.S. 50, is an interesting ghost town of deteriorating old buildings (Stokes Castle, Courthouse, churches, stores, and hotel); *Eureka,* U.S. 50, is another relic of mining days, while *Tuscarora,* on State 226, also exhibits remains of an early mining camp.

Seventeen miles south of Ely, a weird sight in the desert is a row of giant beehive-shaped ovens. This is the *Ward Charcoal Ovens Historic State Monument,* standing as a reminder of early charcoal production used by smelters operating in White Pine County in the late 1800s. Just off Hwy. 93, a little north of Cathedral Gorge State Park, the town of *Pioche* has a "million-dollar courthouse" erected by free-spending miners. *Genoa,* curiously named in honor of the birthplace of Christopher Columbus, and fairly near the shores of Lake Tahoe, has the *Mormon Station State Historical Monument*—a log-cabin stockade that was originally a trading post selling supplies to emigrants passing along the California trail. It shortly thereafter became the first permanent settlement in Nevada. On display here are such relics as a cradle, hand carved by Snowshoe Thompson (who lies buried in the town cemetery), a pair of bearskin gloves worn by one of the early stagecoach drivers, a Bible carried on the pony express, and part of the first overland telegraph. May 1 through Sept. 30. Daily, 9–7. Closed Oct. 1 through Apr. 30. Free. A short ride from Carson City will take you to the *Ft. Churchill Historic State Monument*—ruins of an early fort established near the Carson River in 1860 to protect the pioneers from Indian raids.

INDIANS. There is much Indian heritage in Nevada. *Valley of Fire State Park,* north of Las Vegas, has outstanding examples of Indian petroglyphs. *Winnemucca* was named for a famous Paiute Indian chief who governed that tribe in the mid-1860's. *Battle Mountain* is named for an Indian-emigrant battle that occurred in 1857. *Indian Springs,* midway between Las Vegas and Tonopah, was once an old Indian rancheria and campsite on the emigrant trail; today it is an Air Force base. *Ft. Churchill Historic State Monu-*

ment, outside Silver Springs, displays the ruins of an early fort established in 1860 to protect the pioneers from Indian raids. In the *Jarbridge Wild Area* way up north in the state is a portion of the *Western Shoshone Indian Reservation* with headquarters at Owyhee. Two Indian reservations of definite tourist interest are the *Carson City Indian Colony,* just south of Carson, and the *Pyramid Lake Reservation* at Nixon, just south of Pyramid Lake, northeast of Reno. This is a ranching area, with an interesting trading post, a gift shop, and a counter restaurant. Also worth seeing is the *Stillwater Reservation* near Fallon.

MUSEUMS AND GALLERIES. In Carson City the Nevada State Museum, 600 N. Carson St. (885–4810), has a gun room, a large Indian collection, a fluorescent room (eerie displays of minerals that fluoresce under ultraviolet light), a historical room (loaded with practical and sentimental relics and heirlooms of pioneer Nevadans), the Virginia and Truckee Room (objects relating to the old-time railroad that served Virginia City and the Comstock during the bonanza days), and the Mint Room, a reminder that the whole museum was once a mint, as well as a fascinating, authentic model mine in the basement. Closed hols. Free. In Elko, the Northeastern Nevada Museum, 1515 Idaho St., in a brand-new building, has Indian artifacts, natural history, and library. Closed New Year's, Thanksgiving, and Christmas. Free. The Churchill County Museum, S. Main St., Fallon, has many interesting collections. Free.

The Mackay School of Mines at the University of Nevada in Reno (784–6987) is particularly interesting for its memorabilia depicting methods and occurrences in the mining history of the state. Closed Sun. and academic holidays. Free. Also in Reno, the Nevada State Historical Society Museum, 1650 N. Virginia St. (789–0190), has Indian and pioneer artifacts. Research library. Free.

ART: The Church Fine Arts Building on the University of Nevada campus, in Reno, shows the works of (nationally recognized) local and regional artists; they maintain their permanent collection and feature changing exhibitions. Walt McNamara and Ben Cunningham works are shown here. Closed weekends. Free. The Artists Co-op Gallery, 627 Mill Rd., Reno, handles regional artists' works: oils, watercolors, pen and wash drawing. The Sierra Nevada Museum of Art, at 549 Court St. (329–3333), is Nevada's only fine art museum.

Las Vegas has about two dozen art galleries throughout the city, plus a large number of galleries in the Strip hotels. Various shows are held year round at the Grant Hall Art Gallery at the University of Nevada, 4505 Maryland Parkway, and at Las Vegas Art Museum, 3333 W. Washington (647–4300).

Special Interest: Carson City has a *Fire Museum,* above the Carson Fire House, Curry & Musser Sts. Mementos of Nevada's early days and a collection of Currier and Ives fire-fighting prints.

In Las Vegas the *Museum of Natural History* offers a good introduction to the surrounding desert environment. Featured are displays involving vegetation, wildlife, and Indian artifacts. University of Nevada, 4624 Maryland Pkwy. (739–3381). No admission fee. The Clark County Community College in North Las Vegas features a *Planetarium* with topical programs (643–6060).

In Reno: The *Fleischmann Atmospherium-Planetarium* at the University of Nevada (784–4811) features fabulous displays projected by special 350-degree cameras on an overhead dome. The programs cover astronomy, ecology, oceanography, and meteorology. Adm.: adults $2.75; children and seniors $1.75. Harold's Club has an excellent little *Museum of Western Americana* (mostly historic weapons and firearms) on its second floor. Open 24 hrs. daily. *Harrah's Automobile Collection,* Glendale Ave., Sparks (786–3232), is a must for the antique car buff.

MUSIC. Community concert series are held in the fall and winter in Reno, Carson City, and Las Vegas. Concerts of various types are also frequently presented during the season on the Reno and Las Vegas campuses of the university. The Department of Music, University of Nevada in Las Vegas, presents concerts twice monthly by their chamber orchestra, chorus, and string quartet. Afternoons. No admission charge. The UNLV Master Series brings in artists of international caliber on a regular basis, and Caesars Palace often offers rock or pop artists in their open air theater. And at the university, the Artemus Ham Concert Hall has a regular schedule of symphonic events. The beautiful $4.2 million structure seats 2,000 and is a reflection of the cultural growth of the Las Vegas community.

STAGE AND REVUES. Apart from the spectacular hotel and casino shows to be found at Lake Tahoe, Reno-Sparks, and Las Vegas, many little theater groups are active—at both campuses of the university; in Reno and Las Vegas there are excellent small theater groups. You can catch performances all year-round at the *Judy Bayley Theater,* University of Nevada in Las Vegas—Shakespeare, Bernard Shaw, Brecht, Dylan Thomas. Other theater groups in the Las Vegas area are: *Las Vegas Little Theatre,* 2228 Spring Mountain Rd.; *Clark County Community College* theater group, 3200 E. Cheyenne, N. Las Vegas. Stage performances are also given around the state in such towns as Elko and Fallon.

NIGHTCLUBS. If there is one thing upon which Las Vegas has a solid claim, it is the reputation of being the entertainment capital of the world. Who would deny it? With no less than 4 million-dollar spectaculars, 9 hotels featuring major entertainment headliners, two ice shows, a Broadway musical and play—as well as numerous smaller shows—all playing simultaneously on the three-and-one-half mile stretch of boulevard known as the "Strip," that hackneyed phrase is anything but empty. Some extravaganzas can boast of costing more than $10 million and having a cast of more than 100; performers can earn as much as $300,000 a week. Stage effects run the gamut from fiery earthquakes, rainstorms, live tigers, trapeze artists, disappearing swimming pools, skating rinks, and ship sinkings, all the way to octopuslike stages that swing way out over the audience's heads.

But what people remember most are the girls—endless lines of gorgeous girls, most of them topless, although some of the shows offer one performance a week that is "family-oriented" (with tops). There are more chorus girls in Las Vegas who are members of the American Guild of Variety Artists than in any other city in the world. They come to Las Vegas from everywhere.

Some hotels present dinner shows at about 8 P.M., then a late cocktail show around midnight. A number of hotels have no dinner show and present two cocktail shows, one at about 8 P.M. and the other at midnight. Some hotels also offer a third show on Saturday night. Reservations are recommended at all shows, and hotel guests are of course given preference at the hotel showrooms. The average cost of a "headliner" or extravaganza show is $20–$25 a person, which includes dinner or cocktails.

All the top entertainment in Las Vegas is not necessarily in the big showrooms. To keep the fun going, all the hotels have, in addition, shows in the lounges that also provide a continuous stream of name entertainment from dusk until dawn. Usually the lounge show is available for the price of two drinks.

Las Vegas entertainment is anything but stereotyped. Competition is so keen among hotel and club producers, in fact, that few of them can (or will!) say a month or two ahead of time who will be appearing on their stages. While one house will hold an extravaganza for a year or more, another will showcase a whole stream of top stars.

The south shore of Lake Tahoe and the Reno-Sparks areas are also great for year-round nightclub entertainment.

BARS. In Las Vegas, tops for atmosphere and views are the *Top o' the Mint* (go up in its glass elevator), at 2nd and Fremont and the *Top o' the Strip* at the *Dunes Hotel.* In Reno, the *Corner Bar* at the *Riverside Hotel* is the traditional meeting place. *Harold's 7th Floor Bar* at So. Tahoe, and *Harvey's Top*

of the Wheel Bar have excellent views. In Virginia City, bars abundant with atmosphere are the *Delta,* the *Crystal Bar,* and the *Bucket of Blood.*

LIQUOR LAWS. They couldn't be simpler. No restrictions on hours for legal drinking, nor on where drinks and bottles can be ordered and consumed. No sales to minors, however—age limit is 21.

CASINOS. While much of Nevada is uninhabited, in the cities, you can hardly go anywhere without at least hearing the whir-rattle-clunk of a one-armed bandit, the popular name for slot machines. They're at the airplane, train, and bus terminals, at restaurants, grocery stores, even gas stations. The most opulent casinos, however, are at Las Vegas, Lake Tahoe, and Reno. All are open around the clock, many are also resort-type hotels, and nearly all offer nearly continuous entertainment in their lounges during the night and early morning hours, as well as elaborate nightclubs. Entrance to the casinos is free, and anyone over the age of 21 can gamble.

Las Vegas leaders along the Strip, a carnival-like, glittering, three-and-one-half mile next to I–15, are *Caesars Palace,* the *Desert Inn,* the *Dunes,* the *Riviera,* the *Sahara,* the *Sands,* the *Stardust, El Rancho,* the *Frontier,* the *Holiday Inn,* the *Landmark,* the *Las Vegas Hilton, Bally's Grand* (formerly the MGM Grand), the *Tropicana, Circus Circus,* the *Hacienda,* the *Flamingo Hilton,* the *Maxim,* the *Marina* and the *Aladdin.* (For details, see under *Hotels* and *Dining Out.*) You can walk from one to the other but nobody does. Everyone drives, or takes taxis.

Games of chance include 21, craps, roulette, black-jack, baccarat, keno, poker and, of course, the increasingly popular slot machines. A not-so-known fact: pretty cocktail waitresses hover about the tables, offering free drinks to the more serious-looking players. You don't *have* to order liquor. You can just have a Coke if you would rather. There is something about the casinos that makes you terribly thirsty, and glad of this special service. Most of the above-named casinos also maintain (very close to the playing rooms) bountiful buffet tables, where you can have a bargain breakfast, lunch or dinner for less than $4.

Outstanding casinos in downtown Las Vegas (Fremont St.) are the *Mint, Fremont, Four Queens, Union Plaza, Sundance, Binion's Horseshoe, California,* and the most beautiful of them all, the *Golden Nugget.* A little out of the downtown area on Boulder Hwy. are the *Showboat* and *Sam's Town.*

The downtown is called Casino Center. It's only three blocks long, but twelve hotels and casinos stand side by side, giving out so much light (by day *and* by night) that it is actually brighter here than New York's Times Square! Many visitors find this part of Las Vegas more "real" than the Strip. The big-name stars do not work here, but many gamblers feel the downtown casinos have better odds. The best view of the downtown "Glitter Gulch" area can be had from the second floor restaurant level of the *Union Plaza* or from the glass-enclosed elevator to the *Top of the Mint.*

The major casinos at Lake Tahoe are *Harrah's, Caesars Tahoe, Harvey's,* and the *Sahara Tahoe* on the south shore, and *Nevada Lodge, Hyatt Lake Tahoe* and the *Cal-Neva Lodge* on the north shore.

Reno casinos, which, like those of Las Vegas, feature big-name entertainers and plenty of neon lighting, include *Harrah's, Bally's Grand, Reno Hilton, Circus Circus, Harold's Club, Comstock, Eldorado, Pioneer, Pick Hobson's Riverside* and in nearby Sparks, *John Ascuaga's Nugget.*

If the din of the casinos is earsplitting, the sight of them from the street (or the air) makes your eyes sore, especially in Las Vegas, where the casino signs, in a wild spectrum of colors, flash, blink, revolve, oscillate, soar, plunge, spiral, tower, zoom—do anything, in short, but stand still.

OREGON

The Sedate Frontier

by
RALPH FRIEDMAN

Portland

Portland is not only Oregon's largest but also its sole metropolitan city. As such, it is the proper starting point for tours of the state. But first, Portland itself invites exploration.

The best way to see the "City of Roses" is to take the fifty-mile "Scenic Drive," whose most convenient starting point is the Visitors Information Center at 26 S.W. Salmon (503–222–2223); inside, free maps and guide sheets.

The Scenic Drive leads motorists to the summit of three hills—Council Crest, Rocky Butte, and Mt. Tabor (an extinct volcano)—which afford awesome panoramas of Oregon and Washington. Clearly visible from these vantage points are Mt. Ranier, the volcanic Mt. St. Helens, and Mt. Adams, all in Washington; and the great peaks of the Oregon Cascades: Mt. Hood, Mt. Jefferson, and the Three Sisters.

Other attractions on the Scenic Drive are the International Rose Test Gardens, Rhododendron and Azalea Test Gardens, and Peninsula Park's Sunken Gardens; Reed College, which has turned out more Rhodes Scholars than either Yale, Harvard, or Chicago, and whose reputation for intellectual freedom is worldwide; the fun-in-learning Oregon Museum of Science and Industry (OSMI); the World Forestry

Center; the Portland Zoo, with its elephants and streamlined Zooliner, which carries riders on a mile-long journey through Washington Park; Japanese Gardens; Hoyt Arboretum; the opulent Pittock Mansion; and past many old homes and through some of the city's most beautiful neighborhoods.

For music lovers, summer concerts are given at Washington Park, and other city parks also resound to the lilt of music. "Pops" concerts are presented at the Civic Auditorium, and Reed College is host to the Summer Chamber Music Concerts.

A number of stage companies in Portland present a wide variety of stagefare. (See *Stage and Revues.*) Foremost is the Portland Civic Theatre, whose Summer Repertory company is comprised of paid professionals. There are also special performances of the Children's Theatre.

Be sure to visit the Portland Art Museum, with a collection of Northwest Indian artifacts, African art, classical antiquities, silver, paintings, and sculpture.

Portland's biggest event is its Rose Festival, an annual celebration since 1909. The fiesta, generally held the second week of June, is as various as a Mardi Gras—the Rose Show; the Golden Rose Ski Tournament (on the slopes of Mt. Hood, 62 miles east); numerous cultural, carnival, and outdoor stage entertainment activities—and it is climaxed by the Grand Floral Parade, which draws floats and bands from as far as 1,500 miles away.

Short Excursions from Portland

One of the beauties of Portland is that it is possible to get out into the country from any part of town within twenty minutes at most. The motorist can head in any direction and find a wealth of scenery and outdoor recreational facilities. (For those without cars, touring companies offer various tours.)

The Oregon coast, with all its wonders, is a leisurely two-hour drive from here; the boiling falls of the Willamette, at Oregon City, are twelve miles south of town; and scenic Lake Oswego is halfway between Portland and Oregon City.

Champoeg State Park, in an area that figured prominently in the early settlement of the Oregon Country, has two fine museums and acres of grassy, forested terrain overlooking the Willamette. Champoeg lies thirty minutes from Portland by car and can be reached from Interstate 5 (the north-south freeway), or roads branching off Oregon 99E and Oregon 99W.

The Columbia River Gorge, east of Portland, is lanced by two roads, an expressway at water level and the Scenic Route, via Crown Point. The expressway, rimming the "Great River of the West," has turnoffs for several recreation points, including Rooster Rock State Park, a Columbia River beach and picnic ground.

The shimmering Crown Point road passes eleven waterfalls within a stretch of ten miles, among them the 620-foot-high Multnomah Falls, second highest in the United States. The route also provides access to eight state parks.

In addition, the Scenic Route encompasses some of the most impressive views to be found along the entire 1,200-mile stretch of the Columbia River. At Crown Point, the mighty stream, squeezed in a vise

PORTLAND DOWNTOWN

PORTLAND DOWNTOWN

Points of Interest

1) Art Museum
2) City Hall
3) Civic Auditorium
4) Civic Theater
5) Court House
6) Hotel Benson
7) Imperial Hotel
8) Japanese Garden
9) Memorial Coliseum
10) Muitomah Civic Stadium
11) Opera
12) Oregon Historical Society
13) Oregon Museum of Science & Industry
14) Physicians & Surgeons Hospital
15) Portland Motor Hotel
16) Portland State University
17) Post Office
18) Sheraton Motor Inn
19) Washington Park
20) Zoo

between the basaltic cliffs of Washington and Oregon, breaks through the last barrier of the Cascades and heads unhindered for the open sea.

Bonneville Dam, the most westerly of all the Columbia dams, lies beyond Rooster Rock State Park and Crown Point, yet it is only thirty-five miles from Portland. The sight of the Bonneville locks raising and lowering vessels, and of the salmon pools, where the fighting fish lunge up riffles to continue upstream, awes visitors old and young.

When all is said, however, the most spectacular tour of the Portland area is the up-the-mountain-and-down-to-the-river Mt. Hood Loop Drive. The trip takes about seven hours to complete and is worth every minute.

The motorist should follow US 26 (Powell Boulevard in east Portland) to Government Camp. Then, as a side trip, he should climb the scented slope of Mt. Hood to Timberline Lodge. You can go higher up Mt. Hood, but only on a Sno-Car; and from the lodge some of the grandest panoramas in Oregon paint the sky. From Government Camp, follow Oregon 35 (impassable during winter) for a winding, kaleidoscopic journey through some of the state's most enchanting countryside.

The route passes through lush forests splashed by waterfalls and through Oregon's rich apple highlands, with Mt. Hood almost always in sight. Reaching Hood River, the motorist returns to Portland by way of the Columbia River expressway.

Although Ft. Vancouver National Historic Site is actually in the state of Washington, it is a Greater Portland tourist attraction, being only ten miles from the heart of the city. The historic site is being reconstructed on the exact location of the Hudson's Bay Company fort, which flourished from 1825 to 1849. Artifacts unearthed when the site was excavated, together with Indian relics and dramatic graphic aids, are skillfully arranged to present a picture history of the post, which played such a prominent role in the early years of the Oregon Country.

Oregon's Magnificent Coast

Of all sections of Oregon, the coast is the most famous and the most visited. It has often been termed the most scenic marine border drive in the world, and for good reason none who sees it is disappointed.

Take hundreds of miles of shore fronting the Pacific, fill with rolling sand dunes, mouths of swift rivers, fresh-water lakes, craggy cliffs, toppled mountainsides, battered headlands, hills bursting with greenery, secret coves, deep inlets, picturesque lighthouses, broad beaches, herds of sea lions, grassy state parks, millions of wildflowers, leaping waterfalls—and you have the Oregon coast.

To the purple-shadowed range skirting the shore and the virgin stands of giant firs, add the unsurpassed vistas of surf and sea—and you have one of the nation's grandest terrains. Add to all of this a salubrious climate, fabulous fishing, the taste of world-famous cheese in the valley where it is produced, colorful seashore towns, and a wealth of recreational opportunities—and the pleasure is doubled.

Almost all of the tideland of the coast belongs to the people; only a few miles are privately owned. More than thirty state parks, including the choicest scenic spots, are reserved for public use. In addition, there are many national forest camps.

It is a bit ironic, perhaps, that the most scenic and historical route linking Portland to the coast should be the longest and most time-

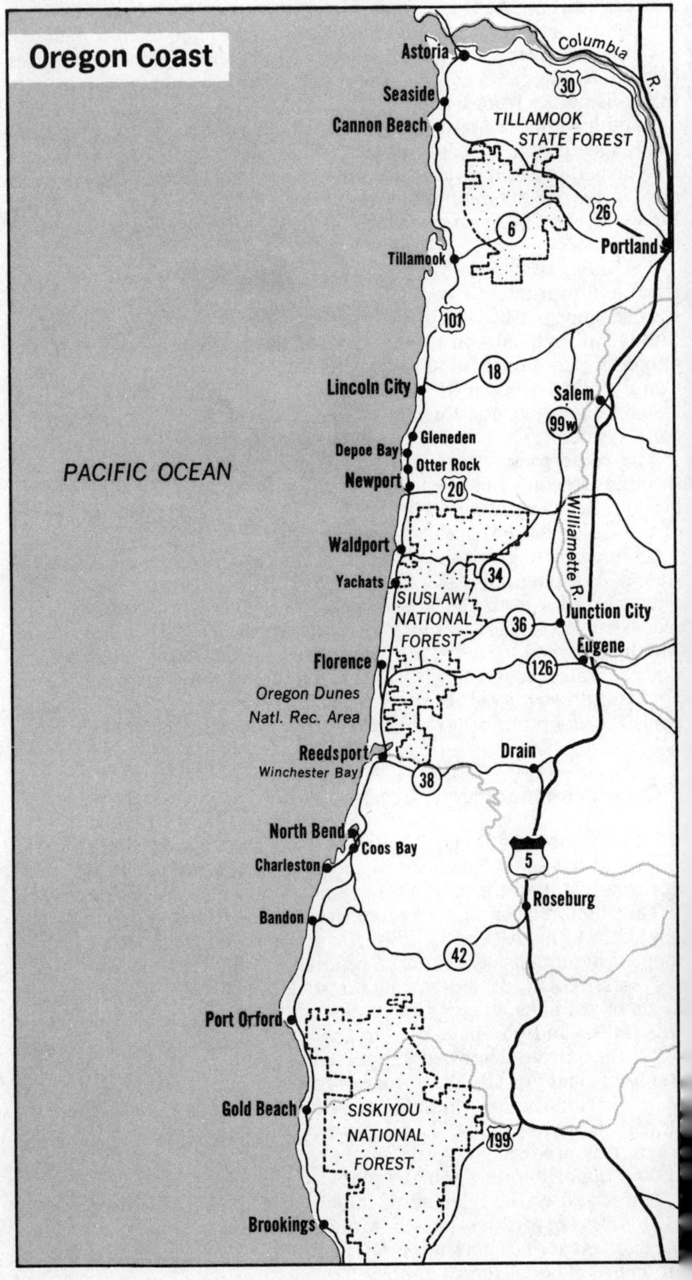
Oregon Coast
Astoria
Columbia R.
30
Seaside
Cannon Beach
TILLAMOOK STATE FOREST
26
6
Portland
Tillamook
101
18
Lincoln City
Salem
99w
Gleneden
Depoe Bay
Otter Rock
PACIFIC OCEAN
Newport
20
Willamette R.
Waldport
34
Yachats
SIUSLAW NATIONAL FOREST
36
Junction City
Eugene
Florence
126
Oregon Dunes Natl. Rec. Area
Reedsport
Winchester Bay
Drain
38
North Bend
Coos Bay
Charleston
5
Roseburg
Bandon
42
Port Orford
Gold Beach
SISKIYOU NATIONAL FOREST
199
Brookings

consuming; nevertheless, US 30, which skirts the Columbia River, is a storybook way to reach Astoria (the northern terminal of the littoral). On the other hand, US 26, the more popular route, is also the most crowded.

The towns along the lower Columbia—St. Helens, Ranier, Columbia City, Catskanie, and Westport—have from their founding depended upon the woods and the river for their livelihood. There is in the mist that comes up from the river and down from the hills a nostalgic twinge of steamboat whistles, donkey engines, and planked streets. At Ranier, a bridge spans the river, to Longview, Washington. At Westport, a small ferryboat crosses the great stream to Cathlamet, Washington. At St. Helens, Courthouse Square is a tintype of the days when the hearts of the towns were pressed against the river. (Today the commercial sections are closer to the modern highway than to the old river.) Behind the courthouse there is a front-on clear view of volcanic Mt. St. Helens. At Columbia City, the more-than-100-year old Caples House, built by a pioneer doctor on the banks of the Columbia, has been opened as a museum; a mile west of Clatsop Crest a county road leads to a pale ghost town, Clifton, where a cannery once throbbed and where the houses on stilts have slid into the river; at Knappa, a backcountry paved road winds to Brownmead a child of destiny and an orphan of progress. The store is closed, the old schoolhouse is a barn, the Grange hall sits silent.

Astoria sits at the mouth of the Columbia River—its northern shore is the southern border of Washington. In 1966 a spectacular 4.1-mile-long toll bridge ($1.50 per car and passengers) was completed, crossing to Megler. This did away with the colorful ferryboats and the bottlenecks that sometimes caused long waits at ferry landings. Astoria's history is inscribed in a pictorial frieze on the 125-foot-high Astoria Column, atop Coxcomb Hill. A circular stairway of 166 steps climbs to the top. (Not recommended for those with weak hearts.) The view from the high platform encompasses the ocean, the river, Young's Bay, the Coast Range, farms, woods, and hamlets.

"Williamsburg of the West"

"Oldest American City of the Missouri" is what Astoria calls itself. It possesses, in this respect, many firsts, including the first post office west of the "Big Muddy." Local historians claim that there has been "more history made within twenty miles of Astoria than all the rest of Oregon put together." This claim is disputed by others elsewhere, but Astoria is so steeped in history that some citizens would like to turn the city into a "Williamsburg of the West."

The first white man to set foot in this area landed in 1792, after Captain Gray's *Columbia* crossed the bar of the river. Ft. Clatsop was built nearby. A representation of Ft. Astoria, built in 1811, is downtown. The Columbia River Maritime Museum dramatizes, through exhibits going back two centuries, Astoria's sea and river history. At the waterfront, below the museum, *Old Lightship 88,* which came 'round the Horn in 1908 and for many years was stationed at the Columbia's mouth, is a tourist attraction now. The Flavel House, a cupola-topped, three-story Victorian mansion put up in 1883, has been restored to shades of its former glory.

Astoria is dotted with mid-and-late-nineteenth-century homes, all of them photogenic and most of them on a "walking tour." For a list, check at Chamber of Commerce or Astor Library.

Astoria draws breath and substance from the sea. This is made obvious by the city's colorful fishing fleet, its bustling Fisherman's Wharf, and its marine traffic.

For many decades Astoria was the largest city on the Oregon coast. Then it went through 17 years of population erosion. Lately it has made a slight comeback and now numbers about 10,000 people—second to Coos Bay, with a population of some 14,000.

Four miles below Astoria is Ft. Clatsop National Memorial, the restored stockade of the Lewis and Clark Party. The reconstruction was built after a sketch that Clark made in late 1805 on the elkskin cover of his field book. Footpaths lead to the camp spring, whose waters still flow sweet and pure, to the boat landing on the Lewis and Clark River, and toward the coast. A visitors' center at the memorial contains a graphic, historical presentation of the Lewis and Clark expedition from start to finish. There are movies and colored slides to view, and daily lectures are given in the Audio-Visual Room.

A short drive west of Astoria is Ft. Stevens, built in 1864, and abandoned a century later. The battery pits, redoubts, and nineteenth-century streets, houses, and barns are still there, tintypes of an earthier time. The Communications Center of the batteries is now a colorful museum.

Through the former military reservation and adjacent Ft. Stevens State Park, a road leads to the south jetty of the Columbia, where the seascape and surf-fishing attract hundreds of summer visitors daily. The park, largest state park in northwestern Oregon, has more than 600 campsites and trailer spaces, many overlooking lovely Lake Coffenbury. The lake is only a short stroll from ocean surf, where waders frolic around the diminishing remains of the *Peter Iredale,* a British bark stranded on the beach during a heavy storm in the autumn of 1906.

Small (population 1,000), off-the-highway Gearhart, 16 miles south of Astoria, was for long the convention center of the northern Oregon coast, though now there are too many convention centers to say that one is really dominant. But Gearhart is still a nice place to convene, because of its carefree, casual atmosphere and the golf course across from the convention site.

Oregon's Finest Beach

Seaside, two miles farther south, has the finest beach in the state, boasting in addition a two-mile-long concrete promenade. More people swim in the ocean here than anywhere else on the Oregon coast. There are also more tourist facilities—and their variety is legion—than in any town twice its size. The "Miss Oregon" pageant is staged here, as is the state's best-known marathon run. Once a hurdy-gurdy town, Seaside is now quite sophisticated, with smart malls, excellent restaurants, and new, large hotels. For years Seaside was the chief resort community in Oregon, but is now getting stiff competition from other towns.

Cannon Beach, eight miles south—and as far south on the coast as the Lewis and Clark party reached—is best known for its offshore Haystack Rock, one of the mightiest monoliths in the Northwest.

A decade ago Cannon Beach was a rather sleepy village, but it has in a few years burst into an art settlement, with shops of painters, sculptors, and artisans, and with health-foods and antique stores as popular as cafés and supermarkets. During July and August the Theater Arts Department of Portland State University stages plays, from the light to the classic, at the Coaster Theater, formerly a skating rink.

Oswald West State Park, 7.5 miles onward, honors a famous political maverick, a colorful, independent governor who fought successfully to preserve the beaches as a public heritage.

The road, US 101, rounds a spectacular cliff on the face of Neah-Kah-Nie Mountain (which the Tillamook Indians called "The Place of the Fire Spirit") and continues on to Manzanita Junction, 0.5 miles below the park honoring Governor West. A paved road leads one mile to the village of Manzanita, which is flanked by seven miles of fine sand beaches.

In the 12 miles between Manzanita Junction and Rockaway, the road passes through the sea-scoured fishing village of Nehalem, curves along Nehalem Bay, and rubs up against Wheeler, once a gusty fish-packing town and now best known for its regional hospital.

Rockaway is another beach resort—a sea bedroom of Portland—with accommodations ranging from the princely to the pauperish.

Between Rockaway and Tillamook, about 15 miles, is Barview Jetty Community Park (excellent fishing); Garibaldi, whose fishing fleet at the boat basin is a romantic forest of masts; and the Tillamook Cheese Factory (tours and free samples).

Tillamook is the center of a rich dairy section, laced by rivers that have been diked, giving the area the name of "Little Holland." Pioneer Museum, a block from the main street, is one of the most professionally arranged museums in all Oregon, and the wildlife dioramas, the work of the late great naturalist Alex Walker, are unequaled in the Pacific Northwest.

A 19-mile Loop Drive out of Tillamook leads to Cape Meares, with its lighthouse and great Sitka spruce known as the "Octopus Tree"; to Oceanside and its Three Arch Rocks, a bird refuge and home to a herd of sea lions; and to sea-scrubbed Netarts. Fourteen miles along the Loop Drive the visitor can go south instead of returning to Tillamook. This road south touches sand dunes; farmsteads that look like a bit of Iowa; gloomy moors that seem to come out of nineteenth-century British novels; Cape Lookout, beloved by painters, campers, and sea birds; viewpoints that open the sea and littoral to full dimension; Cape Kiwanda, a sculptured headland flanking a sprightly cove and shimmering beach; and Pacific City, whose general-store building was once a stage-coach stop and later a hideout for rum runners.

Three miles from Pacific City, US 101 is rejoined. (Go north five miles to the Nestucca River, considered by many fishermen to be the finest fishing stream in the state. Some Chinook are taken, but the catch is chiefly silver salmon.)

Seven miles south of the Pacific City Junction lies Neskowin, an affluent resort community best known for its golf course. Six miles down the highway turn right for Cascade Head. This five-mile road leads to the gateway to Cascade Head, a 1,400-foot promontory jutting out into the Pacific. The southwesternmost portion of it was purchased in 1969 by The Nature Conservancy for preservation as a natural area. The 300-acre Cascade Head natural area includes high meadows, a rainforest area with coniferous trees up to 200 feet in height, and steep, rocky cliffs down which waterfalls plunge into the reaching sea.

Another short jog—four miles—south to the Lincoln City Information Center. This is the beginning of Lincoln City, made up of five small, once-independent towns in the "20 Miracle Miles," now a showplace of tourist attractions.

At Kernville, a brief drive south from Lincoln City, Oregon 229 cuts southeast from US 101 and winds 31 miles to US 20, following the enchanting Siletz River for much of the way.

Salishan, a mile below Kernville, is the innkeeper's Taj Mahal of the Oregon coast. The swankiest resort in the state, the prime convention center of the coast these days, and containing a fine collection of coastal art, Salishan Lodge, at Gleneden Beach, to most Oregonians spells the finest in taste and the highest in price.

In the five miles between Salishan and Depoe Bay there are three excellent state parks; Gleneden, Fogarty Creek, and Boiler Bay. When migrating whales come up or down the coastal waters, one of the best places to observe them is at Boiler Bay.

Depoe Bay, long-settled but incorporated only in 1973, is, geographically, the most exciting town on the coast. It overlooks a rockbound bay, usually jammed with fishing boats. From a sidewalk adjoining US 101 you can see the Spouting Horn, a gap in the rocks through which the tide races upward in a geyser of spray.

Two miles south of Depoe Bay, US 101 encounters the north junction of the Otter Crest Scenic Loop, which rejoins the highway at Otter Rock, after winding along the rugged shore to Otter Crest View Point.

Ocean-Gazing at Otter Crest

Otter Crest Wayside, 1.6 miles south of the junction, is a must stop for anyone who wants to appreciate the glory of the Oregon coast and imbibe a heady draught of beauty. From the 50-car parking area on the promontory, miles of scalloped, battered, gossamer coastline are visible. The Lookout, 500 feet above the sea on Cape Foulweather, faces Oregon's most photographed seascape. Large observatory telescopes are available. Sometimes, focusing on offshore rocks, one sees more than the riled or rhythmic ocean: namely, white sea lions, Oregon penguins, and sea turkeys.

Devil's Punch Bowl, in the town of Otter Crest, is a wave-worn, bowl-shaped rock where incoming tides pour through openings in the deep, round cauldron to boil up, then retreat.

Agate Beach, six miles below the Lookout, gained fame initially for its agate hunting, then for its beach panorama, lastly for being the home of famed composer Ernest Bloch, who died in 1959.

A mile northwest of Agate Beach stands Yaquina Light Station, whose 95-foot tower is the highest of the coast lighthouses.

Newport, three miles south of Agate Beach, was once the social center of the Oregon coast. On the highway, Newport is a modern, neat city. At the town's western edge, some of the most interesting regional houses, facing the sea, may be found. But the real picturesqueness of Newport lingers on in old Bay Front, a waterfront section with seafood restaurants, pubs, old wharfside buildings, and fishing boats.

Within and very close to Newport are Lincoln County Historical Museum, in a log structure back of the Visitors' Information Center, at 555 S.W. Coast Hwy.; Underseas Garden, 267 Bay Blvd., the finest indoor marine life show on the Oregon coast; Wax Museum, across the street from the Underseas Garden; Old Yaquina Bay Lighthouse, established in 1871 and now somewhat restored as a museum; and, across the picturesque Yaquina Bay Bridge, the Mark Hatfield Marine Science Center of Oregon State University, a museum and aquarium designed to key viewers to an awareness of the beauty and frailty of the ocean.

Between Newport and Waldport, for 16 miles, US 101 parallels the beach, affording varied seascapes and abundant recreational opportunities by and at the beach. Four state parks and two waysides are located in this stretch.

From Yachats to Florence, 26 miles, the road becomes a winding, swirling, pirouetting, breathless, roller-coastering ribbon, climbing up and zooming down hills and rimming the cliffs plunging to the sea. Motorists are advised to pull off the highway at one of numerous turnouts if they want to enjoy viewing in safety.

The area between Yachats and Florence is a camper's paradise—no fewer than seven state parks and forest camps. There are also in this stretch several fresh-water lakes—for boating, swimming, and fishing.

Cape Perpetua Forest Camp, 2.6 miles south of Yachats, is worth a pause. A trail declines to Devil's Churn, a deep-wrought fissure where the sea rushes in like a wounded whale and spouts furiously.

Across the highway, a good road serpentines two miles up to Cape Perpetua, 800 feet above sea level. The view from the top is probably the most awesome on the Oregon coast; a breathtaking vista of wave-fringed beaches broken by headlands and by offshore rocks strewn below the forested hills.

At Cape Perpetua Visitor Center, a movie, *Forces of Nature,* and a dramatic diorama introduce the interested to the "living museum" that is the Oregon coast.

Heceta (pronounced *Heh-see-ta)* Head, a spectacular headland named for Captain Bruno Heceta, early Spanish explorer, is best known for its lighthouse, built in 1894.

A mile beyond is Sea Lion Caves, one of the most popular commercial tourist attractions on the coast. An elevator takes visitors down to a huge marine cave, in which a large herd of Steller sea lions make their home.

Florence, on the Siuslaw River, is the shopping center of a beautiful lake and sand-dunes area. In spring and early summer rhododendrons run riot over hills and lowlands.

Honeyman Park and the Dunes

Little more than three miles south of Florence is what is probably Oregon's most used state park, Jessie M. Honeyman. It has 316 campsites and 66 trailer spaces, electric stoves, showers, laundry, boat ramp, and many other facilities, including an outdoor theater. Day-use facilities include picnic tables, toilets, and bathhouses. The 522-acre tract includes a dense forest, swarms of rhododendrons, Cleawox Lake, and a part of Woahink Lake. Trails lead from the park into the cool forest or up to the undulating sand dunes.

The dunes area, extending south about 50 miles to the Coos Bay country, is now the Oregon Dunes National Recreation Area, Oregon's only one of this kind. (For enchanting contrast, the size of the dunes area is almost the same as that of the inland lakes region. These lakes are bounded on the west by Oregon's "Coastal Sahara" and on the east by unspoiled forests.)

The dunes, mutable and mysterious, rise to heights of more than 250 feet. Commercial sand buggies—motorized vehicles that range in size from jeep to bus—grind across the dunes with absolute safety. Drivers halt frequently to permit passengers to take pictures.

Reedsport, 17 miles below Honeyman State Park, is entered by the Umpqua River Bridge. A bit east, the Umpqua receives the Smith River, named for Mountain Man Jedediah Smith, first white man to cross the Sierra Nevada and first white man to reach Oregon from California by land.

The Douglas County-owned Salmon Harbor, at Winchester Bay, is four miles south of Reedsport. Though the harbor is but a few blocks off the national highway, it seems many miles removed from US 101. Motels are as close to the fishing boats as a single block—and the small cafes and grocery and other stores seem to belong to a down-to-the-sea coastal village a long way from big cities. Excursion salmon-fishing boats are numerous here—along with older, larger, and more colorful commercial craft. But if you don't want to go out to sea, you can sit on a bench overlooking the harbor and enjoy what can only be described as bustling serenity.

A mile below Winchester Bay, along the bay road, stands Umpqua Lighthouse—seemingly built for cameras.

Seven miles south of Winchester Bay is the turnoff to Lakeside—a mile off US 101. Here, on fish-famous Tenmile Lakes, the burgeoning community of retired and young actives has it all: scenery, serenity, and neatness in every way.

Myrtlewood Country

Mile-long McCullough Bridge, 11 miles down from Lakeside Junction, spans the channel of Coos Bay and leads into North Bend, a virile lumber town. This is myrtlewood country, and by taking drives off the main road, to the southeast, you will see the myrtle groves. They grow nowhere else in the nation.

The hub of the myrtle area is Coquille (pronounced *Kokeel*), 17 miles south of Coos Bay, reached via US 101 and 42.

Millicoma Myrtle Grove Park, 17 miles northeast of Coos Bay, via Eastside and Allegany, on a county-paved road, affords a splendid opportunity to see these rare trees close up.

From here, continue six miles to Golden and Silver Falls State Park, with two waterfalls, each dropping down a brow of the Coast Range.

The town of Coos Bay, contiguous to North Bend, claims to be the world's largest lumber-shipping port, but the town has been badly hit by the recent slump in lumber prices. The harbor is as colorful as the wharves of Portland. North Bend boasts Coos County Museum, Simpson Park, and unique Pony Village Shopping Center. Coos Bay is distinguished by its factory-shop House of Myrtlewood.

Three Capes

The prime scenic package in the Coos Bay-North Bend area is the Charleston-Cape Arago excursion. Charleston, eight miles from either Coos Bay or North Bend, is famed for its sports fishing, calendar art ambience, and pristine South Slough Estuary, an environmental jewel. Within six miles south of Charleston are clustered three of Oregon's grandest state parks: Sunset Bay, Shore Acres, and Cape Arago. All face the rolling sea and look out over the gnarled, twisting, storm-battered coastal cliffs. Shore Acres has an unusual botanical garden. Bandon, 18 miles from Coos Bay, via US 101, or 17 miles west of Coquille, via Oregon 42S, is the "Cranberry Capital of Oregon" and a major cheese production town. Two good tourist attractions are nearby: a trout hatchery and an old, abandoned lighthouse, the latter at the north jetty of the Coquille River, in Bullards Beach State Park. In summer, melodramas and olios are presented at the Sawdust Theater, Coquille.

Between Bandon and the Cape Blanco turnoff, 23 miles, is West Coast Game Park, where deer, goats, and sheep eat out of your hand, and there are other animals, exotic and domestic. A nursery trail winds through trees to fun learning exhibits.

A side road leads westward six miles to Cape Blanco and its 1870-built lighthouse. The cape was the first geographic feature in Oregon named by a white man (Spanish Captain Martin D'Aquilar in 1603) and is the most westerly point of Oregon.

Port Orford, six miles below the Cape Blanco junction, was long a shipping port for the famed Port Orford cedar. Just south of town is Battle Rock, an aborted headland. In 1851 William Tichenor, a sea captain, and later the founder of the town, brought his small sailing vessel, the *Sea Gull,* into waters close by, landed nine men, and sailed away. The next day, June 10, the local Indians, who resented white intrusion, attacked and forced the newcomers onto a large rock. Thanks to their single, small cannon, the whites held off several charges, and when the Indians had relaxed their vigilance, the whites fled to the nearest settlement north. Battle Rock is now a state park.

Wild sea otters, airlifted from Alaska's Aleutian Amchitka Island starting in 1970, are now rarely seen around the rocks south of Battle Rock.

Humbug Mountain, six miles south, rises 1,748 feet steeply out of the sea. In a fine state park, shaded by alders and maples, campers are close to sweeping sea-views.

Seven miles south is Prehistoric Gardens, a rain-forest "lost world" of life-size replicas of dinosaurs and other prehistoric animals that once roamed these parts.

Gold Beach, 15 miles south, received its name from minerals found on the beach sands. It sits at the mouth of the Rogue River, which, next to the Columbia, is the most famous stream to enter the Pacific in the coterminous U.S. Northwest. A mile north of city center, at Wedderburn, power craft make daily runs up the Rogue. The most popular part of this very popular tourist attraction is the 64-mile round trip to Agness, where lunch may be purchased at one of two lodges. Less in demand but more thrilling is the 104-mile round trip on the untamed Rogue to a remote lodge. (Overnight accommodations if desired, or come back same day.)

Cape Sebastian, seven miles south of Gold Beach, is a 700-foot-high sheer headland jutting abruptly into the Pacific. The state park, aswarm with wildflowers, has many hiking trails.

Mack Arch, 6.5 below, is a 325-foot-high arch rock one-eighth of a mile offshore. The arch is about 100 feet clear of the water.

Within the next 15 miles, to Brookings, some of the grandest scenery along the entire Pacific coast is visible, including Whaleshead Beach, where at incoming tide the rock formation offshore resembles a whale spouting. Spectacular indeed are the views from 350-foot-high Thomas Creek Bridge, higher than San Francisco's Golden Gate Bridge.

Brookings, six miles above the California state line, boasts two state parks: Harris, on the seashore, for overnight camping; and Azalea, a natural park abounding in wild azaleas.

To the Rogue River Valley

There is no direct road from lower southwestern Oregon to southern Oregon across the Coast Range. People from Brookings who want to visit the Rogue River Valley first drive 54 miles through California before reentering Oregon.

But the drive, taking the cutoff 3 miles south of Smith River, California, to US 199, is a delightful one, following the splashing Smith River through thick stands of redwood and Douglas fir.

The first town back in Oregon is Cave Junction, 14 miles above the California line. Cave Junction is the gateway to Oregon Caves National Monument, "The Marble Halls of Oregon." The monument consists of a group of weirdly beautiful caverns at an elevation of 4,000 feet in the heart of the Siskiyou Mountains. The "Chateau," rising six stories from the floor of the canyon, blends with the forest and moss-covered ledges of the surrounding country.

At the landing, overlooking the dining rooms on the third floor, visitors are amazed to hear—and see—the falls of the mountain stream that wends its way across the room, tumbles out of the building, and skips toward the sea. The caves are 20 miles southeast of Cave Junction, on one of Oregon's shortest roads, State 46.

Close to Cave Junction, on US 199, are Woodland Deer Park, a zoo, except for the deer, who bound up to anyone carrying cones of food and eat out of the hand without nibbling or biting the fingers; Kerbyville Museum, which occupies a house built in 1878; ghost gold diggings of more than a century ago and well off the beaten path; and the turnoff to Kalmiopsis Natural Area (17 miles from turnoff), one of the least-known wilderness areas on the Pacific coast and containing some of the most rugged and inaccessible terrain in Oregon. No vehicles; only trails—which are too rough for horses.

Grants Pass, at the confluence of US 199 and Interstate 5, the great north-south expressway, is 30 miles east of Cave Junction. It sits on the banks of the Rogue River and is the takeoff point for runs down the frothing, whitewater stream; runs range from a few hours to five days (to Wedderburn, on the Pacific), with overnight stops made at rustic river lodges.

The turbulent Hellgate and other impressive sections of the rushing, rocky Rogue may be seen close up by driving west on a county road to Galice, 20 miles, give or take a turn, from Grants Pass.

Side Trip to the Southeast

Before returning to Portland, travelers who want to see the new Oregon are strongly advised to first visit Medford and Ashland before heading north.

Though the freeway continues south, it is suggested that motorists shun-pike to Medford. There are two possibilities. The first is to follow Oregon 99 through the towns of Rogue River and Gold Hill to Medford, 30 miles. The alternative is the 38-mile Oregon 238, threading the old-fashioned, charming Applegate Valley. This is a restful, unhurried way to get from Grants Pass to Medford.

En route to Medford via Oregon 238—five miles west of Medford, in fact—is Oregon's most picturesque historical settlement, Jacksonville, founded on the heels of a gold rush in the early 1850s, and looking today like a copper plate of the past. This legendary town was dying and disintegrating when its citizens decided to refurbish the settlement. Now, in vigorous pursuit of the old, they have brought back to life a nineteenth-century Western portrait. Despite the recent migration of the arty and the suburbanites (of Medford), Jacksonville's population is still only about 2,000.

The town's City Hall was the Maury and Davis General Store when it was built in 1856. The Brunner Building, where women and children took refuge during the Indian raids of 1855, is now the local library. The Orth Building, which in 1872 housed a butcher shop, furniture store, and funeral parlor, is now a business establishment.

In 1884 Jacksonville built a sumptuous courthouse. In 1927, however, the seat of the county government was moved to Medford. Rather than let the courthouse go to waste, it was turned into a museum—and with outstanding success. Admission is free and facilities are made available for researchers.

The century-plus-old McCully House is now open as a doll museum. Also open for tourist viewing are the C. C. Beekman mansion, with its contents nearly intact, and the Beekman Bank, which had been closed from 1880 to 1962. If a miner of 1870 could walk into the Beekman Bank today he would recognize the equipment, signs, and pictures.

The Methodist Church, built in 1854, is the oldest Protestant church in Oregon still used as a house of worship. The Catholic Church, built in 1858, is also still operational. The Odd Fellows Hall, whose upstairs was turned into a synagogue by Jewish pioneers, is intact. The United States Hotel, opened in 1880, has been refurbished. (For many years it had been abandoned to dusty ghosts—or ghostly dust.) Today part of it is occupied by a bank branch, and concerts of the Peter Britt Music and Arts Festival are staged in the air-conditioned ballroom of the hotel.

Britt, one of Jacksonville's most illustrious citizens, traveled in 1852 across the plains and established here the first photographic studio in the Northwest, perhaps in all the West. He was the first man to photograph Crater Lake and many of the region's rivers, forests, and mountains. On another note, Britt was the first serious horticulturist in southern Oregon. He planted the pear tree that is credited with being the ancestor of the multi-million-dollar orchard industry in these parts, and his landscaped gardens became the showplace of the Rogue Valley. A replica of Britt's studio is a prized exhibit in the Jacksonville Museum.

Medford and Crater Lake

Medford, five miles from Jacksonville, is the largest city in southern Oregon. It is the center of a vast recreational area and of fruit-packing industries and orchards. Medford is also the most popular western gateway to Crater Lake National Park. The drive can easily be made in two hours and passes, via Oregon 62, through bewitching forests and meadowlands.

The lake, the focal point of Oregon's only national park, is a more-than-21-square-mile caldera, formed when Mt. Mazama, a 15,000-foot-high volcano, literally blew its top. Walls towering 500 to 2,000 feet

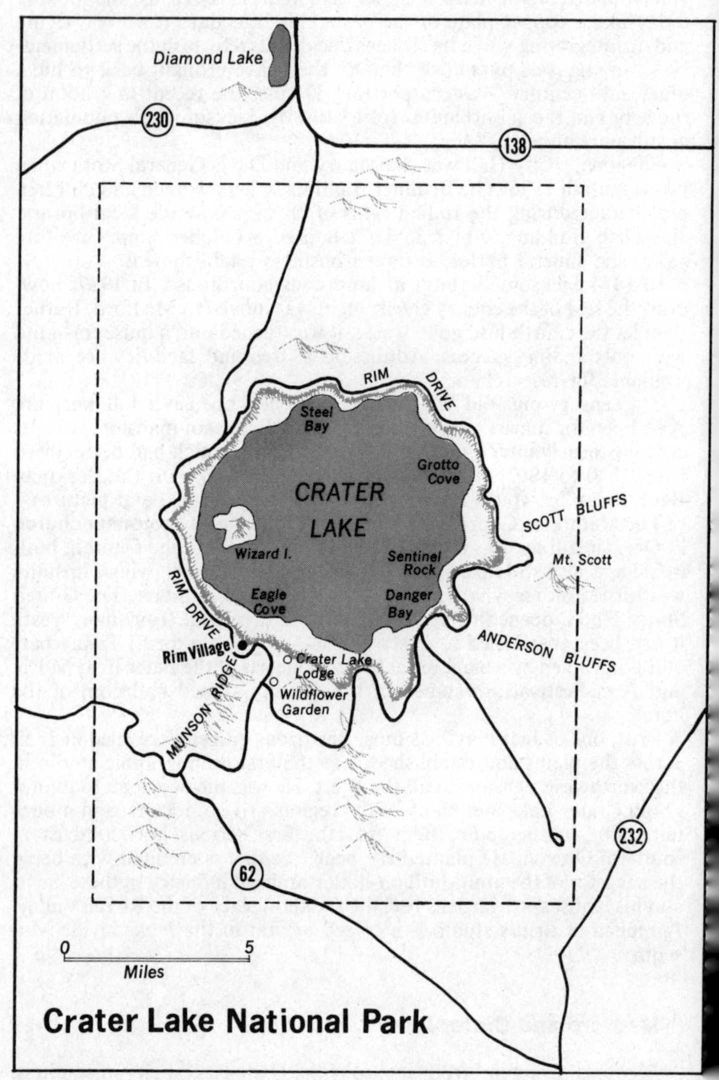

Crater Lake National Park

above the water, accented by rugged prominences, enfold the 6,177-foot-elevation lake. Crater Lake is 1,932 feet deep, and the water temperature seldom varies. Melting snows furnish water for the crater, but there is no apparent outlet.

Two Disneylike islands, Phantom Ship and Wizard Island, provide even greater beauty and interest to the lake. Most unusual is the water's color, the bluest of blue. It makes all other "blue" lakes appear anemic in color.

The 35-mile Rim Drive reaches all points of interest around the crater and has numerous turnouts. Each morning a Ranger naturalist leads a caravan around the lake, pausing often to talk about the geological phenomena and historical record. A sightseeing bus also makes a daily trip around the lake, with stops for viewing and picture taking.

Passenger Launches circle the lake or go directly to Wizard Island and the Phantom Ship. A park naturalist goes along on some of the trips each day.

Shakespeare in Ashland

Ashland, home of America's first Elizabethan theater, is 12 miles south of Medford. It is also the seat of Southern Oregon College, whose gentle campus looks up to the scowling hills of the Siskiyou Range. The plays of the annual Oregon Shakespearean Festival are performed in a magnificent replica of the Globe Theater, in a corner of Lithia Park, a soothing, stimulating fairy wood. The stage love affair with the Bard of Avon was started in 1935 by the late Angus Bowmer, then a young faculty member of the tiny normal school at Ashland (now Southern Oregon College). Ashland now presents plays on a year-round basis, in two indoor theaters, both imaginatively built. Modern drama is performed in the Angus Bowmer Theater. Every year the festival gains broader national and international recognition. A plaza, adjoining the park, has two fountains of lithia water, piped in from mineral springs. Almost everyone takes at least one sip.

Between Medford and Ashland, at Phoenix, is the Samuel Colver House, built in 1855 of logs sheathed with sawed lumber. It has been a stagecoach stop, inn, distillery, and antique shop.

Northward to Portland, we return again to Grants Pass, pausing for sightseeing at the settlements of Gold Hill and Rogue River, between Medford and Grants Pass, a half-hour drive on the freeway.

Gold Hill was the scene of an early southern Oregon gold discovery. Remains of old gold mines can be seen on Nugget Butte, due north of town. The original town stood on the north side of the railroad tracks, and some of the old houses still remain.

Between Gold Hill and Rogue River is the oldest house in Southern Oregon, which served for a brief period in 1855 as Fort Birdseye, a settlers stockade; a portfolio of Rogue River views; and the Oregon Vortex, a commercial "House of Mystery" that continues to puzzle optically illusioned tourists. The building was originally the assay office for a gold-mining company.

The town of Rogue River is sited in an idyllic location in the shimmering Rogue River Valley. The big annual event is the National Rooster Crow on the last Saturday in June. Teeming with visitors from spring into mid-autumn is nearby Valley of the Rogue State Park—with fine campground, boat ramp to Rogue, and complete picnic facilities.

A short side trip around the town exposes travelers to a valley, a covered bridge, an arboretum, the Rock Point Stage Station (1863) and the Rock Point Bridge, named for the rock formation in the river below.

North to Logging Country

From Grants Pass we will avoid the freeway, Interstate 5, as often as possible, and stay with the slower-paced but more revealing US 99.

Twenty-one miles north, at the small, haphazard hamlet of Wolf Creek, there is a hostelry that has been in continuous operation since its founding in 1857. Wolf Creek Inn is the oldest hotel in Oregon and its structure has changed little. According to legend, President Hayes slept here. Ditto Jack London, Sinclair Lewis, Joaquin Miller, and a host of other notables. It is now part of the State Parks system.

The 43-mile stretch to Winston includes Canyonville, a picturesque trade town that developed as a station on the California-Oregon stage route in the 1850s, and Myrtle Creek, an earthy logging burg. Winston is home of the World Wildlife Safari, where you drive your own car among Asian and African animals.

Roseburg, eight miles north of Winston, is one of the great lumber cities of Oregon. Mt. Nebo, across the Umpqua River from the business center, was the place, according to local legend, where the mythical hero logger Paul Bunyan paused on his busy way with Babe, his blue ox. Douglas County Museum, in the fairgrounds, has won high awards for its architectural styling and presentation of displays. Roseburg is the gateway to the North Umpqua River wonderland Diamond Lake and, from this part of the state, Crater Lake. There are few river drives on the continent as unspoiled, as laden with eye-pleasing scenery and as uncluttered as the drive along the North Umpqua.

Oakland, 16 miles north of Roseburg, seems to be a living picture from an 1890 album. The town has a museum but really doesn't need one; the whole town is a museum.

Cottage Grove, 40 miles north of Oakland, has a railroad covered bridge, which locals claim is the only one of its kind in the nation; a footbridge across the Coast Fork of the Willamette; Pioneer Museum, in a nineteenth-century Catholic church; and some intriguing vintage houses, including the Dr. Snapp House, with its witch's-hat front. The town is the portal to the Bohemia Mining District, where only dirt roads probe deep into the mountains for old mines and ghost towns. Prize tourist attraction in Cottage Grove is a 34-mile round-trip train ride on the Oregon Pacific Eastern Railroad into the foothills of the Cascades, following the route of Row (rhymes with *cow*) River. Passenger cars dating back to the 1920s are pulled by a 1914 steam locomotive called *The Goose*.

Springfield, 18 miles north of Cottage Grove, is on the banks of the McKenzie River, as lovely and deceptive a stream as races down from the Central Cascades. The river has been tamed for the first 20 miles up Oregon 126, but after Leaburg Dam it is as wild as a bucking bronco.

American astronauts preparing for lunar flights have explored and experimented on the massive lava beds near McKenzie Pass, 75 miles east of Springfield. The panorama at the pass is most incongruous and awesome: in the foreground is the dead sea of lava; in the background the blazing snow peaks of the Cascades.

Eugene, which practically connects with Springfield, is Oregon's second largest city and the seat of the University of Oregon. The university Art Museum, on the campus, is visited by scholars from all parts of the world. The university library contains an extensive Oregon historical collection, including thousands of documents and raw field work compiled and collected by W.P.A. researchers during the Great Depression. On campus, there is also a Museum of Natural History. Saturday Market, with its carnival air, rustic flavor, and broad range of attractions—from food to magic—is a weekly celebration. Stalls and tables are set up early, and people pour in from town and hinterland. At the Willamette Science and Technology Center, you can talk to a friend on a laser telephone, fight a simulated forest fire on a computer screen, and view the stars and planets in the comfort of an easy chair. A panorama of Eugene, the Willamette Valley, and the surrounding mountains unfolds from atop Skinner's Butte.

Straddling the Willamette

Junction City, 14 miles north of Eugene, was for decades an important market place, because of its position at the joining of Oregon 99W and Oregon 99E. But construction of the freeway, 10 miles distant, dealt the town a shattering blow. It has recovered, however, through an annual four-day Scandinavian Festival. At Junction City there are these two main shunpiking roads: Oregon 99W and Oregon 99E, geographically so designated because of their relationship to the Willamette River.

Let us first explore 99W. Twenty-six miles north, through peaceful farmlands, stands Corvallis, seat of Oregon State University. Like Eugene, it is a tree-shaded, middle-class city, but whereas Eugene is regarded as liberal, Corvallis has a long tradition of conservatism. Of interest here: Natural History Museum, Horner Museum (devoted to Oregon history), Herbarium and Entomological Collection, and Geological and Paleontological Collection.

The road from Corvallis to Monmouth, 21 miles, leads through zesty, sweet, uncluttered meadows, gobbling up the distance in big sweeps. Monmouth, an old farm town, is draped around Western Oregon College. Unlike many college towns, however, Monmouth maintains a rural motif.

Independence, two miles east, was one of the celebrated "trail's end" settlements on the Old Oregon Trail. It was also once one of the largest hop towns in the state. Though small and slow-gaited, Independence retains little of its pioneer vintage. In most of Oregon the slogan seems to be: Make way for the moderns; the past belongs in the museums.

McMinnville, 25 miles north of Monmouth on Oregon 99W, is the seat of Linfield College, established in 1857 as the western extension of Baptist education. For Portlanders, McMinnville has one chief distinction: it is the turnoff to the shortest and easiest road across the Coast Range to the beaches.

Lafayette, six miles up the highway, is one of the oldest towns in the state. A mile east is the Amos Cook House, built in 1850. A mile west of Pioneer Cemetery still stands a house that was lived in for several years by Abigail Scott Duniway, coworker with Susan B. Anthony in the cause of women's suffrage, and a distinguished person in her own right. Three miles west on Bridge St. is the Trappist Abbey of Our Lady of Guadalupe—the only one in Oregon; there are only 12 in the country. Visitors are welcome.

Newberg, nine miles onward, is best known for its Minthorn House. In the mid-1880s Herbert Hoover lived here with his uncle, Dr. H. J. Minthorn. The home has been restored to the way it looked when Hoover spent five years here. A small second-story bedroom holds young Hoover's bed, dresser, chamber pot, and washbowl. Less than a mile from the Hoover House is George Fox College, founded in 1885 by the Society of Friends as Pacific Academy. Hoover was a member of the first class.

Newberg is the key western gateway to historic Champoeg State Park, a 15-minute drive from the center of town. Outside the park is the Robert Newell House, built in 1852 and restored in 1959 with mid-nineteenth-century furnishings. It is now a museum.

Twenty-three miles beyond Newberg is the city center of Portland.

An Alternate Trip Northward

The first interesting point on Oregon 99E from Junction City is Harrisburg, four miles north. It is an old Willamette River town, with many early touches still present. Riverboats landed here, just two blocks from the highway. A slow cruise around town will reveal many old stores and houses.

Shedd, 14 miles north, is a somnolent burg which lost its push when the automobile replaced the horse. But a mile and a half east of town, on the Plainview Road, is Oregon's oldest and most charming industrial plant, the Thompson Mill (1856). Certainly, it is one of the most photogenic man-made settings in all the state, sitting on a mill pond graced by lithe ducks.

Thirteen miles north is Albany, on the banks of the Willamette. Though the city is not a lumbering town of any real significance, it is host to the annual, virile, daredevilish World Timber Carnival. Contestants come from as far as Australia.

Albany is the gateway to a storied, historic land of old, weather-worn towns, covered bridges, churches steeped in pioneer lore, and a Willamette River ferry (at Buena Vista). The main street of Jefferson, a placid settlement of 1,700, is a gallery of nineteenth-century structures. Brownsville, an early woolen-mill town, is seeking to revive the glorious days of its "mauve decade" of the 1890s by false-fronting stores and businesses. Its Moyer House (1881), built in the Italian-villa style popular at the time, is one of the most magnificent nineteenth-century homes anywhere in Oregon. A mile away, Atavista Farm, a house built in 1875, is as resplendent as the Moyer House. A few miles out of Scio, there stands on a silent knoll Providence Pioneer Church, built as Baptist in 1854 by a sturdy band of moralists headed by Elder Joab Powell, pioneer circuit rider and one of the most colorful figures in Oregon's ministerial lore. Among other accomplishments, he delivered the shortest invocation on record when he was chaplain of the state legislature: "Lord, forgive them, for they know not what they do." Quaint Sodaville, appearing to be a hundred years back in time, is the site of Oregon's first state park, Sodaville Springs, though the springs dried up long ago. Inside the no-longer-used covered bridge at Crawfordsville, youngsters rest their horses on a hot day and old men gather in the shade to talk about days past. Covered bridges seem to encircle

Crabtree. The county park at Waterloo, on the South Santiam, has all the flavor of a calendar-art fishing hole.

Salem, the state capital, is 24 miles north of Albany. Murals depict the state's history and from the Capitol dome—above the murals—there is a marvelous overlook of the Willamette Valley and the Cascade foothills. Bush House, an 1876 Victorian mansion, is open to the public as a museum. Near it is Bush Barn Art Center (Salem Art Museum), which sponsors exhibits of Northwest artists. On the grounds of the old Thomas Kay Woolen Mills, Twelfth and Ferry Streets, stand what could be the two oldest buildings in Oregon, the Jason Lee House and Parsonage, both reputedly built in 1841 by Jason Lee, first missionary in Oregon and the most controversial religious figure in the state's history. He died in the East but his body was returned to Salem.

Salem is the gateway to history and recreation. For history, there is the Catholic church at St. Paul, oldest in the state, and, a short drive away, the Catholic church at St. Louis, a crossroads settlement without a post office, store, or gas station. Then there is the Spring Valley Presbyterian Church, a few miles from Lincoln, a famous river landing in the days when steamboats plied the Willamette. The church was built in 1859 and that same year the bell, which was sent from England 'round the Horn, was put up. Farther on, Friends Church (1894) overlooks the Currier and Ives village of Scotts Mills. South of Silverton is the 1851-constructed Geer House, where the illustrious cartoonist Homer Davenport spent much time at the home of his grandparents. Quartzville in the mid-1860s was a feverish gold town, with 500 claims filed and 1,000 inhabitants. Within a decade, Quartzville had become a ghost town. A second gold rush, in the 1890s, brought it back to life, but by 1902 the ghost had returned. People still flock to the area to pan for gold in the legendary creeks of yore but nothing is left of Quartzville now except some markers. Still, it's a great place to picnic. North and northeast of Mehama are spectacular, seldom seen waterfalls; the Elkhorn Valley sparkles with not-easy-to-find geologic and water excitement.

For recreation there is the entire North Santiam River, always cool and clean and refreshing; Detroit Lake and its large state park; Foster and Green Peter reservoirs, and Silver Falls State Park, with its 14 waterfalls.

Somewhere between historical and ceremonial is the Mt. Angel Abbey, in the town of Mt. Angel, a Benedictine community established here in 1884. One of the finest views of the Willamette Valley is from the parking lot.

Twenty-six miles beyond Salem, on 99E, is Aurora, built as a "Christian cooperative community" in the 1850s. Some of the "colony" houses still stand, and are still occupied. Most famous is the Keil House, a large three-story building with a two-deck porch. Ox Barn (1862) has been restored as a museum. Behind it is Steinbach Pioneer Cabin, relocated and somewhat remodeled. To the north of the Ox Barn is the Kraus Family House, donated by descendants of a pioneer family. In the 1970s Aurora also gained a reputation as an antique shop town.

Three miles onward is Canby, whose business district is about half a mile west of the highway and, in the fashion of many old towns, along the railroad track. Canby's distinction is the Canby Ferry, three miles west. It is one of the three ferries on the Willamette River (the others are at Wheatland and Buena Vista). No charge for passengers. Some people park their cars on the "waiting turnout" off the road and ride back and forth for hours, enjoying the serenity and the breeze.

To most scholars, Oregon City, nine miles north of Canby, is the state's most historic city. The town was first called Willamette Falls, the settlement being located where the river drops 42 feet from a basaltic ledge. Oregon City was the first community incorporated west of the Missouri River, was Oregon's first provisional and territorial capital, and can boast of many more firsts as well.

Dr. John McLoughlin, the "White-Headed Eagle" of the Hudson's Bay Company's Columbia District, built a colonial-style frame house in 1845–46 near the river. In 1909 the house was moved to a park that McLoughlin had almost six decades earlier presented to Oregon City. Today the McLoughlin House is a National Historic Site. Next to the McLoughlin House is the Barclay House, built in 1846 by Dr. Forbes Barclay, surgeon at Ft. Vancouver and close friend of McLoughlin. In 1937 the Barclay House was moved from the site of the present Masonic Temple to McLoughlin Park.

Oregon City is built on three distinct terraces, or benches, on the sheer bluff along the east bank of the Willamette. The Municipal Elevator, downtown, lifts pedestrians 90 feet from the business section to the lower residential level. There is no charge, and each rider is given a lifetime pass signed by the mayor.

Across the bridge from Oregon City is the turnoff to a fascinating river attraction. A paved walk leads to Willamette Falls Locks, opened in 1873 and still much used.

Portland's city center lies 12 miles north of Oregon City.

Exploring Eastern Oregon

The road due east of Portland, along the Columbia River, is Interstate 84.

For tourists, the first point of significant interest is Multnomah Falls, 24 miles from the heart of Portland. Second highest in the United States (620-foot drop in two steps), the falls are set in a sylvan glen against the basaltic cliffs of the Columbia River Gorge.

There is another way to reach Multnomah Falls, by way of the Scenic Route—once US 30. This narrow, zigzagging road was once the main national highway; today it is for sightseeing only. The route is sprayed with lofty waterfalls, state parks, and dense thickets, and hairpins around Crown Point, which affords the grandest panorama of the Columbia River Gorge.

Five miles beyond Bonneville Dam is a full-faced view of Beacon Rock, supposedly the second highest monolith in the world. Named by Lewis and Clark for obvious reasons, the great rock is now the "anchor" of a Washington state park. Trails lead to the top.

Hood River, 23 miles farther, is the packing and shipping center of the apple- and cherry-rich Hood River Valley, and the southern portal to the Mt. Hood Loop Drive.

One of Oregon's loveliest bodies of water, Lost Lake, is 20 miles southeast of Hood River, reached by county and forest roads. Towering above the lake is Mt. Hood, dominating a blue and green canvas of sky and earth.

The Dalles, 21 miles east, was described by Lewis and Clark as "the great [Indian] mart of all this country." The name of the city is derived from the French word for "flagstone" and was used by the French-

Canadian *voyageurs* to define the now submerged river rapids, flowing swiftly through a narrow channel over flat basaltic rocks. Today The Dalles is a bustling city of more than 11,000, the shopping and financial center for grain growers and grain elevators, orchard growers, packing houses, and stock ranchers.

The city was the site of Old Ft. Dalles, established in 1850. The only remaining building of the post, the Surgeon's Quarters, is now an historical museum. The original Wasco County Courthouse, built in 1859, has been restored as a museum. Free admission.

The museum sits almost at the foot of The Dalles Dam, a key unit in the comprehensive development of water resources of the Columbia River and its tributaries. A lake, formed by the dam, extends 24 miles upstream to John Day Dam. (The lake is really the river, tranquilized and rendered harmless.)

Side Trip to Washington State

Twenty miles east of The Dalles, at Biggs Junction, a toll bridge crosses the river to Washington State. Try this for a fascinating side trip. On a bluff 800 feet above the Columbia sits Maryhill Castle, a three-story rectangular structure built by Samuel Hill and dedicated in 1926 by Queen Marie of Rumania. The castle is now a rather ornate museum. Three miles east of the castle is Hill's Stonehenge Memorial—to the dead soldiers of World War I. The memorial, stark as the bony fingers of death, is a weird apparition on the naked, desolate hills, staring mournfully at the river. Hill meant his memorial to be a true reproduction of the great ruins on England's Salisbury Plain, but his best effort turned out to be an imperfect copy, as precise observations have discovered. Eleven miles north of Maryhill is the town of Goldendale, to which thousands of persons from all parts of the continent flocked in early 1979 to watch the eclipse, the town's Observatory Hill being in the direct path of the phenomenon.

Five miles east of Biggs Junction, back in Oregon, is John Day Dam, completed in 1968. It then became the second biggest power producer in the world, topped only by Bratsk, on the Angara River in the Soviet Union. The lake created by John Day Dam forced removal, 29 miles east, of the town of Arlington, a hamlet of 500, to higher ground. In essence this meant the building of a complete new—and modern—settlement.

The terrain back of the river is now arid, and the farther east one goes the less the river seems to lend itself to the land. Forty miles beyond Arlington, Interstate 84 leaves the Columbia and begins to bend south toward grainlands and wastelands. Roads branching south, state roads 19, 74, and 207, are paved paths through the wheat basket of Oregon. They touch, or come close to, old homesteads, homesteader ghost towns, bizarre rock formations and canyons, sculptured hills, and fossil beds. Near Echo Junction, five miles south of Interstate 84 on Oregon 207, are ruts of the old Oregon Trail. The country road from here to Echo, eight miles, parallels the route of the covered wagons.

Twenty-five miles east of the turnoff to Echo Junction is Pendleton, the largest city in eastern Oregon, and the home of the internationally renowned Pendleton rodeo.

The Pendleton Round-Up

The four-day Pendleton Round-Up and Happy Canyon Days, held each mid-September, transform the city into a western camp of horses, cowpokes, cowgirls, and ranch wear. All the leading rodeo contestants in the United States and Canada compete here. The Round-Up has more events than most rodeos, and the sophisticated watchers, who number in the thousands, applaud moves that escape the amateur eyes of tenderfeet.

The 51-mile stretch to La Grande is a delightful drive, sweeping breezily over the Blue Mountains as though the road were a boulevard (which it is). It was not so easily negotiated by the covered wagons, which were lucky to make seven miles a day in this terrain. But the overlanders found the Blue Mountains much more to their liking than they did the Burnt Hills to the east, which they described as thirsty, hellishly hot, agonizing, and a maddening ordeal. At least the Blue Mountains had water, wood, and grass. One of the favorite campsites on the old Oregon Trail is now Emigrant Springs State Park, 24 miles east of Pendleton.

La Grande is the seat of Eastern Oregon College, the cultural stage of the area, and marketplace of the lush Grande Ronde Valley, whose tall green grass and rich soil dazzled the Oregon Trailers. Later, many could not understand why the pioneers had not stopped here to settle.

It is 65 miles from La Grande to Enterprise, seat of Wallowa County, on Oregon 82. But the drive itself is an adventure, for it passes through sparkling vales, rides a high slope of the Blue Mountains, follows the acrobatic Wallowa River, and then breaks into the green plains of the Wallowa Valley, dotted by farmsteads that are long on utility and short on frill.

At Elgin, Minam, and the town of Wallowa, roads or trails lead into the mountains, to primitive areas, or to seldom-traveled, eye-striking canyons and fast rivers.

Enterprise, 2,000 population, might be just another small town, but the Wallowa peaks, thundering above the spread-out settlement, give the county seat a pictorial eloquence scarcely matched in the West. (Scenic side trips out of Enterprise include the 40 miles to Buckhorn Springs and the 120-mile loop trip, which visits a hatful of spectacular canyons.)

"Oregon's Switzerland"

Six miles south of Enterprise is Joseph, a quaint little hamlet that looks as though it had just sleepwalked into the twentieth-century. As is the case with Enterprise, there are several drives out of Joseph that will not soon be forgotten. The first is the 108-mile round trip to Hat Point Lookout Tower. View-points on the last 19 miles going up and the first 19 miles going back reveal stunning vistas of the Wallowa and Seven Devils Mountains and of the deep, awesome Imnaha Canyon. From 6,982-foot-high Hat Point, the visitor looks down on Hells Canyon, deepest gorge in the continent. Hat Point is 5,706 feet above the Snake River, which looks like a blue trough twisted in a maze of eroded hills.

The second extraordinary tour is the Upper Imnaha River Canyon loop, an all-day trip of about 140 miles—from Joseph and back. There

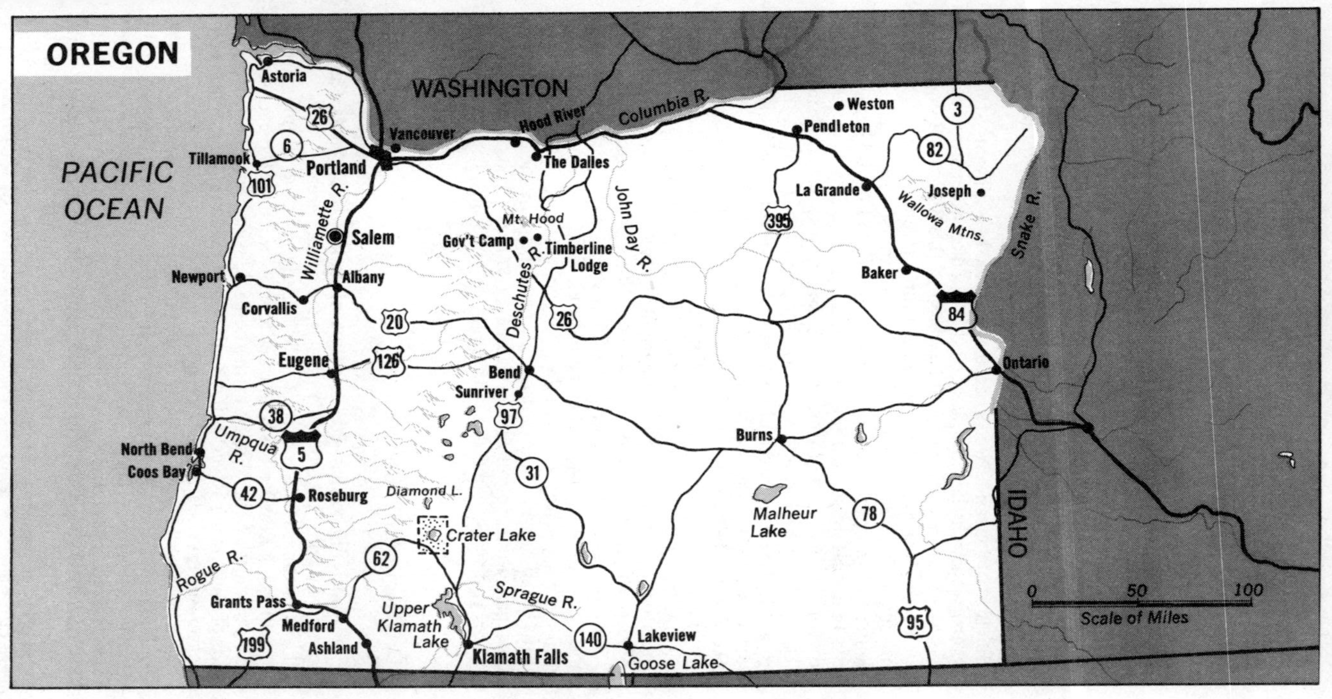
OREGON
PACIFIC OCEAN
WASHINGTON
IDAHO
Astoria
Tillamook
Portland
Vancouver
Hood River
The Dalles
Columbia R.
Mt. Hood
Gov't Camp
Timberline Lodge
Salem
Williamette R.
Albany
Newport
Corvallis
Eugene
Deschutes R.
John Day R.
Bend
Sunriver
North Bend
Coos Bay
Umpqua R.
Roseburg
Diamond L.
Crater Lake
Rogue R.
Grants Pass
Medford
Ashland
Upper Klamath Lake
Klamath Falls
Sprague R.
Lakeview
Goose Lake
Burns
Malheur Lake
Weston
Pendleton
La Grande
Joseph
Wallowa Mtns.
Baker
Snake R.
Ontario
0
50
100
Scale of Miles
3
82
395
84
26
6
101
20
126
26
97
38
5
42
31
62
78
95
140
199

is only one place on this trip where there is a store or gas station, and few ranches lie below the high, rock-ribbed mountains, with their precipitous rimrock. But about halfway between Joseph and Imnaha, a frontier settlement, there are a group of Forest Service campgrounds.

Wallowa Lake, six miles south of Joseph, is a precious emerald reflecting snow-capped peaks. For the grandeur of its environs, it has few peers.

Wallowa Lake State Park is a complete recreational campground in a pleasant wooded area.

A mile south of the state park is the High Wallowas Gondola Lift. Gondolas rise 3,700 vertical feet to 8,020-foot Mt. Howard in 15 minutes. Trails from the tramway terminal on Mt. Howard lead to view points that show the many faces of the Wallowa Mountains and the Wallowa Valley.

Back at La Grande we proceed south on I–84. Twenty-four miles onward we reach the turnoff to Anthony Lakes Recreation Area—21 miles west. The six lakes, 7,100 feet high in the Elkhorn Range of the Blue Mountains, are the headwaters of three rivers. In recent years the Anthony Lakes have gained enormous popularity among campers.

Nine miles from the Anthony Lakes turnoff on I–84 is Haines, which has a fine local museum, though the population is less than 400. Radium Hot Springs, an old-time mineral spa, is just out of Haines.

Baker, 11 miles farther, was born during the gold rush in the 1860s, though the Oregon Trail had for years passed through what is now the heart of the city. The state's largest gold-nugget display—valued at $20,000—can be seen at the U.S. National Bank. Baker rose to eastern Oregon bigness on the strength of its railroad yards, lumber markets, and marketing facilities. But in recent years the economy has undergone attrition, and Baker's population is now only about 10,000.

Few of the gold camps of yore survive. Most of them are reached out of Sumpter, 26 miles southwest of Baker. A day's exploration and ghosttown prowling will take the curious visitor to Bourne, Granite (until recently Oregon's smallest incorporated town), Greenhorn, Whitney, Susanville, and Galena, all prominent in their day. Take a sluice pan along (purchasable at Baker) and try your luck on any stream; you might come up with color, as the miners used to say.

Driving to Hells Canyon

The most impressive side trip out of Baker is to Hells Canyon, regarded by some as Oregon's most spectacular area.

The first phase of the drive to Hells Canyon is the 42-mile stretch to Richland, a Powder River market town of about 180 persons. With the open faces of the Wallowas in the background and the glistening fields of the Powder River Valley under their shadows, the country that Oregon 86 traverses is sheer delight.

At Richland the state road curves uphill to Halfway, which, with 375 people, has some modest motel facilities. Halfway was a kind of nothing-ever-happens outland town until construction on the Snake River dams started. Cows and horses meandered in the streets, nobody ever locked their doors, strangers invited you up to their porches for chats as you strolled past their houses, everything shut down at eventide. Dam construction made a boom town of Halfway, but after the dams were completed the construction workers moved on, and the town, a little richer and a little dizzier, returned, or sought to return, to its old ways.

(A must side trip out of Halfway is to Cornucopia, 11 miles north on a county road. Out of its 30 miles of underground workings came more than half of Oregon's gold output. Founded in 1885, the town was going strong until Oct. 31, 1941, when the mines were suddenly closed. Within 24 hours, practically all the 700 inhabitants pulled out. Cornucopia is the largest gold ghost town in Oregon.)

The state highway, Oregon 86, rolls on for 17 miles beyond Halfway, reaching Oxbow Dam, on the Snake. From Oxbow a paved road north, on a shelf above the stream, goes 25 miles to Hells Canyon Dam at the gateway to the "real" or "box" chasm, where the black, beetling walls erupt [illegible],000 feet, reach a bench, then soar 2,000 feet to a second bench. Hells Canyon Park, on the reservoir en route to the dam, has trailer-camper hookups, with water and electricity. Also, flush toilets, picnic tables, boat ramps, dock.

Jet boats, shooting the boiling rapids, penetrate the canyon for seven miles below the dam. The most spectacular "looking up" scenery is in this section. For latest information on Hells Canyon and Snake River trips, write: Baker Chamber of Commerce, Baker, OR 97814.

Far from the Madding Crowd

Returning to Baker, we head southeast again. The road to Ontario, 73 miles, is not a pretty drive; for the most part the country is barren and scorched. Ontario is quite warm in summer. Temperatures of 100 are not uncommon. The town is the hub of a large sugar-beet industry, and probably more migratory workers come to eastern Malheur County than to any other part of Oregon.

There are two major side trips out of Ontario. The first is to Lake Owyhee, 50 miles, and reached by way of Oregon 201 and well-marked county roads. Next to Crater Lake, Owyhee (pronounced *O-why-hee*) is without equal in Oregon when it comes to enfolding terrain. The Grand Canyonesque formations include fluted cliffs, redstone pinnacles, jagged rocks that look like ghostly ships, high-spired towers that appear in the distance to be Arabian castles, blood-red battlements, and bottom slope swellings that conjure up the image of elephant feet in motion.

The 53-mile-long man-made lake, created by the construction of 450-foot-high Owyhee Dam, second highest in the world when it was completed in 1932, is relatively unknown, even to Oregonians west of the Cascades. There are no settlements along the lake, and the few scattered cabins, occupied by summer tenants who yearn to be far from the madding crowd, are without electricity, running water, or plumbing. But at the north end of the lake there is a resort of sorts, which has a store, a café, cabins and boats to rent; and two miles from the resort is Lake Owyhee State Park, with a fine campground, picnic ground, and boat ramps.

The one- to seven-mile-wide lake, which is really a reservoir of the ghostly Owyhee River, is best known for its bass and crappie fishing and its motor-boat racing along the lower part.

The second don't-miss-it exploration out of Ontario is the 140-mile round trip to Succor Creek Canyon and Leslie Gulch. (South on Oregon 201 through Nyssa and Adrian and then, 10 miles below Adrian, on a dirt road.)

Beyond Adrian there are no cafés, stores, motels, or gas stations. There is a state park in Succor Creek Canyon, 19 unimproved campsites near scenic rock formations, a creek, and thunderegg beds. And trailers camp at the far end of Leslie Gulch, on the eastern shore of Lake Owyhee.

The spectacular Succor Creek Canyon is only a preface to the seven-mile-long Leslie Gulch, reached from a side road below Succor Creek. The formations of Leslie Gulch, which some visitors hold comparable in beauty and color to Utah's Bryce Canyon National Park, suggest a thousand images, and the color spectrum seems to run from one end of the other.

If you return from the Leslie Gulch road and continue south, in four miles you will come to Rockville, whose two-room schoolhouse is the cultural, political, and social center for the scattered ranchers of this vast area.

Seven miles on, the dirt road runs out at Malloy Ranch, surrendering to US 95, which has just entered Oregon from Idaho. Ten miles below Malloy Ranch is a turnoff west to Cow Lakes (with a relatively primitive campground) and Jordan Craters, the results of rather recent volcanic action. The lava beds are quite fascinating, but watch your step lest you tumble into a pit.

Eight miles below the turnoff to Cow Lakes and Jordan Crater is Jordan Valley, the largest Basque community in the state. With a population of only 460, Jordan Valley is also the largest town in an area of thousands of square miles. But the town, because of its isolation, has motels, garages, gas stations, restaurants, grocery stores—with the very modern (motels) mixed up with the very old (grocery stores). The opening of a mine across the Idaho state line quadrupled the population and presented Jordan Valley with multiple municipal problems and the creation of a 2-man police department. The police department created its own image of notoriety around the state and adjoining Idaho with its mass-issuance of traffic tickets. A chunk of the money went to the police chief, who in 1979 had a bigger income than the president of the United States. But, hit by adverse publicity, the city council changed the situation and now everything in Jordan Valley is back to normal.

At Jordan Valley it seems a long way from anywhere, but if you really want a sense of adventure, or isolation, try the 35-mile road to Three Forks. You can be there all week and not see another soul. (Don't try the backcountry trails to McDermitt: you can be wandering for a month and not see a soul.)

Interesting trips out of Jordan Valley are to the former town of Danner, the tiny settlement of Arock (pronounced *A-rock*) and to Silver City, Idaho, a ghost town that was once a large, feverish mining camp. A mile out of Jordan Valley a ranchhouse sits half in Oregon and half in Idaho.

You can get to Burns from Jordan Valley by following US 95 and Oregon 78. It's a distance of 138 miles, with the largest settlement between consisting of fewer than 20 people—if that much. You won't see many houses or trees or cars—and at one stretch it's 55 miles between gas, food, and water—but you'll sure see a lot of mind-boggling wasteland.

Westward, Ho!

At Ontario we turn our trail westward, setting off on US 20 for the long haul across eastern Oregon.

The road between Ontario and Burns—130 miles—rides the high desert, where trees and green fields are seldom seen and where juniper and bunchgrass cover the silent plains and ghostly hills. The only steadfast companion to the road is the barbed wire of fences designed to keep cattle, wherever they graze, from wandering onto the highway. Here and there are the pathetic mementos of failure in this dry, wind-blown land: homesteaders' cabins.

Beyond Vale, the county seat, 16 miles out of Ontario, the land begins to look as if you've seen it before, in a cinema or TV Western. Twenty-two miles from Vale is Harper, big in these parts because it has a grocery store, tavern-café, and garage, with a service station only a mile away. Twelve miles north of Harper, on a paved road, is Westfall, until recently the only post office in the U.S.A. without a single resident in the community. Westfall was a mighty lively town about 65 years ago, but it's all ghost now, except for the old general store long abandoned but now a "community" hall for the far-spread settlers of the valley.

Juntura, 34 miles west of Harper, is a popular stop for motorists who want to break up the long ride between Ontario and Burns. Juntura has about 50 people, but it looks much bigger, because it has a couple of gas stations, a store, a café, and a garage.

Sixteen miles down the road to Burns is the turnoff to Drewsey. Drive three miles north and you'll come to Drewsey, known in the blood-and-thunder pioneer days as Gouge Eye, for reasons easily understood. Drewsey is Western in character to the bone, though it has a service station which doesn't seem to belong in this horse-opera country.

Fifteen miles from the Drewsey turnoff is Stinkingwater Pass, which indicates what the pioneers thought of the mineral waters found around here.

It's three miles to Buchanan, a lonely store, and then 21 miles to Burns, the great metropolis of the high desert, with fine motels (with swimming pools, yet!), restaurants, stores, doctors, a hospital, and a weekly paper that boasts that it "covers Harney County like the sage." But, hit hard by the slump in the lumber economy, Burns has experienced massive unemployment. As a result, many families have left town, and the population has dropped from 3,500 to below 2,900.

Off the Road to Big Sky Country

Burns is the gateway to Oregon's "Big Sky" country, an immense area of sageland, great cattle ranches, rimrock buttes and silent hamlets, spreading out from the slopes of the 50-mile long, 9,354-foot high Steens Mountain.

For most persons the 250-mile loop tour is too long. Suggested, instead, is a drive to Frenchglen, 60 miles south of Burns, a night spent at the Frenchglen Inn, and a return to Burns the following morning. En route to Frenchglen—most of the road is paved—a splendid side trip begins at the turnoff to Malheur National Wildlife Refuge, 25.5 miles south of Burns, on Oregon 205.

Frenchglen, with 21 persons, give or take a few, is the largest settlement of the cattle country south of Burns. The hamlet contains a hotel (probably the most colorful in Oregon) and a general store. The inn serves meals and the general store has a gas pump. Though the inn has only eight rooms, it seldom hangs out the "No Vacancy" sign—if it has one. Most of the overnighters are bird watchers, who spend their days at the Refuge.

From Burns, our eastern Oregon tour continues westward 26 miles on US 20 to the junction of US 395. Turn onto 395 and drive south, through seemingly never-ending expanses of sage ripples and rimrock hills.

Twenty-nine miles below the junction is Wagontire, a settlement of two, or sometimes three or four. For lovers of solitude, this is a fine place to spend the evening, in the midst of the desert. The nights are peaceful, under a sky pregnant with stars and with the calls of birds and wildlife echoing across the velvet darkness.

Fifty miles below Wagontire is one of the largest fault escarpments in the world, Albert Rim. Extending 19 miles along the east edge of the road and kaleidoscopic Lake Albert, the Rim rises, wall-like, 2,000 feet above the plateau and has an 800-foot lava cap ending in a sheer precipice.

Where the Geysers and Antelope Play

Less than an hour's easy drive south of Albert Rim lies Lakeview. At Hunter's Hot Springs, about three miles north of the city center (and on our road into Lakeview), an oddity that brings almost every newcomer up short flares up on the right side of the highway. This is *Old Perpetual,* the only continuously spouting geyser in Oregon. Steam pressure flings a column of water, at 200 degrees Fahrenheit, to a height of 60 feet.

Lakeview, at 4,800-foot altitude, is regarded as the "tallest town in Oregon." The residents, who sport wide-brimmed hats, "string" ties, and sometimes cowboy boots, like the moniker. Maybe it makes them feel tall in the saddle—in their brand-new cars.

There is one side trip of keen tourist interest from Lakeview. It is to Hart Mountain National Antelope Refuge, whose headquarters is 60 miles northeast. (Follow US 395 north five miles, turn east, then north at the Adel Junction, and continue on through Plush.)

A side trip of lesser dimension but with its own peculiar charm is a drive 15 miles south on US 395 to New Pine Creek and Goose Lake. New Pine Creek straddles both Oregon and California, with the post office in Oregon. There are two other towns that spread across state lines, the post offices of McDermitt (US 95) and Denio (Oregon 205 and Nevada 140) being in Nevada. In fact, the White Horse Inn, in McDermitt, is in both states, with the slot machines being in Nevada and the sleeping rooms in Oregon. (Slot machines are prohibited in Oregon.)

Goose Lake, which laps the skirt of New Pine Creek and extends deep into California's Modoc County, is a phantasmagoria in liquid, with unstalked hills and haunting horizons. Somehow, when the none-too-numerous tourists are gone, it seems appropriate that this strange lake is on the flypath of large flocks of geese, whose tremulous calls reflect the eerie mood. Apart from New Pine Creek there is not a settlement close to the lake, and after New Pine Creek no road is within reaching distance of the water. Oregon has a state park on the lakeshore, with a campground, picnic facilities, and boat ramp.

Before leaving Lakeview you might want to visit Schminck Museum, which displays relics of pioneer days. From Lakeview we turn west again and take Oregon 140 to Klamath Falls, 96 miles away. There are several hamlets along the road for gas, and some inviting camping and picnic sites as the pike prances through welcome forests and along cool streams before descending into a valley.

Klamath Falls, which the natives call "K Falls," is the second largest city east of the Cascades, with luxurious motels and restaurants. It is a key lumber, railroad, and agricultural center, and seat of Oregon Technical Institute. Link River, less than one mile long, lies entirely within the city and is locally heralded as the world's shortest river. Discounting the inverse hyperbole, the river is an enchanting scene from May through August, when large numbers of pelicans soar above the river or silently float on it and adjacent Lake Ewauna. From the Lake Ewauna bridge there is a stirring view of Upper Klamath Lake.

Points of interest within Klamath Falls: Klamath County Museum, in old National Guard building: Klamath Art Association Gallery, at Main and Riverside; Favell Museum of Western Art and Indian Artifacts; and Baldwin Hotel, 31 Main, now a museum. The hotel is an official historic site, and justly so. It has 32 hollow Western brass beds, 36 wood-burning stoves, early-day commodes, a Quaker spinning wheel, a 150-year-old mahogany sleigh bed, a seventeenth-century cast-iron bed, an Aladdin's lamp more than 100 years old, and cheval dressers.

Now, from Klamath Falls, we head north, on US 97. The highway swings around the eastern shore of Upper Klamath Lake, always a picture of surprises. Among the waterfowl that frequent the lake are huge-beaked, snow-white pelicans. Twenty-five miles north of Klamath Falls the national highway comes abreast of Oregon 62. A half-hour drive on the state road brings the motorist to Crater Lake National Park. A short distance beyond the north end of the park is one of Oregon's most popular recreation areas, Diamond Lake.

Five miles beyond the junction, back on US 97, is Collier State Park, a logging museum of the early timber days, with a Paul Bunyanesque flavor. Across the road there is trout fishing in Spring Creek and Williamson River, with camping and picnic sites on the banks.

If you have missed the turnoff to Crater Lake, there is another opportunity 31 miles above Collier State Park. From here Oregon 138 travels 15 miles straight as an arrow to enter the national park from the north.

Twenty-five miles on, Oregon 58 empties into US 97. This road, which passes or comes close to such famous Cascade lakes as Crescent and Odell, to Diamond Peak Wilderness, to three large aquatic reservoirs, and to Salt Creek Falls, which leaps 286 feet from an overhanging cliff into an emerald gorge near the headwaters of the Willamette River, was for many years the fastest and most convenient highway from Portland to Klamath Falls, or vice versa. But with the completion of Interstate 5, the great north-south freeway, many people now reach Klamath Falls from Portland by driving Interstate 5 to Gold Hill or Medford and taking Oregon 140, a fast and very scenic mountain road (it touches beautiful Lake of the Woods and skirts the western borders of Upper Klamath Lake) to Klamath Falls.

But there is more scenery ahead, so we continue on up US 97. In 31 miles we reach the turnoff east to Newberry Crater. A paved road of ten miles reaches this dead volcano of spectacular proportions.

Oregon's Volcanic Heartland

Newberry Crater's huge, trackless obsidian flow, the scores of deep cones scattered around the slopes, the shining cliffs, and 65-foot Paulina Creek Falls provoke gapes and questions. But the crater is best known now for the two recreational lakes in its massive caldera: Paulina and East. Both are renowned for trout fishing.

Back on US 97, continue nine miles to the Sunriver turnoff and drive two miles west to Sunriver, a grandiose resort complex. There seems to be everything here: tennis, golf, putting green, bicycle trails, saunas, boat dock on the Deschutes River, boats, fishing, nature tours. In the last few years Sunriver has become the convention center of central Oregon.

Return to US 97, cross the road and continue east on a forest road for ten miles to Lava Cast Forest. What you see here is a strewn mass of lava casts, shaped as though of plaster, in the form of trees. Actually, these were trees that were engulfed by a lava flow, and before the wood burned out, the lava cooled sufficiently to mold. Wear heavy shoes and rough clothing and watch your step.

Once again on US 97, two more miles to another turnoff—to Lava River Caves State Park. Eons ago, a flow of molten lava, pouring out from under the cooled and hardened surface, cored a tunnel a mile long, 50 feet wide, and 35 feet high. There is lantern rental for the purposes of exploration.

Up US 97 a mile to the turnoff to Lava Butte Visitor Center. Wind up the 5,016-foot-high butte, the center of the 8,983-acre Lava Butte Geological Area, encompassing central Oregon's lava domain. The butte was formed by an eruption in a fissure extending from Newberry volcano a millennium or two ago. The prominent cone is the most popular site of Oregon's "Moon Country." The entire Oregon Cascades is seen from the observatory. A trail from the observatory around the butte's crater takes 15 minutes to stroll and is marked with explanatory signs.

Seven miles up US 97, beyond the turnoff to Lava Butte Visitor Center, is the turnoff to Arnold Ice Cave. A gravel road winds 12 miles southeast to the cave, whose floor is covered with ice the year around.

It is four miles from the Arnold Ice Cave turnoff to Bend, and when Bend has been reached, one is at the gateway to wilderness areas, high lakes, swift streams, and waterfalls—all in the Central Cascades.

From the knob of Pilot Butte (a state park), the city is clearly delineated, and a dozen Cascade peaks, blazing white above the hazy blue forest and ocher plain, confront the eye. The butte received its name from early emigrants, who from the top of the cinder cone, 511 feet above the plateau, charted their wagon-train courses.

Located on the banks of the Deschutes River, Bend is one of Oregon's handsomest cities, with fine parks around the river and Mirror Lake.

Bend is the gateway to several interesting trips off the highway. One is to Tumalo Falls, 17 miles west. The 97-foot cataract is deep in a pine forest, near a small Forest Service campground.

Another—and one of the most impressive explorations in the state—is Century Drive, also known as the Cascades Lake highway. This 97-mile loop trip passes through high and rugged mountains, touches lava flows and high lakes, reservoirs, and waterfalls, meets the source of the Deschutes River, and looks at the Crane Prairie Reservoir Osprey Management Area, first of its kind in the nation. About 50 to 75 nests of the fish hawk—often mistaken for the bald eagle—are scattered through the 10,600-acre area. There are numerous campgrounds and two resorts (at Elk Lake and Cultus Lake) on this drive. Pack trains for safaris into the Three Sister Wilderness make up at Elk Lake Lodge.

Redmond, 16 miles north of Bend, is regionally renowned for Petersen's Rock Garden, seven miles southwest of town, and Reindeer Ranch, two miles west, on Cregon 126. The rock garden is an incredible construction of rock-lined lagoons, castles, Statue of Liberty, bridges, and fairytale themes, using native rocks and petrified wood. At Reindeer Ranch, the reindeer are as close to you as the other side of the fence. (They are used chiefly as commercial exhibits during the Thanksgiving and Christmas seasons, being hauled to points hundreds of miles away in air-conditioned vans.)

Rockhounds will be intrigued by a trip via Oregon 126 to Prineville (19 miles from Redmond), site of their National Pow Wow. Public claims of 740 acres are open for work there. Crook County Court House is a page from the Old West, and the log-cabin Prineville Museum is well stocked with pioneer artifacts.

Six miles above Redmond, at Terrebonne, on US 97, a paved road leads almost three miles eastward to Smith Rock State Park. The little-heralded park is a "must" for anyone interested in spectacular rock and canyon formations. Three miles north of Terrebonne (on US 97) the Crooked River Gorge is spanned by a bridge. The gorge is 400 feet wide and 304 feet deep, with vertical walls. Seventeen miles onward lies Madras, gateway to Pelton Dam, Round Butte Dam, Lake Simtustus, and Cove Palisades State Park.

Construction of Round Butte Dam created Billy Chinook Lake, into which poured the Deschutes, Crooked, and Metolius rivers. The lake, which covers 3,600 acres of pumice, lava, and basalt canyons, has 60 miles of shoreline and is part of the new Cove Palisades State Park. Each of these absorbing places is within half an hour's drive from Madras. At Madras we turn west by north onto US 26 for the last, long lap of our eastern Oregon tour.

Indian Hospitality and Health Spas

Fourteen miles from Madras is Warm Springs, administrative center of Warm Springs Reservation. Turn north and drive ten miles to Kah-nee-ta, a resort operated by the Indians. The skylight *nee-sha* (motel units) are artistically decorated. In an Indian encampment scene tepees are for rent. They have no furniture, but tepee lovers—mostly children—don't mind. Kah-nee-ta has hot baths, the largest swimming-pool complex in Oregon, hiking trails, riding horses, a golf course, a fine restaurant, new convention facilities, picnic grounds, and sites for trailers.

From Warm Springs to Portland is 100 miles on US 26, a comfortable two-hour drive. The road first gallops over the high, arid plateau, with the terrain subtly changing from almost no vegetation to clumps of grass, bushes, tiny trees, bigger trees, and then tall trees—an exciting metamorphosis.

Leaving the hot plateau, the road winds through cool, shimmering woods. Emerging on Mt. Hood's towering image, in a few miles, it reveals the grandest Oregon peak in innumerable angles and moods. Then US 26 sweeps down the western slope of the Cascades, runs through wooded hamlets, rich valleys that must have inspired the Oregon Trailers who came this way, and enters Portland, our starting point for both state tours.

PRACTICAL INFORMATION FOR OREGON

HOW TO GET THERE. Commercial transportation facilities range from barely fair to excellent. **By Plane.** Portland, which has about half of the state's population in its metropolitan area, is served by *Alaska, American, Continental, Delta, Eastern, Hawaiian Air, Horizon, Northwest Orient, PSA, San Juan, Sunworld, TWA, United, United Express* and charter lines *Flight International* and *Great American.* From Portland's modern International Airport, visitors reach the city only by taxis; fare from airport to downtown (Hilton Hotel), $20.

By Train. Only Amtrak serves Portland. Three trains daily to and from Seattle. One train daily from Portland direct to Los Angeles, with stops in the key cities along the route. One train daily from Los Angeles to Portland, with same stops. Direct daily service from the east is along the Union Pacific tracks, following I–84, with stops at the major towns along the way.

By Bus. Two transcontinental lines (Greyhound and Trailways) have service to Portland.

By Car. From the east Interstate I–84 enters from Idaho at Ontario. From California you can take Interstate 5 to the state line below Ashland or the scenic US 101 to Astoria. I–5 runs from Portland to Seattle. From Reno, take US 395 to Lakeview, in Central Oregon.

ACCOMMODATIONS. Oregon has many fine local hotels and motels in addition to those operated or franchised by the larger regional and national chains. While price and luxury generally go hand-in-hand, the traveler will often find excellent accommodations and facilities in the moderate and inexpensive price groups. Seasonal rate fluctuations are more common along the coast and in some of the other prime tourist areas while in the larger cities prices tend to remain relatively constant the year round. Hostelries listed here are given in order of price category, highest first, under each city or town heading. Cities are listed in alphabetical order. Price categories are based on double occupancy without meals. *Deluxe,* $50 and up; *Expensive,* $40–50; *Moderate,* $30–40; *Inexpensive,* $30 and under. For a more complete explanation of hotel and motel categories see *Facts at Your Fingertips* at the front of this volume.

Private *bed & breakfasts* are sprouting up everywhere. For listings, write: Northwest Bed and Breakfasts, Inc., 610 SW Broadway, Portland, OR 97201 (243–7616).

There are a number of charming country inns in Oregon, many far off the beaten path. For a listing, write: Unique Northwest Country Inns, 4000 West Cliff Drive, Hood River, OR 97031.

All state telephone numbers have area code 503.

ALBANY. Best Western Pony Soldier Motor Inn. *Expensive.* Immaculate, attractive units, some with refrigerators. Heated pool. Senior discount. Restaurant adjacent. 315 Airport Rd. S.E., Albany 97321 (928–6322).

Takeena Lodge. *Moderate.* Comfortable 79-unit facility, with 9 2-bedroom units. Near Albany airport. Heated pool; restaurant; cocktail lounge with entertainment. 1212 S.E. Price Rd., Albany 97321 (926–6031).

ASHLAND. Windmill's Ashland Hills Inn. *Expensive–Deluxe.* With lots of extras, including heated pool, therapy pool, putting green, and tennis. Coffee shop, restaurant and lounge with entertainment. Proper born-to-the-manner setting for Shakespearean Festival. 2525 Ashland St., Ashland 97520 (in Oregon 1–800–452–5315; outside Ore. 1–800–547–4747).

Best Western Bard's Inn Motel. *Expensive.* A medium-size, two-level motel just two blocks from the Shakespearean Theater, and convenient to business center and college. Restaurant. Heated pool. Seasonal rates. 132 N. Main St., Ashland 97520 (482–0049).

Chanticleer Inn. *Expensive.* Large 60-year-old bungalow in quiet residential neighborhood, filled with French country charm. 120 Gresham St., Ashland 97520 (482–1919).

Columbia Hotel. *Moderate* Charming European style with old-fashioned elegance, 1½ blocks to classic theaters. 22 rooms. Winter rates. 262½ E. Main St., Ashland 97520 (482–3726).

Knight's Inn Motel. *Inexpensive–Moderate.* Medium-size inn with pool, restaurant, and lounge, located on State Highway 66. Seasonal rates. 2359 Hwy. 66., Ashland 97520 (482–5111).

ASTORIA. City Center Motel. *Expensive.* On US 101 close to heart of business district. Restaurants close. Popular with commercial travelers. 250 1st, Astoria 97103 (325–4211).

Thunderbird Inn. *Expensive–Deluxe.* Large motel affording fine view of Columbia River and marina. Seafood restaurant and bar on premises. Seasonal rates. 400 Industry St., Astoria 97103 (325–7373).

Dunes Motel. *Expensive.* Medium-size motel, two and three levels, with well-equipped units. Seasonal rates. 288 W. Marine Dr., Astoria 97103 (325–7111).

Rosebriar Bed & Breakfast Inn. *Expensive.* Opened in summer of 1983. 8 units; very homey. 636 14th St., Astoria 97103 (325–7427).

BAKER. Best Western Sunridge Inn. *Expensive.* Large, excellent motel with well-appointed units, heated pool, beautiful grounds, meeting and banquet facilities, restaurant and lounge. One Sunridge Ln., Baker 97814 (523–6444).

El Dorado Motel. *Moderate.* 56 units, with restaurant, pool, Jacuzzi. Well-tended. 695 E. Campbell St., Baker 97814 (523–6494).

Oregon Trail Motel. *Moderate.* Medium-size downtown motel with heated pool and saunas. Restaurant handy. One of the old, comfortable and easy-going motels on the Oregon Trail. 211 Bridge St., Baker 97814 (523–5844).

Royal Motor Inn. *Moderate.* Comfortable, medium-size motel with heated pool and central location. Well-maintained. 2205 Broadway, Baker 97814 (523–6324).

Western Motel. *Inexpensive.* Small motel with playground area for youngsters who need to work off some energy. Pets OK. 3055 10th St., Baker 97814 (523–3700).

BANDON. Spindrift. *Deluxe.* Bed and breakfast in lovely home 40 ft. above long, sandy beach. 2990 Beach Loop Dr., Bandon 97411 (347–2275).

Inn at Face Rock. *Expensive–Deluxe.* Artistic interior design. Comfortable, crackling fire, and gorgeous sea views. 3225 Beach Loop Rd., Bandon 97411 (347–9441).

Sunset Motel. *Moderate.* A medium-size Beach Loop Road motel with some family-size housekeeping units and lovely ocean views. Seasonal rates. 1755 Beach Loop Rd., Bandon 97411 (347–2453).

BEAVERTON. Greenwood Inn. *Deluxe.* Large motor inn with two heated pools, exercise room, restaurant, cocktail lounge, all on premises. 10700 S.W. Allen Blvd., Beaverton 97005 (643–7444).

Nendels Beaverton West. *Expensive.* Large motel between Beaverton and Portland with efficiency units and swimming pool. Restaurant adjacent. 13455 S.W. Tualatin Valley Hwy., Beaverton 97005 (643–9100).

Value Inn–Beaverton. *Moderate.* A medium-size motel with Olympic-size heated swimming pool. Restaurant near. 12255 S.W. Canyon Rd., Beaverton 97005 (646–4131).

Satellite Motel. *Inexpensive.* Medium-size motel affording comfortable units, some with kitchens. Laundry facilities available. Heated pool. 13295 S.W. Canyon Rd., Beaverton 97005 (646–2155).

BEND. *See also* Sunriver. **Inn of the Seventh Mountain.** *Expensive–Deluxe.* At this lovely Century Drive location, 7 miles west of Bend and about 15 miles from Mt. Bachelor, you will find a variety of resort facilities. Huge three-story inn affords choice of hundreds of units, many one-room as well as larger suites, with fireplace and balcony. More than half of the 300 units have kitchen facilities. Recreation and relaxation offerings include heated pools, whirlpool, wading pool, sauna, playground, tennis, putting green, roller skating, ice skating, and river rafting. Miniature golf and riding also available, as well as transportation to ski area. Dining room, cocktails, banquet facilities. Seasonal rates. Box 1207, Bend 97709 (382–8711). (In Oregon, 1–800–452–6810; western states, 1–800–547–5668).

Rock Springs Guest Ranch. *Deluxe.* 6 miles northwest on U.S. 20, then 3 miles west. 1 to 3-room cottage-like units, each with porch. Heated pool, wading area; boats, fishing; playground, children's program; lighted tennis courts. Clear air and magnificent scenery. 2-day min. stay. 64201 Tyler Rd., Bend 97701 (382–1957).

Best Western Entrada Lodge. *Expensive.* Small, quiet, immaculately clean, this motel is located in a wooded area 4 miles west of Bend on scenic Century Drive, about 18 miles east of Mt. Bachelor ski area. Heated pool, sauna, free after-ski refreshments during ski season. Full breakfast served daily. Ski bus and lift tickets available. Box 975, Bend 97709 (382–4080).

Red Lion Motel. *Expensive.* Comfortable and attractive medium-sized motel with heated pool and whirlpool. Restaurant nearby. 849 NE 3rd St., Bend 97701 (382–8384).

Riverhouse Motor Inn. *Expensive.* Large, luxurious motel with private balconies or patios overlooking the Deschutes River. Heated pool, saunas, whirlpool. Coin laundry available. Dining room, cocktails, entertainment. 3075 N Hwy. 97, Bend 97701 (389–3111).

Thunderbird Motel. *Expensive.* Large, well-furnished two-story motel, with heated pool, saunas, and restaurant adjoining. 1415 NE 3rd St., Bend 97701 (382–7011).

Maverick Motel. *Moderate.* Comfortable units on two levels, with pool, restaurant, and lounge. Noted for its quiet and friendliness. 437 NE 3rd St., Bend 97701 (382–7711).

Royal Gateway Motel. *Moderate.* Smaller motel some units with kitchens. Restaurant near. Seasonal rates. Charming make-yourself-at-home kind of place. 475 SE 3rd St., Bend 97701 (382–5631).

Westward Ho Motel. *Moderate.* Medium-size motel with comfortable, attractive units, some family-size units with kitchens. Heated indoor pool. Play area. Pleasant well-furnished, immaculate. You're made to feel welcome from arrival to departure. 904 SE 3rd St., Bend 97701 (382–2111).

Rainbow Motel. *Inexpensive.* Smaller motel offering a few units with kitchens, and complimentary coffee. Playground area. 154 NE Franklin St., Bend 97701 (382–1821).

Tom Tom Motor Inn. *Inexpensive.* Spartanly furnished but comfortable 10-unit facility. Restaurant at hand. 3600 N. Hwy. 97, Bend 97701 (382–4734).

BIGGS. Best Western Riviera Motel. *Expensive.* Medium-size motel with heated pool, and a few two-room units. Restaurant near. Well-maintained. Star Route, Wasco 97065 (739–2501).

BOARDMAN. Best Western Nugget Motel. *Moderate.* Comfortable units, heated pool, and restaurant handy. Box 79, Boardman 97818 (481–2375).

Riverview Motel. *Moderate.* Smaller motel with very comfortable accommodations; several two-room units for large families. Box 25, Boardman 97818 (481–2775).

BROOKINGS. Best Western Brookings Inn. *Moderate–Expensive.* Medium-size motel on north end of town. Very comfortable units, some family-size and with restaurant on premises. Handy to ocean beaches and to rivers. Seasonal rates. Box 1139, Brookings 97415 (469–2173).

Spindrift Motor Inn. *Inexpensive–Moderate.* Just north of town on US 101, with exciting ocean views close by. 35 immaculate units. Restaurant adjacent. Reservation deposit required. Fills up early in summer. Senior discount. Box 6026, 1215 Chetco Ave., Brookings 97415 (469–5345).

BURNS. Best Western Ponderosa Motel. *Moderate.* 577 W. Monroe. Medium-size, two-level motel, with a few two-room units. Heated pool. Restaurant adjacent. 1.4 m. west of town, on US 395 & US 29 (573–2047).

City Center Motel. *Inexpensive.* Small, cozy. Pets welcome. In-room movies. Centrally located. 73 W. Monroe (573–2001).

CANNON BEACH. Best Western Surfsand Resort. *Deluxe.* Beachfront location for this medium-size motel, with well-appointed units of one to three rooms, makes this a choice spot to stay. Some kitchens, some fireplaces, many private lanais, patios with beach view. A few larger apartments for up to 6 persons at higher rates, for minimum of 3-night stay. Heated indoor pool, therapy pool. Seasonal rates. Box 219, Cannon Beach 97110 (436–2274).

Land's End Resort Motel. *Deluxe.* Medium-sized motel with ocean front, fireplaces, kitchen. Near store. 263 W. 2nd, Cannon Beach 97110 (436–2264).

Surfview Hallmark Resort. *Deluxe.* A bit south, on Beach Loop, this somewhat smaller motel offers many units with fireplaces, several 2-room and 3-room units, several units with kitchens, as well as heated pool, playground, and beach access. Opposite Haystack Rock, one of great attractions of Oregon Coast. 1400 S. Hemlock, Cannon Beach 97110 (436–1566).

Tolovana Inn. *Moderate–Deluxe.* Large establishment on beachfront with wide choice of accommodations in one-and two-room units, and even some two-bedroom apartments. Heated indoor pool, sauna, coin laundry available. Restaurant adjacent. Wide range of rates depending on facilities desired. Box 165, Tolovana Park 97145 (436–2211).

Cannon Village Motel. *Moderate.* Great ocean views. Desirable for families. Kitchens, play area, near store. Small eight-unit motel with excellent local reputation. 3163 S. Hemlock St. Tolovana Park 97145 (436–2317).

CASCADE LOCKS. Scandian Motor Lodge. *Moderate.* Attractive, medium-size motel with delightful view of scenic Columbia River Gorge and very comfortable units. Sauna available. Restaurant and lounge near. Box 398, Cascade Locks 97014 (374–8417).

CAVE JUNCTION. Junction Inn. *Moderate.* Large, well-appointed motel on the Redwood Highway, with heated pool, playground, and restaurant. Seasonal rates. Jct., US 199 & 0 46, Cave Junction 97523 (592–3106).

CHARLESTON. Capt. John's Motel. *Moderate.* This medium-size motel is located at the Small Boat Basin near Coos Bay, and affords convenient access to boating facilities. Some kitchens. Restaurant near. 8061 Kingfisher Dr., Charleston 97420 (888–4041).

CHRISTMAS VALLEY. Christmas Valley Desert Inn. *Moderate.* On Oregon's ghostly high desert. Artifact hunting and rockhounding nearby. Christmas Valley 97638 (576–2262).

COOS BAY. *See also* Charleston *and* North Bend.

Thunderbird Inn. *Deluxe.* Large motel with spacious units; many two-room suites. Heated pool. Restaurant and lounge. 1313 N. Bayshore Dr., Coos Bay 97420 (267–4141).

Best Western Holiday Motel. *Moderate–Expensive.* Large motel in center of town with attractively appointed units and restaurant adjoining premises. Just one block from covered shopping mall. Indoor pool, spa, fitness center. Seasonal rates, 411 N. Bayshore Dr., Coos Bay 97420 (269–5111).

Timberlodge Motel. *Moderate.* Medium-size motel on Highway 101. Free morning coffee delivered. Restaurant open 24 hours on weekends. Seasonal rates. 1001 N. Bayshore Dr., Coos Bay 97420 (267–7066).

Southsider Motel. *Moderate.* Small 11-unit motel with intimate ambiance. Courtesy coffee, courteous treatment. 1005 S. Broadway, Coos Bay 97420 (267–2438).

CORVALLIS. Best Western Country Kitchen Motel. *Deluxe.* Medium-size motel about a mile from Oregon State University campus, and north of the business center. Mostly one-room units, but a very few 2-room units. Heated pool. Dining room, coffee shop, lounge. 800 NW 9th St., Corvallis 97330 (753–7326).

Nendels Inn. *Expensive.* Large, multi-story motel, with fine, comfortable units including many one- and two-bedroom suites. Heated pool. Dining room, lounge, entertainment. Senior discount. 1550 NW 9th St., Corvallis 97330 (753–9151).

Shanico Motor Inn. *Moderate–Deluxe.* Heated pool, 2-bedroom units, movies. Adjacent restaurant. 1113 NW 9th, Corvallis 97330 (754–7474).

COTTAGE GROVE. Village Green Motor Hotel. *Deluxe.* A large, renowned recreation spot and motel on spacious, beautifully landscaped grounds. Tastefully, furnished rooms, some suites with fireplaces. Heated pool, wading pool, playground, tennis, jogging track. Airstrip near. Coffee shop, gourmet dining room, cocktail lounge, entertainment. Seasonal rates. Box 277, Cottage Grove, 97424 (942–2491).

CRATER LAKE. Crater Lake Lodge. *Expensive.* A lodge-type hotel offering rooms with or without shower or bath, as well as several rustic cottages with minimum conveniences. Restaurant and cafeteria as well as dining room, cocktail lounge. Evening programs, launch and bus trips at extra charge. Open summer months only. Crater Lake, 97604 (594–2511).

DEPOE BAY. Holiday Surf Lodge. *Expensive.* Large, with kitchens, honeymoon suite, conference rooms. 939 NW Hwy. 101, Depoe Bay 97341 (765–2133).

Channel House. *Moderate–Deluxe.* At the entrance to Depoe Bay, one block off US 101. Member of Unique Northwest Inns. Solidly perched on rocky ocean front, affording ideal views of ocean, storms and whales. Sport fishing, library, community breakfast room (gourmet breakfast included in rates). Restaurant. Box 56, Depoe Bay 97341 (765–2140).

Whale Cove Inn. *Moderate to expensive.* Small, picturesque motel south of town. Restaurant and lounge. Fantastic views. Star Route South, Box 1–X; Depoe Bay 97341 (765–2255).

Arch Rock Motel. *Moderate.* Small, family size, with warm atmosphere. Box 251, Depoe Bay 97341 (765–2560).

ENTERPRISE. Ponderosa Motel. *Moderate.* Electric heat, free coffee, beautiful scenery. 102 SE Greenwood, Enterprise 97828 (426–3186).

Wilderness Inn. *Moderate.* Comfortable lodgings in new motel. Sauna. Restaurant with beer and wine available nearby. 301 W. North St., Enterprise 97828 (426–4535).

EUGENE. Valley River Inn. *Deluxe.* One of the most luxurious inns in the area, this huge establishment, about a mile northwest of the city, has a number of units with balconies overlooking the river, as well as heated pool, sauna, whirlpool. Some larger units available. Dining room, cocktail lounge, entertainment. Box 10088, Eugene 97440 (687–0123).

Best Western Greentree Motel. *Expensive.* Quiet, medium-sized facility, tastefully furnished. Heated pool, some kitchens, senior discount. 1759 Franklin Blvd., Eugene 97403 (485–2727).

Best Western New Oregon Motel. *Expensive.* At south end of business district, just across from University of Oregon, this large motel provides the conveniences of a heated pool, restaurant adjoining premises, and a few two-room units. Seasonal rates. 1655 Franklin Blvd., Eugene 97440 (683–3669).

Holiday Inn of Eugene. *Expensive.* A large motor inn northeast of Eugene. Comfortable units, heated pool, dining room, coffeeshop, cocktail lounge. 225 Coburg Rd., 97401 (342–5181).

Red Lion Inn. *Expensive.* Large, lovely rooms exquisitely furnished. Some with patio or balcony overlooking artfully landscaped grounds. Heated pool, whirlpool. Some 2-bedroom units. Dining room, lounge, entertainment, coffee shop. 3280 Gateway Rd., Springfield 97477 (726–8181).

Shilo Inn. *Expensive.* Fine large establishment two miles north. Heated pool, dining room, coffeeshop, and cocktail lounge. Kitchenette facilities. 3350 Gateway Rd., Eugene 97401 (747–0332).

Thunderbird Motor Inn. *Expensive.* Another large motor inn, with many units with private balconies. Heated pool, dining room, coffeeshop, lounge, entertainment. Seasonal rates. 205 Coburg Rd., 97401 (342–5201).

Friendship Inn. *Moderate.* Medium-size, with heated pool. Pets ok. Restaurant adjacent. Clean and cozy. 1857 Franklin Blvd., Eugene 97403 (342–4804).

Motel Orleans. *Moderate.* South of Eugene, near suburban Creswell. 72 units, free laundromat, family restaurant, parking; special access rooms for handicapped; heated pool; all queen-size beds. Delightful social climate. Children 10 and under stay free with parents. Creswell 97426 (895–3341).

Village Inn Motel. *Moderate.* Large, well-kept. Heated pool, putting green, restaurant. 1875 Mohawk Blvd., Springfield 97477 (747–4546).

Budget Host Motor Inn. *Inexpensive.* Sparkling clean, cheery. 1190 W. 6th Ave., Eugene 97402 (342–7273).

Continental Motel. *Inexpensive.* Close to University of Oregon, hospitals, restaurants. Family rooms available. 390 E. Broadway, Eugene 97401 (343–3376).

Downtown Motel. *Inexpensive.* In heart of city and close to University of Oregon. Gracious management. 361 W. 7th Ave. 97401 (345–8739).

Eugene Motor Lodge. *Inexpensive.* Medium-size motel with heated pool. Close to downtown mall. Near restaurants. Convenient to University of Oregon. 476 E. Broadway, Eugene 97401 (344–5233).

The Timbers Motel. *Inexpensive.* Comfortably furnished motel with central location; convenient to bus depot, mall and restaurants.

66 Motel. *Inexpensive.* Medium-size motel with comfortable units. 755 E. Broadway, Eugene 97401 (342–5041).

FLORENCE. Driftwood Shores Surfside Resort. *Expensive–Deluxe.* Large inn with all units facing ocean. Private balconies. Many units with kitchens, several larger suites. Laundromat. Heated pool, therapy pool, saunas. Dining room and cocktail lounge. 3 miles north of Florence. Seasonal rates. 88416 First Ave., Florence 97439 (997–8263).

Americana Motel. *Expensive.* Two miles north of town. Kitchen facilities. Restaurant nearby. Senior discount. 3829 Hwy. 101 N. (997–7115).

Le Chateau Motel. *Moderate.* Hwy. 101 at 10th. Medium-size motel with just about all the conveniences offered by many larger establishments. Heated pool.

Recreation room. Sauna. Putting green. Coin laundry. Restaurant nearby. Seasonal rates. 1084 Hwy. 101 (997–3481).

GEARHART. Gearhart by the Sea Condominiums. *Deluxe.* This is an apartment-style hostelry, with family-size units of two and three bedrooms, with kitchens, some with fireplace and balcony. On ocean front. Snack-shop, bar, pool, golf available. Seasonal rates. NW Marion Ave. at Clubhouse, Gearhart 97138 (738–8331).

GLENEDEN BEACH. Salishan Lodge. *Deluxe.* Unique resort complex whose architecture and landscaping, sprawling gracefully over the Salishan Hills, blend with the natural beauty of the coastal area. Every unit—1-room or 2-room—has fireplace and private balcony as well as covered carport. Elegant dining room, pleasant coffee shop, bar-cocktail lounge. Indoor heated pool, saunas, hydro-therapy pool, gyms. Playground, 18-hole golf course, driving range, indoor and outdoor tennis courts. Nature trails invite exploration. Works of top Northwest artists on display here. Seasonal rates. Hwy 101, Gleneden Beach 97388 (in Oregon, 800–452–2300; in continental USA, 800–547–6500).

GOLD BEACH. Tu Tu' Tun Lodge. *Deluxe.* Small, luxurious, this resort seven miles east of Gold Beach is located on the Rogue River, and provides secluded atmosphere without sacrificing comfort and convenience. Units overlook river, have private patios or balconies. Modified American Plan. Heated pool. Pitch and putt. Boat dock and ramp, fishing. River excursion boat makes daily stop here. Dining room, cocktail lounge. Library. Airport transportation from Gold Beach private airport. Open only May through October. 96550 North Bank Rd., Gold Beach 97444 (247–6664).

Best Western Inn of The Beachcomber. *Expensive–Deluxe.* Medium-size motel with spacious accommodations. Ocean-front location. Heated indoor pool and sauna. Seasonal rates. 1250 S. Hwy. 101, Gold Beach 97444 (247–6691).

Jot's Resort. *Expensive–Deluxe.* This large inn located north of Rogue River Bridge affords delightful river view from balconies of most of its units, several larger (two-bedroom) units, many with kitchen facilities. Heated pool. Coin laundry. Marina, fishing available. Tour boat stops here daily on way into Rogue River Wilderness Area. Restaurant, cocktail lounge. Seasonal rates. Box J, North Bank Rd., Gold Beach 97444 (247–6676).

Ireland's Rustic Lodges. *Moderate–Deluxe.* Individual rustic cottages of one or two rooms, located on well-landscaped grounds, provide the charm of this small facility. Fireplaces in most units. Box 774, Gold Beach 97444 (247–7718).

Ebbtide Motel. *Moderate.* South of town, this small motel offers comfortable rooms, some larger suites. Seasonal rates. 775 S. Ellensburg Ave. (Hwy. 101), Gold Beach 97444 (247–6635).

Singing Springs Resort. *Moderate.* At Agness, 1-hour drive or 2 hours by boat on beautiful Rogue River. Seven units; kitchens. Restaurant and gift shop. A memorable off-the-beaten-path facility. Agness 97406 (247–6162).

GRANTS PASS. Best Western Riverside Inn. *Deluxe.* Large motor inn overlooking the Rogue River, with comfortable one- or two-room units, two heated swimming pools, therapy pool, dining room, cocktail lounge. Boat dock; river rafting and fishing. Outdoor dining in summer. Seasonal rates. 971 SE 6th St., Grants Pass 97526 (476–6873).

Rodeway Inn. *Expensive.* Large, plush. Heated pool and therapy pool. Restaurant on premises. Relaxing atmosphere. Senior discount. Handicapped facilities. 111 Agness Ave., (476–1117).

Colonial Motor Inn. *Moderate.* 61 sparkling units. Htd. pool. Restaurant few steps away. In-room movies. Senior discount. 1889 NE 6th St.; Grants Pass 97526 (479–8301).

Galice Resort. *Moderate.* At Merlin, 16 miles NE, on Rogue River. Small. Restaurant. Pets allowed. 11744 Galice Rd., Merlin 97532 (476–3818).

Motel Del Rogue. *Moderate.* An excellent choice. Tree-shaded grounds along Rogue River 3½ miles east of Grants Pass. Units overlook river. 2600 Rogue River Hwy. Grants Pass 97526 (479–2111).

Redwood Motel. *Moderate.* Small, comfortable motel north of town, with heated pool, and playground for active youngsters to unwind in. Some units with kitchens. Seasonal rates. 815 NE 6th St. Grants Pass 97526 (476–0878).

Eygptian Motel. *Inexpensive.* Very comfortable motel with quiet units in shaded location, set back from highway. Family-size units and units with kitchens available. Heated pool. Restaurant nearby. 728 NW 6th St. Grants Pass 97526 (476–6601).

GRESHAN. Coachman Inn. *Moderate.* Moderately large motel with comfortable large units; family size units also available. Heated pool. Restaurant & lounge adjacent. Handy to golf course, shopping center, and dog racing. 1545 NE Burnside, Gresham 97030 (666–9545).

HERMISTON. J & L Motel. *Inexpensive.* Medium-sized motel operated in homelike fashion. Restaurants near. Rooms scrupulously kept. 425 N. First St., Hermiston 97838 (567–5583).

The Way Inn. *Inexpensive.* A neat, comfortable 30-unit motel with heated pool. Pets OK. Senior discount. 635 S. Hwy. 395, Hermiston 97838 (567–5561).

HILLSBORO. Dunes Motel. *Moderate.* Comfortable basic units with restaurant mearby. 452 SE 10th, Hillsboro 97123 (648–8991).

Park Dunes Motel. *Moderate.* 24-hour desk in 60-unit facility. Restaurant adjacent. queen-size beds, in-room coffee. 622 SE 10th, Hillsboro 97123 (640–4791).

HOOD RIVER. Columbia Gorge Hotel. *Deluxe.* This elegant 1920s country inn overlooks Columbia River. Memorable. 4000 W. Cliff Dr., Hood River 97031 (386–5566).

Hood River Inn. *Expensive–Deluxe.* Very comfortable units built along the Columbia River. Heated pool, playground, boat dock. Dining room, coffee shop, cocktail lounge. Jct., I–84 & SR 35 (386–2200).

Meredith Gorge Motel. *Moderate.* View of Columbia River makes units at this motel most appealing. Some kitchens. 4300 Westcliff Dr., Hood River 97031 (386–1515).

JOHN DAY. Dreamers Lodge Motel. *Moderate.* Mountain View Country Club. In-room movies. Senior discount. 144 N. Canyon Ave., John Day 97845 (575–0526).

John Day Sunset Inn. *Moderate.* Largest motel in county, with 44 units. Suites, heated indoor pool, restaurant. 390 W. Main, John Day 97845 (575–1462).

JOSEPH. The Bed, Bread, and Trail Inn. *Expensive.* Small, intimate facility looking up to Wallowa Mountains and in heart of historic town. 700 S. Main St., Joseph 97846 (432–9765).

KLAMATH FALLS. Thunderbird Motel. *Expensive–Deluxe.* Large, two-story motel with very attractive rooms. Heated pool. Restaurant near. 3612 S. 6th St., Klàmath Falls 97603; (882–8864).

Best Western Klamath Inn. *Expensive.* Everything here is king size. Continental breakfast. Valet service. Indoor heated pool. 4061 S. 6th St., Klamath Falls 97603 (800–528–1234).

Molatore's Motel. *Moderate.* Large, two-level motel with well-furnished, well-kept units. Heated pool. Restaurant, cocktail lounge. 100 Main St., Klamath Falls 97601 (882–4666).

Budget Host Inn. *Inexpensive.* Medium-size motel, well-kept units, heated pool. 11 Main St., Klamath Falls 97601 (882–4494).

North Entrance Motel. *Inexpensive.* Located north of town, near hospital and Ore. Tech. Inst., this motel has some family units as well as one-room units, and offers the convenience of a heated pool, playground for youngsters, and some kitchens. 3844 Hwy. 97, Klamath Falls 97602 (884–8104).

LA GRANDE. Best Western Pony Soldier Motor Inn. *Expensive.* Large, very comfortable motel with many conveniences, including heated pool, sauna, exercise room. Delightful courtyard. Restaurant near. Hwys. 82 & 84, La Grande 97850 (963–7195).

Royal Motor Inn. *Moderate.* Medium-size motel with comfortable units, a few two-room units, some refrigerators. Restaurants nearby. 1510 Adams, La Grande 97850 (963–4154).

LAKE OSWEGO. Best Western Sherwood Inn. *Expensive.* Medium-size motel five miles south of Portland, with heated indoor pool, saunas, restaurant, and cocktail lounge. 15700 SW Upper Boones Ferry Rd., Lake Oswego 97034 (620–2980).

LAKEVIEW. Skyline Motor Lodge. *Moderate.* Newer facility with comfortable units, restaurant nearby. 414 N. G St., Lakeview 97630 (947–2194).

Lakeview Lodge Motel. *Moderate.* Quiet location off highway. Free in-room movies. Some kitchens. 301 N. G St., Lakeview 97630 (947–2181).

LINCOLN CITY. The Inn at Spanish Head. *Deluxe.* Huge, 10-story inn built against a cliff on the oceanfront. Variety of rooms and suites available, some with kitchens, most with ocean view, many with balconies, fireplaces. Coin laundry. Heated pool, sauna, and beach. Recreation room. Restaurant, cocktails, entertainment. Seasonal rates. 4009 S. Hwy. 101, Lincoln City 97367 (in Oregon, 800–452–8127; in WA, ID, NV, UT, & N CA, 800–547–5235; elsewhere call collect 503–996–2161).

Surftides Beach Resort. *Deluxe.* At this large oceanfront resort, rates vary depending on the season as well as the type of accommodation sought. Many units with balconies, fireplaces. A few suites. Two heated pools—one outdoor, one indoor—plus sauna, therapy pool, adult exercise room. Tennis available. Beach, playground. Laundry facilities. Dining room, bar. 2945 N. Jetty St., Lincoln City 97367 (994–2191).

Nendels Cozy Cove Motel. *Expensive–Deluxe.* Smaller oceanfront motel has some family-size units, kitchens, woodburning fireplaces. Saunas, sundecks, children's play area. Seasonal rates. 515 NW Inlet Ave., Lincoln City 97367 (994–2950).

Nordic Motel. *Expensive–Deluxe.* 2133 N.W. Inlet Ave. Moderate-size new motel with an ample number of units with kitchens or "efficiencies" for heating up in-room sips or snacks. Heated pool and saunas, too, in this beachfront place with ocean view. 2133 NW Inlet, Lincoln City 97367 (994–8145).

Coho Inn. *Expensive.* Medium-size motel overlooking ocean, many units with balconies or patios, some kitchenettes, some fireplaces. Seasonal rates. 1635 NW Harbor, Lincoln City 97367 (994–3684).

Sailor Jack's Oceanfront Motel. *Expensive.* Medium-size motel on sandy beach, offering delightful ocean views. Sauna. Some units with kitchens, fireplaces. Seasonal rates. 1035 N. Harbor, Lincoln City 97367 (994–3696).

Westshore Oceanfront Motel. *Expensive.* Medium-size facility with sparkling interiors. Low bank beach access. Fireplaces, kitchens. Cribs available. Quiet location off Hwy. 101, Near restaurants. 3127 S. Anchor Ave., Lincoln City 97367 (996–2001).

"D" Sands Motels. *Moderate–Deluxe.* Moderately large, with kitchens in all units, and indoor heated pool for all-weather use. Seasonal rates. 171 SW Hwy. 101, Lincoln City 97367 (994–5244).

Shilo Inn. *Moderate–Deluxe.* Oceanfront resort with 188 rooms. Indoor swimming and therapy pool. Guest laundry. The latest in luxury. 1501 NW 40th St., Lincoln City 97367 (994–3655).

Nidden Hof. *Moderate.* Kitchens, in-room movies. Ocean view; low bank beach access. Handicapped facilities. Seasonal rates. 136 NE Hwy. 101, Lincoln City 97367 (994–8155).

City Center Motel. *Inexpensive.* Short walk to beach. Near restaurants. 1014 NE Hwy. 101, Lincoln City 97367 (994–2612).

MADRAS. Juniper Motel. *Moderate.* Compact 20-unit facility. Pets welcome. Kitchens. Friendly management. 414 N. Hwy 26, Madras 97741 (475–6186).

Master Host Motor Inn. *Moderate.* 48 tidy units. Pool. Casual atmosphere. 203 4th St., Madras 97741 (475–6141).

McMINNVILLE. Safari Motel. *Moderate.* Medium-size motel a mile north of town, with heated pool, restaurant and lounge. 345 N. Hwy 99W, McMinnville 97128 (472–5187).

MEDFORD. Jacksonville Inn. *Deluxe.* At historic Jacksonville, 5 miles west on Oregon 238. Built in 1863 in Oregon's first gold town. Rooms in authentic Western motif. Gourmet dining, cocktail lounge. Great way to see Oregon's most interesting town. 175 E. California St., Jacksonville 97530 (899–1900).

Red Lion Inn. *Deluxe.* Large, two-level, comfortably furnished motel in center of town. Two heated pools. Coffeeshop, dining room, lounge, entertainment. Airport transportation available. Seasonal rates. 200 N. Riverside, 97501 (779–5811).

Best Western Medford Inn. *Expensive.* All the comforts of a really fine, large motel. A small number of two-room units. Heated pool. Restaurant open 24 hours. Cocktail lounge. 1015 S. Riverside, 97501 (773–8266).

Best Western Pony Soldier Motor Inn. *Expensive.* 72-unit full service facility. Senior discount. Restaurant adjacent. Affluent ambience. 2340 Crater Lake Hwy. 97504 (779–2011).

Shilo Inn. *Expensive.* Medium-size motel, well-appointed. Sauna, spa; pets welcome. 2111 Biddle Rd. 97501 (770–5151).

Capri Motel. *Moderate.* Smaller motel offers kitchen facilities, swimming pool, at modest rates. 250 Barnett Rd. 97501 (773–7796).

Best 4 Less Village Inn. *Inexpensive.* Family units. Kitchenettes, pool. Low commercial and weekly rates. 722 N. Riverside, 97501 (773–5373).

Cedar Lodge. *Inexpensive.* Medium-size motel with heated pool and restaurant close at hand. 518 N. Riverside, 97501 (773–7361).

NEWPORT. Embarcadero Resort Hotel. *Deluxe.* Very large new motor inn with variety of accommodations including one-room and two-room units and family-size apartments. Balconies overlooking Yaquina Bay. Fireplaces in many units. Laundry facilities. Heated indoor pool, saunas, therapy pool, marina, boat ramp, fishing and crabbing facilities, outdoor cooking and barbecues. 1000 SE Bay Blvd., Newport 97365 (265–8521—toll free in Oregon, 800–452–8567).

Newport Hilton. *Deluxe.* Luxury hotel on oceanfront, three miles north on US 101. Beach, heated pool, sauna. Dining room, lounge with entertainment. 3019 N. Coast Hwy., Newport 97365 (265–9411).

Windjammer Hallmark Resort. *Deluxe.* Beach-front motel, very comfortable units, some with fireplaces, some kitchenettes. Restaurant nearby. 744 SW Elizabeth, Newport 97365 (265–8853).

Moolack Shores Motel. *Expensive.* A true ocean hostelry; small, secluded, on the beach. Fireplaces, beamed ceilings, kitchens. Ideal for the romantic. Star Route N, Box 420 (265–2326).

Whaler Motel. *Expensive.* Well-maintained property with 61-units, each with ocean view. Kitchenettes, fireplaces available. 155 SW Elizabeth (800–433–4360, in Oregon; 800–433–9444, out-of-state).

Penny Saver Motel. *Moderate.* Many repeats in this 46-unit facility. Close to beach and restaurants. Seasonal rates. 710 N. Coast Hwy., Newport 97365 (265–6631).

NORTH BEND. *See also* Coos Bay.

Pony Village Motor Lodge. *Moderate.* Large, two-level motel with comfortable units, located at distinctive Pony Village Shopping Center. Dining room and cocktail lounge. Pets OK. Eight blocks west of US 101 on Virginia Ave., North Bend 97459 (756–3191).

ONTARIO. Tapadera Motor Inn. *Expensive.* Large motel with lovely, comfortable units in garden setting. Heated pool, restaurant, cocktail lounge. 725 Tapadera Ave., Ontario 97914 (889–8621).

Colonial Motor Inn. *Moderate.* 74 units; Heated indoor pool; whirlpool. Restaurant adjacent. 761 Tapadera Ave., Ontario 97914 (889–9615).

Holiday Budget Motel. *Moderate.* Large, two-story motel, with comfortably furnished units, heated pool, free in-house movies. Restaurant, cocktail lounge. 615 E. Idaho, Ontario 97914 (889–9188).

Plaza Motel. *Moderate.* Neat, cozy 23-unit facility near restaurants. 1144 SW 4th Ave., Ontario 97914 (889–9641).

Shaw Motel. *Inexpensive.* Kitchens, pets OK, near restaurants, well-attended. 589 N. Oregon St., Ontario 97914 (889–8658).

OREGON CAVES. Oregon Caves Chateau. *Expensive.* Beautiful mountain locale at Oregon Caves National Monument. All rooms with bath in both lodge and cottages. Guided tours through Oregon Caves depart from lodge. Coffee shop, dining room, bar. Open mid-June through early September. Box 128, Cave Junction 97523 (592–3400).

OREGON CITY. International Dunes. *Moderate.* Large motel with choice accommodations, queen-size beds, outdoor heated pool, restaurant, and lounge. Overlooks Willamette River. 1900 Clackamette Dr., Oregon City 97045 (655–7141).

Poolside Motel. *Moderate.* A good family motel, with lots of kitchen units, all-year indoor heated pool, restaurants near. 19240 McLoughlin Blvd., Oregon City 97045 (656–1955).

OTTER ROCK. Inn at Otter Crest. *Deluxe.* Built on a wooded headland jutting into the sea, this mammoth resort facility provides elegant units of varying sizes, each with private balcony affording magnificent ocean view. Some units with fireplaces, some kitchens. Heated pool, sauna, four tennis courts, miniature golf, volleyball, badminton, recreation room. Direct beach access. Mini-buses from registration area to rooms, electric tramway from units to conference center, restaurant and lounge. Nature trails. Dining room, cocktail lounge, entertainment, dancing. Box 50, Otter Rock 97369 (765–2111).

PENDLETON. Red Lion Inn—Indian Hills. *Deluxe.* Large motel with spacious units, some balconies, a few two-room units. Heated pool. Coffee-shop, dining room, lounge, entertainment. 303 SE Patawa Rd. 97801 (276–6111).

Tapadera Motor Inn. *Expensive.* Medium-size motel located in city center, with popular restaurant and cocktail lounge on premises. 105 SE Court 97801 (276–3231).

Imperial 400 Motor Inn. *Moderate.* Medium-size, two-story motel, well maintained. Heated pool. Restaurant near. 201 SW Court 97801 (276–5252).

Pendleton TraveLodge. *Moderate.* Medium-size facility, with standard comforts and heated pool, too. 310 SE Dorion, 97801 (276–6231).

Ranch Motel. *Inexpensive.* Restaurant, kitchens, pool, air conditioning. 50-unit facility simply but neatly furnished. I–84 & Barnhart, 97801 (276–4711).

PORTLAND. *See also* Beaverton, Gresham, Hillsboro, Lake Oswego, Oregon City, Tigard, Tualatin.

Best Western Flamingo Motel. *Deluxe.* Large, two-level motel with spacious rooms. Family units with kitchens. Coffee shop, dining room, lounge, banquet facilities. Heated pool. Free airport transportation. 9727 N.E. Sandy Blvd., 97220 (255–1400).

Chumaree Comfortel. *Deluxe.* Very comfortable units at this large motor inn 5 miles east of downtown. Convenient to airport. Suites available; some units with fireplaces and spas. Heated pool, sauna, in-room movies. 8247 N.E. Sandy Blvd., 97220 (256–4111).

Heathman Hotel. *Deluxe.* Luxurious rooms, furnishings, service—the works. Valet parking. SW Broadway at Salmon, right downtown. 97205 (in Oregon call collect: 241–4100; outside Oregon, 800–551–0011).

Marriott Hotel. *Deluxe.* A huge facility overlooking the Willamette River offers full range of small and large units and suites, heated indoor pool, therapy pool, exercise room, sauna. Two restaurants and a lounge. City tennis facilities across from hotel. 1401 S.W. Front, 97201 (226–7600 or 800–228–9290).

Nendels Motor Inn-Airport. *Deluxe.* Large motor inn near Portland International Airport. Heated pool, whirlpool. Suites available. Restaurant, lounge, entertainment. Free airport transportation. 7101 N.E. 82nd Ave., 97220 (255–6722).

Portland Hilton Hotel. *Deluxe.* Large, downtown, modern facility combining the personal services of a hotel and the conveniences of a motor inn. Family rates, in-room coffee. Three restaurants, including one on the 23rd floor where patrons enjoy a dramatic view of the city. Coffee shop, lounge with entertainment, heated pool, sauna. Pay garage parking. Airport transportation available. 921 S.W. 6th Ave., 97204 (226–1611 or 800–445–8667).

Ramada Inn. *Deluxe.* Large motel with the many guest features offered by this chain. No extra charge for children under 18 in the same room with parents. Heated indoor pool, steambaths, dining room, cocktail lounge. Room service. Near Coliseum and Lloyd Center. 10 N. Weidler, 97212 (239–9900).

Red Lion Inn-Columbia River. *Deluxe.* Lavish, glittering, three-story motel with glassed-in elevator shaft so you can see and be seen as you ride to your floor. Located on Columbia River, with many units affording river view. Free parking, outdoor heated pool, sauna. Suites complete with wet bar and Jacuzzi bathtubs available. Room service. Full-menu coffeeshop plus formal dining room, cocktail lounge, nightly entertainment. Free airport transportation. 1401 N. Hayden Island Drive., 97217 (283–2111).

Red Lion Inn-Lloyd Center. *Deluxe.* Large, multi-story hotel located at Lloyd Center, near airport, five minutes from downtown. Large selection of accommodations, including some with lanais at poolside. Some suites. Heated pool. Family rates. Garage. Two restaurants, coffeeshop, cocktail lounge, entertainment. 1000 NE Multnomah, 97232 (281–6111).

Red Lion Motor Inn-Jantzen Beach. *Deluxe.* Huge waterfront facility 4 miles north of town off I–5, with many large and small units; many balconies have views of Columbia River. Heated pool, whirlpool, boating, tennis. Restaurants, lounge, entertainment. Airport transportation. 909 N. Hayden Island Drive, 97217 (283–4466).

Red Lion Motor Inn-Portland Center. *Deluxe.* Beautiful facility, very comfortable rooms, near Portland Center and downtown. Suites available. Free parking. Heated pool, restaurant, cocktail lounge with entertainment. Airport transportation. 310 S.W. Lincoln, 97201 (221–0450).

RiverPlace Alexis Hotel. *Deluxe.* New luxury hotel at the fringe of downtown. Pets OK. Restaurant. Cocktail lounge, entertainment. 1510 SW Harbor Way, 97201 (228–3233).

Riverside Inn. *Deluxe.* Large, conveniently located downtown motor hotel, just west of Morrison Bridge, with some units overlooking Willamette River. Free parking. Restaurant, coffee shop, cocktail lounge. Room service. Meeting room. No charge for children under 12 in same room with parents. 50 S.W. Morrison, 97204 (221–0711).

Sheraton Inn-Portland Airport. *Deluxe.* Large motor inn adjoining Portland International Airport. Variety of larger units and suites in addition to one-room units. Some rooms with steam baths. Heated indoor pool, exercise room; dining room, coffee shop, lounge with entertainment. Airport transportation. 8235 N.E. Airport Way, 97220 (281–2500).

Shilo Inn-Lloyd Center. *Deluxe.* New facility near both Lloyd Center and Memorial Coliseum. Sauna. Restaurant near. 1506 N.E. 2nd Ave., 97232 (231–7665 or 800–222–2244).

The Westin Benson. *Deluxe.* A large, elegant downtown hotel with many luxuries. Rooms richly furnished with over-sized beds. Family rates. Pay parking in garage. Two dining rooms, cocktail lounge, entertainment. Meeting and display rooms. 309 S.W. Broadway, 97205 (228–2000).

Mallory Motor Hotel. *Expensive–Deluxe.* A large, well-furnished, well-kept, quiet, older hotel, handy to downtown yet away from busiest area. Free parking. Restaurant, cocktail lounge. Across from Civic Theater, 729 S.W. 15th Ave., 97205 (223–6311).

Best Western Fortniter Motel. *Expensive.* Family-size suites with kitchens available, as well as one-room units. Laundry room. Guests have free use of facilities at athletic club nearby, including Olypmic-size pool, gym, saunas. Free airport transportation. 4911 N.E. 82nd Avenue, 97220 (255–9771).

Best Western Kings Way Inn. *Expensive.* Five-story motel with well-furnished rooms. Near Lloyd Center and Memorial Coliseum, not far from downtown. Suites and studios available. Saunas, therapy pool, restaurant. 420 N.E. Holladay St., 97232 (233–6331).

Best Western Sherwood Inn. *Expensive.* Immaculate medium-size motor inn. Heated indoor pool, sauna, pets OK. Senior discount. In suburban area. 15700 S.W. Upper Boones Ferry Rd., 97223 (620–2980).

Corsun Arms Motor Hotel. *Expensive.* Medium-size, multi-story motel offering "a complete apartment for the price of a room." In quiet residential area near Civic Stadium, with view of Portland from attractive roof garden and sun deck. 809 S.W. King, 97205 (226–6288).

Cosmopolitan Hotel. *Expensive.* Large multi-story motor inn, near both downtown and Lloyd Center. Particularly well-appointed. Some suites, some two-room units. Rooftop swimming pool. Gorgeous view of Portland and environs from rooftop dining room and lounge; dancing, entertainment, too. 1030 N.E. Union Ave., 97232; (235–8433).

Hyatt Lodge. *Expensive.* Near downtown and Lloyd Center. Heated pool. Restaurant opposite. 431 N.E. Multnomah, 97232 (233–5121).

Imperial 400 Motor Inn. *Expensive.* Medium size motel with family units as well as one-room units. Heated pool. Restaurant nearby. Close to Lloyd Center and Memorial Coliseum. 518 N.E. Holladay, 97232 (234–4391; out-of-town reservations, 800–368–4400).

Red Lion Inn-Coliseum. *Expensive.* Across from Memorial Coliseum, this very large motor inn is within easy reach of Lloyd Center and downtown as well. Heated pool. Coffee shop, restaurant, cocktail lounge, entertainment. 1225 N. Thunderbird Way, 97212 (235–8311).

Shilo Inn-Portland Airport. *Expensive.* Near Portland International Airport. Large motel with heated pool, sauna. Some large kitchen units available. Coin laundry. Weekly and monthly rates available. 3328 N.E. 82nd Ave., 97220; (256–2550 or 800–222–2244).

Sunnyside Inn. *Expensive.* Adjacent to Kaiser Sunnyside Hospital and off Oregon 205. Also near giant shopping center. Jct., 0 205 & Sunnyside Rd. 97015 (800–547–8400 or 652–1500).

Imperial Hotel. *Moderate–Deluxe.* A large, well-kept hotel in the heart of Portland. Free parking. Oversized beds in every room. Meeting facilities. Popular coffee house and bar. 400 S.W. Broadway, 97205 (228–7221).

Caravan Motor Hotel. *Moderate.* Medium-size motel with wide choice of accommodations, including executive suites and family-size units. Room service. 24-hour desk service. Restaurant and cocktail lounge. Heated pool. 2401 S.W. 4th. Ave. (226–1121).

Chalet Motel. *Moderate.* Small, two-level motel with satellite television. Snack shop and restaurants nearby. In Milwaukie, south of Portland. 8900 S.E. McLoughlin Blvd., 97222 (654–3181).

Chumaree Motel/Eastport. *Moderate.* Comfortable, medium-size motel in southeast area, near Eastport Plaza shopping center. Special ramps and specially equipped rooms for handicapped. Reserved parking spaces for handicapped, too. 4512 S.E. 82nd, 97266 (774–8876).

City Center Motel. *Moderate.* Medium-size motel on east side of town, with family units available. Patio, sun deck. Restaurants nearby. 3800 N.E. Sandy Blvd., 97232 (287–1107).

Hallmark Motel. *Moderate.* Medium-size motel, with some family units with kitchens. Small heated pool. Cozy atmosphere. Restaurant and lounge nearby. 4810 N.E. Sandy Blvd., 97213 (282–7711).

Jade Tree Motel. *Moderate.* In lively shopping district. Nicely maintained units. 3939 N.E. Hancock, 97212 (288–6891).

Motel 6. *Moderate.* This chain operates motels nationwide, and specializes in standardized, comfortable units at minimal, standard rates. The two motels in this area have heated outdoor pool, vending room where soft drinks may be purchased, and each is located near restaurants. Portland: 3104 S.E. Powell Blvd., 97202 (238–0600).

Rose Manor Motel. *Moderate.* Medium-size, two-level motel at edge of business district, with family units, kitchens, in-room movies. Heated pool, spacious grounds. Restaurant and cocktail lounge. 4546 S.E. McLoughlin Blvd., 97202 (236–4175).

Scandia Lodge. *Moderate.* Off I–5 at Barbur exit; 5 miles south of downtown. A splash of luxury in the twinkling lights of the city. Heated pool, kitchenettes, 1 and 2 bedroom suites. 10450 S.W. Barbur Blvd., 97219; (244–0151).

Sixth Avenue Motel. *Moderate.* Frequented by visitors of the Veterans Hospital and Oregon Health Science Center, this motel maintains a neat, friendly, and understanding atmosphere. Senior citizen rates. 2221 S.W. 6th, 97201 (226–2979).

Capri Motel. *Inexpensive.* Five miles east of Portland city center, this motel offers comfortable rooms, heated pool, and is close to restaurants. Airport just a few minutes away. 1530 N.E. 82nd Ave., 97220 (253–1151).

Danmoore Hotel. *Inexpensive.* At edge of business section, quiet and convenient, this older hotel is still considered a comfortable, friendly place by its patrons. Inexpensive dining room. 1217 S.W. Morrison, 97205 (227–1243).

Portland Rose Motel. *Inexpensive.* Near Veterans Hospital. Weekly rates. Wheelchair units; kitchens. 8920 SW Barbur Blvd., 97219 (244–0107).

Union Ave. Motel. *Inexpensive.* Smaller motel north of Portland, between Portland and Vancouver, Wash. Well off highway, quiet, some units with kitchens. 59 N.E. Gertz Road at Union Avenue, 97211 (285–3909).

PORT ORFORD. Sea Crest Motel. *Inexpensive–Expensive.* Quiet location, well off highway, ocean view. Comfortable units. Seasonal rates. In one of most scenic areas of state. Box C, Port Orford 97465 (332–3040).

PRINEVILLE. Ochoco Inn. *Moderate.* Medium-size motel, two stories, well-equipped. Restaurant, cocktail lounge. Pioneer Museum, swimming, tennis, bowling all nearby. 123 E. 3rd St., Prineville 97754 (447–6231).

Carolina Motel. *Inexpensive.* Smaller motel, comfortable, some kitchens. Laundry facilities. Lack of lavishness compensated for by small-town friendliness. 1050 E. 3rd, Prineville 97754 (447–4152).

City Center Motel. *Inexpensive.* No-frills, neat, convenient facility near heart of town. Pets welcome. 509 E. 3rd, Prineville 97754 (447–5522).

REDMOND. Redmond Inn. *Moderate.* Lots of conveniences here, including pool, nearby restaurant and lounge; some units with kitchens. 1545 Hwy. 97 S., Redmond 97756 (548–1091).

86 Corral Motel. *Moderate.* Medium-size motel with a few two-room units, some with refrigerators. Restaurant, cocktail lounge nearby. 517 W. Birch, Redmond 97756 (548–4591).

Village Squire Motel. *Moderate.* Smaller motel with comfortable units. 629 S. 5th St., Redmond 97756 (548–2105).

REEDSPORT. Tropicana Motel. *Moderate.* Medium-size motel offering comfortable sleeping units. Heated pool. Restaurant, lounge nearby. Seasonal rates. 1593 Highway Ave., Reedsport 97467 (271–3671).

ROCKAWAY. Silver Sands Motel. *Expensive.* Medium-size motel on beach; several larger units with kitchenettes, fireplaces, balconies. Playground, heated indoor pool. Seasonal rates. 2nd & Pacific, Rockaway 97136 (355–2206).

Surfside Motel. *Moderate–Deluxe.* Smaller beachfront motel, units of varying sizes, some with fireplace, some with kitchenette. Heated indoor pool. Seasonal rates. Hwy. 101 N., Rockaway 97136 (355–2312).

ROSEBURG. Best Western Douglas Inn Motel. *Expensive.* Downtown motel, affording easy walking access to restaurants and other mid-town conveniences. Free in-room movies. Seasonal rates. 511 SE Stephens St., Roseburg 97470 (673–6625).

Windmill Inn. *Expensive.* Heated pool, sauna, whirlpool, pets ok, restaurant, cocktails, airport transportation. Some balconies, 1450 Mulholland Dr., Roseburg 97470 (673–0901).

Master Host Motor Inn. *Moderate.* Large motel with some suites, some kitchen units available. About 1½ miles northwest of city center. Heated pool. Restaurant near. Seasonal rates. 427 NW Garden Valley Blvd., Roseburg 97470 (673–5561).

Budget 6 Motel. *Inexpensive.* All the essentials in tidy form. Small pets OK. Pool. 1067 NE Stephens, Roseburg 97470 (673–5556).

Casa Loma Motel. *Inexpensive.* Small, compact, neat units on main drag. Restaurants near. 1107 NE Stephens, Roseburg 97470 (673–5569).

Sycamore Motel. *Inexpensive.* Small motel with some two-room units, and a few with kitchenettes, at extra charge. Seasonal rates. 1627 SE Stephens, Roseburg 97470 (672–3354).

SALEM. Chumaree Comfortel. *Deluxe.* Lavish in every way. Heated indoor pool, saunas, whirlpool. Restaurant, lounge, entertainment. 3301 Market St. NE, 97301 (370–7888).

Best Western New Kings Inn. *Expensive.* Large, comfortable rooms. Heated indoor swimming pool, therapy pool, wading pool, saunas. Coin laundry. Restaurant nearby. Seasonal rates. 3658 Market St. NE, 97301 (581–1559).

Best Western Pacific Highway Inn. *Expensive.* This medium-size motel offers conveniences such as a playground, and special facilities for the handicapped. Close to State Fairgrounds, Chemeketa Comm. College and golfing. Restaurant adjoining. 4526 Portland Rd. NE, 97305 (390–3200).

City Center Motel. *Moderate.* Medium-size, two-level motel with comfortable sleeping units. Coin laundry. Restaurant nearby. 510 Liberty St. SE, 97301 (364–0121).

Tiki Lodge. *Moderate.* Medium-size motel, two-story, with well-kept units. Heated pool, sauna, waterbeds. Restaurant nearby. 3705 Market St. NE. 97301 (581–4441).

Motel 6. *Inexpensive.* Not elaborate but neatly utilitarian and the price is right for those who want no more than a good night's sleep. 2250 Mission St. SE, 97301 (588–7191).

Traveler's Inn. *Inexpensive.* Medium-size, simple, neat. Pool. 3230 Portland Rd. NE, 97301 (581–2444).

SEASIDE. Ebb Tide. *Deluxe.* Three-level motel at ocean front, with one- and two-room sleeping units, many kitchenettes, most units with fireplaces. Heated indoor pool, whirlpool, and sauna. 300 N. Promenade, Seaside 97138 (738–8371).

Hi-Tide Motel. *Expensive–Deluxe.* On oceanfront. Gas-burning fireplaces, refrigerators. Heated indoor pool, whirlpool. 30 Ave. G, Seaside 97138 (738–8414).

Sundowner Motor Inn. *Moderate–Expensive.* Near beach and the best ocean swimming in Oregon. Sauna, 2 kitchens. Impressive views. 125 Ocean Way, Seaside 97138 (738–8301).

SUNRIVER. Sunriver Lodge and Resort. *Deluxe.* Outstanding resort located 15 miles south of Bend, off US 97, in magnificent natural forest setting. Ample and varied accommodations and recreational facilities. Well-equipped one-room units and variety of larger suites and separate houses up to 3-bedrooms, with kitchens, fireplaces, view decks, etc. Heated pools, wading pool, saunas, tennis, golf, putting green, riding, bike trails, footpaths, playground, boats and boat dock, fishing, nature tours. Transportation to Mt. Bachelor ski area. Laundry, grocery, service station. Restaurant and cocktail lounge, entertainment. Coffee shop. Seasonal rates. Box 3609, Sunriver 97707 (593–1221).

THE DALLES. Portage Inn. *Deluxe.* Large motel 2½ miles east of city, near The Dalles Bridge. Sleeping units and some larger suites. Heated pool. Dining room, cocktail lounge. Seasonal rates. 3223 N.E. Frontage Rd., The Dalles 97058 (298–5502).

Tapadera Motor Inn. *Expensive.* Large, well-kept, multi-story motel at city center, with heated pool, restaurant and cocktail lounge. 112 W. Second, The Dalles 97058 (296–9107).

Tillicum Motor Inn. *Moderate.* Largest motel in town. Coin laundry, heated pool, restaurant adjacent. Pets welcome. 2114 W. Sixth, The Dalles 97058 (298–5161).

Shamrock Motel. *Inexpensive.* Clean, comfortable, smaller motel, close to city center, restaurants. 118 W. 4th, The Dalles 97058 (296–5464).

TIGARD. Best Western Tualatin Inn. *Expensive.* Fairly large motel about 10 miles south of Portland, with heated pool, sauna, and therapy pool. Restaurant and lounge nearby. 17993 S.W. Lower Boones Ferry Rd., Tigard 97223 (620–2030).

Tigard Inn Motel. *Moderate.* Moderately-large motel 8 miles southwest of Portland, with comfortable units, heated pool, and restaurant near. 11455 S.W. Pacific Hwy., Tigard 97223 (246–8451).

TILLAMOOK. Best Western Mar-Clair Motel. *Expensive.* Medium-size, two-level motel with comfortable units, a few with kitchens. Heated pool. Restaurant on premises. Seasonal rates. 11 Main Ave., Tillamook 97141 (842–7571).

El Rey Sands Motel. *Moderate.* Smaller motel with more modest rates. Comfortable units. Restaurant at hand. Seasonal rates. 815 Main Ave., Tillamook 97141 (842–7511).

TIMBERLINE. Timberline Lodge. *Deluxe.* An historic landmark on the south slope of Mt. Hood at 6,000 feet. Built in 1937, this renowned three-story mountain resort offers a variety of comfortable rooms and suites. Year-round outdoor heated pool. Rope tows, chairlifts, ski school, ski shop, snack bar, cafeteria open weekends, formal dining room, cocktail lounge. The 40-foot fireplace in lobby is a cozy spot on a chilly night. Seasonal rates. Government Camp 97028 (226–7979).

TUALATIN. Nyberg Inn. *Expensive.* Large motel 12 miles south of Portland, has heated pool, playground, in-room movies, dining room, dancing, cocktail lounge. Senior discount. Pets accepted. 7125 S.W. Nyberg Rd., Tualatin 97062 (692–5800).

UMATILLA. Nendels Inn. *Expensive.* Near McNary Dam, 3 miles off US 730 and 395. Water sports, golfing on the grounds. Restaurant, heated pool. So quiet you can hear the river run. (922–4871).

Tillicum Motor Inn. *Moderate.* Large motel with comfortable units, several two-room units, a number with kitchens. Laundry available. Heated pool. Restaurant and lounge nearby. 1481 6th St., Umatilla 97882 (992–3236).

WALDPORT. Bayshore Inn. *Moderate.* Lovely, large motel 3¼ mile away from Highway 101, but easily reached. On Alsea Bay, near ocean. Comfortable rooms. Outdoor heated pool, game room, special playhouse for children. Dining room, cocktail lounge, entertainment. Waldport 97394 (563–3202).

WARM SPRINGS. Kah-nee-ta Village and **Kah-nee-ta Lodge.** *Deluxe.* Two sections (a mile apart) of same resort complex which spreads out over 564,000 acres owned by the Confederated Tribes of the Warm Springs Indian Reservation. Kah-nee-ta is actually 10 miles north of the town of Warm Springs. Although rates in the plush Lodge and Village suites range well into the *Deluxe* category, large families can be accommodated very inexpensively in the unique, 20-foot-diameter teepees (with no facilities) which can be rented for the night. Hot springs provide naturally-warm, mineral-rich waters for the enormous swimming pool, children's pool and 'minnow' wading pool, usable year-round. In addition there are Roman-style mineral baths, massage room, golf, riding stable, bike paths. Babysitting available. Two restaurants, two cocktail lounges (one at pool). Box K, Warm Springs 97761 (553–1112 or 800–831–0100).

YACHATS. Fireside Motel. *Moderate–Expensive.* Moderate-size motel with comfortable units located away from highway. Quiet rooms, some offering ocean view. Seasonal rates. P.O. Box 313, Yachats 97498 (547–3636).

YOUTH HOSTELS. There are fewer lodgings for young people traveling in Oregon on limited budgets than there were a few years ago. Rates have also increased, and some places which once were available are simply not open any more. Smaller cities and towns are less likely to have such facilities.

In Portland, the *YWCA,* 1111 S.W. 10th Ave., rents to women only. Single rooms (with wash basin and shared bath on floor) are $17.44, and there are also hostel rooms, shared by two people, where lodgings are $8.72 per night per person if linens are needed, or $7.63 if person has her own sleeping bag.

In Ashland, *The Ashland Hostel,* 150 N. Main, is internationally chartered, and provides true European travel ambiance. Bicyclists and hikers welcome. Nonmembers: $7.

And at Coos Bay there is *The Sea Gull Youth Hostel,* in the Presbyterian Church at 438 Elrod, which operates summers only.

Additional youth hostels, all reasonably priced are at Bandon (347–9533); Cave Junction (592–3203); Newport (265–9816); Portland (236–3380); Prospect (560–3795); St. Helens (397–0014) and Springfield/Eugene (726–5012).

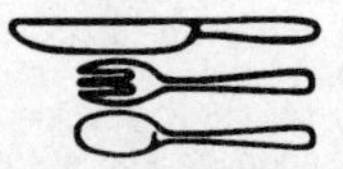

RESTAURANTS. Dining out in Oregon means an opportunity to savor fresh salmon and other seafood, as well as river-fresh fish from the state's many streams. The all-time favorites—steak, fried chicken, and prime rib roasts—are also easily found almost anywhere in the state. Many foreign favorites may also be found, and the exotic treats of Oriental, European, Middle East, and Polynesian cooks have made dining out in Oregon a cosmopolitan experience. The restaurants listed here are primarily those which have particularly distinguished themselves in regard to specialties or established a reputation for food and service. In addition the traveler should note the restaurants mentioned in connection with hotels and motels, where convenience and fine dining are often combined. Restaurants are listed in order of price category. Price categories and ranges for a complete dinner are: *Deluxe:* $14 and up; *Expensive:* $10–$14; *Moderate:* $5.50–$9.50; *Inexpensive:* Under $5. A la carte meals would, of course, cost more, as would the inclusion of wine or other alcoholic beverages with the meal.

ALBANY. Myrl's Chuck Wagon. *Moderate.* Home-style cooking in a leisurely, informal atmosphere. 2125 Pacific Blvd. SW (926–6177).

ASHLAND. Chateaulin Restaurant Français. *Expensive.* Delightful French cuisine set off by French country décor. 50 E. Main St. (482–2264).

ASTORIA. Drop Anchor. *Moderate.* A local favorite. Non-smoking area. Full portions excellently prepared. Children's menu. Tidy, good service. 11 W. Marine Dr. (325–3031).

Pier 11 Feed Store Restaurant. *Moderate.* Dine on cioppino peppered eye rib while watching seals frolic and freighters glide by. 77 11th St. (325–0279).

BEAVERTON. Pavillion (Greenwood Inn). *Expensive.* A gourmet dining experience for any meal. Salad umberto and steak provide a solid base for a memorable meal. Bar. 10700 SW Allen (626–4550).

BEND. Pine Tavern. *Moderate to expensive.* Well-known restaurant with delightful colonial atmosphere. Pot roast and prime rib are menu staples. Dining room looks out upon parklike grounds with pond. Bar. 967 NW Brooks (382–5581).

Frieda's. *Moderate to expensive.* Good hearty American steaks and seafood with a touch of German-style cookery here and there. Families encouraged. Children's menu available. Cocktails and lounge. 1955 NE Division (382–3790).

Le Bistro. *Moderate to expensive.* Delightful French specialty restaurant and lounge. French sidewalk cafe atmosphere, surrounded by walls of an old church. Closed Mon. Reservations advised. 1203 NE 3rd St. (389–7274).

BROOKINGS. Flying Gull. *Inexpensive to moderate.* One of the largest seafood menus on the Oregon Coast. Cheery place. 1153 Chetco (469–5700).

BURNS. Pine Room Cafe. *Moderate to deluxe.* General menu in delightful surroundings. Children's portions. Bar. Monroe & Egan Sts. (573–6631).

CHARLESTON. The Portside. *Moderate to deluxe.* At Charleston Harbor. Strong on seafoods. Try Travite Pochée Sauce Aurore (poached trout with cream saffron sauce and shrimp meat). Small Boat Basin (888–5544).

CORVALLIS. Nearly Normals. *Moderate.* Vegetarian cuisine. Complete breakfast menu. Nightly specialties. Surprises mixed with good cheer and innovative dining. Cosmopolitan atmosphere in college town. 109 NW 15th (752–3509).

The Night Deposit. *Moderate.* Fine dining in an old bank building. Entertainment nightly. 143 SW 2nd (754–0450).

COTTAGE GROVE. Iron Maiden. *Expensive.* At the Village Green Motor Hotel. A gourmet cuisine for those who enjoy a varied Continental/American menu. Coquilles St. Jacques and lobster thermidor are but two of many specialties. Village Loop—Exit 174 (942–2491).

The Cottage. *Moderate.* Nourishing food in an innovative solar building. Clean, courteous atmosphere. 2915 Row River Rd. (942–3091).

EUGENE. Coburg Inn. *Expensive to deluxe.* Five miles north of Eugene, in a building that once was a nineteenth-century residence, diners enjoy gas-lit atmosphere and unusual beef, chicken, and seafood specialties. Desserts are extra, so if you have a sweet tooth the tab may move into the *Deluxe* category. Children's menu. Bar. 209 Willamette St. N (484–0633).

Excelsior Café. *Expensive.* Another excellent eating place set in an old home with a distinct European air. But the food is fine, blending some of the best in Middle East, French, and Mediterranean dishes. Again, desserts are extra, and likely to up the price of the meal into the *Deluxe* bracket, especially if you decide on one of the salad specials instead of the one that comes with the dinner. Sunday brunch here is another specialty gaining fame for the café. 745 E. 13th (342–6963).

Mazzi's. *Moderate.* Pizza experts around these parts often use Mazzi's as a standard by which to judge others. 3377 E. Amazon Dr. (681–2252).

Moreno's Mexico. *Moderate.* The name tells you the menu, but the recipes and combinations are delightfully original, and the locale, an old home close to downtown, adds zest. 433 E. Broadway (343–5612).

GLENEDEN BEACH. Gourmet Dining Room (Salishan Lodge). *Deluxe.* Careful attention to details and an outstanding dining room staff make dinner a memorable experience. Continental cuisine includes such delicacies as Le Boeuf Bourguignon, Roast Duckling Bigarade, as well as a variety of other *haute cuisine* specialties of beef, lamb, chicken, and seafood. On US 101 (764–2371).

Sun Room Coffee Shop. *Moderate to expensive.* Salishan's delightful coffeeshop offers breakfast, lunch, and dinner in pleasant surroundings, with the outdoors everywhere you look. On US 101 (764–2371).

GOLD BEACH. Rod 'n Reel Club. *Expensive.* Seafood dishes are a specialty in the Rogue River mouth dining room. Try Admiral's Delight—fresh grilled oysters and baked lobster tail. North of Rogue River Bridge (247–6823).

HILLSBORO. Anthony's Old-Fashioned Eatery. *Moderate.* Antique atmosphere that gives dining a gaslight touch. Cozy, 19th-century ambiance. Heaped-plate meals, homemade cornbread. Everything but singing waiters. 6440 SE 10th (640–2024).

HOOD RIVER. Stonehedge. *Expensive.* Located away from town, on a hilltop reached via a short stretch of dirt road, this fine restaurant fills an old mansion with sounds of happy gourmets dining on salmon meuniére or roast duckling in wine or sweetbreads of veal. Again, desserts are extra, but hard to resist. 3405 Cascade Dr. (386–3940).

JOHN DAY. The Old Timer Cafe. *Moderate to expensive.* Famous among cowmen for its juicy one-pound sirloin steaks and salad bar. 241 W Main (575–2528).

KLAMATH FALLS. El Gringo's Mexican Restaurant. *Moderate.* Everything Mexican style, including the El Toro 16-oz. T-bone steak. 4545 S. 6th St. (882–7657).

LA GRANDE. Rangler Family Steakhouse. *Moderate.* Locally prominent for its substantial food and efficient service. 1914 Adams (963–0351).

LAKEVIEW. The Indian Village. *Moderate.* Indian decor, and exhibit of Indian dress and artifacts worthy of finest museums. Tasty, general menu. 508 N. 1st (947–2833).

LINCOLN CITY. Bay House. *Moderate.* Charming view of Siletz Bay combines with such exquisite dishes as Bay House Oysters Sauté for a visual and palatable experience.5911 SW Hwy. 101 (996–3222).

Road's End Dory Cove Restaurant. *Moderate.* Chowder, fish and chips, clam strips, salmon, steak—this place has all the goodies, served in a soft-tone "roadside inn" atmosphere. 5819 Logan Rd. (994–5180).

Mo's. *Inexpensive to moderate.* Seafood at Mo's—their clam chowder is famous in the area—is almost synonymous with going to Lincoln City for some people. 860 SW 51st (996–2535).

MEDFORD. Mon Desir Dining Inn. *Expensive.* Located about three miles from Medford, in Central Point, this restaurant has an excellent reputation for the finest in food and service. Children's menu. Bar. 4615 Hamrick Rd., in Central Point (664–6661).

NEWPORT. The Moorage at Embarcadero. *Expensive.* Nautical setting overlooking Yaquina Bay. Fantastic dining. Best single bargain on Coast may be their Friday night seafood buffet. Everything—and more—for a fair price. 1000 SE Bay Blvd (265–8521).

Mo's. *Inexpensive-Moderate.* Newport is the original home of this famous seafood spot, and it now has two—the original and an "Annex." Some folks love Mo's so much they just follow it along the coast. Lincoln City to Otter Rock to Newport. Frequently there's a long line to get in, so don't wait until you're starved. 622 NW Bay Blvd. (265–7512).

NORTH BEND. Hilltop House Restaurant. *Expensive.* Dining with a view of Coos Bay Harbor. Suggested for the discriminating diner. Abalone Steak Amandini. Broiled Australian Rock Lobster Tails and Tornedos of Beef. (756–6515).

Fisherman's Grotto. *Inexpensive.* In Pony Village. Fish and chips, shrimp, scallops, clams, chowders—delicious in all respects. (756–0341).

OAKLAND. Tolly's Deli. *Moderate.* Great food surrounded by exquisitely displayed antiques in charming downtown Oakland. A real Oregon find. In center of one-street business district (459–3796).

ONTARIO. East Side Cafe. *Moderate.* Both Oriental and American dishes are featured, and you have a wide variety of choices. Bar, dancing. 105 S.E. 2nd St. (881–1374).

PENDLETON. Tapadera Restaurant. *Expensive.* Prime rib dinners draw patrons to this popular restaurant located on grounds of Tapadera Inn. 725 Tapadera Ave. (889–8621).

PORTLAND. Rating restaurants is, at best, a subjective business, and obviously a matter of personal taste. It is, therefore, difficult to call a restaurant "the best," and hope to get unanimous agreement. The restaurants listed below are our choices of the best, followed by a list of other recommended restaurants.

Editors' Choices

Jake's Famous Crawfish. Locally famous since 1892 for crawfish, steamed clams, and other fresh seafood. It's a Portland landmark, and no one who likes seafood should leave town without having had dinner here at least once. Trout stuffed with almonds and crab or scallops sauteed with mushrooms well may bring you back for an encore. *Expensive.* 401 S.W. 12th Ave. (226–1419).

London Grill. The only thing ordinary about this restaurant is its name. This is dining in splendor with all that the phrase implies. Waiters and captains provide the perfect pace for a leisurely meal. Fine menu, well prepared. Pork tenderloin a l'Indienne (with curry) and cornish hen with madiera sauce provide proof of the pudding. *Deluxe.* 309 S.W. Broadway (295–4110).

Old Country Kitchen. The best beef in Portland. All steaks are guaranteed, unless you order one well done, in which case you deserve what you get. The mammoth 72-ounce steak, served with salad and baked potato, is free to you if you can finish it all. (They rarely have to pay off). *Expensive.* 10519 S.E. Stark Street (252–4171).

The Old Spaghetti Factory. If there is any restaurant in Portland that is a fun place, it is this one. Everyone enjoys—all ages. Setting is enhanced by interior, loaded with early 20th century artifacts. The Food—spaghetti dishes with wide selection of sauces—is as pleasurable as the service. *Moderate.* 0715 SW Bancroft (222–5375).

The Organ Grinder. It's not just the pizza that draws people here, although it's good and ample, and a family of four can feast on a huge one at small expense. Great salad bar, too. But where else can you see the world's largest organ in action, with approximately 2,400 different pipes ranging in size from building-high to inches small? All this and music, bubbles floating in the air, old-time silent movies, and even a real organ grinder and monkey. There's never a dull moment and when that organ plays full blast, you can feel the building rock! Not a place for quiet tête-á-tête, but an experience both old and young will giggle about for months. *Inexpensive.* 5015 S.E. 82nd Street (771–1178).

McCormick & Schmick's Restaurant. Gourmet dining in nostalgic atmosphere, in Old Town. A Yuppy favorite. Interior seems to come out of gaslight era. Diners seem to linger longer here, because of "innocent age" atmosphere. *Expensive.* 235 S.W. 1st Ave. (224–7522).

Sumida's Restaurant. The inside resembles a modest Japanese country inn. Sumida's is the next best thing to being in rural Japan. Delicious food, friendly and folksy service. The "sleeper" of Portland. *Moderate.* 6744 N.E. Sandy Blvd. (287–9162).

Other Recommended Restaurants

Couch Street Fish House. *Deluxe.* Located in Portland's "old town," this establishment offers seafood and beverages in old-time style and splendor. You'll have a choice of 25 fish entrees. 105 N.W. 3rd Avenue (223–6173).

Genoa. *Deluxe.* This is the Northern Italian relative of the below-mentioned L'Auberge, and is as fine and exclusive in its own right. Seven-course dinner. Wines and aperitifs extra. Reservations a must. 2832 S.E. Belmont (238–1464).

L'Auberge. *Deluxe.* Small, extremely fine restaurant with authentic French cuisine, consisting of complete six-course dinner with choice of three entrées. Coq au vin and rack of lamb are typical choices. Wine and champagne available. 2601 NW Vaughn (223–3202).

Trader Vic's. *Expensive to deluxe.* Polynesian to the core, augmented by Chinese oven cookery and curry. Buttery Fly Steak and Javanese Sate inspire return. At the Benson Hotel, downtown. Broadway & Stark, downtown (295–4130).

Bart's Wharf & Marina. *Expensive.* Overlooking the Columbia River. Boasting "live lobsters" and noted particularly for its seafood. A prestige place. 3894 NE Marine Dr. (288–6161).

Bush Garden. *Expensive.* Authentic Japanese cuisine served in forty individual dining rooms. Open tables, too. Sukiyaki is the house favorite. Japanese decor. 900 SW Morrison (226–7181).

Jade West. *Expensive.* Fine Chinese and Continental cuisine, served at lunch and dinner. Sesame chicken and pressed duck both have their champions. 122 S.W. Harrison (226–1128).

John's Meatmarket. *Expensive.* Steak and seafood in relaxing surroundings. Dungeness crabs provide an attractive alternate to steak. Cocktail lounge and piano bar. 115 N.W. 22nd Ave. (223–2119).

Sweet Tibbie Dunbar. *Expensive.* The posh of a grand English country estate, spiced with a Moll Flanders flavor. Try Tibbie Dunbar's Special Cioppino. 718 N.E. 12th Ave. (232–1801).

Rusty Pelican. *Moderate to expensive.* Attractive restaurant on bank of Willamette River. Emphasis on fresh seafood. Dancing, entertainment. 4630 S.W. Macadam (222–4630).

Zapata's. *Moderate-Expensive.* The flavor of Mexico—in food, atmosphere, music. Strolling mariachis. Excellent, charming service. 2917 SW Kelly (222–6677).

Dan & Louis Oyster Bar. *Moderate.* Shellfish, seafood, seafood salads are specialties of this informal restaurant where patrons can view display of boating artifacts. A la carte menu entrées include shrimp, scallops and oysters from the owner's private beds. Children's portions. 208 SE Ankeny (227–5906).

Hamburger Patti's. All advertising is word of mouth—and the joint is jammed. Fabulous hamburgers, fries, and whatever else is served. 2401 NE Fremont (287–3655).

Henry Thiele's. *Moderate.* Long known for its excellence. German dishes hit the bull's-eye for gourmets. 2305 W. Burnside (223–2060).

Omelets and Such. *Moderate.* Leans toward omelets, pancakes and steaks, but also strong on veal, chicken and spaghetti. Crisp salad bar. 10711 N.E. Halsey (254–7391).

Rose's. *Moderate.* Nobody, but nobody, serves more super-colossally huge corned beef and pastrami sandwiches or higher, lighter, more calorie-crammed cakes and Viennese pastries than Rose's. Full course dinners too. Suggestion: try cornucopia Nasher's Plate. 315 N.W. 23rd Ave., or Rose's East, 12329 N.E. Glisan St. (227–5181 and 254–6546).

Tortilla Flats. *Moderate.* Some who claim to know say this is the best Mexican food this side of the close-to-the-border towns on the U.S. side. Anyhow, the menu offers lots of choice and several original variations of what is standard Mexican-style fare elsewhere. And if you order judiciously, you may even have dinner in the *Inexpensive* price range here. 9010 S.E. 82nd Ave. (777–[illegible]).

Old Wives' Tales. *Moderate.* Feminist restaurant with emphasis on organic foods. Fine European desserts. Children's playroom. 1300 E. Burnside (238–0470).

The Pagoda. *Inexpensive to moderate.* Specialists in Chinese cuisine. Swift, courteous service and delicious food. 3839 N.E. Broadway (288–5788).

Poor Richard's Restaurant. *Inexpensive.* American-Colonial decor provides background for diners to enjoy variety of steaks and seafood. In Hollywood shopping district at 3907 N.E. Broadway. Two-for-the-price-of-one steak dinners is institutional here. (288–5285).

Red Robin. *Inexpensive.* Gourmet burger spot; every kind conceivable. 2020 S.W. Morrison. SW 20th Pl. & W. Burnside (222–4602).

Sizzler. *Inexpensive.* Best salad bar bargain in town. Great meal: soup & salad. Senior discount. 3737 S.E. 82nd (774–0132).

ROSEBURG. Gay 90's Delicatessen. *Moderate.* Fantastic sandwiches, salads, soups, shakes, sundaes—in unpretentious setting. 630 W. Fairhaven (672–5679).

SALEM. The Inn At Orchard Heights. *Expensive.* 695 Orchard Heights (378–1780). Steak and seafood to suit most connoisseur palates, with some sinfully tempting desserts.

Prime Country. *Expensive.* A favorite of legislature lobbyists, who ought to know about privileged dining. Substantial food and proper service in airy setting. 3815 State (362–1129).

The Spaghetti Warehouse. *Moderate.* The name tells you the menu. Family dining at family prices. 420 Commercial S.E. (588–2112).

SEASIDE. Crab Broiler. *Moderate to expensive.* The seafood here is splendid, but so are the other menu items. Bar. Three miles south of town, where Highways 26 and 101 meet. (738–5313).

Norma's. *Moderate.* In downtown mall, near beach. Decor adds charm to seafoods that bear Norma's magic touch. Gourmet dining at plebian rates. 20 N. Columbia (738–6170).

COFFEE HOUSES AND OUTDOOR CAFES. *Carnival Restaurant,* in Portland, at 2805 Sam Jackson Park Road, is a charming self-service eatery south of downtown where customers can choose either indoor or outdoor tables at which to enjoy inexpensive sandwiches, pastries, coffee, milk, or soft drinks. And at *Victoria's Nephew,* 212 S.W. Stark in Portland, a variety of delicious breads are available for sandwiches overflowing with homemade goodness which, in fine weather, can be enjoyed at sidewalk café tables as well as within the charming little shop. And, if you want this kind of informal atmosphere but the weather doesn't cooperate, try the many food purveyors at the Galleria, 921 S.W. Morrison, where you can have Greek souvlaki at the *Souvlaki Shop* or bagels and cream cheese and lots of other "outrageous sandwiches" dished up by *Barney Bagel & Suzy Creamcheese.* Eat inside these little shops or take your goodies with you, to munch at one of the tables outside in the corridor, or just walk and browse while observing the shops and shoppers. Every street corner in downtown Portland seems to have a hot dog or other luncheon cart. They are wheeled into position about 11 A.M. and pushed away about 2 P.M. Each vendor seems to have a specialized frankfurter. The carts have gained the attention of junior executives up against inflation.

HOW TO GET AROUND. *By air:* Almost every Oregon city of 10,000 or more has some kind of commercial air service. Every town, however small, seems to have an airfield, and private planes are for hire in Portland and elsewhere in the state. Three commuter airlines are based at Portland's International Airport: Horizon, San Juan, and United Express. They cover key cities throughout the state.

By car: Oregon has a highway system rated among the best in the nation. And it's all toll-free. The main north-south route, running from the California line below Ashland to the Columbia River at Portland, is now at least four-lane and, as Interstate 5, zips through the great heartland of the state without encountering a single stoplight. Interstate 84 enters from Idaho at Ontario, swings north through Baker, and at La Grande turns west. Forty-five miles later, at Boardman, it meets the Columbia River, which it follows to Portland. The route for touring Oregon's scenic coast is US 101, from California to Astoria at the mouth of the Columbia. From Portland the most popular highways to the coast are US 26, Oregon 6, and Oregon 18. All bridges across the Columbia River, except at Portland and Ranier, charge tolls (50¢ to $1.50 for car and passengers). There is a toll ferry across the Columbia, at Westport. The last three ferries across the Willamette River, at Canby, Wheatland, and Buena Vista, are no longer free; vehicles are charged $1 each.

Car rentals: Hertz and Avis have car rental offices in airports and in town at Eugene, Klamath Falls, Medford and Portland. Hertz has offices in Astoria, Bend, Corvallis, North Bend, Pendleton, Redmond, Salem, and Sun River.

By bus: Practically all major cities are reachable by bus. Portland's municipal bus system, Tri-Met, costs 85¢ within the city, with transfers free; senior citizens, 25¢ except rush hours, transfers free. However, with Tri-Met in financial difficulty, fares are sure to increase.

TELEPHONES. The area code for all points in Oregon is 503.

TOURIST INFORMATION SERVICES. Headquarters for travel and tourist information is the Economic Development Department, Tourism Division, 595 Cottage St., N.E., Salem, OR 97310; tel.: toll free outside Oregon 800–547–7842; toll free inside Oregon 800–233–3306. The State of Oregon has six Welcome Centers to aid travelers. They are located near the following port-of-entry towns: Ontario, I–84 (east); Klamath Falls, US 97 (southcentral); Ashland, I–5 (south); Brookings, US 101 (southwest); Astoria, US 101 (north near the Astoria bridge); Portland, I–5 (north and near the Interstate bridge). Season of operation is from May 1 to Oct. 30. Oregon has 13 Travel Infocentres, strategically located at points along I–5, I–84, US 101, and US 97. These open-wall gazebo structures provide information on scenic and recreational attractions as well as commercial messages of travel-related services. Open 24 hours a day, they are unmanned, but telephones connecting directly with the operator enables users to make collect calls for accommodations, reservations and other business. The displays include state, regional and local maps along with listings of nearby manned information centers where travel literature is available. Tourist information services are offered at more than 45 centers located in local chamber of commerce offices throughout the state. Travelers can look for the blue directional signs adjacent to the major highways for reference to the centers. The Portland Visitors Service is at 26 S.W. Salmon (503–222–2223).

The Oregon Dept. of Fish and Wildlife, 506 S.W. Mill St., Portland, Oregon 97208 (503–229–5222), provides voluminous and detailed materials. For data on the Oregon Coast, write: The Oregon Coast Assn., P.O. Box 670, Newport, Oregon 97365 (503–336–5107). For information on the Central Oregon area write: Central Oregon Recreation Assn., Bend, Oregon 97701; on Northeast Oregon write to: Northeast Oregon Vacationland, P.O. Box 308, La Grande, Oregon 97850.

For not-found-anywhere-else information about hundreds of off-the-beaten path places, see *Oregon for the Curious* ($5.95, Caxton Printers, Caldwell, Idaho 83605).

SEASONAL EVENTS. Most of the more than ten million tourists attracted to Oregon each year come between late spring until early fall, when weather is best suited to travel and outside activities (except skiing).

If top attractions were selected from Oregon's crowded calendar of events, the seasonal favorites would probably be the Portland Rose Festival, in June; the Oregon Shakespearean Festival, from early June into late October, in Ashland; World Championship Timber Carnival, at Albany, in early July; Scandinavian Festival, at Junction City, in mid-August; the State Fair, at Salem, in late August and early September; Oktoberfest, at Mt. Angel, in mid-September; the Pendleton Round-Up and Happy Canyon Pageant, in Pendleton, also in mid-September; and the Mt. Hood Festival of Jazz, on the campus of Mt. Hood College, near Gresham.

Other popular attractions, a notch or two below the giants, include the Blossom Festival at Hood River, in April; Pacific Northwest Championship All-Indian Rodeo at Tygh Valley, and All-Indian Rodeo at Klamath Falls, all in May; Lebanon Strawberry Festival, Rockhound Pow Wow at Prineville, All Rockhound Pow Wow Club of America dig at Madras, Beachcomber Days at Waldport, and High Desert Fiddlers Contest, at Burns, North Bend Air Show, at North Bend, '62 Days Celebration, in Canyon City, and Sandcastle Contest, at Cannon Beach, all in June; St. Paul Rodeo at St. Paul, Festival of the Arts, at Lake Oswego. Bohemia Mining Days at Cottage Grove, Antique Powerland Farm Fair at Brooks, Oregon Coast Music Festival at Coos Bay, and Britt Dance Festival and Britt Bluegrass Festival at Jacksonville, all in July; Springfield Broiler Festival, and the Threshing Bee and Draft Horse show at Dufur, all in August; Indian-Style Salmon Bake at Depoe Bay, Charlie Tuna Festival, in Charleston, Alpenfest at Wallowa Lake, and all in September.

For celebrations of flora, consider these: Pear Blossom Festival at Medford (April), Azalea Festival at Brookings-Harbor (May), Pea Festival at Milton-Freewater (May), Strawberry Festival at Lebanon (May), Rhododendron Festival at Florence (May), Fleet of Flowers Memorial Service at Depoe Bay (May), and Wild Blackberry Festival at Cave Junction (August).

The state is rich in cultural events. In addition to professional performances by visiting artists and the Oregon Symphony Orchestra, there are plays and musicals staged by colleges, universities, and communities. Pop concerts in many towns, the Music by Moonlight Festival in Portland at the city parks all through the summer, and summer theaters at Ashland, Eugene, Coquille, and Cannon Beach, as well as Portland. There are also these: Wallowa County Festival of Arts at Enterprise (May), Arts Festival at Pendleton (May), Very Special Arts Festival for the Handicapped at Monmouth (May), Umpqua Valley Arts Festival, at Roseburg (June), Big River Band Festival at Arlington (June), Summer Festival of Music at Eugene (late June; early July), Willamette Midsummer Jazzfest, in Albany (July), Oregon Coast Music Festival at Coos Bay (July), Arts Festival at Roseburg (July), Square Dance Festival, at Diamond Lake (July), Bluegrass Festival at Klamath Falls (August), Peter Britt Music and Arts Festival at Jacksonville (August), Oktoberfest at Mt. Angel (September), Folk Art Festival at Salem (October).

Almost every town seems to have a rodeo. In addition to those mentioned, at Pendleton, Tygh Valley, and St. Paul, there are these (to name the most prominent or colorful): in June: Sisters Rodeo at Sisters and South Douglas Rodeo, at Myrtle Creek; in July, Emerald Empire Round-Up at Eugene, Elgin

Stampede at Elgin, Molalla Buckeroo at Molalla, Crooked River Round-Up at Prineville, Chief Joseph Days at Joseph; in August: Deschutes County Rodeo at Redmond, Grant County Rodeo at John Day, Morrow County Rodeo at Heppner; in September: Harney County Rodeo, at Burns, and Sherman County Rodeo at Moro.

Drawing from a wide area are the Portland International Rose Show, in June, and the Portland International Livestock Exposition, in October.

For horse shows not connected with fairs or festivals, there's the Treasure Valley Horse Show and Sale at Ontario, the Arabian Horse Breeders Association show at the Fairgrounds in Salem; and the Morgan Horse Show at the Fairgrounds in Salem, in April; the Arabian Horse Show at Prineville, colorful Classic Horse Show at State Fairgrounds in Salem, and Appaloosa Horse Show at Roseburg, in May; 4-H Horse Show at Corvallis, Appaloosa Horse Show at the Salem Fairgrounds, State of Jefferson Horse Show at Central Point and Arabian Horsebreeders Show at the Salem Fairgrounds in June; the Cascade Arabian Horse Show, the Oregon Appaloosa Horse Show, and the Morgan Horse Association or Oregon Show, all in the State Fairgrounds at Salem and Columbia Morgan Horse Show at the Salem Fairgrounds in July; Morrow County Open Horse Show at Heppner, and AHAO All Arabian Horse Show at Salem, in August; and Arabian Horse Shows at Grants Pass and Eugene, Appaloosa Horse Show at Eugene, and So. Oregon-No. Calif. Paint Horse Show, at Central Point, in September. The National Donkey and Mule Show is held in Eugene in mid-August.

There is Dairy Goat Show in Portland in April; a Lamb Fair in Scio in May; a Livestock Show in Tygh Valley and a Hog Show in Island City in June; and a Pygmy Goat Show in Canby in July.

Portland stages an All-Breed Dog Show in July, and there are AKC Dog Shows in Klamath Falls, Roseburg, and Medford in September.

Many other shows of all kinds are held in conjunction with fairs and festivals.

(Some of the smaller seasonal events can change dates or cancel on short notice, and sometimes without publicity, so to keep as current as possible, write to Economic Development Department, Tourism Division, 595 Cottage St., N.E., Salem, OR 97310 for latest edition of *Oregon Events*).

TOURS. The visitor who drives to the state—or rents a car here—is best off with a do-it-yourself tour service, selecting specific areas or attractions and then plotting a course. For guides, confer with the Oregon Tourism Division (see Tourist Information Services, above), the Automobile Club of Oregon, and the book *Oregon for the Curious.*

The Gray Line (226–6755) has absorbed all its competitors and offers these tours: Mt. Hood Loop, 8½ hours; City of Portland Tour, 7 hours; West Side City Tour, 3 hours; Northern Oregon Coast; 8 hours; Japanese Gardens, Portland, 3 hours; Columbia River Gorge bus-boat combination, 7 hours. All Tours depart from the Imperial Hotel, 400 S.W. Broadway, Portland, where the Gray Line has its office.

Yachts-O-Fun Cruises has Columbia Gorge and Willamette River cruises on scheduled basis. 5215 N. Emerson, Portland 97217 (289–6665).

Columbia Gorge Sternwheeler has 2-hour cruises through Columbia Gorge, starting from Cascade Locks, 606 NW Front, Portland 97209 (223–3928). Bold Duck Riverboat Trips has a daily 2-hour cruise and a 3-hour Saturday and Sunday dinner cruise aboard its sternwheeler on the Coquille River, upstream from Pacific Ocean. Rt. 1, Box 2029, Bandon 97411 (347–3942).

Oregon Pacific & Eastern RR offers 35-mile trips into the Cascade Mountains aboard its steam locomotive train, "The Goose." Box 565, Cottage Grove 97424 (942–3368).

Sisters, in Central Oregon, has several outstanding tours, including a trek into the wilderness using llamas as pack animals. (Write: Sisters Chamber of Commerce, 340 S.W. Cascade, Sisters, OR 97759.)

Wilderness trips using Alaska malamutes as pack and sled dogs are offered year-round by Wilderness Freighters, 2166 SE 142nd Ave., Portland, 97233 (761–7428).

SPECIAL-INTEREST TOURS. There are several jetboat tours up the whitewater Rogue River from Wedderburn, near Gold Beach on the southern Oregon Coast. (Reservations for overnight trips advised.) *Rogue Mail Boats* leave from the mail boat dock, ¼-mile upstream from the north end of the bridge. Jet boats for the 6-hour, 64-mile early trip leave daily at 8:30 P.M., May 1-Nov. 1, with afternoon trips (2:30 P.M. to 8 P.M.) available July through Labor Day daily, weather and passenger volume permitting. Two-hour lunch stop at Lucas Pioneer Lodge or Singing Springs Resort at tiny upriver hamlet of Agness on morning tour, and two-hour dinner stop at same places on afternoon tour. (Price of meal not included in fare.) For 104-mile trip, leave mail boat dock at 8 A.M., return to dock at 3:30 P.M. (Price of lunch not included in fare.) For a 2-day trip, overnight arrangements can be made for a stay at a wilderness lodge. Write: Rogue Mail Boat Service, Inc., Box 1165, Gold Beach, OR 97444 (503–247–0225). *Jerry's Rogue River Jet Boat Trips* leave from boat basin at the Port of Gold Beach, south side of the river. A 6-hour, 64-mile trip departs daily at 8:30 A.M., May 15–Oct. 15; a 5½ hour tour takes off daily at 2:30 P.M. July 1–Labor Day weekend. There is a 2-hour food stop at Agness; price of meals not included. The 104-mile trip to Paradise Bar leaves 8 A.M. May 15–Oct. 15 daily, returns to Gold Beach at 4 P.M. Luncheon orders taken at dock for smorgasbord at Paradise Bar or Barbarian Lodge; price of meal not included in fare. Overnight accommodations with all meals available upon request; early reservations advised. Write: *Jerry's Rogue River Jet Boat & Wild River Trips,* Box 1011, Gold Beach, OR 97444 (503–247–7601).

Six-hour raft trips that challenge Hellgate Canyon on the Rogue begin at Paul Brooks's Raft Trip HQ, 12221 Galice Rd., Merlin, 16 miles from I–5. Lunch $40 adults; $30 children under 13. Write: Paul Brooks Raft Trips, Box 638, Merlin, OR 97532 (503–476–8051).

From Grants Pass, on I–5, there are a large number of boat trips, varying from a few hours to several days, down the Rogue River. For a list of the more than 25 outfitters, write: Rogue River Adventures, Visitors and Convention Bureau, Box 970, Grants Pass, OR 97526 (800–547–5927). For a list of licensed guides (for boating, hunting, fishing, etc.) in SW Oregon, write: Rogue River Guides Assn., P.O. Box 792, Medford, OR 97501. Most of the trips are 2½-hour jetboat runs, to a fearsome canyon called Hellgate, and back. (Inquire at Chamber of Commerce, Grants Pass, OR 97526.) *Irv Urie,* famous river guide, offers a wide variety of Rogue River trips, from half-day and 1-day salmon fishing on the Upper Rogue to 3-and 4-day rubber raft and 4-day summer-run steelhead fishing trips through the Wild Section of the Rogue. Write: Irv Urie, 900 Murphy Rd., Medford, OR (503–779–3798). *Rogue River Hellgate Excursions* has 75-mile "Rough Water Trips" to Hellgate Canyon, with lunch stop at Galice, an historical mining town. Write: Hellgate Excursions, Box 982, Grants Pass, OR 97526 (503–479–7204). A 6-day, 5-night *Owyhee River Float Trip* with camping, fishing, swimming and hiking is offered three times in the spring. Write: Hells Canyon Navigation Co., Box 145, Oxbow, OR 97840 (503–785–3352). *Orange Torpedo Trips* provide guided inflatable kayaking on the Rogue and Deschutes Rivers. These trips are strenuous. Write: Orange Torpedo Trips, P.O. Box 1111, Grants Pass, OR 97527 (503–479–5061). Lute Jerstad, of Himalayan fame, has 3–5 day trips on the Owyhee, Grande Ronde, Deschutes, Snake and Rogue. Write: *Lute Jerstad Adventures,* Box 19537, Portland, OR (503–244–4364). Veteran guide *Jim Cunningham* offers raft trips on the deep green McKenzie River. Write: Vida, OR 97488 (503–896–3750).

River Trails rents canoes and rafts for 1-day trips down the Sandy River (east of Portland). Canoes and rafts transported to your starting point. At end of drift, complimentary rides available back to your car. These are not guided tours but were conceived for people who prefer to participate in an encounter with nature. Write: River Trails, 336 E. Columbia St., Troutdale, OR 97060 (503–667–1964).

Exploration Cruise Lines in Portland runs a spectacular 6-night cruise up the Columbia and Snake Rivers, which includes a jet-boat ride through Hell's Canyon. Sightseeing stops are made at historic spots. The luxury vessel, more akin to an ocean liner than a river craft, runs as far upstream as Lewiston, Idaho. Write: Exploration Cruise Lines, 1500 Metropolitan Park Building, Seattle, WA 98101 (800–426–0600).

Oregon River Outfitters have float trips through Hells Canyon of the Snake River. Write: 1715 Winter S.E., Salem, OR 97302 (503–363–2074).

Numerous fishing, boating and hunting trips are offered by experienced, all-out-ready-to-please guides and packers of this state. For a brochure of who and what is available, write: Oregon Guides & Packers Association, Box 3797, Portland, OR 97208. For an excellent, free guide of special-interest tours in Oregon, write: Tourism Division, Economic Development Dept., 595 Cottage St. N.E., Salem, OR 97310.

Oregon River Experiences runs participatory "Row It Yourself" and "Paddle Raft" trips on the Owyhee, Deschutes, Grande Ronde and Rogue. Geological and wildlife education. Write: Oregon River Experiences, Inc., 1935 Hayes St., Eugene, OR 97405 (503–342–3293).

GARDENS. In Portland, the Rose City, visit Washington Park for *International Test Gardens,* free, and *Japanese Gardens,* nominal fee; *Rhododendron Test Garden,* at S.E. 28th Ave. and Woodstock (free); and *Sunken Gardens,* in Peninsula Park, 6400 N. Albina (free); *Hoyt Arboretum,* 4000 S.W. Fairview Blvd., a wildlife sanctuary. Portland is a city of lovely private gardens and lawns; just drive around the town, especially in the Laurelhurst and Alameda neighborhoods, on the east side, and in the hills west of downtown. Near Redmond, in Central Oregon, *Petersen's Rock Garden* is a fantasy of rock and petrified wood construction. Free. *Shore Acres State Park,* southwest of Coos Bay, is an old estate with unusual botanical gardens. *Azalea State Park,* in Brookings, on the southern Oregon Coast, is a botanical glory. Spring pushes up wild strawberry blossoms, purple and yellow violets, and wild cherry and crabapple blooms, partitioned by bushes of five varieties of native azaleas. Free. Throughout western Oregon there are a number of distinctive commercial gardens, all free and hospitable to visitors. Examples: *Greer Gardens,* in Eugene; and Strahms Lillies, near Brookings, with over 300 varieties of lillies growing indoors and out.

NATIONAL PARKS AND FORESTS. More than one-fourth of Oregon is covered by national forests, comprising about 17.5 million acres of gross area within unit boundaries and about 15.6 million acres of National Forest system lands, out of a total land area of 61,641,600 acres. (Water area, excluding Pacific coastal waters, is 666 square miles.) The fame and lure of the single national park, *Crater Lake,* more than makes up for its solitary position. The deep, brilliantly blue basin, encircled by stark lava cliffs, often brings gasps of awe from visitors and even leaves travel writers without adequate adjectives. It was created thousands of years ago when Mt. Mazama, a 15,000-foot volcano, erupted and formed a crater now filled by the 1,932-foot-deep lake. First seen by white men in 1853, no one has yet found the outlet for the lake, which is fed by melting snows. Drives through the 250-square-mile park, especially the 35-mile route around the rim, bring a succession of spectacular views: Wizard Island, a symmetrical cone rising 760 feet above the surface of the lake; Phantom Ship, a mass of lava resembling a ship under sail; Llao Rock, a lava flow on the north rim that fills an ancient glacial valley. The view from Cloudcap, on the east rim, is considered the best of many excellent views. There are many fine mountain viewpoints, but even the athletic are apt to be short of breath after climbing to the top of 8,060-foot Garfield Peak or to the 8,926-foot lookout station atop Mt. Scott. The northern entrance drive, off Oregon 138, opens about June 14, and Rim Drive about July 4. Overnight accommodations, meals, garage and gasoline services are available from about June 15 to September 15. In addition to the 75-room lodge there are sleeping cottages. (Sites in the campground, if available, are included in the vehicle fee.) There are daily lectures by park naturalists, guided drives and hikes, and geological exhibits. During the off-season the coffee shop serves skiers. Reached by Oregon 62 from Medford (I–5), Oregon 138 from Roseburg (I–5), or off US 97 onto Oregon 138, Oregon 232, and Oregon 62.

The *Siuslaw National Forest,* divided into two major areas along the coast, contains the Oregon Dunes National Recreation Area, which was established in 1972 with 31,566 acres. The undulating dunes cover everything in their path, even forest, but conservationists are attempting stabilization with beachgrass and broom. The Forest Service's Cape Perpetua Visitor Center offers a free color motion picture, "Forces of Nature," which describes the geologic life of the coast and the effect of waves, wind, and weather on her rugged beauty. Exhibits, nature trails, and camping and picnicking facilities round out Perpetua's offering. From here the vacationer can travel north, south, east . . . and a few feet west . . . to enjoy the approximately 40 campgrounds and picnic areas of the Siuslaw National Forest.

Located in the southwest corner of Oregon, the *Siskiyou National Forest* embraces rugged terrain, heavily timbered mountainsides and bold, rocky cliffs that rise abruptly from the sea. The famous Rogue River (one of a handful of National Wild and Scenic Rivers in the U.S.) and the Illinois River systems bisect the National Forest and offer unparalleled fly fishing for native trout, including the fighting sea-run steelhead. There are about 30 campgrounds and picnic areas in the Siskiyou National Forest.

For the back-country hiker, the Kalmiopsis Wilderness, in this National Forest, provides opportunity to explore a rough, wild, and untamed land of unique beauty and fascination. The Kalmiopsis Wilderness is a botanist's paradise. But absolutely check with the District Ranger at Grants Pass or at the Ranger Station at Brookings—before starting off for the Kalmiopsis. It is easy to get lost there, and only the hardy should consider the venture. Be sure to carry water, map and compass.

Along the Cascade Mountain range are *Mt. Hood, Willamette, Deschutes, Umpqua, Rogue River,* and *Winema* national forests. Mt. Hood, east, of Portland, offers hiking, climbing, and skiing. The Mt. Hood Loop Highway encircles the 11,235-foot peak, Mt. Hood, highest peak in Oregon and an Oregon Trail beacon. The forest extends from the Columbia River on the north to Mt. Jefferson on the south and from the foothills just beyond the suburbs of Portland to the plateau country of central Oregon, with lakes, waterfalls, hot springs, and glaciers on its 1,108,264 acres. Snow buggies take tourists from Timberline Lodge, at 6,000-foot altitude, to above 9,000 feet on Oregon's highest mountain. Oddly enough, some wilderness areas, particularly Mt. Hood, are in danger of being overcrowded by people.

Other ski areas on Mt. Hood are Ski Bowl, Summit, Cooper Spur, and Mt. Hood Meadows. (Timberline is the only one with overnight facilities.)

The 1,796,704 acres of the *Willamette National Forest* are the most heavily timbered in the nation. Access to the Mt. Jefferson, Mt. Washington, and Diamond Peak wild areas and to the Three Sisters Wilderness Area is by foot or horseback only, and on some trails horses are not permitted. There is a constant struggle, regarding this national forest and others, between conservationists and commercial interests. The *Umatilla,* with 1,189,747 acres, and the Wallow and Whitman, with a combined total of 2,376,051 acres, cover much of northeastern Oregon. Together they provide more than 100 camp areas, and recreation from swimming to skiing.

Fees for improved campsites range from $3 to $15, but there is no charge for campgrounds that lack drinking water or other facilities.

For detailed information, write: U.S. Forest Service, Box 3623, Portland, OR 97208 (503–221–2877).

For individual forests: *Deschutes National Forest,* 1645 Hwy. 20 E., Bend, OR 97701 (503–388–2715). *Fremont National Forest,* 524 N G St., Box 551, Lakeview, OR 97630 (503–947–2151). *Malheur National Forest,* 139 N.E. Dayton, John Day, OR 97845 (503–575–1731). *Mt. Hood National Forest,* 2955 N.W. Division, Gresham, OR 97030 (503–666–0700). *Ochoco National Forest,* Federal Bldg., Prineville, OR 97754 (503–447–6247). *Rogue River National Forest,* Federal Bldg., Medford, OR 97501 (503–776–3600). *Siskiyou National Forest,* Box 440, Grants Pass, OR 97526 (503–479–5301). *Siuslaw National Forest,* Box 1148, Corvallis, OR 97339 (503–757–4480). *Umatilla National Forest,* 2517 S.W. Hailey, Pendleton, OR 97801 (503–276–3811). *Umpqua National Forest,* Federal Office Bldg., Roseburg, OR (503–672–6601). *Wallowa-Whitman National Forest,* Box 907, Baker, OR 97814 (503–6391). *Willamette*

National Forest, Box 10607, Eugene, OR 97440 (503–687–6522). *Winema National Forest,* Post Office Bldg., Klamath Falls, OR 97601 (503–883–6714).

STATE PARKS AND FORESTS. The State Parks and Recreation Division maintains more than 200 Parks, Waysides, Recreation Areas and historic sites totaling more than 92,000 acres. These areas provide over 6,000 picnic sites, 5,500 campsites, and an unlimited variety of outdoor recreation activities. The parks—50 of which have overnight camping facilities—are found in every part of Oregon; some, in the remote areas, are sparsely occupied, while parks on the coast and at popular lakes are sometimes filled up weeks in advance. (Many parks have rest rooms that are accessible to handicapped persons). With a minimum of commonsense planning one can travel slowly through Oregon and put up at a state park every night. Every major city is within easy driving distance of at least one state park.

Starting in the far northwest corner of the state, the visitor can stop at *Fort Stevens,* 10 miles west of Astoria. Built in 1864 to guard the Columbia against the possible threat of Confederate gunboats, it was fired on by a Japanese submarine in 1942, the only mainland U.S.A. military installation to suffer this fate in World War II. Fort Stevens State Park is a coastal lake area with beach access near historic Fort Stevens, boat ramps to four lakes, swimming, fishing, and clamming. The campground of the 3,670-acre park contains 262 tent campsites, 120 improved sites, 213 trailer sites, and 225 picnic sites, hot showers, laundry rooms, trailer dumping station, outdoor theater, trails, and group camp facilities. Traveling 20 miles south, the tourist is at *Ecola State Park,* where members of the Lewis and Clark expedition came in early 1806 to obtain blubber and oil from a grounded whale. There are fine sea views; sea-lion and bird rookeries are located on offshore rocks, and deer roam the park at will. A section of the Oregon Coast Trail, for hikers only, touches the Ecola State Park as part of the northern most segment of the trail, 64 miles between the Columbia River and Tillamook Bay. Eventually the trail will extend the entire length of the coast between the Columbia River and the California line.

Cape Meares State Park, named after Captain John Meares, an early British explorer who roamed the waters of the Pacific Northwest, is 10 miles west of Tillamook off US 101. The park features a lighthouse, built in 1890 and recently restored, and the Octopus Tree, a giant sitka spruce famed for its massive candelabra branching.

Farther south, 12 miles below Tillamook, is *Cape Lookout,* an unusually scenic area of Sitka spruce, with a fine ocean beach and a headland projecting 1.5 miles into the ocean. Favorite viewing is of a sea-bird rookery, with thousands of California murres in nesting season. The 1,946-acre park has picnic facilities with electric stoves available and an overnight camp with 197 tent campsites, 53 trailer sites, 121 picnic sites, showers, laundry facilities, and group camps.

The everchanging sand dunes provide the recreational backdrop at *Jessie M. Honeyman State Park,* 2.5 miles south of Florence. Gorgeous rhododendrons seem to weave between the sand-dune area and a magnificent coastal lake. The 522-acre park contains 241 tent campsites, 75 improved campsites, 66 trailer sites, 107 picnic sites, hot showers, laundry room, trailer dumping station, and group camp facilities.

Humbug Mountain State Park, 6 miles south of Port Orford on US 101, has a virgin forest, trout streams, sandy beach, swimming, fishing, electric stoves, and 32 picnic sites. The overnight camp has 75 tent campsites, 30 trailer sites, showers, and laundry rooms. Humbug Mountain, climbed by a winding trail, rises to an elevation of 1,750 feet, and the seascapes from the top are spectacular. (The state park is at the foot of the mountain.)

In the Willamette Valley, *Champoeg State Park,* 28 miles south of Portland, has 48 improved campsites, 317 picnic sites, boat dock, and a museum of historical relics along the Willamette River where the Oregon provisional government was formed in 1843.

Cameras come out at *Sivler Falls State Park,* 15 miles south of Silverton, where the largest concentration of waterfalls in the country is located. Five of the 14 falls are more than 100 feet, the highest being 178 feet. Good trails lead to all falls. There are picnic facilities, day-use lodges, and campground.

A logging museum is the main attraction at *Collier State Park,* 30 miles north of Klamath Falls on US 97. Located at the confluence of Spring Creek and the Williamson River under a canopy of mature ponderosa pine, the park provides good fishing in both streams. Facilities include 79 picnic sites, with electric stoves available, and an overnight camp with 18 tent campsites and 50 trailer sites.

In the northeastern corner of Oregon, 6 miles south of Joseph, *Wallowa Lake State Park,* where Nez Percè Indians dwelt for centuries, provides beaches, boating, camping (89 tent campsites and 121 trailer sites), picnicking (169 sites), and acres of lush meadow. There are pack trains and hiking trips into the high mountains close at hand.

Comparatively recent is Stewart State Park, on the south side of Lost Creek Lake in southern Oregon, 35 miles north of Medford off Oregon 62. The park has 721 land acres and 190 acres of water surface, a 201-unit campground with bathhouses, playgrounds, a picnic area, boat ramps, a swimming beach and a 140-boat docking facility.

State parks are found at fantastic seascapes, in swarms of azaleas hundreds of years old, by the driftwood foreshore that is a paradise to beachcombers, along rivers and lakes, at the side of lighthouses, in the forest primeval, in a rare myrtle grove, on the banks of the world's shortest stream, covering the unusual bog-loving Darlingtonia, on the rim of a bowl where the ocean thunders in through a cavern, along the old Oregon Trail, at a pioneer homesteader reunion site, by dams and reservoirs, at the entrance to awesome Grand Canyonesque formations, near the site of an ancient Indian burial ground, on a juniper-covered promontory, on the shore of a backcountry reservoir, at the edge of a canyon 400 feet wide and 304 feet deep, at the foot of fossil deposits estimated to be 30 million years old, high in the mountains, deep in the desert, near the tumult of the masses, and far from the madding crowds.

On weekends and holidays there is a $1 day use fee (to include picnic facilities and boat launching) at the following parks: Shore Acres, Rooster Rock, Benson, Silver Falls, Cahmpoeg, McIver, Armitage, Detroit Lake, Ecola, Ft. Stevens, Cape Lookout, Tumalo, and Tou Velle.

Overnight camping is permitted in State Parks in areas designated for camping with length of stay at any one park limited to 10 days in any 14-day period from mid-May through Labor Day; also limited to 14 out of every 18 days from Sept. 15 through May 14. At parks with camper registration booths, campsites are assigned by the attendant. Check out time is 2:30 P.M. daily.

Although camping rates change, the following may approximate reality:

Trailer campsite—$9 per night. Facilities include hookups for water, electricity, and sewage disposal at each site, with a table, stove, and access to a modern utility building containing toilets, showers, and laundry facilities.

Improved campsite—$8 per night. Facilities include water supply and electric hookups at each site, plus a table, stove, and access to a modern restroom or a utility building with toilets, showers, and laundry facilities.

Tent campsite—$7 per night. Facilities include a tent site with a table, stove, water, and access to a nearby rest station with flush toilets.

Primitive campsite—$5 per night. Facilities include a table and stove but water and sanitary facilities may be some distance from the site.

(At all overnight parks, there is either an added charge per extra vehicle per night or extra vehicles are not permitted. Boat moorage is $2 per night.)

Note: Most campgrounds charge an additional $2 per night for motor vehicles not licensed in Oregon.

Campsite reservations are available at 13 Oregon State Parks from Memorial Day weekend through Labor Day weekend. Reservations may be made by all park users, regardless of residence, by letter or in person at the park where the reservation will be utilized.

A $9 advance deposit ($3 non-refundable) must accompany each reservation request sent to the specific state park. Reserved campsites must be claimed by 6 P.M. of the first day of the reservation period, except Friday and Saturday, when a reserved campsite will be held until 9 P.M.

Campsite reservations may be made at the following state parks:

Beachside (563–3023) Box 1350, Newport, OR 97365.
Beverly Beach (265–7655) Star Route North, Box 684, Newport, OR 97365.
Cape Lookout (842–2200) 13000 Whiskey Creek Rd. W., Tillamook, OR 97141.
Detroit Lake (854–3333) Box 549, Detroit, OR 97342.
Devils Lake (994–3737), 1452 N.E. 6th, Lincoln City, OR 97367.
Fort Stevens (861–1671), Hammond, OR 97121.
Harris Beach (469–4774), 1655 Hwy 101, Brookings, OR 97415.
Honeyman (997–8484) 84505 Highway 101, Florence, OR 97439.
Prineville Reservoir (447–7676) Prineville Lake Rt., Box 1050, Prineville, OR 97754.
South Beach (867–6611), Box 1350, Newport, OR 97365.
Sunset Bay (888–9200) 13030 Cape Arago Hwy., Coos Bay, OR 97420.
The Cove Palisades (546–3591 or 546–4681) Route 1, Box 60 CP, Culver, OR 97734.
Wallowa Lake (432–5181), Route 1, Box 323, Joseph, OR 97846.

The State Park Campsite Information Center is in operation Monday through Friday, 8 A.M. to 4:30 P.M., beginning on the first Monday in March and continuing to Labor Day. The information system enables campers to make toll-free telephone calls from anywhere in Oregon to a special number in Salem, in order to receive current information on the availability of campsites in Oregon's State Parks. To assist campers wishing to cancel reservations they cannot use, the Campsite Information Center also accepts cancellations for reserved campsites. However, campsite reservations can be made only at the individual parks listed above.

Toll free telephone calls to the Campsite Information Center may be made from anywhere within Oregon by dialing 1–800–452–5687. Portland and out-of-state residents should call 503–238–7488.

Further information about the reservation and information systems is available by writing: Oregon State Parks, 525 Trade St. S.E., Salem, Oregon 97310 (503–378–3605).

While the main season of use for overnight camping is from mid-April through October, 13 state parks remain open all year. These parks are Beverly Beach, Bullards Beach, Cape Lookout, Champoeg, Fort Stevens, Harris Beach, Jessie M. Honeyman, Valley of the Rogue, Farewell Bend, Hilgard Junction, Washburne, Loeb, and Nehalem Bay.

More than 60 rest areas are located on the major highways throughout the state. Most Rest Areas provide rest stations, drinking water, and picnic tables under shade trees or sun shelters.

The *Oregon State Forestry Department* has under its own name, or manages for state schools, a total of more than 785,000 acres of forest land, spread throughout the state. 2600 State St., Salem, OR 97310 (503–378–2562).

CAMPING. Campsites for public use are spread throughout the state, with the largest number in the most scenic areas, such as the Oregon Coast and the mountains. There are 5,455 tent and trailer sites in the 49 overnight *state parks* alone. (*See section above.*) The *U.S. Forest Service* has 639 campgrounds, with 10,256 tent and trailer sites. The nearly 300 Oregon county parks have over 1,100 campsites, as well as more than 4,350 picnic units. The *Bureau of Land Management* (BLM) operates 19 recreation sites where fees of from $2–$6 are charged for single unit camping, and 56 recreation sites (for day use only) which are free. Best sites: Fishermen's Bend, Alsea Falls, Yellowbottom, Susan Creek, Cavitt Creek and Loon Lake. There are 7 recreational sites that charge groups for day use, and 2 that have a fee for overnight group use. For list of sites, write: Bureau of Land Management, Box 2965, Portland, OR 97208. (503–231–6274).

The *Corps of Engineers* administers only 2 overnight camping areas—Pine Meadows ($5 per night) and Plymouth ($7 per night). For list of all campgrounds, write: U.S. Army Corps of Engineers, Box 2946, Portland, OR 97208. (503–221–6021).

The *Oregon State Forestry Department* operates 13 campgrounds with 250 picnic sites.

Over 50 public recreation sites have been provided by private power and timber companies in Oregon. These parks total 3,500 acres and offer over 500 picnic sites and 650 campsites, as well as the usual range of outdoor recreation activities.

In addition, there are KOA Kampgrounds in all parts of the state, including at or near these towns: Ashland, Bandon/Port Orford, Bend, Cascade Docks, Creswell/Eugene, Sunny Valley (Grants Pass area), Klamath Falls, Lincoln City, Madras, Medford/Gold Hill, Sisters and Salem.

For detailed information on camping in Oregon, write: Tourism Division, Economic Development Department, 595 Cottage St., N.E., Salem, OR 97310.

TRAILER TIPS. Many of the better parks are designed only for stationary mobile homes, and the number of commercial sites reserved for overnight trailers, RVs, and campers is limited. With hundreds of national, state, and county campgrounds able to accommodate trailers, most trailerists seek private parking only in or near cities. Within Portland or close to it are: *Fir Grove Trailer Park,* 5541 N.E. 72nd Ave. (252–9993); *Trailer Park of Portland,* 6645 S.W. Nyberg, Tualatin (692–0225); *Cedar Shades Trailer Park,* 7120 N.E. Killingsworth (254–1692); *Lawn Acres Mobile Home Park,* 11421 S.E. 82nd (654–5739); and *Rolling Hills Mobile Terrace,* 20145 N.E. Sandy Blvd., Troutdale (666–7282). *Twin Firs Mobile Home & R.V. Park,* 15656 S.E. Division (761–8210); and Portland *Mobile Home Park,* 9000 N.E. Union (285–1617). All telephones have area code 503.

FARM VACATIONS AND GUEST RANCHES. A guest ranch vacation in Oregon offers relaxation and excitement for every member of the family. Accommodations and recreational opportunities are as diversified as the state, with each ranch offering something a little different. Activities range from tennis to hayrides. And, some of the ranches are open year-round, catering to skiers and snowmobilers as well as swimmers. All Oregon guest ranches do share some of the same characteristics. Each of the ranches listed below has its own stable with horses available for trail rides or pack trips. (Contact ranches directly for additional information.)

Take It Easy Ranch Resort, located between Crater Lake National Park and Klamath Falls off Oregon 62. On site of historic Fort Klamath, where Klamath Indian and old fort artifacts are still being discovered. Fly-fishing in nearby springs, creeks, lakes, and river is featured attraction. Horses for rides on meadows and Winema National Forest trails. Family game room, general store. Accommodations: modern, fully equipped cabins comfortably hold 30 to 35 persons. Main lodge includes dining area. Open for hunters. Write: Take It Easy Ranch Resort, Box 408, Fort Klamath, OR 97626 (503–381–2328). *Paradise Ranch Inn.* outside scenic Grants Pass in southwestern Oregon, is noted for its clear streams and tall Douglas firs. It's a bed and breakfast inn with horseback riding available at local stables, Rogue River raft trips, tennis courts, swimming pool and fishing. Transportation provided from local airport. Special instructions on living in and utilizing untrammeled nature. Write: Paradise Ranch Inn, 7000 Monument Drive, Grants Pass, OR 97526 (503–479–4333). *Hidden Valley Horse Ranch,* between Baker and La Grande in northeastern part of state, is novel because it is a dude ranch *exclusively* for boys and girls, 9 to 16. Instructions in riding, fishing, trapping, archery, boating and swimming. Comfortable quarters, good food, smogless (and beautiful) scenery. Write: Hidden Valley Horse Ranch, North Powder, OR 97867 (503–898–2377). *Flying M Ranch,* approximately 50 miles southwest of Portland. Catered picnics for groups up to 80 persons and "campouts" are specialties. Trail rides, fishing, tennis, and swimming. Facilities include recreation game room, banquet rooms. Besides campsites, lodging facilities include two-story log lodge and three-double-bed Harp cabin. Planned group activities welcomed. Airstrip on ranch. Write: Bryce and Barbara Mitchell, Route 1, Box 95C, Yamhill, OR 97148 (503–662–3222).

Rock Springs Guest Ranch, 10 miles northwest of Bend and adjacent to Deschutes National Forest. Horseback riding in nearby wilderness areas. Two official size tennis courts. Heated pool. Fishing on ranch and in nearby streams. Play area and recreation for children. Ranch lodge plus modern cottages with fireplaces. Off-season cottage rentals. Accommodation for conference groups by arrangement with ranch. Write: Rock Springs Guest Ranch, 64201 Tyler Rd., Bend, OR 97701 (503–382–1957). *Lake Creek Lodge,* between Black Butte and Camp Sherman in Metolius River resort area, 12 miles northwest of Sisters and 34 miles northwest of Bend. Trail rides into surrounding Deschutes National Forest. Fishing in nearby Metolius River. Swimming in creek-fed pool. Tennis court and children's play area. Housekeeping cottages for two to eight persons and two-bedroom hotel cottages surround pool. Year-round with seasonal rates available. Write: Glenna Grace, Lake Creek Lodge, Sisters, OR 97759 (503–595–6331). *Blue Mountain Hot Springs Guest Ranch,* located in historic John Day ranching country, 10 miles southeast of Prairie City and at edge of Malheur National Forest land near Strawberry Mountain Wilderness Area of Blue Mountains. Horseback rides on wilderness trails. Fishing in wilderness streams, lakes. Outside pool heated by natural warm mineral springs. Country-style lodge with accommodations for families. Write: Helen Ricco, Star Route, Prairie City, OR 97876 (503–820–3744). *Baker's Bar M Ranch,* 31 miles northeast of Pendleton on Umatilla River. On the site of historic Bingham Springs Resort and adjacent to Umatilla National Forest in northeastern Oregon's Blue Mountains. Wide variety of family recreation. Stable of 50 horses. Pool heated by natural warm springs. Recreation barn for games and dancing. Eight rooms in hand-hewn log ranch house built in 1864, four suites in Homestead annex, two large cabins for family groups. Season: June 1 through Sept. 30. Write: Baker's Bar M Ranch, Route 1, Box 263, Adams, OR 97810 (503–566–3381). *The Horse Ranch,* secluded year-round resort located within boundaries of Eagle Cap Wilderness Area in northeastern Oregon's Wallowa Mountains. Accessible only by private airplane or charter (from Enterprise) or by eight-mile pack trip. Horses for sightseeing rides, pack and fishing trips to high alpine lakes. Other recreation: bird and deer hunting, cross-country skiing, snowshoeing tours. Specialized summer pack and fall hunting trips arranged. Log cabins with fireplaces. Write: The Horse Ranch, Box 26, Joseph, OR 97846 (503–432–9171).

Flying Arrow Resort, in alp-like basin. Cottages along Wallow River surrounded by green lawn and big trees. Magnificent views from the sundeck. Walk to the trailhead of the 300,000-acre Eagle Cap Wilderness Area from your cottage. Horseback riding; guided tours into the wilderness. Miniature golf, hiking, swimming, water skiing. Learn flint knapping, fire-making, snaring, fish smoking, Indian legends and culture. Nearby Teepee Village Market offers furs and wool things, quilts, baskets, buckskin, and beadwork. Write: Flying Arrow Resort, Rt. 1, Box 370, Joseph, OR 97846 (503–432–4061.)

Howard Prairie Lake Resort, on Howard Prairie Lake, is situated in the Cascades between two mountain ridges at 4,500-foot elevation. It is approximately 6 miles in length, with several islands providing inlets and bays, which are favorites of fishermen and make the lake quite attractive. The lake abounds with natural food and is acclaimed by fishers as one of the finest rainbow-trout lakes in the West. It also has a good reputation for catfish. Bank and jetty fishers find choice spots for their angling chairs. Water skiing, sailing, and swimming are popular as are horseback riding and hunting for Indian artifacts. Write: Howard Prairie Lake Resort, Johnston Stores, Medford, OR 97501 (503–773–3619 or 482–1979).

In addition, Oregon boasts several fine fishing lodges, such as: *Morrison's Lodge,* on the banks of the Rogue River, 16 miles from Grants Pass. The lodge offers both housekeeping cottages and American Plan accommodations. (All accommodations from Sept. 15 through November are American Plan.) Housekeeping units can be served on American or European plan. Two bedrooms, living room, dining area, kitchen, bath, carport, and completely furnished with linen and utensils. Air-conditioned in summer, with a fireplace for spring and autumn. One-, two-, three-, and four-day raft trips can be taken from the lodge. Write: Morrison's Lodge, 8500 Galice Road, Merlin, OR 97532. *Tu Tu Tun Lodge,* 7 miles up Rogue River from Gold Beach, on US 101. American Plan. Lounge area, dominated by huge stone fireplace, overlooks the terrace, heated swimming pool, and the Rogue River. Many of the menu items are from fine, old, and almost forgotten recipes. Between meals, snacks are always available. Lodge guests provide their own fishing equipment. Minor fishing tackle items and fishing license may be purchased at the lodge. Guides are available through the lodge for river and ocean fishing. Your catch will be cared for by Tu Tu Tun, either held for you fresh or frozen for shipping. Write: Tu Tu Tun Lodge, Route 1, Box 365, Gold Beach, OR 97444.

HEALTH SPAS. Natural warm-water and mineral springs spurt and leak from the ground at many spots of Oregon, especially in the central and eastern parts of the state. At *Kah-nee-ta* on the Warm Springs Indian Reservation, plush cabins or tepees holding up to 10 can be rented. Day visitors can swim in Olympic-size pools and enjoy mineral and mud baths. *Blue Mountain Hot Springs Guest Ranch,* 10 miles southeast of Prairie City, has weekly rates that include meals and fishing and swimming privileges. *Radium Hot Springs,* at Haines, 12 miles north of Baker, has no housing accommodations. Vehicles use the campground at night. Swimming in the 50' X 120' pool. Restaurant motel close by. *Breitenbush Community,* 10 miles from Detroit, OR, off 224, has hot tubs, natural hot pools, a sauna. Cascade scenery and hiking. All meals vegetarian. Children adored here. *Jackson Hot Springs,* 2 miles north of Ashland, on Oregon 99, is in the heart of the beautiful Rogue Valley. The modern 50' X 100' swimming pool is filled with 82°–84° F mineral water from the original Jackson Hot Springs. Changed every third or fourth day. Private rooms for hot mineral tub-baths available. All cabins equipped with electric kitchens, excellent beds, electric or gas heaters in bedrooms; private baths. Laundry facilities. Utility hookups for mobile homes, campers, travel trailers.

SUMMER SPORTS. Exposure to towering mountains, dense forests, broad beaches, swift streams, and winding waterways makes sportsmen out of Oregon residents and visitors alike. So much recreational variety is available that no one activity is more than a seasonal favorite.

Beachcombing for shells and rocks and Japanese glass floats and *driftwood collecting* seem almost an occupation along the entire coast.

Bicycling. Oregon's bike routes extend down the coast, down the Willamette Valley, across the state, and in many interior areas. Contact the Tourism Division, Oregon Economic Development Department, 595 Cottage St. N.E., Salem, OR 97310 (800–547–7842).

Boating: All kinds on lakes and scenic rivers. *Water skiing* also popular. Area between Yachats and Florence fine for acquatics. Motor boating good at Owyhee Dam (Oregon 201). Also Wallowa Lake, 78 miles east of La Grande.

Fishing draws more than half a million fishermen a year to 46,000 miles of trout angling streams and more than 1,000 lakes. Principal game fish taken in coastal streams are chinook and silver salmon, steelhead and cutthroat trout, striped bass, and shad. Fishing conditions and regulations change rapidly; for latest information write Oregon Dept. of Fish & Wildlife, 506 S.W. Mill, Portland, OR 97208.; 229–5222.

Golfing: Oregon boasts over 130 golf courses, with 29 in the Portland area. The links are active all year in mild western areas. Most courses are open to public play, and Easterners especially will be surprised by the uncrowded first tees. According to *Golf Digest,* the best courses are: Gearhart G.C., Gearhart, windy, flat, seaside course; West Delta Park G.C., Portland, a Robert Trent Jones course; Pleasant Valley G.C., Clackamas, with a view of Mt. Hood from all holes; Bowman's Mt. Hood G.C., Wemme, hilly year-round golf and ski resort; Salishan Golf Links, Gleneden Beach, narrow, nicely landscaped, overlooking Pacific; Sunriver G.C., Sunriver large resort complex.

Hiking and Packing: Natural sites are the numerous national forests and primitive areas. Backpacking hikes are popular in the high country of central and eastern Oregon. Indian-style hikes at Kah-nee-ta (US 26), and at Rooster Rock State Park in Columbia River Gorge, east of Portland.

Horseback Riding: Fine resources in all areas. Organized packhorse trips appeal to many through the mountainous country of central and eastern Oregon. Other areas: Warm Springs, Kah-nee-ta, Rooster Rock State Park (east of Portland).

Hunting: The best game hunting is in the mountain country of central and eastern Oregon, and birds are also more plentiful east of the Cascades. Deer are widely scattered, with quite a few Pronghorns mixed in. Bighorn sheep are taken in special hunts on Hart Mountain in September, and mountain goats are sought in the Eagle Gap Wilderness Area in late August and early September. For hunting regulations, contact Oregon Dept. of Fish & Wildlife, 506 S.W. Mill, Portland, 97208 (229–5222).

Mountain Climbing: Most climbers are attracted by 11,235-foot Mt. Hood, east of Portland. But the Alpinelike peak can be dangerous for the inexperienced or unprepared, and only highly skilled and fully equipped groups should consider winter ascents, when conditions can quickly change from brilliant sunshine into a nightmare of arctic wasteland without warning. Even in summer, climbers should check equipment, obtain an experienced leader, and register the climb.

Windsurfing. Oregon's latest participatory sport is windsurfing. Experts say the Columbia Gorge is one of the best places in the world for that sport. Write: Windsurfing, 4 Fourth St., Hood River 97031 (386–5787).

Swimming: Most popular spa swimming is at Kah-nee-ta, on the Warm Springs Indian Reservation. Timberline Lodge (at 6,000-foot elevation on Mt. Hood) has an all-weather, open-air swimming pool. Most popular coastal swimming is at Seaside. Most popular river swimming is at Rooster Rock State Park (a half-hour drive from Portland) on the Columbia. Fresh-water lakes between Yachats and Florence, on the sand-dune strip of the coast, are also frequented. Because of relatively little warm water in Oregon, the lakes and streams are not crowded with swimmers. Each town of 5,000 or more (and sometimes less) has a municipal swimming pool, generally in a (or the) city park. *Ocean beaches* are fine for hiking and sunbathing (when the sun is bright) and also provide clam digging and crabbing.

WINTER SPORTS. *Skiing.* The top winter sport in Oregon, with 14 downhill areas in operation from November well into the summer.

Oregon's snow covers a variety of terrain and scenery, giving skiers endless choices of forest-lined trails and wide, open spaces.

The volcanic Cascade range hosts most of the state's downhill ski traffic. For over 50 years, skiers have been attracted to the heavily snow-blanketed slopes of *Mt. Hood,* Oregon's highest peak at 11,235 feet. Today, 3 major areas, 2 smaller facilities, and 2 snow play areas provide snow recreation from early November until at least June 30 and usually even later on the upper snowfields of the mountain.

Farther south along the eastern slope of the Cascades in the vast Central Oregon vacationland, *Mt. Bachelor,* with 5 double lifts and 5 triple lifts, is vying to become the leading ski area in Oregon and generally has snow when most other areas don't.

Hoodoo Ski Bowl on Santiam Pass, on the crest of the Central Oregon Cascades, is a long-time favorite among beginners and intermediate skiers from the Willamette Valley.

One of the Pacific Northwest's largest ski schools serves skiers on *Mt. Ashland* in southwest Oregon's scenic Siskiyou range on the Oregon-California border. The Mt. Ashland area, along with the *Spout Springs* and *Anthony Lakes* areas in Eastern Oregon's granitic Blue Mountains, offers plenty of the dry, powder variety of snow.

Miles of ski touring trails have contributed to the rapid growth of cross-country skiing and snowshoeing in Oregon. Most of the state's established trails are located on Forest Service land, particularly in the Mt. Hood, Willamette, Deschutes, Winema, Rogue River, Wallowa, Whitman, and Umatilla National Forests. A 35-mile ski touring trail also leads visitors around the rim of Crater Lake in Crater Lake National Park.

Several of the state's major areas are involved in ski vacation packages with nearby resort facilities. Details and further information on Oregon ski packages are available to persons living outside Oregon by toll-free telephone, 1–800–547–4901.

A sampling of ski package costs along with information on schedules, lift rates, facilities, and locations are included in a colorful ski brochure published by the Economic Development Department. Brochures published by the state's major ski areas also are available from Tourism Division, Economic Development Dept., 595 Cottage St., N.E., Salem, OR 97310.

There are several indoor ice skating rinks open all year round in the Portland area. The best known is at Lloyd Center. Ice skating on frozen lakes and at many winter resorts in the state are increasingly popular. Open horse-drawn sleighs are part of the winter recreation scene in many parts of Oregon. Rides in Sno-Cats are another way to enjoy the winter terrain. *Skijoring*—an easy form of skiing, either using a horse to tow you along trails or over frozen lakes, or behind a snowmobile, is gaining acceptance. Most resorts use a snowmobile rather than a horse. *Paulina Lake* in central Oregon has miles and miles of trail for every level of snowmobiles. *Diamond Lake* has over 200 miles of snowmobiling trails. Winter nature hikes are offered in many areas.

SPECTATOR SPORTS. *Baseball.* The Portland Beavers play their Pacific Coast League home games at Multnomah Stadium. Eugene, Salem, Bend, and Medford field baseball teams in the Northwest League. *Basketball.* The Portland Trailblazers of the National Basketball Association keep on packing in crowds at Memorial Coliseum. Oregon and Oregon State are hosts to the Far-West Class tourney, held over the Christmas season at Portland's Memorial Coliseum. Outstanding college and university basketball teams in the state include the University of Oregon, at Eugene; Oregon State University, at Corvallis; Portland State University, the University of Portland, and Lewis and Clark College, at Portland; Willamette University, at Salem; Linfield College, at McMinnville; and Pacific University, at Forest Grove. *Football.* Oregon plays its home games at Eugene and Oregon State at Corvallis. On occasion, OSU plays in Portland, but Multnomah Stadium these days is the home of Portland State University and local high school games. Practically all secular colleges and universities field football teams. *Soccer.* Portland no longer has a professional soccer team but the sport has caught on in the high schools and parks. Rugby is also catching on, and its champions claim it will some day supersede soccer and football in popularity. *Golf.* Top male Northwest golfers come to Portland in May for the handsome-purse Giusti Memorial Golf Classic. Top women golfers from around the nation visit Portland in fall for the Open Golf Tournament on the L.P.G.A. tour. The ladies' purse is higher than the men's. *Hockey.* The Portland Winter Hawks of the Western Hockey League play their home games in Memorial Coliseum. *Horse Racing.* There are no gambling casinos or legal slot machines in Oregon, so the betting urge impels thousands to go to Portland Meadows for horse racing from mid-Oct. through April. Post times: Sat., Sun., and holidays, 1:30 P.M.; Fri., 7 P.M. *Greyhound Racing.* From early May into Sept., the dogs chase the mechanical rabbit at Multnomah Kennel Club, 12 miles east of Portland. Every day but Sun. and Mon. Post time, first race: 7:30 P.M. Sat. matinee, 1 P.M. The seasons are changed each year, so for the most current schedules, write Tourism Division/Economic Development Dept., 595 Cottage St., N.E. Salem, OR 97310.

Rodeos. See *Seasonal Events.* For specific up-to-date information (dates change from year to year and sometimes from month to month), write: Tourism Division/Economic Development Dept., 595 Cottage St., N.E., Salem, OR 97310.

SHOPPING. Whatever one can purchase anywhere else in the United States can be bought in Portland—or so it would seem from the almost stupefying variety of stores. Downtown not only has major department stores and specialty stores of a wide range, but the fringes of downtown, especially along the diminishing Skid Road, are being filled with the shops of innovative artisans. Portland has so many shopping centers, large and small, that a common expression here is that the city is "overshopulated." *Lloyd Center* is not only one of the largest shopping centers in America but is noted for its unusual landscaping and cultural and recreational facilities, especially its ice rink. *Jantzen Mall,* on the site once occupied by a venerable amusement park, is as modernistic as the nearby Columbia River is historic. *Washington Square,* west of town and designed to capture the patronage of the middle-class denizens of one of the fastest-growing counties in the country, has a clutch of major department stores.

Competing with downtown Portland retailers are several major discount stores, but with price competition on the one hand and inflation on the other, it's a matter of reading the ads.

Several firms specialize in imports but none approaches in factory dimension the several piled-high floors of *Import Plaza,* at the north edge of downtown.

For open-air browsing, try the weekend *Saturday Market* just north of downtown, and near the river. Some of the liveliest off-beat shops and boutiques are interspersed with and at the edge of skid row. Between the winos there is the wine of romance. The restaurants are also deliberately different, set up in a sort of sod hut-candlelight motif.

Legions of Portlanders seem to do a lot of their shopping at garage and basement sales and scour the small towns of the lower Willamette Valley for auction houses and secondhand stores.

Hitching on to the fast locomotive of nostalgia, antique stores have sprung up everywhere. You will find them in every town, village, and hamlet, and on state and county roads between settlements.

Outside of Portland, shopping centers seem to be in every town of 10,000 or more (and sometimes less). The biggest is Valley Center, across the Willamette River from Eugene. Much of Eugene's downtown is now a pedestrian mall, with benches, a fountain, and some artistic design pattern. Here is the "Athens of Oregon," with culture sometimes running rampant. *Fifth Street Public Market* sells baked goods, fresh produce, and handcrafted items by skilled artisans from the forested hills. Saturday is *Market Day* on the parking lot of the Lane County Court House.

At Cottage Grove, the 1912-built *Cottage Grove Hotel* has been restored as a charming complex of 10 specialty shops.

Coos Bay, on the coast, also has a downtown pedestrian mall, where shoppers can rest on benches under shade trees as they ponder how to stretch the dollar. At North Bend, adjacent to Coos Bay, local wood products were used to create *Pony Village,* a shopping center whose atmosphere combines the rural with the urban.

Made in Oregon, a glinty shop at the Portland International Airport, sells only what its name says.

The most authentic indigenous products, made of myrtlewood, are found in western Oregon and particularly on the central Oregon coast; semiprecious stones, particularly agates and thunder eggs, are found all over the state, and seashells on the Oregon Coast.

WHAT TO DO WITH THE CHILDREN. There are a thousand things for children to enjoy free in Oregon: building sand castles, collecting driftwood, and looking for Japanese glass floats, agates, and shells on the beaches of the Oregon coast; rockhounding throughout the state; swimming in lakes and rivers; hiking forest trails; communing with nature high and low; looking at waterfalls and wildflowers and caves and canyons and Indian pictographs; splashing in Portland's hip Forecourt Fountain; angling for a trout at Small Fry Lake (14 is the upper age limit) seven miles southeast of Estacada; goggling at the geyser at Lakeview; tracing the stream to the hot mineral outlets at Austin Hot Springs, on the upper Clackamas River, out of Estacada; watching the fishing boats come in at Astoria, Depoe Bay, Warrenton, Newport, and a lot of other coastal ports; trying to spot a whale or sea otter in Pacific waters; looking up at the giant redwoods and Douglas firs; browsing through county museums; running over sand dunes; seeing the elk and deer at Ecols State Park, near Cannon Beach; climbing to the towers of lighthouses; playing on an extinct volcano; walking through huge lava fields; counting the waterfalls along the Columbia River Scenic Route, east of Portland; seeing cattle "push" cattle in central and eastern Oregon; taking enough pictures to last a lifetime. Then there are the rodeos and the sand-dune buggy rides, with costs for children seldom more than $1.

The Portland Municipal Parks system has daily children's programs during the summer months, including story hours, nature hikes, dancing classes, carnivals, fly casting, golf, and picnics.

The Salem and Eugene city parks' recreation programs include similar fare.

The Portland Zoo, 4001 S.W. Canyon Rd., is famous for its elephants, but it has a lot of other species of the animal kingdom, too. Daily, 10 A.M.-dusk a 30-minute train ride through Washington Park on the Zooliner fascinates kids of all ages. The fun-in-learning *OMSI* (Oregon Museum of Science and Industry), next door to the Zoo, is the great people's school in the Portland area. Many special attractions for children. *Portland Civic Theatre,* at the edge of downtown, has its own *Children's Theatre,* with productions specifically staged for the kids. (See *Stage and Revues.*) World Forestry Center, a small walk from OMSI and the Zoo, will tell children more about trees than a dozen books could—especially if the kids listen to the Talking Tree. Portland Children's Museum, 3037 S.W. 2nd, has local history relics, toys, dolls, miniatures, live animals. Jan.–Aug. and Oct.–Dec., Mon.-Fri. 10–6; Sat., 10–3. Free.

At Astoria, kids (and adults) can climb without cost the 166 steps leading to the top of the Astoria Column (the views are fantastic); board the old lightship *Columbia,* the key feature of the Columbia River Maritime Museum; and go through Ft. Clatsop National Memorial, a replica of the log stockade built by Lewis and Clark in late 1805 (no charge).

At Bend, see thousands of waterfowl (many tame enough to be hand-fed) at Drake City Park.

Near Bend, leg the information trail at Lava Butte, look into Lava River Caves, gaze with awe on the Lava Cast Forest.

Watch the fish go up the fish ladders at Bonneville Dam. (And stop in at any fish hatchery to see the eggs-to-maturity cycle of salmon and trout.)

At Woodland Deer Park, Cave Junction, at West Coast Game Park, near Bandon, and at Western Deer Park, near Sheridan, deer eat out of hands—and there are a lot of other animals around to keep any child from being bored.

At Cottage Grove, ride up Row River on *The Goose,* a steam locomotive train that takes off from The Village Green on a 2-hour, 34-mile round-trip. Daily at 2 P.M., July 1-Labor Day; Sat., Sun. and holidays at 2 P.M., mid-May to June 30 and Labor Day to mid-Sept.

At Depoe Bay, The Aquarium is famous for its ham-it-up seals. There are many other kinds of marine life there, too. And the shell shop, one of the best on the Coast, will enchant the junior set. Open daily. Free.

Sea Lion Caves, 11 miles north of Florence, is home to wild sea lions. An elevator descends into the caves. Open daily daylight hours; closed Dec. 25. Fee.

Kids of all ages will be thrilled on the 64-mile round-trip or 104-mile round-trip up the Rogue River from Wedderburn, near Gold Beach. (See *Special Interest Tours.*)

From Grants Pass, I–5, jet or drift boat excursions down the Rogue River to Hellgate Canyon should keep everyone awake. (See *Special Interest Tours.*)

At Horseworld, Seaside, on the Coast, kids can ride gentle horses along the beach or on forest trails. Open daily. "Play Barn" at Horseworld has supervised child care while the parents and older kids are horseback riding.

The whole town of Jacksonville, which started as a gold camp, is a museum, and children with curious minds will delight in the tintype buildings and the shops of artisans. It's a real cool place—past and present. The Doll Museum, located in the mid-nineteenth-century McCully House, 240 California St., Jacksonville; has a fantastic collection of dolls on display. July, Aug., daily, 10:30 A.M.–5 P.M. Winter hours irregular.

Lions, zebras, impalas, elephants, giraffes, and many other animals at home on the African plains are easily viewed at the *Wildlife Safari,* near Winston. The ride through the uncaged "jungle" delights youngsters.

Seal Gulch, at Seal Rock, on the coast, is a chainsaw Disneyland, where kids get the "Old West" feeling in a colorful village sculpted by a chainsaw.

Newport is a treasure chest for children. There's no admission fee to the Marine Science Center or Oregon State University, with its aquarium and museum, and only a nominal fee to visit Old Yaquina Bay Lighthouse, built in 1871, and furnished in period. Wander along gusty, briny Front Bay, with its fishing boat excitement and seagulls free-wheeling over the bustling wharves and streets. Daily, 11–6. Fee. Underseas Garden, on Bay Front, offers unobstructed views of sea plants and animals through large underground window. Daily, 10 A.M.–9 P.M., June 1–Aug. 31; 10 A.M.–5 P.M. rest of year. Fee. The Wax Works, directly across the street from the Underseas Garden, features wax figures, including faces of the past and present, fairyland characters, and horror figures. Daily, 10 A.M.–9 P.M. in summer, Mon.-Fri.; 10 A.M.–5 P.M. rest of year. Fee.

In Oregon City children will get a kick out of receiving a free Lifetime Pass, signed by the mayor, after riding the Municipal Elevator. Across the Willamette River, at West Linn, they will find the century-old boat locks picturesque.

Prehistoric Gardens, 12 miles south of Port Orford, presents life-sized replicas of dinosaurs and other prehistoric monsters in a rain-forest setting. Daily, 8 A.M.–dusk. Fee. Stone Age Park, 7 miles north of Port Orford, and also on US 101, houses Indian artifacts and a mineral collection featuring a display of fluorescent rocks. Adjacent are reindeer, geese, and ducks. There's also a nature trail and a waterlily garden. In other words, a lot to take in for the scientifically-minded youngster. Daily, 8 A.M.–8 P.M., closed in winter. Fee.

Petersen's Rock Garden, 7 miles from Redmond, contains several acres of unusual and colorful rock gardens. Bridges, terraces, and replicas of historic structures are built of rock and petrified wood. A delightful place to picnic. Daily, 7 A.M.–9 P.M., May 15–Aug. 31; 7 A.M.–dusk, rest of year. Donations.

Enchanted Forest, 7 miles south of Salem, on I–5, features storybook characters in a wooded setting. Daily, 8:30 A.M.–dusk, May 1–Oct. 31. Fee.

At Wallowa Lake the children are in for a real, up, up and away thrill. A gondola lift climbs to the 8,020-foot level on Mt. Howard. Daily, 10 A.M.–5 P.M., May 1–Sept. 30, weather permitting. Fee.

At the Wildlife Safari, 6 miles south of Roseburg, off I–5 (use Winston-Coos exit), lions, tigers, and other African and Asian animals roam freely inside fenced enclosures. Drive through in your own car. It'll be one long point-to for and by the children. Open daily, daylight hours. Fee.

One of the least-known and most exciting places to take children is Pacific Northwest Live Streamers, 3 miles east of Molalla (30 miles southeast of Portland). Oil-and-coal-burning scale-model steam-locomotive-drawn trains run over the tracks, a paddle wheeler churns on the slough of the Molalla River, a rowboat is for use in a Huckleberry Finn pond, there's plenty of soft grass to roll on, and picnic trees are sited under shade trees. And it's all free! Open Sundays in summer.

HISTORICAL SITES AND MUSEUMS. There are Oregon towns, some only a few ghostly buildings shivering in a banshee wind, that are museums in themselves. These include Andrews, Ashwood, Bourne, Brownmead, Chitwood, Clifton, Cornucopia, Drewsey, Elk City, Friend, Golden, Cranite, Hardman, Klondike, Lonerock, Mayger, Richmond, Sodaville, Sparta, Sumpter, and Susanville.

Four much more viable communities—Albany, Astoria, Jacksonville, and Oakland—are loaded with 19th-century buildings. Contact the chambers of commerce for self-guided walking tours: Albany Visitors Bureau, Box 548, Albany, OR 97321 (926–1517); Astoria Area Chamber of Commerce, Box 176, Astoria, OR 97103; Jacksonville Chamber of Commerce, Box 33, Jacksonville,

OR 97530 (899–8118); Oakland Chamber of Commerce, Box 788, Oakland, OR 97462 (459–3796).

Historical

Astoria: *Museum of Clatsop County Historical Society,* in old city hall.

Columbia River Maritime Museum. Nautical displays and maritime library. 1792 Marine Dr., Astoria 97103 (325–2323).

Ft. Clatsop National Memorial. Museum and reconstruction of the fort built by Lewis and Clark in late 1805. Rt. 3, Box 604-FC, Astoria 97103 (861–2471).

Aurora: *Aurora Colony Ox Barn Museum.* Log cabin and colony home containing pioneer artifacts and items of historical interest. Second & Liberty Sts., one block from 99E. Aurora 97002 (678–5754).

Champoeg Visitors Center, in Champoeg State Park. Best museum on Oregon white settlement in this area. Near entrance to park. 8329 Champoeg Rd. NE, Aurora 97002 (678–1251).

Robert Newell House, at edge of Champoeg State Park. Reconstructed home of Robert "Doc" Newell, famous mountain man and founder of the pioneer community of Champoeg. 8089 Champoeg Rd. NE, Aurora 97002 (678–5537).

Bend: *Oregon High Desert Museum.* A living cultural center dedicated to ecology. 59800 S. Hwy. 97, Bend 97702 (382–4754).

Brooks: *Antique Powerland Museum.* Antique steam, gas, and other farm equipment. 3995 Brooklake Rd. NE, at Brooks turnoff from I–5, Brooks 97305 (393–2424).

Brownsville: *Linn County Museum* and *Moyer House,* the latter an Italian villa style, built in 1881, with all original furnishings. Park St., Brownsville 97327 (466–3390).

Burns: *Harney County Museum.* Memorabilia and artifacts of Indians, sod-busters, and ranchers. 18 W D, Burns 97720 (573–2636). Pete French Round Barn, 57 miles southeast of Burns. The last remaining structure of a once-great cattle empire. Nearby is *Frenchglen Hotel,* pioneer hostel in 1880s decor. Rooms, meals available. Frenchglen 97736 (493–2825).

Canby: *Canby Depot Museum.* Oregon's oldest railroad station, built in 1873, adjoins Clackamas County Fairgrounds. Box 160, Canby 97013 (260–2980).

Canyon City: *Herman and Eliza Oliver Museum.* Well-displayed relics of early Gold Rush days. On grounds are log cabin home of famed poet Joaquin Miller and a mining camp jail that was spirited away from its original site up in the mountains. Canyon City 97820 (575–0547).

Cascade Locks: *Cascade Locks Museum.* Steamboat displays in early home of lockkeeper. Marine Park, Cascade Locks 97014 (374–8290).

Central Point: *Crater Rock Museum.* Indian artifacts, crystal and gold displays, petrified wood, agates, honeybees. 2002 Scenic Ave., Central Point 97502 (664–1355).

Corvallis: *Horner Museum of Oregon State University.* Thousands of items of Oregon historical interest occupy basement of Gill Coliseum. Corvallis 97331 (754–2951).

Echo: *Echo Museum.* This museum is worth a visit if only to appreciate the marble and wrought-iron architecture of this National Register of Historic Places site. The Oregon Trail passed through present Echo and crossed the Umatilla River at "Emigrant's Crossing," and the museum reflects Oregon Trail life.

Eugene: *Lane County Historical Museum,* on county fairgrounds, in pioneer building. Well-documented and displayed artifacts of early settlers. 1853 Lane County Clerk's Building adjacent. 740 W 13th Ave, Eugene 97402 (687–4239).

Museum of Natural History, on University of Oregon Campus. Showcase of Oregon's natural heritage, displays of archaeology, geology, and biology. Eugene 97403 (686–3024).

Willamette Science and Technology Center. Exhibits on physics, biology, and computer science in addition to a weekend planetarium show. 2300 Centennial Blvd., Eugene 97401 (484–9027).

Florence: *Indian Forest.* Oregon Coast's finest Indian trading post. Authentic full-size Indian dwellings. A-frame trading post contains handmade Indian arts and crafts, including Navajo rugs, Pagago baskets, Hopi pottery, Acoma pottery, Zuni beadwork, kachinas, sand paintings, Indian books and dolls, and more. 88493 Hwy. 101 North, Florence 97439 (997–3677).

Forest Grove: *Old College Hall.* Located in center of Pacific University campus. Built in 1850, this New England hall houses a reception room, chapel, and pioneer museum. Oldest building devoted to education in Oregon. Pacific University, Forest Grove 97116 (357–6151, ext. 2455).

Fort Klamath: *Old Fort Klamath.* Established and garrisoned by the Oregon Volunteer Cavalry in 1863 to protect Southern Emigrant Trains from Indian attack and maintain peace in the region during the Civil War. The fort played an important role in the 1864 Peace Treaty of "Council Grove" and in the conduct of the 1872–73 Indian Modoc War, including its use as the site for Modoc War trials and executions. The frontier post is located on Crater Lake Hwy. 62, 44 miles north of Klamath Falls. Fort Klamath 97626.

Fossil: *Fossil Historical Museum.* Indian and pioneer homesteader artifacts. Fossil 97830.

Glenwood: *Trolley Park.* A live museum of old-time trolleys (from three continents) and railroad passenger cars. Star Route, Box 1318, Glenwood 97120 (357–3574).

Gold Hill: *House of Mystery,* also called *Oregon Vortex.* A spherical field of force, half above ground and half below, and, by reason of this, the affected area is a circle. To Indians, the area was known as the Forbidden Ground, a place to be shunned. Sardine Creek Road, Gold Hill 97525 (855–1543).

Haimes: *Eastern Oregon Museum.* The Museum building, former gymnasium of Haines High School, is 4 blocks east of Main St. in Haines, which is old US Hwy. 30, now US 237. Excellent collection of memorabilia dating from Oregon Trail days. Authentic turn-of-century parlor, 1870s kitchen, gold-rush camp bar, and more. Haines 97833.

Hood River: *Hood River County Historical Museum.* The museum leads the visitor by historic steps from the area's earliest inhabitants to the founding of white settlement in 1854 and the development of Hood River Valley as a world-famous fruit center. Post Marina Park, Hood River 97031 (386–6772).

Independence: *Heritage Museum,* in former First Baptist Church. Independence was one of the best-known "End of the Oregon Trail" towns and its museum is strong on post-Oregon Trail life. 3rd & B Sts., Independence 97351 (838–4989).

Jacksonville: The entire town is a living museum, and all places recognized as museums are close together. *Jackson County Museum,* in old Jacksonville Courthouse. Two large floors of exhibits depicting the history of Jackson County. *Children's Museum,* where children can touch and learn about our pioneer past. *U.S. Hotel,* constructed during Jacksonville's gold-rush era, houses a ballroom and a host of exhibits, including a century-old dentist's office, a millinery, and harness makers shop. *Beekman Bank.* Built in 1863, the bank was operational until 1912. Most of the furnishings exhibited are original. *C.C. Beekman House.* Constructed in 1876. Beekman was a banker, a gold freighter, and a Wells Fargo agent. *Catholic Rectory.* Constructed as a private residence in 1861, Catholic Rectory was later used as a parish house by St. Joseph's Catholic Church. *The Doll Museum,* in 1860 McCully House. Make all queries to Southern Oregon Historical Society, Box 480, Jacksonville 97530 (899–1847).

John Day: *Kam Wah Chung & Co. Museum,* adjacent to City Park. The building, constructed as a trading post on the Dalles Military Road in 1866–67, served as a center for the Chinese community in Eastern Oregon until the early 1940s. The original building now contains thousands of artifacts and relics that illustrate the many former uses of the site—as a general store, pharmacy, doctor's office, Chinese temple, and home. John Day 97845.

Kerby: *Kerbyville Museum.* Traces history of the region, starting with discovery of gold in 1851. Kerby 97531 (592–2076).

Klamath Falls: *Klamath County Museum.* The theme of the museum is "telling the story of Klamath County," and it does it well. 1451 Main St., Klamath Falls 97601 (882–2501, ext. 208).

Baldwin Hotel Museum. Hotel, as it was at turn-of-century. 31 Main St., Klamath Falls 97601 (882–2501, ext. 209).

Favell Museum of Western Art and Indian Artifacts. Exquisite museum with beautiful displays. 125 W Main, Klamath Falls 97601 (882–9996).

La Grande: *Walter Pierce Museum* of Eastern Oregon College. Indian artifacts and pioneer relics. La Grande 97850 (963–2171).

Lakeview: *Schminck Memorial Museum.* Thoughtful, artistic displays of south-central Oregon. 128 S E St., Lakeview 97630 (947–2239).

Newberg: *Hoover-Minthron House.* Boyhood home of Herbert Hoover built in 1881. 115 S River St., Newberg 97132 (538–6629).

Dr. John C. Brougher Museum, in Brougher Hall, George Fox College. Items relating to early Friends (Quakers), Pacific College (now George Fox), Newberg and Northwest pioneer history, artifacts from missionary work around the world. Newberg 97132 (538–8383).

Newport: *Underseas Gardens.* Marine life viewed through portholes below the sealine. On colorful Bay Front. Newport 97365.

Mark O. Hatfield Marine Science Center. Exhibits of sea life, marine-science displays. In summer, free movies and lectures. Marine Science Drive, Newport 97365 (867–3011).

Lincoln County Historical Museum. Pioneer Artifacts in log building. S.W. 9th & Fall, Newport 97365 (265–7509).

The Wax Works. Directly across street from Undersea Gardens. Wax imagery of past, present, and future. 250 S.W. Bay Blvd., Newport 97365 (265–2206).

Old Yaquina Bay Lighthouse. One of the Coast's oldest lighthouses, turned into a museum. At south end of Newport, off US 101. Write State Parks and Recreation Division, Salem 97310 (378–6305).

North Bend: *Coos County Historical Museum.* Displays of loggers, fishers, and farmers of Coos County. At north end of city, just off US 101. North Bend 97459 (756–4613).

Oakland: The entire village retains a 19th-century atmosphere. Visitors who enjoy the nostalgia might stop into *Tolly's* for a tasty and inexpensive meal.

Oregon City: *Clackamas County Historical Society,* in 1907 house. 15 period rooms. 603 Sixth St. Oregon City 97045 (655–2866).

End of the Oregon Trail Interpretive Center. A visitors center to better explain the arduous trail journey and the welcome site of Oregon City. Fifth & Washington Sts., Oregon City 97045 (655–6896).

McLoughlin House. 11th National Historic Site. Home of "Father of Oregon," Fr. John McLoughlin, Chief Factor of Hudson's Bay Co., 1824–46. Operated by McLoughlin Memorial Assn., 713 Center St., Oregon City 97045 (656–5146).

Philomath: *Benton County Historical Museum.* In Philomath College building since 1867. Historical exhibits relating to the history of Benton County, art exhibits. 11th & Main., Philomath 97370 (929–6230).

Port Orford: *Prehistoric Gardens.* In Oregon's rain forest. A "lost world" of recreated, life-size replicas of dinosaurs and other prehistoric animals among the primitive plants that grow so profusely in this area. 36848 Hwy. 101 South, Port Orford 97465 (332–4463).

Portland: *Oregon Historical Society.* Oregon Historical display and library. 1230 SW Park, Portland 97205 (222–1741).

Oregon Museum of Science and Industry (OMSI). One of the finest, warmest, fun-in-learning museums in nation. 4015 SW Canyon Rd., Portland 97221 (222–2828).

World Forestry Center. Complex consists of large exhibit hall and two annex buildings containing multi-purpose halls and woodworking shop. All the structures, inside and out, are stunning examples of wood construction at its best. 4033 S.W. Canyon Rd., Portland (228–1367).

Pittock Mansion. Opulent French Renaissance house overlooking city. Lavishly furnished. 3229 N.W. Pittock Dr., Portland 97210 (221–1730).

John Palmer House. Gorgeous 1890 house, a highly ornamented example of Victorian architecture. Rooms filled with high Victorian antiques. Bed and breakfast. 4314 N. Mississippi Ave., Portland 97217 (284–5893).

The Old Church. Oldest standing church in Portland, on its original site, and turned into arts and public affairs center as well as community meeting hall. 1422 SW 11th, Portland 97201 (222–2031).

Prairie City: *De Witt Museum.* Early mining and ranching equipment. Box 577, Prairie City 97869 (820–3605).

Prineville: *Prineville Museum.* In log cabin, Pioneer Park. Artifacts of early homesteader life. Prineville, 97754 (447–5627).

Roseburg: *Lane House.* Home of Gen. Joseph Lane, first territorial governor of Oregon. 544 SE Douglas St., Roseburg 97470 (459–1393).

Douglas County Museum. Award-winning structure features displays of pioneer logging equipment and steam traction engine. Fairgrounds. Roseburg 97470 (440–4507).

Salem: *Criterion School.* Rural schoolhouse used from 1912 to 1925. Moved from near Maupin, Oregon, in 1975 and restored. Open during the Oregon State Fair each year. Operated by Oregon Dept. of Education, Salem 97310 (378–8429).

School for the Deaf Museum. Old furniture, records, and memorabilia of the Oregon State School for the Deaf. 999 Locust St. Salem 97303 (378–3825).

Mission Mill Village. Original site of the Thomas Kay Woolen Mills established in 1889. Now houses museum of the pioneer woolen industry. Included in the village are the Jason Lee Home & Parsonage (1841), John D. Boon Home (1847), Pioneer Presbyterian Church (1858), restored water power system, and more. 13th and Mill St., Salem 97301 (585–7012).

Marion Museum of History. Noteworthy display of annals of Marion County. In Northwest corner of Mission Mill Village, 1313 Mill St., Salem 97301 (364–2128).

Jason Lee Home and Parsonage. The two oldest buildings in Oregon, both reputedly built in 1841, stand near the pioneer Thomas Kay Woolen Mill, 12th & Ferry Sts., in Salem.

Asahel Bush House. Italianate mansion, 1878. Home of Democratic leader, newspaper editor, territorial and state printer and banker. Original wall papers, marble fireplaces, original and period furnishings. 600 Mission St., SE. Salem 97301 (363–1825).

The Dalles: *Fort Dalles Museum.* Surgeon's quarters of old Ft. Dalles, cavalry post with genuine mid-19th century atmosphere. 15th and Garrison St., The Dalles 97058 (296–2231).

Tillamook: *Pioneer Museum.* Finest wildlife dioramas in state. Excellently displayed pioneer relics. Across from county courthouse, downtown. Tillamook 97141.

Woodburn: *Jessie Settlemier House.* Queen Anne Mansion, built in 1889. Period rooms. 355 N Settlemier Ave. Woodburn 97071 (982–9363).

INDIANS. Oregon has four main groupings: *Klamath,* in south-central; *Umatilla,* near Pendleton in northeastern part; *Confederated Tribes of the Warm Springs Reservation* (Paiute, Wasco, and Warm Springs), occupying a half-million-plus-acre swath of generally arid land about 100 miles southeast of Portland; and the *Siletz,* on the Coast, who regained tribal status in 1977 and were given deeds to about 4,000 acres of federal land.

For all practical purposes the state contains two reservations: the Umatilla and the Warm Springs. The 85,000-acre Umatilla is much the smaller and poorer, and there seems to be little planning for the future; the atmosphere is depressed. The Warm Springs Indians have a long-range program to develop industry, elevate their standard of living, educate their youth, and put themselves into the mainstream of the dominant culture while trying to maintain and revive their ancestral traditions and crafts.

The Warm Springs Indians have done much to attract the tourist dollars of the whites, building a plush resort, Kah-nee-ta, a hot springs spa, with luxurious lodge, cabins, tepees, camp sites, trailer sites, elegant restaurant, Indian Crafts shop, mineral baths, massage room, Olympic-size swimming pool complex, miniature golf course. Spa also has horseback riding, fishing, hiking trails, bicycling trails. Current events are held in the lodge, built to attract conventions.

Special events on and near the reservation are the Warm Springs Rodeo, in April; the Root Festival, in the spring, usually around April; the Tygh Valley Celebration in connection with the All-Indian Rodeo there, in May; Parade and

Indian dances, on the Fourth of July; the Huckleberry Festival, sometime in August, depending on when the berries ripen; and Labor Day Rodeo and Indian Dancing, in September. In late May there is another All-Indian Rodeo, staged at Klamath Falls. The Umatillas have a Lincoln's Birthday celebration in February; a Root Festival in late April or May; Veterans' Day celebration and Thanksgiving Week Pot Luck Dinner, in November; and Christmas Celebration, with dancing, in December. Indians participate in Chief Joseph Days, centered around a rodeo at Joseph, in late July. An Indian tepee village is part of the Pendleton Round-Up and Happy Canyon Pageant, held in Pendleton in mid-September.

ART MUSEUMS AND GALLERIES. Coos Bay: *Coos Art Museum.* Gaining a reputation as focal point for Southwest Oregon art. 235 Anderson, Coos Bay 97420 (267–3901).

Coquille: *Coquille Valley Art Association.* Permanent and changing exhibitions of paintings and textiles by state artists. 587 N Elliott, Coquille 97423 (396–3294).

Corvallis: *Corvallis Art Center.* Changing exhibits at Oregon State University. 700 S.W. Madison, Corvallis 97333 (754–1551).

Enterprise: *Wallowa Valley Arts Council.* Center of art for the Wallowa Valley; magnet for expatriates to the Wallowa Mountains. Box 306, Enterprise 97828 (432–8901).

Eugene: *Art Museum,* University of Oregon, Eugene 97403 (686–3027). *Maude Kerns Art Center.* Quality exhibits of regional and contemporary fine art and craft. 1910 E. 15th Ave., Eugene 97403 (345–1571).

Klamath Falls: *Favell Museum of Western Art and Indian Artifacts.* Originals of some famous Western artists. 125 W. Main, Eugene 97601 (882–9996).

Lincoln City: *Lincoln City Art Guild* displays top Northwest painters. 4840 S.E. Hwy 101, Lincoln City 97367 (996–3403).

Portland: *Portland Art Museum.* Northwest Indian artifacts collection of antiques, silver, paintings, and sculpture. Also famous paintings from around the world often on loan here. 1219 SW Park, Portland 97201 (226–2811).

Roseburg: *Umpqua Valley Arts Center.* A cultural facility specializing in the development of regional artists. 1624 W. Harvard Blvd., Roseburg 97470 (672–2532).

Salem: *Bush House and Bush Barn Art Center.* Gallery and collection of costumes, decorative arts. 600 Mission St. SE, Salem 97302 (363–4714).

SPECIAL-INTEREST MUSEUMS. Portland: *Oregon Museum of Science and Industry (OMSI).* A plethora of varied exhibits and how-to-do-it operations that surely has something of interest for everyone. Open daily. Nominal fee. *World Forestry Center,* near OMSI and Zoo. The best "trees" museum in the state. Open daily. Nominal fee. Astoria: *Columbia River Maritime Museum.* The best of its kind by far in Oregon. Open daily May-Sept. Nominal fee. Lightship, docked at pier, but part of Maritime Museum, open only in summer. Nominal fee. Corvallis: *Natural History Museum.* Oregon State University. Many specimens of birds and animals. Open daily except Sunday; closed mid-June through Sept. Closed holidays. Free. Glenwood: *Trolley Park.* Ride trolleys from three continents in lovely wooded area. Open daily in summer. Fee. Klamath Falls: *Collier State Park Logging Museum* (30 miles north of Klamath Falls). A veritable history of early-day logging in Oregon. Open daily. Free. Newport: Oregon State University *Marine Science Center.* Exhibits of sea life and marine-science displays. Open daily. Closed Christmas and New Year's. Free. *Old Yaquina Bay Lighthouse.* A true, unvarnished picture of an early-day lighthouse. Climb to the top, where the light was. Open Tues.-Sun. June–Sept.; Fri.-Sun. Oct.-May. Fee. Aurora: *Champoeg State Park Museum.* Steamboat wheels and mementos of founders of Provisional Government of Oregon. Open daily May-Sept.; Fri.-Sun., Oct.-April. Free. Silverton: *Mikkelson Farm* (one mile out of town, on Pine St.). Largest collection of steam-engine threshers in Pacific Northwest. Open daily. Free.

WINERIES. Among Oregon wineries that are free for visiting are: *Bjelland Vineyards,* Rt. 4, Box 931, Roseburg, (503–679–6950); *Amity Vineyards,* Rt. 1, Box 348-B, Amity (503–835–2362); *Century Home Wines,* Rt. 2, Box 111, Newberg (503–538–6710); *The Eyrie Vineyards,* 935 East 10th Ave., McMinnville (503–864–2410); *Hillcrest Vineyard,* 240 Vineyard Lane, Roseburg (503–673–3709); *Honeywood Winery,* 501 14th St. S.E., Salem (503–362–4111); *Oak Knoll Winery,* Rt. 6, Box 184, Hillsboro (503–648–8198); *Elk Cove Vineyards,* Rt. 3, Box 23, Gaston (503–958–7760).

MUSIC. Since 1949, a summertime *Music by Moonlight* program of free concerts sponsored by the Portland Park Bureau has been held at Washington Park. Performances generally include folk-dance recitals, jazz concerts, drum and bugle corps, musical plays, and ballet. Starting time: 8:30 P.M. Other city parks offer summer band concerts on a flexible schedule, weekdays as well as weekends, daytime as well as evening. From late July to mid-August.

The Portland Opera Association, featuring famous singers, presents four operas during its annual season, which starts at the end of Sept. and runs thru May. All operas are performed three times: Sat., Wed., Sat. Performances start at 8 P.M. at the Civic Auditorium. Tickets for all operas go on sale at the Civic Auditorium and Portland Opera ticket office the day after Labor Day. Season schedules may be obtained by writing to: Portland Opera Association, 1530 S.W. 2nd Ave., Portland, OR 97201. (241–1407).

The Oregon Symphony Orchestra, during its concert season from Sept. through June, presents 12 classical triples, Sun., Mon. and Tues. evening concerts, starting Sun. at 7:30 P.M. and Mon. and Tues. at 8:00 P.M. In addition, there are a series of 6 "Pops" concerts, on Sun., Mon. and Tue. Starting time 3 P.M. and 8 P.M. on Sundays; 8 P.M. Mon. and Tue. There is also a family concert series, Sun. afternoons at 3 P.M. Oct. through May. 813 S.W. Alder, Portland 97205 (228–4296).

Chamber Music Northwest presents a series of Summer Chamber Music Concerts at Reed College and Catlin Gable School, consisting of 25 performances during a five-week season in June and July with 30 nationally and internationally acclaimed artists. Check with Chamber Music Northwest, for concert dates. Suite 418, 421 SW 6th, Portland 97204 (223–3202).

Statewide, the biggest musical happening is held at the historic gold mining town of Jacksonville, 16 days each August, starting early in the morning. The *Peter Britt Music Festival* is aimed to coincide with the Shakespearean Festival at nearby Ashland. The music festival presents the work of a selected composer performed by string and woodwind groups, soloists, and vocalists. At the University of Oregon campus, Eugene, the *Summer Festival of Music* is a 2-week series of orchestra and choral concerts featuring nationally acclaimed guest artists. In late June and early July. Since 1983, opera has been presented at the downtown Hult Center of Performing Arts in Eugene.

STAGE AND REVUES. In the summer the focus of attention is on the *Oregon Shakeapearean Festival,* in Ashland, which presents matinee and evening performances in a replica of the Globe Theater in beautiful Lithia Park and in an indoor theater from early June to early October. Two theaters, approaching year-round schedules, present modern plays. For additional information on the Festival, write: Shakespeare, Box 605, Ashland, OR 97520.

The 1926-founded *Portland Civic Theatre,* 1530 S.W. Yamhill, at the edge of the downtown district, offers a varied fare, classic to contemporary, including musicals, all through the year, both on its main stage and Blue Room "theater-in-the-round." From Sept. to June, performances Thurs., Fri., Sat., Sun. nights, and in the Summer Repertory, June, July, and Aug., the company performs Thurs., Fri., Sat. and Sun. nights. Curtain time is 8 P.M. From Oct. to May there are also intermittent Sat. morning and matinee performances of the *Children's Theatre.* On the first Tue. of every month from Oct. thru May, at 10:30 A.M., the *Theatre Guild* presents readings of play excerpts, poetry, etc. Admission to all performances is quite reasonable. Portland 97205.

New Rose Theater innovatively presents plays year-round in the basement of the Masonic Hall, 1119 S.W. Park.

Willamette Repertory Theater (S.W. First and Salmon), staging performances Thursday thru Sunday, is strong on popular, modern drama and concentrates on long stage runs. Four plays are presented each year with nationally known directors.

Storefront Actors Theatre, 6 S.W. 3rd Ave. (in renovated skid row porno film house), Portland, presents innovative "way-out" revues and plays the year round. Five productions a year, including three originals. Thurs., Fri., and Sat. evenings, 8 P.M.

Community Theatre of the Cascades, in Bend, draws finest talent in central Oregon to stage summer productions of varied theatrical fare in one of finest natural settings in state.

In the Medford Area, old-time melodrama and olio theatre are presented during the summer months at the Minshall Theatre, 101 Talent Ave.

The Coaster Theater, at Cannon Beach (on the Coast), is the summer program for students at Portland State University's Theater Arts Department. Performances Thurs. through Sat., starting at 8:30 P.M. During winter, Cannon Beach residents put on their own productions, including Dickens at Christmas time, at the theater and are initiating year-round theater fare.

In Coquille, the community-enterprise *Sawdust Theater* stages melodramas and olios every Sat., May 29–Sept. 4.

At Cave Junction, the *Valley Players Theatre Group* performs from June through Sept. at Illinois Valley festivals.

Grants Pass came of artistic age with its exuberant *Barnstormers Little Theater.*

Close to Portland, at Forest Grove, *Theatre-in-the Grove* operates from a building on the main drag. Forty miles south of Portland, at McMinnville, *The Gallery Players of Oregon* (150 Linfield Ave.) range the gamut of drama. Fifty miles south of Portland, at Salem, the *Pentacle Theatre,* with its own building on the outskirts of the state capital, has an exciting theater-in-the-round during the warm months.

Farther down the Willamette Valley, Albany has a *Civic Theater* and the *Eugene Very Little Theatre* (2350 Hilyard St.) has shown stagecraft ingenuity. The city's Hult Center for the Performing Arts is the site of many offerings by Eugene's proliferating drama, music and dance groups.

On the Coast, theatrical groups, comprised chiefly of happy, enthusiastic amateurs who perform their labors of love mainly in the summer are: *The Little Theater on the Bay,* Coos Bay; and the *Northcoast Repertory Theatre,* Astoria.

East of the Cascades is the new *Community Theater* of Klamath Falls.

Throughout the state, excellent stage presentations are offered by colleges and universities. Central Oregon Community College, at Bend, is equally strong on musicals and drama; Mount Hood Community College, at Gresham, has a fine repertory group; the University of Oregon, at Eugene, provides opportunities for serious-minded, stage-oriented students with a varied schedule; Oregon State University, at Corvallis, is bursting into prominence with presentations at its Mitchell Playhouse; and Lewis and Clark College and the University of Portland, at Portland, have done notable experimentation in stagecraft.

Then, of course, there are the small town groups, such as the *Bandon Playhouse* in Bandon (population 2,450).

NIGHTLIFE. Portland (and other Oregon) night clubs have a high mortality rate, so a popular place today may be empty or less entertaining tomorrow. The following were alive and in high gear at presstime:

Mary's Club, 129 S.W. Broadway, downtown, has Japanese food, days, and topless dancers, nights, to go with wine, beer, and pinball machines.

Taylor's Viewpoint, 8102 N.E. Killingsworth, draws people for its dancing and live entertainment as well as dining. *BeBop USA* swings all week, with complimentary buffet, at 11753 S.W. Beaverton Hwy. *Sylvia's,* 5115 N.E. Sandy

Blvd., has dinner show run on repertory theater concept. *The Drum,* 14601 S.E. Division, has live Western music and dancing nightly. *Key Largo,* 31 N.W. 1st Ave., has dining, dancing, and live entertainment nightly. *Peppertree* at Holiday Inn/Portland Airport, 8349 N.E. Columbia Blvd., zings with live entertainment nightly. *Boiler Room* in the Steamers Restaurant of the Rodeway Inn at the Airport, 8247 N.E. Sandy, is disco-happy 7 nights a week. Right outside the airport, *The Showplace Lounge* at the Sheraton-Portland Airport has soft music to relax weary travelers. *Darcelle XV,* 208 N.W. 3rd Ave., in Old Town, draws an off-beat crowd with its array of female impersonators. At suburban Beaverton, the *Pavilion,* in the Greenwood Inn, 107 S.W. Allen Blvd., presents up-and-coming talent. A novelty of sorts is *City Nightclub,* 624 S.W. 13th, downtown, a favorite of the financial district yuppies.

At Lincoln City, on the Oregon Coast, there are casual dining and candlelight dancing in the *Cedar Tree* at Salishan Lodge during the summer season; and "over-the-waves" dancing in the lounge of the *Surftides Beach Resort.* North up the coast an easy drive, *River Sea Inn* in Wheeler has "Sunset Live Dinner Theatre." The Crab Tree Broiler, near Cannon Beach, has a lovely *Fireside Lounge* outside a beautiful Japanese garden.

Elsewhere in the state, Bliss Steak Ranch, in Eugene, has a video screen in its *Red Dog Saloon* for sports watching. If you have a horse along, you can tie it to the hitching rail. Dancing nightly in the *Bunkhouse Cocktail Lounge.* At Grants Pass, *Shepp's Sportsman Inn* offers dancing every night, with live music weekends in its lounge by a waterfall. In central Oregon, *Owl's Nest Cocktail Lounge* in the Sunriver Lodge, at Sunriver, 15 miles South of Bend on US 97, looks up to the snow-covered Cascades. On the southern Oregon Coast, there is dockside dancing in the *Sea Horse Lounge* in Sporthaven, at Brookings. Over on the other side of the state, on the shore of the Snake River, which separates Oregon from Idaho, *Moore's Alley* in Ontario has entertainment nightly in a 1910-period lounge. *The Riverhouse Motor Inn Lounge* in Bend is the center of swinging sophistication in central Oregon.

BARS. You can get high before your first highball when perched in the *Agate Bar* at the Top of the Cosmos, Cosmopolitan Hotel, 1030 N.E. Union Ave., in Portland. So as not to distract anyone from the spectacular view of Portland at night, illumination comes from beneath the polished agate table and bar tops. An even more awesome view of the city is from *Panorama,* on the 23rd—and top—floor of the Hilton Hotel, in the heart of downtown Portland. *Piccadilly Bar,* at the Benson Hotel, on Broadway near Burnside, downtown Portland, has everything of sophisticated London but the fog. *Stanich Ten Till One Tavern,* 4915 N.E. Fremont, Portland, has the most fabulous hamburgers in town (one—exotically put together—is a full meal) and good cheer that has made tour guides out of residents in the area from visitors: "How do I get to Stanich's?" *Produce Row Cafe,* 204 S.E. Oak, Portland, has been described as the "beer drinker's beer drinking heaven." Eleven varieties of beer are on tap, 5 American & 6 European. Twenty-three varieties of domestic bottled beer and 22 imported varieties from 11 countries. *Hospital Pub,* 2845 S.E. Stark, has nightly live music, blues jam Mon. nights, large dance floor, no cover, big screen TV, and pool tables. *Goose Hollow Inn,* 1927 S.W. Jefferson, is the Greenwich Village showplace of Portland, where people gather to be seen and see as well as eat and drink. Monday has been set aside for nonsmokers. Most talked-about of the Portland-area bistros is *Earthquake Ethel's Roadhouse,* at 2970 S.W. Cedar Hills Blvd., Beaverton, adjoining Portland from the west. The legend is that Ethel's is built on a fault, but if there was an earthquake, who could tell it? There are 3 dance floors, 2 bars, more than 20,000 lights, 52 power amplifiers and 72 speakers in this wall-to-wall dancing nocturnal circus. Ethel's has inexpensive drinks, a dazzling light show, and enough noise to drown out an air raid. *Helvetia Tavern,* on Helvetia Road off Sunset Road (U.S. 26), about 30 minutes' drive from Portland, has the best hamburgers in the state. The beer is also good—and everything inexpensive—but the backcountry cosmopolitan charm is best of all. The people are their own amusement, better than the jukebox, the pool table, and the Wed. night bingo. Folks, from big city celebrities to simple folk who want to go safely adventuring, drive as far as 100 miles to get here. You can't miss the tavern; it's the only business in Helvetia, which otherwise boasts all of two houses. *Rock Creek Tavern,* in a former blacksmith shop west of Portland, is a magnet for the younger set. There are many colorful taverns outside Portland, especially in the small logging and cowtowns. In Hines, *The Egan Tavern* has been doing business in Hines since 1882. *The Gatehouse,* in Eugene, competes with University of Oregon athletics by offering pool, air hockey and football. In Silverton, *Wooden Nickel Tavern,* on the road to Mt. Angel, draws happy-seekers from the several towns around. In central Oregon, right in downtown Bend, the *Ore House Bar & Grill* has live entertainment nightly. At *Woody's Place,* in Baker, mountain vacationers mix with city folks and ranchers for jovial companionship. In south central Oregon, in Lakeview, *Round-Up Tavern* has a lively logging-country atmosphere. In Paisley, the *Pioneer Saloon* has a cattle drive atmosphere in a cowspread valley town.

LIQUOR LAWS. Minimum age for consumption of any alcoholic beverage in Oregon is 21. Bottled hard liquor is sold only at liquor stores. Beer and wine of less than 21 percent alcohol content can be bought at grocery stores. Taverns, open until 2:30 A.M., sell beer and wine to consume and take out. Cocktails are served at licensed bars, usually open until 2:30 A.M. Helpful hint for those who have passed their 21st birthday but don't look it, or for those who don't have driver's license: Motor Vehicles Dept. issues ID cards without cost. If you're an Oregon driver, no other ID but driver's license with photo is needed. Drivers' licenses with photos from other states are valid.

UTAH

The Outdoor Amphitheater

by
HARRY E. FULLER, JR.

Harry Fuller has lived for twenty-two years in Salt Lake City, where he is an editorial writer for the Salt Lake Tribune.

Salt Lake City

Salt Lake City's greatest single attraction for visitors is the Temple Square area. This is the sacred ground of Mormonism. Here, on two ten-acre blocks flanking Main Street, in the middle of town, are the central religious shrines of Latter-Day Saint worship. The Temple block, on the west, is surrounded by a 15-foot-high masonry wall. On the grounds stand the Temple, Museum, Tabernacle, Seagull Monument, Assembly Hall and Visitors Center. Curbside parking is available around Temple Square.

Guided tours are offered on the Temple grounds every half-hour. On the itinerary is the Tabernacle, which houses the famous Temple Square pipe organ and from where Sunday Tabernacle Choir concerts are broadcast. This is an elongated structure with rounded ends that resembles a grounded dirigible. It is actually 250 feet long and 150 feet wide. Its vaulted self-supporting roof is 70 feet from the floor. Completed in 1867, the building can seat over 5,000 and is used for the church's biannual conferences. It also served many years as a cultural center, where the Utah Symphony presented its season and visiting concert artists performed. Those programs are now presented in the city's new concert hall at the Salt Palace Center sport and convention complex.

As an auditorium, the Tabernacle is known for its remarkable acoustics, although you can get an argument from different performers about whether the sound-carrying qualities are really helpful. In any case, no listener misses much. The choir, 375 mixed voices, was organized in the early 1850's and can be heard free during its Thursday evening rehearsals as well as on Sundays, when the formal program is presented in its entirety.

South of the Tabernacle is Assembly Hall, a gray, granite structure seating 2,000, which also doubles as a lecture hall and place of worship. Facing the hall's east entrance is the Seagull Monument, said to be America's only historic monument to birds. It commemorates "The Miracle of the Gulls." In 1848 swarms of crickets descended from the mountain slopes to devour the pioneers' crop, the food that would protect them from famine the following winter. All eradication methods were insufficient and after the Mormons turned to prayer, flocks of seagulls appeared from the west, gorging themselves on crickets and rescuing the situation from certain disaster. Seagulls instantly earned an honored place in Mormon tradition.

Temple Square also holds monuments to the martyred Joseph Smith, the prophet, and his brother Hyrum, and the Three Witnesses Monument, with bronze bas-relief of the trio who testified that an angel showed them the golden plates from which the Book of Mormon was translated. A pedestaled statue of Brigham Young stands outside the Temple Square, at its southeast corner, in the intersection of Main St. and South Temple St.

Dominating Temple Square is the Temple itself, which is closed to non-Mormons. Although there are six other LDS temples in Utah, the Salt Lake City version has a majesty and singularity about it denied the others. Its architectural style is imprecise. Some have called it "Mormon Gothic," and the appearance is not dissimilar from Europe's Middle Ages cathedrals. And yet it departs from that design, too. In any case, the building was dedicated in 1893, exactly forty years to a day after ground was broken for the foundation. Granite for its 167-foot-high walls was quarried from the nearby mountains and first dragged by oxen and mules to the building site. Later, rails were used for transportation. At each end of the 163-foot-long, 100-foot-wide edifice rise three spire-tipped towers, the highest, 204 feet in the air, centered above the east façade. Balanced on that point is a gilded statue of the angel Moroni, heralding toward the east with a long-stemmed trumpet. According to Joseph Smith, it was Moroni, pronounced Mo-rown-eye, who led him to the golden plates engraved with hieroglyphics described as "Reformed Egyptian." Smith testified that with heavenly aid he was allowed to translate the record into English. Two years of laborious writing became the Book of Mormon. By 1830, Smith had six followers and the beginning of the Church of Jesus Christ, which eventually lengthened into the Church of Jesus Christ of Latter-Day Saints.

SALT LAKE CITY

Points of Interest

1) Beehive House
2) Brigham Young's Grave
3) Brigham Young Statue
4) Cathedral of the Madeleine
5) City County Building
6) Council Hall
7) University of Utah and Museum of Natural History
8) Hansen Planetarium
9) Memory Grove
10) Mormon Temple
11) Pioneer Memorial Museum
12) Promised Valley Theater
13) Saint Mark's Cathedral
14) Salt Palace and Concert Hall
15) Seagull Monument
16) State Capitol
17) Tabernacle & Assembly Hall
18) Utah Governor's Mansion
19) Utah State Historical Society

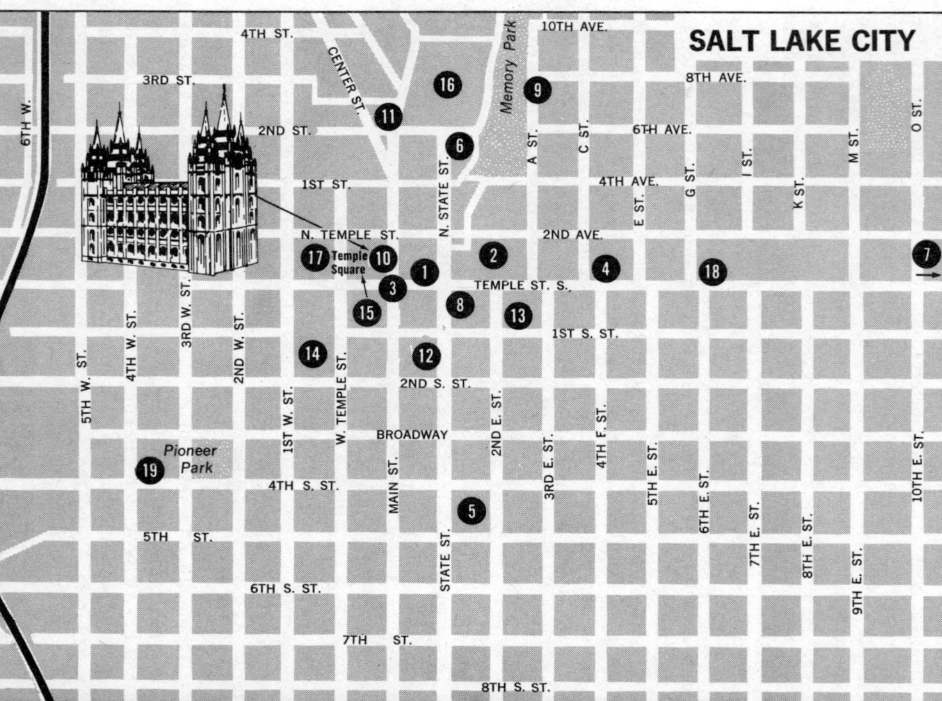

Capitol Hill

Salt Lake City is the state's capital city and Capitol Hill is worth a visit. It is reached on State Street, moving under restored Eagle Gate, marking the original entrance to Brigham Young's northside estate. On the hill, city dwellers used to gather wood from the prophet's grounds. Now forty acres are carefully landscaped around the granite and marble statehouse and office building. Completed in 1914, the copper-domed Capitol was designed for largely ceremonial uses, although it contained chambers for two houses of the bicameral legislature, the five-member State Supreme Court and the governor's office. Extensive interior remodeling has made space for administrative agencies. Expanding state government also led to construction in the late 1950's of an office building, north, across a plaza from the older structure. The capitol's first-floor hallway is lined with showcases exhibiting the qualities of every Utah county, mostly by region. Though sometimes slightly outdated, the displays are accurate enough to be instructive.

A favorite attraction is the original Mormon Meteor, the piston-driven car in which Ab Jenkins set endurance records at the Bonneville Speedway some forty years ago. The speedway is about 120 miles west of Salt Lake City and in the Great Salt Lake Desert. It still hosts drivers and their crews attempting to set every imaginable land speed mark, in rocket cars, stock engine vehicles and motorcycles. The activity grows brisk toward summer's end, when the salt flats have dried to a table-top firmness, and continues until weather conditions force a halt, usually by November.

Skiing Around Salt Lake City

A central exhibit in the Capitol display consists of a large relief map of the state, shaped by the U.S. Forest Service. The mountain terrain around Salt Lake City stands out conspicuously, indicating why, in 1962, the city was selected as this country's nominee for the 1964 Winter Olympics. Skiing is the area's chief winter pastime. East from the city, up two adjacent canyons are four ski areas that rival any in the U.S. for snow depth and consistency. Big Cottonwood Canyon leads to Solitude and Brighton. Little Cottonwood Canyon, a few miles farther south, trails up the mountain side to Snowbird and famed Alta. All operate a complex of chair lifts, but Snowbird features an aerial tramway that ferries skiers and sightseers to the top of 11,000-foot-high Hidden Peak. The 2,900-foot trip takes about six minutes, and each of two cars carries 125 passengers in warm, dry enclosures. Snowbird is a year-round resort, with a village consisting of hotel, restaurant and condominium accommodations. It hosts conventions throughout most of the year.

On the east side of the mountains, Salt Lake City residents have been skiing at Park City for more than a decade. Originally a mining town, Park City made a comeback from "ghost" status when its recreational potential was discovered. Developers have since filled vacant property with new condominium groupings, close to skiing in winter and golf courses and tennis courts in summer. Downtown Park City has retained much of its old mining character. As a "Gentile" town, Park City differs markedly from other Utah communities. Its streets are two-lane, it has more former saloons on the Main Street and its past is charred by horrendous fires that repeatedly leveled homes, stores, bars, churches and schools. Most of the mine owners, who took their riches from hills around Park City, lived in Salt Lake City. Today, remaining homes built by these mineral kings can be seen lining South Temple Street east of Brigham Street. One, belonging to the Thomas Kearns family, was eventually deeded to the state and served as the governor's mansion. In the 1950's it was transferred to the Utah Historical Society for use as an office and a library when a new governor's residence was built. In 1977, the State Legislature authorized the governor's family to move back into the old Kearns mansion following its renovation, completed in 1980.

"This Is the Place"

South Temple is a good street to follow east from downtown. It leads to the University of Utah, laid out on a fine vantage point from which to view the city below. The campus, set on 1,500 acres, was animated by a massive building program during the 1960's. New structures and landscaping created a particularly engaging combination at the institution's southern half, which embraces pleasant walkways and fountains. The north half is older, the original campus, but well cared-for and a portal to nostalgia. It also contains a highly regarded Museum of Natural History, housed in the university's former library. Guided tours are available. The school of architecture maintains a Fine Arts Museum, and the school's various theaters and auditoriums produce year-round drama, ballet, popular music festivals and classical recitals. Ballet West, a professional troupe supported by the intermountain region, was homebased at the university until it obtained new facilities in downtown Salt Lake City. On the campus edge, the Art Barn provides new showings of contemporary paintings, drawings, photography, sculptures and industrial art about every three weeks. The university's teaching hospital is nationally acclaimed, the only one between Denver and the West Coast. Its researchers have excelled in bone, blood and organ transplant work. Worldwide attention focused here in 1982 when Barney Clark became the first recipient of an entirely artificial heart. The University Hospital and Medical Center is state-supported and was made possible by substantial federal financing. The campus has always been aware of the U.S. Government. At its back is the 9,000-acre Fort Douglas Military Reservation, complete with barracks, officers quarters and parade grounds. Much was declared surplus by the Pentagon and deeded to the state, to serve the university and other purposes. One of the other uses will be to enlarge Pioneer Trail State Park, which is south of the university and approximately at the spot where Brigham Young is supposed to have uttered his famous line, "This is the place," after emerging from Emigration Canyon overlooking Salt Lake Valley.

More precise historians quote Brigham as actually saying: "It is enough. This is the right place. Drive on!" And he knew exactly where he was going. That had been decided after advanced parties reported back about the prospects near the Great Salt Lake. In any case, the park has a "This is the Place Monument," a stone shaft and flanking extensions decorated by bronze figures of such early area explorers as Jim Bridger, Father Escalante and General John Fremont. The State Parks & Recreation Division has developed a Pioneer Village on the park area grounds. Nearby stands a visitors center with murals telling the story of the Mormon migrations. Opposite the monument is Salt Lake City's Hogle Zoological Gardens, a well-stocked, neatly kept zoo.

Below the zoo, south on Wasatch Boulevard, is a shopping center fairly typical of many that dot neighborhoods in the Salt Lake Valley. At least five are indoor "shopping malls," the most unique located at 7th East and 5th South. It is called Trolley Square because it is in converted streetcar barns dating back to 1908. Tastefully remodeled for functional purposes, this shopping mall boasts more than 120 tenants, ranging from specialty stores, snack bars and a farmers market to restaurants and night spots. Six small, but comfortable theaters operate in the adjacent building. The location is marked by a gold-painted and iron-ornamented water tower. Light bulb trimming gives the tank and its embellishments a special night-time appearance. Trolley Square is an extraordinary example of commercial recycling.

America's First Department Store

New enclosed shopping malls flank upper Main St. in downtown Salt Lake City. The latest is Crossroads Mall, directly opposite the historical ZCMI Mall. The initials stand for Zion's Cooperative Mercantile Institution. It was Brigham Young's answer to storekeepers who seemed to be profiteering among the early, struggling Mormon settlement in Salt Lake Valley. In 1868 he simply put the Church in the retailing business and neutralized the competition. As it evolved, ZCMI is claimed by some to be America's first department store. Whatever the fact on that score, ZCMI is Utah's leading department store today and its new downtown building devoured the old structure, which was actually a collection of stores at the corner of Main Street and South Temple. Retained, however, as part of the new building's façade, is the cast-iron front that decorated ZCMI's Main Street entrances for decades. Another compromise between old and new can be seen on 1st South between Main and West Temple Streets. This short block was "renovated" in 1970, given new sidewalks, a median strip planted with seedling trees and stone benches at the corners. Yet the street lighting shines from vintage candelabra lamp posts, deliberately installed to retain a dated, but ageless, ingredient. This street leads to the new Salt Lake County civic auditorium, called the Salt Palace. It seats 14,000 in the main arena and has 30 smaller meeting and exhibition rooms, as well as a little theater. A separate fine arts and concert hall stands north of the main building.

Advent of the Salt Palace has transformed the city's downtown west side. A restaurant and specialty shop compound, entitled Arrow Press Square, blossomed from three aged, rejuvenated brick buildings opposite the Salt Palace on West Temple. Five new hotels were constructed in the immediate vicinity. All in all, the effect has been a wholesome one. A National Basketball Assn. team, the Utah Jazz, and a minor league hockey team, the Golden Eagles, use the arena through the winter season. The building's versatility accommodates circuses, track meets, concerts and rodeos. It has become the modern home of the Pioneer Days rodeo.

Logan

Logan, at the junction of US 91 and 89, is the commercial hub of northeastern Utah. It is the location of Utah State University, original-

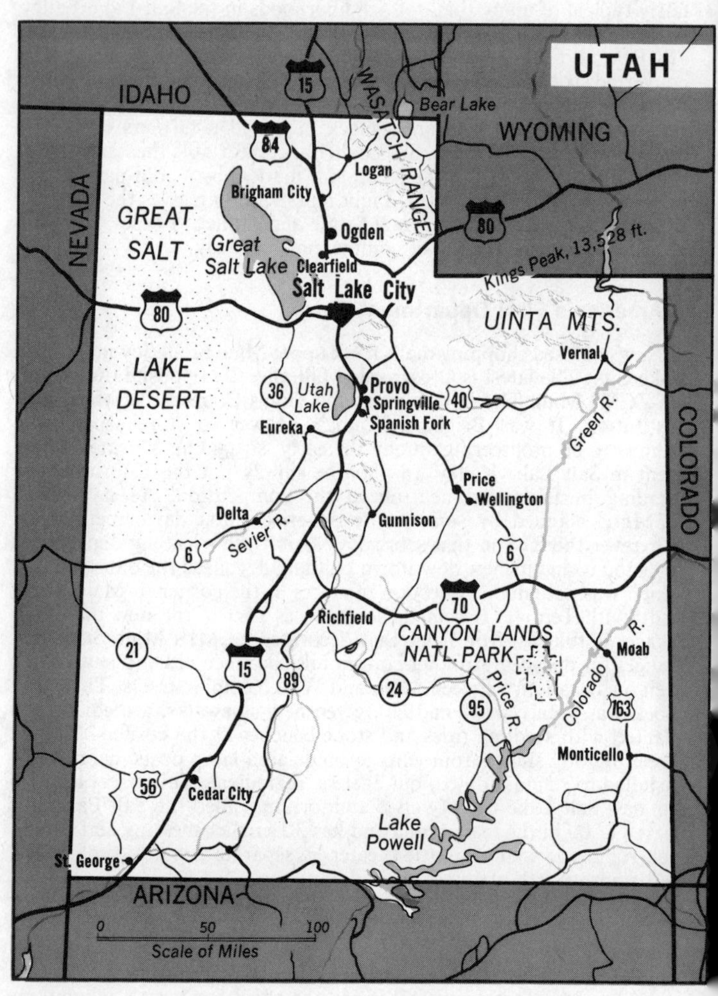
UTAH
IDAHO
WYOMING
NEVADA
COLORADO
ARIZONA
15
84
80
WASATCH RANGE
Bear Lake
Logan
Brigham City
Ogden
Clearfield
GREAT SALT
Great Salt Lake
Salt Lake City
Kings Peak, 13,528 ft.
UINTA MTS.
Vernal
LAKE DESERT
36
Utah Lake
Provo
Springville
Spanish Fork
40
Eureka
Green R.
Price
Wellington
Delta
Gunnison
Sevier R.
6
70
Richfield
CANYON LANDS NATL. PARK
21
89
24
95
Price R.
Colorado R.
Moab
163
Monticello
56
Cedar City
Lake Powell
St. George
0
50
100
Scale of Miles

ly limited to agricultural and forestry studies, which currently offers other courses as well, and boasts nationally ranked football and basketball teams. Logan also has one of Utah's seven Mormon temples, a stone-hewn structure, finely landscaped and flower decorated during summer months.

Nine miles south and sixteen miles east of Logan, through Hyrum on State 101, a rare encounter is staged every winter. The Utah Wildlife Division has established, at a place called Hardware Ranch, an elk feeding station. The animals, mostly cows and an occasional lame bull, congregate in the snow to survive on daily alfalfa handouts. Visitors are transported into the midst of the herd by horse-drawn sleighs. It's a singular experience, mingling with five hundred seldom-seen creatures, approachable only because of their hunger.

Another entry to Utah known by the mountain men is along the present Interstate 80. It leads, after a junction at Echo, forty-three miles beyond Wyoming, to either Ogden or Salt Lake City. The I–80 branch traverses stunning Weber Canyon on its way to Ogden. Near Morgan, the super highway gives travelers an opportunity to view Devil's Slide, two parallel slabs of limestone twenty feet apart and forty feet high sticking to the mountain side. It helped conjure many Indian legends.

The Coming of the Railroad

Ogden, thirty-three miles north of Salt Lake City, is Utah's third largest city with 64,000 residents. It was also planned by Brigham Young, but, after the arrival of transcontinental rails in 1868, Ogden gained the reputation as a railroad town. It was, during those track-laying days, a brawling, free-for-all hot spot, causing the Mormon population considerable unease.

Now the city is a quieter commercial and industrial center, beneficiary of a new church temple and home of Weber State College, a four-year vocational and liberal arts school. With the help of an active industrial development program and several federal installations—Hill Air Force Base and an Internal Revenue Service computer center and Regional Forest Service office—Ogden continues to progress. The Browning brothers, inventors of automatic weapons, were from Ogden. The John M. Browning Armory and Firearms Museum displays eighty-six original and production models of Browning rifles, pistols and machine guns.

On I–15, northwest from Ogden, in an especially tranquil setting, is Brigham City, given a space-age boost by missile industry firms located nearby. Via Brigham City, off State 83, motorists can visit one of Utah's latest National Historic Sites—the Golden Spike site at Promontory. It features a tourist center and replicas of two engines used during the driving of the last spike which completed America's first transnation railroad. During summer months the 1869 ceremony is reenacted at the Golden Spike National Historic Site as the finale to a film, narration and tour of the museum.

The Northern Tier

Doubling back, through Brigham City toward Ogden, travelers can encounter a collection of bird management areas around bays on the east-central portion of Great Salt Lake. At Willard Bay State Park, summer regattas for both power and sail boats are held annually.

Utah's northern tier fluctuates dramatically, from the Great Salt Lake Desert on the western hand and the High Uintas Wilderness Area on the east. This magnificent slab of the Uinta Mountains, the only continental range running east and west, contains Utah's loftiest point —Kings Peak, 13,528 feet high. It is also the preferred terminal for backpackers and campers. Mirror Lake resort touches the wilderness area at its eastern extremity and can be reached on U–150 as soon as the road is cleared of snow, sometime in late spring. Uinta mountain lakes and streams are a hardy fisherman's challenge.

Fishing in northeastern Utah can be successful without being strenuous, especially at Flaming Gorge Reservoir behind Flaming Gorge Dam. This is a delightful outdoor offering tucked into the northern and most eastern corner of Utah, approximately 75 miles due north from Vernal. Previously a hunter and fisherman rendezvous, Vernal has also become the center for oil field development. The area has another distinction—prehistoric fossil remains at Dinosaur National Monument, 20 miles east of Vernal, where visitors can actually watch workmen patiently unearth bones of long-extinct giant reptiles. At Vernal, the state maintains the Field House of Natural Science, an exhibit of local geological features, prominent Utah scenes—not always up to date—and ancient Indian artifacts. This is Indian country.

The main highway between Vernal and Salt Lake City is US 40, which passes through the Uintah and Ouray Indian Reservation. The principal towns along this stretch are Roosevelt and Duchesne, but about seven miles east of Roosevelt is a modest experiment in contemporary Indian self-sufficiency. The Bottle Hollow Resort, a motel complex built alongside a 450-acre reservoir, is owned and operated by the Ute Indian Tribe. It derives its name from a previous custom of locals pitching empty liquor bottles into a natural depression in the brush dotted landscape between settlements at Roosevelt and Ft. Duchesne. The resort advertises ceremonial Indian performances and has a trading post dealing in native artwork and craft specialties.

On farther, closer to Salt Lake City, US 40 passes two more large fishing holes, Starvation and then Strawberry Reservoir, impounded sources of irrigation water also stocked with trout. Beyond, at Heber City, a left turn off US 40 leads to Provo along US 189. A right turn, staying with 40 to I–80, leads to Salt Lake City. Delaying at Heber City isn't a bad idea.

Heber is a familiar Mormon name, but the place could have easily been called Basel or Tavaness, anything from the Swiss foothills, as this is what the Heber Valley resembles. And it did to the Mormon converts from Switzerland who settled there. Directly west lies 22,000-acre Wasatch Mountain State Park, a hiking, camping and picnicking wayside that includes a 27-hole golf course nestled in a crisp Alpine setting.

Railroad Run

During summer months and also from Thanksgiving to New Year's Day, a steam engine known as the Heber Creeper hauls passengers from Heber City through Provo Canyon to Deer Creek Dam. The round trip meanders through meadowland, along streams and reservoirs while penetrating a mountain pass. It's a quaint way to sightsee.

Bridal Veil Falls is a double cataract that splashes in steep descent down Provo Canyon's sheer mountain walls. It's viewable from alongside US 189, and by a thrilling 1,228-foot tramway ride in summer. Provo Canyon is one of the principal passes slicing through the Wasatch Range and, most of the way, it follows Provo River, a premier trout stream. Also off US 189 in Provo Canyon is Sundance Resort, a development led by film actor Robert Redford. It features skiing during the winter and camping or horseback riding through the other seasons.

US 189 is an old, narrow road, but preferred by conservationists attempting to prevent a planned widening and straightening project. Whatever the outcome, the highway will still lead to Provo, Utah's second largest city.

Provo and BYU

Located at the foot of 11,000-foot-high Provo Peak, the city is typically Mormon, with clean, wide streets and well-tended landscaping. It is a combination farming, education and industrial center. The Mormon Church's biggest and best college campus graces Provo—Brigham Young University. Handsome and sprawling after a massive 1960's construction program, BYU, or "The BY," as it is colloquially called by many Utah admirers, attracts a 25,000-member student body from LDS families throughout the U.S. and foreign countries. Its rigid, and obeyed, code of conduct rivals its nationally ranked athletic teams for far-flung recognition. BYU administrators make a point of avoiding federal financing.

A U.S. Government decision to scatter basic industry during World War II gave the area around Provo a steel mill. Now owned and operated by the Columbia-Geneva Division of the U.S. Steel Corp., the mill has provided steady employment for over forty years, also persistent air pollution. Protecting air and water has been a problem in this area.

Utah Lake, twenty-three miles long north to south and ten miles wide, ripples just west of Provo. It is Utah's largest fresh-water lake. And while much of the water is fit for boating, fishing and water-skiing, parts are termed a health hazard by state officials. The culprit is sewage, being treated, but not under full control before it finds the lake. A wise swimmer looks first for posted warnings. The situation hasn't discouraged Saratoga, a lakeside amusement park that attracts sizable crowds all summer long.

Just south of Provo, on US 89, lies Springville, also called Art City. The honorary title goes with Springville's Art Museum, which contains an acclaimed collection of paintings and sculpture. In April, the permanent display is enhanced with an annual exhibit by nationally known artists.

To the north, near Lehi, is Timpanogos Cave National Monument. Located in American Fork Canyon, the cleverly lighted caves were formed by a now-vanished underground river. The monument headquarters and visitor center on US 92 is open year-round, and the setting is spectacular. The cave is at the head of a long, uphill walk not recommended for the aging or infirm.

Gateway to Southern Utah

Provo could be considered the gateway to southern Utah, the point from which the state gradually changes, becoming less populated, not as arable, with but a few exceptions, nonindustrialized, and cross-cut by geologic extremes.

Colorado River Canyon Country

Sixty-one square miles in area, Capitol Reef National Park is slick-rock country with canyons and cliffs. The road moves along the base, encountering spurs and graded trails leading to impressive Grand and Capitol Gorges, Chimney Rock, Hickman Natural Bridge, petrified forests and Indian petroglyphs engraved on stone 1,200 years ago.

The Capitol Reef escarpment marks the southern boundary of Wayne Wonderland, a desert region of canyons, basins and sheer cliffs, the most awesome work produced by natural upheaval and erosion. Here stand Cathedral Valley, Capitol Dome, Hickman Bridge, and the surrealistic Valley of the Goblins. Ask about road conditions before exploring these sites in standard model cars.

After departing the park, State 24 winds to Hanksville, the now-renowned Robbers Roost headquarters, made famous by the film "Butch Cassidy and the Sundance Kid." Yes, they were actual early-day Utah outlaws and this was their hideaway country. It is, today, a well-traveled way toward Lake Powell and the Glen Canyon National Recreation Area. Southwest from Hanksville, State 95 drops to a junction with State 276, which finally reaches Bullfrog Basin at lakeside. There are marinas and overnight facilities at the basin.

An alternate course follows State 95 to a river crossing at Hite. As long as the road is passable, this way leads to Natural Bridges National Monument, three gigantic rock spans and cliff ruins in tranquil high desert, dotted by piñon and juniper growth. East and north lies a section of the Manti-La Sal National Forest, and directly east a fork in State 95 leads to either Blanding, north, or Bluff, south. Blanding is larger, with 3,100 people, and closer to Monticello, which is the actual center of the region's tourist activity. But Bluff is a more interesting tiny community with a dramatic past. It is the first white settlement in southeastern Utah, an oasis reached in 1879 by a Mormon party after an epic winter trek across the canyon harshness. From Bluff it's possible to boat through whitewater rapids of the San Juan River to Mexican Hat, named for a nearby sombrero-shaped rock. Also north on State 261 outside Mexican Hat, the nine-mile sidetrip to an overlook above the Goosenecks of the San Juan is worth taking. The river has carved a narrow canyon 1,500 feet deep, in a sequence of horseshoe bends. Water must flow six miles to proceed one.

East of Bluff are the widely scattered prehistoric ruins of Hovenweap National Monument. South from Mexican Hat, on US 163, travelers enter the northern rim of the 25,000-square-mile Navajo Indian Reservation, largest in the U.S. Here, on the Utah-Arizona border, is awesome, incredible Monument Valley. Mile after mile, the pavement passes huge red sandstone buttes, pillars, columns and needles soaring more than one thousand feet above the wide desert floor. The unforgettable shapes have been given such names as Totem Pole, Castle, Stagecoach, Brigham's Tomb and Mitten Buttes. Indians still spend summers amid these wonders, living much as their ancestors did centuries ago. The Navajos have created Monument Valley Tribal Park, taking in 96,000 acres. It offers an observation building, Indian crafts center, campgrounds, fourteen miles of passable roads and guided tours to sections in special big-wheeled vehicles.

Returning through Monticello, US 163 meets Moab, another tourist base camp. The Old Testament name is misleading these days. Moab bustles, often with Hollywood film companies, shooting outdoor scenes on location. They headquarter in Moab and search surrounding terrain for likely background to go with westerns, desert dramas and, yes, Biblical enactments. Scenes from "The Greatest Story Ever Told" were shot outside Moab. The desired "authenticity" isn't difficult to find.

In the 1950's, Moab enjoyed a different kind of drama. Uranium was discovered nearby and, while it lasted, the mining and prospecting was frenetic. Located above the confluence of the Green and Colorado Rivers on the Colorado, Moab makes the most of its river country. Various boat tours are available at the landings, including a night ride that takes sublime advantage of shapes formed on gorge walls with high-powered flood lights.

Arches and Towers

Crossing the Colorado River, US 163 passes Arches National Park, featuring a 114-square-mile area with rock spires, pinnacles and narrow fins pierced by 88 naturally formed openings. One is a 291-foot bridge, the largest known natural arch. Paved roads reach the finest specimens, but some walking is necessary to see rock-formed skyscrapers of Park Avenue, Landscape Arch, Devil's Garden and whimsical Delicate Arch. Called Schoolmarm's Britches by local cowhands, the last is the most beautiful and remarkable of the bunch. Rising more than one hundred feet high, it stands alone and unsupported in a setting of slick-rock domes, with the gorge of the Colorado River and the 12,000-to-13,000-foot peaks of the La Sal Mountains in the distance.

Castleton Towers and Fisher Towers are two other areas of unique rock formations northeast from Moab. They can be visited by a black-topped road through the multi-hued Colorado River gorge.

Canyonlands National Park envelops the confluence of the Colorado and Green Rivers and exhibits the greatest variety of rock sculpture found anywhere on earth. Elevations range from 3,700 feet in the depths of Catarac Canyon to over 6,000 feet on the plateau rims. Between both a half-billion years of the planet's life are apparent in countless folds, warps, shifts and tilts. Canyonlands, established as a national park in 1964, is still fairly untamed. The more intrepid visitors can explore it satisfactorily on Jeep roads, but other autos are advised to proceed with advance knowledge about conditions ahead. Local pilots have offered sightseeing flights over the area and information on such possibilities is available at the Arches Visitor Center.

For a less expensive bird's-eye view of the Canyonlands region, a black-topped county road leads west from US 163, north of Moab, to Dead Horse Point State Park, a magnificent overlook on the Colorado gorge. Also, a graded road veers away from the Dead Horse Point approach southwest across the plateau to appropriately titled Island in the Sky, ending at Grand View Point. This jutting promontory provides a giddy, 2,500-foot-high view of the merging Colorado and Green Rivers.

US 163 continues north to I–70, built through country never before crossed by road or trail. Scenery this opened up is typical of the entire area. The 235-mile trip from here to Salt Lake City is usually made on US 50–6, branching north from I–70, through Green River and Price. At Green River, the annual Friendship Cruise is launched in late May. Power boats of every description, conveying groups that vary from sightseers to fishermen to outdoors enthusiasts to purely revelers, compose the armada. Their destination is Moab, which is usually reached the second day out, total elapsed time depending on the boatman's skill.

Price and Helper are centers of Utah's coal-mining industry. Most Utah miners came from non-Mormon stock and the coal communities are no exception. They evidence a firm individuality verging on truculence toward the predominantly LDS settlements. In the past, Price was known to openly defy state laws restricting liquor sold in bars. A former mayor, J. Bracken Lee, who subsequently became a two-term Utah governor and then mayor of Salt Lake City, once arrested state liquor control officers in Price, claiming they had no jurisdiction interfering with municipal matters. Price is also the home of Eastern Utah College, formerly Carbon College, a two-year state institution.

Farther South

Southern Utah is, for its population, particularly blessed with state colleges. Others include Snow College at Ephraim and Southern Utah College at Cedar City. The Cedar City campus has developed as a center for arts instruction. This extends through painting, metal work and drama. Utah's summer Shakespearean Festival is held on the college campus every year in July.

Cedar City, on I–15, 260 miles south of Salt Lake City, is also a recreation and tourist center. It reclines on the western edge of the Dixie National Forest and is within eighteen miles of Cedar Breaks National Monument. Farther east, on State 14, then north on US 89, Bryce Canyon National Park drops away in a multi-hued extravaganza. One of Utah's several ski resorts, Brian Head, is less than a one-hour drive, depending on road conditions, from Cedar City. The facility, with chair lifts rising above 10,000-foot elevations, is a favorite with skiers from Nevada, Arizona and even California.

Zion National Park is located directly south of Cedar City, off I–15 and then along state routes that take motorists through small prime Mormon settlements named Toquerville, LaVerkin and Virgin. A tranquil, wooded camping site east of Cedar City off State 14 is Navajo Lake. The lake is cold enough for good trout fishing and big enough for boating. The area around it is being "found," and fast acquiring vacation cabin sites. Another rediscovery is taking place at St. George in the southwest corner of Utah.

St. George has Dixie State College and was a favorite wintering retreat for Brigham Young. His two-story winter home, an echo from New England, has been restored as a Utah State Park museum. Lately, condominium developers have done well at St. George, with accommodations for retirees, weekend recreation seekers and tourists traveling at a leisurely and stylish pace. The permanent community, 13,000 at the last census, started with a cotton mission sent to the Virgin River Valley by Brigham Young in 1861. The pioneers endured considerable hardship, but managed to succeed. Utah's first Mormon temple, white stucco surrounded by desert palms, was erected at St. George in 1871.

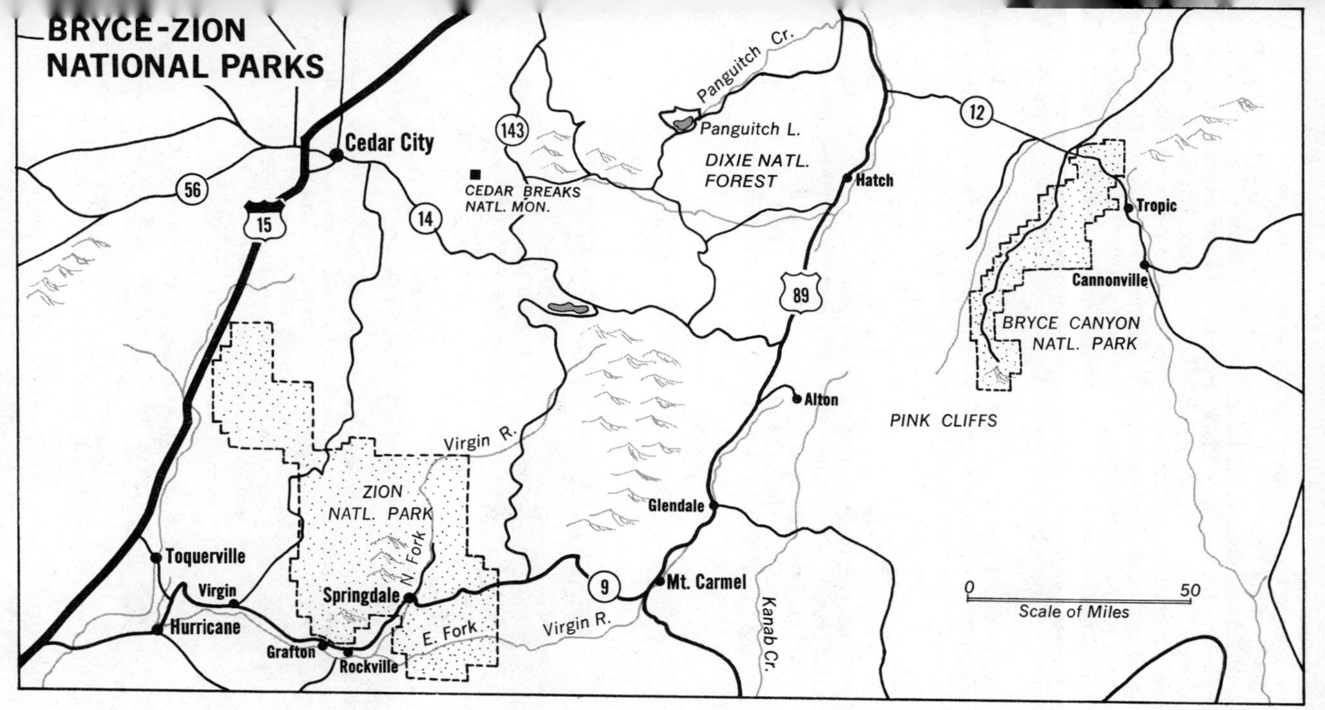
BRYCE-ZION
NATIONAL PARKS
Cedar City
56
15
143
14
CEDAR BREAKS
NATL. MON.
Panguitch Cr.
Panguitch L.
DIXIE NATL.
FOREST
Hatch
12
89
Tropic
Cannonville
BRYCE CANYON
NATL. PARK
Alton
PINK CLIFFS
Virgin R.
ZION
NATL. PARK
N. Fork
Glendale
Toquerville
Virgin
Springdale
9
Mt. Carmel
Hurricane
E. Fork
Virgin R.
Grafton
Rockville
Kanab Cr.
0
50
Scale of Miles

Early vineyards once produced quality Utah wine around St. George until a burst of abstinence wiped the industry out.

North of town rise the cool, forested Pine Valley Mountains, topped by 10,325-foot-high Signal Point. Five miles west from St. George is Dixie State Park at Santa Clara, featuring the formidable native sandstone home built in 1862 by Jacob Hamblin, an outstanding Mormon explorer and missionary to the Indians. No one was more familiar with the obscure trails of southern Utah. Hamblin devoted almost half a century to keeping the peace between Indian tribes and white settlers. He died in 1886 while on the run from officers arresting polygamists. Southwest from Santa Clara, the highway passes through the Shivwits Indian Reservation, winding over the Beaver Dam Mountains as high as 4,800 feet.

An eastward route from St. George leads past Zion National Park on State 15 to a junction with US 89 on its way south to Kanab. Kanab has been called "Hollywood's backyard" because of the countless outdoor films photographed in its vicinity. The credits run from the early "Drums Along the Mohawk," to the more recent "Planet of the Apes." Parry Lodge in Kanab was made famous by the interviews with movie stars conducted there. Scenery around Kanab is literally "too magnificent to be real." The Moqui Indian caverns are located five miles north of town, displaying the largest fluorescent mineral exhibit in the United States. Immediately south of Kanab, the small Kaibab Indian Reservation hugs the state line in Arizona. The settlement, accessible from US 89 after that highway exits Utah, is exactly 305 miles beyond Salt Lake City and 71 miles away from the north rim of Grand Canyon.

PRACTICAL INFORMATION FOR UTAH

HOW TO GET THERE. *By car:* I–80, probably the most heavily traveled transcontinental highway, passes through Salt Lake City. From the north I–84 runs southeast through Salt Lake from Portland, Oregon. I–15 comes from the Los Angeles area through Cedar City, Utah, and up to Salt Lake. *By air:* Salt Lake City is the major terminal. Among the long-distance carriers serving it are *American, Continental, Delta, Eastern, Northwest Orient, TWA,* and *United.*

By train: Amtrak's *California Zephyr* runs from Denver to Salt Lake City, on the route previously used by the *Denver and Rio Grande Zephyr.* Amtrak's *Desert Wind* connects Salt Lake City and Los Angeles. The *Pioneer* connects Salt Lake City with Seattle, through Ogden and Boise.

By bus: Greyhound offers the major service to Utah (Salt Lake City is the busiest terminal), but the region is also served by numerous other lines including Crown Transit, Linea Azul, Sun Valley and Bremerton-Tacoma.

HOTELS AND MOTELS in Utah are relatively inexpensive. Their highest rates will be in effect for the "in-season" period which, according to the locale, is either ski time (November through April) or the summer months that bring tourists to the national parks and forest lands. These are the rates we have used to compile our categories.

Based on double occupancy, the rate categories for Utah are: *Deluxe,* over $70; *Expensive,* $50–$70; *Moderate,* $35–$50; and *Inexpensive,* under $35.

Note: Utah area code is the same for all numbers listed below: 801.

ALTA. Alta Peruvian Lodge. *Expensive.* Alta, UT 84092 (742–3000). A fine ski resort. Fireplace, library, dining room, heated outdoor pool.

Rustler Lodge. *Expensive.* Alta, UT 84092 (742–2200). Family rates, cafe, bar, sauna, rec room.

BEAVER. Beaver TraveLodge. *Moderate.* 605 N. Main St., Beaver, UT 84713 (438–2409). 41 units, family suites, in-room movies, restaurant, gas station.

Best Western Paice Motel. *Moderate.* 161 S. Main St., Beaver UT 84713 (438–2438). Cable TV, sauna, spa, gym.

Quality Inn. *Moderate.* 1450 N. 300 W., Beaver, UT 84713 (438–2484). Indoor pool, helicopter landing pad for skiers.

DeLano Motel. *Inexpensive.* 480 N. Main St., Beaver, UT 84713 (438–2418). Ten units, cable TV, senior discount, pets allowed.

BLANDING. Best Western Gateway. *Moderate.* 88 E. Center St., Blanding, UT 84511 (678–2278). Cafe nearby, pets allowed, pool, playground.

Blanding Motel. *Inexpensive.* 92 W. Center St., Blanding UT 84511 (678–2514). Kitchenettes.

Cliff Palace Motel. *Inexpensive.* 132 S. Main St., Blanding, UT 84511 (678–2264). Central location.

BLUFF. Mokee Motel. *Inexpensive.* Bluff, UT 84512 (672–2217). Beautiful cliff view, cafe nearby.

Recapture Lodge & Tours. *Inexpensive.* Bluff, UT 84512 (672–2281). Geologist-guided tours and river trips leave from here. Cafe nearby.

BRIAN HEAD. Accommodation Station, Write to Box F, Cedar City, UT 84720 (572–9705), for information on condo rentals and skiing. Or call *Brian Head Reservations Center* (677–2042) for motel accommodations.

Brian Head Royale TraveLodge. *Inexpensive.* Brian Head UT 84719 (677–2222). Lounge, jacuzzi, restaurant.

BRYCE CANYON. Best Western Ruby's Inn. *Expensive.* Bryce, UT 84717 (834–5341). Closest accommodation to Bryce Canyon. Ski trails, senior discount.

Bryce Canyon Pines. *Moderate.* Bryce, UT 84717 (834–5336). On US 12.

CEDAR CITY. Quality Inn. *Expensive.* 18 S. Main St., Cedar City, UT 84721 (586–2433). Cable TV and movies, oversize beds. No elevator. Cafe nearby. Airport shuttle.

Best Western Town & Country Inn. *Moderate.* 200 N. Main St., Cedar City, UT 84720 (586–9911). Some of the best food in town.

Comfort Inn. *Moderate.* 250 N. 1100 W., Cedar City, UT 84720 (586–2082). Cable TV, pool. Free Continental breakfast.

Holiday Inn. *Moderate.* 309 N. 200 W., Cedar City, UT 84720 (586–8888). Sauna, whirlpool, in-room movies, some non-smoking rooms.

Rodeway Inn. *Moderate.* 281 S. Main St., Cedar City, UT 84720 (586–9916). Cable TV, sauna, family units. Children under 17 free.

TraveLodge. *Moderate.* 479 S. Main St., Cedar City, UT 84720 (586–9471).

COALVILLE. Blonquist Motel. *Moderate.* 99 S. Main St., Coalville, UT 84017 (336–2451).

DUCHESNE. Ell's Motel. *Inexpensive.* 220 E. Main St., Duchesne, UT 84021 (738–2433). Kitchenettes, cable TV and HBO, queen size beds. Restaurant nearby.

Gateway Motel. *Moderate.* 136 E. Main St., Duchesne, UT 84021 (738–2491). Cable TV and HBO.

FILLMORE. El Ana Motel. *Inexpensive.* 50 N. Main St., Fillmore, UT 84631 (743–5350). Kitchen units, in-room coffee.

Fillmore Motel. *Moderate.* 61 N. Main St., Fillmore, UT 84631 (743–5454). Kitchenettes, cafe nearby.

Best Western Paradise Inn. *Moderate.* 800 N. Main St., Fillmore, UT 84631 (743–6895). Service station, cafe nearby.

GREEN RIVER. Best Western River Terrace. *Expensive.* One mile east on US 6, 50. Box B, Green River, UT 84525 (564–3401). On river. Heated pool. Patios and balconies.

Bookcliff Motor Inn. *Moderate.* 395 E. Main St., Green River, UT 84525 (564–3406). 99 rooms, cable TV, game room, 24-hr. restaurant.

Cottage Motel. *Inexpensive.* 60 E. Main St., Green River, UT 84525 (564–8187). 31 rooms, cable TV, family units.

HEBER CITY. Green Acres National 9 Inn. *Moderate.* 989 S. Main St., Heber City, UT 84032 (654–2202). 24-hr. cafe nearby.

The Homestead. *Moderate.* 700 N. Homestead Dr., Heber City, UT 84032 (654–1102). Reservations necessary. A resort-type motel, heated spring-fed pools, pony rides, tennis, putting green, horseback riding. Beautiful grounds.

Wasatch Motel. *Inexpensive.* 875 S. Main St., Heber City UT 84032 (654–3090). Spring-fed heated pool, cafe nearby.

KANAB. Four Seasons. *Moderate.* 36 N. 300 W., Kanab, UT 84741 (644–2635). King and queen size beds, cable TV.

K-Motel. *Moderate.* 300 S. 100 E., Kanab, UT 84741 (644–2611). Family units, kitchenettes.

Parry Lodge. *Moderate.* 89 E. Center St., Kanab, UT 84741 (644–2601). Many Hollywood stars have stayed here while making movies in this colorful area, the "Hollywood of Utah."

Red Hills Best Western. *Moderate.* 125 W. Center St., Kanab, UT 84741 (644–2675). Cable TV, some family units, restaurant nearby.

LOGAN. Center Street B & B. *Moderate to Expensive.* 169 E. Center St., Logan, UT 84321 (752–3443). Victorian mansion in center of town. Continental breakfast.

Baugh Motel. *Moderate.* 153 S. Main St., Logan, UT 84321 (752–5220). Bridal suite, fireplaces.

Alta Motel. *Inexpensive.* 51 E. 500 N., Logan, UT 84321 (752–6300). Cafe nearby, playground.

MEXICAN HAT. Canyonlands Motel. *Moderate.* Mexican Hat, UT 84531 (683–2230). Cafe nearby, pets allowed.

San Juan Friendship Inn. *Moderate.* Hwy. 163, Mexican Hat, UT 84531 (683–2220). On San Juan River. Restaurant and lounge.

MOAB. Apache Motel. *Moderate.* 166 S. 400 E., Moab, UT 84532 (259–5727). HBO, AA approved.

Best Western Green Well. *Moderate.* 105 S. Main St., Moab, UT 84532 (259–6151). Cafe.

Bowen Motel. *Moderate.* 169 N. Main St., Moab, UT 84532 (259–7132). Queen size beds, kitchenettes.

Landmark Motel. *Moderate.* 168 N. Main St., Moab, UT 84532 (259–6147). 35 units, AAA approved.

Rustic Inn Motel. *Inexpensive.* 120 E. 1st St., S., Moab, UT 84532 (259–6177). Cable TV and HBO, waterbeds, family suites.

The Virginian. *Inexpensive.* 70 E. 200 St. S., Moab, UT 84532 (259–5951). 20 units near US 191. Cable TV. Pets allowed.

MONTICELLO. Canyonlands 6 Motel. *Moderate.* 197 N. Main St., Monticello, UT 84535 (587–2266). Sauna, whirlpool, queen size beds.

Triangle H Motel. *Inexpensive.* 160 E. US 666, Monticello, UT 84535 (587–2274). One- and two-bedroom units. Restaurant nearby.

NEPHI. Best Western Sunset Inn. *Moderate.* 1025 S. Main St., Nephi, UT 84648 (623–0624). 40 rooms, restaurant.

Safari Motel. *Inexpensive.* 413 S. Main St., Nephi, UT 84648 (623–1071). Cable TV and HBO.

OGDEN. Hilton Hotel. *Expensive.* 247 24th St., Ogden, UT 84401 (627–1190). Ogden's finest hotel. Three restaurants, indoor swimming pool.

Best Western High Country Inn. *Moderate.* 1335 W. 12th St., Ogden, UT 84401 (394–9474). King and queen size beds, waterbeds, in-room movies, bridal suite, handicapped facilities.

Holiday Inn. *Moderate.* 3306 Washington Blvd., Ogden, UT 84401 (399–5671). Health club, meeting room, bar.

Orleans. *Inexpensive.* 1825 Washington Blvd., Ogden, UT 84401 (621–8350). Restaurant, barber shop, satellite TV. Some kitchens. Laundry room.

TraveLodge. *Inexpensive.* 2110 Washington Blvd., Ogden, UT 84401 (394–4563). Movies, game room.

ORDERVILLE. Orderville Motel. *Inexpensive.* On US 89. Box 86, Orderville, UT 84758 (648–2271). Seven units, some kitchens. Restaurant nearby.

PANGUITCH. Best Western New Western. *Moderate.* 2 E. Center St., Panguitch, UT 84759 (676–8876). Queen size beds. Cafe nearby.

Sands Motel. *Moderate.* 390 N. Main St., Panguitch, UT 84759 (676–8874). Oversize beds, pool, color TV.

PARK CITY. *Park City Reservations,* 1790 Bonanza Dr., Park City, UT 84060 (649–9598), will arrange for condo and motel rentals for skiiers.

Park City Resort Lodging, 1515 Park Ave., Park City, UT 84060 (649–6368), can arrange for condos and motels near the slopes.

The Yarrow. *Deluxe to Expensive.* 1800 Park Ave., Park City, UT 84060 (649–7000). Ski packages, golf privileges, tennis. Restaurant and bar.

Best Western Landmark Inn. *Expensive.* 6560 N. Landmark Dr., Park City, UT 84060 (649–7300). Near I–80. Some suites, refrigerators. Laundry, pool, restaurant.

PRICE. Best Western Greenwell. *Moderate.* 655 E. Main, Price, UT 84501 (637–3520). Restaurant, gift shop and pool.

Carriage House Inn. *Moderate.* 590 E. Main St., Price, UT 84501 (637–5660). Indoor pool and spa, 42 rooms, cable TV and HBO, restaurant.

Crest Motel. *Inexpensive.* 625 E. Main St., Price, UT 84501 (637–1532). 85 units, family suites, cable TV.

PROVO. Best Western Rome Inn. *Moderate.* 1200 S. University Ave., Provo, UT 84601 (373–0060). Free continental breakfast, family units, king and queen size beds.

Chez Fontaine Bed & Breakfast. *Moderate.* 45 N. 300 E., Provo, UT 84601 (375–8484). A turn-of-the-century inn filled with pioneer furniture.

Colony Inn. *Moderate.* 1380 S. University Ave., Provo, UT 84601 (374–6800). Saunas, cable TV.

Excelsior Hotel. *Moderate.* 101 W. 100 N., Provo, UT 84601. Saunas, exercise room, two restaurants, non-smoking rooms, cable TV.

Holiday Inn. *Moderate.* 1460 S. University Ave., Provo, UT 84601 (374–9750). Jacuzzis, across from golf course, restaurant.

The Pullman Bed & Breakfast. *Moderate.* 415 S. University Ave., Provo, UT 84601 (374–8141). In a lovely old home, close to BYU.

TraveLodge. *Inexpensive.* 124 S. University Ave., Provo, UT 84601 (373–1974). Near the university, restaurant.

RICHFIELD. Best Western Executive Inn. *Expensive.* 333 N. Main St., Richfield, UT 84701 (896–6476). Cocktail lounge, restaurant, dancing. Airport shuttle.

Best Western High Country Inn. *Moderate.* 145 S. Main St., Richmond, UT 84701 (896–5481). Honeymoon suites.

Rodeway Inn. *Moderate.* 69 S. Main St., Richmond, UT 84701 (896–5491). Cable TV and HBO, restaurant. Pets allowed.

ROOSEVELT. Bottle Hollow Inn. *Moderate.* Ft. Duchesne, on US 40, six miles east of Roosevelt, Box 70, Roosevelt, UT 84021 (722–2431). Water sports, entertainment. Owned, run by Ute Indian Tribe. Tennis, bowling, playground. Tribal museum.

Frontier Motel & Grill. *Inexpensive.* 75 E. 2 E., Roosevelt, UT 84021 (722–4613). Cable TV, queen size beds, restaurant.

SALT LAKE CITY. Marriott. *Deluxe.* 75 South West Temple, Salt Lake City, UT 84104 (531–0800). Restaurant, lounge, liquor store, sauna. Special weekend rates.

Westin Hotel Utah. *Deluxe.* Main at South Temple, Salt Lake City, UT 84111 (531–1000). Barber shop and beauty salon. Shuttle bus to airport.

Hilton Hotel & Inn. *Deluxe.* 150 West 500 S., Salt Lake City, UT 84101 (532–3344); and 5151 Wiley Post Dr., Wylie, at the airport (539–1515). Restaurant, lounge, 24-hour coffeeshop.

Airport Inn International. *Expensive.* 2333 West North Temple, Salt Lake City, UT 84116 (539–0438). In-room jacuzzis, cable TV, restaurant.

Little America Motel. *Expensive.* 500 S. Main St., Salt Lake City, UT 84111 (363–6781). Combination of a motel and a highrise, with different rates for each. Indoor pool, sauna, exercise room, entertainment, 24-hr. coffeeshop.

Sheraton Triad Hotel & Towers. *Expensive.* 255 South West Temple, Salt Lake City, UT 84104 (328–2000). Bar, entertainment, ski packages.

Embassy Suites. *Expensive.* 600 South West Temple, Salt Lake City, UT 84104 (359–7800). All two-room suites. Wet bars, microwaves, complimentary breakfast, indoor pool, sauna, restaurant.

Flying J. *Moderate.* 715 West North Temple, Salt Lake City, UT 84116 (363–0062). Cafe, pool, oversize beds. Shuttle bus.

Orleans Inn. *Moderate.* 325 South 300 E., Salt Lake City, UT 84111 (521–3790). Kitchens, restaurant, cable TV.

Radisson Hotel. *Moderate.* 161 West 6th S., Salt Lake City, UT 84101 (521–7373). Restaurant and lounge. Convention facilities.

Regent Hotel. *Moderate.* 458 West 5300 S., 84101 100 rooms, indoor pool, cable TV, restaurant, airport shuttle, 5 miles from downtown.

TraveLodge Salt Palace. *Moderate.* 215 West North Temple, Salt Lake City, UT 84103 (532–1000). Restaurant, sauna. 24-hr. movies, bridal suite.

Super 8 Motel. *Inexpensive.* 616 South 200 W., Salt Lake City, UT 84101 (534–0808).

Colonial Village Motel. *Inexpensive.* 1530 S. Main St., Salt Lake City, UT 84111 (486–8171). Pool, next door to a popular German restaurant.

Deseret Inn Motel. *Inexpensive.* 50 West 5th S., Salt Lake City, UT 84101 (532–2900). Pool, extra-large beds, room service.

Eller Bed & Breakfast. *Inexpensive.* 164 S. 900 East, Salt Lake City, UT 84012 (533–8184). Historic Victorian home, Continental breakfast.

Imperial 400 Motel. *Inexpensive.* 476 S. State St., Salt Lake City, UT 84111 (533–9300). Next to the Salt Palace and opposite a park.

Scenic Motel. *Inexpensive.* 1345 Foothill Dr., Salt Lake City, UT 84108 (582–1527). Cafe nearby.

SNOWBIRD. The Lodge at Snowbird. *Deluxe.* Snowbird, UT 84092 (742–2222). Skiing, tennis, hiking, kitchens, fireplaces, balconies, saunas, cafe.

ST. GEORGE. Hilton Hotel & Inn. *Expensive.* 1450 S. Hilton Inn Dr., St. George, UT 84770 (628–0463). Wet bars, fireplaces, patios, restaurant and pool.

Best Western Coral Hills. *Moderate.* 125 E. St. George Blvd., St. George, UT 84770 (673–4844). Jacuzzi suites, saunas, spas, putting green, waterbeds, non-smoking rooms.

Four Seasons Motor Inn. *Moderate.* 747 E. St. George Blvd., St. George, UT 84770 (673–4804). Highly rated, two restaurants, putting green, in-room steambaths.

Holiday Inn. *Moderate.* 850 S. Bluff St., St. George, UT 84770 (628–4235). Tennis courts, game room, exercise room, miniature golf, putting green, cable TV.

Lamplighter Inn. *Moderate.* 107 W. St. George Blvd., St. George, UT 84770 (673–4679). Cable TV, queen size beds.

Regency Inn. *Moderate.* 770 E. St. George Blvd., St. George, UT 84770 (673–6119). King and queen size beds, jacuzzi and saunas, cable TV, kitchenettes. Restaurant nearby.

Rodeway Inn. *Moderate.* 260 E. St. George Blvd., St. George, UT 84770 (673–6161). King and queen size beds, family suites.

TraveLodge East. *Moderate.* 175 N. 1000 East St., St. George, UT 84770 (673–4621). Suites, pool, cable TV. 24-hour cafe, Pets allowed.

Dixie Palms. *Inexpensive.* 185 E. St. George Blvd., St. George, UT 84770 (673–3531). Oversize beds, cable TV, two kitchenettes. Cafe nearby.

VERNAL. Sheraton Inn. *Expensive.* 1684 W. Hwy. 40, Vernal, UT 84078 (789–9550). Best accommodations in Vernal.

Antlers Best Western. *Moderate.* 423 W. Main St., Vernal, UT 84078 (789–1202). Pool, playground, satellite TV.

Best Western Dinosaur Inn. *Moderate.* 251 E. Main St., Vernal, UT 84078 (789–2660). Hot tub, bathroom phones, cafe.

Split Mountain Motel. *Moderate.* 1015 Hwy. 40 E., Vernal, UT 84078 (789–9020). Queen size beds.

Diamond Hills Motel & Gardens. *Inexpensive.* 590 W. Main, Vernal, UT 84078 (789–1754). Restaurant. Pets allowed.

WENDOVER. Wendover Best Western. *Expensive.* 809 St. Hwy., Wendover, UT 84083 (665–2211). Gambling just over the state line in Nevada, cable TV and HBO, jacuzzi and steam room.

ZION NATIONAL PARK. Zion Lodge. *Expensive.* Hwy. 9, five miles N. of Zion National Park S. entrance (772–3231). For reservations contact *TW Services,* Box 400, Cedar City, UT 84720 (586–7686). Cabins and motel. Open May–Oct. Nature program, spectacular views.

Bumbleberry Inn. *Moderate.* 897 Zion Park Blvd., Springdale, UT 84767 (772–3224). Just outside the park. Famous pie in the restaurant. Sauna.

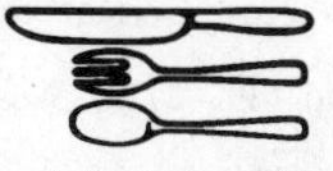

RESTAURANTS. There is nothing different or unique about Mormon cooking. Statewide restaurant quality has improved considerably since tourism developed into such a big, booming business. It's possible to discover an especially tasty cuisine in out-of-the-way locations, but don't count on it. Salt Lake City, however, is beginning to acquire a kitchen. The going is slow because liquor laws discourage heavy investment in grand cafes or exclusive type restaurants. But specialty places, offering French, Spanish and German dishes, are increasing. Seafood, believe it or not, is found fresh and well prepared in several Salt Lake City dining rooms. Some of the best menus will be found up nearby canyons or south of the city.

Restaurant price categories are as follows: *Deluxe* \$20 up; *Expensive* \$15–20; *Moderate* \$10–\$15; and *Inexpensive* under \$10.

BRIGHAM CITY. Maddox Ranch House. *Moderate.* Two miles S. of Brigham City on US 89 (723–8545). Western atmosphere, famous fried chicken. Baked goods.

Idle Isle. *Inexpensive.* 24 S. Main St. (734–9062). Prime rib and seafood. Soda fountain.

CEDAR CITY. Sullivan's. *Expensive.* 8 S. Main St. (586–6761). In Best Western Motel. Salad and potato bar. Steak and lobster.

China Garden. *Moderate.* 170 N. Main St. (586–6042). Chinese/American food and take-out.

Sugarloaf. *Moderate.* 281 S. Main St. (586–6593). In-house bakery.

La Tajada Steak & Seafood House. *Moderate.* 86 S. Main St. (586–6761).

GREEN RIVER. Oasis Cafe. *Moderate.* 118 W. Main St. (564–3475). Seafood, chicken, steaks.

HEBER CITY. High Country. *Moderate.* 1050 S. Main St. (654–2022). Homestyle cooking, halibut, prime rib.

KANAB. Chef's Palace. *Expensive.* 151 W. Center St. (644–5052). Home-cooked food, family dining, prime rib. Salad bar.

Parry Lodge. *Moderate.* 89 E. Center St. (644–2601). Prime rib, beer and wine. Closed Nov. to mid-April.

Territorial Inn. *Moderate.* 85 S. 200 W. (644–5744). Steak and seafood.

LOGAN. The Cottage. *Expensive.* 51 W. 200 South (752–5260). Rustic building, open-air dining. Sunday brunch.

The Bluebird. *Moderate.* 19 N. Main St. (752–3155). A locally popular restaurant that makes its own candy and ice cream.

Gia's. *Moderate.* 119 S. Main St. (752–9384). Fine Italian food, strolling violinist.

MOAB. Arches Dining Room. *Moderate.* 182 S. Main St. (259–7141). Salad bar, American cuisine. Children's menu.

Grand Old Ranch House. *Expensive.* N. Hwy. 163 (259–5753). On the National Registry of Historic Places. Prime rib, steaks, seafood, German dishes, Sunday brunch.

Sundowner. *Moderate.* N. Hwy. 163 (259–5201). Steaks, prime rib, ranch-style dining.

Calico Kitchen. *Inexpensive.* 56 E. 300 S. (259–8710). Smorgasbord.

OGDEN. Bistro 1900. *Expensive.* Ogden Hilton, 258 25th St. (399–3709). Fine French and Italian cuisine.

Hunter's. *Expensive.* Radisson Hotel, 2510 Washington Blvd. (627–1900). Excellent food in an attractive atmosphere.

Bavarian Chalet. *Moderate.* 4387 Harrison Blvd. (479–7561). German cooking in old-world atmosphere.

Mansion House. *Moderate.* 2350 Adams Ave. (392–2225). German and American food, homemade bread and pastries.

Prarie Schooner Steak House. *Moderate.* 445 Park Blvd. (392–2712). Western atmosphere. Dine in covered wagons. Steaks, prime rib.

Ye Lion's Den. *Moderate.* 3607 Washington Blvd. (399–5804). Steaks, prime rib, seafoods, all in an olde-English atmosphere.

Star Noodle Parlor. *Inexpensive.* 225 25th St. (394–6331). Chinese and American menu.

PARK CITY. Adolph's. *Expensive.* 1541 Thames Canyon Dr. (649–7177). Swiss atmosphere and food.

Car 19. *Expensive.* 438 Main St. (649–9338). Mostly steaks served in an old railroad car.

Janeaux's. *Expensive.* 306 Main St. (649–6800). Gourmet fare, duck, cordon bleu.

Grub Steak. *Moderate.* Prospector Square (649–8060). Steaks, seafood, prime rib, large salad bar.

Baja Cantina. *Inexpensive.* 1284 Empire Ave. (649–2252). A wild Mexican restaurant.

A Horse of a Different Color. *Moderate.* 596 Main St. (645–7883). International gourmet fare.

PRICE. Robintino's. *Moderate.* 700 Price River Dr. (637–2295). Italian food and steaks, also pizza.

Window's Cafe. *Moderate.* Radisson Inn, US 50 and 6 (637–8880). Prime rib a speciality. Children's menu. Cocktail lounge.

China City. *Inexpensive.* 350 E. Main St. (637–8211). Chinese and American menu.

PROVO. Adrian's. *Expensive.* 101 W. 100 North (377–4700). In Excelsior Hotel. Continental cuisine. Beer and wine. Sunday brunch.

First Wok. *Moderate.* 1425 S. State St. (373–7203). Peking-style Chinese food.

Joe Vera's. *Moderate.* 250 W. Center St. (375–6714). Mexican food.

La France. *Moderate.* 463 N. University Ave. (377–4545). Authentic French cuisine; owners from the Riviera.

RICHFIELD. South China Cafe. *Moderate.* 141 N. Main St. (896–9007). Chinese and American food and take-out.

ROOSEVELT. Frontier Grill. *Moderate.* 65 S. 200 E. (722–3669). Homestyle cooking.

ST. GEORGE. Andelin's Gable House. *Expensive.* 206 E. St. George Blvd. (673–6796). Excellent food. Prime rib a specialty.

Hilton Inn. *Expensive.* 1450 S. Hilton Inn Dr. (628–0463). Excellent food during the week and a famous Sunday brunch.

Dick's Cafe. *Moderate.* 114 E. St. George Blvd. (673–3841). Open since 1935. Western atmosphere, 3.2 beer. Gift shop.

Mushroom Farm. *Moderate.* 212 N. 900 E St. George Blvd. (673–6047). Pioneer atmosphere and old-time music. Country, seafood, and gourmet dishes.

Peppelars. *Moderate.* 850 S. Bluff (628–4235). Homemade bread and pastries, prime rib, lobster. Famous Sunday brunch.

Ronnie's. *Inexpensive.* 482 W. St. George Blvd. (628–4190). "World's Greatest Buffalo Burgers."

Los Hermanos. *Inexpensive.* 46 W. St. George Blvd. (628–5989). Northern Mexican food. Try the seafood salad.

SALT LAKE CITY. We begin our coverage of Salt Lake restaurants with a few editor's choices. Rating restaurants is, at best, a subjective business. These are not presented as absolutely "the best" but as our choices of places among the best where we might take friends. A list of other recommended restaurants follows.

Editors' Choices

Devereaux. *Deluxe.* Devereaux Plaza Triad Center (575–2000). In a restored 19th-century mansion, this restaurant is the centerpiece of a multi-million dollar office, apartment, and shopping-center development at 3rd West between North and South Temple. Varied menu, from chicken and beef to pork and pasta. Well worth a visit.

La Caille at Quail Run. *Deluxe.* 9565 Wasatch Blvd., Sandy (942–1751). The kind of country atmosphere that only the wealthy can produce, often with fires burning brightly in the huge fireplaces. Local residents regularly make the drive out of the city to enjoy the home baking, fresh flowers, and candlelit atmosphere. Sunday Basque dinner. Call first for reservations.

The New Orleans Cafe. *Moderate–Expensive.* 200 S. 307 W. (363–6573). Distinctively different for Salt Lake City, this downtown restaurant conveys an authentic Louisiana atmosphere, with superbly prepared Creole and Cajun entrees. Live Dixieland melodies on Friday and Saturday nights and at Sunday brunch. The menu changes daily but usually features shrimp creole, oyster stew, fried catfish, creole gumbo, and redfish pecan.

The Roof. *Expensive.* Westin Hotel South Temple & Main (531–1000). This dining experience in elegant but subdued surroundings, atop the Westin Hotel, affords a magnificent view of Temple Square. Live piano accompaniment completes the setting for superb dining.

Thirteenth Floor. *Expensive.* 161 W. 600 S. (364–7013). Soup is served in individual tureens, and loaves of hot bread accompany every meal. There's also a great view of the entire Salt Lake Valley. Steaks and prime rib are the staples of the menu.

Other Recommended Restaurants

La Fleur de Lys. *Deluxe.* 165 S. West Temple (359–5753). Sweetbreads, roast pheasant, and live lobsters cooked to order. Posh atmosphere and fine service.

Log Haven. *Expensive.* Mill Creek Canyon (272–8255). Varied menu with a mountain setting overlooking a lake. They bake their own bread. Reservations required.

Diamond Lil's. *Moderate–Expensive.* 1528 W. North Temple (533–0547). In a frontier western atmosphere created by restored 100-year-old buildings. Prime rib and steak specialties are graced by generous portions of homemade bread. The period-piece saloon also is worth a visit.

Finn's. *Moderate–Expensive.* 2675 Parley's Way (466–4682). Off the beaten tourist path but worth finding for its tasty fare. Homemade bread and pastries.

Ho Ho Gourmet. *Moderate–Expensive.* 1504 S. State St. (487–7709). A pleasant dining experience for oriental-food lovers. Cantonese and Mandarin favorites, prepared as they would be in Hong Kong.

Market Street Broiler. *Moderate–Expensive.* 258 S. 1300 East (583–8808). Restored historic fire station. Fresh seafood and baked goods.

Old Salt City Jail. *Moderate to Expensive.* 460 S. 10th East. (355–2422). Old-time country jail decor. Steak, seafood, salad bar.

The Cedars. *Moderate.* 154 E. 200 S. (364–4096). Authentic Armenian, Lebanese, and Morrocan fare. From felafel with sesame seed sauce to stuffed grape leaves.

Litza's. *Moderate.* 716 E. 400 S. (359–5352). Italian menu.

Ristorante Della Fontana. *Moderate.* 336 S. 400 E. (328–4243). In addition to Italian food, there are representative dishes from many Mediterranean countries, with a dinner normally running to a full seven courses. The dining room is an old church, complete with fountain and ornately carved interior.

The Hawaiian. *Inexpensive.* 2920 Highland Dr. (486–5076). Chinese and Polynesian food to the accompaniment of a Hawaiian thunderstorm.

La Morena. *Inexpensive.* 3 Triad Center (575–7100). Good authentic Mexican food.

Spaghetti Factory. *Inexpensive.* Trolley Square (521–0424). Great family dining in a fun setting.

SPRINGDALE. Bumbleberry Inn. *Moderate.* 897 Zion Park Blvd. (772–3224). Baron of beef and famous bumbleberry pie.

VERNAL. Vernal Mine Co. *Moderate–Expensive.* 1360 W. US 40 (789–4514). Popular spot for prime rib, seafood. Entertainment. Reservations a must.

HOW TO GET AROUND. By car. The Interstates (I–70 and I–80 east-west, I–84 northwest, and I–15 north-south) are the primary means of communication where there are long distances between towns. State roads crisscross the rest of the state except in truly desolate areas like the Great Salt Lake Desert to the west of Salt Lake City.

By Plane. From Salt Lake City, *Sky West* flies to Cedar City and St. George. There is also charter service from Salt Lake City to local airports near Zion, Bryce and Canyonlands National Park.

By Train. Ogden and Salt Lake City are on the *Amtrak* line.

By Bus. All the major cities and towns in Utah have good bus service. *Greyhound, Sun Valley* and *Mid-Continental* are some of the carriers.

TOURIST INFORMATION. Detailed information about anything in the state may be obtained from the Utah Travel Council, Council Hall, Capitol Hill, Salt Lake City 84114. Tel. (801) 533–5681.

TELEPHONES. The area code throughout Utah is 801.

SEASONAL EVENTS. Utah keeps busy year round with entertainment, cultural, sporting and festival events. As with most states, winter month attractions are mostly indoor, of a cultural nature and not quite as plentiful as spring, summer and fall activities. The more urban the setting, the more versatile the annual events calendar.

January: In Salt Lake City, the drama season is still in full swing, with productions at *Hale Center Theater* and *Brickyard Plaza.* Auditorium events are held year round in Salt Lake City's municipal coliseum, *The Salt Palace.* It is home for the International Hockey League team, the Salt Lake Golden Eagles and National Basketball Assn. Utah Jazz. At Park City, the *Silver Wheel Theatre* presents old-fashioned melodrama. Winter resort specials include the *Color Country Winter Classic* at Brian Head ski area and the *U.S. Film and Video Festival* at Park City.

February: *Babcock Theatre* at the University of Utah presents drama and music performances during the month. Ballet West performances are staged in Salt Lake City's restored *Capitol Theatre,* as well as Utah Opera Co. productions. Pro hockey and basketball will continue in Salt Lake City. Heber City puts on *snowmobile and dog sled races*

March: Special events centers at University of Utah in Salt Lake City, Utah State University, at Logan, Weber State University, Ogden, and Brigham Young University, Provo, usually hold public programs varying from concerts to pop artists. The *Mormon Festival of Art* is usually conducted at Brigham Young University. Hockey, basketball near season's end in Salt Lake City, and Park City holds its annual *snow sculpture festival.*

April: *Springville Museum of Art,* Springville, holds its annual national art exhibit. *Utah Symphony* and *Ballet West* spring gala at Utah State University. The annual *jeep safari* rendezvous in Moab—bring your own jeep. Brian Head Ski Resort holds its spring fiesta. The *Dixie College Rodeo* is held at St. George. *Indian Days* events at Bluff.

May: *Golden Spike Celebration* at Brigham City; *Smithfield Health Days,* Smithfield; *Black and White Days,* Richmond; *Cache Dairy Festival,* Logan; annual *Ute Indian tribal bear dances* at Whiterocks; *Green River Friendship Cruise,* 180 miles from Green River to Moab. *Widowmaker Motorcycle Hill Climb* near Provo.

June: *The Lagoon* amusement park opens for the summer season near Farmington. Park City hosts the *Vaughn Angel Bicycle Race.* Delta offers their annual *Renaissance Faire,* in City Park. The *Golden Spike Fiddlers' Contest and Bluegrass Festival* occurs in Ogden, while the *Utah Scottish Festival and Highland Games* are held in Salt Lake City. Rodeos at Price, Lehi and Pleasant Grove are usually produced during June. As is the *Dinosaurland Art Festival* at Vernal. *Canyonlands Festival and Rodeo,* late June, Moab.

July: Annual celebrations are in high gear. *Days of '47,* marking the Mormon's arrival in what became Utah, are observed in most communities near and on the 24th, with parades, rodeos and pageants. Also, there are *The Ute Stampede,* Nephi; the *Mormon Miracle Pageant.* The Utah Shakespeare Festival, Cedar City, July 10-Aug. 30 *Kamas Valley Fiesta,* Kamas; *Dinosaur Roundup,* Vernal. and the *Oriental Festival,* Salt Lake City.

August: *County fairs* are prevalent, in Heber City, St. George, Salt Lake City, Logan, Tremonton, Nephi, Parowan, Farmington, Manti. Provo's *Hot Air Balloon Festival* colors the sky and speed trials get underway at the Bonneville Salt Flats. Park City *Art Festival; Railroaders Festival,* Brigham City; *Bluegrass Festival,* Roosevelt.

September: Park City stages an outstanding Labor Day program including mining skill contests and rugby matches. *Bi-Run-Yah Triathalon,* Moab; *Golden Arc Marathon,* Blanding to Bluff. *Peach Days Art Festival* at Brigham City and the *Cache Valley Threshing Bee,* featuring old-fashioned steam-driven machinery, is held at College Ward, *Southern Utah Folklife Festival* relives pioneer days at Zion National Park.

October: *Golden Eagles* hockey and *Utah Jazz* basketball starts another season. The *Hansen Planetarium* in Salt Lake City also launches a new season. Snowbird's *Oktoberfest* is in full swing through mid-month.

November: *Golden Spike livestock show,* Ogden; Christmas parades in major cities throughout the state. College and university football games conclude their season. *Temple Square Christmas Lighting,* Salt Lake City. *Heber City Turkey Shoot;* Santa Clara *Rodeo.*

December: An international *Christmas celebration* is held at Ogden's municipal gardens, *Utah Symphony* and *Ballet West* launch season in Salt Lake City. The Salt Lake Oratorio Society's annual performance of "The Messiah" is performed in the Salt Lake City Tabernacle. On Saturdays, cutter races are held at Tremonton.

TOURS. Few tours are confined to the state itself. But many companies that conduct tours of the region include trips into Utah. Those services operating within the state generally restrict themselves to particular areas and cover certain attractions rather than the full locale.

Gray Line Motor Tours, Hotel Temple Square, 553 W. 100 S., Salt Lake City, UT 84101 (801–521–7060) conducts short trips in and around Salt Lake City. The company also runs shuttles to Alta and Snowbird ski resorts up Little Cottonwood Canyon out of Salt Lake City and tours to Bryce Canyon National Park, Zion National Park and Cedar Breaks National Monument, as well as a Canyonland tour.

Western Leisure Inc. (532–2113) schedules tours of Salt Lake City, the Bonneville Salt Flats and Park City. *Scenic West Tours* (572–2717) makes trips to the Great Salt Lake/Kennecott Copper Mine and Timpanogas Cave National Monument/Bridal Falls from Salt Lake City. *Greater Salt Lake Tours* (523–3664) arranges a 3-hour Chuckwagon Barbecue in Emigration Canyon, along the Pioneer Trail.

NATIONAL PARKS AND MONUMENTS. The five national parks in the state of Utah offer much in the way of outdoor living for hardy travelers who enjoy roughing it. **Bryce Canyon National Park** is located in the southwest part of the state. Its multicolored layers of limestone and clay produce a quilted effect that is enhanced by the rays of the sun. Bryce Canyon itself is particularly impressive, as are Yellow Creek, Willis Point and Rainbow Point. There are 35 miles of roads in the park, but some sections are accessible only on a mule or horse. For those without cars, the park provides transportation at a nominal charge. The Rim Road trip will cover most points of interest. In addition to a hotel and lodge the park has improved camp sites. Camping time is limited. Bryce Canyon also has a well-organized museum with lectures and illustrations explaining the origins of its outstanding features.

At **Zion National Park,** the emphasis is also on natural beauty. But while at Bryce most of the viewing is down, at Zion it is up. At the entrance visitors pass between two enormous colored monoliths, indicating what is to come. After entering the "gate," visible in the distance is the famous Bridge Mountain, so named because of a natural rock bridge high on the crest. Past this is a succession of rainbow-hued rock formations including Streaked Wall and the Mountain of the Sun. Driving north to the road's end leads to the Great White Throne and The Organ. The green, wooded canyon and murmuring river combine with majestic temples and towers to make this a magnificent showcase of natural splendor. Hiking trails lead to such places as Emerald Pool and the Hidden Canyon. Swimming in the Virgin River is an unforgettable experience. A hotel, cabins and campsites offer accommodations for extended stays. Many Jeep camp tours are available for a good, close look at Utah's newest National Park—*Canyonlands.* They can be engaged at Moab, Blanding or Monticello. This park is divided roughly into the Needles District at the southern end and the Island in the Sky at the northern end. Between the two are fascinating formations in The Maze, Land of Standing Rocks, Doll House, Salt Creek, Horseshoe Canyon and White Rim. In the south lies Chesler Park, a secluded valley completely ringed by fingers of rock jutting skyward.

Arches National Park, north of Moab, has five distinct sections, all unique in geology and scenery. The Windows Section is centrally located. Courthouse Towers is in the southern end, Klondike Bluffs at the northernmost point and Devils Garden and Delicate Arch fill the rest of the northern section. The park gets its name from the 89 erosion-formed natural arches scattered around its interior.

Stone portals and bridges are found in **Capitol Reef National Park,** a slender stretch of sightseeing country about midway between Bryce and Canyonlands. It also contains petrified forests and artifacts left by pre-Columbian Indians of the Fremont culture. It is named for the gigantic, domed formations, capped with white sandstone and resembling the nation's capitol. They are part of the Waterpocket Fold, a 100-mile-long bulge in the earth's surface that contains depressions eroded in the rock and capable of holding thousands of gallons of rain water. In the north end, on cliffs behind the peach orchards at Fruita, are petroglyphs carved by ancient Indians. Outlaws, including the infamous Butch Cassidy, knew the area as a perfect hideout.

In addition to the national parks, Utah has nine national monuments. On State Route 14, near Cedar City, is **Cedar Breaks National Monument,** red, yellow, and purple rock country decorated with a profusion of wild flowers in season. Near Point Supreme are full service camp facilities, an information center and a museum explaining the various natural surroundings.

Dinosaur National Monument is particularly fascinating. East of Vernal in north-eastern Utah, entire prehistoric skeletons have been excavated intact by several archeological institutions. Some are kept at a small museum in the monument for visitors to inspect. Many canyons remain unexplored, but it's possible to ride big rubber rafts on safe guided trips through such perilous-sounding places as Split Mountain Canyon and Whirlpool.

Natural Bridges National Monument takes its name from three rock bridges visible from White Canyon. In cave dwellings, open to the public, a fine, sweeping view of the area is possible. This monument is in southeastern Utah, approachable on U–95 or U–261 off US 163.

Hovenweep National Monument, southeast of Blanding, preserves pueblos, cliff dwellings, and dams of prehistoric Pueblo Indians. Camping and hiking are popular here. Ranger Station at Square Tower Trailhead.

On the Navajo Indian Reservation is **Rainbow Bridge National Monument.** It features a fantastic natural bridge which is now only a quarter mile away from the rising waters of Lake Powell. Eventually, as the reservoir water reaches maximum levels, boats will be able to move even closer.

Timpanogos Cave National Monument, in north-central Utah, east of Lehi in American Fork Canyon, features sidewall scenes of white and pink crystals enclosing stalagmites and stalactites shimmering in artificial lighting. The caves, open from May to October, are reached by a strenuous one-and-a-half-mile hike.

Golden Spike National Historic Site, at Promontory in Northern Utah, marks the completion point of America's first transcontinental railroad. A museum at the site also tells the country's cross-nation railroad story.

Flaming Gorge National Recreation Area in northeastern Utah offers water sports and fishing in Flaming Gorge Reservoir. Two visitor centers are open May to September. Lodges, campgrounds and cabins are available.

Glen Canyon National Recreation Area encompasses most of the 150,000-acre Lake Powell, on the Colorado River. Fishing and houseboating are popular, and the scenery (lake, sky, and red sandstone cliffs) is spectacular. The main gateway to the area is Page, Arizona, but the lake lies mostly in Utah.

STATE PARKS. There are 48 state parks in Utah, the largest are Snow Canyon, Dead Horse Point and Wasatch Mountain.

Snow Canyon (5,688 acres), five miles northwest of St. George in the southwest corner of the state, is formed by a large gorge cut out of multi-colored sandstone. There are facilities for both recreational vehicles and tents. Open all year.

Dead Horse Point (4,627 acres) is an area of deep gorges and mesas. Dead Horse Point itself rises about 2,000 feet above the Colorado. Located 34 miles southwest of the town of Moab. There are tent and recreational vehicle spaces and flush toilets. Open all year.

Wasatch Mountain (22,000 acres), near Heber City southeast of Salt Lake City, has trailer hookups, tent spaces, fishing and hunting. There is a golf course nearby. In Heber City is the Wasatch Mountain Railway which chugs along a 3-hour trip through Heber Valley, Provo Canyon and Bridal Veil Falls.

FARM VACATIONS AND GUEST RANCHES. There are not as many guest ranches in Utah as in some of the other "Old West" states, but the ones here have some of the most spectacular scenery in the country. **Diamond Valley Ranch,** 12 miles north of St. George at Veyo (574–2281) offers horseback riding, hunting, camping, and pack trips. Write Box 712, St. George, UT 84770.

Bottle Hollow at Fort Duchesne is owned and operated by Ute Indians. You can take it easy around the modern lodge and pool or take guided trips into the Green River Wilderness.

On the Navajo Reservation in the Monument Valley area is **Gouldings Trading Post and Lodge.** You can take guided jeep tours through this almost unbelievable country of towering mesas and pinnacles and precipitous gorges.

FISHING AND HUNTING. Generally, Utah's **fishing** season starts the Saturday closest to June 1 and runs through November. However, some 200 waters are open year round. The state's most popular and regularly caught fish is the rainbow trout. Frequently taken from many waters are brook, native cutthroat, brown, Mackinaw or lake trout, grayling, largemouth and white bass, bluegill, channel catfish and walleyed pike.

Two large man-made lakes furnish spectacular opportunities for anglers—Flaming Gorge in northeastern Utah and Lake Powell in southern Utah. The state has other reservoirs and several streams, running through high mountain country and down along valley floors, joining sizable rivers, and all are sport for fishermen. These include the Provo, Weber and Logan Rivers; streams in Big Cottonwood Canyon, the High Uinta Mountains and most of the state's national forests. Non-resident licenses good for a year cost $40. A five-day adult tourist license is $15, a one-day tourist license, $5. Non-residents under 12 may fish without a license provided they are accompanied by a licensed angler and their catch is counted in the adult's daily limit.

Limits are: trout, salmon, 8 fish, except in some counties a bonus of 6 cutthroat and/or brook trout; grayling, 8 fish; Bonneville cisco, 30 fish, Bear Lake only; Largemouth and smallmouth bass in the aggregate, 6 fish; white bass, no limit; crappie, 50 fish, but in Lake Powell, no limit; Northern pike, 6 fish except in Provo River, where the limit is 2; whitefish, 10 fish; channel cat, 8.

Hunting is widely practiced in Utah, whether for deer, elk, antelope, jack rabbits, badgers, woodchucks and gophers or quail, pheasant, chukar partridge, ducks and geese. The large mule deer has been stocked around the state wherever browse and competition for the range allows. For years the annual harvest, attracting hunters from throughout the west, has averaged 100,000 deer. A nonresident big game license costs $120 for one deer, either sex.

Quail is best hunted in Washington County and the Uintah Basin while ring-necked pheasants can be found throughout central Utah during a short season in early November. Marshes along lakes and rivers are usual ambush sites for ducks and geese. Non-resident waterfowl and small-game licenses cost $40. Minimum age for hunting big game is 16, for waterfowl and game birds, it's 12.

SUMMER SPORTS. Utah is a wonderland for outdoor recreation, a land of wide-open spaces, magnificent scenic variety and matchless natural wonders. Tennis and golf courses seem to be everywhere and for hardy individualists, possibilities for fishing, hunting, camping, hiking, horseback riding, swimming, water-skiing and boating abound. Water slides are appearing along the Wasatch Front, between Ogden and Provo.

Trails are excellent for **hiking** in Utah's national forests for short trips or several weeks backpacking. Long pack trips are advised to use guide services on the Colorado Plateau and High Uintahs Wilderness Area. An especially memorable hike is the 20-mile walk through Zion National Park's Virgin Narrows. The hike starts several miles below Navajo Lake in the Dixie National Forest and concludes at the bottom of a foot path in Zion National Park. Guide information at the park is available for this spectacular hike.

Jeeping is a popular way to see ghost towns, Indian ruins and spectacular rock formations. The Mexican Hat area, Canyonlands, and Arches National Park provide excellent trails. *Lin Ottinger's Tours,* 137 Main St., Moab, UT 84532 (259–7312), can arrange trips.

River running is a fast growing lure in Utah. These trips, in large unsinkable rubber rafts, carry thrill enthusiasts through rough water on the San Juan, Green and Colorado Rivers. Charter arrangements can be made at Moab, Green River, Bluff and Mexican Hat. For information on them, contact *Utah Guides & Outfitters,* Box 21242, Salt Lake City, UT 84121 (801–943–6707).

House boating, water-skiing and **sailing,** can be enjoyed on Utah's several man-made reservoirs and lakes. In addition to Flaming Gorge, Lake Powell, Great Salt Lake, Bear Lake and Utah lake, there are Strawberry, Pineview, Scofield, Deer Creek, Rockport, East Canyon, Otter Creek, Steinaker and Bottle Hollow Reservoirs. For information about renting houseboats on Lake Powell, contact Del E. Webb Recreational Properties, 3800 N. Central Ave., Box 29040, Phoenix, AZ 85038 (602–278–8888).

There are 45 public **golf courses** in operation around Utah. Many are nestled in unique mountain or desert settings. The state maintains one, at Wasatch Mountain State Park, near Midway in Wasatch County.

SKIING. Utah has some of the finest skiing facilities in the country. For information on areas, accommodations, and costs, write to Utah Ski Planner, Utah Travel Council, Council Hall, Capitol Hill, Salt Lake City, UT 84114 (801–533–5681). Here are some of the best: *In Cedar City:* Brian Head Ski Resort. Excellent powder and alpine skiing (See Cedar City listing) *In Beaver:* Elk Meadows, a new resort with two chairlifts, natural open bowls and cut trails. Mt. Holly Ski Resort. A good family resort. *Ogden Valley:* Nordic Valley Ski Resort. Well-groomed and uncrowded runs. Powder Mountain Ski Resort. 31 runs on three mountains, two double chairs and one triple chair. Snowbasin Ski Resort. In operation since the early 40s, with more than 40 runs. *In Salt Lake City:* Alta Ski Resort. A full-service resort, up to 10,500 feet in altitude. Eight double chair lifts. Snowbird Ski Resort. A full-service resort with modern hotel. Ten chairlifts. Brighton Ski Resort. A great family area for beginners and experts. Solitude Ski Resort, 32 runs and bowls, five chairlifts. *In Park City,* Utah's newest ski area: Deer Valley Ski Resort. Eight triple chairs, one double, and 41 runs. Park City Ski Area. The largest ski area in Utah, with 12 high-performance chairlifts. Parkwest Ski Resort. The locals' favorite. Sundance Ski Resort, Provo Canyon. Yes, this is the one that is owned by Robert Redford. 30 runs, two doubles, and two triples.

SPECTATOR SPORTS. The National Basketball Assn. Utah Jazz and minor International Hockey League team, Golden Eagles, play at the Salt Lake City Salt Palace through the late fall, winter and early spring. The University of Utah in Salt Lake City, Brigham Young University in Provo, Utah State University at Logan, and Weber State in Ogden have full athletic schedules, and the Salt Lake Gulls, play minor league baseball at Derks Field in Salt Lake City.

MUSEUMS AND GALLERIES. Price: *College of Eastern Utah Prehistoric Museum,* City Hall (637–5060). Dinosaur skeletons and Indian artifacts. **Brigham City:** *Brigham City Museum-Gallery,* 24 N. 3rd W. (723–6769). Art and historic exhibits concerning history of the area. **Vernal:** *Utah Field House of Natural History,* 235 E. Main St. (789–3799). Dinosaur gardens, museum with fossils, Indian artifacts, minerals. **Salt Lake City:** *Church Museum of History and Art,* 45 North West Temple (531–3310). Paintings and important historical documents of the Mormon religion. *Genealogical Library,* 35 North West Temple (531–2331). The largest of its kind in the world and open to all at no charge. *Pioneer Memorial Museum,* 300 N. Main St. (581–6961). A treasure trove of frontier relics. *University of Utah Fine Art and Natural History Museums.* On the university campus (581–6927). **Provo:** *Bean Life Science Museum.* On the BYU campus (378–5051). Utah wildlife. In **Fairview:** *Museum of Art & History,* 85 N. 100 East (427–9916). Relics of the Old West. Large woodcarving collection.

HISTORIC SITES. Utah is a perpetual history lesson, with special locations to underline the text. St. George has the first Mormon temple built in Utah as well as Brigham Young's winter home, now a state park museum. Other pioneer homesteads are preserved in the area, particularly the *Jacob Hamblin Home* at Santa Clara.

The oldest house, the *Miles Goodyear Cabin,* is on display in Ogden. Built around 1841, the log-hewn house was used by the first white family settling permanently in what became Utah.

The town of Fillmore is the original Territorial Capital and retains the 1855 building that accommodated the state's first legislative sessions. It's now a museum.

Salt Lake City is packed with historic reminders. Prominent among them are *Lion House,* Brigham Young's office, and *Beehive House,* right next door, which was one of his homes. Also, there's "This is the Place" monument, the *Daughters of the Utah Pioneers Museum* and *Council Hall.* The last two are on Capitol Hill. The *Salt Lake City and County Building,* on Washington Square, is an original and still used for local government purposes. The inside has been extensively remodeled, the second-floor walls are lined with vintage photographs and blueprints. The outside walls are being completely reconditioned, a job that is expected to take 20 years.

Ghost town prowling has become a popular Utah pastime, principally because there are so many abandoned settlements throughout the state and because it's another enjoyable way to see the countryside. Stephen L. Carr, in a 1972 publication, listed 150 ghost towns marking Utah's landscape. A good many are deserted mining camps, but some are former agricultural centers. Among the more interesting are Mercur and Ophir in Tooele County; Rockport,

Summit County, Blacks Fork, Summit County; Rainbow, Uintah County; Scofield, Carbon County; Latuda, Carbon County; Eureka, Juab County; Mamoth, Juab County; Spring City, Sanpete County; Frisco, Beaver County; Cove Fort, Millard County; Osiris, Garfield County; Silver Reef, Washington County. In Pine Valley, Washington County, due north of St. George stands a dignified old two-story church, a magnificent example of meeting house construction common a century ago. But standing as it does, isolated, yet still useful, it is one of rural Utah's most poignant sights.

MUSIC. The Tabernacle on Temple Square in Salt Lake City is home of the world-famous *Mormon Tabernacle Choir.* The Choir can be heard free on Thursday evening rehearsals or on Sundays for the formal performance. The Tabernacle was host to visiting symphonies and home of the *Utah Symphony.* However, such performances are now conducted in Symphony Hall, built on the grounds of the Salt Palace.

LIQUOR LAWS. Utah's liquor control laws beg the visitor's patience. Beer is the only alcoholic beverage served in all public bars. And it is the 3.2 variety. Certain licensed restaurants also serve 2-ounce "mini-bottles" of the most commonly preferred cocktail or highball liquor. But they can only be ordered with food. That applies to wine as well. Private clubs, however, can serve mini-bottle mixed drinks whether food is also served or not. Visitors can purchase a temporary private club membership, and local visitors' bureaus will often supply a list of private clubs. Almost all public eating and drinking establishments permit customers to carry their own liquor to the table or bar, commonly called "brown bagging." And remember, in public restaurants, waiters and waitresses aren't permitted to fetch, open or mix mini-bottles. That all must be done by the customer. Mix will be served, a set-up is provided, and most good restaurants will chill wine brought to the establishment. Retail liquor is only sold in state stores, or package agencies. The legal age is 21 and, for the most part, strictly enforced.

WASHINGTON

The Mountains and the Sea

by
BYRON FISH and ARCHIE SATTERFIELD

Washington is really two states in one. In the west, a mild maritime climate with abundant rainfall nourishes vast evergreen forests that stretch from mountains to sea. East of the Cascades, the lack of rainfall has created arid landscapes, treeless and sparsely populated for the most part, where wheat and irrigated crops thrive.

While trees and mountains dominate the west, water is the other major feature. Dotted with islands, the vast inland sea of Puget Sound extends from the Strait of Juan de Fuca southward to the state capital at Olympia.

In addition to creating the beautiful scenery, these natural features shape the vacation experience. Outdoor recreation—fishing, boating, hiking, river running, horseback riding, skiing, and camping—heads the list for most visitors.

Water and timber shaped the state's history as well. British Captain George Vancouver sailed into Puget Sound in 1792, naming many of the mountains and waterways. Moving north from Oregon, the Hudson's Bay Company came in search of furs, followed by settlers looking for good farmland and timber to build ships. Although Washington became a state in 1889, it really came into its own as the major supply center and debarkation point for the Klondike gold rush in 1898.

EXPLORING SEATTLE

Seattle is a rarity among big cities—it grows more attractive with the years in spite of urban sprawl. In recent years, the "flight" to the suburbs has subsided. Instead, renovating old homes in the center of the city, or buying condominiums and co-ops in the heart of town, has become common. On the other hand, people still can buy pleasant homesites not far from town and become the first occupants of the land.

Downtown Seattle's answer to the challenge of suburbs and their shopping centers has been a constant upgrading, with plantings, fountains, sculpture, malls, imaginative urban parks, and preservation-renewal of two historic areas and the waterfront. Bus drivers collect no fare in the downtown area—everyone rides free. One result has been that Seattleites repeatedly read national magazine articles describing their city as "the most liveable." They can't decide whether to be smug, or alarmed that such praise will bring a crowd and less liveability.

The central skyline changes each year as 30-to-76-story buildings go up. The Space Needle, built for the World's Fair in 1962, was called the tallest structure in town, but it was soon topped by the 50-story Sea-First Bank Building. The L.C. Smith Tower, correctly bragged about by two generations as "the tallest building west of the Mississippi," is now a quaint little spire peering up at its neighbors.

Skyscrapers with thousands of feet of new office space are visual proof that Seattle is indeed the paperwork capital of the Pacific Northwest. Their height also means that, as in San Francisco, the easiest way to go is up. The central city is narrow-waisted, squeezed in against hills by its Puget Sound harbor, Elliott Bay. Lake Union, the city's back-door, freshwater harbor, lies just to north. South, the land was once a tideflat. Now it is occupied by rail lines, warehouses, trucking companies, machinery manufacturers and, along the waterfront, the piers and giant cranes of the shipping business. Seattle's aerospace activities get the publicity locally and nationally, but the maritime industry accounts for more jobs. East lies Lake Washington, the other half of the water girdle that squeezes the city's waistline.

The best way to see this all at once and get oriented to the city's layout is from the observation platform at the 500-foot level of the Space Needle at the Seattle Center. If you are downtown you can get there in two minutes for a 60¢ fare on the Monorail. (Its terminal is at the Westlake Mall.) The Space Needle (elevator fare) is not the only spectacular vantage point; but it is the only one that presents a 360-degree panorama.

The central business district lies to the south. There used to be a hill between it and the Space Needle, but it was dumped into Elliott Bay years ago. To save later confusion, first note that downtown is different from the main pattern of avenues north-south, and streets east-west. The pioneers laid out the first avenues parallel to the waterfront, so downtown faces southwest toward the bay.

Ocean-going ships used to moor right downtown. Today you'll see the working port at the southern end of Elliott Bay, where the Duwamish River flows in. The residential area southwest across the water is

West Seattle, and the extreme point at the entrance to the bay is Alki, where the first settlers landed in 1851. Early the next year they found the deeper harbor along the present waterfront and moved to it to start the city.

The state ferries coming and going to the west across Puget Sound are bound for Bremerton, back in a mainland channel of the Kitsap Peninsula, and to closer Bainbridge Island, where many commuters live. Backing the whole scene are the Olympic Mountains.

Seattle Center is laid out directly below. Queen Anne Hill, to the north, blocks a view of what is down behind it, the ship canal whose locks connect salt water with Lake Union, seen to the right of the hill. Lake Washington, which forms the entire eastern boundary of the city, is over other hills. Northeast, on the canal between the two lakes, is the University of Washington and its accompanying business district.

The backdrop on the east side is the Cascade Range, with Mount Rainier looming on the southerly horizon and, farther away, toward the north end, 10,778-foot Mount Baker.

Back to earth. Downtown Seattle has three built-in shows that run all year, most busily from mid-spring through October. They are the Pioneer Square Historic District, the Pike Place Public Market, and the waterfront. They can be reached by foot or by free city bus from the main hotels, and they cost nothing except what you may decide to pay for food, drink, a boat ride, or an aquarium admission.

The Waterfront

The biggest circus is the waterfront. After the maritime trade moved down the harbor to modern facilities, people and fun moved in. Don't allow less than half a day on foot if you are really going to savor this section. It stretches some 19 blocks, from Pier 51 at the foot of Yesler to Pier 70 at the end of Broad Street, and up to Pier 91 on a foot path.

Pier 51 is approximately where the city began, with Henry Yesler's pier and sawmill. Actually that site is now a couple of blocks inland, near Pioneer Square and the totem pole, as a result of landfills. South of Pier 51 is an old-fashioned pergola marking the first city-owned dock for the Harbor Patrol; and the Alaska State Ferries pier. The ferries sail north twice a week in the summer, once a week in the winter, and since they are conditioned and repaired in Seattle, their blue funnels with the seven stars of the Big Dipper are often seen there.

At the street end of Pier 51 is the unusual, widely-known Ye Olde Curiosity Shop, a mixture of souvenir store and museum, that has been in existence (with one move) since 1899.

State ferries load and unload at Pier 52, and its second-level open walkways on each side afford waterfront viewpoints. (For more about the ferries, see "How to Get Around.") Pier 52's predecessor was Colman Dock, long the terminal for traffic up and down the Sound back when roads were few. Passengers and freight were carried by a "Mosquito Fleet" of small steamers that called at dozens of otherwise isolated villages and brought back farm produce.

North of 52 is Fire Station No. 5, a great curiosity to inlanders because it houses waterborne "firetrucks," boats designed to protect Seattle's many miles of shoreline buildings and capable of pouring thousands of gallons of seawater a minute through their "cannon" nozzles. The fireboats are periodically seen in the bay when they go out to test their equipment, or to greet Tall Ships or cruise ships that call

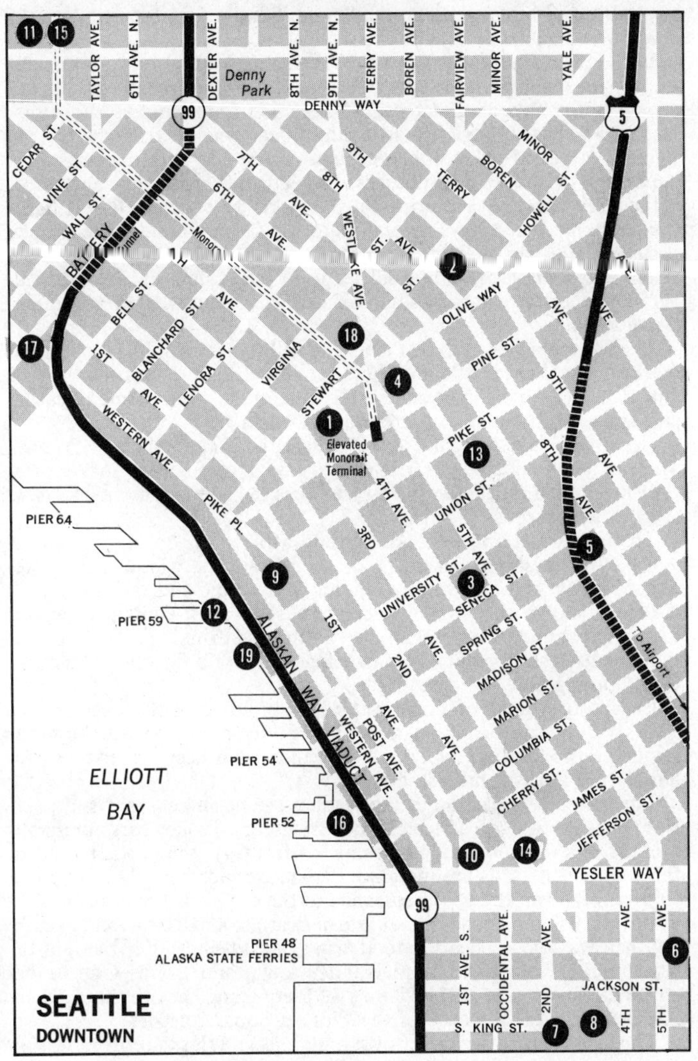

Points of Interest:

1) Bon Marché
2) Central Bus Terminal
3) Four Seasons Olympic Hotel
4) Frederick & Nelson
5) Freeway Park
6) International District
7) Kingdome
8) King Street Station (Amtrak)
9) Pike Place Market
10) Pioneer Square
11) Seattle Center
12) Seattle Public Aquarium
13) Seattle Sheraton
14) Smith Tower
15) Space Needle
16) State Ferry Terminal
17) Waterfront Terminal
18) Westin Hotel
19) Waterfront Park

on Seattle and other cities on the Sound. Station 5 and its exhibits are open to the public from 1 to 9 P.M.

In the blocks on north there are numerous seafood restaurants and snack bars opening on the street. Except in the worst weather there are people eating outside under heated canopies. Large import shops display goods bazaar style. Sight-seeing boats operate from here. (See "Tours".) Pier 57 offers public fishing. A new city park has walkways built over the water, and observation platforms. Also new and novel is the aquarium (fee) featuring Pacific Northwest marine life. It has a sunken dome that allows spectators to walk around under the surface so fish outside can watch them through the glass. In other sections sea otters and seals lead as normal a life as is possible in captivity (no performances), and along with live specimens in tanks, there are educational exhibits.

The Schwabacher Wharf, Pier 58, is still remembered in a historical marker. The *Portland* landed here on July 17, 1897 with its "ton of gold," news of which set off the Klondike rush, transformed Seattle, and made its name known around the world.

Canadians have bought Pier 69, where the excursion ships *Princess Marguerite* and *Vancouver Island Princess* dock for runs to Victoria, B.C. in summer (see *Tours,* below), as does the new catamaran *Victoria Clipper* which runs year-round.

The Edgewater Inn (see "Hotels and Motels") is on Pier 67, and if you have a bayside room and want to fish out the window, the hotel will go along with the gag by lending you a pole and tackle.

Pier 70's huge warehouse was converted into a self-contained bazaar. It runs the gamut of shops, galleries, eating and drinking places. Across the street is the popular, open-evenings-only, Old Spaghetti Factory. (See "Dining Out.")

Except for a small oil dock, waterfront buildings end at Pier 70, but a newly-built trail leads on north along the shore, toward the monstrous grain elevators, which stand beside such deep water they can handle the largest tankers afloat.

The railroad tracks under the viaduct are not-much-used spurs left from days when they carried cargo to freighters. Trolley cars purchased in Australia run up and down the waterfront. At the northern end of this stretch, the rails are mainline. If you wonder how they got there so invisibly from the south entrance to the city, it is because some 75 years ago, when railroads meant life or death to small cities and usually got their way, young Seattle stood firm against being cut up by right-of-ways. It held out for a tunnel under town, and got it. One tunnel entrance can be seen in the vicinity of Pier 64 and the other near King Street Station, at the edge of the Pioneer Square district.

The viaduct between downtown buildings and the waterfront was an aesthetic mistake, Seattleites now admit, but there is no gainsaying it furnishes a fast-flowing freeway that by-passes the city center.

Farmer's Market

A number of cities include a "farmer's market" in their list of attractions, but none has the historic background of Seattle's, nor the fervent, emotional support of citizens who went to the polls to vote money to preserve it.

The market began in 1907 when the city issued permits to farmers to sell their produce off wagons parked in Pike Place. As time went on, too many wagons showed up and the city built stalls which it allotted for a small fee on the basis of daily drawings.

Pike Place became a Seattle phenomenon, an amiable madhouse of vendors hawking their wares (including seafood) and willing to haggle over price—a quite unAmerican practice that astounded visitors.

The fading of nearby farmlands into subdivisions and commercial zoning, the addition of non-local produce (bananas, grapefruit and California vegetables to keep counters in business during the winter), the leasing of otherwise unused space for the sale of nonagricultural products, and a city decision to subdue so much shouting and bargaining, somewhat changed the original character of the market.

The buildings had aged, so planners blithely wrote off the market in an urban renewal plan. That's when Seattle voters said "NO" and decreed it to be a historical asset. Most of the buildings have been restored and the complex also is newly connected by stairs and elevator to the waterfront park. The market continues as the place to find fresh octopus, bulk spices, every kind of cheese, arts and crafts, small restaurants with the menus of various nations, home brew supplies, old books and records, fresh vegetables, fruit, meat, seafood—you name it.

Skid Road or the Pioneer District

The term "Skid Road" originated in Seattle for a logical reason. Oxen or horses dragged timber down off the hill to Yesler's mill and wharf at the village center. The skidroad consisted of small logs placed crossways to the path and greased, a method widely used in the woods before the advent of steam donkey engines and later diesel-powered skidders.

By the 1890s Victorian brick buildings had sprouted on the site; and with the Klondike gold rush the area just to the south of them, a former tideflat whose fill included a lot of sawdust, became the saloon and red-light district. During the first decades of the century city business gradually moved north into newer buildings, and the original center deteriorated. The old Skidroad became known for its dubious character and (with cheap rents) as the place where men went when they were down on their luck.

New buildings began creeping back down the streets, demolishing old structures in their path. As they approached Pioneer Square, Seattle arrived of an age to become interested in its heritage. The upshot was a preservation movement that progressed into an official declaration of a protected "Pioneer District" (sounds better than "Skidroad") whose landmark is the totem pole in Pioneer Square, a triangle at First and Yesler.

The district takes in eighteen blocks and by now includes pedestrian malls, arcades, shops of all descriptions, and some fashionable restaurants. You can't tell what's inside a building by its antique exterior; you have to explore. The best way to learn all the history is by an Underground Tour (See Tours).

This was the jump-off point for the Klondike (Yukon Territory) and Alaska gold rushes. It is the southern terminus of the Klondike Gold Rush National Historical Park. The "park" is the route from Seattle through Skagway and Chilkoot and White Passes to Dawson, Yukon. The park service has an interpretative center at 117 Main that tells the story of Seattle's role as supplier for the gold rush, and provides information to travelers heading North.

Adjoining the Pioneer District on the east is Chinatown. The Chinese are outnumbered by other races and the area was renamed the "International District" but tradition keeps that name from sticking. What with Pioneer Square developments and the nearby stadium, Kingdome, this district also is reviving. It contains the top Chinese and Japanese restaurants. Two colorful events are Chinese New Year and the Japanese Bon Odori street dances in August. Tours of the area (reservations required) begin at 628 S. Washington.

The domed stadium's name is from the local county, King, but it is also king-size, the building itself encompassing ten acres. It has the world's largest self-supporting roof (no posts to sit behind). Among the superlatives applied to the Kingdome is that "you could put the Rome Stadium inside it, lions, Christians, chariots and all." It has daily tours, with senior citizens charged the same rate as children.

The 1962 World's Fair never really ended in Seattle. Its legacy, the fairgrounds now called Seattle Center, has as many visitors as ever, to the Space Needle, theaters, Coliseum, exhibition halls, Seattle Art Museum's contemporary gallery, rides, shops, the old Food Circus renamed Center House, and the exhibits of Pacific Science Center.

The free show at Hiram Chittenden Locks, better known as the Ballard Locks, rates with the rest. Allow more time than you expected to spend watching boats go up and down between saltwater Shilshole Bay and the freshwater lakes. You also can watch fish going up the ladder, through glass from a viewing room. There are neatly landscaped grounds, and a new interpretive center has been added. On the way to the locks you'll see the fishing fleet's marina, south shore just west of the Ballard bridge.

For the motorist there are four scenic drives called Trident Tours. Follow the street signs with Neptune's fork, and you will see all parts of the city.

Excursions from Seattle

The ferry boats that connect the northwest Washington mainland with seven big islands and the Kitsap and Olympic peninsulas do more than provide essential commuter service; they are means of exploration. Capacity for automobiles ranges from 40 to 206. Hot meals and snacks are served at lunch counters on most runs.

The longest and most spectacular regular ferry run begins at Anacortes, about 75 miles northwest of Seattle, and weaves through the San Juan Islands to Sidney, above Victoria, B.C.

Anacortes is reached by I–5 to Mount Vernon and Wash. 536. But a far more scenic, though slower, path to Anacortes traverses two islands, Whidbey and Fidalgo. The southern gateway to Whidbey is the ferry from Mukilteo to Columbia Beach, and the road north is Wash. 525, which becomes Wash. 20 midway up the island.

Approximately 50 miles long, Whidbey Island is the largest island in Puget Sound and the longest in the United States. Here, rhododendrons, Washington's state flower, reach heights of 20 to 30 feet. Homes of early settlers dot the shores. In recent years, a number of bed-and-breakfast inns have opened in and around the little country town of Langley on the south end of the island. Oak Harbor is the most important town. Ft. Casey is a former coast artillery post, whose long guns are now for tourist viewing.

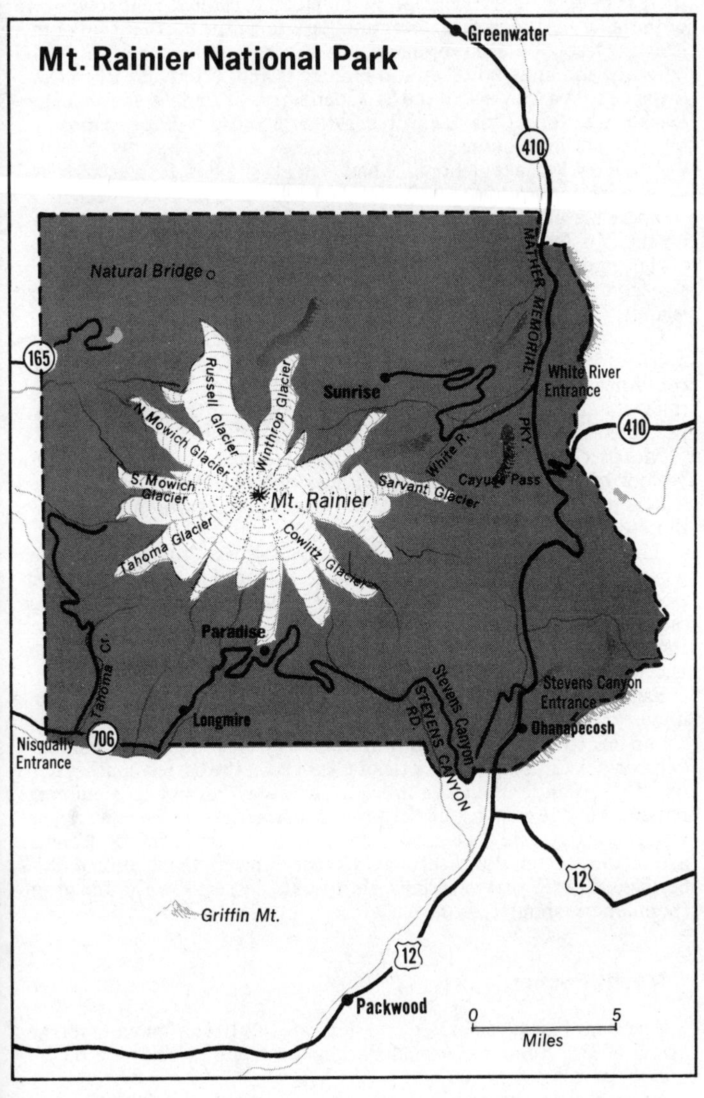
Mt. Rainier National Park
Greenwater
410
Natural Bridge
165
Russell Glacier
Winthrop Glacier
N. Mowich Glacier
S. Mowich Glacier
Tahoma Glacier
Mt. Rainier
Cowlitz Glacier
Sarvant Glacier
Sunrise
White R.
Cayuse Pass
MATHER MEMORIAL PKY.
White River Entrance
410
Paradise
Tahoma Cr.
Longmire
Nisqually Entrance
706
Stevens Canyon
STEVENS CANYON RD.
Stevens Canyon Entrance
Ohanapecosh
12
Griffin Mt.
12
Packwood
0
5
Miles

Between Oak Harbor and Ft. Casey is Coupeville, where stands Alexander's Blockhouse, built as a defense against Indians. Actually, there is more: Coupeville is a museum piece, a restored 1875 town. One of the state's finest parks, Deception Pass, is on the northern tip of this island. Deception Pass bridge spans a gorge notorious for its tidal currents, and links Whidbey and Fidalgo Island. From here it is a short distance to Anacortes and the San Juan ferry. Enroute, a short sidetrip leads to the top of the 1,270-foot Mt. Erie and a view of islands and mainland, all directions.

The ferry touches at Lopez, Shaw, Orcas, and San Juan Islands and skirts many more of the 172 isles that comprise this archipelago.

There are eight state parks with campgrounds (no trailer hookups) on the San Juan Islands, and the state owns 42 undeveloped islands, all but one of which are accessible by boat only. These isles range in size from 134 acres down to less than an acre. (If you use one of these islands, carry your garbage back with you.)

Orcas Island, in the San Juans, possesses the most vacation resorts and best beaches. Its Moran State Park contains picnic grounds, 124 campsites, four trout-stocked lakes, miles of foot paths cutting through thick stands of virgin forest, and an abundance of game and bird life, protected under state law.

Moran's Mt. Constitution rises 2,400 feet above sea level. From a 50-foot rock tower atop the butte, hundreds of miles of island-dotted waters are visible. To the east, Mt. Baker rears its white dome above the high Cascades.

San Juan was the site of the bloodless "Pig War" of 1859. It began when British settlers, claiming the island belonged to the Crown, wanted to try in Victoria an American farmer who had shot a British-owned pig. For twelve years the island was occupied by both American and British military forces. Finally the dispute was settled, sustaining the U.S. claim to the San Juans.

San Juan Island National Historic Park, in two sections, recalls the unnasty war, in which not a life was lost except that of the pig. English Camp lies 10 miles from Friday Harbor. The blockhouse, commissary, and barracks still stand. American Camp is on the barren southeastern tip of the island, about five miles from Friday Harbor. No buildings remain, but the vestiges of the principal American defense works are well preserved. The park is open daily from sunrise to sunset. Rangers are on duty from June through October and at the National Park Service office all year in Friday Harbor, the largest town in the group (population: about 1,200).

Mount Rainier

The state's most celebrated and highest (14,410 feet) mountain takes up all of Mt. Rainier National Park. (For details, see section on *National Parks.*)

From Seattle, drive to Enumclaw, then east on US 410 up the western slope of the Cascades 41 miles to the Cayuse Pass "Y." (Shortly before you get to Cayuse Pass, a park road winds nineteen miles to Sunrise, a 6,400-foot high campground "looking straight up the mountain." The dead-end road, usually not open until July, keeps it from being heavily visited, but Sunrise enthusiasts rate it as Rainier's most inspiring spot.) At Cayuse Pass it is worth driving several miles up the Chinook Pass highway for views of Mt. Rainier from its east side, and south along the Cascade Range. Return to the "Y" and drive south fifteen miles to Stevens Canyon entrance. The park road goes 21 all-which-way miles to Paradise, whose inn is above 5,400 feet. This is the principal destination and stopping point for all tours, many of which turn around here after arriving from the other direction, through Sunshine Point (Nisqually), the longtime main entrance at the southwest corner of the park. From Nisqually it is about an hour-and-a-half to Tacoma and two hours to Seattle via Eatonville and Puyallup.

PRACTICAL INFORMATION FOR SEATTLE

HOW TO GET THERE. By Plane. Because Seattle is the closest American city to Alaska and Japan, it is served well by airlines that use Seattle-Tacoma International (Sea-Tac) Airport as a port of entry. While the fallout of airline deregulation continues, there are a number of relatively stable airlines serving Seattle from both foreign and domestic cities: *Alaska Airlines, American, Braniff, British Airways, Canadian, Continental, Delta, Eastern, Finnair, Hawaiian Air, JAL, Mexicana, Northwest Orient, PSA, Pan American, SAS, Thai, TWA* and *United.* Commuter airlines include *Horizon* and *San Juan.*

By Bus. As with most cities, *Greyhound* and *Continental Trailways* are the major companies. Trailways serves cities along the I–5 corridor. Greyhound serves all cities along its routes.

By Train. Amtrak serves Seattle. From the east come the *Empire Builder* (from Chicago via St. Paul, Spokane, and Portland), *The Pioneer* (from Chicago via Salt Lake City, Ogden, Boise, and Portland); from the south, the *Coast Starlight* (from Los Angeles), and *Mount Rainier* (daily service between Seattle and Portland).

By Car. The two major corridors to Seattle from everywhere else are I–5, which runs from the Canadian border to the Mexican border; and I–90, which begins at Seattle (or ends there, depending on the direction you are traveling) and heads east toward the Atlantic. I–5 gets you to Vancouver; British Columbia; and Portland, Oregon. I–90, which points east, takes you skiing at Snoqualmie Summit, and to Spokane.

By Boat. *Sitmar Cruises* uses Seattle as a port for its Alaska cruises. The city has become a port of call for other cruise lines repositioning their ships in spring and fall, and serves as the southern terminus for Alaska Marine Highway ferries.

ACCOMMODATIONS. The half-century-old Olympic, with its aura of early-day elegance, reopened several years ago as the Four Seasons Olympic, with most of the rooms remodeled, many enlarged to suites, and the entrance and lobby restored to their original opulence. All others in the deluxe category are sleek and relatively new, both downtown and at the Seattle-Tacoma International Airport. A growing number are in Bellevue, separated from Seattle on the east by Lake Washington but easily reached by two floating bridges. (A semi-rural suburb 30 years ago, Bellevue is now an independent city of 80,000 population.) As elsewhere, hotels and motels are arranged alphabetically by price range based on double occupancy. They are: *Deluxe* $90 and up; *Expensive* $60–$90; *Moderate* $40–$60; *Inexpensive* under $40. Those listed are typical but, especially in the less expensive categories, represent only a fraction of the rooms available. Note: all area codes are 206.

Since a single "Seattle" listing would lump together motels and restaurants up to 30 miles apart, they have been put into "central," "north," "south" and "east" categories. Through Seattle, "Motel Strip" is along old Highway 99—Aurora Avenue north of the city center and Pacific Highway South, toward the airport. Biggest suburban cities surrounding Seattle are Edmonds, Lynnwood, Mountlake Terrace and Bothell to the north; Kirkland and Bellevue east across

Lake Washington; Renton, Tukwila, unincorporated Burien and Des Moines to the south, along with Kent, Auburn and Federal Way.

Central Seattle

Alexis Hotel. *Deluxe.* 1007 1st Ave., Seattle 98104 (624–4844). European-style elegance. 54 rooms. Concierge.

Crowne Plaza Hotel. *Deluxe.* 6th Ave. and Seneca, 98101 (464–1980). I–5 Seneca-Union exit. One of the newer hotels in downtown Seattle, conveniently located near freeway, shopping, and entertainment.

Four Seasons Olympic. *Deluxe.* 411 University, 98101 (621–1700). Grand old hotel restored to its former elegance. Concierge, shops, valet parking, health club, fine dining.

Seattle Sheraton Hotel and Towers. *Deluxe.* 1400 N. 6th Ave., 98101 (621–9000). Corner 6th and Pike. City's largest hotel in heart of downtown. Concierge, suites, award-winning restaurant, extensive art collection.

Sorrento Hotel. *Deluxe.* 900 Madison, 98104 (622–6400). Small, intimate hotel completely renovated to become one of Seattle's showplaces. Perched on a steep hill above downtown, has wonderful views of Puget Sound and Olympic Mountains. Dining room, cocktail lounge, suites.

The Warwick. *Deluxe.* 401 Lenora, 98121 (443–4300). Corner 4th and Lenora. Hotel on northern edge of downtown district. Modest on the outside, luxurious inside. Indoor pool, sauna, exercise room.

Westin Hotel. *Deluxe.* 1900 5th Ave., 98101 (728–1000). 5th and Westlake. Its twin circular towers are a downtown landmark and provide stunning views of water and mountains. Some suites. Pay garage. Cafe, dining rooms (including Trader Vic's), and cocktail lounge with entertainment.

Best Western Executive Inn. *Expensive.* 200 Taylor Ave. N., 98109 (448–9444). Medium-size motor hotel, north of downtown near the Seattle Center. Restaurant, entertainment.

Camlin Hotel. *Expensive.* 1619 9th Ave., 98101 (682–0100). Corner Pine. Classic older hotel newly remodeled. Cloud Room rooftop restaurant commands fine views. Pool, parking lot.

Inn at the Market. *Expensive.* 86 Pine St., 98101 (443–3600). The city's newest lodging, in heart of Pike Place Market, has flavor of a European country inn. Complimentary breakfast. Dozens of restaurants nearby.

Mayflower Park Hotel. *Expensive.* 405 Olive Way, 98101 (623–8700). Corner of 4th Avenue. Wonderfully situated in heart of downtown shopping area. Just a few blocks from Pike Place Market. Covered parking, Restaurant, bar.

Meany Tower Hotel. *Expensive.* 4507 Brooklyn Ave. N.E., 98105 (634–2000). In the University district, this large hotel offers 155 corner rooms with views of Lake Washington and mountains. Parking lot, coffeeshop, dining room.

Best Western Continental Plaza Motel. *Moderate.* 2500 Aurora Ave. N., 98109 (284–1900). Motor inn of 2- and 4-story buildings comprising units of varying sizes. Many with lake and mountain views. Some with refrigerators, a few with water beds, some with kitchens at extra charge. Coffeeshop. Seasonal rates.

Downtown TraveLodge. *Moderate.* 2213 8th Ave., 98121 (624–6300). Attractive, convenient motel. Restaurant nearby. No pets.

Edgewater Inn. *Moderate.* 2411 Alaskan Way 98121 (728–7000). Attractive 4-story motor inn hanging over Puget Sound on Pier 67. Guests can fish from their windows. Coffeeshop, dining rooms, cocktail lounges, entertainment. Wide range of accommodations.

TraveLodge by the Space Needle. *Moderate.* 200 6th Ave. N., 98109 (441–7878). As its name implies, motel is near to Seattle Center and all its attractions. Pool. No pets. Seasonal rates.

University Inn. *Moderate.* 4140 Roosevelt Way N.E., 98105 (632–5055). Large motor inn near the University of Washington campus. Many kitchenettes. Laundry, pool.

University Plaza Hotel. *Moderate.* 400 N.E. 45th, 98105 (634–0100). Just off I–5 at the N.E. 45th exit. Large motor inn near University of Washington. Some suites. Some refrigerators. Pool, dining room, lounge, and entertainment.

Vance Downtown Hotel. *Moderate.* 620 Stewart St., 98101 (441–4200). Convenient downtown hotel with garage. Popular grill and Cedar Room. Cocktail lounge.

Bridge Motel. *Inexpensive.* 3650 Bridge Way N., 98103 (632–7835). Rather small motel situated a block east of the north end of the Aurora Bridge. Some units with beautiful views of the city, Lake Union, and mountains.

City Center Motel. *Inexpensive.* 226 Aurora Ave. N., 98109 (441–0266). Comfortable, conveniently located between downtown and Seattle Center. Some kitchenettes, some with two rooms. Coin laundry.

Marco Polo Motel. *Inexpensive.* 4114 Aurora Ave. N., 98103 (633–4090). 2-story motel with 1- and 2-room units. Some with kitchen facilities at extra charge.

North Seattle

Ramada Inn. *Expensive.* 2140 N. Northgate Way, 98133 (365–0700). Large motel near Northgate Shopping Mall. Pool, restaurant and lounge adjacent.

Best Western Landmark Inn. *Moderate.* 4300 200th S.W., Lynnwood (775–7447). Just off I–5. Large motor inn with variety of accommodations. Some rooms with steam baths. Very good restaurant, coffeeshop, lounge with entertainment. Indoor pool, whirlpool.

Rodeside Lodge. *Moderate.* 12501 Aurora Ave. N., 98133 (364–7771). Large motel two miles west of I–5. Some suites, two-bedroom units. Features heated pool, spa, sauna, exercise room. Dining room and restaurant. Senior rates.

Black Angus Motor Inn. *Inexpensive.* 12245 Aurora Ave. N., 98133 (363–3035). Part of extensive Black Angus restaurant chain founded in Seattle. Motel offers comfortable rooms, on-site restaurant, usual amenities.

Thunderbird Motel. *Inexpensive.* 4251 Aurora Ave. N., 98103 (634–1213). An attractive, smaller motel, very accessible to downtown area. Some 2-bedroom units with kitchenettes at extra charge.

South Seattle

Hilton Airport. *Deluxe.* 17620 Pacific Highway S., 98188 (244–4800). One of three Hiltons in Seattle area, with amenities expected of its name. Dining room, coffeeshop, lounge, entertainment. Swimming and wading pools. Pets allowed. Courtesy car to airport.

Marriott. *Deluxe.* 3201 S. 176th St., 98188 (241–2000). The newest Sea-Tac hotel and one of the finest in the area.

Holiday Inn of Sea-Tac. *Expensive.* 17338 Pacific Highway S., 98188 (248–1000). Large hotel with friendly atmosphere. Large revolving restaurant on top serves excellent dinners. Young waiters/waitresses furnish the entertainment. Coffeeshop, lounge with entertainment. Pool, car to airport.

Hyatt Seattle. *Expensive.* 17001 Pacific Hwy. S., 98188 (244–6000). Very large motor inn with broad choice of accommodations. Some suites with refrigerators. Pool, saunas, coffeeshop, dining room. Lounge is popular with local people for entertainment and dancing. Car to airport.

Red Lion Inn/Sea-Tac. *Expensive.* 18740 Pacific Highway S., 98188 (246–8600). Very large motor inn with wide choice of accommodations. Dining rooms and coffeeshops. Lounge with entertainment. Also Maxi's Restaurant and lounge on top of the tower. Pools, saunas. Transportation to airport.

Sheraton Renton Inn. *Expensive.* Box 487, Renton, 98057 (226–7700). 800 Rainier Ave. S. Large motor inn, conveniently situated in Renton, a few minutes' drive from airport. Some 2-room units and suites. Pool, dining room, coffee shop, lounge, entertainment. Transportation to and from airport.

Doubletree Inn. *Moderate–Expensive.* 205 Strander Blvd., 98188 (246–8220). Large motor inn in Southcenter Shopping Complex, a short drive from the airport. Wide choice of units, some with refrigerators, some with steam baths. Several suites. Dining room, coffee shop, lounge with entertainment. Playground, pool. Pets allowed.

Jet Motel. *Moderate.* 17300 Pacific Highway S., 98188 (244–6255). Large 3-level motor inn. Restaurant, cocktail lounge with dancing and entertainment.

Indoor and outdoor pools, exercise room, whirlpool, sauna. Courtesy car to airport.

Sandstone Inn. *Moderate.* 19225 Pacific Highway S., 98188 (824–1350). 2-level motor inn with one and two room units, several with kitchenettes. Lounge and excellent 24-hour restaurant. Pets allowed. Free parking for "fly-away" guests. Airport transportation.

Vance Airport Inn. *Moderate.* 18220 Pacific Highway S., 98188 (246–5535). Large 5-story motor inn. Attractively furnished rooms. Restaurant, lounge with dancing and entertainment. Pool, sauna, whirlpool.

Imperial Inn. *Inexpensive.* 17108 Pacific Highway S., 98188 (244–1230). Medium-size motel. Some units with kitchenettes. Pool, car to airport. Pets allowed. Restaurant next door.

West Wind Motel. *Inexpensive.* 110 Rainier Ave. S., Renton 98055 (226–5060). In Renton city center. Several units with kitchenettes at extra charge. Adjacent restaurant.

East Seattle

Red Lion Inn-Bellevue. *Expensive–Deluxe.* 300 112th Ave., Bellevue 98004 (455–1300). Largest hotel in Bellevue, adjacent to I–405 in downtown area. Two restaurants, banquet facilities, pool, suites.

Best Western Greenwood Hotel. *Expensive.* 625 116th Ave. N.E., Bellevue 98004 (455–9444). I–405 N.E. 8th exit. Large motor inn. Some suites with fireplaces. Panache Restaurant, lounge, entertainment. Pool.

Holiday Inn-Bellevue. *Expensive.* 11211 Main St., Bellevue 98004 (455–5240). Large motor inn in downtown Bellevue. Pool, pets ok. Gourmet restaurant, "Jonah and the Whale," very popular with locals. Lounge, entertainment.

Red Lion/Bellevue Center. *Expensive.* 818 112th Ave. N.E., Bellevue 98004 (455–1515). Large facility with comfortable, attractive rooms. Some with fireplaces and kitchenettes. Several suites. Restaurant and lounge with entertainment.

Holiday Inn–Issaquah. *Moderate.* 1601 12th Ave. N.W., Issaquah 98027 (392–6421). Off I–90 near Lake Sammamish State Park. Comfortable motor inn with many amenities. Wading and swimming pools, sauna, whirlpool, putting green. Coin laundry. Restaurant, lounge, and entertainment.

Eastgate Motel. *Inexpensive.* 14632 S.E. Eastgate Way, 98007 (746–4100). Small. Some units have kitchenettes, some with two rooms. No pets. Near shopping centers.

Overlake Silver Cloud Motel. *Inexpensive.* 15304 N.E. 21st St., Redmond 98052 (746–8200). Newer motel in suburban shopping area. Some rooms have refrigerators. Coin laundry. Whirlpool, exercise room. No pets. Restaurant adjacent.

HOSTEL. The Seattle **YMCA,** 909 Fourth Ave., Seattle, WA 98104 (382–5000), is a member of the American Youth Hostels Association. It is located within a few blocks of the Pike Place Market, Pioneer Square, Chinatown, and the Monorail. For additional information, contact the Washington State Council of the American Youth Hostels, 419 Queen Anne Ave. N., # 108, Seattle, WA 98109 (281–7306).

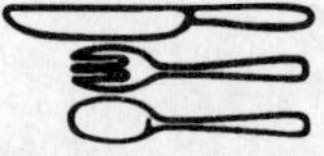

RESTAURANTS. During the past 20 years Seattle has moved its culinary rating up from "undistinguished" to "none better." There is fierce competition for a gourmet reputation among dozens of restaurants. There are hundreds of cafes and restaurants in the area and new ones are opening all the time. We have chosen but a few of them. Very great eating places are to be found in the hotels and motels but have not usually been listed separately.

Restaurants, large and small, abound on the waterfront, ranging in price from inexpensive to deluxe. There is seafood, of course, but other specialties are also represented. This strip is best explored on foot.

While at the Seattle Center, a visit to the Center House's Food Circus Court offers a chance to sample a wide range of international snacks.

Chinatown is a great place to explore. There are numerous Chinese, Japanese, and Filipino cafes and restaurants in all price ranges. In the Pioneer Square Area are many snack shops and sidewalk cafes. The Pike Place Market has a number of ethnic cafes and restaurants as does the Broadway District on Capitol Hill.

In the University District, one finds coffeeshops and little cafes. In the Ballard area, look for home-style Scandinavian cafes.

Among the many fast food and take-out chains are Kentucky Fried Chicken, McDonalds, Herfy's, Skipper's Seafood 'N Chowder House, Shakey's Pizza, Dairy Queen, Jack-in-the-Box, Taco Time, Taco Bell, Pizza Haven, Godfather's Pizza, Ivar's Seafood Bars, Burgermaster, and Burger King.

We list city restaurants first, followed by a selection of good restaurants in the suburbs. Price categories for a complete dinner, excluding tax, tip, and drinks, and ranges are: *Deluxe,* $20 and up; *Expensive,* $15–$20; *Moderate,* $10–$15; and *Inexpensive;* under $10.

Canlis. *Deluxe.* 2576 Aurora Ave. N. (283–3313). Wonderfully friendly and relaxing restaurant with a la carte menu and generous portions. The chef, presiding over a flaming pit, turns out steaks as ordered, also seafood and lamb. Sparkling view of the lights reflected in Lake Union. Piano bar.

City Loan Pavilion. *Deluxe.* 206 First Ave. S. (623–4167). Owner Francois Kissel, holder of a Culinary Olympics medal, offers a classic French menu based on fresh, local fish, meats, produce, and herbs. Lively, romantic setting.

Dominique's Place. *Deluxe.* 1927 43rd Ave. E. (329–6620). French cuisine lovingly prepared and served in an atmosphere resembling a French auberge. Specialties include lamb rack medallions, roast duck, venison, and veal. Dominique's sauces are famous.

Fuller's. *Deluxe.* Seattle Sheraton Hotel, 1400 6th Ave. (621–9000). Top-rated gourmet restaurant featuring nouvelle cuisine. Emphasis on Northwest ingredients. Stunning art collection of some of the region's finest artists including museum-quality glass from Pilchuck School.

Mirabeau. *Deluxe.* 1001 4th Ave. (624–4550). Continental cuisine high atop the city on the 46th floor of the Fourth Avenue Plaza Building. Excellent views of Puget Sound and city.

Rossellini's Four-10. *Deluxe.* 4th and Wall (728–0410). A Seattle institution named for its former location at 410 Union. This is where lots of the locals go for an elegant, expensive dinner. No better service, food, or wine. Valet parking.

Space Needle Restaurant. *Deluxe.* Seattle Center (443–2100). Revolving restaurant 500 feet above Seattle Center with the best dining view in town. Northwest cuisine. Emerald Suite for gourmet dining.

Labuznik. *Expensive–Deluxe.* 1924 1st Ave. (682–1624). Near Pike Place Market. Eastern European restaurant is one of Seattle's finest. Specialties include roast duck and veal Orloff.

13 Coins. *Expensive.* 125 Boren Ave. N. (682–2513). New York-style "after-theatre" restaurant in Furniture Mart Building. Somewhat difficult to find. Huge servings in categories from plain to exotic. Open 24 hours. Locally popular. Another 13 Coins is at 18000 Pacific Highway S., near Sea Tac International Airport.

Adriatica. *Expensive.* 1107 Dexter N. (285–5000). Remodeled 1920s house, overlooking Lake Union, is the setting for Mediterranean cuisine. Specialties are calamari with Greek garlic sauce, lamb marinated in zinfandel wine, and mixed grill. Top-floor bar, with fine views, is popular gathering spot.

Clipper's. *Expensive.* Mayflower Park Hotel, 405 Olive Way (623–8700). Quiet, elegant dining. Specialties are baby back ribs with plum sauce and fettucini con pollo. Weekend brunch.

F. X. McRory's. *Expensive.* Occidental S. and S. King St. (623–4800). Vast restaurant in Pioneer Square near the Kingdome. Seats 350 at a time. Perhaps the loudest restaurant in town, but intentionally so. Premium meat and oyster bar. Infinite number of liquor selections.

Hiram's at the Locks. *Expensive.* 5300 34th N.W. (784–1733). If one gets hungry while visiting Hiram Chittenden Locks, this is a great place to eat. Get a table with a view of the constant activity at the Locks. An experience in both dining and viewing.

Jake O'Shaughnessey's. *Expensive.* 100 Mercer St. in the Hansen Baking Complex (285–1897). Gold-rush days decor and a menu limited to that of the original Jake O'Shaughnessey who opened a restaurant in Seattle in 1897. House specialty is "saloon beef," loin encased in salt and cooked for ten hours. An interesting bar—Irish coffee a specialty. Friendly, informal restaurant, not far from Seattle Center.

Le Tastevin. *Expensive.* 19 W. Harrison (283–0991). Unexcelled French cuisine served by professionals. Exceptional wine cellar. Lunch and dinner, full bar.

McCormick and Schmick's. *Expensive.* 1103 1st Ave. (623–5500). Dark wood paneling and emerald carpeting, staff in white aprons and black bow ties give this seafood restaurant a San Francisco atmosphere.

Prego. *Expensive.* Atop the Stouffer Madison Hotel, 515 Madison (583–0300). Fine Northern Italian cuisine. Extensive wine list.

Ray's Boathouse. *Expensive.* 6049 Seaview Ave. N.W. (789–3770). Although fire destroyed this Seattle landmark in 1987, it is being rebuilt for the 1988 season. Known as one of the city's finest seafood restaurants, it's on Shilshole Bay at the entrance to the Ship Canal.

Ivar's Acres of Clams. *Moderate.* Pier 54 on Alaskan Way (624–6852). Long-time Seattle family favorite newly remodeled. Located near Washington State Ferry dock, with great views of water traffic and Olympic Mountains. Huge variety of fresh seafood. Children's menu.

Ivar's Salmon House. *Moderate.* 401 N.E. Northlake Way (632–0767). The building, a reproduction of an Indian longhouse, houses artifacts collected by owner. Dugout canoes hang from ceiling, old photographs and other memorabilia decorate walls. Full-course salmon dinners are prepared Indian-style over open alderwood fires. Children's portions. Buffet lunch, cocktails.

Maximilien-in-the-Market. *Moderate.* In Pike Place Market (682–7270). French market cafe. The chef shops here, food is fresh from the stalls and prepared with special flair. Watch the harbor activity as you dine.

The Phoenicia. *Moderate.* 100 Mercer St. (285–6739). Newly relocated, locally popular restaurant serving Mideast and Balkan dishes, including lamb, seafood, curries, and vegetarian dinners.

Stuart Anderson's Black Angus. *Moderate.* 15820 1st Ave. S. (244–5700). Several other locations in Seattle area. Top-quality beef. Excellent chefs who prepare it to order. House specialty is steak and lobster. Lounge with entertainment and dancing.

Triple's. *Moderate.* 1200 Westlake N. (284–2535). Upbeat waterfront dining on Lake Union, just north of downtown. Emphasis on fresh Northwest cuisine.

Andy's Diner. *Inexpensive–Moderate.* 2963 4th Ave. (624–4097). In complex consisting of seven railroad passenger cars, guests eat in an atmosphere recalling early years of dining on the rails. Choices are limited to prime quality beef. Great family atmosphere.

Gretchen's Of Course. *Inexpensive.* 1513 6th Ave. (467–4006). Also 1111 3rd Ave. (467–4002). Imaginative selection of breakfast and lunch items to eat in or take out. Good, hearty food.

Guadalajara Restaurants. *Inexpensive.* 1429 4th Ave. (622–8722). Also 1718 N. 45th (632–7858), 5923 California S.W. (932–2803). Expertly prepared Mexican food. Imported and domestic wines and beer.

King's Table. *Inexpensive.* 1545 N.W. Market St. (784–8955). Also 16549 Aurora N. (542–5665); 10001 Lake City Way (523–1331); 2222 California St. (937–2999). Family place, with children under 10 charged according to age. Large selection of entrees and salads, served buffet style. Lunch and dinner.

Old Spaghetti Factory. *Inexpensive.* Elliott and Broad St. (441–7724). Family food and fun in restored warehouse. 19th-century decor, antiques in lobby and bar. Metal bedstands form booths, and even an old Birney streetcar is used for seating. Choice of sauces, plus salad, sourdough bread, beverage, and spumoni for dessert. Dinners only.

Tai Tung. *Inexpensive.* 659 S. King St. (622–7372). Old-time Chinese restaurant with dozens of selections. Popular with locals. Good for families.

Tokyo Teriyaki. *Inexpensive.* 372 Roy St. (282–0393). Near Seattle Center. Small menu, featuring beef and chicken teriyaki served with salad and rice. Bargain prices. Good pre-theater choice.

In the Suburbs

Anthony's Home Port. *Expensive–Deluxe.* 135 Lake St., Kirkland (822–0225). Pleasant restaurant on waterfront. Very good food, carefully prepared. View lounge. Sunday brunch.

Cafe de Paris. *Expensive–Deluxe.* 109 Main St., Edmonds (771–2350). Near ferry dock in Edmonds. Outstanding gourmet menu. Plan to make it a leisurely, special dining experience. French and domestic wines.

Jonah and the Whale. *Expensive–Deluxe.* In Holiday Inn, 11211 Main St., Bellevue (455–5240). Award-winning gourmet restaurant with elegant surroundings.

Benjamin's. *Expensive.* 10655 N.E. 4th. (454–8255). On the ninth floor of Seattle Trust Building in Bellevue. One of the few restaurants with a view toward Seattle. Large menu with chicken, pasta, and seafood.

Cafe Juanita. *Expensive.* 9702 N.E. 120th Pl., Kirkland (823–1505). Known throughout the Puget Sound area for its outstanding Italian food, imaginatively prepared. Specialties include spiedini misto, pollo ai pistacci, and homemade pasta. Owner Peter Dow makes his own wine, sold only at his restaurant.

13 Coins. *Expensive.* 18000 Pacific Highway S., in the Sea-Tac Office Building on Airport Strip (243–9500). Open kitchen so customers can watch chefs working with their frying pans over hot flames. Generous relish trays, great food and desserts. Comfortable lounge.

Angelo's. *Moderate.* 1830 130th N.E., Bellevue (883–2777). Off-the-beaten track, serving traditional Italian cuisine in comfortable, intimate setting.

Brusseau's. *Moderate.* 117 5th Ave. S., Edmonds (774–4166). Small neighborhood cafe with bakery is a Northwest trendsetter in serving fresh, local foods and wine. Breakfast and lunch. Weekend breakfasts are popular.

Casa Lupita. *Moderate.* 437 108th N.E., Bellevue (453–9795). Hearty Mexican food served in pleasant setting.

Morgan's Lakeplace. *Moderate.* 2 Lake Bellevue Drive, Bellevue (455–2244). Emphasis on fresh Northwest cuisine at this comfortable, very popular waterside Bellevue restaurant. Attentive service.

Stuart Anderson's Black Angus. *Moderate.* 95 Airport Way, Renton (226–9600). 1411 156th N.E., Bellevue (746–1663). This well-known chain has restaurants throughout Puget Sound area. All have very good food served in comfort and privacy. All have lounges, entertainment, and dancing. No cover charge.

Andy's Tukwila Station. *Inexpensive.* 16200 West Valley Rd., Renton (235–1212). Complex of railroad cars make up this restaurant. Same good food and drinks as the downtown Andy's.

Mandarin Garden. *Inexpensive.* 40 E. Sunset Way, Issaquah (392–9476). One of area's finest Chinese restaurants, tucked away in this Seattle suburb, 20 miles east of downtown. Owner Andy Wang prepares authentic Mandarin, Szechuan, and Hunan dishes, with fresh ingredients purchased daily at Pike Place Market.

HOW TO GET AROUND. By Plane. For intrastate flights, see same heading under general information for the state.

Car rental: At Sea-Tac Airport alone, 16 firms vie for business. Motels, hotels, and the telephone directory can steer you to still more, downtown and in the suburbs.

By Ferry. Washington State's fleet of ferries is part of the state highway system. All but one route is across Puget Sound, which is not very wide but it forms an efficient barrier to westbound roads for about 90 miles along I–5. The only bridge crossing Puget Sound itself (no toll) is at Tacoma.

South to north, the ferry routes are Tacoma to Tahlequah, Vashon Island; Fauntleroy (southwest Seattle) to Vashon and on to Southworth on the Kitsap Peninsula; Pier 52 in downtown Seattle to Bremerton, and another route to Winslow on Bainbridge Island; Edmonds, 15 miles north of Seattle, to Kingston at the north end of Kitsap Peninsula; Mukilteo, southwest of Everett, to Columbia Beach, Whidbey Island; and Keystone, Whidbey Island, to Port Townsend. Bainbridge and Whidbey islands are connected to the mainland by bridges, but not anywhere near their ferry landings.

From Anacortes, ferries run to the San Juan Islands, and one trip extends to Sidney, B.C. on Vancouver Island. A Canadian ferry runs frequently to Vancouver Island from Tsawwassen, just north of the border and west of Blaine.

Crossing times are from 15 minutes (Tacoma-Tahlequah) to one hour (Seattle–Bremerton). Reaching various San Juan islands takes from 45 minutes to an hour and 45 minutes. To Sidney it is 3½ hours. Ages 5–11 and 65–up ride half fare. There are round-trip excursion fares that allow time ashore before return.

By Bus. Metro Transit (information: 447–4800) runs not only city buses but routes all over the county. It is one of the best transit systems in the United States. Most schedules are frequent. The no-fare zone in the downtown area is from Sixth Avenue to the waterfront, and from South Jackson to Battery Streets. Beyond, to the city limits, fare is 55¢ non-rush hours; 65¢ during rush hour; 85¢ and $1.00 for outside city. A Metro line goes to and from Tacoma, stopping at Sea-Tac Airport. It's not Metro, but from the airport Gray Line runs the Airport Express, much cheaper than taxis.

Outbound, pay when you get off; inbound, when you board. You must have exact change. With a pass from the Metro office, Exchange Bldg., Second & Marion, senior citizens (65 or older) can ride anywhere for 20¢. The Monorail runs from Fifth and Stewart to Seattle Center, non-stop. Fare is 60¢.

TOURIST INFORMATION. The Seattle-King County Convention and Visitors Bureau is the basic source of information for the area, and the organization's walk-in information center, at the corner of Seventh Avenue and Stewart Street, has brochures, schedules, and information for all over the city, county, and state. Address: 666 Stewart St., Seattle, WA 98101 (447–7273).

Twice a year the bureau publishes a Coming Events Calendar, one for September through February, the other for February through September.

MUSEUMS AND GALLERIES. Historical: *Museum of History and Industry,* 2161 E. Hamlin (324–1125). History of Pacific Northwest from time of the Indian, transportation and fire engines, aerospace exhibits, fashions, and furnishings. Maritime collection of figureheads, ships' bells, ship models; dioramas and specimens of wild life.

Art: *Charles and Emma Frye Art Museum,* 704 Terry (622–9250). Large collection of Munich School paintings, 1850–1900; American School, 19th and 20th centuries. Free. *Seattle Art Museum,* Volunteer Park (625–8900). Exceptional collections in all fields of Asian art; pre-Columbia collection; European and American paintings. *Seattle Art Museum Pavilion,* Seattle Center. Rotating exhibits, generally contemporary art. *Henry Art Gallery,* U. of Washington (543–2280). 19th- & 20th-century American and European paintings; contemporary prints and American ceramics; modern Japanese folk pottery. Newest on the institution scene is the Bellevue Art Museum, in Bellevue Square Mall (454–6021). Permanent collection, rotated on exhibit, and juried shows as well.

As elsewhere, private galleries and craft shops have been springing up faster than they fade away. You find them everywhere. Among those well-established are *Kirsten, Woodside/Braseth, Francine Seders, Linda Farris, Penryn,* and *Stonington. The Silver Image* is devoted to photography, and *The Snow Goose* has Eskimo art. For others and what they present, see Friday editions of the newspapers, when more than 100 galleries are listed.

Special Interest: *Pacific Science Center,* Seattle Center (443–2880). Exhibits primarily math, space, astronomy, and physical science, with developing programs in life science and Northwest Indians. *Thomas Burke Memorial Washington State Museum,* U. of Washington (543–5590). Unique collection of Northwest Coast Indian material; ethnology of the Pacific Rim; geology and paleontology of the Pacific Rim; zoology; human evolution. Free. *Wing Luke Memorial Museum,* 407 7th Ave. S. (623–5124). Rotating exhibits emphasize Chinese history and culture. In Kirkland, a suburb of Seattle, Kirkland Historical Museum has exhibits of several old ships. *Museum of Flight,* 9494 E. Marginal Way S. (764–5720), is a world-class museum with a brand-new Great Gallery displaying 30 full-size historic aircraft. *Nordic Heritage Museum.* 3014 N.W. 67th in Seattle (789–5707). Interesting exhibits dealing with the city's Scandinavian community. *Suquamish Museum* (598–3311), on the Kitsap Peninsula west of Seattle, provides a fascinating look at the Indians who settled in the Puget Sound area. Take the Washington State Ferry to Winslow on Bainbridge Island.

TOURS. (For ferry touring, see *How to Get Around.*) *Seattle Harbor Tours* runs a one-hour, narrated trip around Elliott Bay, Seattle's waterfront, leaving from Pier 56 on the downtown waterfront, mid-April to October. Canadian Pacific has two daily summertime cruises from Seattle's Pier 69 to Victoria aboard the *Princess Marguerite* and the *Vancouver Island Princess.* It's a four-and-a-half-hour trip each way.

There is a new catamaran service from Pier 69 to Victoria; the *Victoria Clipper* operates two roundtrips daily in summer, one the rest of the year (448–5000). While in Victoria there is the choice of two sightseeing tours, world-famous "Butchart Gardens" or "Sealand of the Pacific," with afternoon tea at the Empress Hotel. Mid-May through mid-Sept.

A trip to Tillicum Village on Blake Island runs from spring through fall, twice a day. You go by sightseeing boat from Pier 56 on Seattle's downtown waterfront. The captain points out points of interest on the 45-minute trip. Tour Tillicum Village longhouse, with its Indian carvings and totem poles. Indian-made handicrafts available at the curio shop. Salmon is barbecued the way the Indians did it centuries ago on 5-foot cedar stakes over an open alder fire. Menu includes Tillicum hot bread and wild blackberry cream tarts. North Coast Indian dances are after-dinner entertainment. For information, call 329–5700.

Gray Line of Seattle offers a wide variety of tours in and around Seattle. Its 2½ hour "Discovery City Tour of Seattle" takes in Chinatown, the world's first concrete floating bridge, the arboretum, the University campus, and the Metropolitan Tract, new glass and steel downtown skyline. Year-round.

The "Adventure Water Tour," a 2¼ hour cruise aboard Gray Line's double-decked *Sightseer* boat, includes a cruise through Seattle's busy harbor, from salt-water to freshwater, via Government Locks to Fisherman's Terminal and Lake Union. May through Sept. A combination of the "Discovery" and "Adventure Water" tours takes 4½ hours.

Underground Tour is an off-beat 1½ hour guided walking tour of 5 blocks, both above and below ground, in the Pioneer Square area. A fire in 1889 destroyed much of Seattle, and the city took the opportunity to improve the waterfront and rebuild streets 10 to 18 feet higher than they had been. Blocks of stores and sidewalks became subterranean, and eventually were forgotten for several decades. For information call 682–1511.

Chinatown tours also go afoot. Call 624–6342 for reservations. Starting point is 628 S. Washington St. The Kingdome has three daily tours except when some event is in progress.

The self-guiding, drive-yourself *Trident Tours* provide the easiest and most inexpensive method of seeing the Seattle area for visitors with cars. Brochures for these tours are available at all hotels, and most rental-car agencies. *Skagit Hydroelectric Project Tours* are offered by Seattle City Light from mid-June to Labor Day. They begin at the tour center in Diablo, on State 20 (North Cascades Highway). The package includes a ride up the 500-foot incline railway, a 4½-mile boat trip to Ross Dam, a tour of the dam and a big meal—all the chicken you can eat. Total cost during the 1987 season was $18. Reservations are required. Write Skagit Tours, City Light Bldg., 1015 Third Ave., Seattle 98104, or call, 625–3030.

Probably the most popular surface tour out of Seattle is Gray Line's *Mt. Rainier National Park Tour.* "The Around the Mountain Sightseeing Tour," as it is called, completely encircles the mountain, with 2 hours for passengers to explore along the trails, take in the Visitor Center, and enjoy lunch at Paradise Inn. Tour starts at 9 A.M.; completes at 6 P.M. May through Sept. For information call 624–5813.

Northwest Trek, six miles north of Eatonville on Wash. 161, is a 600-acre zoo allied to Tacoma's. Animals native to the Northwest roam freely-bison, deer, elk, moose, mountain sheep, and many others. Visitors ride around on propane-propelled trams with guides explaining the tour. Also nature trails. Great for families. Senior citizens get a reduced rate. Open daily from end of February through October; reduced hours in November and December. Call 832–6116.

GARDENS. *U. of Washington Arboretum,* along Lake Washington Blvd., south of the campus. Roads wind through 250 acres of extraordinary plantings, bringing blooms throughout most of the year. The delicate *Japanese Tea Garden,* which encompasses four acres in the Arboretum, is the largest of its kind outside Japan. Free guided tours. Call 543–8800 for times. *Woodland Park Zoological Gardens* covers about 95 acres and includes an extensive rose garden. Seattle has 45 parks, each of which has a bit of garden. There's an early-day conservatory at *Volunteer Park,* site of the Seattle Art Museum. At the *Carl S. English, Jr. Gardens* at Hiram Chittenden Locks, you can pick up a self-guiding tour brochure at the Interpretive Center. *Freeway Park,* in the center of town, is a garden consisting of huge planter boxes and waters. It "lids" the I–5 freeway and is quite unusual.

SPORTS. Because of the mild winter climate, most outdoor recreations go on the year-round in the lowlands, including golf and even skin diving; and determined skiers can find usable snow in the high mountains eight months of the year. *Boating:* Canoes to yachts, motorized or for sailing; rented, chartered, or on tours; on lakes or in Puget Sound; with or without pilot—all are available. Some 30 charter, tour, and rental firms are listed in the yellow pages of the Seattle telephone directory. *Bicycle Riding:* One popular place for this is the 2.8-mile public track around Green Lake. Rent bikes at Gregg's, 7007 Woodlawn N.E. And watch out for joggers. Alki has a rental shop and miles of streets marked for cyclers. The Bicycle Center is close to the Burke-Gilman Trail. *Fishing:* In parks or by designated public access to otherwise private lakes. Bass, perch and crappie, and cutthroat, silver, and rainbow trout are the principal species taken. License is needed in freshwater, and for salmon and clams in saltwater.

Boathouses at Ballard, in West Seattle, and in suburban Puget Sound shore towns rent boats and gear. *Golf:* Seattle has three municipal courses, 18–27 holes. There are a dozen 18-hole public courses in the immediate suburbs, plus some 9-hole courses and private clubs with exchange privileges for visiting members of other clubs. *Hiking:* Many trails in and around the city. Myrtle Edwards Park is a 2-mile path along Elliott Bay. Nature trails in Arboretum-Foster Island, Seward, Schmitz, Lincoln and Discovery Parks. Burke-Gilman Trail runs 12½ miles from north side of Lake Union to Kenmore, north end of Lake Washington. *Picnicking:* Allowed in almost all city and county parks. All have tables and benches and some have stoves. *Swimming:* Both city and county have numerous beaches, freshwater and saltwater. There are nine municipal pools and several commercial indoor pools, but in many cases the out-of-town visitor has a heated pool at his motel. *Tennis:* City parks have many courts, some of which are lighted at night.

SPECTATOR SPORTS. Completion of the West's first domed stadium made Seattle eligible to have major league baseball and football teams. (For all sports schedules, consult the daily papers or the Seattle-King County Convention and Visitors Bureau Information Center.) *Baseball:* Seattle Mariners, playing at the Kingdome, are in the American League. *Basketball:* Seattle Supersonics, in National Basketball Association, play in the Coliseum. Top college contests are at the University of Washington Hec Edmundson Pavilion, and Seattle University plays at the North Court of Connolly Center on campus. Seattle Pacific, an independent, plays at Royal Brougham Pavilion on the SPC campus. *Football:* Seattle Seahawks, National Football League, play in the Kingdome. University of Washington Huskies often draw capacity crowds in 55,000-seat stadium. *Auto Racing:* Three tracks in the region are Seattle International Raceways, at Kent; Evergreen Speedway, at Monroe; and the Puyallup Raceway Park. *Horse Racing:* Season at Longacres, in Renton, is from April to October. *Hydroplane Racing:* The big unlimiteds compete on Lake Washington in early August, to end Seafair. *Hockey* and *soccer* are occasional events in Seattle, and you will have to watch local papers for the existence or nonexistence of these sports.

SHOPPING. Seattle's central shopping district covers six blocks, from Seneca to Stewart streets, between First and Seventh avenues, and includes the Monorail Terminal and numerous good hotels. Browsers delight in its high-fashion shops, antique galleries, china shops, men's and women's specialty shops, pastry shops, and dozens of others. *Frederick & Nelson,* 5th and Pine; and *The Bon,* 4th & Pine, are the best-known large department stores. *Nordstrom,* 5th and Pine, specializes in high-quality apparel for men, women, and children. Top quality is offered at plush. *I. Magnin,* 6th & Pine. *Eddie Bauer,* Rainier Concourse, is famous for its outdoor equipment for campers, hunters, fishermen, backpackers, and climbers. Long-established *Shorey Book Store,* 110 Union, specializes in old books and maps and in Northwest history. It also has a branch in the Pioneer Square area, which is full of small shops of every description, running strongly to handcrafts and imports.

Scattered throughout the downtown area and in the so-called *International District* are small shops specializing in ivory, furs, lacquer ware, silver, silks, carpets, handmade furniture, glass, china, leather, and other imports. In the basement of Center House at Seattle Center is the *International Bazaar,* and nearby is *Hansen Baking Co.,* whose name is a non-sequitur. It used to be a bakery but is now a collection of restaurants and shops of all kinds. See description of the waterfront under *Exploring Seattle* for shops in that area.

There are many sophisticated shops in the *University District,* a living area reflecting the diversity of the more than 30,000 students from many countries who populate the campus. There is a genuinely cosmopolitan air on University Way, more familiarly known as "The Ave." Understandably, this district has a congregation of bookstores. Among the many shopping malls surrounding the city, the largest are *Northgate, Alderwood, Bellevue Square,* and *Southcenter,* with branches of many of downtown's leading stores.

CHILDREN'S ACTIVITIES. There is an abundance of parks and beaches. The most unusual playground is Gas Works Park, north side of Lake Union. You'll never see another one like it, nor happier children as they clamber over and into what was once industrial equipment. Ferry rides and the Monorail appeal to youngsters. There's Green Lake, with boats, bikes, and fishing gear to rent and with swimming both indoors and out. Playgrounds and picnic areas are scattered throughout the parks. Seattle Center, with the Space Needle; the Pacific Science Center, where the child can see more than 100 special exhibits, an amusement area; puppet shows and children's plays at the Piccoli Theater; Then, in another part of Seattle, there's Lake Washington Ship Canal and locks—and Woodland Park Zoo, with its children's zoo. On the waterfront is the Marine Aquarium.

Tillicum Indian Village on Blake Island (See *Tours*) is a family experience.

MUSIC. The Seattle Symphony Orchestra is among the best in the nation. It presents a long season at Seattle Center Opera House, and a number of special performances. The Seattle Opera Association has drawn raves from critics throughout the world. The Northwest Chamber Orchestra, which performs eight "concert pairs" from September to May, has a loyal following.

There's a Gilbert & Sullivan Society and an outstanding Seattle Youth Symphony. Pacific Northwest Ballet is a professional resident ballet company. Touring orchestras, singers, dancers, and other performers add to the full bill.

STAGE AND REVUES. A Seattle newspaper's list of stage events was chosen at random. It showed 12 theaters in action Fri.-Sun., and some for all week. All companies were professional or semi-pro, based in the area and presenting a whole season. The two biggest are Seattle Repertory Theater at Seattle Center, and A Contemporary Theater (ACT). Among others are the Pioneer Square, Empty Space, Intiman, Poncho Theater, and Bathhouse. Touring companies appear in several theaters. The University of Washington has three theaters, Glenn Hughes (Playhouse), Penthouse, and the Meany Theatre. The Fifth Avenue presents occasional road shows of Broadway hits in a restored rococo theater.

The best way for a visitor to find out what is going on currently is to consult the Friday entertainment sections of the two Seattle dailies. The *Times'* section is called "Tempo" and the *Post-Intelligencer's* is "What's Happening." A third source is "Seattle Guide," a free weekly found at hotels, motels, Seattle-King County Convention and Visitors Bureau Information Center, and elsewhere. *The Weekly* is a fourth source.

This advice also applies to *Nightclubs and Bars* and to *Museums and Galleries.* The two newspapers list where the entertainers are, and what exhibits are in progress at which galleries.

NIGHTCLUBS & BARS. State law requires that any place licensed to pour liquor by the drink must also serve food—that is, to enough customers to prove its substantial business is being a restaurant or cafe. (The law is not applicable to taverns dispensing only beer and wine.) Therefore there are no saloons as such, nor nightclubs devoted only to drinking, dancing, and floorshows. However, that situation has not slowed activities very much. The restaurant side may close by 9 or 10 P.M., but the bars are open until 2 A.M. More than 100 places in the Seattle area have live entertainment, ranging from a single pianist to floor shows.

The big hotels feature much the same thing in conjunction with their bars and lounges, both downtown and at the *Airport Strip.* Several downtown spots put on cabaret-style entertainment. In smaller nightspots, "entertainment" may mean featured soloists or an act during dancing intermissions.

Just drinking and listening to sometimes too-loud music can be done in any cocktail lounge, anywhere. Residents tend to take their guests—and visitors seek out—places that are distinctive to the area. (The same can be said for eating, but as noted above, all the lounges are in restaurants.) Half a dozen "sky rooms" on a top floor are popular. Numerous restaurants face Puget Sound, and more look out on Lake Union. Some have views of the fishing fleet and half a dozen others are at marinas. Similar spots ring Lake Union and are dotted along Lake Washington.

EXPLORING WASHINGTON

The state's main south-north freeway, I–5, follows much the same route as did the pioneers, from Vancouver, Washington to Puget Sound cities. It continues to Vancouver, B.C. US 101, the coastal route, crosses a 4.1-mile-long toll bridge from Astoria, Oregon, into Washington. It runs all the way up from Southern California, then does a somersault over the northern end of the Olympic Peninsula, to head south again and end its journey in Olympia.

The Cascade Range divides the state in half and into different climates, vegetation and, to some extent, different ways of thinking. Six passes lead through the mountains, one of them carrying the main trail, I–90, a fast freeway from Seattle to Spokane and on to the east. It crosses Snoqualmie Pass, next to the lowest gap at 3,022 feet.

Those who take the lowest one don't realize they are crossing a pass at all. Wash. 14 follows the Columbia River. Nevertheless there is a point midway in the gorge that marks the change from west side to east side. The Columbia is perhaps the only river in the world that managed to cut its way directly through a major mountain range rather than follow easier routes downhill.

The newest and most northerly highway is Wash. 20, which passes through the North Cascades National Park, described under "Parks." Warmed up to jump mountains, it wanders on through the rumpled Okanogan Highlands to Newport, on the Idaho border north of Spokane.

US 2 begins (or ends) in Everett, and crosses 4,061-foot Stevens Pass. It goes through Wenatchee and provides the closest access to Grand Coulee Dam on its way to Spokane. Once the main east-west route (until I–90 was built), it is still mostly two lanes.

Between Yakima and the west side there is a choice of two passes. Thirteen miles out of Yakima, Wash. 410 splits off from US 12 to go over 5,440-foot Chinook Pass, a beautiful drive but usually closed in winter. US 12 itself uses 4,500-foot White Pass, which is generally kept open. Either pass connects with highways to Seattle and Tacoma, and to I–5 south of Chehalis. They tap Mount Rainier National Park as a bonus.

The east-side Columbia Basin is criss-crossed with fast highways heading in all compass directions. Here are the main routes:

Eastbound from Yakima, US 12 goes through the Tri-Cities—Richland, Kennewick, and Pasco—and on to Walla Walla and Clarkston, bordertown with Lewiston, Idaho. A freeway, I–82, runs from Ellensburg to Prosser. In the future it will replace US 12 to Tri-Cities, then go south to join I–80N as it speeds from Portland to Pendleton and on east.

US 97 goes from Oroville, on the Canadian border, to Mexico. In Washington it links Okanogan, Wenatchee, Ellensburg, Yakima, Toppenish, and Goldendale. On the Oregon side of the Columbia River it crosses I–80N—another handy tie-in for loop trips. US 395 connects I–80N on a diagonal to Spokane, by way of Tri-Cities and Ritzville (where it also becomes I–90).

For Easterners, it should be noted that "freeway" is to be taken literally. There are no toll roads in the West. Occasionally you hear the word "expressway," but it is used merely as a synonym for freeway, a divided arterial crossed only by over- or under-passes. A "limited access" highway hasn't quite passed the tests to become a genuine freeway. Lanes often are divided, but occasionally there is a plain old turnoff, crossroad, or a speed zone that may include a traffic signal.

Southwest Entrance

The winding coastal route, US 101, is popular with visitors who are really sightseeing. They choose it, coming or going, because of the spectacular Oregon Coast it follows in that state. The toll bridge from Astoria ends at Megler, where there is a choice of taking US 101 north or turning right on Wash. 401 to pick up Wash. 4 to Longview and I–5. The last half of this route is usually in sight of the Columbia. A reviving, historical town on the way is Cathlamet, which dates to 1846 as a trading post. A bridge-and-ferry combination connects, via Puget Island, to Oregon.

Longview, the first planned community in the Northwest, began strictly as a lumber-company town but is now quite diversified, especially in retailing. At Longview a bridge crosses the Columbia to Rainier, Oregon. Kelso, a mile from Longview, is on I–5.

Back at Megler, if you follow US 101 you arrive immediately in Washington's distinctive southwest corner. It is a long drive away for most of the state's residents because they must circle down around Willapa Bay to reach Long Beach Peninsula. From one to four miles wide, it stretches 28 miles north between ocean and bay. The ocean beach is hard-packed sand, and cars are driven on it. Some of them also are lost there, by drivers who squirrel around too close to the water or who don't watch the incoming tide.

Activities include surf fishing there and, oddly enough, also in elongated lakcs. Accommodations and trailer spaces are abundant, although they may fill up in the summer. The first town, Seaview, is shoulder-to-shoulder with the town of Long Beach, once a great summer spa for Portlanders, who were carried there by sidewheel steamboats and a short spur railroad from a landing at Ilwaco, inside the mouth of the Columbia.

Willapa National Wildlife Refuge is on the east side of the peninsula. You have to walk a bit to get to the shore of the refuge to see the migratory birds and waterfowl. At Nahcotta visitors are welcome at the Northwest Oyster Farm plant; see how oysters are planted and harvested. Oysterville, founded in 1854, was once the richest and most famous town on the Peninsula—and for 30 years was the seat of Pacific County, before that honor (with all the jobs involved) was stolen by South Bend. In Oysterville are Clarke Rhododendron Nursery, with an international reputation for its shrubs, and Cranguyma Farms, almost equally famous for its azaleas, holly, and cranberry products. Beyond Oysterville the road ends at Leadbetter Point, another wildlife refuge.

Two miles south of Seaview, on Wash. 103, is Ilwaco, popular with ocean and Columbia River fishermen. Like Long Beach, it, too, has nostalgic touches in its old residential section.

A short distance west of Ilwaco is Ft. Canby State Park, with 60 trailer hookups and excellent picnic grounds. The nearby North Jetty is occupied by fishermen on many a summer day. Not far from the park are two lighthouses: North Head and Canby Light on Cape Disappointment. This area, where the Columbia River empties into the Pacific, earned the name "Graveyard of the Pacific" because of the many ships wrecked here.

Between Ilwaco and Megler is Ft. Columbia State Park. The fort was one of three military posts established at the mouth of the Columbia River during the Spanish-American War. The 554-acre area includes old buildings and gun batteries. The museum contains Indian and pioneer relics, pictures, dioramas, and ship relics relating to the explorations of the region. The park has no campground but has tables and stoves for picnicking. Included in the park is the D.A.R. House Museum, home of a former commanding officer.

Leaving the Long Beach area, US 101 swings around the east side of Willapa Bay, once the home of small native oysters which were shipped in great quantities to San Francisco when that city was reveling in the glory days of the California gold rush. The native oysters mysteriously died out but were replaced, several decades ago, by seeding a larger oyster from Japan. They thrived. If you want them by the pound, fresh from the water, stop at the Coast Oyster Co. plant in South Bend, the town that stole the county seat from Oysterville. It has a historical museum also worth a stop.

Four miles beyond South Bend is bigger Raymond, a moribund lumber town. Wash. 105 goes off left around the north shore of Willapa Bay to the ocean, and although US 101 gets to Aberdeen in half the distance, 105 is much more interesting. (This loop is described later, as an extension of the Olympic loop.)

Many motorists do continue on 101 to the Olympic Peninsula. However, if your destination is Puget Sound, watch for the Wash. 107 exit, 15 miles north of Raymond. It is a shortcut to Montesano, where it joins US 12, a fast limited-access highway to Olympia and I–5 on north to Seattle.

The I–5 Mainline

Busy I–5, crossing the Columbia from Portland to Vancouver, Wash., is tapped as it heads north by highways leading to all other parts of the state, but its main devotion is to through traffic to destinations the motorists want to reach as soon as possible. At Vancouver there is a state visitors' information center alongside the highway. No matter how much of a hurry you are in, the Fort Vancouver National Historic Site deserves at least an hour's stop. Here the Hudson's Bay Company had its most prominent post in the West. From 1825 until 1846 the fort and its factor, Dr. John McLoughlin, represented civilization in the Pacific Northwest. Products were manufactured, and trade was carried on with Mexican California, Russian Alaska, and Hawaii.

Then the 1846 treaty put Fort Vancouver on American soil. McLoughlin went to Oregon City, where his home is also a National Historic Site. Fire destroyed the fort, but it is now being reconstructed. An excellent interpretive center overlooks the site. Nearby Vancouver Barracks is a military post started in 1848.

Thirty-two miles north of Vancouver is Kalama, small but a grain-loading port on the Columbia. The weird, monstrous stack that then comes in sight across the river, blinking lights around its top and puffing steam, is the Trojan nuclear power plant, built by private companies.

I–5 goes past Kelso, where the Wash. 4 cross-over from US 101 ends. Ten miles farther north, at Castle Rock, Wash. 504 leads east towards Mt. St. Helens, which blew its top in May, 1980, after being dormant for 123 years. The massive eruption killed 65 persons and deposited ash nearly a foot deep in parts of eastern Washington. A new visitor center for the Mt. St. Helens National Monument opened in late 1986 on Wash. 504, across from Seaquest State Park. The best way to view the volcano is to take "flight-seeing" charters from the Kelso airport or from the small town of Toledo, just off I–5.

Eleven miles short of Chehalis, I–5 has a juncture with US 12, the quickest route (from the south) to Mt. Rainier National Park and the eastern side of the state. To see the park, turn off US 12 at Morton to Elbe, 17 miles on Wash. 7, then turn right on State 706 to the park's main entrance.

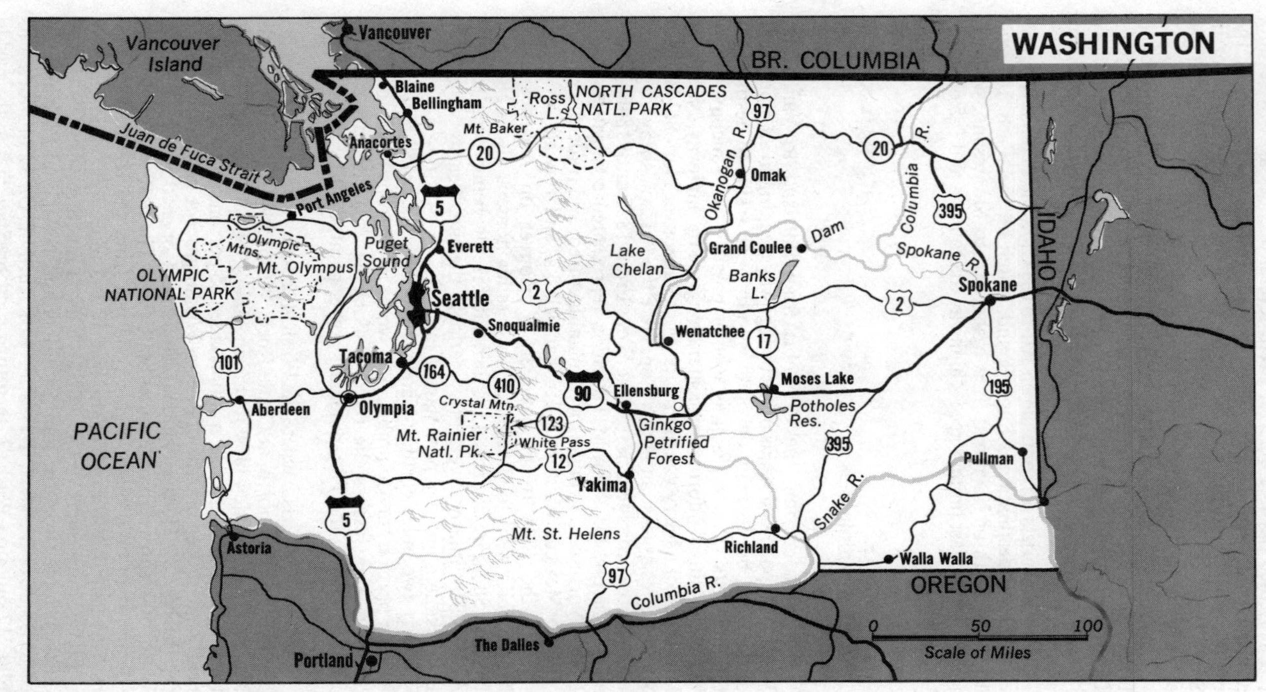
WASHINGTON
BR. COLUMBIA
IDAHO
OREGON
Vancouver
Vancouver Island
Juan de Fuca Strait
Port Angeles
Anacortes
Blaine
Bellingham
Mt. Baker
Ross L.
NORTH CASCADES NATL. PARK
Omak
Okanogan R.
Columbia R.
Grand Coulee Dam
Banks L.
Spokane R.
Spokane
Pullman
Walla Walla
Snake R.
Moses Lake
Potholes Res.
Wenatchee
Lake Chelan
Ellensburg
Ginkgo Petrified Forest
Richland
Columbia R.
Yakima
Mt. St. Helens
White Pass
Crystal Mtn.
Mt. Rainier Natl. Pk.
Snoqualmie
Everett
Seattle
Puget Sound
Tacoma
Olympia
Aberdeen
Olympic Mtns.
Mt. Olympus
OLYMPIC NATIONAL PARK
PACIFIC OCEAN
Astoria
Portland
The Dalles
5
20
97
395
195
2
17
90
12
123
410
164
101
0 50 100
Scale of Miles

At Mary's Corner, two miles from I–5, is Jackson Courthouse, built as a home by John R. Jackson in 1844. It was used as a stopping place by immigrants headed north and in 1850 was converted into a courthouse. The building is a state landmark, revered for its "antiquity." Also on US 12 are two dams, Mayfield and Mossyrock, whose reservoirs offer camping, picnicking, and fishing.

If you continue on I–5, Chehalis is next. Three miles west of the freeway, on Wash. 6 which runs to Grays Harbor, is Claquato Church, built in 1858, the oldest Protestant church in the state. The bronze bell was cast in Boston in 1857 and shipped around Cape Horn. If you want to take a break in Chehalis, it offers either Recreation Park, or Alexander Park, on the Chehalis River. Swimming and picnicking facilities.

Centralia is four miles north on I–5. Its first residents were a Missourian, J. G. Cochran, and his Negro slave, George Washington. Cochran freed his slave and then adopted him to protect the man, and George Washington became a principal founder of the settlement first known as Centerville, then as Centralia. In Ft. Borst Park is Ft. Borst Blockhouse, built in 1855 for defense against the Indians. In 1919 an Armistice Day clash between American Legion members and those of the Industrial Workers of the World led to shootings, a lynching and the arrest of many persons suspected of "radicalism," which meant labor organizing. For many years Centralia suffered a boycott from labor sympathizers and would like to omit that page from its history.

Millersylvania State Park, 16 miles north of Centralia near an I–5 turnoff, is one of the most popular parks in the state. It has almost 200 campsites and more than 50 trailer hookups and is one of the best-equipped parks in Washington, with tables and stoves, kitchens, hot showers, a boat launch, mooring for boats, swimming, fishing, hiking trails, all at a lake.

Back on I–5, in ten miles you're in Olympia.

The Capital

Olympia is the state capital. Lumber and shipping played a part in Olympia's development, too, but despite its fairly extensive role as a port and transshipment terminal, the city has remained basically a state governmental center. There are alternating periods of bustle and quiet, depending upon whether the legislature is in session. Incorporated in 1859, the city withstood several attempts by other localities to have the site of the capital shifted. Dominating the city's horizons to the northwest and east, respectively, are the peaks of the Olympic Mountains and Mt. Rainier.

On the meticulously landscaped Capitol grounds, Japanese cherry trees bloom about the third week in April. With summer comes the full color of the sunken rose garden. The Capitol greenhouse is open to the public. The Legislative Building, the central one in the Capitol group, is famed for its 287-foot dome, fourth highest of its kind in the world and resembling the Capitol in Washington, D.C. An incongruous and somewhat annoying aspect of visiting these public grounds is that you must pay to park on them.

Points of interest in Olympia include the State Capitol Museum, with its separate museums of history, natural history, and art; St. Martin's College Museum; and Crosby House, a furnished house built in 1860 by the grandparents of singer Bing Crosby.

Tumwater, 3 miles south of Olympia on I–5, is of interest for its history and type of industry. The first American settlement north of the Columbia River was established here in 1845. A granite marker on the west bank of the Deschutes River, notes the spot where the first settlers, including a black family, put down roots. But Tumwater is better known these days for the Olympia Brewing Company, open for tours. Adjacent to the brewery is Tumwater Falls Park. Self-guiding trails here take the visitor through springtime blooms of rhododendron and azalea. With playground and picnic facilities, the park is a very good place for a luncheon pause.

Tacoma

Tacoma is 30 miles northeast of Olympia. Much of the mileage between the two cities is taken up, on both sides of I–5, by Fort Lewis and McChord Air Force Base. They are among the largest permanent military installations in the United States.

Lumber and shipping were, and continue to be, the major reasons for Tacoma's growth as a city. The first sawmill was built by a Swedish settler, Nichalas De Lin, in the early 1850s. Today industrial giants operate huge plants in Tacoma, and millions of board feet of lumber are used in the manufacture of pulp, paper, plywood, cartons, and furniture. The most visible landmark in Tacoma these days is the Tacoma Dome, an attractive wooden structure painted in shades of blue and situated next to I–5. Though smaller than Seattle's Kingdome, it has successfully attracted sporting events, rock concerts, and major exhibitions.

The city's main business area overlooks Commencement Bay, a fine deep-water harbor that handles millions of tons of shipping annually. Along the bay and its tidal flats are several hundred industrial plants whose products range from chemicals to railroad cars. The bay, an extension of Puget Sound, is the city's eastern shoreline boundary. On the west is a body of water called The Narrows, and Tacoma is, in effect, a peninsula town jutting into these connecting waters. As a result, boating and fishing are highly popular.

The Tacoma Narrows Bridge, which carries Wash. 16 across the Narrows from the Kitsap Peninsula, had a famous predecessor. The original span swayed so much and so often that it earned the nickname "Galloping Gertie" before it collapsed in 1940. Gertie's trouble-free replacement was completed in 1950. It is 5,450 feet long, including its approaches, and its center span of 2,800 feet is one of the longest suspension spans in the country.

In common with many American citics, Tacoma was hard hit by the rise of suburban shopping centers, in this case to the east and south of town. Downtown was left with few department stores and only one first-class hotel. It has tried valiantly to make its main business streets more attractive, turning one into a pedestrian mall and connecting two hillside avenues with the first municipally owned escalators in the nation. Old City Hall, a distinctive landmark, has been converted into shops and eating places, and seeing how it was done is worth the visit. Restoration of other buildings is in progress.

A marked 2-hour tourist trail affords visitors a convenient way to see Tacoma. The Kla-how-ya Trail (the word means "welcome" in the Chinook Indian language) starts at 9th and A streets in the heart of the downtown section. Marking the start of the trail is a 105-foot-high totem pole carved from a single cedar tree by Alaskan Indian artists.

Kla-how-ya points of interest include Wright Park, a botanical conservatory with more than 1,000 labeled trees of many varieties and a large collection of orchids and tropical plants, and the State Historical Society Museum, with its illuminated photographic murals and displays relating to Indian, pioneer, and Alaskan cultures.

The most interesting of Tacoma's 44 parks is also on the Kla-how-ya Trail. Point Defiance Park, at the northernmost extension of the city, has more than 600 acres of flower gardens, virgin forestland, a Children's Farm Animal Zoo, a bathing beach on Commencement Bay, a deep-sea aquarium, and a fine otter display. The Natural Habitat Aviary displays birds from all over the world. An ambitious plan is afoot to expand a small zoo into a major one.

There is also a lot of history at Point Defiance Park. Parts of the SS *Beaver,* first steamship on the Pacific Coast, are here for viewing. Camp Six is an outdoor museum of old-time logging equipment, with original bunkhouses, five steam donkey engines, a 110-foot spar tree, and a Lidgerwood skidder. The work-worn steam Shea locomotive gives passengers rides. The park is also the site of Ft. Nisqually. Built by Hudson's Bay Company in 1833 at a point south of the city, this old installation was moved to the park and restored in 1934. Two of the buildings (the factor's house and the granary) are original structures, and many original items, such as hand-forged hardware, were incorporated into the replicas of other structures.

Adjacent to the east entrance to Point Defiance Park is the ferry slip for the crossing to Tahlequah on the south end of Vashon Island.

For the artistically minded, Tacoma has Handforth Gallery, Tacoma Art Museum (founded in 1891), and the Kittredge and Hill Art Galleries, on the University of Puget Sound campus.

Puyallup Valley, with its renowned bulb farms, is only a 15-minute drive east of Tacoma on US 410. The valley is a major center of the production of tulip, iris, and daffodil bulbs. Every April the Puyallup Valley Daffodil Festival is held jointly in Tacoma, Puyallup, Sumner, and Orting. Southwest of the city is Steilacoom, oldest incorporated city in the state (1853) and once the seat of Pierce County. A small county ferry runs to residential Anderson Island, and to McNeil Island, formerly a federal penitentiary. A scramble among public agencies and private developers ended when the island became a maximum-security state prison. Nearby is Fort Steilacoom, 1849–1868, next door to Western Washington State Hospital.

Northwest from Tacoma, across the Narrows Bridge on Wash. 16, is Gig Harbor, devoted to fishing and pleasure boats, and arts and crafts studios. The town surrounds a cozy bay.

It is about 30 miles from Tacoma to Seattle, and although it is not apparent from the I–5 freeway, the scattered suburbs of the two cities overlap. The same is true for 30 miles beyond Seattle to Everett. This is the heart of the Puget Sound megapolis, where two-thirds of the state's population lives.

The Olympic Peninsula

The "gateway" to Olympic Peninsula and the national park is wherever you start on the loop. If you do the whole US 101 circle by way of Hood Canal, more than 400 miles, the longest but most complete way is from Seattle to Bremerton or Southworth by ferry, then down to the tidewater end of Hood Canal; or from Tacoma, across the Narrows Bridge to pick up the extreme end of the Canal at the same point. If you are in Olympia, you can start on US 101 and get to Hood Canal much faster.

Washington has been a pioneer in floating bridges; the Lacey B. Murrow floating bridge from Seattle to Mercer Island (now known simply as the Mercer Island bridge) was the first in the state. It was joined in the early 1960s by the Hood Canal floating bridge, which stayed in place for 17 years before breaking apart in a storm in February 1979. It is back together now, and apparently much stronger than before.

From Olympia, it is less than a 30-minute drive up US 101 to Shelton. Between Olympia and Shelton are commercial coves that produce thousands of gallons per year of the world's smallest oyster. Oysters are important to the economy, but so are Christmas trees. In recognition of its annual million-dollar crop of these traditional beauties, Shelton calls itself "Christmas Town." The Simpson Timber Company plant welcomes visitors from June 15 through Labor Day.

Ten miles onward US 101 meets Hood Canal. Nearby is Potlatch State Park, with small but pleasant campgrounds for tents and trailers.

Hood Canal (Vancouver named it "Hood's Channel") separates the Kitsap Peninsula from the Olympic Peninsula, but it is an arm of Puget Sound and not an actual canal. It stretches south from Admiralty Inlet, the entrance to Puget Sound, and ends in a fishhook curve back to the northeast, a total distance of some 75 miles. US 101 winds along its shore for about 60 miles.

Five miles north of Potlatch State Park is the village of Hoodsport. From here, you can turn west and drive seven miles to Lake Cushman State Park, near Cushman Dam. There are good fishing, resort and camping facilities.

Back at Hoodsport you may want to tour the salmon hatchery before driving on 4 miles to Lilliwaup. Dosewallips State Park is just below the village of Brinnon. About six miles on, you can turn off US 101 onto a side road that leads five miles to Mt. Walker, for enormous vistas of the Olympics, the Cascades and Hood Canal. A splendid time to come is in June, when rhododendrons sweep right up to the 2,804-foot summit of Mt. Walker.

By any routes to the Olympic Peninsula, you arrive at Discovery Bay. Take Wash. 113 north 13 miles to Port Townsend, one of the most fascinating cities in the state. During the last decades of the nineteenth century it was one of the most posh cities on the West Coast. The people here claim that Port Townsend contains the best collection of Victorian architecture north of San Francisco—and they may be right. You can pick up at the Tourist Information Center a city guide that will route you past all the points of historic and exotic interest, including a Chinese Tree of Heaven, which an emperor of China presented to the city more than 100 years ago. Rothschild House is a restored late nineteenth-century house furnished in period. The Jefferson County Historical Society Museum and Library is housed in the 1891 City Hall building, with pioneer exhibits, Indian artifacts, and one room devoted to Ft. Worden (a mile north of town). Port Townsend is a rapidly growing center for art and culture, with a Rhododendron Festival in mid-May. Point Wilson Lighthouse (1870) stands where the Straight of Juan de Fuca turns to form Admiralty Inlet, which leads into Puget

Sound. Old Ft. Townsend State Park, three miles south of the city, has historical charm.

If you had arrived in Port Townsend by ferry, you still would be headed for Discovery Bay and US 101.

It is 11 miles more to Sequim (pronounced *Skwim*), the center of the peninsula's "Sunshine Belt." Because it is on the sheltered lee side of the Olympic Mountains, Sequim gets little rain—considering that it is in western Washington. Its annual rainfall averages 16 inches a year, about eight inches less than Port Angeles, only 17 miles away, and the farmers irrigate.

About five miles north of Sequim via a paved road is Dungeness on Juan de Fuca Strait. This once-busy fishing village gave its name to the North Pacific coast's most delectable crabs. Near Dungeness is the Olympic Game Farm. You can tour it on foot or by car. (Special prices for kids and senior citizens.) However, earnest believers in Walt Disney "true life" nature movies should be warned that they may be disillusioned. Here live all the creatures trained to perform for Disney and other TV and movie companies that produce pictures featuring animals supposedly in the wild—Grizzly Adams' bear and all the rest who have ever appeared on a screen. Some 80 "nature" films have been made with these animals.

The largest city on the Olympic Peninsula, Port Angeles is an important fishing town. Its Salmon Derby, held there every Labor Day weekend, is one of the big events of the Peninsula. At Ediz Hook, a natural sandpit forming the city harbor, there are places to picnic, and a boat launch. Visitors are welcome to tour the U.S. Coast Guard Air Rescue Station at Ediz Hook. Pioneer Memorial Museum, 2800 Hurricane Ridge Road, is at Olympic National Park Headquarters, where you can brief yourself about the park. There's a log cabin of the 1890s, a large relief model of Olympic National Park, and botanical, geological, and biological exhibits.

There is year-round ferry service from Port Angeles to Victoria, on Vancouver Island. Black Ball, a private line, runs once a day in winter, twice during "shoulder seasons," and four times daily in summer.

The Olympic National Park

Port Angeles is also the gateway to Olympic National Park, a lush wilderness of thick rain forests (spruce, fir, and cedar), wildlife (65 species), alpine flower meadows, glaciers, lakes, and streams, all cradled in a rugged mountain fastness. Yearly rainfall on the western slopes of the park exceeds 140 inches and centuries of such heavy rains have promoted the growth of towering trees, many of them more than 200 feet high and more than ten feet in diameter. The park contains the largest known specimens of Douglas fir, red cedar, western hemlock, and Alaska cedar. Equally impressive are the mountains within the park's boundaries. Mt. Olympus, at nearly 8,000 feet, is the highest; many others rise above 7,000 feet. Just east of Port Angeles the Heart O' the Hills Highway leads to 5,228-foot Hurricane Ridge, where there are awesome views of Juan de Fuca Strait, Vancouver Island, and the Olympic peaks. A summit lodge is open daily through the summer but has no overnight accommodations. Park naturalists give talks and lead nature walks throughout the day.

For other tremendous views, leave US 101 about six miles east of Port Angeles and twist up a mountain road to 6,000-foot Deer Park.

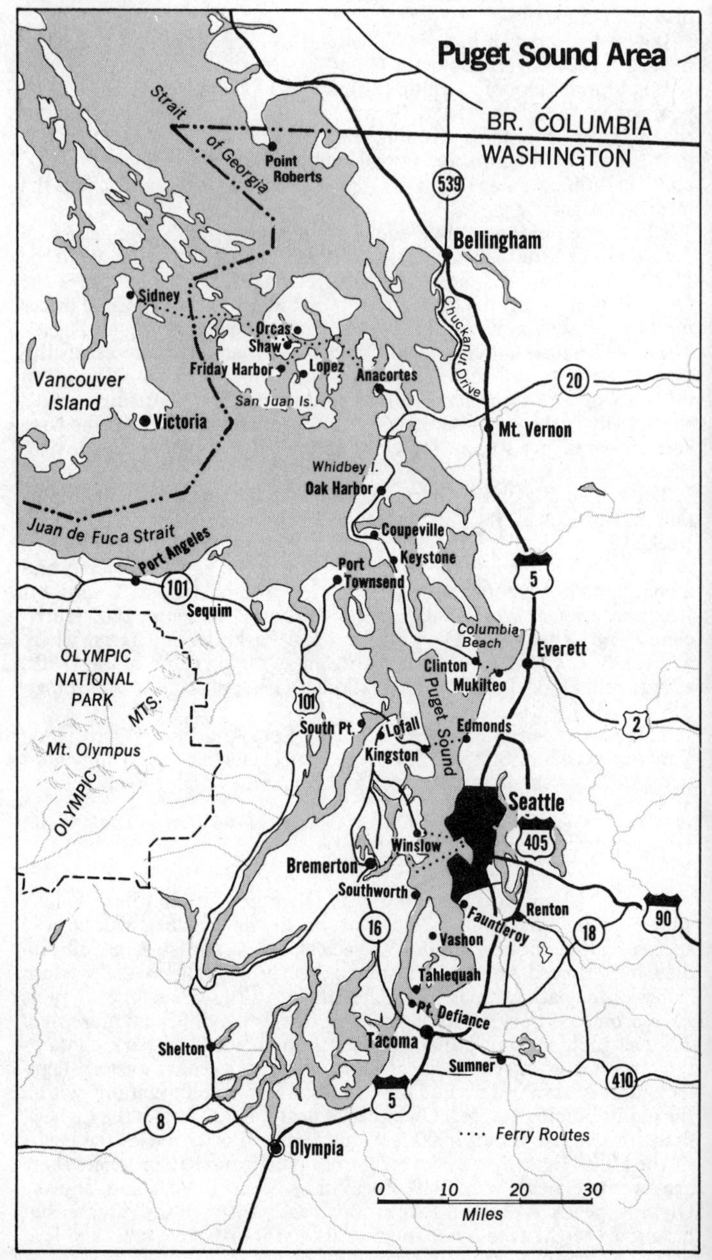
Puget Sound Area
BR. COLUMBIA
WASHINGTON
Strait of Georgia
Point Roberts
539
Bellingham
Chuckanut Drive
Sidney
Orcas
Shaw
Friday Harbor
Lopez
Anacortes
San Juan Is.
20
Vancouver Island
Victoria
Mt. Vernon
Whidbey I.
Oak Harbor
Juan de Fuca Strait
Coupeville
Port Angeles
Keystone
Port Townsend
101
5
Sequim
Columbia Beach
Everett
OLYMPIC NATIONAL PARK
Clinton
Mukilteo
Puget Sound
101
2
MTS.
South Pt.
Lofall
Edmonds
Mt. Olympus
Kingston
OLYMPIC
Seattle
405
Winslow
Bremerton
Southworth
Renton
90
16
Fauntleroy
18
Vashon
Tahlequah
Pt. Defiance
Tacoma
Shelton
Sumner
410
5
8
Ferry Routes
Olympia
0 10 20 30
Miles

Not well understood by out-of-state visitors is that relatively few miles of US 101 are in the national park. Only nine dead-end roads enter the park elsewhere, and then just barely. The broad views of what is inside are from the two vantage points described above. The National Park Service charges $3 per vehicle for access to the Hoh River Road and Hurricane Ridge.

Under plans proposed by the National Park Service, 92 percent of the Olympic National Park will be designated wilderness area. The service proposes to take 834,890 of the park's nearly 900,000 acres and preserve them as "a pristine and undisturbed part of our natural inheritance." The wilderness designation would apply to three areas—two strips along the Pacific Ocean and the heart of the main park on the Olympic Peninsula. The federal Wilderness Act provides that the only facilities in wilderness areas will be "the minimum required for public enjoyment, health and safety, preservation and protection of the features."

West of Port Townsend are three fine lakes, Aldwell, Sutherland, and Crescent. Lake Crescent is inside the national park and has one seasonal concession lodge and one all-year resort, Log Cabin, on private land. There are two campgrounds. From the Visitor Center, midway along the south shore, a nature trail leads to Marymere Falls, a 90-foot cascade.

A few miles beyond the lake a newly improved road takes off US 101 and runs parallel to the Soleduck River to Sol Duc Hot Springs, an early-century resort that has been renovated in recent years.

Twelve miles beyond the Sol Duc turnoff, US 101 arrives at Sappho, a former rough-and-tumble logging camp named, for some reason, for a poetess of ancient Greece. An interesting side trip can be made from Sappho to Clallam Bay, which lies 17 miles north via a county road. Clallam Bay is an old lumber town on the shore of Juan de Fuca Strait, but it is not the reason for detouring north.

From Clallam Bay, Wash. 112 follows the coast 21 miles to the town of Neah Bay, on the Makah Indian Reservation. The Makahs, whose canoe-building culture is closely related to that of the southeastern Alaska and Vancouver Island Indians, were once known for their fierceness and prowess as whale hunters. Today Neah Bay has quite a reputation among sports fishermen after salmon. The Makahs also derive some income from handicrafts, which are sold at local shops. A new attraction is a museum featuring the archaeological treasures from Ozette (see below).

From Neah Bay, intrepid sightseers can follow a quiet road out of town and through wooded terrain for about seven miles. From where the road ends, a path—perhaps a thousand yards long—snakes through a forest glade to a cliff. This is the tip of Cape Flattery, often called the most northwesterly point of the coterminous United States. (However, Cape Alava, 15 miles south, is the most western point by a few hundred feet) From the cliff of Cape Flattery you see, across a trough of turbulent Pacific water, a large, high rock, on top of which is a lighthouse and several houses. This is Tatoosh Island, where until recently lighthouse keepers and their families lived. Now the light is automated.

On the way to Neah Bay there is really an unusual sidetrip from a sidetrip. Just west of Sekiu (another center for salmon fishing) a road leads off left, 20 miles to Lake Ozette and Cape Alava. You can't go any farther west in the continental United States than Alava, and Ozette was where the tide of immigration stopped in the 1890s. The Klondike gold rush of 1898 drew most of the homesteaders away, and the land went back to wilderness. Lake Ozette is in the Olympic National Park, and the coast north for 7-plus miles recently has been added to the park.

You have to hike three miles on a boardwalk to the cape, where archeologists made a very important find, an Indian village that had been buried beneath an air-tight clay slide that preserved artifacts that went back centuries to before the time white men arrived. Thousands of artifacts from the dig have gone on display at Neah Bay.

The Rain Forest

On the main Olympic Loop road, US 101 bends south to Forks, an important center in the logging industry of the Olympic Peninsula. Within 15 miles of Forks are six top rivers for rainbow trout, cutthroat, steelhead, and King salmon.

Two miles north of Forks a paved road takes off from US 101 to wind west 14 miles to La Push, a rambling coastal village on the Quillayute Indian Reservation. La Push is a home for sports and commercial fishing boats, in a setting of offshore rocks, sandy beaches hemmed by wind-twisted trees, foaming surf, and far vistas. Driftwood and agates are found along the beach, and booming waves can bring in a lot of other things.

Return to Forks and follow US 101 for 13 miles south to a turnoff east. This road, which runs for 18 miles following the Hoh River, is an entrance to Olympic National Park and is a good way to see the rain forest, where moss drapes the branches of trees and forms a thick carpet underfoot. Immense ferns also grow in the light dimly filtered through the overhead canopy. At the end of the paved road are camping facilities and self-guiding nature trails. Botanical, geological, and biological exhibits are on display at the Visitor Center.

Ten miles below the Hoh Valley turnoff, US 101 enters a dozen miles of the Olympic National Park's Pacific Coast strip. About a mile south of Ruby Beach, a roadside viewpoint faces Destruction Island and a lighthouse famous along the coast. The lighthouse keeper once had to haul kerosene up the 94-foot tower every night. But today the lighthouse is completely automated—more efficiency, less strain, less romance.

This part of the Washington coast is strewn with grotesque offshore formations. Between the Destruction Island viewpoint and Kalaloch, seven miles south along US 101, there are more impressive seascapes. The driftwood-strewn beaches are only a short walk from the road, with trail entrances announced by signs on the highway. Camping and lodge accommodations are available at Kalaloch.

Six miles south of Queets a road leads 14 miles along the Queets River to another part of the rain forest, with camping at the end of the road.

On US 101 you come to Lake Quinault. Roads on both sides of the lake, north and south, pass lake resort accommodations to penetrate more rain forest.

Now far inland, US 101 turns south again. At Humptulips, 18 miles south of Quinault, you can take a road leading to Copalis Beach, 17 miles away, or proceed south 22 miles to Grays Harbor, where the cities of Hoquiam and Aberdeen are centers of lumbering and fishing.

However, there's a new road to the north end of the ocean beaches. It goes off to the right soon after you pass Neilton, south of Amanda

Park (Lake Quinault). Gravel but wide and hard-packed, the road is inside the Quinault Reservation, and is a compromise for a shorter route along the coast from Queets south. The Indians said "no trespassing" when the state tried to build that highway. Four miles along the new road there is an interesting federal fish hatchery with a visitors' center—but that's all you will see in the 20 miles to Moclips.

Moclips, Pacific Beach, Copalis Beach, and Ocean City date back to when they were resort towns away out on the Pacific coast. Some of their "resort" cabins are still in use, but scattered along the shore are also some new, very fancy lay-outs. Between Ocean City and Ocean Shores is a wonderful state park.

Ocean Shores was a real-estate project that began some 20 years ago with full ballyhoo. Today you don't know whether to laugh or cry about it. It is laid out for miles with unused streets, lots, canals, and an occasional residence. At the same time it does have top-notch resort-type motels, a golf course, and a marina for charter fishing. (See Resorts.) It was recently incorporated as a city. Buses prowl its streets and connect to Hoquiam and Aberdeen.

One last side trip to the sea from inland US 101: At Aberdeen take Wash. 105 for 22 miles to Westport, near the southwest tip of Grays Harbor. (The bay was named for the first American to visit this part of the coast, Captain Robert Gray, a mariner out of Boston who sailed across the bar into the harbor in 1792—the same year, and on the same voyage, that he entered the Columbia River, becoming the first white person to find the Great River of the West.)

Westport is one of the great salmon fishing ports of Washington, with a fishing fleet of more than 500 commercial, charter, and pleasure boats harbored in a sheltered cove. Clam digging is popular, and the beaches near Westport are perused for shells and driftwood. Twin Harbors State Park, two miles south of Westport, is the most popular ocean front park on the Washington coast. Grayland, three miles south of the park, is a cranberry district center. From here you can cut across Wash. 105 to Raymond (see "Southwest Entrance").

From Aberdeen, a 47-mile drive east via US 12 and Wash. 8 leads back to Olympia and completes the circuit of the Olympic Peninsula.

North by West to the Border

Interstate 5 between Seattle and Vancouver, B.C. is truly an international highway. Canadians, among the world's most traveling people, are heading south. Because of the exchange rate, Canadian coins are not accepted by merchants. Canadian currency is discounted and the best exchange rate, either side of the border, is at banks.

Heading north are all the Americans making an easy trip "abroad." Seattle looks upon Vancouver and Victoria as two of its interesting suburbs and expects its visitors to take in either one or both of them. Vancouver, about the size of Seattle, has the same attitude toward the other two. Victoria gets tourists from both big cities and is glad of it.

The first stop off I–5 is at Everett, 30 miles north of Seattle. At 44th St. and Rucker Ave., an 80-foot totem pole carved by Tulalip Chief William Shelton honors Patkanim, a great Indian chief of the Salishes. Snohomish County Historical Society Museum, in Legion Park, is located in an abandoned Indian Council building.

From Everett it's a short drive west to Mukilteo, where you can board a ferry to Whidbey Island, described earlier.

A summer trip that draws city residents who want to wander in the mountains by car, starts at Lake Stevens, five miles east and north of Everett. Continue north to Wash. 92 (which comes off Wash. 9), and then eight miles to Granite Falls. The road eastward meanders through the hamlets of Robe and Verlot, skirts 5,324-foot Mt. Pilchuck, eases into the massive Mt. Baker National Forest and follows the Stillaguamish River toward 7,790-foot Sloan Peak (dwarfed by nearby 10,541-foot Glacier Peak), to arrive at Barlow Pass. Four miles up a dead-end road is Monte Cristo, a ghost mining town that started in 1889 and petered out by 1909.

The main road goes down to the Sauk River and comes to Darrington, a logging town whose early residents were largely North Carolina "tarheels." From Darrington, Wash. 530 returns to I–5 along the North Fork of the Stillaguamish.

Going north from Everett, there's another alternate to I–5. Fifteen miles north, turn off the freeway onto Wash. 530 and in five miles you will reach Stanwood. A road takes you across a bridge to Camano Island, which has a large state park on the shores of Saratoga Passage.

Heading on from Stanwood to Mount Vernon, Wash. 530 rejoins I–5. Mount Vernon is a pleasant city surrounded by the rich agricultural land of the lower Skagit River valley. The highway west to Anacortes also gives access to Bayview State Park and, to the south, La Conner, a picturesque town on Skagit Bay next door to the Swinomish Indian Reservation. The Swinomish Tribal Celebration is held July 3–4.

Four miles north of Mount Vernon is Burlington, the turnoff point to Wash. 20, the North Cascades Highway. Five miles east of Burlington on Wash. 20 is Sedro Woolley, and from here you can go north on Wash. 9 to Deming on Wash. 542. It's a shortcut to Mt. Baker. This is dairy and tulip country, and "Little Holland" with mountainous background scenery. In many other states, Wash. 9 would be a major tourist drive.

Back at Burlington, there's a choice of following I–5 to Bellingham or a slower road, Wash. 11. Its first seven miles, from Burlington to Edison, won't send you into ecstasy but the next 13 miles, from Edison to the outskirts of Bellingham, were long known as the most spectacular marine drive on the state's inland coasts. People used to drive to Bellingham just to see this cliff-hanging stretch of highway known as Chuckanut Drive. It follows Sanich and Chuckanut Bays and passes Larrabee State Park seven miles south of the city.

Overlooking Puget Sound and the San Juan Islands, Bellingham is within view of both the Olympic Mountains and the Cascades, in which Mt. Baker is dominant—and next to Mt. St. Helens, the hottest of the Cascade's volcanoes. Drive up Sehome Hill, on the campus of Western Washington University for vistas of Bellingham Bay and the San Juan Islands. (On a clear day you can see Vancouver Island.) For picnicking, there's Fairhaven Park, on Chuckanut Drive, at the southern entrance to the city. Bloedel-Donovan Park, three miles east of Lake Whatcom, has a picnic area, a playground, and a "swimming hole." Whatcom Museum of History and Art, in a former city hall built in 1892 (a good example of late Victorian civic architecture), has a large collection of regional exhibits.

Bellingham celebrates its reputation as a flower-area hub with a Blossomtime Festival in mid-May. (No one should come to Bellingham in the springtime without driving out to the tulip fields around Lynden and Everson. The Ski to Sea Festival Memorial Day Weekend starts at Mt. Baker, ends at Puget Sound, and includes skiing, running, bicycling, canoeing, and sailing. From June through August, a steam train runs Tues. and Sat. from Wickersham, four miles east of Lake Whatcom.

The city is close to the partly offshore Lummi Indian Reservation. The Lummi Stommish, held in June at the reservation village of Marietta, is highlighted by Indian canoe races, dancing, and a salmon bake.

Blaine, on Drayton Harbor, is best known (apart from being a port of entry for Canadians) for its Peace Arch State and Provincial Park—handsomely landscaped grounds, with a well-equipped picnic area.

There is one place else in this "far corner" on American soil that you can reach by driving north, odd as that may seem. This is Point Roberts, a village on the Strait of Georgia.

When the mapping party settled on the U.S.-Canadian boundary, it followed a straight line, and so "amputated" Point Roberts, which was just south of the line. So the village gets practically all of its service from Canada, and American goods are trucked, sealed, 30 miles through British Columbia and back into Washington.

Birch Bay State Park, ten miles south of Blaine, on Birch Bay, is 172 acres, with a large campground and hookups for more than 50 trailers. Swimming, fishing, clamming, hiking.

From Blaine you can drive east to saunter through the streets of marketplace Lynden. Another eight miles east, Wash. 9 goes north five miles to Sumas, another town on the Canadian border. Sumas is a popular entry point for Americans bound for the Trans-Canada Highway, headed east. They short-cut to Wash. 9 out of Burlington or Bellingham.

Undoubtedly the most scenic trip out of Bellingham is to Mt. Baker, 58 miles east. Mt. Baker is seen much of the way, and you can understand why to the Indians it was the Great White Watcher and to Francisco Eliza it was El Montana de Carmelo (he saw in the long white slopes an imagery of the flowing robes of Carmelite nuns).

A mile past the village of Glacier, on Wash. 542, try Glacier Creek Road for superb views of Mt. Baker and the multihued face of Coleman Glacier. Turn onto Wells Creek Road, a few miles along; in half a mile you'll be at Nooksack Falls, whose thundering seems to shake the trees. Mt. Baker ski area, near the end of the road, offers nearly year-round skiing.

Although Baker is the drawing card, 9,127-foot Mt. Shuksan, just behind it at road's end, steals the scene for photographers.

North Cascades

Washington's newest major road is the North Cascades Highway, which links the Puget Sound area to the north-central part of the state. Although Wash. 20 was primarily completed to provide a shorter route between these two sections of the state, it has become a prime tourist road because of its abundance of scenery.

From I–5 at Burlington, turn east on Wash. 20. The first few miles are pastoral, through the Skagit River Valley to Sedro Woolley. The next 23 miles to Concrete also pass through farmlands, but gradually forests and peaks come into view. At Concrete a lesser road north leads to Baker Lake, formed by Upper Baker Dam. (Lake Shannon, below, is formed by Lower Baker Dam.) Baker Lake is really away from it all, except for all the other people who are there to get away from it all.

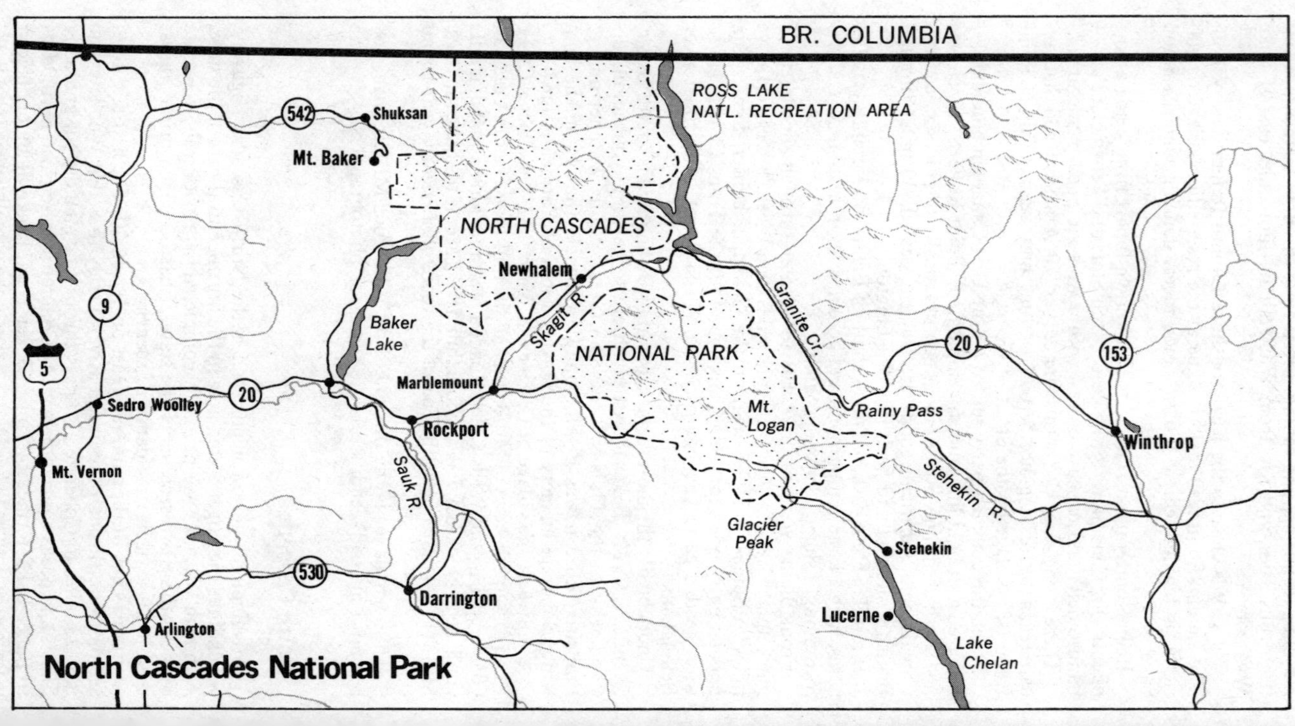

North Cascades National Park

The lake is in Mt. Baker National Forest, and Mt. Baker covers a chunk of the skyline. Campsites are plentiful and good, and for those who don't have tents and campers and trailers, some cabins are available for rent. Trout fishing is good enough to attract a lot of anglers.

Wash. 20 rolls on past Concrete for seven miles to Rockport, where there is a state park with a small campground. Rockport and nearby Marblemount are the largest settlements you will meet now for more than 100 miles. Fill up on gas, buy whatever groceries you need.

The dream of a road across the North Cascades began with a search for gold. Until the feverish prospectors arrived in 1858, the only white men to venture into the wilderness were a few hardy trappers.

That gold activity lasted about a year. The country was too isolated, the terrain too rugged, the weather too fierce. For about twenty years the area was silent again. Then, in 1880, gold was "rediscovered" in the upper Skagit headwaters and the rush was on. But once again the rush was short-lived and once again, the lack of adequate transportation was blamed. Most of the year it was impossible to bring in supplies; the rest of the time it was extremely difficult.

Continued agitation by the miners and cattlemen of the Okanogan Valley for the state to build a wagon road across the North Cascades resulted in several surveys. In 1893 the legislature appropriated all of $20,000 to build 200 miles of road from Bellingham Bay to the Okanogan Valley by way of the old gold country—$100 a mile for a road through one of the wildest and most rugged sections in the entire United States!

Three years later a board of examiners judged Cascade Pass, to the south of Wash. 20, as the most feasible route, and work was started. But the next year slides and washouts ruined whatever construction had been done. Then, for more than thirty years, there was practically no activity.

Bits and pieces of road were worked on during the 1930s by the Public Works Administration and Civilian Conservation Corps. Using rudimentary equipment, compared to today's arsenal of machinery, they finally extended the Cascade River Road to its present terminus, still a long way from the Okanogan Valley. But the gravel road, southeast of Marblemount, leads to some very scenic country. From the end of the 25-mile-long road there is a trail that will take the hiker through Cascade Pass to Lake Chelan. Two campgrounds are along the road.

With the close of World War II, interest in a route across the North Cascades was revived. A route was settled upon, and in 1960 construction began. Ten years later it was possible to go from the Okanogan Valley to Puget Sound on a rather direct line, all things considered. There is a stretch of 75 miles where there are no facilities, and this section between Ross Dam and Mazama is closed in the winter.

Newhalem, east of Marblemount, is the gateway to the Ross Lake Recreation Area. Seattle City Light begins its tours at the tour center in Diablo. (For information on the recreation area, see *National Parks;* for information on Seattle City Light tours, see *Tours.*) There's also a lake-tour boat.

Places worth a pause are the roadside overlooks above Diablo Dam, with views of Ross Dam and Ross Lake. At Rainy Pass a 1.4-mile trail leads to Lake Ann, and the Pacific Crest National Scenic Trail crosses the highway. Whistler Basin Viewpoint, a couple of miles farther on, provides a view of alpine meadows and avalanche areas.

Washington Pass Overlook, at about 5,500 feet, is the most popular stop. A road leads half a mile from the highway to a parking and picnic area. The nearby viewpoint looks down to Early Winters Creek and up to the needle peaks of 8,876-foot Silver Star Mountain and Snagtooth Ridge; to Cooper Basin and Early Winters Spire and Liberty Bell Mountain. Lots of color film is shot here.

In the next 17 miles there are three Forest Service campgrounds: Lone Fir, Klipchuck, and Early Winters. All three accommodate some tents, and Klipchuck and Lone Fir have space for some trailers.

(On the west side of the highway there are only two camps, Goodell Creek and Colonial Creek, both operated by the National Park Service.) There's also a campground at Newhalem.

The first settlement on the east slope of the Cascades is Mazama, still an outpost hamlet, though it has grown since completion of the road.

Harts Pass

For the most adventurous of side trips, you might try the 20-mile drive from Mazama to 6,197-foot Harts Pass. In 1890 there was quite a gold rush to the Harts Pass area. Four miles northwest a town called Barron had a hotel, post office, dance hall and the usual run of saloons. But the ore turned out to be low-grade, and in 1907 the whole town was abandoned. There are a lot of old mines around, and those who explore the area are cautioned to stay out of the tunnels, buildings and trestles, most of which aren't safe.

Probably the best single point to see the wilderness from is Slate Point Lookout, three miles beyond Harts Pass. The 360-degree panorama takes in several hundred square miles, from Mt. Baker on the west, through the glaciated valleys of the Pasayten Wilderness, to the many-toned eastern horizon, and to snowy Glacier Peak in the south.

The road to Harts Pass from Mazama was hewn out to serve the 1890 miners. Trailers are permitted to go up the road only for 10 miles—so that gives you an idea of what the pike is like.

Winthrop, about 12 miles east of Mazama, has through renovation become an "Old West" town, with false-front buildings and all the trappings. Owen Wister, who wrote *The Virginian,* lived here for a while. To hear the locals talk, you would think that the locale of the book was Winthrop and the Methow Valley. But it wasn't, of course, as everybody in eastern Wyoming will tell you.

The population of Winthrop is only about 500, but on a summer day at least a thousand people seem to be on the street. Nostalgia may yet ruin Winthrop. Shaffer's Museum, the home of Guy Waring, founder of Winthrop, displays mementos of the past. A nearby state park is Pearrygin Lake.

Visitors are welcome at the fish hatchery operated by the U.S. Fish and Wildlife Service, a short distance out of Winthrop.

Twisp, about 13 miles south of Winthrop, is the largest town in the rustic, homespun Methow Valley, with approximately 800 population.

Here Wash. 20 continues its eastward journey through the Okanogan Highlands, and Wash. 153 takes you south along the Methow River to Pateros on the Columbia, where it picks up US 97. This is the usual loop for sightseers, down to Wenatchee and back to the west side via US 2.

Between Wenatchee and Pateros is a highly popular recreation area. Lake Chelan, more than 50 miles long and only one to two miles wide, occupies a deep valley naturally dammed at its lower end. Its extreme depth is 1,600 feet, which puts the bottom 400 feet below sea level.

Stehekin, deep in the mountains at the upper end of the lake, is reached only by hiking, seaplane or boat. Hikers get there through Cascade Pass in the North Cascades National Park. Ever since the early century a daily mailboat has run to Stehekin, and excursionists take it up in the morning and return in the afternoon.

The town of Chelan is rife with tourist accommodations, most of them reserved well in advance during summer. Seven miles west of town is Lake Chelan State Park, also likely to be jammed on weekends.

A bridge crosses the Columbia just below Chelan. State highway 151, following the east bank to Wenatchee, runs tamely along an orchard-forested bench. US 97 skirts basaltic cliffs and occasionally passes through orchards in small valleys that break through the Columbia's west side walls. It arrives in Wenatchee five miles sooner than the eastside road.

Through Stevens Pass

This second-oldest highway pass (the first one opened to automobile traffic was Snoqualmie) has its western terminus in Everett. From Seattle, the shortcut is from Bothell to Monroe on State 522, then up the Skykomish River valley on US 2.

The settlements along the way, Sultan, Startup, Gold Bar and Index, began in a flurry of mining activities but logging became more important. They also benefited from being railway points on the Great Northern, and from dairying in intermittent stretches of the valley.

Just beyond Index, a charming town, motorists pause to look at two waterfalls, Sunset and Eagle, and to stare in awe at the sheer granite face of Mt. Index. It is "impossible" to climb, so naturally a lot of mountaineers have scaled it from that side.

Skykomish is the last settlement on the west side and the last town for nearly 60 miles. It has the political distinction of being the only one on US 2—because of a highway jog—that is in King County along with Seattle.

Stevens Pass, 4,061 feet, is a ski area. Far underground, in an 8-mile tunnel, longest in the nation, trains cross this divide.

Twenty miles down the east slope, a turn-off at Cole's Corner onto Wash. 207 leads to Lake Wenatchee four miles away. There is a pleasant state park at the near end of the 7-mile lake.

Leavenworth, 16 miles beyond Cole's Corner, surprises travelers not prepared for the sight. The town was stagnating, so it face-lifted itself into a Bavarian village. Now scads of tourists stop to take pictures and maybe shop or have lunch. Leavenworth was early into skiing, with international jumping tournaments. The record (since surpassed elsewhere) was 284 feet, which is still a long time to hang up there in the air.

Leavenworth is the gateway to the Wenatchee National Forest, largest in the state, and it also marks the western boundary of the great Wenatchee apple country, which spreads over three counties. Peshastin, Dryden, Cashmere, and Monitor are all apple towns. In Cashmere the Liberty Orchards Company, which manufactures candy with local fruit content, offers free tours and samples of Aplets, Cotlets, and Fruitlets. Well worth visiting in Cashmere, too, is the Willis Carey Historical Museum, with the reconstruction of a pioneer village and an outstanding collection of Indian artifacts.

Near Peshastin there is a merger of US 2 and US 97 which has come over Swauk Pass from I–90, splitting off at Teanaway just east of Cle Elum. This is an alternate route from Seattle to Wenatchee (and which oldtimers still refer to as the "Blewett Pass" road because it used to go over that divide). Eleven miles from US 2 there's an arrastra beside the highway—a stone on which miners ground ore a century ago when they were working the gold creeks.

From Cashmere, a 15-minute drive on US 2–97 brings you to Wenatchee, "Apple Capital of the World." Thousands of carloads of apples leave yearly for all parts of the country from the railroad marshaling yard, "Appleyard." The city is located above the Columbia River, near its confluence with the Wenatchee River. In spring, when the apple trees are in full white blossom, and in autumn, when the apples are a glowing red, the area's orchards are dazzling. The Washington State Apple Blossom Festival, held in late April or early May, is noted for its elaborate, colorful floats. Wenatchee also has the distinction of being situated at the geographical center of the state.

Northcentral Washington Museum, at 127 S. Mission, houses memorabilia dealing with the early Indians. Ohme Gardens, on a hillside three miles north off US 97, has various shrubs, plants, flowers, and Northwest trees on its artistically wrought five acres. Visit the lookout tower for panoramic views of the area. People come to Wenatchee just to visit Ohme Gardens and to see Rocky Reach Dam, seven miles north of the city, on US 97.

Rocky Reach is an educationally entertaining museum. You can see fish, as they swim upstream in the 1,350-foot-long fish ladder, from an underwater gallery. The Information Center has a Columbia River Indian exhibit of tools and other artifacts (all found in excavating the region now flooded by the dam) that trace life along the river back more than 10,000 years. A movie and lecture are presented daily throughout the year. And it's all free, with the best wishes of the publicly-owned Chelan County Public Utility District.

The 57 miles of US 97 between Wenatchee and Pateros is the loop link between the North Cascades Highway and US 2.

At Wenatchee, US 2 crosses the Columbia, swings north along the river for ten miles, then climbs onto the wheat-growing plateau in the northwest corner of the Columbia Basin. Waterville is the main town in the 52-mile stretch to Coulee City, and the crossing of upper Moses Coulee is the only topographical excitement.

Coulee City was once a cowboy-and-stagecoach town far out in the sagebrush. Now it has a 30-mile lake at its front door, and is the crossroads for attractions off US 2 both north and south. Wash. 155 follows the lake north to Coulee Dam.

Grand Coulee Dam

Grand Coulee Dam is a man-made wonder of the world, and visitors have made it an unofficial monument. The Bureau of Reclamation built a shaded grandstand for the comfort of visitors, and gives lectures at a nearby small-scale model of the project. The dam is 5,223 feet across and rises 550 feet from bedrock. Nearly half its volume is below the waters of the river. Construction began in 1933, and the dam, incorporating more than 10 million cubic yards of concrete, was completed in 1941. It is more than four times the bulk of Egypt's Great Pyramid. Its reservoir, named Franklin D. Roosevelt Lake, stretches 151 miles behind the dam to the Canadian border. Coulee Dam National Recreation Area, on the shores of the lake, has about 25 campgrounds.

The dam is at the head of the Grand Coulee, a chasm 52 miles long and up to five miles wide. Its rock walls, streaked with red and green hues, tower a thousand feet high in some places along its length. The coulee, or channel in the rock, was formed by the flood waters of a mighty glacier which once blocked the original bed of the Columbia River and forced the river to carve a new channel. When the glacier receded, the river returned to its old course and size, leaving the coulee dry. The dam is at the point where the river originally broke through to form the coulee. Its mammoth pumps irrigate about 2,000 square miles of land with waters from the huge reservoir.

Just southwest of Coulee City, on Wash. 17, is a geological phenomenon, the sheer cliffs of Dry Falls. An overlook provides a view of these scarred walls, where the Columbia River once formed a waterfall with an uninterrupted drop of 417 feet and a width of five miles. The cataract was many times greater than Niagara Falls. It dried up when the glaciers receded. Dry Falls Interpretive Center contains ancient artifacts and exhibits telling the story of the creation of Dry Falls and other coulees.

Dry Falls is at the north end of Sun Lakes State Park, in the extension of Grand Coulee. This 19-mile walled canyon holds a chain of clear lakes. You will find every facility here: cabins, campsites, trailer sites, boating, golfing, fishing, horseback riding, and hiking trails, as well as a cave shaped by a prehistoric rhinoceros when it was buried under lava.

Wash. 17 comes out of Grand Coulee at the town of Soap Lake. The lake it faces is highly mineralized and the wind kicks up "soap suds." This, of course, gave the water an early-day reputation of having therapeutic value.

From Soap Lake, highways connect to the upper Basin cities of Ephrata and Moses Lake on Interstate 90. For any trip that includes Coulee Dam and a loop south from US 2, Wash. 17 through the Grand Coulee is the most interesting highway.

Going east from Coulee City on US 2, you are back in semi-arid wheat country all the way to Spokane. Motorists westbound from Spokane to Coulee Dam can take a shortcut, Wash. 174, at Wilbur, midway between Davenport and Coulee City. Davenport is an old-time wheat town with the Lincoln County Historical Society Museum. Outside the building is a collection of antique farm machinery.

After Davenport it is 32 miles to Spokane on US 2.

Roads to the northern part of the state start in both Wilbur and Davenport.

The Okanogan Highlands

The northern part of Washington is rumpled from its seacoast to the Idaho border. Where the Cascades leave off on their east side, rugged up-and-down country continues. Known as the Okanogan Highlands, four rivers run south through it to the Columbia, and their valleys are the main routes of transportation, now as in the past.

Historically this has been cattle, sheep, mining, logging and Indian country. The Colville Reservation takes in everything north of the Columbia from the Okanogan River to Lake Roosevelt, and extends north halfway to the Canadian border.

Access to all these valleys was (and is) by roads north from US 2 or from Spokane by way of two additional rivers. Ranchers had their dirt roads over the humps between valleys, but an improved highway was a long time in coming. The only one that goes the whole way through, east-west, is Wash. 20 (which we left earlier at Twisp). It crosses or joins the north-south arterials, thus providing a potential loop to the "outside" from any of them.

The westernmost river valley is the Methow, entered by Wash. 20 when it finishes its run as the North Cascades Highway. As described earlier, the Methow flows down to Pateros on the Columbia.

The next river east is the Okanogan, with US 97 running through its valley. Coming up from Wenatchee, US 97 passes through Pateros to Brewster. Five miles north, on a county road, is an earth station with a 97-foot-diameter antenna. It receives and transmits information to satellites in orbit. A visitor center is open daily mid-March to mid-October.

If you want to see another mighty power-plant barrier on the Columbia River, take Wash. 173 from Brewster to Bridgeport and Chief Joseph Dam. On the reservoir above it is a marina and Bridgeport State Park.

Wash. 17 takes you back north to US 97, and at the junction is Ft. Okanogan State Park. Here at the confluence of the Okanogan and Columbia Rivers an outpost was built in 1811. It was first to fly the American flag in what is now the state of Washington. Dioramas and exhibits in the museum concern early fur trading in the Pacific Northwest.

US 97 follows the Okanogan River through the town of Okanogan to Omak, this region's biggest city with a population around 4,500. A hectic rodeo, the Omak Stampede, is held annually in August.

The town also is a gateway to the Colville Indian Reservation. Wash. 155 goes through open pine country to Nespelem, "capital" of the reservation. Here is where Chief Joseph, the great leader of the Nez Percé, ended his days. When their land in northeastern Oregon was taken from them, Joseph led his people on a long trek, brilliantly outmaneuvering the pursuing U.S. troops. The Indians were captured just before reaching sanctuary in Canada, and never were allowed to return to their native Wallowa Valley.

Wash. 155 goes south from Nespelem to Coulee Dam. (Fishing in the reservation's streams and lakes requires a license from the Indians.)

Back on US 97, the highway continues up the Okanogan through cattle ranches with wide meadows, cottonwood, aspen and pine. Along the way secondary roads lead west into the Okanogan National Forest and its many recreation areas. Outstanding among them is Conconully Lake and its state park.

Passing through Tonasket, US 97 arrives in Oroville, a port of entry just short of the Canadian border. Oroville got its name from early-day placer miners but the gold is now in fruit and in recreational opportunities. The town is at the south end of long Lake Osoyoos, which stretches across the international boundary. Lake Osoyoos State Park adjoins Oroville, and at nearby Wannacut there's a small but long-established resort and guest ranch, Sun Cove.

Continuing into British Columbia, Highway 97 gives access to the province's sunny eastside lake resorts, to B.C.'s east-west Highway 3, and farther north, to the Trans-Canada Highway that passes through Banff.

The third river coming out of the Okanogan Highlands is the Sanpoil, which makes its lonely way through the Colville Indian Reservation. It is reached from Wilbur on US 2. A free ferry takes cars across Lake Roosevelt to Keller, which had to be transplanted when the reservoir submerged its former site on the north bank of the Columbia. There is only one other village in the 53 miles to Republic, north of the reservation.

Republic, surrounded by hills, pine forests and lakes (there's a state park at Curlew Lake) is a mining town that dates from 1896. For its history, visit the Ferry County Historical Society Museum.

Wash. 21 continues north another 32 miles to Danville on the Canadian line, and immediately across the border connects to B.C. 3, the east-west arterial. (If here and at Lake Osoyoos you notice you are in the Okanagan region, don't charge the sign-painters with an error. The Canadians spell it differently.)

Lake Roosevelt, the dammed-up Columbia, marks the eastern boundary of the Okanogan region but the Selkirk Mountains begin there and continue the pattern, with two or more river valleys paralleling the others. The main difference is that these two run in a northerly direction, the Colville to meet the Columbia at Kettle Falls, and the Pend Oreille, in the extreme northeast corner of the state, to join it just north of the Canadian border.

To follow Lake Roosevelt, take Wash. 25 out of Davenport on US 2. It picks up the lake at Miles, the site of old Fort Spokane, built at this corner of the Spokane Indian Reservation in 1881 so the troops could keep an eye on the Spokanes, and the Colvilles across the river. No trouble arose and the fort was soon abandoned. Several buildings remain and a small museum tells the fort's history. There are three campgrounds in the vicinity, and a boat ramp.

The highway on north, generally in the Coulee Dam Recreation Area, passes through a number of villages and is often in sight of the lake. In 57 miles it reaches Kettle Falls, another town that had to move to higher ground ahead of the rising reservoir (which also eliminated the falls). Nearby is St. Paul's Mission, established by Jesuits in 1846. The site is preserved in a state historical park.

Above Kettle Falls the Columbia changes slowly from being a lake and shows a current again. Wash. 25 follows it to the border and connects to B.C. 3 near Trail.

Kettle Falls may be small but it is quite a crossroads. Both the Kettle River and the Colville enter the Columbia here. US 395 goes up the Kettle to join B.C. 3 just across the border. In the other direction, US 395 follows the Colville's shallow valley for half of the 92 miles south to Spokane.

The easternmost river, the Pend Oreille, comes out of Idaho at Newport and runs north through the lumber town of Ione, and Metaline Falls to the border, where it too connects to B.C. 3. Near the boundary are Crawford State Park with Gardner Cave, the state's only large limestone cavern, and on the B.C. side, Boundary Dam.

It is in the Pend Oreille valley that Wash. 20 begins (or ends) its cross-hatch route through the Okanogan Highlands, tying into all the other valley highways.

When Wash. 20 stops being the North Cascades Highway and leaves the Methow valley at Twisp, the 30 miles over to Okanogan is called the Loup Loup Trail, a name that harks back to the days when "trail" was literal. It gives access to the Loup Loup ski area, and to campgrounds on a sideroad to Conconully.

From Okanogan to Tonasket. Wash. 20 takes second billing to US 97, traveling the same route, but then it parts company and heads east 41 miles through another section of the Okanogan National Forest to Republic. After that it climbs 5,575-foot Sherman Pass, the highest highway pass in the state in spite of those in the Cascades, and descends to Kettle Falls.

For the ten miles to Colville it must share the road with US 395. Colville is the biggest town in the northeast corner of the state and the site of Ft. Colville, 1859–1882. The Stevens County Historical Society has mementos from those days.

Wash. 20 now gets to finish its job alone. Tapping campgrounds in the Colville National Forest, it arrives at Tiger on the Pend Oreille River and heads south toward Spokane, 70 miles away. It never gets there. Instead, it chases the river over to Newport on the Idaho line and ends its journey. Through traffic goes straight ahead to Spokane on Wash. 211 and US 2.

Hub of the Inland Empire

We now have arrived in Spokane three times, by way of US 2, Wash. 20 (almost) and US 395. It is time we stopped in the city.

Depending upon which statistics are used, Spokane is either the second or the third largest city in Washington. Within city limits it outranks Tacoma, 175,000 to 155,000. In metropolitan area population, Tacoma was credited with 397,600 to Spokane's 303,800 in 1975 census estimates. However, Tacoma lives in the shadow of a neighboring city more than three times as large, whereas Spokane reigns over a realm that stretches for hundreds of miles around. It has good reason for calling itself the capital of an "Inland Empire."

It is not an old city, dating only to the 1870's, but it was center-stage during the glory days of railroad building, and until the Klondike gold rush put Seattle on the map, probably was the best known city in the state.

With no challenge to its position, Spokane let decades pass without any great modernization, and time rubbed it over with a somewhat grubby appearance. Then the city aroused itself to a major effort, the Expo '74 World's Fair. It cleared away a lot of eyesores in the center of town and created a park on the riverbanks above Spokane Falls. Aside from the improvement in looks, it gained an Opera House, a Convention Center and other permanent facilities, including some updated hotels.

Spokane has more than 60 parks and gardens, including the famous Duncan Gardens and Japanese Tea House in Manito Park. Its museums include Cheney Cowles Memorial Museum, West 2316–1st Ave., with an art gallery and a regional history museum. Ft. Wright College Historical Museum, West 400 Randolph Rd., with items relating to the military occupancy of the fort (1899–1958), and the restored St. Michael's Chapel, dating from 1882; and Clark Mansion, W. 2208 Second, an elegant old residence with Tiffany glass, carved woodwork, murals and period furniture. Campbell House, a late-nineteenth-century mansion of 19 rooms and 10 fireplaces that has been restored to its elegant time, adjoins the Cheney Cowles Memorial Museum. The Crosby Library, at Gonzaga University, 502 Boone, contains memorabilia donated by Bing Crosby to his alma mater. Nearby is the outstanding Museum of Native American Cultures at East 200 Cataldo Ave.

Spokane Falls, on the Spokane River, in the heart of the business district, is illuminated during the spring, when the water is high. The best view is from the nearby Monroe Street Bridge. The central plaza, downtown, is a superbly designed shopping area, with sidewalk malls and small specialty shops.

The 28-mile City Loop Drive, marked by signs, is a good way to explore the highlights of Spokane. The drive, starting at Howard and Riverside, in the heart of the downtown area, takes in High Drive Parkway, Manito Park, Cliff Park (built around an ancient volcanic island), and Gonzaga University. Mount Spokane, 25 miles northeast of the city, is the highest point in the "Inland Empire." This 5,878-foot peak is at the center of Mt. Spokane State Park, the largest in the state, with almost 21,000 acres. The park offers a view in the summer and winter sports in the winter. An unpaved road ascends to the peak, but an easier way to make the ascent is by chair lift.

Riverside State Park, a few miles from the city center, and spread on both banks of the Spokane River, has a large campground. Odd volcanic formations within the park, such as the one called "Bowl and Pitcher," fascinate most everyone. The park also commemorates Spokane House, built in 1810, the first white settlement in what became the State of Washington. An interpretive center at the far north end of the park explains the history of this fur-trading post.

There are ten public golf courses in and around the city. South of Spokane are dozens of small lakes for swimming and fishing, little known to anyone but area residents. A short distance to the east are the big lakes of Northern Idaho, which Spokane looks upon as part of its suburbs—with some justice—because it has the population to support the resorts.

Interstate 90

The way I–90 is laid out, it runs not only from Seattle to Spokane, but from Spokane to Seattle. That's a good arrangement, because many visitors enter the state from Idaho and almost the first thing they come to is Spokane.

In earlier years the westbound drive across the state perplexed newcomers. There were trees around Spokane, pines nicely sprinkled about in open woods. Some 25 or 30 miles out of town, though, they disappeared quite abruptly, leaving the landscape brown and bare. Hills and mountains retreated to dim blue lines on distant horizons. There was rich wheatland around Ritzville, but then the desert took over again, mile after mile through sagebrush, with only an occasional small coulee to break the sandy flats. Any farm or village with a few shade trees appeared to be almost an oasis.

After about four hours of this, sight of the Columbia came as another shock. The river flowed in a somber canyon whose walls were stark brown rock, and beyond lay arid rolling hills, seemingly forever.

By now the puzzled newcomers were wondering, "Why in the world is this called 'the Evergreen State'?"

In another 30 miles they would enter the green basin around Ellensburg and see the Cascade Range ahead. From there on, their question would be answered.

Even today, without knowing how the Columbia Basin looked before Coulee Dam's irrigation water had time to take effect, first-time visitors are likely to be a bit surprised. They hadn't realized Washington has so much space not taken up by forests or mountains. And except for Moses Lake, neither is this part of the state much devoted to tourism. Fast highways fan out in all directions from I–90, across the Basin (as a look at a road map discloses) but the main business of Basin towns is agriculture. Wheat and potatoes comprise the biggest crops. Sugar beets rated right with them until 1979 when the rug was yanked from under the industry. The state's refineries quit and beet farmers were forced into other crops—whether temporarily or for good depends upon the future economics of domestic sugar.

Ritzville is still the rich wheat center, where farmers deal in family businesses whose dollar value is in the six and seven figure range. As you near Moses Lake, the big installation north of the highway is a sugar refinery, closed in 1979.

Moses Lake (the city) was a crossroads called Neppel, but with the coming of water it sprawled along the highway as a boom town, then settled down to being the mid-Basin's supply center. Among the supplies are motel rooms. Two dams form holding reservoirs west and south of the city. On the lakes are two state parks, Moses Lake (picnicking and swimming) and Potholes, where everyone launches a boat and goes prowling and fishing among hundreds of small sand islands. South of Potholes Reservoir is the Columbia National Wildlife Refuge, where innumerable ponds formed by irrigation seepage furnish homes for wildfowl and fish.

I–90 heads west from Moses Lake in a straight line for 23 miles, then swings south to cross the Columbia. Near the bend in the highway is a small town started by a fellow who thought the state ought to have a town called George, Washington. On Feb. 22 George makes a point of serving all comers cherry pie.

You cross the Columbia at Vantage. Here is Ginkgo Petrified Forest State Park, with about 7,000 acres of ginkgo fossils, the fossilized wood of this 15-million-year-old tree. The petrified remains also include those of sequoias up to 10 feet in diameter, oaks six feet in diameter, a 100-foot spruce, and a 50-foot maple. More than 200 kinds of petrified wood are displayed in the museum, and a Trail of Petrified Logs winds through this strange forest. Ginkgos, incidentally, still thrive in other areas. There is no campground at the park, but there is a nice picnic area at the museum.

Wanapum Dam is dimly within sight, downriver, from Vantage. Its Tour Center has mementos from early Indian, trapper, miner, and pioneer homestead days to present times. Inside an underwater viewing room you can watch the salmon go by (March to November) as they work their way upstream to spawning beds.

Ellensburg, the seat of Kittitas County, is the home of Central Washington State College. The community reputation, however, is that of a cow-country town. There are many cattle ranches in the area, and Ellensburg's rodeo, held in early September, is topped—in tradition—only by the Pendleton (Oregon) Round-Up.

The first town west, twenty-two miles, is Cle Elum, a coal town. The Cle Elum Historical Society Museum, in the old Bell Telephone Co. building, has pioneer items, a telephone exhibit, and a mining display.

About halfway between Cle Elum and 3,022-foot Snoqualmie Pass, a distance of thirty-one miles, is Lake Easton State Park, with 100 tentsites, picnic grounds, fishing and swimming. At the summit of Snoqualmie Pass there is a warren of ski areas, all jammed on propitious winter days. Down the west slope the first town is North Bend, 22 miles away. From there it is 29 miles to mid-Seattle.

The Southeast Corner

That was a fast trip from Spokane to Seattle on I–90. Or anyway, about six hours without too many pauses along the road. Now let's suppose you were not in that much of a hurry to get to Seattle and would rather explore the southeast corner of the state.

South of Spokane, US 195 leads through farm country, punctuated by drowsy hamlets. At Rosalia, 31 miles south, is the Steptoe Battlefield Memorial, a 26-foot granite shaft commemorating a battle here between the United States Army and warriors from several Indian tribes. In May of 1858, Colonel Edward J. Steptoe set out with 158 dragoons and two howitzers from Ft. Walla Walla to punish the Palouse Indians and their allies, who had been staging raids in the Walla Walla Valley. He narrowly missed staging a preview of Custer's Last Stand. Pinned down after a running battle with Coeur d'Alenes, Yakimas, Nez Perce, Palouse and Spokane Indians (about 1,000 of them, compared to his 158 men), the colonel managed to slip away during the night and race ahead of his pursuers back to safety. Shocked by the defeat, the Army set out in earnest four months later and routed the tribal allies. Among their glorious victories, they caught and slaughtered 700 Indian horses out east of present-day Spokane. Colonel George Wright reasoned that Indians afoot couldn't chase colonels nearly as fast as they did Steptoe.

The town named after Colonel Steptoe is 17 miles farther south on US 195. This area of rolling hills is the Palouse wheat country, which reputedly produces more grain per acre than any major area in the world.

A 4½ mile drive northeast from Steptoe, via a county road, leads to Steptoe Butte State Park. The butte rises 3,613 feet, but looks higher because of the relative flatness of surrounding terrain. A road leads to the summit, and the view takes in the entire Palouse country. From the town of Steptoe, follow US 195 south nine miles to Colfax, the commercial hub of the North Palouse River Valley. Perkins House here, owned by the Whitman County Historical Society, is an 1885 Victorian mansion and the first house built in Colfax. A log cabin is also on the property.

US 195 continues to Clarkston. On the way is Pullman, home of Washington State University. The school had its beginnings as a land-grant college, built on a plateau above the business section. On campus are the Nuclear Research Reactor and Albrook Hydraulics Laboratory. For tours, inquire at the Office of Information, 448 French Administration Building. Also open free to visitors are the Charles R. Conner Museum, with its display of several hundred mounted birds and animals, and the Washington State University Herbarium, with 260,000 dried plant specimens. The town itself is at the eastern edge of the wheat belt. On three sides are the treeless hills of the Palouse wheatlands, rolling as a billowy sea. A few miles east are the forested foothills of Idaho's Moscow Mountains. The city is seven miles from the Idaho line.

US 195 ends at Clarkston, whose big neighbor across the Snake River in Idaho is Lewiston. Clarkston always has been a favored residential area and now it appears to have a bright future in the recreation field. A dam on the Snake River put it at the head of a long lake. Parks are being developed and marinas are growing. Thrilling jetboat excursions up-river into Snake's Hells Canyon take off from here.

The highway from Colfax southwest to Walla Walla is Wash. 127, which joins US 12 35 miles west of Clarkston. A longer route is to take Wash. 26 at Dusty. It runs through less-than-gentle wheatlands to Washtucna, where you turn south on Wash. 260–261. The road descends through grazing lands, following the path of the Mullan Road, hacked out in 1860. Nine miles down Wash. 261 there is the entrance to Palouse Falls State Park, where the mighty falls plunge deep into a mammoth rimrock basin before swirling through the canyon to froth into the Snake River.

Six miles below the park, archaeologists of Washington State University discovered in 1968 the remains of a 10,000-year-old prehistoric man, oldest in the Western Hemisphere. The find was made at Marmes Rock Shelter, now covered by the waters of a reservoir. Before you cross the bridge spanning the Snake River, ponder that Lewis and Clark stood on the north shore of the Snake on their way westward in 1805. The new Lyons Ferry State Park, on an arm of the reservoir, is a pleasant place for pondering, camping and swimming. Wash. 261 connects with US 12 between Dayton and Pomeroy. Dayton is a trim, neat canning town and one of the homes of the "Jolly Green Giant" of television renown. Depending on the season, the day, and who is around to act as a guide, you may be able to tour the plant.

Five miles west on US 12 is Lewis and Clark Trail State Park. Here, on its return trip in 1806, the party of trailblazers camped in a grove of pines on the banks of the Touchet River. There are about 30 tent sites in the park.

Waitsburg, four miles west, is a restful-looking town of shaded streets and large homes. It is in one of the most fertile farming regions in the state, and its residents harvest wheat, peas, and asparagus.

As US 12 rolls into the Walla Walla Valley, the view opens to embrace broad expanses of level fields fringed by gently rolling hills. Twenty-one miles south of Waitsburg, the road enters Walla Walla, the largest city in southeastern Washington.

Walla Walla's Many Waters

Walla Walla, the town subjected to many jokes about having been named twice, actually derives its name from an Indian word meaning "many waters," which is borne out by the town's location: Mill Creek runs through the business district; the Walla Walla River lies to the south; the Touchet River is north of town; and the Columbia River is only 30 miles to the west. In addition, the valley is laced by many lesser streams. It has often been said that Walla Walla has a patrician atmosphere, but the town's history has been western to the core.

Two highly disparate institutions give prominence to Walla Walla; one is the state penitentiary, the other is Whitman College. The latter is Washington's oldest institution of higher learning, dating back to 1859. It was originally founded as a seminary by Cushing Eells, a Congregational missionary. He named the school after his friend, Dr. Marcus Whitman, who, with his wife and twelve other persons at their mission, was slain by Cayuse Indians in 1847. Among the many distinguished alumni of Whitman College is Supreme Court Justice William O. Douglas. The Whitman Memorial Museum on the campus numbers among its displays the diary of Mrs. Narcissa Whitman and the journal of John Mullan, builder of the Mullan Road. Carnegie Center, an art museum at 109 South Palouse, has changing exhibits and a crafts shop.

Ft. Walla Walla Park, at the southwestern edge of town, along Garrison Creek has trees to camp under and lots of grass to romp on. The park contains a replica of Ft. Walla Walla, built in 1856, with the pioneer buildings of the village furnished in period style. The Chamber of Commerce will be glad to give you a copy of their walking tour brochure so you can see the city, with all its history, on an easy walk around town.

Six miles west of town on US 12 is a turnoff to Whitman Mission National Historic Site, where the Whitmans established Wai-i-lat-pu Mission in 1836. The name is Indian for "place of rye grass." The mission ruins have been excavated, a millpond and irrigation ditch have been restored, and excavated articles are displayed in a museum at the site. The Visitor Center contains a graphic record of the mission and the work of the Whitmans. From the memorial shaft atop a small, easily climbed hill, there are views of the Walla Walla River, the valley and, to the south, the mystic haze of the Blue Mountains.

US 12 follows the Walla Walla River 24 miles west to its confluence with the Columbia River at Wallula Gap. At this point the Columbia is a mile wide. Near here stood old Ft. Walla Walla, built in 1817. The highway swings northwest, following the bend of the river, 16 miles to Pasco. At the edge of Pasco the Snake River pours into the Columbia. Here, too, is Sacajawea State Park and Museum. The park was named for the young Shoshone mother who was the only female on the Lewis and Clark expedition. You can tour Ice Harbor Dam, nine miles east of Pasco and off Wash. 124. Lake Sacajawea, formed by the dam, is a key recreational area in these parts, offering camping, boating, picnicking, water skiing, swimming, and fishing.

US 12 crosses the Columbia River from Pasco to Kennewick, one of the Tri-Cities, and continues seven miles to the third of these, Richland. Before World War II, Richland was a sleepy little burg, four miles off the highway. The town had a general store and, as late as 1940, a population of fewer than 250. Then came the Manhattan Project—the supersecret development of the atomic bomb—and Richland was changed for all time. The Hanford Atomic Works were built nearby, on the Columbia River, and many of the workers were moved to Richland for reasons of security. The town has been booming ever since. Its population now is about 28,000. Hanford Science Center, in the Federal Building, has intricate displays, models, and animated exhibits illustrating the development and uses of atomic energy.

The Fruit Bowl

The main highway to Seattle from Tri-Cities is US 12. In the Yakima valley it is trying, in off-and-on-again style, to become part of I–82, a freeway connecting I–80N (in Oregon, headed for Portland) and east-west I–90 across the center of Washington. Since I–80N is a major arterial from the Midwest, up through Idaho, a good many travelers also arrive in Washington from this southeast corner.

The Yakima valley holds some of the richest agricultural land in the country. Long known for its apples, soft fruit and vegetables, its grapes and wineries are now rapidly growing in reputation. Among other products are hops and mint.

The towns in the valley are numerous and long-established. At Toppenish (on Wash. 22, which parallels US 12 on the south side of the river), US 97 goes south through Satus Pass and Goldendale to I–80N;

and Wash. 220 runs due west 20 miles to White Swan on the Yakima Indian Reservation. Seven miles farther, at road's end, is Ft. Simcoe State Park.

Fort Simcoe was an Army post from 1865 to 1895, and from then until 1923 an Indian agency and school. The dry climate preserved it well and five of the original buildings remain, including a log blockhouse and the commanding officer's two-story house. It is the state's most authentic example of a frontier military outpost.

Yakima, second largest city in eastern Washington, is the agricultural capital of the region, with blocks of produce warehouses and processing plants. It is also a tourist center—its abundant motels feature pools for sun-seekers from the west side of the state. On weekends from April to September, old interurban trolleys make sightseeing trips in the city and out into the countryside. The Yakima Valley Historical Museum in Franklin Park is one of the best in the state. It includes a fine wagon collection and books and furnishings from Supreme Court Justice William O. Douglas' office. In spring and again in the fall there is a short horseracing season at Yakima Meadows.

The fastest way to reach Seattle from Yakima is to take a freeway, I–82 (also known as US 97 here) to Ellensburg, and then I–90 west to Seattle.

Travelers who really want to find the best scenery are advised to choose Wash. 821 to Ellensburg. It winds along the Yakima River canyon and reveals many formations you won't see on the freeway.

Two Passes: Chinook and White

Two alternate routes to Seattle from Yakima are by way of 4,500-foot White Pass or 5,440-foot Chinook Pass. They both start west as US 12, into the Naches River valley, but four miles beyond Naches 410 continues along the river. It climbs the Cascades slope, following northwestward a pioneer pack trace, the Naches Pass Trail, hacked out in 1853. It was a rough route for wagons and was abandoned in favor of the Chinook Pass route, which was less direct but far more practical. Fifty-one miles after splitting off US 12, Wash. 410 reaches Chinook Pass, having touched six National Forest campgrounds along the way.

Back at the highway split, US 2 switches to the Tieton River. It passes Tieton Dam, which has created a large lake in the center of the Tieton Recreation Area, popular with boating, fishing, and swimming enthusiasts. Within ten miles is Clear Lake, with similar attractions. Five miles farther on is White Pass, a ski area and the site of the chair lift to the summit of Pigtail Peak. Look to the south for 8,201-foot Goat Rock, in a wilderness area. Other peaks rise to more than 7,000 feet. This is the habitat of the mountain goat; the landscapes range from glaciers to mountain meadows clustered with rare alpine flowers.

Thirteen miles beyond White Pass, US 12 meets Wash. 123 at the southeastern edge of Mt. Rainier National Park. (If you continue west on US 12, it is about seventy-five miles to I–5, south of Chehalis). Wash. 123 climbs to 4,630-foot Cayuse Pass, three miles west of Chinook Pass. Here Wash. 123 gives way to Wash. 410, which continues north through the park. Forty-one miles beyond the pass it reaches Enumclaw. It is about 25 miles on Wash. 410 to Tacoma. Or, at Enumclaw, you can take Wash. 169 and in an hour or less be in Seattle.

The Columbia Gorge

The other "pass" through the Cascade Range was mentioned at the beginning of *Exploring Washington.* The Columbia River kept chewing out its channel as the mountains rose, and kept this pass to less than 100 feet in elevation. (The Cascade Crest Trail reaches the river midway between Bonneville and Bingen-White Salmon.)

The fast track is I–80N on the Oregon side, but the Washington highway has scenic advantages and it is not much slower. You can pick up Wash. 14 at Tri-Cities and follow it clear to Vancouver, Wash. but the popular section is the Gorge itself. Motorists make a loop trip by using US 97 through Goldendale, seat of Klickitat County. Goldendale gained the greatest publicity in its history in February 1979. It was the only town with an observatory in the path of a total solar eclipse.

US 97 intersects Wash. 14 and then crosses the Columbia on a bridge. East of the junction is John Day Dam, another massive hydroelectric structure. Shortly before US 97 reaches the bridge a sideroad leads to a strange sight—a replica of England's Stonehenge. Sitting on a cliff above the Columbia, it is Samuel Hill's memorial to Klickitat County men who died in World War I. There is no caretaker or admittance fee.

Downriver on Wash. 14, and equally at odds with its surroundings, is the Maryhill Museum of Fine Arts. It also was built by Sam Hill, multimillionaire son-in-law of James J. Hill, builder of the Great Northern Railway. A palace in the middle of nowhere, high above the Columbia, it was started in 1914 and "dedicated" (to nothing in particular) in 1926 by Queen Marie of Romania. It was named for Mary Hill, Sam's wife, but they never lived there.

Hill died in 1931, specifying in his will that the mansion was to become a museum and leaving to it some remarkably diverse collections. Rembrandt, Van Dyck, Monet and Rodin are represented in the art galleries, along with American paintings, firearms, boat models, French mannequins, a very good American Indian collection and—to top it off—Queen Marie's coronation gown and other personal possessions.

Washington's Columbia River highway (14) runs on to Horsethief State Park, on a bay backed up by The Dalles Dam just below it. The dam submerged Celilo Falls, traditional fishing spot for the Indians, and the village of Wishram. Indians came from 100 or more miles around to fish and trade there. It was okay, though, to steal horses when opportunities arose.

Bingen is on the river highway, with White Salmon on the hill just above it. Bingen was named for the German city on the Rhine, in a wine-producing area. This one also has some vineyards and recently has dressed itself up to look like an old-fashioned German town.

Sidetrip: Wash 141 goes north from here, 22 miles to Trout Lake with unobstructed views of 12,307-foot Mt. Adams on the way. A road continues into Gifford Pinchot National Forest and the lava tube ice caves. One, entered by a ladder, is 400 feet long. Why ice forms in such caves would require too long an explanation here.

Back on the Columbia River highway, it proceeds west through the Gorge. At the Bridge of the Gods, you can cross into Oregon, to the town of Cascade Locks and Bonneville Dam. Six miles farther is Beacon Rock State Park, whose great attraction is the second largest monolith in the world (the largest is Gibraltar). For centuries Beacon Rock was a landmark to Indians and then to white explorers, settlers, and rivermen. The view from the top, reached by a winding staircase, is from 900 feet above the river.

One of the best ways to see the Columbia and its tributary, the Snake, is by boat. From May through September, Exploration Cruise Lines runs six-night round trips from Portland to Lewiston at the head of navigation on the Snake.

At Camas, Crown Zellerbach Corp. produces Chiffon and Zee paper products. From Camas, it is 14 miles to Vancouver. And that's where we came in.

PRACTICAL INFORMATION FOR WASHINGTON

HOW TO GET THERE. The gateway for many travelers to Washington is Seattle. See "How to Get There" in the Seattle Practical Information. If you are not going to Seattle, you can fly to Spokane on *Northwest, Alaska, PSA,* or *United* as well as a number of regional carriers. *Amtrak* trains also stop in Spokane. *Greyhound* has extensive routes in the state, while *Trailways* only offers interstate service to Seattle.

Many travelers drive into the state. The major interstates are I–5 and I–90. I–84 runs just south of the border with Oregon.

By Ferry. Black Ball runs between Victoria, British Columbia (on Vancouver Island), and Port Angeles. Alaska State Ferries connect Southeast Alaska and Seattle twice a week in winter and once a week in summer. Washington State Ferries operate from Sidney near Victoria on Vancouver Island to Anacortes, 90 miles north of Seattle. A toll ferry on the Columbia River operates between Cathlamet and Westport, Oregon.

ACCOMMODATIONS. Hotels and motels equal to those of Seattle in comfort and facilities often cost less in other parts of the state. Resort areas may have off-season rates. Accommodations are listed alphabetically by town and by price category. The categories, based on the cost of a double room, are *Deluxe,* \$50 and up; *Expensive,* \$40–\$50; *Moderate,* \$30–\$40; and *Inexpensive,* \$30 and under.

ABERDEEN. Red Lion Motel. *Deluxe.* 521 W. Wishkah, Aberdeen 98520 (532–5210). Medium-size motel at south end of town. 5 kitchens at extra charge. Pool. Pets OK. Restaurant nearby.

Nordic Inn. *Moderate.* 1700 S. Boone, Aberdeen 98520 (533–0100). Medium-size motel at southern edge of town on Wash. 105. 2-story motel, units with in-room sauna, fine restaurant. Cocktail lounge, entertainment.

Olympic Inn. *Moderate.* 616 W. Heron, Aberdeen 98520 (533–4200). Double-story motel with nicely furnished rooms. Some suites and efficiencies available. Restaurant near.

TraveLure Motel. *Inexpensive.* 623 W. Wishkah, Aberdeen 98520 (532–3280). Centrally located, smaller motel with 1- and 2-room units. Seasonal rates.

ANACORTES. Anacortes Inn. *Expensive.* 3006 Commercial, Anacortes 98221 (293–3153). Medium-size motel. Some kitchens available at extra charge.

Cap Sante Inn. *Expensive.* 906 9th St., Anacortes 98221 (293–0602). Small, 2-story downtown lodging, close to waterfront. Pets allowed.

San Juan Motel. *Expensive.* 1103 6th St., corner O, Anacortes 98221 (293–5105). Many of the 27 units have kitchens, some suites. Small pets allowed.

Ship Harbor Inn. *Expensive.* 5316 Ferry Terminal Rd., Anacortes 98221 (293–5177). Some rooms with marine view. Kitchenettes at extra charge. Restaurant nearby.

BELLEVUE. See "Seattle-East," above.

BELLINGHAM. Nendel's Motel. *Deluxe.* 714 Lakeway Dr., Bellingham 98225 (671–1011). Large, newly renovated motel at north end of town. Covered recreation area with indoor pool. Restaurant, lounge.

BLAINE. Inn at Semiahmoo. *Deluxe.* 9500 Semiahmoo Pkwy., Blaine 98230 (371–5100). New luxury 200-room waterfront resort focuses on Arnold Palmer-designed golf course and marina. Two lounges, two restaurants, recreational center.

Pony Soldier Motor Inn. *Expensive.* 215 Samish Way, Bellingham 98225 (734–8830). Large, 3-level motel with variety of accommodations. Some units with refrigerators, some with balconies. Pool. Restaurant adjacent.

BREMERTON. Bayview Inn. *Deluxe.* 5640 Kitsap Way, Bremerton 98312 (373–7349). Large, split-level motel overlooking bay. Most units with balconies. Pool, covered recreation area. No pets. Fine restaurant, cocktail lounge, and entertainment.

Best Western Westgate Inn. *Moderate–Expensive.* 4303 Kitsap Way, Bremerton 98312 (377–4402). Large, 2-story motel with choice of 1-, 2-, and 3-room units, many with kitchens at extra charge. Pool, playground. Pets allowed. Laundry, picnic tables, and grill. Restaurant adjacent.

Chieftain Motel. *Moderate.* 600 National Ave., Bremerton 98312 (479–3111). Medium-size motel on 3 levels. Units with electric fireplaces and balconies, a few with kitchen facilities at extra charge. Pool.

Bremerton Super 8 Motel. *Moderate.* 5068 Kitsap Way, Bremerton 98312 (377–8881). 77-unit motel east of town. Pets OK. Restaurant nearby.

CENTRALIA. Econo Lodge. *Moderate.* 702 Harrison Ave., Centralia 98531 (736–2875). 93-unit motel off I–5. Some rooms with jacuzzi. Pool. Restaurant nearby.

Lake Shore Motel. *Inexpensive.* 1325 Lake Shore Dr., Centralia 98531 (736–9344). Medium-size motel on small lake, just off I–5. North of town. 1- and 2-room units. Boating, swimming, and fishing in season. Playground. 24-hr cafe adjacent, bar.

Park Motel. *Inexpensive.* 1011 Belmont, Centralia 98531 (736–9333). North edge of town. 2-level motel offers convenience and comfort. A few kitchens at extra charge. Restaurant nearby.

CHEHALIS. Best Western Pony Soldier Motor Inn. *Moderate–Expensive.* 122 Interstate Ave., Chehalis 98532 (748–0101). South of town off I–5. Large, well-furnished motel. Some units with refrigerators. Pool. Restaurant next door.

Cascade Motel. *Inexpensive.* 550 S.W. Parkland Dr., Chehalis 98532 (748–8608). Medium-size motel at south edge of town. With attractive units, some with balconies.

CHELAN. See also Stehekin. **Campbell's Lodge.** *Deluxe.* 104 W. Woodin Ave., Chelan 98816 (682–2561). In center of town. Large motel with several buildings along Lake Chelan. Two pools, therapy pool, beach, fishing, boat dock at extra charge. Seasonal rates. Restaurant, cocktails. Advance deposit required.

Caravel Motor Hotel. *Deluxe.* Box 1509, Chelan 98816 (682–2715). 1 block west of town on U.S. 97. Medium-size 2-story motel on lakefront. 1- and 2-room units. Pool, boat moorage, playground. No pets. Some kitchens. Seasonal rates. Reservation required.

Darnell's Resort Motel. *Deluxe.* Box 506, Chelan 98816 (682–2015). ¼ mile north of town on lake. 38 units with balconies facing lake. Most units have kitchens. Pool, marina, fishing and other water sports. Tennis courts, exercise room. No pets. Open April to October. Seasonal rates. Weekly rates available in summer.

CLARKSTON. Best Western Rivertree Inn. *Expensive.* 1257 Bridge St., Clarkston 99403 (758–9551). Medium-size motel. Half the units have kitchens at an extra charge. Pool. Restaurant near.

Nendel's Motel. *Moderate–Expensive.* 222 Bridge St., Clarkston 99403 (758–1631). Large motel near downtown. Some units have refrigerators. Pool. Fee for pets.

COLVILLE. Benny's Panorama Motel. *Inexpensive–Moderate.* 915 S. Main, Colville 99114 (684–2517). On U.S. 395. Medium-size 2-level motel.

COPALIS BEACH. Iron Springs Beach Resort. *Deluxe.* Box 207, Copalis Beach 98535 (276–4230). Unique oceanfront resort with individual cottages scattered upon wooded hillside. Each has fireplace, kitchen, living and bed rooms. Covered swimming pool. Reservations must be for at least 3 nights during season. 3 miles no. of Copalis Beach.

Beachwood Resort. *Expensive–Deluxe.* Box 116, Copalis Beach 98535 (289–2177). On Wash. 109. At this small attractive resort, family-size units overlook ocean. With fireplaces and kitchens. 3-day minimum reservation required in season.

COULEE DAM. Coulee House Motel. *Expensive–Deluxe.* 110 Roosevelt Way, Coulee Dam 99116 (633–1101). View of the dam. Some 2-room units and suites. Some refrigerators. Pool, restaurants, cocktail lounge.

Ponderosa Motel. *Moderate.* 10 Lincoln St., Coulee Dam 99116 (633–2100). 34-unit motel on SR 155. View of dam from every room. Restaurant nearby.

COUPEVILLE. Captain Whidbey Inn. *Deluxe.* 2072 W. Captain Whidbey Rd., Coupeville 98239 (678–4097). 24 antique-furnished rooms in historic madrona log inn overlooking Penn Cove. Also cottages with fireplaces. Boats available. Fishing, swimming, playground. Pets allowed in cottages. Wellknown restaurant adjoins (see "Dining Out" section).

CRYSTAL MOUNTAIN. Crystal Mountain Resort. *Deluxe.* Crystal Mountain 98022 (663–2265). 2-story ski lodge in village. Restaurant adjacent. No pets. Seasonal rates.

ELLENSBURG. Accommodation rates are usually higher during the rodeo.

Best Western Ellensburg Inn. *Deluxe.* 1700 Canyon Rd., Ellensburg 98926 (925–9801). Large 2-story motel with pool, playground, coffee shop, dining room, cocktail lounge with entertainment.

Regalodge. *Moderate.* 300 W. 6th St., Ellensburg 98926 (925–3116). Medium-size downtown motel. Indoor pool. Pets allowed. 2 blocks to restaurant.

Harold's Motel. *Inexpensive–Moderate.* 601 N. Water, Ellensburg 98926 (925–4141). Medium-size 2-story motel, downtown. Pool. Free parking. Seasonal rates.

Rainbow Motel. *Inexpensive.* 1025 Cascade Way, Ellensburg 98926 (925–3544). Small motel with some kitchenettes, no utensils. Half are two-bedroom units. No pets. Playground.

ENUMCLAW. King's Motel. *Inexpensive.* 1334 Roosevelt Way E., Enumclaw 98022 (825–1626). Small motel just a mile east of town and set well back from highway. 2-levels, several units with kitchen facilities. Pool. Restaurant adjoining.

EPHRATA. Ephrata TraveLodge. *Moderate.* 31 Basin S.W., Ephrata 98823 (754–4651). Well-furnished small downtown motel. Heated pool. No pets.

EVERETT. Everett Pacific Hotel. *Deluxe.* 3105 Pine St., Everett 98201 (339–3333). 250-room lodging with indoor pool, jacuzzi, and exercise room. Dining room, lounge, entertainment.

Holiday Inn Seattle North. *Deluxe.* 101 128th St. S.W., Everett 98204 (745–2555). Just off I–5. Large 2-level motel with many conveniences. Pool and wading pool in covered recreation area. Coffee shop, dining room, cocktail lounge with entertainment. Pets OK.

Royal Motor Inn. *Moderate.* 952 Hwy. 99N, Everett 98201 (259–5177). Medium-size 2-story motel. A few units with kitchens at extra charge. Pool, restaurant adjacent.

Topper Motel. *Inexpensive–Moderate.* 1030 N. Broadway, Everett 98201 (259–3151). 32-room motel, some with kitchens at extra charge. Several 2-room units. Restaurant nearby.

Motel 6. *Inexpensive.* 10006 Evergreen Way, Everett 98204 (355–1811). South of town on Highway 99. Large motel with the usual "6" accommodations. Pool.

FORKS. Kalaloch Lodge. *Deluxe.* Star Rt. 1, Box 1100, Forks 98331 (962–2271). Oceanfront resort on wild coast. Motel, cabins, and lodge units. Restaurant. Year-round activities.

FRIDAY HARBOR. Friday Harbor Motor Inn. *Expensive–Deluxe.* 410 Spring St., Friday Harbor 98250 (378–4351). 72-unit motel near ferry, marina, restaurants. Some kitchens. Seasonal rates.

Island Lodge at Friday Harbor. *Expensive–Deluxe.* 1016 Guard St., Friday Harbor 98250 (378–2000). Small motel on outskirts of town, with hot tub and sundeck.

GOLDENDALE. Ponderosa. *Inexpensive.* 775 U.S. 97N, Goldendale 98620 (773–5842). Small motel on north city limits. Some with kitchens. Small pets allowed. Interesting cafe and bar next door.

HOQUIAM. Westward Lodge. *Moderate.* 910 Simpson Ave., Hoquiam 98550 (532–8161). Large motel with some kitchenettes, some suites, and 2-room units. Restaurant nearby.

Sandstone Motel. *Inexpensive–Moderate.* 2424 Aberdeen Ave., Hoquiam 98550 (532–4160). Small and pleasant, with restaurant nearby.

KALAMA. Columbia Inn Motel. *Moderate.* 602 N. Frontage Rd., Kalama 98625 (673–2855). Off I–5. Clean, simply furnished units on two levels. Interesting restaurant featuring Indian artifacts and souvenirs next door.

KELSO. Thunderbird Motor Inn. *Deluxe.* 510 Kelso Dr., Kelso 98626 (636–4400). Large 2-story motel. Pool, dining room, coffee shop. Cocktail lounge with entertainment. Some suites. Pets allowed.

Motel 6. *Inexpensive.* 106 Minor Rd., Kelso 98626 (636–3770). Medium-size comfortable motel with usual "6" simplicity. Pool. Small pets allowed. Cafe across the street.

KENNEWICK. see "Tri-Cities."

LA PUSH. La Push Ocean Park Resort. *Moderate–Expensive.* Box 67, La Push 98350 (374–5267). Medium-size motel and cabins on beach near Olympic National Park. Area is home to the Quillayute Indians. Modern units, all with complete kitchens. Beautiful scenery, great beachcombing, surf fishing. Off-season and senior-citizen rates.

Shoreline Resort. *Inexpensive.* La Push 98350. (374–6488). Fully equipped modern cottages facing the ocean beach. Prices vary according to size of unit. Trailer park with some hookups. Seasonal rates.

LEAVENWORTH. Haus Rohrbach. *Deluxe.* 12882 Ranger Rd., Leavenworth 98826 (548–7024). Bed-and-breakfast inn on outskirts of town, modeled after an Austrian chalet. Swimming pool, hot tub, hiking trails.

Der Ritterhof Motor Inn. *Moderate.* Hwy. 2, Leavenworth 98826 (548–5845). 38-unit motel with view rooms, suites with balcony and kitchenettes. Pool and jacuzzi. Pets allowed. Good restaurants nearby.

LONG BEACH. Anchorage Motor Court. *Expensive–Deluxe.* Rt. 1, Box 581, Long Beach 98631 (642–2351). Small oceanfront lodging. Most units have kitchens. Fireplaces with wood supplied.

Shaman Motel. *Expensive–Deluxe.* 115 S.W. 3rd, Long Beach 98631 (642–3714). Medium-size city-center 2-story motel. Ocean view from many units, several fireplaces, kitchen facilities in many units. Pool, restaurant near. Seasonal rates.

Chautauqua Lodge. *Moderate–Deluxe.* 304 14th N.W., Long Beach 98631 (642–4401). 180-unit oceanfront motel. Many units with fireplaces and efficiencies. Indoor pool, whirlpool, sauna. Recreation room with ping-pong, pool tables. Dining room, lounge with live entertainment. Pets allowed.

Our Place at the Beach. *Moderate–Expensive.* 309 South Blvd., Long Beach 98631 (642–3793). Small motel. Many rooms with ocean view, some with fireplaces. Fitness center with sauna, steam, 2 spa pools, exercise room.

LONGVIEW. Lewis and Clark Motor Inn. *Moderate.* 838 15th Ave., Longview 98632 (423–6460). Small lodging, some units with refrigerators. Pets OK. Restaurant nearby.

Town Chalet Motor Hotel. *Inexpensive.* 1822 Washington Way, Longview 98632 (423–2020). Downtown. Some kitchens. Pets allowed. Cafe nearby.

LOPEZ ISLAND. The Islander Lopez. *Expensive–Deluxe.* Fisherman Bay, Lopez Island 98261 (468–2233). Medium-size 2 level motel. Some units with kitchen facilities. Pool, therapeutic pool, marine with boats and motors available, fishing. Coffee shop, dining room, bar. Seasonal rates. On west side of island. Reservations advised.

MOCLIPS. Hi Tide Ocean Beach Resort. *Deluxe.* Box 308, Moclips 98562 (276–4142). Modern fully-equipped suites with kitchens, private lanais. Panoramic ocean view. Pets extra.

Ocean Crest Resort. *Moderate–Deluxe.* Sunset Beach, Moclips 98562 (276–4465). Medium-size resort motel situated on bluff overlooking the Pacific. Accommodations available in cottages or 1- to 3-level motel. Some rooms have balconies, fireplaces, and kitchens. Indoor heated pool, saunas. On weekends, minimum reservation is 2 days; holidays, 3 days.

Moonstone Beach Motel. *Moderate–Deluxe.* Box 156, Moclips 98562 (276–4346). Small motel right on the beach. Every unit has beach view. 1–2 bedroom units with kitchens. Pets extra.

Moclips Motel. *Inexpensive–Moderate.* Box 8, Moclips 98562 (276–4228). Medium-size motel with range of prices and facilities. Completely furnished housekeeping units, 50–100 ft. from the beach. Good beachcombing. Ocean view.

MOSES LAKE. Best Western Hallmark Inn. *Expensive–Deluxe.* 3000 Marina Dr., Moses Lake 98837 (765–9211). Large 2-story motel overlooking lake. Some rooms with balcony. Pool, sauna, tennis courts. Room service. Restaurant, bar, entertainment, dancing. Pets limited.

Interstate Inn. *Moderate.* 2801 W. Broadway, Moses Lake 98837 (765–1777). Medium-size. Pool, airport transportation. Restaurant nearby.

Moses Lake TraveLodge. *Moderate.* 316 S. Pioneer Way, Moses Lake 98837 (765–8631). Medium size with some suites, some wheelchair units. Restaurant nearby. Park adjacent.

Maples Motel. *Inexpensive.* 1006 W. 3rd Ave., Moses Lake 98837 (765–5665). Medium-size motel with heated pool, well-kept units. One mile W. on business Rte. 90.

MT. RAINIER NATIONAL PARK. Gateway Inn. *Moderate–Deluxe.* Ashford 98304 (569–2506). Small cottages, some with fireplaces. Restaurant, cocktails. Pets OK. Reservations required during season. S.W. entrance to park.

Paradise Inn. *Moderate–Deluxe.* Mt. Rainier Guest Services, Star Route, Ashford 98304 (569–2275). Grand old mountain lodge within the park. No pets. Dining room, coffee shop, bar. Guided hikes and naturalist. Reservations.

Mountain View Lodge Motel. *Inexpensive–Deluxe.* Box 525, Packwood 98361 (494–5555). Half mile E. of Packwood on U.S. 12. Small motel with cottages and units in 2-story building. A few kitchens at extra charge. Pool, playground.

MT. VERNON. Nendel's Inn. *Moderate–Expensive.* 2009 Riverside Dr., Mount Vernon 98273 (424–4141). Large motel with king or queen size beds, suites with hot tubs. Heated pool, restaurant, lounge, room service.

NEWHALEM. Diablo Lake Resort. *Expensive.* Box 194, Rockport 98283. Ask Everett operator for Newhalem. Lakeshore housekeeping cottages of 2, 3, or 4 rooms each. Snack bar, groceries. Boat ramp, dock, boats, fishing. Cruise boat at no extra charge. One mile off Wash. 20, across Diablo Dam. Restaurant on premises.

OAK HARBOR. Auld Holland Inn. *Moderate–Expensive.* 5861 Wash. 20, Oak Harbor 98277 (675–2288). Small motel with some kitchen units at extra charge. Pool, tennis, playground.

Queen Anne Motel. *Moderate.* 1204 W. Pioneer Way, Oak Harbor 98277 (675–2209). Downtown motel with indoor pool, restaurant, bar. A few kitchens at extra charge.

OCEAN CITY. Pacific Sands Motel. *Expensive.* Route 4, Box 585, Ocean City 98569 (289–3588). Wash. 109, about ½ mi. N. of town. Small motel, direct access to beach. Some units with fireplaces, most have kitchens. Pool, playground. Extra charge for pets. Seasonal rates.

OCEAN SHORES. Canterbury Inn. *Deluxe.* Box 310, Ocean Shores 98569 (289–3317). 3-story motel on beach. 1- to 3-room housekeeping units overlooking ocean. Many with fireplaces, some with balconies. Indoor heated pool. Seasonal rates.

Grey Gull Condominium Motel. *Deluxe.* Box 1417, Ocean Shores 98569 (289–3381). 3-level motel with ocean-view kitchen units, fireplaces. Restaurant nearby. Heated pool, sauna. Seasonal rates.

Royal Pacific Motel. *Expensive–Deluxe.* Ocean Shores Blvd., Ocean Shores 98569 (562–9748). Kitchen and fireplace in every unit.

Polynesian Resort. *Expensive–Deluxe.* Box 998, Ocean Shores 98569 (289–3361). Large 3-story motel overlooking ocean. Some units with fireplaces, some balconies, most with kitchens. Indoor pool, restaurant, bar. Seasonal rates.

Discovery Inn. *Expensive.* 1031 Discovery Ave. S.E., Ocean Shores 98569 (289–3371). Medium-size motel near marina. Over half of units have kitchens. Some with fireplaces. Recreation room, barbecue grill, pool. Pets OK. Cafe nearby. Charter boats available at marina.

OLYMPIA. Westwater Inn. *Expensive–Deluxe.* 2300 Evergreen Park Dr., Olympia 98502 (943–4000). Large motor inn overlooking state capitol and lake.

Many units with balconies, some suites with refrigerators and whirlpool baths. Pool, dining room, coffee shop, cocktail lounge, entertainment.

Best Western Aladdin Motor Inn. *Expensive.* 900 Capitol Way, Olympia 98501 (352–7200). Large motor inn halfway between the capitol and downtown. Some units have refrigerators. Pool, dining room, cocktails. Pets allowed. Under-building parking if desired.

Tyee Motor Inn. *Expensive.* 500 Tyee Dr., Tumwater 98502 (352–0511). 3¾ mi. S. of town. Large motor inn with pleasant decor. Some private therapeutic pools available in cabana suites. Heated pool. Restaurant, bar, entertainment.

Governor House. *Expensive.* 621 S. Capitol Way, Olympia 98501 (352–7700). 6-story downtown motor inn. Parking lot. Pool, coffee shop, dining room, cocktail lounge, entertainment.

Carriage Inn Motel. *Moderate.* 1211 S. Quince, Olympia 98501 (943–4710). 2-story motel with pool, 5 blocks from state capitol, 6 blocks from city center. Restaurant nearby. No pets.

Golden Gavel Motor Hotel. *Moderate.* 909 Capitol Way, Olympia 98501 (352–8533). Medium-size 2-story downtown motel, just 3 blocks north of capitol. Restaurant nearby. No pets.

Motel 6. *Inexpensive.* 400 W. Lee St., Tumwater 98501 (943–5000). The usual modest, clean rooms of this chain. Pool. Pets OK. Cafe nearby.

OLYMPIC NATIONAL PARK. Lake Crescent Lodge. *Expensive–Deluxe.* Star Route 1, Box 11, Port Angeles 98362 (928–3211). 20 mi. W. of Port Angeles on U.S. 101. 2-story motor inn with cottage units. Lovely, quiet spot on lakeshore. Some lodge rooms with central bath, some fireplaces. Swimming, hiking, fishing, boats available.

Lake Crescent Log Cabin Resort. *Moderate–Expensive.* 6540 E. Beach Rd., Port Angeles 98362 (928–3325). Smaller rustic resort on sunny side of lake. Variety of accommodations, including housekeeping units. Beautiful setting. Lodge has snack bar, dining room, cocktails. Playground, fishing, swimming. Boats, motors, canoes. Fee for use. Seasonal rates.

Sol Duc Hot Springs Resort. *Moderate–Deluxe.* Box 2169, Port Angeles 98362–0283 (327–3583). Long-established, newly remodeled rustic resort 12 miles from U.S. 101. On trailheads leading into the Olympics. Comfortable units, some kitchens. New cabins have full baths, others no tub or shower. Pools, mineral baths. Coffee shop, restaurant. Small store. Open mid-May to mid-September.

OMAK. Motel Nicholas. *Moderate–Expensive.* 527 E. Grape Ave., Omak 98841 (826–4611). Small motel north of city center. Refrigerators in most units, some two-bedroom units with kitchens.

ORCAS ISLAND. Rosario Resort. *Deluxe.* Eastsound 98245 (376–2222). South of Eastsound. Huge resort occupying 1,300-acre historic estate. Wide range of accommodations, single rooms to spacious suites, most rooms with bay view, some with garden view. Heated pools, indoor and outdoor adult pools, therapy pool, children's pool, sauna. Tennis, lawn games, boating, boat dock, boat and motor rentals, fishing, waterskiing. Coffee shop, dining room, cocktail lounge, entertainment. Seasonal rates. Reservations required.

Outlook Inn. *Deluxe.* Box 210, Eastsound 98245 (376–2581). 35 rooms in refurbished century-old inn, with one modern unit overlooking the water. Restaurant.

OROVILLE. Sun Cove Resort and Guest Ranch. *Deluxe.* Rt. 2, Box 1294, Oroville 98844 (476–2223). Fifteen mi. N.W. of Tonasket off U.S. 97. Small resort with variety of recreational facilities in lovely lake and mountain setting. Heated indoor pool. Fishing, lake swimming, boat dock. Boats and horses available at extra charge. Cafe. Reservations required.

OTHELLO. Aladdin Motor Inn. *Moderate.* 1020 E. Cedar, Othello 99344 (488–5671). Large 2-story motel. Pool, bar. Restaurant near.

Cabana Motel. *Inexpensive–Moderate.* 665 Windsor, Othello 99344 (488–2605). Large motel close to center of town. Some units have kitchenettes at extra charge. Pool.

PACIFIC BEACH. Sandpiper Beach Resort. *Expensive–Deluxe.* Box A, Pacific Beach 98571 (276–4580). Medium-size motel with units right on the beach. All nicely furnished with kitchens. Some have fireplaces. Almost all are set up for large families or groups. Advance reservations advisable.

PASCO. See "Tri-Cities."

PORT ANGELES. See also "Olympic National Park."

Red Lion Bayshore. *Deluxe.* 221 N. Lincoln St., Port Angeles 98362 (452–9215). Large waterfront inn with lovely view of harbor and Juan de Fuca Strait. Pool. Fine Haguewood Restaurant, bar.

Aggie's Inn. *Expensive–Deluxe.* 602 E. Front St., Port Angeles 98362 (457–0471). Some suites, some kitchenettes. Indoor pool, sauna. Good restaurant, bar, entertainment. Pets allowed.

Hill Haus Motel. *Moderate–Deluxe.* 111 E. 2nd St., Port Angeles 98362 (452–9282). Medium-size 3-story motel on bluff overlooking harbor. Some suites with kitchens. Cafe nearby.

Uptown Motel. *Moderate–Deluxe.* 101 E. 2nd, Port Angeles 98362 (457–9434). Medium-size multilevel motel, 1- and 2-room units, away from highway. Some units with kitchen facilities at extra charge.

Aircrest Motel. *Moderate–Expensive.* 1006 E. Front St., Port Angeles 98362 (452–9255). Smaller motel, comfortable units, east side of town.

PORT LUDLOW. The Resort at Port Ludlow. *Deluxe.* 781 Walker Way, Port Ludlow 98365 (437–2222). Large resort and motor inn. Wide range of units, most affording view of bay. Pool, sauna, playground. Squash and tennis courts, water skiing, fishing. Full-service marina, boat and motor rentals. Harbormaster Restaurant offers boat moorage, entertainment, varied menu. Seasonal rates.

PORT TOWNSEND. Bishop Victorian. *Deluxe.* 714 Washington St., Port Townsend 98368 (385–6122). 13 suites, Victorian decor, some two-bedroom units and kitchens. Downtown location, near restaurants and ferry dock.

Port Townsend Motel. *Deluxe.* 2020 Washington St., Port Townsend 98368 (385–2211). Small motel situated away from highway. Comfortable 1- and 2-room units with view of mountains and waterway.

PROSSER. Prosser Motel. *Inexpensive.* 206 6th St., Prosser 99350 (786–2555). Small motel with comfortable units in shady, quiet area. Some kitchen units at extra charge.

PULLMAN. Nendel's Motor Lodge. *Moderate–Expensive.* S.E. 915 Main, Pullman 99163 (332–2646). Large 2-story motel across from Washington State University Campus. Heated pool, restaurant, bar. No pets.

PUYALLUP. Motel Puyallup. *Inexpensive–Moderate.* 1412 S. Meridian St., Puyallup 98371 (845–8825). Medium-size motel with king- and queen-size and water beds. Adjacent 24-hour restaurant, guest laundry and one-day valet service. Near fairgrounds."

QUINAULT. Lake Quinault Lodge. *Deluxe.* Box 7, Quinault 98575 (288–2571). Two miles E. of U.S. 101, south shore Lake Quinault. Historic medium-size lakeshore inn. Some units with fireplaces. Indoor pool, therapy pool, health spa, saunas. Lake swimming, boat dock, boat and motor rentals, fishing, putting green. Dining room, cocktail lounge, entertainment. Seasonal rates.

Rain Forest Resort. *Expensive–Deluxe.* Rt., 1, Box 40, Quinault 98575 (288–2535). Complete resort, with motel, fully equipped cabins, restaurant, RV hook-ups, general store, laundry facilities. Boat and fishing tackle rentals. Beautiful spot for nature lovers. Indian fishing license required on lake and lower river.

RAYMOND. Maunu's Mountcastle Motel. *Inexpensive–Moderate.* 524 3rd St., Raymond 98577 (942–5571). Medium-size downtown motel with 1- and 2-room units. A few kitchens at extra charge.

RENTON. See "South Seattle."

RICHLAND. See "Tri-Cities."

SEAVIEW. Shelburne Inn. *Deluxe.* Box 250, Seaview 98644 (642–2442). Small charming 1890s Victorian bed-and-breakfast hotel with antique decor. Excellent restaurant.

SEDRO WOOLLEY. Skagit Inn Motel. *Moderate.* 1977 Wash. 20, Sedro Woolley 98284 (856–6001). Medium-size motel with both 1- and 2-room units, some with kitchen facilities at extra charge. Restaurant near.

SEQUIM. Sequim West Motel. *Moderate–Expensive.* 740 W. Washington St., Sequim 98382 (683–4144). 2-story motel, 1- and 2-room units, some suites. Units with kitchenettes at extra charge. Restaurant on premises. Seasonal rates.

SHELTON. Shelton Super 8 Motel. *Moderate.* 6 Northview Circle, Shelton 98584 (426–1654). Medium-size motel with restaurant nearby. Pets accepted.

SILVERDALE. Best Western Silverdale Hotel & Resort. *Deluxe.* 3963 Bucklin Hill Rd., Silverdale 98383 (698–1000). Large resort features rooms with balconies and view of the water. Tennis courts, pool, beach.

SKYKOMISH. Skylark Motel. *Inexpensive.* Box 117, Skykomish 98288 (677–2261). On U.S. 2, south end of Skykomish River Bridge, 17 miles west of Stevens Pass. Small motel on 2 levels. Many units with refrigerators, 4 upstairs units share bath. Some kitchenettes at extra charge.

SPOKANE. Cavanaugh's Inn at the Park. *Deluxe.* W. 303 N. River Dr., Spokane 99201 (326–8000). Waterside inn on Spokane River overlooking Riverfront Park. Heated pools, exercise room, tennis court, putting green. Restaurants, entertainment.

Cavanaugh's River Inn. *Deluxe.* N. 700 Division St., Spokane 99202 (326–5577). Large motor inn with restaurant, bar, live music. Sauna, tennis courts, three swimming pools. Near Riverfront Park.

Holiday Inn Downtown. *Deluxe.* 110 E. 4th Ave., Spokane 99202 (838–6101). Large downtown 5-story motel just off I–90. Heated pool, dining room, bar.

Holiday Inn West. *Moderate–Deluxe.* W. 4212 Sunset Blvd. 99204 (747–2021). On Business 90. Large 2-level motel west of city. Heated pool, airport car, putting green. Dining room, cocktail lounge, entertainment.

Ramada Inn. *Deluxe.* Box 19228, Spokane 99219 (838–5211). Large motel with attractively decorated rooms, some suites. 2 private pools, heated pool, sauna. Dining room, cocktail lounge, entertainment. Near Spokane International Airport.

Red Lion Motor Inn. *Deluxe.* Box 3385, Spokane 99220 (924–9000). I–90 at Sullivan Rd. exit. Large 2-level motor lodge, 8 ½ miles east of city, on spacious grounds. Attractively furnished, many rooms with private balconies. Airport limousine available. Heated pool, coffee shop, bar, gourmet dining.

Ridpath Hotel and Motor Inn. *Deluxe.* 515 W. Sprague Ave., Spokane 99210 (838–2711). One of Spokane's best-known hotels with motor-inn accommodations. Lanais, heated pool, garage, coffee shop, dining rooms, bar. Ankeny's on the top floor is one of city's top dining and dancing spots.

Sheraton-Spokane Hotel. *Deluxe.* N. 322 Spokane Falls Court, Spokane 99220 (455–9600). Large downtown hotel next to Convention Center and Riverfront Park. Close to opera house, downtown shopping. Coffeeshop, restaurant, lounge, entertainment, dancing. Pool, tennis.

Gateway Hotel. *Expensive–Deluxe.* E. 923 3rd Ave., Spokane 98202 (535–9000). Large motor hotel in city center. Indoor pool, restaurants, lounge, entertainment.

Quality Inn Spokane House. *Moderate–Expensive.* Box 91, Spokane 99210 (838–1471). Located at 4301 W. Sunset Hwy. 3-level medium-size motor inn overlooking city west of town. Heated pool, sauna, par-3 golf, airport car. Coffee shop, bar, and fine Spokane House Restaurant.

Lincoln Center Motor Inn. *Moderate.* 827 1st Ave., Spokane 99204 (456–8040). Large downtown motel with pool, restaurant. Pets OK.

Tiki Lodge. *Moderate.* W. 1420 2nd Ave., Spokane 99204 (838–2026). Medium-size 2-story motel. Small heated pool, restaurant.

Shangri-La Motel. *Inexpensive–Moderate.* W. 2922 Government Way, Spokane 99204 (747–2066). Small motel off I–90 with 2- and 3-bedroom units, some with kitchens at extra charge.

West Wynn Motel. *Inexpensive–Moderate.* W. 2701 Sunset Blvd., Spokane 99204 (747–3037). Medium-size 2-level motel, comfortable large units, some kitchens. Heated indoor pool, playground, some covered parking, restaurant.

Motel 6. *Inexpensive.* S. 1508 Rustle St., Spokane 99204 (838–6401). Large no-frills motel typical of this chain. Pool.

STEHEKIN. North Cascades Lodge. *Expensive–Deluxe.* Box W, Chelan 98816 (682–4711). Situated at the head of Lake Chelan, this rustic complex is the food, lodging, and transportation concession for the National Park Service. The lodge consists of sleeping and housekeeping facilities in single units and a 2-story building. Beautiful setting backed by the North Cascade Alps. Accessible only by boat, plane, or hiking. (The boat, *Lady of the Lake,* leaves Chelan every day in summer, every other day in winter.) Dining room, coffee shop, grocery store, photo shop. There is a boat rental concession and Park Service interpretive center. Reservation deposit required. Open all year.

SUNNYSIDE. Best Western King's Way Inn. *Moderate.* 408 U.S. 12, Sunnyside 98944 (837–7878). Medium-size motel with pool.

Town House Motel. *Inexpensive.* 509 U.S. 12, Sunnyside 98944 (837–5500). Small motel with playground. Pets OK. Restaurant nearby.

TACOMA. Holiday Inn by the Dome. *Expensive–Deluxe.* 1425 E. 27th St., Tacoma 98421 (383–5566). Large new motel. Exercise room, pool, whirlpool. Dining room, coffee shop, cocktail lounge with entertainment.

Sheraton Tacoma Hotel. *Deluxe.* 1320 Broadway Plaza, Tacoma 98402 (572–3200). Elegant, large downtown hotel. Many rooms have mountain and water views. Dining rooms (including a rooftop one with views of Mt. Rainier), coffee shop, cocktail lounge, entertainment. Airport transportation. No pets.

Tacoma Dome Hotel. *Deluxe.* 2611 E. "E" St., Tacoma 98421 (572–7272). Large motel adjacent to Tacoma Dome. Sauna, exercise room. Dining room, coffee shop, cocktail lounge, entertainment.

Nendel's Motor Inn. *Expensive.* 8702 S. Hosmer, Tacoma 98444 (535–3100). Off I–5. Very comfortable rooms, singles, suites. Dining room and lounge. Adjacent to golf course. Pool.

Butler's Heritage Inn. *Expensive.* 6802 S. Sprague Ave., Tacoma 98409 (475–5900). South Tacoma off I–5. Large 2-story motel with excellent facilities. Some units with steam baths, some large suites. Pool, dining room, cocktail lounge with entertainment.

Doric Tacoma Motor Hotel. *Expensive.* 242 St. Helens Ave., Tacoma 98402 (572–9572). Large downtown hotel with 2-story annex, some suites. Pool, coffee shop, dining room, lounge. Gift shop, limousine to airport.

Quality Inn. *Expensive.* 9920 S. Tacoma Way, Tacoma 98499 (588–5241). 2-level motel with 1- and 2-room units. Coffee shop, dining room. Some kitchens at extra charge.

Royal Coachman Motor Inn. *Expensive.* 5805 Pacific Hwy. E., Tacoma 98424 (922–2500). Large motel at Fife exit, north of Tacoma. Restaurant adjacent.

Sherwood Inn. *Moderate.* 8402 S. Hosmer, Tacoma 98444 (535–3200). Large 3-story motel, minutes from Tacoma Mall. Pool, wading pool, coffee shop, restaurant, bar, entertainment.

Motel 6. *Inexpensive.* 5201 20th St. E., Fife 98424 (922–6612). North off I–5. Large 2-story motel. Pool. Adjacent cafe.

TRI-CITIES (Kennewick, Richland, and Pasco). **Cavanaugh's Motor Inn.** *Deluxe.* 1101 Columbia Center Blvd., Kennewick 99336 (783–0611). Large, attractive lodging. Some suites. Pool, whirlpool. Dining room, cocktails, entertainment.

Hanford House Thunderbird. *Deluxe.* 802 George Washington Way, Richland 99352 (946–7611). Large 2-story motel on shore of Columbia River. Wide choice of units, suites, poolside units with lanais. Pool, putting green, boat dock, boat rentals available, water skiing. Poolside service, coffee shop, dining room, bar, entertainment. Playground, recreation room, airport limousine.

Holiday Inn. *Deluxe.* 1515 George Washington Way, Richland 99352 (946–4121). Large motel with varied accommodations. Family plan. Pool, playground. Pets OK. Room and poolside service. Coffee shop, dining room, bar, entertainment.

Red Lion Inn. *Deluxe.* 2525 N. 20th Ave., Pasco 99301 (547–0701). Very large property with attractive grounds, two pools, two restaurants, lounge, entertainment."

Clover Island Motor Inn. *Moderate–Expensive.* 435 Clover Island, Kennewick 99336 (586–0541). Large motel with usual accommodations. Pool, restaurant.

Nendel's Motor Inn. *Moderate–Expensive.* 2811 W. 2nd Ave., Kennewick 99336 (735–9511). Large downtown motel. Some kitchenettes at extra charge. Pool. Pets extra. Restaurant nearby.

Bali Hi Motel. *Moderate.* 1201 George Washington Way, Richland 99352 (943–3101). Medium-size 2-level motel with pleasant grounds. Pool. Restaurant nearby.

UNION. Alderbrook Inn. *Deluxe.* Union 98592 (898–2200). Large resort on Hood Canal. Units include nicely furnished family-sized cottages with kitchens. Dock, swimming, boats, sauna, whirlpool, golf, tennis. Dining at the inn. (See "General Information" under "Resorts.") Reservations required. No pets.

VANCOUVER. Red Lion Inn at the Quay. *Deluxe.* 100 Columbia St., Vancouver 98660 (694–8341). Large motel at waterfront. Many units with dramatic view of Interstate Bridge and Columbia River. Pool, 3-level inn with coffee shop, dining room, bar, entertainment. Boat dock. Extra charge for pets.

Residence Inn-Vancouver Mall. *Deluxe.* 8005 N.E. Parkway Dr., Vancouver 98662 (253–4800). Complete living facilities includes bedroom, living room and kitchen, some fireplaces. Pool, sport court.

Shilo Inn–Downtown. *Deluxe.* 401 E. 13th St., Vancouver 98660 (573–0511). Much the same accommodations as below, though larger.

Shilo Inn–Hazel Dell. *Expensive.* 13206 Hwy. 99, Vancouver 98665 (573–0511). Large motel. Some kitchenettes and suites. Coin laundry, pool, whirlpool, sauna, steamroom. Pets extra. Restaurant nearby.

Salmon Creek Motel. *Moderate.* 11901 N.E. Hwy. 99, Vancouver 98686 (573–0751). Small motel off I–5 with some 2-bedroom units and kitchens.

Aloha Motel. *Inexpensive.* 708 N.E. 78th St., Vancouver 98665 (574–2345). Large 2-story motel, 3 miles north of town. Pool, playground, restaurant nearby. Pets OK.

WALLA WALLA. Best Western Pony Soldier Motor Inn. *Expensive.* 325 E. Main, Walla Walla 99362 (529–4360). Large downtown inn near Whitman College. Complimentary breakfast, pool.

Walla Walla TraveLodge. *Moderate–Expensive.* 421 E. Main, Walla Walls 99362 (529–4940). Medium-size lodge. Pool. No pets.

Imperial Inn. *Inexpensive–Moderate.* 305 N. 2nd Ave., Walla Walla 99362 (529–4410). Medium-size motel with some kitchens. Pool. Restaurant nearby.

WASHOUGAL. Brass Lamp Motor Inn. *Moderate.* 544 6th St., Washougal 98671 (835–8591). Smaller motel, many conveniences. Several units with kitchen facilities at extra charge. Pool, saunas, health spa. Restaurant nearby.

WENATCHEE. Thunderbird Motor Inn. *Deluxe.* 1225 N. Wenatchee Ave., Wenatchee 98801 (663–0711). Large, attractive units with balconies. Some suites. Heated pool, coffee shop, restaurant, bar, entertainment.

Chieftain Motel. *Expensive.* 1005 N. Wenatchee Ave., Wenatchee 98801 (663–8141). Larger 2-level motor inn. 1- and 2-room units, executive suite. Salesman display room, hospitality room. Pool, Chieftain Restaurant, cocktail lounge, entertainment.

Holiday Lodge. *Moderate–Expensive.* 610 N. Wenatchee Ave., Wenatchee 98801 (663–8167). 2-story motel with 60 soundproofed units. Pool.

Avenue Motel. *Moderate.* 720 N. Wenatchee Ave., Wenatchee 98801 (663–7161). Medium-size motel, 1- and 2-room units, some kitchen facilities at extra charge. Pool, restaurant nearby.

Uptowner Motel. *Moderate.* 101 N. Mission, Wenatchee 98801 (663–8516). Some suites available. Saunas, pool, whirlpool. Despite its name, motel is downtown.

Imperial Inn. *Inexpensive.* 700 N. Wenatchee Ave., Wenatchee 98801 (663–8133). 41 comfortable units with pool. No pets. Restaurant nearby.

Scotty's Motel. *Inexpensive.* 1004 N. Wenatchee Ave., Wenatchee 98801 (662–8165). Medium-size 2-level motel, 1- and 2-room units. Pool, saunas, restaurant nearby.

WESTPORT. Chateau Westport. *Deluxe.* Box 349, Westport 98595 (268–9101). Wash. 205, 3 blks. S. of Coast Guard Lighthouse. Large 4-story motel, small units, suites, some units with kitchen facilities, some with balconies and fireplaces. Heated indoor pool, charter boats.

Islander Motel. *Deluxe.* Box 488, Westport 98595 (268–9166). Medium-size motel. Pool, wading pool, charter boats. Coffee shop, dining room, cocktail lounge, entertainment. Seasonal rates.

Coho Motel. *Moderate.* 2501 Nyhus St., Westport 98595 (268–0111). Medium-size motel. Runs a large fleet of charter boats. Units include 1- and 2-bedroom suites. Restaurants near. Ask manager about best beachcombing spots. Seasonal rates.

Windjammer Motel. *Moderate.* Box 1315, Wesport 98595 (268–9351). Small, quiet motel on E. Pacific Ave., with some refrigerators, 2-bedroom units, kitchens. No pets.

WHITE PASS. Village Inn. *Deluxe.* Star Route, White Pass 98937. Medium-size lodging at summit near skiing area. Some fireplaces, suites, kitchens.

WINTHROP. Sun Mountain Lodge. *Deluxe.* Box 1000, Winthrop 98862 (996–2211). 9 mi. W. off Wash. 20. 2-story resort complex atop Sun Mountain with magnificent view of Methow Valley and Cascades. Smaller units and suites. Pool, therapeutic pool, tennis, putting green, boat dock with boats available.

Fishing, hunting, trap-shooting, pack trips. Cross-country ski trails. Dining room, bar, entertainment. Seasonal rates.

Holiday Inn. *Deluxe.* 9th St. and Yakima Ave., Yakima 98901 (452–6511). Large pleasant 3-level motor inn. Pool, restaurant, cocktail lounge, entertainment. Wheelchair units. Room service.

Thunderbird Motor Inn. *Deluxe.* 1507 N. 1st, Yakima 98901 (248–7850). Large motor inn with many services. Pool, sauna. Some 2-room units and suites. Coffee shop, restaurant, bar, entertainment.

Towne Plaza. *Deluxe.* N. 7th St. and E. Yakima Ave., Yakima 98901 (248–5900). Large 2-story motor inn. 1- and 2-room units, many with balconies or lanais. Coffee shop, dining room, lounge, entertainment. Poolside service. Recreation room. No pets.

Yakima TraveLodge. *Expensive.* 110 S. Naches, Yakima 98901 (453–7151). Some 2-room units. Pool. Seasonal rates.

YAKIMA. Best Western Tapadera Motor Inn. *Moderate.* 12 Valley Mall Blvd., Yakima 98903 (248–6924). Large motel at Union Gap. Pool, restaurant. Pets allowed. Seasonal rates.

Colonial Motor Inn. *Moderate.* 1405 N. 1st, Yakima 98901 (453–8981). Medium-size motel off I–82. Water beds, indoor pool, hot tubs. Restaurant nearby.

Cabana Motel. *Inexpensive–Moderate.* 1900 N. 1st Ave., Yakima 98901 (452–7111). Medium-sized motel, king-size and water beds. Pool. Mini golf course.

Motel 6. *Inexpensive.* 1104 N. 1st St., Yakima 98901 (452–0407). Large 2-story motel with the usual "6" decor and facilities. Pool.

HOSTELS. The establishment of youth hostels is a comparatively recent event in Washington State. American Youth Hostels can be found at Fort Columbia Hostel at Chinook, Birch Bay Hostel at Blaine, Fort Flagler Hostel at Nordland, The Lodge Youth Hostel at Ashford, Carnation Home Hostel at Carnation, Elite Hotel at Friday Harbor on San Juan Island, Doe Bay Village at Olga on Orcas Island, Vashon Home Hostel on Vashon Island and the Seattle/YMCA in Seattle. For information on the above listed hostels and others now being developed, write or call Washington State Council, American Youth Hostels, 419 Queen Anne Ave. N., #108, Seattle, WA 98109 (206–281–7306).

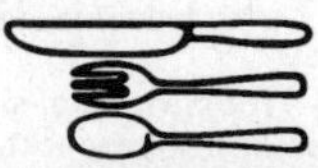

RESTAURANTS. As is true everywhere, the best hotels have one or more restaurants and so do the expensive motor inns. Quality is expected and prices are commensurate. Since restaurants of this type are run in connection with lodging, no attempt to list them has been made here or in the Seattle section. Those suggested below are only a few whose main business is food, and that have kept customers pleased for a number of years. Price ranges for dinner are *Expensive,* $15 up; *Moderate,* $9–$15; and *Inexpensive,* under $9. However, in all categories dessert usually is extra, and often coffee or tea. Also add sales tax and the usual tip.

ABERDEEN. Bridges Restaurant. *Moderate–Expensive.* 112 N. G St. (532–6563). A very nice downtown restaurant with children's menu. Prime rib and seafood specialties. Lounge.

Nordic Inn Restaurant. *Moderate–Expensive.* 1700 S. Boone (533–0100). Wide variety, with commensurate range in prices. Pleasant decor with Viking theme. Children's menu. Entertainment in lounge.

BELLEVUE. See "Seattle-East."

BELLINGHAM. Chuckanut Manor. *Moderate–Expensive.* 302 Chuckanut Drive in Bow (766–6191). 15 miles south of Bellingham. Specializing in prime ribs, steaks, seafood, home baking. Sit at windows overlooking bay. Bar, entertainment, dancing some evenings.

Dirty Dan Harris'. *Moderate–Expensive.* 1211 11th (676–1011). Specializing in prime rib and local seafood. 1880s decor. Cocktails.

High Country. *Moderate–Expensive.* Top of Bellingham Tower. 119 N. Commercial (733–3443). Fine dining with views of city, Mt. Baker, the San Juans. Steaks, chicken, seafood.

M'sieurs. *Moderate–Expensive.* 130 E. Champion (671–7955). Intimate, classic dining. Menu features fresh local products, especially seafood and vegetables. Great variety of pasta.

King's Table Buffet. *Inexpensive.* 1530 Ellis (676–8288). Buffet with special prices for children and seniors. Large selection of salads, entrees, desserts.

BREMERTON. Hearthstone. *Moderate–Expensive.* 4312 Kitsap Way (377–5531). Excellent view of the waterfront from paneled dining room. Specialties include fresh salmon in season, other seafood, and steaks. Cocktail lounge with entertainment and dancing.

CAMAS–WASHOUGAL. Parker House. *Moderate.* 56 1st St. (835–2167). Beautiful view of Columbia River from your table. Favorite dining spot of Vancouverites for delicious seafood and steaks. Children's menu. Lounge and entertainment.

CHEHALIS. Mary McCrank's Dinner House. *Moderate–Expensive.* 2923 Jackson Hwy. (748–3662). A tradition in dining. Home-style cooking, delightful surroundings, interesting display of antique dishes. Popular restaurant with farmhouse atmosphere.

CHELAN. Campbell House Restaurant. *Moderate–Expensive.* 104 W. Woodin (682–2561). Fine restaurant housed in a Historical Landmark building furnished with beautiful antiques. On Lake Chelan at Campbell's Lodge. Lounge, children's menu.

COUPEVILLE. The Captain Whidbey. *Moderate–Expensive.* 2072 W. Capt. Whidbey Island Road (678–4097). 3 miles north of town on Penn Cove overlooking the water and docks. Unique turn-of-the-century madrona log, building decorated with antiques. Crabs, oysters, clams are specialties, also prime ribs.

ELLENSBURG. Casa de Blanca. *Inexpensive–Moderate.* 1318 S. Canyon Rd. (925–1693). Mexican food plus American specialties, prime rib, steak.

McCullough's. *Inexpensive–Moderate.* 402 N. Pearl (925–6545). Located in historic building. International cuisine.

EVERETT. Pelican Pete's. *Moderate.* 1722 W. Marine View Drive (252–3155). Waterfront restaurant in Everett Marina Village. Fresh seafood, locker-aged beef, pasta, gourmet burgers.

LEAVENWORTH. Edelweiss Bavarian Restaurant. *Moderate.* 843 Front St. (548–7015). As attractive as its name. Serving authentic Bavarian dishes, apple strudel for dessert. Lounge and usually old-country entertainment.

LONGVIEW. Henri's. *Moderate–Expensive.* 4545 Ocean Beach Hwy. (425–7970). Well-prepared continental cuisine served in French atmosphere. Good wine selection. Bar.

King's Table Buffet. *Inexpensive.* 970 14th. (425–4070). Serving one-price buffet with special prices for children and seniors. Large selection of salads, entrees, desserts.

OCEAN SHORES. Home Port. *Inexpensive–Moderate.* Point Brown Avenue (289–2600). Pleasant restaurant open for breakfast, lunch, and dinner. Seafood and steaks. Large salad bar.

OLYMPIA. Carnegie's. *Moderate–Expensive.* 7th and Franklin (357–5550). Seafood, prime rib, poultry, veal served in the former Carnegie Public Library. Original bookshelves in dining room and bar. Two fireplaces. Open for lunch and dinner.

Olympia Oyster House. *Inexpensive–Expensive.* 320 W. 4th (943–8020). Waterfront restaurant noted for seafood, particularly the famous tiny Olympia oyster. Also tender steaks and prime rib. Bar.

Falls Terrace. *Inexpensive–Moderate.* 106 Deschutes Way in Tumwater (943–7830). Overlooking Tumwater Falls near Olympia Brewery. Continental and American cuisine. Children's menu.

Migel's. *Inexpensive–Moderate.* 4611 Tumwater Valley Dr. (352–1575). South of Olympia in Tumwater. Restaurant adjoins the Tumwater Valley Golf Club. Mexican and American cuisine served in pleasant surroundings. Children's menu.

The Trails. *Inexpensive–Moderate.* 7842 Trails End Dr. S.E. (753–8720). Across from airport. 27-acre equestrian restaurant and entertainment complex. Western-style steaks, seafood.

PORT ANGELES. Haguewood's Restaurant. *Moderate–Expensive.* In the Red Lion Bayshore Inn at 221 N. Lincoln St. (457–0424). Dungeness cracked crab is a specialty at this waterfront restaurant overlooking Strait of Juan de Fuca. Wide selection of other menu items and own baked goods. Bar.

C'est Si Bon. *Moderate–Expensive.* 2300 Hwy. 101 E. (452–8888). Elegant French restaurant with a view. Cocktails, lounge. Open for dinner only. Reservations advised.

The Greenery. *Inexpensive–Moderate.* 117B E. First (457–4112). Wide selection of menu items for breakfast, lunch and dinner. Specialties include pasta, chicken and seafood sautees, and salads. Locally popular. Reservations advised.

Traylor's Restaurant. *Inexpensive–Moderate.* 3320 U.S. 101 E. (452–3833). Family restaurant for over a quarter of a century. Known for fish and chips. Also seafood and aged beef. Open for breakfast, lunch, dinner.

PORT LUDLOW. The Harbormaster. *Moderate–Expensive.* In the Resort at Port Ludlow, 781 Walker Way (437–2222). Wonderful water view from this fine restaurant. Well-prepared food from varied menu. Children's menu. Lounge, entertainment, boat moorage. Reservations required.

PULLMAN. Hilltop Restaurant. *Moderate.* In Hilltop Motor Inn on the Colfax Hwy. (334–2555). Situated on hilltop overlooking town and W.S.U. campus. Beef and seafood specialties. Bar.

The Seasons. *Inexpensive–Moderate.* 215 Paradise S.E. (334–1410). One of city's older homes is site of this restaurant. International cuisine prepared to order. No bar, but wine and Washington beers available.

PUYALLUP. Anton's. *Moderate–Expensive.* 3207 E. Main (845–7569). Near Puyallup River bridge. Varied choice of entrees, well served. Children's menu. Lounge and entertainment. Reservations advised.

SEQUIM. Casoni's. *Moderate.* U.S. 101 at Carlsborg Rd. (683–4144). Small restaurant serving innovative Italian cuisine using homemade pasta.

3 Crabs. *Inexpensive–Moderate.* 101 Three Crabs Rd. in Dungeness (683–4264). Famous for seafood dishes—crab, clams, geoduck, oysters. Modest little restaurant but well worth the seven-mile drive north from center of town. On water's edge with view of Dungeness Spit.

SPOKANE. Ankeny's. *Moderate–Expensive.* Atop the Ridpath Hotel at 515 W. Sprague Ave. (838–2711). View dining at one of the city's finest restaurants. Cocktails, lounge, entertainment, dancing. Reservations advised.

Patsy Clark's. *Moderate–Expensive.* W. 2208 2nd Ave. (838–8300). Dinner and Sunday brunch in historic turn-of-the-century Spokane mansion built for well-known mining tycoon. Continental menu features rack of lamb, roast duck Amaretto, seafood. Valet parking.

Spokane House. *Moderate–Expensive.* In Quality Inn Spokane House, 4301 W. Sunset Hwy. (838–1475). Long-time Spokane favorite known for fine steak, prime rib, seafood dinners. Sunday brunch. Perched on hill overlooking the city, it also offers outdoor dining.

Chapter XI. *Inexpensive–Expensive.* 105 E. Mission Ave. (326–0466); Also 9304 N. Division (467–7011). Known for well-prepared prime rib, steaks, tiger shrimp, served in a rustic setting. Huge salad bar. Cocktails, lounge.

C. I. Shenanigan's. *Inexpensive–Moderate.* N. 332 Spokane Falls Court (455–5072). On banks of Spokane River. Varied menu featuring fresh seafood, oyster bar, dry-aged beef, pasta. Outdoor deck service. Lounge serves Northwest wine and beer.

Clinkerdagger, Bickerstaff & Pett's. *Inexpensive–Moderate.* 621 W. Mallon St., in the Old Flour Mill overlooking the Spokane River and Riverfront Park (328–5965). Prime rib, seafood served in a setting resembling an old English inn. Open for lunch and dinner.

Culpepper Cattle Co. *Inexpensive–Moderate.* E. 511 3rd (624–2203). Steaks and barbecue are featured in this Western-style restaurant.

Sea Galley. *Inexpensive–Moderate.* N. 1221 Howard (327–3361). Featuring a wide variety of seafood, also steaks and prime rib. Open for lunch and dinner. Children's menu. Cocktails, lounge.

Old Spaghetti Factory. *Inexpensive.* S. 152 Monroe (624–8916). Family dining at reasonable prices. Specialty is pasta served with a variety of sauces. Turn-of-the-century decor.

Stuart Anderson's Black Angus. *Inexpensive.* 510 N. Lincoln (328–8120). One of a chain of restaurants with reputation for well-prepared beef, including steaks and prime rib. Also seafood and chicken. Cocktails, lounge. Open for lunch and dinner.

TACOMA. Cliff House. *Expensive.* 6300 Marine View Dr. (927–0400). Dine with beautiful view of Commencement Bay and Mt. Rainier at this long-time Tacoma favorite. Known for its Fish Kettle and other seafood. Open for lunch, dinner, Sunday brunch.

Rose Room. *Expensive.* On the 26th floor of the Sheraton Tacoma Hotel at 1320 Broadway Plaza (572–3200). Elegant dining for special occasions. Watch the sun set on Mt. Rainier. Classic continental cuisine.

E. R. Rogers. *Moderate–Expensive.* 1702 Commercial in neighboring Steilacoom (383–8600). Restored 1894 Victorian mansion is setting for relaxing dining. Seafood, poultry dishes, along with prime rib. Drive out for dinner or Sunday brunch.

Johnny's Dock. *Moderate–Expensive.* 1900 East D, six blocks north of the Tacoma Dome (627–3186). Famous restaurant known for fine steaks and fresh seafood. View of waterway and Union Station. Extensive wine list. Also sells its own seasonings all over the country.

Lakewood Terrace. *Moderate–Expensive.* In the Best Western Lakewood Motor Inn at 6125 Motor Ave. S.W. (588–5215). Popular with locals. Serves steak and seafood specialties. Children's menu. Sunday brunch. Lounge and entertainment. Reservations advised.

Bavarian. *Inexpensive–Expensive.* 294 N. K St. (627–5010). German food served in rustic Bavarian inn setting. Combination plate includes rouladen and sauerbraten. Extensive list of German wines. Weekend entertainment.

Barbecue Pete's. *Inexpensive–Moderate.* 1314 E. 72nd. (535–1000). Great barbecued ribs a specialty here. Lunch and dinner. Lounge.

Fujiya. *Inexpensive–Moderate.* 1125 Court "C" (627–5319). Outstanding Japanese sushi bar/restaurant tucked away in Tacoma Center, near Sheraton

Tacoma. Japanese owner/chef prepares authentic teriyaki, tempura, other traditional dishes. Saki and imported beers.

Bloch's. *Inexpensive.* 1128 Broadway (627–3400). Also in Tacoma Center in downtown area. Known for outstanding prime rib, hickory-smoked ham, breast of turkey sandwiches. Cocktails and beer.

Old Spaghetti Factory. *Inexpensive.* 1735 Jefferson St. (383–2214). Interesting antique decor. Large choice of spaghetti sauces. Children's menu. Lounge, cocktails, variety of wines.

Stuart Anderson's Black Angus. *Inexpensive.* 9905 Bridgeport Way S.W. in Lakewood (582–6900). Choice beef served "as you like it." Also seafood and chicken. Lunch and dinner. Full bar, entertainment, dancing.

VANCOUVER. Eaton's Hilltop Restaurant. *Inexpensive–Moderate.* 10808 N.E. 18th St., at Mill Plain Exit off I–205 (256–5472). View of Mt. St. Helens and the Cascades. Specializes in steaks, chicken, seafood in garden setting. Lounge. Reservations advised.

The Holland. *Inexpensive–Moderate.* 109 W. 17th St. (694–1521). A Vancouver institution for over 50 years. Family dining for breakfast, lunch, dinner. Homemade bread and desserts.

The Crossing. *Inexpensive–Moderate.* 900 W. 7th St. (695–3374). Steaks, prime rib, seafood served in classic railway cars. Sunday brunch.

King's Table Buffet. *Inexpensive.* 616 N.E. 81st Ave. (574–3455). One-price buffet for lunch and dinner. Large assortment of salads, entrees, desserts. Special prices for children and seniors.

HOW TO GET AROUND. By Plane. *Horizon* flies from Seattle-Tacoma International Airport to Wenatchee, Yakima, Pasco, Walla Walla, Pullman, Moses Lake, and Spokane. *San Juan* serves Port Angeles, Bellingham, and the San Juan Islands. *Harbor Airlines* flies to Whidbey Island. Numerous charter planes for business trips, fishing, or sightseeing fly from Boeing Field (between Sea-Tac and downtown Seattle), from Renton Aviation, Lake Union, and Kenmore Air Harbor, the latter a major seaplane base.

TOURIST INFORMATION. A visitor information center is open all year on I–5 near the interstate bridge in Vancouver. Centers are open in summer on I–5 at Blaine, just south of the customs station on the Canadian boder; at Oroville on US 97, also near the Canadian border: at Megler, on US 101, at the north end of the Asotia bridge, near Ridgefield 14 miles north of Vancouver, and near Maryhill State Park and the Sam Hill Bridge on US 97.

Questions about tourist attractions and facilities are handled quickly by the Tourism Development Division, General Administration Building, Olympia, WA 98504 (586–2088; 800–544–1800 for the travel book "Destination Washington"). Local maps, guides, information on resorts, etc., can be obtained from the chamber of commerce in the area you plan to visit. The U.S. Forest Service, Regional Office, Box 3623, Portland, OR 97208, supplies a directory of campgrounds, trails, etc. in National Forests. For camping on state lands with limited facilities write Washington State Dept. of Natural Resources, Public Lands Building, Olympia, WA 98501. For information on Mt. Rainier National Park write the Superintendent, Mt. Rainier National Park, Longmire, WA 98397; on Olympic National Park, Superintendent, Olympic National Park, Port Angeles, WA 98362; on North Cascades National Park, Superintendent, North Cascades National Park, Sedro Woolley, WA 98284; Washington State Parks, State Parks and Recreation Commission, P.O. Box 1128, Olympia, WA 98504. Hunting and fishing regulations are supplied by the Washington State Game Dept., 600 N. Capitol Way, Olympia, WA 98504.

SEASONAL EVENTS. Because of the mild weather, the festival season starts early in Washington as the state's many flowers break into full bloom. Most of the best-known festivals are built around the blossoms—daffodils in early April, apple blossoms in late April, rhododendrons and lilacs in May. The most popular parades are flecked with flowers—daffodils at Tacoma, Puyallup, and Sumner, apple blossoms at Wenatchee, and lilacs at Spokane. The late summer and early fall are filled with fairs and rodeos—the most famous being the Ellensburg Rodeo.

Here are samples of these and numerous other excuses for holding a festival:

March: Driftwood Show, Grayland; Columbia Center Art Show, Kennewick.

April: Puyallup Valley Daffodil Festival, at Puyallup, Tacoma, Sumner, and Orting; Apple Blossom Festival, Wenatchee; Holland Happening (flower celebration), Oak Harbor; International Plowing Match, Lynden.

May: (First Saturday) opening day of yachting season, parade of boats, Seattle; Granger Cherry Festival, Granger; Lilac Festival, Spokane; Blossomtime Festival, Bellingham; Rhododendron Festival, Port Townsend; Mason County Forest Festival, Shelton; Colorama Rodeo, Grand Coulee; Norwegian festivals in Ballard, Poulsbo and other towns; Ski to Sea Festival in Bellingham.

June: Salty Sea Days, Everett; Logging Show, Deming; Lummi Stommish Water Festival, Lummi reservations;

July: Pow Wow and Rodeo, Toppenish; Loggerodeo, Sedro Woolley; Swinomish Tribal Celebration, La Conner; 4th of July celebrations in most cities, big or little, throughout the state. Tri-City Water Follies, Pasco, Kennewick, and Richland; Seafair and Seafair Grand Parade, Seattle; Pacific Northwest Arts and Crafts Fair, Bellevue; Bear Festival, McCleary; Hydroplane races, Kennewick.

August: Seafair continues into August, ending with hydroplane races on Lake Washington, Seattle; Omak Stampede and Suicide Race, Omak; Logger's Jubilee, Morton; Salmon Derby Days, Port Angeles; Festival of Bon Odori in the International Settlement, Seattle; Makah Days (Indian), Neah Bay.

September: Ellensburg Rodeo, Ellensburg; Bumbershoot Festival, Seattle Center; Milk Fund Salmon Derby, Seattle; Odessa Deutches Fest, Odessa; Autumn Leaf Festival, Leavenworth; Western Washington Fair, Puyallup.

October: Scandinavian Festival, Tacoma; Oktoberfest, Pasco.

December: Christmas Lighting Ceremony, Leavenworth; Christmas Around the World, Seattle.

County and regional fairs are held from late July through September. Rodeos are held in conjunction with most east-side county fairs and some western Washington fairs.

Arts and crafts shows are held from late March into early September.

GARDENS. Bellingham: *Fairhaven Park,* on Chuckanut Dr. at southern entrance to town, has lovely rose gardens. Blaine: *Peace Arch State Park,* at Canadian border, highlighted by rare flowers and shrubs. Olympia: *State Capitol* grounds and conservatory. Spokane: *Manito Park* has formal Duncan Gardens, city park nursery, Rose Hill, and Japanese Tea House. Tacoma: *Wright Park* has botanical conservatory; *Point Defiance Park* has rose gardens. Wenatchee: *Ohme Gardens* has large collection of northwest shrubs, plants, and flowers. From the lookout tower there are panoramic views of the area. Open Apr. 15–Oct. 15. Fee.

NATIONAL PARKS. Washington has three, including the fourth oldest one to be set aside (1899), Mount Rainier National Park. Rising to 14,410 feet, most of it from sea level, Rainier keeps everyone reminded of its presence for 100 miles around it. Residents speak reverently of it as "The Mountain." In sheer aloof majesty, The Mountain chooses when to show itself, remaining invisible while sunshine falls on lesser areas, and looming awesomely in the sky on otherwise cloudy days. If, as a visitor, The Mountain benignly reveals itself to you, you have been favored.

Mt. Rainier National Park: Mt. Rainier, an ice-clad, dormant volcano, stands on the western edge of the Cascade Range. Its gleaming mantle of ice is composed of more glaciers than there are on any other single mountain in the United States south of Alaska. The national park is the best-known tourist attraction in Washington (though not the most visited). More than 300 miles of hiking trails encircle the mountain.

During the summer, the wildflower fields provide a striking contrast to the mountain's glaciers. Wildlife includes mountain goats, bear, deer, and elk. Many of them are seen in the flower belt, which is above the 5,000-foot forest elevation. (Don't regard any of these animals as harmless.) Visitor centers are located at Longmire Park Headquarters, in the southwest corner; at Ohanapecosh, at the southeast entrance; at Sunrise, on the northeast side of the mountain; and at Paradise, due south of the mountain. The National Park Inn, at Longmire, is open from early May to mid-October; Paradise Inn, mid-June until Labor Day. For rates and reservations, write: Mt. Rainier Guest Services, Star Route, Ashford, WA 98304. There are no overnight accommodations at Sunrise or Ohanapecosh, but they are available near the park at Ashford, Packwood, White Pass, Crystal Mountain, and Enumclaw. Park activity includes mountain climbing with guide service, riding, hiking, fishing, and guided nature tours. Camping, tenting, and trailering allowed in designated sites. Cats and dogs on leash only. Campgrounds are open throughout the park in summer on a first come, first served basis. Stays are limited to 14 days a season. Sunshine Point Campground at the Nisqually Entrance is the only one open all year. There are no trailer utility hookups in the park, but there is a trailer dumping station at Cougar Rock Campground. All camping areas have water and toilet facilities. For park information, write Superintendent, Mount Rainier National Park, Ashford, WA 98304 (206–569–2211).

Olympic National Park, is a 1,400-square-mile jumble of glacier-studded mountains, coniferous rain forests, lakes and streams. Roosevelt elk, black-tailed deer, bear, raccoon, and skunk roam their feeding grounds, and about 140 species of birds have been identified in a variety of habitats. There are only a few peaks above 7,000 feet, with Mt. Olympus the highest at 7,965 feet. These figures, though, are deceiving—the mountains rise from near sea level. The park, pristine and rugged, has about 60 glaciers. Most of the lakes, however charming, are small, the largest (Crescent), being only 10 miles long and 1½ miles wide.

The park also includes a 60-mile-long, primitive strip of Pacific Ocean coastline, with rocky headlands and beaches. Seals are frequently seen in the water or on the offshore rocks. (Between the main part of the park and the coastal strip is the *Olympic National Forest* and a rich agricultural valley.) The Quinault Indian Reservation is to the south of the coastal strip. The rain forests are on the west side of the Olympic Peninsula and chiefly along the Hoh, Queets, and Quinault rivers. A yearly rainfall of 140 inches is not uncommon here. (In contrast, the northeast side of the Olympic Peninsula is one of the driest on the Pacific Coast outside of southern California.) Within the rain forests, some Douglas fir and Sitka spruce attain a height of nearly 300 feet and a diameter of 8 feet or more. Western hemlocks also attain heights and diameters greater than in areas of less precipitation.

More than 600 miles of trails lead through the park and provide hikes of from a few minutes to several weeks. Probably no other national park offers such contrasts in hiking—from glaciers and blizzard-ridden mountain peaks to dense, perpetually shaded jungles. Mountain climbers must check in with the rangers; only the experienced should attempt the peaks. Points of special interest include trails leading to beach adventure along the Ocean Strip and the spectacular view from Hurricane Ridge, reached by a fine highway off US 101, near Port Angeles. There are concession-operated cabins, lodges, and trailer parks at Sol Duc Hot Springs, Lake Crescent, La Push, and Kalaloch. For information, write: Superintendent, Olympic National Park, 600 E. Park Ave., Port Angeles, WA 98362 (206–452–4501).

All campsites are on a first come, first served basis. Some campgrounds at lower elevations are open all year, but high-elevation areas are covered by snow from early November to early July. The park has 3 visitor centers—Pioneer Memorial Museum, near Port Angeles (open all year); Storm King Visitor Center, at Lake Crescent; and Hoh Rain Forest Visitor Center, southeast of

Forks. Lectures, campfire talks, exhibits, and tours are provided by the National Park Service. Check visitor centers for details, interpretive publications, and maps. There is a charge of $3 per vehicle for access to the Hoh River Road and Hurricane Ridge.

North Cascades National Park, established by Congress in 1968, has four distinct units—North and South Units of the Park, and Ross Lake and Lake Chelan National Recreation Areas. The 1,053-square mile area, designed to conserve an exceptionally wild and beautiful part of the extensive North Cascades mountain range near the Canadian border, has alpine scenery unmatched in the coterminous 48 states; deep-glaciated canyons, more than 300 glaciers, hundreds of jagged peaks, hanging valleys, waterfalls and icefalls, skyblue lakes nestled in glacial cirques, frigid streams that vein the wilderness, and vegetation regions that range from rain forest to dry shrubland. Ross Lake NRA also contains three dams—Ross, Diablo, and Gorge Lakes—which provide electrical power for Seattle. Ross Lake is 24 miles long and 2 miles across at its greatest width. Diablo Lake and Gorge Lake are much smaller.

Camping is not of the luxury type. Colonial Grounds and Goodell are developed, drive-in campgrounds off Wash. 20 in Ross Lake NRA, but a number of small ones are reached only by boat. There are no campgrounds in the North Unit of the national park, and only 2 in the South Unit. Lake Chelan NRA has about 5 campgrounds. In addition to the named lakes, there are many small mountain and valley lakes, and so many streams that no count has been made of them. The principal game fish are rainbow, Eastern brook, Dolly Varden, and cutthroat trout. Swimming is not suggested—the waters of the lakes and rivers are quite chilly. Even in August, water activities are mainly confined to boating and fishing.

This park is described in the North Cascades Highway Section and also in connection with Lake Chelan. For further information, write: Superintendent, North Cascades National Park, Sedro Woolley, WA 98284 (206–855–1331).

National Recreation Areas (in addition to Ross Lake and Lake Chelan): *Coulee Dam National Recreation Area.* This area stretches from the Canadian border to the Grand Coulee Dam on the Columbia River. Recreation is basically wateroriented: swimming, water skiing, sailing, fishing, motorboating, but it is not greatly developed commercially. The camping is good. At the dam there is a Visitor Center, museum, and campgrounds. The nearest town is Grand Coulee, a mile from the great dam. The area is open all year but is too cold for water recreation from late fall to spring.

National Heritage Parks: San Juan Island National Historic Park. Site of the comic-opera "Pig War" between the U.S. and the British. Both countries claimed possession of the island following the Treaty of 1846. The British set up camp on the north end of the island, and the Americans established a base at the south end. The dispute, which was more serious in Washington and London than on the island, where the officers invited each other to dinner, was finally resolved by Kaiser Wilhelm I of Germany in 1872. Mementos of the almost-war everyone avoided form the basis of this national historic park. The island is reached by auto-ferry from Anacortes, about 75 miles north of Seattle.

National Historic Sites: Whitman Mission National Historic Site, 7 miles from Walla Walla (US 12). The 98-acre area, which has a Visitor Center, museum, and picnic area, is described under Walla Walla in "Exploring Washington." The same is true of Fort Vancouver National Historic Site at Vancouver, Wash.

National Forests: Washington had completely within its boundaries seven national forests—until Mt. Baker and Snoqualmie were combined—and parts of two other national forests, comprising more than 9 million acres. They hold more than a million acres of land designated as National Forest Wilderness. There are five such Wilderness Areas. *Glacier Park,* in Mt. Baker and Wenatchee National Forests, *Goat Rocks,* in Gifford Pinchot and Snoqualmie; *Mount Adams,* in Gifford Pinchot; *Pasayten,* in Mt. Baker and Okanogan. Added in 1976 was Alpine Lakes Wilderness, some 392,000 acres mostly in the Wenatchee National Forest. All national forests have campgrounds, hundreds of miles of trails and a great variety of lakes, streams and wildlife.

Colville National Forest, is in northeastern Washington. Roads leading to it are US 395 and Wash. 20, 25, 31, and 251. Nearby towns are Colville, Kettle Falls, and Republic, Wash., and Grand Forks, British Columbia, Canada. Attractions include 151-mile-long, 82,000-acre Roosevelt Lake; an old mission near Kettle Falls; huckleberries and mushrooms; large mule deer; lake and stream fishing and the Chewalah Peak Winter Sports Area (renamed 49 Degrees North).

Gifford Pinchot National Forest stretches from the Columbia River on the south, along the Cascade Range, to the edge of Mount Rainier National Park on the north. Near the western edge of the forest is 8,400 foot Mt. St. Helens and near the eastern border is 12,307-foot Mt. Adams. Roads leading to the forest region are US 12 and Wash. 504, branching off I–5, and Wash. 141 up from White Salmon on the Columbia. The Cascade Crest Trail extends through this national forest. Attractions are many lakes; the remains of Mt. St. Helens; Wind River Nursery; lake and stream trout fishing; huckleberry fields (stay out of Yakima Indian Reservation); saddle and pack trips; and mountain climbing.

Mt. Baker-Snoqualmie National Forest borders on British Columbia, includes Mt. Baker, Mt. Shuksan and Glacier Peak, and extends south to Mt. Rainier. A big chunk of land was taken from the Baker region to create North Cascades National Park. Roads approaching the northern part from I–5 are Wash. 542, 20, 530 and 92. Wash. 542 goes from Bellingham to Mt. Baker and 9,127-foot Mt. Shuksan. The Cascade Crest Trail passes through the length of this forest (and on through Gifford Pinchot into Oregon). The Snoqualmie section is the national forest closest to Seattle and Tacoma. From I–5 it is reached by US 2, US 12, I–90 and Wash. 410. Attractions include the scenic Chinook and White Pass highways, and views of Mt. Rainier from various angles. The summit of the Cascades is the general eastern boundary of this forest, and there are winter sports areas at three of the passes.

Okanogan National Forest, in north-central Washington, is a multiple-use forest, with thousands of cattle and sheep grazing in its meadows. The forest is reached by US 97, Wash. 153, and Wash. 20. Nearby towns are Brewster, Okanogan, Omak, Twisp, and Winthrop. The forest is bounded on the west by North Cascades National Park and linked to it by Wash. 20. Part of Pasayten Wilderness Area is in the forest. Attractions include snow peaks, alpine meadows, lake and stream fishing, boating, saddle and pack trips, mountain climbing, and winter sports.

Olympic National Forest, borders Olympic National Park on the east, south, and northwest. Only one main highway approaches either the forest or the park: US 101. Nearby towns are Aberdeen, Forks, Olympia, Port Angeles, and Shelton. Attractions include dense rain forests, giant trees, snow peaks, a myriad of lakes and streams, salmon and steelhead fishing, scenic drives, and deer, bear, cougar, and elk.

Wenatchee National Forest stretches along the eastern slope of the Cascades. A portion of Glacier Peak Wilderness Area is included. US 2 and 97 lead to the forest and both enter it, with US 2 crossing it east to west. Attractions include elongated Lake Chelan, snow peaks; good fishing streams; alpine meadows; rare wildflowers in Tumwater Botanical Area; Lake Wenatchee; saddle and pack trips; and winter sports. For National Forest recreation information in Washington, call 206–442–0170.

STATE PARKS. Washington has more than 70 state parks where camping is allowed (generally including RV's and trailers). The largest, from the standpoint of sites, are: *Twin Harbor,* 3 miles south of Westport (Wash. 105); *Deception Pass,* north end of Whidbey Island (Wash. 20); *Alta Lake,* 2 miles northwest of Pateros (US 97); *Sun Lakes,* 6 miles south of Coulee City (Wash. 17, off US 2); *Millersylvania,* 11 miles south of Olympia, off I–5; *Lake Chelan,* 9 miles west of Chelan (US 97) and, *Lake Wenatchee,* off US 2, nine miles north of Leavenworth.

The big ones are most likely to be full on summer week-ends, while the lesser-known parks are uncrowded. Reservations are required at 11 of them. You can check campsite availability by calling the Parks & Recreation Commission toll free in-state at 1–800–562–0990. (The service is in operation only during the busy summer season.) Out-of-state call 206–586–2543. You can write to the Commission at 7150 Cleanwater Lane, Olympia, WA 98504–5711.

Don't plan an arrival after 10 P.M. or before 6:30 A.M. in the summer. Gates close.

Palouse Falls, 17 miles southeast of Washtucna (Wash. 26), is in an ancient coulee, through which the Palouse River plunges in fury before it finds its way to the nearby Snake River. No camping, but shortly downstream, at the confluence with the Snake, is the new Lyons Ferry park with all facilities.

Potholes Lake, on a reservoir just south of Moses Lake (I–90), was created by the construction of O'Sullivan Dam and Reservoir. The park has innumerable islands, the tops of sand dunes. Although the park has accommodations for tents and trailers, many families enjoy camping on a "desert island" and have a ball fishing, swimming, boating, and water skiing.

Riverside, 3 miles downriver from Spokane, along the Spokane River, boasts an excellent campground and generally fair fishing. Hiking trails lead to places that seem quite far removed from the big and nearby city of Spokane.

Sacajawea, near the confluence of the Snake and Columbia rivers, 5 miles southeast of Pasco (US 12, 395), is one of the several marked Lewis and Clark campsites in Washington and was named for the Indian woman who was part of the expedition. Swimming, fishing, boating. No campground, but numerous accommodations nearby.

Sun Lakes, (mentioned previously), in the desert country of central Washington, is a veritable oasis. Well-developed facilities for swimming, fishing, boating, golf. Picnic areas. Campground for tents and trailers.

Twanoh, 15 miles northeast of Shelton (US 101), is near the south end of Hood Canal. Dock and boat-launching for saltwater waterway. Swimming in sunwarmed water. Fills up on summer week-ends.

Because of its inland waters and islands—and forethought—Washington has more marine parks (56) than all the other states put together, which fits in with its highest-per-capita ownership of boats. Most of the marine parks are not developed, but they are reserved for seagoing explorers who want to put ashore and camp.

CAMPING OUT. There are campgrounds all through the state. See information under *"State Parks," National Forests,* and *National Parks.* For detailed information on state parks, write to Tourism Development Division. Campgrounds are located at *KOA Kampgrounds:* Bay Center, Burlington, Concrete, Ellensburg, Gig Harbor (near Tacoma), Ilwaco, Kent (near Seattle), Leavenworth, Lynden, Olympia, Port Angeles, Spokane, Vantage, Winthrop, and Yakima. For campsites along Roosevelt Lake, write: Coulee Dam National Recreation Area, Box 37, Coulee Dam, WA 99116 (or pick up a brochure at Information Center at dam). A number of the largest lumber and power companies in Washington provide facilities available to the general public. See chambers of commerce for campgrounds in area.

TRAILER TIPS. The term "RV" now lumps together travel trailers, motor homes, and campers. Many state and national parks have spaces set aside for them, with hookups. Forest Service campgrounds also are open for their use but generally do not provide any special facilities. Most small towns have trailer parks for overnighters, particularly along the ocean coast and other resort areas where they actively invite even short stays.

It is tougher for transients in the vicinity of large cities, where "mobile" homes cluster in residential "parks" and never move. Consult the campgrounds and recreational vehicle parks listings in the yellow pages for current information.

GUEST AND DUDE RANCHES. Strictly speaking, "dude ranches" began as working outfits, even if today they keep only a few head of cattle for atmosphere. They accept reservations for a week or more, usually quite well in advance. "Guest ranches" (there's a distinction, at least to dude ranchers) may be based on some old ranch houses, but were either converted or built-to-order for guests, who generally stay for a few days or a weekend. Some take in overnighters. Running a guest ranch is one of those ideas that appeal to families—for a while. You might write to the Washington State Tourism Division for a list of those currently in business.

One long-established dude ranch in the old tradition is Hidden Valley Ranch near Teanaway Junction, Star Route 2, Cle Elum, WA 98922. Riding horses, fishing, hay rides, rodeo grounds, tucked away amid fascinating coulees, pine trees, and brown hills.

Sun Cove Resort & Guest Ranch is aptly named—a little of each. It is on a sunny, pleasant place set in an appropriately western scene on Wannacut Lake near Oroville. Horses, swimming, fishing. Oroville's ZIP is 98844.

Dude ranch, guest ranch, or resort, whatever it is called—Washington has a special kind. The principal activity is riding high mountain trails with a packer and guide. The oldtimer in the business is Double "K" Mountain Ranch, Goose Prairie, WA 90929. Reserve well in advance, and think twice if you have acrophobia. From some trails you look *down* on mountain goats.

A couple of well-established ranches are for boys and girls. Flying Horseshoe Ranch, Rt. 2, Cle Elum, WA 98922, offers horsemanship, swimming, hiking, camp-outs, crafts, and games. Aqua Barn Ranch, Maple Valley Highway, Renton, WA 98055, runs all year. Summer day-camps are for 5-day periods, with horses and swimming.

RESORTS. "Resort" is a word anyone can use on the sign naming his place. The facilities may be run-down cabins for fishermen merely holing up until dawn. In the middle, there are many very pleasant, if small, resorts that deserve the name. They are scattered throughout the state. So are some luxurious lay-outs, golf courses and all, open to the public—but whose origin and main business was (or still is) to sell real estate and condominiums.

Among the long-established resorts in the deluxe classification, five are on the west side of the state. They are: *Alderbrook Inn,* near Union on Hood Canal. 18-hole PGA golf course. Cottages have 2 bedrooms, living room, fireplace, kitchen. Lodge with rooms and dining room. *The Resort at Port Ludlow,* on a bay off Admiralty Inlet. 212 rooms and suites, restaurant and lounge, marina, beach club, tennis, 18-hole public golf course, conference center.

Lake Quinault Lodge on the lakeshore at the edge of Olympic National Park. Oldtimer, all seasons. Hiking, fishing, boating, trail riding, indoor pool. *Rosario Resort Hotel,* Orcas Island (San Juans). Was once the mansion of a millionaire shipbuilder. Pools, tennis, marina, boat rentals, fishing, gardens, pipe-organ concerts.

Ocean Shores, on the Pacific beach at the north entrance to Grays Harbor, is described in the Olympic Peninsula loop trip. Accommodations run from motel to deluxe inn. Genuine "resort" qualifications are met by the *Canterbury Inn,* the *Polynesian,* and the *Grey Gull,* beachside neighbors.

Sun Mountain Lodge is on the east side, near Winthrop and the North Cascades Highway. It is perched on a hilltop with a sweeping view in all directions. Pool, tennis, hiking, horseback riding, and in winter, cross-country skiing.

Newest on the resort scene is the *Inn at Semiahmoo,* a luxurious waterfront complex off I–5 near the Canadian border.

HISTORICAL MUSEUM. Auburn: *White River Valley Historical Society Museum,* 918 H St. S.E. (939–2783).

Bellingham: *Whatcom Museum of History and Art,* 121 Prospect St. (676–6981).

Bremerton: *Kitsap County Museum.* Washington and Byron streets, Silverdale. (692–1949). *Naval Shipyard Museum,* 120 Washington Ave. (479–7447).

Cashmere: *Willis Carey Historical Museum,* East Sunset Hyw. (782–3230).

Eastsound, Orcas Island: *Orcas Island Historical Society Museum.* (376–4849).

Fort Lewis: *Fort Lewis Military Museum.* I–5, Exit 119 (967–7206).

Friday Harbor: *San Juan Historical Society Museum,* 405 Price St. (378–4587).

Goldendale: *Klickitat County Historical Society Museum,* 127 W. Broadway (773–4303).

Moses Lake: *Adam East Museum,* 5th and Balsam Sts.

North Bend: *Snoqualmie Valley Historical Museum,* 4th and N. Ballarat (888–3200).

Olympia: *State Capitol Museum,* 211 W. 21st Ave. (753–2580).

Port Angeles: *Pioneer Memorial Museum,* 3002 Mt. Angeles Rd. (452–4501).

Port Townsend: *Jefferson County Historical Society Museum,* City Hall Bldg., Madison and Wall Sts. (385–1003). *Rothschild House,* Franklin and Taylor Sts. (385–2722).

Pullman: *Charles R. Conner Museum,* Washington State University campus (335–4527).

Puyallup: *Ezra Meeker Mansion,* 321 E. Pioneer (848–1770). *Frontier Museum,* 2301 23rd Ave. S.E. (845–4402).

Snoqualmie: *Puget Sound Railway Historical Association* (888–3030).

Spokane: *Cheney Cowles Memorial Museum,* W. 2316 1st Ave. (456–3931). *Museum of Native American Cultures,* E. 200 Cataldo Ave. (326–4550).

Tacoma: *Washington State Historical Society Museum,* 315 N. Stadium Way (593–2830).

Vancouver: *Clark County Historical Museum,* 1511 Main St. (695–4681). *Ulysses S. Grant Museum,* 1106 E. Evergreen Blvd. (694–4002).

Wenatchee: *North Central Washington Museum,* 127 S. Mission St. (662–4728).

HISTORIC SITES. Ellensburg: *Olmstead Place Heritage Site,* 4 mi. east of town. 1875 log cabins furnished with items used in pioneer days by Olmstead family. **Hoquiam:** *Hoquiam's "Castle"* has been declared a state and national historic site. The beautifully restored 20-room mansion is an antique fancier's delight. **Mary's Corner** (12 mi. south of Chehalis): *John R. Jackson Cabin,* built in 1840s. **Port Angeles:** *Clallam Indian Longhouse,* in Lincoln Park. **Port Gamble:** Town established in 1863 is registered as a National Historic Landmark. **Port Townsend:** Site of *Old Fort Townsend,* 3 mi. south of town. *Fort Worden,* turn-of-the-century coastal defense fort, 1 mi. north of town. **Spokane:** Site of *Spokane House,* built in 1810 by the North West Company, and the first white settlement in what was to become Washington state. Free. A history museum in Riverside State Park, near town, has exhibits relating to the early fur-trading post. **Suquamish:** Site of *Old Man House* (Ol-e-man in Chinook jargon). A longhouse for communal living. Chief Seattle's grave in cemetery adjoining St. Peter's Church. A very old cemetery where both whites and Indians were buried. **Waitsburg:** 1806 campsite of Lewis & Clark party in *Lewis & Clark State Park,* 5 mi. east of town. **Wallula:** Site of *Fort Walla Walla,* which stood at bend of Columbia from 1818 to 1855, as fur-trading and distributive post.

INDIANS. Washington State has many Indian reservations—some so small it takes researcher's skill to seek them out, and two that contain more than one million acres each. The tongue-twisting tribal names in the Pacific Northwest provide clues that can't be missed: Hoh, Makah, Ozette, Quillayute, Quinault, Chehalis, Lummi, Muckleshoot, Nisqually, Nooksack, Puyallup, Skokomish, Squaxin, Swinomish, Tulalip, Spokane, Yakima.

Six of the reservations in Washington are on the coast, 13 along Puget Sound, and the others inland, including the huge Yakima and Colville units. The Colville Reservation, where the famed Chief Joseph of the Nez Percé is buried, stretches eastward from the Cascades above the Columbia River. The other million-acre reservation, the Yakima, lies in southcentral Washington, bounded in part by the Cascades and Horse Heaven Hills. The 141,000-acre Spokane reservation, adjoining the Colville on the east, has extensive mineral deposits and two active uranium mines.

The Washington tribes put on more than two dozen festivals, dances, and special events each year. Many are now as much for the benefit of tourists as for tribal members, but they do at least provide a link with the Indians' cultural past and are often a colorful spectacle.

Prominent Indian events are listed earlier in this section, under *Seasonal Events.*

In recent years, three fine Indian museums have opened around the state. They are different from traditional historical museums in that they present history from the Indian's view and are well worth a visit. Spokane, in eastern Washington, has the Museum of Native American Cultures at E. 200 Cataldo Ave. In Toppenish, south of Yakima, in the central part of the state, is the Yakima National Cultural Center on U.S. 97. On the Kitsap Peninsula, reached by ferry across Puget Sound, is the newest of the three, the Suquamish Museum.

HUNTING AND FISHING. Hunting. The big-game animals are deer, elk, black bear, moose, bighorn sheep, cougar, and mountain goats. Hunters annually harvest about 40,000 deer and 9,000 elk. The 300 goats taken are on permits issued by public drawings. In five counties, bears are considered predators and the season is always open on them. About 1,000 are killed each year. Principal game birds are pheasants, ducks, geese, grouse, quail, and partridge, and among them they furnish an annual bag of well more than a million birds. Rabbit hunting averages an annual harvest of about 30,000. Hunting season on one game or another is open all year somewhere in the state, although fall and winter are the busiest. Age limit for a license is 18, unless the youngster has completed a firearms training course. Licenses are purchased from sport stores, or request an application from the Game Department. For further information contact the Wildlife Management Division, Department of Game, 600 N. Capitol Way, Olympia, WA 98504 (753–5728).

Fishing: In rivers that run into saltwater, the great game fish is the steelhead, a large seagoing trout, for which a license is required. It is caught in winter, but trout fishing goes on from mid-April to the end of October. There are 8,000 lakes in the state, with trout, bass, and other whitefish. In saltwater, salmon fishing is at its peak in summer. Westport (Grays Harbor), Ilwaco (mouth of the Columbia River), and Neah Bay and Sekiu (outer end of the Strait of Juan de Fuca) are the most popular centers for charter boats and equipment. However, Port Angeles and many other coastal towns have boathouses. A beach sport at Long Beach Peninsula and on the coast north of Grays Harbor is digging for the delicate-shelled razor clam. There is a limit per day per person of the first 15 gathered.

For license fees and regulations on shellfish, bottom fish, salmon, and sturgeon, write Dept. of Fisheries, Room 115, General Administration Bldg., Olympia, WA 98504, (753–6600). For steelhead and other trout, bass, crappie, catfish and other information, write Fisheries Management Division, Dept. of Game, 600 N. Capitol Way, Olympia, WA 98504 (753–5713).

SUMMER SPORTS. Facilities for family activities are found throughout the state, especially in the larger towns, though even towns of 2,000 people have tennis courts, bowling alleys, swimming pools (or nearby facilities), and plenty of places for bicycling.

Golf: In all, there are nearly 200 courses. Since all chambers of commerce list them among tourist attractions, the state has discontinued its golf brochure.

Hiking: You can set foot on a trail within an hour's drive of any city in the state, and the only limit to how far you go is time and endurance. The mountain trails vary from easy 3-mile walks to rugged backpack trips not recommended for beginners. The lengthiest routes are the Cascade Crest Trail along the summit of the range from British Columbia to Oregon (230 miles, airline), and the crossing of the Olympic Peninsula by Olympic National Park trails.

Horseback riding: Available at dude ranches and in various National Forest areas, where packers still contract some work for the Forest Service. These are hard to keep track of, year to year, because helicopters may have displaced them. On the other hand, horses for rent pop up around developing resort areas each season. Make local inquiry.

Mountain-climbing: Mountains stand on fully half the area of the state, and vary from 2,000-foot hills to 14,410-foot Mt. Rainier—which you must climb with a guide unless you can give convincing proof of mountaineering experience. There are peaks with trails to the top and some that never have been scaled. Stick to trails unless you are fully equipped and know what you are doing. The high ones have glaciers on them, and a few climbers die every summer from overconfidence.

WINTER SPORTS. *Skiing:* The season runs from late December to April, and at some areas, when there's been a heavy-snow winter, there's enough snow left over for Fourth of July races and summer training. Ski areas abound in Washington, from west to east. Cross-country skiing is enjoying a new surge of popularity.

Among the outstanding ski areas are *Alpental, Snoqualmie Summit,* and *Ski Acres,* 46 to 50 miles E. of Seattle on I–90; *Crystal Mountain,* 64 miles S.E. of Tacoma on Wash. 410; *Stevens Pass,* 60 miles E. of Everett on US 2; *White Pass,* 50 miles W. of Yakima on US 12; *Mt. Baker,* 60 miles E. of Bellingham on Wash. 542; *Mt. Spokane,* 34 miles N.E. of Spokane; 49° north at Chewelah (45 miles N. of Spokane on US 395); *Mission Ridge,* 12 miles S. of Wenatchee.

Smaller areas with pomas and rope tows are *Leavenworth, Badger Mountain* near Waterville, *Hurricane Ridge* out of Port Angeles, *Loup Loup* between Twisp and Okanogan and *Sitzmark* at Tonasket. *Sun Mountain,* near Winthrop, is gaining note as a place for cross-country skiing.

"Ski-erized" rental cars with ski racks, snow tires, chains, scrapers, and antifreeze are available at Seattle-Tacoma and Spokane International Airports and regional airports at Wenatchee and Yakima. Many of the ski resorts can also be reached by bus.

Skating: Unique to the state is the outdoor Pavilion in Spokane's Waterfront Park. Open mid-November to mid-April. Indoor rinks are found in a few other cities.

SPECTATOR SPORTS. (Other than in Seattle). *Baseball:* Tacoma and Spokane have teams in the Pacific Coast League. Walla Walla, Bellingham and Everett have teams in the Northwest League. Clarkston shares with Lewiston, Idaho, a team in the Northwest League. *Football:* Washington State University, at Pullman, is a member of the Pacific Coast Conference, and plays such powers as Southern California, U.C.L.A., Stanford, and the University of Washington regularly. Some of its "home" games are played in Spokane. *Basketball:* Washington State and smaller universities and colleges furnish a good brand of the collegiate game. *Horse Racing:* Playfair, at Spokane, has a season that runs from June into October. Yakima Meadows season starts in April and runs to May. (See also Seattle Spectator Sports.) *Rodeo:* Anywhere in eastern Washington, any weekend throughout the summer and into fall, you are likely to find a rodeo in progress. They range from home-town affairs which spectators watch from their cars as well as from bleacher seats, to the big league Ellensburg Rodeo over Labor Day weekend. A number of rodeos also are held in the western part of the state, but they tend to be out of context in their setting and are not as colorful.

Logger Sports: These are western Washington's equivalent of the rodeo, and they, too, come in all sizes from small-town events to major competitions at Shelton, Sedro Woolley, and Morton. (See Seasonal Events.) As in a rodeo, "loggerodeo" is based on jobs that traditionally went with the work—sawing, chopping, tree topping, log rolling—even if modern methods have replaced them.

SHOPPING. In Spokane, the *Crescent Department Store,* at 710 W. Riverside, is the heart of the second city's shopping district. Seattle-based Nordstrom, the apparel store, is at W. 724 Main Ave. The ever-popular *Bon Marché* is at Main and Wall. Yakima has a new shopping mall, downtown, and the Tri-Cities have a big new shopping center. Tacoma's old City Hall, recently renovated, holds a number of small shops. On the island towns of Puget Sound and along the Olympic Peninsula there are many artisans working in generally small but colorful shops. On the Indian-reservation towns you can buy Indian-made artifacts.

CHILDREN'S ACTIVITIES. Even most of the small cities have parks and playgrounds for rest stops. With 3,000 miles of saltwater coast, Washington is a great place for beachcombing and peering at the creatures in tidal pools. At Mt. Baker and Mt. Rainier, nothing excites youngsters more than getting to throw a snowball in July. There are many rodeos and Indian celebrations. Boating goes on in lakes, rivers, Puget Sound and around ocean harbors—the simplest form of it being to take a ferry ride to Victoria, B.C., the San Juan Islands or round-trip on Puget Sound.

All those "stone trees" from *Gingko Petrified Forest* at Vantage are fascinating. Tacoma's *Point Defiance Park* has a "Never-Never Land" and a farm animal zoo for children. On summer weekends there are old-fashioned train rides there, at Snoqualmie east of Seattle, and at Lake Whatcom near Bellingham.

Seattle has the largest zoo. *Northwest Trek* at Eatonville is a branch of the Tacoma zoo. Animals roam freely, viewed from quiet motor trams. Near Sequim is *Olympic Game Farm* where famous animal characters are kept and filmed for TV and Disney nature movies. Walk through with guide or drive around the extensive compound. And of course, with all the state's mountains, forests and open rangeland, there is always a chance of seeing bears, deer and smaller animals in the wild.

MUSIC AND STAGE. The *Spokane Symphony Orchestra's* season is from October to May. It performs in the Opera House and features leading guest artists. *Spokane Civic Theater* puts on plays and musicals in its own 335-seat Civic Theater, September through June. A steady flow of visiting artists is presented at the 2,700-seat Opera House—top names and roadshows, in drama, music and dancing. (See also *Seattle Information.*)

BARS AND LIQUOR LAWS. Legal hours for cocktail lounges and taverns are 6 A.M. to 2 A.M. Hard liquor and wine are sold at state stores, Monday through Saturday. Hours are generally noon to 8 P.M., but stores in the bigger cities may open earlier and close later, and some stay open on holidays. (Beer and wine can be purchased in taverns and grocery stores.) Under state monopoly, Washington has the highest liquor prices in the nation. Cocktail lounges are always found at a licensed restaurant (state law, see also Seattle Information). Minimum drinking age is 21.

WYOMING

The Cowboys Still Ride

Wyoming is still Cowboy Country. That means cattle and horses, branding and riding. Rodeos remain Big! (There are more than eighty in the state each year.) And of course, interest in the many Indian tribes who have called this territory home remains high.

During mid-July the Sheridan-Wyo. Rodeo, one of the oldest in the country, takes place. Sheridan is the headquarters for the Bighorn National Forest, covering 1,107,670 acres. There are at least 38 campgrounds and many picnic spots in the forest. Fishing and hunting expeditions can be arranged, as can saddle and pack pleasure trips deep into the wilderness area. The area saw many Indian battles, and several battlesites remain.

Drive on to Dayton, via I–90 and US 14, and take a look at one of the finest cattle and horse regions of the West. Genuine western hospitality reigns in Dayton, where the locals like to use first names as soon as you're introduced and want you to reciprocate. Near Dayton, Tongue River Cave, with its underground river and narrow tunnels, is a mecca for experienced spelunkers in search of adventure.

Buffalo Bill Land

From Dayton drive over the summit of the Big Horn Mountains along US 14 to Greybull, where US 20 and 16 join for the journey to Yellowstone National Park, the first and the largest in the U.S. park system. En route the town of Cody, at 5,002-foot elevation, can be visited. Check in at a working or dude ranch for a few days of rest and unhurried sightseeing amid awesome scenery. An equestrian statue of the great scout, "Buffalo Bill" Cody, looks down the main street of the town that he founded and named. Mementos of the famed Westerner are on exhibit in the Buffalo Bill Historical Center, which includes Cody's boyhood home, and a replica of the old Cody ranch. The Center features 4 museums. Cody was born in LeClaire, Iowa, but his house was taken apart and re-erected here. In July, visitors flock to the area for the Cody Stampede, an exciting rodeo. The Whitney Gallery contains one of America's greatest collections of western art.

From Cody to Yellowstone National Park is fifty-three miles via US 14, 16, and 20, known collectively as the "Buffalo Bill Scenic Hiway to Yellowstone." Open from May until Oct. 1, this hard-paved road snakes west through the Shoshone Canyon, tunnels its way beneath Rattlesnake Mountain, and affords sweeping panoramic views of the Buffalo Bill dam and canyon. There are spacious parking places where stops can safely be made to better appreciate the view and to take pictures.

The highway passes lush western ranch country through the Shoshone Valley, plunges into the Shoshone National Forest, then twists through the Absaroka mountains where such strange and colorful rock formations as the Chinese Wall, Laughing Pig Rock, and Devil's Elbow, the Camel, the Palisades, Chimney Rock, and Holy City are found in the area known as the Playgrounds of the Gods. Finally, the road enters Yellowstone Park and continues past Lake Eleanor, Sylvan Lake, to reach Yellowstone Lake, the largest high-altitude lake in the United States.

So vast is Yellowstone National Park—about 3,472 square miles—that weeks on end would be needed to explore all of its scenic and varied attractions. No other national park embraces so many of nature's masterpieces. Most outstanding among the park's many natural wonders are the world's largest geyser basins and the thundering falls and canyon of the Yellowstone River.

Nowhere else in the West will you find so large a wildlife sanctuary. Powerful binoculars can afford a safe, close look at bear, elk, buffalo, moose, deer, and antelope. Although the black bear may appear amiable, they are extremely dangerous, and it is strictly against park regulations to feed or approach them.

An excellent highway system swings close to many of the prominent sights, but accommodations within the park, including campgrounds, are far from adequate during the height of the summer season. Early reservations at the hotels, lodges, and inns are a necessity.

Yellowstone National Park has five entrances. From the north, by way of Livingston, and Gardiner, Montana, I–90, US 10 and 89; from the northeast, by way of Billings and Cooke City, Montana, I–90, US 10 and 212; from the east by way of Cody, Wyoming, US 14, 16 and 20; from the south by way of Jackson, Wyoming, and Grand Teton National Park, US 26, 89, 191, 189, and 287; and from the west by way of West Yellowstone, Montana, US 20 and 191.

From the east entrance the highway passes volcanically formed Yellowstone Lake, whose sparkling blue waters invite a tour of its 110-mile shoreline. Scenic cruisers operate daily during the summer, and from their decks the wildlife and waterfowl can be observed in a truly natural setting virtually unchanged since fur trappers discovered the lake more than a hundred years ago.

On past the lake, the road leads to Fishing Bridge Junction, where anglers attempt to lure the large trout that abound there (permit required—free at visitor centers or ranger stations). Rustic cabin accommodations are available 2 miles south of the lake.

Scenic Treasures of Yellowstone

Starting out from Fishing Bridge, go north on the road leading to Canyon Village at Canyon Junction. This circle tour offers some of the park's outstanding scenery and passes near good accommodations.

At Canyon Junction is one of the park's most spectacular sights, the magnificent Grand Canyon of the Yellowstone. This 24-mile-long, 1,200-foot-deep gorge is a visual delight. Countless shades of red and ochre within the canyon are enhanced by the emerald green of the surrounding forest. There are also two waterfalls, one twice as high as Niagara, that will thrill you. While the canyon and the falls may be viewed and photographed from several angles, Inspiration Point on the north rim and Artist Point across the gorge are popular vantage points.

Mt. Washburn, rising 10,317 feet, is on your right as you drive the nineteen miles from Canyon Village to Tower Junction. The road slips through Dunraven Pass at an elevation of 8,859 feet before dropping a couple of thousand feet to Tower Fall, where the Roosevelt Lodge provides excellent rustic accommodations. Pause here to enjoy horseback expeditions, cookouts, and the fun of riding on a stagecoach.

Mammoth Hot Springs, at the north entrance, is just about eighteen miles from Tower Junction and is but one more scenic spectacular in a region literally filled with them. The impressive travertine terraces of these fabled springs are sometimes vividly colored, sometimes snow white. If you want to spend some time here, there are accommodations at the Mammoth Hot Springs Hotel and Cabins.

Having reached the top of the loop at Mammoth Hot Springs, the route swings down twenty-one miles to Norris Junction, then fourteen miles to Madison Junction, and finally sixteen miles to Old Faithful.

Old Faithful

Nowhere in the world can match Yellowstone for the variety of geysers. Some erupt in rage and fury spewing thousands of gallons of water over one hundred feet in the air, others merely splash up a few inches.

And most beloved of them all is Old Faithful.

Old Faithful is one of the gathering points for all visitors to the park, and no one leaves until he has seen this geyser shoot its 5,000–8,000 gallons of steaming water high into the air. It "blows" on the average of 22 times a day and has not missed a performance in over eighty years. In the Old Faithful Visitor Center is a geyser diagram which explains in detail just what goes on beneath the ground to cause this phenomenon. Old Faithful Inn is hard pressed to take care of the demands for accommodations, and reservations must be made in advance.

If you have an appetite for more geysers there are many others around the Old Faithful area, like "Grotto," "Beehive," and "Lone Star." Leaving Old Faithful southbound, take the 17-mile drive from Old Faithful to West Thumb Junction, where the Grant Village Campground offers camping facilities.

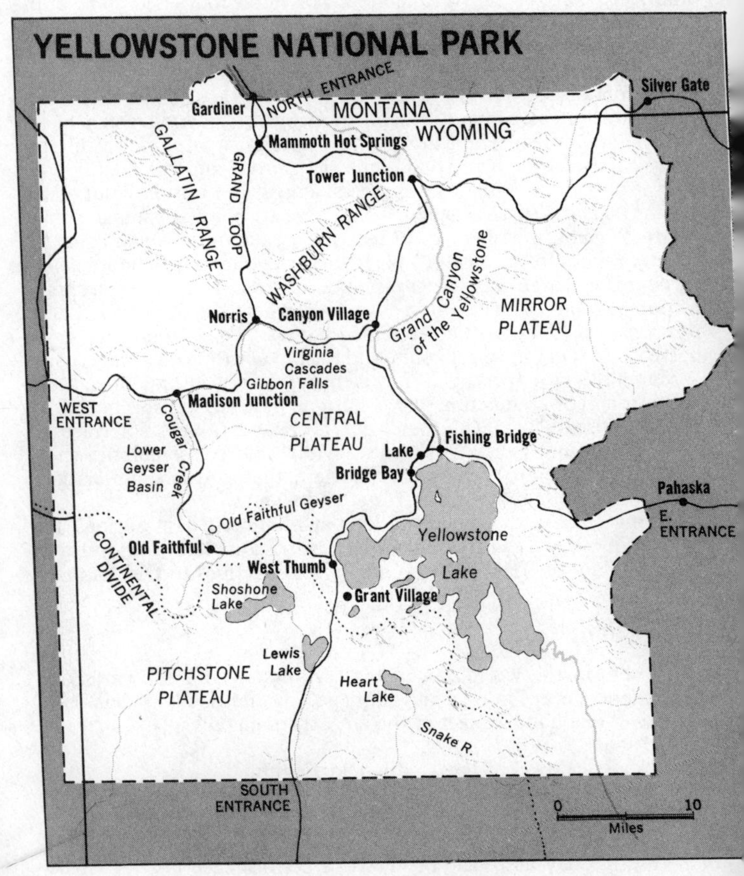
YELLOWSTONE NATIONAL PARK
NORTH ENTRANCE
Gardiner
MONTANA
WYOMING
Silver Gate
Mammoth Hot Springs
GALLATIN RANGE
GRAND LOOP
Tower Junction
WASHBURN RANGE
Grand Canyon of the Yellowstone
MIRROR PLATEAU
Norris
Canyon Village
Virginia Cascades
Gibbon Falls
Madison Junction
WEST ENTRANCE
Cougar Creek
CENTRAL PLATEAU
Fishing Bridge
Lake
Bridge Bay
Lower Geyser Basin
Pahaska
E. ENTRANCE
Old Faithful Geyser
Old Faithful
CONTINENTAL DIVIDE
West Thumb
Yellowstone Lake
Shoshone Lake
Grant Village
Lewis Lake
PITCHSTONE PLATEAU
Heart Lake
Snake R.
SOUTH ENTRANCE
0
10
Miles

From West Thumb to Bridge Bay and the start of this loop is a distance of twenty-one miles. In Bridge Bay there are two worthwhile points of interest: the Bridge Bay Marina, capable of handling two hundred boats, and the Lake Lodge, with every facility, including a hospital.

Visitors to the park interested in seeing its remotest areas can do so by either hiking or on horseback. There're some 1,000 miles of trails in the Park, including some short ones. You will need a pair of sturdy, comfortable hiking boots, and it's best to break them in before arriving at the park.

For the experienced horseback rider there are more than nine hundred miles of paths. Horses may be rented, but all horseback trips into the wilderness areas must be accompanied by a guide.

You can visit Yellowstone from May through October and from mid-December to mid-March. There are always accommodations open in the communities that surround the Park. In winter, all wheeled vehicles are prohibited. Access is possible by snow coach or snowmobile, and this winter trip into the Park is spectacular.

Grand Teton National Park

Grand Teton National Park, 485 square miles packed with some of this country's best mountain, valley, and lake scenery, can be easily reached over a 22-mile stretch of smooth highway, US 89 & 287. Even though the area is compact the traveler here can spend several weeks, with each day revealing something new in scenic views and recreational offerings.

Scattered throughout Teton National Park are a variety of facilities and campgrounds. You can spread your bedroll on the ground, pitch your tent, find a simple tent village with the tents already pitched for you, use the marina on 26,000-acre Jackson Lake, or enjoy the more comfortable surroundings at one of the lodges.

One of the most interesting and varied ways of touring the park is to hedge-hop from one accommodation to another. After the rustic log cabins of Colter Bay Village it is a short move on to Jackson Lake Lodge. Here you have a choice of 385 luxurious rooms spread in the lodge itself and in adjacent cottages. In the Lodge's main lounge a ceiling-to-floor picture window frames the lake and the Grand Teton Range. Dining facilities include coffee shop, dining room and room service. A few steps away is the Olympic-sized pool.

Moving on from Jackson Lake Lodge be sure to take the Teton Park Road to Jenny Lake Lodge, one of the most luxurious accommodations in the park. There are also campgrounds and excellent fishing sites; most of the trails through the mountains start at this location.

At Colter Bay or Jackson Lake Lodge, saddle up and jog along astride a gentle mare through the piney woods and breathe in the sweet, clean air of early morning. The long ride (over three hours) ends with a bountiful breakfast of bacon and eggs to sate the big appetite you've worked up.

A beautiful lodge, dining room and lounge, and rustic motel units have been built at Signal Mountain Lodge. The Lodge is famous for its western menu. Grocery store, gift shop, and filling station serve the visitor. Fishing guides for Jackson Lake are available from the marina. The Lodge operates its own river float trips.

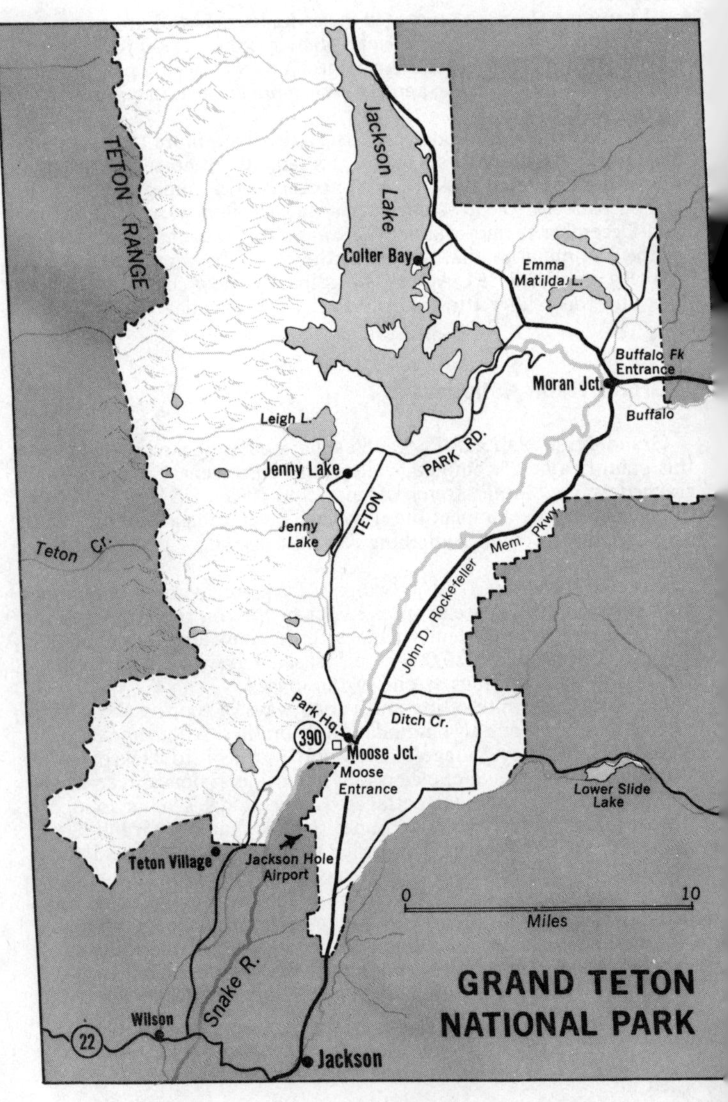
TETON RANGE
Jackson Lake
Colter Bay
Emma Matilda L.
Buffalo Fk Entrance
Moran Jct.
Buffalo
Leigh L.
Jenny Lake
TETON PARK RD.
Jenny Lake
Teton Cr.
John D. Rockefeller Mem. Pkwy.
Park Hq.
390
Ditch Cr.
Moose Jct.
Moose Entrance
Lower Slide Lake
Teton Village
Jackson Hole Airport
0
10
Miles
Snake R.
Wilson
22
Jackson
GRAND TETON NATIONAL PARK

Motor through the park first to familiarize yourself with the various areas so you can revisit and spend more time at those you find especially appealing. Then park your car and take to the trails, either on foot or on horseback, for intimate and uninterrupted views of the natural beauty of the region.

Each of the six major routes traversing the park offers an entirely different set of attractions. You might find that some trails are too long and arduous to be followed on foot so rent one of the docile, sure-footed horses and settle back on the creaky leather for a relaxing ride through the dramatic scenery that characterizes Grand Teton. Other trails, shorter and less rugged, can be appreciated on foot. And, for the truly adventurous, there are combination horseback-and-foot trails that end at the dizzying height of 11,000 feet on the Static Peak Divide. Many a mountain climber has been lured to the summit.

If the lowlands are your ticket, try the Lakes Trail, which hugs the lakes at the bottom of Teton range. Branching out from this point, three other routes cut deeply into the canyon territory. Death Canyon, Cascade Canyon, and Indian Paintbrush Canyon, with their incredibly steep walls and myriads of wildflowers, are thrilling to behold. If you are lucky, you may catch a glimpse of an elk or coyote or any of the other wild animals that inhabit the region.

Skyline Trail and Teton Glacier Trail into the highlands are unforgettable visual experiences, but you should not attempt them alone or before mid-June or after mid-September. Before starting out, check in with officials. Mountain climbing is taught in the Park at a fee for those who lack experience but would like to try it.

If water is your element, float trips down the Snake River are available at the Lake or at Jackson. These exciting trips take either a half or a full day and include a picnic lunch. Along the route the majestic Bald Eagle may be seen high in the trees in one of his few remaining natural habitats. You travel past the historic Menor's Ferry at Moose.

You may visit the Grand Teton National Park all year long with facilities open at Signal Mountain Lodge.

Gateway to the Tetons and the National Parks is Jackson, just fourteen miles from Moose, on a straight highway through the majestic Teton Mountains. Located at the southern entrance to the parks, Jackson is headquarters for the Bridger-Teton National Forest, an area of 1,701,000 acres of wilderness land bordering on both Grand Teton and Yellowstone National Parks. This resort community offers year-round recreational opportunities. The town and nearby countryside abound with dude ranches, motels and entertainment centers, good fishing and hunting, and three exceptional ski slopes: Snow King, Jackson Hole, and Targhee. There is also a Robert Trent Jones championship 18-hole golf course and a modern airport.

For those whose interests are culture and history Jackson offers both. On the one hand it remains entirely Western, and on the other boasts many art galleries, fine shops, a summer Fine Arts Festival, summer symphony, and summer stock theater.

Arts Festival in the Mountains

With camera in tow, summer or winter, board the chair lift at Jackson and ride to the crest of Snow King Mountain some two thousand feet above. Or look out the 50-foot-high lobby windows of the Snow King Inn and watch the skiers slaloming down Kelley's Alley.

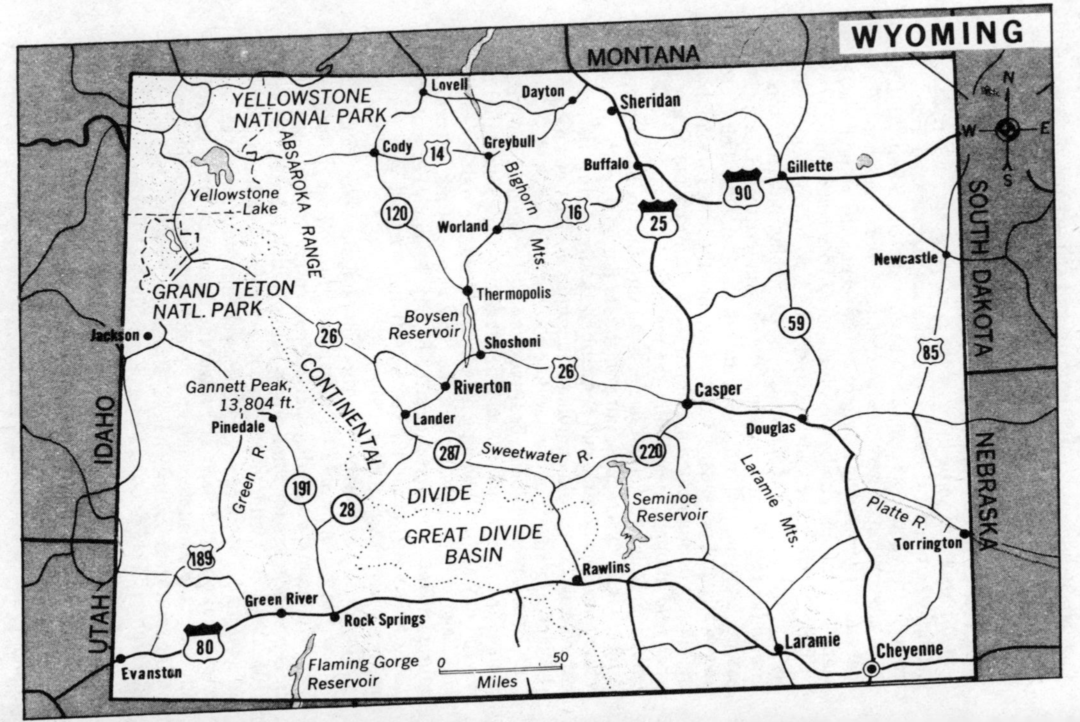
WYOMING
MONTANA
SOUTH DAKOTA
NEBRASKA
IDAHO
UTAH
N
E
S
W
YELLOWSTONE NATIONAL PARK
Lovell
Dayton
Sheridan
Cody
14
Greybull
Buffalo
Gillette
90
ABSAROKA RANGE
Yellowstone Lake
120
Bighorn Mts.
16
25
Worland
Newcastle
GRAND TETON NATL. PARK
Thermopolis
59
Boysen Reservoir
Jackson
26
Shoshoni
85
26
Riverton
Casper
Gannett Peak, 13,804 ft.
CONTINENTAL
Lander
Douglas
Pinedale
287
Sweetwater R.
220
Green R.
191
DIVIDE
Laramie Mts.
28
Seminoe Reservoir
Platte R.
GREAT DIVIDE BASIN
Torrington
189
Rawlins
Green River
Rock Springs
80
Laramie
Cheyenne
Evanston
Flaming Gorge Reservoir
0
50
Miles

A scenic aerial tramway ride leaves from Teton Village, part of the Jackson Hole Ski area just twelve miles west of Jackson on the Wilson-Moose road. Teton Village consists of hotels, chalets, lodges, and condominiums. The Ski Tram here rises 4,139 feet in an almost vertical ascent to Rendezvous Peak. The ride takes ten minutes and offers a panoramic view of the Teton Range. Jackson Hole is Wyoming's premier ski area.

Over scenic Teton Pass west of Jackson there is another ski area in Wyoming, Grand Targhee Village. Targhee has some of the finest, earliest, and latest snow in the West. Unless you're delayed by blizzards, it takes an hour to get there from Jackson.

For the non-skier, Jackson Hole Country offers recreational opportunities which include cutter racing, snowmobiling, and ice skating. Cutter races usually are held during January and February; finals held on the weekend of George Washington's birthday.

From Jackson you may choose to complete this loop tour back to Cheyenne via Rock Springs. If so, take US 189 and 191 south and stop off at Pinedale.

This community is off the beaten track, and after the crowds in Yellowstone and Grand Teton you'll find a slower tempo. It is the gateway to the Bridger–Teton Wilderness and the farthest incorporated town from a railroad. Pinedale is a true western cowtown and is surrounded by working cattle ranches. To the east are Wyoming's highest and most massive mountains, the Wind River Range. If you like fishing and big-game hunting settle in here for a while and it won't be long before you'll have your limit. There are more than one thousand lakes and streams. Six large lakes are accessible by road. In the quiet retreats of the Bridger-Teton National Forest, there are many choice campsites. In Pinedale itself are modern motels, dude ranch accommodations, and restaurants.

One hundred miles farther south is Rock Springs, a thriving sheep-raising community. Beneath the surface of this town of about 19,000 is a bituminous coal deposit of tremendous proportions. From Rock Springs take I–80 east back to Cheyenne.

Another route from Jackson to Cheyenne lies through Casper. Take US 26 and 89 to Moran Jct., then US 26 and 287 south, with a stopover in Dubois, the Rock Capital of the Nation.

The Dubois area, located on the upper Big Wind River and surrounded on three sides by Shoshone National Forest, is one of the richest places in the nation for prospectors and rockhounds. Found in the region are gem quality agatized opalized woods, pine and fir cone replacements, amethyst lined trees and limb casts, and all types of high grade agate.

Two Tribes with One Reservation

Bordering the Dubois area is the big Shoshone and Arapahoe Indian Reservation. In July, first the Shoshone and then the Arapahoe Indians hold their sun dances. Dressed in full costume, they dance continuously for three days and nights without taking food or water. US 287 and 26 passes through the reservation, where the Indians tend their horses and cattle or irrigate their haylands. On your way to Dubois note Crowheart Butte, a State Monument commemorating the scene of the great battle between the Shoshone and the Crow tribes.

Continuing on US 26 and 287 from Dubois, the town of Lander, one of Wyoming's oldest communities, is worth a stopover for those making a leisurely exploration of the state. Sometimes called the place where the rails end and the trails begin, Lander is a great place to fish, hunt, and mountain climb. Sinks Canyon State Park is nearby.

Or follow US 26 into Riverton. Located in the center of the Reservation, the Riverton Museum has Indian displays and pioneer-days memorabilia. There are three Indian Missions in this vicinity: St. Stephens on State 789, St. Michael's Mission at Ethete, and Fort Washakie, the Indian headquarters in Fort Washakie.

Laramie and Cheyenne

Laramie, at an altitude of more than 7,000 feet, offers an invigorating climate and clean, clear air. Nearly a century old, the town has flourished since its inception as a station on the Union Pacific Railroad line. Its name, immortalized in Wild West literature, movies, and television, was taken from one of its first settlers, Jacques La Ramie.

A short jaunt from Laramie is historic Fort Sanders, a stopping place for Western pioneers and Mormons. Forging west, they followed the Overland Trail, now commemorated in the Laramie vicinity with stone markers. Traveling the smooth, well-developed highways of today, it is difficult to appreciate the hardship of crossing this rugged terrain in a prairie schooner.

Visitors are invited to inspect the University of Wyoming's sprawling, landscaped campus. The college has some 9,000 students and an outstanding Geological Museum and Western History library with almost 700,000 volumes.

From Laramie to Cheyenne, the state capital, I–80 swings past one of the highest points along the entire Lincoln Highway. A good photo stop is the Ames Monument, located about two miles off US 30 on a marked road. This 65-foot pyramid was erected in honor of the Ames Brothers who helped finance the Union Pacific.

Cheyenne, now a peaceful, prosperous 47,000-inhabitant community, was known as "Hell on Wheels" in the days of the Old West. This spirit is revived once a year, usually during the last full week of July, at Cheyenne Frontier Days. At Frontier Park, the nation's top cowboys muster all their skill, strength, and sheer nerve to try to stay astride the backs of bucking steers and horses. For tickets, write: Cheyenne Frontier Days Committee, P.O. Box 2666, Cheyenne, Wyo. 82003.

While in Cheyenne, visit the Capitol Building. Guided tours of the Gold Dome are available during June to August, but the panoramic view is worth a visit anytime. The State Museum, located on Central Avenue at 23rd Street, exhibits archeological and historical treasures of Wyoming and the Old West. The Frontier Days Old West Museum boasts a large collection of horsedrawn vehicles and old sleighs.

PRACTICAL INFORMATION FOR WYOMING

HOW TO GET THERE AND AROUND. By Plane. *United* flies to Casper, Cody, Cheyenne, Gillette, and Sheridan. *Continental* services Casper, Cheyenne, Jackson Hole, and Rock Springs. *Delta* has flights to Casper, Cheyenne, Jackson Hole, and Rock Springs. *Mesa Air Shuttle* is a local commuter service.

By Car. I–80 crosses southern Wyoming entering from Nebraska in the east and leaving into Utah in the west. I–25 passes into the state from Colorado in the south. I–90, from Montana in the north and South Dakota in the east, serves the northern part of Wyoming.

By Bus. *Greyhound* provides transportation to and within Wyoming. *Zenetti Bus Lines* connects Rock Springs, Lander, and Riverton. *Jackson–Rock Springs Stages* also provide intrastate service.

ACCOMMODATIONS. The larger towns in Wyoming have excellent hotel and motel accommodations; most have parking facilities, restaurants, and bars. Rates are usually higher in summer, though some have special family rates. Cost figures generally are for the minimum or moderate priced rooms, unless a range is indicated. Listings are in order of price category.

The price categories, based on the cost of a double room, will average as follows: *Super Deluxe,* over $110; *Deluxe,* $60–110; *Expensive,* $50–60; *Moderate,* $40–50; and *Inexpensive,* under $40. No meals are included in these prices. All area codes are 307.

AFTON. Mountain Inn. *Deluxe.* Highway 89, Rt. 1, 83110 (886–3156). Pool. Golf nearby.

The Corral. *Expensive–Moderate.* 161 Washington, 83110 (886–5424). Group of rustic cabins in the heart of the Star Valley cheese country. Children's playground. Has AAA listing.

ALTA. Grand Targhee Resort. *Deluxe–Expensive.* 12 mi. E. on county road in the Teton Mountains near Driggs, Idaho, (800–443–0637). One of Wyoming's leading ski resorts. Early and late snow. Open summers. Swimming pool. One-, one-and-a-half, and two-level condominiums.

BUFFALO. Best Western Cross Roads Inn. *Expensive.* I–90, Exit 58. Box 639, 82834 (684–2256). A 60-unit motel just off the interstate. Dining room, cocktail lounge, swimming pool. Meeting rooms. Pets accepted.

Canyon Motel. *Moderate–Inexpensive.* 997 Fort St., 82834 (684–2957). Pool. Some kitchens. Free coffee and cable TV.

Keahey's Motel. *Moderate–Inexpensive.* 350 N. Main, 82834 (684–2225). Very nice. Some cooking units. Old-time hospitality. In the historic downtown.

Z-Bar Motel. *Inexpensive.* 626 Fort St., 82834 (684–5535). Well kept. Weekly rates in winter. AAA approved.

CASPER. Best Western East. *Expensive.* 2325 E. Yellowstone Hwy., 82601 (234–3541). Heated pool. Parking. Restaurant next door.

Casper Hilton Inn. *Deluxe.* I–25 & Rancho Rd. at North Poplar, 82601 (266–6000). One of Wyoming's plushest hostelries. 238 rooms. All services. Two restaurants.

Holiday Inn. *Deluxe–Expensive.* 300 West F St., Box 3500, 82601 (235–2531). Plush accommodations.

Imperial "400." *Moderate.* 400 E. "A" St., 82601 (1–800–368–4400). Motel with large, well-appointed rooms and heated pool. Most credit cards.

Showboat Motel. *Moderate.* 100 W. "F" St., 82601 (235–2711).

Super 8 Lodge. *Moderate to Inexpensive.* 3838 CY Ave., 82601 (1–800–843–1991). 68 rooms. Gift shop.

CHEYENNE. Hitching Post Inn. *Deluxe to Expensive.* 1700 W. Lincolnway, 82001 (638–3301). Long a Wyoming landmark near the downtown area. Large attractive rooms, indoor and outdoor pools, sauna, gourmet "Carriage Court" dining room, coffee shop, cocktail lounge, beauty salon, gift shop, outdoor tennis.

Holiday Inn Holidome. *Expensive.* 204 W. Fox Farm Rd., 82001 (1–800–HOLIDAY). 250 rooms plus meeting facilities.

Holding's Little America. *Expensive.* 2800 W. Lincolnway, 82001 (634–2771). 1½ mi. west at jct. I–80 and I–25. Just west of the city limits, this motor hotel conforms to other "Little America" establishments in Wyoming, Arizona, and Utah. Almost 200 elaborate rooms and suites. Wyoming Best Western establishment. Heated pool, coffee shop, dining room and cocktail lounge. Antiques and curios.

Stage Coach Motel. *Moderate–Inexpensive.* 1515 W. Lincolnway, 82001 (634–4495). I–80 Business & U.S. 30. Cable TV, pets OK.

Super 8 Motel. *Moderate–Inexpensive.* 1900 W. Lincolnway, 82001 (635–8741). Highway 30 West. Popular with truckers.

Sapp Bros. Friendship Inn. *Inexpensive.* 3350 E. I–80 Service Rd., Exit 370, 82001 (632–6600). 40 rooms, laundry, restaurant.

CODY. Holiday Inn Convention Center. *Deluxe–Expensive.* 1701 Sheridan Ave., 82414 (587–5555). A complete motel combined with one of the Cody-country's historic attractions. Dining room, cocktail lounge, swimming pool, meeting rooms. Gift shop.

Sunrise Motor Inn. *Deluxe–Expensive.* 1407 8th St., 82414 (587–5566). Medium-sized motel with large, well-furnished rooms, heated pool, and putting green. A Best Western establishment.

Bill Cody's Ranch Inn. *Expensive.* 25 miles west on US 14, 16, and 20. Box 1390, 82414 (587–2097). Outdoor recreation nearby. Fishing, skiing.

Buffalo Bill Village. *Expensive–Moderate.* 1701 Sheridan Ave., 82414 (587–5544). Large group of Western cabins, a trailer parking area, playground, heated pool, and western entertainment. Famous for chuckwagon dinners.

Absaroka Mountain Lodge. *Moderate.* Box 168, Wapiti, (587–3963). In the Wapiti Valley, this small, rustic motel is located on a rushing mountain stream. Dining room and large Western lobby with stone fireplace.

Wigwam Motel. *Inexpensive.* 1701 Alger Ave., 82414 (587–3861). TV.

DOUGLAS. Holiday Inn. *Expensive.* 1450 Riverbend Dr., 82633 (800–HOLIDAY). Pool, restaurant, all amenities.

Chiefton Motel. *Inexpensive.* 815 E. Richards St., 82633 (358–2673). A 20-unit motel. Close to several restaurants.

DUBOIS. Stagecoach Motor Inn. *Moderate.* Box 216, 82513 (455–2303). West side on main highway. In the best tourist tradition. Family atmosphere.

Branding Iron Motel. *Inexpensive.* 401 W. Ramshorn St., 82513 (1–800–341–8000). 1½ blks. west on US 26, 287. In the heart of a western town. Nearby cafe and cocktail lounge. Log cabin units.

EVANSTON. Best Western Dunmar. *Expensive.* Box 768, 82930 (789–3770). At west entrance of Hwys. 30 and I–80. Free transportation to airport, bus and train stations. Complimentary breakfasts; pool; restaurant and lounge nearby.

Pine Gables B & B Inn. *Moderate–Expensive.* 1049 Center St., 82930 (789–2069). 1880s inn located in the historic district. Continental breakfast.

Vagabond Motel. *Moderate.* 212 Hwy. 30E (789–2902). A well-established Friendship Inn. Playground, pets. Cafe nearby.

Super 8. *Moderate to Inexpensive.* 70 Hwy 30E (1–800–843–1991). Restaurant and mini-mart next door.

GILLETTE. Best Western Sands Motor Lodge. *Expensive.* 608 E. 2nd St., 82716. (800–528–1234). Spacious, well-appointed rooms with balconies, dining room, cocktail lounge, coffee shop, heated pool.

Holiday Inn. *Expensive.* 2009 S. Douglas Hwy. 82716 (686–3000). A three-story, 160-unit motel with convention facilities and all amenities. Night club.

Western Traveler's Motel. *Inexpensive.* 2011 Rodgers, 82716 (686–1230). 50 rooms, TV, pets OK.

GRAND TETON NATIONAL PARK—JACKSON. The central reservations and information number for the Jackson Hole area is 800–443–6931.

Alpenhof. *Deluxe.* Box 288 Teton Village, 83025 (307–733–3242). Full-service resort lodge at base of Rendezvous Mountain. Skiing, horseback riding. Excellent restaurant. Heated pool, sauna.

Americana Snow King Resort. *Deluxe.* 400 E. Snow King Ave., Jackson, 83001 (307–733–5200). Restaurant, bar. Pool, sauna, Jacuzzi. Sport shops and ski rental. At base of Snow King Mountain.

Jenny Lake Lodge. *Super Deluxe.* Box 240, Moran 83013 (733–4647). Rustic lodge and log cabins nestled under the Tetons at Jenny Lake. Fishing, horseback riding, hiking, and more.

Jackson Lake Lodge. *Expensive.* Box 240, Moran, 83013 (307–543–2855). In Grand Teton National Park. Landscaped grounds with pleasing views of the lake and of Tetons. Hiking, rafting, horseback riding.

Trapper Motel. *Moderate–Expensive.* 235 N. Cache Dr., Jackson, 83001 (733–2648). 28 well-kept rooms near center of town. Cable TV, handicapped facilities, laundry room. Restaurants and shops nearby.

Colter Bay Village. *Moderate.* Box 240, Moran, 83013 (307–543–2855). In Grand Teton National Park. Log cabins with attractive view of Grand Tetons. Hiking, rafting, horseback riding.

GREEN RIVER. Mustang Motel. *Moderate.* 550 E. Flaming Gorge, 82935 (875–2468). Various types of rooms. Coffee shop, cocktail lounge, meeting room. Open all year.

Walker's Motel. *Inexpensive.* 680 W. Railroad, 82935 (875–3567). Several modest units for economy travelers. No credit cards.

GREYBULL. K-Bar Motel. *Inexpensive.* 300 N. 6th St., 82426 (765–4426). 20 units. Open all year.

LANDER. Holiday Lodge. *Moderate.* 210 McFarlane Dr., 82520 (332–2511). At intersection US 26, 287 on south edge of Lander. Golf privileges.

Pronghorn Lodge. *Moderate.* 150 E. Main St., 82520 (800–442–6172). Clean rooms, TV. Restaurant.

Maverick Motel. *Moderate.* 808 Main St., 82520 (332–2821). A small, well-appointed motel with coffee shop.

LARAMIE. Chutes Inn. *Expensive.* Hwy I–80 and 287, Box 850, 82070 (742–6611). Newly decorated rooms, pool. Restaurant, weekend entertainment.

Ramada Inn. *Expensive.* 1503 S. 3rd St., 82070 (742–3721). 80 units. New dining room, cocktail lounge, meeting and banquet room.

Circle S Motel. *Moderate.* 2440 Grand, 82070 (745–4811). On the east edge of town, with attractively landscaped ground and pleasant rooms. Heated pool.

Wyoming Motel. *Moderate.* 1720 Grand, 82070 (742–6633). Friendly motel across the street from the University.

Friendship Inn Downtown Motel. *Moderate to Inexpensive.* 165 N. 3rd St., 82070 (742–6671). 30 clean units. Central.

Super 8. *Inexpensive.* I–80 & Curtis St., 82070 (1–800–843–1991). Popular with tourists.

LITTLE AMERICA. Best Western Holding's Little America Motel. *Expensive.* I–80, Exit 68. Box 1, 82929 (875–2400). A large oasis in the middle of the desert. Large, warm rooms, dining room. Coffee shop and cocktail lounge.

MEDICINE BOW. Virginian Hotel/Motel. *Inexpensive.* 404 Lincoln Hwy., 82329 (379–2377). Wyoming landmark. Dining room, coffee shop and cocktail lounge.

NEWCASTLE. Best Western Fountain Motor Inn. *Expensive.* Jct. 16 & 85, 82701 (746–4426). Heated pool, pets. Free Continental breakfast. Cafe nearby. Most major credit cards.

Morgan Motel. *Inexpensive.* 205 S. Spokane, 82701 (746–2715). TV, phones, pets OK.

Sage. *Inexpensive.* 1227 S. Summit, 82701 (746–2724). Small, well-furnished motel with free coffee in the rooms, color TV.

RAWLINS. Bel Air Inn. *Expensive–Moderate.* 23rd at Spruce. (800–528–1234). A sleek 122-unit motel. Heated pool. Good restaurant and bar. Popular with airline personnel. A Best Western property.

Holiday Inn. *Expensive.* 1801 E. Cedar, 82301 (324–2783). New, large, and reliable. All amenities.

Quality Inn. *Expensive.* 2222 E. Cedar, 82301 (324–6615). Dining and coffee shop, lounge.

Bridger Inn. *Inexpensive.* 1902 E. Cedar, 82301 (324–2737). TV, near cafe.

RIVERTON. Best Western Sundowner II. *Expensive.* 1616 N. Federal, 82501 (856–6503). 60-room motel with many amenities. Restaurant on premises.

Thunderbird Motel. *Moderate.* 302 E. Fremont, 82501 (856–9201). Medium-sized with well-furnished rooms.

Hi-Lo Motel. *Inexpensive.* 414 N. Federal Blvd., 82501 (856–9223). 23 nice rooms, senior discount.

ROCK SPRINGS. Best Western Outlaw Inn. *Deluxe.* 1630 Elk St., 82901 (362–6623). Old West motif, spacious rooms, large interior arcade, indoor heated pool, cocktails, dining. Leading local inn.

Holiday Inn. *Deluxe.* Indoor-outdoor pool, tennis, cafe, bar. Free airport bus.1675 Sunset Dr., 82901 (800-HOLIDAY).

Quality Inn. *Expensive.* 2518 Foothill Blvd., 82901 (362–9600). Restaurant, lounge, pool.

Nomad Inn. *Moderate.* 1545 Elk, 89901 (362–5646). Well-restored hotel, heated pool, playground, pets limited, free coffee.

SARATOGA. Saratoga Inn. *Expensive.* Box 869, 82331 (326–5261). Just across the river in Saratoga. Located on the North Platte River, golf course, tennis. Dining room, cocktail lounge.

Cary's Sage & Sand Motel. *Moderate.* 311 S. 1st St., 82331 (326–8339). Small, clean.

SHERIDAN. Sheridan Center Motor Inn. *Expensive.* 612 N. Main St., 82801 (800–528–1234). Large Best Western establishment. Dining room, cocktail lounge. Banquet, meeting rooms. Swimming pool. Two blocks from business district.

Trails End Motel. *Moderate.* 2125 N. Main St., (672–2477). Small, attractive motel with an indoor pool.

The Mill Inn Motel. *Inexpensive.* 2161 Coffeen Ave., 82801 (672–6401). Former historic flour mill.

THERMOPOLIS. Holiday Inn of the Waters. *Expensive.* In Hot Springs State Park, 82443 (800–HOLIDAY). Pool, dining room, coffee shop, cocktail lounge, banquets and convention center. Mineral baths. Fishing.

Best Western Moonlighter Motel. *Expensive–Moderate.* 600 Broadway. 82443 (864–2321). Pool; tennis, hunting, fishing, restaurant and lounge nearby.

TORRINGTON. Kings Inn. *Expensive to Moderate.* 1555 S. Main St., 82240 (523–4011). Highly rated Best Western motel.

Western Motel. *Moderate.* Hwy 26 W., 82240 (532–2104). A 20-unit motel with color TV in all rooms. Pools.

WHEATLAND. Motel West Winds. *Moderate.* 1765 South Rd., 82201 (322–2705). Pleasant.

Vimbo's Motel. *Moderate.* South of town (322–3843). A free shuttle to airport. Restaurant.

WORLAND. Best Western Settlers Inn. *Moderate.* 2200 Big Horn Ave., 82401 (347–8201). Queen-size beds.

Sun Valley Motel. *Moderate.* 500 N. 10th, 82401 (347–4251). A 25-unit motel with attractive rooms.

Sun Valley Motel. *Inexpensive.* 500 N. 10th St., 82401 (347–4251). 24 rooms with cable TV. Pets OK.

YELLOWSTONE NATIONAL PARK. Canyon Village. *Expensive.* TW Services, Yellowstone National Park, 82190 (307–344–7311). Rustic cabins, with cafeteria. Horseback riding and park touring possible.

Mammoth Hot Springs Hotel. *Expensive.* TW Services, Yellowstone National Park, WY 82190 (307–344–7311). Park headquarters. Near major geothermal activity. Comfortable rooms in older lodge. Attractive restaurant.

Old Faithful Inn. *Expensive.* TW Services, Yellowstone National Park, WY 82190 (307–344–7311). Across from the famous geyser. Attractive restaurant. Open winter and summer, with reservations only.

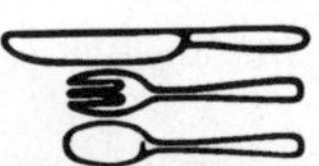

RESTAURANTS. People in Wyoming are not particularly interested in exotic cuisine, so steak-and-potatoes are often the best fare to be found. Beef is somewhat cheaper here than in some other states, and the cuts are quite good. Native trout is excellent and usually well prepared. The following list is just a selection; for other worthwhile restaurants, check the accommodations list. Restaurants are listed alphabetically by town. The price categories, based on the cost of a full meal for one without beverage, tax, or tip included, are: *Deluxe,* $25 and up; *Expensive,* $16–24; *Moderate,* $11–15, and *Inexpensive,* $7–10.

BUFFALO. Corell's Mexican Steer. *Moderate.* 610 Hart, on Hwy. 16 (684–7814). Good meats. Family restaurant. Cocktails.

CASPER. Gourmet Room. *Expensive.* 123 W. E. St. (235–5713). Bar, butcher shop, bakery. Veal and chicken specialties. Dancing and entertainment.

Benham's. *Expensive.* 739 North Center (234–4531). Businessman's lunches and charcoal-broiled steaks.

Goose Egg Inn. *Expensive.* West of Casper (473–8838). A tradition for family dining.

Wyatt Cafeteria. *Inexpensive.* 601 Wyoming Blvd. (266–2257). Good value for family dining.

CHEYENNE. Carriage Court Inn. *Expensive.* 1600 W. Lincolnway (638–3301). An excellent gourmet restaurant at the Hitching Post motor hotel (see *Hotels*). Specialties: veal dishes, flambé entrees. Fine wine list.

China Dragon. *Moderate.* Warren and 17th (635–7775). Cocktails. Sunday brunch.

Poor Richard's. *Moderate.* 2233 E. Lincolnway (635–5114). Beef and seafood.

Owl Inn. *Moderate to Inexpensive.* 3919 Central Ave. (638– 8578). Good American cooking, from fried chicken to chicken-fried steak.

Kings Table Buffet. *Inexpensive.* 3451 E. Lincolnway. Nice variety of food. Large seating area.

CODY. Green Gables. *Expensive.* 937 Sheridan Ave., US 14, 16, 20 (587–4640). Dinner smorgasbord; pancakes a specialty.

Irma Grill. *Moderate.* 1192 Sheridan Ave. (587–4221). This restaurant, located in the hotel "Buffalo Bill" Cody built, has Old West atmosphere. Specialties are steak, prime ribs, and trout.

La Comida. *Moderate.* 1385 Sheridan Ave. (587–9556). American and Mexican food. Popular.

GILLETTE. The Squire. *Moderate.* At Gillette Ave. and 4th St. (682–9684). Cocktails. Closed Sundays.

JACKSON. Alphenhof. *Deluxe.* (733–3462). European restaurant at Teton Village. Seafood, veal. Reservations advised.

Jenny Lake Lodge. *Expensive.* Box 250 (733–2811). Awards for international cuisine. Summer only.

The Open Range. *Expensive.* Box 1249, on the town square (733–3544). Some continental dishes, good prime rib and T-bone. Locally well-known.

Pioneer Room. *Moderate to Inexpensive.* Box 250 (733–2811). Three home-cooked meals a day.

LANDER. Miner's Delight. *Deluxe.* (332–3513). A ghost town out of Lander off US 28. A local tradition. Continental cuisine includes crepes, escargots, coq au vin. Atmosphere of the Old West. By reservation only.

The Commons Restaurant. *Moderate.* 170 E. Main (332–5129). Friendly family restaurant. Children's menu, senior discount.

Husky Cafe. *Inexpensive.* Hwy 287 South (332–4628). "Homestyle." Opens at 5:30 A.M. for early risers.

LARAMIE. Dr. Finefrock's Table. *Expensive.* 209 S. 3rd St. (742–7310). Wide range of interesting entrees, crab, veal, lamb. Excellent appetizers and desserts. Long wine list. Grill.

MORAN. Signal Mountain Lodge. *Moderate.* (733–5470). 31 mi. north of Jackson on the shore of Jackson Lake in Teton National Park. Full view of the Grand Tetons. Offers excellent food in the dining room. Housekeeping rooms available.

RAWLINS. Bel-Air Inn. *Moderate.* 2301 W. Spruce, US 30, I–80 Business (324–2737). Large portions. Western fare. Handsome decor.

RIVERTON. The Broker Restaurant. *Expensive.* 203 E. Main St. (856–0555). Great atmosphere in an old hotel. Roast Duck and prime rib are featured. Reservations advised.

SARATOGA. Wolf Hotel Restaurant. *Expensive.* 101 E. Bridge (326–5525). Excellent cornfed prime ribs.

SHERIDAN. Golden Steer. *Expensive.* 2071 N. Main (674–9334). Known for good char-broiled steaks.

Historic Sheridan Inn. *Expensive to Moderate.* 856 Broadway (672–5861). Dining in an old, historic inn. Well-known for prime rib and steak. Worth a detour.

JB's. *Inexpensive.* 1294 Coffeen Ave. (672–7050). Family chain restaurant. Salad bar, breakfast bar.

WORLAND. Washakie Grill. *Moderate.* 544 Big Horn, US 20 (347–4244). A Western hotel from times gone by, but the lounge and dining room are modern. The steak, prime ribs, and lamb chops served here are excellent, and the service is fast.

TOURIST INFORMATION. For all Wyoming travel, vacation resort, and camping information write for brochures from Wyoming Travel Commission, Cheyenne, WY 82002. For information call 1–800–225–5996.

SEASONAL EVENTS. *Cheyenne Frontier Days:* This is the world's largest rodeo. During the last full week in *July,* over one thousand professional cowboys descend on Cheyenne to compete for some $500,000 in prize money. And in addition to the rodeos, there are parades, nationally known entertainment figures (particularly country and western), carnival, dancing, Indians, band concerts, free chuck wagon breakfasts, and chuck wagon races, and even Western art exhibits. With good reason, this has been called the "Daddy of 'em All."

Other famous Wyoming rodeos include *Lander Pioneer Days and Parade* and *Cody Stampede,* the first week in July, *the Fremont County Fair* during the third week of August at Riverton, the *Wyoming State Fair* the last week of August at Douglas, *Central Wyoming Fair and Rodeo* late July to early August in Casper, and Laramie *Jubilee Days,* with world-championship roping, in mid-July.

Jackson celebrates *Old West Days* in late May. Cody puts on a *Frontier Festival* late June. The *Green River Rendezvous Pageant,* on the second Sunday of July at Pinedale, relives the days of the mountain men. Another Mountain Man Rendezvous, along with a Black Powder Shoot, takes place at Fort Bridger in early September.

Almost every Wyoming community holds a pageant, rodeo, or western event during the summer. One of the biggest events is the Wyoming State Fair held in Douglas in late August. The *Wyoming Travel Commission* can tell you what events will coincide with your vacation.

Worland celebrates a 2-day *Oktoberfest* the third weekend in Sept. Winter activities range from January dog-sled races in Teton Village to cutter races in Jackson, as well as many ski races. In December, Riverton holds its Christmas parade.

TOURS. Package tours in the park areas can be arranged through the Jackson Lake Lodge at Moran, Wyoming; Yellowstone Park Company at Mammoth, Wyoming; or Old West Tours in Jackson. Also, check with the Wyoming Travel Commission. Travel tours, summer and winter sports can be arranged through the Americana Snow King Resort in Jackson. Lander Tours guides excursions along old military and cattle trails (332–5011).

SPECIAL-INTEREST TOURS. Geological, historical, scenic tours available in both Yellowstone and Grand Teton National Parks. Wyoming's national monuments are worth seeing. They are *Fossil Butte,* off U.S. 30, and *Devil's Tower,* a spectacular volcanic rock near Hulett off US 14. Devil's Tower was this country's first national monument. It was set aside by President Roosevelt in 1906. It is perhaps most famous for its place in the movie *Close Encounters of the Third Kind.*

Many dude ranches and outfitters offer pack trips, float trips and guided hikes, particularly in Wyoming's mountain regions. For a list of guides, write the state travel commission.

GARDENS. The University of Wyoming campus: Beginning about May 15 and extending until about September 15, the campus is a blaze of flowers. Landscaping is spectacular. Many varieties of trees. Botanical gardens. Visitors are welcome. No charge. Locale: Laramie, Wyoming.

NATIONAL PARKS. *Yellowstone National Park.* Two-million-acre Yellowstone is the nation's first and largest national park. Located in the northwestern corner of Wyoming, it is a scenic wonderland of spouting geysers, steaming hot springs, magnificent waterfalls, beautiful lakes, towering mountains, big game, wildlife, birds, fishing and, of course, the inevitable bear (don't pet him, he's not tame). Yellowstone is open part of the winter, too. Take a "Snow Coach" trip through the south entrance to Old Faithful Lodge. Old Faithful geyser spouting on a frosty day, the most famous of Yellowstone's 10,000 hydrothermal features, is unsurpassed. For conditions in the park, year-round, call 307–344–7381 or 307–543–2559.

Grand Teton National Park. Just south of Yellowstone lies another great national park, known as the "American Alps." Jackson Lake reflects the spectacular beauty of the Teton Mountains. Unspoiled wilderness areas start at the roadside. Even the untrained can hike these mountain trails and gasp at undreamed-of views. Lakes and rivers, fabulous fishing, hiking, boating, square dancing, and real western, mountain pleasures abound. The quaint western town of Jackson is nearby. In winter, ski at Snow King Mountain, Teton Village, or Grand Targhee in the Tetons. Fish through the ice on Jackson Lake. Float the Snake River in summer. Snowmobile into the winter wonderland. For park information, call 307–733–2880 or 307–543–2851.

John D. Rockefeller, Jr. Parkway, fills the gap between Yellowstone and Teton National parks. Beautiful forested land, camping, hot springs, wilderness horseback riding.

Wyoming has seven National Forests. Among them are the Black Hills in northeastern Wyoming, Medicine Bow in the southeast, Bridger, Shoshone, and Teton in northwestern Wyoming, and the Big Horn National Forest in north central Wyoming.

Each forest has wilderness and primitive areas, hundreds of campsites, all the wonders of the mountain West. Fishing streams abound, snowcapped mountains, wildlife. If you plan to utilize the national forest be sure and obtain a recreation sticker. Write to Shoshone National Forest, Cody, Wyoming; Bridger-Teton National Forest, Jackson, Wyoming; Big Horn National Forest, Sheridan; Medicine Bow National Forest, Laramie.

Fossil Butte National Monument, located near Kemmerer in southwest Wyoming, contains a rich concentration of fossils which illustrates the evolution of freshwater fishes—reminders of the great oceans that once covered this portion of the state. The Butte amounts to a living classroom for studies of ancient life and its evolution.

STATE PARKS. Wyoming also has ten state parks. **Buffalo Bill State Park** is an hour's drive from the east gate of Yellowstone National Park on the north shore of Buffalo Bill Reservoir. It offers complete picnicking and day-use facilities plus minimum camping facilities. The adjacent dam, a prototype for world arch dam construction, features excellent trout fishing, as do the north and south forks of the Shoshone River that feed it. A commercial concession, campground, trailer park, and marina are also available.

Boysen State Park is located in central Wyoming and can be reached by driving either north or west of Shoshone on US 20 or 26. The park is surrounded by the Wind River Indian Reservation, home grounds for the Shoshone and

Arapahoe tribes. Day-use and overnight camping facilities are offered, and the reservoir and the river provide trout and walleye fishing and other popular watersports activities.

Sinks Canyon State Park. In a spectacular mountain canyon ten miles southwest of Lander, this park is one of the newest additions to the Wyoming park system. Here are hiking trails, nature walks, scenic overlooks, and countless glacier-fed pools and swirling eddies. Fishing is excellent. As an added attraction the river disappears into a gaping canyon wall cave and reappears in a crystal-clear trout-filled spring pool. Campsites are limited. Lander has several campgrounds.

Seminoe State Park is surrounded by giant dunes of white sand, miles of sagebrush, thousands of pronghorn antelope and sage grouse. Located near Seminoe Reservoir twenty-eight miles from Sinclair, the area offers excellent beaches, fishing and camping. The closeby "Miracle Mile" of the North Platte River got the name for its reputation for trout fishing.

Keyhole State Park is four miles north of I–90 between Sundance and Moorcroft, along the southeastern shore of Keyhole Reservoir and within sight of Devil's Tower. Antelope, deer, and wild turkeys are common in this area, and the reservoir offers excellent fishing for trout, walleye, catfish, and perch. The water is warm, and camping and picnic sites are readily available.

Glendo State Park, four miles east of the town of Glendo, is the best developed area in Wyoming's park system. There are excellent day-use facilities, a complete commercial concession, cabin, trailer court, and marina operation, and some of the finest boating and trout fishing in the state. Arrive early on weekends to be assured of getting picnic and campsites.

Guernsey Lake State Park, a few miles west of Guernsey on US 26, is located on the shores of one of Wyoming's most attractive reservoirs. High bluffs surround the park and block the wind so the water is always warm for the swimmer and water-skier. Historically, this is the country of the Oregon Trail, and the State Park Museum has full information. Complete day-use facilities are available, but camping space is limited, and fishing is poor due to the lake's annual draining.

Curt Gowdy State Park is located in the foothills of a mountain range separating Cheyenne and Laramie amid massive granite towers, rocky soils, and timbered slopes. Granite Reservoir and Crystal Lake offer fishing opportunities, and a variety of winter sports. The hills around the lakes invite the hiker, rockhound, and, in winter, the snowmobiler.

Hot Springs State Park, on the edge of Thermopolis, features hot springs, indoor/outdoor pools, a state-owned bathhouse and lodgings.

HOT SPRINGS. *Washakie Plunge,* south of Fort Washakie on the Wind River Indian Reservation. *Jackalope Warm Springs Plunge* on State 94 near Douglas. *Saratoga Hot Springs,* near Saratoga on State 130 and *Hot Springs State Park,* Thermopolis.

CAMPING OUT. Wyoming has literally hundreds of campgrounds offering everything from minimal to complete facilities. Yellowstone Park and adjacent Teton and Shoshone counties offer many campsites but only on a first-come, first-served basis. Reservations are accepted only for large organized groups such as the Boy Scouts.

Special regulations governing food storage apply at most Wyoming campsites to avoid trouble with the many bears. All food or similar organic material must be kept completely sealed in a vehicle or camping unit that is constructed of solid, non-pliable material, or, alternately, may be suspended at least ten feet above the ground and four feet horizontally from any post or tree trunk. The cleaner the camp, the less chance there is of being bothered by bears.

For complete information about the location and facilities of campgrounds in Wyoming, contact the Wyoming Travel Commission, in Cheyenne, Wyoming 82002 (307–777–7777).

FARM VACATIONS AND GUEST RANCHES. Wyoming is famous for its great variety of guest (dude) ranches. A selection of those available is included here; complete information is available from the Wyoming Travel Commission, Cheyenne, Wyoming 82002.

CM Ranch, six miles from Dubois. Located in the Wind River Mountains amid beautiful scenery and rushing streams where the atmosphere is completely remote. Separate cabins with private baths. Furnishing family vacations since 1927; children and teenagers are especially welcome. There are square dances, riding, fishing, hunting (in season), and pack trips. Open for summer guests and hunters. CM Ranch, Dubois, Wyoming 82513 (307–455–2331).

Crossed Sabres, 4 miles from Yellowstone. Summers. Pack trips, cabins, float trips, horses. At Wapiti, Box WTC, 82450 (307–587–3750).

Rafter Y Ranch, in the Big Horn Mountains near Buffalo. Riding, swimming, fishing. Working cattle ranch. Box 19, Banner, Wyoming 82832.

The Valley Ranch, 40 miles southwest of Cody, is known for its homelike atmosphere. Famous since 1892. Fishing, pack trips, wrangler school, hay rides, square dances, games. An ideal family vacation spot. On Valley Ranch Road, West Cody, Wyoming 82414.

The same formula—good food, good riding, good clean air—can be had at many more Wyoming dude ranches. Among them: The *Grizzly Ranch,* half-way between Cody and Yellowstone National Park; the *Lazy L & B Ranch,* outside Dubois, 82513; and the *Heart Six Guest Ranch,* near Jackson Hole.

Triangle X Ranch, north of Jackson in Teton National Park, just a mile off US 26. Fall hunting and outfitting. Summer river outings, horseback riding, packing. Winter cross-country skiing, snowmobiling, touring. A family ranch, children are welcome. Triangle X Ranch, Moose, Wyoming 83012 (307–733–5500 or 733–2183). For more information: Dude Ranchers Association. Tie-Siding, WY 82084.

Outfitters: Big-game hunting for elk, moose, deer, pronghorn antelope, bighorn sheep, and bear abound in Wyoming. Many are found in remote wilderness areas where hiring of an outfitter is a must. Wyoming has more than two hundred outfitters; all are required to be licensed.

SUMMER SPORTS. *Boating:* The numerous lakes and reservoirs provide ample opportunity for boating recreation. The Bridger National Forest, Flaming Gorge National Recreation Area, Grand Teton National Park, and all the Wyoming State Parks, offer particularly good boating waters. Raft and canoe trips down the rivers are popular, but care should be taken to explore the waters thoroughly before heading out. River rafting trips are available.

Float Trips: Wyoming offers a great number of outfitters and firms that specialize in river trips. Among the more prominent firms: Heart Six Float Trips, Box 70, Moran, 83013; National Park Float Trips, Box 411, Jackson, 83001, and Triangle X Trips, Moose, 83012.

Fishing: Wyoming's 20,000 miles of streams and over 264,000 acres of lakes provide unlimited fishing possibilities. Trout is king, but there are many other species of game fish. A five-day fishing license costs $10. The highly-detailed Wyoming Fishing Guide is available from the Wyoming Game & Fish Dept., Cheyenne 82002.

Hunting: There are seasons for pronghorn antelope, moose, elk, whitetail and mule deer, and bighorn sheep. For complete hunting and fishing information, contact the Wyoming Game and Fish Commission, Cheyenne, Wyoming 82002. For guide service contact Skinner Bros., Box B, Pinedale, 82941.

Horseback riding and pack trips: Available throughout the state, particularly at dude ranches and in the Bighorn National Forest, Grand Teton and Yellowstone National Parks.

Mountain Climbing: Contact Jackson Hole Mountain Guides, Teton Village, Wyoming, 83025 (733–4979).

WINTER SPORTS. Skiing is a favorite winter sport, and Wyoming has some great ski areas, including the famous Jackson Hole ski area with its Teton Village and Snow King at Jackson, White Pine north of Pinedale, Snowshoe Hollow east of Afton, Sundance Mt. south of Sundance, Hogadon Basin near Casper, Meadowlark east of Worland between Ten Sleep and Buffalo, Sleeping Giant at the edge of Yellowstone National Park.

Targhee is an attractive ski resort in the Tetons. Snowmobiling and ski touring are popular, especially out of Dubois and Jackson Hole. Or tour Yellowstone National Park in the winter in snow coaches.

SPECTATOR SPORTS. By far the most popular and prevalent spectator sport in Wyoming is the rodeo; nearly every community sponsors at least one. The major events, however, are these: *Cody Night Rodeo,* mid-Jun to Sept., nightly except Sun; *Cheyenne Frontier Days,* during the last full week in July; *Central Wyoming Fair and Rodeo* at Casper, late July to early Aug.; *Lander Pioneer Days* and *Cody Stampede* over the 4th of July weekend; the *Fremont County Fair,* third week in Aug. at Riverton; and the *Wyoming State Fair,* the last week of Aug. at Douglas.

Stock car and motorcycle races are frequent, and the state championships stock car races are held early in Sept. at Gillette.

Registered *quarter-horse racing* at Meadowlark Downs at Riverton.

CHILDREN'S ACTIVITIES. Both Yellowstone and Grand Teton National Parks are a paradise for children. The National Elk Refuge is situated between Jackson and Grand Teton National Park. Visitors are guided through the world's largest Elk herd in horsedrawn sleighs from late December to March, daily. At Yellowstone, along with the geysers, hot springs, and bubbling paint pots, there are game preserves where youngsters can see thousands of elk and hundreds of bear, buffalo, moose, deer, mountain sheep, and antelope in a near-natural habitat. Beware the Yellowstone bear who appears cute and cuddly, but is actually a dangerous wild animal who has lost his fear of man. *Under no circumstances should the bears be fed.*

The parks afford children the chance to frolic in the waters and along the nature trails while enjoying the clean, fresh mountain air.

Geological tour to the bottom of an old oil well, near Newcastle.

Rodeos, including Little Britches Rodeos where younger cowboys compete, take place in nearly every Wyoming community of any size and offer thrills and excitement to young and old alike. The Cheyenne Frontier Days (last full week of July) offers special children's programs.

Indian dances such as those seen at Jackson and Jackson Lake Lodge are performed in full ceremonial dress by the Indians native to Wyoming.

Stagecoaches, pulled by 4-horse teams, leave Roosevelt Lodge in Yellowstone and bounce over forest and sagebrush trails. Covered wagons depart from Jackson for 2, 4- and 6-day treks, gear furnished.

MUSEUMS AND GALLERIES. The state of Wyoming boasts more than 70 museums. Among them: The *Buffalo Bill Historical Center* at Cody features several excellent museums of western lore including *The Whitney Gallery of Western Art.* The Buffalo Bill Museum contains the guns, saddles, painting, furniture, letters, personal effects, and a valuable trophy collection of the famed William F. Cody, "Buffalo Bill." The Whitney Gallery features original art of such figures as Frederic Remington, George Catlin, Alfred Jacob Miller, and Charles M. Russell. A Plains Indian Museum wing has received accolades.

Bradford Brinton Memorial Museum: This working ranch near Big Horn has a fine collection of pioneer western art, Indian relics, and sculpture. Guided tours begin in the main ranch house and nearby buildings, the horse and carriage barns, and a "trophy" lodge near the main entrance. Western artists Frank Tenney Johnson and Charles M. Russell, among others, are featured.

The *University of Wyoming:* The Geological Museum in Laramie has many exhibits, including restored dinosaurs, fossil fish, prehistoric mammoth. Coe Library contains a western lore museum, a contemporary art museum, and many valuable archives.

Other Western and pioneer museums can be found at Buffalo, Casper, Fort Bridger, Fort Laramie, Green River, Greybull (rock collection), Kemmerer, Newcastle, Rawlins, Thermopolis. And Lander has its *Fremont County Pioneer Museum.*

In Cheyenne, the *Wyoming State Museum* offers displays of mountain men, railroad memorabilia, a cowboy cabin, saddles, minerals and gems, Indian and early-day western relics. A military uniform and button collection. The *National First Day Cover Museum* was opened in 1979. Unique and valuable stamps and first edition covers, original art. The *Werner Wildlife Museum* in Casper has displays of wildlife, including species indigenous to Wyoming and an African collection. Cheyenne's Frontier Days *Old West Museum* should not be missed, with its massive array of horsedrawn carriages and sleighs.

In Jackson, the centrally located Jackson Hole museum displays many guns of the area, contains a large collection of hand-forged knives, mounted deer antlers, and pioneer and trapper relics. The museum also has dioramas. In the nearby Grand Teton National Park, the *Indian Arts Museum* can be found at the Colter Bay Visitor Center. The museum offers an insight into Indian beadmaking and other arts. Lectures and films and other activities.

HISTORIC SITES. Fort Laramie: One of Wyoming's most famous historical sites is Fort Laramie on US 26 in southeastern Wyoming, which makes it an interesting "first stop" in the state when entering from the east. Trappers built the original fort in 1834 and named it after Jacques LaRamie, a French fur trapper killed by the Indians in 1820. Later they sold it to the American Fur Company, who then sold it in 1849 to the U.S. Government. For many years it was headquarters for U.S. Cavalry units and protected the pioneer from marauding Indians. A number of peace treaties with the Indians were signed at Fort Laramie. Abandoned in 1890, it was declared a National Monument by President Roosevelt in 1938. Much of Fort Laramie has been restored, and there are more than twenty historical structures. "Old Bedlam," which served as the bachelor officers' quarters, is now completely restored and open to the public.

South Pass City State Historical Site: Gold discoveries were first reported in 1842 in the South Pass area some thirty miles southeast of Lander. Of course, Lander wasn't there at the time. Nobody came to the district, except a few trappers, until 1867 and 1868, mainly because the Indians of that region fought fiercely against encroachment on their lands. This was the scene of Wyoming's only major gold strike. For several years mining boomed, but gradually died out after 1870. An authentic western gold ghost town remains, much as it was nearly one hundred years ago. The Carissa and Duncan mines may be seen. There is also a museum. Neighboring Atlantic City also contains many historical sites, including old Carpenter Hotel.

The Oregon Trail, the Mormon Trail, and the original Pony Express Route pass near South Pass City.

Forts: Fort Bridger, built in 1842–43 by the trapper and guide Jim Bridger, is located in Fort Bridger State Park in southwestern Wyoming and has been largely restored. Fort Caspar (on the outskirts of the city of Casper) has many pioneer and Indian relics preserved in a museum, and part of the old fort has been restored. Fort Fetterman is near Douglas; Fort Sanders, near Laramie; Jenny's Stockade near Newcastle; Fort Bonneville near Pinedale; Fort Mackenzie near Sheridan; Fort Phil Kearny near Story in the Sheridan area; Fort Stanbaugh near Atlantic City; Fort McKinney near Buffalo; Fort D. A. Russell near Cheyenne; Fort Steele near Sinclair. Travelers should inquire for directions at the chamber of commerce in cities located nearest these famous forts of the West.

Pioneer Sites: St. Mary's Stage Station and the historical marker where ninety Mormons perished in a blizzard and were ravaged by wolves may be reached from South Pass City (inquire there). The first cabin built by a white man in Wyoming is at Bessemer Bend (inquire at Casper Chamber of Commerce). Buffalo Bill Statue (inquire at Cody). Charcoal kilns (inquire at Evanston). Big Sandy Stage Station (inquire at Farson). Register Cliff with names of early pioneers and early graves (inquire at Guernsey). Hole-in-the-wall Gang (inquire at Kaycee). Crowheart Battle, where Chief Washakie cut out the heart of the Crow chief and saved his people (inquire at Riverton). First oil well in Wyoming at Dallas (inquire at Lander). Spanish Diggings, prehistoric quarries (inquire at Lusk). Ghost town Cambria (inquire at Newcastle). Father DeSmet's first Catholic Mass in Wyoming (inquire at Pinedale.) Independence Rock (Father DeSmet called it the "Register of the desert"). First Masonic Lodge meeting (1862) at Independence Rock. Site of Sweetwater Stage Station (inquire at Casper). Medicine Lodge, near Hyattville, archaeological site has 30,000-year-old petroglyphs. Trapper's Rendezvous point (inquire at Riverton). Early ghost coal mine camps (inquire at Kemmerer and Rock Springs). Oregon Trail Ruts (inquire at Guernsey). Teapot Dome (inquire at Casper). The Big Teepee ranch home (inquire at Shoshone). Fetterman Massacre, monument near Buffalo.

INDIANS. Arapahoe and Shoshone Indians preserve many of their native customs on one of the nation's largest reservations, the Wind River Agency in Fremont County. Two Indian missions still operate on the reservation—St. Stephen's Jesuit Mission near Riverton and St. Michael's Mission near Ethete in the heart of the reservation. Chief Washakie, the famous Shoshone, is buried here and so is Sacajawea, the Shoshone girl Indian scout for the Lewis and Clark Expedition. It is now the Indian Agency headquarters. Tours of the reservation can be arranged there, or at the Chambers of Commerce in Riverton or Lander. More than 5,000 Indians live on the reservation. A favorite spot to start a tour is at Paul Hines General Store on US 287, fifteen miles northwest of Lander. Meanwhile, during Frontier Days, the Southern Plains Indians perform their traditional dances.

During summer many Indian celebrations, traditional Sun Dances and Powwows are held. Inquire for the dates.

The Arapahoe, fierce and fearless warriors, were among the last Indians to submit to a reservation. The Shoshone is famed for his horsemanship. Many are cattle ranchers. Both tribes provide sterling bronc busters and race horses for rodeos in Wyoming. A visit to the reservation is a must for Wyoming tourists.

Shoshone and Arapahoe Indian craft may be found at Fort Washakie on the Reservation, at Riverton and Lander. Museums in Lander and Riverton offer exhibits on Indian history and folk lore. And Indian pictographs and petroglyphs survive on sandstone cliffs.

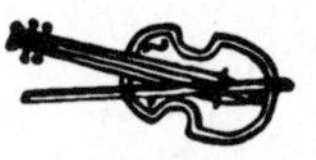

MUSIC. In mid-July Teton Village in Jackson Hole hosts the 6–week *Grand Teton Music Festival.* In past years concerts have included symphonic and chamber pieces. The Watermelon Concerts, so-called because after the performance the audience and musicians sit down to discuss the performance over large slices of watermelon, have been very popular.

The *Concert Hall* in the Fine Arts Center of the University of Wyoming at Laramie hosts numerous concerts and music festivals throughout the year. Their Walcker pipe organ, designed in Germany especially for the college, is one of the largest tracker organs in the United States.

In Casper, the *Civic Symphony Orchestra* performances are worth a combined symphony-skiing trip during the winter months. Casper's new Events Center, with 10,000 seats, hosts everything from concerts to rodeos and wrestling.

Cheyenne and Lander also offer some musical events.

STAGE AND REVUES. Wyoming, once considered culturally deprived, boasts an ever-increasing variety of theatrical entertainment. The University of Wyoming at Laramie has a *Fine Arts Center* whose theatrical section not only provides space for the legitimate theater but also a teaching center. In Jackson, the *Jackson Hole Opera House,* and *Dirty Jack's* offer theatrical and melodrama productions throughout the summer, as do the *Pink Garter Theatre* and the *Playhouse Theatre.* And Casper, Cody, Sheridan, and Lander all have *Little Theaters.* In Cheyenne, the seasonal *Little Theater,* at the historic Atlas Theater, produces melodrama in July and August.

LIQUOR LAWS. Wyoming bars open at 6 A.M. and close at 2 A.M. except Sunday, when it's noon to 10 P.M. Minimum drinking age is nineteen. Liquor may be sold over bars either by drink or the bottle, in cocktail lounges and in dining rooms by the drink, and in any liquor stores by the bottle. No state permit is required.

Index

Accommodations. *See* Hotels and motels; Youth accommodations
Adventureland, CA, 84
Albany, OR, 326
Ambos Nogales, AZ, 54–55
American Indians. *See* Indians, American
Amtrak, 5–6
Apache Indians, 47–49
Arches National Park, UT, 399
Architecture, in Nevada, 303–304
Arizona, 13–72
- American Indians in, 14, 16, 47–49, 69
- auto rental in, 65
- auto travel in, 32–57
- auto travel to, 57
- boating in, 70
- bus travel in, 65
- bus travel to, 57
- camping in, 68
- children's activities in, 70–71
- cliff dwellings in, 37, 39
- fishing in, 70
- gardens in, 69–70
- ghost towns in, 47–48
- golf in, 70
- guest ranches in, 69
- historic sites in, 71
- hotels and motels in, 57–63
- hunting in, 70
- liquor laws in, 72
- map of, 15
- museums and galleries in, 69–70
- music in, 72
- national forests in, 68
- national monuments in, 67–68
- national parks in, 66–67
- nightlife in, 72
- northern, 36–37
- plane travel to, 57
- restaurants in, 63–65
- seasonal events in, 65–66
- shopping in, 72
- skiing in, 70
- Spanish heritage of, 16–17
- state parks in, 68
- telephones in, 65
- tennis in, 70
- theater in, 72
- tourist information in, 65
- tours in, 71
- trailers in, 69
- train travel to, 57
- youth accommodations in, 27

Art exhibits. *See* Museums and galleries
Arts festivals, in Wyoming, 503, 505
Ashland, OR, 323
Astoria, OR, 313–314
Auto clubs, 1, 2–3, 4
Auto rentals
- in Arizona, 65
- in Idaho, 232
- in Los Angeles, 86
- in Oregon, 362

Auto travel, 4–5
- in Arizona, 32–57
- to Arizona, 57
- in desert, 5
- in Idaho, 212–222, 232
- to Idaho, 223
- in Los Angeles, 100
- in Montana, 253–265, 272
- to Montana, 266
- in mountains, 5
- in Nevada, 285–287, 296
- to Nevada, 287
- in Oregon, 309–340, 362
- to Oregon, 340

Auto travel (*continued*)
to Phoenix, 24
in San Diego, 110
in San Francisco, 174
to Seattle, 427
to Southern California, 138
in Utah, 393–402, 411
to Utah, 402
in Washington, 329, 418–496
in Wyoming, 507

Backpacking, 9
Bars. *See also* Nightclubs; Nightlife
in Idaho, 251–252
in Los Angeles, 107
in Nevada, 306–307
in Oregon, 386–387
in San Francisco, 177
in Seattle, 438
in Washington, 496
Beachcombing, in Oregon, 373
Beaches
in Los Angeles, 103
in San Diego, 118
in Southern California, 124
Bed-and-breakfasts, 7–8
Berkeley, CA, 181
Berlin-Ichthyosaur State Park, NV, 286
Bicycling
in Oregon, 373
in San Diego, 119
in Seattle, 436
in Southern California, 157
Big Sky country, in Oregon, 335–336
Billings, MT, 256–257
Blackfeet Indians, 263
Boating
in Arizona, 70
in Idaho, 216–217, 241
in Montana, 281
in Northern California, 207
in Oregon, 373
in San Diego, 119
in Seattle, 436
in Southern California, 157
in Utah, 415
in Wyoming, 516
Boat tours, in Idaho, 233
Boat travel
in Nevada, 296
in Northern California, 200
to Seattle, 427
Boise, ID, 210–212
map of, 211
Brigham Young University, 397
British visitors, 3
Bryce-Zion National Park, UT, 400
map of, 401
Bus travel
in Arizona, 65
to Arizona, 57
in Idaho, 232
to Idaho, 223
in Los Angeles, 86
in Montana, 272
to Montana, 266
in Nevada, 296
to Nevada, 287
in Oregon, 364
to Oregon, 342
to Phoenix, 24
to San Diego, 110
in San Francisco, 174
to San Francisco, 168
in Seattle, 434
to Seattle, 427
to Southern California, 138
in Utah, 411
to Utah, 402
to Washington, 470
in Wyoming, 507
Butte, MT, 259

Cable cars, in San Francisco, 174–175
California
map of, 160–161
California, Northern, 162–209
boating in, 207
boat travel in, 200
camping in, 203–204
casinos in, 207
children's activities in, 208–209
drinking laws in, 207
farm vacations in, 204–205
ferries in, 174
fishing in, 208
gardens in, 207

golf in, 208
guest ranches in, 204–205
health spas in, 205
historic sites in, 206
horseback travel in, 200
hotels and motels in, 193, 195–197
liquor laws in, 207
missions in, 206–207
museums and galleries in, 205–206
music in, 207
national and state parks in, 202–203
plane travel in, 200
restaurants in, 197–200
seasonal events in, 200–202
skiing in, 207, 208
spectator sports in, 208
theater in, 207
tourist information in, 200
tours in, 206
train travel in, 200
white water sports in, 208
wineries in, 187, 189
youth hostels in, 197

California, Southern, 73–161
auto travel to, 138
backcountry of, 126–127
beaches, map of, 124
bicycling in, 157
boating in, 157
bus travel to, 138
camping in, 152–153
casinos in, 156
children's activities in, 158–159
fishing in, 156–157
gardens in, 155–156
golf in, 157
guest ranches in, 144–145
health spas in, 145–146
hiking in, 157
historic sites in, 154
horseback riding in, 158
hotels and motels in, 139–144
jai alai in, 158
liquor laws in, 156
missions in, 125–127, 155
museums and galleries in, 153–154
music in, 156
national forests in, 151
national parks in, 150–151
north coast of, 135–136
plane travel to, 138
restaurants in, 146–148
seasonal events in, 148–150
skiing in, 158
south coast of, 122–126
spectator sports in, 158
state parks in, 151–152
surfing in, 157
swimming in, 157
tennis in, 158
theater in, 156
tourist information in, 148
tours in, 154
trailers in, 153
train travel to, 138
water sports in, 156–157

Camping, 10
in Arizona, 68
in Idaho, 239
in Montana, 275–276
in Nevada, 300–301
in Northern California, 203–204
in Oregon, 370–371
in Southern California, 152–153
in Washington, 491
in Wyoming, 515

Cannon Beach, OR, 314–315
Canoeing, 9
Canyonlands National Park, UT, 399
Cape Arago, OR, 318–319
Cape Blanco, OR, 319
Cape Sebastian, OR, 319

Casinos
in Nevada, 307
in Northern California, 207
in Southern California, 156

Cheyenne, WY, 506

Children's activities
in Arizona, 70–71
in Idaho, 246
in Montana, 281–282
in Nevada, 303
in Northern California, 208–209
in Oregon, 376–378
in Phoenix, 30
in San Francisco, 179
in Seattle, 437

Children's activities (*continued*)
in Southern California, 158–159
in Washington, 496
in Wyoming, 517
Chinook Pass, WA, 468
Cliff dwellings, in Arizona, 37, 39
Coal Canyon, AZ, 42–43
Coeur d'Alene, ID, 217
Coffeehouses and cafes, in Oregon, 361–362
Colorado River Canyon, UT, 398–399
Columbia Gorge, WA, 469–470
Convention sites, in Idaho, 240
Costs, 3–4
Crater Lake National Park, OR, 321–323
map of, 322
Custer Battlefield National Monument, MT, 256

Death Valley, CA, 132–133
Death Valley, NV, 286
Desert driving, 5
Disneyland, 84–85, 103
Dude ranches, in Washington, 491–492

Expenses, 3–4

Farm vacations, 10
in Montana, 276–277
in Nevada, 301
in Northern California, 204–205
in Oregon, 371–373
in Utah, 414
in Wyoming, 516
Ferries
in Northern California, 174
in Seattle, 424, 433–434
in Washington, 426, 470
Fishing, 9
in Arizona, 70
in Idaho, 242
in Montana, 279–280
in Nevada, 302
in Northern California, 208
in Oregon, 373
in San Diego, 119–120
in Seattle, 436
in Southern California, 156–157
in Utah, 414–415
in Washington, 494
in Wyoming, 516
Flagstaff, AZ, 37
Float trips, in Wyoming, 516
Fort Defiance, AZ, 44–45
Fort Peck, MT, 254
Frontierland, CA, 84

Galleries. *See* Museums and galleries
Gardens
in Arizona, 69–70
in Los Angeles, 102
in Northern California, 207
in Oregon, 366
in Phoenix, 30
in San Diego, 117
in San Francisco, 176
in Seattle, 436
in Southern California, 155–156
in Washington, 487
in Wyoming, 514
Gates of the Mountains, MT, 262–263
Ghost towns
in Arizona, 47–48
in Montana, 259–260
Glacier National Park, MT, 263–266, 273
map of, 264
Golf, 9
in Arizona, 70
in Idaho, 241
in Los Angeles, 102
in Montana, 281
in Nevada, 302
in Northern California, 208
in Oregon, 373
in Phoenix, 30
in San Diego, 119
in San Francisco, 178
in Seattle, 436
in Southern California, 157
in Utah, 415
in Washington, 494
Grand Canyon, AZ, 35–36
map of, 33
Grand Coulee Dam, WA, 458–459
Grand Teton National Park, WY, 501–503
map of, 502
Great Falls, MT, 262

Guest ranches
in Arizona, 69
in Idaho, 240
in Montana, 276–277
in Nevada, 301
in Northern California, 204–205
in Oregon, 371–373
in Southern California, 144–145
in Utah, 414
in Washington, 491–492
in Wyoming, 516

Handicapped travelers, 11–12
in Los Angeles, 100
in San Diego, 117
Harts Pass, WA, 456–457
Health spas
in Nevada, 301
in Northern California, 205
in Oregon, 339–340
in Southern California, 145–146
Helena, MT, 260
map of, 261
Hells Canyon, OR, 332–333
Hiking, 9
in Nevada, 302
in Oregon, 373
in Seattle, 436
in Southern California, 157
in Utah, 415
in Washington, 494
Historic sites
in Arizona, 71
in Idaho, 248–250
in Los Angeles, 104
in Montana, 278–279
in Nevada, 304
in Northern California, 206
in Oregon, 378–382
in Phoenix, 31
in San Diego, 120
in San Francisco, 175
in Southern California, 154
in Utah, 416–417
in Washington, 493
in Wyoming, 519
Hollywood, CA, tours in, 101–102
Honeyman Park, OR, 317–318
Hoover Dam, 34
map of area around, 299
Horseback riding, 9
in Nevada, 302
in Oregon, 374
in San Diego, 120
in Southern California, 158
in Washington, 494–495
in Wyoming, 516
Horseback travel, in Northern California, 200
Hotels and motels, 6–8. *See also* Youth accommodations
in Arizona, 57–63
in Idaho, 223–230
in Las Vegas, 288, 290–291
in Los Angeles, 87–95
in Montana, 266–270
in Nevada, 287–288, 290–293
in Northern California, 193, 195–197
in Oregon, 340–356
in Phoenix, 24–26
in San Diego, 110–115
in San Francisco, 168–171
in Seattle, 427–430
senior-citizen discounts at, 1–2, 7
in Southern California, 139–144
in Utah, 402–407
in Washington, 470–482
in Wyoming, 507–511
Hot springs
in Idaho, 240–241
in Montana, 275
in Wyoming, 515
House boating, in Utah, 415
Hunting, 10
in Arizona, 70
in Idaho, 242
in Montana, 280–281
in Nevada, 302
in Oregon, 374
in Utah, 415
in Washington, 494
in Wyoming, 516

Ice skating, 10
in Oregon, 375
in Washington, 495
Idaho, 210–252
American Indians in, 234–235
auto rentals in, 232
auto travel in, 212–222, 232
auto travel to, 223
bars in, 251–252

Idaho (*continued*)
boating in, 216–217, 241
bus travel in, 232
bus travel to, 223
camping in, 239
children's activities in, 246
convention sites in, 240
eastern, 218–220
fishing in, 242
golf in, 241
guest ranches in, 240
historic sites in, 248–250
hotels and motels in, 223–230
hot springs in, 240–241
hunting in, 242
liquor laws in, 251
map of, 214
museums and galleries in, 246–248
national forests in, 235–237
nightclubs in, 251
plane travel to, 222
restaurants in, 230–231
river boat trips in, 216–217
seasonal events in, 232–233
shopping in, 245
skiing in, 242–245
spectator sports in, 245
state parks in, 238–239
theater in, 250
tourist information in, 232
tours in, 233–234
trailers in, 239
train travel to, 222
youth accommodations in, 230
Imperial Valley, CA, 127–128
Indian reservations, in Arizona, 38, 39, 40
Indians, American
in Arizona, 14, 16, 47–49, 69
in Idaho, 234–235
in Montana, 263, 275
in Nevada, 304–305
in Oregon, 339, 382–383
in Washington, 493–494
in Wyoming, 497, 505–506, 519
Insurance, 2–3

Jai alai, in Southern California, 158
Jogging
in Los Angeles, 102
in San Diego, 119
Jordan Valley, OR, 334

Kaibab National Forest, AZ, 34
Kayaking, 9
Kingman, AZ, 34
Kings Canyon National Park, 135
Klamath Falls, OR, 337

Lake Mead National Recreation Area, AZ, 32–33
map of, 299
Lake Pend Oreille, ID, 217
Lake Tahoe area, 193, 287
map of, 194
Laramie, WY, 506
Lassen Volcanic National Park, CA, 192–193
Las Vegas, NV, 283, 285
hotels and motels in, 288, 290–291
map of, 289
restaurants in, 294–295
Lehman Caves, NV, 287
Liquor laws, 9
in Arizona, 72
in Idaho, 251
in Montana, 282
in Nevada, 307
in Northern California, 207
in Oregon, 387
in Southern California, 156
in Utah, 417
in Washington, 496
in Wyoming, 520
Logan, UT, 393, 395
Los Angeles, CA, 73–80
auto rentals in, 86
auto travel in, 100
bars in, 107
beaches in, 103
bus travel in, 86
gardens in, 102
golf in, 102
handicapped travelers in, 100
historic sites in, 104
hotels and motels in, 87–95
jogging in, 102
map of, 74–75, 81

museums and galleries in, 76–80, 104–105
music in, 105–106
parks in, 102
plane travel to, 86
restaurants in, 95–99
shopping in, 106–107
show farms in, 83–84
spectator sports in, 103
stadiums in, 77, 79
studio tours in, 101–102
taxis in, 87
telephones in, 100
tennis in, 102
theater in, 107
theme parks in, 103–104
tourist information in, 99–100
tours in, 100–102
train travel in, 86–87
zoos in, 102

Marin County, CA, 181–184
map of, 182
Medford, OR, 321
Missions
in Arizona, 53–54
in Northern California, 206–207
in San Diego, 121
in Southern California, 125–127, 155
Mission San Juan Capistrana, CA, 125
Mission San Xavier del Bac, AZ, 53–54
Missouri River, 254
Mojave Desert, 130–131
Montana, 253–282
American Indians in, 263, 275
auto travel in, 253–265, 272
auto travel to, 266
boating in, 281
bus travel in, 272
bus travel to, 266
camping in, 275–276
children's activities in, 281–282
farm vacations in, 276–277
fishing in, 279–280
ghost towns in, 259–260
golf in, 281
guest ranches in, 276–277
historic sites in, 278–279
hotels and motels in, 266–270
hot springs in, 275
hunting in, 280–281
liquor laws in, 282
map of, 255
museums and galleries in, 277–278
music in, 282
national parks and forests in, 273–274
plane travel in, 272
plane travel to, 266
restaurants in, 271–272
rock hunting in, 281
seasonal events in, 273
skiing in, 281
state parks in, 275
tennis in, 281
theater in, 282
tourist information in, 273
tours in, 279
trailers in, 276
train travel in, 272
train travel to, 266
Monterey, CA, 184–187
map of, 185
Mountain climbing, 9
in Oregon, 374
in Washington, 495
in Wyoming, 516
Mountain driving, 5
Mt. Rainer National Park, WA, 426–427
map of, 425
Museums and galleries
in Arizona, 69–70
in Idaho, 246–248
in Los Angeles, 76–80, 104–105
in Montana, 277–278
in Nevada, 305
in Northern California, 205–206
in Oregon, 378–382, 383
in Phoenix, 29, 31
in San Diego, 121–122
in San Francisco, 175, 176
in Seattle, 434–435
in Southern California, 153–154
in Utah, 416
in Washington, 492–493
in Wyoming, 517–518

Music
- in Arizona, 72
- in Los Angeles, 105–106
- in Montana, 282
- in Nevada, 305–306
- in Northern California, 207
- in Oregon, 384
- in Phoenix, 31
- in San Diego, 122
- in San Francisco, 176–177
- in Seattle, 437–438
- in Southern California, 156
- in Utah, 417
- in Washington, 496
- in Wyoming, 519

Napa, CA, 187–189
National forests
- in Arizona, 68
- in Idaho, 235–237
- in Montana, 273–274
- in Nevada, 297–298
- in Oregon, 366–368
- in Southern California, 151

National monuments
- in Arizona, 67–68
- in Utah, 412–414

National parks
- in Arizona, 66–67
- in Montana, 273–274
- in Nevada, 297–298
- in Oregon, 366–368
- in Northern California, 202–203
- in Southern California, 150–151
- in Utah, 412–414
- in Washington, 487–490
- in Wyoming, 497–503, 514

Navajo cliff dwellings, 41–42
Nevada, 283–307
- American Indians in, 304–305
- architecture in, 303–304
- auto rentals in, 296
- auto travel in, 285–287, 296
- auto travel to, 287
- bars in, 306–307
- boat travel in, 296
- bus travel in, 296
- camping in, 300–301
- casinos in, 307
- children's activities in, 303
- farm vacations in, 301
- fishing in, 302
- golf in, 302
- guest ranches in, 301
- health spas in, 301
- hiking in, 302
- historic sites in, 304
- horseback riding in, 302
- hotels and motels in, 287–288, 290–293
- hunting in, 302
- liquor laws in, 307
- map of, 284
- museums and galleries in, 305
- music in, 305–306
- national parks and forests in, 297–298
- nightclubs in, 306
- plane travel in, 296
- plane travel to, 287
- restaurants in, 293–296
- seasonal events in, 296–297
- shopping in, 303
- skiing in, 302
- spectator sports in, 302
- state parks in, 298, 300
- swimming in, 301
- theater in, 306
- tourist information in, 296
- tours in, 285, 297
- trailers in, 301

Nightlife. *See also* Bars
- in Arizona, 72
- in Idaho, 251
- in Nevada, 306
- in Oregon, 385–386
- in Phoenix, 32
- in San Francisco, 177
- in Seattle, 438

North Cascades Highway, 453, 455–456
North Cascades National Park, WA
- map of, 454

Northern California. *See* California, Northern

Oakland, CA, 179–181
Ogden, UT, 395
Okanogan Highlands, WA, 459–462
Old Faithful Geyser, 499

Olympia, WA, 443–444
Olympic National Park, WA, 447, 449–450
Olympic Peninsula, WA, 445–447
Oregon, 308–387
American Indians in, 339, 382–383
auto rentals in, 362
auto travel in, 309–340, 362
auto travel to, 340
bars in, 386–387
beachcombing in, 373
bicycling in, 373
boating in, 373
bus travel in, 362
bus travel to, 340
camping in, 370–371
children's activities in, 376–378
coast of, 311–313
coffeehouses and cafes in, 361–362
eastern, 328–329
farm vacations, 371–373
fishing in, 373
gardens in, 366
golf in, 373
guest ranches, 371–373
health spas in, 339–340, 373
hiking in, 373
historic sites in, 378–382
horseback riding in, 374
hotels and motels in, 340–356
hunting in, 374
ice skating in, 375
liquor laws in, 387
map of, 331
mountain climbing in, 374
museums and galleries in, 378–382, 383
music in, 384
national parks and forests in, 366–368
nightclubs in, 385–386
plane travel in, 362
plane travel to, 340
restaurants in, 358–361
seasonal events in, 363–364
shopping in, 376
skiing in, 374–375
spectator sports in, 375
state parks and forests in, 368–370
swimming in, 374
telephones in, 362
theater in, 384–385
tourist information in, 362–363
tours in, 364–366
trailers in, 371
train travel to, 340
windsurfing in, 374
wineries in, 3[illegible]
youth accommodations in, 356
Oregon City, OR, 328
Oregon Shakespearean Festival, 323
Otter Crest, OR, 316

Packing, 2
Pack trips, in Wyoming, 516
Palm Springs, CA, 128–130
Parks. *See also* National parks; State parks
in Los Angeles, 102
in San Diego, 117
Pasadena, CA, 80, 82
Pendleton Round-Up, OR, 330
Pets, traveling with, 6
Phoenix, AZ, 20–23
auto travel to, 24
bus travel to, 24
children's activities in, 30
gardens in, 30
golf in, 30
historic sites in, 31
hotels and motels in, 24–26
map of, 21
museums and galleries in, 29, 31
music in, 31
nightlife in, 32
plane travel to, 24
restaurants in, 27–29
seasonal events in, 29
shopping in, 31–32
spectator sports in, 30
tennis in, 30
theater in, 31
tourist information in, 29
tours in, 29–30
train travel to, 24
weather in, 23–24
zoos in, 30
Picnicking, in Seattle, WA, 436
Plane travel
to Arizona, 57

Plane travel (*continued*)
to Idaho, 222
to Los Angeles, 86
in Montana, 272
to Montana, 266
in Nevada, 296
to Nevada, 287
in Northern California, 200
in Oregon, 362
to Oregon, 340
to Phoenix, 24
to San Diego, 110
to San Francisco, 168
in Seattle, 433
to Seattle, 427
to Southern California, 138
in Utah, 411
to Utah, 402
in Washington, 486
to Washington, 470
in Wyoming, 507
Portland, OR, 308–309
map of, 310
Provo, UT, 397, 398
Puget Sound area, WA
map of, 448

Rafting, 9
Rain forest, WA, 450–451
Racquetball, in San Diego, 120
Ranches. *See* Guest ranches
Reno, NV, 193
hotels and motels in, 292
map of, 194
restaurants in, 295
Resorts, in Washington, 492
Restaurants, 4, 8–9
in Arizona, 63–65
in Idaho, 230–231
in Los Angeles, 95–99
in Montana, 271–272
in Nevada, 294–297
in Northern California, 197–200
in Oregon, 358–361
in Phoenix, 27–29
in San Diego, 115–116
in San Francisco, 171–174
in Seattle, 430–433
in Southern California, 146–148
in Utah, 407–410
in Washington, 482–486
in Wyoming, 511–513
River boat trips, in Idaho, 216–217
River running, in Utah, 415
Rock hunting, in Montana, 281
Rodeos, 9
in Wyoming, 497
Rogue River Valley, OR, 320, 323
Roseburg, OR, 324
Rowboating, in San Deigo, 119

Sacramento, CA, 191
Sailing
in San Diego, 119
in San Francisco, 178
in Utah, 415
Salem, OR, 327
Salmon River, 213, 215
Salt Lake City, UT, 388–393
map of, 390
San Diego, CA, 107–122
auto travel in, 110
beaches in, 118
bicycling in, 119
bus travel to, 110
fishing in, 119–120
gardens in, 117
golf in, 119
handicapped travelers in, 117
historical sites in, 120
horseback riding in, 120
hotels and motels in, 110–115
jogging in, 119
map of, 108
missions in, 121
museums and galleries in, 121–122
music in, 122
parks in, 117
plane travel to, 110
racquetball in, 120
restaurants in, 115–116
rowboating in, 119
sailing in, 119
scuba diving in, 119
snorkeling in, 119
spectator sports in, 120
swimming in, 120
taxis in, 110
tennis in, 119
theater in, 122
tourist information in, 116

tours in, 117
train travel to, 110
trolleys in, 110
windsurfing in, 119
zoos in, 118–119
San Francisco, CA, 162–184
auto travel in, 174
auto travel to, 168
bars in, 177
bus travel in, 174
bus travel to, 168
cable cars in, 174–175
children's activities in, 179
ferries in, 174
gardens in, 176
golf in, 178
historic sites in, 175
hotels and motels in, 168–171
map of, 164–165
museums and galleries in, 175, 176
music in, 176–177
nightlife in, 177
plane travel to, 168
restaurants in, 171–174
sailing in, 178
seasonal events in, 200–202
shopping in, 178–179
spectator sports in, 178
tennis in, 178
theater in, 177
tourist information in, 174
tours in, 176
train travel to, 168
youth hostels in, 171
San Gabriel, CA, 80, 82
Santa Barbara, CA, 136–137
Scottsdale, AZ, 23
hotels and motels in, 26–27
Scuba diving, in San Diego, 119
Seaside, OR, 314
Seasonal events
in Arizona, 65–66
in Idaho, 232–233
in Montana, 273
in Nevada, 296–297
in Northern California, 200–202
in Oregon, 363–364
in Phoenix, 29
in San Francisco, 200–202
in Southern California, 148–150
in Utah, 411–412
in Washington, 487
in Wyoming, 513
Seattle, WA, 419–424
auto rentals in, 433
auto travel to, 427
bars in, 438
bicycling in, 436
boating in, 436
boat travel to, 427
bus travel in, 434
bus travel to, 427
children's activities in, 437
farmer's market in, 422–423
ferries in, 424, 433–434
fishing in, 436
gardens in, 436
golf in, 436
hiking in, 436
hotels and motels in, 427–430
map of, 421
museums and galleries in, 434–435
music in, 437–438
nightlife in, 438
picnicking in, 436
plane travel in, 433
plane travel to, 427
restaurants in, 430–433
shopping in, 437
skid road in, 423
spectator sports in, 436–437
swimming in, 436
tennis in, 436
theater in, 438
tourist information in, 434
tours in, 435–436
train travel to, 427
waterfront of, 420, 422
youth accommodations in, 430
Sequoia National Park, 135
Shopping
in Arizona, 72
in Idaho, 245
in Los Angeles, 106–107
in Nevada, 303
in Oregon, 376
in Phoenix, 31–32
in San Francisco, 178–179
in Seattle, 437
in Washington, 496

Shoshone and Arapahoe Indian Reservation, WY, 505
Show farms, in Los Angeles, 83–84
Sierra Nevada, CA, 134
Skiing, 1, 9
in Arizona, 70
in Idaho, 242–245
in Montana, 281
in Nevada, 302
in Northern California, 207, 208
in Oregon, 374–375
in Utah, 391, 415–416
in Washington, 495
in Wyoming, 517
Snorkeling, in San Diego, 119
Snowmobiling, 9
Southern California. *See* California, Southern
Spectator sports
in Idaho, 245
in Los Angeles, 103
in Nevada, 302
in Northern California, 208
in Oregon, 375
in Phoenix, 30
in San Diego, 120
in San Francisco, 178
in Seattle, 436–437
in Southern California, 158
in Utah, 416
in Washington, 495
in Wyoming, 517
Spokane, WA, 462–463
Stadiums, in Los Angeles, 77, 79
State forests, in Oregon, 368–370
State parks
in Arizona, 68
in Idaho, 238–239
in Montana, 275
in Nevada, 298, 300
in Northern California, 202–203
in Oregon, 368–370
in Southern California, 151–152
in Utah, 414
in Washington, 490–491
in Wyoming, 514–515
Stevens Pass, WA, 457–458
Studio tours, in Los Angeles, 101–102
Summer sports, 9. *See also* Bicycling; Boating; Fishing; Golf; Hiking; Horseback riding; Mountain climbing; Sailing; Swimming; Tennis; Windsurfing
Sun Valley, ID, 220
map of, 221
Surfing. *See also* Windsurfing
in Southern California, 157
Swimming, 9
in Nevada, 301
in Oregon, 374
in San Diego, 120
in Seattle, 436
in Southern California, 157

Tacoma, WA, 444–445
Taxis
in Los Angeles, 87
in San Diego, 110
Telephones
in Arizona, 65
in Los Angeles, 100
in Oregon, 362
in Utah, 411
Tennis, 9
in Arizona, 70
in Los Angeles, 102
in Montana, 281
in Phoenix, 30
in San Deigo, 119
in San Francisco, 178
in Seattle, 436
in Southern California, 158
Theater
in Arizona, 72
in Idaho, 250
in Los Angeles, 107
in Montana, 282
in Nevada, 306
in Northern California, 207
in Oregon, 384–385
in Phoenix, 31
in San Diego, 122
in San Francisco, 177
in Seattle, 438
in Southern California, 156
in Washington, 496
in Wyoming, 520
Theme parks, in Los Angeles, 103–104
Tipping, 10–11
Tombstone, AZ, 56–57

Tourist information
in Arizona, 65
in Idaho, 232
in Los Angeles, 99–100
in Montana, 273
in Nevada, 296
in Northern California, 200
in Oregon, 362–363
in Phoenix, 29
in San Diego, 116
in San Francisco, CA, 174
in Seattle, 434
in Southern California, 148
in Utah, 411
in Washington, 486
in Wyoming, 513
Tours
in Arizona, 71
in Idaho, 233–234
in Los Angeles, 100–102
in Montana, 279
in Nevada, 285, 297
in Northern California, 206
in Oregon, 364–366
in Phoenix, 29–30
in San Diego, 117
in San Francisco, CA, 176
in Seattle, 435–436
in Southern California, 154
in Utah, 412
in Wyoming, 513–514
Trailer camps and parks
in Arizona, 69
in Idaho, 239
in Montana, 276
in Nevada, 301
in Oregon, 371
in Southern California, 153
in Washington, 491
Train travel, 5–6
to Arizona, 57
to Idaho, 222
in Los Angeles, 86–87
in Montana, 272
to Montana, 266
to Nevada, 287
in Northern California, 200
to Oregon, 340
to Phoenix, 24
to San Diego, 110
to San Francisco, 168
to Seattle, 427
to Southern California, 138
in Utah, 411
to Utah, 402
Transportation. *See* Auto rental; Auto travel; Boat travel; Bus travel; Ferries; Plane travel; Taxis; Train travel
Trolleys, in San Diego, 110
Tuba City, AZ, 41–42
Tucson, AZ, 49–53
map of, 50

Utah, 388–417
auto travel in, 393–402, 411
auto travel to, 402
bus travel in, 411
bus travel to, 402
farm vacations in, 414
fishing in, 414–415
golf in, 415
guest ranches in, 414
hiking in, 415
historic sites in, 416–417
hotels and motels in, 402–407
house boating in, 415
hunting in, 415
liquor laws in, 417
map of, 394
museums and galleries in, 416
music in, 417
national parks and monuments in, 412–414
plane travel in, 411
plane travel to, 402
restaurants in, 407–410
river running in, 415
sailing in, 415
seasonal events in, 411–412
skiing in, 391, 415–416
spectator sports in, 416
state parks in, 414
telephones in, 411
tourist information in, 411
tours in, 412
train travel in, 411
train travel to, 402
water-skiing in, 415

Valley of Fire State Park, NV, 285–286
Virginia City, MT, 258
Volcanic area, OR, 338–339

Walla Walla, WA, 466–467
Washington, 329, 418–496
American Indians in, 493–494
auto travel in, 438–470
bars in, 496
bus travel to, 470
camping in, 491
children's activities in, 496
dude ranches in, 491–492
ferries in, 470
fishing in, 494
gardens in, 487
golf in, 494
guest ranches in, 491–492
hiking in, 494
historic sites in, 493
horseback riding in, 494–495
hotels and motels in, 470–482
hunting in, 494
ice skating in, 495
liquor laws in, 496
map of, 442
mountain climbing in, 495
museums and galleries in, 492–493
music in, 496
national parks in, 487–490
plane travel in, 486
plane travel to, 470
resorts in, 492
restaurants in, 482–486
seasonal events in, 487
shopping in, 496
skiing in, 495
spectator sports in, 495
state parks in, 490–491
theater in, 496
tourist information in, 486
trailers in, 491
youth accommodations in, 482
Water-skiing, in Utah, 415
Water sports, 9. *See also* Boating; Fishing; Sailing; Swimming; Windsurfing
in Northern California, 208
in San Diego, 119–120
in Southern California, 156–157
White Pass, WA, 468
White water sports, in Northern California, 208
Willamette River, OR, 325–326
Windsurfing
in Oregon, 374
in San Diego, 119
Wineries
in Northern California, 187, 189
in Oregon, 384
Winter sports, 9–10. *See also* Hunting; Ice skating; Skiing
Wyoming, 497–520
American Indians in, 497, 505–506, 519
arts festivals in, 503, 505
auto travel in, 507
boating in, 516
bus travel in, 507
camping in, 515
children's activities in, 517
farm vacations in, 516
fishing in, 516
float trips in, 516
gardens in, 514
guest ranches in, 516
historic sites in, 519
horseback riding in, 516
hotels and motels in, 507–511
hot springs in, 515
hunting in, 516
liquor laws in, 520
map of, 504
mountain climbing in, 516
museums and galleries in, 517–518
music in, 519
national parks in, 497–503, 514
pack trips in, 516
plane travel in, 507
restaurants in, 511–513
rodeos in, 497
seasonal events in, 513
skiing in, 517
spectator sports in, 517
state parks in, 514–515
theater in, 520
tourist information in, 513
tours in, 513–514

Yakima Valley, WA, 467–468
Yellowstone National Park, WY, 497–501
map of, 500

Yosemite National Park, CA, 189–191
  map of, 190
Youth accommodations, 10
  in Arizona, 27
  in Idaho, 230
  in Northern California, 197
  in Oregon, 356
  in San Francisco, 171
  in Seattle, 430
  in Washington, 482

ZCMI (Zion's Cooperative Mercantile Institution), UT, 393
Zoos
  in Los Angeles, 102
  in Phoenix, 30
  in San Diego, 118–119